ORGANIZATION THEORY AND DESIGN

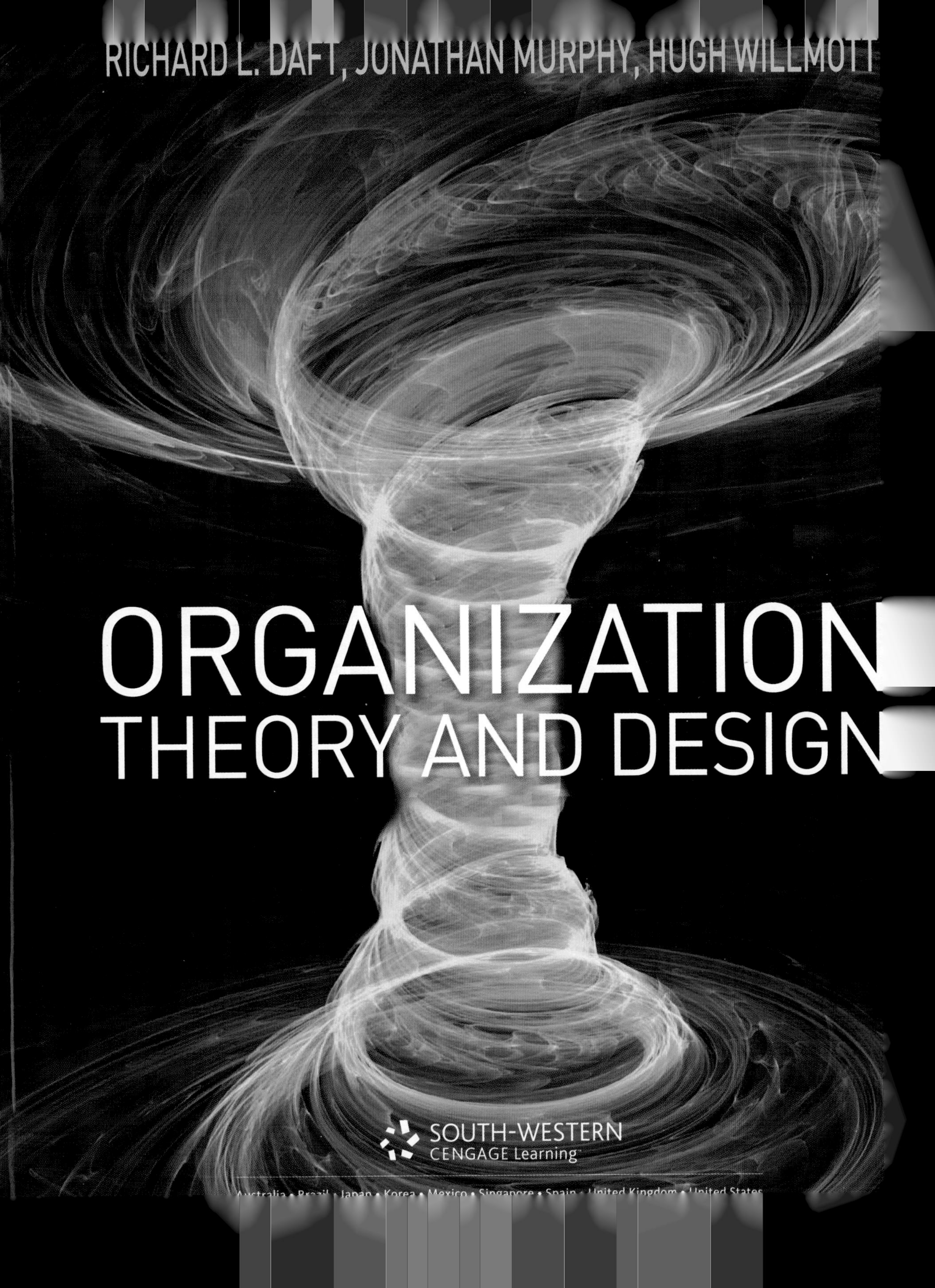
RICHARD L. DAFT, JONATHAN MURPHY, HUGH WILLMOTT
ORGANIZATION
THEORY AND DESIGN
SOUTH-WESTERN
CENGAGE Learning
Australia • Brazil • Japan • Korea • Mexico • Singapore • Spain • United Kingdom • United States

Organization Theory and Design

Richard L. Daft, Jonathon Murphy and Hugh Willmott

Publishing Director: Linden Harris
Publisher: Thomas Rennie
Development Editor: Linda Dhondy
Content Project Editor: Alison Cooke
Head of Manufacturing: Jane Glendening
Senior Production Controller: Paul Herbert
Marketing Manager: Amanda Cheung
Typesetter: Pre-Press PMG
Cover design: Adam Renvoize
Text design: Design Deluxe

For product information and technology assistance, contact **emea.info@cengage.com**.

For permission to use material from this text or product, and for permission queries, email **clsuk.permissions@cengage.com.**

This work is adapted from Organization Theory and Design, 9th Edition by Richard L. Daft, published by SOUTH-WESTERN, a division of Cengage Learning, Inc. © 2007.

British Library Cataloguing-in-Publication Data
A catalogue record for this book is available from the British Library.

ISBN: 978-1-84480-990-5

Cengage Learning EMEA
Cheriton House, North Way, Andover,
Hampshire, SP10 5BE, United Kingdom

Cengage Learning products are represented in Canada by Nelson Education Ltd.

For your lifelong learning solutions, visit **www.cengage.co.uk**

Purchase your next print book, e-book or e-chapter at **www.CengageBrain.co.uk**

Printed by Seng Lee Press, Singapore
1 2 3 4 5 6 7 8 9 10 – 11 10 09

BRIEF CONTENTS

CONTENTS

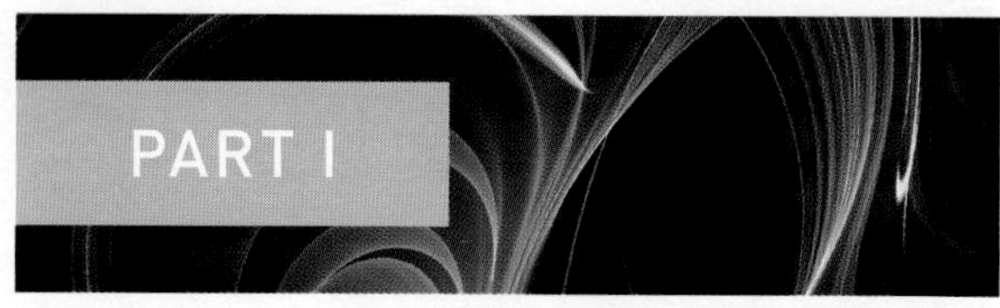

PART I

INTRODUCTIONTO ORGANIZATIONS 1

PART II

ORGANIZATIONAL PURPOSE AND STRUCTURAL DESIGN 47

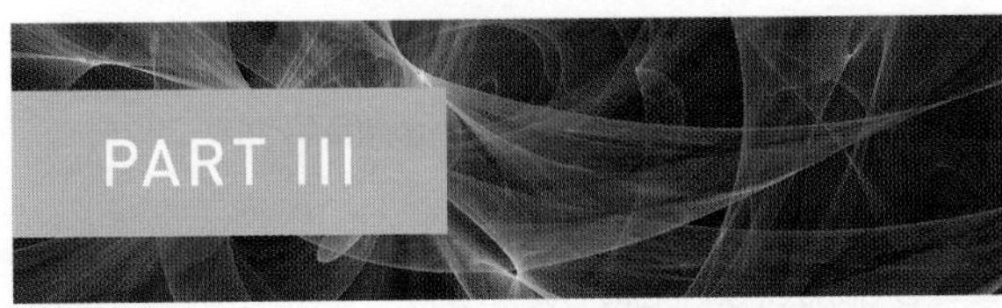
PART III

PART IV

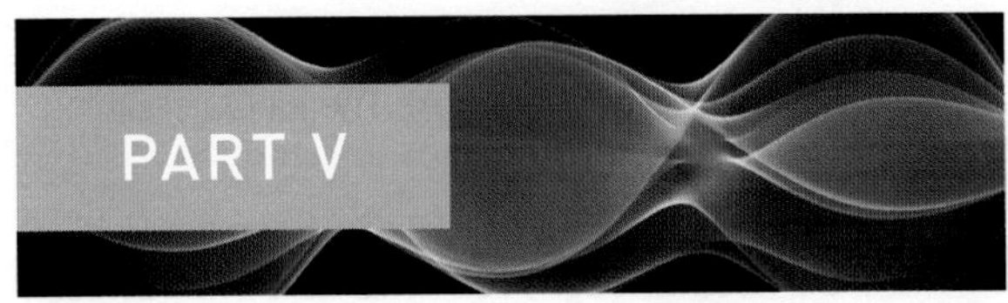
PART V

INTEGRATIVE CASES 579

LIST OF INTEGRATIVE CASES, CASES AND EXHIBITS

INTEGRATIVE CASES

LIST OF CASES FOR ANALYSIS

LIST OF EXHIBITS

PREFACE

Our vision for the first edition of *Organization Theory and Design* prepared specifically for students in Europe, the Middle East and Africa (EMEA) is to explore contemporary issues in organization design using both classic ideas and theories and mobilizing some critical thinking, in a way that helps students understand different approaches to management. The first EMEA edition incorporates a number of significant changes and additions to the enormously successful version sole authored by Professor Daft and now in its 10th US edition. These changes include: updates to every chapter that incorporate the most recent ideas, new case examples, new book reviews, new end-of-chapter cases and new end-of-book integrative cases as well as a counterpoint feature which is described in more detail below.

Jonathan Murphy and Hugh Willmott join Richard Daft as co-authors of this edition of *Organization Theory and Design*. The text has been substantially rewritten to address contemporary concerns for an international audience. Throughout this new text, examples are drawn from global sources, reflecting different issues and best practices faced by managers working in national and international business, public sector, and non-profit environments around the world.

Changing World – Changing Organizations

The international crisis that hit economic activity around the world beginning in 2007 has raised fundamental questions about the international economic order, and has challenged earlier assumptions about organizational design. It has become clear that the period of US dominance of the world economy, in place since the end of the Second World War, is in the process of change. New economic powers like China and India are growing rapidly and seem likely to overtake the former economic powers in America, Europe, and Japan, within the next generation. In addition, a number of major multinational corporations are in decline, a phenomenon that was brought home in striking fashion by the bankruptcy of two of the United States' Big Three automakers, General Motors and Chrysler, in 2009. These companies will continue to exist in some form, but it is clear that US-headquartered manufacturing MNCs are no longer unrivalled in organizational innovation and entrepreneurial dynamism. In the auto-industry and in other areas, notably electronics, powerful competitors have emerged, particularly from Asia-Pacific, where Japanese and Korean automakers have proved more than a match for the lumbering Big Three. There has also been a shift – particularly within the advanced economies – away from manufacturing and towards services, particularly tied to the dramatic development of information technology. This new EMEA edition of *Organization Theory and Design* reflects this changing business environment, with greater focus on service-delivering organizations, as well as much more geographic diversity in the organizations we discuss and explore.

The economic changes that have been occurring since the 1970s – brought to a head by the post-2007 economic crisis – reflect the decline of a form of production based on large multinationals whose sheer size and available resources enabled them to set the standard for business practice throughout their industries.

International economic liberalization combined with advances in information and communication technologies mean that companies do not need to be enormous in order to compete internationally. We shall see in the text that numerous smaller, more agile companies, often based in emerging economies in the Asia-Pacific, have been able to grow rapidly, and have in many cases outstripped the former market leaders in the developed countries. These companies are embedded in distinctive (non-Western) cultures and they incorporate practices that have proven highly effective. These newcomers have humbled many industry giants whilst other well-established companies have adapted and flourished in new conditions nurtured by globalization and market liberalization.

These developments have served to underscore the key yet repeatedly overlooked, insight that *there is no single, effective way of designing and managing an organization*. When we look around the world, we see very different organizations, designed on highly divergent principles and philosophies, succeeding in both national and international markets. British firms controlled by private equity funds with a very short term profit-maximizing perspective operate cheek-by-jowl with Japanese companies that plan generations ahead. Western multinational corporations that are constantly looking to sell off 'non-core' assets compete against sprawling Asian conglomerates that are happy to incorporate an ever-burgeoning range of apparently disconnected product ranges; extending for example from tomato paste to air conditioners. Similarly, organizations with very different management styles coexist in the global business environment. Many successful companies have highly developed human resource departments, where hiring is carried out on the basis of 'scientific' assessments including batteries of psychometric tests and rigorous multi-stage hiring panels, and where every staff member has a multi-faceted, multi-year development plan. In other, equally competitive corporations, new employees may be brought onboard through connections with the founding family, or a short interview with the CEO, who relies entirely on intuition in making key hiring decisions. While there is no doubt that some information important to organizations can be gathered and analyzed systematically and scientifically, many other factors will remain unknowable, or even more significantly, subject to very different cultural interpretations.

Differing interpretations, and the uncertainties that they cause, affect the contemporary organization not only in terms of its own planning and decision-making, but also in how it is perceived from the outside, which in turn has a substantial effect on the resources available to the organization and the possibilities of it achieving its objectives. As we have seen in several boom and bust cycles of the 'dot-com' sector, the valuation of companies and their ability to raise capital can soar and plunge within days or weeks, whereas the actual work being carried out by the company, and the quality of its technicians and engineers, is unchanged. Perceptions, therefore, change material reality for organizations no less than the reality of organizations, including their strengths and weaknesses, drives perceptions of organizations.

But what does this philosophic-sounding insight mean for managers? First of all, it is extremely important to be able to be self-reflective. The way that we see things is different from the way others see things, and the way we see ourselves is different from the way others see us. The better that this lesson is learned, the more likely we will be able to succeed in our objectives. Secondly, our efforts to exert control over our internal and external environments are likely to be partially successful at best. The potency and scope of management control should not be exaggerated as unexpected and unscheduled developments and events disrupt the best laid plans. Appreciating the limits of executive intervention and control encourages the development of a more facilitating and adaptable, rather than controlling, approach. It can also help reduce stress levels as the unforeseen becomes less surprising and threatening. Thirdly, it points to the importance of developing an ability to understand more intuitively and respond more skillfully to change, rather than relying upon techniques and procedures which hold out the overblown promise of rendering the future predictable.

How have these new insights been incorporated in this textbook? First of all, we have tried to avoid simple and one-size-fits-all answers. Students often hope to find a single simple answer (if nothing else, it promises to reduce uncertainties and stress associated with writing assignments and revising for exams). But, as we have stressed, there is no single best way to design an organization, and no single best way to manage. These are *contingent* on circumstances, capacities, and in no small measure, on chance – which should come as no great surprise as the same ill/logic applies to our own life-histories and 'choices'. We have sought to provide was some, necessarily partial, illumination of how different organizations have dealt with diverse issues, as well as the pros and cons of their decisions, again bearing in mind that every situation is distinctive and dynamic.

In line with this way of looking at organizational problems, we have included a Counterpoints feature in this edition. Its purpose is to challenge conventional wisdom and thereby stimulate reflection. The main body of the text concentrates primarily upon 'mainstream' or traditional ways of looking at organizations. As you will encounter these as a practitioner as well as in other courses you are taking, it is important to understand traditional management thinking and theories. The Counterpoints are intended to signal the existence of alternative ways of looking at organization theory and design – recall what we said earlier about different perceptions. By providing brief commentaries on traditional management perspectives, we highlight their (inevitable) limitations as a reliable basis for advancing, or at least broadening, your understanding of organization design. Our hope is that the Counterpoints will help bridge the gap between a traditional approach to studying organization and management, in which a single view of 'best practice' tends to be emphasized, and a newer, diverse and flexible way of looking at issues. The latter, as we have said, encourages ways of approaching problems from different angles in a more open way that does not presuppose definitively 'right' and 'wrong' approaches. In organizations decisions usually have to be made based on such differing and sometimes conflicting perspectives, and thus the Counterpoint feature is consistent with the differences of understanding and values encountered in real-life organizations.

Major challenges currently face world leaders, including the senior executives of corporations. Not least of these is the role of corporations in relation to climate change and, even more fundamentally, to the sustainability of the contemporary economic order. Climate change will increasingly disrupt supply-chains and economic security – problems that reach to the core of corporate activity. The bigger picture is one of material questions about sustainability. How is the spread of an affluent, resource-depleting life-style to emerging economies to be reconciled with the finite availability of natural resources? Corporations are eagerly entering and developing emerging markets but can their improved material well-being be enabled without a corresponding, radical shift in consumption patterns in the affluent, developed world? What roles – benign or malevolent – will corporations play in addressing issues of climate change and sustainability issues – issues that are of such key importance to the welfare of future generations? To what extent can the pursuit of profitable growth – which is what corporations are traditionally designed to deliver – be reconciled with demands for 'global justice' in the form of a more equitable and sustainable distribution of wealth?

These are not questions that this text addresses directly. Indeed, there is a chasm between traditional thinking about organization design and the question of how corporations might be (re)designed to make them 'fit' for the purpose of achieving ecological efficiency (e.g. attaining a zero carbon footprint) or the systematic alleviation of poverty. We have taken a small step in this direction in the Counterpoints feature insofar as this is responsive to mounting criticisms of the ethics of business. These criticisms have become more pointed in light of corporate malfeasance which contributed to, and has been exposed by, recent economic crises. The reputation and credibility of corporations and their leaders has been badly damaged and it is not easy to see how it will be restored. A number of Counterpoints identify practices where the corporate interest (for example in data gathering on customers) is poorly aligned with public and customer expectations of business conduct and public good. But, beyond these issues, there is the larger question of whether corporations will contribute to the solution, or simply exacerbate the problem, of climate change and sustainability. Is the mantra of corporate social responsibility (CSR) a superficial response to a deepening crisis of trust in corporations or is it the beginning of a reinvention of corporations – will the leopard evolve to change its spots? There are few clear cut answers to such key issues – notably the tensions between profitable growth and public service, and between ecologically sustainable growth and pressures for business expansion. That is what makes the study of organization design of such critical practical importance as well as intellectually challenging as an area of study.

Distinguishing Features of the first EMEA Edition

Many students in a typical organization theory course do not have extensive work experience, especially at the middle and upper management levels, where organization theory tends to be consciously applied. Therefore, to help engage students in the world of organizations, this book contains a number of special learning features: Look Inside chapter introductions, Book Marks, the Leading by Design feature, In Practice examples, end-of-chapter and integrative cases for student analysis, as well as the Counterpoint feature discussed in the previous section.

Look Inside The Look Inside feature introduces chapters by exploring examples of companies that have faced the organizational design issues featured in that chapter. Many of the Look Inside organizations have enjoyed success, but others have struggled despite imaginative responses to organizational challenges. These cases show that in a turbulent business environment, failure may be due to factors outside the control of management, rather than because of bad decisions or poor management skills. Look Inside examples include companies from around the world including Philips NV, Starbucks, Nokia, H&M, Interpol, Boots PLC, Toyota, and Lenovo.

Book Marks Book Marks are a unique feature of the *Organization Theory and Design* text. The Book Marks are short reviews of books that address current issues of concern for managers. They offer an introduction into the wider management literature that addresses real-life challenges of contemporary organizations, encouraging students and practical managers to extend their reading on organizational theory and design. In this EMEA edition a number of new reviews of particular European and global interest have been included, such as *Cradle to Cradle: Remaking the Way We Make Things*, *Managing Sceptically: A Critique of Organizational Fashion* and *Business as Unusual: My Entrepreneurial Journey – Profits with Principles.*

New Case Examples This edition contains a balance of case examples from different parts of the world as well as many new examples to illustrate theoretical concepts. All examples are based on real organizations. We look at companies from emerging economies, like South Africa's *Transnet*, *Johor Corporation* of Malaysia,

Chile's *Codelco*, and India's *Tata Group*. European organizations are a particular focus, with discussion of corporations such as Sweden's *H&M*, Germany's *Continental*, Britain's *Virgin Group*, Spain's *Zara*, and the European *EADS* aerospace consortium. The success of Asia-Pacific organizations is also examined, through numerous examples such as *Toyota* and *Sony* of Japan, Korea's *Samsung* and *SK Telecom*, and Australia's *Oroton*.

Leading by Design The Leading by Design feature highlights organizations that have applied new design ideas, based both on contemporary management thinking and the availability of new information and communication technologies. Typically, these organizations have undergone a major shift in organization design, strategic direction, values, or culture as they strive to be more competitive in today's turbulent global environment. Many of the Leading by Design examples illustrate company transformations toward knowledge sharing, empowerment of employees, new structures, new cultures, the breaking down of barriers between departments and organizations, and the joining together of employees in a common mission. Once again, the Leading by Design examples for this edition have been drawn from across the world. New cases include the *Rolling Stones*, *Acer Computers*, and *Singapore Airlines*.

In Practice These cases illustrate theoretical concepts in organizational settings. A number of new In Practice cases have been included, including *Apotex*, Inc of Canada, *Benpres* from Phillipines, UK's *Bedlam Puzzles*, and the Anglo-Dutch *Unilever*.

Manager's Briefcase Located in the chapter margins, this feature tells students how to use concepts to analyze cases and manage organizations.

Text Exhibits Frequent exhibits are used to help students visualize organizational relationships, and the artwork has been redone to communicate concepts more clearly.

Summary and Interpretation The summary and interpretation section tells students how the chapter points are important in the broader context of organizational theory.

Case for Analysis A number of new cases were commissioned from prominent business scholars, mainly from leading European business schools. These are tailored to chapter concepts and provide a vehicle for student analysis and discussion.

Integrative Cases The integrative cases at the end of the text are positioned to encourage student discussion and involvement, and cover cross-cutting themes that have been addressed in the text. Particular attention has been paid to selecting integrative cases from a diverse range of geographical and organizational settings, from profiling AirAsia's rapid growth through to the challenges facing public sector organizations such as the Liverpool City Council.

ABOUT THE AUTHORS

RICHARD L. DAFT

Richard L. Daft, Ph.D., is the Brownlee O. Currey, Jr., Professor of Management in the Owen Graduate School of Management at Vanderbilt University. Professor Daft has served on the editorial boards of *Academy of Management Journal, Administrative Science Quarterly,* and *Journal of Management Education.* He was the Associate Editor-in-Chief of *Organization Science* and served for three years as associate editor of *Administrative Science Quarterly.*

Professor Daft has authored or co-authored 12 books, including *Management* (Cengage/South-Western, 2010), *The Leadership Experience* (Cengage/South-Western, 2008), and *What to Study: Generating and Developing Research Questions* (Sage, 1982). He also published *Fusion Leadership: Unlocking the Subtle Forces That Change People and Organizations* (Berrett-Koehler, 2000, with Robert Lengel). He has authored dozens of scholarly articles, papers, and chapters.

Professor Daft has been involved in management development and consulting for many companies and government organizations, including the American Banking Association, Bell Canada, National Transportation Research Board, NL Baroid, Nortel, TVA, Pratt & Whitney, State Farm Insurance, Tenneco, the United States Air Force, the United States Army, J. C. Bradford & Co., Central Parking System, Entergy Sales and Service, Bristol-Myers Squibb, First American National Bank, and the Vanderbilt University Medical Center.

JONATHAN MURPHY

Jonathan Murphy is Lecturer in International Management and Organizational Analysis at Cardiff University, Wales, UK. He has combined academic study of management with professional practice in the areas of democracy and good governance. Jonathan is author of *The World Bank and Global Managerialism* (Sage, 2008), as well as numerous articles and book chapters on international management, non-profit sector, and international development issues. He is Associate Editor of *Critical Perspectives on International Business*, the first international management journal with an explicitly critical focus. He holds a doctorate in management from the Judge Business School at Cambridge University, UK.

Jonathan has worked for many years as a consultant in the area of democratic development, with clients including the United Nations, the World Bank, USAID, Britain's Department for International Development, and the European Union. Jonathan is frequently called upon to deliver international training on management and development of democratic institutions, in recent years in locales as varied as Sudan, Brussels, and Ghana. He has worked as a development and democracy expert in over twenty countries on four continents and is globally acknowledged for his expertise in parliamentary development. Prior to embarking on his academic and consulting career Jonathan worked mainly in Canada, first as a manager in non-profit organizations and later as a senior official with the Canadian parliament.

Jonathan's current main research focus is studying global business practices, as well as the emergence of globalized social formations. He is undertaking a multi-year research project in India that examines the interplay between traditional social practices and international business. Case studies include youth working in international call centres, and sanitation workers from traditionally oppressed 'castes'.

HUGH WILLMOTT

Hugh Willmott is Research Professor of Organization Studies at Cardiff Business School. He has previously held professorial positions at the Universities of Cambridge and Manchester and has been a visiting professor at the Universities of Copenhagen, Innsbruck, Lund and Uppsala. He has served on the editorial boards of *Adminstrative Science Quarterly*, *Accounting, Organizations and Society*, *Journal of Management Studies* and. He is currently serving on the boards of *Academy of Management Review* and *Organization Studies*, and is an Associate Editor for *Organization*.

Professor Willmott has authored or co-authored 21 books including *Introducing Organisational Behavior & Management* (co-edited with David Knights – Cengage Learning, 2007), *Job Redesign* (with David Knights), *Making Quality Critical* (with Adrian Wilkinson – Routledge, 1995), *Changing Managers and Managing Change* (with Mahmoud Ezzamel, Chris Green and Simon Lilley – Chartered Institute of Management Accountants - 1995), *Managing Knowledge* (with Craig Prichard, Richard Hill and Michael Chumer – Macmillan, 2000) , *Fragmenting Work: Blurring Organizational Boundaries and Disordering Hierarchies* (with Michael Marchington, Damian Grimshaw and Jill Rubery – Oxford University Press, 2004) and *The Oxford Handbook of Critical Management Studies* (with Mats Alvesson and Todd Bridgman – Oxford University Press, 2009).

Professor Willmott's consultancy experience is also wide ranging. It includes work for the European Commission on New Management Practices and the Use of New Information and Communication Technologies; the preparation of a report on the impact of organization structure on the design of information systems for the Defence Scientific Advisory Council (DSAC); inputs to IBM's 'Knowledge Management' programme and the Scottish Top Management Forum; advising Universities about their research strategies including a major strategic review of Uppsala University; and consulting with national and international companies regarding their restructuring programmes. Teaching-related activity has included involvement in programmes for the World Health Organization, McKinsey and Ernst and Young.

ACKNOWLEDGMENTS FOR THE FIRST EMEA EDITION

Textbook writing is a team enterprise, and no more so than this text which is a thorough revision of Richard Daft's original *Organization Theory and Design*, focused on the requirements of students studying within EMEA. The extensive revisions were carried out by two new co-authors, Jonathan Murphy and Hugh Willmott. In addition to the three authors, this first EMEA Edition has integrated ideas and hard work from many people to whom we are grateful. Robin Klimecki of Cardiff University greatly aided the process by cross-checking data accuracy and identifying potential new cases. Reviewers made an important contribution that has greatly strengthened the book. They praised many features, were critical of things that didn't work well, and offered valuable suggestions.

Dirk Akkermans, Assistant Professor, Department of International Economics and Business, Faculty of Economics and Business, University of Groningen

John Cullen, Department of Business & Law, National University of Ireland Maynooth

Robert Finnigan, Associate Lecturer, Bradford University School of Management

Anni Hollings, Principal Lecturer, Staffordshire University Business School

Theo Lynn, Lecturer, DCU Business School, Dublin City University

Henrik B. Sorensen, Associated Professor, Department of Economics and Management, University of Aarhus

We would also like to thank the team of international academics that contributed case studies prepared specifically for this textbook:

Mehdi Boussebaa, University of Oxford

Helga Drummond, University of Liverpool

Kate Kenny, University of Cambridge

Glenn Morgan, University of Warwick

Yuri Narayen, VU University Amsterdam

Cliff Oswick, Queen Mary University of London

Tuomo Peltonen, University of Oulu

Craig Prichard, Massey University

Maxine Robertson, Queen Mary University of London

Renee Scheerman, VU University Amsterdam

Henrik B. Sorensen, University of Aarhus

Brian Tjemkes, VU University Amsterdam

The team at Cengage UK deserves special mention. Tom Rennie guided us through the entire process with grace, patience, and professionalism. Linda Dhondy did sterling work as Development Editor, keeping the people and project on schedule while solving problems creatively and quickly.

The publisher also thanks the various copyright holders for granting permission to reproduce material throughout the text. Every effort has been made to trace all copyright holders, but if any issues remain outstanding the publisher will be pleased to make the necessary arrangements at the first opportunity. Please contact the publisher directly.

WALK THROUGH TOUR

A Look Inside cutting-edge examples of organization theory in practice within a wide range of organizations

Briefcase pithy insights provide guidance on how to analyze cases and manage organizations

In Practice practical illustrations of the text's surrounding theory in practice

Bookmark highlights of key issues impacting modern management

CHAPTER 1 ORGANIZATIONS AND ORGANIZATION THEORY 7

LEADING BY DESIGN

The Rolling Stones

They may be old, but they keep on rocking and rolling after more than 40 years in the music business. The Rolling Stones have enjoyed phenomenal commercial success in recent decades, generating billions of dollars in revenue from record sales, song rights, concert tickets, sponsorships and merchandising.

The Rolling Stones group was recently cited as one of the world's ten most enduring organizations, according to a study commissioned by Booz Allen Hamilton. One reason for the Stones' success is that the band operates like an effective global business organization. The Stones have set up a solid organizational structure, with different divisions to run different aspects of the business, such as touring or merchandising. At the top of the organization is a core top management team made up of the four band members: Mick Jagger, who acts as a sort of CEO, Keith Richards, Charlie Watts and Ronnie Wood. This core team manages a group of somewhat autonomous yet interlocking companies that include Promotour, Promopub, Promotone and Musidor each dedicated to a particular part of the overall business. At times, depending on what's happening in the organization, each company might employ only a few dozen people. When the band is touring, on the other hand, head count goes way up and the organization resembles a flourishing start-up company. Jagger himself keeps a close eye on the market-price range for concert tickets so that the band can keep their prices competitive. That sometimes means cutting costs and increasing efficiency to make sure the organization turns a profit.

The Stones also recognize the importance of interorganizational partnerships, cutting sponsorship deals with big companies such as Sprint, Anheuser-Busch and Microsoft, which reportedly paid $4 million for the rights to 'Start Me Up' for the launch of Windows 95. And they hire lawyers, accountants, managers and consultants to keep in touch with changes in the environment and manage relationships with customers (fans), partners, employees, record companies, promoters and tour sites. Jagger learned from the early days that creativity and talent aren't enough to ensure success – in the mid-1960s, the band was selling millions of records but still living hand to mouth. Today, effective control systems and widespread information sharing make sure that doesn't happen.

'You don't start to play your guitar thinking you're going to be running an organization that will maybe generate millions,' Jagger says. Yet by understanding and applying organization theory, the Rolling Stones have become one of the most successful organizations ever in the music industry – and the wealthiest rock 'n' roll band on the planet.

Source: Andy Serwer, 'Inside the Rolling Stones Inc.', *Fortune* (September 30, 2002), 58–72; and William J. Holstein, 'Innovation, Leadership, and Still No Satisfaction', *The New York Times* (December 19, 2004), Section 3, 11.

corruption scandal that has become a diplomatic crisis.[10] Lax financial and management controls at France's giant Société Générale financial services company allowed a junior trader to gamble away over a billion euros in company funds.[11] Scandals are not confined to corporations. Britain's Revenue and Customs agency managed to lose personal data on 25 million citizens – nearly half the entire population – somewhere in the mail system.[12] Pick up any major newspaper on almost any day, and there will be a story about some corporation, government department or even entire administration embroiled in some form of 'sleaze'.

While executives and officials are inclined to insist that it is a few bad apples or a single junior employee involved in all the wrongdoing, the ordinary citizen is quickly forming the opinion that all executives and senior managers are crooks.[13] The public is disillusioned with such 'leadership', and leaders – corporate and political – are under pressure to hold their organizations and employees to higher standards of ethics and competency.

Leading by Design cutting-edge examples of organizations undergoing major change within the turbulent global environment

CHAPTER 8 INFORMATION TECHNOLOGY AND CONTROL 321

they are accessible to anyone in the firm who needs them. In addition, having these systems as part of the intranet means new features and applications can easily be added and accessed through a standard browser.

Intranets can improve internal communications and unlock hidden information. They enable employees to keep in touch with what's going on around the organization, quickly and easily find information they need, share ideas and work on projects collaboratively. The most advanced intranets are linked into the proprietary systems that govern a company's business functions. Portable devices like the BlackBerry and netbooks (see Chapter 7) allow on-the-move employees to stay in touch anywhere in the world, downloading information and filing reports from hotel rooms and airport departure lounges, with data instantly available across the company.[37,38]

COUNTERPOINT 8.5

The usefulness of intranets depends upon the preparedness of employees to share and regularly update (rather than hoard) information, and also their willingness to use an impersonal channel rather than informal networks and word of mouth which are often richer and more nuanced in what they can provide. If information requires little interpretation or finesse, then an intranet can be useful so long as information is easy to find. Otherwise, intranets may be used infrequently and fall into disuse. **Discuss**

See online COUNTERPOINT 8.13

Enterprise Resource Planning

Another recent approach to information management helps pull together various types of information to see how decisions and actions in one part of the organization affect other parts of the firm. A growing number of companies are setting up broad-scale information systems that take a comprehensive view of the organization's activities. These enterprise resource planning (ERP) systems collect, process and provide information about a company's entire enterprise, including order processing, product design, purchasing, inventory, manufacturing, distribution, human resources (HR), receipt of payments and forecasting of future demand.[39] An ERP system can serve as the backbone for an entire organization by integrating and optimizing all the various business processes across the entire firm.[40]

Such a system links all of these areas of activity into a network, as illustrated in Exhibit 8.6. When a salesperson takes an order, the ERP system checks to see how the order affects inventory levels, scheduling, HR, purchasing and distribution. The system replicates organizational processes in software, guides employees through the processes step-by-step and automates as many of them as possible. For example, ERP software can automatically produce an accounts payable cheque as soon as a clerk confirms that goods have been received in inventory, send an online purchase order immediately after a manager has authorized a purchase or schedule production at the most appropriate plant after an order is received.[41]

The world's biggest and best-known travel guidebook company, Australia-based Lonely Planet, has grown from producing a stapled guide to budget travel across Asia in 1973, to selling 6 million guidebooks with 500 different titles a year, publishing in 14 different languages. For a long time the company just grew organically, adding new titles and publishing profits as it went along. But the sheer size of the business and its varied activities meant that important information inevitably fell off the table, and that led to costly errors. By 2003, in the wake of declining sales, Lonely Planet had to lay off staff for the first time. David Sadler, finance and operations director for Lonely Planet's Europe, Middle East and Africa (EMEA) region, was put in charge of developing an ERP system that could improve efficiency by

Counterpoint/Online Counterpoint deliberately provocative viewpoints that generate debate and encourage multiple perspectives for rounded learning

36 PART I INTRODUCTION TO ORGANIZATIONS

Summary and Interpretation

One important idea in this chapter is that organizations have been conceived as systems that either adapt to, or exert control over, the environment as a means of pursuing the goals of their dominant stakeholders. When understood in this way, different parts of the organization – identified as the technical core, technical support, administrative support and management are seen to perform key subsystem functions of production, maintenance, management, adaptation and boundary spanning.

The primary focus of analysis for organization theory is not the psychology of individual employees but, rather, their activities as organizational members. That is why this book is less directly concerned with topics such as supervision or the motivation of employees which are the mainstay of courses on organizational behaviour. Greater attention is paid here to how behaviour in organizations, which includes the supervision and motivation of employees, is shaped within the structure of social relations in which it occurs. Accordingly, our focus is upon the characteristics and dynamics of this structure – how they are influenced by the wider environment, and how key decisions makers attempt to manage their environment by designing effective structures. Students of this structure have conceived of its aspects and dimensions in terms of degrees of formalization, specialization, hierarchy of authority, centralization, professionalism, personnel ratios, size, organizational technology, environment, goals and strategy and culture. All of them have been invoked to offer conceptual handles for analyzing organizations and informing actions within them.

Many types of organizations exist. One important distinction is between for-profit businesses, in which managers direct their activities toward earning money for the company, and nonprofit organizations, in which managers direct their efforts toward generating some kind of social impact. Managers strive to design organizations to achieve what they deem to be effective and/or efficient. But their meaning and pursuit is often contested because different stakeholders have different priorities that they want the organization to satisfy. In the end, the priorities that are pursued will reflect the outcomes of negotiations between stakeholders, with the most privileged and well resourced of these – owners and creditors in corporations – being able to exert the greatest influence upon how organizational goals are defined and pursued. There is nothing natural or inevitable about this but a significant change – for example, in the direction of social enterprise, mutuality and sustainability – would require a shift in the balance of power accompanying organized resistance to entrenched forms of organization.

As the context of organizations becomes more turbulent and complex, managers and organizations face a range of intertwined challenges which include coping with globalization; maintaining high standards of ethics and social responsibility; achieving rapid response to environmental changes, organizational crises or new customer expectations; shifting to a technology-based workplace; and supporting diversity. These challenges are tending to prompt a shift away from highly structured systems based on a mechanical model toward looser, more flexible systems based on a more organic model. At the very least, less rigid elements are being incorporated into structured, hierarchical systems with the intention that improved communications and responsiveness will reduce costs, improve competitiveness and thereby produce added value for shareholders. One symptom of this change is the interest in redesigning companies toward the ideal of the 'learning organization' in which a premium is placed upon developing a more horizontal structure, more empowered employees, greater sharing of information, a collaborative form of strategy, and a culture that enables more rapid adaptation to changing circumstances.

Summary highlight the key learning points and how they can be applied to organizational settings

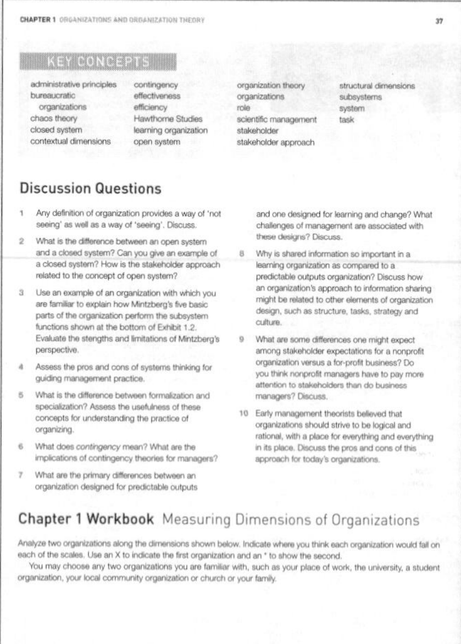
CHAPTER 1 ORGANIZATIONS AND ORGANIZATION THEORY 37

KEY CONCEPTS

administrative principles
bureaucratic organizations
chaos theory
closed system
contextual dimensions
contingency
effectiveness
efficiency
Hawthorne Studies
learning organization
open system
organization theory
organizations
role
scientific management
stakeholder
stakeholder approach
structural dimensions
subsystems
system
task

Discussion Questions

1 Any definition of organization provides a way of 'not seeing' as well as a way of 'seeing'. Discuss.

2 What is the difference between an open system and a closed system? Can you give an example of a closed system? How is the stakeholder approach related to the concept of open system?

3 Use an example of an organization with which you are familiar to explain how Mintzberg's five basic parts of the organization perform the subsystem functions shown at the bottom of Exhibit 1.2. Evaluate the stengths and limitations of Mintzberg's perspective.

4 Assess the pros and cons of systems thinking for guiding management practice.

5 What is the difference between formalization and specialization? Assess the usefulness of these concepts for understanding the practice of organizing.

6 What does *contingency* mean? What are the implications of contingency theories for managers?

7 What are the primary differences between an organization designed for predictable outputs and one designed for learning and change? What challenges of management are associated with these designs? Discuss.

8 Why is shared information so important in a learning organization as compared to a predictable outputs organization? Discuss how an organization's approach to information sharing might be related to other elements of organization design, such as structure, tasks, strategy and culture.

9 What are some differences one might expect among stakeholder expectations for a nonprofit organization versus a for-profit business? Do you think nonprofit managers have to pay more attention to stakeholders than do business managers? Discuss.

10 Early management theorists believed that organizations should strive to be logical and rational, with a place for everything and everything in its place. Discuss the pros and cons of this approach for today's organizations.

Chapter 1 Workbook Measuring Dimensions of Organizations

Analyze two organizations along the dimensions shown below. Indicate where you think each organization would fall on each of the scales. Use an X to indicate the first organization and an * to show the second.

You may choose any two organizations you are familiar with, such as your place of work, the university, a student organization, your local community organization or church or your family.

Key Concepts highlighted throughout with a detailed glossary at the back of the text

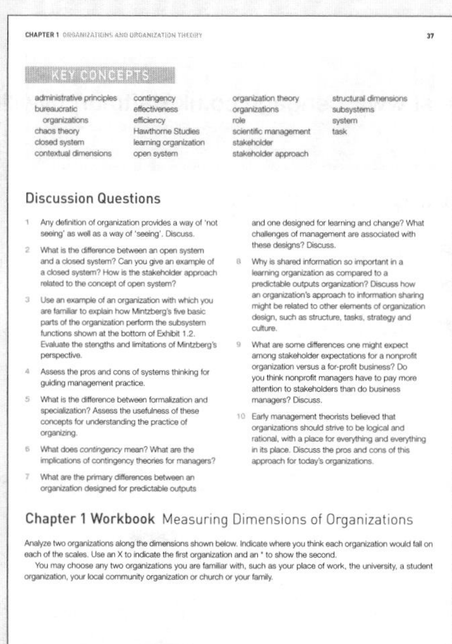

KEY CONCEPTS

administrative principles
bureaucratic organizations
chaos theory
closed system
contextual dimensions
contingency
effectiveness
efficiency
Hawthorne Studies
learning organization
open system
organization theory
organizations
role
scientific management
stakeholder
stakeholder approach
structural dimensions
subsystems
system
task

Discussion Questions

1 Any definition of organization provides a way of 'not seeing' as well as a way of 'seeing'. Discuss.
2 What is the difference between an open system and a closed system? Can you give an example of a closed system? How is the stakeholder approach related to the concept of open system?
3 Use an example of an organization with which you are familiar to explain how Mintzberg's five basic parts of the organization perform the subsystem functions shown at the bottom of Exhibit 1.2. Evaluate the strengths and limitations of Mintzberg's perspective.
4 Assess the pros and cons of systems thinking for guiding management practice.
5 What is the difference between formalization and specialization? Assess the usefulness of these concepts for understanding the practice of organizing.
6 What does contingency mean? What are the implications of contingency theories for managers?
7 What are the primary differences between an organization designed for predictable outputs and one designed for learning and change? What challenges of management are associated with these designs? Discuss.
8 Why is shared information so important in a learning organization as compared to a predictable outputs organization? Discuss how an organization's approach to information sharing might be related to other elements of organization design, such as structure, tasks, strategy and culture.
9 What are some differences one might expect among stakeholder expectations for a nonprofit organization versus a for-profit business? Do you think nonprofit managers have to pay more attention to stakeholders than do business managers? Discuss.
10 Early management theorists believed that organizations should strive to be logical and rational, with a place for everything and everything in its place. Discuss the pros and cons of this approach for today's organizations.

Chapter 1 Workbook Measuring Dimensions of Organizations

Analyze two organizations along the dimensions shown below. Indicate where you think each organization would fall on each of the scales. Use an X to indicate the first organization and an * to show the second.

You may choose any two organizations you are familiar with, such as your place of work, the university, a student organization, your local community organization or church or your family.

Discussion Questions carefully prepared questions help tease out the key issues

CASE FOR ANALYSIS

Breed's Tipping Point: Headed towards Success or Failure?

By Brian Tjemkes, Renee Scheerman & Yuri Narayen, *VU University Amsterdam*

Breed: A Creative Communications Agency

On 23 May 2008 Breed was officially recognized by the Dutch KvK, six months later than the company started doing business. As Lisa Varkevisser, one of the members joked: 'We chose to use a cooperative as a legal form, because it is relatively easy and quick to incorporate, but it took us half a year to make Breed official.' Breed is a creative agency settled in Amsterdam, centre of the communication and commercial field in the Netherlands. Its core businesses are to accomplish marketing and communication; they sell products and services related to advertising, concept development of events, commercials, online business and they initiate activities pertaining to art, culture and music. Breed consists of six founding members; Scott van der Velden, Cyril Stom, Marcel Ossendrijver-Bisschops, Lisa Varkevisser, Edward den Ouden and Jean Pierre Kin.

Breed's Start-Up

The rent of business space on 1 September 2007 in the Maple Leaf factory was the starting point of Breed. During September and October 2007 the six members of the Breed cooperative met each other frequently. All of them knew one another from previous jobs at various advertising and communication agencies. Together the six founders of Breed hit upon the idea of starting a company in which freelancers were united.

On the 1st of January 2008 Breed officially became a company. In this month Breed got their first order; developing a web portal for The Ster (foundation of ether commercials). Because Breed acquired its first order, the 'terms and conditions' had to be written. This was the first official document signed by a client. Fuelled by this instant success, other organizational matters also demanded decision-making; at that time, Breed's legal form was unclear, a website was non-existent, as well as the requirement for a brochure to promote the company. Breed only existed based on the informal connection between the members. The cooperative UA as a legal form was established on the 26th of February 2008. A cooperative is an 'autonomous association of persons united voluntarily to meet their common economic, social and cultural needs and aspirations through a jointly-owned and democratically-controlled enterprise' UA means that members are locked out for liability and that no recover rights exist on the Breed members (i.e. six founders). It was also decided that the six board members would each receive one-sixth shares of the profits and that Breed always remains intellectual owner of designed concepts. The digital brochure was accomplished on 26th of March 2008. The official Breed web log, www.bestofbreed.nu, went live on 8th of May. On this web log the members update their soul mates, clients and fans about their activities. Although Breed did not yet officially exist for the Dutch government (KvK), the first invoice was sent to The Ster at the end of March. But, it took untill May 23 to complete the 'act and regulation' and the notation at the KvK. After achieving this milestone it was finally possible to hire an accountant. Lacking knowledge and skills on running a business, the members of Breed decided to establish a Board of Advice. The board of advice consisted of three members with organizational, personnel, and legal backgrounds. They had a first meeting on 12th of February 2008 and on the 20th of March 2008 all six core Breed members presented themselves and their business plans to the Board of Advice. With the help of the Board, Breed formulated their business strategy on 20th of May. After these initial activities Breed was ready to start doing business.

Breed's Environment

Breed is a creative communications agency. A creative agency is a company that offers one or many communicative disciplines, like advertising, development of events, commercials, online communication and textual or graphic communications. In the past decade, several developments and trends have been noticeable in the industry of creative communication agencies, contributing to the creation of new agencies, intensified competition, and new strategies.

Case for Analysis chapter-ending cases provide real-world settings for analysis and assessment

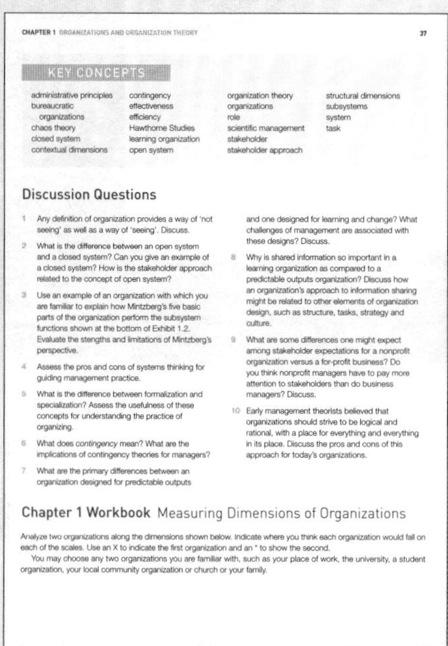

CHAPTER 1 ORGANIZATIONS AND ORGANIZATION THEORY 37

KEY CONCEPTS

administrative principles
bureaucratic organizations
chaos theory
closed system
contextual dimensions
contingency
effectiveness
efficiency
Hawthorne Studies
learning organization
open system
organization theory
organizations
role
scientific management
stakeholder
stakeholder approach
structural dimensions
subsystems
system
task

Discussion Questions

1 Any definition of organization provides a way of 'not seeing' as well as a way of 'seeing'. Discuss.
2 What is the difference between an open system and a closed system? Can you give an example of a closed system? How is the stakeholder approach related to the concept of open system?
3 Use an example of an organization with which you are familiar to explain how Mintzberg's five basic parts of the organization perform the subsystem functions shown at the bottom of Exhibit 1.2. Evaluate the strengths and limitations of Mintzberg's perspective.
4 Assess the pros and cons of systems thinking for guiding management practice.
5 What is the difference between formalization and specialization? Assess the usefulness of these concepts for understanding the practice of organizing.
6 What does contingency mean? What are the implications of contingency theories for managers?
7 What are the primary differences between an organization designed for predictable outputs and one designed for learning and change? What challenges of management are associated with these designs? Discuss.
8 Why is shared information so important in a learning organization as compared to a predictable outputs organization? Discuss how an organization's approach to information sharing might be related to other elements of organization design, such as structure, tasks, strategy and culture.
9 What are some differences one might expect among stakeholder expectations for a nonprofit organization versus a for-profit business? Do you think nonprofit managers have to pay more attention to stakeholders than do business managers? Discuss.
10 Early management theorists believed that organizations should strive to be logical and rational, with a place for everything and everything in its place. Discuss the pros and cons of this approach for today's organizations.

Chapter 1 Workbook Measuring Dimensions of Organizations

Analyze two organizations along the dimensions shown below. Indicate where you think each organization would fall on each of the scales. Use an X to indicate the first organization and an * to show the second.

You may choose any two organizations you are familiar with, such as your place of work, the university, a student organization, your local community organization or church or your family.

Workbook experiential exercises encourage team learning and skills development

1.0

INTEGRATIVE CASE 1.0

CIRCUS OZ (A)

We have to think very carefully about...whether the values and the culture of our organization can engage with the corporate sector in a way that furthers the aims of our company without diluting them.
—Linda Mickleborough, General Manager, Circus Oz

In early 2002, Linda Mickleborough, general manager of Australia's Circus Oz, had to decide how to respond to an offer by its major government sponsor (the Australia Council) to fund the creation of a new position of director of development. The decision should have been an easy one for a number of reasons. First, the Australia Council had strongly encouraged the country's major performing arts organizations to hire development professionals to expand their funding from corporate donors – at least partly as a way to reduce these organizations' reliance on government support. Second, the council was offering to underwrite the cost of the position for a period of two years. Third, Mickleborough had found the ideal candidate for the position in Paul McGill, a senior management consultant at Deloitte & Touche who had done *pro bono* consulting for Circus Oz in the past. During her interview with McGill, his passion for Circus Oz and his excitement about the prospect of developing the company's strategic alliances and partnerships with corporate sponsors was transparent.

The problem for Circus Oz, however, was that a competitive salary for a talented development professional like McGill could easily be close to twice what the highest paid performers or managers at Circus Oz currently received – a fact confirmed by the suggestions offered by the Australia Council about the level of compensation necessary to attract the calibre of person it envisioned in such a position. In its early years, all employees of Circus Oz were paid the same salary. Though this changed over time, even in 2002 the highest paid person earned about 50 per cent more than the lowest paid. Mickleborough was acutely aware of the potential damage a larger disparity might wreak on the company's morale and culture. While Circus Oz had grown professionally, artistically, and financially over the years, this success had been based on deeply held egalitarian and democratic values that had shaped both the artistic and operational practices of the company.

Despite the fact that Paul McGill might easily bring in contributions many times his salary, hiring him at anything close to the going rate seemed to fly in the face of everything Circus Oz stood for. Aside from the concerns about salary, Mickleborough also faced nagging questions about whether McGill's corporate background would fit with, and be accepted by, the rest of the staff at Circus Oz. Anticipating the havoc that such a departure from Circus Oz's bohemian culture and egalitarian wage structure might wreak on the company, Mickleborough recounted the image that her colleague, Artistic Director Mike Finch, had conjured up as they contemplated the type of person who might be hired as a director of development: 'They'll be driving up in a new BMW and dropping in for a couple of hours to hand over the corporate cheque that they'd gathered that week and then cruising off again to the beach house . . . while all the artists and performers are still struggling along on basic equity wages'.

A final complication surrounding the position was the actual decision-making process. As general manager of Circus Oz, Mickleborough was the primary person responsible for dealing with the administrative and financial issues facing the organization. However, consistent with the company's strong egalitarian ethos, its governance was based on norms of broad participation and a tradition of consensus building. Hence, any decision about the development position and/or Paul McGill would have to be approved by the member-dominated board of directors.

Hilary Stockton prepared this case under the supervision of Professor James Phills as the basis for class discussion rather than to illustrate either effective or ineffective handling of an administrative situation. It is intended to be used in conjunction with the videocase *Circus Oz: The Development* Director SI-69V.

Integrative Cases longer cases integrate learning by addressing themes and concepts from across the text

ABOUT THE WEBSITE

Visit the Organizational Theory and Design companion website at **www.cengage.co.uk/daftmurphywillmott** to find valuable teaching and learning material including:

FOR LECTURERS:

- Instructor's Manual
- ExamView Testbank
- PowerPoint Slides
- Additional Case Study Material

FOR STUDENTS:

- Revision Tests
- Flashcards
- Key Concepts

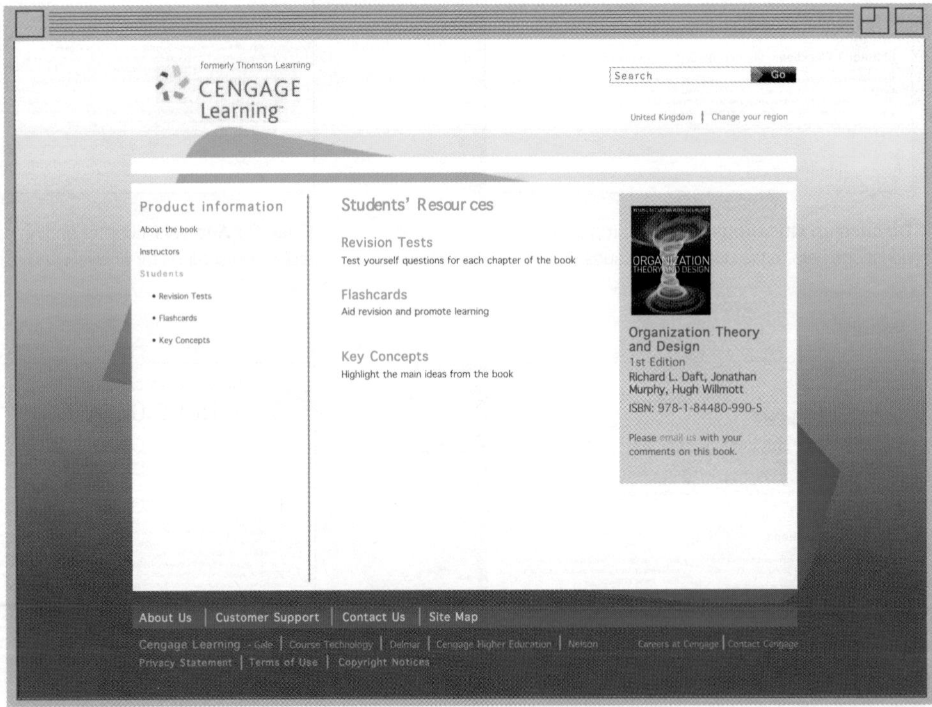

PART I

INTRODUCTION TO ORGANIZATIONS

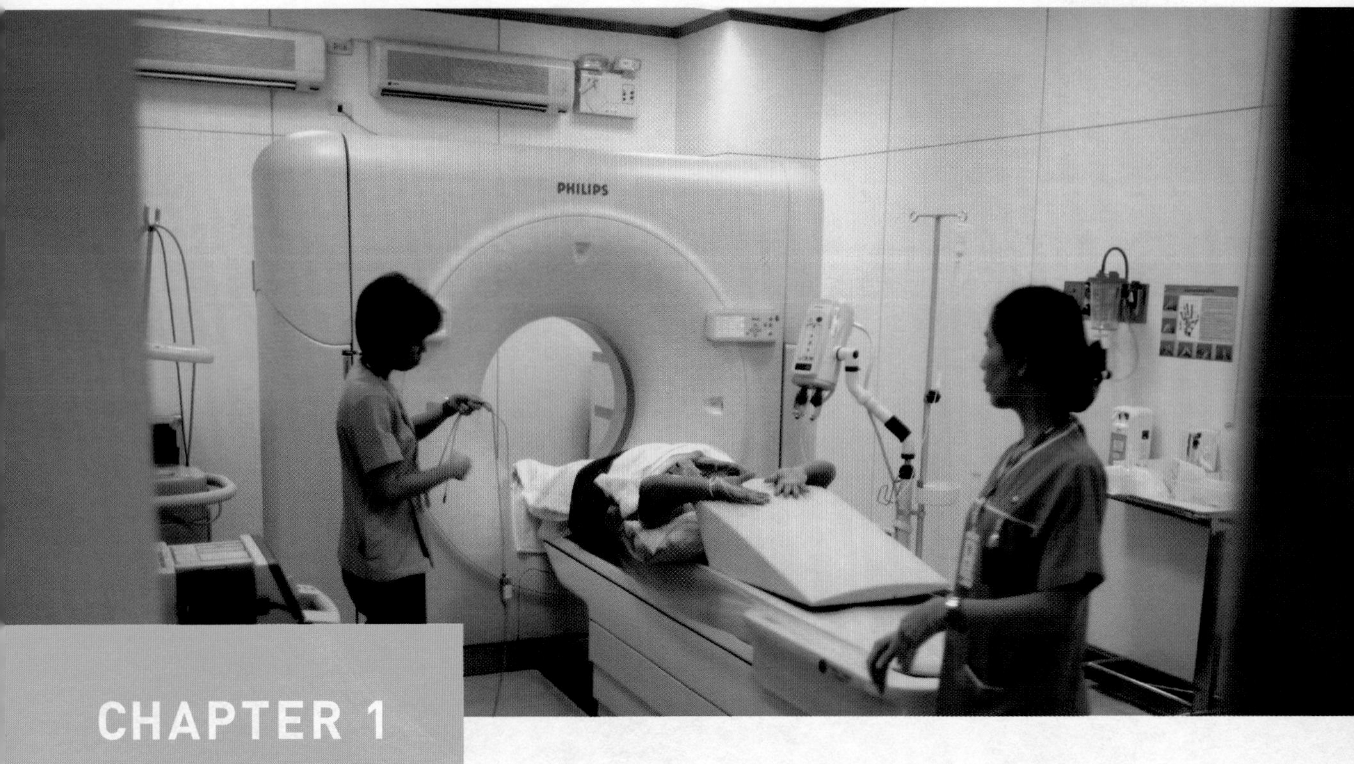

CHAPTER 1

ORGANIZATIONS AND ORGANIZATION THEORY

A LOOK INSIDE

Philips NV

Philips was one of the world's first genuine multinationals. Founded in Eindhoven, Netherlands by Gerard Philips in 1891, the company initially manufactured light bulbs, seizing the opportunity of widespread home and business electrification. Electricity soon brought opportunities for inventing and selling further electrical devices, and during much of the twentieth century, no European company seized market opportunities better than Philips. The relatively small size of Holland's domestic market pushed the company to seek new markets on the continent and eventually beyond. By the mid-1980s, the company was active in fourteen different divisions ranging from the original lighting sector to large appliances and the new field of computers. Philips' product development laboratories were unparalleled, developing cutting edge electrical equipment across the company's vast product range.

But as is often the case in business, at the height of Philips' success, storm clouds were forming on the horizon. Several different factors were beginning to work against the company as it approached its second century.

One issue was the very loose organizational structure that the company was forced to adopt when it internationalized. Before the great era of trade and market liberalization that began in the 1970s, it was simply not possible to centralize functions globally. Indeed, during the Second World War, when Holland was occupied by the German Nazis, international branches of Philips basically operated entirely independently. Even in normal times, companies wishing to enter different countries' markets were typically forced to set up fully functional national units, with their own manufacturing, marketing and distribution systems.

The national units that had to be set up tended to become autonomous power bases. In theory this could have been beneficial, if innovative approaches were developed and tested in one country and then rolled out internationally, as was the case for example for the Anglo-Dutch consumer products firm Unilever.[1] But consumer electronics are different from household products; they are costly to develop, and tend not to require tailoring to individual markets; thus centralized product development tends to be the preferred approach. Autonomy sometimes reached extremes, for example when Philips in North America decided to manufacture early video recorders based on a competitor.

Another problem was bureaucracy and inefficiency. Philips was so successful, for so long, that workers and managers began to see their positions as jobs-for-life. Employment grew and grew, ultimately Philips had over 300,000 employees worldwide. Eindhoven itself was every bit the company town; Philips took on numerous social projects ranging from the Philips library and theatre to the PSV Eindhoven football team, which under Philips' benevolent sponsorship became one of the giants of European club soccer. Philips product development division seemed to lose its knack for creating products that fit customer needs. Its early forays into computers, in particular, were not competitive with either the American giants like IBM and later Compaq, or the emerging brands from the Far East.

By the 1980s, Japan had emerged from its early postwar avatar as producer of cheap copies of western consumer goods. In motorcycles, then the automobile industry, and fatefully for Philips, in electronics, Japan began producing flashy, competitively priced but well-made products. The Matsushita conglomerate, in particular, with brands such as Toshiba, as well as Sony Corporation, began to develop the same kind of positive reputation amongst consumers that Philips once enjoyed, whereas Philips products started to be viewed as expensive and behind the times.

Philips' bottom line suddenly turned red. Despite fitful efforts to cut costs in the late '80s, by 1990 the company had run up an accumulated deficit of $2.6 billion. PSV Eindhoven had won the European Cup in 1988, but on the eve of its hundredth anniversary, its sponsor Philips was in real danger of disappearing underneath this sea of red ink.[2]

Philips turned to a new company president, Jan Timmer, who slashed the company's workforce by 50,000, got out of the computer business altogether, terminated a number of unprofitable joint ventures, and reoriented the company towards Asian production facilities in place of increasingly costly Europe. Timmer's hard-nosed strategy stemmed some but not all the bleeding. In 1996, Sony, Philips biggest competitor, generated sales of $43 billion with 150,000 employees, while Philips managed only $37 billion with almost twice as many workers. In 1996, and once again in 2001, the company changed its top management, but the same cycle of job cuts, divestments, market upticks and then disappointing losses continued. In 2001 the company lost €2.5 billion on sales down 15 per cent from the previous year.[3] The competitive situation was even more dire, as Korean brands like LG had joined the Japanese giants as global competitors, cleaning up the cost-conscious market segment where Sony and Toshiba had a stranglehold on the most affluent customers.

The enigma of Philips was that while the company's engineers brought many of electronic technology's most important innovations to market (for example, the audio cassette, the compact disc *and* the DVD), it didn't seem able to take commercial advantage of the breakthroughs, with Far Eastern companies quickly adopting the most important inventions, and making money out of them where Philips seemed incapable. In the early years of the new millennium, Philips resolved to move away from being a manufacturing-driven company towards one that would be customer-driven, a change in direction that involved a much greater focus on what insiders called 'The Marketing Journey'.[4] Building from this approach, Philips developed the slogan, 'Sense and Simplicity', reflecting not only an external marketing tool but also a new ethos of product development. Products would be innovative, but they also needed to be simple and easy to use. Right across the product spectrum, from mass-market consumer products like electric toothbrushes to the most sophisticated medical equipment like the cardiovascular X-ray, Philips would apply this same approach. Simplicity didn't mean basic, however, but rather well-designed. The company tried innovative approaches like appointing a 'simplicity board' that brought in renowned designers to help the company think 'outside the box' in product development.[5]

From 2004 onwards, Philips' fortunes seemed to be on the upswing. Finally, the company seemed to be doing well with its innovations. Medical systems and consumer electronics sales were up 9 per cent and 10 per cent respectively, but temporary growth blips like that had been seen before. What was more important, sales from newly introduced products rose sharply. In the media area, 70 per cent of sales were of products introduced in the previous two years, unusual for a field with typically long product cycles. Company-wide, the proportion of sales derived from products introduced in the previous two years rose from one-quarter in 2003 to over half in 2006.

From 2005 to 2007, the company won numerous awards for its products from its main dealers, companies like Wal-Mart in the US, Dixons in Britain and Carrefour in Europe. The bottom line picked up too.[6] Group revenues rose an average of over 6 per cent per year between 2003 and 2007, and earnings were up 9 per cent annually in the same period. Share price easily outperformed the Dow Jones index between 2003 and 2007. Finally, brand valuation, a crucial indication of how well a company is able to manage and valorize its intellectual property, rose by 60 per cent to nearly $8 billion in the three years to 2007.

By early 2008, when the company moved to simplify its organizational structure into three core divisions of consumer, healthcare and lighting, the company's future seemed brighter than for a long time. However, Philips still has its detractors. The company still doesn't have a 'segment killer' product like Apple's iPod, nor does it dominate a single product area such as Nokia in the mobile phone business. Some analysts still argue the company has too many brands and thus doesn't leverage a single global name like Nokia and Sony, for example. The next few years will start to tell whether Philips has weathered the storm of the last years of its first century, and can move from strength to strength in its second hundred years, or whether its recent successes are more like rearranging the deckchairs on the *Titanic*.

Organization Theory in Action

Topics

Many of the topics covered in this book are illustrated in the Philips case. Consider, for example, the company's failure to respond to or control such elements as competitors and customers in the fast-paced external environment; its difficulties implementing strategic and structural changes to help the organization attain

Philips NV

Philips was one of the world's first genuine multinationals. Founded in Eindhoven, Netherlands by Gerard Philips in 1891, the company initially manufactured light bulbs, seizing the opportunity of widespread home and business electrification. Electricity soon brought opportunities for inventing and selling further electrical devices, and during much of the twentieth century, no European company seized market opportunities better than Philips. The relatively small size of Holland's domestic market pushed the company to seek new markets on the continent and eventually beyond. By the mid-1980s, the company was active in fourteen different divisions ranging from the original lighting sector to large appliances and the new field of computers. Philips' product development laboratories were unparalleled, developing cutting edge electrical equipment across the company's vast product range.

But as is often the case in business, at the height of Philips' success, storm clouds were forming on the horizon. Several different factors were beginning to work against the company as it approached its second century.

One issue was the very loose organizational structure that the company was forced to adopt when it internationalized. Before the great era of trade and market liberalization that began in the 1970s, it was simply not possible to centralize functions globally. Indeed, during the Second World War, when Holland was occupied by the German Nazis, international branches of Philips basically operated entirely independently. Even in normal times, companies wishing to enter different countries' markets were typically forced to set up fully functional national units, with their own manufacturing, marketing and distribution systems.

The national units that had to be set up tended to become autonomous power bases. In theory this could have been beneficial, if innovative approaches were developed and tested in one country and then rolled out internationally, as was the case for example for the Anglo-Dutch consumer products firm Unilever.[1] But consumer electronics are different from household products; they are costly to develop, and tend not to require tailoring to individual markets; thus centralized product development tends to be the preferred approach. Autonomy sometimes reached extremes, for example when Philips in North America decided to manufacture early video recorders based on a competitor.

Another problem was bureaucracy and inefficiency. Philips was so successful, for so long, that workers and managers began to see their positions as jobs-for-life. Employment grew and grew, ultimately Philips had over 300,000 employees worldwide. Eindhoven itself was every bit the company town; Philips took on numerous social projects ranging from the Philips library and theatre to the PSV Eindhoven football team, which under Philips' benevolent sponsorship became one of the giants of European club soccer. Philips product development division seemed to lose its knack for creating products that fit customer needs. Its early forays into computers, in particular, were not competitive with either the American giants like IBM and later Compaq, or the emerging brands from the Far East.

By the 1980s, Japan had emerged from its early postwar avatar as producer of cheap copies of western consumer goods. In motorcycles, then the automobile industry, and fatefully for Philips, in electronics, Japan began producing flashy, competitively priced but well-made products. The Matsushita conglomerate, in particular, with brands such as Toshiba, as well as Sony Corporation, began to develop the same kind of positive reputation amongst consumers that Philips once enjoyed, whereas Philips products started to be viewed as expensive and behind the times.

Philips' bottom line suddenly turned red. Despite fitful efforts to cut costs in the late '80s, by 1990 the company had run up an accumulated deficit of $2.6 billion. PSV Eindhoven had won the European Cup in 1988, but on the eve of its hundredth anniversary, its sponsor Philips was in real danger of disappearing underneath this sea of red ink.[2]

Philips turned to a new company president, Jan Timmer, who slashed the company's workforce by 50,000, got out of the computer business altogether, terminated a number of unprofitable joint ventures, and reoriented the company towards Asian production facilities in place of increasingly costly Europe. Timmer's hard-nosed strategy stemmed some but not all the bleeding. In 1996, Sony, Philips biggest competitor, generated sales of $43 billion with 150,000 employees, while Philips managed only $37 billion with almost twice as many workers. In 1996, and once again in 2001, the company changed its top management, but the same cycle of job cuts, divestments, market upticks and then disappointing losses continued. In 2001 the company lost €2.5 billion on sales down 15 per cent from the previous year.[3] The competitive situation was even more dire, as Korean brands like LG had joined the Japanese giants as global competitors, cleaning up the cost-conscious market segment where Sony and Toshiba had a stranglehold on the most affluent customers.

The enigma of Philips was that while the company's engineers brought many of electronic technology's most important innovations to market (for example, the audio cassette, the compact disc *and* the DVD), it didn't seem able to take commercial advantage of the breakthroughs, with Far Eastern companies quickly adopting the most important inventions, and making money out of them where Philips seemed incapable. In the early years of the new millennium, Philips resolved to move away from being a manufacturing-driven company towards one that would be customer-driven, a change in direction that involved a much greater focus on what insiders called 'The Marketing Journey'.[4] Building from this approach, Philips developed the slogan, 'Sense and Simplicity', reflecting not only an external marketing tool but also a new ethos of product development. Products would be innovative, but they also needed to be simple and easy to use. Right across the product spectrum, from mass-market consumer products like electric toothbrushes to the most sophisticated medical equipment like the cardiovascular X-ray, Philips would apply this same approach. Simplicity didn't mean basic, however, but rather well-designed. The company tried innovative approaches like appointing a 'simplicity board' that brought in renowned designers to help the company think 'outside the box' in product development.[5]

From 2004 onwards, Philips' fortunes seemed to be on the upswing. Finally, the company seemed to be doing well with its innovations. Medical systems and consumer electronics sales were up 9 per cent and 10 per cent respectively, but temporary growth blips like that had been seen before. What was more important, sales from newly introduced products rose sharply. In the media area, 70 per cent of sales were of products introduced in the previous two years, unusual for a field with typically long product cycles. Company-wide, the proportion of sales derived from products introduced in the previous two years rose from one-quarter in 2003 to over half in 2006.

From 2005 to 2007, the company won numerous awards for its products from its main dealers, companies like Wal-Mart in the US, Dixons in Britain and Carrefour in Europe. The bottom line picked up too.[6] Group revenues rose an average of over 6 per cent per year between 2003 and 2007, and earnings were up 9 per cent annually in the same period. Share price easily outperformed the Dow Jones index between 2003 and 2007. Finally, brand valuation, a crucial indication of how well a company is able to manage and valorize its intellectual property, rose by 60 per cent to nearly $8 billion in the three years to 2007.

By early 2008, when the company moved to simplify its organizational structure into three core divisions of consumer, healthcare and lighting, the company's future seemed brighter than for a long time. However, Philips still has its detractors. The company still doesn't have a 'segment killer' product like Apple's iPod, nor does it dominate a single product area such as Nokia in the mobile phone business. Some analysts still argue the company has too many brands and thus doesn't leverage a single global name like Nokia and Sony, for example. The next few years will start to tell whether Philips has weathered the storm of the last years of its first century, and can move from strength to strength in its second hundred years, or whether its recent successes are more like rearranging the deckchairs on the *Titanic*.

Organization Theory in Action

Topics

Many of the topics covered in this book are illustrated in the Philips case. Consider, for example, the company's failure to respond to or control such elements as competitors and customers in the fast-paced external environment; its difficulties implementing strategic and structural changes to help the organization attain effectiveness; difficulties coping with the problems of large size and bureaucracy; lack of adequate cost controls; and an outmoded corporate culture that stifled innovation and change. These are illustrative of the issues with which organization theory is concerned.

COUNTERPOINT 1.1

Note how these topics tend to take a managerial focus and also to assume that problems are the same for everyone. Those who lost their jobs at Philips might well question this view. They might challenge the legitimacy of a system that resulted in such poor performance. What about the accountability of executives to their employees as well as to their shareholders? Employees bore the brunt of the poor decision-making; but they had little input into the strategic decision-making process. Organization theory extends beyond a managerial perspective to ask more fundamental questions about how and why organizations are designed the way that they are and may also explore alternative designs. Design is reducible to a technical matter; it is an inherently political one that involves the distribution of power and opportunity. Whatever design is calculated to be most efficient or effective, it will reflect the values and priorities of its architects. Implementation of the design will be contingent upon the political will to implement and the capacity to overcome resistance to it. **Discuss**

Of course, the concepts of organization theory are not limited to firms like Philips. All companies and other organizations – from the largest to struggling start-ups – undergo changes that can be illuminated and informed by theories of organization design. Organization theory is no less relevant to public sector and nonprofit organizations, including central and local government departments, Non-Governmental Organizations (NGOs), arts organizations, charities and so on. In different ways, all face challenges comparable to Philips, even if they are accountable to politicians or trusts rather than shareholders, and are generally more influenced by an ethos of public or charitable service rather than private gain.

As an organization manager, keep these guidelines in mind:

Do not ignore the external environment or protect the organization from it. Because the environment is unpredictable, do not expect to achieve complete order and rationality within the organization. Strive for a balance between order and flexibility.

The story of Philips is important because it demonstrates that organizing involves continuous challenges in the face of uncertainty and change. The world does not stop still and no organization – not even tax departments or undertakers – are protected from changes of technologies, conventions, customer preferences, availability of supplies, etc. In this sense, organizations are vulnerable; lessons are not learned automatically, and organizations are only as strong – ethically as well as economically and technically – as their decision makers who take primary responsibility for shaping their structures and cultures. Organizations are not static. Not only are they continuously adapting to shifts in the external environment but they try to control those changes and, in doing so, contribute to changes in the environments of other organizations. Surveys of top executives indicate that coping with rapid change is the most common problem facing managers and organizations.[7] Organizations face the challenge of finding ways of changing themselves and/or changing their environments to become technically, economically and ethically more responsive and effective.

COUNTERPOINT 1.2

The term 'organizations' is repeatedly used in everyday life as well as in this text. How are we to interpret it? When we say 'organizations face challenges' or 'the company failed to . . .' we probably do not mean all the people who work in that organization or company. In fact, organizations are often very diverse with different departments and factions pulling in different directions as well as attempting to cooperate with each other.

Organizations are often also hierarchical and undemocratic. That means that it is only a handful of people who actually determine how 'challenges' are to be 'faced' or how 'failure' is to be addressed. In corporations, executive decision-makers are typically accountable primarily to the owners, or shareholders and creditors. Decisions that they make may pay attention to other stakeholders insofar as they are relevant for the profitable growth of the business. These decisions may also be coloured by executives' own priorities and preferences, including any material or career advantages that flow from the decisions they make.

When reading this book, therefore, it is relevant to take acount of what may be termed the 'political economy' of organizations. **Discuss**

Current Challenges

Some specific challenges are dealing with globalization, maintaining high standards of ethics and social responsibility, responding rapidly to environmental changes and customer needs, managing the digital workplace and supporting diversity.

Globalization With rapid advances in technology and communications, the time it takes to exert influence around the world from even the most remote locations has been reduced from years to only seconds. Markets, technologies and organizations are becoming increasingly interconnected.[8] It is now more feasible for companies to locate different parts of the organization wherever it makes the most business sense: top leadership in one country, technical brainpower and production in other locales, depending upon calculations of where is best for cutting costs, generating revenues and thereby increasing the return on capital invested to shareholders. A related trend is to contract out some functions to organizations in other countries or to partner with foreign organizations to gain global advantage. India's Wipro Ltd. used to sell cooking oils; today, its more than 72,000 employees develop sophisticated software applications, design semiconductors and manage back-office solutions for giant companies from all over the world. Many of Intel's new chip circuits are designed by companies in India and China. These organizations can do the job for 50 to 60 per cent less than companies based in more developed, but more expensive, capitalist economies, creating new advantages as well as increased competitive pressures.[9] Companies large and small are searching for the structures and processes that can help them reap the advantages of global interdependence and minimize the disadvantages.

Ethics and Social Responsibility Issues of ethics and social responsibility – relating to concerns about ecological sustainability, and not just corporate survival – are becoming increasingly important, and corporations, in particular, are being expected to take a lead on addressing these issues. At the same time, the list of executives and major corporations involved in financial and ethical scandals casts a shadow over corporate life. The sordid story of high-flying Enron Corporation, where managers admitted they inflated earnings and hid debt through a series of complex partnerships, was hardly unprecedented but has, hopefully, been a loud wake-up call. Executives profited handsomely from the fraud at Enron, but when the company collapsed, employees and average investors lost billions. Arthur Andersen LLP, the company's auditor, was found guilty of obstruction of justice for improperly shredding documents related to the Enron investigation. Elsewhere, the UK's flagship defence contractor, BAe, has been embroiled in a multi-billion pound

The Rolling Stones

They may be old, but they keep on rocking and rolling after more than 40 years in the music business. The Rolling Stones have enjoyed phenomenal commercial success in recent decades, generating billions of dollars in revenue from record sales, song rights, concert tickets, sponsorships and merchandising.

The Rolling Stones group was recently cited as one of the world's ten most enduring organizations, according to a study commissioned by Booz Allen Hamilton. One reason for the Stones' success is that the band operates like an effective global business organization. The Stones have set up a solid organizational structure, with different divisions to run different aspects of the business, such as touring or merchandising. At the top of the organization is a core top management team made up of the four band members: Mick Jagger, who acts as a sort of CEO, Keith Richards, Charlie Watts and Ronnie Wood. This core team manages a group of somewhat autonomous yet interlocking companies that include Promotour, Promopub, Promotone and Musidor each dedicated to a particular part of the overall business. At times, depending on what's happening in the organization, each company might employ only a few dozen people. When the band is touring, on the other hand, head count goes way up and the organization resembles a flourishing start-up company. Jagger himself keeps a close eye on the market-price range for concert tickets so that the band can keep their prices competitive. That sometimes means cutting costs and increasing efficiency to make sure the organization turns a profit.

The Stones also recognize the importance of interorganizational partnerships, cutting sponsorship deals with big companies such as Sprint, Anheuser-Busch and Microsoft, which reportedly paid $4 million for the rights to 'Start Me Up' for the launch of Windows 95. And they hire lawyers, accountants, managers and consultants to keep in touch with changes in the environment and manage relationships with customers (fans), partners, employees, record companies, promoters and tour sites. Jagger learned from the early days that creativity and talent aren't enough to ensure success – in the mid-1960s, the band was selling millions of records but still living hand to mouth. Today, effective control systems and widespread information sharing make sure that doesn't happen.

'You don't start to play your guitar thinking you're going to be running an organization that will maybe generate millions,' Jagger says. Yet by understanding and applying organization theory, the Rolling Stones have become one of the most successful organizations ever in the music industry – and the wealthiest rock 'n' roll band on the planet.

Source: Andy Serwer, 'Inside the Rolling Stones Inc.', *Fortune* (September 30, 2002), 58–72; and William J. Holstein, 'Innovation, Leadership, and Still No Satisfaction', *The New York Times* (December 19, 2004), Section 3, 11.

corruption scandal that has become a diplomatic crisis.[10] Lax financial and management controls at France's giant Société Générale financial services company allowed a junior trader to gamble away over a billion euros in company funds.[11] Scandals are not confined to corporations. Britain's Revenue and Customs agency managed to lose personal data on 25 million citizens – nearly half the entire population – somewhere in the mail system.[12] Pick up any major newspaper on almost any day, and there will be a story about some corporation, government department or even entire administration embroiled in some form of 'sleaze'.

While executives and officials are inclined to insist that it is a few bad apples or a single junior employee involved in all the wrongdoing, the ordinary citizen is quickly forming the opinion that all executives and senior managers are crooks.[13] The public is disillusioned with such 'leadership', and leaders – corporate and political – are under pressure to hold their organizations and employees to higher standards of ethics and competency.

See online
COUNTERPOINT 1.9

Speed of Responsiveness A third significant challenge for organizations is to respond quickly and decisively to environmental changes, organizational crises and shifting customer expectations. For much of the twentieth century, organizations operated in relatively stable conditions. There was little need to search for new ways to cope with increased competition, volatile environmental shifts or changing customer demands. Today, globalization and advancing technology has accelerated the pace at which organizations in all industries must adapt their internal structures and systems in order to keep rolling out new products and services that are sufficiently competitive.

Companies that relied on mass production and distribution techniques have had to adjust to customer demands, often fuelled by leaner and more nimble competitors, for the tailoring of products and services to their specific requirements. Reflecting the importance attributed to 'customization' and branding, the financial basis of today's economy is *information*, not machines and factories. Intangible assets, including corporations' investments in people as well as financial products, become increasingly important relative to tangible assets. In the mid-1900s tangible assets represented 73 per cent of the assets of nonfinancial corporations in the United States. By 2002, the percentage had shrunk to about 53 per cent, and it continues to decline.[14] Knowledge involved in designing and coordinating the manufacture of products and the delivery of services becomes increasingly important. In this process, it becomes clearer that, ultimately, it is employees and their knowledge, not the means of production or of service delivery, who provide the best chance of organizational prosperity. At the same time, as demonstrated by the Enron and Société Générale scandals, among many others that came to light as a result of the global financial crisis of 2007–2009, the line between making appropriate use of knowledge and indulging in out-and-out gambling with other people's money, or even illegal schemes has become ever more blurred.[15]

COUNTERPOINT 1.3

If this point is accepted, why do you think that employees are typically able to exert so little influence over key corporate decision-making and what are the implications of this for organizational theory and design? **Discuss**

The Digital Workplace Many traditional managers feel awkward in today's technology-driven workplace. Organizations have been flooded by information technology that affects how they are designed and managed. In today's workplace, many employees perform much of their work on computers and may work in virtual teams, connected electronically to colleagues around the world. In addition, organizations are becoming enmeshed in electronic networks. More and more business takes place by digital processes over a computer network rather than in physical space. End-to-end digital supply-chain networks are used to keep in touch with customers, take orders, buy components from suppliers, coordinate with manufacturing partners and ship customized products directly to consumers. This trend toward *disintermediation* – eliminating the middleman often by consuming the unpaid time of the customer who, for example, experiences the frustration of waiting for, and dealing with, responses from call centres – is affecting every industry.[16] These developments mean that leadership in organizations increasingly needs to be technologically savvy as well as responsible for managing a web of relationships that reaches far beyond the boundaries of the physical organization to employees, suppliers, contract partners and customers.[17]

Diversity In advanced capitalist societies, today's average worker is older, and many more women, ethnic minorities and immigrants are seeking job and advancement opportunities. This development brings a variety of challenges, including fully recognizing and embracing diversity, balancing work and family concerns and coping with the differences associated with varying cultural styles. People from diverse ethnic and cultural backgrounds offer varying styles, and managing diversity may be one of the most rewarding challenges for organizations competing on a global basis. Consider the consulting firm McKinsey & Co. In the 1970s, most consultants were American, but by the turn of the twenty-first century, McKinsey's chief partner Rajat Gupta was Indian, and 60 per cent of consultants were from outside the US, coming from forty different countries.[18] But diversity is often the exception rather than the rule. Research has indicated that women's style of working may hold important lessons for success in the emerging global world of the twenty-first century but the glass ceiling which keeps women from reaching positions of top leadership remains in place.[19]

Purpose of This Chapter

The purpose of this chapter is to explore the nature of organizations and organization theory today. The next section begins with a formal definition of organization and then explores introductory concepts for describing and analyzing organizations. Next, the scope and nature of organization theory are discussed more fully. Succeeding sections examine the history of organization theory and design, the development of new organizational forms in response to change and how organization theory can be helpful in managing organizations in a period of massive challenges associated with rapid changes. The chapter closes with a brief overview of the themes to be covered in this book.

What Is an Organization?

Organizations are hard to see. We see a tall building, a computer workstation or a friendly employee; but the whole organization is vague and abstract and may be scattered among several locations, even around the world. We live in an organizational world, one that we tend to take for granted. We hardly notice that we are born in a hospital, have our birth records registered in a government agency, are educated in schools and universities, are raised on food produced in factory farms, are treated by doctors engaged in a joint practice, buy a house built by a construction company, borrow money from a bank, turn to police and fire departments when trouble erupts, receive an array of benefits from government agencies and so on.[20]

Definition

Organizations as diverse as a church, a hospital and a giant corporation like Philips have characteristics in common.

COUNTERPOINT 1.4

When we claim that 'organizations . . . have characteristics in common' it is important to reflect on what we are doing. We are attributing specific, ostensibly shared characteristics to very diverse phenomena. It is rather like saying that all employees have 'characteristics in common' – that is, they all receive payment for their contribution and, therefore, they can be analyzed in the same way. But the nature and the meaning of this payment will likely differ – for example, between a cooperative where the employees co-own and co-control the organization and a privately owned company where most employees have at best a very minimal ownership stake and no significant control. This approach risks overlooking the diversity of organizations. *They are diverse both in their composition and the conditions of their operation.* Diversity tends to be overlooked when it is assumed that one 'model' of organization is equally relevant and successful for grasping the salient features of very different kinds of organization. Or that one, 'dominant' model is readily applicable to all organizations. **Discuss**

The definition used in this book to describe **organizations** is as follows: organizations are (1) social entities that (2) are goal-directed, (3) are designed as deliberately structured and coordinated activity systems, and (4) are linked to the external environment. In the light of the Counterpoint (above) it is worth bearing in mind the particularity of this definition. Like all definitions it has limits that flow from the assumptions that are made – for example, with respect to the extent that goals are rationally determined or broadly shared. Another way to think of a 'goal' is as a notion invoked by executives to convince employees that objectives are shared and rationally deliberated rather than politically defined. See next Counterpoint.

COUNTERPOINT 1.5

It is worth stressing that this is simply one possible definition that is potentially misleading as well as illuminating.

'Social entities' This is a key point as it indicates that organizations are cultural and political as well as economic phenomena. They are 'social' all-the-way-down. To regard organizations as equivalent to machines or as technologies is to invite disaster. Organizations comprise people who, in contrast to material entities, **interpret** their situations and are capable of ignoring or **resisting**, collectively and individually, often in subtle and difficult-to-control ways, demands that are made of them.

Goal-directed This element of the definition emphasizes how activity in organizations is highly instrumental (e.g. to get paid, acquire a skill or gain in status) rather than intrinsically meaningful. That is to say, such activity is strongly influenced by individuals' calculations concerning the most effective means of achieving their ends or 'goals', whatever these may be. The idea that organizations are 'goal-directed' may be taken to imply that there is a single, consensually agreed goal. This is misleading in circumstances where there are considerable conflicts between stakeholders and between senior executives about the goal, or goals, that an organization is, or should be, pursuing. To suggest that organizations are goal-directed tends to conceal the extent to which these goals are **contested** and that whatever goal is attributed to an organization is the outcome of processes of negotiation and struggle that result in specific goals being privileged or 'hegemonized', at least for the time being. For this reason, it is necessary to place scare quotes around the idea of 'common' goals or the 'purpose' attributed to an organization.

Designed as deliberately structured and coordinated activity systems In contrast to other human 'activity systems', such as the family, it is likely that the division and coordination of labour in work organizations will be more 'deliberately structured'. For example, there will likely be formal job descriptions and reporting procedures. It would be a mistake, however, to assume that such designs are necessarily effective, or that an intended design is what operates in practice. Designs are frequently a product of ideals and/or compromises that incorporate fondly held beliefs, and they involve more or less participation in their design and cooperation in their operation from those who are expected to make the 'stuctures' work.

Linked to the external environment It is important to appreciate that organizations exist within a wider context or set of conditions. The idea of being 'linked' to the environment does not necessarily grasp the extent to which organizations are part-and-parcel of their 'environments' rather than simply connected to them. The so-called environment is shaped and changed by the organizations that comprise it. It is therefore necessary to place scare quotes around 'external environment'. **Discuss**

The key element of an organization is not a building or a set of policies and procedures; organizations are made up of people and their relationships with one another. An organization exists when people interact with one another. Recent trends in management recognize the importance of human resources, with most new approaches designed to empower employees with greater opportunities to learn and contribute as they work together toward ostensibly 'common' goals.

Managers deliberately structure and coordinate organizational resources to achieve '*the organization's purpose*' (see **Counterpoint 1.5**). However, even though work may be structured into separate departments or sets of activities, most organizations today are striving for greater horizontal coordination of work activities, often using teams of employees from different functional areas to work together on projects. Boundaries between departments, as well as those between organizations, are becoming more flexible and diffuse as companies face the need to respond to changes in the external environment more rapidly. An organization cannot exist without interacting with customers, suppliers, competitors and other elements of the 'external environment' (see **Counterpoint 1.5**). Today, some companies are even cooperating with their competitors, sharing information and technology to their mutual advantage.

Types of Organizations

Some organizations are large, multinational corporations. Others are small, family-owned shops. Some manufacture products such as automobiles or computers, whereas others provide services such as legal representation, banking or medical services. Later in this text, Chapter 7 will look at the distinctions between manufacturing and service technologies. Chapter 9 discusses size and life cycle and describes some differences between small and large organizations.

Another important distinction is between for-profit businesses and *nonprofit organizations*. With the proviso entered in the previous Counterpoint 1.5, the topics in this text are also relevant to nonprofit organizations. However, there are some important differences to keep in mind. The primary one is that the activities of managers in businesses are directed primarily at producing goods and services in order to be earning money for the shareholders of the company, whereas managers in nonprofits do not face this particular constraint but may encounter many others, such as the difficulty in securing funding or raising capital or competing with profit-making businesses. The distinctive characteristics of nonprofit organizations created by this distinction present unique challenges for organizational leaders.[21]

Financial resources for nonprofits typically come from sources such as government grants, private foundation grants and donations, rather than from the sale of products or services to customers. In businesses, managers focus on developing and positioning the organization's products and services in ways that are intended to increase sales revenues. Nonprofit organizations are responsive to demands that are inadequately met by markets. In nonprofits, services are typically provided to nonpaying clients, and a major problem for many organizations is securing a steady stream of funds as well as staff or volunteers to continue operating. Nonprofit managers are often committed to serving a large pool of potential clients with limited income. To serve these clients, they are obliged to keep organizational costs as low as possible and, in order to secure funding, must demonstrate a highly efficient use of resources.[22] As they do not have a conventional 'bottom line', it is more difficult or inappropriate to measure their performance in terms of returns on capital invested, for example. Nonprofits have to measure intangible goals such as 'improve public health' or 'make a difference in the lives of the disenfranchised'.

With these considerations in mind, many of the organization design concepts discussed throughout this book – such as setting goals and measuring effectiveness, coping with environmental uncertainty, implementing effective control mechanisms, satisfying multiple stakeholders and dealing with issues of power and conflict – are of relevance for nonprofit organizations. But, as in the case of for-profit businesses, the concepts and theories must be adapted and revised in relation to an assessment of distinct challenges and operating circumstances.

Importance of Organizations

Only a century ago, there were comparatively few organizations of any size or importance.[23] This chapter's Bookmark examines the rise of the corporation and its contemporary significance. Why have they become so important? Exhibit 1.1 lists seven reasons organizations are important to you and to society. First, organizations bring together resources to generate wealth from the production of goods and services bought by customers that could not be so readily be accomplished by individuals acting on their own or in smaller units. Putting together an aircraft carrier, for example, is an incredibly complex job involving 47,000 tons of precision-welded steel, more than 1 million distinct parts, 900 miles of wire and cable, about 40 million skilled-worker hours and more than 7 years of hard work by the organization's 17,800 employees.[24] Companies are continuously under pressure from shareholders to develop innovative ways of producing and distributing desirable goods and services more efficiently. Two ways are through e-business and through the use of computer-based manufacturing technologies. Redesigning organizational structures and management practices can also contribute to increased efficiency. Organizations create a drive for innovation rather than a reliance on standard products and outmoded ways of doing things.

Organizations adapt to and influence a rapidly changing environment. Consider Google, provider of the Internet's most popular search engine, which continues to adapt and evolve along with the evolving Internet. Rather than being a rigid service, Google is continually adding technological features that create a better service by accretion. At any time, Google's site features several technologies in development so that engineers can get ideas and feedback from users.[25] Some large businesses have entire departments charged with monitoring the 'external environment' and finding ways either to influence demand for its products and services or adapt to changes created by its competitors. Organizations such as Philips, AES Corporation, Heineken Breweries and IBM are involved in strategic alliances and partnerships with companies around the world as well as lobbying governments and regulators and committing enormous sums to the promotion of their brands in an effort to influence the environment and compete on a global scale.

Have you read this book?

The Company: A Short History of a Revolutionary Idea

BY JOHN MICKLETHWAIT AND ADRIAN WOOLDRIDGE

'The limited liability corporation is the greatest single discovery of modern times,' is one conclusion of the concise and readable book, *The Company: A Short History of a Revolutionary Idea* by John Micklethwait and Adrian Wooldridge. Companies are so ubiquitous today that we take them for granted, so it may come as a surprise that the company as we know it is a relatively recent innovation. Although people have joined together in groups for commercial purposes since ancient Greek and Roman times, the modern company has its roots in the late nineteenth century. The idea of a *limited liability company* that was legally an 'artificial person' began with the Joint Stock Companies Act, enacted by the London Board of Trade in 1856. Today the company is seen as 'the most important organization in the world'. Here are a few reasons why:

- The corporation was the first autonomous legal and social institution that was within society yet independent of the central government.
- The concept of a limited liability company unleashed entrepreneurs to raise money because investors could lose only what they invested. Increasing the pool of entrepreneurial capital spurred innovation and generally enriched the societies in which companies operated.
- The company is the most efficient creator of goods and services that the world has ever known. Without a company to harness resources and organize activities, the cost to consumers for almost any product we know today would be impossible to afford.
- Historically, the corporation has been a force for civilized behaviour and provided people with worthwhile activities, identity and community, as well as a paycheck.
- The Virginia Company, a forerunner of the limited liability corporation, helped introduce the revolutionary concept of democracy to the American colonies.
- The modern multinational corporation began in Britain in the third quarter of the 1800s with the railroads, which built rail networks throughout Europe by shipping into each country the managers, materials, equipment and labour needed.

During the past few years, it seems that large corporations have been increasingly in conflict with societies' interests. Yet large companies have been reviled throughout modern history – consider the robber barons at the beginning of the twentieth century – and the authors suggest that recent abuses are relatively mild compared to some incidents from history. Everyone knows that corporations can be scoundrels, but overall, Micklethwait and Wooldridge argue, their force has been overwhelmingly for the cumulative social and economic good.

The Company: A Short History of a Revolutionary Idea, by John Micklethwait and Adrian Wooldridge, is published by The Modern Library.

Through all of these activities, organizations create value for their owners as they deliver goods and services to customers, and provide employment to their staff. Managers are hired to analyze which parts of the operation create value and which parts do not. Ultimately it is this preoccupation that gives shape to how organizations actually cope with and accommodate today's challenges of workforce diversity and growing concerns over ethics and social responsibility, or address the question of how to motivate employees in conditions where job security is absent or under threat. The challenge is to understand organizations in ways that are capable of analyzing and addressing such issues.

EXHIBIT 1.1 Importance of Organizations

Organizations exist to do the following:

1. *Bring together resources to achieve desired goals and outcomes*
2. *Produce goods and services efficiently*
3. *Facilitate innovation*
4. *Use modern manufacturing, service, and information technologies*
5. *Adapt to and influence a changing environment*
6. *Create value for owners, customers and employees*
7. *Accommodate ongoing challenges of diversity, ethics and the motivation and coordination of employees*

Perspectives on Organizations

There are various ways to look at and think about organizations. Two important perspectives are the open-systems approach and the organizational-configuration framework.

Open Systems

One significant development in the study of organizations was the distinction between closed and open systems.[26] A **closed system** design focuses exclusively upon the organization without consideration of its dependence upon or capacity to influence elements comprising its context. In effect, from a closed systems perspective, organizations are conceived as autonomous, effectively sealed off from the outside world. Early management philosophies tended to be closed-system in approach. They took the wider context as a given and assumed the organization could be made more effective through internal design. In principle, the management of a closed system is comparatively easy if the context is stable and unchanging, and therefore predictable. Managerial attention can then be focused exclusively upon the refinement of existing structures – to cope with increases in scale, for example – rather than adapting them to a changing situation.

Open system thinking pays attention to the (open) boundary between the organization and its context. Developing a design that effectively manages the exchanges – of raw materials, people, products, etc. – across this boundary is, in an open systems perspective, considered to be key to survival and prosperity. Organizations are conceived as consumers of resources (inputs) and exporters of resources (outputs). In order to survive and prosper they are impelled to adapt to, or attempt to control, a changing environment. It is necessary to find and obtain needed resources, interpret and act on environmental change, dispose of outputs and control and coordinate internal activities in the face of environmental disturbances and uncertainty. In organizations, it can happen – surprisingly easily – that particular divisions, departments and especially top managers forget that they are part of an open system. They may, for example, isolate themselves within a self-referential culture – a 'bubble' – as they fail to pay attention to what was going on with their employees, customers, suppliers and competitors. It would seem that in our earlier example, Philips suffered through a lack of attention to environmental changes in addition to weak responsiveness to new product opportunities. The relevance of open systems thinking and designs has been underscored in recent years with regard to changes relating to the explosion of the Internet and e-business, growing diversity of the workforce and the opening up of low wage labour economies, such as China and India, and even newer (and lower-cost) entrants to the global economy like Vietnam.

COUNTERPOINT 1.6

Open systems thinking is helpful in reminding us of the interdependencies both between subsystems (e.g. 'production' and 'maintenance') as well as between the organization and what exists beyond its boundaries.

A major limitation of this thinking is that it presents an excessively neat, technical picture of how organizations operate and relate to their environment. It is worth recalling that organizations comprise people who are not necessarily willing to be compliant tools of systems. Nor are the designers of these systems necessarily able to make them operate according to apparently rational specifications.

In practice, organizing, like politics, is 'the art of the possible' based upon the available capacities and capabilities and always at the mercy of 'events'. How people 'fulfil' the 'needs' attributed to subsystems will inevitably depend upon their **own values, priorities and preconceptions.** If a set of subsystems were designed that perfectly met the 'needs' of their system, this would be achieved only by transforming employees into automotons – that is, perfectly formed cogs in a smooth-running machine. That is perhaps the ambition of designs based upon systems thinking but its failure to deal with the practicalities of organizing means that it is unrealized except in the most regimented and oppressive of corporations. And where it is nearly realized, it can be counterproductive as automotons are usually better at following procedures than responding creatively to unexpected events. **Discuss**

Exhibit 1.2 illustrates an open system. Inputs to an organization system include employees, raw materials and other physical resources, information and financial resources. The transformation process changes these inputs into something of value that can be exported back to the environment. Outputs include specific products

EXHIBIT 1.2 An Open System and Its Subsystems

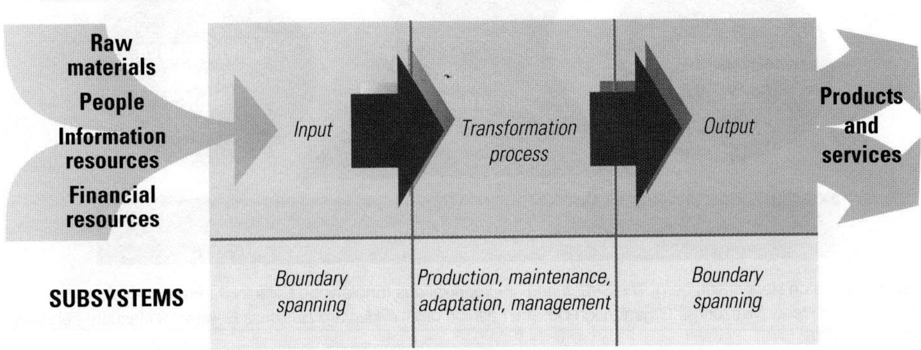

and services for customers and clients. Outputs may also include employee satisfaction, pollution and other by-products of the transformation process.

In systems thinking, each system is understood to comprise several **subsystems**, as illustrated at the bottom of Exhibit 1.2. These subsystems are identified in relation to the specific functions they are conceived to perform for organizational survival – such as production, boundary spanning, maintenance, adaptation and management. For example, in a systems perspective, the production subsystem is understood to produce the product and service outputs of the organization. Boundary subsystems are deemed responsible for enabling exchanges with the external environment. They include activities such as purchasing supplies or marketing products. Maintaining the smooth operation and upkeep of the organization's physical and human elements is understood to be performed by the maintenance subsystem. The adaptive subsystems are said to be responsible for organizational change and adaptation. Management is a distinct subsystem, responsible for coordinating and directing the other subsystems of the organization.

BRIEFCASE

As an organization manager, keep these guidelines in mind:

Design the organization so that the five basic parts – technical core, technical support, administrative support, top management, and middle management – adequately perform the subsystem functions of production, maintenance, adaptation, management and boundary spanning. Try to maintain a balance among the five parts so that they work together for organizational effectiveness.

Organizational Configuration

Systems thinking conceives of different parts of an organization being designed to perform the key subsystem functions illustrated in Exhibit 1.2. Because there are limitations with this thinking (see Counterpoint 1.7), it is necessary to keep these firmly in mind when adopting an approach that relies upon it., One framework proposed by Henry Mintzberg suggests that every organization has five parts.[27] These parts, illustrated in Exhibit 1.3, include the technical core, top management, middle management, technical support and administrative support. These five parts may vary in size and importance depending on an organization's particular environment, its technology and other factors.

Technical Core The technical core includes people who do the basic work of the organization. It performs the production subsystem function and actually produces the product and service outputs of the organization. This is where the primary transformation from inputs to outputs takes place. The technical core is the production department in a manufacturing firm, the teachers and classes in a university and the medical activities in a hospital. This core is complemented by other parts that provide technical and administrative support.

EXHIBIT 1.3 Five Basic Parts of an Organization

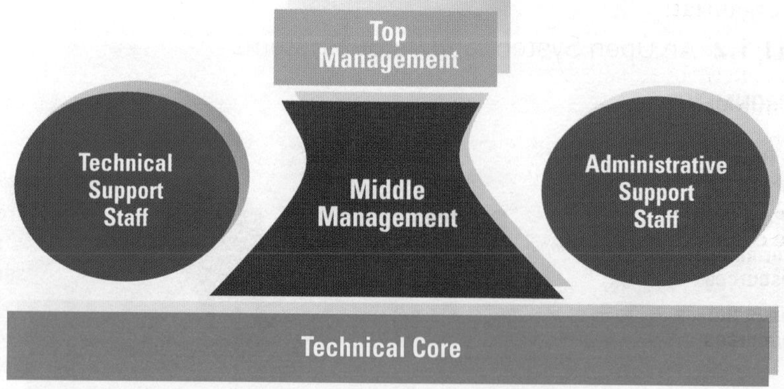

Source: Based on Henry Mintzberg, *The Structuring of Organizations* (Englewood Cliffs, N.J.: Prentice-Hall, 1979), 215–297; and Henry Mintzberg, 'Organization Design: Fashion or Fit?' *Harvard Business Review* 59 (January-February 1981): 103–116.

Technical Support Technical support employees, such as engineers and researchers, scan the environment for problems, opportunities and technological developments. Technical support is responsible for creating innovations in the technical core, helping the organization change and adapt. Technical support includes departments such as technology, research and development (R&D) and marketing research.

Administrative Support The administrative support function is responsible for the smooth operation and upkeep of the organization, including its physical and human elements. This includes human resource activities such as recruiting and hiring, establishing compensation and benefits and employee training and development, as well as maintenance activities such as cleaning of buildings and service and repair of machines. Administrative support functions include the human resource department and maintenance staff.

Management – Top and Middle Management is a function responsible for directing and coordinating other parts of the organization. Top management provides direction, strategy, goals and policies for the entire organization or major divisions. Middle management is responsible for implementation and coordination at the departmental level. In traditional organizations, middle managers are responsible for mediating between top management and the technical core, such as implementing rules and passing information up and down the hierarchy.

See online
COUNTERPOINT 1.10

In real-life organizations, the five parts are not readily distinguishable and they may serve more than one subsystem function. For example, managers coordinate and direct other parts of the system, but they may also be involved in administrative and technical support. In addition, several of the parts are involved in the *boundary spanning* function mentioned in the previous section. For example, in the administrative support realm, human resource departments are responsible for interacting with external as well as internal labour markets to find quality employees; and members of R&D departments work directly with outside organizations to learn about new technological developments.

Dimensions of Organization Design

The systems view pertains to dynamic, ongoing activities within organizations. The next step for understanding organizations is to look at dimensions that describe specific organizational design traits.

Organizational dimensions can be categorized in two types: structural and contextual, illustrated in Exhibit 1.4. **Structural dimensions** provide labels to distinguish some key, internal characteristics of an organization, such as the degree of formalization. They provide a basis for comparing the composition of organizations. **Contextual dimensions** characterize both the organization as a whole, including its size, technology, etc. and the broader organizational setting. To understand and evaluate organizations, it is important to examine both structural and contextual dimensions.[28] These dimensions of organization design interact with one another and can be adjusted to accomplish the purposes listed earlier in Exhibit 1.1.

Structural Dimensions

1 *Formalization* refers to the reliance upon written documentation in the organization. Such documentation relates to procedures, job descriptions,

EXHIBIT 1.4 Interacting Contextual and Structural Dimensions of Organization Design

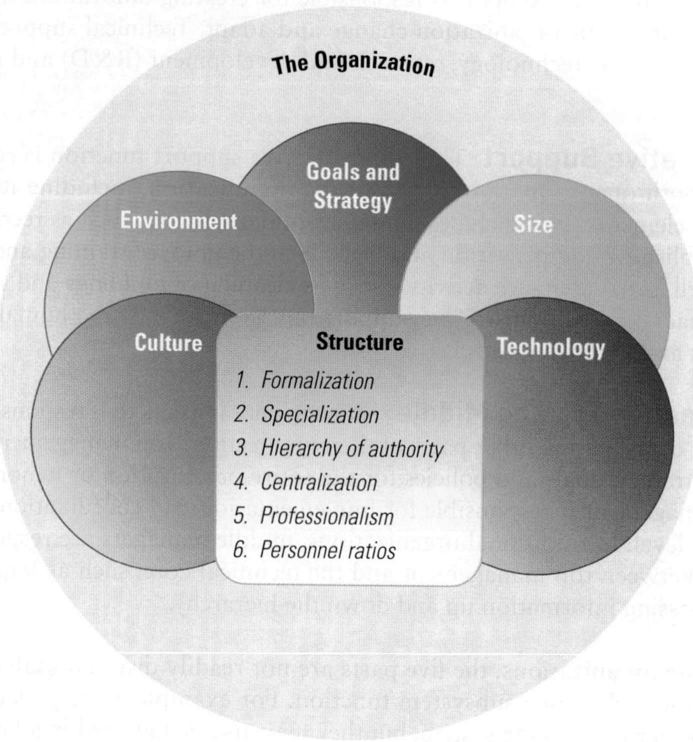

regulations and policy manuals. Larger organizations tend to score high on formalization because they have written rules to authorize and control a wide range of activity A small, family-owned business, in contrast, may have almost no written rules and would be considered 'informal' even if the personal control exercised by its head is rigid and all-encompasing.

2 *Specialization* is the degree to which organizational tasks are subdivided into separate jobs. If specialization is extensive, each employee performs only a narrow range of tasks. High levels of specialization are found on production lines where each worker is expected to become highly adept at repeatedly performing a narrow set of skills. Likewise, the division of labour amongst managers may be highly specialized.

3 *Hierarchy of authority* describes who reports to whom and the span of control for each manager. The hierarchy is depicted by the vertical lines on an organization chart, as illustrated in Exhibit 1.5. The hierarchy is related to span of control (the number of employees reporting to a supervisor). When spans of control are narrow, specialization is high and the hierarchy tends to be tall. When spans of control are wide, the hierarchy of authority will be shorter.

4 *Centralization* refers to the hierarchical level that has authority to make a decision. When decision making is kept at the top level, the organization is centralized. When decisions are delegated to lower organizational levels, it is decentralized. Organizational decisions that might be centralized at head office or decentralized to a particular division or operating unit may include the purchasing of certain types of equipment or the hiring of particular grades of employee.

As an organization manager, keep these guidelines in mind:

Think of the organization as an entity distinct from the individuals who work in it. Describe the organization according to its size, formalization, decentralization, specialization, professionalism, personnel ratios and the like. Use these characteristics to analyse the organization and to compare it with other organizations.

EXHIBIT 1.5 Organization Chart Illustrating the Hierarchy of Authority for a Community Job Training Programme

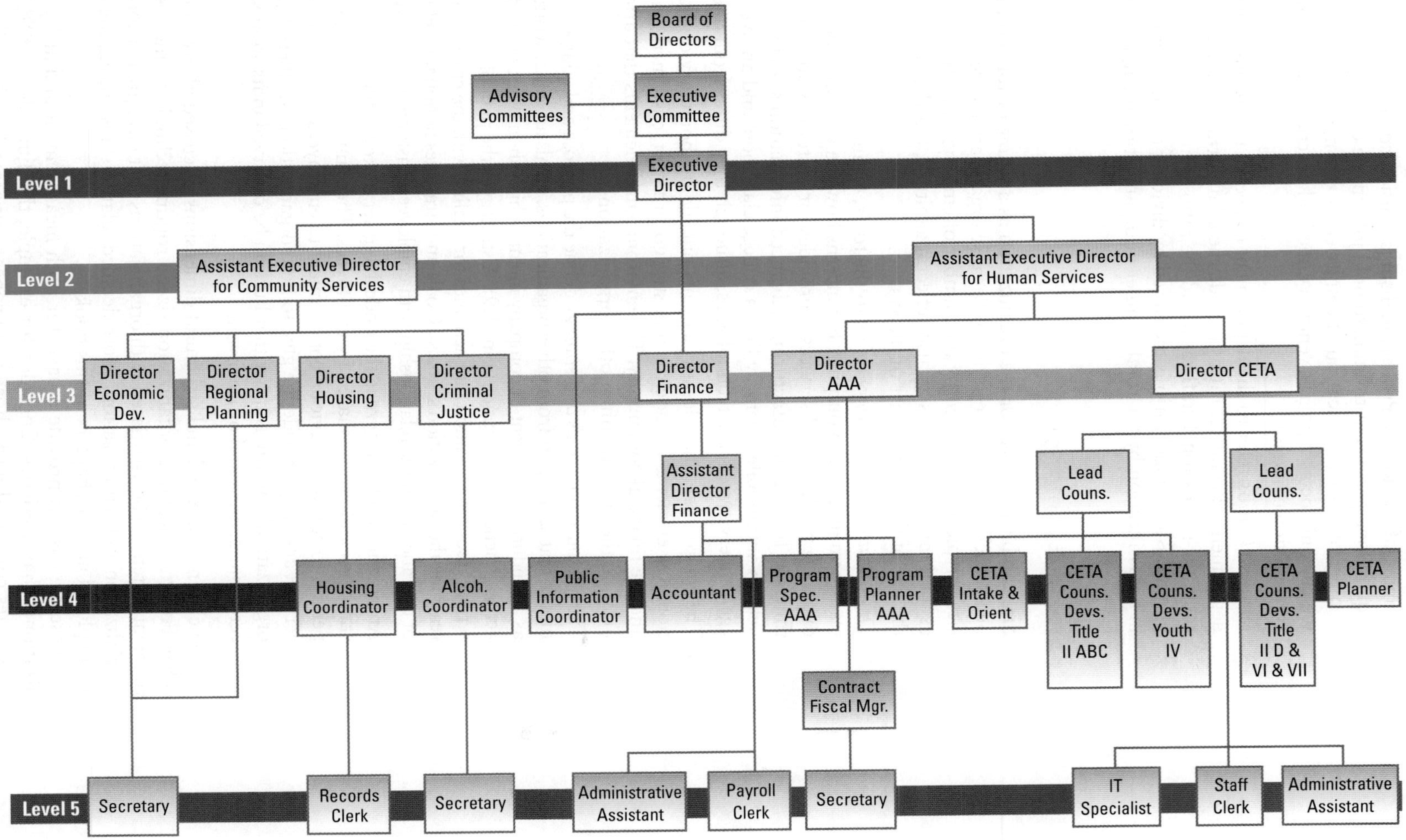

Board of Directors
Executive Committee
Advisory Committees

Level 1
Executive Director

Level 2
Assistant Executive Director for Community Services
Assistant Executive Director for Human Services

Level 3
Director Economic Dev.
Director Regional Planning
Director Housing
Director Criminal Justice
Director Finance
Director AAA
Director CETA
Assistant Director Finance
Lead Couns.
Lead Couns.

Level 4
Housing Coordinator
Alcoh. Coordinator
Public Information Coordinator
Accountant
Program Spec. AAA
Program Planner AAA
CETA Intake & Orient
CETA Couns. Devs. Title II ABC
CETA Couns. Devs. Youth IV
CETA Couns. Devs. Title II D & VI & VII
CETA Planner
Contract Fiscal Mgr.

Level 5
Secretary
Records Clerk
Secretary
Administrative Assistant
Payroll Clerk
Secretary
IT Specialist
Staff Clerk
Administrative Assistant

5 *Professionalism* is the term used to describe the level of formal education and training of employees. Professionalism is considered high when employees require long periods of training to hold jobs in the organization. The average number of years of education of employees is one measure of professionalism, which could be as high as twenty in a medical practice and less than ten in a construction company.

6 *Personnel ratios* refer to the deployment of people to various functions and departments. Personnel ratios include the administrative ratio, the clerical ratio, the professional staff ratio and the ratio of indirect to direct labour employees. A personnel ratio is measured by dividing the number of employees in a classification by the total number of organizational employees.

Contextual Dimensions

1 *Size* can be measured for the organization as a whole or for specific components, such as a plant or division. Because organizations are social systems, size is typically measured by the number of employees. Other measures such as total sales or total assets also reflect magnitude, but they do not indicate the size of the human part of the system.

2 *Organizational technology* refers to the tools, techniques and actions used to transform inputs into outputs. It concerns how the organization actually produces the products and services it provides for customers and includes such things as flexible manufacturing, advanced information systems and the Internet. An automobile assembly line, a college classroom and an overnight package delivery system are technologies, although they differ from one another.

3 The *environment* includes all elements outside the boundary of the organization. Key elements include the industry, government, customers, suppliers and the financial community. The environmental elements that affect an organization the most are often other organizations.

4 The organization's *goals and strategy* define the purpose and competitive techniques that set it apart from other organizations. Goals are often written down as an enduring statement of company intent (which should not be confused with actual practice – see Counterpoint 1.9). A strategy is the plan of action that describes resource allocation and activities for dealing with the environment and for reaching the organization's 'goals'. Goals and strategies notionally define the scope of operations and the relationship with employees, customers, and competitors.

5 An organization's *culture* is the underlying set of key values, beliefs, understandings and norms shared by employees. These underlying values may pertain to ethical behaviour, commitment to employees, efficiency or customer service, and they provide the glue to hold organization members together. An organization's culture is unwritten but can be observed in its stories, slogans, ceremonies, dress and office layout.

The eleven contextual and structural dimensions discussed above influence each other. For example, large organization size, a routine technology and a stable environment all tend to be associated with organizations that have greater formalization, specialization and centralization. More detailed relationships among the dimensions are explored in later chapters of this book.

These dimensions provide a basis for both measurement and analysis of organizational characteristics. Consider, for example, the dimensions of W. L. Gore & Associates compared with those of European supermarket chain Carrefour and governmental non-profit agencies.

W. L. Gore & Associates

When Jack Dougherty began work at W. L. Gore & Associates, Inc., he reported to Bill Gore, the company's founder, to receive his first assignment. Gore told him, 'Why don't you find something you'd like to do.' Dougherty was shocked at the informality but quickly recovered and began interrogating various managers about their activities. He was attracted to a new product called Gore-Tex, a membrane that was waterproof but breathable when bonded to fabric. The next morning, he came to work dressed in jeans and began helping feed fabric into the maw of a large laminator. Five years later, Dougherty was responsible for marketing and advertising in the fabrics group.

Bill Gore died in 1986, but the organization he designed still runs without official titles, orders or bosses. One of the key tenets of the organization is that employees (called associates) figure out what they want to do and where they think they can make a contribution. The company has some 6,000 associates in forty-five locations around the world. The plants are kept small – up to 200 people – to maintain a family atmosphere. 'It's much better to use friendship and love than slavery and whips,' Bill Gore said. Several professional associates are assigned to act as 'sponsors' for new product development, but the administrative structure is lean. Good human relations is a more important value than is internal efficiency. The company has seven times been named one of *Fortune* magazine's '100 Best Companies to Work For in America,' and Gore continues to grow and prosper.

Carrefour

Carrefour is one of the giants in today's global retailing. In 1963, Carrefour pioneered the concept of the *hypermarché*, or hypermarket in English, a concept bringing together the traditional food-based supermarket with the full-range department store, carrying items from clothes to house paint to computers; 'everything under the same roof.' The company, based in France but now operating in 26 different national markets from China to Argentina, is the world's second largest by retail sales after Wal-Mart, with over 10,000 stores worldwide, on four continents. Although in some markets Carrefour operates a number of other chains ranging from convenience stores to cash and carry warehouses, these operations are driven by the supply and distribution systems established for the hypermarket operations. Its hypermarkets all contain about the same product mix of about 60 per cent food and 40 per cent non food, with the specific products sold tailored of course to national tastes. Where Carrefour has expanded through purchasing existing chains, such as Spain's Continente chain, it has usually moved quickly to rebrand the purchased properties with the name, logo, and 'look and feel' of the Carrefour group.

Carrefour's success has been built on following its basic model quite rigidly across national markets. The company's managers are drawn from all its operating countries, but management training places a strong emphasis on creating common corporate values and understanding amongst both managers and shopfloor employees, enabling it to avoid some of the differing visions that so hampered Philips, discussed earlier in this chapter.[29]

Public Sector Organizations and Nonprofits

An even greater contrast is seen in many government agencies or nonprofit organizations that rely heavily on public funding. Nonprofits in the arts sector, for example, are typically staffed by a small number of highly dedicated employees who often find themselves overwhelmed with rules and regulations and swamped by paperwork. Employees who have to implement directives and rule changes often don't have time to read the continuous stream of memos and still keep up with their obligations to their clients.

Exhibit 1.6 provides a pictorial illustration of a number of the structural and contextual dimensions of Gore & Associates, Carrefour and the Wales Millennium Centre, a nonprofit UK regional arts centre. Gore & Associates, a medium-sized manufacturing organization, ranks low with respect to formalization, specialization

EXHIBIT 1.6 Characteristics of Three Organizations

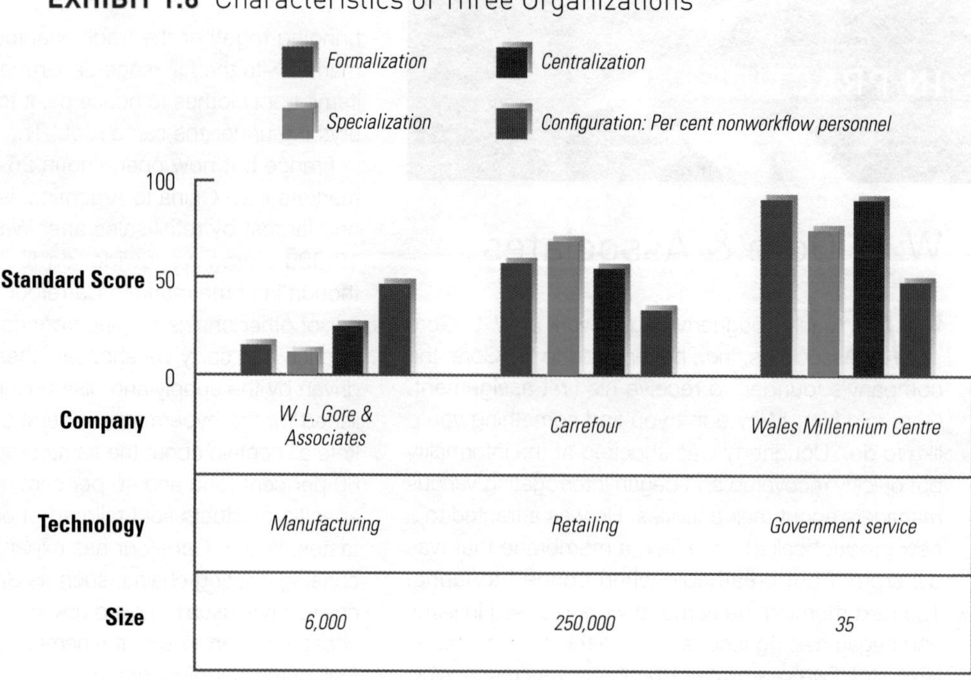

and centralization. A number of professional staff are assigned to nonworkflow activities to do the R&D needed to stay abreast of changes in the fibre industry. Carrefour is much more formalized, specialized and centralized. Cost-cutting to protect market share and increase profitability are of key importance and this is accomplished through standardization and economies of scale: 'growing market share can only be achieved on a consistent basis, if we are always locally the price leader.' The percentage of nonworkflow personnel is kept to a minimum. The Wales Millennium Centre, in contrast to the other organizations, reflects its dependent status within the nonprofit sector. The organisation has to comply with many rules and procedures and different stakeholder demands that are imposed upon it. Most employees are assigned to workflow activities, although a substantial amount of staff time is consumed in providing administration and clerical support.

BRIEFCASE

As an organization manager, keep this guideline in mind:

Consider the needs and interests of all stakeholders when setting goals and designing the organization to achieve effectiveness.

Performance and Effectiveness Outcomes

The whole point of understanding varying perspectives and the structural and contextual dimensions of organizations is to design the organization in such a way as to achieve high performance and effectiveness. At least, it would be difficult to justify the resources devoted to organizations if the outcome were low performance and ineffectiveness. In principle, managers are hired to adjust structural and contextual dimensions and organizational subsystems to most efficiently and effectively transform inputs into outputs and provide value (see Counterpoint 1.10). **Efficiency** refers to the amount of resources used to achieve the organization's goals. It is based on the quantity of raw materials, money and employees necessary to produce a given level of output. **Effectiveness** is a broader term, meaning the degree to which an organization achieves its goals.

COUNTERPOINT 1.7

When reference is made to such things as 'high performance and effectiveness', it is worth asking: effective for who and performance in relation to what criteria? Concerns with ethics and social responsibility suggest that companies have responsibilities that cannot be equated with increasing the returns to their shareholders.

Other performance measures are also important and may ultimately affect their very survival – such as the impact of corporations upon the natural environment, their contribution to improving the quality of life nationally and internationally and the legitimacy that they enjoy amongst the general public upon whom corporations ultimately depend – as employees and consumers.

It is likely that companies will come under increased regulatory and public pressure to broaden their criteria of performance and effective. For example, it may be asked how well they are performing in producing goods and services that are ecologically enhancing and sustainable rather than destructive and degrading, or how they are performing in returning the wealth generated by companies to the communities from where their resources – material and social – are drawn. **Discuss**

Whatever the objective, it relevant to take care in working out how it is going to be achieved. A clear, consensually determined objective accompanied by clear, focused goals and appropriate strategies for their attainment are important elements of successful design. Strategy, goals and approaches to measuring effectiveness will be discussed in detail in Chapter 2. However, as we have already noted, achieving effectiveness is rarely a simple matter because different people want different things For customers, the primary concern is high-quality products and services at a reasonable price, whereas employees are mostly concerned with adequate pay, good working conditions, promotion prospects and job satisfaction. Managers are faced with competing needs and the interests of various stakeholders in setting goals and striving for effectiveness. This idea of balancing the preferences of different groups has been characterized as a **stakeholder approach**. Its claim is to integrate diverse organizational activities by looking at various organizational stakeholders and what they want from the organization. A **stakeholder** is any group within or outside of the organization that has a stake in the organization's performance. The satisfaction level of each group can be assessed as an indication of the organization's performance and effectiveness.[30]

See online **COUNTERPOINT 1.11**

Exhibit 1.7 illustrates various stakeholders and what each group wants from the organization. Organizations frequently struggle to simultaneously satisfy the demands of all groups. A business might have high customer satisfaction, but the organization might have difficulties with creditors or supplier relationships might be poor. Consider the American-headquartered retail chain Wal-Mart. Customers love its efficiency and low prices, but the low-cost emphasis the company uses with suppliers and in relation to employees has caused friction. Some activist groups argue that Wal-Mart's tactics are unethical because they force suppliers to lay off workers, close factories and outsource to manufacturers from low-wage countries operating facilities with poor working conditions. One supplier said clothing is being sold at Wal-Mart so cheaply that suppliers from developed countries in Europe and North America couldn't compete even if they paid their workers nothing. The challenges of managing such a huge organization have also led to strains in relationships with employees and other stakeholder groups, as evidenced by recent gender discrimination suits and complaints about low wages.[31] And then there are other groups affected by company actions – such as communities from where the raw materials used in products sold by Wal-Mart – who do not even appear in Exhibit 1.7.

Stakeholder interests often conflict. In nonprofit organizations, the needs and interests of clients sometimes conflict with restrictions on use of government

EXHIBIT 1.7 Major Stakeholder Groups and What They Expect

funds or contributions from donors. In companies, there is conflict when unions campaign for improved conditions or wage increases that might hurt shareholders' financial returns or prompt a switch to lower-cost suppliers. Demands made by stakeholders other than shareholders and senior executives are likely to meet resistance unless they can be reconciled with increased financial returns – for example, by tying in wage increases to productivity gains or improving reliability from suppliers in return for better treatment. In reality, it is unreasonable to assume that all stakeholders can be equally satisfied or even equally treated. However, if an organization fails to manage the expectations and/or meet the demands of stakeholder groups, it is likely risking its longer term survival – by becoming a take-over target or simply going out of business – as well as failing to live up to its claims to care for its employees and customers as well as its stockholders. Research has shown that the assessment of multiple stakeholder groups is a strong indicator of organizational effectiveness, especially with respect to organizational adaptability.[32] Because profit and nonprofit organizations are generally (but not universally) concerned about their reputations amongst customers, creditors and regulators, they also put considerable resources into shaping and controlling the part of the environment comprising stakeholders' perceptions of their performance.[33]

Managers strive to at least minimally satisfy the interests of all stakeholders. Failure to do so invites disruption and loss of reputation – by suppliers, employees, customers, etc. – which is likely to prove damaging for profitable growth. When any one group becomes seriously dissatisfied, it may withdraw its support and hurt future organizational performance. Satisfying multiple stakeholders can be challenging, particularly as goals and priorities change, as illustrated by the following example.

Conflict and Compromise in the Forest Products Industry

The forest products industry literally underpins our daily lives. Wood and wood products are a crucial part of the homes we live in, especially if our houses are of wood frame construction as in much of Europe and North America. Even if they have an outer shell of brick or concrete, much of the internal framing and finishing is likely to be wood-based. And, despite the growth of electronic media, most of us still access much of our information by picking up books and newspapers, again produced from wood pulp. At the same time, many of us are shocked by visions of some of the world's great forests being logged, whether teak from the Burmese rain forest, or old growth cedar trees on British Columbia, Canada's west coast.

Nowhere are the debates about the forest industry more heated, or the stakes higher, than in Canada. The forest industry is a major job creator in the country, accounting for more than 300,000 jobs directly and 600,000 indirectly. The industry is worth 3 per cent of Canada's GDP annually, and whole communities are entirely dependent on forestry.[34] In 2008 the town of Mackenzie in northern British Columbia faced complete closure when forest products giant Abitibi Bowater indefinitely closed the community's two saw mills and a pulp mill.[35]

At the same time, Canada is home not merely to vast expanses of pristine wilderness, but also one of the world's most active and sometimes militant environmental movements. Greenpeace, the world's best known environmental group, was founded in Canada. During the 1990s, proposals to log old growth forest in Clayoquot Sound in BC led to the largest campaign of civil disobedience in Canadian history, with over 800 environmentalists arrested.[36] In addition to the conflicting perspectives of forest industry companies and workers and environmentalists, much of the country's usable timber is located on lands claimed by the country's indigenous peoples, who tend to share environmentalists' concerns about damage to their homelands, while also wanting to ensure that any development benefits their populations which are easily the poorest in Canada's generally affluent society.[37] Canada's forest products industry, therefore, is working in an extraordinarily complex environment.

After the great conflicts over Clayoquot Sound, some of Canada's more forward looking forest companies decided on a different approach from simply relying on property rights and contract enforcement through the courts. In the late 1990s, MacMillan Bloedel (MacBlo), now part of Weyerhauser, had been running into financial difficulties, caused by decline in Asian markets due to the 'Asian flu' economic downturn, a softwood lumber trade dispute with the US and difficulty selling to Europe because of environmentalists' pressure on European buyers to guarantee that all their wood came from sustainable sources. In 1997 MacBlo's new CEO Tom Stephens decided that the only way he would be able to provide value to his shareholders would be if he adopted a stakeholder approach. Stephens charged his managers to come up with a strategy that would respond to concerns about sustainability by moving to selective logging, reducing the impact of logging on forest land biodiversity, and signing up to the sustainable forestry certification scheme run by the Forest Stewardship Council (FSC). He developed long-term dialogue and partnerships with environmental groups, effectively widening the company's sphere of accountability to include both environmental groups and First Nations communities, as well as its workforce.[38]

Tom Stephens' approach turned out to be the only game in town. Since 2000, the area of forest land certified as managing sustainably has risen tenfold, and major retailers in Europe and North America from B&Q to Hallmark Cards have committed to use wood products sourced exclusively or almost exclusively from independently certified sources like FSC.[39] Although frictions continue between environmental organizations and the forest products industry, these are usually seen on both sides as part of the process of negotiating compromises that will allow forest companies to contribute to the economy while helping to protect the planet for future generations.

The Evolution of Organization Theory and Design

Organization theory is not a collection of facts or an operation manual; it is a way of thinking about, and informing action within, organizations. 'Facts' are, in this sense, contingent upon the particular kind of thinking that goes into specific theories of organization. Different theories of organization – for example, closed systems theories and open systems theories – provide alternative ways to represent and analyze organizations. Each theory makes its own claims about the accuracy and depths of its analysis relative to commonsense views or alternative theories. Drawing upon different theories, organization scholars point to, or suggest the relevance of, diverse features, patterns and regularities which they make available to the rest of us. For this reason, the specific 'facts' generated from the research are not, in practice, as important as the general patterns and insights into the realities of organizing and organizations.

Historical Perspectives

Organization design and management practices have varied over time in response to changes in the larger society.

The modern era of management theory began with the classical management perspective in the late nineteenth and early twentieth century. The emergence of capitalism brought with it the development of the factory system which posed problems that earlier organizations had not encountered. Factories became a new source of wealth creation. Enclosing large numbers of workers in factories, where their productive activity could be more readily controlled, made it possible to extract significant surpluses from their labour. That was because workers could be supervised closely as they performed repetitive but highly productive tasks. By combining workers in factories, goods could be mass produced to reach a mass market, with the prospect of earning a handsome profit on each item sold as a consequence of the long hours and low wages of factory workers. This was not a recipe for good industrial relations and the outcome was the formation of unions and the development of ideologies that demanded fairer treatment and less autocratic forms of control. In turn, the scale of the factories and the competition between producers stimulated interest in how to design and manage work in order to better incentivize cooperation as a means of further increasing productivity and profitability.

The outcome was the so-called '**classical perspective**' which sought to apply rational calculations to turn organizations into efficient, well-oiled machines. This perspective is associated with the development of extended hierarchies and bureaucratic procedures of control. Pioneered by Frederick Winslow Taylor, his principles of **scientific management** postulate that decisions about organizations and job design should be based on a precise, 'scientific' study of individual situations to determine which method of doing a job delivers the greatest output.[40] On this basis, managers standardize procedures for doing each job, select workers with the most appropriate abilities, train them to follow the standard procedures, carefully plan work and provide wage incentives to increase output. Favouritism and amateurism were to be replaced by careful research, meritocracy and standardization.

For example, Taylor studied the unloading of iron from railcars and reloading finished steel for the Bethlehem Steel plant in Pennsylvania, USA, in 1898. He calculated that with 'correct' movements, tools and sequencing, each man was capable of loading 47.5 tons per day instead of the typical 12.5 tons. He also worked out an incentive system that paid each man \$1.85 per day for meeting the new standard, an increase from the previous rate of \$1.15. Finally, he devised a means of

'Scientific management, the charge went, pitted workers against one another, made them claw at each other for the privilege of being one of Taylor's 'first class men'. It broke up the comradely fellow-feeling, the respect of one man for his brother, that lay behind the labour movement at its best . . .

Scientific management was degrading. In reducing work to instructions and rules, it took away your knowledge and skill. In standing over you with a stop-watch, peering at you, measuring you, rating you, it treated you like a side of beef. You weren't supposed to think. Whatever workmanly pride you might once have possessed must be sacrificed on the altar of efficiency, your role only to execute the will of other men paid to think for you. You were a drone, fit only for taking orders.'

R. Kanigel (1997), *The One Best Way: Frederick Winslow Taylor and the Enigma of Efficiency*, New York: Little, Brown and Company, p. 534.

identifying the workers most capable – morally as well as physically – of maximizing their earnings using this system – that is, what Taylor calls his 'first class man'. In Taylor's view, workers sought employment for one reason alone – to earn money. So, he believed that by enabling them to be more productive – by linking output directly to payment – he could reconcile the demands of two key stakeholders: employees who obtained substantially improved wages and shareholders who received massively increased surpluses while ensuring that the basis of this reconciliation was impartial and therefore fair.

However, Taylor's scientific management was based upon closed systems thinking. He overlooked how employees develop a sense of identity and meaning outside of the workplace. Despite a strong interest in earning money from their employment, many were unwilling to accept their treatment as living machines who simply executed repetitive tasks conceived by others and, incentivized to work as rapidly as possible by piece-work payments systems. Nor, when economic conditions changed, were workers willing to accept cuts in their pay in order to preserve surpluses for the owners. An unintended consequence of Taylor's treatment of workers as human machines programmed to be maximally productive was to facilitate their solidarity in opposition to management. Workers, it turned out, would not necessarily do what they were told.

Another subfield of the classical perspective took a broader look at the organization. Whereas scientific management focused primarily on the technical core and its immediate support functions – on the organization of work performed on the shop floor – **administrative principles** looked at the design and functioning of the organization as a whole. For example, Henri Fayol proposed fourteen principles of management, such as 'each subordinate receives orders from only one superior' (unity of command) and 'similar activities in an organization should be grouped together under one manager' (unity of direction). These principles have formed the foundation for many aspects of modern management practice and organization design.

The scientific management and administrative principles approaches provided potent ideas for establishing high productivity and increasing prosperity. Administrative principles in particular contributed to the development of **bureaucratic organizations**, which emphasized designing and managing organizations on an impersonal, ostensibly rational basis by establishing clearly defined authority and responsibility, formal recordkeeping and uniform application of standard rules. Although the term *bureaucracy* has taken on negative connotations, the introduction of bureaucratic characteristics into the sphere of work revolutionized its organization. Notably, it replaced nepotism and other forms of favouritism with impartial processes that were indifferent to rank, gender, colour and so on. It is worth recalling how much red tape and tedious procedure ensures that people are treated equally and are not able to curry favour or queue-jump on the basis of their status. One problem with the classical perspective, however, concerns its limited attention to the social context and human needs.

Early work on industrial psychology and human relations tended to be marginalized by the dominance of scientific management and administrative principles. A major breakthrough occurred with a series of experiments at a Chicago electricity company, which came to be known as the **Hawthorne Studies**. Interpretations of the results of these experiments concluded that positive treatment of employees, even by simply acknowledging their presence and contribution, improved their motivation and productivity. That this had not been widely acknowledge prior to these studies gives a strong indication of the social distance between managers and workers. The Hawthorne Studies laid the groundwork for subsequent work examining 'the human side of enterprise' including leadership, motivation and, more recently the diverse aspects of human resource management. Even so, the classical approach has remained the primary approach to organization design and functioning, at least in contexts where change was minimal or predictable. It was only in the 1970s and early 1980s, as markets for commodities and finance became less stable, and international competition intensified, that the classical approach was challenged by organizations that incorporated alternative design principles, such as teamworking as they came under pressure to achieve increased flexibility, rapid response to the customer, more adaptive and well motivated employees and improved products with shorter life-cycles.[41] Further organizational adaptations and innovations have occurred to exploit the opportunity of the Internet and other advances in information technology and other developments, such as the opening up of China and the ex-Soviet Union, have called for new management perspectives and more flexible approaches to organization design.

As an organization manager, keep these guidelines in mind:

Be cautious when applying something that works in one situation to another situation. All organizational systems are not the same. Use organization theory to identify the appropriate goals, strategy and management systems for each organization.

Don't Forget the Context Principles of scientific management and administrative assume that there is 'one best way' of organizational design. But this 'closed systems' thinking disregards the variability of context. It suggests that the **contingencies** facing the retail division of a conglomerate are equivalent to those of a manufacturing division; or that the same principles are appropriately applied to the design of the financial procedures for an entrepreneurial Internet firm like eBay or Google as that of a large food processing plant. Contingency means that what structure or system is appropriate, or effective, depends upon the particular circumstances or context of its design. For organizations to be effective, this logic suggests, there must be a 'goodness of fit' between the 'structural' and 'contextual' dimensions.[42] What works varies according to circumstances. For example, an inflexible mechanistic approach may be viable in a setting that is unchanging but it cannot be expected to work as effectively in a different, more complex or turbulent setting. Where there is a predictable environment and use of a routine technology, for example, a 'classical' approach based bureaucratic control procedure, a hierarchical structure and formal communication may be viable, at least so long as there is no significant change in the context. But unchanging contexts are becoming less common. For most organizations, at least some aspect of their environment is uncertain and thus demands a degree of innovation and flexibility where more free-flowing management processes are likely to develop. In short, and against the 'one best way' philosophy, a contingent approach suggests that the correct management approach is contingent on the organization's situation.

COUNTERPOINT 1.8

The claim that an approach is 'correct' should be heeded with some caution. Even if a 'good fit' between an organization and its environment is attained this does not necessarily make it 'correct' in the sense of legitimate. It would therefore be better to say that the approach is 'viable'. Whether it is 'correct' will depend upon what evaluation is made of the 'best fit'. It should not be assumed that the pragmatic test of 'best fit' is the only criteria of 'correctness'. So, for example, the 'fit' may be good but the possible negative impact upon the quality of life of employees may lead them to contest its 'correctness'. **Discuss**

Contemporary Organization Design

To a great extent, managers and organizations are still imprinted with the hierarchical, bureaucratic approach that arose more than a century ago. Yet numerous challenges – of globalization, diversity, ethical concerns, rapid advances in technology, the rise of e-business, a shift to knowledge and information as organizations' most important form of capital and the growing expectations of workers for meaningful work and opportunities for personal and professional growth – prompt a questioning of the adequacy of forms of classical thinking. The perspectives of the past do not necessarily provide a road map for steering today's organizations. In the contemporary context, managers are endeavouring to design and orchestrate new responses that, in general, are less mechanical and more organic in formulation.

Newtonian science suggests that the world functions as a well-behaved machine, a view that has underpinned much management thinking about organizations.[43] The science of **chaos theory**, in contrast, suggests that relationships in complex, adaptive systems – including organizations – are nonlinear and made up of numerous interconnections and divergent choices.[44] This is a world full of uncertainty, characterized by surprise, rapid change and confusion. Managers can't measure, predict or control in traditional ways the unfolding drama inside or outside the organization. At the same time, chaos theory also recognizes that this randomness and disorder occurs within certain larger patterns of order. The ideas of chaos theory suggest that organizations should be viewed more as natural systems than as well-oiled, predictable machines.

Many organizations are attempting to shift from strict vertical hierarchies to more flexible, decentralized structures that emphasize horizontal collaboration, widespread information sharing and adaptability. This shift can even be seen in modern armies, once considered the ultimate example of rigid, top-down organizations. Modern armies, much like modern corporations, find themselves fighting a new kind of war that demands a new approach to how it trains, equips and uses soldiers. Fighting a fluid, fast-moving and fast-changing terrorist network means that junior officers in the field who are experts on the local situation have to make quick decisions, learning through trial and error and sometimes departing from standard procedures.

Although the stakes might not be as high, business and nonprofit organizations today also need greater fluidity and adaptability. Many managers are redesigning their companies to become so-called **learning organizations**. The principle of the learning organization is for communication and collaboration to be actively promoted so that everyone is engaged in identifying and solving problems, enabling the organization to continuously experiment, improve and increase its capability. The learning organization is, in principle, based on equality, open information, little hierarchy and a culture that encourages adaptability and participation, enabling ideas to bubble up from anywhere that can help the organization seize opportunities and handle crises. In a learning organization, the essential value is problem solving, as opposed to the traditional organization designed for predictable outcomes.

Efficient Performance versus the Learning Organization

As managers struggle toward the learning organization, they are engaged in changing the structural dimensions of organizations. Exhibit 1.8 compares organizations designed for efficient performance with those designed for continuous learning by looking at five elements of organization design: structure, tasks, systems, culture and strategy. As shown in the exhibit, all of these elements are interconnected and influence one another.

As an organization manager, keep these guidelines in mind:

When designing an organization for learning and adaptation in a turbulent environment, include elements such as horizontal structure, shared information, empowered roles, collaborative strategy and adaptive culture. In stable environments, organizations can achieve efficient performance with a vertical structure, formal information and control systems, routine tasks, competitive strategy and a stable culture.

From Vertical to Horizontal Structure The most common organizational structure, based upon classical principles, has been one in which activities are grouped together by common work from the bottom to the top of the organization. Generally little collaboration occurs across functional departments, and the whole organization is coordinated and controlled through the vertical hierarchy, with decision-making authority residing with upper-level managers. In stable conditions, this structure is consistent with cost-efficient production and in-depth skill development, and the hierarchy of authority provides a sensible mechanism for supervision and control in large organizations. However, in a rapidly changing environment, the absence of delegation results in top executives becoming overloaded with decision-making as they struggle to respond sufficiently rapidly to problems or opportunities.

In the learning organization, the vertical structure that creates distance between managers at the top of the organization and workers in the technical core is, in principle, collapsed if not disbanded. Structure is created around horizontal workflows or processes rather than departmental functions. The vertical hierarchy is dramatically flattened, with perhaps only a few senior executives in traditional support functions such as finance or human resources. Self-directed teams are the fundamental work unit in the learning organization. Boundaries between functions are eroded as teams include members from several functional areas.

From Routine Tasks to Empowered Roles Another shift in thinking relates to the degree of formal structure and control placed on employees in the performance of their work. Recall that scientific management advocated precisely defining each job and how it should be performed. A **task** is a narrowly defined piece of work assigned to a person. In traditional organizations, tasks are broken down into specialized, separate parts, as in a machine. Knowledge and control of tasks are centralized at the top of the organization, and employees are expected to do as they are told. A **role**, in contrast, is a part in a dynamic social system. A role-holder has discretion and responsibility, allowing the person to use his or her discretion and ability to achieve an outcome or meet a goal. In learning organizations, employees play roles in team or departments, and these roles may be continually redefined or adjusted. There are comparatively few rules or procedures, and knowledge and immediate control of tasks are located with workers rather than with supervisors or top executives. Employees are encouraged to take care of problems by working with one another and with customers.

From Formal Control Systems to Shared Information In mechanical designs, formal systems are often implemented to manage the growing amount of complex information and to detect deviations from established standards and

EXHIBIT 1.8 Two Ideal-Type Organization Design Approaches

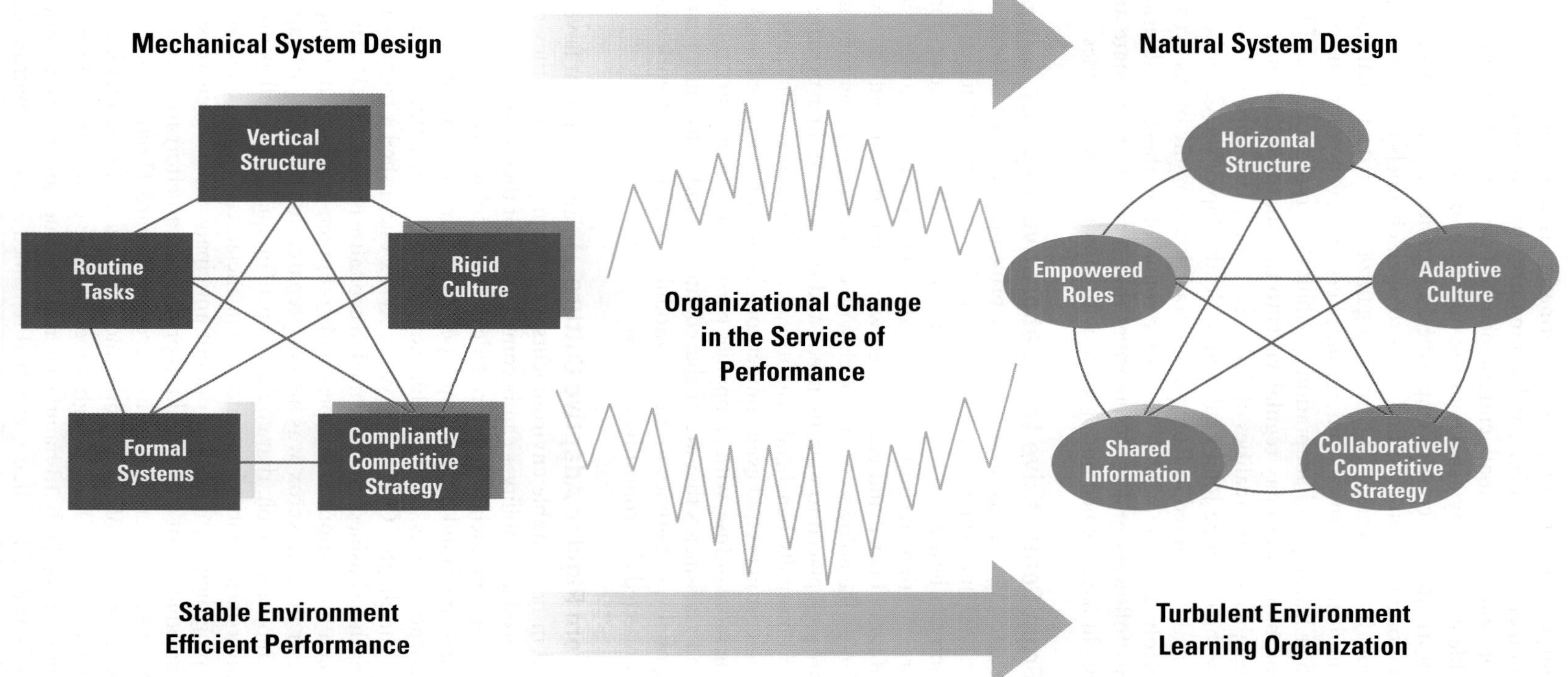

Source: Adapted from David K. Hurst, *Crisis and Renewal: Meeting the Challenge of Organizational Change* (Boston, Mass.: Harvard Business School Press, 1995).

goals.[45] In learning organizations, in contrast, information serves a very different purpose. In principle, much information is accessible and shared in a way that optimizes performance. The learning organization strives to restore the agility and community of a small, entrepreneurial firm in which all employees are knowledgeable about many aspects of the operation of the organization. Rather than using information to control employees, a significant part of a manager's job in a learning organization is to find ways to open channels of communication so that ideas flow in all directions. Learning organizations strive to maintain open lines of communication with customers, suppliers and even competitors in order to enhance their learning and adaptation capabilities. A typical means of leading by example is for managers to pay regular visits to the 'sharp end' of their organizations to gain insights into the realities of daily operations. This approach was used to great effect by the late Pope John Paul II in his leadership of the Catholic Church. Rather than remain cloistered in Rome in the tradition of many of his predecessors, his papacy involved a seemingly never-ending round of on-the-ground visits and dialogue with his followers and representatives that served to rejuvenate an organization that might have seemed out of touch with rapidly changing times.[46]

From Competitive to Collaborative Strategy In organizations designed according to classical, mechanistic principles, strategy is formulated by top managers and imposed on the organization. Top executives think about how the organization can best respond to competition and efficiently use resources. In the learning organization, in contrast, organic design principles demand the accumulated actions of an informed and empowered workforce to contribute to strategy development. Since all employees are in touch with customers, suppliers and new technology, they are well placed to identify needs and solutions and participate in strategy making, and mutually beneficial insights can also be gained from partnerships with suppliers, customers and even competitors. Boundaries between organizations are becoming more diffuse, with companies participating in industry forums to exchange ideas and assessments that are of shared interest, and in forming partnerships to compete globally, sometimes joining in modular or virtual network organizations that are connected electronically.

From Rigid to Adaptive Culture Organizations that have been highly successful in fairly stable environments – for example, where they dominate the market to produce stability – can become victims of their own success when circumstances change and their dominance fades as their culture as well as their mechanical structures are found to be ill-equipped to respond to new challenges. America's Xerox Corporation is a comparable example to that of Philips discussed at the beginning of the chapter. Over many years, Xerox established a highly successful photocopier machine business but this failed to capitalize upon its R&D activity that had spawned such innovations as the personal computer, graphical user interface, Ethernet and laser printer. Xerox was also unprepared for the entry of Japanese rivals, such as Canon and Ricoh, that could compete on quality as well as price. After a disastrous diversification into insurance and financial services, the company recovered by developing digital copiers but did not anticipate either the increased use of email or the introduction of cheap desktop printers. In an effort to reverse the tide, Xerox CEO, Paul Allaire, recruited as his successor Richard Thoman, then Louis Gerstner's right-hand man at IBM. Thoman came to Xerox as president, chief operating officer and eventually CEO, amid high hopes that the company could regain the stature of its glory years. Only 13 months later, as revenues and the stock price continued to slide, he was fired by Allaire, who had remained as Xerox chairman. Allaire and Thoman blamed each other for the failure to successfully implement their strategy. Outsiders, however, believe the failure had much more to do with Xerox's culture. It was resistant to adaptation, and some say that under Allaire it became almost totally paralyzed by politics. Thoman was brought in to shake things up. When he tried, the old guard rebelled. A management struggle developed, with the outsider Thoman and a few allies on one side lined up against Allaire and his group of insiders who were accustomed to doing things the Xeroid way. Ideas and practices that helped attain success were detrimental to effective performance in a rapidly changing environment.

In a more adaptive culture, characteristic of a learning organization, there is, in principle, greater emphasis upon openness, equality, continuous improvement and change. People are encouraged to become aware of the whole system, how everything fits together, and how the various parts of the organization interact with one another and with the environment. Treating everyone with care and respect is intended to create a climate in which people feel safe to experiment, take risks and make mistakes, all of which encourages learning. This whole-system mindset aspires to minimize boundaries within the organization and with other companies. But, as we have already noted, changing in this direction can be painful and effectively resisted by groups determined to defend an approach with which they are comfortable and are better able to manipulate their advantage. One organization that is transforming into a learning organization is Mexico's Cementos Mexicanos (Cemex), which is discussed in the *In Practice* box.

Framework for the Book

As an organization manager, keep this guideline in mind:

Make yourself a competent, influential manager by using the frameworks that organization theory provides to interpret and understand the organization around you.

What topic areas are relevant to organization theory and design? How does a course in management or organizational behaviour differ from a course in organization theory? The topics within the field of organization theory are interrelated. Chapters are presented so that major ideas unfold in logical sequence. The framework that guides the organization of the book is shown in Exhibit 1.9.

Part 1 introduces the basic idea of organizations as social systems and the nature of organization theory.

Part 2 is about strategic management, goals and effectiveness, and the fundamentals of organization structure.

Part 3 considers the various open system elements that influence organization structure and design, including the external environment, interorganizational relationships and the global environment.

Part 4 describes how organization design is related to such factors as manufacturing and service technology, organizational size and life cycle and information and control systems.

Part 5 shifts to dynamic processes that exist within and between major organizational departments and includes topics such as innovation and change, culture and ethical values, decision-making processes, managing intergroup conflict and power and politics.

Plan of Each Chapter

Each chapter begins with an organizational case to illustrate the topic to be covered. Theoretical concepts are introduced and explained in the body of the chapter. Several *In Practice* segments are included in each chapter to illustrate the concepts and show how they apply to real organizations. *Bookmarks* are included in most chapters to present organizational issues that managers face right now. These book reviews discuss current concepts and applications to deepen and enrich your understanding of organizations. The *Leading by Design* examples illustrate the dramatic changes taking place in management thinking and practice. There is no single 'right

Cementos Mexicanos

Cementos Mexicanos (Cemex), based in Monterrey, Mexico, has been making and delivering concrete for nearly a century. But the organization is on the cutting edge of organization design, a model of what it takes to succeed in the complex environment of the twenty-first century.

Cemex specializes in delivering concrete in developing areas of the world, places where anything can, and usually does, go wrong. Even in Monterrey, Cemex copes with unpredictable weather and traffic conditions, spontaneous labour disruptions, building permit snafus, and arbitrary government inspections of construction sites. In addition, more than half of all orders are changed or cancelled by customers, usually at the last minute. Considering that a load of concrete is never more than ninety minutes from spoiling, those chaotic conditions mean high costs, complex scheduling and frustration for employees, managers and customers.

To help the organization compete in this environment, managers looked for both technological and organizational innovations. Leaders call their new approach 'living with chaos'. Rather than trying to change the customers, Cemex resolved to do business on the customers' own terms and design a system in which last-minute changes and unexpected problems are routine.[47]

A core element of this approach is a complex information technology system, including a global positioning satellite system and onboard computers in all delivery trucks, which is fed with streams of day-to-day data on customer orders, production schedules, traffic problems, weather conditions and so forth. Now Cemex trucks head out every morning to cruise the streets. When a customer order comes in, an employee checks the customer's credit status, locates a nearby truck and relays directions for delivery. If the order is cancelled, computers automatically direct the plant to scale back production.

Cemex also made managerial and organizational changes to support the new approach. The company enrolled all its drivers, who had an average of six years of formal schooling, in weekly secondary-education classes and began training them in delivering not just cement but quality service. In addition, many strict and demanding work rules were abolished so that workers had more discretion and responsibility for identifying and rapidly responding to problems and customer needs. As a result, Cemex trucks now operate as self-organizing business units, run by well-trained employees who think like businesspeople. According to Francisco Perez, operations manager at Cemex in Guadalajara, 'They used to think of themselves as drivers. But anyone can deliver concrete. Now our people know that they're delivering a service that the competition cannot deliver.'

Cemex has transformed the industry by combining extensive networking technology with a new management approach that taps into the mindpower of everyone in the company. People at Cemex are constantly learning – on the job, in training classes and through visits to other organizations. As a result, the company has a startling capacity to anticipate customer needs, solve problems and innovate quickly. In addition, Cemex freely shares what it knows with other organizations, even competitors, believing the widespread sharing of knowledge and information is the best way to keep the organization thriving in a world of complexity. This philosophy has helped transform a once-sleepy cement company into a global powerhouse, with 2,200 operating units in 22 countries.[48]

answer' in organizational theory and design. That is not just because different designs may deliver similar outcomes or because the field of organization has not yet reached a sufficient level of maturity. It is because whatever is counted as a 'right answer' implicitly appeals to some particular set of values. An alternative set of values might view a very different answer as 'right', and it not possible to provide values with a rational warrant. Counterpoints are included throughout, which present alternative perspectives on issues discussed in the book. There are two sets of Counterpoints; one printed within the book and the other available online at www.cengage.co.uk/daftmurphywillmott. Each chapter closes with a 'Summary and Interpretation' section that reviews and explains important theoretical concepts.

EXHIBIT 1.9 Framework for the Book

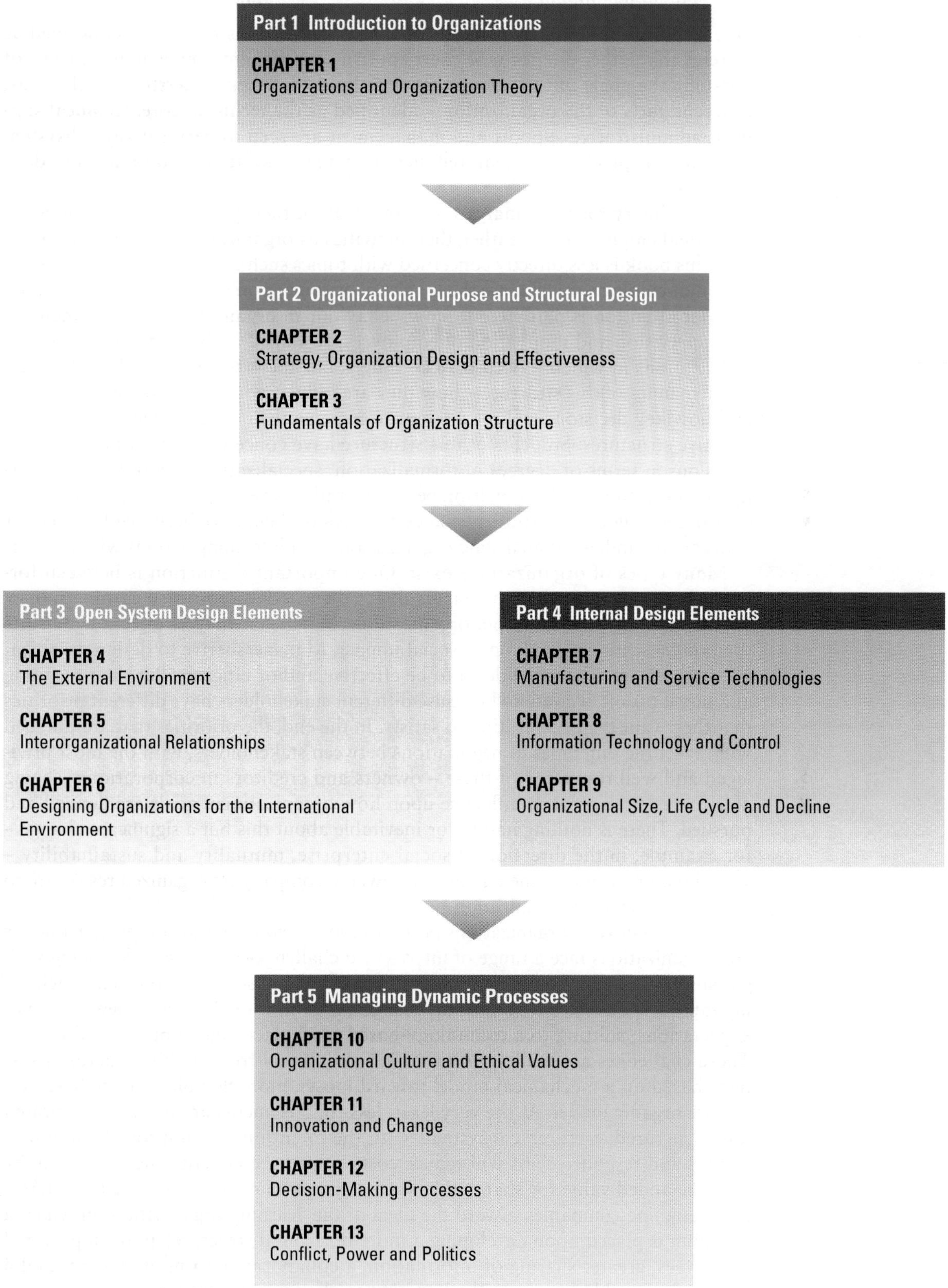

Part 1 Introduction to Organizations

CHAPTER 1
Organizations and Organization Theory

Part 2 Organizational Purpose and Structural Design

CHAPTER 2
Strategy, Organization Design and Effectiveness

CHAPTER 3
Fundamentals of Organization Structure

Part 3 Open System Design Elements

CHAPTER 4
The External Environment

CHAPTER 5
Interorganizational Relationships

CHAPTER 6
Designing Organizations for the International Environment

Part 4 Internal Design Elements

CHAPTER 7
Manufacturing and Service Technologies

CHAPTER 8
Information Technology and Control

CHAPTER 9
Organizational Size, Life Cycle and Decline

Part 5 Managing Dynamic Processes

CHAPTER 10
Organizational Culture and Ethical Values

CHAPTER 11
Innovation and Change

CHAPTER 12
Decision-Making Processes

CHAPTER 13
Conflict, Power and Politics

Summary and Interpretation

One important idea in this chapter is that organizations have been conceived as systems that either adapt to, or exert control over, the environment as a means of pursuing the goals of their dominant stakeholders. When understood in this way, different parts of the organization – identified as the technical core, technical support, administrative support and management are seen to perform key subsystem functions of production, maintenance, management, adaptation and boundary spanning.

The primary focus of analysis for organization theory is not the psychology of individual employees but, rather, their activities as organizational members. That is why this book is less directly concerned with topics such as supervision or the motivation of employees which are the mainstay of courses on organizational behaviour. Greater attention is paid here to how behaviour in organizations, which includes the supervision and motivation of employees, is shaped within the structure of social relations in which it occurs. Accordingly, our focus is upon the characteristics and dynamics of this structure – how they are influenced by the wider environment, and how key decisions makers attempt to manage their environment by designing effective structures. Students of this structure have conceived of its aspects and dimensions in terms of degrees of formalization, specialization, hierarchy of authority, centralization, professionalism, personnel ratios, size, organizational technology, environment, goals and strategy and culture. All of them have been invoked to offer conceptual handles for analyzing organizations and informing actions within them.

Many types of organizations exist. One important distinction is between for-profit businesses, in which managers direct their activities toward earning money for the company, and nonprofit organizations, in which managers direct their efforts toward generating some kind of social impact. Managers strive to design organizations to achieve what they deem to be effective and/or efficient. But their meaning and pursuit is often contested because different stakeholders have different priorities that they want the organization to satisfy. In the end, the priorities that are pursued will reflect the outcomes of negotiations between stakeholders, with the most privileged and well resourced of these – owners and creditors in corporations – being able to exert the greatest influence upon how organizational goals are defined and pursued. There is nothing natural or inevitable about this but a significant change – for example, in the direction of social enterprise, mutuality and sustainability – would require a shift in the balance of power accompanying organized resistance to entrenched forms of organization.

As the context of organizations becomes more turbulent and complex, managers and organizations face a range of intertwined challenges which include coping with globalization; maintaining high standards of ethics and social responsibility; achieving rapid response to environmental changes, organizational crises or new customer expectations; shifting to a technology-based workplace; and supporting diversity. These challenges are tending to prompt a shift away from highly structured systems based on a mechanical model toward looser, more flexible systems based on a more organic model. At the very least, less rigid elements are being incorporated into structured, hierarchical systems with the intention that improved communications and responsiveness will reduce costs, improve competitiveness and thereby produce added value for shareholders. One symptom of this change is the interest in redesigning companies toward the ideal of the 'learning organization' in which a premium is placed upon developing a more horizontal structure, more empowered employees, greater sharing of information, a collaborative form of strategy, and a culture that enables more rapid adaptation to changing circumstances.

KEY CONCEPTS

administrative principles
bureaucratic organizations
chaos theory
closed system
contextual dimensions
contingency
effectiveness
efficiency
Hawthorne Studies
learning organization
open system
organization theory
organizations
role
scientific management
stakeholder
stakeholder approach
structural dimensions
subsystems
system
task

Discussion Questions

1 Any definition of organization provides a way of 'not seeing' as well as a way of 'seeing'. Discuss.

2 What is the difference between an open system and a closed system? Can you give an example of a closed system? How is the stakeholder approach related to the concept of open system?

3 Use an example of an organization with which you are familiar to explain how Mintzberg's five basic parts of the organization perform the subsystem functions shown at the bottom of Exhibit 1.2. Evaluate the stengths and limitations of Mintzberg's perspective.

4 Assess the pros and cons of systems thinking for guiding management practice.

5 What is the difference between formalization and specialization? Assess the usefulness of these concepts for understanding the practice of organizing.

6 What does *contingency* mean? What are the implications of contingency theories for managers?

7 What are the primary differences between an organization designed for predictable outputs and one designed for learning and change? What challenges of management are associated with these designs? Discuss.

8 Why is shared information so important in a learning organization as compared to a predictable outputs organization? Discuss how an organization's approach to information sharing might be related to other elements of organization design, such as structure, tasks, strategy and culture.

9 What are some differences one might expect among stakeholder expectations for a nonprofit organization versus a for-profit business? Do you think nonprofit managers have to pay more attention to stakeholders than do business managers? Discuss.

10 Early management theorists believed that organizations should strive to be logical and rational, with a place for everything and everything in its place. Discuss the pros and cons of this approach for today's organizations.

Chapter 1 Workbook Measuring Dimensions of Organizations

Analyze two organizations along the dimensions shown below. Indicate where you think each organization would fall on each of the scales. Use an X to indicate the first organization and an * to show the second.

You may choose any two organizations you are familiar with, such as your place of work, the university, a student organization, your local community organization or church or your family.

	Formalization	
Many written rules	1 2 3 4 5 6 7 8 9 10	Few rules
	Specialization	
Separate tasks and roles	1 2 3 4 5 6 7 8 9 10	Overlapping tasks
	Hierarchy	
Tall hierarchy of authority	1 2 3 4 5 6 7 8 9 10	Flat hierarchy of authority
	Technology	
Product	1 2 3 4 5 6 7 8 9 10	Service
	External Environment	
Stable	1 2 3 4 5 6 7 8 9 10	Unstable
	Culture	
Clear norms and values	1 2 3 4 5 6 7 8 9 10	Ambiguous norms and values
	Professionalism	
High professional training	1 2 3 4 5 6 7 8 9 10	Low professional training
	Goals	
Well-defined goals	1 2 3 4 5 6 7 8 9 10	Goals not defined
	Size	
Small	1 2 3 4 5 6 7 8 9 10	Large
	Organizational Mindset	
Mechanical system	1 2 3 4 5 6 7 8 9 10	Biological system

Questions

1. What are the main differences between the two organizations you evaluated?
2. Would you recommend that one or both of the organizations have different ratings on any of the scales? Why?

CASE FOR ANALYSIS

Breed's Tipping Point: Headed towards Success or Failure?

By Brian Tjemkes, Renee Scheerman & Yuri Narayen, *VU University Amsterdam*

Breed: A Creative Communications Agency

On 23 May 2008 Breed was officially recognized by the Dutch KvK, six months later than the company started doing business. As Lisa Varkevisser, one of the members joked: 'We chose to use a cooperative as a legal form, because it is relatively easy and quick to incorporate, but it took us half a year to make Breed official.' Breed is a creative agency settled in Amsterdam, centre of the communication and commercial field in the Netherlands. Its core businesses are to accomplish marketing and communication; they sell products and services related to advertising, concept development of events, commercials, online business and they initiate activities pertaining to art, culture and music. Breed consists of six founding members; Scott van der Velden, Cyril Stom, Marcel Ossendrijver-Bisschops, Lisa Varkevisser, Edward den Ouden and Jean Pierre Kin.

Breed's Start-Up

The rent of business space on 1 September 2007 in the Maple Leaf factory was the starting point of Breed. During September and October 2007 the six members of the Breed cooperative met each other frequently. All of them knew one another from previous jobs at various advertising and communication agencies. Together the six founders of Breed hit upon the idea of starting a company in which freelancers were united.

On the 1st of January 2008 Breed officially became a company. In this month Breed got their first order; developing a web portal for The Ster (foundation of ether commercials). Because Breed acquired its first order, the 'terms and conditions' had to be written. This was the first official document signed by a client. Fuelled by this instant success, other organizational matters also demanded decision-making; at that time, Breed's legal form was unclear, a website was non-existent, as well as the requirement for a brochure to promote the company. Breed only existed based on the informal connection between the members. The cooperative UA as a legal form was established on the 26th of February 2008. A cooperative is an 'autonomous association of persons united voluntarily to meet their common economic, social and cultural needs and aspirations through a jointly-owned and democratically-controlled enterprise' UA means that members are locked out for liability and that no recover rights exist on the Breed members (i.e. six founders). It was also decided that the six board members would each receive one-sixth shares of the profits and that Breed always remains intellectual owner of designed concepts. The digital brochure was accomplished on 26th of March 2008. The official Breed web log, www.bestofbreed.nu, went live on 8th of May. On this web log the members update their soul mates, clients and fans about their activities. Although Breed did not yet officially exist for the Dutch government (KvK), the first invoice was sent to The Ster at the end of March. But, it took untill May 23 to complete the 'act and regulation' and the notation at the KvK. After achieving this milestone it was finally possible to hire an accountant. Lacking knowledge and skills on running a business, the members of Breed decided to establish a Board of Advice. The board of advice consisted of three members with organizational, personnel, and legal backgrounds. They had a first meeting on 12th of February 2008 and on the 20th of March 2008 all six core Breed members presented themselves and their business plans to the Board of Advice. With the help of the Board, Breed formulated their business strategy on 20th of May. After these initial activities Breed was ready to start doing business.

Breed's Environment

Breed is a creative communications agency. A creative agency is a company that offers one or many communicative disciplines, like advertising, development of events, commercials, online communication and textual or graphic communications. In the past decade, several developments and trends have been noticeable in the industry of creative communication agencies, contributing to the creation of new agencies, intensified competition, and new strategies.

Trends in the Communication Market

Due to an emphasis on costs and economizing, clients started to use a 'pitch-system' enabling them to have multiple creative agencies apply for one commission. However, the time and efforts necessary to pitch are often not compensated by the client, putting high pressure on the revenues of the creative agencies. Another consequence is that several creative agencies adopted a cost-leadership strategy to meet clients' demands, further reinforcing an already competitive market.

Another trend in the industry is the shift from building client-relationships to the use of project-based orders. Companies used to have a long-lasting relationship with one creative agency. Nowadays, they prefer to let agencies pitch for a project and repeat this process for every project. By using their bargaining power clients are able to realize cost reductions. For instance, they only have to pay a creative agency during the project and to win pitches creative agencies lower their prices. Another reason, however, pertains to changing customer demands requiring that clients invest in creative campaigns to maintain and increase their market shares. Stimulating competition between creative agencies enables clients, at the expense of giving up long-lasting relationships, to obtain state-of-the art creative work.

Online communication has become an important product/service of the creative communications industry. Traditional communication was restricted to commercials on television and radio, graphics and textual communication. In contrast, online communication associates with websites, interactive and digital commercials, banners, online polls, etc. Nowadays, offering multidisciplinary approaches has become a critical success factor. Creative agencies should have knowledge of traditional media as well as online media.

Breed's Competitive Position

Breed is one of many creative agencies in the Netherlands. Most of them are settled in or around Amsterdam. There are a few large players in the market, a couple of small-medium sized companies, and there are numerous freelancers. Creative communication agencies can be arranged by the diversity of communication methods they offer to clients and their attitude towards innovation. With respect to communication methods agencies vary from single disciplinary to multidisciplinary. Possible communicative disciplines are textual or graphic communications, online communication, commercials, production and account managing. A creative agency can offer one of these services, a combination of services or all of these services. Another important distinguishing feature between agencies is their attitude towards developing innovative products and services. Some companies seek a unique position in the market by presenting themselves as highly innovative and proactive. In contrast, other companies position themselves as reactive and conservative. The main competitors of Breed can be organized along these dimensions (see Exhibit 1.10).

Breed is highly innovative and possesses a lot of expertise in different modes of communication. Therefore, Breed considers itself as a pro-active multidisciplinary creative agency (i.e. right-top quadrant in Exhibit 1.10). Competitors, such as 'They' and 'Noise', have adopted similar positioning strategies; however Breed is the smallest firm among them. Most likely, once a client decides to commission an innovative advertising campaign these companies become direct competitors. However, conditional on the communication mode companies specialized in one discipline (i.e. left-top quadrant in Exhibit 1.10) should be considered as competitors as well, because they are expert in one of the disciplines Breed offers. In addition to competitors another important group of players in the market form a threat to Breed: freelancers. A freelancer is an expert in a certain area and can be hired by a company. Some freelancers have united themselves in freelance communities. For example, 'Mach1' is a medium-seized freelance community which focuses on multitask orders. Freelancers or freelance communities should be seen as important competitors for Breed, because they can offer similar expertise, flexibility, price and they have the possibility to adapt their collaboration to fit every order. To conclude, in line with recent developments creative agencies are more and more opting for a multimedia approach. To date however, Breed still has a competitive advantage compared to most companies as Breed is able to combine a multi-disciplinary approach with innovative products and services.

Breed's Competencies and Strategy

To offer state-of-the-art products and services Breed has developed two core competencies providing them with a unique selling point: expertise and flexibility. Due to the members backgrounds Breed possesses a unique combination of know-how and skills. Blending of expertise pertaining to innovative communication methods and state-of-the-art production enables Breed to develop out-of-the-box solutions tailored to clients' demands. For instance,

EXHIBIT 1.10 Matrix of the Position of Creative Agencies

Innovative/Proactive Creative Agencies

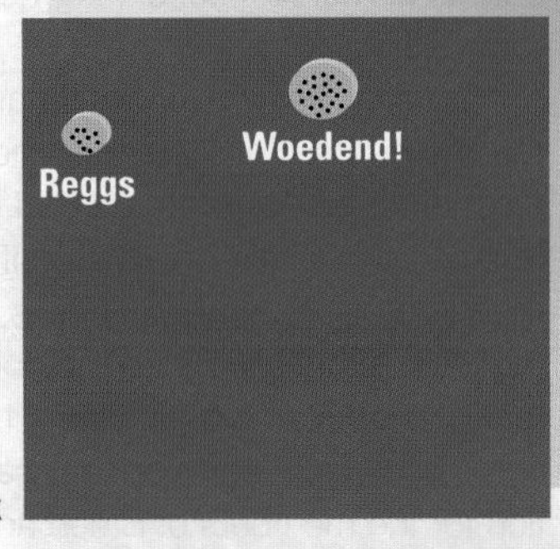

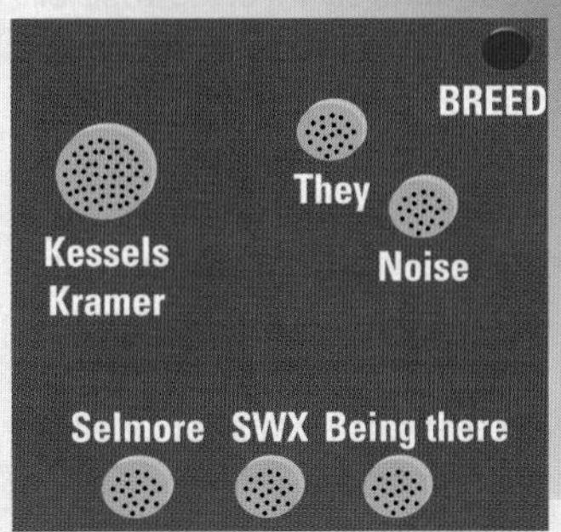

Single-task Creative Agencies

Multi-task Creative Agencies

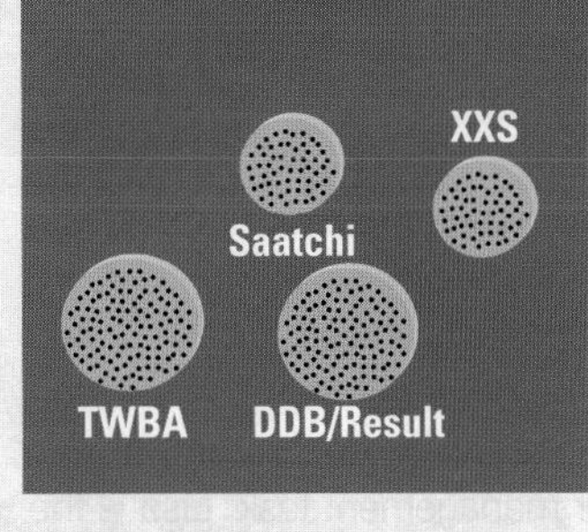

Conservative/Reactive Creative Agencies

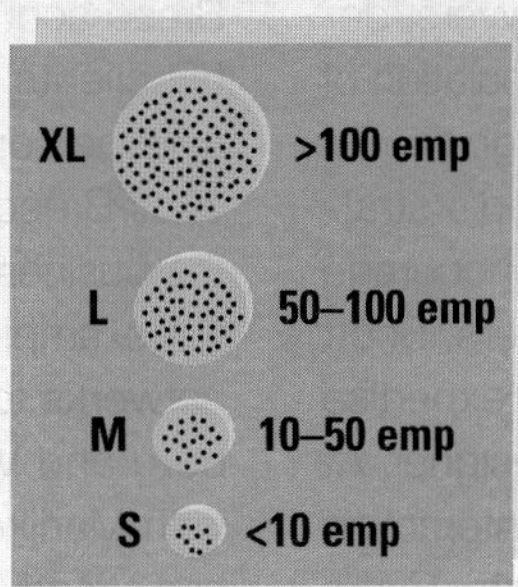

Breed members have expertise in graphics, production, online-businesses, personal relations as well as textual communications, suggesting that all members individually contribute to Breed's success. In addition, if Breed is lacking in-house expertise they are still able to develop unique solutions, as Breed is supported by a strong network of soul mates. Soul mates are people that stand close to the Breed-members and have their own field of expertise. As Breed is a relatively small organization they are fast and flexible in conceptualization and delivery of products. In order to make a product that fits best to the client's demands, they engage in frequent interaction with their clients. Furthermore, as Breed members have different specializations, all members can act autonomously within their projects. That is, decisions are not approved by different managers, but are often taken after quick consultation by the members. This combination of expertise and flexibility distinguishes Breed from its competitors.

Breed tries to distinguish themselves from other creative agencies by offering many products and services, including online communication, commercials, graphic communication and production. As such, their main strategy is best characterized as one of differentiation; however, it is the combination of several strategic decisions that really distinguishes them from other creative communication agencies. Breed's strategy is closely related to Breed's identity and slogan: 'Stay true to yourself'. For instance, Breed decided to only accept orders which they find interesting and reinforces their identity. Another defining characteristic is that Breed actively involves their clients in the conceptualization and production phases. This enables Breed to align concepts with clients' wishes, whereas clients can monitor expenses. Breed also decided that short-term financial gains may not be gained at the expense of long-term creativity, exclusivity and quality. The Breed members believe that their unique products and enthusiasm for every project provides Breed with a stronger market position than their (cost focused) competitors.

Breed's Internal Organization

Breed has a flat organizational structure with six founder members. Within this structure all members are equal and no hierarchical order or leader (i.e. director) has been installed. Breed has a functional structure where all members have different areas of expertise, which depicts their functional discipline. Members inform each other of their projects and try to be informed about the activities of the other members. In addition to their functional specialization, each member has been assigned another management task. Lisa is the account director of Breed, but also takes care of administrative tasks, including contact with lawyers, designing contracts, arranging insurances, formulation of the statutes, terms and conditions, the recognition by the Dutch KvK and the formulation of Breed's strategy. She also takes most responsibility to encourage and control the activities of the other members. Scott functions as the chairman of Breed and his expertise relates to that of art director and motion designer. At Breed, Cyril's task is that of art director and interaction designer. He leads on-line and off-line projects. Cyril's task is also that of treasurer and currently he is occupied with financial tasks, such as sending invoices, making payments and keeping track of hours worked on projects. Edward and J-P are primarily concerned with keeping track of creative developments. Edward is strong at concept design, theme communication and sales promotion, whereas J-P makes creative concepts visual. At Breed Marcel fulfils the functions secretary to the board and producer, as he is mainly concerned with the production of audio and video. However, as production is a very small part of the main activities, Marcel is exploring how he can contribute to Breed.

However, several tensions have emerged between the members. For instance, clients are behind with payments, clients reported that having multiple contact persons within Breed is confusing; information on clients, projects, and finances is disorganized and often tacit. Although, Breed members considered these tensions as start-up problems they started to make some changes. For instance, Lisa wrote a job description for the members of Breed and the core-members of Breed discussed how to assign and specify the responsibilities of the different members. However, to date the assignment of the tasks and responsibilities is not clear, resulting in a situation in which each member feels more or less responsible for different tasks. For instance, although Lisa is primarily responsible for external communication she also deals with internal communication. Furthermore, in July 2008 the Board of Advice was officially dismantled with the exception of only one member of this committee.

Breed's Acquisition of Clients

Breed acquires new orders in two ways. First, potential clients are approached through connections in their personal networks. Due to the work experience of all Breed members, they know different people in the business, which may lead to possible new orders. For example, leads were generated by these personal networks to potential clients, such as Heinz, Peijnenburg and Van Haren. Lisa has also become friends with Marijke Helwegen, a Dutch celebrity. A contact has already led to several orders or links to other people who might have an order for Breed. The Breed members also obtained orders through their advisory board. However, provided with the broadness of the network, relatively few contacts are used to generate orders. Although, clients are approached to ensure that they will remind Breed first when they have an order, the members do not capitalize sufficiently on their networks.

EXHIBIT 1.11 Breed's Organizational Design

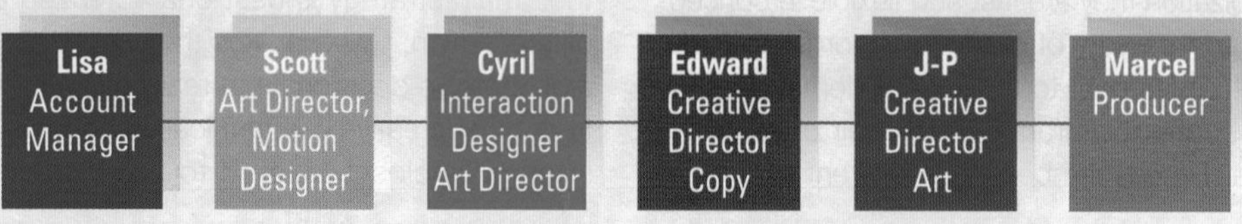

Second, pitches are common practice in the industry to connect clients to creative agencies. The Ster order was, for example, won by a pitch. A pitch is a unique possibility to show to a client what Breed can offer. The Breed members prefer to convince a potential client with a visible product, like a model, a presentation or graphics instead of a description of their ideas. To develop a product for a pitch it is necessary to invest into the idea for the pitch and build the product. However, a disadvantage of a pitch is that the time and effort spend on a pitch can not be charged to the client. It is common practice, however, that a company that loses a pitch receives a compensation of €1000. – and the winner is rewarded by obtaining the order. To deal with the downside of this pitching system Breed decided to (1) only pitch one time per client and (2) deliver a state-of-the-art pitch. Although, this strategy increases risks and costs, it turns out to be a successful strategy, as to date all pitches have been won.

Breed's 'Service Production' Process

The production process of Breed exists of seven stages. The first stage in the service production process is orientation. In this stage the first acquaintance between Breed and the potential client takes place. The second stage in the production process is making an inventory. In this stage among other things the actual strategy, proposition and goals of the client are discussed, inspection of former campaigns takes place, figures and facts are collected and budgets and deadlines are discussed. Furthermore in this stage Breed makes a plan of action and formats a project team which will work on the project. The third stage is the strategy stage. A target group analysis happens in this stage, as well as the arrangement of the goal of the project. Furthermore the client takes care of a briefing of Breed, a closer look at existing means will be discussed and a debriefing by Breed takes place. Finally Breed provides the client with an indication of the costs of the project and makes a plan for the concept design. Concept development is the fourth stage in the production process, in which concept design and elaboration take place. In this stage a briefing of the creation and presentation for the client take place. The fifth stage is pre-production. In this stage Breed visits its clients, preferably on the client's location; the assignment is formalized in detail. That is, it is decided what is going to be produced and how. An interim presentation for the client is performed and a final agreement on the art work is made. The pre-production stage is followed by the production stage. In this stage the actual production of the project happens and the end of this stage means delivery of the products and services. The seventh stage of the production process is the post-production stage. In this stage the production is evaluated and discussed with the client. During the second, third and fourth stages of the production process account management is leading, however across the stages the core-members of Breed are not working independently. They have continuous contact with the project members and they are expected to help one another by discussing their progress and output. Furthermore Breed keeps in touch with the client during the production process.

Breed's Start-up Performance

Project Performance

Since the foundation of Breed, the company has landed several projects. The projects of Breed can be categorized into three groups. The first group consists of projects performed for commercial clients, the second group consists of social projects and the third group consists of Breed initiated projects. The first client of Breed was a big fish already. This client was The Ster and Breed was asked to create and implement a new structured website and develop a strategy and online presentation for The Ster. Breed's first ever invoice was sent to The Ster at the end of March 2008. Breed also created a campaign for Interior Matters in which campaign stickers were glued on cast-off furniture that was placed along the roads as bulky refuse. Other clients of Breed included Mexx, Voedingscentrum and Junkbeat. Concerning social projects Breed has performed activities for Hiphopinjesmoel. Jean Pierre is actively involved in this organization and Breed helps Hiphopinjesmoel with their contacts in the media. Another social project Breed is active in is No Kidding. This is a project which cares about the guiding of derailed youngsters in youth prisons to return into the society. Lisa is active at this organization which is creating a national action plan and communication plan. Thirdly, Breed also developed several of their own projects, which means that Breed is responsible for concept development, financial investments and execution. Examples of such projects are the Minimafair (www.minimafair.com) and Meccabox.

Marketing Performance

During the first year of the life of Breed the company's brand awareness grew very quickly. This resulted in the landing of projects of a couple of big clients. Examples of these clients are the Ster, Voedingscentrum and Mexx. Concerning public relations Breed decided not to invest in all kinds of public relations activities, such as interviews in professional magazines. Their work should speak for itself and do the work for Breed. Breed only wants to make use of public relations if they are sure that project is ready to be taken into public relations. For instance, the project Breed performed for Interior Matters resulted in an article about Breed and this project in the creation publication of the magazine Adformatie. Breed's Minimafair project entered into the media in November 2008 through coverage in the Story (a Dutch gossip magazine) and by several television interviews with Marijke van Helwegen.

Financial Performance

During the second quarter of 2008 Breed had a positive result of €54.912,76. Breed and accountancy company Claus Accountants made a forecast of the results over the period 2008–2010. This forecast shows that over the fiscal years 2008 and 2009 a negative result before tax is predicted. This forecasted negative result is -€22.059,00 in 2008 en -€54.381,00 in 2009. The fiscal year 2010 is the first year that shows a positive forecasted result. This positive result numbers €34.650,00. The forecasted returns in the period 2008–2010 are respectively €60.000,00 in 2008, €880.400,00 in 2009 and €980.400,00 in 2010. The Breed members decided not to give themselves salaries until January 2009, contributing to the positive net result. The gross monthly salary per member of the management will be €9.190,00 in 2009 and 2010 which amounts to a gross yearly salary of €110.277,00. With regard to the number of own projects performed by Breed a forecast of two own projects in the year 2008, and five own projects in both 2009 and 2010 is made. However, it remains uncertain whether Breed has sufficient funds to implement these projects.

Breed's Future

When looking at the future of Breed, it is the ambition of the core members of the company to accomplish growth and become a successful creative agency. This growth is aspired to in several aspects including financial and marketing performance, corporate social responsibility, brand awareness and company size. In the long term, the members plan to terminate their freelance activities and work full time for Breed. They want to hire employees to a maximum of thirty people. Concerning the ambition of growth and becoming a successful creative agency, to date there are some enablers and barriers that may foster or impede Breed's ambitions.

The financial and marketing performance of Breed shows sustainable growth at this moment. Also the brand awareness of Breed is growing, which resulted in attracting several bigger clients. Although this is a positive development for Breed, the core members of Breed are not yet ready to stop their freelance activities and start working for Breed full time at this moment. They do not dare to take this step at present. On the other hand, it is the short term ambition of Breed to realize more paid Breed commissions, so the members can discontinue their freelance activities. The fact that the members of Breed have to divide their time and effort between Breed and their freelance activities negatively affects Breed's success and growth.

The diverging focus of the founding members threatens the chemistry and linkage between the members of the company. It was chemistry that drove their initial decision to start Breed. Whereas initially members worked together very well and complemented each other, currently tension and conflicts are emerging. The member's focus is shifting and they are exploring different directions outside Breed.

Concerns also exist with respect to the organization design. Although the flat structure enables Breed to build on its core competences, it creates all kinds of communication problems and tensions between the members. For instance, frequent discussions and conflicts emerge about members' responsibilities, professionalism of the project organization, lack of information, repeated and redundant contacts with clients and the fact that conflicting agreements are made with clients on products. In addition, due to Breed's motto of equality no member feels responsible for taking care of the long-term strategy of the firm. A leader and leadership are missing, contributing to Breed's lack of focus and direction. In addition to financial performance other performance criteria such as efficiency, creativity and flexibility need to be included into the management information system. Given Breed's ambition to grow, it is likely that more tensions and conflicts can be expected.

The strategy of Breed and the unique Breed identity are two very important grounds for the success of Breed. Especially the slogan 'Stay true to yourself' depicts a unique feature of Breed. For instance, the Breed approach towards pitching reflects their strategy and identity. However, growth may threaten their identity as new members (i.e. staff), clients and stakeholders may have different views. It, therefore, remains a question if the Breed identity and vision, which are essential to continue success, will remain unharmed by the ambition to grow.

▶

To conclude, the future of Breed is quite uncertain. The ambition of Breed to grow and become a successful creative agency is one possible reality as during the start-up phase important decisions were made, including the choice of the company name, logo, legal form, digital brochure, terms and conditions, the website www.bestofbreed.nu and the recognition by the Dutch KvK. However, unexpected barriers also threaten Breed's success, including conflicts between members, difficulties in acquiring new projects, and poor internal and external communication. It is reasonable to conclude that Breed is at a critical tipping point. Therefore, the question is: is Breed headed towards success or failure?

Case Questions

1 Which organization design decisions do you think are particulary relevant for the start-up of a creative communication agency like Breed? Explain why.

2 What explanation can you give for the start-up success of Breed? Consider both the external environment and the internal organization.

3 Given Breed's ambition to grow further, which changes would you recommend to Breed to make in the organization design? Explain your recommendations.

Notes

1. Geoffrey Jones (2005), *Renewing Unilever: Transformation and Tradition,* Oxford, OUP.
2. 'After three years of painful effort, Europe's biggest electronics company is still struggling to get fit', *The Economist*, April 7, 1990, Pg. 99.
3. G. Mahesh and S. Chaudhuri (2004), 'Philips: Restructuring to Make Things Better', ICFAI Business School Case Study 304-330-1, Hyderabad.
4. Sean Meehan (2007), 'The Philips Marketing Journey', IMD Case Study IMD-5-0729.
5. Kerry Capell (2006), 'Thinking Simple At Philips: A panel of outside experts is helping the electronics giant reinvent itself', *Business Week*, December 11.
6. Govind, S., and George, S. (2007), 'Philips, Making Sense of Simplicity', ICFAI Case Study 507-085-1.
7. Harry G. Barkema, Joel A. C. Baum and Elizabeth A. Mannix, 'Management Challenges in a New Time,' *Academy of Management Journal* 45, no. 5 (2002), 916–930. Eileen Davis, 'What's on American Managers' Minds?' *Management Review* (April 1995), 14–20.
8. Barkema et al., 'Management Challenges.'
9. http://www.wipro.com/aboutus/fact_file.htm, accessed on July 8, 2008.
10. Craig Unger, House of cards: From 9/11 to BAE, the Saudis have turned the purchase of political power into a fine art, *The Guardian*, April 15, 2008, Pg. 28; Robert Baer, The Saudis do not give up their secrets, Mr Blair, *The Independent on Sunday*, April 13, 2008, Pg. 50; Jane Wardell, 'Calls to reopen UK inquiry into BAE-Saudi arms deal', Associated Press Worldstream, April 11, 2008; Nick Clark and Stephen Foley, 'BAE chief detained as US turns up heat in bribes case', *The Independent*, May 19, 2008, Pg. 36.
11. 'After JK; Société Générale, *The Economist*, May 31, 2008; Peter Robison, 'When traders go bad; The Société Générale scandal is following a familiar script, *Ottawa Citizen* January 26, 2008, Pg. E3; 'Societe Generale boss admits faults in control systems', *Agence France Presse*, June 10, 2008.
12. Joe Willis, '"Woeful" – Scandal of Lost Data Discs', *The Northern Echo*, June 26, 2008, Pg. 1.
13. David Wessel, 'Venal Sins: Why the Bad Guys of the Boardroom Emerged en Masse', *The Wall Street Journal* (June 20, 2002), A1, A6.
14. Greg Ip, 'Mind Over Matter—Disappearing Acts: The Rapid Rise and Fall of the Intangible Asset,' *The Wall Street Journal* (April 4, 2002), A1, A6.
15. Jim Davis (2003), 'Speculative Capital in the Global Age,' *Race and Class*, 44, 1– 22; Anita Hawser, 'Mergers and Acquisitions: A Dangerous Game', *Global Finance Magazine*, May, 2007, Pg. 4.
16. Bernard Wysocki Jr., 'Corporate Caveat: Dell or Be Delled,' *The Wall Street Journal* (May 10, 1999), A1.
17. Andy Reinhardt, 'From Gearhead to Grand High Pooh-Bah,' *BusinessWeek* (August 28, 2000), 129–130.
18. G. Pascal Zachary, 'Mighty is the Mongrel,' *Fast Company* (July 2000), 270–284.
19. Debra E. Meyerson and Joyce K. Fletcher, 'A Modest Manifesto for Shattering the Glass Ceiling', *Harvard Business Review* (January–February 2000), 127–136; Annie Finnigan, 'Different Strokes', *Working Woman* (April 2001), 42–48; Joline Godfrey, 'Been There, Doing That', *Inc.* (March 1996), 21–22; Paula Dwyer, Marsha Johnston and Karen Lowry Miller, 'Out of the Typing Pool, into Career Limbo', *BusinessWeek* (April 15, 1996), 92–94.
20. Howard Aldrich, *Organizations and Environments* (Englewood Cliffs, N.J.: Prentice-Hall, 1979), 3.
21. This section is based largely on Peter F. Drucker, *Managing the Non-Profit Organization: Principles and Practices* (New York: HarperBusiness, 1992); and Thomas Wolf, *Managing*

a Nonprofit Organization (New York: Fireside/Simon & Schuster, 1990).
22. Christine W. Letts, William P. Ryan and Allen Grossman, *High Performance Nonprofit Organizations* (New York: John Wiley & Sons, Inc., 1999), 30–35.
23. Robert N. Stern and Stephen R. Barley, 'Organizations and Social Systems: Organization Theory's Neglected Mandate', *Administrative Science Quarterly* 41 (1996): 146–162.
24. Philip Siekman, 'Build to Order: One Aircraft Carrier', *Fortune* (July 22, 2002), 180[B]–180[J].
25. Schlender, 'The New Soul of a Wealth Machine', and Keith H. Hammonds, 'Growth Search', *Fast Company* (April 2003), 75–80.
26. James D. Thompson, *Organizations in Action* (New York: McGraw-Hill, 1967), 4–13.
27. Henry Mintzberg, *The Structuring of Organizations* (Englewood Cliffs, N.J.: Prentice-Hall, 1979), 215–297; and Henry Mintzberg, 'Organization Design: Fashion or Fit?' *Harvard Business Review* 59 (January–February 1981), 103–116.
28. The following discussion was heavily influenced by Richard H. Hall, *Organizations: Structures, Processes, and Outcomes* (Englewood Cliffs, N.J.: Prentice-Hall, 1991); D. S. Pugh, 'The Measurement of Organization Structures: Does Context Determine Form?' *Organizational Dynamics* 1 (Spring 1973), 19–34; and D. S. Pugh, D. J. Hickson, C. R. Hinings and C. Turner, 'Dimensions of Organization Structure', *Administrative Science Quarterly* 13 (1968), 65–91.
29. Matthew Curtin, Carrefour's cares, *The Edge Malaysia*, November 1, 2004; John Ryan, 'World-class Retailer – Carrefour drives down the road to domination, *Retail Week*, May 12, 2000, Pg.17; Rozenn Perrigot and Gérard Cliquet, 'Hypermarket Format: Any Future or a Real Need to Be Changed? An Empirical Study of the French, Spanish and Italian markets', paper presented at 5th International Marketing Trends Congress,Venice, 20–21 January 2006; 'Q4 2006 Carrefour S.A. Earnings Presentation – Final', *Fair Disclosure Wire*, March 8, 2007.
30. T. Donaldson and L. E. Preston, 'The Stakeholder Theory of the Corporation: Concepts, Evidence and Implications', *Academy of Management Review* 20 (1995), 65–91; Anne S. Tusi, 'A Multiple-Constituency Model of Effectiveness: An Empirical Examination at the Human Resource Subunit Level', *Administrative Science Quarterly* 35 (1990), 458–483; Charles Fombrun and Mark Shanley, 'What's in a Name? Reputation Building and Corporate Strategy', *Academy of Management Journal* 33 (1990), 233–258; Terry Connolly, Edward J. Conlon and Stuart Jay Deutsch, 'Organizational Effectiveness: A Multiple-Constituency Approach', *Academy of Management Review* 5 (1980), 211–217.
31. Charles Fishman, 'The Wal-Mart You Don't Know—Why Low Prices Have a High Cost', *Fast Company* (December 2003), 68–80.
32. Tusi, 'A Multiple-Constituency Model of Effectiveness'.
33. Fombrun and Shanley, 'What's in a Name?'
34. Forest Products Association of Canada, *Annual Report 2007*, p. 16–17, accessed at http://www.fpac.ca/pdfs/annual_reviews/fpac_annual_review_e_2007.pdf on July 8, 2008.
35. Rod Mickleburgh, 'There's nothing more. The town is dying,' *The Globe and Mail*, May 17, 2008, Pg. S3.
36. Joel Connelly, Conservationists Want to Halt Logging on Clayoquot Sound: Summer of Confrontation in British Columbia, *Seattle Post-Intelligencer*, August 30, 1993, Pg. A1.
37. 'AbitibiBowater to stop logging in Grassy Narrows First Nation territory', Canada NewsWire, June 4, 2008.
38. Winn, Monika and Zietsma, Charlene (2004), 'The war of the woods: a forestry giant seeks peace', *Greener Management International* 48, 21–37.
39. B&Q policy ar http://www.diy.com/diy/jsp/aboutbandq/social_responsibility/BQSRTIMB.PDF, Hallmark at http://www.hallmarkuk.com/files/Sustainability%20Statement%20Nov%2007.pdf, both accessed on July 8, 2008.
40. Ann Harrington, 'The Big Ideas', *Fortune* (November 22, 1999), 152–154; Robert Kanigel, *The One Best Way: Frederick Winslow Taylor and the Enigma of Efficiency* (New York: Viking, 1997); and Alan Farnham, 'The Man Who Changed Work Forever', *Fortune* (July 21, 1997), 114. For a discussion of the impact of scientific management on American industry, government, and nonprofit organizations, also see Mauro F. Guillén, 'Scientific Management's Lost Aesthetic: Architecture, Organization, and the Taylorized Beauty of the Mechanical', *Administrative Science Quarterly* 42 (1997), 682–715.
41. Amanda Bennett, *The Death of the Organization Man* (New York: William Morrow, 1990).
42. Johannes M. Pennings, 'Structural Contingency Theory: A Reappraisal', *Research in Organizational Behavior* 14 (1992), 267–309.
43. This discussion is based in part on Toby J. Tetenbaum, 'Shifting Paradigms: From Newton to Chaos', *Organizational Dynamics* (Spring 1998), 21–32.
44. Based on Tetenbaum, 'Shifting Paradigms: From Newton to Chaos', and Richard T. Pascale, 'Surfing the Edge of Chaos', *Sloan Management Review* (Spring 1999), 83–94.
45. David K. Hurst, *Crisis and Renewal: Meeting the Challenge of Organizational Change* (Boston, Mass.: Harvard Business School Press, 1995), 32–52.
46. 'Freeman: Will White Smoke Blow The Developing World's Way?', *Irish Independent*, April 7, 2005.
47. For more information about Cemex, see http://www.ssireview.org/pdf/2005SU_feature_sandoval.pdf.
48. Thomas Petzinger, *The New Pioneers: The Men and Women Who Are Transforming the Workplace and Marketplace* (New York: Simon & Schuster, 1999), 91–93; and 'In Search of the New World of Work', *Fast Company* (April 1999), 214–220; Peter Katel, 'Bordering on Chaos', *Wired* (July 1997), 98–107; Oren Harari, 'The Concrete Intangibles', *Management Review* (May 1999), 30–33; and 'Mexican Cement Maker on Vergeof a Deal', *The New York Times* (September 27, 2004), A8.

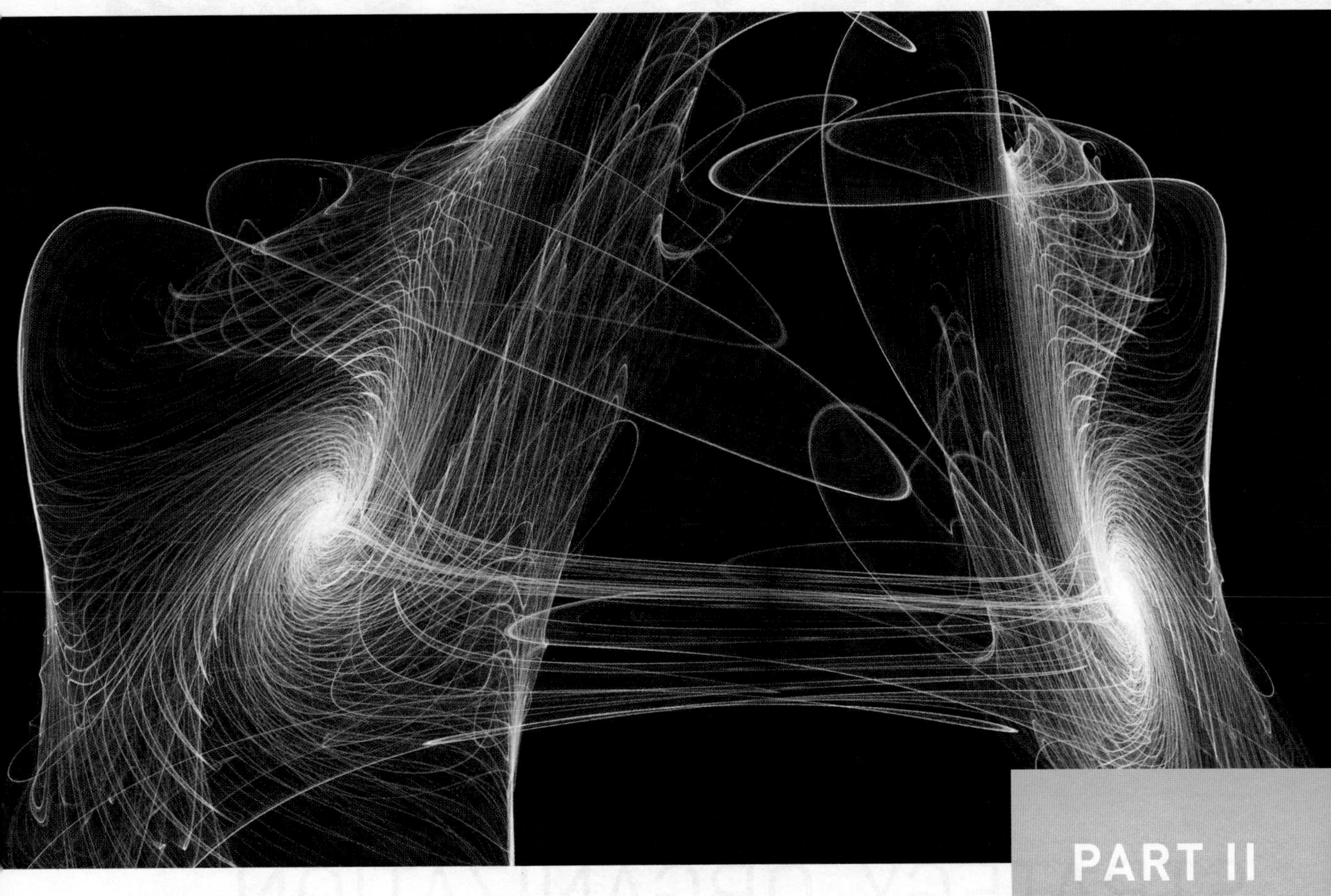

PART II

ORGANIZATIONAL PURPOSE AND STRUCTURAL DESIGN

CHAPTER 2

STRATEGY, ORGANIZATION DESIGN AND EFFECTIVENESS

Starbucks Corporation

Starbucks is one of the world's best known brands. By 2007 the familiar green logo was present in 43 countries, with over 15,000 company-owned and franchised coffee shops around the world.[1] Although several other speciality coffee retailers also established themselves during the 1980s, it was Starbucks that redefined coffee drinking as the emblem of the new class of young urban professionals (yuppies).

The Starbucks phenomenon began in Seattle as a small speciality-coffee retailer, founded in 1971, and named after Captain Ahab's first mate in the book *Moby Dick*. In its early years Starbucks was better known as a coffee bean retailer than coffee shop, but once Howard Schultz took over leadership of the company in 1987, the company never looked back. Starbucks has always pursued a strategy of growth based on promoting its uniqueness. The company doesn't just sell coffee but 'the Starbucks Experience', a phrase that is routinely used in the company's promotional materials, and which is built from its six point mission statement, developed in 1990, that emphasizes a positive work environment, respect for diversity, excellent product quality, satisfied customers, corporate responsibility and profitability. Schultz has steered Starbucks through tremendous growth, but he emphasizes the company's continuing ambitions to tap into various new markets, new customers and new products and services. Schultz's overall goal is to spur greater growth by transforming Starbucks more broadly into a retail chain rather than just a coffee shop. The company's plans for achieving that overall goal include the following:

- Expand the company's food offerings. In 2005, Starbucks began selling lunch in five new markets, bringing to 2,500 the total number of stores offering lunch. Starbucks also successfully tested sales of hot breakfast at its Seattle stores, and has gradually rolled out hot breakfasts elsewhere in the United States.
- Develop the company's entertainment division into a major profit centre. The company's HearMusic brand offers a variety of ways to listen to, and buy music, from traditionally prerecorded CDs to media bars that offer customers the possibility of burning compact discs with their own selection of songs from 15,000 different albums.
- Continue store growth across with world, with 2,500 openings in 2008, and an ultimate goal of 40,000 stores (20,000 in the United States and 20,000 in the rest of the world).[2]

The new goals and plans were a bold push beyond Starbucks' coffee roots. Some observers felt the company's foray into music in particular was a mistake, but Schultz and Donald believed it fit right in with Starbucks' strategy. 'Providing our customers with innovative and unique ways to discover and acquire all genres of great music is another way we are enhancing the Starbucks Experience', said Schultz.[3]

Despite their confidence, by early 2008, many market watchers were worried about Starbucks. On the one hand, the company continued to grow impressively fast, and the company remained very profitable. On the other hand, the company's per-store sales have flattened, and other food chains, especially McDonald's, have begun to fight back effectively. For example, McDonald's has begun offering speciality coffee at many of its stores internationally, at prices significantly below those of Starbucks.[4]

Starbucks' rapid growth beyond its original affluent yuppie target audience, into the more cost-sensitive, blue-collar market, mean the chain's revenues are particularly vulnerable to an economic downturn, such as occurred due to the sub-prime mortgage crisis that enveloped the US in 2007 and then spread around the world. During 2007, Starbucks' shares declined by 50 per cent, leading to pressure from shareholders. On January 8th 2008 Starbucks chairman Howard Schultz acted decisively. He fired Jim Donald as CEO (Donald had spearheaded Starbucks's mass-market drive) and re-assumed the position himself, simultaneously announcing store closures and a reduction in the number of openings in the next year. Schultz's keen market sense had paid off in the past. Would his swift action put Starbucks back on track?

Top managers are responsible for positioning their organizations for success by establishing goals and strategies that can help the organization be competitive as a necessary, but not in itself sufficient, condition of being profitable. An **organizational goal** is a desired state of affairs or outcome that an organization attempts to reach.[5] A goal represents a result or end point toward which it is intended that organizational efforts will be directed. The goals for Starbucks in 2008 included continuing expansion but with more focus than previously, as well as continued diversification into music and a wider food offering. Starbucks's goals aim to reassert the company's differentiation from the competition by creating an overall 'experience'. The choice of goals and strategy affects organization design, as we will discuss in this chapter.

Purpose of This Chapter

Top managers give direction to organizations. They generally exert the greatest influence in setting goals and developing the plans for their organization to attain those goals, although they may operate within a context over which they can exert limited control, at least in the short term. The purpose of this chapter is to help you understand the types of goals that organizations pursue and some of the competitive strategies managers use to reach those goals. We will examine two significant frameworks for determining strategic action and look at how strategies affect organization design. The chapter also describes the most popular approaches to measuring the effectiveness of organizational efforts. To manage organizations well, managers require a clear sense of how to identify and secure effectiveness.

The Role of Strategic Direction in Organization Design

See online COUNTERPOINT 2.9

An organization is created to achieve some purpose, which is decided by the chief executive officer (CEO) and the top management team. In a for-profit business this is generally in consultation with board members, investors and creditors. It is this purpose and direction that shapes how the organization is designed and managed. Indeed, it is widely held that the primary responsibility of top management is to determine an organization's goals, strategy and design, therein adapting the organization to a changing environment.[6] Middle managers are considered to do much the same thing for major departments within the guidelines provided by top management. The relationships through which top managers typically provide direction and then design are illustrated in Exhibit 2.1.

COUNTERPOINT 2.1

One should treat with caution the tendency to represent organization design as a highly rational process which involves careful calculation and proceeds smoothly through a series of stages. In practice, the design of organizations is a messy, political process in which established routines and vested interests are challenged and defended. Uneasy, hybrid compromises are the more normal outcome. There is therefore likely to be some considerable discrepancy and tension between how the design of organizations is represented by top management – for example, as a neat if complex organization chart – and how organizations operate on a day-to-day basis. **Discuss**

EXHIBIT 2.1 Top Management Role in Organization Direction, Design, and Effectiveness

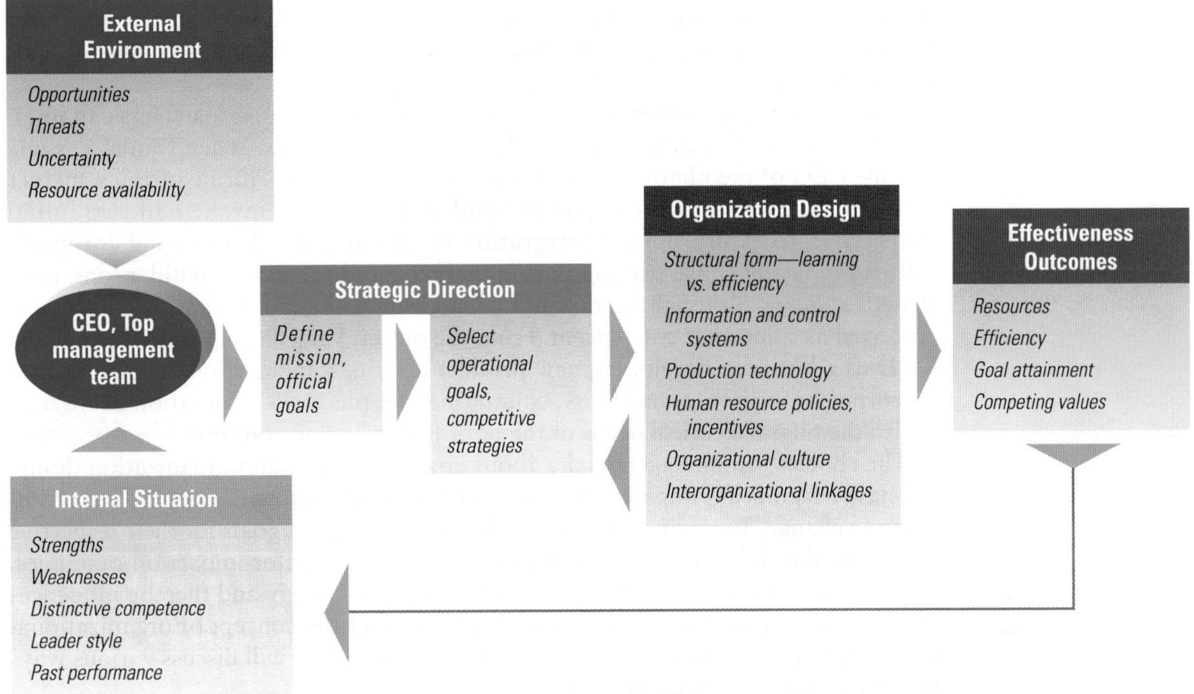

Source: Adapted from Arie Y. Lewin and Carroll U. Stephens, 'Individual Properties of the CEO as Determinants of Organization Design,' unpublished manuscript, Duke University, 1990; and Arie Y. Lewin and Carroll U. Stephens, 'CEO Attributes as Determinants of Organization Design: An Integrated Model,' *Organization Studies* 15, no. 2 (1994), 183–212.

The direction-setting process often involves an assessment of the opportunities and threats in the external environment, including the amount of change, uncertainty and resource availability, which we discuss in more detail in Chapter 4. This includes assessment of internal strengths and weaknesses to define the company's distinctive competence compared with other firms in the industry.[7] The assessment of internal environment includes an evaluation of each department and is shaped by past performance and the leadership style of the CEO and top management team. The process of defining, reaffirming and/or changing the overall mission and official goals is, in principle, a matter of determining the best fit between external opportunities and threats, on the one hand, and internal strengths, including competences, on the other. In this light, specific operational goals or strategies can be formulated to define how the organization is to accomplish what is identified as its overall mission.

In Exhibit 2.1, organization design is presented as reflecting the way goals and strategies are implemented. Organization design is shown as the administration and execution of the strategic plan. Organization direction is seen to be implemented through decisions about structural form, including whether the design of the organization has a learning or an efficiency orientation, as discussed in Chapter 1, as well as choices about information and control systems, the type of production technology, human resource policies, culture and linkages to other organizations. Changes in structure, technology, human resource policies, culture and interorganizational linkages will be discussed in subsequent chapters. Also note the arrow in Exhibit 2.1 running from organization design back to strategic direction. This means that strategies are often made within the current structure of the organization, so that current design constrains or puts limits on goals and strategy.

Finally, Exhibit 2.1 illustrates how managers evaluate the effectiveness of organizational efforts – that is, the extent to which the goals attributed to organizations are realized. This chart reflects the most popular ways of measuring performance, each of which is discussed later in this chapter. It is important to note here that performance measurements feed back into the internal environment, so that past performance of the organization is assessed by top management in setting new goals and strategic direction for the future.

The role of top management is held to be important because managers can interpret the environment differently and develop different goals. When Daniel Vassella became CEO of the pharmaceutical multinational Novartis, formed from a merger between the Swiss-based companies Sandoz and Ciba-Geigy, he had two initial goals. First, to assure smooth integration in an industry where strong corporate cultures typically cause friction during mergers, and second, to build a long-term growth strategy. Although Sandoz and Ciba-Geigy had good reputations, they were perceived as somewhat complacent. From the outset, Vassella emphasized expanded R&D as a basis for developing new product offerings. In addition, he has focused on corporate social responsibility, countering 'big pharma's' reputation as insensitive to the pharmaceutical needs of the poor in developing countries.[8]

The choices top managers make about goals, strategies and organization design can have a significant impact. Remember that goals and strategy are not fixed or immune to change. Top managers and middle managers select goals for their respective units, and the ability to make these choices can have a major impact on outcomes. Organization design is used to implement goals and strategy and thereby influences the prospects of success. We will now discuss further the concept of organizational goals and strategy, and in the latter part of this chapter, we will discuss various ways to evaluate organizational effectiveness.

COUNTERPOINT 2.2

Throughout the book we often focus on private businesses, or corporations, as if they are the only kind of organization. Of course, as we noted in Chapter 1, this is not true. Public sector and non-profit ('third sector') organizations are an important part of the economy in almost every country of the world. Especially in Europe, the public and non-profit sectors can be as large and important as the private sector. For example, in Germany the Catholic welfare association Caritas is the country's largest non-state employer with 350,000 staff,[9] while in most western European countries the public sector accounts for around 40 per cent of GDP.[10] While many aspects of organization theory and design are shared between different economic sectors, there are important differences which we try to highlight throughout the text. **Discuss**

Organizational Purpose

Organizations are maintained, even if they are not deliberately designed in the first instance, to accomplish something. All organizations, including Novartis, Oxford University, Fiat Motors, the Roman Catholic Church, the European Commission, the local dry cleaner and the local grocery store, exist for a purpose. This purpose may be referred to as the overall goal, or mission which emerges from a process of discussion, negotiation and imposition rather than something that is self-evident or 'read off' from reality. Likewise, different parts of the organization establish their own goals and objectives that may be more or less tightly related to what is identified as the overall goal, mission or purpose of the organization. One major distinction is between the officially stated goals, or mission, of the organization and the operative goals that, in practice, are pursued by the organization.

Mission

The overall, officially stated goal attributed an organization is often encapsulated in an explicitly-stated **mission** – the organization's reason for existence. The mission describes the organization's vision, its shared values and beliefs and its reason for being. It can have a powerful impact on an organization.[11] The mission is also sometimes called the **official goals**, referring to the formally-stated definition of business scope and outcomes the organization is trying to achieve. Official goal statements typically define business operations and may focus on values, markets and customers that distinguish the organization. Whether called a mission statement or official goals, the organization's general statement of its purpose and philosophy is often written down in a policy manual and/or the annual report. The mission statement for the American insurance company State Farm is shown in Exhibit 2.2. Note how the overall mission, values and goals are all defined.

One of the primary purposes of a mission statement is to serve as a communication tool.[12] The *mission statement* communicates to current and prospective employees, customers, investors, suppliers and competitors what the organization stands for and what it is trying to achieve. A mission statement communicates to internal and external stakeholders, who may join and be committed to the organization because they identify with its stated purpose. Most top leaders want employees, customers, competitors, suppliers, investors and the local community to look on them in a favorable light, and the concept of legitimacy plays a critical role.[13] The corporate concern for legitimacy is real and pertinent. Consider the accounting firm Arthur Andersen, which was accused of obstructing justice by shredding accounting documents related to the Enron investigation. Once the previously respected global firm lost legitimacy with clients, investors and the public, it was all but dead. From 85,000 employees in 2002, by 2007 Arthur Anderson had a skeleton staff of about 200, working mainly on handling the lawsuits against the company and presiding over its orderly dissolution. In the post-Enron environment of weakened trust and increasing regulation, many organizations face the need to redefine their purpose and mission to emphasize the firm's purpose in more than financial terms.[14]

As an organization manager, keep these guidelines in mind:

Establish and communicate organizational mission and goals. Communicate official goals to provide a statement of the organization's mission to external constituents. Communicate operational goals to provide internal direction, guidelines and standards of performance for employees.

EXHIBIT 2.2 State Farm's Mission Statement

STATE FARM INSURANCE
Our Mission, Our Vision and Our Shared Values

State Farm's mission is to help people manage the risks of everyday life, recover from the unexpected and realize their dreams.

We are people who make it our business to be like a good neighbor; who built a premier company by selling and keeping promises through our marketing partnerships; who bring diverse talents and experiences to our work of serving the State Farm customer.

Our success is built on a foundation of shared values – quality service and relationships, mutual trust, integrity and financial strength.

Our vision for the future is to be the customer's first and best choice in the products and services we provide. We will continue to be the leader in the insurance industry and we will become a leader in the financial services arena. Our customers' needs will determine our path. Our values will guide us.

Source: 'News and Notes from State Farm,' Public Affairs Department, 2500 Memorial Boulevard, Murfreesboro, TN 37131.

Companies where managers are sincerely guided by mission statements that focus on their social purpose, such as Medtronic's 'To restore people to full life and health' or Liberty Mutual's 'Helping people live safer, more secure lives', typically attract better employees, have better relationships with external parties, and perform better in the marketplace over the long term.[15]

COUNTERPOINT 2.3

Although most people agree that mission statements help to focus a company, they are not a panacea for unexpected business downturns, or poor management. Enron, for example, had a mission statement that promised the company would always be 'open and fair' even though corporate managers were ultimately convicted for multi-billion pound fraud![16] While some academic studies have shown companies with mission statements perform better, others have not been able to show such a link. Most likely, it is not so much the mission statement itself that helps a company succeed, but rather the benefit of focusing corporate leadership on defining the organization's purpose.[17] **Discuss**

Operative Goals

Operative goals designate the ends sought through the actual operating procedures of the organization and explain what the organization is actually trying to do.[18] Operative goals describe specific measurable outcomes and are often concerned with the short run. Operative goals may sometimes appear not to be consistent with stated goals. Operative goals typically pertain to the primary tasks an organization must perform, similar to the subsystem activities identified in Chapter 1.[19] These goals concern overall performance, boundary spanning, maintenance, adaptation and production activities. Specific goals for each primary task provide direction for the day-to-day decisions and activities within departments.

Overall Performance Profitability is the most widely accepted benchmark of the overall performance of for-profit organizations. Profitability may be expressed in terms of net income, earnings per share or return on investment. Other overall performance goals are growth and output volume. Growth pertains to increases in revenues over time. Volume pertains to total sales or the amount of products or services delivered. For example, the global truck manufacturer Volvo aims to increase sales by 10 per cent annually over a business cycle, while maintaining a focus on profitability.[20]

Government and non-profit organizations such as social service agencies or trade unions do not usually have profitability goals, but they do have goals that attempt to specify the delivery of services to clients, members or other beneficiaries within specified expense levels. The United States Internal Revenue Service has a goal of providing accurate responses to 85 per cent of taxpayer questions about new tax laws. Growth and volume goals also may be indicators of overall performance in non-profit organizations. Expanding their services to new clients is a primary goal for many social service agencies, such as the UK Samaritans, which provides helpline services to people in crisis.

Resources Resource goals refer to the acquisition of needed material and financial resources from the environment. They may involve obtaining financing for the construction of new plants, finding less expensive sources for raw materials or hiring top-quality technology graduates. Resource goals for the French business school INSEAD include attracting top-notch professors and students. Honda Motor Company has resource goals of obtaining high-quality auto parts at low cost.

For Britain's the Samaritans NGO, resource goals include recruiting dedicated volunteers and expanding the organization's funding base.

Market Market goals relate to the market share or market standing desired by the organization. Market goals are the responsibility of marketing, sales and advertising departments. An example of a market goal is Honda's desire to overtake Toyota Motor Company as the number-one seller of cars in Japan. Honda surpassed Nissan to become number two in Japan, and the Fit subcompact,[21] introduced in 2001, briefly eclipsed the Toyota Corolla as the best-selling car in that market, although the Corolla soon regained top spot.[22] In the toy industry, Canada's Mega Bloks Inc. managed to more than achieve its goal of 30 per cent of the North American construction toy market, and began aggressive international expansion as well as expansion of its product lines. The global giant of the industry, Denmark's Lego, has attempted to stop Mega Blok's growth internationally[23] through both intellectual property lawsuits (mainly unsuccessful) and by refocusing on its core business.[24]

Employee Development Employee development refers to the training, promotion, health and safety and growth of employees. It includes both managers and workers. Strong employee development goals are one of the characteristics common to organizations that regularly show up on lists of the best companies to work for. Spansion, a joint chip-making venture between Japan's Fujitsu and the US-based AMD, has been voted best employer in Asia. Its employees, mainly based in Thailand and China, appreciate the company's commitment to employee development, even though it doesn't necessarily pay the highest wages. Its Singaporean CEO, Loh Poh Chye, says, 'We are always willing to offer training to someone who's motivated, or move someone to a new department, laterally, to work across and up in a new area'.[25]

Innovation and Change Innovation goals refer to internal flexibility and readiness to adapt to unexpected changes in the environment. Innovation goals are often defined with respect to the development of specific new services, products or production processes. 3M Co. has a goal that 30 per cent of sales should come from products that are less than four years old.[26]

Productivity Productivity goals concern the amount of output achieved from available resources. They typically describe the amount of resource inputs required to reach desired outputs and are thus stated in terms of 'cost for a unit of production', 'units produced per employee', or 'resource cost per employee'. Managers at US-based Akamai Technologies, which sells Web content delivery services, keep a close eye on sales per employee to see if the company is meeting productivity goals. Akamai's chief financial officer, Timothy Weller, sees this statistic as 'the single easiest measure of employee productivity'. Embraer, the Brazilian aircraft manufacturer, has gone from being a technologically-advanced though inefficient state-owned company to a high-productivity, profitable manufacturer ranking third in the world in sales in its market category, in little more than a decade. As one of the rapidly-emerging BRIC countries, Brazil is becoming a more costly place to build aircraft, and new competitors such as China and Russia are threatening the company's dominance in the commuter-jet segment. Embraer CEO Frederico Curado is responding by emphasizing productivity: revising production processes, investing in equipment and perfecting lean manufacturing technologies, 'It's a day-to-day battle. This is not a war, and it's over', the 46-year-old engineer said. In addition, the company is hiring staff earlier in their careers, at moderate salary levels.[27] Once the wings and landing gear are attached, each plane is dragged toward the door at two inches

Wegmans

Supermarkets aren't typically considered great places to work. The pay is low, the hours are gruelling, and you don't get much appreciation from anyone. Most supermarkets have annual turnover rates of 19 to 20 per cent and as much as 100 per cent for part-timers. But the situation is different at Wegmans, an American chain of sixty-seven stores in New York, Pennsylvania, New Jersey and Virginia. Annual turnover is just six per cent for full-time employees. About 6,000 Wegmans workers have at least ten years of service, and more than 800 have worked at Wegmans stores for a quarter of a century.

Wegmans is one of the most successful supermarket chains in the United States. Its operating margins are about double that of the other four big chains (Albertson's, Kroger, Safeway and Ahold USA). Sales per square foot are 50 per cent higher than the industry average. An annual survey conducted by Cannondale Associates found that Wegmans beat all other retailers – even Wal-Mart – in merchandising savvy.

Employee commitment and satisfaction is an important factor in Wegmans success, and managers consider meeting goals for employee development just as important as meeting sales, profit or productivity targets. 'You cannot separate their strategy as a retailer from their strategy as an employer', says consultant Darrell Rigby, head of Bain & Company's global retail practice. Hourly wages and annual salaries at Wegmans are among the highest in the industry, but that's only a small part of the story. What really sets Wegmans apart is that it creates an environment and provides the resources to enable employees to develop to their fullest potential. The company has invested $54 million for college scholarships to more than 17,500 full- and part-time employees over the past 20 years. It thinks nothing of sending employees on trips to visit wineries in California or cheesemakers in Italy. 'It's our knowledge that can help the customer', says president Danny Wegman. 'So the first pump we have to prime is our own people.' Employees are empowered to do just about anything to satisfy a customer, without checking with a higher-up. Operations chief Jack DePeters says only half-jokingly that Wegmans is 'a $3 billion company run by 16-year-old cashiers'.

Priming the pump is illustrated by the opening of a new Wegmans store in Dulles, Virginia, where the company spent $5 million on training alone. The company refuses to open a new store until everyone is fully prepared. Wegmans could have easily opened in November 2003, in time for the critical holiday sales season, but chose to wait until February. The emphasis on development over dollars pays off. Wegmans attracts high-quality employees, both for management and store positions. Eighty-six-year-old Robert Wegman, chairman of the company, explains why he's always emphasized employee development goals despite the high costs: 'I have never given away more than I got back.'

Source: Matthew Boyle, 'The Wegmans Way', *Fortune* (January 24, 2005), 62–68.

a minute, with workers moving along with it on a floatlike apparatus. Of course, competitors don't sit still either – Embraer's giant US rival Boeing has a productivity goal to push a 737 jet out of the door in five days, down from the eleven days that it currently takes.[28]

Successful organizations are held to use a balanced set of operative goals. Although profitability goals are important, some of today's best companies calculate that a single-minded focus on bottom-line profits may not be the best way to achieve and maintain outstanding performance. Innovation and change goals are increasingly important, even though they may initially be disruptive leading to a loss of performance measured in financial terms. Employee development goals are relevant for helping to maintain a motivated, committed workforce which can be important for corporate prosperity.

EXHIBIT 2.3 Goal Type and Purpose

Type of Goals	Purpose of Goals
Official goals, mission:	Legitimacy
Operative goals:	Employee direction and motivation
	Decision guidelines
	Standard of performance

The Importance of Goals

Both official goals and operative goals are important for the organization, but they serve very different purposes. Official goals and mission statements describe a value system for the organization that is frequently preoccupied with engendering legitimacy, Operative goals related to key tasks of the organization. Official goals legitimize the organization; operative goals are often more explicit and comparatively well defined.

Operative goals serve several specific purposes, as outlined in Exhibit 2.3. For one thing, goals can provide employees with a sense of direction, so that they know what they are working toward. This can help to motivate employees toward goal accomplishment, especially if employees are involved in setting the targets. The events at Iraq's notorious Abu Ghraib prison provide a negative illustration of the motivating power of goals. Analysts say one of the explanations for the abuse of Iraqi detainees may have been that US soldiers guarding prisoners at Abu Ghraib were under much pressure to meet quotas on the number of interrogations and intelligence reports they generated that they resorted to unethical approaches and even abuse.[29] Managers need to understand the power of goals and targets and use care when setting and implementing them. Another important purpose of goals is to act as guidelines for employee behaviour and decision-making. Appropriate goals can act as a set of constraints on individual behaviour and actions so that employees behave within boundaries that are acceptable to the organization and larger society.[30] They help to define the appropriate decisions concerning organization structure, innovation, employee welfare or growth. Finally, goals provide a standard for assessment. The level of organizational performance, whether in terms of profits, units produced, degree of employee satisfaction, level of innovation or number of customer complaints, requires a basis for evaluation. Operative goals translate officially stated goals, of mission, into more substantive courses of action and means of measuring their attainment.

A Framework for Selecting Strategy and Design

To support and accomplish the direction determined by organizational mission and operative goals, managers select specific strategy and design options that they justify in relation to their relevance for achieving official and operative goals within its competitive environment. In this section, we examine a couple of practical approaches to selecting strategy and design.

A **strategy** is a plan for interacting with the competitive environment to achieve organizational goals. Some managers think of goals and strategies as interchangeable, but for our purposes, *goals* define where the organization wants to go and *strategies* define how it will get there. For example, a goal might be to achieve

15 per cent annual sales growth; strategies to reach that goal might include aggressive advertising to attract new customers, motivating salespeople to increase the average size of customer purchases and acquiring other businesses that produce similar products. Strategies can include any number of techniques to achieve the goal. One important aspect of formulating strategies is choosing whether the organization will perform different activities than its competitors or will execute similar activities more efficiently than its competitors do.[31]

Two models for formulating strategies are the Porter model of competitive strategies and Miles and Snow's strategy typology. Each provides a framework for competitive action. After describing the two models and some newer strategy concepts, we will discuss how the choice of strategies affects organization design.

BRIEFCASE

As an organization manager, keep these guidelines in mind:

After goals have been defined, select strategies for achieving those goals. Define specific strategies based on Porter's competitive strategies or Miles and Snow's strategy typology.

Porter's Competitive Strategies

Michael E. Porter studied a number of businesses and introduced a framework describing three competitive strategies: low-cost leadership, differentiation and focus.[32] The focus strategy, in which the organization concentrates on a specific market or buyer group, is further divided into *focused low cost* and *focused differentiation*. This yields four basic strategies, as illustrated in Exhibit 2.4. To use this model, managers evaluate two factors, competitive advantage and competitive scope. With respect to advantage, managers determine whether to compete through lower cost or through the ability to offer unique or distinctive products and services that can command a premium price. Managers then determine whether the organization will compete on a broad scope (competing in many customer segments) or a narrow scope (competing in a selected customer segment or group of segments). These choices determine the selection of strategies, as illustrated in Exhibit 2.4.

EXHIBIT 2.4 Porter's Competitive Strategies

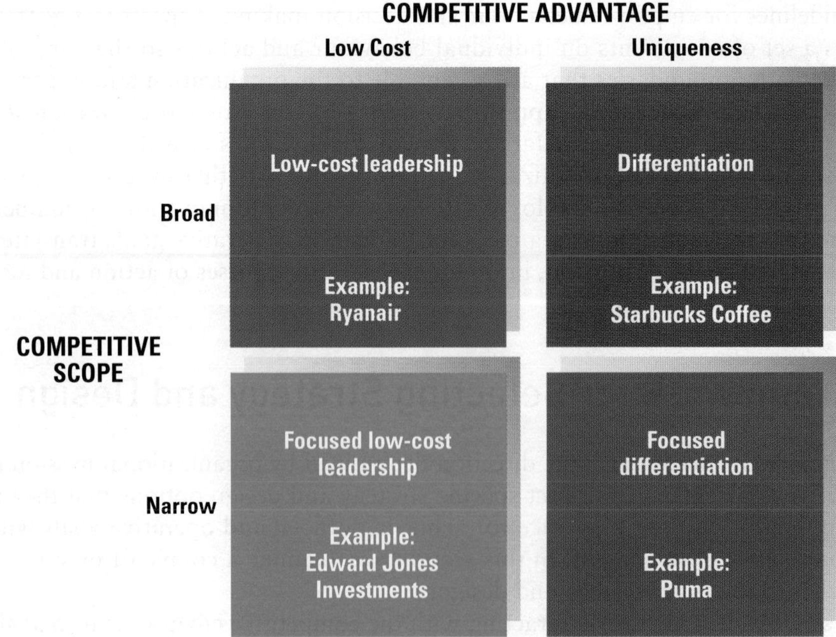

Source: Adapted with the permission of The Free Press, a division of Simon & Schuster Adult Publishing Group, from *Competitive Advantage: Creating and Sustaining Superior Performance* by Michael E. Porter. Copyright © 1985, 1988 by Michael E. Porter.

Differentiation In a **differentiation** strategy, organizations attempt to distinguish their products or services from others in the industry. An organization may use advertising, distinctive product features, exceptional service or new technology to achieve a product perceived as unique. This strategy usually targets customers who are not particularly concerned with price, so it can be quite profitable. Rolex watches, Tommy Hilfiger clothing and Jaguar automobiles are examples of products from companies using a differentiation strategy. Service firms such as the Nationwide Building Society (mortgage bank) in the UK, Four Seasons Hotels and Starbucks Coffee, described in the chapter opening, can use a differentiation strategy as well.

A differentiation strategy can reduce rivalry with competitors and fight off the threat of substitute products because customers are loyal to the company's brand. However, companies must remember that successful differentiation strategies require a number of costly activities, such as product research and design and extensive advertising. Companies that pursue a differentiation strategy need strong marketing abilities and creative employees who are given the time and resources to seek innovations.

Low-Cost Leadership The **low-cost leadership** strategy tries to increase market share by emphasizing low cost compared to competitors. With a low-cost leadership strategy, the organization aggressively seeks efficient facilities, pursues cost reductions and uses tight controls to produce products or services more efficiently than its competitors. One good example of a low-cost leadership strategy is the Irish airline Ryanair.

Ryanair

Fifteen or so years ago, Michael O'Leary took a trip that would change his life – and transform the Irish air carrier Ryanair into Europe's most successful, most profitable airline. O'Leary, who had been brought in as chief executive of Ryanair to save the ailing carrier, flew on American low cost carrier Southwest Airlines and learned the tricks of running a low-cost airline.

O'Leary says of his corporate strategy: 'It's the oldest, simplest formula: Pile 'em high and sell 'em cheap . . . We want to be the Wal-Mart of the airline business. Nobody will beat us on price. EVER.' And sell 'em cheap he does. One industry expert says ticket prices on Ryanair are so inexpensive that it's 'nearly a no-fare carrier'. Ryanair often offers fares across Europe of less than €10 including taxes, although travellers have to be quick on their mouse buttons to catch fares like this, as well as careful to avoid a wide range of 'optional extras' and hidden but unavoidable charges such as a credit card charge for each leg of each flight for each passenger booked.

Ryanair is able to offer low fares because it keeps costs at rock bottom, lower than anyone else in Europe. The company's mantra is cheap tickets, not customer care. The carrier offers no business class, maximizes seating space, turns around an aircraft in 25 minutes rather than the 45 or so required by traditional carriers and doesn't offer travel agent commissions. Most tickets are sold over the Internet, and Ryanair is the largest short-haul carrier in Europe. Instead of giving away snacks or food, Ryanair sells it. Staff costs are kept low too. In one recent year, the airline employed fewer than 2,000 people to fly 24 million passengers a year, while the German carrier Lufthansa employed about 30,000 people to fly 37 million.

Ryanair's passenger numbers continue to grow. They soared from 3.9 million in 1998 to more than 24 million in 2005, and nearly 50 million in 2007.[33] The airline industry is increasingly competitive, other low-cost carriers are encroaching on Ryanair's territory, and soaring fuel prices in 2007 and 2008 were worrying even as confident a CEO as Michael O'Leary. But he knows that Ryanair can beat anyone on price and cost control. As long as the airline keeps its disciplined approach, Ryanair will continue to dominate the European low-cost market.[34]

Although Ryanair is expanding, continuing to add new routes, the low-cost leadership strategy is usually concerned primarily with stability rather than taking risks or seeking new opportunities for innovation and growth. A low-cost position means a company can undercut competitors' prices and still offer comparable quality and earn a reasonable profit. But when prices are already rock-bottom and the company relies upon passengers with limited disposable income, keeping flights full is a testing challenge. If flights cannot be filled, costs are already pared to the bone and novel ways of raising income are not developed, the only way to save cost is to ground the planes – something that Ryanair has done during the recession of 2008 – or to find ways of deriving additional revenues from existing passengers – for example by introducing restrictive baggage allowances and then applying high penalties for exceeding them.

Focus With Porter's third strategy, the **focus strategy**, the organization concentrates on a specific regional market or buyer group. The company will try to achieve either a low-cost advantage or a differentiation advantage within a narrowly defined market. One good example of a focused low-cost strategy is Edward Jones, a brokerage house headquartered in St. Louis in America's Midwest. The firm has succeeded by building its business in rural and small-town America and providing investors with conservative, long-term investments.[35] An example of a focused differentiation strategy is Puma, the German athletic-wear manufacturer. In 1993, when CEO Jochen Zeitz took the helm, Puma was on the brink of bankruptcy. Zeitz, then only 30 years old, revived the brand by targeting selected customer groups, especially armchair athletes and creating stylish shoes and clothes that set design trends. Puma went, 'out of its way to be different', says analyst Roland Könen. Zeitz says Puma decided to be a, 'very sports-fashion brand when at the times everybody talked about sports, and sports performance and functionality. We said well it's about more.' The differentiation strategy worked and sales and profits reflected the change. Puma has been profitable every year since 1994, with sales growing faster than those of competitors.[36] Puma is ranked in the top 25 best-known brands in the US – an achievement in a country where domestic brands tend to predominate. In 2007 the company was acquired at a valuation of $5.3 billion by the French luxury brand conglomerate PPR (formerly Pinot Printemps Redoute), which owns such iconic brands as Gucci and Yves St. Laurent.[37]

When managers fail to adopt a competitive strategy, the organization is left with no strategic advantage, and performance almost inevitably suffers. Porter found that companies that did not consciously adopt a low-cost, differentiation, or focus strategy, for example, achieved below-average profits compared to those that used one of the three strategies. Many Internet companies have failed because they did not develop competitive strategies that would distinguish them in the marketplace.[38] On the other hand, eBay and Google have been highly successful with coherent differentiation strategies. The ability of managers to devise and maintain a clear competitive strategy is one of the defining factors in an organization's success, as further discussed in this chapter's Bookmark.

COUNTERPOINT 2.4

Is it always a good idea to have a powerful, charismatic CEO? In this chapter we have sometimes emphasized the role of powerful CEOs, like Ryanair's Michael O'Leary, Puma's Jochen Zeitz and Starbucks' Howard Schultz. Partly this is because it is always easier to attach ideas and direction to an individual rather than to a management team as a whole.

The achievements of O'Leary, Zeitz and Schultz are real and should be acknowledged. However, strong and charismatic leadership can be a double-edged sword. Researchers are divided about the impact of charismatic leadership on profits; while some have found a positive leadership effect, others have found little or no benefit over organizations driven by bureaucratic leaders who focus on incremental change and following tried-and-true strategies. Rakesh Khurana notes in *Harvard Business Review* that, 'for all the excitement and optimism that are generated by superstar CEOs, the truth remains that the factors affecting corporate performance are varied, highly nuanced, almost frighteningly complex and certainly beyond the power of even the most charismatic leader to influence single-handedly. To pretend otherwise is to grossly oversimplify reality in the hope of finding easy answers.'

It is also important to recognize that charismatic leadership can be a force for harm as well as for good. The case of Enron is an example of the potentially negative impact of charismatic leadership. Top executives including Kenneth Lay and Jeffrey Skilling built a corporate culture that was at the same time ambitious and dynamic, and unethical and ultimately fraudulent. The company's internal culture was so dominated by this leadership that employees felt powerless to 'blow the whistle' on inappropriate business practices.

Some management scholars feel that the current emphasis on charismatic corporate leadership creates an environment where other 'Enrons' can emerge. Dennis Tourish and Naheed Vatcha argue that, 'the increased primacy afforded to shareholder value, the growing power of CEOs and market pressure for speedy results implies the further erosion of cultures that embrace discussion, debate and dissent'.[39] In any event, reliance upon a single individual is a source of vulnerability, especially when circumstances that have favoured his or her skills change. Perhaps success is less related to the skills per se but, rather, to their match with particular contingencies and opportunities. It is also worth noting that Porter's analysis makes no reference to the importance of good fit between a favoured strategy and the capacity (e.g. 'competencies') of the organization. **Discuss**

Miles and Snow's Strategy Typology

Another business strategy typology was developed from the study of business strategies by Raymond Miles and Charles Snow.[40] The Miles and Snow typology is based on the idea that managers seek to formulate strategies that will be congruent with the external environment. Organizations strive for a fit among internal organization characteristics, strategy and the external environment. The four strategies that can be developed are the prospector, the defender, the analyzer and the reactor.

Prospector The **prospector** strategy is to innovate, take risks, seek out new opportunities and grow. This strategy is suited to a dynamic, growing environment, where creativity is more important than efficiency. Historically, FedEx Corporation, the multinational courier firm, has been an innovator in both services and production technology in the rapidly changing shipping, document management and information services industry, and exemplifies the prospector strategy, as have leading high-tech companies, such as Microsoft.

Defender The **defender** strategy is almost the opposite of the prospector. Rather than taking risks and seeking out new opportunities, the defender strategy is concerned with stability or even retrenchment. This strategy seeks to hold onto current customers, but it neither innovates nor seeks to grow. The defender is concerned primarily with internal efficiency and control to produce reliable, high-quality products for steady customers. This strategy can be successful when the organization exists in

Have you read this book?

Managing Sceptically: A Critique of Organizational Fashion

BY HARVIE RAMSAY

In *Managing Sceptically*, Harvie Ramsay takes a close look at many 'innovations' in organization theory and management practice, and finds many of them to be fads that are quickly forgotten and replaced by other new, but often shallow ideas. Some past fads that Ramsay identifies include:

- *Quality circles*: this idea was imported from Japan in the 1970s, and saw its greatest popularity in the early 1980s. The idea was for groups of workers to get together to discuss ways to improve the production process. Within a few years researchers found that any short-term gains were quickly lost. Corporate productivity is embedded in a whole range of social relationships that extend into wider society, and in most cases productivity cannot be fundamentally improved by adopting a single idea from another country
- *Total Quality Management*: a combination of American systems theory and Japanese meticulousness, TQM was intended to ensure organization-wide quality management, resulting in improved products for consumers, as well as better return to shareholders. TQM seems to have been successful mainly when combined with incentive bonuses, suggesting that it did not succeed in improving intrinsic employee motivation. By the mid-1990s, TQM seemed to be reaching the end of its life cycle.
- *Change management*: an approach that aims to structure the change process in an organization from current practices to an improved future. There are numerous change management models, which might include stages such as developing a change management strategy, enrolling senior managers as change leaders, communicating the need for change, training employees in the changed systems, coaching employees to accept and support change and approaches to sustaining the change. However, Ramsay cites one large-scale study that showed only one-third of organizations undertaking change management achieved lasting organizational strengthening.

Ramsay considers different explanations for why organizations continue to seize on new fads and fashions, given the singular lack of evidence for their success. These include the inherent contradiction in business organizations between the means to achieve improved productivity which is largely through building employee commitment, and the appropriation by shareholders of the resultant increased profits. He concludes that there is a tendency for fads to oscillate between 'rationalist' approaches such as Taylorism and 'normative' approaches, each of which generates dysfunctionalities that lead to oscillating paradigm shifts between the two norms.

Ramsay's work is several years old, but the pattern of management fads continues unabated. A highly influential and long-lasting fad for private-public partnerships was generated by David Osborne and Ted Gaebler's 1992 *Reinventing Government*. Although Osborne and Gaebler intended to strengthen public service provision, the result of applying their ideas was often state capture by private interests and the loss of universal public services. Many of the private finance schemes set up as part of the 'reinventing government' movement have proven poor value for money, and a number collapsed during the 2007–2009 global economic crisis, leaving the taxpayer holding the tab.

Source: Faranak Miraftab (2004), 'Public-Private Partnerships: The Trojan Horse of Neoliberal Development?', *Journal of Planning Education and Research*, 24, 89–101.

Source: Warwick Funnell, Robert Jupe and Jane Andrew (2009), *In Government We Trust: Market-Failure and the Delusions of Privatisation*, London, Pluto; David Walker (2008), 'Out with the outsourcers?' *Prospect*, November 20.

'*Managing Sceptically: A Critique of Organizational Fashion*', is Chapter Nine in Stewart Clegg and Gill Palmer (1996), *The politics of management knowledge*, London, Sage.

a declining industry or a stable environment. Paramount Pictures has been using a defender strategy for several years.[41] Paramount turns out a steady stream of reliable hits but few blockbusters. Managers shun risk and sometimes turn down potentially high-profile films to keep a lid on costs. This has enabled the company to remain highly profitable while other studios have low returns or actually lose money.

Analyzer The **analyzer** tries to maintain a stable business while innovating on the periphery. It seems to lie midway between the prospector and the defender. Some products will be targeted toward stable environments in which an efficiency strategy designed to keep current customers is used. Others will be targeted toward new, more dynamic environments, where growth is possible. The analyzer attempts to balance efficient production for current product lines with the creative development of new product lines. Sony Corp. illustrates an analyzer strategy as, increasingly, does Microsoft. Sony's strategy is to defend its position in traditional consumer electronics, but also build a business in the 'integrated home entertainment' market, such as with its innovative Vaio computer.[42] Businesses that have become established and enjoy a degree of market domination often find it difficult to balance retention of market share in the face of more agile competitors while also attempting to exploit opportunities for innovative products.

Reactor The **reactor** strategy is not really a strategy at all. Rather, reactors respond to environmental threats and opportunities in an ad hoc fashion. In a reactor strategy, top management has not defined a long-range plan or given the organization an explicit mission or goal, so the organization takes whatever actions seem to meet immediate needs. Although the reactor strategy can sometimes be successful, it can also lead to failed companies. Some large, once highly successful companies, such as Xerox and Kodak, have struggled, at least partly, because managers failed to adopt a strategy consistent with consumer trends. In recent years, managers at McDonald's, long one of the most successful fast-food franchises in the world, have also been floundering to find the appropriate strategy. McDonald's had a string of disappointing quarterly profits as competitors continued to steal market share. Franchisees grew aggravated and discouraged by the uncertainty and lack of clear strategic direction for the future. Recent innovations such as healthier food options have revived sales and profits, but managers still are struggling to implement a coherent strategy.[43]

The Miles and Snow typology has been widely used, and researchers have tested its validity in a variety of organizations, including hospitals, colleges, banking institutions, industrial products companies and life insurance firms. In general, researchers have found strong support for the effectiveness of this typology for organization managers in real-world situations.[44]

Emerging Concepts in Business Strategy

Strategy is a highly dynamic field. Companies – and management thinkers – are always looking for new approaches that will give them an edge over competition. Typically this involves looking at business opportunities and challenges from an entirely different angle. One interesting new concept is Chan Kim and Renée Mauborgne's Blue Ocean Strategy.[45] Kim and Mauborgne divide up markets into what they call 'red oceans' and 'blue oceans'. Red oceans are market segments that are already being exploited; where strategy is geared towards finding ways to gain an edge over competitors. Although strategy is useful in these areas, as Porter and Miles and Snow discuss, ultimately the red oceans are crowded and returns on strategic innovation will decline over time. By contrast, blue oceans are industries or business ideas that are not currently in existence, and thus the size of blue ocean market space is unknown. If companies can come up with concepts for products or services that meet (or even define) consumers' needs, and which are not currently in the marketplace, they take advantage of the 'blue ocean' space and generate strong profits. The authors conducted a study of business launches in 108 companies, and found that while only 14 per cent were geared to creating blue oceans, these delivered 38 per cent of total revenues and an impressive 61 per cent of total profits.

Another aspect that recent strategy thinkers have considered is the importance of strategy models in start-up companies, where the structure and philosophy imprinted on the organization at its beginning can be a key determinant of success and failure. A major Stanford University study looked at emerging hi-tech companies. James Barron and Michael Hannan, the study leaders, grouped together the differing blueprints that hi-tech entrepreneurs had in mind for their organizations as they were developing them. The five groups were star (recruiting top talent and paying highly), engineering (emphasizing professional commitment), commitment (building a strong family identity to encourage retention), bureaucracy (documented rules and systems for every eventuality), autocracy (hierarchical discipline) and companies with no clear blueprint type. Barron and Hannan found that these founding blueprints had a significant impact on success; the 'commitment' approach was the most successful model.[46]

How Strategies Affect Organization Design

As an organization manager, keep these guidelines in mind:

Design the organization to support the firm's competitive strategy. With a low-cost leadership or defender strategy, select design characteristics associated with an efficiency orientation. For a differentiation or prospector strategy, on the other hand, choose characteristics that encourage learning, innovation and adaptation. Use a balanced mixture of characteristics for an analyzer strategy.

Choice of strategy has implications for internal organization characteristics. In principle, organization design characteristics support the firm's competitive approach. For example, it is likely that a company wanting to grow and invent new products will look and 'feel' different from a company focused on maintaining market share for long-established products in a stable industry. Exhibit 2.5 summarizes organization design characteristics associated with the Porter and Miles and Snow strategies.

COUNTERPOINT 2.5

The models devised by Porter and Miles and Snow, as well as the newer ideas like Blue Ocean strategy, can be analytically useful for distinguishing between different types of strategic orientation. In practice, the picture for any organization is likely to be messier, with hybrid elements and different forms of strategy being pursued for different divisions or product lines. Ultimately, the pursuit of a strategy depends upon the dispositions and capabilities of employees as much as the diagnosis of the environment of the positioning of the organization to exploit it. What type of strategy makes sense as well as how it is pursued will be contingent upon how managers and other employees assess the situation and their capacity to persuade others – suppliers and customers but especially investors – to support their assessment. **Discuss**

With a low-cost leadership strategy, managers take an efficiency approach to organization design, whereas a differentiation strategy calls for a learning approach. Recall from Chapter 1 that organizations designed for efficiency have different characteristics from those designed for learning. A low-cost leadership strategy (efficiency) is associated with strong, centralized authority and tight control, standard operating procedures and emphasis on efficient procurement and distribution systems. Employees generally perform routine tasks under close supervision and control and are not empowered to make decisions or take action on their own. A differentiation strategy, on the other hand, requires that employees be constantly experimenting and learning. Structure is more fluid and flexible, with strong horizontal coordination. Empowered employees work directly with customers and are rewarded for creativity and risk taking. The organization values research, creativity and innovativeness over efficiency and standard procedures.

EXHIBIT 2.5 Organization Design Outcomes of Strategy

Porter's Competitive Strategies	Miles and Snow's Strategy Typology
Strategy: Differentiation **Organization Design:** • Learning orientation; acts in a flexible, loosely knit way, with strong horizontal coordination • Strong capability in research • Values and builds in mechanisms for customer intimacy • Rewards employee creativity, risk taking and innovation **Strategy:** Low-Cost Leadership **Organization Design:** • Efficiency orientation; strong central authority; tight cost control, with frequent, detailed control reports • Standard operating procedures • Highly efficient procurement and distribution systems • Close supervision; routine tasks; limited employee empowerment	**Strategy:** Prospector **Organization Design:** • Learning orientation; flexible, fluid, decentralized structure • Strong capability in research **Strategy:** Defender **Organization Design:** • Efficiency orientation; centralized authority and tight cost control • Emphasis on production efficiency; low overhead • Close supervision; little employee empowerment **Strategy:** Analyzer **Organization Design:** • Balances efficiency and learning; tight cost control with flexibility and adaptability • Efficient production for stable product lines; emphasis on creativity, research, risk-taking for innovation **Strategy:** Reactor **Organization Design:** • No clear organizational approach; design characteristics may shift abruptly, depending on current needs

Source: Based on Michael E. Porter, *Competitive Strategy: Techniques for Analyzing Industries and Competitors* (New York: The Free Press, 1980); Michael Treacy and Fred Wiersema, 'How Market Leaders Keep Their Edge,' *Fortune* (February 6, 1995), 88–98; Michael Hitt, R. Duane Ireland, and Robert E. Hoskisson, *Strategic Management* (St. Paul, Minn.: West, 1995), 100–113; and Raymond E. Miles, Charles C. Snow, Alan D. Meyer, and Henry J. Coleman, Jr., 'Organizational Strategy, Structure, and Process,' *Academy of Management Review* 3 (1978), 546–562.

The prospector strategy requires characteristics similar to a differentiation strategy, and the defender strategy takes an efficiency approach similar to low-cost leadership. Because the analyzer strategy attempts to balance efficiency for stable product lines with flexibility and learning for new products, it is associated with a mix of characteristics, as listed in Exhibit 2.5. With a reactor strategy, managers have left the organization with no direction and no clear approach to design.

Other Factors Affecting Organization Design

Strategy is one important factor that affects organization design. Ultimately, however, organization design is a result of numerous contingencies, which will be discussed throughout this book. The emphasis given to efficiency and control versus learning and flexibility is determined by the contingencies of strategy, environment, size and life cycle, technology and organizational culture. In principle, the organization is designed to achieve a good 'fit' with the contingency factors, as illustrated in Exhibit 2.6.

For example, in a stable environment, a traditional structure that emphasizes vertical control, efficiency, specialization, standard procedures and centralized decision making is more viable, at least from a managerial and technical perspective.

EXHIBIT 2.6 Contingency Factors Affecting Organization Design

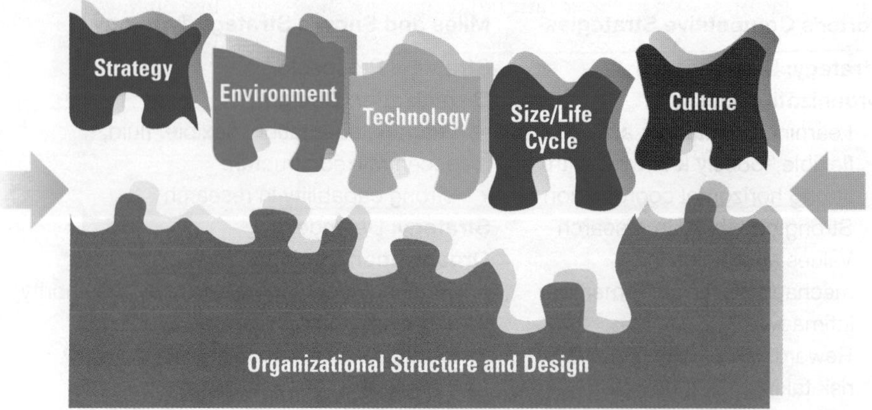

The Right Mix of Design Characteristics Fits the Contingency Factors

If there is minimal turbulence and therefore maximum predictability, the capacity to be adaptable or to encourage new skill development is an unnecessary cost, regardless of how employees may value it. In contrast, a rapidly changing environment may justify, again managerially and technically, a more flexible structure, with strong horizontal coordination and collaboration through teams or other mechanisms. Whether this is welcomed by employees is immaterial from this perspective unless their resistance begins to impede the implementation of a more flexible approach. In general, the demands of the 'the environment' are invoked by managers to justify changes – whether in the direction of increased or reduced flexibility and learning – that are not necessarily welcomed by employees. Environments will be discussed in detail in Chapters 4 and 5. In terms of size and life cycle, young, small organizations are generally informal and have little division of labour, few rules and regulations and ad hoc budgeting and performance systems. Large organizations such as Coca-Cola, Sony or General Electric, on the other hand, have an extensive division of labour, numerous rules and regulations and standard procedures and systems for budgeting, control, rewards and innovation. Size and stages of the life cycle will be discussed in Chapter 9.

Likewise, in principle, design is intended to fit the workflow technology of the organization. For example, with mass production technology, such as a traditional automobile assembly line, an emphasis upon formalization, specialization, centralized decision making and tight control is to be expected. An e-business, on the other hand, might engender a more informal and flexible design. Technology's impact on design will be discussed in detail in Chapters 7 and 8. A final contingency that affects organization design is corporate culture. An organizational culture that values teamwork, collaboration, creativity and open communication among all employees and managers, for example, might struggle to co-exist with a tight, vertical structure and strict rules and regulations. The role of culture is discussed in Chapter 10.

One responsibility of managers is to design organizations that fit the contingency factors of strategy, environment, size and life cycle, technology and culture. Finding the right fit leads to organizational effectiveness, whereas a poor fit can lead to decline or even the demise of the organization.

COUNTERPOINT 2.6

Managers have multiple agendas that are not necessarily consistent with fitting the design of organizations to contingency factors. Assessing these factors as well as balancing them involves judgement as much as calculation. And judgements are likely to be coloured by managers' preconceptions, theories and vested interests.

There is also a danger of assuming that design is the key to success when it may be that other factors – such as the capacity to dominate a market (e.g. by branding or the construction of high barriers to entry) by virtue of a monopoly position – that better account for a level of performance that is (mis)attributed to an organization's technical 'effectiveness'. For example, it is unlikely that a carrier that does not enjoy Ryanair's dominant position could derive a substantial income stream from applying the same credit card charges and excess baggage charges. **Discuss**

Assessing Organizational Effectiveness

Understanding organizational goals and strategies, as well as the concept of fitting design to various contingencies, is a first step toward understanding organizational effectiveness. Organizational goals are a way of representing the reason for an organization's existence and the outcomes it seeks to achieve. The next few sections of the chapter explore the topic of effectiveness and how effectiveness is measured in organizations.

Recall from Chapter 1 that organizational effectiveness was conceived as the degree to which an organization realizes its goals.[47] *Effectiveness* is a broad concept. It implicitly takes into consideration a range of variables at both the organizational and departmental levels. Effectiveness evaluates the extent to which multiple goals – whether official or operative – are attained.

Efficiency is a more limited concept that refers to the internal workings of the organization. Organizational efficiency is the amount of resources used to produce a unit of output.[48] It can be measured as the ratio of inputs to outputs. If one organization can achieve a given production level with fewer resources than another organization, it would be described as more efficient.[49]

Sometimes efficiency is congruent with effectiveness. In other organizations, efficiency and effectiveness are less closely related. An organization may be highly efficient but fail to achieve its goals because it makes a product for which there is no demand. Likewise, an organization may achieve its profit goals but be inefficient.

Overall effectiveness is difficult to measure in organizations. Organizations are large, diverse and fragmented. They perform many activities simultaneously, pursue multiple goals and generate many outcomes, some intended and some unintended.[50] Managers determine what indicators to measure in order to gauge the effectiveness of their organizations. One study found that many managers have a difficult time with the concept of evaluating effectiveness based on characteristics that are not subject to hard, quantitative measurement.[51] However, top executives at some of today's leading companies are finding new ways to measure effectiveness, including the use of such 'soft' indications as 'customer delight' and employee satisfaction. A number of approaches to measuring effectiveness look at which measurements managers choose to track. These *contingency effectiveness approaches*, discussed in the next section, are based on looking at which part of the organization managers consider most important to measure. Later, we will examine an approach that integrates concern for various parts of the organization.

Contingency Effectiveness Approaches

Contingency approaches to measuring effectiveness focus on different parts of the organization. Organizations bring resources in from the environment, and those resources are transformed into outputs delivered back into the environment, as shown in Exhibit 2.7. The **goal approach** to organizational effectiveness is concerned with

EXHIBIT 2.7 Contingency Approaches to the Measurement of Organizational Effectiveness

External Environment		
Resource Inputs	Organization: Internal activities and processes	Product and Service Outputs
Resource-based approach	Internal process approach	Goal approach

the output side and whether the organization achieves its goals in terms of desired levels of output.[52] The **resource-based approach** assesses effectiveness by observing the beginning of the process and evaluating whether the organization effectively obtains resources necessary for high performance. The **internal process approach** looks at internal activities and assesses effectiveness by indicators of internal health and efficiency.

Goal Approach

The goal approach to effectiveness consists of identifying an organization's output goals and assessing how well the organization has attained those goals.[53] This is a logical approach because organizations do try to attain certain levels of output, profit or client satisfaction. The goal approach measures progress toward attainment of those goals. For example, in 2000, the United Nations set eight Millennium Development Goals to improve the quality of life in the world by the year 2015, including such targets as reducing infant mortality by two-thirds, halving the number of people suffering from hunger and ensuring all children complete basic education. By 2007, most of the goals were on track in most developing countries.[54]

Indicators The important goals to consider are operative goals. Efforts to measure effectiveness have been more productive using operative goals than using official goals.[55] Official goals, associated with mission, tend to be abstract and difficult to measure. Operative goals reflect activities the organization is actually performing.

One example of the existence of multiple goals is from a survey of US business corporations.[56] Their reported goals are shown in Exhibit 2.8. Twelve goals were listed as being important to these companies. Although the survey was conducted more than two decades ago, these twelve goals continue to be critical objectives for most businesses. These goals represent outcomes that cannot be achieved simultaneously. They illustrate the array of outcomes organizations attempt to achieve.

EXHIBIT 2.8 Reported Goals of US Corporations

Goal	% Corporations
Profitability	89
Growth	82
Market share	66
Social responsibility	65
Employee welfare	62
Product quality and service	60
Research and development	54
Diversification	51
Efficiency	50
Financial stability	49
Resource conservation	39
Management development	35

Source: Adapted from Y. K. Shetty, 'New Look at Corporate Goals,' *California Management Review* 22, no. 2 (1979), 71–79.

Usefulness The goal approach is used in business organizations because output goals can be readily measured. Business firms typically evaluate performance in terms of profitability, growth, market share and return on investment. However, identifying operative goals and measuring performance of an organization are not always easy. Two problems that must be resolved are the issues of multiple goals and subjective indicators of goal attainment.

Since organizations have multiple and conflicting goals, effectiveness often cannot be assessed by a single indicator. High achievement on one goal might mean low achievement on another. Moreover, there are department goals as well as overall performance goals. A full assessment of effectiveness takes into consideration several goals simultaneously.

The other issue to resolve with the goal approach is how to identify operative goals for an organization and how to measure goal attainment. For business organizations, there are often objective indicators for certain goals, such as profit or growth. However, when quantitative data is not available, subjective assessment is needed for other goals, such as employee welfare or social responsibility. Someone has to go into the organization and learn what the operative goals are by talking with the top management team. Once goals are identified, subjective perceptions of goal attainment have to be used when quantitative indicators are not available. Managers rely on information from customers, competitors, suppliers and employees, as well as their own intuition, when considering these goals.

See online
COUNTERPOINT 2.10

Resource-based Approach

The resource-based approach looks at the input side of the transformation process shown in Exhibit 2.7. It assumes organizations must be successful in obtaining and managing valued resources in order to be effective. From a resource-based perspective, organizational effectiveness is defined as the ability of the organization, in either absolute or relative terms, to obtain scarce and valued resources and successfully integrate and manage them.[57]

Volkswagen

Volkswagen was the first European car manufacturer to develop a genuinely mass-market vehicle, the famous VW Beetle, originally launched in 1938, and still in production in an updated version. After the end of the Second World War Volkswagen rapidly expanded, through Beetle sales, acquisition of several other European marques and global expansion. However, by the end of the 1990s the original Beetle's long run was over, and the models that replaced it had mixed reputations for consumer appeal, quality and reliability. In comparison with Toyota, Volkswagen's cars seemed tired and outdated, and the perception was reflected in Volkswagen's global sales, which fell below Toyota.

In the early years of the twenty-first century Volkswagen revamped its product line-up, and initial sales results were promising; global year-on-year sales were up 8.5 per cent in 2007. The company's new management developed an ambitious strategy to catch up with Toyota globally. By 2012, it plans to sell 8 million cars globally, up 29 per cent from 2007, and each of the company's brands and national units have been expected to set similarly ambitious targets; its US subsidiary is hoping to triple its US sales to 1 million automobiles over the next decade.

The outlook for Volkswagen is generally promising, and the company is back on track to challenge Toyota, an effort that is focused by the ambitious growth targets. However, an emphasis on sales goals could lead to short term success at the expense of solid long-term growth. For example, some of the company's short-term success has been in high-performance vehicles; it will be increasingly difficult to manufacture and sell these cars in both Europe and North America over the next few years given high fuel prices and heightened environmental sensitivities among car buyers. In addition, some industry experts note that volume sales are in small cars, which generate much smaller profit margins than larger vehicles. Thus even if Volkswagen met its sales targets it might still have a negative impact on profitability.[58] This might be a welcome prospect for employees and managers as it promised increased job security and career progression. But, in an increasingly financialized global economy, Volkswagen are likely to struggle to attract continuing capital investment to finance their ambitious plans unless growth is matched by profitability. From an investors' perspective, growth *per se* or outselling Toyota is not a priority unless, for example, it enables Volkswagen to attract the most able employees and enjoy greater benefits of economies of scale as a means of improving profitability.

Indicators Obtaining and successfully managing resources is the criterion by which organizational effectiveness is assessed. In a broad sense, indicators of effectiveness according to the resource-based approach encompass the following dimensions:

- Bargaining position – the ability of the organization to obtain from its environment scarce and valued resources, including financial resources, raw materials, human resources, knowledge and technology
- The abilities of the organization's decision makers to perceive and correctly interpret the real properties of the external environment
- The abilities of managers to use tangible (e.g. supplies, people) and intangible (e.g. knowledge, corporate culture) resources in day-to-day organizational activities to achieve superior performance
- The ability of the organization to respond to changes in the environment

Usefulness The resource-based approach is valuable when other indicators of performance are difficult to obtain. In many not-for-profit and social welfare organizations, for example, it is hard to measure output goals or internal efficiency. Regional development agencies typically market their regions on the basis of the bundle of diverse resources they have available to potential companies.[59] Some for-profit organizations also use a resource-based approach. Shared service firms, as well as shared service units within larger companies, aim to concentrate a range of complementary skills sets together, thus permitting the efficient centralization of specific activities for multiple internal or external clients. Shared services are part of the trend towards business process re-engineering, outsourcing and offshoring. Companies such as India's Tata Consulting Services (TCS) offer companies custom-designed solutions. N. Ganapathy Subramaniam, President of TCS's financial solutions arm, notes that his company has, 'experience in consulting, business process outsourcing, engineering and IT infrastructure services and our goal is to provide clients with the right set of capabilities for the right problems at the right time'.[60]

Although the resource-based approach is valuable when other measures of effectiveness are not available, it does have shortcomings. For one thing, the approach may not adequately consider the organization's link to the needs of customers in the external environment, although the absence of a strong link indicates a lack of resource in this area (of marketing) that could be remedied. A superior ability to acquire and use resources is important only if resources and capabilities are used to achieve something that meets a demand in the environment. Critics have argued that the approach assumes stability in the marketplace and fails to adequately consider the changing value of various resources as the competitive environment and customer needs change but, again, attentiveness to changing markets may be incorporated into the second element of the resource-based approach listed above.

Internal Process Approach

In the internal process approach, effectiveness is measured as internal organizational health and efficiency. An effective organization has a smooth, well-oiled internal process. Employees are focused and satisfied. Department activities mesh with one another to ensure high productivity. This approach does not consider the external environment. The important element in effectiveness is what the organization does with the resources it has, as reflected in internal health and efficiency. In principle, the internal process could be very smooth but poorly aligned to the shifting demands of the market.

Indicators One indicator of internal process effectiveness is the organization's economic efficiency. However, the best-known proponents of a process model are from the human relations approach to organizations. Writers including Chris Argyris, Warren G. Bennis, Rensis Likert and Richard Beckhard have all worked extensively with human resources in organizations and emphasize the connection between human resources and effectiveness.[61] Writers on corporate culture and organizational excellence have stressed the importance of internal processes. Results from a study of nearly 200 US secondary schools showed that both human resources and employee-oriented processes were important in explaining and promoting effectiveness in those organizations.[62]

There are seven indicators of an effective organization as seen from an internal process approach:

1. Strong corporate culture and positive work climate
2. Team spirit, group loyalty and teamwork
3. Confidence, trust and communication between workers and management
4. Decision making near sources of information, regardless of where those sources are on the organizational chart

As an organization manager, keep these guidelines in mind:

Use the goal approach, internal process approach and resource-based approach to obtain specific pictures of organizational effectiveness. Assess competing values to obtain a broader, more balanced picture of effectiveness.

5 Undistorted horizontal and vertical communication; sharing of relevant facts and feelings

6 Rewards to managers for performance, growth and development of subordinates and for creating an effective work group

7 Interaction between the organization and its parts, with conflict that occurs over projects resolved in the interest of the organization.[63]

Usefulness The internal process approach is important because the deployment of resources and harmonious internal functioning are ways to assess organizational effectiveness. Today, most managers believe that committed, actively involved and satisfied employees and a positive corporate culture are important indicators, if not direct measures, of effectiveness. For example, the giant aerospace company Boeing has struggled partly because internal processes were not functioning smoothly. Although technical processes for building planes had improved to meet competition from Airbus and emergent smaller players like Embraer as described earlier, human relations and corporate culture were in some disarray. Hiring, promotion and compensation practices were under fire. Twenty-eight thousand female employees filed law suit charging that the company systematically pays women less than men. Depositions described a hostile work environment, including groping and offensive language on the part of male colleagues and bosses. CEO Harry Stonecipher was forced to resign in 2005 because of improprieties related to an affair with a female executive. These internal human resources issues, combined with ethics scandals related to Boeing's external environment, have seriously damaged the company. Subsequent CEOs Alan Mullaly and Scott Carson have led a turn-around of the company's fortunes through empowering employees, re-emphasizing innovation and building a strong product strategy.[64]

In contrast to Boeing's turbulence, Four Seasons Hotels, an international luxury chain of hotels with headquarters in Toronto, Canada, has been able to maintain smooth internal processes. Treating employees well is considered key to the organization's success.[65] Workers at each hotel select a peer to receive the Employee of the Year award, which includes an expenses-paid vacation and a $1,000 shopping spree. Internal processes are particularly important for hotel chains because so many employees have contact with customers, and any one of them who is disgruntled and unfocused on customer satisfaction could potentially spoil customers' experience.[66]

The internal process approach also has shortcomings. Total output and the organization's relationship with the external environment are not evaluated. Another problem is that evaluations of internal health and functioning are often subjective, because many aspects of inputs and internal processes are not quantifiable.

An Integrated Effectiveness Model

The three approaches – goal, resource-based, internal process – to organizational effectiveness described earlier all have something to offer. The **competing values model** tries to balance a concern with different kinds and aspects of effectiveness rather than focusing on one approach. The competing values model acknowledges that organizations do many things have many outcomes.[67] It combines several indicators of effectiveness into a single framework.

The model is based on the assumption that there are disagreements and competing viewpoints about what constitutes effectiveness. Managers sometimes disagree over which are the most important goals to pursue and measure. In addition, stakeholders have competing claims on what they want from the organization, as described in Chapter 1. One tragic example of conflicting viewpoints and competing interests comes from the

US space agency NASA. After seven astronauts died in the explosion of the space shuttle *Columbia* in February 2003, an investigative committee found deep organizational flaws at NASA, including ineffective mechanisms for incorporating dissenting opinions between scheduling managers and safety managers. External pressures to launch on time overrode safety concerns with the *Columbia* launch. As Wayne Hale, the NASA executive charged with giving the go-ahead for the next shuttle launch, puts it, 'We dropped the torch through our own complacency, our arrogance, self-assurance, sheer stupidity and through continuing attempt[s] to please everyone'. NASA is an extremely complex organization that operates not only with different viewpoints internally but also from the US Congress, the president and the expectations of the American public.[68]

The competing values model takes into account these complexities. The model was originally developed by Robert Quinn and John Rohrbaugh to combine the diverse indicators of performance used by managers and researchers.[69] Using a comprehensive list of performance indicators, a panel of experts in organizational effectiveness rated the indicators for similarity. The analysis produced underlying dimensions of effectiveness criteria that represented competing management values in organizations.

Indicators The first value dimension pertains to organizational **focus**, which is whether dominant values concern issues that are *internal* or *external* to the firm. Internal focus reflects a management concern for the well-being and efficiency of employees, and external focus represents an emphasis on well-being with respect to the environment. The second value dimension pertains to organization **structure**, and whether *stability* versus *flexibility* is the dominant structural consideration. Stability reflects a management value for efficiency and top-down control, whereas flexibility represents a value for learning and change.

The value dimensions of structure and focus are illustrated in Exhibit 2.9. The combination of dimensions provides four approaches to organizational effectiveness,

EXHIBIT 2.9 Four Approaches to Effectiveness Values

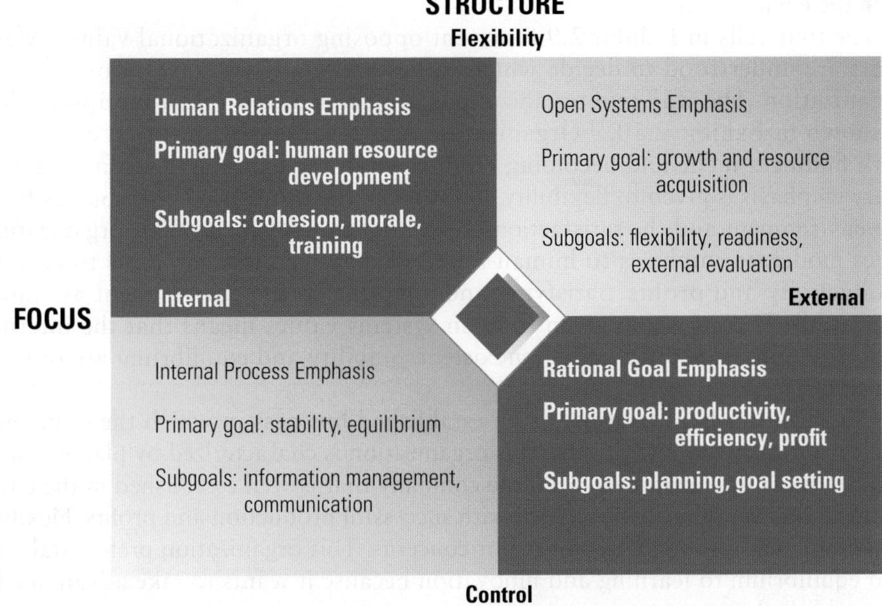

Source: Adapted from Robert E. Quinn and John Rohrbaugh, 'A Spatial Model of Effectiveness Criteria: Toward a Competing Values Approach to Organizational Analysis,' *Management Science* 29 (1983), 363–377; and Robert E. Quinn and Kim Cameron, 'Organizational Life Cycles and Shifting Criteria of Effectiveness: Some Preliminary Evidence,' *Management Science* 29 (1983), 33–51.

which, though seemingly different, are closely related. In real organizations, these competing values can and often do exist together. Each approach reflects a different management emphasis with respect to structure and focus.[70]

A combination of external focus and flexible structure leads to an **open systems emphasis**. Management's primary goals are growth and resource acquisition. The organization accomplishes these goals through the subgoals of flexibility, readiness and a positive external evaluation. The dominant value is establishing a good relationship with the environment to acquire resources and grow. This emphasis is similar in some ways to the resource-based approach described earlier.

The **rational goal emphasis** represents management values of structural control and external focus. The primary goals are productivity, efficiency and profit. The organization wants to achieve output goals in a controlled way. Subgoals that facilitate these outcomes are internal planning and goal setting, which are rational management tools. The rational goal emphasis is similar to the goal approach described earlier.

The **internal process emphasis** is in the lower-left section of Exhibit 2.9; it reflects the values of internal focus and structural control. The primary outcome is a stable organizational setting that maintains itself in an orderly way. Organizations that are well established in the environment and simply want to maintain their current position would reflect this emphasis. Subgoals include mechanisms for efficient communication, information management and decision-making. Although this part of the competing values model is similar in some ways to the internal process approach described earlier, it is less concerned with human resources than with other internal processes that lead to efficiency.

The **human relations emphasis** incorporates the values of an internal focus and a flexible structure. Here, management concern is for the development of human resources. Employees are given opportunities for autonomy and development. Management works toward the subgoals of cohesion, morale and training opportunities. Organizations adopting this emphasis are more concerned with employees than with the environment.

The four cells in Exhibit 2.9 represent opposing organizational values. Managers are understood to decide which values and goals will take priority in the organization. The way two organizations are mapped onto the four approaches is shown in Exhibit 2.10.[71] Organization A is a young organization concerned with finding a niche and becoming established in the external environment. Primary emphasis is given to flexibility, innovation, the acquisition of resources from the environment and the satisfaction of external constituencies. This organization gives moderate emphasis to human relations and even less emphasis to current productivity and profits. Satisfying and adapting to the environment are more important. The attention given to open systems values means that the internal process emphasis is practically nonexistent. Stability and equilibrium are of little concern.

Organization B, in contrast, is an established business in which the dominant value is productivity and profits. This organization is characterized by planning and goal setting. Organization B is a large company that is well established in the environment and is primarily concerned with successful production and profits. Flexibility and human resources are not major concerns. This organization prefers stability and equilibrium to learning and innovation because it wants to take advantage of its established customers.

Usefulness The competing values model makes two contributions. First, it integrates diverse concepts of effectiveness into a single perspective. It incorporates

EXHIBIT 2.10 Effectiveness Values for Two Organizations

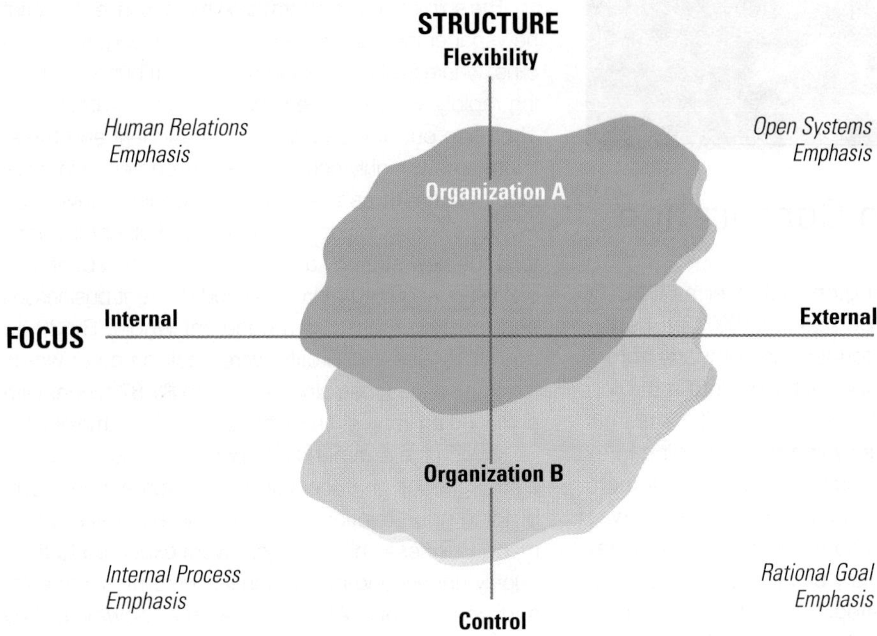

the ideas of output goals, resource acquisition and human resource development as goals the organization tries to accomplish. Second, the model calls attention to effectiveness criteria as management values and shows how opposing values exist at the same time. Managers must decide which values they wish to pursue and which values will receive less emphasis. The four competing values exist simultaneously, but not all will receive equal priority. For example, a new, small organization that concentrates on establishing itself within a competitive environment may not be in a position to give attention to developing employees as priority is given to addressing the demands of the external environment.

COUNTERPOINT 2.7

It may be misleading to suggest that managers can 'decide which values they wish to pursue' as such decisions are constrained by their entrenched preconceptions, vision and priorities as well as by the pressures upon them to meet the immediate demands of investors, customers or suppliers. It is also questionable whether any organization can afford to ignore 'current productivity and profits', especially in the Anglo-American business zone where short-term profits are a primary indicator of managers' effectiveness . . . and survival. It may be that a business plan for a recently established organization will focus upon getting established and gaining visibility and reputation. But it is likely that these concerns are considered to be indicators of future profitability. Immediate profitability is sacrificed in the expectation that building reputation and capability will pay future dividends. Even in the many cases where businesses are established for non-financial reasons – for example, the entrepreneur is passionate about a product or a service and/or is interested primarily in being their own boss – the survival of the business (and thus the realization of the non-financial dreams) will depend upon securing continuing external investment or generating sufficient surpluses to plough back into the development of the business. **Discuss**

The Thomson Corporation

When Richard Harrington took over as CEO of the Thomson Corporation in 1997, he began a process that has transformed the company from a fabled Canadian newspaper publisher into a thriving information services enterprise. Today, Thomson is a leader in electronic publishing and providing integrated information solutions to corporate customers in a variety of industries. The line of newspapers was sold. Managers rebuilt Thomson into an organization providing a wide variety of information products and services to four strategic market groups: Legal and Regulatory, Learning, Financial and Science and Healthcare. In 2007, Thomson sold its Learning arm to a private equity group, Cengage, publishers of this book.

The shift into digital information made sense. The print newspaper industry appears to be in a long, slow, decline, whereas electronic information distribution is growing rapidly. However the new goals and strategy took Thomson out of the business it knew best and thrust it into a new, highly competitive environment. Financial results suffered as the company acquired new businesses, new knowledge, new skills and other resources to fit the new strategy and goals. Thomson spent several years acquiring more than 200 different businesses and melding them into a coherent whole. By 2006, both revenues and profits were back on an upwards track: revenues rose nine percent to $1.87 billion, with profits up an impressive 57 per cent to $390 million.[72]

Making the revamped company successful required a strong focus on understanding customer needs and building good relationships with the external environment. Business unit managers were expected to thoroughly understand their potential customers, markets, and competitors. At the same time, however, they also had to make the internal people changes. As a knowledge-based organization, Thomson considers employee development and a unified corporate culture fundamental to the company's success.[73]

The dominant values in an organization often change over time as organizations experience new environmental demands or new top leadership. The above example describes the dominant effectiveness values for the Thomson Corporation, Canada's best-known media company.

The picture of Thomson mapped onto the competing values framework would look very much like Organization A in Exhibit 2.10. The company's transformation required a strong open systems emphasis with fairly strong emphasis on human relations as well. The rational goal emphasis and internal process emphasis are much weaker. Adapting to the environment and understanding and meeting customer needs are much more important now than internal control and cost efficiency, but this emphasis could change in the future.

COUNTERPOINT 2.8

Is top management really able to set clear strategic direction? We all like to feel that we are in control of our lives, and there is an expectation – reflected in this chapter – that top managers will be able to fundamentally shape the direction of their companies. However, just as individuals' lives frequently take unexpected turns, the same is true of corporations and their leadership.

Sometimes in retrospect a top manager's long-term strategy may appear to be clear – and of course it is in her or his interest to represent it in such a way – but things are often much less certain on a day-to-day basis. Even the most strategy-oriented managers such as Thomson's Harrington, for example, seem to have changed direction. As we saw, Thomson divested its Learning division in 2007, but earlier in Harrington's tenure he had substantially expanded Thomson Learning through acquisitions such as Macmillan Library Reference USA and Capstar, an academic testing and assessment business. Then, in late 2007, Thomson and the leading news agency Reuters agreed to merge, a move that could be interpreted as radically shifting Thomson's direction back towards a more traditional news focus, albeit not print newspaper publication.

Perhaps more important than the details of strategic direction is the *image* of strategic clarity and decisive leadership. Leaders such as Richard Harrington and Puma's Jochen Zeitz project an aura of competence and vision. If inconsistencies and shifts are successfully glossed over or effectively rationalized, investors are provided with a sense of assurance that the company and their human resources and financial assets are in good hands. **Discuss**

Summary and Interpretation

This chapter discussed organizational goals and the strategies that top managers use to help organizations achieve those goals. Goals specify the mission or purpose of an organization and its desired future state; strategies define how the organization will reach its goals. The chapter also discussed the impact of strategy on organization design and how designing the organization to fit strategy and other contingencies can lead to organizational effectiveness. The chapter closed with an examination of the most popular approaches to measuring effectiveness, that is, how well the organization realizes its purpose and attains its desired future state.

Organizations are widely held to exist for a well-defined purpose; and top managers are seen to define a specific mission or task to be accomplished. The mission statement, or official goals, makes explicit the purpose and direction of an organization. Official and operative goals are a key element in organizations insofar as they establish legitimacy with external groups and set standards of performance for participants.

Managers develop or rationalize strategies to describe the actions they deem to be required to achieve goals. Strategies may include any number of techniques to achieve the stated goals. Two models for formulating strategies are Porter's competitive strategies and the Miles and Snow strategy typology. The formal process of organization design is represented as a process of assessing and fitting the structure of the organization to the contingencies that it faces, thereby securing enhanced organizational effectiveness.

Difficulties of defining and assessing organizational effectiveness reflect the complexity of organizations as a topic of study. No easy, simple, guaranteed measure will provide an unequivocal assessment of performance. Organizations perform diverse activities – from obtaining resource inputs to delivering outputs. Contingency approaches use output goals, resource acquisition or internal health and efficiency as the criteria of effectiveness. The competing values model aspires to provide a balanced approach that considers multiple criteria simultaneously. Organizations can be assessed by evaluating competing values for effectiveness. No approach is suitable for every organization, but proponents of each approach identify advantages that others are seen to lack.

From the point of view of managers, the goal approach to effectiveness and measures of internal efficiency may be found to be useful when measures are available. Factors including top-management preferences, the extent to which goals are assessed to be measurable, and the scarcity of environmental resources may influence the selection and use of effectiveness criteria. In nonprofit organizations, where internal processes and output criteria are often not quantifiable, resource acquisition may be the best available indicator of effectiveness. From the point of view of people outside the organization, such as academic investigators or government researchers, the competing values model of organizational effectiveness may be compelling and helpful. This model acknowledges different areas of focus (internal, external) and structure (flexibility, stability) and allows for managers to appreciate how approaches – human relations, open systems, rational goal or internal process – may be combined in order to give priority to the values to which they subscribe and the priorities that they privilege.

KEY CONCEPTS

analyzer
competing values model
defender
differentiation
focus
focus strategy
goal approach
human relations emphasis
internal process approach
internal process emphasis
low-cost leadership
mission
official goals
open systems emphasis
operative goals
organizational goal
prospector
rational goal emphasis
reactor
resource-based approach
strategy
structure

Discussion Questions

1 Discuss the role of top management in setting organizational direction.

2 How might a company's goals for employee development be related to its goals for innovation and change? To goals for productivity? Can you discuss ways these types of goals might conflict in an organization?

3 What is a goal for the class for which you are reading this text? Who established this goal? Discuss how the goal affects your direction and motivation.

4 What is the difference between a goal and a strategy as defined in the text? Identify both a goal and a strategy for a campus or community organization with which you are involved.

5 Discuss the similarities and differences in the strategies described in Porter's competitive strategies and Miles and Snow's typology.

6 In what ways is the Blue Ocean strategy different from the approaches described by Porter, and Miles and Snow?

7 To what extent do mission statements and official goal statements provide an organization with genuine legitimacy in the external environment? Discuss.

8 Suppose you have been asked to evaluate the effectiveness of the police service in a medium-sized city. Where would you begin, and how would you proceed? What effectiveness approach would you prefer and why?

9 What are the advantages and disadvantages of the resource-based approach versus the goal approach for measuring organizational effectiveness?

10 What are the similarities and differences between assessing effectiveness on the basis of competing values versus the stakeholder approach described in Chapter 1? Explain.

11 A noted organization theorist once said, 'Organizational effectiveness can be whatever top management defines it to be'. Discuss.

Chapter 2 Workbook Identifying Company Goals and Strategies*

Choose three companies, either in the same industry or in three different industries. Search the Internet for information on the companies, including annual reports. In each company look particularly at the goals expressed. Refer back to the goals in Exhibit 2.8 and also to Porter's competitive strategies in Exhibit 2.4.

	Goals from Exhibit 2.8 articulated	Strategies from Porter used
Company #1		
Company #2		
Company #3		

Questions

1 Which goals seem most important?

2 Look for differences in the goals and strategies of the three companies and develop an explanation for those differences.

3 Which of the goals or strategies should be changed? Why?

4 *Optional:* Compare your table with those of other students and look for common themes. Which companies seem to articulate and communicate their goals and strategies best?

Chapter 2 Workshop Competing Values and Organizational Effectiveness*

1 Divide into groups of four to six members.

2 Select an organization to 'study' for this exercise. It should be an organization for which one of you has worked, or it could be the university.

3 Using the exhibit 'Four Approaches to Effectiveness Values' (Exhibit 2.9), your group should list eight potential measures that show a balanced view of performance. These should relate not only to work activities, but also to goal values for the company.

4 How will achieving these goal values help the organization to become more effective? Which values could be given more weight than others? Why?

5 Present your competing values chart to the rest of the class. Each group should explain why it chose those particular values and which are more important. Be prepared to defend your position to the other groups, which are encouraged to question your choices.

*Adapted by Dorothy Marcic from general ideas in Jennifer Howard and Larry Miller, *Team Management*, The Miller Consulting Group, 1994, p.92.

CASE FOR ANALYSIS

JP Carpets

By Henrik Sørensen, *Aarhus University*

In the spring of 1995 one of Dan Carpets' employees, Jean Pelletier, decided to start up his own business. He established JP Carpets in the small town of Val-des-Marnes. Neither the management nor the employees of Dan Carpets were surprised by his decision, because Dan Carpets had been going through a long period of problems and conflicts. Pelletier ('JP') had long voiced his dissatisfaction with what was going on in the company. As a person who emphasized working in the most appropriate and efficient manner, he simply could not live with the present situation.

After heavy criticism of Dan Carpets' management, Pelletier had reached the conclusion that its managers simply could not effectively manage the company. He believed that its (matrix) structure was totally inappropriate and had given several examples of how its working spirit was, in fact, destructive. 'We cooperate ourselves to death' was one of JP's favourite mottoes.

On several occasions he had shown that the company lost orders because its employees found it more important to cooperate than to produce and deliver the carpets, which its customers (primarily interior design shops, private customers or public institutions) wanted. Furthermore, the company structure with two managing directors did not function at all. Very often they gave contradictory orders and directives to the staff, and to avoid facing the ensuing problems, they simply let the employees choose their own (and sometimes more suitable) production method. As the employees did not have sufficient knowledge of the company's customers and their needs, their decisions often turned out wrong and did not stand up to reality. Both sides feeling responsible for the poor decisions, management and employees easily agree to forget the whole matter, only to see the same problem surface again shortly after.

In JP's opinion it was hard to believe that Dan Carpets' management was unaware of the company's problems, and often he saw their reactions as a sign of panic. Thus, when Dan Carpets had to deliver a major order to a large medical company last year — with the company logo printed in two colours — JP had realized that no one actually knew exactly what the medical company had ordered. The product manager of the carpet division said that the medical company had ordered a carpet in two colours sharply contrasting with each other, which was an expensive production procedure. As opposed to this, the marketing manager believed that Dan Carpets was free to decide which colours to use. After three days of discussion, in which the whole order could have been produced, the two managers approached the top management and proposed that the manager losing the argument should leave the company. Top management was also unwilling to solve the conflict, saying that, 'When a company has a matrix structure, the competent managers must get used to making difficult decisions and try to find joint solutions'.

The heads of the linoleum, wooden floor and vinyl departments supported the head of the carpet department, while the functional managers for design, production and finance supported the marketing manager. A minor disagreement about the specifications of the order from the medical company had turned into a giant internal fight about who was to take decisions at the company, and ever since this fight nobody in the management group had been talking together.

The most obvious solution would have been to send the medical company a number of proposals as to how the order could be executed and let them decide. However, out of fear of not being able to deliver the order, the managing director had decided to produce the carpets in totally different colours. Subsequently his decision turned out to be disastrous: the colour composition of the carpets was very similar to a competitor's colours. When the medical company received the carpets, they sent the whole lot back to Dan Carpets. Furthermore, the medical company ordered some new carpets from one of Dan Carpets' competitors.

JP had been vocal in criticizing both the company and its management, calling their actions panicky and poorly thought through. It was clear to him that they were not able to manage the company and that another organizational structure, with a different management team, and thus a reorganization of the entire company was needed.

As time went by, Dan Carpets employees turned out to be quite reasonable. They were prepared to forget the whole matter and move on in order to make the company function despite the conflicts within the management group. On his own initiative, a member of the carpet division staff had thus visited the medical company to explain why everything went wrong with their order. He did not mention the ongoing conflict in the management group, but gave as explanation that the original order form had been lost, which was basically true.

Another example of the good intentions of the employees was that although the management group continued to wage war and disagree on almost everything, the employees handled all practical matters in the company. People said more or less openly that the management spent their time fighting internally while the employees made the company function. Everybody avoided asking their superiors about anything, as chances were that things would go wrong when the management group interfered. Of course this situation was untenable in the long run, and when a similar problem arose six months later, JP had had enough of the company.

He went to the managing director immediately, and in very clear terms he explained to him that the entire management of Dan Carpets was totally incompetent and incapable of managing a company of this size. 'We have pure chaos here, and although you see it, you do nothing to change the situation', he commented harshly. The managing director could only agree with him. 'I have therefore decided to start up on my own. I have hired 15 people from your carpet division, so they will be leaving Dan Carpets along with me.' JP left the managing director quite shaken and alone in his office.

JP starts his own company

The new company was established less than 3 months after JP's harsh exchange of words with Dan Carpets' managing director. There were no competition clauses limiting the activities of JP and his 15 new employees in their new company JP Carpets, so they immediately started competing with Dan Carpets in one of the latter's most important business areas.

Without any noticeable efforts on the part of Pelletier or his employees, a number of Dan Carpets' customers switched to JP Carpets. They simply said that Dan Carpets was too chaotic to deal with.

JP had no ambitions about making his new company too big. JP Carpets retained its original 15 employees, who got along well together. It was very strong in the manufacturing and development fields, so more and more customers found out about the qualities of JP's carpets. The company developed a skill for finding special market niches in the carpet industry.

JP Carpets had no formal structure. Staff often solved their problems by informal communication, or after Pelletier had ranted loud enough until people sat down and sorted out the issue. Having solved the problem, however, no one harboured a grudge against each other as had been the case in Dan Carpets. One major strength of JP Carpets was that whenever a customer needed a new carpet, one of the employees was appointed 'project owner' – meaning that this person followed the customer from order entry to carpet delivery. This way the customers felt that they always got custom-designed solutions, and in the event of any problems with their order, they always knew whom to contact.

Many employees felt that the main reason for JP Carpets' success was the close contact to their customers, but the only administrative member of the staff, Lise Boisvert, disagreed. She believed that the flexible way JP planned production was the secret behind JP Carpets' success.

'If we had not invested in new advanced production technologies, if we didn't have such a strong company spirit and desire to develop new products for our customers and to search for more advanced production equipment, our company would not have survived, let along flourished', she said.

At several Friday meetings – where Jean Pelletier and his employees talked about the past week – there had been intense discussions of how JP Carpets was earning its money. Lise Boisvert had mentioned that when comparing JP Carpets with several of its large French competitors, the latter all had some advantages compared to JP. They could scope the whole market for customers, quickly shift to new products, and all had professional sales staff.

Their bureaucratic structure allowed them to enhance the efficiency of every function down to the smallest detail, unlike a small company like JP Carpets. Besides, she pointed out, as soon as a large company had sales problems because of saturation of the home market, it just started exporting – something that would have been beyond JP Carpets.

JP's problems become clearer

Very few staff at JP had noticed what Lise had pointed out. This was due to several things. Lise Boisvert was the only person working in the administration, which left her all alone with the administrative problems. Customers not paying their bills or suppliers not getting paid were all Lise's problem. A proper administrative department was badly needed at JP Carpets. New procedures for control and follow-up of accounts, and some form of financial controls also had to be implemented as soon as possible.

The need for better financial controls was highlighted by UJP Carpets' many liquidity problems in the second half of 1998. For some time then, a lot of expenses had had to be paid before the company could invoice its customers. This was not a sign of falling revenues, as throughout the financial year profits as a percentage of company sales were still high. However, the profit margin was falling, but only Lise Boisvert realized this.

Lise had great difficulty gaining Jean Pelletier's attention in order to explain the seriousness of their situation. She understood that she was working in an environment of almost solely male employees (including all their male jargon), and that the production was considered the most important part of the company, but she could not accept that Pelletier made no effort to understand what she was telling him regarding the company accounts and financial control. 'My professional pride was hurt', she says.

She decided to quit her job. One Friday meeting when there was not much on the agenda, and everybody thought they could sit and relax over a few beers, she let loose, announcing that she intended to leave the company because of its extremely weak financial management. She said that in future she foresaw a lot of trouble between the companies' employees. She knew that JP was very intent on good leadership and employee relations and hope this would spur him into action.

JP jumped up, surprised and shocked. Lise continued talking, disclosing that JP Carpets' profits were lower than during the start-up years of the company. This made several of the employees wrinkle their foreheads, and although they normally never raised difficult company matters with JP, one of them got up and said that lately he had noticed a definite lack not only in spirit, but also in efficiency of the employees.

Suddenly JP realized that the motivation level within the JP family (as he called all the employees of the company) was declining. The company was not yet in a deep crisis, because it was still making a profit, but he was concerned because for the first time the employees were questioning his way of running the company and his style of leadership. Furthermore, Lise was right, the figures showed that profits were falling.

This whole discussion started at the same time as some of the big competitors were gearing up to take on JP Carpets, and a few had even prepared a coordinated competition effort against Pelletier's firm.

One of Dan Carpets' initiatives was to lower the price of its carpets, JP Carpets' sole business area, to almost the level of their production costs while raising the profit margins in other less price-sensitive product areas. This meant that Dan Carpets could offer considerably lower prices, while maintaining total company profits.

Dan Carpet had replaced its management, and the new managers had shown very efficient in 'cleaning up' the company in only nine months, firing all the product and functional managers, who they saw as just stirring up trouble. In organizational terms the management of the company had given up the matrix structure and divided the company into four subsidiaries, each with separate responsibility for the carpet, linoleum, wooden floor and vinyl production. They had also got rid of several employees with bad attitudes, and the company was now more customer-oriented. All four subsidiaries had introduced new advanced production facilities, using computerized inventory controls for the purchase of raw materials, so that these arrived at the company at the exact time when they were needed in the production process. Large IT supported systems also controlled deliveries to customers.

JP did not know what to do. Soon it became apparent that he was unable to effectively control the work performance of his employees. Little by little the company had almost 30 employees, which meant that JP no longer had the same close contact with everybody as before. Daily problems were not being solved because people had to wait until JP got the time to help them. He went from one problem to another, so much so that he felt he was functioning as the corporate 'fire extinguisher'. One consequence of all the firefighting was that no one was assessing the company's production facilities and whether they were competitive with the rest of the carpet industry. It became more and more apparent that JP was now an older man, and that he didn't have the energy to grasp the problems and deal with them. The employees were quite openly talking about a management crisis at JP Carpets, saying that if the company was to survive, 'the old man' had to resign.

JP's problems grow bigger

In January 2007 JP Carpets had an unannounced visit from the tax authorities, who had identified that there was something seriously wrong with the company's accounting. JP Carpets had few or no accounting procedures or financial controls, as Lise Boisvert had acknowledged. The result was that the company had fallen behind with its tax remittances and was liable for a hefty fine. Even JP could now see that something had to be done.

After the visit from the tax authorities everything suddenly moved very quickly. JP acknowledged that he no longer was able to effectively manage the company. One morning in March 2007 he called together all employees and told them that his life's work –JP Carpets – had for quite some time had major problems with its finances. It had outdated technology and it was being outstripped by its competitors.

JP announced that he had therefore decided to leave the daily management of the company to what he called 'a professional managing director'. A management consultancy had been recruited to find a new managing director before April 1. The employees applauded JP's decision, believing that now everything would be better.

However, they were in for a shock when on April 1 the new managing director called everybody together to tell them how he would revolutionize the company. He would take the following three measures:

1 Give the company a divisional structure and hire 30 new salesmen.
2 Introduce new technology.
3 Form a number of inter-organizational relations.

1 Give the company a divisional structure and hire 30 new salesmen

The new managing director started explaining what he planned to do in each of his three target areas. He began by confirming that he believed JP Carpets' problems were caused fundamentally by its organizational structure. 'We are in a situation where we have to begin competing with the big companies within our business area, and to do this we need a divisional structure. My reason for hiring 30 more salesmen is that I want us to be much more active in sales and marketing, not only on the home market, but also as a step towards building up an export division.

'By introducing a divisional structure we shall have a much clearer delineation of responsibilities in the company, and we all know we are in dire need of that. The daily operations of JP Carpets today are characterized by nothing but emergencies. We never seem to plan ahead. With the new structure a number of division managers will be appointed, all from outside the company.'

In his message to the employees the new managing director mentioned other advantages of a divisional structure. He also paid special attention to the role of the new top management: 'I would like the top management to be less visible in the daily running of the company than it is today, not due to lack of interest, but because it should focus its efforts on market surveillance, which needs to be much more important in our business planning. Furthermore we must be prepared to buy, merge and sell companies at the right moment, and this will be another of the top management's primary tasks.'

'We will make sure middle managers, i.e. the heads of divisions, get more responsibility, and that they are more involved in staff management than they are today. Each division will be an independent profit centre, giving the middle managers increased independence as well as greater responsibility. It will be up to each division to determine to what extent their employees should be rewarded, for instance with bonus schemes.

'The 30 new sales people will be hired and incorporated in the new divisional structure. From now on we have to compete more directly with the big companies.'

2 Introduction of new technology

'The introduction of new technology is a must. It will revolutionize the entire company', the new managing director continued. He revealed that JP's production technology must match that of the competition, and that this would make the company's production much more flexible. 'The reason why we cannot compete with the big companies today is that we have made no investments in new technology whereas others realized many years ago that needed to develop and implement a technology action plan. With the introduction of new technology, each division will be able to quickly respond to new customer demands.

'We need to redevelop our just-in-time agreements with our suppliers, who have gradually become too lax. They claim to live up to the JIT systems but the truth is that we have built up big inventory stockpiles. This means that the suppliers can easily live up to their JIT agreements. Each division needs its own logistics manager.

'Furthermore we need to implement computer-aided manufacturing (CAM) systems within the next two years. In our construction department we should use only well-known and well-established computer-based design systems enabling us to change product lines quickly according to customer wishes.

'In our production department the entire production process needs to be automated using the CAM systems where technology supports production. This relies of course on CAD systems being used in the construction department.'

Denis Lalonde, one of the more capable employees JP Carpets and certainly an internal candidate for one of the new middle manager positions, asked the new managing director whether he was absolutely certain that a divisional structure would be able to handle the advanced production technology. Slightly shaken by the question, the managing director answered that this was a problem they had to look into later. Lalonde spoke up again saying that it was important to make as few organizational changes as possible, and that the new director did not seem to have considered the connection between the two.

The new managing director said to Lalonde and the other employees: 'Please give me a chance. I come to JP with great ideas. Of course, I cannot give a detailed account of how everything will work right now, but I am sure we will be one of the winners in the European carpet business.' Without commenting further on Lalonde's criticism, the managing director went on to Part 3.

3 Form a number of inter-organizational relations

The new managing director pointed out that henceforth it would be vital to strengthen ties between the company and its customers, suppliers and not least its competitors. He said it was his philosophy that JP should try to manoeuvre itself into a position where it was less vulnerable to hostile actions by the big companies. In order to do that it needed to stop challenging them directly, and instead try to show them that there is room for everybody in the industry. 'As long as you show respect towards each other, your clients and your markets, it is better to cooperate than to fight', he said. 'You are very welcome to start spreading this message whenever you are in contact with clients, suppliers or competitors. In order to make this cooperation strategy work, we have to develop a clearer and better defined company strategy stating our basic corporate values.'

When the new managing director had presented his three proposals, about half the employees applauded enthusiastically, while the other half seemed less convinced. The director, who thought that he had made a pretty good impression, was surprised by this lukewarm reaction on the part of a good proportion of the staff.

Amelie Amyotte, another of the company's young stars, gave voice to the doubters' concerns 'We are happy to see that something is happening in the company now, but on the other hand we are also worried. It seems strange first to introduce a divisional structure and then to introduce advanced production technology. It seems a bit ill-considered.

'If I could be a bit critical, and I think you would want me to be honest, I am very surprised to see that you want to raise such high barriers between the different divisions. What makes JP Carpets a well-run company today is the close contact between all employees, and especially between the present management and the employees. As far as I can see, you want to erect barriers not only between the employees, but also the employees and the management. In my opinion this will result in more and more serious conflicts not only between employees and management, but also among employees.

'Further, I am very worried that you are not presenting any drawbacks to all your proposals. In life change seldom brings only benefits. I think you need to be more specific about where difficulties and problems may arise. By doing that you would show us that you are realistic about possible future problems. For instance, I would like to know what disadvantages can be expected with the divisional structure, and how you propose to solve them as they arise.'

The managing director answered that he couldn't reel off all the problems which may arise, but that it was his job to foresee future problems. He came with an open and positive mindset, hoping that the employees felt the same way. It was his job to overcome resistance to change and to make sure that the company's employees exploited the potential of new organizational structures, new technology and new strategies to the full. He also needed to ensure that the employees learned to cooperate with other companies. 'Even if it has to be done by force', was the last volley he fired at the astounded employees.

Now Jean Pelletier spoke up: 'Dear friends. JP Carpets is my life's work. With your help I built up a large and profitable company. We have run into some problems which can best be solved by my retirement and the employment of a professional manager. Please support him in his work! Continue to be good employees and be constructive. The process of change we are now going through must not be jeopardized because of misguided resistance to change. I am sure the new managing director of the company will ensure that there will be a positive learning and working environment within the company.'

Now all the employees applauded their old manager, who turned and said goodbye to the new managing director. Both hoped that the company would be changed for the better, but they were also well aware of all the problems and pitfalls that lay ahead.

Case Questions

1 What were the main problems at Dan Carpets, that led JP to leave and establish his own firm?

2 Why did JP Carpets initially succeed, but ultimately run into difficulties?

3 If you were the new managing director, how would you manage Amelie Amyotte and Denis Lalonde?

4 The new managing director outlined a three point plan. What is the rationale behind each of the points and what are the advantages and disadvantages of each?

CASE FOR ANALYSIS

The University Art Museum

By Peter F. Drucker

Visitors to the campus were always shown the University Art Museum, of which the large and distinguished university was very proud. A photograph of the handsome neoclassical building that housed the museum had long been used by the university for the cover of its brochures and catalogues.

The building, together with a substantial endowment, was given to the university around 1912 by an alumnus, the son of the university's first president, who had become very wealthy as an investment banker. He also gave the university his own small, but high-quality, collections – one of Etruscan figurines, and one, unique in America, of English pre-Raphaelite paintings. He then served as the museum's unpaid director until his death. During his tenure he brought a few additional collections to the museum, largely from other alumni of the university. Only rarely did the museum purchase anything. As a result, the museum housed several small collections of uneven quality. As long as the founder ran the museum, none of the collections were ever shown to anybody except a few members of the university's art history faculty, who were admitted as the founder's private guests.

After the founder's death, in the late 1920s, the university intended to bring in a professional museum director. Indeed, this had been part of the agreement under which the founder had given the museum. A search committee was to be appointed; but in the meantime a graduate student in art history, who had shown interest in the museum and who had spent a good many hours in it, took over temporarily. At first, Miss Kirkoff did not even have a title, let alone a salary. But she stayed on acting as the museum's director and over the next 30 years was promoted in stages to that title. But from the first day, whatever her title, she was in charge. She immediately set about changing the museum altogether. She catalogued the collections. She pursued new gifts, again primarily small collections from alumni and other friends of the university. She organized fund raising for the museum. But, above all, she began to integrate the museum into the work of the university.

When a space problem arose in the years immediately following World War II, Miss Kirkoff offered the third floor of the museum to the art history faculty, which moved its offices there. She remodeled the building to include classrooms and a modern and well-appointed auditorium. She raised funds to build one of the best research and reference libraries in art history in the country. She also began to organize a series of special exhibitions built around one of the museum's own collections, complemented by loans from outside collections. For each of these exhibitions, she had a distinguished member of the university's art faculty write a catalogue. These catalogues speedily became the leading scholarly texts in the fields.

Miss Kirkoff ran the University Art Museum for almost half a century. But at the age of 68, after suffering a severe stroke, she had to retire. In her letter of resignation she proudly pointed to the museum's growth and accomplishment under her stewardship. 'Our endowment', she wrote, 'now compares favorably with museums several times our size. We never have had to ask the university for any money other than our share of the university's insurance policies. Our collections in the areas of our strength, while small, are of first-rate quality and importance. Above all, we are being used by more people than any museum of our size. Our lecture series, in which members of the university's art history faculty present a major subject to a university audience of students and faculty, attracts regularly three hundred to five hundred people; and if we had the seating capacity, we could easily have a larger audience. Our exhibitions are seen and studied by more visitors, most of them members of the university community, than all but the most highly publicized exhibitions in the very big museums ever draw. Above all, the courses and seminars offered in the museum have become one of the most popular and most rapidly growing educational features of the university. No other museum in this country or anywhere else', concluded Miss Kirkoff, 'has so successfully integrated art into the life of a major university and a major university into the work of a museum'.

Miss Kirkoff strongly recommended that the university bring in a professional museum director as her successor. 'The museum is much too big and much too important to be entrusted to another amateur such as I was forty-five years ago', she wrote. 'And it needs careful thinking regarding its direction, its basis of support, and its future relationship with the university.'

The university took Miss Kirkoff's advice. A search committee was duly appointed and, after one year's work, it produced a candidate whom everybody approved. The candidate was himself a graduate of the university who had then obtained his Ph.D. in art history and in museum work from the university. Both his teaching and his administrative record were sound, leading to his current museum directorship in a medium-sized city. There he converted an old, well-known, but rather sleepy museum to a lively, community-oriented museum whose exhibitions were well publicized and attracted large crowds.

The new museum director took over with great fanfare in September 1981. Less than 3 years later he left – with less fanfare, but still with considerable noise. Whether he resigned or was fired was not quite clear. But that there was bitterness on both sides was only too obvious.

The new director, upon his arrival, had announced that he looked upon the museum as a 'major community resource' and intended to 'make the tremendous artistic and scholarly resources of the museum fully available to the academic community as well as to the public'. When he said these things in an interview with the college newspaper, everybody nodded in approval. It soon became clear that what he meant by 'community resource' and what the faculty and students understood by these words were not the same. The museum had always been 'open to the public' but, in practice, it was members of the college community who used the museum and attended its lectures, its exhibitions and its frequent seminars.

The first thing the new director did, however, was to promote visits from the public schools in the area. He soon began to change the exhibition policy. Instead of organizing small shows, focused on a major collection of the museum and built around a scholarly catalogue, he began to organize 'popular exhibitions' around 'topics of general interest' such as 'Women Artists through the Ages'. He promoted these exhibitions vigorously in the newspapers, in radio and television interviews, and, above all, in the local schools. As a result, what had been a busy but quiet place was soon knee-deep with schoolchildren, taken to the museum in special buses that cluttered the access roads around the museum and throughout the campus. The faculty, which was not particularly happy with the resulting noise and confusion, became thoroughly upset when the scholarly old chairman of the art history department was mobbed by fourth-graders who sprayed him with their water pistols as he tried to push his way through the main hall to his office.

Increasingly, the new director did not design his own shows, but brought in traveling exhibitions from major museums, importing their catalogue as well rather than have his own faculty produce one.

The students, too, were apparently unenthusiastic after the first six or eight months, during which the new director had been somewhat of a campus hero. Attendance at the classes and seminars held at the art museum fell off sharply, as did attendance at the evening lectures. When the editor of the campus newspaper interviewed students for a story on the museum, he was told again and again that the museum had become too noisy and too 'sensational' for students to enjoy the classes and to have a chance to learn.

What brought all this to a head was an Islamic art exhibit in late 1983. Since the museum had little Islamic art, nobody criticized the showing of a traveling exhibit, offered on very advantageous terms with generous financial assistance from some of the Arab governments. But then, instead of inviting one of the university's own faculty members to deliver the customary talk at the opening of the exhibit, the director brought in a cultural attaché of one of the Arab embassies in Washington. The speaker, it was reported, used the occasion to deliver a violent attack on Israel and on the American policy of supporting Israel against the Arabs. A week later, the university senate decided to appoint an advisory committee, drawn mostly from members of the art history faculty, which, in the future, would have to approve all plans for exhibits and lectures. The director thereupon, in an interview with the campus newspaper, sharply attacked the faculty as 'elitist' and 'snobbish' and as believing that 'art belongs to the rich'. Six months later, in June 1984, his resignation was announced.

Under the bylaws of the university, the academic senate appoints a search committee. Normally, this is pure formality. The chairperson of the appropriate department submits the department's nominees for the committee who are approved and appointed, usually without debate. But when the academic senate early the following semester was asked to appoint the search committee, things were far from 'normal.' The Dean who presided, sensing the tempers in the room, tried to smooth over things by saying, 'Clearly, we picked the wrong person the last time. We will have to try very hard to find the right one this time.'

He was immediately interrupted by an economist, known for his populism, who broke in and said, 'I admit that the late director was probably not the right personality. But I strongly believe that his personality was not at the root of the problem. He tried to do what needs doing, and this got him in trouble with the faculty. He tried to make our museum a community resource, to bring in the community and to make art accessible to broad masses of people, to the blacks and the Puerto Ricans, to the kids from the ghetto schools and to a lay public. And this is what we really resented. Maybe his methods were not the most tactful ones – I admit I could have done without those interviews he gave. But what he tried to do was right. We had better commit ourselves to the policy he wanted to put into effect, or else we will have deserved his attacks on us as "elitist" and "snobbish".'

'This is nonsense', cut in the usually silent and polite senate member from the art history faculty. 'It makes absolutely no sense for our museum to become the kind of community resource our late director and my distinguished colleague want it to be. First, there is no need. The city has one of the world's finest and biggest museums, and it does exactly that and does it very well. Secondly, we have neither the artistic resources nor the financial resources to serve the community at large. We can do something different but equally important and indeed unique. Ours is the only museum in the country, and perhaps in the world, that is fully integrated with an academic community and truly a teaching institution. We are using it, or at least we used to until the last few unfortunate years, as a major educational resource for all our students. No other museum in the country, and as far as I know in the world, is bringing undergraduates into art the way we do. All of us, in addition to our scholarly and graduate work, teach undergraduate courses for people who are not going to be art majors or art historians. We work with the engineering students and show them what we do in our conservation and restoration work. We work with architecture students and show them the development of architecture through the ages. Above all, we work with liberal arts students, who often have had no exposure to art before they came here and who enjoy our courses all the more because they are scholarly and not just "art appreciation". This is unique and this is what our museum can do and should do.'

'I doubt that this is really what we should be doing', commented the chairman of the mathematics department. 'The museum, as far as I know, is part of the graduate faculty. It should concentrate on training art historians in its Ph.D. program, on its scholarly work and on its research. I would strongly urge that the museum be considered an adjunct to graduate and especially to Ph.D. education, confine itself to this work, and stay out of all attempts to be "popular", both on campus and outside of it. The glory of the museum is the scholarly catalogues produced by our faculty, and our Ph.D. graduates who are sought after by art history faculties throughout the country. This is the museum's mission, which can only be impaired by the attempts to be "popular", whether with students or with the public.'

'These are very interesting and important comments', said the Dean, still trying to pacify. 'But I think this can wait until we know who the new director is going to be. Then we should raise these questions with him.'

'I beg to differ, Mr. Dean', said one of the elder statesmen of the faculty. 'During the summer months, I discussed this question with an old friend and neighbour of mine in the country, the director of one of the nation's great museums. He said to me: "You do not have a personality problem; you have a management problem. You have not, as a university, taken responsibility for the mission, the direction, and the objectives of your museum. Until you do this, no director can succeed. And this is your decision. In fact, you cannot hope to get a good director until you can tell that person what your basic objectives are. If your late director is to blame – I know him and I know that he is abrasive – it is for being willing to take on a job when you, the university, had not faced up to the basic management decisions. There is no point talking about who should manage until it is clear what it is that has to be managed and for what."'

At this point the Dean realized that he had to adjourn the discussion unless he wanted the meeting to degenerate into a brawl. But he also realized that he had to identify the issues and possible decisions before the next senate meeting a month later.

Case Questions

1 What do you see as the fundamental problem facing the University Art Museum? Is it the selection of a new director, or something more fundamental?

2 If you were the Dean, how would you go about designing a process to decide the future direction of the University Art Museum?

3 Everyone seemed to agree that the departed director was an abrasive character. But do you think any director could have managed the museum more successfully? If so, how?

4 To what extent do you think the current problems of the University Art Museum can be traced back to the foundation of the museum in 1912?

Notes

1. http://www.starbucks.com/aboutus/Company_Factsheet.pdf
2. Starbucks Inc. Annual Report 2006, available at http://media.corporate-ir.net/media_files/irol/99/99518/reports/StarbucksAnnualReport.pdf.
3. Steven Gray, 'Starbucks Brews Broader Menu; Coffee Chain's Cup Runneth Over with Breakfast, Lunch, Music', *The Wall Street Journal* (February 9, 2005), B9; Andy Serwer, 'Hot Starbucks to Go', *Fortune* (January 26, 2004), 60–74; Jean Patteson, 'Warm Hues Hot for Fall; Call It the Starbucks Influence, as Designers Serve Colours from Latte to Espresso Spiked with Vibrant Blues'. *Orlando Sentinel* (February 10, 2005), E1; 'Starbucks' Continues Successful Expansion of Music Experience', *Business Wire* (February 9, 2005), 1; and Monica Soto Ouchi, 'No Roast, Just Thanks to Can-Do Coffee Man', *Seattle Times* (February 10, 2005), A1.
4 Janet Adamy, 'McDonald's to take on a weakened Starbucks', Associated Press wire, January 7, 2008.
5. Amitai Etzioni, *Modern Organizations* (Englewood Cliffs, N.J.: Prentice-Hall, 1964), 6.
6. John P. Kotter, 'What Effective General Managers Really Do', *Harvard Business Review* (November–December 1982), 156–167; Henry Mintzberg, *The Nature of Managerial Work* (New York: Harper & Row, 1973).
7. Charles C. Snow and Lawrence G. Hrebiniak, 'Strategy, Distinctive Competence and Organizational Performance', *Administrative Science Quarterly* 25 (1980), 317–335.
8. 'Strong R&D Medicine is the Drug of Choice for Fast-Growing Pharma', *Irish Independent*, September 9, 2004; Alison Maitland, 'A leader striving for the perfect bedside manner', *Financial Times*, November 28, 2001, page 1; David Pilling, 'What the Doctor Ordered', *Financial Times*, October 12, 1998, page 1; Bill Griffeth, Maria Bartiromo, 'Novartis: CEO and Chairman Interview', *CEO Wire* January 2, 2006.
9. Helmut K Anheier (2002), The third sector in Europe: Five theses, Civil Society Working Paper 12, London, LSE.
10. Klein, P. (2006), *Economics Confronts The Economy*, London, Edward Elgar, p. 228.
11. Forest R. David and Fred R. David, 'It's Time to Redraft Your Mission Statement', *Journal of Business Strategy* (January–February 2003), 11–14; John Pearce and Fred David, 'Corporate Mission Statements: The Bottom Line', *Academy of Management Executive* 1, no. 2 (May 1987), 109–116; and Christopher Bart and Mark Baetz, 'The Relationship Between Mission Statements and Firm Performance: An Exploratory Study', *Journal of Management Studies* 35 (1998).
12. Barbara Bartkus, Myron Glassman and R. Bruce McAfee, 'Mission Statements: Are They Smoke and Mirrors?' *Business Horizons* (November–December 2000), 23–28.
13. Mark C. Suchman, 'Managing Legitimacy: Strategic and Institutional Approaches', *Academy of Management Review* 20, no. 3 (1995), 571–610.
14. Kurt Eichenwald, 'Miscues, Missteps and the Fall of Andersen', *The New York Times* (May 8, 2002), C1, C4; Ian Wilson, 'The Agenda for Redefining Corporate Purpose: Five Key Executive Actions', *Strategy & Leadership* 32, no. 1 (2004), 21–26.
15. Bill George, 'The Company's Mission is the Message', *Strategy & Business*, Issue 33 (Winter 2003), 13–14; Jim Collins and Jerry Porras, *Built to Last: Successful Habits of Visionary Companies* (New York: HarperBusiness, 1994).
16. Chris Penttila, 'Missed Mission', Entrepreneur Magazine, May 2002, at http://www.entrepreneur.com/magazine/entrepreneur/2002/may/51106.html.
17. Fred David (1989), 'How Companies Define Their Mission', *Long Range Planning*, volume 22, 90–97; Carolyn Strong (1997), 'The question we continue to ask: How do organizations define their mission?' *Journal of Marketing Practice: Applied Marketing Science*, Volume 3, 268–283; Jatinder Sidhu (2003), 'Mission Statements: Is it Time to Shelve Them?', *European Management Journal*, 21, 439–446; Chris Bart (2004), 'Innovation, mission statements and learning', *International Journal of Technology Management,* 27, 544–567; Barbara Bartkus, Myron Glassman and Bruce McAfee (2006), 'Mission Statement Quality and Financial Performance', *European Management Journal*, 24, 86–94.
18. Charles Perrow, 'The Analysis of Goals in Complex Organizations', *American Sociological Review* 26 (1961), 854–866.
19. Johannes U. Stoelwinder and Martin P. Charns, 'The Task Field Model of Organization Analysis and Design', *Human Relations* 34 (1981), 743–762; Anthony Raia, *Managing by Objectives* (Glenview, Ill.: Scott, Foresman, 1974).
20. Volvo AG Annual Report 2006, page 13, at http://www.volvo.com/NR/rdonlyres/90719C03-4AC1-4DFA-BB93-2E6150E8670A/0/070319_volvo_engelsk_150dpi.pdf.
21. Known as the Honda Jazz in Europe.

22. Japan Automobile Dealers Association, December 6, 2006, cited at http://www.shiotsu-autotrade.jp/blog/?p=9.
23. Ivar Ekman, Lego braces for big changes, *International Herald Tribune*, July 2, 2005, oage 9; Bernard Marotte, 'Top court quashes Lego bid against toy rival', *Globe and Mail*, November 18, 2005, B5.
24. Alex Taylor III, 'Honda Goes Its Own Way,' *Fortune* (July 22, 2002), 148–152; Joseph Pereira and Christopher J. Chipello, 'Battle of the Block Makers', *The Wall Street Journal* (February 4, 2004), B1.
25. Cris Prystay, 'Why a Small Company in China Was Named Asia's Best Employer', Wall Street Journal Asia Online, April 24 2007; Michael Kanellos, 'Memory maker looks to new tech for turnaround', *C-Net news.com*, November 28 2007; Eileen Lian, 'Devotion to their staff puts companies on top', *South China Morning Post*, May 12 2007, 24.
26. Michael Arndt, '3M: A Lab for Growth?' *BusinessWeek* (January 21, 2002), 50–51.
27. Doreen Hemlock, 'Brazilian jet maker Embraer soars', *South Florida Sun-Sentinel*, November 25, 2007; Q1 2007 Embraer-Empresa Brasileira de Aeronautica S.A. Earnings Conference Call, *Fair Disclosure Wire*, May 15, 2007.
28. Kim Cross, 'Does Your Team Measure Up?' *Business2.com* (June 12, 2001), 22–28; J. Lynn Lunsford, 'Lean Times: With Airbus on Its Tail, Boeing is Rethinking How It Builds Planes', *The Wall Street Journal* (September 5, 2001), A11.
29. Christopher Cooper and Greg Jaffe, 'Under Fire: At Abu Ghraib, Soldiers Faced Intense Pressure to Produce Data', *The Wall Street Journal* (June 1, 2004), A1, A6.
30. James D. Thompson, *Organizations in Action* (New York: McGraw-Hill, 1967), 83–98.
31. Michael E. Porter, 'What Is Strategy?' *Harvard Business Review* (November–December 1996), 61–78.
32. Michael E. Porter, Competitive Strategy: Techniques for Analyzing Industries and Competitors (New York: Free Press, 1980).
33. Datamonitor, January 7, 2008.
34. Alan Ruddock, 'Keeping Up with O'Leary', *Management Today* (September 2003), 48–55; Jane Engle, 'Flying High for Pocket Change; Regional Carriers Offer Inexpensive Travel Alternative', *South Florida Sun Sentinel* (February 13, 2005), 5; 'Ryanair is Top on Net', *The Daily Mirror* (February 3, 2005), 10; and 'Ryanair Tops 2m Passengers', *Daily Post* (February 4, 2005), 21.
35. Richard Teitelbaum, 'The Wal-Mart of Wall Street', *Fortune* (October 13, 1997), 128–130.
36. CNN interview transcript, Puma CEO and Chairman Jochen Zeitz, September 28 2006 at http://edition.cnn.com/2006/BUSINESS/07/06/boardroom.zeitz/; Holger Elfes, 'Puma strengthens ties with its parent, *International Herald Tribune*, p. 16; FD (Fair Disclosure) Wire', Interim 2007 PPR (ex. Pinault Printemps Redoute) Earnings Conference Call', August 31, 2007.
37. Kevin J. O'Brien, 'Focusing on Armchair Athletes, Puma Becomes a Leader', *The New York Times* (March 12, 2004), W1.
38. Michael E. Porter, 'Strategy and the Internet', *Harvard Business Review* (March 2001), 63–78; and John Magretta, 'Why Business Models Matter', *Harvard Business Review* (May 2002), 86.
39. Dennis Tourish and Ashly Pinnington (2002), 'Transformational leadership, corporate cultism and the spirituality paradigm: An unholy trinity in the workplace?', *Human Relations*, 55, p: 147–172; Rakesh Khurana (2002), 'The Curse of the Superstar CEO', *Harvard Business Review*, 80(9), 60–67; Dennis Tourish and Naheed Vatcha (2005), 'Charismatic Leadership and Corporate Cultism at Enron: The Elimination of Dissent, the Promotion of Conformity and Organizational Collapse', *Leadership*, 1, pp. 455–480.
40. Raymond E. Miles and Charles C. Snow, *Organizational Strategy, Structure, and Process* (New York: McGraw-Hill, 1978).
41. Geraldine Fabrikant, 'The Paramount Team Puts Profit Over Splash', *The New York Times* (June 30, 2002), Section 3, 1, 15.
42. 'Miles and Snow: Enduring Insights for Managers: Academic Commentary by Sumantra Ghoshal', *Academy of Management Executive* 17, no. 4 (2003), 109–114.
43. Pallavi Gogoi and Michael Arndt, 'Hamburger Hell', *BusinessWeek* (March 3, 2003), 104–108; and Michael Arndt, 'McDonald's: Fries with That Salad?' *BusinessWeek* (July 5, 2004), 82–84.
44. 'On the Staying Power of Defenders, Analyzers and Prospectors: Academic Commentary by Donald C. Hambrick', *Academy of Management Executive* 17, no. 4 (2003), 115–118.
45. W. Chan Kim and Renée Mauborgne (2005), 'Blue Ocean Strategy: From Theory to Practice', *California Review of Management,* 47, 105–121; C. Kim and R. Mauborgne (2005), *Blue Ocean Strategy: How to Create Uncontested Market Space and Make the Competition Irrelevant,* Cambridge, MA, Harvard Business School Press.
46. Baron, J.N., and Hannan, M.T. (2002), 'Organizational blueprints for success in high-tech start-ups', *California Management Review*, Vol. 44 No.3, pp. 8–36.
47. Etzioni, *Modern Organizations,* 8.
48. Etzioni, *Modern Organizations*, 8; and Gary D. Sandefur, 'Efficiency in Social Service Organizations', *Administration and Society* 14 (1983), 449–468.
49. Richard M. Steers, *Organizational Effectiveness: A Behavioral View* (Santa Monica, Calif.: Goodyear, 1977), 51.
50. Karl E. Weick and Richard L. Daft, 'The Effectiveness of Interpretation Systems', in Kim S. Cameron and David A. Whetten, eds., *Organizational Effectiveness: A Comparison of Multiple Models* (New York: Academic Press, 1982).
51. David L. Blenkhorn and Brian Gaber, 'The Use of 'Warm Fuzzies' to Assess Organizational Effectiveness,' *Journal of General Management*, 21, no. 2 (Winter 1995), 40–51.
52. Steven Strasser, J. D. Eveland, Gaylord Cummins, O. Lynn Deniston and John H. Romani, 'Conceptualizing the Goal and Systems Models of Organizational Effectiveness —

Implications for Comparative Evaluation Research', *Journal of Management Studies* 18 (1981), 321–340.

53. James L. Price, 'The Study of Organizational Effectiveness', *Sociological Quarterly* 13 (1972), 3–15.
54. United Nations Millennium Declaration, Resolution 55/2, September 18 2000, at http://www.un.org/millennium/declaration/ares552e.pdf; *United Nations Millennium Development Goals Report - 2007*, at http://www.un.org/millenniumgoals/pdf/mdg2007.pdf.
55. Richard H. Hall and John P. Clark, 'An Ineffective Effectiveness Study and Some Suggestions for Future Research', *Sociological Quarterly* 21 (1980), 119–134; Price, 'The Study of Organizational Effectiveness'; and Perrow, 'Analysis of Goals'.
56. Y. K. Shetty, 'New Look at Corporate Goals', *California Management Review* 22, no. 2 (1979), 71–79.
57. The discussion of the resource-based approach is based in part on Michael V. Russo and Paul A. Fouts, 'A Resource-Based Perspective on Corporate Environmental Performance and Profitability', *Academy of Management Journal* 40, no. 3 (June 1997), 534–559; and Jay B. Barney, J. L. 'Larry' Stempert, Loren T. Gustafson and Yolanda Sarason, 'Organizational Identity within the Strategic Management Conversation: Contributions and Assumptions', in *Identity in Organizations: Building Theory through Conversations*, David A. Whetten and Paul C. Godfrey, eds. (Thousand Oaks, Calif.: Sage Publications, 1998), 83–98.
58. Jan Drazan, 'VW Group's YTD Sales Up 8.5 per cent Y/Y; Decision on New North American Plant to Be Made by Mid-2008', World Markets Research Centre *Global Insight*, November 16, 2007; Mark Phelan and Jewel Gopwani, 'Audi ready to break 1-million mark with new lineup', *Detroit Free Press*, January 13, 2008; Jesse Snyder, 'VWoA's 1 million sales goal: Get real; Quality and image help keep VW brand in its place', *Automotive News*, November 5, 2007 p.14.
59. Enrico Valdani and Fabio Ancarani (2001), 'Marketing Places: A Resource-Based Approach and Empirical Evidence from the European Experience', SDA Bocconi, Research Division Working Paper No. 01/55.
60. AT Kearney, Inc, (2008), *Success through Shared Services – From Back Office Functions to Strategic Drivers*, Chicago, AT Kearney, at http://www.atkearney.com/shared_res/pdf/Shared_Services_S.pdf; Alan Duerden, 'Commercial services strategy support', The Banker, December 1, 2007; Alan Rodger, 'AnalystWatch: Another Ground-Breaking Year for TCS', Computerwire, December 24, 2007; Elizabeth Ferrarini, 'Shared Services', *Computerworld*, November 27, 2000.
61. Chris Argyris, *Integrating the Individual and the Organization* (New York: Wiley, 1964); Warren G. Bennis, *Changing Organizations* (New York: McGraw-Hill, 1966); Rensis Likert, *The Human Organization* (New York: McGraw-Hill, 1967); and Richard Beckhard, *Organization Development Strategies and Models* (Reading, Mass.: Addison-Wesley, 1969).
62. Cheri Ostroff and Neal Schmitt, 'Configurations of Organizational Effectiveness and Efficiency', *Academy of Management Journal* 36 (1993), 1345–1361; Peter J. Frost, Larry F. Moore, Meryl Reise Louis, Craig C. Lundburg and Joanne Martin, *Organizational Culture* (Beverly Hills, Calif.: Sage, 1985).
63. J. Barton Cunningham, 'Approaches to the Evaluation of Organizational Effectiveness', *Academy of Management Review* 2 (1977), 463–474; Beckhard, *Organization Development*.
64. Mike Lewis, 'New Boeing leader a big part of company's turnaround', *Seattle Post-Intelligencer*, September 6, 2006; James Wallace, 'Boeing leader ousted', *Seattle Post-Intelligencer*, March 8, 2005.
65. Roger Martin, 'How he thinks', *Canadian Business*, Winter 2007–2008¸ p. 78.
66. Stanley Holmes, 'A New Black Eye for Boeing?' *BusinessWeek* (April 26, 2004), 90–92; Robert Levering and Milton Moskowitz, 'The 100 Best Companies to Work For', *Fortune* (January 24, 2005), 72–90.
67. Eric J. Walton and Sarah Dawson, 'Managers' Perceptions of Criteria of Organizational Effectiveness', *Journal of Management Studies* 38, no. 2 (2001), 173–199.
68. Beth Dickey, 'NASA's Next Step', *Government Executive* (April 15, 2004), 34+.
69. Robert E. Quinn and John Rohrbaugh, 'A Spatial Model of Effectiveness Criteria: Toward a Competing Values Approach to Organizational Analysis', *Management Science* 29 (1983), 363–377.
70. Regina M. O'Neill and Robert E. Quinn, 'Editor's Note: Applications of the Competing Values Framework', *Human Resource Management* 32 (Spring 1993), 1–7.
71. Robert E. Quinn and Kim Cameron, 'Organizational Life Cycles and Shifting Criteria of Effectiveness: Some Preliminary Evidence', *Management Science* 29 (1983), 33–51.
72. Grant Robertson, 'Private equity eyes Thomson unit; Company begins review of bidders for division worth up to $6-billion', *Globe and Mail*, February 9, 2007, B3; Richard Blackwell, 'Deal would create world's largest market data firm', *The Globe and Mail*, May 5, 2007, B5; Wednesday; Peter Healy, 'Thomson Learning to become Cengage', *The Stamford Advocate, Conn*. July 25, 2007; *History of the Thomson Corporation* at http://www.thomson.com/about/history/. BBC News, 'Reuters agrees to Thomson buyout', at http://news.bbc.co.uk/1/hi/business/6656525.stm; Barrie McKenna 'Richard Harrington', *The Globe and Mail*, May 9, 2007, page B6.
73. Larry Bossidy and Ram Charan, *Confronting Reality: Doing What Matters to Get Things Right* (New York: Crown Business, 2004), Chapter 9, 153–168.

CHAPTER 3

FUNDAMENTALS OF ORGANIZATION STRUCTURE

GM España

GM España (formerly Opel España) is the Spanish subsidiary of the global auto giant General Motors, based near the northern Spanish city of Zaragoza. While US auto manufacturers, including GM, are facing increasingly difficult market conditions in their home base due to competition from Asian car builders, global operations had been performing well, at least until the global downturn that hit manufacturing industry everywhere starting in 2007/2008. One of GM's survival strategies is based on continuing its international growth as it rebalances its activities towards growing markets outside the United States. The Zaragoza plant is GM's largest in Europe, with 7,600 staff and annual capacity of around 400,000 vehicles, and makes the high-selling Corsa and the Meriva minivan.

Consumer expectations are becoming increasingly sophisticated and differentiated. In the early days of car manufacture, Henry Ford was famously quoted as saying of his Model T, 'the customer can have any colour he wants so long as it's black'.[1] Nowadays, consumer preferences are key. Car buyers demand fashionable interiors and exteriors, technological innovation, a variety of product options to fit individual needs and high quality at reasonable prices. In addition, competition from other manufacturers has intensified, and customers have a range of high quality, competitively priced alternatives.

This increasingly demanding business environment is leading car companies to adopt various new production models, including what is termed *agile manufacturing*.[2] Agile manufacturing departs from the traditional mass production approach, focusing on highly customized manufacturing, producing vehicles as and when customers require them, rapidly changing production to meet new demands and marketing a wide variety of products and product options to satisfy an increasingly diverse and knowledgeable customer base.

GM España has spent considerable time and effort tailoring its physical plant, equipment, organizational structure and management systems to meet these challenges and to allow continued growth and profitability. For the launch of fourth-generation Opel Corsa D in 2006, managers brought in experts from GM's International Technical Development Centre in Germany to design more efficient and flexible production. The strategy emphasized the need for integrated improvements. Equipment innovations included expanded use of robots in production, and new paint-spraying machinery that produces higher quality finish and fewer environmental emissions.[3] Production processes and procedures were streamlined. Central to the production redesign, however, were improvements in organizational design.

Organizational design is centred around teamwork practices designed to build empowerment, involvement and motivation of employees, from top management to the shop floor. From the beginning, the new Corsa's design was based on the integration of production, engineering and marketing managers in the development team.[4] This teamwork approach extends into the manufacturing process, where flexible manufacturing systems are based on a modular approach. The modular approach allows the end-customer to select from a wide range of standardized options so that the car that rolls off the production line is the one that the consumer has chosen. Like many other manufacturers, GM España relies increasingly on the outsourcing of various parts of the vehicle. Again, the company is moving towards modular outsourcing, so that rather than subcontracting numerous small components, suppliers provide whole modules, such as steering assemblies, which are then incorporated into the car at the Zaragoza plant. Major suppliers, too, were involved in the Corsa design process from the earliest stage, ensuring that potential problems were smoothed out before full production began.

Managers responsible for the design and redesign of organizations have used various structural alternatives to help them achieve their purpose and goals. Nearly every organization undergoes structural reorganization at some point to help meet new challenges. Structural changes reflect new strategies or respond to changes which, in Chapter 2, were conceived as 'contingency factors', such as environment, technology, size and life cycle and culture. In general, the effectiveness of a traditional directive, authoritarian management style has been increasingly criticized for its lack of responsiveness and 'agility' and there has been increased experimentation with more flexible, teamwork-based approaches in an effort to improve decision making and put resources in places where they are assessed to produce the greatest value.[5]

Purpose of This Chapter

This chapter introduces basic concepts of organization structure and shows how to design a structure as it is drawn up on organization charts. First we define a structure and provide an overview of structural design. Then, an information-processing perspective explains how to design vertical and horizontal linkages to provide needed information flow. Basic design options are then presented, followed by strategies for grouping organizational activities into functional, divisional, matrix, horizontal, virtual network or hybrid structures. The final section examines how the application of basic structures depends on the organization's situation and outlines the symptoms of structural misalignment.

See online COUNTERPOINT 3.7

Organization Structure

There are three key components in the definition of **organization structure**:

1. Organization structure designates formal reporting relationships, including the number of levels in the hierarchy and the span of control of managers and supervisors.
2. Organization structure identifies the grouping together of individuals into departments and of departments into the total organization.
3. Organization structure includes the design of systems to ensure effective communication, coordination and integration of efforts across departments.[6]

These three elements of structure refer to both vertical and horizontal aspects of organizing. For example, the first two elements are the structural *framework*, which include the vertical hierarchy.[7] The third element pertains to the pattern of *interactions* among organizational employees. An ideal structure encourages employees to provide horizontal information and coordination where and when it is needed.

As an organization manager, keep these guidelines in mind:

Develop organization charts that describe task responsibilities, reporting relationships and the grouping of individuals into departments. Provide sufficient documentation so that all people within the organization know to whom they report and how they fit into the total organization picture.

Organization structure represented visually in organization charts

It isn't possible to see the internal structure of an organization the way we might see its manufacturing tools, offices or products. Although we might see employees going about their duties, performing different tasks and working in different locations, a way to show the structure underlying all this activity is through the organization chart. The organization chart is the visual representation of a whole set of underlying activities and processes in an organization. Exhibit 3.1 shows a sample organization chart.

The concept of an organization chart, showing what positions exist, how they are grouped and who reports to whom, has been around for centuries.[8] Diagrams outlining church hierarchy can be found in medieval churches in Spain. However, the

EXHIBIT 3.1 A Sample Organization Chart

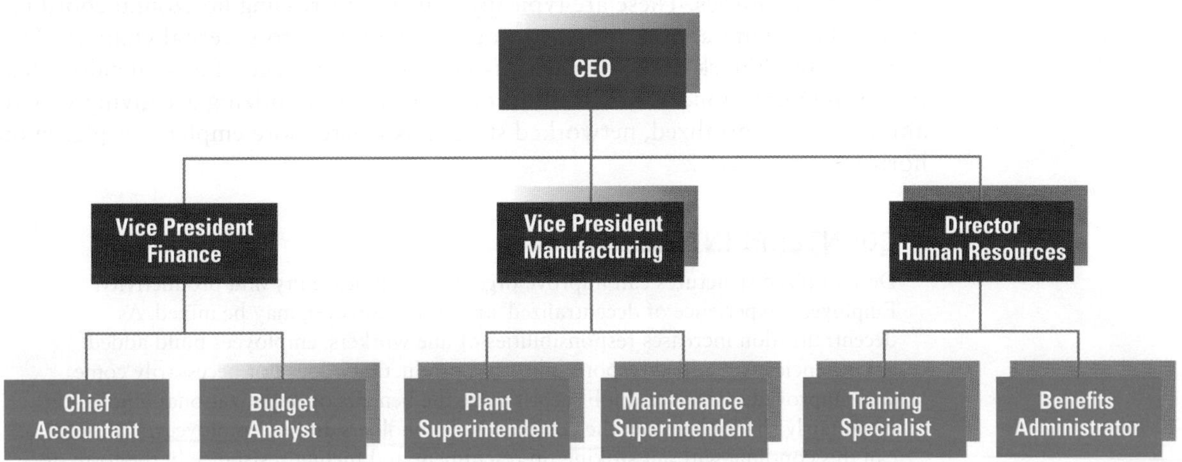

contemporary use of the organization chart for business stems from the Industrial Revolution, and especially from the emergence of large scale steam railways in the mid nineteenth century. As we discussed in Chapter 1, as work grew more complex and was performed by greater and greater numbers of workers, there was a pressing need to develop ways of managing and controlling organizations. The earliest development of business organizational charts seems to have been in American railways, as a response to safety issues. After two passenger trains collided in Massachusetts in 1841, the public demanded better control of the operation. As a result, the Board of Directors of the Western Railroad took steps to outline 'definite responsibilities for each phase of the company's business, drawing solid lines of authority and command for the railroad's administration, maintenance and operation'.[9]

COUNTERPOINT 3.1

An organization chart is only so many lines and boxes on a piece of paper. The organization chart indicates the structure of control but its enactment and realization depends upon the employees who provide the behavior. Its purpose is to provide a common frame of reference that, in general and above all, asserts and reinforces a hierarchical relationship of domination between executives at the apex, managers in the middle levels and workers at the base. If all employees can be encouraged to accept this hierarchy as something that is a necessity rather than politically imposed or expedient, then the goals of the organization determined by executives will more likely be realized through the actions of employees. The chart is not only a technical guideline to encourage people to work together but a powerful political symbol whose acceptance implies deference to its demands. **Discuss**

The type of organization structure that grew out of these efforts to draw lines of command in the late nineteenth and early twentieth centuries was one in which the CEO was placed at the top and everyone else was arranged in layers down below, as illustrated in Exhibit 3.1. It indicates how thinking and decision making are to be carried out by those at the top, and the physical work is performed by employees who are organized into distinct, functional departments. This structure became increasingly entrenched in business, nonprofit and military organizations during the twentieth century. However, such a structure is not always effective, particularly in rapidly changing environments, and a variety of alternative structures have been devised to be more flexible and to increase involvement of all the organization's employees. These are typically aimed at increasing horizontal coordination and communication and encouraging adaptation to external changes. This chapter's Bookmark asks whether business is on the verge of a tremendous historic transformation, in which traditional forms of organizing are giving way to alternative decentralized, networked structures where more emphasis is placed on horizontal processes.

COUNTERPOINT 3.2

Decentralized structures can improve organizational flexibility and productivity. Employee's experience of decentralized structures, however, may be mixed. As decentralization increases responsibilities of line workers, employees build added competencies. Yet added responsibility and productivity does not necessarily come with improved salaries and job security. Are the benefits of organizational innovation being fairly shared between the company's shareholders and its employees?[10] If not, can this continue without stoking up resentment and fueling resistance in the form of psychological distancing, withdrawal of goodwill, organized opposition, individual sabotage and so on? **Discuss**

In this chapter, we will examine five basic structural designs and show how they are reflected in the organization chart.

Information-Processing Perspective on Structure

In this perspective, the organization design is conceived to provide both vertical and horizontal information flow as necessary to accomplish the organization's overall goals. If the structure doesn't fit the information requirements of the organization, people either will have too little information or will spend time processing information that is not vital to their tasks, thus reducing effectiveness.[11] However, there is an inherent tension between vertical and horizontal mechanisms in an organization. Whereas vertical linkages provide the mechanism for control, horizontal linkages are designed for coordination and collaboration, processes that can reduce top management control.

COUNTERPOINT 3.3

Note that a vertical division of labour is associated with control in *the name of efficiency*, and not necessarily with the delivery of enhanced efficiency or effectiveness. At the extreme, the autocratic CEO may exert control through the micro-management of activities so that no significant decision is made without his or her agreement. Such control will likely produce a backlog of decision-making and delayed decisions that are based upon a distant and limited understanding of the specific circumstances. What is true of the autocratic CEO is also true, to a degree, of all organizations with a structure where those 'at the top' become remote from what is happening 'at the bottom'. The problems are compounded when senior management teams either assume that they are omniscient or rely upon managers who live in fear of providing unwelcome information. **Discuss**

Organizations can choose whether to orient toward a traditional organization design, which emphasizes vertical communication and control, or toward a contemporary learning organization, which emphasizes horizontal communication and

Have you read this book?

The Future of Work: How the New Order of Business Will Shape Your Organization, Your Management Style and Your Life

BY THOMAS W. MALONE

Organizations are experiencing tremendous change, and Thomas W. Malone suggests in his book *The Future of Work* that they are on the verge of a fundamental shift that could be 'as important to business as the shift to democracy has been for government'. Rigid, highly centralized vertical hierarchies, he says, will essentially be a thing of the past as organizations move to flexible decentralized forms of organizing based on horizontal work processes. Command-and-control management and top-down decision making will give way to empowered teams of employees focused on specific workflows and processes, working across organizational boundaries and making their own decisions based on up-to-the-minute information.

The Brave New World of Work

Malone describes several decentralized management structures and provides numerous examples of organizations that are experimenting with new forms of organizing and innovative management techniques. Here are some of Malone's key points about the future of work:

- *Information technology is the key driver of the transformation*. The falling cost of communication is making the distribution of power away from the corporate suite both inevitable and desirable. Outsourcing information work to India, for example, is possible because digital communication with India is so cheap, as is labour in India. In the same way, accessible information makes it possible for any lower-level employee to plan his or her work more effectively, network and get advice from people anywhere, and make good decisions based on accurate information.
- *Managers will move from command-and-control to coordinate-and-cultivate*. To coordinate is to organize work so that good things happen, whether managers are 'in control' or not. To cultivate means to bring out the best in employees with the right combination of control and freedom. W. L. Gore, the maker of Gore-Tex fabric, lets people decide what they want to do. Leaders emerge based on who has a good idea and can recruit people to work on it. AES, one of the world's largest electric power producers, coordinates and cultivates so well that it lets low-level workers make critical multimillion-dollar decisions about such things as acquiring new subsidiaries.
- *Every organization needs standards*. Many people think clear standards are incompatible with flexibility and decentralization. Malone points out, though, that when employees have guidelines and standards within which to make decisions and take action, they can do their jobs with greater freedom and authority. Consider eBay, which has more than 430,000 people who make their primary living as sellers on the site. eBay managers have no direct control over those 430,000 people, yet they've established clear standards and guidelines for trading that maintain order and accountability.

The Transition Years

Malone, a professor at MIT's Sloan School of Management, acknowledges that hierarchy and centralization continue to provide tremendous advantages for some companies in today's economy. In addition, for most organizations, centralized and decentralized structures and management systems will coexist well into the future. Yet, he is convinced that, ultimately, rigid hierarchical centralized structures will be consigned to the dustbin of history.

The Future of Work: How the New Order of Business Will Shape Your Organization, Your Management Style and Your Life, by Thomas W. Malone, is published by Harvard Business School Press.

EXHIBIT 3.2 The Relationship of Organization Design to Efficiency versus Learning Outcomes

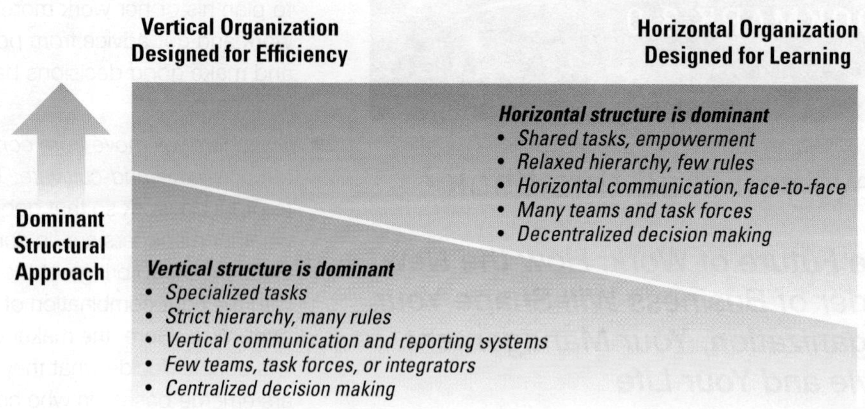

coordination. Exhibit 3.2 compares organizations designed for control with those designed for learning. An emphasis on control is associated with specialized tasks, a hierarchy of authority, rules and regulations, formal reporting systems, few teams or task forces and **centralized** decision making, which means problems and decisions are funnelled to top levels of the hierarchy for resolution. An emphasis on learning is associated with shared tasks, a relaxed hierarchy, few rules, face-to-face communication, many teams and task forces and informal, **decentralized** decision making. Decentralized decision making means decision-making authority is pushed down to lower organizational levels. Organizations may have to experiment to find the correct degree of centralization or decentralization to meet their needs. Some of the most successful 'new economy' companies such as Google operate on a highly decentralized model giving employees great freedom to collaborate and innovate.[12] At the same time, even in a decentralized company a basic hierarchical structure usually remains in place even though it may be overlaid and obscured by an emphasis upon horizontal coordination. At the very least, shareholders require assurance that the use of their assets is 'under control' as well as being deployed as effectively as possible by ensuring agility and responsiveness to emerging opportunities and challenges, as discussed in the Oracle case below. Increasingly, information technologies are used to monitor performance, ideally in real time, thereby facilitating centralized as well as decentralized communication to keep control of the diverse operations of global corporations. For example, Mexico's Cemex, discussed in Chapter 1, has installed computers with broadband internet connections into employees' homes, all linked to the company's intranet portal.[13]

See online COUNTERPOINT 3.8

Managers are always searching for the best combination of vertical control and horizontal collaboration, centralization and decentralization, taking advantage of communications advances to perfect interaction both vertically and horizontally.

Vertical Information Linkages

Linkage is defined as the extent of communication and coordination among organizational elements. **Vertical linkages** are used to coordinate activities between the top and bottom of an organization and are designed primarily for control of the organization. Employees at lower levels are expected to carry out activities consistent with top-level goals, and top executives must be informed of activities and accomplishments at the lower levels. Organizations may use any of a variety of structural devices to achieve vertical linkage, including hierarchical referral, rules, plans and formal management information systems.[14]

Hierarchical Referral The first vertical device is the hierarchy, or chain of command, which is illustrated by the vertical lines in Exhibit 3.1. If a problem arises that employees don't know how to solve, it can be referred up to the next level in the hierarchy. When the problem is solved, the answer is passed back down to lower levels. The lines of the organization chart act as communication channels.

Rules and Plans The next linkage device is the use of rules and plans. To the extent that problems and decisions are repetitious, a rule or procedure can be established so employees know how to respond without communicating directly with their manager. Rules provide a standard information source enabling employees to be coordinated without actually communicating about every task. A plan also provides standing information for employees. The most widely used plan is the budget. With carefully designed budget plans, employees at lower levels can be left on their own to perform activities within their resource allotment.

Vertical Information Systems A **vertical information system** is another strategy for increasing vertical information capacity. Vertical information systems include the periodic reports, written information and computer-based communications distributed to managers. Information systems make communication up and down the hierarchy more efficient. Vertical information systems are an important component of vertical control at software-maker Oracle.

In today's world of corporate financial scandals and ethical concerns, many top managers are considering strengthening their organization's linkages for vertical information and control. The other major issue in organizing is to provide adequate horizontal linkages for coordination and collaboration.

Horizontal Information Linkages

Horizontal communication overcomes barriers between departments and provides opportunities for coordination among employees to achieve unity of effort and organizational objectives. **Horizontal linkage** refers to the amount of communication and coordination horizontally across organizational departments. Its importance is articulated by comments made by Lee Iacocca when he took over the ailing Chrysler Corporation in the 1980s.

What I found at Chrysler were thirty-five vice presidents, each with his own turf ... I couldn't believe, for example, that the guy running engineering departments wasn't in constant touch with his counterpart in manufacturing. But that's how it was. Everybody worked independently. I took one look at that system and I almost threw up. That's when I knew I was in really deep trouble ... Nobody at Chrysler seemed to understand that interaction among the different functions in a company is absolutely critical. People in engineering and manufacturing almost have to be sleeping together. These guys weren't even flirting![15]

During his tenure at Chrysler (now DaimlerChrysler[16]), Iacocca pushed horizontal coordination to a high level. Everyone working on a specific vehicle project – designers, engineers, and manufacturers, as well as representatives from marketing, finance, purchasing, and even outside suppliers – worked together on a single floor so they could constantly communicate.

Horizontal linkage mechanisms often are not drawn on the organization chart, but they invariably form some element of organization structure. The following

As an organization manager, keep these guidelines in mind:

Provide vertical and horizontal information linkages to integrate diverse departments into a coherent whole. Achieve vertical linkage through hierarchy referral, rules and plans and vertical information systems. Achieve horizontal linkage through cross-functional information systems, direct contact, task forces, full-time integrators and teams.

Oracle Corporation

In an era of decentralization and empowerment, Larry Ellison, CEO of Oracle, the global database management company, doesn't hesitate to proclaim his belief in stronger vertical control. Oracle got in trouble some years ago because sales managers around the globe were cutting backroom deals or hammering out private, individualized compensation agreements with salespeople in different countries. Today, all the terms, including sales contracts and commissions, are dictated from the top and spelled out in a global database. In addition, Ellison requires that all deals be entered into the database so they can easily be tracked by top managers.

The Internet plays a key part in Ellison's vertical information and control systems, by offering the power to centralize complex operations while also rapidly disseminating information all over the world. Oracle uses its own suite of Internet software applications that work together on a global basis. All employees do their work via the Internet, enabling Ellison to carefully track, analyze and control the behaviour of each unit, manager and employee. Although many managers weren't happy with the stronger top-down control, Ellison believed it was necessary to effectively manage a sprawling global corporation that was beginning to behave more like a bunch of separate companies. In addition, the system helps to circulate and ensure implementation of standard rules and procedures across divisions. According to Chief Marketing Officer Mark Jarvis, this ultimately provides for greater freedom for lower levels and prevents the hierarchy from becoming overloaded. 'Once we have a standard set of global business practices', Jarvis notes, 'the [managers] can be allowed more scope for decision making within the broad framework'.

Oracle's 2004 acquisition of PeopleSoft, as well as other, smaller acquisitions, has increased the complexity of the organization, but Ellison and other top managers are focused on smooth integration through the use of vertical information systems. The company is working on developing a super-suite of software applications that combines the best features of products from Oracle, PeopleSoft and J.D. Edwards and will allow for standardization and centralization across the enterprise. Oracle hopes that the new super-suite, dubbed Project Fusion, will allow its customers to automate an entire global infrastructure so that everything is linked and compatible and managers can get the information they need to effectively control the organization.[17] Project Fusion suffered lengthy delays, however, underlining the difficulties inherent in complete vertical integration.[18]

devices are structural alternatives that can improve horizontal coordination and information flow.[19] Each device enables people to exchange information.

Information Systems A significant method of providing horizontal linkage in today's organizations is the use of cross-functional information systems. Computerized information systems can enable managers or frontline workers throughout the organization to routinely exchange information about problems, opportunities, activities or decisions. For example, Siemens uses an organization-wide information system that enables 450,000 employees around the world to share knowledge and collaborate on projects to provide better solutions to customers. The information and communications division recently collaborated with the medical division to develop new products for the healthcare market.[20]

Some organizations also encourage employees to use the company's information systems to build relationships all across the organization, aiming to support and enhance ongoing horizontal coordination across projects and geographical boundaries. In 2007, The Samaritans, a UK charity which runs telephone helplines and other services for people in emotional distress, adopted a specially tailored Customer Management System (CRM) that consolidates information about its

17,000 volunteers, its financial supporters, as well as business partners. The system will permit the organization's staff to work more efficiently, making linkages between different 'customers' of the organization in a way that was not possible before. Thus, for example, its business partners could be asked to launch an appeal for volunteers within their companies.[21]

Direct Contact A higher level of horizontal linkage is direct contact between managers or employees affected by a problem. One way to promote direct contact is to create a special **liaison role**. A liaison person is located in one department but has the responsibility for communicating and achieving coordination with another department. Liaison roles often exist between engineering and manufacturing departments because engineering has to develop and test products to fit the limitations of manufacturing facilities. At Johnson & Johnson, CEO William C. Weldon set up a committee made up of managers from research and development (R&D) and sales and marketing. The direct contact between managers in these two departments enables the company to set priorities for which new drugs to pursue and market. Weldon also created a new position to oversee R&D, with an express charge to increase coordination with sales and marketing executives.[22] Another approach is to locate people close together so they will have direct contact on a regular basis.

Task Forces Liaison roles usually link only two departments. When linkage involves several departments, a more complex device such as a task force is required. A **task force** is a temporary committee composed of representatives from each organizational unit affected by a problem.[23] Each member represents the interest of a department or division and can carry information from the meeting back to that department.

Task forces can be an effective horizontal linkage device for temporary issues. They endeavour to solve problems by direct horizontal coordination and reduce the information load on the vertical hierarchy. Typically, they are disbanded after their tasks are accomplished or superceded.

Task forces have been used for everything from organizing the annual company picnic to solving expensive and complex manufacturing problems. One example is the Executive Automotive Committee formed by DaimlerChrysler CEO Jürgen Schrempp. This task force was set up specifically to identify ideas for increasing cooperation and component sharing among Mercedes, Chrysler and Mitsubishi (in which DaimlerChrysler owns a 37 per cent stake). The task force started with a product road map, showing all Mercedes, Chrysler, Dodge, Jeep and Mitsubishi vehicles to be launched over a 10-year period, along with an analysis of the components they would use, so task force members could identify overlap and find ways to share parts and cut time and costs.[24]

Full-time Integrator A stronger horizontal linkage device is to create a full-time position or department solely for the purpose of coordination. A full-time **integrator** frequently has a title, such as product manager, project manager, programme manager or brand manager. Unlike the liaison person described earlier, the integrator does not report to one of the functional departments being coordinated. He or she is located outside the departments and has the responsibility for coordinating several departments, or even, in the case below, in integrating internal departments, suppliers and customers.

Kalmar Industries is the world's leading supplier of cargo handling equipment to ports, terminals and intermodal facilities, and is a subsidiary of the Finland-headquartered, globally-present Cargotec Corporation. Kalmar provides customized cargo solutions to large scale customers, with 2006 sales of about €1.2 billion.

As in many modern manufacturing enterprises, most of Kalmar's production is outsourced, with the company heavily involved in system integration, liaising closely both with suppliers and customers to ensure delivery and support of the customized product.[25] Kalmar's managers realized that although the company had strong relationships with its suppliers and customers, there were many inefficiencies due both to communications misunderstandings and logistical costs of manufacturing items in separate locations and transporting them to Kalmar for assembly. In order to respond to this issue, Kalmar established Product Supply Centres (PSCs), where key suppliers co-located their production facilities for specific Kalmar products. This approach allowed Kalmar to respond much more quickly and effectively to customers' specific requests.[26]

An integrator or integrating department can be responsible for an innovation or change project, such as coordinating the design, financing and marketing of a new product. An organization chart that illustrates the location of project managers for new product development is shown in Exhibit 3.3. The project managers are drawn to the side to indicate their separation from other departments. The arrows indicate project members assigned to the new product development. New Product A, for example, has a financial accountant assigned to keep track of costs and budgets. The engineering member provides design advice, and purchasing and manufacturing members represent their areas. The project manager is responsible for the entire project. He or she sees that the new product is completed on time, is introduced to the market, and achieves other project goals. The horizontal lines in Exhibit 3.3 indicate that project managers do not have formal authority over team members with respect to giving pay raises, hiring or firing. Formal authority rests with the managers of the functional departments, who have formal authority over subordinates.

EXHIBIT 3.3 Project Manager Location in the Structure

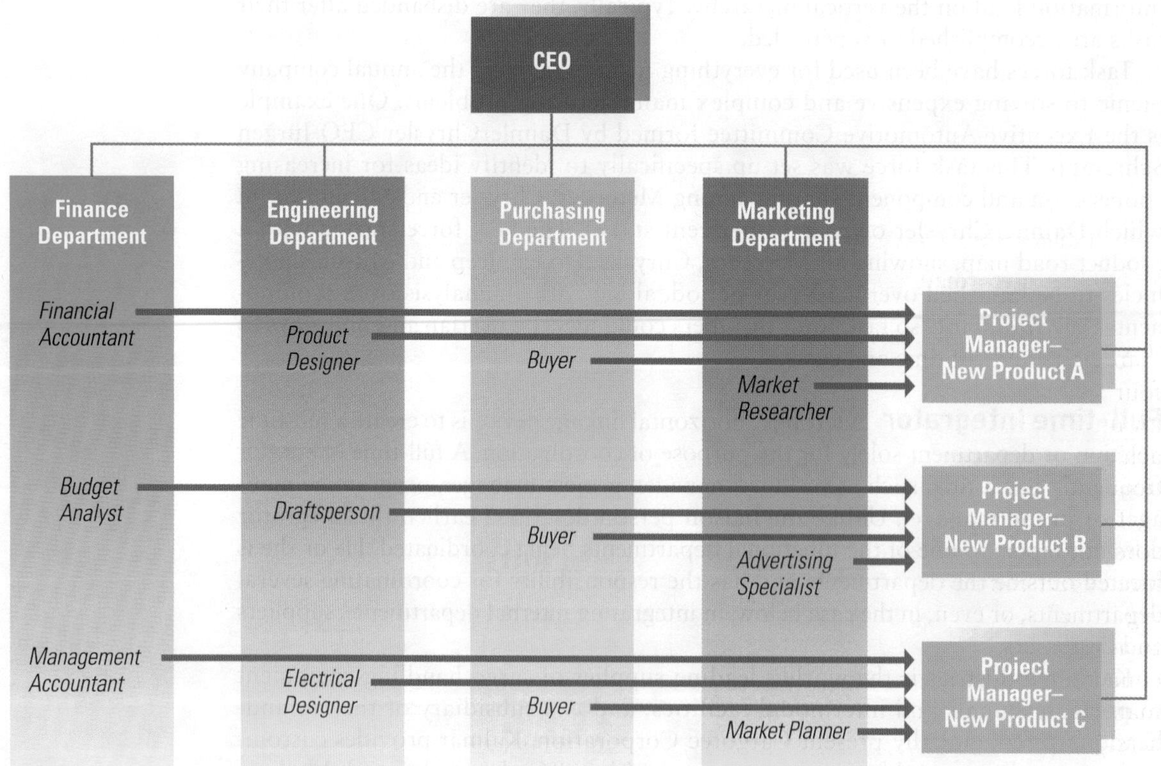

Integrators in most companies have a lot of responsibility but little authority. The integrator has to use expertise and persuasion to achieve coordination. He or she spans the boundary between departments and must be able to get people together, maintain their trust, confront problems and resolve conflicts and disputes in the interest of the organization.[27]

Teams Project teams tend to be the strongest horizontal linkage mechanism. **Teams** are permanent task forces and are often used in conjunction with a full-time integrator. When activities among departments require strong coordination over a long period of time, a cross-functional team is often the solution. Special project teams may be used when organizations have a large-scale project, a major innovation or a new product line.

Imagination Ltd., Britain's largest design firm, relies heavily upon teamwork. At the beginning of each project, Imagination puts together a team of designers, writers, artists, marketing experts, information specialists and representatives of other functional areas to carry out the entire project from beginning to end. Hewlett-Packard's Medical Products Group uses *virtual cross-functional teams*, made up of members from various countries, to develop and market medical products and services such as electrocardiograph systems, ultrasound imaging technologies and patient monitoring systems.[28] A **virtual team** is one that is made up of organizationally or geographically dispersed members who are linked primarily through advanced information and communications technologies. Members frequently use online collaborative technologies to work together, rather than meeting face to face.[29]

As an organization manager, keep this guideline in mind:

Recognize that the strongest horizontal linkage mechanisms are more costly in terms of time and human resources but are necessary when the organization needs a high degree of horizontal coordination to achieve its goals.

Volvo, the Sweden-headquartered truck manufacturer, has an enviable reputation for innovative management practices, and particularly with fostering strong teamwork. The Dutch researchers Ben Kuipers and Marco de Witte took a close look at teamwork at Volvo's cab manufacturing plant in Umeå in northern Sweden to better understand how successful teamwork develops, what they call in*Volvo*ment. They identified four dimensions to teamwork:

- Job enlargement: encouraging employee multifunctionality and thus the elimination of inefficiency within the team
- Job enrichment: the redesign of the supervision system to delegate management responsibilities to the team members
- Cooperation: members work together as a team, building on communication and a sense of shared responsibility
- High performance: the team is able to work together to resolve nonroutine issues, requiring collaborative innovation.

Unlike some other studies of teamwork, Kuipers and de Witte found that these four aspects of teamwork don't occur sequentially, one after the other, but through an interconnected process. They showed that the higher the level of teamwork achieved, the better quality of product, higher productivity and employee satisfaction. Truly a win-win.[30]

See online
COUNTERPOINT 3.9

Teambuilding has become so important to companies that it has spawned a whole new business opportunity in teamwork development. Many organizations hire expert companies to support the teambuilding process. Often, the teambuilding includes some physically challenging activities that require close collaboration to achieve success, such as sailing a boat together, overcoming an outdoor obstacle course or even performing a daredevil circus act. Airbus, the European aeroplane manufacturer, has management staff working in several different countries who rarely meet face to face, so building team spirit is a challenge. At a recent annual away day, the company hired a teambuilding company, Blue Hat, which organized

EXHIBIT 3.4 Ladder of Mechanisms for Horizontal Linkage and Coordination

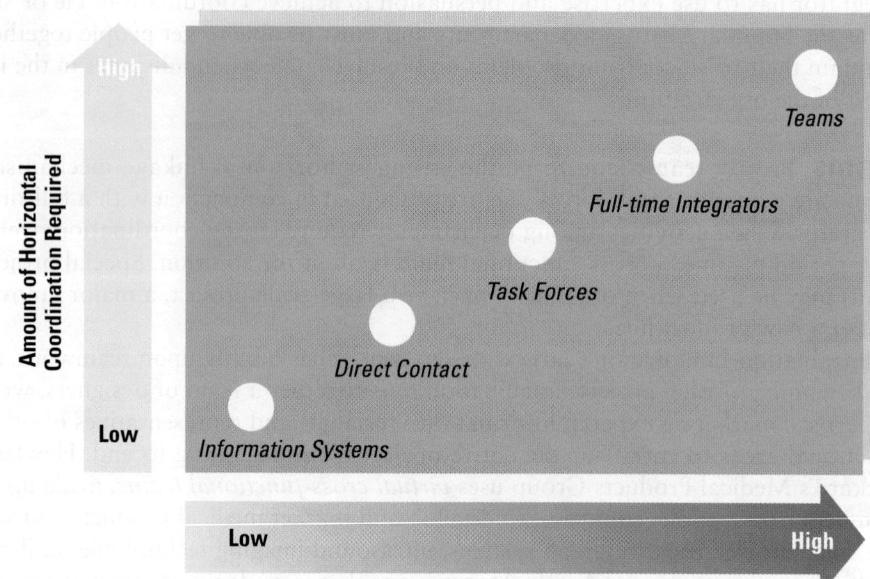

a 'Da Vinci Code Challenge' in which small teams had to work together to find the famous chalice and elixir of life.[31]

Exhibit 3.4 summarizes the mechanisms for achieving horizontal linkages. These devices represent alternatives that managers can select to increase horizontal coordination in any organization. The higher-level devices provide more horizontal information capacity, although the cost to the organization in terms of time and human resources is greater. If horizontal communication is insufficient, departments will find themselves out of synchronization, resulting in inefficiency and ineffectiveness.

Organization Design Alternatives

Overall, the design of organization structure indicates three things – required work activities, reporting relationships and departmental groupings.

Required Work Activities

Departments are created to perform tasks considered important to the company. For example, in a manufacturing company, work activities are organized into a range of functions, such as a human resource department to recruit and train employees, a purchasing department to obtain supplies and raw materials, a production department to build products, a sales department to sell products and so forth. As organizations grow larger, their organizational structure often becomes more complex as more and more different functions are added. For example, before the 1980s many companies had large divisions ('pools') of secretarial staff. Today, most employees do much of their own administrative work so secretaries have been replaced with information technology departments that ensure the smooth operation of the computers and networks used to create and transmit data within and beyond the company.

Reporting Relationships

Hierarchical reporting relationships, often called the *chain of command*, are represented by vertical lines on an organization chart. The chain of command is typically an unbroken line of authority that links all persons in an organization and shows who reports to whom. Although organizations have emphasized flattening of hierarchy in recent years, this typically reflects a reduction in the number of vertical levels rather than an absence of hierarchy.

Departmental Grouping Options

Options for departmental grouping, including functional grouping, divisional grouping, multifocused grouping, horizontal grouping and virtual network grouping, are illustrated in Exhibit 3.5. **Departmental grouping** affects employees because they share a common supervisor and common resources, are jointly responsible for performance, and tend to identify and collaborate with one another.[32] For example, a credit manager's perspective might well change if she moves from the finance department to the marketing department. As a member of the marketing department, the credit manager would work more closely with salespeople, understanding the importance of increasing sales and thus becoming more willing to see credit as a sales tool than when she was located in the finance department.

Functional grouping places together employees who perform similar functions or work processes or who bring similar knowledge and skills to bear. For example, all marketing people work together under the same supervisor, as do manufacturing and engineering people. All people associated with the assembly process for generators are grouped together in one department. All chemists may be grouped in a department different from biologists because they represent different disciplines.

Divisional grouping means people are organized according to what the organization produces. All people required to produce toothpaste – including personnel in marketing, manufacturing, and sales – are grouped together under one executive. In many large conglomerates, some product or service lines have entirely separate identities from that of the parent company. For example, the French-headquartered Accor group of hotels.

Multifocused grouping means an organization embraces two structural grouping alternatives simultaneously. These structural forms are often called matrix or *hybrid*. They will be discussed in more detail later in this chapter. An organization may need to group by function and product division simultaneously or perhaps by product division and geography.

Horizontal grouping means employees are organized around core work processes, the end-to-end work, information and material flows that provide value directly to customers or support strategic development. All the people who work on a process are brought together in a group rather than being separated into functional departments. Frequently, new product development is organized through horizontal and/or cross-functional groups, ensuring for example that product design takes into account manufacturing challenges. India's first sport utility vehicle, the Mahindra Scorpio, was developed through the work of a cross-functional team of 120 staff from across the company.[33] Horizontal groupings are often implemented in addition to traditional vertical working relationships. In the West African state of Senegal, for example, representatives of the various government agencies involved in

EXHIBIT 3.5 Structural Design Options for Grouping Employees into Departments

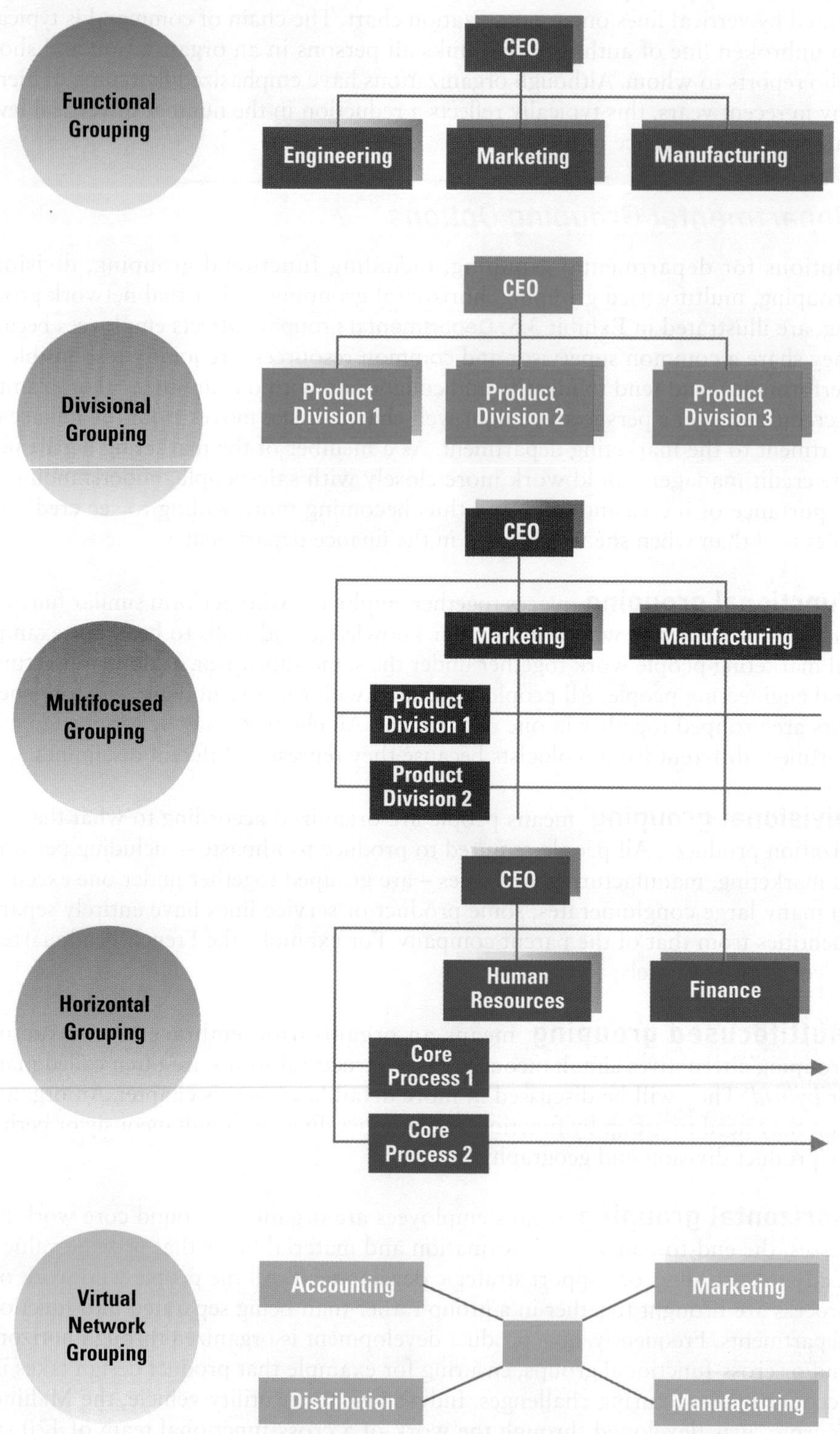

Source: Adapted from David Nadler and Michael Tushman, *Strategic Organization Design* (Glenview, Ill.: Scott Foresman, 1988), 68.

agricultural sector management form part of an 'inter-professional committee' that ensures coordinated agricultural policy and programming.[34] Horizontal grouping may be adopted in civil society organizations to fit with the egalitarian ethos of the members. For example, the Argeninian Movimiento de Trabajadores Desocupados Solano (MTD Solano) is a network of unemployed people dedicated to improving the circumstances of the unemployed and other people people in Argentina. In line with its members' belief that social inequality is the cause of their problems, MTD Solano rejects a leadership hierarchy and operates through horizontal groupings of different groups of social activists.[35]

Virtual network grouping is the most recent approach to departmental grouping. With this grouping, the organization is a loosely connected cluster of separate components. In essence, departments are separate organizations that are electronically connected for the sharing of information and completion of tasks. Departments can be spread all over the world rather than located together in one geographical location. In recent years there has been a rapid increase in the use of this type of organizational structure, implemented through the reengineering of business processes. Business process outsourcing (BPO) is an example where organizational functions such as customer service can actually be placed outside the firm, and even in another part of the world.

The organizational forms described in Exhibit 3.5 provide the overall options within which the organization chart is drawn and the detailed structure is designed. Each structural design alternative has significant strengths and weaknesses, to which we now turn.

Functional, Divisional and Geographical Designs

Functional grouping and divisional grouping are the two most common approaches to structural design.

Functional Structure

In a **functional structure**, activities are grouped together by common function from the bottom to the top of the organization. All engineers are located in the engineering department, and the vice president of engineering is responsible for all engineering activities. The same is true in marketing, R&D, and manufacturing. An example of the functional organization structure was shown in Exhibit 3.1 earlier in this chapter.

With a functional structure, all human knowledge and skills with respect to specific activities are consolidated, providing a valuable depth of knowledge for the organization. This structure is most effective when in-depth expertise is critical to meeting organizational goals, when the organization needs to be controlled and coordinated through the vertical hierarchy, and when efficiency is important. The structure can be quite effective especially if there is little need for horizontal coordination. Exhibit 3.6 summarizes the strengths and weaknesses of the functional structure.

The functional structure can improve economies of scale by concentrating specialists in groups in a common location and sharing facilities. Producing all products in a single plant, for example, may strengthen a financial case for the plant to acquire the latest machinery. Constructing only one facility instead of separate facilities for each product line can reduce duplication and waste. The functional structure may

EXHIBIT 3.6 Strengths and Weaknesses of Functional Organization Structure

Strengths	Weaknesses
1. Allows economies of scale within functional departments 2. Enables in-depth knowledge and skill development 3. Enables organization to accomplish functional goals 4. Is best with only one or a few products	1. Slow response time to environmental changes 2. May cause decisions to pile on top, hierarchy overload 3. Leads to poor horizontal coordination among departments 4. Results in less innovation 5. Involves restricted view of organizational goals

Source: Adapted from Robert Duncan, 'What Is the Right Organization Structure? Decision Tree Analysis Provides the Answer,' *Organizational Dynamics* (Winter 1979), 429.

also promote in-depth skill development of employees. Employees are exposed to a range of functional activities within their own department.[36]

The potential shortcoming of the functional structure is a slow response to environmental changes that require coordination across departments. The vertical hierarchy can become isolated and/or overloaded. Decisions pile up as top managers lack effective means of coordination across specialist functions. A functional structure may also impede innovation when this requires coordination.

Many small and medium-sized organizations in which the focus is upon core competencies, operate with a functional structure. Consider the *In Practice* case of Real Hotel Company Ltd., a medium-sized UK-based hotel chain, active in Britain and Europe. Real Hotels has made losses for several years, and in 2006 its top management decided to reorganize into a clear functional structure as one of a series of steps designed to bring the company back into the black.

BRIEFCASE

As an organization manager, keep these guidelines in mind:

When designing overall organization structure, choose a functional structure when efficiency is important, when in-depth knowledge and expertise are critical to meeting organizational goals, and when the organization needs to be controlled and coordinated through the vertical hierarchy. Use a divisional structure in a large organization with multiple product lines and when you wish to give priority to product goals and coordination across functions.

Functional Structure with Horizontal Linkages

During the late years of the twentieth century, criticism of extended hierarchical structures promoted a shift toward flatter, more horizontal structures, as business activities become more complex and companies identified the potential for restructuring business processes to achieve synergies. Organizations may compensate for the vertical functional hierarchy by installing horizontal linkages, as described earlier in this chapter. Managers may improve horizontal coordination by using information systems, direct contact between departments, full-time integrators or project managers (illustrated in Exhibit 3.3), task forces or teams. One interesting use of horizontal linkages occurred at Karolinska Hospital in Stockholm, Sweden, which once had forty-seven functional departments. Even after top executives cut that down to eleven, coordination was still inadequate. The team set about reorganizing workflow at the hospital around patient care. Instead of bouncing a patient from department to department, Karolinska now envisions the illness to recovery period as a process with 'pit stops' in admissions, X-ray surgery and so forth. The most interesting aspect of the approach is the new position of nurse coordinator. Nurse coordinators serve as full-time integrators, troubleshooting transitions within or between departments. The improved horizontal coordination dramatically improved productivity and patient care at Karolinska.[37] Karolinska is effectively using horizontal linkages to overcome some of the disadvantages of the functional structure.

The Real Hotel Company PLC

When Michael Praeger took over as CEO of the Real Hotel Company in early 2007, he knew he had a difficult task on his hands. His previous experience with several international chains would stand him in good stead on the hotel side of the business, but the company needed radical action to halt years of poor financial performance and failed restructuring efforts.

The Real Hotel Company is a British-headquartered company with its main business operating budget to mid-range hotels. Since being founded as Friendly Hotels in the mid-80s by the iconic hotelier Henry Edwards, in the late 1990s the company secured the European master franchise for the global chain of budget hotels, Choice Hotels International, meaning the company was operating over 300 hotels across the continent. The business almost immediately went into the red and Henry Edwards left the company he had founded. Despite a dizzying series of name changes, capital raising efforts, hotel refurbishments, attempts to sell out and even a near bankruptcy in 2001, the business never produced satisfactory results. By the time Michael Praeger arrived, the company had already decided to exit the franchise agreement with Choice Hotels, which it successfully did in late 2006. But with the great majority of company-operated hotels now gone, the hybrid functional-geographic management structure seemed top-heavy. Furthermore, the company now needed to focus on building its own brands, which had been a lower priority while the company was trying to manage all the Choice Hotel franchises.

Praeger slimmed down the management structure, eliminating the geographic divisions in favour of functional divisions. He gave up development of Sleep Inn, a brand that had never really caught on, and focused most of the company's efforts on the new Purple Hotel label – a contemporary brand that would appeal to a younger clientele interested in value, but also style. Real Hotels invested heavily in its sales and marketing division, and pondered exiting completely from the traditional budget sector. The company now had a manageable portfolio of properties and a simple functional management structure.

In early 2008, revenues started to pick up. However, with the onset of a serious recession during 2008, all the efforts proved too little, too late, and in January 2009 Real Hotels was forced to call in the administrators. The chain was carved up, with big competitors like Travelodge picking up the most profitable properties. Was Praeger's strategy flawed, or did the global economic situation mean that the turnaround never had much chance of success?[38]

In 2004, Karolinska merged with another large hospital. Some progress has been made in effectively integrating the hospitals, particularly in the area of IT, but integration problems remain. In today's rapidly changing organizational environment, managers are constantly challenged to adapt and redesign organizational structures and systems to meet new operational challenges.[39]

Divisional Structure

The term **divisional structure** is used here as the generic term for what is sometimes called a *product structure* or *strategic business units*. With this structure, divisions can be organized according to individual products, services, product groups, major projects or programmes, divisions, businesses or profit centres. The distinctive feature of a divisional structure is that grouping is based on organizational outputs.

The difference between a divisional structure and a functional structure is illustrated in Exhibit 3.7. The functional structure can be redesigned into separate product groups, and each group contains the functional departments of R&D, manufacturing, accounting and marketing. Coordination across functional departments

EXHIBIT 3.7 Reorganization from Functional Structure to Divisional Structure at Info-Tech

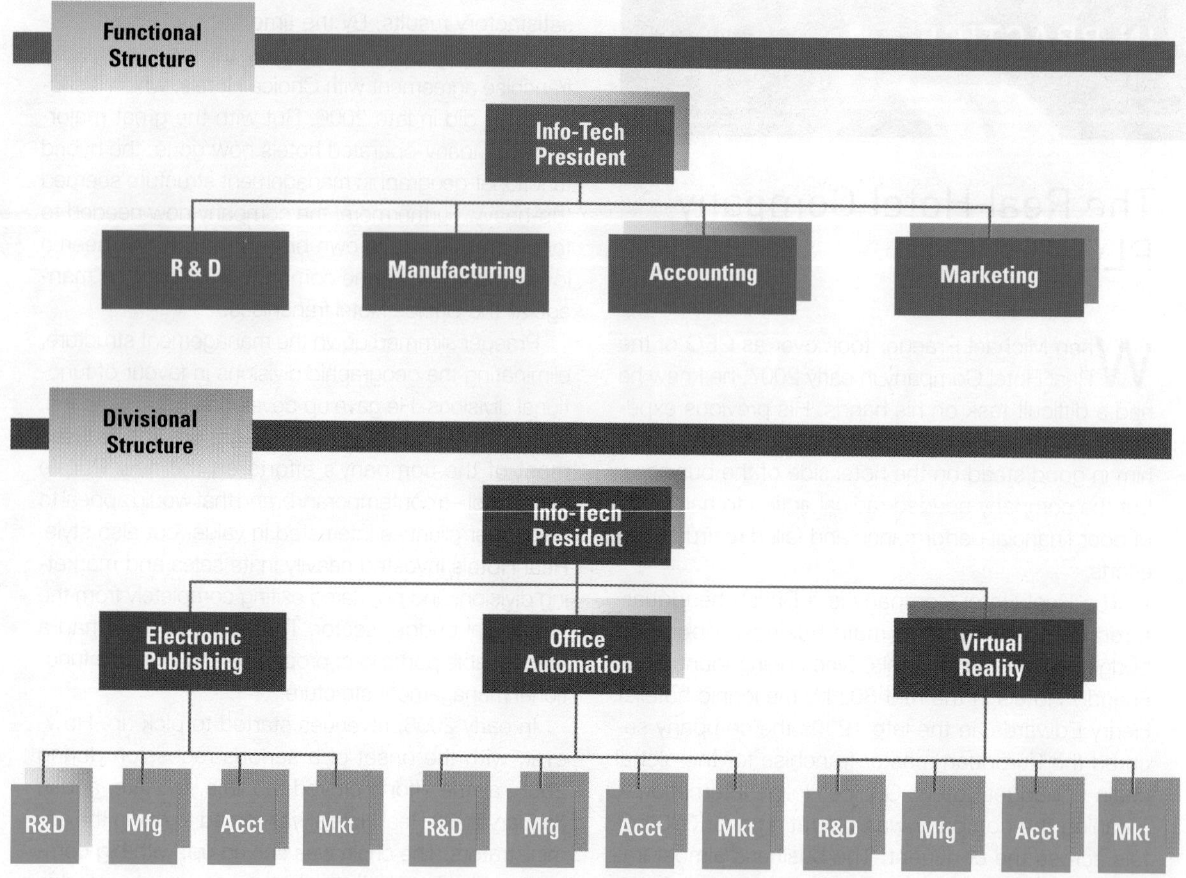

within each product group is maximized. The divisional structure promotes flexibility and change because each unit is smaller and can adapt more flexibly to opportunities and threats. Moreover, the divisional structure *decentralizes* decision making as the lines of authority converge at a lower level in the hierarchy. The functional structure, by contrast, is *centralized* as it forces decisions all the way to the top before a problem affecting several functions can be resolved.

Strengths and weaknesses of the divisional structure are summarized in Exhibit 3.8. The divisional organization structure is excellent for achieving coordination across functional departments. It works well when organizations can no longer be adequately controlled through the traditional vertical hierarchy, and when goals are oriented toward adaptation and change. Giant, complex organizations such as Nestlé, General Electric and India's Tata Corporation are subdivided into a series of smaller, self-contained organizations for better control and coordination. In these large companies, the units are sometimes called divisions, businesses or strategic business units. The structure at Johnson & Johnson includes 204 separate operating units, including McNeil Consumer Products, makers of Tylenol; Ortho Pharmaceuticals, which makes Retin-A and contraceptive pills; and J & J Consumer Products, the company that manufactures globally-known brands such as Johnson's Baby Shampoo and Band-Aids. Each unit is a separately chartered, autonomous company, although operating under the guidance of Johnson & Johnson's corporate headquarters.[40]

Many government organizations use a divisional structure. The British National Health Service has made extensive organizational changes in order to meet

EXHIBIT 3.8 Strengths and Weaknesses of Divisional Organization Structure

Strengths	Weaknesses
1. Suited to fast change in unstable environment 2. Leads to customer satisfaction because product responsibility and contact points are clear 3. Involves high coordination across functions 4. Allows units to adapt to differences in products, regions, customers 5. Best in large organizations with several products 6. Decentralizes decision making	1. Eliminates economies of scale in functional departments 2. Leads to poor coordination across product lines 3. Eliminates in-depth competence and technical specialization 4. Makes integration and standardization across product lines difficult

Source: Adapted from Robert Duncan, 'What Is the Right Organization Structure? Decision Tree Analysis Provides the Answer,' *Organization Dynamics* (Winter 1979), 431.

service-improvement targets such as the requirement that Emergency Department patients will receive treatment within a specified time. Harrap and Gillies describe how one hospital reorganized from many small departments into five large divisions, each equipped with clear criteria for success and headed by a member of the senior management team.[41] The world-leading software company Microsoft uses a divisional structure to develop and market its different products.

The divisional structure has several strengths that are of benefit to Microsoft.[42] This structure is in principle responsive to fast changing, unstable conditions and can provide high product or service visibility. Each product line 'belongs' to a specific division, so customers can more easily identify and reach the right division to resolve any issues they have. In principle, each product can adapt to requirements of individual customers or regions. The divisional structure is typically adopted in organizations that have multiple products or services and enough personnel to staff separate functional units. At firms like the Dutch-headquartered Philips Electronics (see *A Look Inside* in chapter one), the US-based Johnson & Johnson pharmaceutical and personal hygiene company and Microsoft, decision making is pushed down to the lowest levels. Each division is small enough to respond rapidly to changes in the market. Often, European firms favour greater decentralization to both product and geographic divisions than is the case with North American corporations.

One disadvantage of using divisional structuring is the loss of economies of scale. Instead of fifty research engineers sharing a common facility in a functional structure, ten engineers may be assigned to each of five product divisions. The critical mass required for in-depth research can be lost, and physical facilities have to be duplicated for each product line. Another problem is that product lines become separate from each other, and coordination across product lines can be difficult. An executive from Johnson & Johnson said, 'We have to keep reminding ourselves that we work for the same corporation'.[43] Excessive decentralization at Philips Electronics has been blamed for depriving the company of a coherent and comprehensive response to the onslaught of Japanese electronics goods from the 1970s onwards, with the result that Philips lost its dominant position in the European market.[44]

From the early years of this century, Microsoft began losing ground to Google. On the other hand Microsoft, with its divisional structure, had effectively

Microsoft

Bill Gates co-founded Microsoft in 1975 and built it into the most profitable technology company in the world. But as the company grew larger, the functional structure was just too slow and inflexible for a large organization operating in the fast-moving technology industry. Employees began complaining about the growing bureaucracy and snail's pace decision making.

To speed things up and better respond to environmental changes, in 2002 top executives created seven business units, the Information Worker business, Microsoft Business Solutions (MBS), the Home and Entertainment Division, the Mobile and Embedded Devices Division, the Windows Client, Windows Server and the Tools group, built around the company's major products . . . Each division was run by a general manager and contained most of the functions of a stand-alone company, including product development, sales, marketing and finance. The division system was further streamlined three years later when the seven units were replaced by three core divisions, the Windows, MSN and Server groups became the *Microsoft Platform Products and Services Division*; the Information Worker and MBS groups were merged into the *Microsoft Business Division*; and the Mobile and Embedded Devices, and the Home and Entertainment division became the *Microsoft Entertainment and Devices Division*.[45]

What really made the new structure revolutionary for Microsoft was that the division heads were given the freedom and authority to run the businesses and spend their budgets as they see fit to meet goals. The general managers and chief financial officers for each division set their own budgets and manage their own profit and loss statements. Previously, the two top executives, Bill Gates and Steven Ballmer, were involved in practically every decision, large and small. Managers of the divisions are charged up by the new authority and responsibility. One manager said he feels 'like I am running my own little company'.[46]

countered competitive software, Google represented a new business model driven through search engine revenues. Without a coordinated approach, competitive threats can emerge from unexpected sources like this, and businesses may find themselves poorly placed even to identify the threat, let alone develop an effective response.

Companies such as Sony and Xerox have a large number of divisions and can have severe problems with horizontal coordination. It has been alleged that Sony lost out in the business of digital media products, despite its early advantage with the Walkman device, partly because of poor coordination. Apple's iPod quickly captured 60 per cent of the US market versus only 10 per cent for Sony's Walkman range. The digital music business depends on seamless coordination. Sony's Walkman was unable to recognize some of the music sets made with early versions of the company's SonicStage software introduced in 2001. It wasn't until version 3.4 of SonicStage that compatibility was achieved – demonstrating a disconnection with the company's division selling music downloads. By 2007, Sony had decided to wind down its music download division, having lost the battle with Apple. In response to difficulties such as this, Sony has moved decisively to more effectively integrate its disparate product divisions.[47]

Unless effective horizontal mechanisms are in place, a divisional structure can be inefficient and unresponsive. One division may produce products or programs that are incompatible with products sold by another division. Customers are frustrated when a sales representative from one division is unaware of developments in other divisions. Task forces and other linkage devices may be introduced to coordinate across divisions. A lack of technical specialization is also a problem in a divisional structure. Employees may identify with the product line rather than with a functional specialty. R&D personnel, for example, tend to be employed to undertake research to benefit a particular product line rather than basic research to benefit the entire organization.

Geographical Structure

Another basis for structural grouping is the organization's users or customers. The most common structure in this category is geography. Each region of the country may have distinct tastes and preferences. Each geographic unit includes all functions required to produce and market products or services in that region. This structure is particularly common in large NGOs and other civil society organizations that depend upon a close connection with volunteers, supporters and/or clients at the local level such as the UK's Citizen's Advice Bureaus, Alcoholics Anonymous and most political parties frequently use a type of geographical structure, with a central headquarters and semi-autonomous local units. The national or international headquarters organization provides brand recognition, coordinates fund-raising services and handles some shared administrative functions, while day-to-day control and decision making is decentralized to a greater or lesser extent to local or regional units.[48]

Multinational corporations (MNCs) often create self-contained units for different countries and parts of the world. As MNC's integrate acquisitions into corporate structure, they often move from discrete functional units that were formerly stand-alone businesses, towards geographic coordination. For example, in 2008, Kingfisher, the UK-headquartered multinational home renovation supplies retailer, best known for its B&Q stores, responded to disappointing performance in some of its units by establishing three geographic units, representing UK, France and Other Countries, each headed by a senior executive. These managers were charged with turning their region into a profit centre by strictly controlling costs and focusing on maximizing profits from existing retail space.[49] Some years ago, California's Apple Computer reorganized from a functional to a geographical structure to facilitate manufacture and delivery of Apple computers to customers around the world. Exhibit 3.9 contains a partial organization structure illustrating the geographical thrust. At Apple this structure was introduced to focus managers and employees on specific geographical customers and sales targets.

The strengths and weaknesses of a geographic divisional structure are parallel to those of the divisional organization characteristics listed in Exhibit 3.8. The geographic division can adapt to specific conditions of its own country or region, and employees may identify with regional goals rather than with the overall corporate vision. Horizontal coordination within a region may be emphasized rather than linkages across regions or to the head office, and this can detract from overall corporate synergies. This is true both for national firms with regional divisions, and for multinational firms with national or regional units around the world.

Matrix Structure

Sometimes, a **matrix structure** is developed in an effort to give equal emphasis and attention to product and function, or product and geography. The matrix is more likely to be introduced when, say, technical expertise and product innovation and change are assessed to be of equal importance. When it is assessed that functional, divisional and geographical structures combined with horizontal linkage mechanisms are not working effectively, the matrix may be adopted as a remedy.

EXHIBIT 3.9 Geographical Structure for Apple Computer

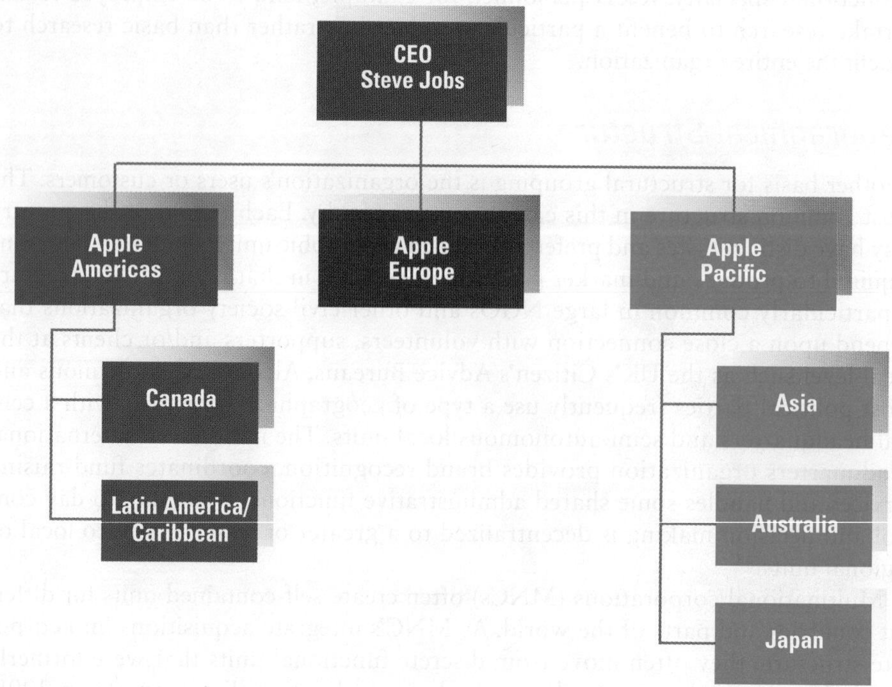

Source: Apple Computer, Inc. regions of the world, http://www.apple.com/find/areas.htm, April 18, 2000.

The matrix is a strong form of horizontal linkage as, in principle, it enables two objectives to be pursued simultaneously, as shown in Exhibit 3.10. In this structure, product managers and functional managers, for example, have equal authority within the organization, and employees report to both of them. The matrix structure is similar to the use of full-time integrators or product managers described earlier in this chapter (Exhibit 3.3), but within the matrix structure, the product managers (horizontal) are given formal authority equal to that of the functional managers (vertical).

Conditions for the Matrix

A dual hierarchy may seem an unusual way to design an organization as it contradicts the classical principle of unity of command, but it can be a workable structure, particularly when one or more of the following conditions is met:[50]

- *Condition 1.* Pressure exists to share scarce resources across product lines. The organization is often medium sized and has a moderate number of product lines. There are pressures for the shared and flexible use of people and equipment across the product lines. For example, the organization is not large enough to assign engineers full-time to each product line, so engineers are assigned part-time to several products or projects.
- *Condition 2.* Environmental pressures exist for two or more critical outputs, such as for in-depth technical knowledge (functional structure) and frequent new products (divisional structure). The dual pressure requires sharing of power is needed between the functional and product sides of the organization, and a dual-authority structure is needed to maintain that balance.
- *Condition 3.* The environmental domain of the organization is both complex and uncertain. Frequent external changes and high interdependence between

EXHIBIT 3.10 Dual-Authority Structure in a Matrix Organization

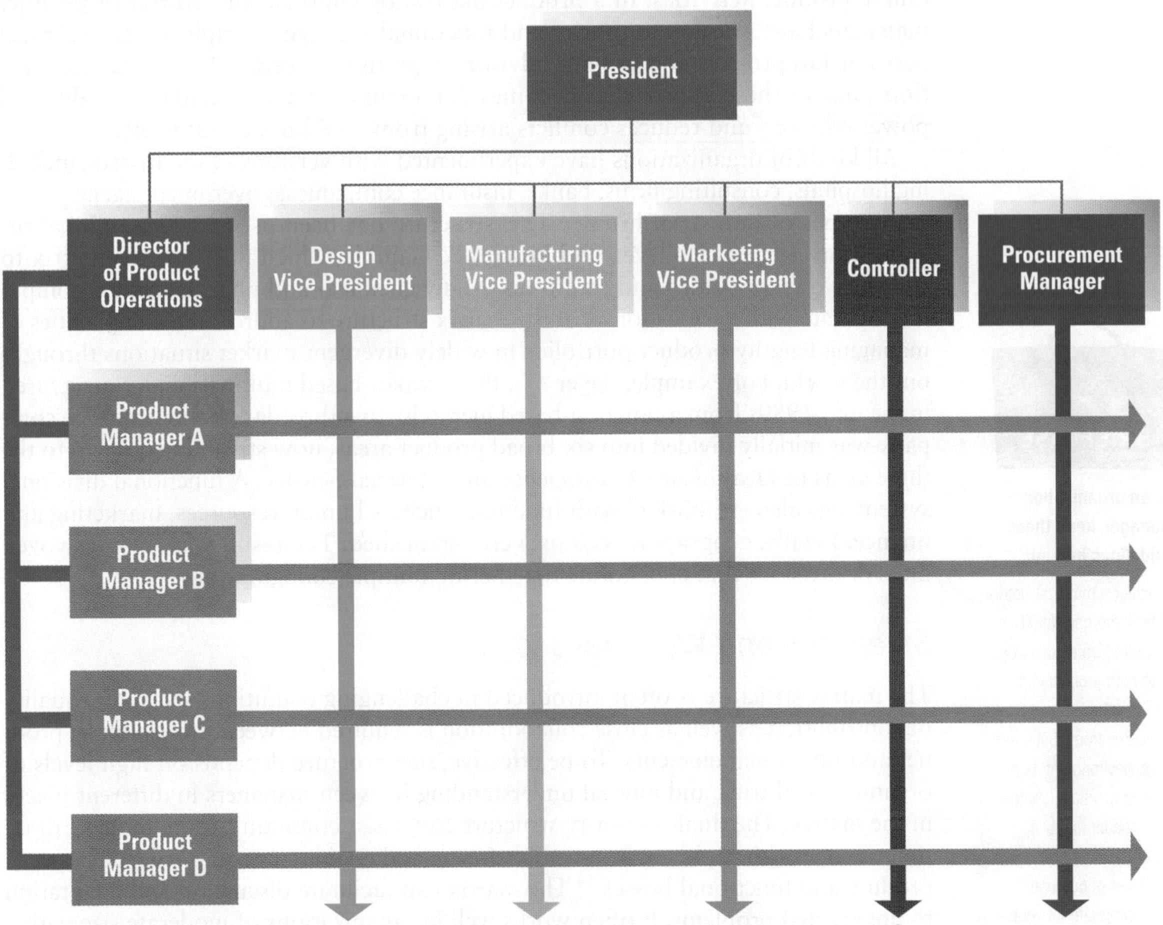

President

Director of Product Operations

Design Vice President

Manufacturing Vice President

Marketing Vice President

Controller

Procurement Manager

Product Manager A

Product Manager B

Product Manager C

Product Manager D

departments require a large amount of coordination and information processing in both vertical and horizontal directions.

In principle, a dual-authority structure can help ensure a balance between vertical and horizontal aspects of organizations.

Referring again to Exhibit 3.10, assume the matrix structure is for a clothing manufacturer. Product A is footwear, product B is outerwear, product C is night clothes and so on. Each product line serves a different market and customers. As a medium-size organization, the company must effectively use people from manufacturing, design and marketing to work on each product line. There are not enough designers to warrant a separate design department for each product line, so the designers are shared across product lines. Moreover, by keeping the manufacturing, design and marketing functions intact, it allows for employees to develop the in-depth expertise to serve all product lines efficiently.

The matrix formalizes horizontal teams along with the traditional vertical hierarchy and tries to give equal balance to both. However, the matrix may shift one way or the other. Many companies have found a balanced matrix hard to implement and maintain because one side of the authority structure often dominates. For employees, serving two masters can prove a confusing and excessively demanding experience. As a consequence, two variations of matrix structure have evolved – the **functional matrix** and the **product matrix**. In a functional matrix, the functional bosses have primary authority and the project or product managers simply coordinate product activities. In a product matrix, by contrast, the project or product managers have primary authority and functional managers simply assign technical personnel to projects and provide advisory expertise as needed. For many organizations, one of these approaches becomes dominant as it accommodates established power relations and reduces conflicts arising from dual lines of authority.[51]

All kinds of organizations have experimented with versions of the matrix, including hospitals, consulting firms, banks, insurance companies, government agencies and many types of industrial firms.[52] This structure has been used by large, global organizations such as Unilever, and Procter & Gamble, which fine-tune the matrix to suit their own priorities and traditions. Many chemical and pharmaceutical companies operate with various forms of the matrix structure to address the complexities of managing lengthy product portfolios in widely divergent market situations throughout the world. For example, Bayer AG, the German-based multinational, restructured in the mid-1980s from a function-based hierarchy to a three-layered matrix. The company was initially divided into six broad product areas, now streamlined down to the three areas of HealthCare, CropScience and Material-Science. A functional divisional system was also established with functions such as human resources, marketing and finance. Finally, geographic regions were established. The result was 19 interwoven units or divisions that collaborate together in multiple configurations.[53]

BRIEFCASE

As an organization manager, keep these guidelines in mind:

Consider a matrix structure when the organization needs to give equal priority to both products and functions because of dual pressures from customers in the environment. Use either a functional matrix or a product matrix if the balanced matrix with dual lines of authority is not appropriate for your organization.

Strengths and Weaknesses

The matrix structure is often introduced in challenging conditions when an equality of contribution as well as close collaboration is required between, for example, product and functional elements. To be effective, the structure depends on high levels of organizational trust and mutual understanding between managers in different places in the matrix. The dual-authority structure can assist communication and coordination to cope with rapid environmental change and enables an equal balance between product and functional bosses.[54] The matrix can facilitate discussion and adaptation to unexpected problems. It often works well in organizations of moderate size with a few product lines. Exhibit 3.11 summarizes the strengths and weaknesses of the matrix structure based on what we know of organizations that use it.[55]

EXHIBIT 3.11 Strengths and Weaknesses of Matrix Organization Structure

Strengths	Weaknesses
1. Achieves coordination necessary to meet dual demands from customers 2. Flexible sharing of human resources across products 3. Suited to complex decisions and frequent changes in unstable environment 4. Provides opportunity for both functional and product skill development 5. Best in medium-sized organizations with multiple products	1. Causes participants to experience dual authority, which can be frustrating and confusing 2. Means participants need good interpersonal skills and extensive training 3. Is time consuming; involves frequent meetings and conflict resolution sessions 4. Will not work unless participants understand it and adopt collegial rather than vertical type relationships 5. Requires great effort to maintain power balance

Source: Adapted from Robert Duncan, 'What Is the Right Organization Structure? Decision Tree Analysis Provides the Answer,' *Organizational Dynamics* (Winter 1979), 429.

CNH Global NV[56]

CNH was formed in the late 1990s through a merger of the construction and agricultural equipment companies Case and New Holland. It is the world's largest company in its market segment. One third of all combine harvesters and backhoe loaders, and one quarter of all tractors and skid steer loaders sold worldwide are built by CNH, a majority-owned subsidiary of the Italian vehicle manufacturer Fiat SpA.

CNH managers wanted to benefit from the economies of scale that could be leveraged from such a large company with many common elements in its products, while at the same time retaining the ability to tailor its products to different customer needs and desires in its different markets across ther world. It aimed to achieve this through a 'multi-brand, multi-channel' strategy while establishing a global product development platform. Put simply, this meant producing a variety of lines for different markets from a few large production facilities. In order to succeed there had to be a close, interactive relationship between the marketing and sales teams on the one hand, who were close to customers, and the production experts on the other. CNH put in place matrix accountability to structures to support this interactivity between the product and geographic managers.

CNH has been largely successful in its efforts, despite facing challenging market conditions at times. The company is rated highly for employee satisfaction, despite closing several production facilities while moving towards global production platforms.

A significant disadvantage of the matrix is that employees sometimes experience dual authority, reporting to two bosses and juggling conflicting demands. This can be frustrating and confusing, especially if roles and responsibilities are not clearly defined by top managers.[57] Working effectively in a matrix demands excellent interpersonal and conflict-resolution skills. The matrix also forces managers to spend a great deal of time in coordinating meetings.[58] If managers do not adapt to the information and power sharing processes required to secure the benefits of the matrix, the system will underperform and fall into disrepute as employees revert to an earlier structure or develop 'work-arounds' that shadow and further disrupt the matrix. Managers must collaborate with one another rather than rely on vertical authority in decision making. An example of a successful matrix design is discussed above:

See online
COUNTERPOINT 3.10

Horizontal Structure

A recent approach to organizing, considered in Chapter 2, is the **horizontal structure**, which organizes employees around core processes. Organizations may be prompted to move toward a horizontal structure as a consequence of an intervention like total quality management or a procedure called reengineering. **Reengineering**, or *business process reengineering*, involves the redesign of a vertical organization along its horizontal workflows and processes. A **process** refers to an organized group of related tasks and activities that work together to transform inputs into outputs that create value for customers.[59] Reengineering aspires to change the way managers think about how work is done. Rather than focusing on narrow jobs structured into distinct functional departments, reengineering emphasizes core processes that cut horizontally across the organization and involve teams of employees working together to serve customers. Examples of processes include order fulfilment, new product development and customer service.

A good illustration of process engineering is the redesign of customer services at the Vale of Glamorgan Council, a medium sized local government in Wales, UK. The council provides citizens with a range of services ranging from waste disposal to administration of planning and building regulations. In the past, citizens had to reach a specific department in order to make a complaint or arrange an appointment. It was often hard to reach the right person, and both staff and citizens wasted time leaving phone messages back and forth. After studying the problem and getting feedback from service users, the council reorganized the way it does business. Its OneVale initiative established a centralized customer contact centre in conjunction with a computerized information management system. Now, anyone needing to deal with the Council calls the contact centre, whose staff are empowered to deal with simple enquires and complaints themselves, and can set up appointments for all the Council's different departments. The council's phone lines are open late into the evening, and the Vale of Glamorgan has won awards for innovation and customer satisfaction (see Exhibit 3.12).[60]

When an organization is reengineered to a horizontal structure, all the people throughout the organization who work on a particular process (such as customer service, claims handling or order fulfilment) have better access to one another so they can communicate and coordinate their efforts. The horizontal structure reduces the vertical hierarchy and erodes old departmental boundaries. This approach is generally facilitated by the use of information and communication technologies as well as by changing attitudes to work flexibility that have occurred in the workplace and the business environment over the past 25 years. Computerization and Internet connectivity permits wide-ranging integration and coordination. Customers expect faster and better service, and employees may have the opportunity to develop new skills, and assume more responsibility.

EXHIBIT 3.12 OneVale Initiative

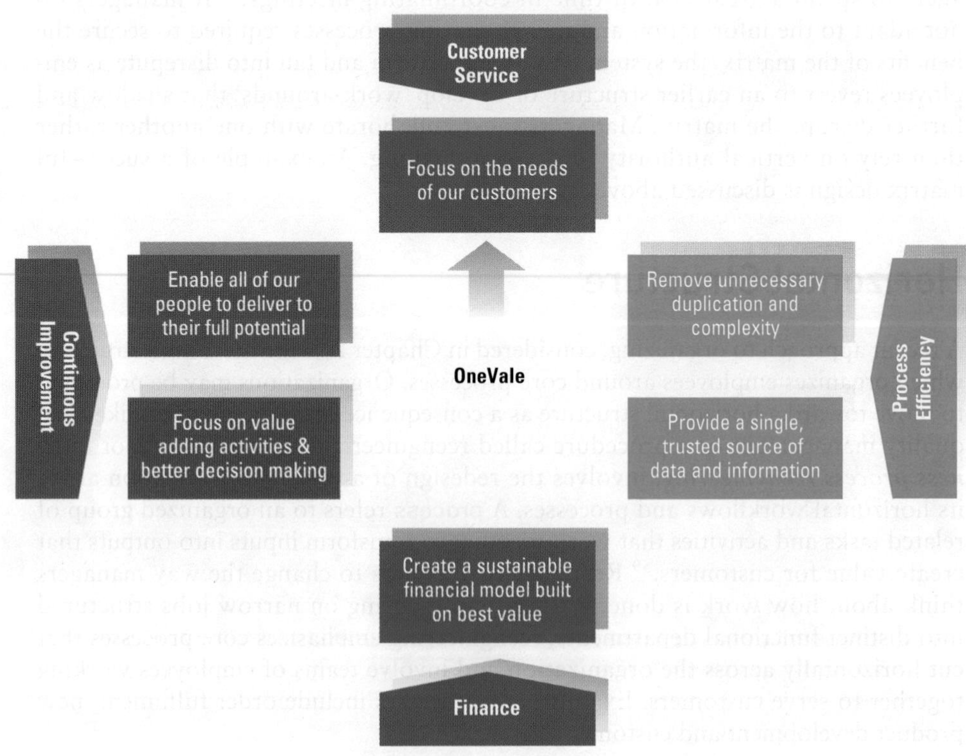

Organizations mired in a vertical mindset where each function or department operates within a separate 'silo' have a hard time meeting these challenges. Thus, numerous organizations have experimented with horizontal mechanisms such as cross-functional teams to achieve coordination across departments or task forces to accomplish temporary projects. Increasingly, organizations are shifting away from hierarchical, function-based structures to structures based on horizontal processes.

COUNTERPOINT 3.4

It would be misleading to suggest that such changes are easily or smoothly introduced or that they are always welcomed by customers or employers. Contacting call centres can be a frustrating and unsatisfactory for customers and employees alike. Change is often driven by the objective of making savings rather than improving service. Or, service improvements are anticipated but an emphasis on cost reduction or a lack of vision results in poor service and disenchanted employees. Call centres can be 'designed' in various ways – at worst, there are those that mirror highly fragmented organizations, where callers wait in queues without any information and are then passed around to different employees who never give their name; and at best there are those that deal with calls promptly, courteously and are trained to manage the process – that is, take care of the handling of each call or 'case' from initial contact to its resolution. **Discuss**

Characteristics

An illustration of a company reengineered into a horizontal structure appears in Exhibit 3.13. Such an organization has the following characteristics:[61]

As an organization manager, keep these guidelines in mind:

Consider a horizontal structure when customer needs and demands change rapidly and when learning and innovation are critical to organizational success. Carefully determine core processes and train managers and employees to work within the horizontal structure.

- Structure is created around cross-functional core processes rather than tasks, functions or geography. Thus, boundaries between departments are obliterated.
- Self-directed teams, not individuals, are the basis of organizational design and performance.
- Process owners have responsibility for each core process in its entirety. For example, until the 1990s, most Britons bought houses through building societies, a kind of financial cooperative. Banks were just not set up to smoothly handle all the different elements that go in to mortgage approval. Prospective buyers had to visit several different departments of the bank to arrange the loan, arrange the legal paperwork, obtain mortgage insurance etc., with delays of weeks if not months. As the property market became more competitive, Barclays Bank realized that if it wanted to build its mortgage business, it had to offer a comprehensive, one-stop service. It brought together all the different expertise and signing authority into a single department, allowing the process to be greatly streamlined. Now, most buyers receive a formal offer within 24 hours, with money often transferred into their account within a week. Barclays crystallized this new business process into its Home Finance Division. Both approvals and, crucially, profits, rose substantially, and Barclays consolidated its position among the top ten mortgage lenders in the UK.[62]
- People on the team are given the skills, tools, motivation and authority to make decisions central to the team's performance. Team members are cross-trained to perform one another's jobs, and the combined skills are sufficient to complete a major organizational task.

See online COUNTERPOINT 3.11

EXHIBIT 3.13 A Horizontal Structure

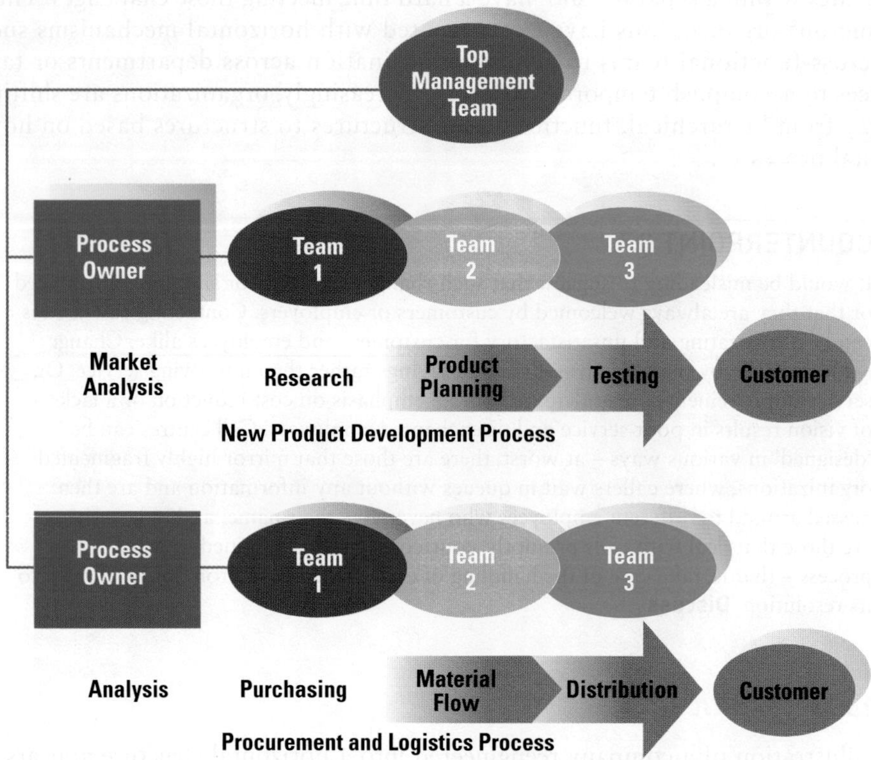

Source: Based on Frank Ostroff, *The Horizontal Organization* (New York: Oxford University Press, 1999); John A. Byrne, 'The Horizontal Corporation,' *BusinessWeek* (December 20, 1993), 76–81; and Thomas A. Stewart, 'The Search for the Organization of Tomorrow,' *Fortune* (May 18, 1992), 92–98.

- Teams have the freedom to think creatively and respond flexibly to new challenges that arise.
- Customers drive the horizontal corporation. Effectiveness is measured by end-of-process performance objectives, based on the goal of bringing value to the company's stakeholders including customers and investors.
- The culture is one of openness, trust and collaboration, focused on continuous improvement. The culture values employee empowerment, responsibility and well-being.

See online COUNTERPOINT 3.12

Avaya Ireland, a hi-tech telecommunications firm is featured in the *In Practice* text box on the next page. Avaya, successfully shifted to a flexible, less hierarchical model in order to meet the needs of diverse customers and a rapidly changing product mix.

Strengths and Weaknesses

As with all structures, the horizontal structure has weaknesses as well as strengths. Some of the main strengths and weaknesses of the horizontal structure are listed in Exhibit 3.14.

The most significant strength of the horizontal structure is that it can dramatically improve flexibility and responsiveness. The structure tends to direct attention toward the customer, leading to greater customer satisfaction as well as improvements in productivity, speed and efficiency. In addition, because there are no boundaries between functional departments, employees can take a broader view of organizational goals

Avaya Ireland

Avaya Ireland is part of the global Avaya corporation, one of the many offspring of the giant AT&T telecommunications business that was broken up in the 1980s into smaller, more flexible and more entrepreneurial entities. Avaya specializes in manufacture of networking components, key building blocks of today's information society. Ireland is one of the main European centres for the computer industry, so Avaya Ireland had a dual advantage of location and growing demand for its product sector. Despite this positive market situation, the company languished through the 1980s and early 1990s. The company was run by a rigid functional hierarchy, with poor cross-functional communication. Costs were high compared with competitors and other subsidiaries of the Avaya group, and staff morale was poor. Avaya Ireland was in real danger of closing. In the mid-1990s top managers realized that they had to adapt to the times or the company would die. A management steering group was established to animate a process of internal dialogue, called Engaging our People. The highly inclusive, and often difficult process identified four main areas of weakness, communications, training, the manager/employee relationship and lack of teamwork. An action plan, based on the Business Excellence Model[63] was developed. Structural changes to realize the company's vision entailed replacing the rigid organizational hierarchy with cross-functional teams focused on core products, from conception, through production to end-user support. Armed with this new focus, the company was able to contain costs while improving product quality. Avaya invited customers to visit the plant and meet its new product-focused cross-functional teams. This was a highly successful initiative – customers saw that the Avaya had an open culture and knowledgeable staff. Satisfaction with the company's networking products soared. In 1998 Avaya won the Irish Business Excellence overall award, and two years later a prize at the European Quality Awards as well as becoming one of the first Irish companies to be awarded ISO9001 certification. The change-driving steering group remains in place, and Avaya Ireland continues to win high marks for customer service and innovation. The company has now moved strongly into the related high-growth area of voice over internet protocol (VOIP) telephony.[64]

EXHIBIT 3.14 Strengths and Weaknesses of Horizontal Structure

Strengths	Weaknesses
1. Promotes flexibility and rapid response to changes in customer needs 2. Directs the attention of everyone toward the production and delivery of value to the customer 3. Each employee has a broader view of organizational goals 4. Promotes a focus on teamwork and collaboration 5. Improves quality of life for employees by offering them the opportunity to share responsibility, make decisions, and be accountable for outcomes	1. Determining core processes is difficult and time consuming 2. Requires changes in culture, job design, management philosophy, and information and reward systems 3. Traditional managers may baulk when they have to give up power and authority 4. Requires significant training of employees to work effectively in a horizontal team environment 5. Can limit in-depth skill development

Sources: Based on Frank Ostroff, *The Horizontal Organization: What the Organization of the Future Looks Like and How It Delivers Value to Customers* (New York: Oxford University Press, 1999); and Richard L. Daft, *Organization Theory and Design*, 6th ed. (Cincinnati, Ohio: South-Western, 1998), 253.

rather than being focused on the goals of a single department. The horizontal structure promotes an emphasis on teamwork and cooperation, so that team members share a commitment to meeting common objectives. Finally, the horizontal structure can improve the quality of life for employees by giving them opportunities to share responsibility, make decisions and contribute significantly to the organization.

A potential weakness of the horizontal structure is that it can harm rather than help organizational performance, unless managers carefully determine which core processes are critical for bringing value to customers. Simply defining the processes around which to organize can be difficult. In addition, shifting to a horizontal structure requires significant changes in culture, job design, management philosophy and information and reward systems, and can therefore be complicated, time consuming and thus costly. Traditional managers may baulk at having to share elements of power and authority, and find it difficult to learn to exercise leadership through team facilitation. Employees have to be trained to work effectively in a team environment, and they may be suspicious of the company's motives in dismantling overt hierarchy or hostile to its disruptive impact upon valued routines. Finally, because of the cross-functional nature of work, a horizontal structure can limit in-depth knowledge and skill development unless measures are taken to enable employees opportunities to maintain and build technical expertise.

Virtual Network Structure

The virtual network structure extends the concept of horizontal coordination and collaboration beyond the boundaries of the traditional organization. Many of today's organizations farm out some of their activities to other companies. **Outsourcing**, which means the contracting out of aspects of work (e.g. manufacturing, information technology or credit processing), to other companies is a significant trend in many industries that has implications for organization structure.[65] Accenture, for example, handles all aspects of information technology for the British food retailer J. Sainsbury's. Companies in countries such as India and Malaysia, as well as European sites such as Scotland and Eastern Europe manage call centre and technical support for multinational corporations including financial companies, computer vendors and mobile phone companies. Entire chunks of aeroplanes manufactured by Canada's Bombardier and Brazil's Embraer are engineered and built by outside contractors, often outside Canada and Brazil respectively. Fiat Auto is involved in multiple complex outsourcing relationships with other companies handling logistics, maintenance and the manufacturing of some parts.[66]

These interorganizational relationships reflect a significant shift in organization design. An increasing number of organizations take outsourcing to the extreme and create a virtual network structure. With a **virtual network structure**, sometimes called a *modular structure*, the firm subcontracts many or most of its major processes to separate companies and coordinates their activities from a small headquarters organization. Nowadays fashionwear companies like Nike frequently produce none of their own clothing, focusing instead on building brand value through comprehensive marketing efforts and exercising tight control over their suppliers. The virtual network structure has become much more feasible as a result of advances in information and communication technologies.[67]

How the Structure Works

The virtual network organization may be viewed as a central hub surrounded by a network of outside specialists. Rather than being housed under one roof or located within one organization, services such as accounting, design, manufacturing, marketing and distribution are outsourced to separate companies that are connected electronically to a central office. Organizational partners located in different parts of the world may use secure networking to exchange data and information so rapidly and smoothly that a loosely connected network of suppliers, manufacturers and distributors can look and act like one seamless company. The virtual network form can also incorporate a free-market style to replace the traditional vertical hierarchy. In this case, contractors can be brought into and released from the system to meet changing needs.

With a network structure, the hub maintains control over processes in which it has difficult-to-imitate capabilities and transfers other activities – along with the decision making for, and operational control over, those activities – to other organizations who are specialists. These organizations organize and accomplish their work using their own ideas, assets, and tools.[68] The idea is that a firm can concentrate on its 'core competence' – what is key to its survival – and contract out everything else to companies with distinctive competence in those specific areas, thereby in principle enabling the organization to do more with less.[69] The network structure is often advantageous in reducing costs for start-up companies, such as Dicole, a Finnish IT firm that works with companies to implement Web 2.0 technologies, featured in the *In Practice* box below.

As an organization manager, keep this guideline in mind:

Use a virtual network structure for extreme flexibility and rapid response to changing market conditions. Focus on key activities that give the organization its competitive advantage and outsource other activities to carefully selected partners.

Leveraging Web 2.0: Dicole Ltd

Virtual networking is made possible by new technologies, and the ever-expanding universe of virtual communication creates new opportunities almost daily. Companies small and large are exploring ways to build virtual networks and strengthen collaboration across the globe, using the boundless potential of Web 2.0, and particularly new thinking in virtual communications. Dicole, a Finnish start-up, works with companies to leverage Web 2.0 potential, offering a dizzying variety of potential and permutations.

One of the simplest forms of virtual communication is the Wiki, a word that comes from the Hawaiian for 'fast', and involves working collaboratively and in real-time on a single text. Wikipedia, the online collaborative encyclopedia, is the best known example of wiki technology, but wikis are used increasingly within companies for internal communication, and increasingly for technical documentation of work processes. As employees become more familiar with wikis, they are being used to develop product manuals and instructions for end users outside the company. Similarly, the same technology used to create YouTube, the popular site for uploading, viewing and sharing video clips, can be used to transfer knowledge within a company quickly and cheaply. Large companies such as IBM use technology similar to that underpinning the social networking site Facebook to help employees to get to know and understand each other – over 400,000 IBM employees have their own pages on the company's 'Blue Pages', which can include photos, employees' places in the IBM hierarchy, contact information and even their own weblogs.

While many companies use versions of wikis, blogs and Facebooks, Dicole works with its customer organizations to combine the various technologies together in a tailor-made approach to virtual network communications, which it has branded Dicole Knowledge Work Environment.[70]

The concept can be taken even further through the product development technique called *crowdsourcing*, where social networking technologies are used to develop new products. Many different approaches have been tried. One example is Threadless (www.threadless.com), a Chicago-headquartered t-shirt company that invites anyone to submit t-shirt designs. If the design is selected, the designer is paid an up-front fee and a commission depending on the number of t-shirts sold with that design.[71]

Strengths and Weaknesses

Exhibit 3.15 summarizes the strengths and weaknesses of the virtual network structure. One of the major strengths is that even quite small organizations can be truly global, drawing on resources worldwide to achieve the best quality and price and then selling products or services worldwide just as easily through subcontractors. The network structure also enables new or small companies to develop products or services and get them to market rapidly without huge investments in factories, equipment, warehouses or distribution facilities. The ability to arrange and rearrange resources to meet changing needs and best serve customers gives the network structure flexibility and rapid response. New technologies can be developed quickly by tapping into a worldwide network of experts. The organization can continually redefine itself to meet changing product or market opportunities. A final strength is reduced administrative overhead. Large teams of staff specialists and administrators are not needed. Managerial and technical talent can be focused on key activities that provide competitive advantage while other activities are outsourced.[72]

The virtual network structure also has a number of weaknesses.[73] The primary weakness is a potential lack of control associated with taking decentralization to the extreme. Managers do not have all operations under their jurisdiction and must rely on contracts, coordination and negotiation to hold things together. This can also mean increased time spent managing relationships with partners and resolving conflicts, which can be especially complex if partners are operating in different contents, many time zones away. Communications technologies have greatly reduced effective distance, but there is no substitute for face-to-face negotiations when complex, serious issues arise.

A problem of equal importance is the risk of failure if one organizational partner fails to deliver, has a plant burn down or goes out of business. Managers in the headquarters organization have to act quickly to spot problems and find new arrangements. Finally, from a human resource perspective, employee loyalty can be weak in a network organization, both because of concerns over job security and because developing a cohesive corporate culture is difficult between far-flung units or outsourced functions. Employees may feel that they could be replaced at any

EXHIBIT 3.15 Strengths and Weaknesses of Virtual Network Structure

Strengths	Weaknesses
1. Enables even small organizations to obtain talent and resources worldwide 2. Gives a company immediate scale and reach without huge investments in factories equipment, or distribution facilities 3. Enables the organization to be highly flexible and responsive to changing needs 4. Reduces administrative overhead costs	1. Managers do not have hands-on control over many activities and employees 2. Requires a great deal of time to manage relationships and potential conflicts with contract partners 3. There is a risk of organizational failure if a partner fails to deliver or goes out of business 4. Employee loyalty and corporate culture might be weak because employees feel they can be replaced by contract services

Sources: Based on Linda S. Ackerman, 'Transition Management: An In-Depth Look at Managing Complex Change,' *Organizational Dynamics* (Summer 1982), 46–66; and Frank Ostroff, *The Horizontal Organization* (New York: Oxford University Press, 1999), Fig 2.1, 34.

time by contract services. Turnover may be higher because emotional commitment between the organization and employees is low. With changing products, markets and partners, the organization may need frequently to reshuffle employees to get the correct mix of skills and capabilities.

Hybrid Structure

As a practical matter, many structures in the real world do not exist in the pure forms we have outlined in this chapter. Organizations often use a **hybrid structure** that combines characteristics of various approaches tailored to specific strategic needs. Most companies combine characteristics of functional, divisional, geographical, horizontal and/or network structures to take account of the relative strengths and weaknesses of these structures in their own particular business.

As an organization manager, keep these guidelines in mind:

Implement hybrid structures, when needed, to combine characteristics of functional, divisional and horizontal structures. Use a hybrid structure in complex environments to take advantage of the strengths of various structural characteristics and avoid some of the weaknesses.

One type of hybrid that is often used is to combine characteristics of the functional and divisional structures. When a corporation grows large and has several products or markets, it typically is organized into self-contained divisions of some type. Functions that are important to each product or market are decentralized to the self-contained units. However, some functions that are relatively stable and require economies of scale and in-depth specialization are also centralized at headquarters.

Sony Europa is the European arm of the Japanese electronics giant, Sony Corporation. The company has been active in Europe since 1960, and has enjoyed success across the continent due to the famed high quality of Sony products. However, the company's involvement in Europe developed in an unplanned way, with marketing offices and manufacturing plants growing up in many different countries. Country managers, by default, became leaders of mini-empires, and there was little cross-European coordination. The weaknesses of this approach could be overlooked while Sony was growing, but as the company faced stiffer competition on both price and quality from the 1990s, company leaders realized a more strategic and coordinated approach to organizational structure was needed. Successive efforts by Sony's top management to introduce some coordination resulted in establishment of business units that grouped together consumer electronics, business and professional products and OEM products geared to industrial purchasers. While this improved coordination, each division had its own functional units such as HR, marketing and logistics, detracting from possible cost synergies and overall corporate identity. In 2002, Sony Europa's new president Mike Tsurumi established a hybrid structure which retains product divisions, but centralizes the functional areas of HR, Finance, Sales, Marketing and infrastructure[74] (see Exhibit 3.16 as applied to Marketing). A hybrid structure such as this is often preferred over the pure functional, divisional, horizontal or virtual network structure because it can provide some of the advantages of each and overcome some of the disadvantages.

Applications of Structural Design

Each type of structure is applied in different situations and is intended to address different demands. In describing the various structures, we touched briefly on conditions such as environmental stability or change and organizational size that are related to structure. Each form of structure – functional, divisional, matrix, horizontal, network, hybrid – represents a tool that can make an organization more or less effective, depending on the exigencies of the situation and the capacity of the structure to respond effectively to their often conflicting demands.

EXHIBIT 3.16 New Structure of European Marketing Introduced During the Era of Mike Tsurumi

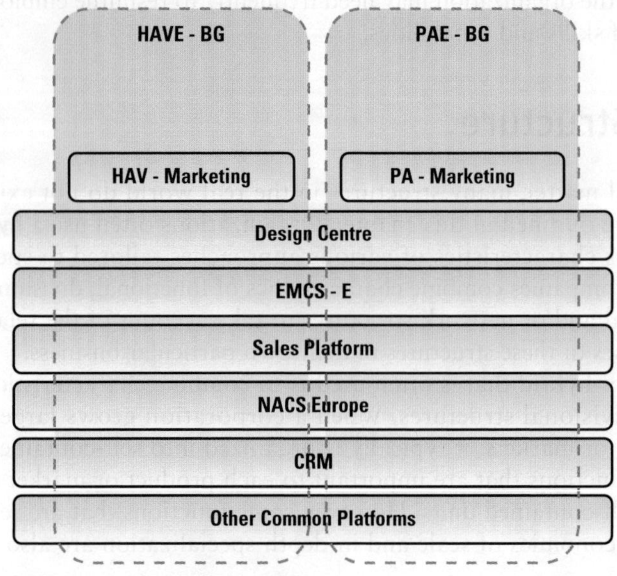

Key:
HAVE = Home Audio Visual Europe
PAE = Personal Audio Europe
EMCS = Engineering Manufacturer Customer Service, Europe
NACS = Network Applications Content Solutions
CRM = Customer Relationship Management
BG = Business Group

Reproduced with permission of Prof. Paul Sparrow: http://www.lums.lancs.ac.uk/files/hr/10044.pdf

Structural Alignment

One of the most important roles of top managers in structural design is finding the right balance between vertical control and horizontal coordination, depending on the constantly changing needs of the organization. Vertical control tends to be associated with goals of efficiency and stability, while horizontal coordination is associated with learning, innovation and flexibility. Exhibit 3.17 shows a simplified continuum that illustrates how structural approaches are associated with vertical control versus horizontal coordination. The functional structure is most appropriate when managers believe that efficiency in meeting organizational goals can be achieved through coordination by vertical hierarchy. However, the narrow focus on specific outcomes that vertical hierarchy tends to produce can be insufficiently flexible to account for rapidly changing pressures in a complex business environment.

As an organization manager, keep these guidelines in mind:

Find the correct balance between vertical control and horizontal coordination to meet the needs of the organization. Consider a structural reorganization when symptoms of structural deficiency are observed.

At the opposite end of the scale, more horizontal structures are more appropriate when innovation is a priority. In this case, continuous coordination among functions fosters organizational learning. The horizontal structure enables organizations to differentiate themselves and respond quickly to changes, but often at the expense of short-term efficiency. The virtual network structure offers even greater flexibility and potential for rapid response by allowing the organization to add or subtract pieces as needed to adapt and meet changing demands and challenges, as well as searching the world for lower costs and increased productivity. Exhibit 3.17 also shows how other types of structure defined in this chapter – functional with horizontal linkages, divisional and matrix – represent intermediate steps on the organization's path to cost-efficiency,

EXHIBIT 3.17 Relationship of Structure to Organization's Need for Efficiency versus Learning

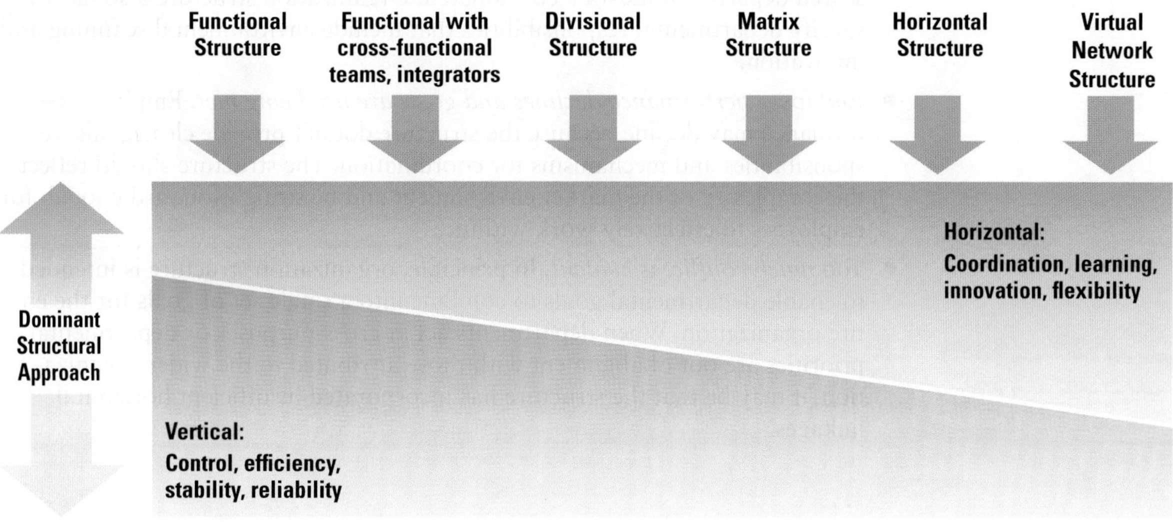

innovation and learning. The exhibit does not include all possible structures, but it illustrates how organizations attempt to balance competing priorities and demands.

COUNTERPOINT 3.5

In this chapter we have presented a range of formal schemas of design, In practice, however, organizations are ongoing projects in which elements and remnants of different structures are overlapped and overlaid. The result is more of a patchwork than a 'hybrid' that is the product of successive efforts to mitigate for the limitations or weaknesses ascribed to a previous structure. Nor should it be overlooked that structures are generally imposed from the top, sometimes mainly to signal the arrival of a new CEO or management team with 'fresh ideas', and they then encounter resistance which moderates their impact and (in)effectiveness. **Discuss**

Symptoms of Structural Deficiency

Top executives periodically evaluate organization structure to determine whether it is appropriate to changing conditions and aspirations. Many organizations try one organization structure and then reorganize to another structure in an effort to develop a better fit between executive aspirations, internal reporting relationships and the external environment.

The following are **symptomatic of structural deficiency.**[75]

- *Decision making is delayed or lacking in quality.* Decision makers may be overloaded because the hierarchy funnels too many problems and decisions to them. Delegation to lower levels may be insufficient. Another cause of poor-quality decisions is that information may not reach the correct people. Information linkages in either the vertical or horizontal direction may be inadequate to ensure decision quality.
- *The organization does not respond innovatively to a changing environment.* One reason for lack of innovation is that departments are not coordinated horizontally. The identification of customer needs by the marketing

department and the identification of technological developments in the research department must be coordinated. Organization structure also has to specify departmental responsibilities that include environmental scanning and innovation.

- *Employee performance declines and goals are not being met.* Employee performance may decline because the structure doesn't provide clear goals, responsibilities and mechanisms for coordination. The structure should reflect the complexity of the market environment and be straightforward enough for employees to effectively work within.
- *Too much conflict is evident.* In principle, organization structure is intended to enable departmental goals to combine into a single set of goals for the entire organization. When departments act at cross-purposes or departmental priorities are out of alignment with those attributed to the wider organization, it may be that the structure has incorporated insufficient horizontal linkages.

COUNTERPOINT 3.6

Although these problems may arise from 'stuctural deficiency' that can be corrected by the techical fix of structural redesign, the problems may also be endemic to capitalist work organizations. Decision-making may be delayed because senior managers anticipate that their jobs or career prospects are threatened by change. Innovation may be slow because it poses a threat to established 'empires' within the organization. Declines in employee performance may be associated with frustration and dissatisfaction in, ultimately, being treated as a disposable commodity or, at least, with insufficient dignity as changes are introduced (or imposed) without genuine consultation or adequate understanding of their counterproductive effects. Conflicts between individuals, groups, departments and divisions may arise from the basic understanding that responding to the demands of shareholders and/or customers is not necessarily compatible with improving the wages and conditions (e.g. pensions) of particular groups of employees. **Discuss**

Summary and Interpretation

Organization structure is intended to accomplish two things. It seeks to provide a framework of responsibilities, reporting relationships and groupings, and it is intended to provide mechanisms for linking and coordinating organizational elements into a coherent whole.

Managers make a strategic choice as they orient toward a traditional organization design which emphasizes vertical linkages such as hierarchy, rules and plans or toward a contemporary learning organization, which emphasizes horizontal linkages through cross-functional information systems, direct contact between managers across department lines, temporary task forces, full-time integrators and teams.

Alternatives for grouping employees and departments into overall structural design include functional grouping, divisional grouping, multifocused grouping, horizontal grouping and network grouping. With functional and divisional structures, managers also use horizontal linkage mechanisms to complement the vertical dimension and achieve integration of departments and levels into an organizational whole. With a horizontal structure, activities are organized horizontally around core work processes. A virtual network structure extends the concept of horizontal coordination and collaboration beyond the boundaries of the organization. Core activities are performed by a central hub while other functions and activities are outsourced to contract partners. The matrix structure attempts to achieve an equal balance between the vertical and horizontal dimensions of structure. Organizations rarely exist in these pure forms. Instead, hybrid varieties evolve that incorporate more or less coherent blends of organizing activity that can be analyzed in terms of the various structural types examined in this chapter.

KEY CONCEPTS

centralized
decentralized
departmental grouping
divisional grouping
divisional structure
functional grouping
functional matrix
functional structure
horizontal grouping
horizontal linkage
horizontal structure
hybrid structure
integrator
liaison role
matrix structure
multifocused grouping
organization structure
outsourcing
process
product matrix
reengineering
symptoms of structural deficiency
task force
teams
vertical information system
vertical linkages
virtual network grouping
virtual network structure
virtual team

Discussion Questions

1 What is the definition of *organization structure*? Does organization structure appear on the organization chart? Explain.

2 How do rules and plans help an organization achieve vertical integration?

3 When is a functional structure preferable to a divisional structure?

4 Large corporations tend to use hybrid structures. Why?

5 What are the primary differences between a traditional organization designed for efficiency and a more contemporary organization designed for learning?

6 What is the difference between a task force and a team? Between liaison role and integrating role? Which of these provides the greatest amount of horizontal coordination?

7 What conditions usually have to be present before an organization should adopt a matrix structure?

8 The manager of a consumer products firm said, 'We use the brand manager position to train future executives'. Do you think the brand manager position is a good training ground? Discuss.

9 Why do companies using a horizontal structure have cultures that emphasize openness, employee empowerment and responsibility? What do you think a manager's job would be like in a horizontally organized company?

10 How is structure related to the organization's need for efficiency versus its need for learning and innovation? How can managers tell if the structure is out of alignment with the organization's needs?

11 Describe the virtual network structure. Why do you think this is becoming a good structural alternative for some of today's organizations?

Chapter 3 Workbook You and Organization Structure

To better understand the importance of organization structure in your life, do the following assignment. Select one of the following situations to organize:

- A copy and printing shop
- A travel agency

- A sports rental (such as skis or snowboards) in a resort area
- A bakery

Background

Organization is a way of gaining some power against an unreliable environment. The environment provides the organization with inputs, which include raw materials, human resources and financial resources. There is a service or product to produce that involves technology. The output goes to clients, a group that must be nurtured. The complexities of the environment and the technology determine the complexity of the organization.

Planning Your Organization

1. Write down the mission or purpose of the organization in a few sentences.
2. What are the specific tasks to be completed to accomplish the mission?
3. Based on the specifics in number 2, develop an organization chart. Each position in the chart will perform a specific task or is responsible for a certain outcome.
4. You are into your third year of operation, and your business has been very successful. You want to add a second location a few kilometres away. What issues will you face running the business at two locations? Draw an organization chart that includes the two business locations.
5. Five more years go by and the business has grown to five locations in two cities in the same country. How do you keep in touch with it all? What issues of control and coordination have arisen? Draw an up-to-date organization chart and explain your rationale for it.
6. Twenty years later you have seventy-five business locations in five European countries. What are the issues and problems that have to be dealt with through organizational structure? Draw an organization chart for this organization, indicating such factors as who is responsible for customer satisfaction, how you will know if customer needs are met and how information will flow within the organization.

Adapted by Dorothy Marcic from 'Organizing', in Donald D. White and H. William Vroman, *Action in Organizations*, 2nd ed. (Boston: Allyn and Bacon, 1982), 154, and Cheryl Harvey and Kim Morouney, 'Organization Structure and Design: The Club Ed Exercise', *Journal of Management Education* (June 1985), 425–429.

CASE FOR ANALYSIS

Aquarius Advertising Agency

The Aquarius Advertising Agency is a middle-sized firm that offered two basic services to its clients: (1) customized plans for the content of an advertising campaign (for example, slogans and layouts) and (2) complete plans for media (such as radio, TV, newspapers, billboards and Internet). Additional services included aid in marketing and distribution of products and marketing research to test advertising effectiveness.

Its activities were organized in a traditional manner. The organization chart is shown in Exhibit 3.18. Each department included similar functions.

Each client account was coordinated by an account executive who acted as a liaison between the client and the various specialists on the professional staff of the operations and marketing divisions. The number of direct communications and contacts between clients and Aquarius specialists, clients and account executives and Aquarius specialists and account executives is indicated in Exhibit 3.19. These sociometric data were gathered by a consultant who conducted a study of the patterns of formal and informal communication. Each intersecting cell of Aquarius personnel and the clients contains an index of the direct contacts between them.

Although an account executive was designated to be the liaison between the client and specialists within the agency, communications frequently occurred directly between clients and specialists and bypassed the account executive. These direct contacts involved a wide range of interactions, such as meetings, telephone calls, e-mail messages and so on. A large number of direct communications occurred between agency specialists and their counterparts in the client organization. For example, an art specialist working as one member of a team on a particular client account would often be contacted directly by the client's in-house art specialist, and agency research personnel had direct communication with research people of the client firm. Also, some of the unstructured contacts often led to more formal meetings with clients in which agency personnel made presentations, interpreted and defended agency policy and committed the agency to certain courses of action.

Both hierarchical and professional systems operated within the departments of the operations and marketing divisions. Each department was organized hierarchically with a director, an assistant director, and several levels of authority. Professional communications were widespread and mainly concerned with sharing knowledge and techniques, technical evaluation of work and development of professional interests. Control in each department was exercised mainly through control of promotions and supervision of work done by subordinates. Many account executives, however, felt the need for more influence, and one commented:

Creativity and art. That's all I hear around here. It is hard as hell to effectively manage six or seven hot-shots who claim they have to do their own thing. Each of them tries to sell his or her idea to the client, and most of the time I don't know what has happened until a week later. If I were a despot, I would make all of them check with me first to get approval. Things would sure change around here.

The need for reorganization was made more acute by changes in the environment. Within a short period of time, there was a rapid turnover in the major accounts handled by the agency. It was typical for advertising agencies to gain or lose clients quickly, often with no advance warning as consumer behaviour and lifestyle changes emerged and product innovations occurred.

An agency reorganization was one solution proposed by top management to increase flexibility in this unpredictable environment. The reorganization would be aimed at reducing the agency's response time to environmental changes and at increasing cooperation and communication among specialists from different departments. The top managers are not sure what type of reorganization is appropriate. They would like your help analyzing their context and current structure and welcome your advice on proposing a new structure.

Adapted from John F. Veiga and John N. Yanouzas, 'Aquarius Advertising Agency', *The Dynamics of Organization Theory* (St. Paul, Minn.: West, 1984), 212–217, with permission.

EXHIBIT 3.18 Aquarius Advertising Agency Organization Chart

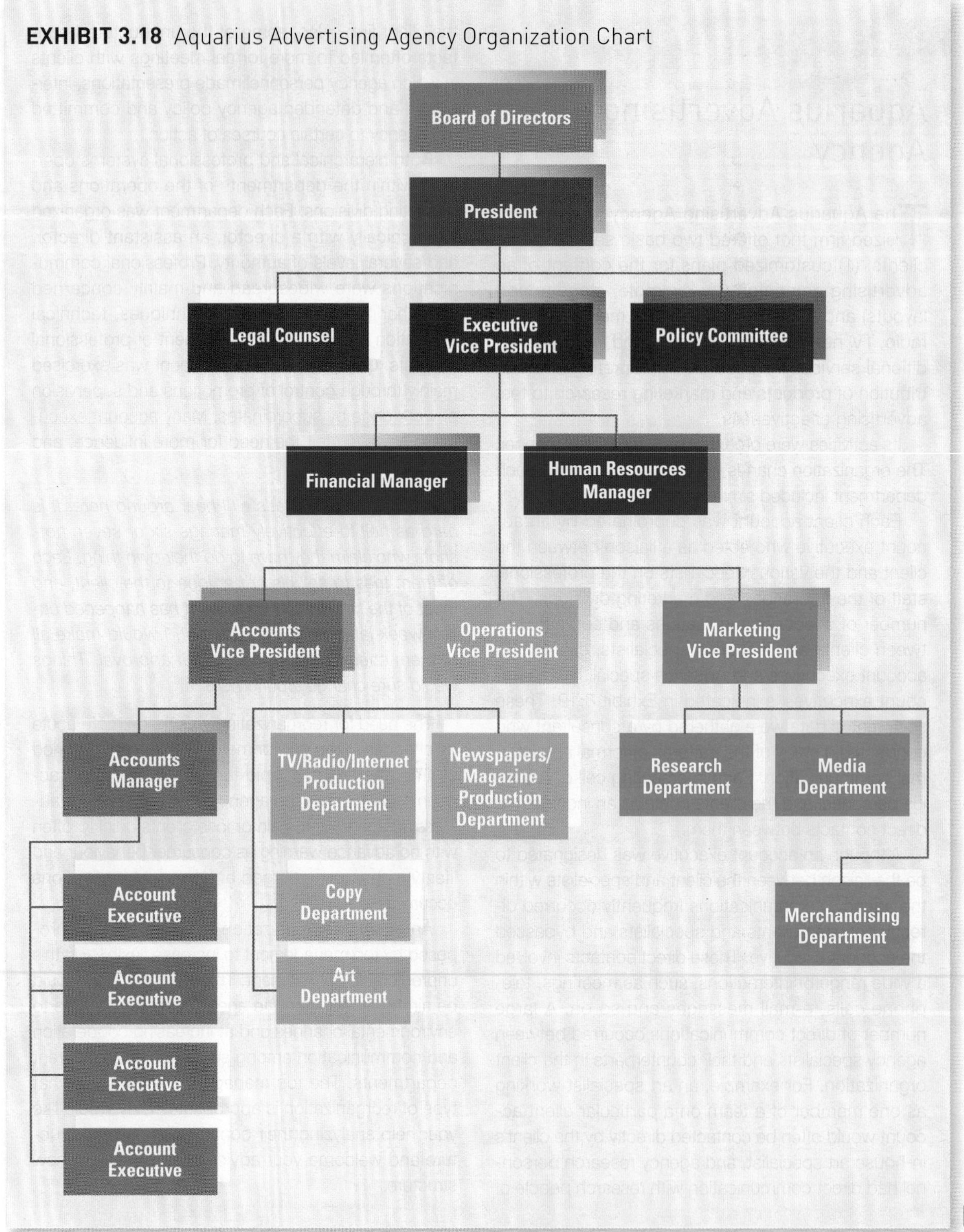

EXHIBIT 3.19 Sociometric Index of Aquarius Personnel and Clients

	Clients	Account Manager	Account Executives	TV/Radio Specialists	Newspaper/Magazine Specialists	Copy Specialists	Art Specialists	Merchandising Specialists	Media Specialists	Research Specialists
Clients	X	F	F	N	N	O	O	O	O	O
Account Manager		X	F	N	N	N	N	N	N	N
Account Executives			X	F	F	F	F	F	F	F
TV/Radio Specialists				X	N	O	O	N	N	O
Newspaper/Magazine Specialists					X	O	O	N	O	O
Copy Specialists						X	N	O	O	O
Art Specialists							X	O	O	O
Merchandising Specialists								X	F	F
Media Specialists									X	F
Research Specialists										X

F = Frequent – daily
O = Occasional – once or twice per project
N = None

Notes

1. 'Henry Ford would just love Toyota: Car makers' strategy for market share', *Strategic Direction*, Volume 21 Number 4 2005, pp. 25–27.
2. E. Bartezzaghi, 'The evolution of production models: is a new paradigm emerging?'*International Journal of Operations and Production Management*, 19, 2, 1999, 229–250.
3. 'GM updates Zaragoza plant for new Corsa'. *just-auto.com*, July 27, 2006.
4. Daniel Vázquez-Bustelo and Lucía Avella, 'Agile manufacturing: Industrial case studies in Spain', *Technovation*, October 2006, Vol. 26 No. 10, 1147b

5. Daniel J. Wakin, 'With Shifting Needs and Ebbing Resources, Church is Reorganizing', *The New York Times* (January 4, 2004).
6. John Child, *Organization* (New York: Harper & Row, 1984).
7. Stuart Ranson, Bob Hinings and Royston Greenwood, 'The Structuring of Organizational Structures', *Administrative Science Quarterly* 25 (1980), 1–17; and Hugh Willmott, 'The Structuring of Organizational Structure: A Note', *Administrative Science Quarterly* 26 (1981), 470–474.
8. This section is based on Frank Ostroff, *The Horizontal Organization: What the Organization of the Future Looks Like and How It Delivers Value to Customers* (New York: Oxford University Press, 1999).
9. Stephen Salsbury, *The State, the Investor and the Railroad: The Boston & Albany, 1825–1867* (Cambridge: Harvard University Press, 1967), 186–187.
10. Gideon Kunda, (1992), *Engineering Culture: Control and Commitment in a High-Tech Corporation,* Philadelphia, Temple University Press; Hugh Willmott (1993), 'Strength is Ignorance; Slavery is Freedom: Managing Culture in Modern Organizations', *Journal of Management Studies* 30, 515–552; James R. Barker (1993), 'Tightening the Iron Cage: Concertive Control in Self-Managing Teams', *Administrative Science Quarterly*, 38, 408–437.
11. David Nadler and Michael Tushman, *Strategic Organization Design* (Glenview, Ill.: Scott Foresman, 1988).
12. Beardsley, Scott C.; Johnson, Bradford C.; Manyika, James M. 'Competitive advantage from better interactions', *McKinsey Quarterly*, 2006 (2), 52–63.
13. 'The Cemex Way', *The Economist*, June 16, 2001.
14. Based on Jay R. Galbraith, *Designing Complex Organizations* (Reading, Mass.: Addison-Wesley, 1973), and *Organization Design* (Reading, Mass.: Addison-Wesley, 1977), 81–127.
15. Lee Iacocca with William Novak, *Iacocca: An Autobiography* (New York: Phantom Books, 1984), 152–153.
16. In 2007 Daimler agreed to sell its Chrysler unit on to Cerebrus Capital Management: The New York Times on the Web, Micheline Maynard and Mark Landler, 'Chrysler Group to Be Sold for $7.4 Billion', *New York Times*, May 14.
17. G. Christian Hill, 'Dog Eats Dog Food. And Damn If It Ain't Tasty', *Ecompany Now* (November 2000), 169–178; 'Country Managers: From Baron to Hotelier'; Rochelle Garner and Barbara Darrow, 'Oracle Plots Course', *CRN* (January 24, 2005), 3; and Anthony Hilton, 'Dangers behind Oracle's Dream', *Evening Standard* (February 11, 2005), 45.
18. 'Is Fusion Beyond Oracle's Reach?', *IT Week*, April 23, 2007, page 9; Richard Waters, 'Departure of executive may delay Oracle plan', *Financial Times*, October 17, 2007.
19. Based on Galbraith, Designing Complex Organizations.
20. 'Mandate 2003: Be Agile and Efficient', *Microsoft Executive Circle* (Spring 2003), 46–48.
21. Jay Galbraith, Diane Downey and Amy Kates, 'How Networks Undergird the Lateral Capability of an Organization – Where the Work Gets Done', *Journal of Organizational Excellence* (Spring 2002), 67–78.
22. Amy Barrett, 'Staying on Top', *BusinessWeek* (May 5, 2003), 60–68.
23. Walter Kiechel III, 'The Art of the Corporate Task Force', *Fortune* (January 28, 1991), 104–105; and William J. Altier, 'Task Forces: An Effective Management Tool', *Management Review* (February 1987), 52–57.
24. Neal E. Boudette, 'Marriage Counseling; At DaimlerChrysler, A New Push to Make Its Units Work Together', *The Wall Street Journal* (March 12, 2003), A1, A15.
25. Mike Danilovic and Mats Winroth (2006) 'Corporate manufacturing network: from hierarchy to self-organising system', *International Journal of Integrated Supply Management*, Vol. 2, 1–2, 106–131.
26. Keith Naughton and Kathleen Kerwin, 'At GM, Two Heads May Be Worse Than One', *Business Week* (August 14, 1995), 46.
27. Paul R. Lawrence and Jay W. Lorsch, 'New Managerial Job: The Integrator', *Harvard Business Review* (November–December 1967), 142–151.
28. Charles Fishman, 'Total Teamwork: Imagination Ltd.', *Fast Company* (April 2000), 156–168; Thomas L. Legare, 'How Hewlett-Packard Used Virtual Cross-Functional Teams to Deliver Healthcare Industry Solutions', *Journal of Organizational Excellence* (Autumn 2001), 29–37.
29. Anthony M. Townsend, Samuel M. DeMarie and Anthony R. Hendrickson, 'Virtual Teams: Technology and the Workplace of the Future', *Academy of Management Executive* 12, no. 3 (August 1998), 17–29.
30. Kuipers, Ben S. and de Witte, Marco C. (2005) 'Teamwork: a case study on development and performance', *The International Journal of Human Resource Management*, 16:2, 185–201.
31. 'Smells like team spirit', *Management Services Journal*, Winter 2005, 28–31.
32. Henry Mintzberg, *The Structuring of Organizations* (Englewood Cliffs, N.J.: Prentice-Hall, 1979).
33. Dutta, S and Regani, S. (2005) 'Project Scorpio: The Making of India's First Indigenous Sports Utility Vehicle', ICFAI Center for Management Research, Case 605-005-1. Accessed at http://www.ecch.com/casesearch/view_pdf.cfm?id=62428&folder=20052&ref=605-005-1.
34. Jean Bonnal and Massimo Rossi (2005), *Understand, analyze and manage a decentralization process: The RED-IFO Model and its use*, Rome, FAO, 63–67.
35. Dina Khorasanee (2007), 'Resistance as "creation": a new sociability in Argentina', *Development in Practice*, 17, 765–774.
36. Based on Robert Duncan, 'What Is the Right Organization Structure?' *Organizational Dynamics* (Winter 1979), 59–80; and W. Alan Randolph and Gregory G. Dess, 'The Congruence Perspective of Organization Design: A Conceptual Model and Multivariate Research Approach', *Academy of Management Review* 9 (1984), 114–127.
37. Rahul Jacob, 'The Struggle to Create an Organization for the 21st Century', *Fortune* (April 3, 1995), 90–99.
38. 'The Real Hotel Co – Preliminary Results', *Thomson Financial News*, April 29, 2008; 'CHE Hotel Group

Plc – Final Results PR Newswire UK Disclose, April 25, 2007', 'Hotel chain chairman to step down' *The Independent* (London), July 17, 1998; Damian Reece, 'Radisson and London Plaza to buy CHE', *Sunday Telegraph*, December 16, 2001, p. 2, CHE Hotels rejigs management to save 1 mln stg annually, *AFX.COM*, January 25, 2007; Emma Rowley, 'Hotels Group Goes Into Administration', January 21, 2009.

39. 'Hur stort kan ett sjukhus bli?', *Sjukhuslakaren*, 06 / 2005, at http://www.sjukhuslakaren.org/605_karolinska.html.
40. Amy Barrett, 'Staying On Top'; Joseph Weber, 'A Big Company That Works', *BusinessWeek* (May 4, 1992), 124–132; and Elyse Tanouye, 'Johnson & Johnson Stays Fit by Shuffling Its Mix of Businesses', *The Wall Street Journal* (December 22, 1992), A1, A4.
41. Nick Harrop and Alan Gillies (IT, culture, context: Emergency department modernisation can inform the NHS information programme, *International Journal of Public Sector Management*, 20, 272–284.
42. Based on Duncan, 'What Is the Right Organization Structure?'
43. Weber, 'A Big Company That Works'.
44. Alan Rugman and Richard Hodgetts (2001), 'The End of Global Strategy', *European Management Journal*,19, 333–343: 337.
45. 'Microsoft Realigns for Next Wave of Innovation and Growth', Microsoft Corporation Press Release, September 20, 2005, accessed at http://www.microsoft.com/presspass/press/2005/sep05/09-20ExecChangesPR.mspx.
46. Robert A. Guth, 'Midlife Correction; Inside Microsoft, Financial Managers Winning New Clout', *The Wall Street Journal* (July 23, 2003), A1, A6; and Michael Moeller, with Steve Hamm and Timothy J. Mullaney, 'Remaking Microsoft', *BusinessWeek* (May 17, 1999), 106–114.
47. Mariko Sanchanta, 'Vital signs at Sony as a talking cure takes effect' *Financial Times*, January 17, 2008, 13.
48. Maisie O'Flanagan and Lynn K. Taliento, 'Nonprofits: Ensuring That Bigger Is Better', *McKinsey Quarterly*, Issue 2 (2004), 112ff.
49. Kingfisher PLC – Final Results 2007, *Thomson Financial News*, March 27 2008.
50. Stanley M. Davis and Paul R. Lawrence, *Matrix* (Reading, Mass.: Addison-Wesley, 1977), 11–24.
51. Erik W. Larson and David H. Gobeli, 'Matrix Management: Contradictions and Insight', *California Management Review* 29 (Summer 1987), 126–138.
52. Davis and Lawrence, *Matrix,* 155–180.
53. Bayer Annual Management Report 2006, accessed at http://www.annualreport2006.bayer.com/en/bayer_management_report_2006.pdfx; Sigurt Vitols, 'Shareholder Value, Management Culture and Production Regimes in the Transformation of the German Chemical-Pharmaceutical Industry', Discussion Paper P 02–902, Wissenschaftszentrum Berlin für Sozialforschung, August 2002; *PBIRG Perspective*, Volume 3, Number 1, 2001.
54. Lawton R. Burns, 'Matrix Management in Hospitals: Testing Theories of Matrix Structure and Development', *Administrative Science Quarterly* 34 (1989), 349–368.
55. Robert C. Ford and W. Alan Randolph, 'Cross-Functional Structures: A Review and Integration of Matrix Organizations and Project Management', *Journal of Management* 18 (June 1992), 267–294; and Duncan, 'What Is the Right Organization Structure?'
56. CNH Third Quarter 2007 Net Income Up 82 Percent From 2006, Marketwire, October 23, 2007; Morosini, P; Huber, H; Khandpur, D; Linguri, S (2005), 'CNH Global Construction Equipment: Building a New Global Organization Across Boundaries', ESMT European School of Management & Technology, Case number 306-136-1.
57. Carol Hymowitz, 'Managers Suddenly Have to Answer to a Crowd of Bosses' (In the Lead column), *The Wall Street Journal* (August 12, 2003), B1; and Michael Goold and Andrew Campbell, 'Making Matrix Structures Work: Creating Clarity on Unit Roles and Responsibilities', *European Management Journal* 21, no. 3 (June 2003), 351–363.
58. Christopher A. Bartlett and Sumantra Ghoshal, 'Matrix Management: Not a Structure, a Frame of Mind', *Harvard Business Review* (July–August 1990), 138–145.
59. Michael Hammer, 'Process Management and the Future of Six Sigma', *Sloan Management Review* (Winter 2002), 26–32; and Michael Hammer and Steve Stanton, 'How Process Enterprises *Really* Work', *Harvard Business Review* 77 (November–December 1999), 108–118.
60. 'Right People, Right Place, Right Time', *Excellence Wales*, Welsh Local Government Association case study, available at http://www.wlga.gov.uk/download.php?id=1135&l=1; Alaistair McLennan, 'LLPG: feel the difference!', *GeoConnexionUK News*, April/May 2007, pp 38–39.
61. Based on Ostroff, *The Horizontal Organization*, and Richard L. Daft, *Organization Theory and Design*, 6th ed. (Cincinnati, Ohio: South-Western, 1998), 250–253.
62. Frank Ostroff, *The Horizontal Organization*, Oxford, Oxford University Press, 1999, pp 115–130; Council of Mortgage Lenders (UK), 'Largest Mortgage Lenders – 2006', accessed at http://www.cml.org.uk/cml/filegrab/1MM10.XLS?ref=2772.
63. http://www.qube.ac.uk/QuBE/toolbox/qualbriefs/briefBusExcellence.pdf.
64. 'Calling Time On Telcos', *Business and Finance Magazine,* October 7, 2004; Graham Dwyer and Ciaran Doyle, 'Strategic Change at Avaya Ireland', Irish Management Institute case study 302-147-1.
65. Melissa A. Schilling and H. Kevin Steensma, 'The Use of Modular Organizational Forms: An Industry-Level Analysis', *Academy of Management Journal* 44, no. 6 (2001), 1149–1168; Jane C. Linder, 'Transformational Outsourcing', *MIT Sloan Management Review* (Winter 2004), 52–58; and Denis Chamberland, 'Is It Core or Strategic? Outsourcing as a Strategic Management Tool', *Ivey Business Journal* (July–August 2003), 1–5.
66. Denis Chamberland, 'Is It Core or Strategic?'; Philip Siekman, 'The Snap-Together Business Jet',

Fortune (January 21, 2002), 104[A]–104[H]; Keith H. Hammonds, 'Smart, Determined, Ambitious, Cheap: The New Face of Global Competition', *Fast Company* (February 2003), 91–97; Kathleen Kerwin, 'GM: Modular Plants Won't Be a Snap', *BusinessWeek* (November 9, 1998), 168–172; and Giuseppe Bonazzi and Cristiano Antonelli, 'To Make or To Sell? The Case of In-House Outsourcing at Fiat Auto', *Organization Studies* 24, no. 4 (2003), 575–594.

67. Schilling and Steensma, 'The Use of Modular Organizational Forms'; Raymond E. Miles and Charles C. Snow, 'The New Network Firm: A Spherical Structure Built on a Human Investment Philosophy', *Organizational Dynamics* (Spring 1995), 5–18; and R. E. Miles, C. C. Snow, J. A. Matthews, G. Miles and H. J. Coleman Jr., 'Organizing in the Knowledge Age: Anticipating the Cellular Form', *Academy of Management Executive* 11, no. 4 (1997), 7–24.
68. Paul Engle, 'You *Can* Outsource Strategic Processes', *Industrial Management* (January–February 2002), 13–18.
69. Don Tapscott, 'Rethinking Strategy in a Networked World', *Strategy & Business* 24 (Third Quarter, 2001), 34–41.
70. Tommi Rantanen, *University 2.0,* Helsinki, University of Technology Institute of Strategy and International Business, 2007; Teemu Arina, 'Blogs as Reflective Practice', conference, paper presented at Online Educa Berlin 2006, November 29–December 1, 2006.
71. Stuart Luman, Open Source Softwear, *Wired Magazine*, 13 June 2005; Mark Weingarten, 'Project Runway' for the t-shirt crowd', *Business 2.0 Magazine*, June 18, 2006.
72. Miles and Snow, 'The New Network Firm'; Gregory G. Dess, Abdul M. A. Rasheed, Kevin J. McLaughlin and Richard L. Priem, 'The New Corporate Architecture', *Academy of Management Executive* 9, no. 2 (1995), 7–20; and Engle, 'You *Can* Outsource Strategic Processes'.
73. The discussion of weaknesses is based on Engle, 'You *Can* Outsource Strategic Processes'; Henry W. Chesbrough and David J. Teece, 'Organizing for Innovation: When Is Virtual Virtuous?' *Harvard Business Review* (August 2002), 127–134; Dess et al., 'The New Corporate Architecture'; and N. Anand, 'Modular, Virtual and Hollow Forms of Organization Design', working paper, London Business School, 2000.
74. Werner Braun, Mark Wilcox and Paul Sparrow, 'Sony Europe – the leadership journey: Case a: a history of change', Lancaster University Management School Centre for Performance-led HR Case Study Series 2007 Stewart Clegg and Toyohiro Kono, 'Trends in Japanese Management: An Overview of Embedded Continuities and Disembedded Discontinuities', *Asia Pacific Journal of Management*, 19, 269–285, 2002.
75. Based on Child, *Organization*, Ch. 1; and Jonathan D. Day, Emily Lawson, and Keith Leslie, 'When Reorganization Works', *The McKinsey Quarterly*, 2003 Special Edition: The Value in Organization, 21–29.

PART III

OPEN SYSTEM DESIGN ELEMENTS

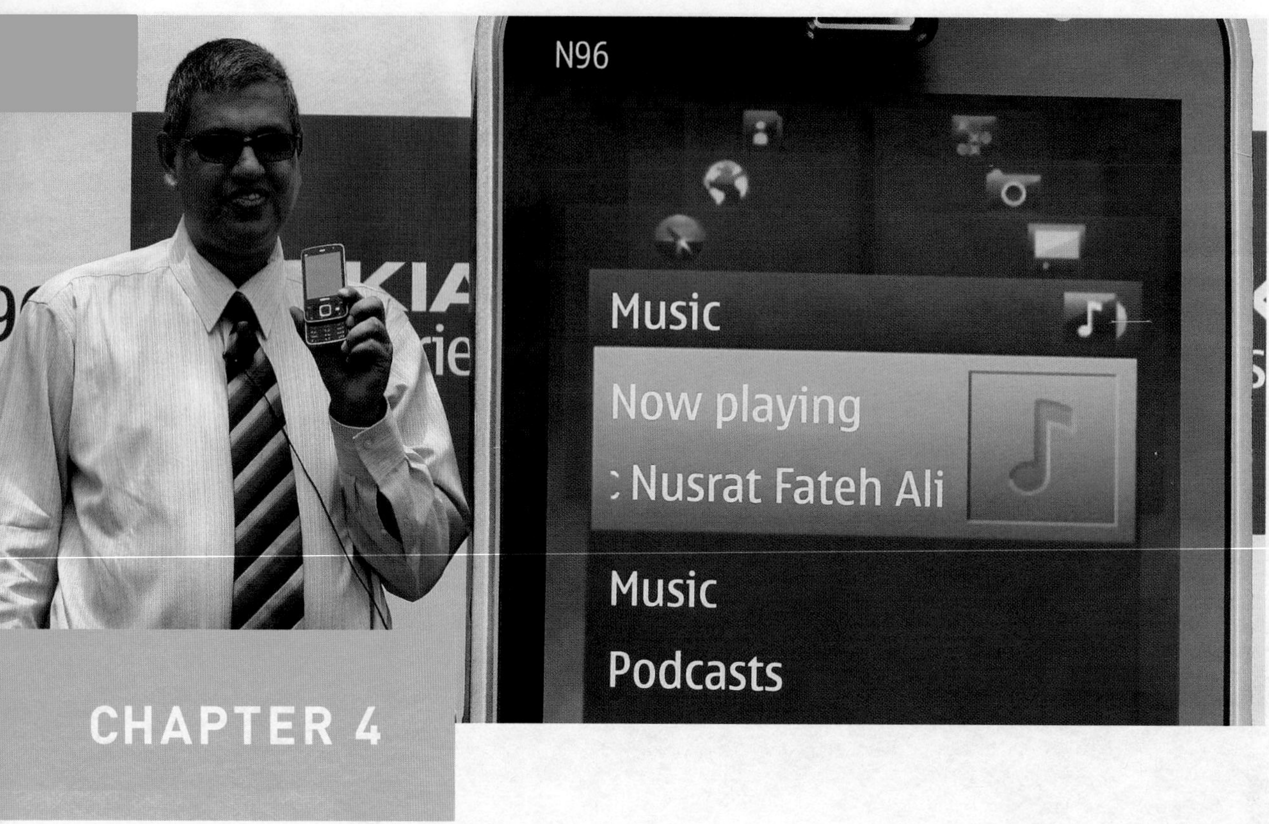

CHAPTER 4

THE EXTERNAL ENVIRONMENT

Nokia

Nokia's reign as the world's leading mobile phone manufacturer began in 1998, and the giant Finnish company looked poised to establish as dominant a position in its business as Microsoft had achieved in PC software, and IBM once had in computers. But by 2004, Nokia had hit serious turbulence, losing nearly a fifth of its 35 per cent global market share. Revenue growth shifted into reverse and the stock took a nosedive.

What went wrong? For one thing, Nokia missed the hottest growth sector in the first years of the new millennium, the expanding market for midrange models with cameras and high-resolution colour screens Nokia's leaders chose instead to pump hundreds of millions of euros into the development of 'smart phones' that allow users to surf the web, play video games, listen to music and watch movies or television shows. The problem was that in their first few years these new phones were too complicated, bulky and expensive for many consumers, who began turning instead to cheaper, stylish models from Motorola, Samsung and Siemens. The clamshell design, in particular, which allowed users to fold the phone in half when it wasn't in use, helped fuel a new cellphone boom in Europe and North America. Nokia also neglected some of its biggest customers. Mobile operators such as Orange SA, France Telecom's wireless unit, pushed for customized phones with special features that their customers wanted, but Nokia was slow to respond. 'Their attitude was that, given their size, they didn't need to listen to us', said an executive at one European mobile operator.

These missteps allowed rivals to gobble up market share. To get Nokia back on track, its top management prioritized the introduction of a competitive range of new midrange phones, slashed costs on low-end models for developing countries, and promised mobile operators to tailor phones to their specifications. Nokia also continues to invest heavily in higher-end phones that feature advanced software and allow users to send and receive emails, and surf the web, just like a computer. From 2005 Nokia's market share rebounded sharply, as the clamshell phones went out of fashion, high end phones shrunk to a pocketable size, and consumers finally warmed to the extra functionality internet phones provide. By 2007, market share was back up above 33 per cent of a much bigger global market, and the company's profit graph was rising impressively. It seemed that, despite some hiccups, Nokia's gamble on cutting edge technology had paid off.[1]

Many companies, like Nokia, face tremendous uncertainty in dealing with the external environment. The only way a high-tech company like Nokia can continue to grow is through innovation, yet unless the company makes products that people want to buy, the huge investments in research and development will not pay off.

Some companies get surprised by shifts in the environment and are unable to quickly adapt to new competition, changing consumer interests or innovative technologies. The music business has been particularly impacted by the shift to digital distribution of recorded music, and hard-to-combat piracy. Iconic record stores in many countries have disappeared or been forced to completely change the focus of their business in order to survive. The Virgin group sold off its music stores, while US-based Tower Records and Canada's Music World filed for bankruptcy,[2] and many smaller retail music chains have simply disappeared, in the wake of Apple's iPod and other new channels that allow music lovers to download just what they want. In the airline industry, major carriers have been pummelled by budget competitors. Belgium's flagship Sabena, and Switzerland's Swissair have both gone out of business, replaced by smaller and leaner carriers; Swissair's successor was eventually purchased in 2005 by the German-based carrier Lufthansa.[3] Meanwhile, during the 1990s and 2000s Ireland's Ryanair and the US budget carrier Southwest Airlines grew exponentially, until their low fare model was itself put in question by soaring fuel prices.[4] It is impossible for companies to avoid external shocks, but the well-structured, flexible company will be in a better position to emerge relatively unscathed from turbulence than rigid and top heavy organizations.[5]

Numerous factors in the external environment cause turbulence and uncertainty for organizations. The external environment, including international competition and events, is the source of major threats confronting today's organizations. The environment often imposes significant constraints on the choices that managers make for an organization.

Purpose of This Chapter

The purpose of this chapter is to develop a framework for assessing environments and how organizations can respond to them. First, we will identify the organizational domain and the sectors that influence the organization. Then, we will explore two major environmental forces on the organization – the need for information and the need for resources. Organizations respond to these forces through structural design, planning systems and attempts to change and control elements in the environment.

The Environmental Domain

In a broad sense the environment is infinite and includes everything outside the organization. However, the analysis presented here considers only those aspects of the environment to which the organization is sensitive and must respond to survive. Thus, **organizational environment** is defined as all elements that exist outside the boundary of the organization and have the potential to affect all or part of the organization.

The environment of an organization can be understood by analyzing its domain within external sectors. An organization's **domain** is the chosen environmental field of action. It is the territory an organization stakes out for itself with respect to products, services and markets served. Domain defines the organization's niche and defines those external sectors with which the organization will interact to accomplish its goals.

The environment comprises several **sectors** or subdivisions of the external environment that contain similar elements. Ten sectors can be analyzed for each organization: industry, raw materials, human resources, financial resources, market, technology, economic conditions, government, sociocultural and international. The sectors and a hypothetical organizational domain are illustrated in Exhibit 4.1. For most companies, the sectors in Exhibit 4.1 can be further subdivided into the task environment and general environment.

BRIEFCASE

As an organization manager, keep these guidelines in mind:

Organize elements in the external environment into ten sectors for analysis: industry, raw materials, human resources, financial resources, market, technology, economic conditions, government, sociocultural and international. Focus on sectors that may experience significant change at any time.

COUNTERPOINT 4.1

What is taken to be the 'environment' is always selected and interpreted by organizational members. They inevitably have particular agendas and priorities, leading them to emphasize some features and neglect others. In other words, the 'environment' is enacted, not given. In this sense, the environment is 'chosen'. But 'choice' is shaped and constrained by established agendas and perceptions that are difficult to change. Also there are numerous aspects of the 'environment' – such as fluctuations in interest rates or commodity prices – over which even the most resourceful executives can exercise very limited choice or control. Nonetheless, 'the environment' is subject to diverse interpretations or 'readings'. It is evident that, for example, Nokia executives 'read' the environment in a different way to those at Samsung. The decisions of Nokia executives (e.g. to concentrate on smart phones and neglect the middle market) effectively created an environment for other companies that successfully identified and exploited the opportunities presented to them. **Discuss**

EXHIBIT 4.1 An Organization's Environment

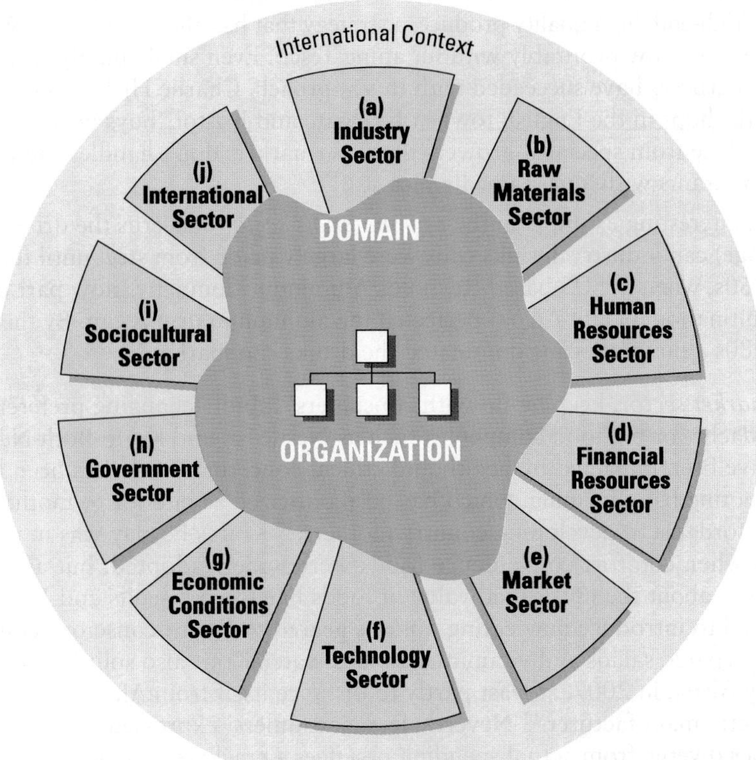

(a) Competitors, industry size and competitiveness, related industries
(b) Suppliers, manufacturers, real estate, services
(c) Labour market, employment agencies, universities, training schools, employees in other companies, unionization
(d) Stock markets, banks, savings and loans, private investors
(e) Customers, clients, potential users of products and services
(f) Techniques of production, science, computers, information technology, e-commerce
(g) Recession, unemployment rate, inflation rate, rate of investment, economics, growth
(h) City, state, federal laws and regulations, taxes, services, court system, political processes
(i) Age, values, beliefs, education, religion, work ethic, consumer and green movements
(j) Competition from and acquisition by foreign firms, entry into overseas markets, foreign customs, regulations, exchange rate

Task Environment

The **task environment** includes sectors with which the organization interacts directly and that have a direct impact on the organization's ability to achieve its goals. The task environment typically includes the industry, raw materials and market sectors, and perhaps the human resources and international sectors.

The following examples illustrate how each of these sectors can affect organizations:

- In the industry sector, traditional food retailers are being challenged by hypermarkets run by companies such as France's Carrefour, Britain's Tesco and US-based Wal-Mart, all of which also carry a wide range of clothes and other non-food items that typically enjoy a higher mark-up. This shift is forcing traditional food retailers to find new ways to compete. One strategy is to focus on high-end, high quality produce, a strategy that has allowed Britain's Waitrose chain to grow profitably without aping Tesco. Even small, highly specialized grocers have succeeded with this approach. Charlie Hicks, a greengrocer with shops in the English towns of Reigate and Bristol, 'buys only top-quality produce from specialist growers the supermarkets don't handle, and provides restaurants with 'unashamedly nice stuff'.[6,7]

- An interesting example in the *raw materials sector* concerns the drinks (beverage) can industry. Drinks cans were largely made from steel until the mid-1960s, when the US-based Reynolds Aluminum Company (now part of the multinational giant Alcoa) perfected the aluminium drinks can. By the mid-1980s aluminium cans dominated the drinks can market.[8,9]

In the *market sector*, keeping up with consumers' rapidly changing preferences is a real headache for big food companies such as Nestlé SA and Kraft. Both Nestlé and Kraft have been impacted by health and ethical concerns. Nestlé has been targeted for promoting baby formula, which has been criticized as inferior to mother's milk, and unaffordable to developing country mothers.[10] Kraft's heyday was in the 1960s and 70s when comfort convenience foods were widely adopted, but as concerns were raised about the nutritional value of foods like Oreo biscuits and Jell-O, Kraft was forced to introduce new eating options geared to health-conscious consumers, such as prepared salads and vitamin-enhanced water. Kraft also split from its parent company Altria, in 2007, at least partly to distance itself from Altria's role as a major cigarette manufacturer.[11] Nevertheless, consumers' expressed preferences may sometimes diverge from actual spending practices – crackers, biscuits and processed cheese remain major money-spinners for Kraft.

- The *human resources sector* is of significant concern to every business. In particular, managers in companies in both developed and developing countries worry about shortages of skilled workers. Industry leaders in countries as diverse as Canada and Thailand are urging their national governments to invest heavily in education and skills, in order to meet the challenges of the globalized economy. Gwyn Morgan, the former CEO of Canada's EnCana, one of the world's largest oil and gas companies, says that Canada needs to accept more highly skilled immigrants, as well as doing a better job in its education system and in training workers on-the-job.[12] Similarly, Thai business leaders have urged their government to invest more in education and skills training if the country is to achieve its ambition of becoming the 'Detroit of Asia'; Asia's manufacturing hub for the automobile industry.[13,14]
- For most companies today, in whatever country, the *international environment* is crucial. Offshoring is a major issue, with companies in both the developed economies of Europe and North America, and emerging economies throughout the world, trying to maximize the possibilities globalization provides to produce in low-cost economies and sell in high value markets. China and India have become major locales for low-cost manufacturing and service industries, respectively, although many other countries from Vietnam to South Africa are also getting in on the global restructuring of business processes. The growing strength of Asian economies, in particular, is allowing emerging economy companies like Taiwan's Acer, India's Ranbaxy and China's Huawei to establish themselves as big players and respected brand names in developed country markets.[15]

General Environment

The **general environment** includes those sectors that might not have a direct impact on the daily operations of a firm but will indirectly influence it. The general environment often includes the government, sociocultural, economic conditions, technology and financial resources sectors. These sectors affect all organizations eventually. Consider the following examples:

COUNTERPOINT 4.2

It is analytically helpful to break down the environment into 'sectors' as this makes it easier to grasp its key elements. But it is important to appreciate how aspects of these elements are interconnected and interdependent. 'Sectors' do not exist except as a heuristic device. What exists is a complex mix of properties (e.g. natural resources, technologies) and practices, labelled 'environment'. To simplify and order this complexity, analytical tools – like 'sectors' have been devised. But this way of seeing is also a way of not seeing. **Discuss**

- In the *government sector*, European Union (EU) environmental and consumer protection legislation impacts both domestic European and foreign firms. For example, one rule requires chemical makers doing business in EU countries to run safety and environmental impact tests on more than 30,000 chemicals, a process that could cost these companies more than €5 billion. Other regulations require companies to pick up the tab for recycling the products they sell in the EU. To an increasing extent, the regulatory environment is becoming global, as national governments model cutting edge practices from other jurisdictions.[16,17]
- Shifting demographics is a significant element in the *sociocultural sector*. In most developed countries, the population is aging rapidly, affecting both human resource practices and markets. Population mobility has expanded rapidly, with people drawn from poorer parts of the world to the wealthier countries of Europe and North America in search of economic opportunity. They bring their tastebuds and entertainment preferences with them, leading to market fragmentation and a plethora of niche opportunities from ethnic foods to narrowcast communications. Congolese delicacies are on sale in many Belgian supermarkets, just as British food stores now have special aisles for Polish food,[18] and in the United States, entire supermarkets have been converted to all-Hispanic *supermercados* to compete with Hispanic merchants.[19]
- General *economic conditions* often affect the way a company does business. Germany's two most celebrated daily newspapers, the *Frankfurter Allgemeine Zeitung* and the *Süddeutsche Zeitung*, expanded pell-mell during the economic boom of the late 1990s. When the economy crashed, both papers found themselves in dire financial circumstances and had to cut jobs, close regional offices, scrap special sections and cut out customized inserts.[20]

The *technology sector* is an area in which massive changes have occurred in recent years, from digital music and video on demand to advances in cloning technology and stem-cell research. One technology having a tremendous impact on organizations is online software allowing people to easily communicate with the world through online versions of diaries, known as Web logs, or *blogs*. By late 2007, one study found that 120,000 new blogs were being created each day. While most are read by few people beyond friends and family, slick and focused sites can attract thousands. Corporations that fail to respond to customer concerns can easily become the target of 'viral' campaigns conducted through blogs that can gather together these disgruntled customers and negatively impact the corporation's image.[21]

- All businesses have to be concerned with *financial resources*, but they are 'make or break' for many entrepreneurs starting a new business. In expansionary times, capital can be relatively easy to raise, but when prospects suddenly darken, entrepreneurs can be left high and dry. In early 2007, aviation veteran and entrepreneur Tim Lee announced ambitious plans for a new Wales-based European budget airline, flyforbeans.com, copying Irish-based Ryanair's successful formula. But oil prices, one of the major cost factors for airlines, soon began to rise dramatically. Financing negotiations stalled, and one year later the airline was still just a dream.[22]

International Context

As discussed earlier in this chapter, distinctions between foreign and domestic operations have become increasingly irrelevant. For example, in the auto industry, Ford owns Sweden's Volvo automobile manufacturing operations, while Germany's Daimler owned US big-three auto manufacturer Chrysler for several years until selling a majority stake to a private equity firm in 2007.[23] Toyota, which has overtaken America's General Motors as the world's largest automaker, is a Japan-based company, but almost half of its worldwide production is outside Japan (see Exhibit 4.2)[24] Increasingly, corporations, no matter their home, are engaged in partnerships and alliances with other firms all around the world. These increasing global interconnections represent both opportunities and threats for organizations. The international dimension of organization theory and design will be covered in detail in Chapter 6.

The growing importance of the international sector means that the environment for all organizations is becoming extremely complex and extremely competitive. However, every organization faces uncertainty domestically as well as globally. Consider how changing elements in the various environmental sectors have created uncertainty for advertising agencies such as the US-based Ogilvy & Mather.

EXHIBIT 4.2 Toyota 2006 Worldwide Production Figures

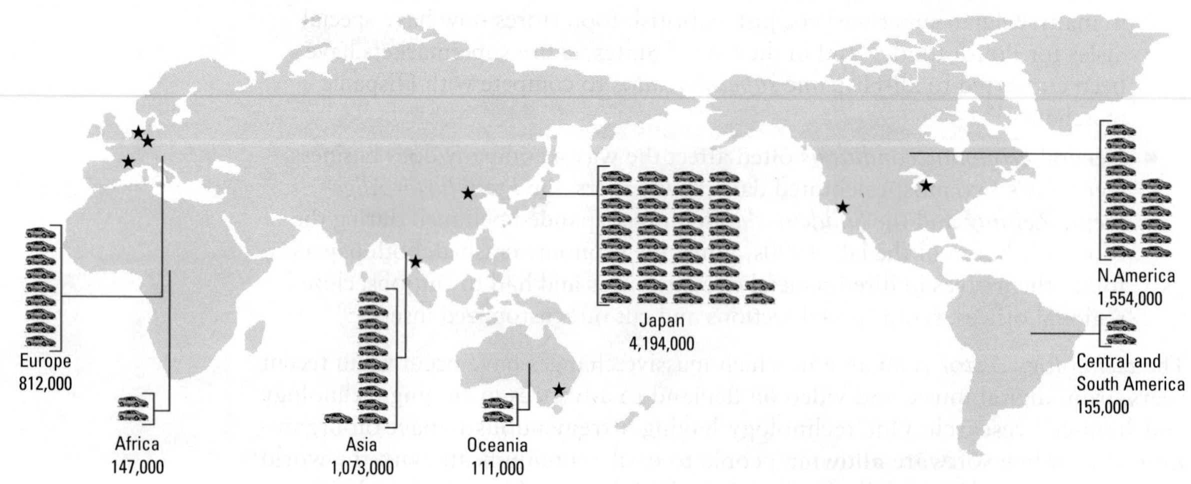

(Source: http://www.toyota.co.jp/en/about_toyota/manufacturing/worldwide.html on June 18, 2008. Reproduced with permission.)

Ogilvy & Mather

It was a sad day in the advertising industry when Ogilvy & Mather, one of the most respected advertising agencies on New York's Madison Avenue, was reduced to competing for business in a live online auction. The company had already been bought out by Britain's WPP consortium in 1989. Now its very survival seemed in doubt.

The world has changed dramatically since Ogilvy & Mather's founder David Ogilvy made deals with corporate CEOs over golf games and could reach 90 per cent of the American public with a prime-time commercial on network television. Today, agency executives frequently have to bargain with people from their client's procurement department, who are used to beating down suppliers on the price of cardboard boxes or paper bags.

The economic decline that followed the 'dot-com crash' and the September 11, 2001 terrorist attacks led to the worst advertising recession in the United States in more than half a century. Marketing budgets were often the first to be cut. Worldwide, advertising spending declined seven per cent in 2001. US-based agencies laid off 40,000 employees, nearly 20 per cent of their workforce. Corporations began striking much less generous deals with their advertising agencies. Instead of the 15 per cent commission they used to pay on media purchases, many corporate procurement departments require agencies to itemize their labour costs and justify all the expenses they are billing the client. This knock-on effect of wider political and economic disturbances is compounded by a transformation in the communications industry. In most countries of the world, up until the 1980s, advertising agencies could reach most people through a handful of TV stations and newspapers, Now, there are hundreds of television channels catering to every conceivable taste and subgroup in the population, traditional newspapers are on the decline and a plethora of new media are cropping up. Corporations are clamouring for more innovative low-key approaches, such as product placements in video games or products integrated into television shows and music events, as well as lower-cost options such as direct mail and Internet advertising. Yet many agencies have been slow to adapt, still clinging to the notion that costly primetime television commercials will pay off.

The combination of weak economic conditions, media fragmentation, new technologies and changing habits had the advertising industry reeling. As Ogilvy & Mather's CEO, Shelly Lazarus, said of the first few years of the twenty-first century, 'These have not been the best years.'[25] However, the company restructured to take account of new communication technologies, and was able to bounce back, winning both awards and big new contracts around the world in 2006 and 2007. Industry magazine *PR Week* said of the firm, 'Ogilvy PR is one of the few agencies that has a meaningful presence in every global region, and multi-region wins for the firm in 2006 show that its wayfarer spirit is providing great returns'.[26]

Advertising agencies aren't the only organizations that have had to adapt to massive shifts in the environment. In the following sections, we will discuss in greater detail how companies can cope with and respond to environmental uncertainty and instability.

Environmental Uncertainty

How does the environment influence an organization? The patterns and events occurring in the environment can be described along several dimensions, such as whether the environment is stable or unstable, homogeneous or heterogeneous, simple or complex; the *munificence*, or amount of resources available to support the organization's growth; whether those resources are concentrated or dispersed; and the degree of consensus in the environment regarding the organization's intended domain.[27] These dimensions boil down to two essential ways the environment influences organizations: (1) the need for information about the environment and (2) the need for resources from the environment. The environmental conditions of complexity and change create a greater need to gather information and to respond based on that information. The organization also is concerned with scarce material and financial resources and with the need to ensure availability of resources.

See online
COUNTERPOINT 4.8

Environmental uncertainty refers primarily to those factors that an organization deals with on a regular, day-to-day basis. Recall the earlier discussion of the general environment and the task environment. Although general environmental factors – such as economic conditions, social trends or technological changes – can create uncertainty for organizations, determining an organization's environmental uncertainty generally means focusing on aspects of the *task environment*, such as how many elements the organization deals with regularly, how rapidly these elements change and so forth. To assess uncertainty, each sector of the organization's task environment can be analyzed along dimensions such as stability or instability and degree of complexity.[28] The total amount of uncertainty felt by an organization is the uncertainty accumulated across environmental sectors.

Organizations must cope with and manage uncertainty to be effective. **Uncertainty** is created by decision makers not having sufficient information about environmental factors, and consequently being unable to accurately predict external changes. Uncertainty increases the risk of failure for organizational responses and makes it difficult to assess costs and probabilities associated with decision alternatives.[29] The remainder of this section will focus on the information perspective, which is concerned with uncertainty created by the extent to which the environment is simple or complex and the extent to which events are stable or unstable. Later in the chapter, we discuss how organizations control the environment to acquire needed resources.

See online
COUNTERPOINT 4.9

COUNTERPOINT 4.3

If uncertainty is a result of insufficient information, it is impossible to assess its scope and significance. It is debatable if uncertainty arises from a lack of information as it is also a matter of how the available information is evaluated. If senior executives are highly risk-averse, there will never be sufficient information to overcome their intransigence and indecision. It is also questionable whether organizations can be managed on a rational basis – in the sense of waiting for information to become available in order to satisfactorily map or predict changes in the environment. Uncertainties are a function of the willingness to take risks as much as they are related to an insufficiency of information. **Discuss**

Simple–Complex Dimension

The **simple–complex dimension** concerns environmental complexity, which refers to heterogeneity, or the number and dissimilarity of external elements relevant to an organization's operations. The more external factors that regularly influence the organization and the greater number of other companies in an organization's domain, the greater the complexity. A complex environment is one in which the organization interacts with and is influenced by numerous diverse external elements. In a simple environment, the organization interacts with and is influenced by only a few similar external elements.

See online
COUNTERPOINT 4.10

Aerospace firms such as Europe's Airbus and America's Boeing operate in a complex environment, as do universities. Universities span a large number of subjects or technologies and are continually buffeted by social, cultural and value changes.

Have you read this book?

Cradle to Cradle: Remaking the Way We Make Things

BY WILLIAM MCDONOUGH AND MICHAEL BRAUNGART

In this chapter we have discussed the environment in which operate, and the impact it has upon them. No environment is more important, of course, than the physical environment, whose well-being is a precondition not just for successful business but for the survival of humanity. William McDonough, an American architect, and Michael Braungart, a German chemist, believe that both business and environmentalists often misunderstand the challenge of true sustainability, which they believe lies in the design process.

Working with instead of against the natural environment

To start with, say McDonough and Braungart, we need to better understand the living earth. Although environmentalists often argue that we must reduce waste, the authors point out that the natural earth itself 'wastes', except in a productive way. Most trees, for example, shed their leaves every year, but we wouldn't dream of calling this wasteful, because we understand that the dead leaves provide nutrient for rejuvenating the soil and making it fertile for new growth, from which McDonough and Braungart gleaned the principle that waste=food. Product and service design needs to build from the intelligence of natural systems, so that business and the earth can healthily co-exist.

When the City of Hannover, Germany, found out it was going to host the 2000 World's Fair, the event planners invited McDonough and Brautigan to come up with a set of sustainability principles that would govern the Fair's design and operations. These Hannover principles have gone on to become a manifesto for intelligent, sustainable, industrial design:

1 Insist on rights of humanity and nature to co-exist in a healthy, supportive, diverse and sustainable condition.
2 Recognize interdependence. The elements of human design interact with and depend upon the natural world, with broad and diverse implications at every scale. Expand design considerations to recognizing even distant effects.
3 Respect relationships between spirit and matter. Consider all aspects of human settlement including community, dwelling, industry and trade in terms of existing and evolving connections between spiritual and material consciousness.
4 Accept responsibility for the consequences of design decisions upon human well-being, the viability of natural systems and their right to co-exist.
5 Create safe objects of long-term value. Do not burden future generations with requirements for maintenance or vigilant administration of potential danger due to the careless creation of products, processes or standards.
6 Eliminate the concept of waste. Evaluate and optimize the full life-cycle of products and processes, to approach the state of natural systems, in which there is no waste.
7 Rely on natural energy flows. Human designs should, like the living world, derive their creative forces from perpetual solar income. Incorporate this energy efficiently and safely for responsible use.
8 Understand the limitations of design. No human creation lasts forever and design does not solve all problems. Those who create and plan should practice humility in the face of nature. Treat nature as a model and mentor, not as an inconvenience to be evaded or controlled.
9 Seek constant improvement by the sharing of knowledge. Encourage direct and open communication between colleagues, patrons, manufacturers and users to link long term sustainable considerations with ethical responsibility, and re-establish the integral relationship between natural processes and human activity.

One key sustainable technology is harnessing natural power, and in particular solar energy, which operated the natural world long before we developed an addiction for fossil fuel power. To an increasing extent, the search for 'alternative fuels' is focusing on solar, wind and tide energy, which are genuinely renewable, rather than bio-fuels; usually crops like palm oil, that deprive citizens of developing countries of crucial land on which to grow food crops, and create harmful greenhouse gas emissions when burned.

McDonough and Braungart have been involved in numerous industrial design projects that have put their principles into practice. Here are just two examples:

- The Swiss furniture manufacturer Rohner and the textile design company DesignTex came up with a hardwearing textile for covering furniture that is both environmentally safe and so easily recyclable that it can simply be put in the ground when no longer needed, where it quickly turns into nutritious plant mulch.
- Alain Duval of Québec, Canada's Victor Innovatex was proud of his company's reputation for high quality textiles, but he wanted to do something of wider environmental benefit. While polyester, a key synthetic fibre, is recyclable, the recycling process typically results in a lower value product. For example, used polyester is often turned into speed bumps to reduce traffic speed. Though this is better than throwing it straight into the landfill, it is part of a downward value spiral that is ultimately not sustainable. Victor Innovatex redesigned the polyster production process to the molecular level, choosing components that are all recyclable, as well as a catalyst that is environmentally safe. The Eco-Intelligent Polyester that came out of their research is the first infinitely recyclable polyester, a product that can be endlessly recycled into new polyester when it wears out.

William McDonough and Michael Braungart (2002), *Cradle to Cradle: Remaking the Way We Make Things,* New York, North Point Press; http://www.mcdonough.com/principles.pdf, accessed on April 14, 2009.

Universities also must cope with multiple and ever-changing government regulations, competition for top students and leading academics and scarce financial resources for many programmes. They deal with funding agencies, professional and scientific associations, alumni, parents, foundations, politicians, community residents, international agencies, donors and corporations. This large number of external elements makes up the organization's domain, creating a complex environment. On the other hand, a family-owned hardware store in a small town is in a relatively simple environment. The store does not have to deal with complex technologies or extensive government regulations. Human resources are typically not a problem because the store is run by family members and part-time help. The main external elements of real importance are a few competitors, suppliers and customers.

See online **COUNTERPOINT 4.11**

Stable–Unstable Dimension

The **stable–unstable dimension** refers to whether elements in the environment are dynamic. An environmental domain is stable if it remains the same over a period of months or years. Under unstable conditions, environmental elements shift abruptly. Environmental domains seem to be increasingly unstable for most organizations. This chapter's Bookmark examines the volatile nature of today's business world and gives some tips for managing in a fast-shifting environment.

Instability may occur when competitors react with aggressive moves and countermoves regarding advertising and new products, as happened with Nokia, described in the chapter opening. Sometimes unpredictable events create unstable conditions. These can range from the global – ranging from the sudden spike in world oil prices and the global credit crunch in 2007 and 2008 – to the local, such as the 2006 outbreak of salmonella poisoning in the UK, caused by unsanitary conditions in Cadbury's Mars Bar manufacturing plant.[30] Today, anti-corporate and 'culture jamming' (see Adbusters and 'hate sites' on the World Wide Web, such as Ihatestarbucks.com, http://www.orangeproblems.co.uk, and www.killercoke.org) are an important source of instability. One estimate puts the number of anti-corporate websites on the internet at over 10,000.[31] In addition, freewheeling bloggers can destroy a company's reputation virtually overnight. Kryptonite's reputation in bicycle locks plummeted after a web log was posted claiming that the locks could be opened with a Bic pen. After 10 days of blogging, Kryptonite announced a free product exchange that would cost it about $10 million.[32]

Although environments are more unstable for most organizations today, an example of a traditionally stable environment is a public utility such as a provider of water, gas, or electricity.[33] For many years, demand and supply factors for public utilities were stable, often operating either as regulated monopolies or as state-owned enterprises. Gradual increase in demand tended to occur, but were easily predicted over time. Toy companies, by contrast, typically have an unstable environment. Hot new toys are difficult to predict, a problem compounded by the encroachment of new technologies like video games. Adding to the instability for toymakers is the changing retail market, with hypermarkets like France's Carrefour and Wal-Mart/Asda undercutting even the biggest specialist toy retailers. Toy manufacture has also been impacted by internationalization of the business process, with much manufacture offshored to China and elsewhere in Asia.[34]

COUNTERPOINT 4.4

Stable environments may be a thing of the past. Even public utilities are feeling the impacts of rapid transformation in business processes, including the break-up of monopolies in the energy market; the British consumer for example is able to select from any of dozens of different gas and electricity suppliers. The tendency towards financialization,[35] including the ever-more innovative packaging of business components into instruments for resource mobilization and speculation, can create opacity and instability, where the line between ingenuity and criminality can seem hazy as best, as the infamous cases of Enron and Société Générale seem to demonstrate.[36] **Discuss**

Framework

The simple–complex and stable–unstable dimensions are combined into a framework for assessing environmental uncertainty in Exhibit 4.3. In the *simple, stable* environment, uncertainty is low. There are only a few external elements to contend with, and they tend to remain stable. The *complex, stable* environment represents somewhat greater uncertainty. A large number of elements have to be scanned, analyzed and acted upon for the organization to perform well. External elements do not change rapidly or unexpectedly in this environment.

Even greater uncertainty is felt in the *simple, unstable* environment.[37] Rapid change creates uncertainty for managers. Even though the organization has few external elements, those elements are hard to predict, and they react unexpectedly to organizational initiatives. The greatest uncertainty for an organization occurs in the *complex, unstable* environment. A large number of elements impinge upon the organization, and they shift frequently or react strongly to organizational initiatives. When several sectors change simultaneously, the environment becomes turbulent.[38]

Beer distributors function in a simple, stable environment. Demand for beer changes only gradually. The distributor has an established delivery route, and supplies of beer arrive on schedule. Universities, home appliance manufacturers and insurance companies are in somewhat stable, complex environments. A large number of external elements are present, but although they change, changes are gradual and predictable.

See online COUNTERPOINT 4.12

Toy manufacturers are in simple, unstable environments. Organizations that design, make and sell toys, as well as those that are involved in the clothing or music industry, face shifting supply and demand. Most e-commerce companies focus on a specific competitive niche and, hence, operate in simple but unstable environments

EXHIBIT 4.3 Framework for Assessing Environmental Uncertainty

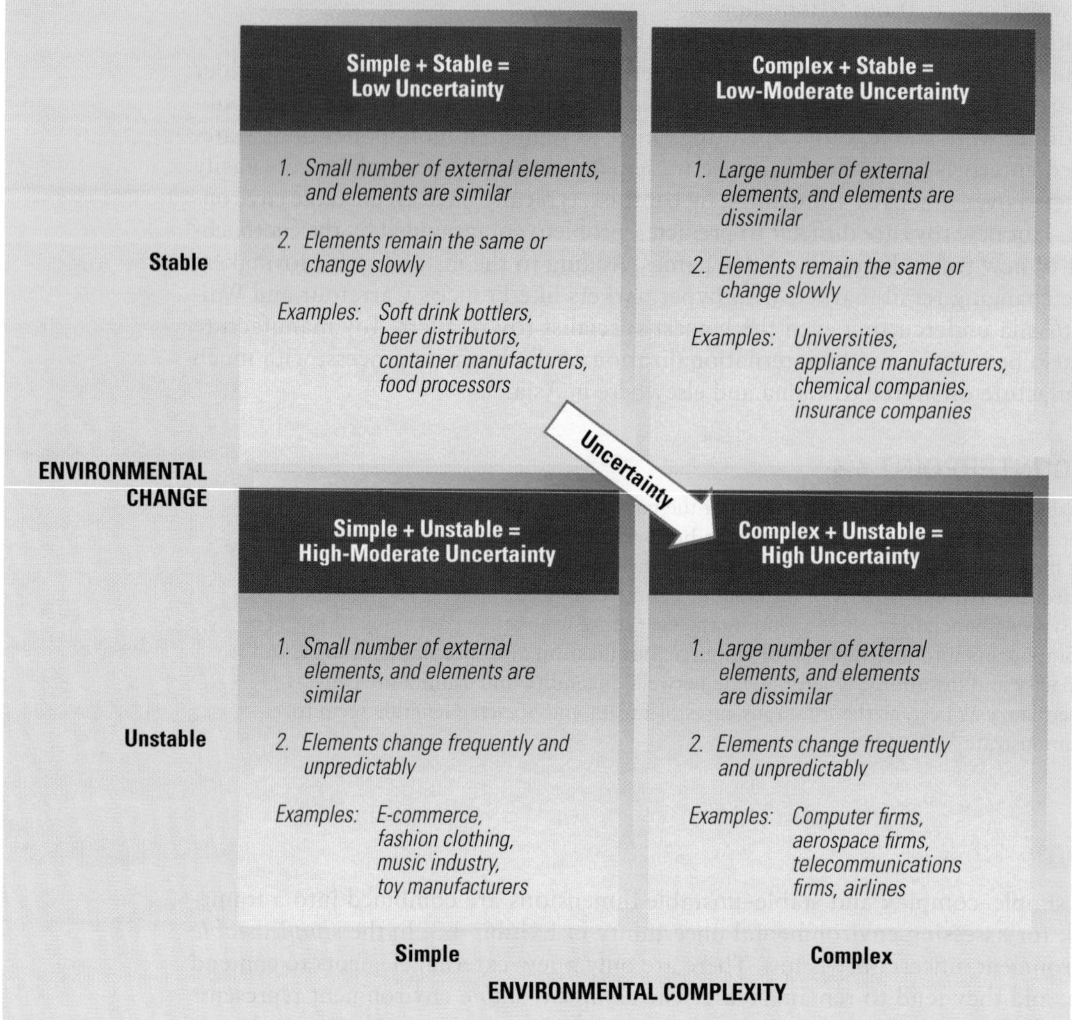

Source: Adapted and reprinted from 'Characteristics of Perceived Environments and Perceived Environmental Uncertainty,' by Robert B. Duncan, published in *Administrative Science Quarterly* 17 (1972), 313–327, by permission of The *Administrative Science Quarterly*. Copyright © 1972 by Cornell University.

as well. Although there may be few elements to contend with – e.g. technology, competitors – they are difficult to predict and change abruptly and unexpectedly.

The telecommunications industry and the airline industry face complex, unstable environments. Many external sectors are changing simultaneously. In the case of airlines, in just a few years they have been confronted with the multiplication of security measures due to the threat of terrorism, the influx of low cost carriers like Ryanair, large tax increases on air travel and dramatic fluctuations in the price of jet fuel.[39]

Adapting to Environmental Uncertainty

Once you see how environments differ with respect to change and complexity, the next question is, 'How do organizations adapt to each level of environmental uncertainty?' Environmental uncertainty represents an important contingency for organization structure and internal behaviours. Recall from Chapter 3 that organizations best equipped to face uncertainty generally have a more horizontal structure as this encourages cross-functional communication and collaboration to adapt to environmental change. In this section we discuss in more detail how the environment affects organizations. An organization in a stable and comparatively certain environment will tend to be managed and controlled differently from an organization in an uncertain environment with respect to positions and departments, organizational differentiation and integration, control processes and future planning and forecasting. A key to organizational effectiveness and prosperity is developing an appropriate fit between the elements of internal structure and salient features of the external environment.

Positions and Departments

As the complexity and uncertainty in the external environment increases, the number of positions and departments within the organization also tends to increase, which in turn increases internal complexity. This relationship is part of being an open system. Each sector in the external environment requires an employee or department to deal with it. The human resource department deals with people who want to work for the company. The marketing department finds customers. Procurement employees obtain raw materials from perhaps hundreds of suppliers. The finance group deals with bankers and venture capitalists. The legal department works with the courts and government agencies. Most companies have added information technology departments to deal with the increasing complexity of computerized information and knowledge management systems, and many have created e-business departments to handle electronic commerce.

Government also responds to environmental uncertainty by changing its structures. Terrorist threats have led many countries to strengthen their border controls through merging agencies that previously worked largely independently.[40]

Buffering and Boundary Spanning

The traditional approach to coping with environmental uncertainty was to establish departments or roles to buffer or absorb its effects upon the 'technical core' of organizations.[41] The technical core comprises those people who perform the production subsystem function and actually produces the product and service outputs of the organization (see Chapter 1). Buffer departments and roles support and service the technical core by taking care of the flows of materials, resources and money between the environment and the organization. They enable the technical core to function efficiently. For example, the purchasing department buffers the technical core by stockpiling supplies and raw materials. The human resource department buffers the technical core by handling the uncertainty associated with finding, hiring and training production employees.

The approach of buffering is somewhat static and defensive. Some organizations are attempting to remove or reduce the buffers in a way that exposes the technical core to the uncertain environment. Potentially, this has the benefit of adapting the core more directly to its environment as emphasis is placed upon being well-connected to customers and suppliers rather than ensuring the stability of the established technical core. For example, the American farm machinery manufacturer John Deere has assembly-line workers visiting local farms to determine and respond to customer concerns. The computer software industry has made involving consumers in product testing a routine activity, with 'alpha' and 'beta' versions of products under development provided free to enthusiast in return for feedback on product flaws and areas for improvement.[42]

As an organization manager, keep these guidelines in mind:

Scan the external environment for threats, changes and opportunities. Use boundary-spanning roles, such as market research and competitive-intelligence departments, to bring into the organization information about changes in the environment. Enhance boundary-spanning capabilities when the environment is uncertain.

Boundary-spanning roles link and coordinate an organization with key elements in the external environment. Boundary spanning is primarily concerned with the exchange of information to (1) detect and bring into the organization information about changes in the environment and (2) send information into the environment that presents the organization in a favourable light.[43]

Keeping in direct touch with what is going on in the environment can facilitate greater responsiveness to market changes and other developments. A study of high-tech firms found that 97 per cent of competitive failures resulted from lack of attention to market changes or the failure to act on vital information.[44] To detect and bring important information into the organization, boundary personnel scan the environment. For example, a market-research department scans and monitors trends in consumer tastes. Boundary spanners in engineering and research and development (R&D) departments scan new technological developments, innovations and raw materials. Boundary spanners prevent the organization from stagnating by keeping top managers informed about environmental changes. Often, the greater the uncertainty in the environment, the greater the importance of boundary spanners.[45]

See online COUNTERPOINT 4.13

One new approach to boundary spanning is **business intelligence**, which refers to the high-tech analysis of large amounts of internal and external data to spot patterns and relationships that might be significant. For example, the US company Verizon uses business-intelligence to actively monitor customer interactions so that it can catch problems and fix them almost immediately.[46] Tools to automate the process have been one of the hottest areas of software development in recent years, with global spending on business intelligence software of over $5 billion in 2007.[47]

COUNTERPOINT 4.5

Sometimes the line between business intelligence and espionage is a thin one. Verizon, along with AT&T and a host of less well-known companies, also make their expertise available, at a fee, to state intelligence services such as America's CIA. Questions have been raised about the appropriateness of outsourcing national intelligence, about whether companies involved in both business and national security intelligence-gathering have an unfair business advantage, and whether there is proper public scrutiny of privatized intelligence gathering.[48] **Discuss**

Business intelligence is related to another important area of boundary spanning, known as *competitive intelligence* (CI). The Society of Competitive Intelligence Professionals has its own academic journal and its membership of 3,000 has more than doubled since 1997. Colleges and universities in North America and Europe are setting up degree programmes in CI to respond to the growing demand for these professionals in organizations.[49,50] Competitive intelligence gives top executives a systematic way to collect and analyze public information about rivals and use it to make better decisions.[51] Using techniques that range from Internet surfing to digging through trash cans, intelligence professionals dig up information on competitors' new products, manufacturing costs or training methods and share it with top leaders.

In today's turbulent environment, many successful companies involve everyone in boundary-spanning activities. People at the grass-roots level are often able to see and interpret changes or problems sooner than managers, who are typically more removed from the day-to-day work.[52] At Canada's Cognos corporation, which sells planning and budgeting programmes to large corporations, any of the company's 3,500 employees can submit scoops about competitors through an internal Web site called Street Fighter. Each day, R&D and sales managers pore over the dozens of entries. Good tips are rewarded with prizes.[53,54]

The boundary task of sending information into the environment to represent the organization is used to influence other people's perception of the organization. In the marketing department, advertising and sales people represent the organization to customers. Purchasers may call on suppliers and describe purchasing needs. The legal department informs lobbyists and elected officials about the organization's needs or views on political matters. Many companies set up their own Web pages to present the organization in a favourable light. For example, to counteract sites that criticize their business practices in developing countries, Nike and Shell, among many others, have created Web sites specifically to tell their side of the story.[55,56]

All organizations have to keep in touch with the environment. Zara, the Spain-headquartered clothing chain featured below in the *In Practice* text box, keeps its finger on the pulse of fashion, becoming the world's biggest fashion retail chain, with shops in 56 countries, only 30 years after its formation in 1975.

Differentiation and Integration

Another response to environmental uncertainty is the amount of differentiation and integration among departments. Organizational **differentiation** is 'the differences

Zara

Amancio Ortega Gaona lives quietly in a modest apartment in La Coruna, Spain, but he has lived one of the most dramatic rags-to-riches stories in modern business. Gaona started in the rag trade at 14 as a junior assistant in a shirt store, but now owns a majority stake in Inditex, the family-controlled holding company of which Zara is the biggest asset. Gaona has succeeded in the fickle fashion business by being able to respond to changing fashions by producing new clothes lines within four to six weeks.[57] Zara's success is all the more remarkable because unlike most of its competitors (see H&M, profiled in Chapter 6), Zara outsources little of its production to low cost developing countries.

Zara's managers for each of its product lines keep their eyes peeled for new fashion opportunities, for example copying one of singer Madonna's costumes from a major international tour and having the product on sale before the end of the tour. Sensitivity to the external environment extends to pricing policy. Rather than operating on a cost-plus basis, Zara sets its prices according to its image and market position in different countries; in Spain the company is a price leader, while in North America it is seen as a premium brand and prices are accordingly higher. Typically, Zara prices its clothes below the best known brands like Gap, but above more mass market retailers such as H&M in Europe and Old Navy in North America.

Like all successful companies, Zara knows its customers well and tailors its offer to meet their expectations, 'Zara's objective is not that consumers buy a lot but that they buy often and will find something new every time they enter the store', says a senior company manager. Unlike other fashion retailers, Zara spends very little on advertising. Instead, the company ensures it has good, highly visible high street locations. Its store managers are expected to know their customers well, their paycheques are partly based on the accuracy of their sales predictions. The close attention Zara pays to its customers means the chain has a much lower level of new product failures, about one per cent, than the industry average of at least ten per cent.

Zara is in a difficult business; fashion tastes are notoriously fickle. However, its close attention to its external environment means it is better equipped than many of its competitors to react effectively to external threats and opportunities.[58]

in cognitive and emotional orientations among managers in different functional departments, and the difference in formal structure among these departments'.[59] When the external environment is complex and rapidly changing, organizational departments become highly specialized to handle the uncertainty in their external sector. Success in each sector requires special expertise and behaviour. Employees in an R&D department thus have unique attitudes, values, goals and education that distinguish them from employees in manufacturing or sales departments.

COUNTERPOINT 4.6

A risk associated with this approach is the creation of 'silos' so that uncertainties are handled – assessed and addressed – in a fragmented manner. It can easily be assumed that some other department is handling an issue; or there wasteful duplication between departments as a consequence of a lack of coordination. To some degree the horizontal forms of communication and coordination discussed in Chapter 3 mitigate such risks. **Discuss**

A study by Paul Lawrence and Jay Lorsch examined three organizational departments – manufacturing, research and sales – in ten corporations.[60] This study found that each department evolved toward a different orientation and structure to deal with specialized parts of the external environment. The market, scientific and manufacturing sub-environments identified by Lawrence and Lorsch are illustrated in Exhibit 4.4. Each department interacted with different external groups. The differences that evolved among departments within the organizations are shown in Exhibit 4.5. To work effectively with the scientific sub-environment, R&D had a goal of quality work, a long time horizon (up to five years), an informal structure and task-oriented employees. Sales was at the opposite extreme. It had a goal of customer satisfaction, was oriented toward the short term (two weeks or so), had a very formal structure, and was socially oriented.

One outcome of high differentiation is that coordination among departments becomes difficult. More time and resources must be devoted to achieving coordination when attitudes, goals and work orientation differ so widely.

EXHIBIT 4.4 Organizational Departments Differentiate to Meet Needs of Subenvironments

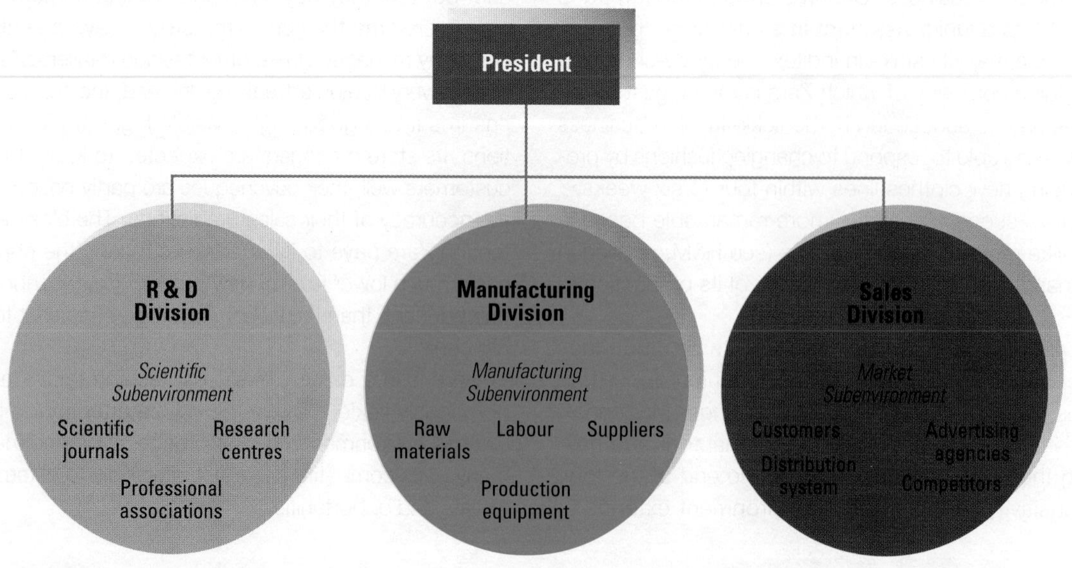

EXHIBIT 4.5 Differences in Goals and Orientations among Organizational Departments

Characteristic	R&D Department	Manufacturing Department	Sales Department
Goals	New developments, quality	Efficient production	Customer satisfaction
Time horizon	Long	Short	Short
Interpersonal orientation	Mostly task	Task	Social
Formality of structure	Low	High	High

Source: Based on Paul R. Lawrence and Jay W. Lorsch, *Organization and Environment* (Homewood, Ill.: Irwin, 1969), 23–29.

Integration is the quality of collaboration among departments.[61] Formal integrators are often required to coordinate departments. When the environment is highly uncertain, frequent changes require more information processing to achieve horizontal coordination, so integrators become a necessary addition to the organization structure. Sometimes integrators are called liaison personnel, project managers, brand managers or coordinators. As illustrated in Exhibit 4.6, organizations with highly uncertain environments and a highly differentiated structure assign about 22 per cent of management personnel to integration activities, such as serving on committees, on task forces or in liaison roles.[62] In organizations characterized by very simple, stable environments, almost no managers are assigned to integration roles. Exhibit 4.6 shows that, as environmental uncertainty increases, so does differentiation among departments; hence, the organization must assign a larger percentage of managers to coordinating roles.

Lawrence and Lorsch's research concluded that organizations perform better when the levels of differentiation and integration match the level of uncertainty in the environment. Organizations that performed well in uncertain environments had high levels of both differentiation and integration, while those performing well in less uncertain environments had lower levels of differentiation and integration.

As an organization manager, keep these guidelines in mind:

Match internal organization structure to the external environment. If the external environment is complex, make the organization structure complex. Associate a stable environment with a mechanistic structure and an unstable environment with an organic structure. If the external environment is both complex and changing, make the organization highly differentiated and organic, and use mechanisms to achieve coordination across departments.

Organic versus Mechanistic Management Processes

Another response to environmental uncertainty is the amount of formal structure and control imposed on employees. Tom Burns and G. M. Stalker observed twenty UK industrial firms and discovered that external environment was related to internal management structure.[63] When the external environment was stable, the internal organization tended to be characterized by rules, procedures and a clear hierarchy of authority. Organizations were formalized. They were also centralized, with most decisions made at the top. Burns and Stalker called this a **mechanistic** organization system.

EXHIBIT 4.6 Environmental Uncertainty and Organizational Integrators

Industry	Plastics	Foods	Container
Environmental uncertainty	High	Moderate	Low
Departmental differentiation	High	Moderate	Low
Percent management in integrating roles	22%	17%	0%

Source: Based on Jay W. Lorsch and Paul R. Lawrence, 'Environmental Factors and Organizational Integration,' *Organizational Planning: Cases and Concepts* (Homewood, Ill.: Irwin and Dorsey, 1972), 45.

EXHIBIT 4.7 Mechanistic and Organic Forms

Mechanistic	Organic
1. Tasks are broken down into specialized, separate parts.	1. Employees contribute to the common tasks of the department.
2. Tasks are rigidly defined.	2. Tasks are adjusted and redefined through employee teamwork.
3. There is a strict hierarchy of authority and control, and there are many rules.	3. There is less hierarchy of authority and control, and there are few rules.
4. Knowledge and control of tasks are centralized at the top of the organization.	4. Knowledge and control of tasks are located anywhere in the organization.
5. Communication is vertical.	5. Communication is horizontal.

Source: Adapted from Gerald Zaltman, Robert Duncan, and Jonny Holbek, *Innovations and Organizations* (New York: Wiley, 1973), 131.

In rapidly changing environments, the internal organization was much looser, free-flowing and adaptive. Rules and regulations often were not written down or, if written down, were ignored. People had to find their own way through the system to figure out what to do. The hierarchy of authority was not clear. Decision-making authority was decentralized. Burns and Stalker used the term **organic** to characterize this type of management structure.

Exhibit 4.7 summarizes the differences in organic and mechanistic systems. As environmental uncertainty increases, organizations tend to become more organic, which means decentralizing authority and responsibility to lower levels, encouraging employees to take care of problems by working directly with one another, encouraging teamwork and taking an informal approach to assigning tasks and responsibility. Thus, the organization is more fluid and is able to adapt continually to changes in the external environment.[64]

The learning organization, described in Chapter 1, and the horizontal and virtual network structures, described in Chapter 3, are organic organizational forms that are used by companies to compete in rapidly changing environments. The American brand Guiltless Gourmet, which sells low-fat tortilla chips and other snack foods with healthy ingredients, shifted to a flexible network structure to remain competitive when large companies like Frito Lay entered the low-fat snack-food market. The company redesigned itself to become basically a full-time marketing organization, while production and other activities were outsourced. An 18,000-square-foot plant in Austin was closed and the workforce cut from 125 to a handful of core people handling marketing and sales promotions. The flexible structure helped Guiltless Gourmet to adapt quickly to changing market conditions, but ultimately it didn't stop the company from being swallowed up by the food and consumer products giant R.A.B Holdings.[65,66]

Planning, Forecasting and Responsiveness

The whole point of increasing internal integration and shifting to more organic processes is to enhance the organization's ability to respond quickly to sudden changes in an uncertain environment. It might seem that in an environment where everything is changing all the time, planning is useless. However, in uncertain environments, planning and environmental forecasting, especially the exploration of different possible scenarios and responses, becomes *more* important as a way to keep the organization geared for a coordinated, speedy response. Japanese electronic giants such as Toshiba and Fujitsu, for example, were caught off guard by a combination of nimble new competitors, rapid technological change, deregulation, problems in Japan's banking system and the sudden end of the 1990s technology boom. Lulled into complacency by years of success, Japan's industrial electronics companies were unprepared to respond to these dramatic changes and lost billions.[67]

When the environment is stable, the organization can concentrate on current operational problems and day-to-day efficiency. Long-range planning and forecasting are not needed because environmental demands in the future will be the same as they are today.

With increasing environmental uncertainty, planning and forecasting become more important, but also more difficult.[68] Planning can soften the adverse impact of external shifts. Organizations that have unstable environments often establish a separate planning department. In an unpredictable environment, planners scan environmental elements and analyze potential moves and countermoves by other organizations. Planning can be extensive and may forecast various *scenarios* for environmental contingencies. With scenario building, managers mentally rehearse different scenarios based on anticipating various changes that could affect the organization. Scenarios are like stories that offer alternative, vivid pictures of what the future will look like and how managers will respond. Royal Dutch/Shell Oil has long used scenario building and has been a leader in speedy response to massive changes that other organizations failed to perceive until it was too late.[69] Nevertheless, some scenarios cannot be predicted, or even if they could be predicted, there may be little a company can do in order to avoid negative outcomes except for getting out of that business and finding another. For example, no airline could have predicted the havoc that would be caused in their industry by the terrorist attack on New York's World Trade Centre on September 11, 2001.[70]

Planning cannot substitute for other actions, such as effective boundary spanning and adequate internal integration and coordination. Organizations that are most successful in uncertain environments are those in which close attention is paid to the environment so they can spot threats and opportunities, and where intelligence is shared in a digestible and meaningful manner, thereby enabling relevant organizational members to respond swiftly and effectively.

See online
COUNTERPOINT 4.14

Framework for Organizational Responses to Uncertainty

The ways environmental uncertainty influences organizational characteristics are summarized in Exhibit 4.8. The change and complexity dimensions are combined and illustrate four levels of uncertainty. The low uncertainty environment is simple and stable. Organizations in this environment have few departments and a mechanistic structure. In a low-to-moderate uncertainty environment, more departments are needed, along with more integrating roles to coordinate the departments. Some planning may occur. Environments that are moderate-to-high-uncertainty are unstable but simple. Organization structure is organic and decentralized. Planning is emphasized and managers are quick to make internal changes as needed. The high uncertainty environment is both complex and unstable and is the most difficult environment from a management perspective. Organizations are large and have many departments, but they are also organic. A large number of management personnel are assigned to coordination and integration, and the organization uses boundary spanning, planning and forecasting to enable a high-speed response to environmental changes.

EXHIBIT 4.8 Contingency Framework for Environmental Uncertainty and Organizational Responses

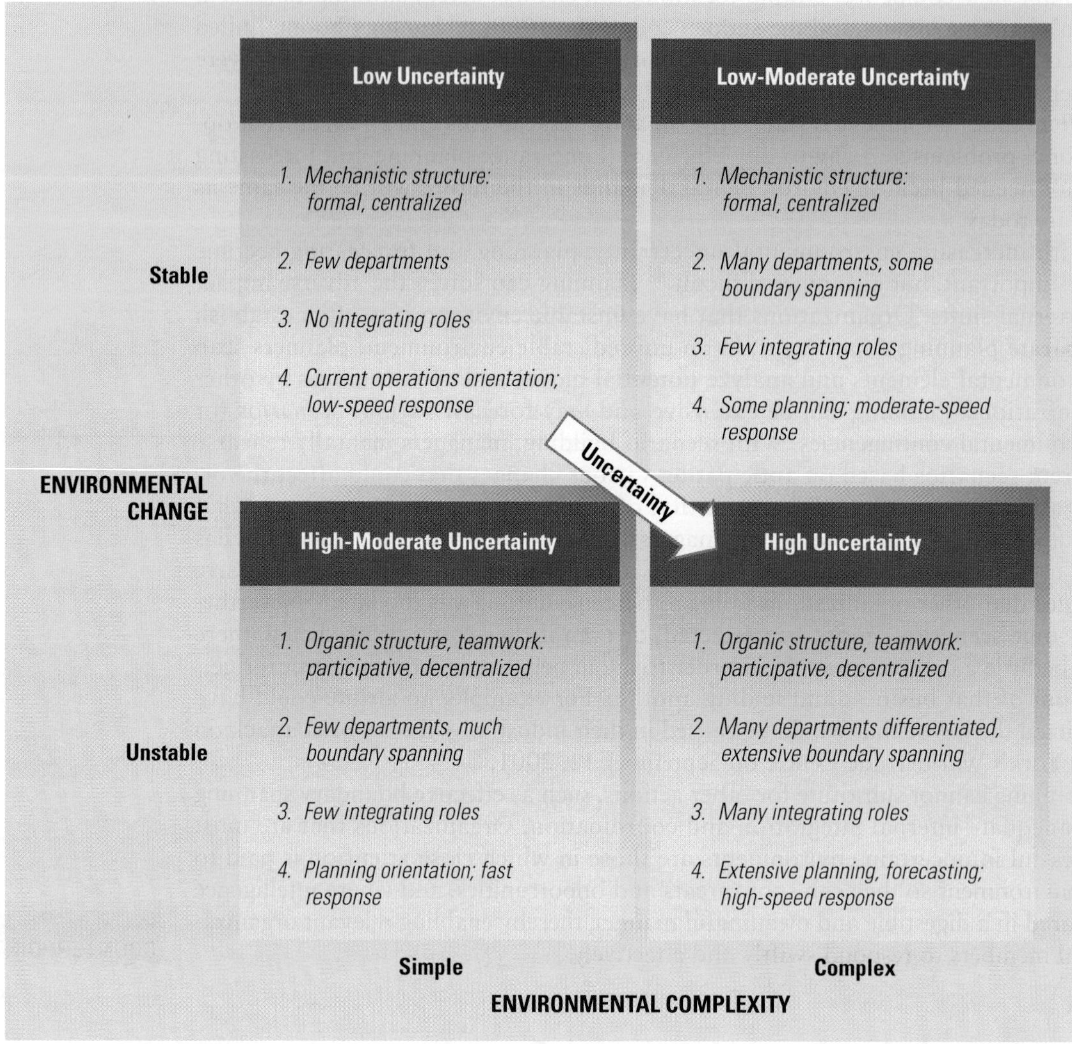

Resource Dependence

Thus far, this chapter has described several ways in which organizations adapt to the lack of information and to the uncertainty caused by environmental change and complexity. We turn now to another characteristic of the organization-environment relationship that affects organizations; the need for material and financial resources. The environment is the source of scarce and valued resources essential to organizational survival. Research in this area is called the *resource-dependence perspective*. **Resource dependence** means that organizations depend on the environment but strive to acquire control over resources to minimize their dependence.[71] Organizations are vulnerable if vital resources are controlled by other organizations, so they try to be as independent as possible. Organizations do not want to become too vulnerable to other organizations because of negative effects on performance.

See online COUNTERPOINT 4.15

Although companies like to minimize their dependence, when costs and risks are high they may team up to share scarce resources and be more competitive on a global basis. Formal relationships with other organizations present a dilemma to managers. Organizations seek to reduce vulnerability with respect to resources by developing links with other organizations, but they also like to maximize their own autonomy and independence. Organizational linkages require coordination,[72] and they reduce the freedom of each organization to make decisions without concern for the needs and goals of other organizations. Interorganizational relationships thus represent a tradeoff between resources and autonomy. To maintain autonomy, organizations that already have abundant resources will tend not to establish new linkages. Organizations that need resources will tend to be more willing to give up independence to acquire those resources.

Dependence on shared resources gives power to other organizations. Once an organization relies on others for valued resources, those other organizations can influence managerial decision making. When a large company like Nokia, Citroen or Toshiba forges a partnership with a supplier for parts, both sides benefit, but each loses a small amount of autonomy. For example, some large companies are now putting strong pressure on their suppliers to lower costs. Suppliers often have few alternatives but to go along.[73] In much the same way, dependence on shared resources gives advertisers power over print and electronic media companies. For example, as newspapers face increasingly tough financial times, they are less likely to run stories that are critical of advertisers.

Though newspapers insist advertisers don't get special treatment, studies show that it is rare for a newspaper to severely criticize a major advertiser.[74] The American NGO Fairness and Accuracy in Reporting (FAIR) scrutinizes links between corporate advertisers and newspaper coverage.[75,76] FAIR particularly singles out the case of Wal-Mart, which has received what FAIR believes is excessively positive media coverage at the same time as it is one of the country's largest advertisers.[77] In some countries, the relationship between advertising and editorial content can be very direct; in 2003 India's biggest-circulation English-language newspaper, *The Times of India*, started accepting money from advertisers for publishing sponsored, but undeclared, editorial content.[78]

As an organization manager, keep these guidelines in mind:

Reach out and control external sectors that threaten needed resources. Influence the domain by engaging in political activity, joining trade associations and establishing favourable linkages. Establish linkages through ownership, strategic alliances, cooptation, interlocking directorates and executive recruitment. Reduce the amount of change or threat from the external environment so the organization will not have to change internally.

Controlling Environmental Resources

In response to the need for resources, organizations try to maintain a balance between linkages with other organizations and their own independence. Organizations maintain this balance through attempts to modify, manipulate or control other organizations.[79] To survive, the focal organization often tries to reach out and change or control elements in the environment. Two strategies can be adopted to manage resources in the external environment: (1) establish favourable linkages with key elements in the environment and (2) shape the environmental domain.[80] Techniques to accomplish each of these strategies are summarized in Exhibit 4.9. As a general rule, when organizations sense that valued resources are scarce, they will use the strategies in Exhibit 4.9 rather than go it alone. Notice how dissimilar these strategies are from the responses to environmental change and complexity described in Exhibit 4.8. The dissimilarity reflects the difference between responding to the need for resources and responding to the need for information.

Establishing Interorganizational Linkages

Ownership Companies use ownership to establish linkages when they buy a part of or a controlling interest in another company. This gives the company access to technology, products or other resources it doesn't currently have.

EXHIBIT 4.9 Organizing Strategies for Controlling the External Environment

Establishing Interorganizational Linkages	Controlling the Environmental Domain
1. Ownership	1. Change of domain
2. Contracts, joint ventures	2. Political activity, regulation
3. Cooptation, interlocking directorates	3. Trade associations
4. Executive recruitment	4. Illegitimate activities
5. Advertising, public relations	

A greater degree of ownership and control is obtained through acquisition or merger. An *acquisition* involves the purchase of one organization by another so that the buyer assumes control. A *merger* is the unification of two or more organizations into a single unit.[81] In the steel industry, Mittal Steel merged with Luxemburg's Arcelor. Acquisition occurred when Germany's Daimler bought the ailing Chrysler Corp., and when US retail giant Wal-Mart purchased Britain's Asda supermarket chain. These forms of ownership can reduce uncertainty in an area important to the acquiring company. In the past few years, there has been a huge wave of acquisition and merger activity in the telecommunications industry, reflecting the tremendous uncertainty these organizations face. The acquisition of Britain's Orange mobile phone network by France Telecom is discussed in this chapter's *In Practice* box.

Formal Strategic Alliances When there is a high level of complementarity between the business lines, geographical positions or skills of two companies, the firms often go the route of a strategic alliance rather than ownership through merger or acquisition.[82] Such alliances are formed through contracts and joint ventures.

Contracts and joint ventures reduce uncertainty through a legal and binding relationship with another firm. Contracts come in the form of *licence agreements* that involve the purchase of the right to use an asset (such as a new technology) for a specific time and *supplier arrangements* that contract for the sale of one firm's output to another. Contracts can provide long-term security by tying customers and suppliers to specific amounts and prices. For example, the Italian fashion house Versace has forged a deal to license its primary asset – its name – for a line of designer eyeglasses. McDonald's has successfully grown in developing countries, where traditional supplier networks might not be present. As the former Soviet Union's economy was transforming in the late 1980s, McDonald's set up operations in Moscow. At the beginning, it had to produce its own ingredients in Russia, but the company worked with emerging private suppliers to establish quality control and production reliability in return for guaranteed markets for their products.[83,84] Large retailers such as American-headquartered Wal-Mart, Britain's Tesco and France's Carrefour are gaining so much clout that they can almost dictate contracts, telling manufacturers what to make, how to make it and how much to charge for it. The changing balance of power in the production value chain has been studied by the sociologist Gary Gereffi, whose work is discussed in Chapter 6.

Joint ventures result in the creation of a new organization that is formally independent of the parents, although the parents will have some control.[85] In a joint venture, organizations share the risk and cost associated with large projects or innovations. AOL created a joint venture with Venezuela's Cisneros Group to smooth its entry into the Latin American online market. IBM formed a joint venture with USA Technologies Inc. to test Web-enabled washers and dryers at American colleges and universities. Traditional coin-operated technology will be replaced with an IBM

Orange and France Telecom

Worldwide, the telecommunications industry is changing perhaps more rapidly than any other industry. Perhaps the most revolutionary of the changes in the telecom sector is 'convergence'. This describes the interweaving of broadcast, telecommunications and electronic media, and their delivery through a single modality, whether by telephone wire, by cable or even wirelessly. The opportunities and risks driven by convergence are enormous, and have led to great shake-ups in all areas of the communications industry. Convergence, in turn, has been driven by technological advances, including but not restricted to the development of the internet, wireless telecommunications and satellite broadcasting.

Mobile telephony took off in the late 1990s. An early response to expanding communications opportunities was a dramatic bidding war for mobile telephone operator licences and networks, which were seen as tremendous revenue generators. Smaller players like Britain's Orange were eyed hungrily by larger telecom operators, especially those that were lagging behind in the rush to mobile. France Telecom, which had until recently been France's state-owned telephone monopoly, had a small mobile arm but with mobiles seeming to be the wave of the future, in 2001 it pounced for Orange, with its reputation for innovation in both technology and marketing: 'This type of merger is becoming increasingly common and we expect to see many more in the coming months as the big old incumbents are forced to form partnerships with the emerging new players in order to stay ahead of the pack', said telecom veteran Gary Gibbs.[86]

Orange quickly established itself as one of the major global brands in the mobile phone industry, but with the pace of change in the sector accelerating rapidly, that was just the beginning. France Telecom continued to expand geographically, with operations in more than two dozen countries, and 170 million customers by 2008. Like its competitors, France Telecom invested heavily in digital convergence, both through acquisitions and greenfield development in broadband internet, online video gaming and television broadcasting.[87] In 2006 France Telecom decided to rebrand most of its global services under the Orange label, including Wanadoo, the largest broadband provider in Europe. Despite the dizzying pace of France Telecom's growth, many analysts believe it has squeezed the creative juice out of Orange, making it a vehicle of a giant corporation, rather than quirky and innovative in the way that Apple has achieved.[88] This highlights one of the great dilemmas of mergers and acquisitions in the converged universe: size and service breadth are needed to win customers, but the price can be depersonalized service and consequently customer dissatisfaction. It's a challenge being faced throughout the telecommunications sector; Virgin Media, the full-service communications company created in 2007 through a merger between the Virgin mobile and broadband operator and NTL/Telewest Cable in the UK, faced both competitive challenges and customer service issues.[89]

micropayment system that allows students to pay by swiping an ID card or pushing a code on a cell phone. They can log onto a Web site to see if a machine is available and have an e-mail sent when a load is done.[90,91]

Cooptation, Interlocking Directorates **Cooptation** occurs when leaders from important sectors in the environment are made part of an organization. It takes place, for example, when influential customers or suppliers are appointed to the board of directors, such as when the senior executive of a bank sits on the board of a manufacturing company. As a board member, the banker may become psychologically coopted into the interests of the manufacturing firm. Community leaders also can be appointed to a company's board of directors or to other organizational committees or task forces. These influential people are thus introduced to the needs of the company and are more likely to include the company's interests in their decision making.

An **interlocking directorate** is a formal linkage that occurs when a member of the board of directors of one company sits on the board of directors of another company. The individual is a communications link between companies and can influence policies and decisions. When one individual is the link between two companies, this is typically referred to as a **direct interlock**. An **indirect interlock** occurs when a director of company A and a director of company B are both directors of company C. They have access to one another but do not have direct influence over their respective companies.[92] Recent research shows that, as a firm's financial fortunes decline, direct interlocks with financial institutions tend to increase. Financial uncertainty facing an industry also has been associated with greater indirect interlocks between competing companies.[93]

Executive Recruitment Transferring or exchanging executives also offers a method of establishing favourable linkages with external organizations. Senior officials often move between government and private industry. Companies like to hire former senior officials and politicians who can both provide them advice on the processes of securing contracts or getting needed approvals, and provide introductions to key decision-making officials. For example, the former minister responsible for the British state health service, Patricia Hewitt, was hired as 'special consultant' by the world's largest chain of chemists, Alliance Boots, and the largest private owner of hospitals in the UK, in January 2008. She also took a non-executive directorship of British Telecom (BT) having previously been instrumental, as Minister at the Department of Trade and Industry, in the creation of Ofcom, the all-in-one regulator for telecoms and the media, including the appointment of its chairman, Lord Currie.[94]

Some politicians and journalists argue that this practice is inherently wrong, because it provides 'connected' companies with an unfair advantage.[95] In many countries there are rules such as a 'cooling off' period after someone leaves the public service, before they are allowed to take this type of lobbying position. The same issue arises in the private sector where companies are naturally unenthusiastic about their executive moving to competitors with inside knowledge, and clauses are often inserted in contracts limiting managers' freedom to jump ship to a competitor. Nevertheless, as long as the practice is lawful, companies wishing to maximize their chances of winning contracts and getting projects approved will continue to hire well-connected executives. Having channels of influence and communication between organizations, both in the public and private sectors, serves to reduce financial uncertainty and dependence for an organization.

Advertising and Public Relations A traditional way of establishing favourable relationships is through advertising. Organizations spend large amounts of money to influence the taste of consumers. Advertising is especially important in highly competitive consumer industries and in industries that experience variable demand. *The Economist* is a global publication appealing to executives looking for concise but sharp analysis of world events and business challenges. With the rise of the Internet and an explosion in news sources, many magazines have faced declining circulation. However, in the decade that Helen Alexander served as CEO between 1997 and 2008, the magazine's circulation doubled, mainly by protecting its elite brand. In conjunction with the advertising agency AMV, *The Economist* has built an image that encourages its readers to see themselves as intelligent and successful, a campaign that has been described as one of the best in the past twenty years. One ad says, 'It's lonely at the top, but at least there's something to read'. Alexander's successor has a solid brand to build on, but will need to keep a close eye on the magazine's positioning in the rapidly changing media and business environment.[96,97]

Public relations is similar to advertising, except that stories often are free and aimed at public opinion. Public relations people cast an organization in a favourable light in speeches, in press reports, and on television. Public relations attempts to shape the company's image in the minds of customers, suppliers and government officials. For example, in an effort to survive in this antismoking era, some tobacco companies have launched aggressive public relations campaigns touting smokers' rights and freedom of choice.

Controlling the Environmental Domain

In addition to establishing favourable linkages to obtain resources, organizations often try to change the environment. We will discuss four techniques for influencing or changing a firm's environmental domain.

Change of Domain The sectors described earlier in this chapter are not fixed. The organization decides which business it is in, the market to enter, and the suppliers, banks, employees and location to use, and this domain can be changed.[98] An organization can seek new environmental relationships and drop old ones. An organization may try to find a domain where there is little competition, no government regulation, abundant suppliers, affluent customers and barriers to keep competitors out.

See online
COUNTERPOINT 4.16

Acquisition and divestment are two techniques for altering the domain. Canada's Bombardier, maker of Ski-Doo snowmobiles, began a series of acquisitions to alter its domain when the snowmobile industry declined. CEO Laurent Beaudoin gradually moved the company into the aerospace industry by negotiating deals to purchase Canadair, Boeing's deHaviland unit, business-jet pioneer Learjet and Short Brothers of Northern Ireland.[99] In 2007, Britain's Virgin Group decided to get out of the declining music retailing business by selling its Virgin Megastores, even though back in the 1980s and 1990s the stores had made founder Richard Branson's brash Virgin brand uniquely recognizable on Britain's high streets. After a management buyout the stores were rebranded Zavvi, refocusing on the expanding video games sector. Early results were positive, but eventually Zavvi fell victim to the global financial crisis, validating Branson's decision to divest the Virgin Megastores.[100]

Political Activity, Regulation Political activity includes techniques to influence government legislation and regulation. Political strategy can be used to erect regulatory barriers against new competitors or to squash unfavourable legislation. Corporations also try to influence the appointment to agencies of people who are sympathetic to their needs.

Microsoft has become one of the biggest and most sophisticated lobbying organizations in the world spending $9 million in 2007 lobbying the US federal government alone. Microsoft has had to defend itself around the world against allegations of misusing its dominant position in computer operating system and office software. It has lobbied hard against proposed legislation in both Europe and North America that would severely restrict its ability to protect its dominant position, for example by forcing Microsoft to 'unbundle' some of its non-core add-ons like multimedia players, and making it easier for competitors to produce software compatible with Microsoft products. One key issue on which Microsoft has lobbied successfully is for its version of 'open' office software to be certified as a global standard by the International Standardization Organization (ISO), although countries opposing Microsoft appealed the 2008 decision. Once certified, Microsoft would be permitted to sell its software to governments, in Europe and elsewhere, that require open software in which some of its internal code can be customized to meet customer needs and permit third-party add-ons.[101] Microsoft's lobbying effort has been global; in order to win the ISO vote against European opposition, it enlisted a number of developing country governments to become active in the organization and support its point of view.[102] Large pharmaceutical companies such as Merck and Wyeth frequently engage in political activity to influence government regulatory agency decisions regarding generic drugs or other changes that might weaken their organization's power and control.[103,104]

The global retail giant Wal-Mart long steered clear of politics but in recent years has been adding lobbyists to the payroll and becoming heavily involved in political activity.

Trade Associations Much of the work to influence the external environment is accomplished jointly with other organizations that have similar interests. For example, in most countries, businesses have powerful associations that lobby legislators, influence new regulations and develop public relations campaigns. These

Wal-Mart

In the late 1990s, Wal-Mart discovered a problem that could hamper its ambitious international expansion plans – US negotiators for China's entry into the World Trade Organization had agreed to a thirty-store limit on foreign retailers doing business there. Worse still, executives for the giant retailer realized they didn't know the right people in Washington to talk to about the situation.

Until 1998, Wal-Mart didn't even have a lobbyist on the payroll and spent virtually nothing on political activity. The issue of China's entry into the WTO was a wake-up call, and Wal-Mart began transforming itself from a company that shunned politics to one that works hard to bend public policy to suit its business needs. Hiring in-house lobbyists and working with lobbying organizations favourable to its goals has enabled Wal-Mart to gain significant wins on global trade issues.

In addition to concerns over global trade, Wal-Mart has found other reasons it needs government support. The company has been fighting off challenges from labour unions in the United States and elsewhere. For example, the United Food and Commercial Workers International Union helped Wal-Mart employees file a series of complaints about the company's overtime, health care and other policies with the US National Labour Relations Board, leading to dozens of class-action lawsuits (in which a large group, or class, of litigants collectively bring a claim to court). Wal-Mart in turn poured millions of dollars into a campaign that presses for limits on awards in class-action suits and began lobbying for legislation that bars unions from soliciting outside of retail stores. Although that legislation failed, top executives were pleased with their lobbyists' progress. Its spending on American lobbyists has risen rapidly, from $1.6 million in 2005 to $2.5 million in 2006, and $4 million in 2007.

Wal-Mart's lobbying activities are not restricted to the US. When the company decided it wanted to expand into the United Kingdom, it lobbied then Prime Minister Tony Blair to loosen British planning regulations governing development of large new supermarkets. A few months later, Wal-Mart purchased the British chain Asda. Similarly, the company has been pressing hard, and with some success, for relaxation of India's restrictions against foreign-owned stores, seeking a share of a potentially enormous market in that emerging economy.[105] In addition to hiring lobbyists and working with other organzations, many CEOs believe they should do their own lobbying. CEOs have easier access than lobbyists and can be especially effective when they do the politicking. Political activity is so important that 'informal lobbyist' is an unwritten part of almost any CEO's job description.[106]

exist on both a national and an industry-wide level. For example, R&D, the association of major pharmaceutical manufacturers in Canada, has engaged in a long and largely effective campaign to restrict availability of generic medications in the country, holding up the carrot of increased investment in pharmaceutical research and development, and effectively hampering development of the country's domestic generic medication industry.[107]

By pooling resources, business organizations can both fund larger lobbying campaigns than they could otherwise afford, and shield themselves from the criticism of self-interest if companies lobbied directly for changes to benefit them. Small businesses are particularly dependent on industry and national associations to represent their interests, as most small businesspeople have neither the time nor the money to drop their work and lobby politicians.

Illegitimate Activities Illegitimate activities represent the final technique companies sometimes use to control their environmental domain. Certain conditions, such as low profits, pressure from senior managers, or scarce environmental resources, may lead managers to adopt behaviours not considered legitimate.[108] Many well-known companies have been found guilty of unlawful or unethical activities. Examples include payoffs to foreign governments, illegal political contributions, promotional gifts and wiretapping. At formerly high-flying companies such as Enron and WorldCom, managers disguised financial problems through complex partnerships or questionable accounting practices. In the defence industry, the intense competition for sales of weapons systems has led some companies to do almost anything to get an edge. BAE, the major British weapons manufacturer, has made up to $2 billion dollars in payments over the past twenty years to the personal bank account of a leading member of the Saudi Arabian government, at the same time as the company secured an $80 billion contract to supply Saudi Arabia with fighter jets and other military equipment. The British government was pressured by Saudi Arabia to stop its investigation into this questionable practice, and in 2006, former Prime Minister Tony Blair decided to drop the investigation on political grounds. However Britain's High Court ordered a full judicial review of the government's actions in 2008, stating that, 'No one, whether within this country or outside, is entitled to interfere with the course of our justice'. In addition, the United States arrested several BAE executives on suspicion of having broken American anti-corruption laws in the same matter.[109]

COUNTERPOINT 4.7

Although cases of outright fraud such as occurred at Enron are well-publicized, a wider issue relates to excessively easy-going relationships between corporations and government regulators that permits issues such as 'rogue trading' and excessively risky business strategies to flourish, especially in the financial sector whose scope is extending far beyond traditional banking to take in 'securitization' and 'marketization' of business areas such as utility and commodity markets. Particularly during economic boom periods, regulators may not be attuned to the risk of major failure, accepting overly optimistic projections by corporate executives. In retrospect, for example, the business model used by Britain's Northern Rock bank, which funded its mortgage lending on international money markets rather than on savings invested with the company, was highly susceptible to any general downturn in economic conditions. British regulators had quietly warned the bank, but allowed it to continue operating until the model collapsed like a pack of cards due to the credit squeeze of 2007, potentially costing British taxpayers many billions of pounds to prop up the institution.[110] Similarly, sometimes quite junior traders at financial institutions feel encouraged or even pressured to take risks in their trading portfolios. When things go badly wrong, as happened at France's Société Générale in 2007, or the Singapore trading office of Barings Bank in 1995, blame is often focused on a single employee. A closer examination of this type of case usually reveals that ethical and compliance weaknesses are endemic in the corporation's culture, and that regulators are far too willing to take the word of a company's managers that all is well.[111] **Discuss**

One study found that companies in industries with low demand, shortages and strikes were more likely to be convicted for illegal activities, implying that illegal acts are an attempt to cope with resource scarcity. Some nonprofit organizations have been found to use illegitimate or illegal actions to bolster their visibility and reputation as they compete with other organizations for scarce grants and donations.[112]

Organization–Environment Integrative Framework

The relationships illustrated in Exhibit 4.10 summarize the two major themes about organization–environment relationships discussed in this chapter. One theme is that the amount of complexity and change in an organization's domain influences the

EXHIBIT 4.10 Relationship between Environmental Characteristics and Organizational Actions

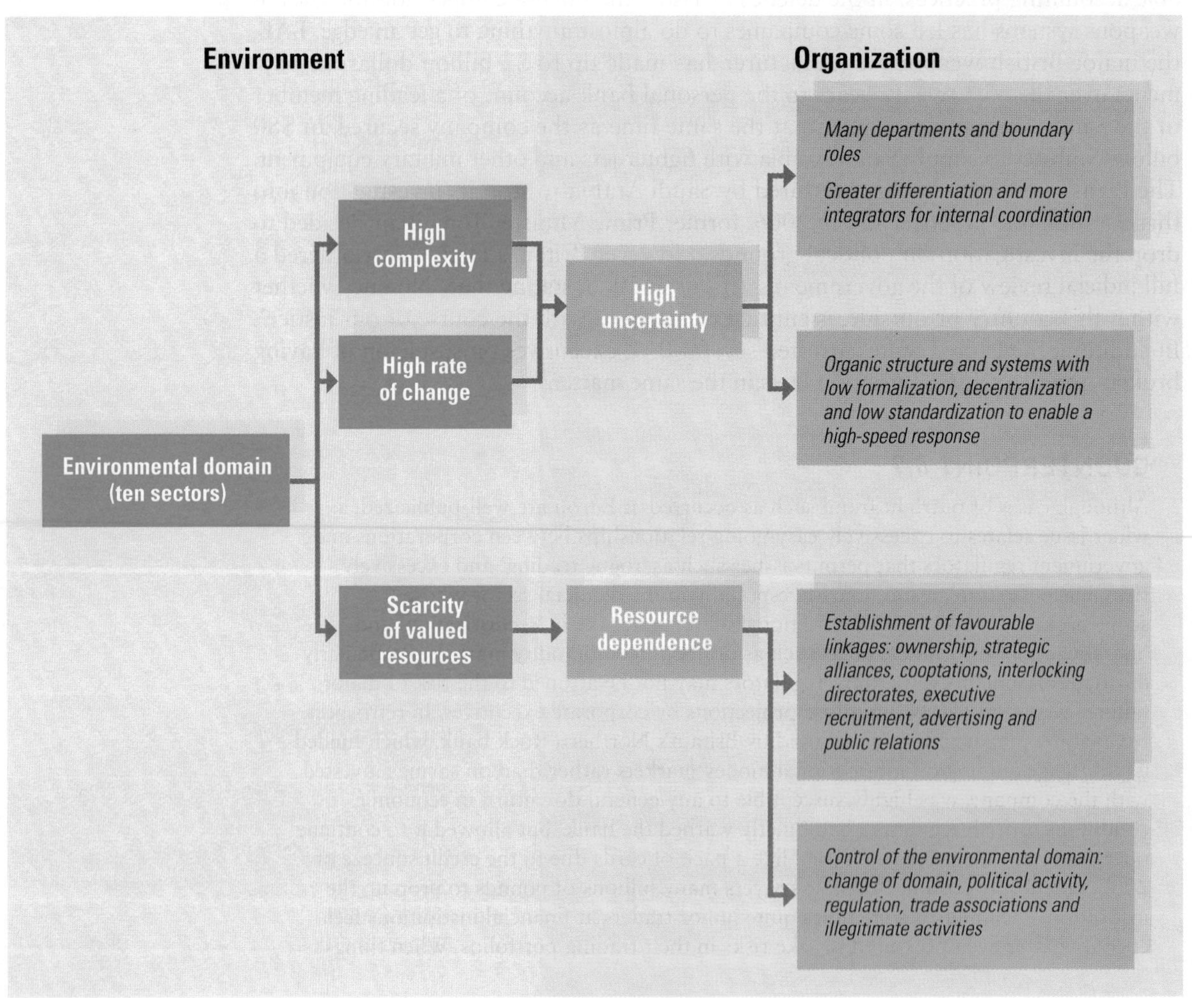

need for information and hence the uncertainty felt within an organization. Greater information uncertainty is resolved through greater structural flexibility and the assignment of additional departments and boundary roles. When uncertainty is low, management structures can be more mechanistic, and the number of departments and boundary roles can be fewer. The second theme pertains to the scarcity of material and financial resources. The more dependent an organization is on other organizations for those resources, the more important it is to either establish favourable linkages with those organizations or control entry into the domain. If dependence on external resources is low, the organization can maintain autonomy and does not need to establish linkages or control the external domain.

Summary and Interpretation

Organizations are open social systems. All but the smallest organizations are involved with hundreds of external elements. The change and complexity in environmental domains have major implications for organization design and action. Most organizational decisions, activities and outcomes can be traced to perceived changes in the external environment.

Organizational environments differ in terms of uncertainty and can be conceptualized in terms stable – unstable and simple – complex dimensions. Specific departments and functions are created to deal with uncertainties. Boundary-spanning roles provide information about the environment.

Resources are allocated to departments that will plan, deal with specific environmental elements and integrate diverse internal activities. Strategic alliances, interlocking directorates, executive recruitment or advertising and public relations can all serve to minimize risk and maintain a supply of scarce resources. Other techniques for controlling the environment include a change of the domain in which the organization operates, political activity, participation in trade associations and perhaps illegitimate activities.

Two important themes in this chapter are that organizations adapt to their environments and endeavour to control their effects. Such control is more feasible for large organizations that command many resources but organizations with fewer but more critical resources may be more nimble and innovative in ways that elude the reach of their less agile competitors.

KEY CONCEPTS

boundary-spanning roles
buffering roles
business intelligence
cooptation
differentiation
direct interlock
domain
general environment
indirect interlock
integration
interlocking directorate
mechanistic
organic
organizational environment
resource dependence
sectors
simple–complex dimension
stable–unstable dimension
task environment
uncertainty

Discussion Questions

1 Define *organizational environment*. Would the task environment of a new Internet-based company be the same as that of a government welfare agency? Discuss.

2 What are some forces that influence environmental uncertainty? Which typically has the greatest impact on uncertainty – environmental complexity or environmental change? Why?

3 Why does environmental complexity lead to organizational complexity? Explain.

4 Discuss the importance of the international sector for today's organizations, compared to domestic sectors. What are some ways in which the international sector affects organizations in your city or community?

5 Describe differentiation and integration. In what type of environmental uncertainty will differentiation and integration be greatest? Least?

6 Under what environmental conditions is organizational planning emphasized? Is planning an appropriate response to a turbulent environment?

7 What is an organic organization? A mechanistic organization? How does the environment influence organic and mechanistic structures?

8 Why do organizations become involved in interorganizational relationships? Do these relationships affect an organization's dependency? Performance?

9 Assume you have been asked to calculate the ratio of staff employees to production employees in two organizations – one in a simple, stable environment and one in a complex, shifting environment. How would you expect these ratios to differ? Why?

10 Is changing the organization's domain a feasible strategy for coping with a threatening environment? Explain.

Chapter 4 Workbook Organizations You Rely On

Below, list eight organizations you somehow rely on in your daily life. Examples might be a restaurant, a clothing or CD store, a university, your family, the post office, the telephone company, an airline, a pizza shop that delivers, your place of work and so on. In the first column, list those eight organizations. Then, in column 2, choose another organization you could use in case the ones in column 1 were not available. In column 3, evaluate your level of dependence on the organizations listed in column 1 as Strong, Medium, or Weak. Finally, in column 4, rate the certainty of that organization being able to meet your needs as High (certainty), Medium, or Low.

Organization	Backup Organization	Level of Dependence	Level of Certainty
1.			
2.			
3.			
4.			
5.			
6.			
7.			
8.			

Questions

1 Do you have adequate backup organizations for those of high dependence? How might you create even more backups?

2 What would you do if an organization you rated high for dependence and high for certainty suddenly became high-dependence and low-certainty? How would your behaviour relate to the concept of resource dependence?

3 Have you ever used any behaviours similar to those in Exhibit 4.9 to manage your relationships with the organizations listed in column 1?

Adapted by Dorothy Marcic from 'Organizational Dependencies', in Ricky W. Griffin and Thomas C. Head, *Practicing Management*, 2nd ed. (Dallas: Houghton Mifflin), 2–3.

CASE FOR ANALYSIS

Kongstrup Machine Factory*

By Henrik Sørensen, *Aarhus University*

Kongstrup Machine Factory was established in 1894. The company's activities since then have primarily involved the development, production and sale of agricultural machinery. The organisational structure of the company can best be described as a traditional functional structure appropriate for the relatively few product items developed and produced by the company from its early years. Although the company's organisation has evolved from a simple structure to a functional structure, the company has still managed to maintain a strong focus on development – a focus established early in the history of the company. Today the company is owned by a handful of large investors (funds and venture enterprises).

In the mid 1970s, Kongstrup's management made a strategic decision to concentrate on production of self-propelled combine harvesters ('combines') and, subsequently, the strategy was further adjusted to also include manufacture of grain handling equipment. These strategic changes were realized through acquisitions, but the company had doubts about relying entirely on the acquisition approach and consequently also entered into a number of strategic alliances. The experiences with the strategic alliances were very positive, whereas the picture presented by acquisitions was much less encouraging.

The company also discussed the option of outsourcing development services, meaning that another company would be contracted and paid to carry out product development. The company's management remained particularly unsure about how to organise the continued development of the company's resources and skills. They were convinced that the development strategy would depend on the characteristics of the available resources and skills – meaning that no standard development approach could be planned. Indecision about development strategy has as a result persisted to the current day.

In the late 1980s, the market for combines declined, leading to large production overcapacity. In 1989, 13,700 combines were sold in Europe – a figure that decreased to 9,800 in 1990. The crisis was mainly attributable to high uncertainty in the agricultural sector, particularly due to changes anticipated in EU agricultural policy coming out of the GATT negotiations. However, the industry presumed that the bottom was reached at a sale of 9,800 combines and, from today's perspective, this appears to be correct.

At the beginning of the 1980s, Kongstrup's focus on self-propelled combines resulted in the development of a completely new generation of medium-sized combines. At that time, they sold about 500 machines a year, but had capacity for twice as many. The principal market was Denmark closely followed by Sweden, Great Britain and Norway. But they did not have any systematic sales to other export markets due, among other things, to limited financial resources.

Within the industry, there is a strong relationship between the sale of combine harvesters and presence of service centres. The company decided that the maximum distance between a customer and a service centre should be approximately 25 km. The fine-meshed distribution network in principal markets cannot be financially justified by the sale of combines alone, but is regarded as an product extension. Kongstrup chose – despite the high costs involved – to maintain this service.

The future prospects of Kongstrup were therefore in some doubt and, by 1986, the company found it logical to join forces with another company through a cooperative agreement.

Cooperation and strategic opportunities

Several options were considered: including Multos Biancos (MB), Case International Harvester and Valmet. Neither MB nor Valmet had its own production of combines at that point in time. MB had previously owned three large combine factories, but these had been based on mass production and as a result of a sales crisis had become highly unprofitable and were consequently closed down. MB was not fully convinced that their product range should include combines.

At this time, MB was a large Brazilian company with a consolidated turnover of approximately 1.5 billion dollars. MB's organization was mostly structured as a divisional structure. The company produced a full range of tractors with production primarily located in

France, Brazil and North America. Nevertheless, the company was only in the 'second division' when it came to production of agricultural machinery, with the three giants being Ford-Fiat, John Deere and Case International Harvester.

To Kongstrup, the advantages of cooperating with MB would be direct access to various export markets through MB's large geographical market spread. Kongstrup also expected to see sales more than double in the short run. The following aspects were crucial for Kongstrup's choice of MB: (i) access to certain types of customers among the partner's contacts, (ii) reduced overcapacity and (iii) the opportunity to rationalize. Likewise access to MB's product range provided benefits through cross-branding and promotion. In addition there were potential competitive advantages of cooperating instead of competing and access to the partner's management competencies, production skills and financial resources.

Furthermore, MB had a good international reputation and a comprehensive, efficient organization. Another strong point was its well-structured sales organisation in Western Europe. The product range was not state-of-the-art, but Kongstrup believed that they could contribute significantly to the partnership through their product development and innovations, thus assuring a leading market position for the alliance. Finally, MB would achieve the advantage of having their product range supplemented without having to expand their organization and in this way strengthen an otherwise weak research and development department (a deficiency created by the company's organisational structure).

Entering into cooperation with MB did involve the risk of dependency for Kongstrup by 'placing all its eggs in one basket'. Other concerns involved the different goals of the two partners in relation to the alliance, and the unequal strengths of the two partners in terms of size and financial resources. In addition, there was a risk of Kongstrup losing its own identity, as the new cooperation partner's strength lay in the distribution chain and consequently it could demand Kongstrup develop new combines whose development needs did not match the resources and competencies available in Kongstrup. Overall, therefore, it was somewhat uncertain whether the partnership would be successful.

During the negotiations, it was clear that Kongstrup's motive for entering into the cooperation was to gain market access, while MB's motive was to gain access to Kongstrup's development and innovation of new combines, as their own R&D department was lagging behind the rest of the industry. In the end, a cooperation agreement was signed and the partnership soon turned out to be very successful.

Cooperation

As mentioned, MB was strong in sales and the financial statements showed positive trends in the proceeding years (see the table above), while the concerns that had initially expressed regarding the cooperation quickly turned out to be unfounded.

Generally, combines are divided into categories ranging from 1 to 10, depending on size. By 2008, the product range of Kongstrup comprised sizes 4 to 9, with Kongstrup's offices and production facilities located in Hillerstorp, close to Gävle in Sweden, where they only build large combines in sizes 6 to 9. The smaller sizes (4 and 5) were built by another partner, EMBRO, in Belgrade in Serbia. This partner manufactures approximately 1/3 of all Kongstrup combines. The Serbian company is an independent combine factory to which Kongstrup has supplied technology, design and production equipment. Before this cooperation, EMBRO only produced outdated models and EMBRO intended to convert the entire production to Kongstrup models, another indication of the great strength of Kongstrup in the field of research and development.

The Kongstrup department dealing with production of combines employs 415 hourly paid employees and 122 salaried employees. The table below shows the turnover of the (combine) factory in Hillerstrop.[1]

2002	2003	2004	2005	2006	2007	2008
100	108	111	120	123	125	131

2002=100

As can be seen, turnover has been increasing steadily in recent years and this trend is expected to continue, with 80% of total turnover coming from exports.

Kongstrup has a wide net of parts suppliers while MB buys 85% of Kongstrup's production. In relation to sales, Kongstrup is therefore highly dependent on MB and another company, Case International Harvester, which itself buys various components from Kongstrup.

[1] The table has been indexed to a 2002 base of 100, in order to avoid disclosing the actual figures for competitive reasons

Kongstrup's market strength is focused on Sweden, Norway, Great Britain and Denmark. In Sweden, Norway and Great Britain its market share represents approximately 12–14% and in Denmark approximately 30%. A market share of less than 10% is held in the remaining parts of Europe. All over Europe, except for Denmark and Sweden, distribution of finished combines is handled by MB under the Kongstrup brand name.

The main competitors of Kongstrup are CLAAS, Massey Fergusson, John Deere, Ford-Fiat, Case International Harvester, Deutch Fahr and Leverada, who are all financially strong corporations. Kongstrup is definitely the smallest of the major players. Among other reasons, this is because the other producers have wider product ranges. Several competitors are subsidiaries of very large multinational corporations.

Catastrophe

The cooperation with MB continued to flourish up until late 2008 when an event occurred with catastrophic consequences for the partnership.

MB was involved in other business activities that unexpectedly impacted the two companies' cooperation. The company had considerable interests in the mining industry in Chile, which suddenly racked up huge financial losses as a result of commodity price fluctuations due to the global financial crisis. This development imposed a heavy financial burden on MB, with the result that the company suspended its payments to Kongstrup. New owners arrived at MB, who immediately announced they were willing to continue the cooperation between Kongstrup and MB on the combines project.

However, Kongstrup did not have the same faith in MB's new owners – a distrust which would turn out to be well founded. Kongstrup noticed irregularities in MB's orders for certain spare parts. Where the company would previously order between 10–15 spare part items, they now suddenly ordered 50–60 items. This made Kongstrup suspect that MB was producing other types of combines, which would obviously be in conflict with the cooperation agreement.

During the autumn of 2008, Kongstrup paid MB a surprise visit that confirmed Kongstrup's suspicion. MB was developing and testing its own copies of Kongstrup's most popular product – a definite breach of contract. MB had become capable of developing Kongstrup's most popular products owing to their knowledge of Kongstrup's products and the development of a very keen awareness of how to internalise knowledge from strategic alliances. All this had been a very conscious process and action on the part of MB.

Thus, Kongstrup informed MB that the cooperation would be terminated with immediate effect if MB did not stop the production of combines. Three meetings were then held between the companies, which resulted in MB offering to dismiss the managing director if Kongstrup would agree to continue the cooperation. MB's board of directors claimed that they had had the best intentions from the start, but had been misled by a corrupt and opportunistic director. Kongstrup feared, however, that MB's production of combines had been ordered by the board of directors and consequently they suspected that dismissal of the managing director would be fruitless. Kongstrup therefore decided to break off its cooperation with MB.

Organisational and strategic crisis

Breaking up the partnership caused huge problems at Kongstrup. Probably the biggest problem was that all distribution and sales activities were in complete ruins after the cancellation of the cooperation agreement. The situation was desperate.

Kongstrup's sales manager Bjarte Ottosen decided to plan for the future by examining the sales performance of the preceding year in order to better understand prospects for the newly independent Kongstrup. The first issue that became clear was that the existing – functional – structure of Kongstrup was not efficient at all. It had been obvious to many employees for some time – some might say for too long – that the company did not have an appropriate organizational structure. Among other things, this was made clear by the company's clumsy attempts to deal with an increasingly comprehensive product range, but also by the fact that the strategic alliance with MB had made such demands on the organization that it could hardly keep up. Naturally, what Ottosen feared the most was that Kongstrup now had to take over the distribution and sale of combines – something that would just reinforce the existing organizational weaknesses – whose inappropriateness would just become even more pronounced. There was little doubt that the cancellation of the alliance with MB would throw Kongstrup into an organizational crisis.

Even though Ottosen believed that an organizational crisis was imminent, both the managing director Henrik Larsen and the production manager Ulla Hedman were convinced that the functional structure would surely continue to prove its worth, not least because they believed Kongstrup could benefit from the advantages in international markets of the functional structure. In particular, they believed the division of labour provided decisive advantages, but they felt another benefit was that the individual department managers would always be managing a team of people who used the same resources. The fact that the departments worked closely together within each function and thereby developed the same values and standards had proved to be very useful. Furthermore, thus far the company had only experienced a limited number of strategic problems.

At the same time, the fact that the company did not have much experience in handling crises was a serious problem for Kongstrup. They were unable to predict the consequences of their actions, and in some cases it had been necessary to change key decisions as soon as they were implemented.

In addition to the problems of the organisational structure, it also became clear that Kongstrup had never considered which strategy to use in its customer relations. It had seemed so easy for Kongstrup to just leave the sale of combines to MB, while they only had to think about manufacture.

The sales manager Ottosen was familiar with both Porter's and Miles and Snow's methods of strategic planning, and he was convinced that the so-called low-cost strategy was the most appropriate one. The reason why he was so confident was the number of competitors and that many of the combine producers were in fact producing the same thing. So the only usable competition parameter for a company in the combine industry appeared to be price.

Furthermore, the analyses of Ottosen and managing director Larsen primarily saw the company as producing only for a domestic market. The basis for this conclusion was that Kongstrup was a Swedish company with a primary market in Scandinavia – a market with more or less the same structure in all the Nordic countries. This meant that they did not really see themselves as an exporting company, but more like a company with limited foreign engagements. Many employees also saw this as an absolute strength of the company.

Another advantage of regarding the company as a home-market company was the possibility of competing intensely on prices in the event that some of the larger and more internationally oriented market players started to flex their muscles. On several occasions this proved to be a highly rewarding strategy and from experience they knew that both Danish and Norwegian farmers preferred combines produced in Sweden rather than some of the large international brands. Furthermore, the strategy of ensuring there would never be more than 25 kilometres between the customer and the nearest service centre turned out to be a particularly persuasive argument for Scandinavian farmers and it was a strategy that could not easily be copied by the international companies.

A third advantage of having Scandinavia as their home market was that they achieved many advantages that were generally a decisive factor for global integration. First of all, it was, of course, the argument that it would be much easier to produce products that fitted into the mentioned low-cost strategy. Although the Scandinavian market was the most important one, sale of combines to other international markets was a key reason Kongstrup could produce combines at competitive prices. Sales manager Ottosen's argument was that the units sold in markets other than the Scandinavian market provided economies of scale that helped keep the price down so that production could be made at a lower cost per unit. When Tom Palme, one of his management colleagues, criticized the company's strategic analyses, Ottosen responded that this tactic was similar to that of the big competitors.

Palme had often been critical of the management in Kongstrup and on several occasions he had nearly been fired. So it was no secret, either to Ottosen or Henry Larson, that Palme thought Kongstrup was little more than 'just a small shop with no international clout' as he phrased it. Palme's own clout in the company had been reduced to next to nothing; not least because the other employees did not have the courage to back him up. His negative attitude and opinions were simply too controversial and no one wanted to be identified with him although several employees understood and agreed with some of his views and points.

On several occasions and by using several examples Palme had demonstrated that Kongstrup often reached decisions too late and that the quality of decisions was not good enough. He always created uproar and amusement at staff meetings when he exposed top management for late and inadequate decisions, particularly those decisions that management had first regarded as inspired, but had to abandon, making them a laughing stock.

Moreover, the dissident manager had for some time believed that Kongstrup was essentially a small, ailing company that had avoided risk through joining the strategic alliance. Several years ago, Palme had also pointed out that Kongstrup was incapable of developing new products and only progressed in line with the changes in the surrounding industry. Internally, the organisation was characterized by people going around 'patting management on the back' and as a result the conflict level was so low that there were few challenges to the status quo and widespread complacency.

It should be added that at the staff meeting where he mentioned the low conflict level, Palme also proclaimed that he was the most important employee of company and ought to get a pay raise. His argument was that a company does not need backslappers, but committed employees with the courage to look at the company in new ways; this should be the path to continuous development of the organization. Unsurprisingly, management was fed up with Palme's arrogance, while other employees found the conflict amusing.

Due to the breakdown of the alliance with MB, management did however start to see the situation of Kongstrup in a different light and changed its attitude towards their critical colleague. This was not least due to a closed meeting between managing director Larson and the department managers, where the production manager Ulla Hedman acknowledged that Palme might not be entirely right, but what he said made some sense.

Larson then asked Hedman to specify to what extent the critical employee was right – on a scale from 1 to 100. Her answer: 95. This sent shock waves through the management team, helping to make the top managers realize that they had to pursue a much strengthened international approach.

Accordingly, it was decided that the management team should try to specify a more proactive international strategy, with the purpose of re-positioning Kongstrup and not least to solve the urgent issue of building up new distribution and sales channels. After extensive research, management concluded that fundamentally there were four potential strategies:

1 A multi-domestic strategy;
2 An export strategy;
3 A globalization strategy; and
4 A combination of a globalization strategy and multi-domestic strategy.

(1) Multi-domestic strategy:
This is Kongstrup's current strategy. According to this strategy, differentiation advantages should be achieved adapting the products to the specific market while at the same time gaining a low-cost advantage. This is achieved by (i) transferring core competencies to those countries where they can be exploited most successfully to create both a low-cost advantage and a differentiation advantage and by (ii) creating a global network to handle coordination, enabling foreign and domestic divisions to share skills and core competencies.

The drawback of this strategy is that the two opposing factors – the differentiation advantage and the low-cost advantage – create considerable complexity which inevitably makes it very difficult to control and coordinate what happens. Furthermore, the bureaucratic costs can be high.

(2) Export strategy:
According to this strategy, Kongstrup is to customise the production of combines to each specific market, which requires that the core competencies (and only those) are developed at home and then transferred to the different countries. Then each foreign division takes over the products and they each have their own production departments, R&D departments and marketing departments. The general products will then be customised to the specific markets; this gives the company access to the resources of the individual countries and the different competencies of their work force. Accordingly, this strategy is synonymous with decentralized strategic control.

The main drawback of this strategy is the danger that the individual country subsidiaries will not exchange learning internationally. So if a division in one country develops a special competence, there may be no technology transfer to the divisions of the other countries. The other country's division might not even discover that the customers' requirements have changed. Consequently, every division has to develop their own individual core competencies. This strategy did not present any advantages of scale.

(3) Globalization strategy:
The globalization strategy is a very simple internationalisation strategy. The idea is to see the entire world as your home market. Currently, the company pays little attention to the specifics of individual markets. Standardized products and marketing strategies are followed. The risk of this strategy is that foreign

customers will feel the product and its marketed profile doesn't fit their specific needs.

(4) A combination of globalisation strategy and multi-domestic strategy:
The idea behind the combined globalisation and multi-domestic strategy is to offer the same standardised product in all countries. In other words, there will be no customisation of the combines for the specific customers in the different countries. Production itself is carried out in different countries, but the products are not customized. The core competencies will remain centralized in the parent company. This applies in particular to R&D, production and marketing.

The drawback of this strategy is that the products are not customized for the individual countries, and therefore there is a risk that local suppliers, who are closely familiar with the specific customer requirements, may gain a competitive advantage. Moreover, the strategy involves a high degree of centralization, high bureaucratic costs and high coordination and resource transferring costs.

The task of preparing the new strategy had now been going on for a few months, and management was proud that they could soon present these four internationalization strategies to the employees.

At one of the last management meetings before the presentation of the strategies, the finance manager did express, however, two concerns: His first concern was that although the company had described these four internationalization strategies, the strategies were not supported by an organisational structure. 'If we choose one of the four strategies and then continue with the functional structure, things might go wrong. We need to suggest a structure that supports the strategies.' The rest of the management team agreed. 'Another thing that worries me is which strategy should we choose?' Managing director Henry Larson joined the debate straight away. He immediately started to point out the obvious advantages of the multi-domestic strategy, where you could achieve differentiation advantages by customizing the products to the specific markets while gaining a low-cost advantage at the same time.

Halfdan Eriksson, the finance manager, was not as enthusiastic. 'I don't think we should propose a specific model. We risk making fools of ourselves. Imagine, if we point at one strategy and our critical colleague makes an entirely opposite suggestion that, for obvious reasons, turns out to be the right one and which we overlooked, we would stand a very bad light and he might end up replacing one of us in a top management position. I prefer that we present all four strategies and make some suggestions for relevant structures and let the employees take the discussion on that basis. We know, of course, which strategy we prefer and can always lead the discussion in that direction.'

The other managers widely supported this view. Now Eriksson, feeling secure in his position as number two – right after the managing director – said: 'We agree to involve the employees in the choice of strategy and then we only need to establish coherence between the strategy and the structure. Let us look at the following suggestion':

Strategy	Structure
1. Multi-domestic strategy	Global product structure
2. Export strategy	Global matrix structure
3. Globalization strategy	Global geographic structure
4. Globalization and multi-domestic	International division

The remaining management team carefully studied the suggestion, and all agreed that the management team now had a very good basis for discussing strategy and future structure with the employees. The high spirits that had characterised the top management team over the recent months gained extra strength and the general atmosphere was very positive indeed. Although the alliance with MB had broken down, up to half a year would pass before the customers should feel the impact of this breakdown. This provided Kongstrup with the time to consider which strategy and structure they should implement.

At the beginning of 2009, all employees were summoned to what management called the most important staff meeting in the history of Kongstrup. Everybody knew that the meeting did not concern any potential downsizing or redundancies at Kongstrup, but only that the company should choose a sensible strategy and structure.

Accordingly, there was a friendly atmosphere among the employees and everybody, both the employees and management, was greatly surprised when Palme, the determined critic, tore the proposal to shreds. He argued convincingly that management did not have the 'ability' – the expression he used – to pull Kongstrup out its very difficult situation.

Soon it became clear to the management team that Palme was right. In reply to a question from Henry Larson, the managing director, Palme revealed that he had previously studied organizational theory and if top management would allow him one month, he would present his suggestion to resolve the situation of the company and at the same time initiate management into his analyses and provide documentation for his arguments.

Larson admitted that management had not been done a good enough job of strategic planning, and he would be pleased to let Tom Palme help coordinate the process. Now the question was what Palme would suggest.

Case Questions

1. List the challenges facing Kongstrup after the collapse of the alliance with MB. Which are the most pressing issues in your opinion?
2. It is unusual in many organizations for top management to allow employees significant input into their strategy, as Kongstrup did. What are the advantages and disadvantages of an open approach to decision-making?
3. Was it advisable for Kongstrup top management to permit their critical employee Tom Palme to design a new strategy?
4. If you were Palme and had been given the task of coming up with a new organizational strategy, what strategy would you propose?

Notes

1. Nicholas George, 'Nokia wins back market share to bolster top spot', *Financial Times,* Jan 28 2005 p. 21; Nokia, *Hoover Company Reports* – In depth report, April 29, 2008; Robert Budden 'Handset prices cut in Nokia attempt to claw back sales' *Financial Times*, Apr 29, 2004; p. 15; BBC News, 'Motorola sales close in on Nokia', July 20, 2006, accessed at http://news.bbc.co.uk/go/pr/fr/-/1/hi/business/5197946.stm.
2. Robert Thompson, 'As The World Turns', *Billboard*, March 8, 2008; 'Tower Records Closing; An Iconic Symbol of Music Closes', *ABC News* transcript, December 22, 2006.
3. Don Phillips, 'Switzerland clears sale of airline to Lufthansa', *International Herald Tribune*, March 23, 2005, 13.
4. Dan Milmo, 'Cheap flights boom over, says BA chief as oil hits new high', *Guardian*, 23 May 2008, p.1.
5. Paul Keegan, 'Is the Music Store Over?' *Business 2.0* (March 2004), 115–118; Tom Hansson, Jürgen Ringbeck and Markus Franke, 'Fight for Survival: A New Business Model for the Airline Industry', *Strategy + Business*, Issue 31 (Summer 2003), 78–85.
6. Matthew Boyle, 'The Wegmans Way', *Fortune* (January 24, 2005), 62–68.
7. John Vidal, 'How do you survive as a greengrocer?' *The Guardian* , June 10, 2008, g2 section, p. 3.
8. Dana Milbank, 'Aluminum Producers, Aggressive and Agile, Outfight Steelmakers', *The Wall Street Journal* (July 1, 1992), A1.
9. Myra Pinkham, 'Aluminium Cans – History, Development and Market' Aluminium International Today, April/May 2002 pp. 37–38.
10. See http://www.babymilkaction.org/resources/boycott/nestlefree.html, accessed on June 18, 2008.
11. Kraft Foods Inc., *Hoover's Company Reports* – In-depth report, April 29, 2008.
12. Gwyn Morgan, 'Government, business must step up to ensure Canada Inc.'s recruitment success' *The Globe and Mail* (Canada), April 14, 2008, B2.
13. The Nation (Thailand), 'The government must resist the idea of an economic quick fix' March 6, 2008.
14. Aaron Bernstein, 'The Time Bomb in the Workforce: Illiteracy', *BusinessWeek* (February 25, 2002), 122.
15. Peter Svensson, 'Easing into the US market, one step at a time', The Virginian-Pilot, April 22, 2008, Pg. D5
16. 'European Union Outpaces United States on Chemical Safety' *Science Direct.com*. Retrieved May 2, 2008, from http://www.sciencedaily.com/releases/2007/01/070103110258.htm).
17. Samuel Loewenberg, 'Europe Gets Tougher on U.S. Companies', *The New York Times* (April 20, 2003), Section 3, 6.
18. Katherine Haddon, 'Top British supermarket cashes in on Polish pound', *Agence France Presse* September 11, 2006.
19. Brian Grow, 'Hispanic Nation', *BusinessWeek* (March 15, 2004), 58–70.
20. Mark Landler, 'Woes at Two Pillars of German Journalism', *The New York Times* (January 19, 2004), C8.
21. 'Weblogs Rack Up a Decade of Posts', *BBC News*, December 17, 2007, accessed at http://news.bbc.co.uk/1/hi/technology/7147728.stm on June 18, 2008.
22. Sion Barry, 'Budget flights from Cardiff', Western Mail, June 11, 2007, p.1, see also http://www.flyforbeans.com/blog, accessed on June 18, 2008.
23. Daimler AG (14 May 2007). 'Cerberus Takes Over Majority Interest in Chrysler Group and Related Financial Services Business for EUR 5.5 Billion ($7.4 billion) from DaimlerChrysler', press release retrieved on 6 June 2007.

24. See http://www.toyota.co.jp/en/about_toyota/manufacturing/worldwide.html, acessed on June 18, 2008.
25. Devin Leonard, 'Nightmare on Madison Avenue', *Fortune* (June 28, 2004), 93–108; and Brian Steinberg, 'Agency Cost-Accounting Is under Trial', *The Wall Street Journal* (January 28, 2005), B2.
26. Chua Hian Hou. 'Ogilvy & Mathers Tops Ad Agency Ranking Again: Firm Retains Title on its Good Number of New Client Signings, Slew of Awards Last Year. *The Straits Times (Singapore).* January 15, 2008; *PR Week*, '2007 ABR: Ogilvy Public Relations Worldwide The Outrider', April 23, 2007, accessed at http://www.prweekus.com/2007-ABR-Ogilvy-Public-Relations-Worldwide---The-Outrider/article/56835/ on June 18, 2008.
27. Randall D. Harris, 'Organizational Task Environments: An Evaluation of Convergent and Discriminant Validity', *Journal of Management Studies* 41, no. 5 (July 2004), 857–882; Allen C. Bluedorn, 'Pilgrim's Progress: Trends and Convergence in Research on Organizational Size and Environment', *Journal of Management* 19 (1993), 163–191; Howard E. Aldrich, *Organizations and Environments* (Englewood Cliffs, N.J.: Prentice-Hall, 1979); and Fred E. Emery and Eric L. Trist, 'The Casual Texture of Organizational Environments', *Human Relations* 18 (1965), 21–32.
28. Gregory G. Dess and Donald W. Beard, 'Dimensions of Organizational Task Environments', *Administrative Science Quarterly* 29 (1984), 52–73; Ray Jurkovich, 'A Core Typology of Organizational Environments', *Administrative Science Quarterly* 19 (1974), 380–394; Robert B. Duncan, 'Characteristics of Organizational Environment and Perceived Environmental Uncertainty', *Administrative Science Quarterly* 17 (1972), 313–327.
29. Christine S. Koberg and Gerardo R. Ungson, 'The Effects of Environmental Uncertainty and Dependence on Organizational Structure and Performance: A Comparative Study', *Journal of Management* 13 (1987), 725–737; and Frances J. Milliken, 'Three Types of Perceived Uncertainty about the Environment: State, Effect and Response Uncertainty', *Academy of Management Review* 12 (1987), 133–143.
30. Calie Williams, 'Crisis management', *The Grocer*, October 6, 2007, Pg. 41
31. David Wilson, 'See hate sites as tough love; Going online and venting anger on corporations is an extreme form of caring', *South China Morning Post*, July 5, 2005.
32. Mike France with Joann Muller, 'A Site for Soreheads', *BusinessWeek* (April 12, 1999), 86–90; Kirkpatrick and Roth, 'Why There's No Escaping the Blog'.
33. J. A. Litterer, *The Analysis of Organizations,* 2d ed. (New York: Wiley, 1973), 335.
34. Constance L. Hays, 'More Gloom on the Island of Lost Toy Makers', *The New York Times* (February 23, 2005), http://www.nytimes.com.
35. For an explanation of financialization, see Randy Martin (2002), *The Financialization of Daily Life*, Philadelphia, Temple University Press; introductory chapter available at http://www.temple.edu/tempress/chapters_1400/1615_ch1.pdf.
36. 'Former SEC Chairman Harvey Pitt speaks about illegal trading activity in France and the US', Transcript, *Wall Street Journal Report*, February 3, 2008; John Lanchester, Dicing with disaster, *The Guardian*, January 26, 2008, pg 31.
37. Rosalie L. Tung, 'Dimensions of Organizational Environments: An Exploratory Study of Their Impact on Organizational Structure', *Academy of Management Journal* 22 (1979), 672–693.
38. Joseph E. McCann and John Selsky, 'Hyper-turbulence and the Emergence of Type 5 Environments', *Academy of Management Review* 9 (1984), 460–470.
39. 'Prices Fuel Capacity Cuts; U.S. airlines grounding planes as costs soar, latest cutbacks in troubled domestic market', *Traffic World*, June 16, 2008, Pg. 29.
40. Rey Koslowski, 'Possible Steps Towards an International Regime for Mobility and Security', paper presented at international workshop on Global Mobility Regimes, Stockholm, June 11–12, 2004.
41. James D. Thompson, *Organizations in Action* (New York: McGraw-Hill, 1967), 20–21.
42. Alicia Buller, 'now it's personal', *Revolution* (Brand Republic), September 3, 2007, pg. 30.
43. David B. Jemison, 'The Importance of Boundary Spanning Roles in Strategic Decision-Making', *Journal of Management Studies* 21 (1984), 131–152; and Mohamed Ibrahim Ahmad At-Twaijri and John R. Montanari, 'The Impact of Context and Choice on the Boundary-Spanning Process: An Empirical Extension', *Human Relations* 40 (1987), 783–798.
44. Michelle Cook, 'The Intelligentsia', *Business 2.0* (July 1999), 135–136.
45. Robert C. Schwab, Gerardo R. Ungson and Warren B. Brown, 'Redefining the Boundary-Spanning Environment Relationship', *Journal of Management* 11 (1985), 75–86.
46. Tom Duffy, 'Spying the Holy Grail', *Microsoft Executive Circle* (Winter 2004), 38–39.
47. 'Gartner Says Worldwide Business Intelligence Platform Market Grew 13 Per cent in 2007', June 19, 2008, accessed at http://www.gartner.com/it/page.jsp?id=700410 on July 1, 2008.
48. Harry Hurt III, 'The Business Of Intelligence Gathering', The New York Times, June 15, 2008, p.5.; Tim Shorrock (2008), *Spies for Hire: The Secret World of Intelligence Outsourcing*, New York, Simon & Schuster.
49. Society of Competitive Intelligence Professionals, accessed May 4, 2008 at http://www.scip.org/Membership/content.cfm?itemnumber=2215&navItemNumber=2216; http://www.dmu.ac.uk/faculties/business_and_law/business/marketing/mk_staff_sheilawright.jsp, accessed on June 19, 2008.
50. Pia Nordlinger, 'Know Your Enemy', *Working Woman* (May 2001), 16.
51. Ken Western, 'Ethical Spying', *Business Ethics* (September/October 1995), 22–23; Stan Crock, Geoffrey Smith, Joseph Weber, Richard A. Melcher and Linda Himelstein, 'They Snoop to Conquer', *BusinessWeek* (October 28, 1996), 172–176; and Kenneth A. Sawka, 'Demystifying Business Intelligence', *Management Review* (October 1996), 47–51.

52. Edwin M. Epstein, 'How to Learn from the Environment about the Environment – A Prerequisite for Organizational Well-Being', *Journal of General Management* 29, no. 1 (Autumn 2003), 68–80.
53. 'Snooping on a Shoestring', *Business 2.0* (May 2003), 64–66.
54. Cognos Inc., Hoover's Company Records – In-depth report, April 29, 2008.
55. http://www.shell.com/home/content/responsible_energy/sustainability_reports/dir_shell_sustainability_reports.html.
56. Mike France with Joann Muller, 'A Site for Soreheads', *BusinessWeek* (April 12, 1999), 86–90.
57. Rhymer Rigby, 'Amancio Ortega Gaona: The shy CEO', *World Business,* 27 January 2007.
58. Nirmalya Kumar and Sophie Linguri, 'Fashion Sense', *Business Strategy Review*, Summer 2006, 80–84.
59. Jay W. Lorsch, 'Introduction to the Structural Design of Organizations', in Gene W. Dalton, Paul R. Lawrence and Jay W. Lorsch, eds., *Organizational Structure and Design* (Homewood, Ill.: Irwin and Dorsey, 1970), 5.
60. Paul R. Lawrence and Jay W. Lorsch, *Organization and Environment* (Homewood, Ill.: Irwin, 1969).
61. Lorsch, 'Introduction to the Structural Design of Organizations', 7.
62. Jay W. Lorsch and Paul R. Lawrence, 'Environmental Factors and Organizational Integration', in J. W. Lorsch and Paul R. Lawrence, eds., *Organizational Planning: Cases and Concepts* (Homewood, Ill.: Irwin and Dorsey, 1972), 45.
63. Tom Burns and G. M. Stalker, *The Management of Innovation* (London: Tavistock, 1961).
64. John A. Courtright, Gail T. Fairhurst and L. Edna Rogers, 'Interaction Patterns in Organic and Mechanistic Systems', *Academy of Management Journal* 32 (1989), 773–802.
65. Dennis K. Berman, 'Crunch Time', *BusinessWeek Frontier* (April 24, 2000), F28–F38.
66. 'R.A.B. Holdings, Inc. Announces the Purchase of Certain of the Assets of Guiltless Gourmet, Inc', *Business Wire*, November 6, 2000, accessed on June 30 2008; R.A.B. Holdings Inc. *Hoovers Company Reports – In-depth report*, April 29, 2008.
67. Robert A. Guth, 'Eroding Empires: Electronics Giants of Japan Undergo Wrenching Change', *The Wall Street Journal* (June 20, 2002), A1, A9.
68. Thomas C. Powell, 'Organizational Alignment as Competitive Advantage', *Strategic Management Journal* 13 (1992), 119–134; Mansour Javidan, 'The Impact of Environmental Uncertainty on Long-Range Planning Practices of the US Savings and Loan Industry', *Strategic Management Journal* 5 (1984), 381–392; Tung, 'Dimensions of Organizational Environments', 672–693; and Thompson, *Organizations in Action.*
69. Ian Wylie, 'There Is No Alternative To ...', *Fast Company* (July 2002), 106–110.
70. Trevor Maxwell, 'Legacy of 9/11 attacks: Lost innocence; Employees at Portland's jetport describe a day of terror and changes that resulted in its aftermath', *Portland Press Herald*, September 9, 2007, Pg. A1.
71. David Ulrich and Jay B. Barney, 'Perspectives in Organizations: Resource Dependence, Efficiency and Population', *Academy of Management Review* 9 (1984), 471–481; and Jeffrey Pfeffer and Gerald Salancik, *The External Control of Organizations: A Resource Dependent Perspective* (New York: Harper & Row, 1978).
72. Andrew H. Van de Ven and Gordon Walker, 'The Dynamics of Interorganizational Coordination', *Administrative Science Quarterly* (1984), 598–621; and Huseyin Leblebici and Gerald R. Salancik, 'Stability in Interorganizational Exchanges: Rulemaking Processes of the Chicago Board of Trade', *Administrative Science Quarterly* 27 (1982), 227–242.
73. Kevin Kelly and Zachary Schiller with James B. Treece, 'Cut Costs or Else: Companies Lay Down the Law to Suppliers', *BusinessWeek* (March 22, 1993), 28–29.
74. Wendy Priesnitz, 'Countering the spin', *Natural Life*, November 1, 2007, p. 34.
75. www.fair.org.
76. G. Pascal Zachary, 'Many Journalists See a Growing Reluctance to Criticize Advertisers', *The Wall Street Journal* (February 6, 1992), A1, A9.
77. Peter Hart and Janine Jackson, 'Media Lick the Hand That Feeds Them: Does Wal-Mart's money buy more than ads?', *Extra*, November/December 2005, accessed at http://www.fair.org/index.php?page=2770 on June 30, 2008.
78. Ashar, Hemal (May 11, 2004) Is this journalism? *Mid Day*, accessed at http://ww1.mid-day.com/news/city/2004/may/83022.htm on February 27, 2005; Ninan, Sevanti (2004) 'The leader cons the reader' in Sunil K Poolani (ed) *Rape of News: The ethics (or lack of it) of selling editorial space*, pp 23-26 Mumbai: Frog Books.
79. Judith A. Babcock, Organizational Responses to Resource Scarcity and Munificence: Adaptation and Modification in Colleges within a University (Ph.D. diss., Pennsylvania State University, 1981).
80. Peter Smith Ring and Andrew H. Van de Ven, 'Developmental Processes of Corporative Interorganizational Relationships', *Academy of Management Review* 19 (1994), 90–118; Jeffrey Pfeffer, 'Beyond Management and the Worker: The Institutional Function of Management', *Academy of Management Review* 1 (April 1976), 36–46; and John P. Kotter, 'Managing External Dependence', *Academy of Management Review* 4 (1979), 87–92.
81. Bryan Borys and David B. Jemison, 'Hybrid Arrangements as Strategic Alliances: Theoretical Issues in Organizational Combinations', *Academy of Management Review* 14 (1989), 234–249.
82. Julie Cohen Mason, 'Strategic Alliances: Partnering for Success,' *Management Review* (May 1993), 10–15.
83. Adrian E. Tschoegl (2007), 'McDonald's – Much Maligned, But an Engine of Economic Development', *Global Economy Journal*, 7, article 5; George Cohon (1998), To Russia with Fries, Toronto, McLelland and Stewart.
84. Teri Agins and Alessandra Galloni, 'After Gianni; Facing a Squeeze, Versace Struggles to Trim the Fat', *The Wall Street Journal* (September 30, 2003), A1, A10; John F. Love, *McDonald's: Behind the Arches* (New York: Bantam Books, 1986).
85. Borys and Jemison, 'Hybrid Arrangements as Strategic Alliances'.
86. Iain S Bruce, 'Dial M for merger', *The Sunday Herald*, June 4, 2000, Pg. 2.

87. Ekow Nelson , Rob van den Dam , Howard Kline (2008), 'A future in content(ion): Can telecom providers win a share of the digital content market?', *Journal of Telecommunications Management* 1, Pg. 125–138.
88. Robert Lester, 'Orange; In need of a brighter dawn', *Marketing Week*, December 20, 2007, Pg. 16.
89. Jon Ashworth and Rupert Steiner, 'How Branson set out to slay sky', *The Business*, March 31, 2007; Dave Bailey, 'Glitches Mar Broadband Services' *IT Week*, July 9, 2007, Pg. 26.
90. 'IBM tests Mobile Speech Applictions', IT World. Retrieved May 5, 2008, from http://www.itworld.com/App/85/060224ibmspeech.
91. Ian Katz and Elisabeth Malkin, 'Battle for the Latin American Net', *BusinessWeek* (November 1, 1999), 194–200; 'IBM Joint Venture to Put Laundry on Web', *The Wall Street Journal* (August 30, 2002), B4.
92. Donald Palmer, 'Broken Ties: Interlocking Directorates and Intercorporate Coordination', *Administrative Science Quarterly 28* (1983), 40–55; F. David Shoorman, Max H. Bazerman and Robert S. Atkin, 'Interlocking Directorates: A Strategy for Reducing Environmental Uncertainty', *Academy of Management Review* 6 (1981), 243–251; and Ronald S. Burt, *Toward a Structural Theory of Action* (New York: Academic Press, 1982).
93. James R. Lang and Daniel E. Lockhart, 'Increased Environmental Uncertainty and Changes in Board Linkage Patterns', *Academy of Management Journal* 33 (1990), 106–128; and Mark S. Mizruchi and Linda Brewster Stearns, 'A Longitudinal Study of the Formation of Interlocking Directorates', *Administrative Science Quarterly* 33 (1988), 194–210.
94. http://www.theregister.co.uk/2008/03/13/hewitt_joins_bt/.
95. Paul Waugh, 'Ex-health secretary to work for hospital owner and Boots', *The Evening Standard*, January 18, 2008, pg B6; Simon Hoggart, Slasher takes on lobbyists, *The Guardian*, May 9, 2008, Pg. 14; David Craig and Peter Brooks, *Plundering the Public Sector*, London, Constable.
96. Andrew Davidson, The end of Alexander the great: chief of the world's top magazine quits, *The Australian*, April 28, 2008, Pg. 30; Damian Reece, A rich legacy at Economist, *The Daily Telegraph*, June 23, 2008, Pg. 5.
97. Lee Hawkins Jr. 'GM Seeks Chevrolet Revival', *The Wall Street Journal* (December 19, 2003), B4.
98. Kotter, 'Managing External Dependence'.
99. William C. Symonds, with Farah Nayeri, Geri Smith and Ted Plafker, 'Bombardier's Blitz', *BusinessWeek* (February 6, 1995), 62–66; and Joseph Weber, with Wendy Zellner and Geri Smith, 'Loud Noises at Bombardier', *BusinessWeek* (January 26, 1998), 94–95.
100. Rosie Baker, 'Sounds different', *In Store Marketing*, May 15 2008, Pg. 20; Kelly Macnamara, 'Xmas Misery For Music Store Workers', *Press Association Newsfile*, December 25, 2008.
101. Ken Schachter 'Microsoft Leads Lobbying Largesse', *Redherring.com*, April, 28 2008, retrieved May 5, 2008, from http://www.redherring.com/Home/24187; Kevin J. O'Brien, 'Microsoft format seen becoming a standard; Battle fought over document software', *The International Herald Tribune*, September 4, 2007, Pg. 11; Joab Jackson, 'ISO benches Microsoft OOXML', *Government Computer News*, June 11 2008.
102. Duncan McLeod, Fear and loathing, *Financial Mail* (South Africa), May 30, 2008, Pg. 14; 'Let's Leave it Open', *Indian Express*, March 27, 2008.
103. Matthew K. Wynia, 'Public Health, Public Trust and Lobbying', *American Journal of Bioethics*, June 2007, Pg. 4.
104. Ben Worthen, 'Mr. Gates Goes to Washington', *CIO* (September 2004), 63–72; Gardiner Harris and Chris Adams, 'Delayed Reaction: Drug Manufacturers Step Up Legal Attacks That Slow Generics', *The Wall Street Journal* (July 12, 2001), A1, A10; Leila Abboud, 'Raging Hormones: How Drug Giant Keeps a Monopoly on 60-Year-Old Pill', *The Wall Street Journal* (September 9, 2004), A1.
105. Christopher Hope and James Hall, 'Wal-Mart did lobby Blair over Asda' *The Sunday Telegraph,* January 27, 2008, Pg. 2; 'Retail opportunities in India' *The Herald* (Glasgow), December 28 2006, Pg. 20; 'Wal-Mart keeps raising lobbying budget', *The Myrtle Beach Sun-News* (South Carolina), March 8, 2008, Pg. 2.
106. David B. Yoffie, 'How an Industry Builds Political Advantage', *Harvard Business Review* (May–June 1988), 82–89; and Jeffrey H. Birnbaum, 'Chief Executives Head to Washington to Ply the Lobbyist's Trade', *The Wall Street Journal* (March 19, 1990), A1, A16.
107. Joel Caeusu, 'R&D: Patent protection attracts research to Quebec', *The Montreal Gazette*, April 24, 1999, S10; David Morley, 'Drug companies focus on profits, not people', *Victoria Times Colonist*, April 20, 2004.
108. Anthony J. Daboub, Abdul M. A. Rasheed, Richard L. Priem and David A. Gray, 'Top Management Team Characteristics and Corporate Illegal Activity', *Academy of Management Review* 20, no. 1 (1995), 138–170.
109. Nelson D. Schwartz and Lowell Bergman, 'Payload: Taking Aim At Corporate Bribery', *New York Times*, November 25, 2007, Section 3, Pg. 1; David Hencke, 'Tories join Brown in bid to block fraud investigations', *The Guardian*, April 12, 2008, Pg. 1
110. Nora Colomer, 'UK mortgage lending sees growth', *Asset Securitization Report*, November 27, 2006; Edmund Conway, 'Was stability bridge to blame for wobble?', *The Daily Telegraph*, September 24, 2007, Pg. 5.
111. *The Guardian*, 'Societe Generale scandal: Unanswered questions Who knew what?' January 26, 2008, Pg. 4; Alex Brummer, 'Hammer Blow to City's Reputation', *The Guardian*, February 27, 1995.
112. Barry M. Staw and Eugene Szwajkowski, 'The Scarcity-Munificence Component of Organizational Environments and the Commission of Illegal Acts,' *Administrative Science Quarterly* 20 (1975), 345–354; and Kimberly D. Elsbach and Robert I. Sutton, 'Acquiring Organizational Legitimacy through Illegitimate Actions: A Marriage of Institutional and Impression Management Theories,' *Academy of Management Journal* 35 (1992), 699–738.

CHAPTER 5

INTERORGANIZATIONAL RELATIONSHIPS

Organizational Ecosystems
- Is Competition Dead?
- The Changing Role of Management
- Interorganizational Framework

Resource Dependence
- Resource Strategies
- Power Strategies

Collaborative Networks
- Why Collaboration?
- From Adversaries to Partners

Population Ecology
- Organizational Form and Niche
- Process of Ecological Change
- Strategies for Survival

Institutionalism
- The Institutional View and Organization Design
- Institutional Similarity

Summary and Interpretation

MAN AG

MAN Nutzfahrzeuge AG, the German-based truck, commercial vehicle and engineering equipment manufacturer celebrated its 250th anniversary in 2008. The company's record of innovation is impressive, and includes the invention of the diesel engine (named after a MAN employee, Rudolf Diesel). 2007 was the company's most successful year yet, with new orders up 17 per cent, sales 19 per cent higher at €15.5 billion, and a fifty per cent increase in profits to €1.7 billion.[1] But MAN isn't resting on its laurels. Nearly 90 per cent of the company's sales are in Europe, a mature market with relatively little room for growth. MAN has been engaged in lengthy negotiations about a possible takeover of Scania, its major European competitor, but another main focus is building stronger positions outside Europe.

In 2004, MAN established a major strategic agreement with International Truck and Engine Corp., the truck division of America's Navistar Corporation. The two companies agreed to jointly develop engines and other key components for trucks. They are a perfect match because International doesn't sell in Europe, while MAN is not present in North America. Their first major collaboration, the Maxxforce big bore six cylinder diesel engine launched in 2007, has been such a success that it prompted the American heavy equipment manufacturer Caterpillar to abandon engine manufacture and adopt the engine as standard in its equipment.[2]

In the longer term, MAN is counting on expansion into the rapidly growing emerging markets of countries like India and China. In 2006 the company set up a joint venture with Force Motors, a major Indian manufacturer of commerical vehicles. By 2008 the joint venture was in production mode, with planned output of 16 to 45-tonne trucks expected to grow fourfold from 6,000 vehicles a year to 24,000 by 2010. Significantly, MAN operates a large design facility in Aurangabad, India, with over 100 design engineers. Already, some Indian-manufactured products, such as marine motors, are shipped overseas from India, undoubtedly an indication of future trends in a highly competitive globalized economy. Two of MAN's competitors, Daimler Trucks and Volvo Trucks, have already set up joint venture deals with two Indian domestic vehicle manufacturers, and other companies are queuing up to sign on too.[3] MAN has also set up several joint ventures in China, though progress has been slower than in India, with several JV deals falling through and the company eventually setting up its own manufacturing plant. Nevertheless, MAN engineering director Karl Viktor Schaller says that in 2009 'we are expecting the most growth in India, China and South America'.[4]

Organizations of all sizes in all industries are rethinking how they do business in response to today's chaotic environment. One of the most widespread trends is to reduce boundaries and increase collaboration between companies, sometimes even between competitors. Today's aerospace companies, for example, depend on strategic partnerships with other organizations. Europe's Airbus Industrie and Boeing, the largest US aerospace company, are both involved in multiple relationships with suppliers, competitors and other organizations. Global semiconductor makers have been collaborating while competing for years because of the high costs and risks associated with creating and marketing a new generation of semiconductors.

Global competition and rapid advances in technology, communications and transportation have created amazing new opportunities for organizations, but they have also raised the cost of doing business and made it increasingly difficult for any company to take advantage of those opportunities on its own. In this new economy, webs of organizations are emerging. A large company like France's Renault develops a special relationship with a supplier that eliminates middlemen by sharing complete information and reducing the costs of salespersons and distributors. Several small companies may join together to produce and market noncompeting products. You can see the results of interorganizational collaboration when movies such as *War of the Worlds, The Incredibles* or *Star Wars: The Clone Wars* are launched. Before seeing the movie, you might read a cover story in *Hello*! or *Heat*, see a preview clip or chat live with the stars at an online site such as E online, find action toys being given away at a fast-food franchise and notice retail stores loaded with movie-related merchandise. For some blockbuster movies, coordinated action among companies can yield millions in addition to box-office and DVD profits. In the new economy, organizations think of themselves as teams that create value jointly rather than as autonomous companies that are in competition with all others.

COUNTERPOINT 5.1

Some care should be exercised when using the 'team' metaphor. These are alliances in which the members are very much calculating their own advantage both in joining and remaining and in inducing and pressurizing others to cooperate. Their 'play' may be one of reciprocal exploitaton rather than collective identification with the venture. As a consequences, there are issues of long-term commitment, and many of these collaborations are tentative, conditional and transitory. **Discuss**

Purpose of This Chapter

This chapter explores the most recent trend in organizing, which is the increasingly dense web of relationships among organizations. Companies have always been dependent on other organizations for supplies, materials and information. The question is how these relationships are managed. At one time it was a matter of a large, powerful company like Unilever or General Electric tightening the screws on small suppliers. Today a company can choose to develop positive, trusting relationships. A company like Toyota might decide to create a subsidiary like Lexus, when it wants to create a product that will be a decisive upmarket shift from the family cars for which the company is famous. The notion of horizontal relationships described in Chapter 3 and the understanding of environmental uncertainty in Chapter 4 are leading to the increased formation of horizontal relationships *across* organizations. Organizations can strive to build relationships in many ways, such as appointing preferred suppliers, establishing agreements, business partnering, joint ventures or even mergers and acquisitions.

COUNTERPOINT 5.2

A 'trusting relationship' is not necessarily something that can be 'chosen' as it involves another party whose cooperation is vital. A company may strive to build more trusting relationships but their establishment will depend upon the willingness of the partner and also the ability to sustain trust during testing times – of market downturns, for example. **Discuss**

The sum total of these ideas can be daunting, because it means managers no longer can rest in the safety of managing a single organization. They have to figure out how to manage a whole set of interorganizational relationships, which is a great deal more challenging and complex.

Organizational Ecosystems

Interorganizational relationships are the relatively enduring resource transactions, flows and linkages that occur among two or more organizations.[5] Traditionally, these transactions and relationships have been seen more as a necessary evil to obtain what an organization needs. The presumption has been that the world in business is a zero-sum game – there are simply winners and losers – in which distinct businesses thrive on autonomy and compete for supremacy. On this view, a company may be forced into interorganizational relationships, depending on its needs and the instability and complexity of the environment, but submits to this force out of weakness.

A new view described by James Moore argues conceives of organizations as participants in business ecosystems. An **organizational ecosystem** is a system formed by the interaction of a community of organizations and their environment. An ecosystem cuts across traditional industry lines. Microsoft operates in four major industries: consumer electronics, information, communications and personal computers. Its ecosystem includes millions of customers across many markets internationally, as well as hundreds of suppliers, including companies across the world such as Singapore-based Flextronics, which manufactures the Xbox under contract.[6] Cable companies like Virgin Media in the UK and Comcast in America are offering telephone service, while telephone companies like Deutsche Telekom are investing heavily in the television business.[7] Apple Computer is arguably having greater success as an entertainment and mobile communications company with its iPod, iPhone and iTunes Music Store than it ever had as a computer manufacturer. Apple's success grows out of close partnerships with other organizations, including music companies, consumer electronics firms, cell phone makers, other computer companies and even car manufacturers.[8] Deutsche Telekom and Microsoft, like other business ecosystems, develop relationships with hundreds of organizations cutting across traditional business boundaries. Organizations around the world are embedded in complex networks of confusing relationships – collaborating in some markets, competing fiercely in others. Indeed, research indicates that a large percentage of new alliances in recent years have been between competitors. These alliances influence organizations' competitive behaviour in varied ways.[9]

COUNTERPOINT 5.3

It is notable that the 'ecosystem' does not extend beyond other companies to the natural environment. There is little recognition of companies' dependence upon the biosphere or of the damage they routinely inflict upon it by externalizing their costs upon a 'party' that is unable to press charges. **Discuss**

As an organization manager, keep these guidelines in mind:

Look for and develop relationships with other organizations. Don't limit your thinking to a single industry or business type. Build an ecosystem of which your organization is a part.

Is Competition Dead?

Traditional competition, which assumes a distinct company competing for survival and supremacy with other stand-alone businesses, no longer exists because each organization both supports and depends on the others for success, and perhaps for survival. However, most managers recognize that the competitive stakes are higher than ever in a world where market share can crumble overnight and no industry is immune from almost instant obsolescence.[10] In today's world, a new form of competition is intensifying but it is one that involves clusters of businesses competing with other clusters.[11] The airline industry is a clear example where a number of alliances, which offer international passengers connectivity and convenience, have formed between the major players. The three largest alliances are the Star Alliance, SkyTeam and Oneworld. A more recent development is the formation of alliances between cargo airlines, such as that of WOW Alliance and SkyTeam Cargo.

With coevolution through an alliance or network, it is possible for the whole system to becomes stronger. Companies coevolve through discussion with each other, shared visions, alliances and managing complex relationships.

Amazon and its partners represent a business ecosystem, in which each company depends to some extent on the others and each has the opportunity to grow stronger. For example, Amazon is finding that every new retail partner has its own demands for how its products should be presented and sold. Amazon managers say they welcome the feedback because it enables them to keep improving the site. The retail partners may benefit too, because Amazon keeps a close watch on factors such as how well the retailers are managing delivery, communication and customer service.

Exhibit 5.1 illustrates the complexity of an ecosystem by showing the myriad overlapping relationships in which high-tech companies were involved in 1999. Since then, many of these companies have merged, been acquired, or gone out of business during the dot-com crash of 2000 and 2001. Ecosystems constantly change and evolve, with some relationships growing stronger while others weaken or are terminated.

Amazon.com Inc.

Amazon.com was one of the earliest players in the world of online retailing, opening its virtual bookstore in 1995, before many people had ever heard of the Internet. Since then, Amazon has continued to evolve, from an online bookseller to an online retailer operating sales portals in Canada, the UK, Germany, Japan, France and China, as well as the original US site, with its own vast warehouses of books, DVDs, kitchen appliances and electronics. Amazon is now also a technology provider for other merchants. Today, Amazon sells everything from baby furniture to golf clubs, but its partners own and store most of the inventory. Amazon's Web sites serve as an online shopping mall where retailers set up shop to sell their wares to a vast global market. Amazon has partnerships with hundreds of small and large retailers, including Lovefilm, Hachette Livre and Lands End.

Amazon processes the orders and gets a cut of the sale, but retailers fill the orders from their own warehouses. The arrangement gives Amazon a way to expand into new businesses without making huge investments in inventory and developing the expertise to forecast hot products in multiple categories. As for the retailers, they get access to Amazon's global customer traffic, $100 million-plus annual spend on leading-edge technology and Internet savvy, enabling them to focus on their bricks-and-mortar businesses.[12]

The partnership approach is not without its challenges. Toys 'R' Us, one of Amazon's earliest partners, sued the online firm and stopped selling its products through the company, charging that Amazon violated its contract when it began allowing other retailers to sell products that compete with Toys 'R' Us.[13] Hachette, the largest book publisher in the UK and France, is involved in a bitter and public dispute about the cut taken by Amazon which it claims exceeds 50 per cent of the book price, and which it says Amazon is pressing to increase even further.[14] Some big companies, including Nike, oppose the sale of their goods on Amazon, fearing it might tarnish their premium brands. Amazon, however, insists that in the long run, the web of partnerships will benefit everyone.[15] One manufacturer that eventually agreed is Sony. Sony executives originally refused to authorize Amazon to sell Sony products, but realized they were fighting a losing battle to try and maintain control and exclusivity in the new world of Internet retailing. Today, Sony products are big sellers on the site.[16]

EXHIBIT 5.1 An Organizational Ecosystem (based on 1999 data)

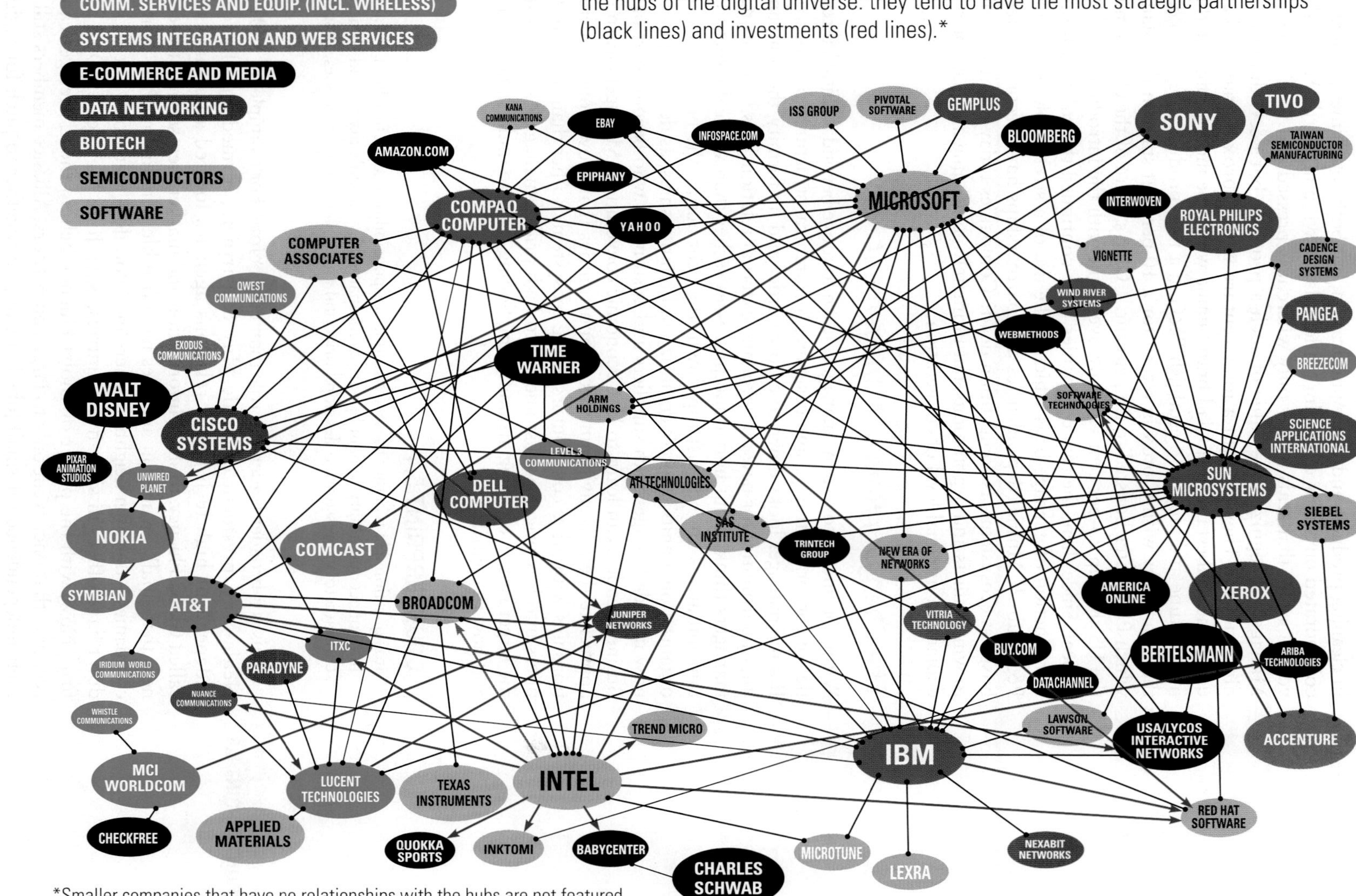

*Smaller companies that have no relationships with the hubs are not featured.

In an organizational ecosystem, conflict and cooperation frequently exist at the same time. Procter & Gamble (P&G) and Clorox are fierce North American rivals in cleaning products and water purification, but both companies profited when they collaborated on a new cling film (called plastic wrap in North America). P&G invented a film that seals tightly only where it is pressed and won't stick elsewhere. Managers recognized the value of such a product, but P&G didn't have a cling film category. They thought a joint venture with Clorox to market the new film under the well-established Glad brand name would be more profitable than investing the time and money to establish P&G in a new product category. P&G shared the technology with Clorox in return for a 10 per cent stake in the Glad business, which P&G later boosted to 20 per cent.[17] Glad's share of the cling film market in the US shot up 23 per cent virtually overnight with the introduction of Glad Press 'n Seal. Since then, the two companies have continued the collaboration with the introduction of garbage bags which make use of a stretchable plastic invented in P&G labs.[18] Mutual dependencies and partnerships have become a fact of life in business ecosystems. Is competition dead? Companies today may use their strength to win conflicts and negotiations, but ultimately continuing any genuine partnership demands a minimal level of cooperation.

The Changing Role of Management

Within business ecosystems managers learn to move beyond traditional responsibilities of corporate strategy and designing hierarchical structures and control systems. If a top manager looks down to enforce order and uniformity, the company is missing opportunities for new and evolving external relationships.[19] In this new world, managers think about horizontal processes rather than vertical structures. Important initiatives are not just top down; they cut across the boundaries separating organizational units. Moreover, horizontal relationships, as described in Chapter 3, now include linkages with suppliers and customers, who become part of the team. Business leaders can learn to lead economic coevolution. Managers learn to see and appreciate the rich environment of opportunities that grow from cooperative relationships with other contributors to the ecosystem. Rather than trying to force suppliers into low prices or customers into high prices, managers strive to strengthen the larger system evolving around them, finding ways to understand this big picture and how to contribute.

COUNTERPOINT 5.4

It is questionable whether these 'traditional responsibilities' are left behind. Established lines of accountability remain but are accompanied by (complexifying and sometimes contradictory) pressures to develop horizontal and collaborative processes. **Discuss**

See online **COUNTERPOINT 5.8**

This is a broader leadership role than ever before. For example, in 2001 Donovan Neale-May, president of Neale-May & Partners, formed an alliance of forty independent high-tech public relations agencies located all around the world, called GlobalFluency, to share information and market their services to acquire business that small, owner-run agencies have trouble winning on their own. 'We have companies – our own neighbours here in Colorado – that won't hire us because we don't have offices in sixty-five countries,' says John Metzger, CEO of a small PR firm. Now, with the power of GlobalFluency behind them, Metzger can share in accounts that once went only to large competitors. Alliance members still maintain their independence for small jobs but can join together to pitch for regional projects or international campaigns. The E3 European Agency Network, comprised of

EXHIBIT 5.2 A Framework of Interorganizational Relationships*

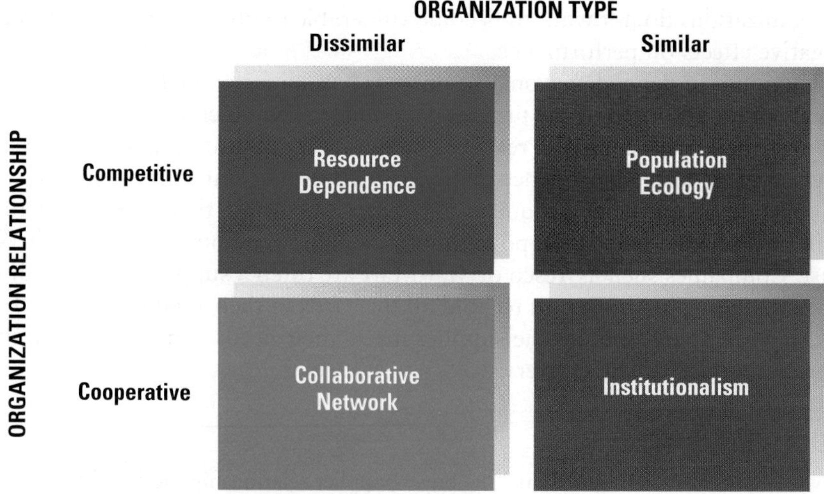

Thanks to Anand Narasimhan for suggesting this framework.

twenty European marketing and communications firms, operates on much the same basis but with a focus on Europe.[20,21]

Interorganizational Framework

Understanding this larger organizational ecosystem is one of the most challenging areas of organization theory. The models and perspectives for understanding interorganizational relationships can be of assistance to managers in developing horizontal management across organizations. A framework for analyzing the different views of interorganizational relationships is in Exhibit 5.2. Relationships among organizations can be characterized by whether the organizations are dissimilar or similar and whether relationships are competitive or cooperative. By understanding these perspectives, managers can assess their environment and adopt strategies to suit their needs. The first perspective is called resource-dependence theory, which was briefly described in Chapter 4. It describes rational ways organizations deal with each other to reduce dependence on the environment. The second perspective is about collaborative networks, through which organizations increase their dependencies upon other organizations to increase value and productivity for both. The third perspective is population ecology, which examines how new organizations fill niches left open by established organizations, and how a rich variety of new organizational forms emerges in response to the changing needs of society. The final approach is called institutionalism and explains why and how organizations legitimate themselves in the larger environment and design structures by borrowing ideas from each other. These four approaches to the study of interorganizational relationships are described in the remainder of this chapter.

Resource Dependence

As described in Chapter 4, **resource-dependence** theory argues that organizations try to minimize their dependence on other organizations for the supply of important resources and try to influence the environment to make resources available.[22] Organizations are conceived to succeed by striving for independence and autonomy.

BRIEFCASE

As an organization manager, keep these guidelines in mind:

Reach out and control external sectors that threaten needed resources. Adopt strategies to control resources, especially when your organization is dependent and has little power. Assert your company's influence when you have power and control over resources.

When threatened by greater dependence, organizations will assert control over external resources to minimize that dependence. Resource-dependence theory argues that organizations do not want to become vulnerable to other organizations because of negative effects on performance.

The amount of dependence on a resource is based on two factors. First is the importance of the resource to the firm, and second is how much discretion or monopoly power those who control a resource have over its allocation and use.[23] With an awareness of resource-dependence theory, executives may pursue strategies to reduce their dependence on the environment and learn how to use their power differences. As will be discussed below, the power differences between buyers and suppliers can be vast. Companies such as Tesco or Wal-Mart are often a supplier's largest, or even only customer. They often seem to hold all the cards in their relationships with suppliers, and are able to ensure the supplier meets their needs, which typically entails low price and fast, timely delivery.

COUNTERPOINT 5.5

Given their success in recent years, the buyer-supplier relationship modelled by Tesco and Wal-Mart might seem to be the preferable position vis-à-vis suppliers. However, as discussed later in this chapter, there has been some backlash against big chain domination, based on issues such as the environmental and long-term financial sustainability of this model, as well as the risk of market monopolization. There is increasing pressure on governments to regulate big chains' behaviour.[24] A recent study by Marjolein et al. of purchaser–supplier relationships in Holland found that the most satisfactory buyer-supplier relationships tended to occur when there was a high level of mutual dependence and interaction.[25] While awareness of the external environment is crucial, it does not necessarily follow that the best way of managing the external environment is to control it. **Discuss**

Resource Strategies

When organizations feel resource or supply constraints, the resource-dependence perspective says they manoeuvre to maintain their autonomy through a variety of strategies, several of which were described in Chapter 4. One strategy is to adapt to or alter the interdependent relationships. This could mean purchasing ownership in suppliers, developing long-term contracts, alliances or joint ventures to lock in necessary resources, or building relationships in other ways. Another technique is to use interlocking directorships, which means boards of directors include members of the boards of supplier companies. Organizations may also join trade associations to coordinate their needs, sign trade agreements or merge with another firm to guarantee resources and material supplies. Some organizations may take political action, such as lobbying for new regulations or deregulation, favourable taxation, tariffs or subsidies, or push for new standards that make resource acquisition easier. Organizations operating under the resource-dependence philosophy will do whatever is needed to avoid excessive dependence on the environment to maintain control of resources and hence reduce uncertainty.

See online COUNTERPOINT 5.9

Power Strategies

In resource-dependence theory, the focus is upon differences of power – for example, between large, relatively independent companies with many options and small suppliers with few options.[26] With the growth of giant retail chains operating through hypermarkets, as well as online portals selling a vast range of goods, power in consumer products has shifted from vendors such as Unilever and Rubbermaid to these even bigger retailers, which can demand – and receive – special pricing deals. Companies like Carrefour, Amazon, Tesco and Wal-Mart have grown so large and powerful that they are in a position to dictate the terms with almost any supplier. Consider Levi Strauss, which for much of its 150-year history was a powerful supplier with a jeans brand that millions of people wanted and retailers were eager to stock. 'When I first started in this business, retailers were a waystation to the consumer,' says Levi's former CEO Philip Marineau, who made the decision to supply to Wal-Mart despite the risks to his company. 'Manufacturers had a tendency to tell retailers how to do business.' But the balance of power has shifted dramatically. In order to sell to the big retailers, Levi Strauss overhauled its entire operation, from design and production to pricing and distribution. The company developed a new lower-priced brand, Levi's Signature, designed to sell through big chain stores like Wal-Mart and Target. Levi jeans used to go from factories to a company-owned distribution centre where they were labelled, packed and sent on to retailers. Now, to meet the discount chains' need to get products fast, jeans are shipped already tagged from contract factories direct to store-run distribution centres, where they are picked up and delivered to individual stores.[27,28] When one company has power over another, it can ask suppliers to absorb more costs, ship more efficiently and provide more services than ever before, often without a price increase. Often the suppliers assess that they have no choice but to go along, and those who fail to do so may go out of business.

The shift to selling through the big box retailers was a partial success for Levi's. Company performance, which had been lagging badly in 2003, picked up. But by 2006 Wal-Mart had cut back on the space it allocated in the store to Levi's products in favour of stocking more 'private label' jeans, which generate a higher profit margin for the retailer. One interpretation is that Wal-Mart used Levi's brand power to bring customers into the store, but once it had them there, it really wanted to sell them higher-margin goods that it sourced itself from low-cost developing countries. Levi's re-examined its strategy. First of all, it found that while the Signature concept worked well in North America and Asia-Pacific, big-box outlets like Wal-Mart were nowhere near as dominant in Europe where the opportunities and benefits of selling the lower cost brand were missing. It stopped selling Signature jeans in Europe. Second, the company found that there were greater profit opportunities in selling through its own Levi's stores. It expanded its chain – both company-owned and franchised – in the US, Europe and Asia-Pacific. Third, the company took note of the rapid growth in consuming power in developing markets in the Asia region, and decided to open 150 Levi brand stores in the region over the next few years.[29] In other words, key to Levi's resurgence was its reduction of dependence upon retail outlets over which it could exert little control. In common with other companies with well-known brand, such as Sony, Apple and Nike, it expanded through its retail outlets that also serve to promote the brand name.

Levi's counter-strategy towards Wal-Mart and the other discount retailers seemed to pay off. The company's results improved steadily between 2006 and 2008. The Signature brand declined in importance to Levi's bottom line, accounting for six per cent of sales in 2007, down from ten per cent in 2005. At its April 2008 briefing with market analysts, company president and CEO John Anderson says, 'We're feeling very good with where things are. Last year was the best year we've had in a decade.' The company expects that by 2011–2013, the bulk of its sales will be outside the US, especially in China, India and Russia.[30]

An ever-shifting environment is also the norm today in other industries. For decades, a few large software companies have dominated the market, creating near-monopoly situations and making it difficult for customers to choose a range of software from different vendors that will work together smoothly on their machines. Those days may be coming to an end. Many companies are considering reducing their dependence upon Microsoft, the market-leader in operating software, in favour of open source software, notably Linux. In addition, government regulators in Europe and the United States have launched a variety of legal actions designed to force Microsoft to make its operating and office systems software more compatible with competitors' add-on products. Several governments in Europe and Asia are requiring software to be written in a standard code that can then be adapted to end-users' needs. In response, Microsoft has revised its strategy. In order to reduce the risks of being pushed out of the market, it is turning over more of its program code to open source software developers, and is also aiming to produce its own version of open source code, allowing it to maintain an edge over its competition.[31]

See online COUNTERPOINT 5.10

Collaborative Networks

In traditional business mythology as has often been taught in North American business schools, the relationship between organizations and their suppliers has been an adversarial one. North American companies are praised for working alone, competing with each other and believing in the tradition of individualism and self-reliance. Nowadays, this simple view of corporate independence, which may always have been an exaggeration of actual business relationships, is being challenged. The **collaborative-network** perspective is an emerging alternative to resource-dependence theory. Companies join together to become more competitive and to share scarce resources. Technology companies join together to produce next-generation products. Large aerospace firms partner with one another, and with smaller companies and suppliers, to design next-generation jets. Large pharmaceutical companies join with small biotechnology firms to share resources and knowledge and spur innovation. Consulting firms, investment companies and accounting firms may join in an alliance to meet customer demands for expanded services.[32] As companies move into their own uncharted territory, they are also racing into alliances.

See online COUNTERPOINT 5.11

Why Collaboration?

Why all this interest in interorganizational collaboration? Major reasons are sharing risks when entering new markets, mounting expensive new programmes and reducing costs and enhancing organizational profile in selected industries or technologies. Cooperation is a prerequisite for greater innovation, problem solving, and performance.[33] In addition, partnerships are a major avenue for entering global markets, with both large and small firms developing partnerships across the world.

International experience shows just how effective interorganizational relationships can be. Asian countries including Japan, Korea and India have long traditions of corporate clans or industrial groups that collaborate and assist each other.[34] European companies often work together closely through cross-shareholdings, interlocking directorships, groupings of associated companies and industrial groups encompassing many different businesses. MAN AG, discussed earlier in this chapter, has a controlling stake in 192 companies across the world, producing commercial vehicles, printing machines, diesel engines and other transport and industrial equipment. It also controls Allianz, the world's third largest insurance group.[35]

North Americans (and US-dominated international institutions like the International Monetary Fund) by contrast have often considered interdependence a bad thing, believing it would reduce competition and hide inefficiencies. However, the experience of collaboration has shown that competition among companies can be fierce in some areas even as they collaborate in others. Interorganizational linkages provide a kind of safety net that encourages long-term investment and risk taking. Companies can achieve higher levels of innovation and performance as they learn to shift from an adversarial to a partnership mindset.[36] In many cases companies are learning to work closely together. Consider the following examples:

- Carlos Ghosn, President and CEO both of France's Renault and Japan's Nissan, has staked his career on building innovative alliances all over the world. After turning Nissan around from a near moribund position to a brief period when the company's profits were higher than Toyota, Ghosn has launched a series of ever more daring alliances, including a Nissan-branded car for the Russian market built in South Korea by a Renault-Samsung tie-up, a sub $3,000 car to be built in India in conjunction with the motorbike manufacturer Bajaj, and a deal whereby Nissan will supply small cars for Chrysler to sell under its brand name, and Chrysler will build pick-up trucks for Nissan to brand and sell. Ghosn frequently makes shareholders nervous with his bold alliances, but he points out that his Nissan-Renault tie-up is the only major auto makers' collaboration that has created rather destroyed shareholder value.[37,38]
- The German-headquartered pharmaceuticals giant Merck has a collaboration programme with the Indian firm Ranbaxy (now part of Japan's Saichi group) for development of anti-viral and anti-tuberculosis medications. Merck has established major research programmes with 44 different companies, universities and research institutions around the word in search of more effective treatments of conditions ranging from cancer to schizophrenia.[39]
- Turkish appliance manfuacturer Arcelik – Europe's third largest appliance builder – is teaming up with New Zealand appliance builder Fisher and Paykel, giving Fisher and Paykel, a high quality but isolated manufacturer, access to the large and growing markets of central and eastern Europe, where Arcelik is strong. In return, Arcelik will be able to tie into the New Zealand firm's top notch engineering and design expertise.[40]

From Adversaries to Partners

Fresh flowers are blooming on the battle-scarred landscape where once-bitter rivalries among suppliers, customers, and competitors took place. A summary of this change in mindset is in Exhibit 5.3. More companies are changing from a traditional adversarial mindset to a partnership orientation. Evidence from studies of such companies as Renault, Toyota and Microsoft indicate that partnering allows reduced cost and increased value for both parties in a predatory world economy.[41,42] Rather than organizations maintaining independence, the new model is based on interdependence and trust. Performance measures for the partnership are loosely defined, and problems are resolved through discussion and dialogue. Managing strategic relationships with other firms has become a critical management skill, as discussed in this chapter's Bookmark. In the new orientation, people try to add value to both sides and believe in high commitment rather than suspicion and competition. Companies work toward equitable profits for both sides rather than just for their own benefit. The new model is characterized by lots of shared information, including electronic linkages for automatic ordering and face-to-face discussions to provide corrective feedback and solve problems. Sometimes people from other companies are on site to enable very close coordination. Partners are involved in each other's product design and production, and they invest for the long term, with an assumption of continuing relations. Partners develop equitable solutions to conflicts rather than relying on legal contractual relationships. Contracts may be loosely specified, and it is not unusual for business partners to help each other outside whatever is specified in the contract.[43]

See online COUNTERPOINT 5.12

For example, AMP, a manufacturer of electronics and electrical connectors (since bought by the US-based multinational Tyco Electronics)[44] was contacted by a customer about a broken connector that posed serious problems. It wasn't even AMP's

EXHIBIT 5.3 Changing Characteristics of Interorganizational Relationships

Traditional Orientation: Adversarial	New Orientation: Partnership
Low dependence	High dependence
Suspicion, competition, arm's length	Trust, addition of value to both sides, high commitment
Detailed performance measures, closely monitored	Loose performance measures, problems discussed
Price, efficacy, own profits	Equity, fair dealing, both profit
Limited information and feedback	Electronic linkages to share key information, problem feedback, and discussion
Legal resolution of conflict	Mechanisms for close coordination, people on site
Minimal involvement and up-front investment, separate resources	Involvement in partner's product design and production, shared resources
Short-term contracts	Long-term contracts
Contract limiting the relationship	Business assistance beyond the contract

Source: Based on Mick Marchington and Steven Vincent, 'Analysing the Influence of Institutional, Organizational, and Interpersonal Forces in Shaping Inter-Organizational Relations,' *Journal of Management Studies* 41, no. 6 (September 2004), 1029–1056; Jeffrey H. Dyer, 'How Chrysler Created an American Keiretsu,' *Harvard Business Review* (July–August 1996), 42–56; Myron Magnet, 'The New Golden Rule of Business,' *Fortune* (February 21, 1994), 60–64; and Peter Grittner, 'Four Elements of Successful Sourcing Strategies,' *Management Review* (October 1995), 41–45.

connector, but the vice president and his sales manager went to a warehouse on a weekend and found replacement parts to get the customer back on line. They provided the service with no charge as a way to enhance the relationship. Indeed, this kind of teamwork treats partner companies almost like departments of one's own organization.[45]

This new partnership mindset can be seen in a number of industries. As discussed above, Microsoft hired the Singapore-based contract manufacturer Flextronics to not only build but also help design Xbox, its electronic game console.[46] Many supermarkets and other retailers rely on key suppliers to help them determine what goes on the store shelves. A large vendor such as Procter & Gamble, for example, analyzes national data and makes recommendations for what products the store should offer, including not just P&G's brands, but products from its competitors as well.[47] A large British company that supplies pigments to the automobile, plastics and printing industries has a long-standing interdependent relationship with a key chemicals supplier, with the two organizations sharing information about their long-term business needs so that any changes in products or processes can benefit both sides.[48]

In this new view of partnerships, dependence on another company is seen to reduce rather than increase risks. Greater value can be achieved by both parties. By being embedded in a system of interorganizational relationships, everyone does better by helping each other. This is a far cry from the belief that organizations do best by being autonomous and independent. Sales representatives may have a desk on the customer's factory floor, and they have access to information systems and the research lab.[49] Coordination is so intimate that it's sometimes hard to tell one organization from another. Consider, in this chapter's *In Practice* box, how Canada's Bombardier and its suppliers were linked together almost like one organization in building the Challenger, a 'super-midsize' business jet that can comfortably fly eight passengers nonstop from coast to coast in North America.

Have you read this book?

Business as Unusual

BY ANITA RODDICK

Often in management texts there is an assumption that there is *one* best way to do business. It is clear that this is untrue, because companies that pursue very different strategies and ways of organizing are often successful in the same industry. In British retailing, for example, Asda and Waitrose have both enjoyed continuing growth, even though they follow almost diametrically opposed management styles. Asda is hierarchical and attempts to impose a uniform corporate culture, while Waitrose is employee-owned, and encourages employee individuality. They can both perform well, albeit targeting different consumer segments.

There are few more striking examples of the different paths to success than that followed by Anita Roddick. From small beginnings in the late 1970s Roddick built her Body Shop into one of the largest and most successful personal care product chains in the world, all the while determined to 'push the limits of business, to change its language, to make it a force for positive change'.

Roddick's autobiography, written not long before her untimely death in 2006, describes her own ascent to success but is above all a ringing indictment of contemporary business practices and a clarion call for change. Roddick explores some of the reasons she has been successful; these include being prepared to ignore and overcome barriers, whether unsympathetic bank managers or those who think women do not make good business leaders. She says many great entrepreneurs were outsiders; many are from immigrant communities. Others, like Roddick, suffered deprivation, whether financial or emotional; Roddick's father died suddenly when she was ten, turning her family life upside down and forcing her to decide her life path for herself. There is typically, she says, a hunger to succeed. This must translate into passion to communicate what is unique about the business, which in Roddick's case included a firm belief that Body Shop's success would contribute not merely to the financial bottom line but would also help further the social and political causes in which she believed so passionately. She underlines her frustration and disgust with mainstream business. Some examples she lists of unacceptable business practices include:

- Footloose business that abandons communities leaving them polluted and jobless.
- The greed of corporate bosses like Disney's Michael Eisner who earns as much in one day as Third World labourers who manufacture Disney-labelled clothing would make in 166 years.
- Unfair trade agreements that allow companies to uproot well-paid, regulated jobs in the US in favour of production facilities on the Mexican side of the US-Mexico border, where labour and environmental protections are almost non-existent.
- The overwhelming impact of consumer advertising, creating a population manipulated to desire ever more ecologically unsustainable possessions, and resulting in both an ecological and a cultural monoculture.

Unlike most business leaders, who tend to demand fewer regulations (sometimes with disastrous effects such as the 2007 sub-prime crisis which was largely caused by inadequate financial regulation), Roddick's prescriptions for making business healthier included more regulation, encouraging consumer consciousness about the products they desire and buy and more responsibility on the part of business leaders. She summarizes her vision as 'spiritual business', the idea that business must act to protect and sustain the world, including 'humans, animals and the Earth itself'. She also demands that:

'Any future business education programme, whether set in a local or global context, must contain the language and action of social justice, human rights, community economics and ethics, as well as the productivity of the human soul.' (p.27)

While Anglo-American business schools tend to teach students to worry only about the bottom line, Roddick emphasizes the *ethical audit*. While there are various versions of this, some only superficial, her version includes a thorough 'values report' that looks at all of Body Shop's relationships, from employees and suppliers to shareholders and to local communities. Based on this report, Roddick's Body Shop developed and implemented an action plan to improve weak points. Another major element of the ethical audit is an environmental audit; a key objective for Body Shop in this area was aiming towards zero emissions, not just from Body Shop itself but also its suppliers and even in turn, their suppliers. An example of Roddick's preparedness to put the public good ahead of narrow business objectives was her campaign against the tyranny of the beauty business. While worries about appearance undoubtedly encourage women to buy more beauty products including those from the Body Shop, Roddick didn't want to get rich on the basis of media and advertising industry-cultivated body insecurity. Under Roddick, the company invested heavily in campaigns warning women against the tyranny of unreasonable expectations around their bodies and self-image.

Roddick readily admits that the company has made mistakes – especially in the United States where Body Shop began by listening to marketing orthodoxy and became sucked in to mass marketing and mall culture, which made it hard for Body Shop to stand out for its unique qualities. After sales slowed in the mid-90s and franchisees started demanding even more concessions to US marketing norms such as constant price discounting. Instead of going down that slippery slope, the Body Shop stopped and looked at itself and its values. It moved out of malls, and focused on urban neighbourhood stores with their own diverse cultures and shopping environments. Bit by bit, the company's US performance improved – by sticking to its values rather than selling out to the bland sameness that has blighted so many aspects of American communities.

The bottom line of Anita Roddick's message to starting entrepreneurs: design organizations your way, with values and a mission you believe in, or don't bother doing it at all.

Business as Unusual, by Anita Roddick, is published by Anita Roddick Books

By breaking down boundaries and becoming involved in partnerships with an attitude of fair dealing and adding value to both sides, today's companies are changing the concept of what makes an organization. The type of collaborative network illustrated by Bombardier is also being used by a growing number of automotive companies, as shown by the examples of Renault, Nissan and their partners discussed earlier in this chapter These companies are pushing the idea of partnership further than ever before, moving somewhat toward a network approach to organization design, as described in Chapter 3.

Bombardier

In an assembly plant on the edge of Mid-Continent Airport in Wichita, a new plane is taking shape as great chunks of it are rolled in and joined together. Not counting rivets, it takes just a dozen big parts – all manufactured elsewhere – to put Bombardier's Challenger business jet (formerly called the Continental) together. Those big subassemblies come from all over the world – the engines from Phoenix in the United States, the nose and cockpit from Montreal, Canada, the mid-fuselage from Belfast, Northern Ireland, the tail from Taichung, Taiwan, the wings from Nagoya, Japan and other parts from Australia, France, Germany and Austria. When production is up to full speed, it takes just four days to put a plane together and get it in the air.

In the past, most executive-jet companies made major parts in-house. For the Challenger, which started commercial service in 2004, Canada's Bombardier instead relied heavily on suppliers for design support and the sharing of development costs and market risks.[50] The company is intertwined with about thirty suppliers, a dozen or so of which have been involved since the design stage. At one point, about 250 team members from Bombardier and 250 from outsider suppliers worked together in Montreal to make sure the design was going to be good for everyone involved. Bombardier invested heavily in bringing the Challenger to market, but suppliers equalled that amount in development costs. In addition to sharing costs, the supplier companies also shared the risks. 'They haven't got a contract that says, "You're going to sell us twenty-five wings a year for the next 10 years." If the market's there, it's there, and if it's not, it's

Pcl#: 88685140 Typ:J4 Tm: WZONE3 Order # 7434823Y Ctn: 1 of 1

Pl#: 1655 Date: 6/10/11 Wve:001 Tote: 88685692 **SLA: 999**

Location	ISBN	Pieces	Description
431-006-030	9781844809905	1	ORGANIZATION THEORY AND D

#00005

SHC: 0

Page: 1 of 1

not', says John Holding, who was in charge of Bombardier's engineering and product development during the development of the Challenger. The results of all the collaboration have been impressive; the Challenger is one of the most successful business jets of all time, with 56 per cent of worldwide deliveries in its sector in 2006.[51]

Integrating partners so that everyone benefits from and depends on the others – and managing this multinational, multicompany endeavour – is no easy task, but with development costs for a new plane reaching more than $1 billion, the partnership approach just makes sense.[52]

Population Ecology

This section introduces a different perspective on relationships among organizations. The **population-ecology perspective** differs from the other perspectives because it focuses on organizational diversity and adaptation within a population of organizations.[53] A **population** is a set of organizations engaged in similar activities with similar patterns of resource utilization and outcomes. Organizations within a population compete for similar resources or similar customers, such as newspaper publishing organizations in Ireland.[54]

Within a population, the question asked by ecology researchers is about the large number and variation of organizations in society. Why are new organizational forms that create such diversity constantly appearing? The answer is that individual organizational adaptation is severely limited compared to the changes demanded by the environment. Innovation and change in a population of organizations take place through the birth of new forms and kinds of organizations more so than by the reform and change of existing organizations. Indeed, organizational forms are considered relatively stable, and the good of a whole society is served by the development of new forms of organization through entrepreneurial initiatives. New organizations meet the new needs of society more than established organizations that are slow to change.[55]

COUNTERPOINT 5.6

What is not explained in population ecology theory is how such changes are 'demanded' by the environment. What accounts for the changes and how are the demands conveyed to organizations? Population ecology theory does not, for example consider how environments are changed politically – by pressures being exerted upon, and by, politicians who change regulations, thereby creating or restricting existing markets and opening up new opportunities. Nor does population ecology pay attention to how organizations comprise much of the 'environment' and actively exert effects on its development. In part, budget airlines have emerged as a consequence of changes in the regulatory environment but their presence and growth has contributed greatly to the development of that environment to which established carriers have struggled to respond. **Discuss**

What does this theory mean in practical terms? It means that large, established organizations often become dinosaurs. As discussed in the previous chapter, many large European airlines that relied on business travellers, protected markets and nationalist loyalty have had tremendous difficulty adapting to a rapidly changing environment including the removal of national barriers to entry and the emergence of a new passenger mass market. Hence, new organizational forms such as Ryanair are emerging that fit the current environment, fill a new niche and, over time, take away business from established companies.

Why do established organizations have such a hard time adapting to a rapidly changing environment? Michael Hannan and John Freeman, originators of the population ecology model of organization, argue that there are many limitations on the ability of organizations to change. The limitations come from heavy investment in plants, equipment and specialized personnel, limited information, established viewpoints of decision makers, the organization's own successful history that justifies current procedures and the difficulty of changing corporate culture. True transformation is a rare and unlikely event in the face of all these barriers.[56]

New organizational forms are emerging all the time. As discussed earlier in this chapter, the advertising industry has generated alliances like E3 European Agency Network and GlobalFluency, responding to the desire of small firms to trade up to bigger contracts. The same process of organizational transformation has occurred from the top down, with large advertising companies restructuring themselves as holding companies like London-headquartered WPP Group with separately incorporated and quasi-independent subsidiaries all over the world, thus getting around client concerns about potential conflict of interest when the same firm is working for competitors in the same business.[57,58] Another recent change is the development of 'corporate universities' within large companies like Motorola in North America, France's Accor, Fujitsu from Japan, Daimler and Volkswagen from Germany and Petrobras in Brazil.[59] Although the definition of corporate university is sometimes stretched to include training activities that companies have been carrying out for many years, there is little doubt that the phenomenon is important and growing. There are estimated to be more than 2,000 corporate universities in North America and another 1,000 in Europe. Emerging economy corporations are jumping on to the bandwagon, too; Wipro and Accenture, two Indian high-tech giants, have both opened corporate universities, as have Bank of China and China Life Insurance Company among many others in China.[60] In the UK, government has endorsed the corporate university phenomenon; the low cost airline Flybe and the rail infrastructure operator Network Rail have each been granted accreditation to award nationally recognized qualifications up to university degree level.[61,62]

As an organization manager, keep these guidelines in mind:

Adapt your organization to new variations being selected and retained in the external environment. If you are starting a new organization, find a niche that contains a strong environmental need for your product or service, and be prepared for a competitive struggle over scarce resources.

According to the population-ecology view, when looking at an organizational population as a whole, the changing environment determines which organizations survive or fail. The assumption is that individual organizations suffer from structural inertia and find it difficult to adapt to environmental changes. Thus, when rapid change occurs, old organizations are likely to decline or fail, and new organizations emerge that are better suited to the needs of the environment.

The population-ecology model is developed from theories of natural selection in biology, and the terms *evolution* and *selection* are used to refer to the underlying behavioural processes. Theories of biological evolution try to explain why certain life forms appear and survive whereas others perish. Some theories suggest the forms that survive are typically best fitted to the immediate environment.

Some years ago, *Forbes* magazine reported a study of American businesses over 70 years, from 1917 to 1987. Have you heard of Baldwin Locomotive, Studebaker or Lehigh Coal & Navigation? These companies were among 78 per cent of the top 100 in 1917 that did not see 1987. Of the 22 that remained in the top 100, only 11 did so under their original names. The environment of the 1940s and 1950s was suitable to Woolworth, but new organizational forms like Wal-Mart became dominant in the 1980s. In 1917, most of the top 100 companies were huge steel and mining industrial organizations, which were replaced by high-technology companies such as IBM and Merck.[63] Two companies that seemed to prosper over a long period were Ford and General Motors, but they are now in deep trouble, partly due to the emergence of global competition in the car industry. No company is immune to the processes of social change. From just 1979 to 1989, 187 of the companies on the *Fortune* 500 list ceased to exist as independent companies. Some were acquired, some merged and some were liquidated.[64] Corporate casualties in British manufacturing industry in the past fifty years have been even more dramatic.[65] Meanwhile, technology continues to change the environment. All over the world, the giant telecommunications monopolies that once decided when, and even if, we might be able to hope to have a landline telephone connection have been outpaced and often nearly eclipsed by mobile phone companies offering an ever expanding range of services on their handsets. The Internet has infiltrated far beyond the office and into everyday lives of citizens; for a new generation of youth, Facebook and YouTube are every bit as important as the pub and radio and TV were for their parents and grandparents.

Organizational Form and Niche

The population-ecology model is concerned with organizational forms. **Organizational form** is an organization's specific technology, structure, products, goals and personnel, which can be selected or rejected by the environment. Each new organization tries to find a **niche** (a domain of unique environmental resources and needs) sufficient to support it. The niche is usually small in the early stages of an organization but may increase in size over time if the organization is successful. If a niche is not available, the organization will decline and may perish.

From the viewpoint of a single firm, luck, chance and randomness play important parts in survival. New products and ideas are continually being proposed by both entrepreneurs and large organizations. Whether these ideas and organizational forms survive or fail is often a matter of chance – whether external circumstances happen to support them. A woman who started a small electronics assembly subcontracting business in Estonia in the 1990s would have had an excellent chance of success. If the same woman were to start the same business in a country with an expensive and declining manufacturing base such as the UK, the chance of success might be far less. Success or failure of a single firm thus is often predicted by the characteristics of the environment as much as by the skills or strategies used by the organization.

Process of Ecological Change

The population-ecology model assumes that new organizations are always appearing in the population. Thus, organization populations are continually undergoing change. The process of change in the population is defined by three principles that occur in stages: variation, selection and retention. These stages are summarized in Exhibit 5.4.

- *Variation*. **Variation** means the appearance of new, diverse forms in a population of organizations. These new organizational forms are initiated by entrepreneurs, established with venture capital by large corporations, or set up by a government seeking to provide new services. Some forms may be conceived to cope with a perceived need in the external environment. In recent years, a large number of new firms have been initiated to develop computer software,

EXHIBIT 5.4 Elements in the Population-Ecology Model of Organizations

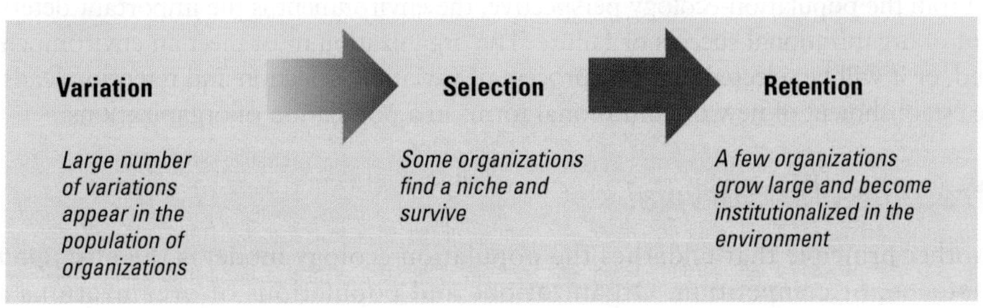

to provide consulting and other services to large corporations and to develop products and technologies for Internet commerce. Other new organizations produce a traditional product such as steel, but do it using minimal technology and new management techniques that allow the company to survive and prosper. Lakshmi Mittal's Ispat Steel purchased declining steel plants in the former Communist bloc and turned them around by focusing on cost and appropriate markets rather than the costly high-technology investments that more traditional western steel producers had proposed.[66] Organizational variations are analogous to mutations in biology, and they add to the scope and complexity of organizational forms in the environment. This chapter's Leading by Design box describes a new organizational form conceived by a British entrepreneur to capitalize on advances in information technology and wireless text messaging.

- *Selection.* **Selection** refers to whether a new organizational form is suited to the environment and can survive. Only a few variations are 'selected in' by the environment and survive over the long term. Some variations will suit the external environment better than others. Some prove beneficial and thus are able to find a niche and acquire the resources from the environment necessary to survive. Other variations fail to meet the needs of the environment and perish. When there is insufficient demand for a firm's product and when insufficient resources are available to the organization, that organization will be 'selected out'. For example, London-based Shazam, described in the Leading by Design box, was launched in mid-2002. If demand for the new service does not continue to grow, or if the company cannot obtain needed resources, the company will be selected out and cease to exist.
- *Retention.* **Retention** is the preservation and institutionalization of selected organizational forms. Institutionalization of an organizational form means that it becomes a general norm in society. Certain technologies, products and services are highly valued by the environment. The organizational form associated with those technologies, products or services may become a dominant part of the environment. Many forms of organization have been institutionalized, such as government, schools, churches and banking institutions. McDonald's, which operates in 119 countries and provides the first job for many teenagers around the world, has become institutionalized in contemporary global life.

See online COUNTERPOINT 5.13

Institutionalized organizations like McDonald's seem to be relatively permanent features in the population of organizations, but they are not permanent in the long run. The environment is always changing, and, if the dominant organizational forms do not or cannot adapt to external change, they will gradually diminish and be replaced by other organizations. McDonald's is struggling partly because it has been most closely associated with increasing concerns about unhealthy fast food.[67,68] British coal mines were once a highly institutionalized part of national life, but as alternative, cleaner forms of fuel came on-stream in the 1950s and 1960s, and cities started restricting use of coal fires as an anti-pollution measure, they entered a downward spiral from which they never recovered.[69]

From the population-ecology perspective, the environment is the important determinant of organizational success or failure. The organization must meet an environmental need, or it will be selected out. The process of variation, selection and retention leads to the establishment of new organizational forms in a population of organizations.

Strategies for Survival

Another principle that underlies the population ecology model is the **struggle for existence**, or competition. Organizations and populations of organizations are

Shazam – It's Magic!

Many people have had the experience of hearing a song they like on the radio or in a dance club and waiting in vain for the DJ to identify it. Shazam, a mobile-phone music service launched in the United Kingdom in August 2002, has come to the rescue. The next time a cell phone user hears that mystery tune, all he or she has to do is dial a four-digit number on the cell phone, let the music play into the handset, and moments later receive a text message with the artist and song title. The user can forward a 30-second clip of the track to friends, or even download the song directly to his or her phone. The song can then be legally copied from the mobile phone to a PC and shared between multiple devices.

Shazam's magic happens through the use of a pattern-recognition software algorithm developed by the company's chief scientist. The algorithm picks out the salient characteristics of a tune and matches them against a massive music database. The company, founded by Californian entrepreneur Chris Barton, calls the process 'tagging', and users in the United Kingdom alone have already tagged more than 5.5 million music tracks. Users can go online and see a list of all the songs they've tagged.

Shazam's success depends on collaborative partnerships with mobile phone companies, major record labels, software companies and others. A partnership with Swiss-based SDC (Secure Digital Container) AG provides the technology that enables a complete 'tag to download' in three simple steps, allowing users to purchase music on the move. A strategic alliance with MTV Japan helped Shazam expand to about 40 million mobile phone subscribers in Japan. Deals with international mobile operators and media companies throughout the United States, Europe, and Asia make Shazam's service available to more than 1 billion mobile phone users worldwide.

The mobile phone companies offer tagging as a premium service to their customers and pay Shazam a cut of the profits. Since tagging promises to drive up call times, most mobile phone companies are interested. And the record labels' interests are served by getting new music in front of consumers. Word-of-mouth recommendations are a powerful means of driving music sales, so the idea of people all over the world forwarding 30-second clips of their new songs has music companies paying attention. The service has proven to be a good predictor of future hits in Britain, so the music industry closely watches Shazam's weekly chart of tagged pre-release tracks.

Shazam is the world's first in music recognition and one of the brightest new ideas in the world of technology. With multiple deals and a presence in twelve countries, it is clear that Shazam is suited to the environment and has found a solid niche. However, managing the complex network of global relationships will be a challenge for managers of the small company, and it remains to be seen if they can take a good idea and build a lasting organization.

Sources: 'SDC Partners with Shazam to Create Simple, Secure Music Download', *M2Presswire* (February 14, 2005), 1; Steve McClure, 'Shazam Works Its Magic', *Billboard* (August 21, 2004), 60; Adam Jolly, 'Going for a Song and Growth', *Sunday Times* (June 13, 2004), 17; Michael Parsons, 'I Got Music, I Got Algorithm', *Red Herring* (May 2002), 54–57; and 'MTV and Shazam Lead Japanese Market Extending Music Recognition Offering to KDDI Subscribers and Expanding Local Music Database', *M2Presswire* (February 16, 2005), 1.

engaged in a competitive struggle over resources, and each organizational form is fighting to survive. The struggle is most intense among new organizations, and both the birth and survival frequencies of new organizations are related to factors in the larger environment. Factors such as size of urban area, percentage of immigrants, political turbulence, industry growth rate and environmental variability have influenced the launching and survival of newspapers, telecommunication firms, railroads, government agencies, labour unions and even voluntary organizations.[70]

In the population ecology perspective, **generalist** and **specialist** strategies distinguish organizational forms in the struggle for survival. Organizations with a wide niche or domain, that is, those that offer a broad range of products or services or that serve a broad market, are generalists. Organizations that provide a narrower range of goods or services or that serve a narrower market are specialists.

In the natural environment, a specialist form of flora and fauna would evolve in protective isolation in a place like Australia, where the nearest major body of land is 2,500 miles away. The flora and fauna are heavily protected. In contrast, a place like Costa Rica, which experienced wave after wave of external influences, developed a generalist set of flora and fauna that has better resilience and flexibility for adapting to a broad range of circumstances. In the business world, Amazon.com started with a specialist strategy, selling books over the Internet, but evolved to a generalist strategy with the addition of music, DVDs, greeting cards and other products, plus partnering with other organizations as an online shopping mall to sell a wide range of products. A company such as the Germany-headquartered Steiff which sells high-end teddy bears,[71] would be considered a specialist, whereas Chad Valley is a generalist, marketing a broad range of toys for boys and girls up to ten years old.[72]

Specialists are generally more competitive than generalists in the narrow area in which their domains overlap. However, the breadth of the generalist's domain serves to protect it somewhat from environmental changes. Though demand may decrease for some of the generalist's products or services, it usually increases for others at the same time. In addition, because of the diversity of products, services and customers, generalists are able to reallocate resources internally to adapt to a

Genentech

California-based Genentech was the world's first biotechnology firm, founded in 1976, and its creation spurred the development of a whole new subset in the pharmaceuticals industry. A wide variety of small biotech firms have been established, with each struggling to find a niche that will enable the company to survive in the volatile, competitive world of drug development and manufacturing.

Genentech spent its early years trying to bring out blockbuster drugs and grow into a company on the scale of pharmaceutical giants like Schering Plough or Merck. But its first potential blockbusters fizzled, and the company's fortunes dwindled. Things began to turn around when Genentech's research director, Arthur Levinson, was appointed CEO. Levinson turned the company in a new direction. Rather than betting the farm on blockbusters, Levinson chose a strategy of developing 'targeted drugs', lucrative new medicines that are aimed at small sets of patients. For example, Herceptin, Genentech's first targeted therapy launched several years ago, is a breast-cancer drug that is prescribed to only the 25 per cent of patients whose tumours reveal a specific genetic characteristic. Other targeted treatments include Rituxan, for treating an immune-cell cancer called non-Hodgkin's lymphoma, and Xolair, a drug approved by the US Food and Drug Administration (FDA) in 2003 as treatment for a type of allergic asthma.

Large drug companies are struggling in an industry that is being threatened by changes in managed care, the expiration of numerous drug patents, and the high cost of new drug development. Many have tried to compete with massive marketing campaigns to make up for the decline in blockbuster drugs. Meanwhile, Genentech is achieving remarkable success with its targeted approach. The company recently jumped ahead of giant pharmaceutical companies to become the top seller of branded anti-tumour drugs in the United States. Genentech has an impressive 13 drugs on the market and twenty more either in clinical trials or awaiting FDA approval.[73]

changing environment, whereas specialists are not. However, because specialists are often smaller companies, they can sometimes move faster and be more flexible in adapting to changes.[74]

See online COUNTERPOINT 5.14

Managerial impact on company success often comes from selecting a strategy that steers a company into an open niche. Consider how Genentech has thrived after a new CEO steered it into a new niche in the pharmaceuticals industry.

Genentech isn't immune from the volatility and uncertainty inherent in the industry, but managers found a niche that put the company on a solid foundation for survival over the long term. CEO Levinson chose a specialist strategy, focusing on specific therapies for relatively small subsets of patients rather than looking for one-size-fits-all blockbuster drugs.

Institutionalism

The institutional perspective provides yet another view of interorganizational relationships.[75] Organizations are highly interconnected. Just as companies need efficient production to survive, the institutional view argues that organizations need legitimacy from their stakeholders. Companies perform well when they are perceived by the larger environment to have a legitimate right to exist. Thus, the **institutional perspective** describes how organizations survive and succeed through congruence between an organization and the expectations from its environment. The **institutional environment** is composed of norms and values from stakeholders (customers, investors, associations, boards, government, collaborating organizations). Thus the institutional view believes that organizations adopt structures and processes to please outsiders, and these activities come to take on rule-like status in organizations. The institutional environment reflects what the greater society views as correct ways of organizing and behaving.[76]

Legitimacy is defined as the general perspective that an organization's actions are desirable, proper and appropriate within the environment's system of norms, values and beliefs.[77] Institutional theory thus is concerned with the set of intangible norms and values that shape behaviour, as opposed to the tangible elements of technology and structure. Organizations must fit within the cognitive and emotional expectations of their audience. For example, people will not deposit money in a bank unless it sends signals of compliance with norms of wise financial management. Consider also your local government and whether it could easily raise property taxes for upgraded refuse collection if residents objected to aspects of the new programme.

Most organizations are concerned with legitimacy, as reflected in the various national and international surveys that rank corporations based on their reputations.[78,79] Many corporations actively shape and manage their reputations to increase their competitive advantage, and managers are searching for new ways to bolster legitimacy in the wake of ethical and financial scandals at such well-known companies as Siemens, Enron and Parmalat. Despite globalization and the presence of worldwide brands like Nike and Coca-Cola, national brands still tend to stand out at both the top and bottom of the rankings. Only Microsoft and McDonald's were mentioned consistently by respondents across Europe, Asia and North America, and McDonald's was mainly ranked poorly due to negative respondent perceptions about the quality of both its food and service. Companies that ranked highest in each country included L'Oreal in France, Porsche in Germany, Virgin Group in the UK and IKEA in Sweden.[80]

Tesco

Tesco is a remarkable British success story. Despite its origins dating back to 1919, the company only really took off in the 1970s, but it has grown massively ever since, in 2007 capturing 30 per cent of the British food budget (double its nearest rival Asda/Wal-Mart), and one pound in every seven spent by Britons in all shops. The company has expanded successfully internationally, with operations in 12 countries. It has increasingly moved into non-food items, moving closer to the Wal-Mart model than a traditional supermarket. Profits have risen annually for the past ten years, reaching £2.7 billion in 2007. In 2007 the company edged past US based Home Depot to become the third largest retailer in the world.

However, whereas in 2003 City analysts were quoted as saying the company had 'not put a foot wrong', five years later Tesco was facing a crescendo of criticism,[81] including (unusually for Britain) its own web 'hate site', www.tescopoly.com. The concerns surround four main issues, each connected to perceptions of the company's excessive – and arguably misused – power. The first relates to Tesco's control of land and power in the town planning process.[82] The company sometimes puts local councils under pressure to allow its stores to open even in rural areas where there is substantial local opposition. It has also been accused of banking land so that its competitors cannot expand (a claim the company vigorously denies).[83] The second issue concerns the company's relationship with producers in the UK and elsewhere. Like Wal-Mart in America, Tesco has the purchasing muscle to be able to do things its way. Some of its products are made in developing countries like Bangladesh, by workers paid very low wages.[84] It has also been accused of keeping farm produce prices so low that farmers have no choice but to follow intensive production methods; argued by animal rights campaigners to be cruel and unhygenic.[85] Tesco also attempts to reduce its tax burden through various offshore holding companies.[86] Finally, the company has responded aggressively to criticism, further reinforcing its image as a corporate bully.[87] Tesco has not yet been seriously damaged by these criticisms, but managers know that how the company is perceived by customers and the public plays a big role in long-term success. Tesco is extremely powerful today, but its power could decline if the company's actions are not considered legitimate and appropriate.

See online **COUNTERPOINT 5.15**

The fact that there is a payoff for having a good reputation is verified by a study of organizations in the airline industry. Having a good reputation was significantly related to higher levels of performance measures such as return on assets and net profit margin.[88]

The notion of legitimacy answers an important question for institutional theorists. Why is there so much homogeneity in the forms and practices of established organizations? For example, visit banks, high schools, hospitals, government departments or business firms in a similar industry, in any part of the country, and they will look strikingly similar. On the other hand, when an organizational field is just getting started, such as in e-commerce, diversity is the norm. New organizations fill emerging niches. However, once an industry becomes established, there is an invisible push toward similarity. *Isomorphism* is the term used to describe this move toward similarity.

The Institutional View and Organization Design

The institutional view also sees organizations as having two essential dimensions – technical and institutional. The technical dimension is the day-to-day work, technology and operating requirements. The institutional structure is that part of the organization most visible to the outside public. Moreover, the technical dimension is governed by norms of rationality and efficiency, but the institutional dimension is governed by expectations from the external environment. As a result of pressure to do things in a proper and correct way, the formal structures of many organizations reflect the expectations and values of the environment rather than the demand of work activities. This means that an organization may incorporate positions or activities (equal employment officer, e-commerce division, chief ethics officer) perceived as important by the larger society to increase its legitimacy and survival prospects, even though these elements may decrease efficiency. For example, many small companies set up Web sites, even though the benefits gained from the site are sometimes outweighed by the costs of maintaining it. Having a Web site is perceived as essential by the larger society today. The formal structure and design of an organization may not be rational with respect to workflow and products or services, but it will help ensure survival in the larger environment.

Organizations adapt to the environment by signalling their congruence with the demands and expectations stemming from cultural norms, standards set by professional bodies, funding agencies and customers. In this way, they obtain approval, legitimacy and continuing support. The adoption of structures thus might not be linked to actual production needs, and might occur regardless of whether specific internal problems are solved. Formal structure is somewhat separated from technical action in this view but this may be the result of routine conformity to established norms and value rather than as a consequence of deliberate planning.[89]

As an organization manager, keep these guidelines in mind:

Pursue legitimacy with your organization's major stakeholders in the external environment. Adopt strategies, structures and new management techniques that meet the expectations of significant parties, thereby ensuring their cooperation and access to resources.

Institutional Similarity

In striving for legitimacy, many aspects of structure and behaviour may be targeted toward environmental acceptance. Interorganizational relationships thus are characterized by forces that cause organizations in a similar population to look like one another. **Institutional similarity**, called *institutional isomorphism* in the academic literature, is the emergence of a common structure and approach among organizations in the same field. Isomorphism is the process that causes one unit in a population to resemble other units that face the same set of environmental conditions.[90]

Exactly how does increasing similarity occur? How are these forces realized? A summary of three mechanisms for institutional adaptation appears in Exhibit 5.5. These three core mechanisms are *mimetic forces*, which result from responses to uncertainty; *coercive forces*, which stem from overtly political influence; and *normative forces*, which result from common training and professionalism.[91]

Mimetic Forces Most organizations, especially business organizations, face great uncertainty. It is not clear to senior executives exactly what products, services or technologies will achieve desired goals, and sometimes the goals themselves are not clear. In the face of this uncertainty, **mimetic forces**, the pressure to copy or model other organizations, occur.

See online COUNTERPOINT 5.16

EXHIBIT 5.5 Three Mechanisms for Institutional Adaptation

	Mimetic	Coercive	Normative
Reason to become similar:	Uncertainty	Dependence	Duty, obligation
Events:	Innovation visibility	Political law, rules, sanctions	Professionalism — certification, accreditation
Social basis:	Culturally supported	Legal	Moral
Example:	Reengineering, benchmarking	Pollution controls, school regulations	Accounting standards, consultant training

Source: Adapted from W. Richard Scott, *Institutions and Organizations* (Thousand Oaks, Calif.: Sage, 1995).

Executives observe an innovation in a firm generally regarded as successful, so the management practice is quickly copied. An example is the proliferation of Wi-Fi hotspots in cafes, hotels and airports. Starbucks was one of the first companies to adopt Wi-Fi, enabling customers to use laptops and handheld computers at Starbucks stores. The practice has rapidly been copied by both large and small companies. Many times, this modelling is done without any clear proof that performance will be improved. Mimetic processes explain why fads and fashions occur in the business world. Once a new idea starts, many organizations grab onto it, sometimes only to learn that the application is difficult and may cause more problems than it solves. This was the case with the recent merger wave that swept many industries. The past two decades have seen the largest merger and acquisition wave in history, but evidence shows that many of these mergers did not produce the expected financial gains and other benefits. The sheer momentum of the trend was so powerful that many companies chose to merge not because of potential increases in efficiency or profitability but simply because it seemed like the right thing to do.[92] Downsizing of the workforce is another trend that can be attributed partly to mimetic forces. Despite some evidence that massive downsizing actually hurts organizations, managers perceive it as a legitimate and effective means of improving performance or, at least, of raising stock price by sending the desired message to financial markets.[93]

Techniques such as outsourcing, reengineering, Six Sigma quality programmes and the balanced scorecard have all been adopted, often without clear evidence that they will improve efficiency or effectiveness. The one certain benefit is that management's feelings of uncertainty will be reduced, and the company's image will be enhanced because the firm is seen as using the latest management techniques. A recent study of 100 organizations confirmed that those companies associated with using popular management techniques were more admired and rated higher in quality of management, even though these organizations often did not reflect higher economic performance.[94] Perhaps the clearest example of official copying is the technique of benchmarking that occurs as part of the total quality movement. *Benchmarking* means identifying which company is best at something in an industry and then duplicating the technique for creating excellence, perhaps even improving it in the process.

The mimetic process works because organizations face continuous high uncertainty, they are aware of innovations occurring in the environment and the innovations are culturally supported, thereby giving legitimacy to adopters. This is a strong mechanism by which a group of banks, or high schools or manufacturing firms begin to look and act like one another.

Coercive Forces All organizations are subject to pressure, both formal and informal, from government, regulatory agencies and other important organizations in the environment, especially those on which a company is dependent. **Coercive forces** are the external pressures exerted on an organization to adopt structures, techniques or behaviours similar to other organizations. As with other changes, those brought about because of coercive forces may not make the organization more effective, but it will look more effective and will be accepted as legitimate in the environment. Some pressures may have the force of law, such as government mandates to adopt new pollution control equipment. Health and safety regulations may demand that a safety officer be appointed. The European Commission has set rules for product warranty that apply in all member states of the European Union.[95] New regulations and government oversight boards have been set up for the accounting industry following widespread accounting scandals.[96]

Coercive pressures may also occur between organizations where there is a power difference, as described in the resource-dependence section earlier in this chapter. Large retailers and manufacturers often insist that certain policies, procedures and techniques be used by their suppliers. When Honda picked Donnelly Corporation to make all the mirrors for its US-manufactured cars, Honda insisted that Donnelly implement an employee empowerment programme. Honda managers believed the partnership could work only if Donnelly learned how to foster collaborative internal relationships.

Organizational changes that result from coercive forces occur when an organization is dependent on another, when there are political factors such as rules, laws and sanctions involved, or when some other contractual or legal basis defines the relationship. Organizations operating under those constraints will adopt changes and relate to one another in a way that increases homogeneity and limits diversity.

Normative Forces The third reason organizations change according to the institutional view is normative forces. **Normative forces** are pressures to change to achieve standards of professionalism, and to adopt techniques that are considered by the professional community to be up to date and effective. Changes may be in any area, such as information technology, accounting requirements, marketing techniques or collaborative relationships with other organizations.

COUNTERPOINT 5.7

'Normative forces' might equally be characterized as institutionalized coercive forces. Their influence is more subtle but no less potent. It might be claimed that 'normative forces' are consensual. But a moment's reflection will reveal that struggles between different groups result in particular norms being established and which also result in these norms being challenged, defended and changed. Within organizations 'culture change' programmes are an example of how executives deploy organizational resources to introduce or strengthen particular kinds of values that they intend to have 'normative force'. **Discuss**

Professionals share a body of formal education based on university degrees and professional networks through which ideas are exchanged by consultants and professional leaders. Universities, consulting firms, trade associations and professional training institutions develop norms among professional managers. People are exposed to similar training and standards and adopt shared values, which are implemented in organizations with which they work. Business schools teach finance, marketing and human resource majors that certain techniques are better than others, so using those techniques becomes a standard in the field. In one study, for example, a radio station changed from a functional to a multidivisional structure because a consultant recommended it as a 'higher standard' of doing business. There was no proof that this structure was better, but the radio station wanted legitimacy and to be perceived as fully professional and up to date in its management techniques.

As an organization manager, keep this guideline in mind:

Enhance legitimacy by borrowing good ideas from other firms, complying with laws and regulations and following procedures considered best for your company.

Companies accept normative pressures to become like one another through a sense of obligation or duty to high standards of performance based on professional norms shared by managers and specialists in their respective organizations. These norms are conveyed through professional education and certification and have almost a moral or ethical requirement based on the highest standards accepted by the profession at that time. In some cases, though, normative forces that maintain legitimacy break down, as they recently did in the accounting industry and the financial sector, and coercive forces are needed to shift organizations back toward acceptable standards.

An organization may use any or all of the mechanisms of mimetic, coercive or normative forces to change itself for greater legitimacy in the institutional environment. Firms tend to use these mechanisms when they are acting under conditions of dependence, uncertainty, ambiguous goals and reliance on professional credentials. The outcome of these processes is that organizations become far more homogeneous than would be expected from the natural diversity among managers and environments.

Summary and Interpretation

At one time, theories and executives tended to regard organizations as 'closed systems' – as autonomous and separate, trying to outdo other companies. Today, there is more support for an 'open systems' view where organizations are seen as part of an ecosystem. The organization may span several industries and will be anchored in a dense web of relationships with other companies. Collaboration becomes an important weapon in the armoury of competition. Indeed, organizations may compete and collaborate at the same time depending on the location and issue. In this business ecosystem, the role of management is changing to include the development of horizontal relationships with other organizations.

Four perspectives have been developed to explain relationships among organizations. The resource-dependence perspective argues that organizations try to avoid excessive dependence on other organizations. In this view, organizations devote considerable effort to controlling the environment to ensure ample resources while maintaining independence. Moreover, powerful organizations will exploit the dependence of small companies. In the collaborative-network perspective, organizations welcome collaboration and interdependence with other organizations to enhance value for both. Many executives are changing mindsets away from autonomy toward collaboration, often with former corporate enemies. The new mindset emphasizes trust, fair dealing and achieving profits for all parties in a relationship.

See online COUNTERPOINT 5.17

The population-ecology perspective explains why organizational diversity continuously increases with the appearance of new organizations filling niches left open by established companies. This perspective says that large companies usually cannot adapt to meet a changing environment; hence, new companies emerge with the appropriate form and skills to serve new needs. Through the process of variation, selection and retention, some organizations will survive and grow while others perish. Companies may adopt a generalist or specialist strategy to survive in the population of organizations.

The institutional perspective argues that interorganizational relationships are shaped as much by a company's quest for legitimacy as by the demand for products and services. The need for legitimacy means that the organization will adopt structures and activities that are perceived as valid, proper and up to date by external stakeholders. In this way, established organizations copy techniques from one another and begin to look very similar. The emergence of common structures and approaches in the same field is called institutional similarity or institutional isomorphism. There are three core mechanisms that explain increasing organizational homogeneity: mimetic forces, which result from responses to uncertainty; coercive forces, which stem from power differences and political influences; and normative forces, which result from common training and professionalism.

Each of the four perspectives represent different lenses through which the world of interorganizational relationships can be viewed and which managers can adopt to address the challenges of change, competition and collaboration with which they grapple. Organizations struggle to reduce dependence and vulnerability; they can thrive through collaborative relationships with others; the slowness to adapt provides openings for new organizations to flourish; and organizations seek legitimacy from the external environment.

KEY CONCEPTS

coercive forces
collaborative network
generalist
institutional environment
institutional perspective
institutional similarity
interorganizational relationships
legitimacy
mimetic forces
niche
normative forces
organizational ecosystem
organizational form
population
population-ecology perspective
resource dependence
retention
selection
specialist
struggle for existence
variation

Discussion Questions

1 The concept of business ecosystems implies that organizations are more interdependent than ever before. From personal experience, do you agree? Explain.

2 How do you feel about the prospect of becoming a manager and having to manage a set of relationships with other companies rather than just managing your own company? Discuss.

3 Assume you are the manager of a small firm that is dependent on a large computer manufacturing customer that uses the resource-dependence perspective. Put yourself in the position of the small firm, and describe what actions you would take to survive and succeed. What actions would you take from the perspective of the large firm?

4 Many managers today were trained under assumptions of adversarial relationships with other companies. Do you think operating as adversaries is easier or more difficult than operating as partners with other companies? Discuss.

5 Discuss how the adversarial versus partnership orientations work among students in class. Is there a sense of competition for grades? Is it possible to develop true partnerships in which your work depends on others?

6 The population-ecology perspective argues that it is healthy for society to have new organizations emerging and old organizations dying as the environment changes. Do you agree? Why would European countries pass laws to sustain traditional organizations and inhibit the emergence of new ones?

7 Explain how the process of variation, selection and retention might explain innovations that take place within an organization.

8 Do you believe that legitimacy really motivates a large, powerful organization such as Wal-Mart? Is acceptance by other people a motivation for individuals as well? Explain.

9 How does the desire for legitimacy result in organizations becoming more similar over time?

10 How do mimetic forces differ from normative forces? Give an example of each.

Chapter 5 Workbook Management Fads

Look up one or two articles on current trends or fads in management. Then, find one or two articles on a management fad from several years ago. Finally, surf the Internet for information on both the current and previous fads.

Questions

1 How were these fads used in organizations? Use real examples from your readings.

2 Why do you think the fads were adopted? To what extent were the fads adopted to truly improve productivity and morale versus the company's desire to appear current in its management techniques compared to the competition?

3 Give an example in which a fad did not work as expected. Explain the reason it did not work.

Chapter 5 Workshop Ugli Orange Case

1 Form groups of three members. One person will be Dr Roland, one person will be Dr Jones and the third person will be an observer.

2 Roland and Jones will read only their own roles, but the observer will read both.

3 Role-play: Instructor announces, 'I am Mr/Ms Cardoza, the owner of the remaining Ugli oranges. My fruit export firm is based in South America. My country does not have diplomatic relations with your country, although we do have strong trade relations.'

The groups will spend about 10 minutes meeting with the other firm's representative and will decide on a course of action. Be prepared to answer the following questions:

a What do you plan to do?

b If you want to buy the oranges, what price will you offer?

c To whom and how will the oranges be delivered?

4 The observers will report the solutions reached. The groups will describe the decision-making process used.

5 The instructor will lead a discussion on the exercise addressing the following questions:

a Which groups had the most trust? How did that influence behaviour?

b Which groups shared more information? Why?

c How are trust and disclosure important in negotiations?

Role of 'Dr Jones'

You are Dr John W. Jones, a biological research scientist employed by a pharmaceutical firm. You have recently developed a synthetic chemical useful for curing and preventing Rudosen. Rudosen is a disease contracted by pregnant women. If not caught in the first four weeks of pregnancy, the disease causes serious brain, eye and ear damage to the unborn child. Recently there has been an outbreak of Rudosen in your state, and several thousand women have contracted the disease. You have found, with volunteer patients, that your recently developed synthetic serum cures Rudosen in its early stages. Unfortunately, the serum is made from the juice of the Ugli orange, which is a very rare fruit. Only a small quantity (approximately 4,000) of these oranges were produced last season. No additional Ugli oranges will be available until next season, which will be too late to cure the present Rudosen victims.

You've demonstrated that your synthetic serum is in no way harmful to pregnant women. Consequently, there are no side effects. The Food and Drug Administration has approved production and distribution of the serum as a cure for Rudosen. Unfortunately, the current outbreak was unexpected, and your firm had not planned on having the compound serum available for 6 months. Your firm holds the patent on the synthetic serum, and it is expected to be a highly profitable product when it is generally available to the public.

You have recently been informed on good evidence that Mr R. H. Cardoza, a South American fruit exporter, is in possession of 3,000 Ugli oranges in good condition. If you could obtain the juice of all 3,000 you would be able to both cure present victims and provide sufficient inoculation for the remaining pregnant women in the state. No other state currently has a Rudosen threat.

You have recently been informed that Dr P. W. Roland is also urgently seeking Ugli oranges and is also aware of Mr Cardoza's possession of the 3,000 available. Dr Roland is employed by a competing pharmaceutical firm. He has been working on biological warfare research for the past several years. There is a great deal of industrial espionage in the pharmaceutical industry. Over the past several years, Dr Roland's firm and yours have sued each other for infringement of patent rights and espionage law violations several times.

You've been authorized by your firm to approach Mr Cardoza to purchase the 3,000 Ugli oranges. You have been told he will sell them to the highest bidder. Your firm has authorized you to bid as high as $250,000 to obtain the juice of the 3,000 available oranges.

Role of 'Dr Roland'

You are Dr P. W. Roland. You work as a research biologist for a pharmaceutical firm. The firm is under contract with the government to do research on methods to combat enemy uses of biological warfare.

Recently several World War II experimental nerve gas bombs were moved from the United States to a small island just off the US coast in the Pacific. In the process of transporting them, two of the bombs developed a leak. The leak is currently controlled by government scientists, who believe that the gas will permeate the bomb chambers within 2 weeks. They know of no method of preventing the gas from getting into the atmosphere and spreading to other islands and very likely to the West Coast of North America as well. If this occurs, it is likely that several thousand people will incur serious brain damage or die.

You've developed a synthetic vapour that will neutralize the nerve gas if it is injected into the bomb chamber before the gas leaks out. The vapour is made with a chemical taken from the rind of the Ugli orange, a very rare fruit. Unfortunately, only 4,000 of these oranges were produced this season.

You've been informed on good evidence that a Mr R. H. Cardoza, a fruit exporter in South America, is in possession of 3,000 Ugli oranges. The chemicals from the rinds of all 3,000 oranges would be sufficient to neutralize the gas if the vapour is developed and injected efficiently. You have been informed that the rinds of these oranges are in good condition.

You have learned that Dr J. W. Jones is also urgently seeking to purchase Ugli oranges and that he is aware of Mr Cardoza's possession of the 3,000 available. Dr Jones works for a firm with which your firm is highly competitive. There is a great deal of industrial espionage in the pharmaceutical industry. Over the years, your firm and Dr Jones's have sued each other for violations of industrial espionage laws and infringement of patent rights several times. Litigation on two suits is still in process.

The federal government has asked your firm for assistance. You've been authorized by your firm to approach Mr Cardoza to purchase 3,000 Ugli oranges. You have been told he will sell them to the highest bidder. Your firm has authorized you to bid as high as $250,000 to obtain the rinds of the oranges.

Before approaching Mr Cardoza, you have decided to talk to Dr Jones to influence him so that he will not prevent you from purchasing the oranges.

By Dr Robert House, University of Toronto. Used with permission.

CASE FOR ANALYSIS

Noble Biotech

By Maxine Robertson & Cliff Oswick,
Queen Mary University of London, UK

Background

NOBLE is a biotechnology company based in Switzerland which develops therapeutics based on human monoclonal antibodies. NOBLE develops products independently and in collaboration with partners (typically large pharmaceutical firms). NOBLE'S primary revenue is from the royalties it receives from a drug it developed and subsequently licensed to a pharmaceutical firm who took on later stage trials and developed the drug through to commercialization. NOBLE has ten further licensed drugs in clinical development, funded by NOBLE's licensees and three proprietary drugs which it is currently developing in-house. NOBLE's expertise lies mainly in preclinical development. Its financial strategy is that all its R&D activities are either to be pre-funded through formal alliances with large pharmaceutical firms or funded from revenues. The strategy is aimed at enabling NOBLE to continue to pursue its own, carefully targeted, proprietary drug discovery programmes in-house. Decisions regarding the funding of any later stage clinical development activity are taken on a case-by-case basis. To date NOBLE has taken only four development programmes into clinical trials itself.

2. The focal innovation project – INFLAM1

INFLAM1 is a drug aimed at tackling an acute respiratory disease which affects approximately eight per cent of Western populations and which continues to increase in prevalence. As such, the drug has the potential to become a 'blockbuster' if it succeeds in development. Blockbuster drugs generate at least $1million each day in revenues and development teams are therefore acutely aware that 'time is money' and speed to market is what matters. However, the team acknowledge that because INFLAM1 is a radical new treatment for the disease, which will change the approach and practices that doctors use in the treatment of this disease, they may experience problems convincing them to allow their patients to participate in clinical trials which could cause delays in development.

The INFLAM1 project is high profile within NOBLE and a new more formalized and professional project management approach has been implemented on INFLAM1 headed up by an external consultant named Donovan Lee. He was chosen because he has considerable experience of managing later stage clinical trials in a large pharmaceutical firm. The INFLAM1 project comprises ongoing pre-clinical research as well as early stage clinical studies. This basic research is being carried out in collaboration with a number of scientists working in universities across Europe and the US who specialize in this scientific area. NOBLE are quite specific in terms of the attributes they look for in academic partners. The Chief Scientific Officer commented

'It's very easy to get disappointed with the quality of some academic research, particularly if you rely too heavily on published material because its often not reproducible. So we tend to work with the people who we think are the best but also hopefully those that are up and coming rather than declining and on the way out. We're very, very selective. We agree on a work plan and what the output's going to be, what the budget's going to be and how it's going to be communicated and published. We try to build up not just specific tasks but a relationship. We have meetings roughly once a quarter and then once a year we get all the experts that we have in respiratory or whatever together for a workshop with a specific agenda and some questions and just get some opinions out of them.'

The Search for a Partner

In September 2006 NOBLE announced that the FDA (the US regulatory agency) had approved a Phase I trial coded INFLAM1-1. The results from this trial in 34 patients reported 9 months later demonstrated that INFLAM1-1 was well tolerated at all doses and no safety concerns were identified. NOBLE's Chief Medical Officer commented at the time: *'We are very optimistic about INFLAM1 as a potential step forward in the treatment for this respiratory disease'*. Hence ten months later NOBLE's Board took the decision to attempt to out-license INFLAM1 that is, to 'sell-on' the developmental drug to a larger firm who would take it through later stage, large scale trials hopefully to commercialization for which Noble would then receive royalties.

This is a very common approach that is used by biotechnology firms who operate in the biomedical sector as they usually only have access to relatively small networks of clinicians. They therefore do not have access to the number of patients required for the much larger scale later stage trials required to gain FDA approval. The CEO, Ed King, thought that it would take around one year to set up a deal with a partner.

Pharmaceutical firms who expressed an interest in partnering were given a non-confidential information pack, about development to-date. The development team produced this and had considerable involvement in supporting partnering negotiations but know nothing of the financial details of the negotiations which were conducted by the business development team. This internal secrecy is quite common in the biotechnology sector where Intellectual Property is very valuable and alliance and partnering activity can significantly raise or lower the share price of biotechnology firms. A shortlist of four potential partners was identified and the development team requested future clinical trials development plans from each. These plans were discussed around three key areas: (i) whether the plans indicated that the potential partner had appropriate expertise to take the product to market efficiently; (ii) whether the plans gave any clues to NOBLE about whether or not to start particular clinical trials in advance of partnering being agreed; (iii) what questions the NOBLE Business Development team should seek potential partners to answer specifically to help them decide on the final partnering agreement.

Whilst partnering negotiations were on-going (and likely to continue for up to nine months) NOBLE still had to keep moving forward with the INFLAM1 project just in case an acceptable partnering deal could not be agreed. Therefore one month later the development team had to make recommendations for in-house future trials to the Board. These recommendations generated significant debate and many tensions. Initially the development team spent a significant amount of their time trying to '*guess*' what potential partners might look for in terms of progress when trying to decide on whether or not to recommend particular trials. This decision was made more difficult by the fact that there did not appear to be any consistency across potential partners about what kind of studies should be done. The Board had explicitly requested the development team to suggest what trials would be critical to the partnering deal but as Donovan Lee commented '*with our knowledge of partners we can't say hand on heart what will be critical as partners don't necessarily know what trials they need*'. Val Lyons, the clinical development manager, was also of the opinion that '*any partner is more than likely going to stop most things that are going on at the point at which they takeover development*'. The team were painfully aware that NOBLE had previously had a bad experience with a partner who took almost a year to get things going and '*then screwed it up*'. The uncertainty created by future partnering for clinical decisions was summarized neatly by the Val: '*In the absence of knowledge about what's happening with partnering we have to assume that we will have fully partnered by the autumn and base our decisions on that*'. The scientific argument for a particular trial could also lead to a different conclusion to an argument based on partnering. As Joe Sommers the Regulatory Manager suggested '*if partnering falls over then our recommendations for clinical trials would be very different. The partnering objective changes things. And if we were going to take it all the way through ourselves as a company, we would do it very differently because we would probably be much more likely to take a scientific approach because what that gives you is the ability to kill the project early if it's really not going well. But we don't want to kill it early until someone's given us a fat cheque*.'

When the development team suggested some options for trials to the Board, they compared them to the trial plans each potential partner had submitted to see whether they '*gave any clues*' as to what trials were likely to be needed for regulatory approval. The Board felt that large pharmaceutical firms would have a far better idea of what was required given their wealth of experience of dealing with the FDA. The problem however was that the plans proposed by each of the potential partners were completely different, with varied combinations of studies proposed. Some of the partners plans were also '*not very well developed*' and some seemed to be at odds with what the development team had suggested would be acceptable from a regulatory standpoint. The major issue for the Board then appeared to be estimating what risk to take on (in terms of committing financial resources to a particular trial when outcomes may not be favourable) for an expected return from the partnering arrangements that were finally agreed. The more robust the evidence for the safety and utility of INFLAM1, the better the financial deal would be with a partner. However, there was a risk that the results of further trials may not be ideal. At worst, that they may jeopardize the partnering agreement by putting the partner off completely, or encourage the partner to hold off and await trial results before proceeding to complete the contractual agreement. As the Board also felt that partners were also likely to stop NOBLE's in-house trials at the takeover point, they felt it was important only to commit to those that can do something '*worthwhile*' in the timeframe. The risk benefit analysis was summarized by Ed King:

'*We're looking at various scenarios for how we will develop the product and what they mean in terms of expenditure, and because we are going to partner the product, we're looking at what is the package of information we're going to give to a partner and how much money will we get back. It's all about if we spend X we get Y back. If we spend Z, we still only get Y back, so why are we spending Z? We're looking at all the scenarios that have been proposed at the moment. The development has to remain optimal for the product because we don't want to stop it or not do things that mean that when someone comes in to pick it up they couldn't continue, so you've got to keep it moving. It's a balance if we don't have to spend X now; we could delay it by six months, then that's preferable. When we make decisions we try and make it as attractive as possible for a partner because we don't want to box them in but there are all sorts of considerations, it's quite complicated.*'

Finally a shortlist of two firms was agreed and these firms went through another round of capability presentations with both the development and business development teams where all of the fine detail about how development would progress and issues such as payments etc. were negotiated. It was agreed that NOBLE would receive payments at particular stages of development and a percentage of royalties would be paid, again in instalments if, and when, the product was successfully commercialized. This is a typical partnering arrangement in the biomedical sector. Eventually Ed King announced internally that NOBLE was going to partner with a firm code named 'Seahorse.' The firm's identity was to remain confidential until the financial agreement had been signed by both parties. This was likely to take a further few weeks. Only then would the announcement be made public. NOBLE's commitment to 'Seahorse' at this point in time was to ensure an effective knowledge transfer of all the data and science pertaining to INFLAM1 over the coming months and to conclude and report the results of a further Phase 1 study INFLAM1-2 which was on-going but had recently stalled.

The INFLAM1-2 trial

Five months into partnering negotiations NOBLE had received FDA approval to commence a further repeat, multiple dose, safety study of INFLAM1 in patients with mild and moderate forms of the disease. The trial known as INFLAM1-2 was to be another safety study to assess tolerability and optimum dosages for patients. This trial was planned to run in the following quarter with three dose groups containing 12 patients per group and a placebo group with six patients (making a total of 42 patients). The team were unsure however whether they would be able to recruit this number of patients from their existing network. Donovan stated confidently to NOBLE's Board at the time that the trial would cost approximately €1.6 million and would take six months to complete without going into detail regarding possible problems with patient recruitment. At a project meeting one month later however the team were still debating how many patients should be included.

The main reason for these ongoing discussions was that the larger the number of patients to be recruited included then the more expensive and lengthy the trial would be. As Donovan had been quite explicit to the Board regarding the time to complete the trial and the costs involved, the team felt that they should be sure to recruit only the patients that were absolutely necessary to provide sufficient data. Karyn, the regulatory manager commented '*We can run this with as few as 24 patients from a regulatory standpoint and we really don't know whether any of the pharma we may partner with on this will want to see the results from a larger trial*'. However, Donovan thought differently and stated to the team '*Let's not forget that the main purpose of this trial is to have a large enough sample to be able to go on to conduct large scale trials in patients with a severe form of the disease. On that basis the magic number for subjects needs to be around 50.*' Further lively discussion ensued across the development team which consisted of representatives from a number of different functions including clinical, regulatory, manufacturing and business development. After 15 minutes Donovan stated '*We might as well stick our finger in the air as to how many patients we need*' as so many different arguments had been made, proposing the optimal number of patients for this study. Finally Donovan suggested that potential partners might also be unsure about patient numbers in a trial of this sort and concluded the discussion *'it's our guess against their guess, so let's stick with 42 – it's the answer to everything isn't it?'* Patient recruitment however turned out to be the least of the development team's problems.

In order to conduct this study the drug needed to be suspended in a solution, then bagged and labelled for each patient, so that it could be administered to the patient intravenously. Further through the development process, the drug would actually be given in much smaller, concentrated doses and the suspension and bagging process would be irrelevant. However suspending in a solution was a requirement in this early trial. A clinical unit in a hospital 100 miles from NOBLE had finally agreed to run the trial but the team had never worked with the doctors there. The suspension was going to be bagged by NOBLE and then delivered to the hospital where patient labels would be added. This however actually constituted an amendment to the manufacturing process for which FDA approval was required. It also came to light that whilst the majority of trials units in hospitals are exempt from the need to have a license to carry out labelling processes, this particular hospital was not exempt and was unlicensed. This was discovered quite late in the day and Val Lyons felt that Bob Scott in manufacturing should have made them aware of this requirement much sooner. The team therefore needed to find a licensed facility that could add the labels to the bags in transit to the hospital where the trial would be conducted.

A firm was eventually found 50 miles away to carry out the labelling. Unfortunately, however, particles were discovered in the suspension when the labelled bags were returned to NOBLE for inspection. No-one had any idea why this had occurred. Clearly however, a solution containing particles could not be intravenously administered to patients as it could cause death! The basic research chemists who generally did not get directly involved in trials at all were called in to try and discover why this had happened. After two weeks at one of the increasingly frequent development team meetings, the chemists could still not agree on what might be causing the formation of particles. Representatives from the clinical trials function were very keen to establish this as soon as possible, reminding everyone at the meeting that every day the trial was delayed then *'another $1million is lost'* but the same sense of urgency was not shared by the chemists. Suggestions were made to delve further into the published literature, perhaps ask other academics to become involved etc. but this was all going to take more time. Eventually two of the three chemists that were present at the meeting decided on a way forward, counter to what had been proposed by another chemist, and stated that they were confident they could solve the problem quickly. Nevertheless at the next development team meeting one week later, the chemists had to admit they were really no further forward. Business development recognised that the INFLAM1-2 trial was now way behind schedule and reluctantly decided to recommend to the Board that 'Seahorse' be informed. Donovan Lee and the rest of the development team were very uncertain how Seahorse would react to this news.

Case Questions

1. The case study demonstrates how technical and business interests often seem to conflict, although in spheres such as the pharmaceutical industry, business and technical requirements must both be satisfied for a product to reach market. Can you list all the technical issues and business issues, and identify which are the most crucial?
2. One key issue that arose was secrecy about the potential partner 'Seahorse'. Why was this an issue and were there alternative ways of dealing with secrecy?
3. Ultimately, the project was badly delayed. Can you suggest ways that product development could have been better organized so as to avoid or at least reduce the delays?

CASE FOR ANALYSIS

Hugh Russel, Inc.

By David K. Hurst

The following story is a personal recollection by David Hurst of the experience of a group of managers in a mature organization undergoing profound change. . . .The precipitating event in this change was a serious business crisis. . . .

When I joined Hugh Russel Inc. in 1979, it was a medium-sized Canadian distributor of steel and industrial products. With sales of CDN$535 million and 3,000 employees, the business was controlled by the chairman, Archie Russel, who owned 16 per cent of the common shares. The business consisted of four groups – the core steel distribution activities (called 'Russelsteel'), industrial bearings and valves distribution, a chain of wholesalers of hardware and sporting goods and a small manufacturing business. . . .

The company was structured for performance. . . . The management was professional, with each of the divisional hierarchies headed by a group president reporting to Peter Foster in his capacity as president of the corporation. Jobs were described in job descriptions, and their mode of execution was specified in detailed standard operating procedures. Three volumes of the corporate manual spelled out policy on everything from accounting to vacation pay. Extensive accounting and data processing systems allowed managers to track the progress of individual operations against budgets and plans. Compensation was performance-based, with return on net assets (RONA) as the primary measure and large bonuses (up to 100 per cent of base) for managers who made their targets.

At the senior management level, the culture was polite but formal. The board of directors consisted of Archie's friends and associates together with management insiders. Archie and Peter ran the organization as if they were majority owners. Their interaction with management outside of the head office was restricted to the occasional field trip. . . .

Crisis

Nine months after I joined the company as a financial planner, we were put 'in play' by a raider and, after a fierce bidding war, were acquired in a hostile takeover. Our acquirer was a private company controlled by the eldest son of an entrepreneur of legendary wealth and ability, so we had no inkling at the time of the roller-coaster ride that lay ahead of us. We were unaware that not only did the son not have the support of his father in this venture but also he had neglected to consult his two brothers, who were joint owners of the acquiring company! As he had taken on $300 million of debt to do the deal, this left each of the brothers on the hook for a personal guarantee of $100 million. They were not amused, and it showed!

Within days of the deal, we were inundated by waves of consultants, lawyers and accountants: each shareholder seemed to have his or her own panel of advisers. After 6 weeks of intensive analysis, it was clear that far too much had been paid for us and that the transaction was vastly overleveraged. At the start of the deal, the acquirer had approached our bankers and asked them if they wanted a piece of the 'action'. Concerned at the possible loss of our banking business and eager to be associated with such a prominent family, our bankers had agreed to provide the initial financing on a handshake. Now, as they saw the detailed numbers for the first time and became aware of the dissent among the shareholders, they withdrew their support and demanded their money back. We needed to refinance $300 million of debt – fast. . . .

Change

The takeover and the subsequent merger of our new owner's moribund steel-fabricating operations into Hugh Russel changed our agenda completely. We had new shareholders (who fought with each other constantly), new bankers and new businesses in an environment of soaring interest rates and plummeting demand for our products and services. Almost overnight, the corporation went from a growth-oriented, acquisitive, earnings-driven operation to a broken, cash-starved company, desperate to survive. Closures, layoffs, downsizing, delayering, asset sales and 'rationalization' became our new priorities. . . . At the head office, the clarity of jobs vanished. For example, I had

Source: Reprinted by permission of Harvard Business School Press. From *Crisis and Renewal: Meeting the Challenge of Organizational Change*, by David K. Hurst (Boston: Harvard Business School Press, 1995), pp. 53–73.

been hired to do financial forecasting and raise capital in the equity markets, but with the company a financial mess, this clearly could not be done. For all of us, the future looked dangerous and frightening as bankruptcy, both personal and corporate, loomed ahead.

And so it was in an atmosphere of crisis that Wayne Mang, the new president (Archie Russel and Peter Foster left the organization soon after the deal), gathered the first group of managers together to discuss the situation. Wayne Mang had been in the steel business for many years and was trusted and respected by the Hugh Russel people. An accountant by training, he used to call himself the 'personnel manager' to underscore his belief in both the ability of people to make the difference in the organization and the responsibility of line management to make this happen. The hastily called first meeting consisted of people whom Wayne respected and trusted from all over the organization. They had been selected without regard for their position in the old hierarchy.

The content and style of that first meeting were a revelation to many! Few of them had ever been summoned to the head office for anything but a haranguing over their budgets. Now they were being told the complete gory details of the company's situation and, for the first time, being treated as if they had something to contribute. Wayne asked for their help.

During that first meeting, we counted nineteen major issues confronting the corporation. None of them fell under a single functional area. We arranged ourselves into task forces to deal with them. I say 'arranged ourselves' because that was the way it seemed to happen. Individuals volunteered without coercion to work on issues in which they were interested or for which their skills were relevant. They also volunteered others who were not at the meeting but, it was thought, could help. There was some guidance – each task force had one person from the head office whose function it was to report what was happening back to the 'center'–and some members found themselves on too many task forces, which required that substitutes be found. But that was the extent of the conscious management of the process.

The meeting broke up at 2:00 a.m., when we all went home to tell our incredulous spouses what had happened. . . .

The cross-functional project team rapidly became our preferred method of organizing new initiatives, and at the head office, the old formal structure virtually disappeared. The teams could be formed at a moment's notice to handle a fast-breaking issue and dissolved just as quickly. We found, for example, that even when we weren't having formal meetings, we seemed to spend most of our time talking to each other informally. Two people would start a conversation in someone's office, and almost before you knew it, others had wandered in and a small group session was going. Later on, we called these events 'bubbles'; they became our equivalent of campfire meetings....

Later, when I became executive vice president, Wayne and I deliberately shared an office so we could each hear what the other was doing in real time and create an environment in which 'bubbles' might form spontaneously. As people wandered past our open door, we would wave them in to talk; others would wander in after them. The content of these sessions always had to do with our predicament, both corporate and personal. It was serious stuff, but the atmosphere was light and open. Our fate was potentially a bad one, but at least it would be shared. All of us who were involved then cannot remember ever having laughed so much. We laughed at ourselves and at the desperate situation. We laughed at the foolishness of the bankers in having financed such a mess, and we laughed at the antics of the feuding shareholders, whose outrageous manners and language we learned to mimic to perfection.

I think it was the atmosphere from these informal sessions that gradually permeated all our interactions – with employees, bankers, suppliers, everyone with whom we came into contact. Certainly, we often had tough meetings, filled with tension and threat, but we were always able to 'bootstrap' ourselves back up emotionally at the informal debriefings afterward. . . .

Perhaps the best example of both the change in structure and the blurring of the boundaries of the organization was our changing relationships with our bankers. In the beginning, at least for the brief time that the loan was in good standing, the association was polite and at arm's length. Communication was formal. As the bank realized the full horror of what it had financed (a process that took about 18 months), the relationship steadily grew more hostile. Senior executives of the bank became threatening, spelling out what actions they might take if we did not solve our problem. This hostility culminated in an investigation by the bank for possible fraud (a standard procedure in many banks when faced with a significant loss).

Throughout this period, we had seen a succession of different bankers, each of whom had been assigned to our account for a few months. As a result of our efforts to brief every new face that appeared, we had built a significant network of contacts within the bank with whom we had openly shared a good deal of information and opinion. When no fraud was found, the bank polled its own people on what to do. Our views presented so coherently by our people (because everyone knew what was going on), and shared so widely with so many bankers, had an enormous influence on the outcome of this process. The result was the formation of a joint company-bank team to address a shared problem that together we could solve. The boundary between the corporation and the bank was now blurred: to an outside observer, it would have been unclear where the corporation ended and the bank began. . . .

Our corporation had extensive formal reporting systems to allow the monitoring of operations on a regular basis. After the takeover, these systems required substantial modifications. For example, we had to report our results to the public every quarter at a time when we were losing nearly 2 million dollars a week! We knew that unless we got to our suppliers ahead of time, they could easily panic and refuse us credit. Hasty moves on their part could have had fatal consequences for the business.

In addition, our closure plans for plants all over Canada and the United States brought us into contact with unions and governments in an entirely different way. We realized that we had no option but to deal with these audiences in advance of events.

I have already described how our relationship with the bankers changed as a result of our open communication. We found exactly the same effect with these new audiences. Initially, our major suppliers could not understand why we had told them we were in trouble before we had to. We succeeded, however, in framing the situation in a way that enlisted their cooperation in our survival, and by the time the 'war story' was news, we had their full support. Similarly, most government and union organizations were so pleased to be involved in the process before announcements were made that they bent over backward to be of assistance. Just as had been the case with the bank, we set up joint task forces with these 'outside' agencies to resolve what had become shared problems. A significant contributor to our ability to pull this off was the high quality of our internal communication. Everyone on the teams knew the complete, up-to-date picture of what was happening. An outside agency could talk to anyone on a team and get the same story. In this way, we constructed a formidable network of contacts, many of whom had special skills and experience in areas that would turn out to be of great help to us in the future.

The addition of multiple networks to our information systems enhanced our ability both to gather and to disseminate information. The informality and openness of the networks, together with the high volume of face-to-face dialogues, gave us an early-warning system with which to detect hurt feelings and possible hostile moves on the part of shareholders, suppliers, nervous bankers and even customers. This information helped us head off trouble before it happened. The networks also acted as a broadcast system through which we could test plans and actions before announcing them formally. In this way, not only did we get excellent suggestions for improvement, but everyone felt that he or she had been consulted before action was taken. . . .

We had a similar experience with a group of people outside the company during the hectic last six months of 1983, when we were trying to finalize a deal for the shareholders and bankers to sell the steel distribution business to new owners. The group of people in question comprised the secretaries of the numerous lawyers and accountants involved in the deal. . . .

We made these secretaries part of the network, briefing them in advance on the situation, explaining why things were needed, and keeping them updated on the progress of the deal. We were astounded at the cooperation we received: our calls were put through, our messages received prompt responses, and drafts and opinions were produced on time. In the final event, a complex deal that should have taken nine months to complete was done in three. All of this was accomplished by ordinary people going far beyond what might have been expected of them. . . .

We had been thrust into crisis without warning, and our initial activities were almost entirely reactions to issues that imposed themselves upon us. But as we muddled along in the task forces, we began to find that we had unexpected sources of influence over what was happening. The changing relationship with the bank illustrates this neatly. Although we had no formal power in that situation, we found that by framing a confusing predicament in a coherent way, we could, via our network, influence the outcomes of the bank's decisions. The same applied to suppliers: by briefing them ahead of time and presenting a reasonable scenario for the recovery of their advances, we could influence the decisions they would make.

Slowly we began to realize that, although we were powerless in a formal sense, our networks, together with our own internal coherence, gave us an ability to get things done invisibly. As we discussed the situation with all the parties involved, a strategy began to emerge. A complicated financial/tax structure would allow the bank to 'manage' its loss and give it an incentive not to call on the shareholders' personal guarantees. The core steel distribution business could be refinanced in the process and sold to new owners. The wrangle between the shareholders could be resolved, and each could go his or her own way. All that had to be done was to bring all the parties together, including a buyer for the steel business, and have them agree that this was the best course to follow. Using our newfound skills, we managed to pull it off.

It was not without excitement: at the last minute, the shareholders raised further objections to the deal. Only the bank could make them sell, and they were reluctant to do so, fearful that they might attract a lawsuit. Discreet calls to the major suppliers, several of whose executives were on the board of the bank, did the trick. 'This business needs to be sold and recapitalized', the suppliers were told. 'If the deal does not go through, you should probably reduce your credit exposure', the deal went through. By the end of 1983, we had new owners, just in time to benefit from the general business recovery. The ordeal was over.

Case Questions

1 What were the initial causes of the difficulties faced by Hugh Russel, Inc.?

2 What are cross-functional project teams and how did they work?

3 What led management to adopt cross-functional teams? Was it inspirational leadership, organizational crisis, or a combination of issues?

4 How did the managers deal with external clients of the company, such as the bank?

5 The case study ended in success. Why do you think the bank agreed to go along with the managers' strategy?

Notes

1. MAN AG, *Annual Report 2007*, Munich.
2. 'International takes wraps off MaxxForce', Fleet Owner, January 1, 2007, Pg. 33; 'Caterpillar Exits Engine Business Enters Work-Truck Market', *Engineering News-Record,* Vol. 260 No. 21, June 23, 2008, Pg. 97; Brezonick, Mike, 'A big step up for International: first in new family of big bore truck diesels to debut in '07; first fruits of alliance with MAN, *Diesel Progress,* Vol. 71 No. 6, June 1, 2005, Pg. 78.
3. 'Force Motors, Man To Form Heavy Trucks JV', *The Economic Times*, November 11, 2005; Roger Houghton, 'Worldwide sales for MAN trucks booming', *Business Day South Africa*, May 10, 2007, Pg. 8 'MAN to ramp up India business', Hindustan Times, May 9, 2008; Eliot Lobo, 'MAN goes upmarket', *Autocar Professional India*, pg. 19; Ravi Krishnan, 'Investors give thumbs down to Eicher-Volvo', *Mint*, December 11, 2007; Ammar Master, 'Daimler Trucks forms JV with Hero Group', *Mint*, December 15, 2007; 'Indian, foreign firms find symbiosis in truck market', *The Nikkei Weekly (Japan)*, November 27, 2006.
4. 'China Truck Makers Face Acid Test', *SinoCast China Transportation Watch,* February 10, 2006; 'MAN Group Opens First Overseas Center in Beijing', *SinoCast China Transportation Watch*, June 15, 2007.
5. Christine Oliver, 'Determinants of Interorganizational Relationships: Integration and Future Directions', *Academy of Management Review* 15 (1990), 241–265.
6. http://www.flextronics.com/en/default.aspx, accessed on July 9, 2008.
7. Crampes, Claude and Hollander, Abraham (2006), 'Triple play time; Bundling competition in ICT industries', *Communications & Strategies*, 63, Pg. 51–71.
8. James Moore, *The Death of Competition: Leadership and Strategy in the Age of Business Ecosystems* (New York: HarperCollins, 1996); Brent Schlender, 'How Big Can Apple Get?' *Fortune* (February 21, 2005), 66–76.
9. Howard Muson, 'Friend? Foe? Both? The Confusing World of Corporate Alliances', *Across the Board* (March–April 2002), 19–25; and Devi R. Gnyawali and Ravindranath Madhavan, 'Cooperative Networks and Competitive Dynamics: A Structural Embeddedness Perspective', *Academy of Management Review* 26, no. 3 (2001), 431–445.
10. Thomas Petzinger, Jr., *The New Pioneers: The Men and Women Who Are Transforming the Workplace and Marketplace* (New York: Simon & Schuster, 1999), 53–54.
11. James Moore, 'The Death of Competition', *Fortune* (April 15, 1996), 142–144.

12. Amazon's spending in new technology increased 41 per cent to 171 $m in 2006 but was expected to slow down in subsequent years: Carrie Flynn 'Amazon to curtail its spending', *New York Times,* October 25, 2006, retrieved May 20, 2008, from http://www.nytimes.com/2006/10/25/technology/25amazon.html.
13. Keith Regan, 'Toys 'R' US Wins Right To End Amazon Partnership', March 3, 2006, Retrieved May 20, 2008, from http://www.technewsworld.com/story/49188.html?welcome=1211372647
14. Edd McCracken, 'Amazon accused of squeezing publisher – Hachette says online giant is making unfair demands', *Sunday Herald*, June 8, 2008; Pg. 24
15. Doug Tsuruoka, 'Amazon Deals Have Short Shelf Life; Retailers Go Their Own Way; Unexpected competition, high cost of platform spur big store chains to cut ties', *Investor's Business Daily*, July 3, 2008
16 Nick Wingfield, 'New Chapter: A Web Giant Tries to Boost Profits by Taking On Tenants', *The Wall Street Journal* (September 24, 2003), A1, A10; and Nick Wingfield, 'Amazon's eBay Challenge', *The Wall Street Journal* (June 3, 2004), B1, B2.
17. Clorox, Hoover's Company Records – In-depth record, May 20, 2008
18. Alice Dragoon, 'A Travel Guide to Collaboration', *CIO* (November 15, 2004), 68–75.
19. Sumantra Ghoshal and Christopher A. Bartlett, 'Changing the Role of Top Management: Beyond Structure and Process', *Harvard Business Review* (January–February 1995), 86–96.
20. Susan Greco and Kate O'Sullivan, 'Independents' Day', *Inc*. (August 2002), 76–83.
21. http://www.e3network.com/default.asp?docId=13028, accessed on July 9, 2008.
22. J. Pfeffer and G. R. Salancik, *The External Control of Organizations: A Resource Dependence Perspective* (New York: Harper & Row, 1978).
23. Derek S. Pugh and David J. Hickson, *Writers on Organizations*, 5th ed. (Thousand Oaks, Calif.: Sage, 1996).
24. James Hall, 'Good For You What About Him? Britain's Powerful Supermarkets Have Been Accused of Bullying Farmers And Food Producers In Order To Keep Costs Low', *The Sunday Telegraph*, August 26, 2007; *OECD Economic Surveys – United Kingdom,* Section V. Product market competition and economic performance, 2004, Pg. 184–243.
25. Marjolein Canils and Cees Gelderman (2005), 'Purchasing strategies in the Kraljic matrix – A power and dependence perspective', *Journal of Purchasing and Supply Management,* 11, Pg. 141–155.
26. This discussion is based on Matthew Schifrin, 'The Big Squeeze', *Forbes* (March 11, 1996), 45–46; Wendy Zellner with Marti Benedetti, 'CLOUT!' *BusinessWeek* (December 21, 1992), 62–73; Kevin Kelly and Zachary Schiller with James B. Treece, 'Cut Costs or Else' *BusinessWeek* (March 22, 1993), 28–29; and Lee Berton, 'Push from Above', *The Wall Street Journal* (May 23, 1996), R24.
27. 'Fitting In; In Bow to Retailers' New Clout, Levi Strauss Makes Alterations', *The Wall Street Journal* (June 17, 2004), A1.
28. 'Levi Makes Alterations To Sew Up Wal-Mart Sales' The State (Columbia, SC), June 20, 2004, Pg. F3; Marquard, William 'Leverage, invest, diversify: the supplier's bargain', *MMR*, Vol. 23 No. 20, December 11, 2006, Pg. 15–19.
29. *FD (Fair Disclosure) Wire*, Q3 2006 Levi Strauss & Co. Earnings Conference Call, October 10, 2006.
30. Ross Tucker, 'Future Face of Levi's: Women's And Overseas Seen As Keys To Growth', *Women's Wear Daily*, April 9, 2008, Pg. 1
31. Pankaj Mishra, 'Microsoft to integrate products with Linux, rival operating tech', *MINT*, August 23, 2007; John Fontana, 'All eyes on how Microsoft pulls off ODF support; Software giant saying right things, but actions will determine if format debate headed in right direction', *Network World*, May 22, 2008, p.19; http://www.iii.org/international/rankings/ accessed on July 10, 2008.
32. Mitchell P. Koza and Arie Y. Lewin, 'The Co-Evolution of Network Alliances: A Longitudinal Analysis of an International Professional Service Network', Center for Research on New Organizational Forms, Working Paper 98–09–02; and Kathy Rebello with Richard Brandt, Peter Coy and Mark Lewyn, 'Your Digital Future', *BusinessWeek* (September 7, 1992), 56–64.
33. Christine Oliver, 'Determinants of Inter-organizational Relationships: Integration and Future Directions', *Academy of Management Review*, 15 (1990), 241–265; Ken G. Smith, Stephen J. Carroll and Susan Ashford, 'Intra- and Interorganizational Cooperation: Toward a Research Agenda', *Academy of Management Journal*, 38 (1995), 7–23; and Ken G. Smith, Stephen J. Carroll and Susan Ashford, 'Intra- and Interorganizational Cooperation: Toward a Research Agenda', *Academy of Management Journal* 38 (1995), 7–23.
34. 'Reviving the economy by freeing corporations', *The Korea Herald*, March 19, 2008.
35. Elfren Sicangco Cruz, 'Globalization and corporate governance', *BusinessWorld*, July 18, 2006, Pg. S1/4.
36. Timothy M. Stearns, Alan N. Hoffman and Jan B. Heide, 'Performance of Commercial Television Stations as an Outcome of Interorganizational Linkages and Environmental Conditions', *Academy of Management Journal* 30 (1987), 71–90; and David A. Whetten and Thomas K. Kueng, 'The Instrumental Value of Interorganizational Relations: Antecedents and Consequences of Linkage Formation', *Academy of Management Journal* 22 (1979), 325–344.
37. Alex Taylor III, 'Just Another Sexy Sports Car?' *Fortune* (March 17, 2003), 76–80.
38. David Kiley, 'Ghosn: 'The U.S. Auto Market Is Not Going to Be Great Again', *Business Week Online*, April 30, 2008; Ian Rowley, 'Underwhelming News for Nissan Investors', *Business Week Online*, January 14, 2008.
39. 'Ranbaxy completes phase II trials for anti-malaria drug' The Press Trust of India July 4, 2008 Friday; http://www.biospace.com/company_profile.aspx?CompanyId=1440, accessed on July 10, 2008.

40. Fisher & Paykel teams up with Turkish company, *The New Zealand Herald*, October 3, 2007.
41. David Magee, *Turnaround: How Carlos Ghosn Rescued Nissan*, (London: HarperCollins, 2003).
42. Myron Magnet, 'The New Golden Rule of Business', *Fortune* (February 21, 1994), 60–64; Grittner, 'Four Elements of Successful Sourcing Strategies'; and Jeffrey H. Dyer and Nile W. Hatch, 'Using Supplier Networks to Learn Faster', *MIT Sloan Management Review* (Spring 2004), 57–63.
43. Peter Smith Ring and Andrew H. Van de Ven, 'Developmental Processes of Corporate Interorganizational Relationships', *Academy of Management Review* 19 (1994), 90–118; Jeffrey H. Dyer, 'How Chrysler Created an American *Keiretsu', Harvard Business Review* (July–August 1996), 42–56; Grittner, 'Four Elements of Successful Sourcing Strategies'; Magnet, 'The New Golden Rule of Business'; and Mick Marchington and Steven Vincent, 'Analysing the Influence of Institutional, Organizational and Interpersonal Forces in Shaping Inter-Organizational Relationships', *Journal of Management Studies* 41, no. 6 (September 2004), 1029–1056.
44. http://www.tyco.com/livesite/Page/Tyco/Who+We+Are/History/? Accessed on July 10, 2008.
45. Magnet, 'The New Golden Rule of Business'; and Grittner, 'Four Elements of Successful Sourcing Strategies'.
46. Pete Engardio, 'The Barons of Outsourcing', *BusinessWeek* (August 28, 2000), 177–178.
47. Andrew Raskin, 'Who's Minding the Store?' *Business 2.0* (February 2003), 70–74.
48. Marchington and Vincent, 'Analysing the Influence of Institutional, Organizational and Interpersonal Forces in Shaping Inter-Organizational Relationships'.
49. Fred R. Blekley, 'Some Companies Let Suppliers Work on Site and Even Place Orders', *The Wall Street Journal* (January 13, 1995), A1, A6.
50. 'Bombardier Challenger 300 Super Midsize Corporate Business Jet' retrieved, May 21, 2008, from http://www.aerospace-technology.com/projects/bombardier/.
51. Marcel van Leeuwen, 'XO JET Orders and Secures Options for a Total of 80 Bombardier Challenger Jets.' September 25, 2007, retrieved May 21, 2008 from http://www.airportbusiness.com/online/article.jsp?id=14570&siteSection=1.
52. Philip Siekman, 'The Snap-Together Business Jet', *Fortune* (January 21, 2002), 104[A]–104[H].
53. This section draws from Joel A. C. Baum, 'Organizational Ecology', in Stewart R. Clegg, Cynthia Hardy and Walter R. Nord, eds., *Handbook of Organization Studies* (Thousand Oaks, Calif.: Sage, 1996); Jitendra V. Singh, *Organizational Evolution: New Directions* (Newbury Park, Calif.: Sage, 1990); Howard Aldrich, Bill McKelvey and Dave Ulrich, 'Design Strategy from the Population Perspective', *Journal of Management* 10 (1984), 67–86; Howard E. Aldrich, *Organizations and Environments* (Englewood Cliffs, N.J.: Prentice Hall, 1979); Michael Hannan and John Freeman, 'The Population Ecology of Organizations', *American Journal of Sociology* 82 (1977), 929–964; Dave Ulrich, 'The Population Perspective: Review, Critique and Relevance', *Human Relations* 40 (1987), 137–152; Jitendra V. Singh and Charles J. Lumsden, 'Theory and Research in Organizational Ecology', *Annual Review of Sociology* 16 (1990), 161–195; Howard E. Aldrich, 'Understanding, Not Integration: Vital Signs from Three Perspectives on Organizations', in Michael Reed and Michael D. Hughes, eds., *Rethinking Organizations: New Directions in Organizational Theory and Analysis* (London: Sage, 1992); Jitendra V. Singh, David J. Tucker and Robert J. House, 'Organizational Legitimacy and the Liability of Newness', *Administrative Science Quarterly* 31 (1986), 171–193; and Douglas R. Wholey and Jack W. Brittain, 'Organizational Ecology: Findings and Implications', *Academy of Management Review* 11 (1986), 513–533.
54. Carol, G.R. and Hannan, M.T. (1989), 'Density Dependence in the Evolution of Populations of Newspaper Organizations', American Sociological Review 54, 524–541.
55. Pugh and Hickson, *Writers on Organizations*; and Lex Donaldson, *American Anti-Management Theories of Organization* (New York: Cambridge University Press, 1995).
56. Michael T. Hannan and John Freeman, 'The Population Ecology of Organizations', *American Journal of Sociology* (March 1977), 929–964
57. Dev Kumar Boojihawon, Pavlos Dimitratos and Stephen Young (2007), 'Characteristics and influences of multinational subsidiary entrepreneurial culture: The case of the advertising sector', *International Business Review*, 16, Pg. 549–572; http:// www.wpp.com/wpp/ accessed on July 11, 2008.
58. Julie Creswell, 'Cisco's Worst Nightmare (And Sun's and IBM's and Nortel's and....)', *Fortune* (February 4, 2002), 114–116.
59. John Walton (2005) 'Would the real corporate university please stand up?' *Journal of European Industrial Training*, 29, pp. 7–20; Matthias Becker, 'Driving ambition: Corporate universities are nothing new, but one manufacturer is hoping its venture will bring it academic credibility, as well as a more highly skilled workforce', *The Guardian*, September 28, 2004, Pg. 16; George Boehmer, 'German group announces corporate university to teach global goals', *Associated Press Worldstream*, August 7, 1998; Steve Coomber, 'Deans' programme goes international', *The Times*, May 14, 2008, Pg. 4.
60. 'Accenture Opens Corporate University in India', *Consulting* 29 April 2008, accessed at http://www.consultingmag.com/articles/710/1/Accenture-Opens-Corporate-University-in-India/Accenture-Opens-Corporate-University-in-India.html on July 11, 2008; 'Wipro Technologies Bags Corporate University Xchange Award', March 28, 2008, accessed at http://www.dailyindia.com/show/228899.php/ on July 11, 2008; 'Loma And China Life Establish China's Largest Corporate University', *Asia Pulse*, February 27, 2004; 'Corporate University', *China Radio International,* 3 April 2007, Accessed at http://english.cri.cn/4026/2007/04/03/44@212015.htm on July 11, 2008.

61. 'Education – 'Dumbing down' provokes fierce reaction', *Human Resources*, March 1, 2008. Pg. 7
62. Thomas Moore, 'The Corporate University: Transforming Management Education' (presentation in August 1996; Thomas Moore is the Dean of the Arthur D. Little University).
63. Peter Newcomb, 'No One is Safe', *Forbes* (July 13, 1987), 121; 'It's Tough Up There', *Forbes* (July 13, 1987), 145–160.
64. Stewart Feldman, 'Here One Decade, Gone the Next', *Management Review* (November 1990), 5–6.
65. Ackroyd S, 2006, 'Aspects of flexible. economic systems: some recent developments in the UK economy', in *Facets of Flexibility*, (eds) Skorstad E. J and Ramsdal H., Ostfold University Press, Oslo, pp 255–*277*.
66. *Murphy, Jonathan (2008), 'International financial institutions and the new global managerial order', Critical Perspectives on Accounting,* 19, 714–740.
67. Eric Schlosser (2002), *Fast Food Nation: The Dark Side of the All-American Meal,* London, Penguin.
68. David Stires, 'Fallen Arches', *Fortune* (April 29, 2002), 74–76.
69. Glyn, Andrew and Stephen Machin (1997), 'Colliery Closures and the Decline of the UK Coal Industry' *British Journal of Industrial Relations,* Volume 35, pp. 197–214.
70. David J. Tucker, Jitendra V. Singh and Agnes G. Meinhard, 'Organizational Form, Population Dynamics, and Institutional Change: The Founding Patterns of Voluntary Organizations', *Academy of Management Journal* 33 (1990), 151–178; Glenn R. Carroll and Michael T. Hannan, 'Density Delay in the Evolution of Organizational Populations: A Model and Five Empirical Tests', *Administrative Science Quarterly* 34 (1989), 411–430; Jacques Delacroix and Glenn R. Carroll, 'Organizational Foundings: An Ecological Study of the Newspaper Industries of Argentina and Ireland', *Administrative Science Quarterly* 28 (1983), 274–291; Johannes M. Pennings, 'Organizational Birth Frequencies: An Empirical Investigation', *Administrative Science Quarterly* 27 (1982), 120–144; David Marple, 'Technological Innovation and Organizational Survival: A Population Ecology Study of Nineteenth-Century American Railroads', *Sociological Quarterly* 23 (1982), 107–116; and Thomas G. Rundall and John O. McClain, 'Environmental Selection and Physician Supply', *American Journal of Sociology* 87 (1982), 1090–1112.
71. http://www.steiffteddybears.co.uk accessed on July 11, 2008.
72. Robert D. Hof and Linda Himelstein, 'eBay vs. Amazon.com', *BusinessWeek* (May 31, 1999), 128–132; and Maria Mallory with Stephanie Anderson Forest, 'Waking Up to a Major Market', *BusinessWeek* (March 23, 1992), 70–73.
73. David Stipp, 'How Genentech Got It', *Fortune* (June 9, 2003), 81–88.
74. Arthur G. Bedeian and Raymond F. Zammuto, *Organizations: Theory and Design* (Orlando, Fla.: Dryden Press, 1991); and Richard L. Hall, *Organizations: Structure, Process and Outcomes* (Englewood Cliffs, N.J.: Prentice-Hall, 1991).
75. M. Tina Dacin, Jerry Goodstein and W. Richard Scott, 'Institutional Theory and Institutional Change: Introduction to the Special Research Forum', *Academy of Management Journal* 45, no. 1 (2002), 45–47. Thanks to Tina Dacin for her material and suggestions for this section of the chapter.
76. J. Meyer and B. Rowan, 'Institutionalized Organizations: Formal Structure as Myth and Ceremony', *American Journal of Sociology* 83 (1990), 340–363.
77. Mark C. Suchman, 'Managing Legitimacy: Strategic and Institutional Approaches', *Academy of Management Review* 20 (1995), 571–610.
78. Jerry Useem, 'America's Most Admired Companies', *Fortune* (March 7, 2005), 66–70; and Survey Results from Harris Interactive and the Reputation Institute, reported in Ronald Alsop, 'In Business Ranking, Some Icons Lose Luster', *The Wall Street Journal* (November 15, 2004), B1.
79. Ronald Alsop, 'Corporate Reputation Survey: Best-Known Companies Aren't Always Best Liked – McDonald's Takes Pounding For Menu Items, Surly Staff; Cheers and Jeers for Microsoft', *The Wall Street Journal*, 15 November 2004 B4.
80. Grahame R. Dowling, 'Corporate Reputations: Should You Compete on Yours?' *California Management Review* 46, no. 3 (Spring 2004), 19–36; Ronald Alsop, 'In Business Ranking, Some Icons Lose Luster'.
81. David Smith and Zoe Wood, 'Are we falling out of love with Tesco?' *The Observer*, June 29, 2008, Pg. 24.
82. 'Tesco "breaching planning laws"', *BBC News*, August 18, 2006, accessed at http://news.bbc.co.uk/2/hi/uk_news/5261844.stm on July 11, 2008. 'Friends of The Earth: New survey spells trouble for Tesco', *M2 Presswire*, June 29, 2007.
83. James Hall, 'Size matters', *The Sunday Telegraph*, April 30, 2006, Pg. 7; 'Tesco giant crushing small traders and suppliers', *Western Mail*, April 26, 2006, Pg. 8.
84. 'Who Pays? How British Supermarkets Are Keeping Women Workers In Poverty', ActionAid, accessed at http://www.actionaid.org.uk/doc_lib/actionaid_who_pays_report.pdf on July 11, 2008.
85. Hugh Fearnley-Whittingstall, 'Kiss me chick', *The Sunday Times,* June 29, 2008, News Review; Pg.1.
86. David Leigh, 'Government outlaws tax avoidance schemes: Tesco says strategy is common practice Offshore companies loophole to be closed', *The Guardian*, June 14, 2008, Pg. 15
87. Jonathan Brown and Martin Hickman, 'Feathers to fly as activists target Tesco bosses' *The Independent*, June 27, 2008.
88. Richard J. Martinez and Patricia M. Norman, 'Whither Reputation? The Effects of Different Stakeholders', *Business Horizons* 47, no. 5 (September–October 2004), 25–32.
89. Pamela S. Tolbert and Lynne G. Zucker, 'The Institutionalization of Institutional Theory', in Stewart R. Clegg, Cynthia Hardy and Walter R. Nord, eds., *Handbook of Organization Studies* (Thousand Oaks, Calif.: Sage, 1996).
90. Pugh and Hickson, *Writers on Organizations*; and Paul J. DiMaggio and Walter W. Powell, 'The Iron Cage Revisited: Institutional Isomorphism and Collective Rationality in Organizational Fields', *American Sociological Review* 48 (1983), 147–160.
91. This section is based largely on DiMaggio and Powell, 'The Iron Cage Revisited'; Pugh and Hickson, *Writers*

on Organizations; and W. Richard Scott, *Institutions and Organizations* (Thousand Oaks, Calif.: Sage, 1995).

92. Ellen R. Auster and Mark L. Sirower, 'The Dynamics of Merger and Acquisition Waves', *The Journal of Applied Behavioral Science* 38, no. 2 (June 2002), 216–244.
93. William McKinley, Jun Zhao and Kathleen Garrett Rust, 'A Sociocognitive Interpretation of Organizational Downsizing', *Academy of Management Review* 25, no. 1 (2000), 227–243.
94. Barry M. Staw and Lisa D. Epstein, 'What Bandwagons Bring: Effects of Popular Management Techniques on Corporate Performance, Reputation and CEO Pay', *Administrative Science Quarterly* 45, no. 3 (September 2000), 523–560.
95. European Commission Directive on Sale of Consumer Goods and Guarantees, available at http://eur-lex.europa.eu/LexUriServ/LexUriServ.do?uri=CELEX:31999L0044:EN:HTML.
96. Jeremy Kahn, 'Deloitte Restates Its Case', *Fortune* (April 29, 2002), 64–72.

CHAPTER 6

DESIGNING ORGANIZATIONS FOR THE INTERNATIONAL ENVIRONMENT

H&M

H&M is a popular shopping stop for many students and other young people in Europe and around the world. The company is well-known for its competitively-priced designer clothing, and has teamed up with some of the world's most famous designers. H&M is expanding aggressively; after conquering Europe in the 1980s and 1990s, the company opened stores across the USA and Canada, and is now beginning a crucial move into China's booming fashion clothing market. H&M is a success story, but the company faces a number of challenges, including tough competition from companies with similar strategies such as Spanish-based Zara, intellectual property battles in several key developing country markets and European Union limits on imports from China, where much of the company's clothing is sourced.

In 1947, the company opened its first shop in Vasteras, a medium-sized city about 100km from Stockholm. Erling Persson, H&M's founder, had visited America, and wanted to import the concept of high volume, low price that he had seen in the States. H&M has long been committed to international expansion. Like many Scandinavian retailers, the company began its internationalization in neighbouring countries, opening in Norway in 1964 and Denmark in 1964. H&M came to the UK in 1976, and by the end of the 1980s had also opened stores in Switzerland, Germany and the Netherlands. In 2000 the company opened its first stores in the United States, and shortly after moved into the new accession states of the European Union. The company has expanded mainly through company-owned stores, but due to local laws has opened a small number of stores in the Gulf region as franchises. Unlike many other companies, H&M resisted opening in China's burgeoning market until recently, but finally opened outlets in Beijing and Shanghai in 2007.

H&M's ambitions to marry mass market accessibility to high design was demonstrated by the company's collaborations in 2004 and 2005 with Karl Lagerfeld and Stella McCartney. In 2004, H&M opened its 1,000th store, and by 2006 had about 1,300 outlets worldwide.

H&M is careful to maintain a positive and modern corporate image. The company publishes and promotes its corporate social responsibility policy, which includes detailed policies in both the social and environmental areas, partners with UNICEF on social projects, and is part of the EU's 'Eco' label programme, which commits to a series of environmentally friendly policies. All of H&M's goods are outsourced, mainly to lower-waged countries, and as Nike and other companies have found to their cost, outsourcing brings the risk of association with unacceptable labour practices as well as broader human rights violations that take place in a number of developing countries. H&M seems well insulated against such criticism. It has a comprehensive audit system for its outsourced factories, and publishes annually a full listing of violations observed and the company's response.

Despite exceptional growth, H&M faces serious challenges. H&M is being outpaced by some other European retailers, especially Spanish-owned Inditex, the operator of the Zara chain, which has overtaken H&M as Europe's largest retailer. In the past ten years, Inditex has quintupled in size, and in 2006 has 2,600 shops, double the number of H&M, in 62 countries, three times as many as H&M. H&M strong concentration in Europe (with over 75 per cent of the chain's sales) could prove a limiting factor for growth, as Europe and particularly the Eurozone is a mature market with relatively slow growth rates compared with developing markets. Europe also has high and rising labour costs.

H&M's ability to insulate itself from high European costs is limited by the EU's reimposition of restrictions on clothing imports from China (the country accounts for about 30 per cent of the company's clothing items). Further, production in the new accession countries of the EU is likely to become more expensive. H&M is planning to expand into China, but too slowly to provide a significant balance to European acitvities. A strategy to open new niche stores in Europe provides the possibility for H&M to continue growing its market share in Europe despite possible saturation of its current brand. The company is also planning to expand its e-commerce activities beyond Scandinavia.

In the next few years, H&M will face the challenge of translating a rapidly growing-brand into a mature marketplace anchor. Generational customer turnover will be an issue, as the managers of the British clothing retailer Marks & Spencer can testify.

H&M needs to retain its current customer base as they become older and their clothing tastes change, while continuing to appeal to its high-spending youth base. The combination of fickle fashion tastes, ever-expanding offshoring opportunities and risks and a highly competitive market segment mean that H&M's managers can't rest for a moment on their past laurels.[1]

Purpose of This Chapter

This chapter will explore how managers design the organization for the international environment. We begin by looking at some of the primary motivations for organizations to expand internationally, the typical stages of international development and the use of strategic alliances as a means for international expansion. Then, the chapter will examine global strategic approaches and the application of various structural designs for global advantage. Next, we will discuss some of the specific challenges global organizations face, mechanisms for addressing them, and cultural differences that influence the organization's approach to designing and managing a global firm. The chapter takes a look at an emerging type of global organization, the *transnational model*, that achieves high levels of the varied capabilities needed to succeed in a complex and volatile international environment. At the end of the chapter we examine organizational designs that derive from the changing nature of globalization. We look at the different growth strategies adopted by *dragon multinationals*, companies, typically from developing countries, whose entire business strategy is built around benefiting from global markets. Finally, we look at *value chains*, another approach to understanding how goods and services are brought to market in a globally-integrated economy.

See online COUNTERPOINT 6.5

Entering the Global Arena

As recently as twenty years ago, many companies could afford to ignore the international environment. Today's companies must consider the global business environment or risk being left behind, or even overrun on their home turf. The world is becoming a unified global field. Extraordinary advancements in communications, technology, and transportation have created a new, highly competitive landscape. Products can be made and sold anywhere in the world, communications are instant and product development and life cycles are growing shorter. No company is isolated from global influence. For many industries, very few countries have large enough markets to sustain large, innovative companies. Even in the United States, still the world's largest market for many goods and services, large companies such as Coca-Cola and Procter & Gamble rely on international sales for a substantial portion of their sales and profits. And communications advances mean that even the smallest companies can be actively involved in international business through exports and online business. The rapid expansion of international activities in the past few years has led some companies, especially from developing countries where markets remain quite small, to operate from the beginning with global markets in mind.

COUNTERPOINT 6.1

There is a risk of overlooking the amount of trade – in raw materials or partially finished goods – that has existed for centuries and gathered pace during the period of industrial imperialism. The 'international environment' has always been an issue for companies involved in importing raw materials (e.g. cotton) and human resources (e.g. slaves) and exporting goods (e.g. fabrics). What has changed is the globalization of potential competitors and the opening up of new markets as a consequence of the loss of monopolies (of supply and provision) associated with colonial rule. **Discuss**

Motivations for Global Expansion

Economic, technological and competitive forces have combined to push many companies from a domestic to a global focus. In some industries, being successful in today's environment means succeeding on a global scale. Three primary factors motivate companies to expand internationally: economies of scale, economies of scope and cheaper production factors.[2]

BRIEFCASE

As an organization manager, keep this guideline in mind:

Consider building an international presence to realize economies of scale, exploit economies of scope or obtain scarce or low-cost production factors such as labour and raw materials.

Economies of Scale Building a global presence expands an organization's scale of operations, enabling it to realize **economies of scale**. Large international organizations are not new, of course. During the imperial era companies like the East India Company, CFAO (The French West African Company) and Canada's Hudson's Bay Company profited from trading with imperial subjects. The Industrial Revolution was another prime motivator for both organizational growth and internationalization. Larger factories could seize the benefits of economies of scale offered by new technologies and production methods. Through large-volume production, industrial giants were able to achieve the lowest possible cost per unit of production. However, for many companies, domestic markets were soon unable to sustain the high level of sales needed to maintain enough volume to achieve scale economies. In an industry such as automobile manufacturing, for example, a company would need a tremendous share of the domestic market to achieve scale economies. Thus, organizations like Ford Motor Company became international early in their histories. Ford, for example, opened its first UK plant in 1911, only eight years after the company was founded in the USA. Economies of scale also enable companies to obtain volume discounts from suppliers, lowering the organization's cost of production.

Economies of Scope A second factor is the enhanced potential for exploiting **economies of scope**. *Scope* refers to the number and variety of products and services a company offers, as well as the number and variety of regions, countries and markets it serves. Having a presence in multiple countries provides marketing power and synergy compared to the same size firm that has presence in fewer countries. For example, an advertising agency or a consultancy firm with a presence in several global markets gains a competitive edge serving large companies that span the globe. Sometimes one large multinational will generate further multinationals. Consider the case of McDonald's, which attempts to standardize its offering through the world. This creates a market opening for a supplier able to supply identical mustard and ketchup packets for its restaurants around the world. A supplier that has a presence in every country that McDonald's serves has an advantage because it provides cost, consistency and convenience benefits to McDonald's, which does not have to deal with a number of local suppliers in each country. Economies of scope can also increase a company's market power as compared to competitors, because the company develops broad knowledge of the cultural, social, economic and other factors that affect its customers in varied locations and can provide specialized products and services to meet those needs. In other words, scope may facilitate forms of learning that can be key to the development of competitive advantage in assessing and exploiting the particularities of new or emergent markets, thereby presenting products or services in ways that seem relevant and valuable.

Low-Cost Production Factors The third major force motivating global expansion relates to **factors of production**. One of the earliest, and still one of the most powerful, motivations for companies to invest outside their home country is the opportunity to obtain raw materials and other resources, notably labour, at the lowest possible cost. In past centuries, slaves were imported to America and elsewhere to cheaply exploit plantations, and the practice of using indentured labour continued in the Dutch colonies until 1941.[3]

Organizations have also long turned overseas to secure cheap materials that were scarce or unavailable where they were needed. Until the development of synthetic rubber in the 1930s, automobile tyres required natural rubber that could not be produced in any of the major automobile producing companies. In the 1920s tyre companies developed rubber plantations in Brazil to supply rubber for tyres for the growing automobile industry, while British and Dutch companies in conjunction with their imperial governments developed new rubber plantations in Asia that eventually came to dominate the worldwide market for natural rubber.

Many companies have viewed other countries as a source of cheap labour. Textile manufacturing in Europe and North America continues to decline as companies shift more and more production to China and other East Asian countries, India, Mexico, Latin America and the Caribbean where labour costs are much lower. Software companies are setting up development centres in India and Russia, apparel and shoe companies outsource production to Asian manufacturers and document processing for credit-card and other banking applications is handled by workers in India, the Philippines and Mexico.

Other organizations have gone international in search of lower costs of capital, sources of cheap energy, reduced government restrictions or other factors that lower the company's total production costs. Companies can locate facilities wherever it is calculated to make the most economic sense in terms of needed employee education and skill levels, labour and raw materials costs and other production factors. Automobile manufacturers such as Toyota, Ford and BMW have built plants in South Africa, Brazil and Thailand, where they can sometimes pay workers less than one-tenth of what workers earn in higher-wage, developed countries. In addition, these countries sometimes offer dramatically lower costs for factors such as land, water and electricity.[4]

Stages of International Development

No company can become a global giant overnight. The shift from domestic to global has traditionally occurred through stages of development, as illustrated in Exhibit 6.1.[5] In stage one, the **domestic stage**, the company is domestically oriented, but managers are aware of the global environment and may want to consider initial foreign involvement to expand production volume and realize economies of scale. Market potential is limited and is primarily in the home country. The structure of the company is domestic, typically functional or divisional and initial foreign sales are handled through an export department. The details of freight forwarding, customs problems and foreign exchange are handled by outsiders.

In stage two, the **international stage**, the company takes exports seriously and begins to think multidomestically. **Multidomestic** means competitive issues in each country are independent of other countries; the company deals with each country individually. The concern is with international competitive positioning compared with other firms in the industry. At this point, an international division has replaced

EXHIBIT 6.1 Four Stages of International Evolution

	I. Domestic	II. International	III. Multinational	IV. Global
Strategic Orientation	Domestically oriented	Export-oriented multidomestic	Multinational	Global
Stage of Development	Initial foreign involvement	Competitive positioning	Explosion	Global
Structure	Domestic structure, plus export department	Domestic structure, plus international division	Worldwide geographical, product	Matrix, transnational
Market Potential	Moderate, mostly domestic	Large, multidomestic	Very large, multinational	Whole world

Source: Based on Nancy J. Adler, *International Dimensions of Organizational Behavior*, 4th ed. (Cincinnati, Ohio: South-Western, 2002), 8–9; and Theodore T. Herbert, 'Strategy and Multinational Organization Structure: An Interorganizational Relationships Perspective,' *Academy of Management Review* 9 (1984), 259–271.

the export department, and specialists are hired to handle sales, service and warehousing abroad. Multiple countries are identified as a potential market.

In stage three, the **multinational stage**, the company has extensive experience in a number of international markets and has established marketing, manufacturing or research and development facilities in several foreign countries. The organization obtains a large percentage of revenues from sales outside the home country. Explosion occurs as international operations take off, and the company has business units scattered around the world along with suppliers, manufacturers and distributors.

The fourth and ultimate stage is the **global stage**, which means the company transcends any single country. The business is not merely a collection of domestic industries; rather, subsidiaries are interlinked to the point where competitive position in one country significantly influences activities in other countries.[6] Truly **global companies** no longer think of themselves as having a single home country, and, indeed, have been called *stateless corporations*.[7] This represents a new and dramatic evolution from the multinational company of the 1960s and 1970s, although few companies are genuinely fully global. Most draw a major proportion of their senior staff from a single country, and tend to retain their corporate headquarters in that country, even though the bulk of their activities may be outside this traditional base.

See online
COUNTERPOINT 6.6

For truly global companies, the entire world is their marketplace. Organization structure at this stage can be extremely complex and often evolves into an international matrix or transnational model, which will be discussed later in this chapter. Companies such as Royal Dutch/Shell, Unilever and Matsushita Electric may operate in more than a hundred countries. The structural problem of holding together this huge complex of subsidiaries scattered thousands of miles apart is immense.

Global Expansion Through International Strategic Alliances

One of the most common ways companies get involved in international operations is through strategic alliances, a strategy that has developed rapidly. Companies in rapidly changing industries such as media and entertainment, pharmaceuticals,

BRIEFCASE

As an organization manager, keep this guideline in mind:

Develop international strategic alliances, such as licensing, joint ventures, partnerships and consortia, as fast and inexpensive ways to become involved in international sales and operations.

biotechnology and software might have hundreds of strategic partnerships with suppliers, partners and distributors.[8]

Typical alliances include licensing, joint ventures and consortia.[9] For example, pharmaceutical companies such as Merck, Eli Lilly, Pfizer and GlaxoSmithKline cross-license their newest drugs to one another to support industrywide innovation and marketing and offset the high fixed costs of research and distribution.[10] A **joint venture** is a separate entity created with two or more active firms as sponsors. This is a popular approach to sharing development and production costs and penetrating new markets. Joint ventures may be with either customers or competitors.[11] A joint venture led by Deutsche Telekom, Sprint and Telecom France, and involving several smaller firms, serves sixty-five countries and functions as a single company to meet the telecommunications needs of global corporations.[12] MTV Networks has joint ventures with companies in Brazil, Australia and other countries to expand its media presence globally.[13]

Manufacturing companies often seek joint ventures to achieve production cost savings through economies of scale or to distribute new technologies and products through another country's distribution channels. The agreement between Toyota and General Motors to construct a Chevrolet plant in California was Toyota's way of distributing its technology to the United States. Caterpillar Inc. and Mitsubishi Heavy Industries Ltd. established a joint venture that enabled Caterpillar to manufacture and sell in Japan and expanded Mitsubishi's export markets.[14]

Another growing approach is for companies to become involved in **consortia**, groups of independent companies – including suppliers, customers and even competitors – that join together to share skills, resources, costs and access to one another's markets. Airbus Industrie, for example, is a consortium made up of French, British and German aerospace companies to successfully compete with Boeing on a global scale.[15] Consortia are often used in other parts of the world, such as the *keiretsu* family of corporations in Japan. In Korea, these interlocking company arrangements are called *chaebol*.

A type of consortia, the global *virtual organization*, is increasingly being used and offers a promising approach to meeting worldwide competition. The virtual organization refers to a continually evolving set of company relationships that exist temporarily to exploit temporary opportunities or attain specific strategic advantages. A company may be involved in multiple alliances at any one time. Oracle, an American software company, is involved in as many as 15,000 short-term organizational partnerships at any time.[16] Some executives believe shifting to a consortia or virtual approach is the best way for companies to remain competitive in the global marketplace.[17] Managers and organizations all over the world are learning to cooperate to achieve competitive advantage on a global scale. This chapter's *In Practice* example, STMicroelectronics NV rapidly grew from two to twenty-seven countries based on the strength of its partnerships with customer organizations.

Designing Structure to Fit Global Strategy

As we discussed in Chapter 3, an organization's structure must fit its situation by providing sufficient information processing for coordination and control while focusing employees on specific functions, products or geographic regions. Organization design for international structure follows a similar logic, with special interest in global versus local strategic opportunities.

Model for Global Versus Local Opportunities

When organizations venture into the international domain, managers strive to formulate a coherent global strategy that will provide synergy among worldwide

STMicroelectronics NV

Based in Geneva, Switzerland, STMicroelectronics NV was created in 1987 by the merger of two money-losing state-owned companies: SGS Microelettronica of Italy and Thomson Semiconductors of France. Since then, the company has partnered its way to a position as the world's fifth-largest computer chip maker and a leader in one of the hottest segments of the chip industry, manufacturing a 'system-on-a-chip' that combines analog functions (such as sound and graphics) together with digital circuitry (such as logic and memory) on a single chip. The system-on-a-chip approach opened a huge market opportunity that very few other companies were prepared to exploit.

Success for STMicroelectronics came, however, not from designing and producing the system-on-a-chip in isolation, but from developing close partnerships with customers to gain a deep understanding of their system designs and unique needs. Partnering began out of necessity, as ST needed to convince customers to replace their complex circuit boards with its system-on-a-chip. One of the earliest major alliances was with US-based Seagate Corporation, the world's largest maker of disk drives. By understanding the company's needs, ST was able to shrink all the components on Seagate's hard disk drive onto one or two custom chips. Being able to produce smaller, cheaper and less power-hungry disk drives enabled Seagate to enter entirely new markets such as laptops and handheld computers. ST's partnership with Seagate has continued, and the company has since established similar close relationships with twelve other telecommunications, computer, automotive and consumer products companies in multiple countries. The partnership between Nokia and ST, for example, has a governance committee made up of senior executives from both companies that meets quarterly to set and measure objectives and evaluate the partnership's performance. Teams from both companies meet regularly to coordinate development, marketing and sourcing of components, and engineers participate in regular *dream days*, where they get together and create wish-list products without interference from management.

By taking a partnership approach, STMicroelectronics now has operations in twenty-seven countries and is able to draw on technological expertise and market understanding from around the world. ST's top managers are working on forming alliances with partners in Asia, where it has very few, to expand its presence in that part of the world.[18]

Using strategic alliances helped STMicroelectronics move from a money-losing operation to year 2000 profits of $1.4 billion on sales of $7.8 billion, although that proved a high-water mark and while revenues continued to grow slowly, profits in the five subsequent years were much more modest. Over the past two decades, ST has evolved into a highly sophisticated global firm that is adept at tapping into knowledge around the world to develop innovative solutions to customers' problems. STMicroelectronics seems to be close to achieving the global stage of development described in Exhibit 6.1. Units around the world carry the name of the city where they're located, and each is viewed as part of a unified global system.[19] The company's corporate headquarters are in Geneva, with strong regional centres in North America and Asia. Production facilities are concentrated in Europe (particularly Italy and France, the founding partners), North America and Asia, with research facilities also located on several continents. The company's core executives remain, however, dominated by nationals of Italy and France.

operations for the purpose of achieving common organizational goals. One dilemma they face is choosing whether to emphasize global integration versus national responsiveness. Managers must decide whether they want each global affiliate to act autonomously or whether activities should be standardized across countries. These decisions are reflected in the choice between a *globalization* versus a *multidomestic* global strategy.

See online
COUNTERPOINT 6.7

The globalization strategy means that product design, manufacturing and marketing strategy are standardized throughout the world.[20] For example, Japanese companies took business away from European and North American competitors by developing similar high-quality, low-cost products for all countries rather than incurring higher costs by tailoring products to specific countries. Black & Decker became much more competitive internationally when it standardized its line of power hand tools. Other products, such as Coca-Cola, are naturals for globalization, because only advertising and marketing need to be tailored for different regions. Frequently, large multinationals employ a global approach for some products and a locally-tailored approach for others; the world's largest food company Nestle, for example, has both local and global brands in its portfolio.

A globalization strategy can help an organization reap economy-of-scale efficiencies by standardizing product design and manufacturing, using common suppliers, introducing products around the world faster, coordinating prices and eliminating overlapping facilities. By sharing technology, design, suppliers and manufacturing standards worldwide in a coordinated global automotive operation, Ford saved $5 billion during the first three years.[21] Even where product contents may vary by country, Nestle can often employ a standardized packaging approach; Nescafe instant coffee's familiar bottle began life in the UK but has been exported around the world.[22]

A **multidomestic strategy** means that competition in each country is handled independently of competition in other countries. Thus, a multidomestic strategy would encourage product design, assembly and marketing tailored to the specific needs of each country. Some companies have found that their products do not thrive in a single global market. The French rarely drink orange juice for breakfast, and in parts of Mexico laundry detergent is more likely to be used to wash dishes, not clothes. Procter & Gamble tried to standardize nappy design, but discovered that cultural values in different parts of the world required style adjustments to make the product acceptable to many mothers. For example, in Italy, designing nappies to cover the baby's navel was critical to successful sales.[23]

See online
COUNTERPOINT 6.8

Different global organization designs, as well, are better suited to global integration or national responsiveness. Recent research on more than 100 international firms based in Spain has provided further support for the connection between international structure and strategic focus.[24] The model in Exhibit 6.2 illustrates a number of structures in relation to their relevance for strategies of global integration and national responsiveness.

Companies can be characterized by whether their product and service lines have potential for globalization, which means advantages through worldwide standardization. Companies that sell diverse products or services across many countries have a globalization strategy. On the other hand, some companies have products and services appropriate for a multidomestic strategy, which means local-country advantages through differentiation and customization.

As indicated in Exhibit 6.2, when forces for both global integration and national responsiveness in many countries are low, simply using an international division with the domestic structure is an appropriate way to handle international business. For some industries, however, technological, social or economic forces may create a situation in which selling standardized products worldwide provides a basis for competitive advantage. In these cases, a global product structure is appropriate. This structure provides product managers with authority to handle their product lines on a global basis and enables the company to take advantage of a unified global marketplace. In other cases, a company can gain competitive advantages through national responsiveness – by responding to unique needs in the various countries in which it does business. For example, people in different countries have very different expectations regarding personal care products such as deodorant or toothpaste. For companies in these industries, a worldwide geographic structure is appropriate. Each country or region will have

EXHIBIT 6.2 Model to Fit Organization Structure to International Advantages

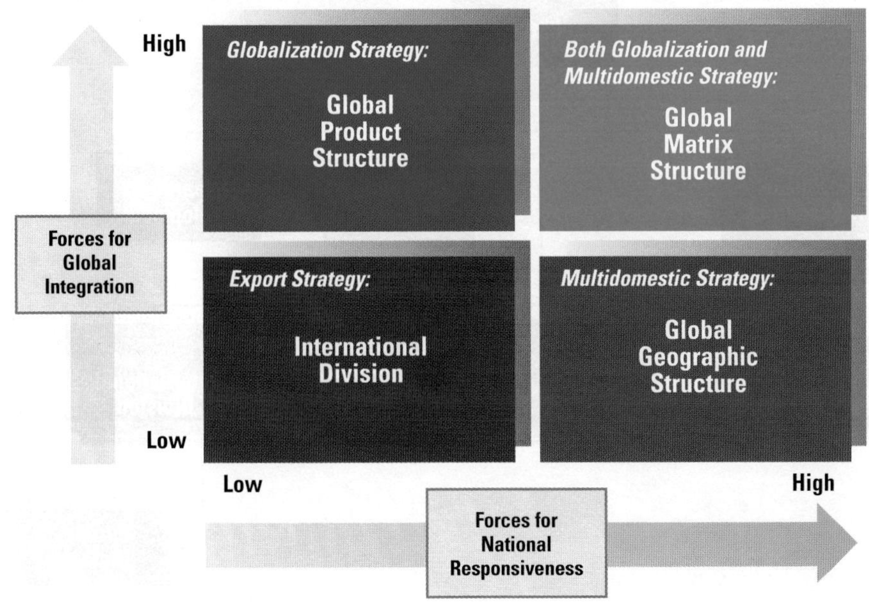

Source: Roderick E. White and Thomas A. Poynter, 'Organizing for Worldwide Advantage,' *Business Quarterly* (Summer 1989), 84–89. Adapted by permission of *Business Quarterly*, published by the Western Business School, the University of Western Ontario, London, Ontario, Canada.

subsidiaries modifying products and services to fit that locale. The advertising firm of Ogilvy & Mather divides its operations into four primary geographical regions because advertising approaches need to be modified to fit the tastes, preferences, cultural values and government regulations in different parts of the world.[25]

European countries frequently have stricter rules on using children for advertising than is the case in the United States, for example. In France children are prohibited from appearing in TV advertising. In several European countries, TV advertising targeted at younger children is not permitted [http://www.easa-alliance.org/]. Other regulations and even voluntary standards vary considerably around the world. Anti-smoking organizations complain that cigarette manufacturers employ advertising techniques in developing countries that would be illegal in most if not all developed countries [http://www.ash.org.uk/html/factsheets/html/fact21.html]. There are major differences between societal attitudes to health advertising between the United States and other developed countries. In the US, pharamceutical companies can widely advertise prescription medicine, whereas in Canada and most of Europe, this is not permitted [http://www.asa.org.uk/asa/codes].[26]

In many instances, such as Nestle mentioned above, companies will need to respond to both global and local opportunities simultaneously, in which case the global matrix structure can be used. Part of the product line may need to be standardized globally, and other parts tailored to the needs of local countries. Let's discuss each of the structures in Exhibit 6.2 in more detail.

International Division

As companies begin to explore international opportunities, they often start with an export department that grows into an **international division**. The international division has a status equal to the other major departments or divisions within

EXHIBIT 6.3 Domestic Hybrid Structure with International Division

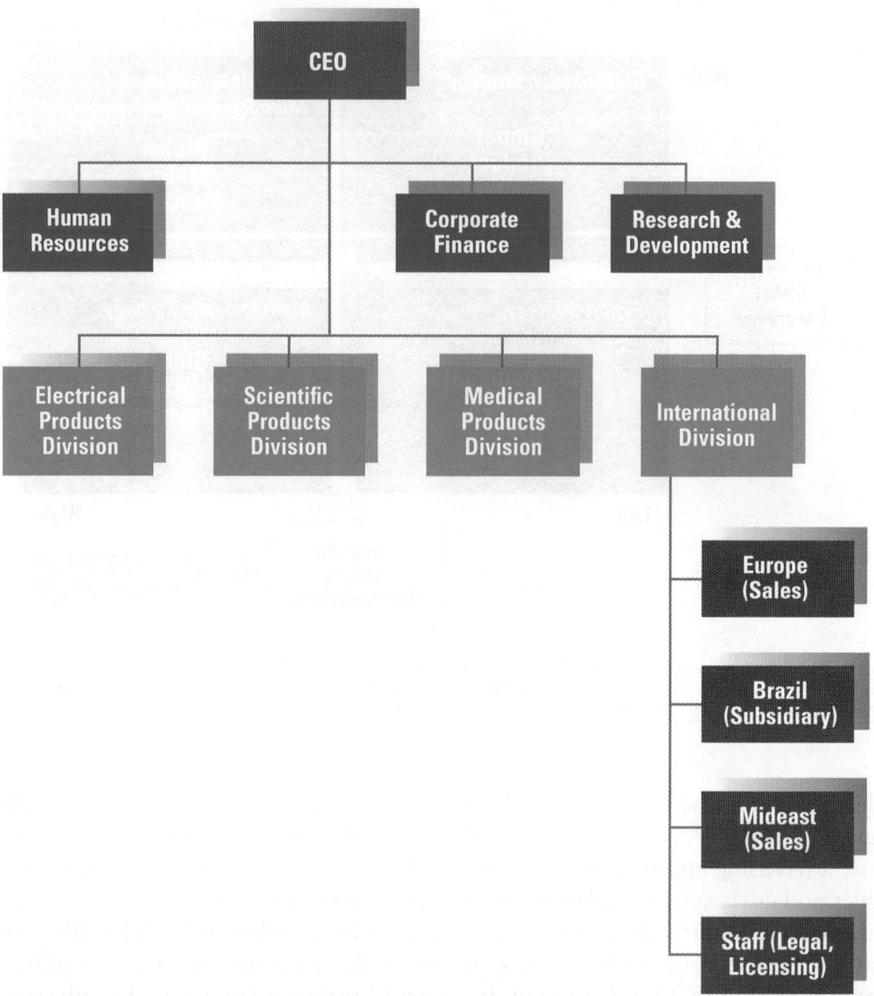

the company and is illustrated in Exhibit 6.3. Whereas the domestic divisions are typically organized along functional or product lines, the international division is organized according to geographic interests, as illustrated in the exhibit. The international division has its own hierarchy to handle business (licensing, joint ventures) in various countries, selling the products and services created by the domestic divisions, opening subsidiary plants and in general moving the organization into more sophisticated international operations.

Although functional structures are often used domestically, they are less frequently used to manage a worldwide business.[27] Lines of functional hierarchy running around the world tend to be associated with inefficiencies and poor coordination at distant units. For example, it is difficult to globally centralize IT functions when operating conditions and human resources capacities vary widely, and local production requires the capacity to mobilize resources from throughout the local unit without each functional unit waiting for approval on the other side of the world. Therefore, a form of product or geographical structure is used to subdivide the organization into smaller units. Firms have traditionally started with an international department and, depending on their strategy, later used product or geographic divisional structures.

Global Product Division Structure

In a **global product structure**, the product divisions take responsibility for global operations in their specific product area. This is one of the most commonly used structures through which managers attempt to achieve global goals because it provides a fairly straightforward way to effectively manage a variety of businesses and products around the world. Managers in each product division can focus on organizing for international operations as they see fit and directing employees' energy toward their own division's unique set of global problems or opportunities.[28] In addition, the structure provides top managers at headquarters with a broad perspective on competition, enabling the entire corporation to respond more rapidly to a changing global environment.[29]

With a global product structure, each division's manager is responsible for planning, organizing and controlling all functions for the production and distribution of its products for any market around the world. The product-based structure is likely to be most appropriate when a division handles products that are technologically similar and can be standardized for marketing worldwide (see Exhibit 6.2). Eaton Corporation, a US-based industrial manufacturer, has used a form of *worldwide product structure*, as illustrated in Exhibit 6.4. In this structure, the automotive components group, industrial group and so on are responsible for manufacture and sale of products worldwide. The vice president international is responsible for coordinators in each region, including a coordinator for Japan, Australia,

EXHIBIT 6.4 Partial Global Product Structure Used by Eaton Corporation

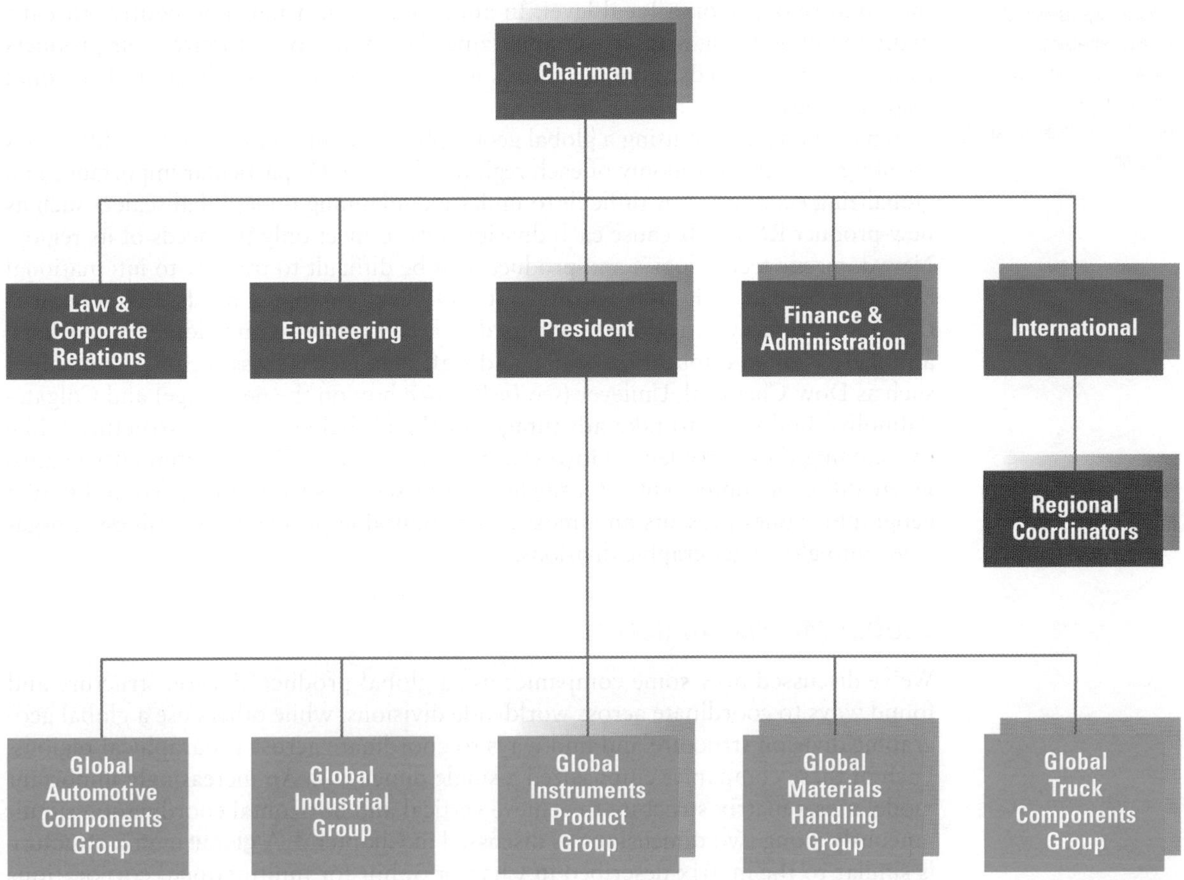

Source: *Based on New Directions in Multinational Corporate Organization* (New York: Business International Corp., 1981)

South America and northern Europe. The coordinators find ways to share facilities and improve production and delivery across all product lines sold in their region. These coordinators provide the same function as integrators described in Chapter 3. The product structure is widely used for standardizing production and sales around the globe, but it can encounter problems when the product divisions do not work well together, competing instead of cooperating in some countries; and some countries may be ignored by product managers. The solution adopted by Eaton Corporation of using country coordinators who have a clearly defined role has helped the company to overcome these potential problems.

BRIEFCASE

As an organization manager, keep this guideline in mind:

Choose a global product structure when the organization can gain competitive advantages through a globalization strategy (global integration). Choose a global geographic structure when the company has advantages with a multidomestic strategy (national responsiveness). Use an international division when the company is primarily domestic and has only a few international operations.

Global Geographic Division Structure

A regionally based organization tends to be developed by companies wishing to emphasize adaptation to regional or local market needs through a multidomestic strategy, as illustrated in Exhibit 6.2. The **global geographic structure** divides the world into geographical regions, with each geographical division reporting to the CEO. Each division has full control of functional activities within its geographical area.

Companies that use this type of structure have typically been those with mature product lines and stable technologies. They can find low-cost manufacturing within countries, as well as meeting different needs across countries for marketing and sales. However, several business and organizational trends have led to a broadening of the kinds of companies that use the global geographic structure.[30] The growth of service organizations has outpaced manufacturing for many years, and services by their nature occur on a local level. In addition, to meet new competitive threats, many manufacturing firms are emphasizing the ability to customize their products to meet specific needs, which requires a greater emphasis on local and regional responsiveness.

Senior management using a global geographic structure may encounter difficulties resulting from the autonomy of each regional division. Of particular importance in a globalizing economy, it is difficult to undertake planning on a global scale – such as new-product R&D – because each division acts to meet only the needs of its region. New domestic technologies and products can be difficult to transfer to international markets because each division thinks it will develop what it needs. Likewise, it is difficult to rapidly introduce products developed offshore into domestic markets; and there is often duplication of line and staff managers across regions. Companies such as Dow Chemical, Unilever (see *In Practice* box on the next page) and Colgate-Palmolive find ways to take advantages of the global geographic structure while overcoming these problems. However, the emergence of global commodity chains, where different components of a single good or service's value are added in different geographic zones presents an almost insurmountable problem for businesses organized into global geographic divisions.

Global Matrix Structure

We've discussed how some companies use a global product division structure and found ways to coordinate across worldwide divisions, while others use a global geographic division structure and find ways to coordinate across geographical regions. Each of these companies emphasized a single dimension. An increasingly important model uses a matrix structure to achieve vertical and horizontal coordination simultaneously along two dimensions as discussed in Chapter 3. A **global matrix structure** is similar to the matrix described in Chapter 3, but for multinational corporations the geographical distances for communication are greater and coordination is more complex.

Unilever

Unilever was one of the first global conglomerates. The modern company emerged from the 1929 fusion of the British-owned Lever Brothers (founders of the famous industrial model town Port Sunlight in northern England) and the Netherlands-based Margarine Unie. Lever Brothers had been operating several factories in the United States as early as the turn of the twentieth century. Unilever, specializing in processed foods and household and beauty products, continued to grow after merger, both through brand acquisitions and brand internationalization, and was one of the fifty largest companies in the world by 2000, with operations in approximately 100 different countries. However, unlike US-based multinational companies that have operated in a relatively stable social and political environment, European-rooted companies like Unilever have had to cope with diverse and rapidly changing operating circumstances across their national operating units.

Unilever's corporate structure is impacted by the complexities of its historical development. In essence the company is a joint venture of two separate units, Unilever NV in the Netherlands, and Unilever PLC UK, although they are so tightly interwoven (identical boards of directors for example) as to be essentially inextricable. Unilever expanded quickly in the United States and became, with Procter & Gamble and Colgate-Palmolive, part of an oligopoly that controlled 80 per cent of the US soap market by the 1930s. The company's revenues were from an early stage geographically widely distributed, with North America, Europe and developing and emerging markets in Africa, Latin America and Asia all substantial earners. Like its American competitior Colgate-Palmolive, Unilever was organized on a global geographic basis. Today, sales in Europe, the Americas and Asia and Africa are all of approxiamtely equal magnitude The North American arm of the firm operated almost autonomously, the European operations reported to the Continental European Group based in Rotterdam, and the other worldwide operations to the Overseas Committee based in London. Under these geographic groupings, national companies operated with a great deal of freedom. Even in Europe during the early years of economic integration, national markets differed greatly due to tariffs, differing retail environments and a patchwork of companies holding different major household product brand names in different countries.

From the early 1960s, Unilever faced severe competition within Europe, particularly from Procter & Gamble, which was perceived as having a more centralized global structure permitting greater strategic purpose. Gradually, Unilever responded by attempting to centralize its European research and marketing operations, with mixed success. Transforming a company that had been assembled from numerous formerly independent companies, with high levels of decentralization, took several years. Unilever moved away from a global geographic structure towards a global matrix, a model that is discussed below. The new organizational structure, combined with the elimination of poorly-performing product units, have restored the company to healthy revenue and profit growth in the first years of the 21st century.[31]

The matrix is effective when pressure for decision-making balances product standardization and geographical localization, and when coordination to share resources is important. For many years, Asea Brown Boveri (ABB), an electrical equipment corporation headquartered in Zurich, used a global matrix structure that worked extremely well to coordinate a 200,000-employee company operating in more than 140 countries. See the *In Practice* box on the next page.

Building Global Capabilities

There are many instances of well-known companies that encounter difficulties transferring successful ideas, products and services from their home country to the international domain. In the 1980s, and 1990s the British-based retailer Marks and

Asea Brown Boveri Ltd. (ABB)

ABB has given new meaning to the notion of 'being local worldwide'. ABB owns 1,300 subsidiary companies, divided into 5,000 profit centres located in 140 countries. ABB's average plant has fewer than 200 workers and most of the company's 5,000 profit centres contain only forty to fifty people, meaning almost everyone stays close to the customer. For many years, ABB used a complex global matrix structure similar to Exhibit 6.5 to achieve worldwide economies of scale combined with local flexibility and responsiveness.

At the top are the chief executive officer and an international committee of eight top managers, who hold frequent meetings around the world. Along one side of the matrix are sixty-five or so business areas located worldwide, into which ABB's products and services are grouped. Each business area leader is responsible for handling business on a global scale, allocating export markets, establishing cost and quality standards and creating mixed-nationality teams to solve problems. For example, the leader for power transformers is responsible for twenty-five factories in sixteen countries.

Along the other side of the matrix is a country structure; ABB has more than one hundred country managers, most of them citizens of the country in which they work. They run national companies and are responsible for local balance sheets, income statements and career ladders. The German president, for example, is responsible for 36,000 people across several business areas that generate annual revenues in Germany of more than $4 billion.

The matrix structure converges at the level of the 1,300 local companies. The presidents of local companies report to two bosses – the business area leader, who is usually located outside the country, and the country president, who runs the company of which the local organization is a subsidiary.

ABB's philosophy is to decentralize things to the lowest levels. Global managers are expected to be generous, patient and multilingual. They work with teams made up of different nationalities and are required to be culturally sensitive. They craft strategy and evaluate performance for people and subsidiaries around the world. Country managers, by contrast, are regional line managers responsible for several country subsidiaries. They cooperate with business area managers to achieve worldwide efficiencies and the introduction of new products. Finally, the presidents of

EXHIBIT 6.5 Global Matrix Structure

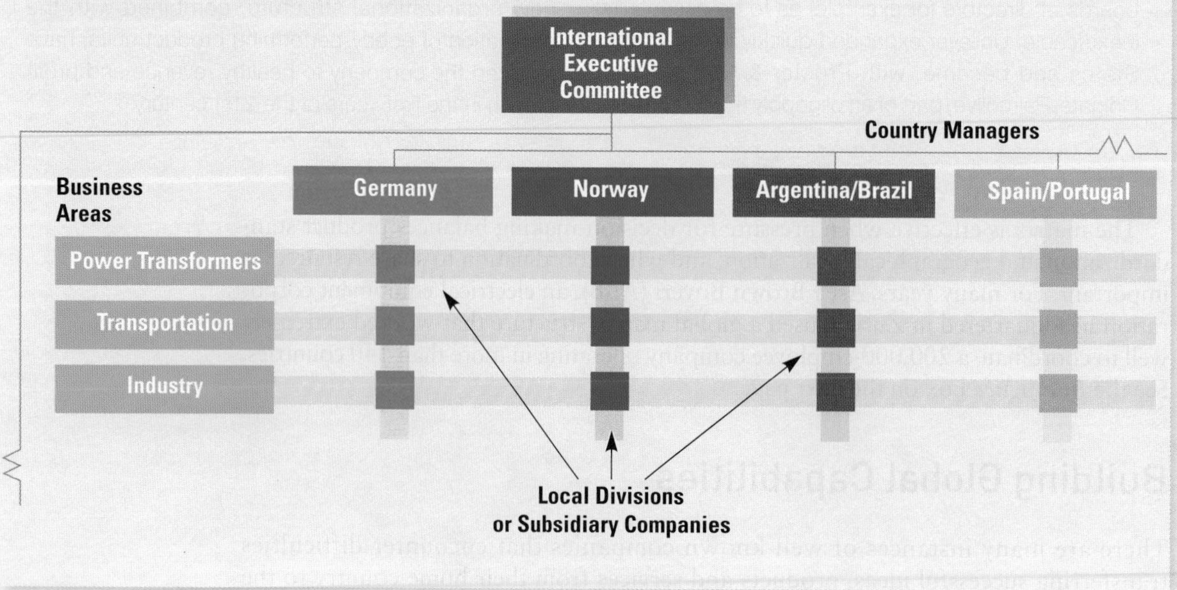

local companies have both a global boss – the business area manager – and a country boss, and their challenge is to coordinate the needs of both.[32]

ABB is a large, successful company that achieved the benefits of both product and geographic organizations through this matrix structure. However, globalization and particularly the rapid emergence of powerful new Asian Pacific economies provided new opportunities and competitive challenges during the 1990s and the 2000s[33] ABB's leaders decided that the matrix model was too unwieldy for rapid response, and transformed the company toward the *transnational model*, an emerging structure for doing business in a globalizing world, which will be discussed later in this chapter.

In the real world of international business, as in the domestic organizational models described in Chapter 3, many international firms apply a *global hybrid* or *mixed structure*, in which two or more different structures or elements of different structures are used. Hybrid structures are typical in highly volatile environments. AT&T's Network Wireless Systems Business Unit, for example, combines functional, geographical and product divisions to respond to the dynamic conditions of the wireless telecommunications industry.[34]

Now, let's look at some of the specific challenges organizations face in the global arena and mechanisms for successfully confronting them.

Spencer expanded throughout Europe and North America. By 2001 the company had decided to almost completely withdraw from overseas retailing, although by 2007 M&S was trying again.[35,36] Wal-Mart's first foray into South America was a disaster, with the company losing $48 billion in its first two years.[37] Hundreds of companies attempted to expand into Russia after the collapse of Communism. Most faced numerous unanticipated problems, and many pulled out incurring large losses.[38] Those that survived had to modify their business practices to accommodate rapidly changing rules and challenges such as corruption.[39] Managers taking their companies international face a tremendous challenge in how to capitalize on the opportunities that the possibility of global expansion presents.

The Global Organizational Challenge

Exhibit 6.6 illustrates the three primary segments of the global organizational challenge facing multinational organizations: greater complexity and differentiation, the need for integration and the problem of transferring knowledge across a global firm. Organizations encounter extremely high levels of environmental complexity in the international domain. Addressing the many differences that occur among countries requires greater organizational differentiation. At the same time, they strive to achieve coordination and collaboration among far-flung units and facilitate the development and transfer of organizational knowledge for global learning.[40]

COUNTERPOINT 6.2

When considering the challenges facing executives, recall that the three segments (see Exhibit 6.6) are highly abstracted elements of highly complex practices. What managers actually do – as contrasted with what textbooks say they should be doing – is conditioned by the legacy of how the challenges have been handled in the past and the politics that constrains as well as enables what can be done today. It is likely that executives will give different amounts of emphasis and attention to the various segments. For example, some will identify knowledge transfer as a top strategic priority whereas others will give much greater emphasis to integration. Needless to say, if each key competitor gave the same balance of emphasis to each of the segments, there would be a loss of competitive advantage to all players. **Discuss**

EXHIBIT 6.6 The Global Organizational Challenge

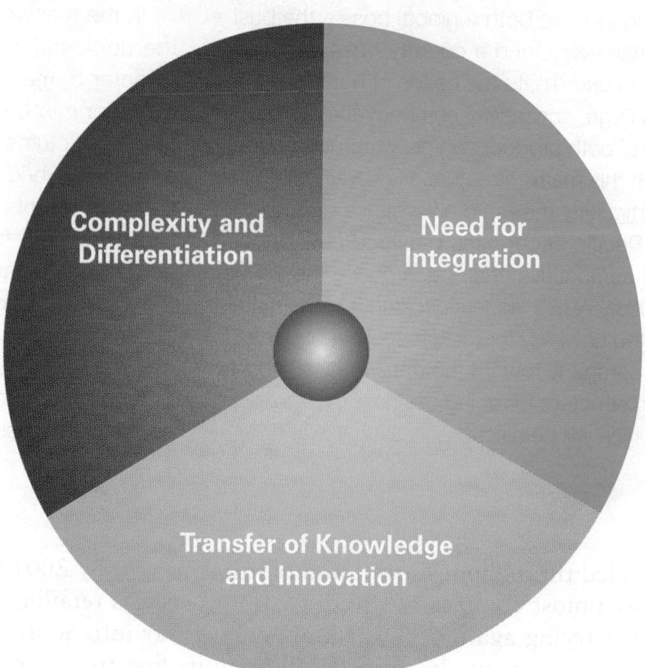

Increased Complexity and Differentiation When organizations enter the international arena, they encounter a greater level of internal and external complexity than anything experienced on the domestic front. Companies are obliged to develop a structure to operate in numerous countries that differ in economic development, language, political systems and government regulations, cultural norms and values and infrastructure such as transportation and communication facilities. For example, although most international firms have their headquarters in wealthier, economically advanced countries, large investments are increasingly being made in emerging economies in Asia, Eastern Europe and Latin America, which offer huge new markets for their goods and services. In the area of e-commerce, the number of Internet users and the amount of online sales are expanding rapidly in these emerging markets. Start-up low-cost airlines in South and South-East Asia now sell their tickets almost exclusively through the Internet, whereas only a few years ago, the internet was unknown to all but a handful of the population.[41]

In addition, a growing number of global consumers are rejecting the notion of homogenized products and services, calling for greater response to local preferences. Even McDonald's, often seen as an ultimate example of standardization for a world market, has found it necessary to respond to local and national differences. In France, where some consumers have been resentful of the fast-food chain's incursion, McDonald's has boosted sales by remodelling restaurants to include features such as hardwood floors, wood-beam ceilings and comfortable armchairs, and by adding menu items such as espresso, brioche and more upscale sandwiches.[42] For religious and cultural reasons, McDonald's in India does not serve serve beef, the mainstay of its menu in North America and Europe.

All this complexity in the international environment is mirrored in a greater internal organizational complexity. Recall from Chapter 4 that as environments become more complex and uncertain, organizations grow more highly differentiated, with many specialized positions and departments to cope with specific sectors in the environment. Top management might set up specialized departments to deal with the diverse government, legal and accounting regulations in various countries, for example. More boundary-spanning departments might be developed to sense and respond to the external environment. In addition, organizations might implement a variety of strategies, a broader array of activities and a much larger number of products and services on an international level in order to meet the needs of a diverse market.

Integration As organizations become more differentiated, with multiple products, divisions, departments and positions scattered across numerous countries, managers face a tremendous integration challenge. As described in Chapter 4, *integration* refers to the quality of collaboration across organizational units. The question is how to achieve the coordination and collaboration that is necessary for a global organization to reap the benefits of economies of scale, economies of scope and labour and production cost efficiencies that international expansion offers. Even in firms operating only in domestic markets, high differentiation among departments requires that more time and resources be devoted to achieving coordination because employees' attitudes, goals and work orientations differ widely. The situation is all the more complex for an international organization, whose operating units are divided not only by goals and work attitudes but by geographical distance, time differences, cultural values and perhaps even language as well. Recall the difficulties Unilever faced in coordinating its activities even in the single European market. Other companies, too, must find ways to share information, ideas, new products and technologies across the organization.

Knowledge Transfer The third piece of the international challenge is for organizations to learn from their international experiences and to exploit that learning so as to create and leverage organizational knowledge. The diversity of the international environment offers extraordinary opportunities for learning and the development of diverse capabilities. Organizational units in each location acquire the skills and knowledge to meet environmental challenges that arise in that particular locale. Much of that knowledge, which may be related to product improvements, operational efficiencies, technological advancements or myriad other competencies, is relevant across multiple countries, so organizations need systems that promote the transfer of knowledge across the global enterprise. One good example comes from Procter & Gamble. Liquid Tide was one of P&G's most successful US product launches in the 1980s, but the product came about from the sharing of diverse international knowledge. Liquid Tide incorporated a technology for helping to suspend dirt in wash water from P&G headquarters in the United States, the formula for its cleaning agents from P&G technicians in Japan and special ingredients for fighting mineral salts present in hard water from company scientists in Brussels.[43]

COUNTERPOINT 6.3

Knowledge may be hidden deliberately in order to preserve jobs or monopolies of expertise, and not just because of cultural differences, etc. Most of the bullet points made opposite suggest that organizations are not simply 'complex' but divided by conflicts of priority amongst different employees and interest groups. Hierarchy may facilitate managerial control but it also tends to frustrate open communication, including the sharing of knowledge. **Discuss**

Statements such as 'Organizations have to find ways to encourage both the development and sharing of knowledge' ring hollow when the sources of resistance to such sharing are unacknowledged or underestimated.

Most organizations tap only a fraction of the potential that is available from the cross-border transfer of knowledge.[44] There are several reasons for this:

- Knowledge often remains hidden in various units because language, cultural and geographic distances prevent top managers from recognizing it exists.
- Divisions sometimes view knowledge as power and want to hold onto it as a way to gain an influential position within the global firm.
- The 'not-invented-here' syndrome makes some managers reluctant to tap into the know-how and expertise of other units.
- Much of an organization's knowledge is in the minds of employees and cannot easily be written down and shared with other units.

Organizations have to find ways to encourage both the development and sharing of knowledge and implement systems for tapping into knowledge wherever it exists to create innovative responses to new challenges.

Global Coordination Mechanisms

Managers meet the global challenge of coordination and transferring knowledge across highly differentiated units in a variety of ways. Some of the most common are the use of global teams, stronger headquarters planning and control and specific coordination roles

Global Teams The popularity and success of teams on the domestic front allowed managers to see firsthand how this mechanism can achieve strong horizontal coordination, as described in Chapter 3, and thus recognize the promise teams held for coordination across a global firm as well. **Global teams**, also called transnational teams, are cross-border work groups made up of multiskilled, multinational members whose activities span multiple countries.[45] Typically, teams are of two types: intercultural teams, whose members come from different countries and meet face to face, and virtual global teams, whose members remain in separate locations around the world and conduct their work electronically.[46] Heineken formed the European Production Task Force, a thirteen-member team made up of multinational members, to meet regularly and come up with ideas for optimizing the company's production facilities across Europe.[47] The research unit of BT Labs has several hundred researchers spread across the United Kingdom and several other countries who work in global virtual teams to investigate virtual reality, artificial intelligence and other advanced information technologies.[48] The team approach enables technologies, ideas and learning in one country to rapidly spread across the firm via the constant sharing of information among team members.

The most advanced and competitive use of global teams involves simultaneous contributions in three strategic areas.[49] First, global teams help companies address the differentiation challenge, enabling them to be more locally responsive by providing knowledge to meet the needs of different regional markets, consumer preferences and political and legal systems. At the same time, teams provide integration benefits, helping organizations achieve global efficiencies by developing regional or worldwide cost advantages and standardizing designs and operations across countries. Finally, these teams contribute to continuous organizational learning, knowledge transfer and adaptation on a global level.

See online
COUNTERPOINT 6.9

Headquarters Planning A second approach to achieving stronger global coordination is for headquarters to take an active role in planning, scheduling and control to keep the widely distributed pieces of the global organization working together and moving in the same direction. In one survey, 70 per cent of global companies reported that the most important function of corporate headquarters was to 'provide enterprise leadership'.[50] In the absence of a strong lead from the centre, highly autonomous divisions can begin to act like independent companies rather than coordinated parts of a global whole. To counteract this, top management may delegate responsibility and decision-making authority in some areas, such as adapting products or services to meet local needs, while maintaining strong control through centralized management and information systems that enable headquarters to keep track of what's going on and that serve to coordinate activities across divisions and countries. Plans, schedules and formal rules and procedures can help ensure greater communication among divisions and with headquarters. They may also foster cooperation and synergy among far-flung units to achieve the goals attributed to an organization in a timely and cost-efficient way. A key role ascribed to top managers is the provision of clear strategic direction that, for example, can guide the activity of far-flung operations and help resolve competing demands from various units.

As an organization manager, keep this guideline in mind:

Use mechanisms such as global teams, headquarters planning and specific coordination roles to provide needed coordination and integration among far-flung international units. Emphasize information and knowledge sharing to help the organization learn and improve on a global scale.

Expanded Coordination Roles Organizations may also implement structural solutions to achieve stronger coordination and collaboration.[51] Creating specific organizational roles or positions for coordination is a possible way to integrate all the pieces of the enterprise to achieve a strong competitive position. In international firms, the role of top *functional managers*, for example, may be expanded to include responsibility for coordinating across countries, identifying and linking the organization's expertise and resources worldwide. In an international organization, the manufacturing manager may give priority to being aware of, and to coordinate with, manufacturing operations of the company in various other parts of the world so that greater manufacturing efficiency is achieved and technology and ideas are shared across units. A new manufacturing technology developed to improve efficiency in Ford's Brazilian operations may be valuable for European and North American plants as well. Manufacturing managers are responsible for being aware of new developments wherever they occur and for using their knowledge to improve the organization. Similarly, marketing managers, human resource managers and other functional managers at an international company are involved not only in activities for their particular location but in coordinating with their sister units in other countries.

See online
COUNTERPOINT 6.10

Whereas functional managers coordinate across countries, *country managers* coordinate across functions. A country manager for an international firm coordinates all the various functional activities to meet the problems, opportunities, needs and trends in the local market, enabling the organization to achieve multinational flexibility and rapid response. The country manager in Venezuela for Unilever's national subsidiary Unilever Andina Venezuela would coordinate everything that goes on in that country, from manufacturing to human resources to marketing, to ensure that activities meet the language, cultural, government and legal requirements of Venezuela. Similarly, the country manager in Ireland or Canada would do the same for those countries. Country managers also contribute to the transfer of ideas, trends, products and technologies that arise in one country and might have significance on a broader scale.

Some organizations create formal *network coordinator* positions to coordinate information and activities related to key customer accounts. These coordinators would enable a manufacturing organization, for example, to provide knowledge and integrated solutions across multiple businesses, divisions and countries for large customers such as the French Carrefour supermarket chain, or Wal-Mart.[52] Top managers in successful global firms may also encourage and support informal networks and relationships to keep information flowing in all directions. Much of an organization's information exchange occurs not through formal systems or structures but through informal channels and relationships. Executives can enhance organizational coordination by supporting these informal networks, giving people across boundaries opportunities to get together, develop relationships and keep in close touch.

Cultural Differences in Coordination and Control

Just as social and cultural values differ from country to country, the management values and organizational norms of international companies tend to vary depending on the organization's home country and history. Organizational norms and values are influenced by the values in the larger national culture, and these in turn influence the organization's structural approach and the ways managers coordinate and control an international firm.

As an organization manager, keep this guideline in mind:

Appreciate cultural value differences and strive to use coordination mechanisms that are in tune with local values. When broader coordination mechanisms are needed, focus on education and corporate culture as ways to gain understanding and acceptance.

National Value Systems

Many studies have attempted to determine how national value systems influence management and organizations. One of the most influential was conducted by Geert Hofstede, who identified several dimensions of national value systems that vary widely across countries.[53,54] Hofstede's five dimensions are Low vs. High Power Distance, Individualism vs. Collectivism, Masculinity vs. Femininity, Uncertainty Avoidance and Long vs. Short-term Orientation.

Two dimensions from Hofstede's model that seem to have a strong impact within organizations are *power distance* and *uncertainty avoidance*. High **power distance** means that people accept inequality in power among institutions, organizations and people. Low power distance means that people expect equality in power. That is to say, they expect to be treated as equals, not as subordinates. High **uncertainty avoidance** means that members of a society feel uncomfortable with uncertainty and ambiguity and thus eagerly support beliefs or programmes that promise certainty and conformity. Low uncertainty avoidance means that people have a comparatively high tolerance for the unstructured, the unclear and the unpredictable.

These value dimensions are reflected within organizations in terms of beliefs regarding the appeal of hierarchy, centralized decision making and control, formal rules and procedures and specialized jobs.[55] In countries that value high power distance, for example, organizations tend to be more hierarchical and centralized, with greater control and coordination from the top levels of the organization. On the other hand, organizations in countries that value low power distance are more likely to be decentralized. A low tolerance for uncertainty tends to be reflected in a preference for coordination through rules and procedures. Organizations in countries where people have a high tolerance for uncertainty typically have fewer rules and formal systems, relying more on informal networks and personal communication for coordination.

This chapter's Bookmark further examines how cultural value patterns influence international organizations.

Some studies have found clear patterns of different management structures when comparing countries in Europe, the United States and Asia, although other studies have found that the firm size and type of business being conducted has a more important impact on organizational structures and management approaches.[56]

Have you read this book?

Cross-Cultural Business Behavior: Marketing, Negotiating and Managing Across Cultures

BY RICHARD R. GESTELAND

Richard Gesteland maintains that heeding the 'two iron rules of international business' is crucial to success in today's global business environment: 'In International Business, the Seller Is Expected to Adapt to the Buyer', and 'In International Business, the Visitor Is Expected to Observe Local Customs'. In his book *Cross-Cultural Business Behavior,* Gesteland explains and categorizes various cultural patterns of behaviour that can help managers follow these rules.

Logical Cultural Patterns

Gesteland outlines four major cultural value patterns, which he calls *logical patterns*, that characterize countries around the world:

- *Deal-Focused vs. Relationship-Focused*. Deal-focused cultures, such as those in North America, Australia, and Northern Europe, are task-oriented, while relationship-focused cultures, including those in Arabia, Africa, Latin America and Asia, are typically people-oriented. Deal-focused individuals approach business in an objective and impersonal way. Relationship-focused individuals believe in building close personal relationships as the appropriate way to conduct business.
- *Informal vs. Formal*. Informal cultures place a low value on status and power differences, whereas formal cultures are typically hierarchical and status-conscious. The unconstrained values of informal cultures, such as those in the United States and Australia, may insult people from formal, hierarchical societies, just as the class-consciousness of formal groups, such as cultures in most of Europe and Latin America, may offend the egalitarian ideals of people in informal cultures.
- *Rigid-Time vs. Fluid-Time*. One part of the world's societies is flexible about time and scheduling, while the other group is more rigid and dedicated to clock-time. Conflicts may occur because rigid-time types often consider fluid-time people undisciplined and irresponsible, while fluid-time people regard rigid-time folks as arrogant, demanding and enslaved by meaningless deadlines.
- *Expressive vs. Reserved*. Expressive cultures include those in Latin America and the Mediterranean. Reserved cultures are those in East and Southeast Asia as well as Germanic Europe. This distinction can create a major communication gap. People from expressive cultures tend to talk louder and use more hand gestures and facial expressions. Reserved cultures may interpret raised voices and gesturing as signals of anger or instability.

A Practical Guide

Geographical-cultural differences, and the potential problems that cross-cultural communication can create, 'impact our business success throughout the global marketplace' argues Gesteland. *Cross-Cultural Business Behavior* 'is intended as a practical guide for the men and women in the front lines of world trade, those who face every day the frustrating differences in global business customs and practices'. By understanding Gesteland's logical patterns of behaviour, managers can adapt to varied cultural values and improve their chances for international success.

Cross-Cultural Business Behavior: Marketing, Negotiating and Managing Across Cultures, by Richard R. Gesteland, is published by Copenhagen Business School Press.

Three National Approaches to Coordination and Control

Let's look at three primary approaches to coordination and control as represented by Japanese, American and European companies.[57] It should be noted that companies in each country use tools and techniques from each of the three coordination methods. However, there are broad, general patterns that illustrate cultural differences.

Centralized Coordination in Japanese Companies When expanding internationally, Japanese-headquartered companies have typically developed coordination mechanisms that rely on centralization. Top managers at headquarters actively direct and control overseas operations, whose primary focus is to implement strategies handed down from headquarters. The senior management teams in different country divisions tend to include some, or many Japanese nationals. This approach enables Japanese companies to leverage the knowledge and resources located at the corporate centre, attain global efficiencies, coordinate across units to obtain synergies, avoid turf battles and maintain a cohesive overall organizational vision. Top managers use strong structural linkages to ensure that managers at headquarters remain up-to-date and fully involved in all strategic decisions. However, centralization has its limits. As organizations expand and divisions grow larger, headquarters can become overloaded and decision making slower. The quality of decisions may also suffer as greater diversity and complexity make it difficult for headquarters to understand and respond to local needs in each region. While the 'Japanese model' has proven highly effective even in various environments with deep national traditions including strong labour unions and a highly structured labour market,[58] it has sometimes encountered difficulties adapting quickly to macroeconomic and market instability.[59]

European Firms' Decentralized Approach A different approach has typically been taken by European companies, as we saw at Unilever and ABB. Rather than relying on strong, centrally directed coordination and control, international units tend to have a high level of independence and decision-making autonomy. Companies rely on a strong mission, shared values, and informal personal relationships for coordination. Thus, great emphasis is placed on careful selection, training and development of key managers throughout the international organization. Formal management and control systems are used primarily for financial rather than technical or operational control. With this approach, each international unit focuses on its local markets, enabling the company to excel in meeting diverse needs. One disadvantage is the cost of ensuring, through training and development programmes, that managers throughout a huge, global firm share goals, values and priorities. Decision making can also be slow and complex, and disagreements and conflicts among divisions are more difficult to resolve.

The United States: Coordination and Control through Formalization US-based companies that have expanded into the international arena have often taken a third direction. Typically, these organizations have delegated responsibility to international divisions, yet retained overall control of the enterprise through the use of sophisticated management control systems and the development of specialist headquarters staff. Formal systems, policies, standards of performance and a regular flow of information from divisions to headquarters are the primary means of coordination and control. Decision making is based on objective data, policies and procedures, which provides for many operating efficiencies and reduces conflict among divisions and between divisions and headquarters. However, the cost of setting up complex systems, policies and rules for an international organization may be quite high. The approach also requires a larger headquarters staff for reviewing, interpreting and sharing information, thus increasing overhead costs. Finally, standard routines and procedures don't always fit the needs of new problems and situations. Flexibility is limited when managers may pay so much attention to systems that they fail to recognize opportunities and threats in the environment.

Clearly, each of these approaches has advantages. But as international organizations grow larger and more complex, the disadvantages of each tend to become more pronounced. Because traditional approaches have been inadequate to meet the demands of a rapidly changing, complex international environment, many large international companies are moving toward a new kind of organization form, the *transnational model* – that is highly differentiated to address environmental complexity yet which in principle offers very high levels of coordination, learning and transfer of organizational knowledge.

COUNTERPOINT 6.4

Great caution needs to be shown in associating certain types of behaviour or even certain types of organizational form with specific cultures. While differences in behaviour can be noted between countries, the origins of these differences tend to be varied and contingent on specific circumstances. Further, culture is a factor in all types of human system, not only nations. Schneider and Barsoux[60] write of 'interacting spheres of culture' in which a variety of cultural factors intersect in working relationships: industry cultures, professional cultures, national cultures, class-based culture, cultures based in ethnicity and religion, gendered cultures etc. Thus, in an international firm, engineers from different countries may share similar working norms and practices despite the fact their 'national cultures' may appear very dissimilar.

The methodology and theoretical assumptions underlying Hofstede's research has been widely critiqued.[61] For example, his reliance on employees from a single company (IBM) introduces a major bias because of the existence of company-specific cultural norms (as noted by Schneider and Barsoux).

At worst, cultural stereotyping can lead to sweeping generalizations about human capacities and compatibilities and can lead to gross misunderstandings and a self-fulfilling prophesy of inter-civilizational conflict whether at the level of the organization or in wider international relations. Samuel P. Huntington's thesis of the 'clash of civilizations'[62] was a key theoretical underpinning to the decision of the George W Bush administration to unleash the United States' disastrous war against Iraq.[63] **Discuss**

The Transnational Model of Organization

The **transnational model** is an organizational form highly adapted to the character of a globalizing economy. It reflects both organizational complexity, with many diverse units, and organizational coordination, with mechanisms for integrating the varied parts. The transnational model is useful for large, multinational companies with subsidiaries in many countries that try to exploit both global and local advantages as well as technological advancements, rapid innovation and global learning and knowledge sharing. Rather than building capabilities primarily in one area, such as global efficiency, national responsiveness or global learning, the transnational model seeks to achieve all three simultaneously. Dealing with multiple, interrelated, complex issues requires a complex form of organization and structure, and a transformative approach in which innovations in one area interrelate with and leverage new ways of looking at, and developing, other aspects of the organization.

The transnational model represents contemporary thinking about the kind of structure needed by complex global organizations such as Philips NV, illustrated in Exhibit 6.7. Headquartered in the Netherlands, Philips has hundreds of operating units all over the world and is typical of global companies such as Unilever, Matsushita or Procter & Gamble.[64]

As an organization manager, keep this guideline in mind:

Strive toward a transnational model of organization when the company has to respond to multiple global forces simultaneously and needs to promote worldwide integration, learning and knowledge sharing.

EXHIBIT 6.7 International Organizational Units and Interlinkages within Philips NV

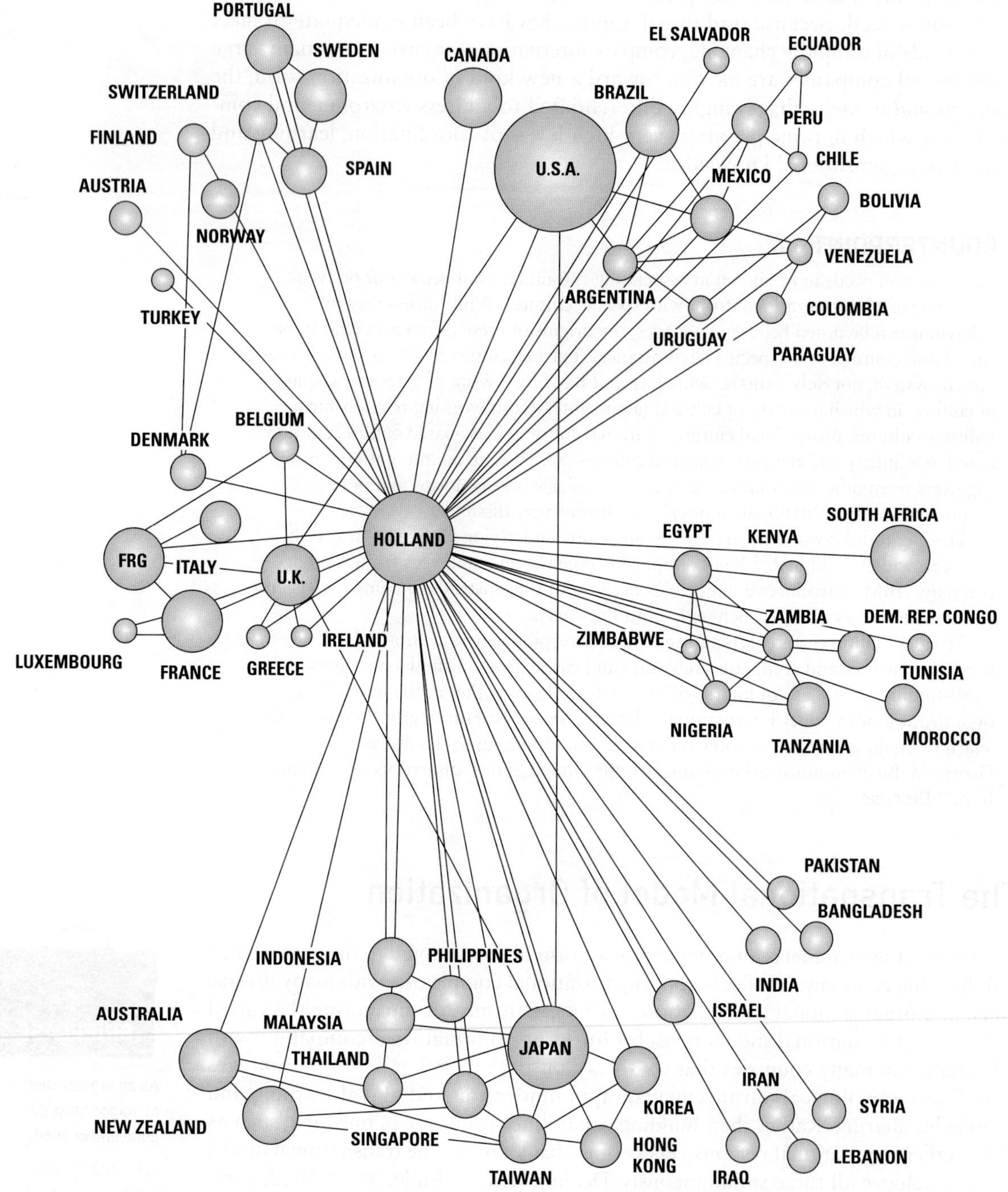

Source: Sumantra Ghoshal and Christopher A. Bartlett, 'The Multinational Corporation as an Interorganizational Network,' *Academy of Management Review* 15 (1990), 605. Used by permission.

The units in Exhibit 6.7 are far-flung. Achieving coordination, a sense of participation and involvement by subsidiaries and a sharing of information, knowledge, new technology and customers is a tremendous challenge. For example, a global corporation like Philips is so large that size alone is a huge problem in coordinating global operations. In addition, some subsidiaries become so large that they no longer fit a narrow strategic role defined by headquarters. While being part of a larger organization, individual units need some autonomy for themselves and need the ability to have an impact on other parts of the organization.

The transnational model addresses these challenges by creating an integrated network of individual operations that are linked together in an effort to achieve the multidimensional goals of the overall organization.[65] The management philosophy is based on *interdependence* rather than either full divisional independence or total dependence of these units on headquarters for decision making and control. Its advocates would say that the transnational model is more than just an organization chart as it necessitates a managerial state of mind, a set of values, a shared desire to make a worldwide learning system work and a flexible and transparent structure for effectively managing such a system. Several characteristics distinguish the transnational organization from other global organization forms such as the matrix, described earlier.

1 *Assets and resources are dispersed worldwide into highly specialized operations that are linked together through interdependent relationships.* Resources and capabilities are widely distributed to help the organization sense and respond to diverse stimuli such as market needs, technological developments or consumer trends that emerge in different parts of the world. However, managers forge interdependent relationships among the various product, functional or geographic units. Mechanisms such as cross-subsidiary teams, for example, compel units to work together for the good of their own unit as well as the overall organization. Rather than being completely self-sufficient, each group has to cooperate to achieve its own goals. Such interdependencies encourage the collaborative sharing of information and resources, cross-unit problem solving and collective implementation demanded by today's competitive international environment. Materials, people, products, ideas, resources and information are continually flowing among the dispersed parts of the integrated network. In addition, managers actively shape, manage and reinforce informal information networks that cross functions, products, divisions and countries.
2 *Structures are flexible and ever-changing.* The transnational operates on a principle of *flexible centralization*. It may centralize some functions in one country, some in another, yet decentralize still other functions among its many geographically dispersed operations. An R&D centre may be centralized in Holland and a purchasing centre located in Sweden, while financial accounting responsibilities are decentralized to operations in many countries. A unit in Hong Kong may be responsible for coordinating activities across Asia, while activities for all other countries are coordinated by a large division headquarters in London. The transnational requires that managers be flexible in determining structural needs based on the benefits to be gained. Some functions, products and geographic regions by their nature may need more central control and coordination than others. In addition, coordination and control mechanisms will change over time to meet new needs or competitive threats.
3 *Subsidiary managers initiate strategy and innovations that become strategy for the corporation as a whole.* In traditional structures, managers have a strategic role only for their division. In a transnational, various centres and subsidiaries can shape the company from the bottom up by developing creative responses and initiating programmes in response to local needs and dispersing those innovations worldwide. Transnational companies recognize each of the worldwide units as a source of capabilities and knowledge that can be used to benefit the entire organization. In addition, environmental

demands and opportunities vary from country to country, and exposing the whole organization to this broader range of environmental stimuli triggers greater learning and innovation.

4 *Unification and coordination are achieved primarily through corporate culture, shared vision and values and management style rather than through formal structures and systems.* The transnational is essentially a horizontal structure. It is diverse and extended, and it exists in a fluctuating environment so that hierarchy, standard rules, procedures and close supervision are not appropriate. Achieving unity and coordination in an organization where employees come from a variety of different national backgrounds, are separated by time and geographical distance and have different cultural norms is more easily accomplished through shared understanding than through formal systems. Top leaders build a context of shared vision, values and perspectives among managers who in turn cascade these elements through all parts of the organization. Selection and training of managers emphasizes flexibility and open-mindedness. In addition, people are often rotated through different jobs, divisions and countries to gain broad experience and become socialized into the corporate culture. Achieving coordination in a transnational organization is a much more complex process than simple centralization or decentralization of decision making and requires shaping and adapting beliefs, culture and values so that everyone participates in information sharing and learning.

See online
COUNTERPOINT 6.11

Taken together, these characteristics facilitate strong coordination, organizational learning and knowledge sharing on a broad global scale. The transnational model is truly a complex and messy way to conceptualize organization structure, but it is becoming increasingly relevant for large, global firms that treat the whole world as their playing field and do not have a single country base. The autonomy of organizational parts gives strength to smaller units and allows the firm to be flexible in responding to rapid change and competitive opportunities on a local level, while the emphasis on interdependency enables global efficiencies and organizational learning. Each part of the transnational company is aware of and closely integrated with the organization as a whole so local actions complement and enhance other company parts.

New Approaches to Global Organizational Design

Dragon Multinationals

The different stages of international organizational development described above are pertinent for international companies building from a domestic base in developed, mature economies. These companies typically have accumulated resources which they can devote to taking advantage of international opportunities. As we saw with the examples of H&M and Unilever, they often develop gradually through stages of international activity, beginning with an export division, then setting up international branches under varying degrees of headquarters supervision, before transforming themselves into the more fully-fledged global and transnational organizations described above.

In the emerging economies, particularly in the Asia-Pacific region, new types of companies have quickly grown, that do not expand from a significant domestic base, but have from their beginnings depended on international and even global markets for growth. Because markets in developing countries are usually relatively small, ambitious companies have little choice but to seek to expand overseas from the beginning. Other reasons for companies to skip the 'domestic' stage include heavily regulated home markets, with few opportunities for developing new businesses. These circumstances have led to the development of what the Australian business professor John Mathews calls 'dragon multinationals'.[66] Companies such as Acer and Mittal Steel exploited the developing global economy as their 'home turf' for rapid business expansion. In fact, for different reasons, both companies had little choice if they wished to become significant business organizations. India's highly regulated steel industry did not permit rapid domestic growth, so Lakshmi Mittal, the son of the owner of Ispat Industries, a medium sized Indian steel firm, hived off a fledgling international division in 1979 and over a fifteen year period parlayed it into the largest steel company in the world, and ultimately a merger with the Luxembourg-based conglomerate Arcelor that put Mittal in charge of the globally dominant Arcelor Mittal corporation.[67] Acer, founded by the Taiwanese entrepreneur Stan Shih, exploited global trade and production networks to create a genuinely global multinational. Shih, who had built Acer into the major Taiwanese computer company, initially aimed to build his international company through acquisitions and expansion in the US, but was severely undercapitalized. On the verge of bankruptcy, in the early 1990s Shih adopted a radically different business growth model, breaking the company down into 'cells' that network together and with outside suppliers and marketers to create multiple profit centres. Deliberately employing a 'fuzzy' organizational design, Acer is ready to transform itself in order to take advantage of the rapidly mutating global hi-tech business (Exhibit 6.8).

Unlike traditional multinationals that build primarily from internal resources, dragon multinationals seek to profit from external resources, through three key strategies: *linkage*, *leverage* and *learning* (Exhibit 6.9). Linkage involves building partnerships and joint ventures to permit access to larger markets. Frequently, as in the case of Acer, these may begin with the dragon multinational in a subordinate role to a more well-established, often western-based multinational. Leverage entails building on global linkages to access necessary knowledge and financial resources for expansion. Learning is the commitment of the organization to improve business understanding and practice through applying knowledge gained from the repeated cycles of linkage and leverage.

EXHIBIT 6.8 Acer's Cellular Structure

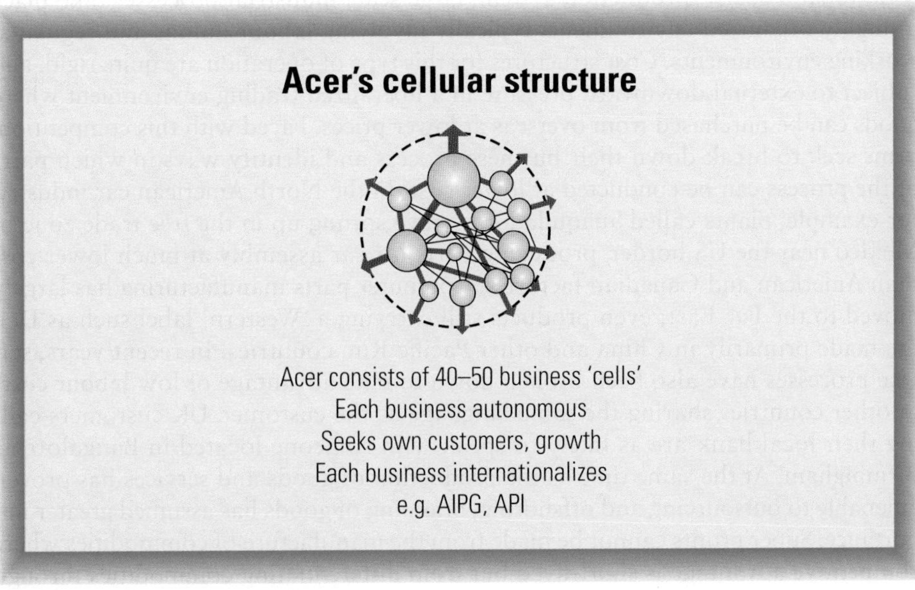

EXHIBIT 6.9 Ingredients of Success

Ingredients of success

Linkage
Links with global players drawn into collaborative networks
Acer: links with TI (DRAMs), IBM

Leverage
Technology leverage from links with advanced firms
Long-term focus: Capabilities enhancement
Securing more from contractual link than revenues

Learning
Repeated application of linkage and leverage
Enhancement of capabilities
Rapid catchup as goal

Source: John Mathews, presentation to United Nations Industrial Development Organization Conference on Competitiveness, Mitwatersrand, South Africa, 2004, Available at http://www.thedti.gov.za/invitations/MathewsSAjune04.ppt.

Value Chains

The potential for dragon multinationals to succeed is substantially based on a major change in the way that business is organized internationally. Although both domestic and multinational firms have always juggled with different levels of vertical integration (the extent to which the entire process of conceiving of a good or service and delivering it to the consumer is carried out directly by the firm), in recent years the business process has been dis-assembled to a far greater extent than had been possible previously. This is both a cause and an effect of globalization. In the traditional 'Fordist' production system, large scale industrial processes take place in highly organized environments typically involving labour unions and regulated working environments. Cost structures for this type of operation are quite rigid, and subject to external downward pressure in a liberalized trading environment where goods can be purchased from overseas at lower prices. Faced with this competition, firms seek to break down their business process and identify ways in which parts of the process can be conducted at lower cost. In the North American car industry, for example, plants called 'maquiladoras' have sprung up in the free trade zone of Mexico near the US border, producing parts for car assembly at much lower cost than American and Canadian factories. Computer parts manufacturing has largely moved to the Far East; even products still carrying a 'Western' label such as Dell are made primarily in China and other Pacific Rim countries. In recent years, service processes have also been broken down to take advantage of low labour costs in other countries sharing the same language as the customer. UK customers calling their local bank are as likely to speak with someone located in Bangalore as Birmingham. At the same time as the production of goods and services has proven amenable to outsourcing and offshoring, branding of goods has assumed greater importance. Super profits cannot be made from the manufacture of commodities where competitive advantage is short-lived but from differentiating commodities through

EXHIBIT 6.10 The Organization of Producer-driven and Buyer-driven Global Commodity Chains

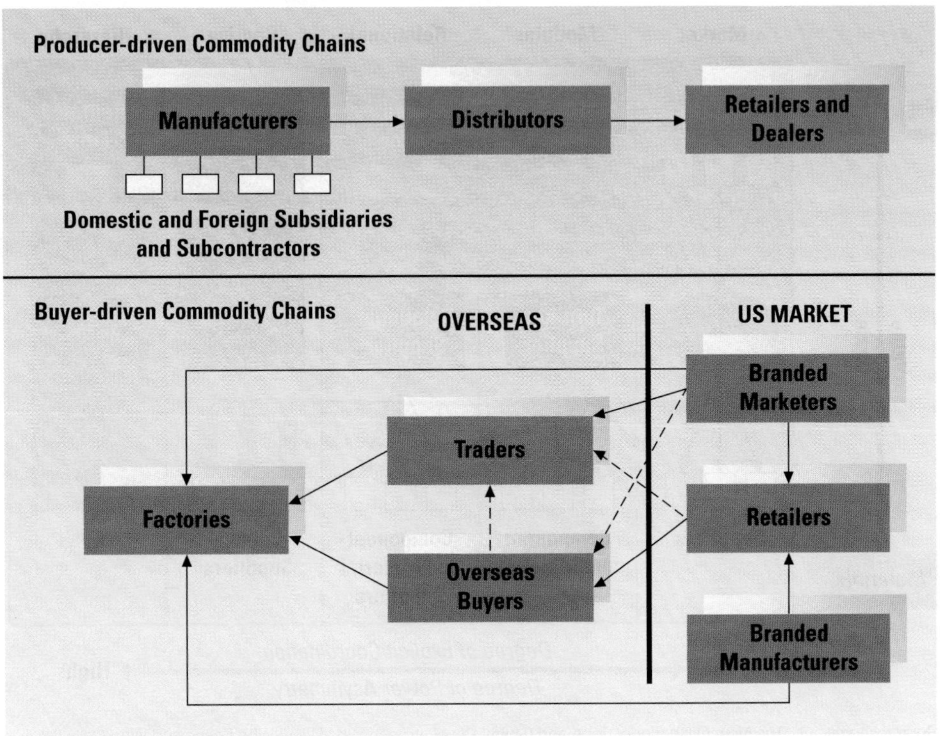

Notes: Solid arrows are primary relationships; dashed arrows are secondary relationships.
Retailers, branded marketers, and traders require full-package supply from overseas factories.
Branded manufacturers ship parts for overseas assembly and re-export to the manufacturer's home market.

branding. Although establishing and maintaining a brand is risky and costly, it can transform a mundane article (e.g. T-shirt or MP3 player) into something prestigious and identity-enhancing. Increasingly, companies in emerging economies are attempting to build globally-recognized brands: for example Hyundai in South Korea, and Lenovo and Haier in China.

The US economic sociologist Gary Gereffi has explored the significance of these developments in his work on global commodity and global value chains. Global chains are a way to look at the creation of value in the economic system. Gereffi notes that offshoring has gradually 'moved up the value chain'. Whereas in the 1960s and 1970s basic production began being offshored, by the 1980s developing country workers had begun providing basic devices such as data processing and customer service. In the 1990s more complex tasks such as medical transcription and business accounting had moved offshore, and as noted above, in the early years of the twenty-first century there are signs that 'top end' skilled work such as design and brand innovation are being offshored. Originally these value chains were mainly driven by 'advanced country' corporations through producer and buyer-driven chains (Exhibit 6.10).

However, as outsourcing and offshoring have gathered pace, the complexity and variety of global value chains has increased, and created broad conflict between corporations in developed and emerging economies as they seek to maintain the largest chare of added value. Gereffi argues that there are as many as five different types of value chain, each with a different dynamic and power relationship between producers and suppliers (Exhibit 6.11).

EXHIBIT 6.11 Five GVC Governance Types

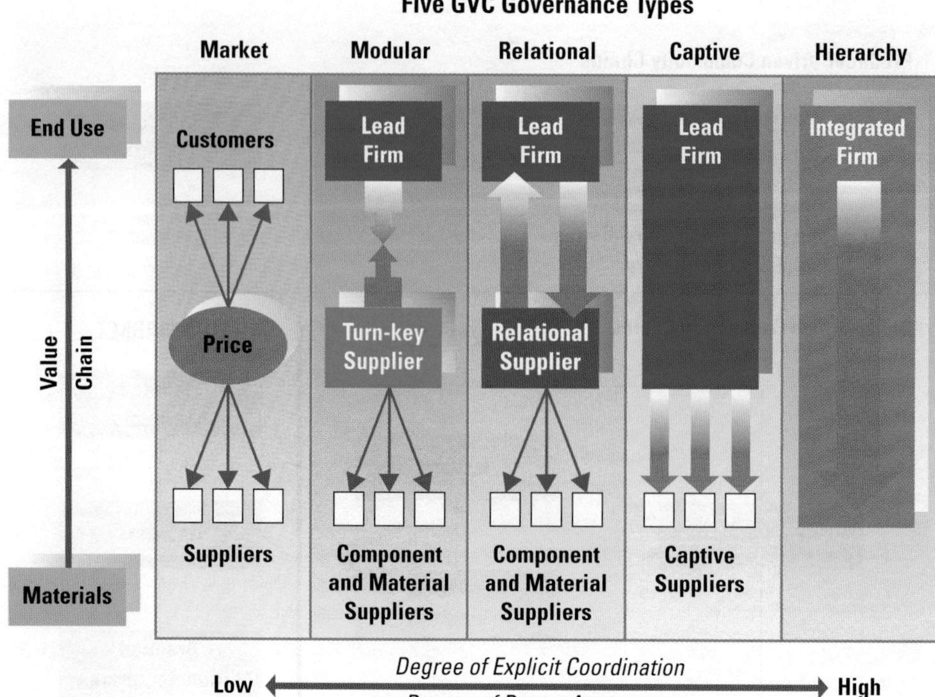

Source: Gereffi, G. 'The New Offshoringof Jobs and Global Development: Who Wins, Who Loses and Who Calls the Shots?' Presentation at Polson Institute for Global Development, Cornell University, October 28, 2005.

The table above describes Gereffi's model of the five different types of value chains that are present in the global economy. These are placed on a scale according to the balance of power (or what Gereffi calls 'governance' within the value chain. In the first case, which fits the traditional model of an open market situation, power is equally balanced between many purchasers and many suppliers. Gereffi suggests that the 'captive' value chain reflects the currently dominant form, where a large retail firm such as Wal-Mart obtains most of its product needs needs from outsourced suppliers, who negotiate with the retail giant from a position of considerable disadvantage. Because they are dependent on the retail giant for much if not all of their revenues, whereas the retailer can usually source from numerous other locations, they are essentially forced to do the bidding of the large retailer, which is typically to drive down cost. Gereffi claims that it is through this mechanism that suppliers have been forced to offshore much of their production to low wage countries such as China.

According to Gereffi, the ability to construct a product across territorial boundaries is a source of instability in both developed countries and emerging economies. Top corporate managers in international businesses need to pay close attention to their place in the value chains, as well as the rapidly changing nature of the chains themselves, as business processes undergo rapid change and restructuring in more and more industries.

Summary and Interpretation

This chapter has examined the design of organizations for complex international environments. Almost every company today is affected by significant global forces. Benefits associated with global expansion were identified as those of economies of scale, economies of scope and access to scarce or low-cost factors of production such as labour, raw materials or land. Each of these can contribute to profitable growth but its realization will depend upon developing a competitive strategy and structure. One popular way to become involved in international operations is through strategic alliances with international firms. Alliances include licensing, joint ventures and consortia.

Organizations have traditionally evolved through four stages, beginning with a domestic orientation, shifting to an international orientation, then changing to a multinational orientation and finally moving to a global orientation that sees the whole world as a potential market. Following this logic, they typically set up an export department, then an international department and eventually develop into a worldwide geographic or product structure. Geographic structures are most effective for organizations that can benefit from a multidomestic strategy, meaning that products and services will do best if tailored to local needs and cultures. A product structure supports a globalization strategy, which means that products and services can be standardized and sold worldwide. Huge global firms might use a matrix structure to respond to both local and global forces simultaneously. Many firms use hybrid structures, by combining elements of two or more different structures to meet the dynamic conditions of the global environment.

Operating on a global scale is not easy. Three aspects of the global organizational challenge are addressing environmental complexity through greater organizational complexity and differentiation, achieving integration and coordination among the highly differentiated units and implementing mechanisms for global learning and knowledge transfer. Common ways to address the problem of integration and knowledge transfer are through global teams, stronger headquarters planning and control and specific coordination roles. Diverse national and cultural values influence the approach to coordination and control. Three broad national approaches were identified: centralized coordination and control typically found in many Japanese-based firms, a decentralized approach common among European firms and the formalization approach often used by US-based international firms. In practice, most companies, no matter their home country, combine elements from each of these approaches. The transnational model, based upon a philosophy of interdependence, offers another approach to coordination where, in principle at least, each part of the organization is aware of and closely integrated with the organization as a whole so that local actions complement and enhance other company parts.

Globalisation has brought new actors onto the global economic stage. Corporations from emerging economies have begun to make a substantial impact in many product and service areas. Their growth patterns tend to be different from those of traditonal multinational corporations that have typically built their international business from domestic bases. For the new 'dragon multinationals', the international environment is their home territory. Their growth strategies from the beginning are based on linkage with other international firms, the leverage of knowledge and resources from these partnerships and a rigorous approach to learning and adaptation.

A connected feature of contemporary globalization is the dissassembling and reorganization of production processes to benefit from cost and skill advantages across territorial boundaries. As different companies from different countries work together to create products and services in a value chain, corporate managers must consistently examine their company's place in the chain, possibilities for increaing the value realization of their part of the chain, and both opportunities and threats presented by the potential for reorganizing that chain.

KEY CONCEPTS

consortia
domestic stage
dragon multinational
economies of scale
economies of scope
factors of production
global companies
global geographic structure
global matrix structure
global product structure
global stage
global teams
global value chain
globalization strategy
international division
international stage
joint venture
multidomestic
multidomestic strategy
multinational stage
power distance
transnational model
uncertainty avoidance

Discussion Questions

1 Under what conditions should a company consider adopting a global geographic structure as opposed to a global product structure?

2 Name some companies that you think could succeed today with a globalization strategy and explain why you selected those companies. How does the globalization strategy differ from a multidomestic strategy?

3 Why would a company want to join a strategic alliance rather than go it alone in international operations? What do you see as the potential advantages and disadvantages of international alliances?

4 Why is knowledge sharing so important to a global organization?

5 What are some of the primary reasons a company decides to expand internationally? Identify a company in the news that has recently built a new overseas facility. Which of the three motivations for global expansion described in the chapter do you think best explains the company's decision? Discuss.

6 When would an organization consider using a matrix structure? How does the global matrix differ from the domestic matrix structure described in Chapter 3?

7 Name some of the elements that contribute to greater complexity for international organizations. How do organizations address this complexity? Do you think these elements apply to an online company such as eBay that wants to grow internationally? Discuss.

8 Traditional values in Mexico appear to support high power distance and a low tolerance for uncertainty. What would you predict about a company that opens a division in Mexico and tries to implement global teams characterized by shared power and authority and the lack of formal guidelines, rules and structure?

9 Do you believe it is possible for a global company to simultaneously achieve the goals of global efficiency and integration, national responsiveness and flexibility and worldwide learning and knowledge sharing? Discuss.

10 Compare the description of the transnational model in this chapter to the elements of the learning organization described in Chapter 1. Do you think the transnational model seems workable for a huge global firm? Discuss.

11 What does it mean to say that the transnational model is based on a philosophy of interdependence?

12 What strategies can companies from emerging economies with limited domestic markets take in order to succeed in the global economy?

13 What are the potential benefits and dangers to a company of offshoring some of its production? What steps would a company's managers need to take in order to determine whether it should offshore, and what aspects of its busness process it should offshore?

14 What are global value chains, and why are they a useful way of looking at production organization today? What might be some options managers could consider if they wanted their corporation to secure a greater proportion of the created value in a value chain?

Chapter 6 Workbook *Where is it made?*

Find three different consumer products, such as a shirt, a toy and a shoe. Try to find out the following information for each product, as shown in the table. To find this information, use Web sites, articles on the company from various business newspapers and magazines, and the labels on the items. You could also try calling the company and talking with someone there.

Product	What country do materials come from?	Where is it manufactured or assembled?	Which country does the marketing and advertising	In what different countries is the product sold?
1				
2				
3				

What can you conclude about international products and organizations based on your analysis?

Chapter 6 Workshop Comparing Cultures

As a group, rent a video of a film made in another country from your own (or, alternately, go to the cinema when a foreign movie is shown). Take notes as you watch the movie, looking for similarities and differences in cultural norms compared to your own. For example, what are the similarities and differences in the following compared to your own cultural norms:

a The way people interact with one another

b The formality or informality of relationships

c The attitudes toward work

d The amount of time people spend on work vs. family

e The connection to family

f How people have fun

Questions

1 What were the key differences you observed in the film's culture versus your own?

2 What are the advantages and disadvantages of using films to understand another culture?

CASE FOR ANALYSIS

Amplifier Consulting: Managing a 'Global' Project

By Mehdi Boussebaa, *University of Oxford &*
Glenn Morgan, *University of Warwick*

April 6, 2006, was a day full of mixed feelings for John Smith, a partner in the UK subsidiary of Amplifier Consulting. John was about halfway through a large-scale international engagement with Global Drinks, a London based multinational beer, wine and spirits company. Global Drinks contracted Amplifier Consulting to re-engineer its European supply-chain organization. A year into the project, however, John found himself struggling to mobilize his firm's resources to deliver the engagement.

After a hectic morning, John retreated from his office on the top floor of a high rise building to meet with an academic from a major business school who was conducting research into the global organization of management consultancies. They met in the lobby and left for a calmer and more anonymous space in a local four-star hotel. After some small talk and light food, John took a deep breath and asked his companion, 'so what do you want to know?' The academic responded, 'I would like to understand how Amplifier Consulting manages global projects, i.e. projects that span multiple subsidiaries of a given client. I must stress here that I am interested in not only the formal aspects of global project management but also, and more importantly, the everyday realities involved in this process, i.e. the problems and challenges faced in the course of delivering global projects.' 'You are talking to the right person', John replied; 'I have been involved in many global projects and have many interesting stories that will interest you. Where do we start?'

Amplifier Consulting

Amplifier Consulting was one of the world's largest and most successful management consultancies. It employed thousands of partners and consultants globally and enjoyed powerful brand awareness in the consulting sector. The firm offered services in a range of areas (including financial management, information technology, strategy development, supply-chain management) and across numerous industries (for instance, banking, manufacturing and retailing). Its client portfolio comprised of many *Fortune* Global 500 corporations as well as numerous government institutions and national companies.

Amplifier Consulting prided itself on being able to service its global clients whenever and wherever they needed assistance. It viewed its strength in the market as a truly global firm with the ability to mobilize knowledge and people across national borders for the benefit of clients. The firm promised its clients to always use 'the best person for the job' on the projects it did for them, assembling project teams 'on the basis of skill and ability rather than geographical location', as John put it. To fulfil this promise, Amplifier had put in place a sophisticated intranet based resourcing system that provided information on the skills, experience, location and availability of all of its consultants. Consultants had access to this information on a worldwide basis and could get involved in projects by contacting the relevant engagement managers who themselves could search for individuals to form their teams.

The Project

John had secured a major contract to re-design Global Drinks' supply-chain on a European level. As part of this engagement, he had to advise the client on which assets it needed in place and which subsidiaries to close down. He also had to advise it on how to restructure its manufacturing, marketing, sales and distribution. Moreover, he had to assist the client with the implementation of his recommendations. Clearly, the fact that the engagement spanned several of the client's subsidiaries meant that John needed a team that could work in multiple countries. John initially thought of creating a global team that would consist of several sub-teams based in each of the major European countries in which work needed to be carried out for the project. Each sub-team would be led by a local partner from that country. Having secured the project, John would be the global client service partner with the responsibility of managing the interface between the client and the other sub-teams involved in the project. Amplifier Consulting portrayed itself as having a unique capability to assemble this kind of team but this image did not stand the test of reality.

The Challenge

How exactly did John assemble his global team to serve his multinational client in multiple countries? The everyday realities of his workplace led John to encounter a major problem: the creation of a global team was at odds with the way in which Amplifier Consulting's offices and the employees within them were evaluated and rewarded for their work. Each national office was a separate profit centre and acted as the source of earnings and career development for the partners and consultants employed in it. Revenue from projects went to the national office which 'owned' the project. This was the basis of the salaries and bonuses received by the consultants and partners. It also funded the quality of the space which the company occupied, the prestige of the address they occupied and the generosity of fringe benefits which they enjoyed, e.g. private health care, pension contributions, expense accounts, etc. Size of revenue and profitability also had a major influence on the size of the organization, the career possibilities and the number of senior manager and partner positions available. Every time a project required a consultant or partner from another office, this created a leakage of revenue and profit from the 'owning' office. John understood this reality well and knew that if he was to maximize his revenue he would have to minimize his dependence on overseas offices. Foreign partners, in particular, would expect to receive a share of his profit in exchange for their work and resources and it was thus better not to request their assistance. As John explained:

> 'If you have got a half-a-million-pound job you may put ten or twenty days into it as a partner. If you bring in another partner in, an expert, who puts in twenty days as well then they take half of the operating profit. Now, although everyone tries to ignore that, it does have an impact in terms of pulling other partners onto a job.'

John was thus faced with a serious dilemma. On the one hand, he needed a global team to offer the best possible service to his multinational client. On the other, he was under pressure to maximize his local profit which could only be achieved by not sharing the workload with foreign partners. He chose to resolve this dilemma by as far as possible ignoring foreign offices and serving the client through his own local office. He thus staffed his team with consultants from the London office. What this meant is that client related work in different countries was not undertaken by offices in those countries but by consultants flying in from the London office. Thus, John's 'global' team was in reality little more than a local team operating internationally.

However, as the project grew in size and scope, John realized that he could no longer rely solely on his local team. The project had become too big for the local team to handle on its own. Moreover, John's team, being British in composition, lacked the cultural and linguistic skills needed to operate in different countries where the client had operations. Although English was considered the *lingua franca* in Global Drinks, at subsidiary level, people did not speak English and even if they did they always preferred to communicate in their own local languages. This made it very difficult for British consultants to do their work in Continental Europe. As John explained,

> 'Language is a factor in Europe... if you drill down into the detail, if you go down to the factory level, they don't speak English and therefore I need to have people with language skills on my project.'

The fact that very few British consultants spoke foreign languages, along with the size-and-scope problem, meant that John had no choice but to add to his local team consultants from other European offices. In doing so, however, he encountered a range of problems. The process of identifying the right consultants in European offices was very time-consuming. In theory, John could use his firm's resourcing system. However, he knew that this system could not guarantee the quality of consultants and that, in any case, the best consultants were often busy on other projects.

John sought to overcome this obstacle by directly contacting his counterparts in the offices from which he needed consultants. The problem, however, was that foreign partners were under the same pressure as he was to maximize their own local profits and were thus reluctant to let their consultants, particularly their 'star consultants', work on a project run by the London office since this meant that they would not be available to work on the projects of the home office. John of course offered to reimburse the salary costs of the borrowed consultants but foreign partners knew that consultants were worth much more than their salaries.

In an attempt to exert some social pressure on European partners, John emphasized that the interest of the client had to come first and that satisfying client needs would, ultimately, benefit the 'global' firm as a whole and, by implication, all partners around the world. However, this client and global-firm rhetoric had little effect in practice since partners were equally concerned with their immediate 'bottom line' which impacted directly on their own financial rewards, status and career. Whilst partners across the world accepted and articulated the discourse of Amplifier Consulting as a global firm, they also knew that in reality the global firm was nothing more than a loose assemblage of local offices, each striving to maximize its own profits.

In particular, partners in the various European offices with which John dealt knew that the idea of the 'global' firm primarily advanced the interests of partners from those economies which had the most multinationals (such as the USA, UK, France and Germany). It was national offices in these countries that had the most opportunities for large profit generating international projects. The big revenues in the firm flowed to these offices. Revenue in other offices by contrast was less. It was dependent on picking up parts of global projects initiated elsewhere and serving domestic clients. The result was a complex set of negotiations and power relations between interdependent offices in Amplifier Consulting as partners sought to meet the expectations of their clients whilst maximizing revenue contributions to their local offices.

It became clear to John in this case that he had no choice but to share some of his profit with overseas partners. He thus offered not only to reimburse the salary costs of the borrowed consultants but also to provide additional compensation to take into account foreign partners' opportunity costs of not deploying home-based consultants on domestic projects. This arrangement was more attractive to European partners but it never fully resolved the problem. Partners from the large offices prioritized their own global projects. John knew that their first tendency when asked to assign him a consultant was to assign somebody who had space in his/her diary, a situation which usually reflected the fact that he or she was considered one of the less effective consultants. He had to bargain hard to get somebody with a good reputation. Similarly, partners from the smaller offices were difficult to deal with as they also wanted to keep their best consultants to work on locally generated projects which constituted their regular and recurrent business.

John attempted to overcome these obstacles by promising that he would reciprocate one day should European offices need British consultants on their own projects though this was problematic as the salary costs of UK consultants were the highest in Europe and thus increased the project costs significantly for projects initiated in other countries (particularly in Central and Eastern Europe). Partners from smaller offices, in particular, did not buy into the reciprocity argument: they knew that British consultants charged out fee rates that none of their domestic clients could afford to pay and that, as a result, it was unlikely that they would be able to borrow consultants from the London office. They also had few global clients to serve and so they were unlikely to be in a position in which they would require the help of British consultants overseas.

After weeks of negotiation, John finally managed to persuade some European partners to release some of their resources. However, John was still never certain that he was getting the most qualified or the most appropriate staff for his project because he knew that foreign partners tended to ring-fence their star consultants and put pressure on them to focus on winning and delivering projects at home. Moreover, some of them refused to assign their consultants to John's project on a full-time basis. More worryingly, some even failed to release the consultants which they had initially promised on the grounds that they were too busy on other projects. All these tactics were familiar to John since he himself had to employ them on occasions in order to prioritize his own projects and profitability.

Thus, whilst John managed to persuade some European partners to collaborate with him on his 'global' project, they tended to be less than fully committed, failing to pull their weight and supply the required consultants. John found himself spending a huge amount of time trying to motivate the various parts of his 'global' team to do their best. He engaged in a great deal of communication with them and spent his life on airplanes travelling to both Global Drinks' subsidiaries and Amplifier's offices across Europe to manage relationships and keep his team together. 'This is about 80 per cent of what I do', John explained.

John was very frustrated by this reality. It significantly limited the extent to which he could freely tap into the resources of his firm's global office network and, as a result, constrained his ability to mobilize firm-wide skills and experience to the benefit of his client, a reality which completely flew in the face of Amplifier's promise to always resource engagements with the 'best person for the job'. He felt it was time to voice his concern within the firm and had thus decided to go a step further by producing a report for other Amplifier partners describing the problem and making recommendations about organizational changes that might be necessary in order to overcome these problems.

Case Questions

John is planning to write a report detailing the problems he has encountered in managing the international project with Global Drinks, and recommending organizational changes that are needed to overcome this problem. Working in groups:

1 Put yourselves in John's shoes. Write a short report (3–4 pages) identifying the key issues and making recommendations for organizational changes to address the problems and permitting Amplifier to operate as a more genuinely global firm.

2 Using the internet and library resources, research whether this problem has occurred in other management consultancies, and write one to two page report on what you find.

Notes

1. Data Monitor, H & M Hennes & Mauritz AB, Company Profile 735, May 2005; June 2006; Sarah Larenaudie, 'Inside the H&M Fashion Machine', *Time*, April 15, 2004, 48-51; H&M, *Facts 2006*, accessed at www.hm.com on May 3, 2008; H&M Annual Report 2005, 2006, accessed at www.hm.com/us/investorrelations/financialreports/annualreports__investorannualreports.nhtml on May 3, 2008; University of Michigan College of Human Ecology, H&M Group Review, 1998, accessed at http://www.hed.msu.edu/internationalretailing/company/H_M/group_review.html on June 6, 2008
2. This discussion is based heavily on Christopher A. Bartlett and Sumantra Ghoshal, *Transnational Management: Text, Cases, and Readings in Cross-Border Management*, 3rd ed. (Boston: Irwin McGraw-Hill, 2000), 94–96; and Anil K. Gupta and Vijay Govindarajan, 'Converting Global Presence into Global Competitive Advantage', *Academy of Management Executive* 15, no. 2 (2001), 45–56.
3. P. Stalker (1994), *The Work of Strangers: A Survey of International Labour Migration*, ILO, Geneva, 13.
4. Todd Zaun, Gregory L. White, Norihiko Shirouzu and Scott Miller, 'More Mileage: Auto Makers Look for Another Edge Farther from Home', *The Wall Street Journal* (July 31, 2002), A1, A8.
5. Based on Nancy J. Adler, *International Dimensions of Organizational Behavior*, 4th ed. (Cincinnati, Ohio: South-Western, 2002); Theodore T. Herbert, 'Strategy and Multinational Organizational Structure: An Interorganizational Relationships Perspective', *Academy of Management Review* 9 (1984), 259–271; and Laura K. Rickey, 'Inter-national Expansion – U.S. Corporations: Strategy, Stages of Development, and Structure' (unpublished manuscript, Vanderbilt University, 1991).
6. Michael E. Porter, 'Changing Patterns of Inter-national Competition', *California Management Review* 28 (Winter 1986) 9–40.
7. William J. Holstein, 'The Stateless Corporation', *BusinessWeek* (May 14, 1990), 98–115.
8. Debra Sparks, 'Partners', *BusinessWeek*, Special Report: Corporate Finance (October 25, 1999), 106–112.
9. David Lei and John W. Slocum, Jr., 'Global Strategic Alliances: Payoffs and Pitfalls', *Organizational Dynamics* (Winter 1991), 17–29.
10. Joseph Weber with Amy Barrett, 'Volatile Combos', *BusinessWeek*, Special Report: Corporate Finance (October 25, 1999), 122; and Lei and Slocum, 'Global Strategic Alliances.'
11. Stratford Sherman, 'Are Strategic Alliances Working?' *Fortune* (September 21, 1992), 77–78; David Lei, 'Strategies for Global Competition', *Long-Range Planning* 22 (1989), 102–109.
12. Cyrus F. Freidheim, Jr., *The Trillion-Dollar Enterprise: How the Alliance Revolution Will Transform Global Business* (New York: Perseus Books, 1998).
13. Ron Grover and Richard Siklos, 'When Old Foes Need Each Other' *BusinessWeek*, Special Report: Corporate Finance (October 25, 1999), 114, 118.
14. Lei, 'Strategies for Global Competition'; Sherman, 'Are Strategic Alliances Working?'
15. Sparks, 'Partners'.
16. Sparks, 'Partners'.
17. Kevin Kelly and Otis Port, with James Treece, Gail DeGeorge and Zachary Schiller, 'Learning from Japan', *BusinessWeek*, (January 27, 1992), 52–60; Gregory G. Dess, Abdul M. A. Rasheed, Kevin J. McLaughlin and Richard L. Priem, 'The New Corporate Architecture', *Academy of Management Executive* 9, no. 3 (1995), 7–20.
18. Lawrence A. Fisher, 'STMicroelectronics: The Metaphysics of a Metanational Pioneer', *Strategy & Business* 28 (Third Quarter 2002), 81–89.
19. Yves Doz, José Santos and Peter Williamson, *From Global to Metanational: How Companies Win in the Knowledge Economy* (Boston: Harvard Business School Press, 2001), 13–15.
20. Kenichi Ohmae, 'Managing in a Borderless World', *Harvard Business Review* (May–June 1989), 152–161.

21. Cesare R. Mainardi, Martin Salva, and Muir Sanderson, "Label of Origin: Made on Earth," *Strategy & Business* 15 (Second Quarter 1999), 42–53; Joann S. Lublin, "Place vs. Product: It's Tough to Choose a Management Model," *The Wall Street Journal* (June 27, 2001), A1, A4.
22. Demetrakakes, P. 'Nestle's packaging wraps up the world', Food & Drug Packaging, October 2004.
23. Gupta and Govindarajan, 'Converting Global Presence into Global Competitive Advantage'.
24. José Pla-Barber, 'From Stopford and Wells's Model to Bartlett and Ghoshal's Typology: New Empirical Evidence', *Management International Review* 42, no. 2 (2002), 141–156.
25. Robert J. Kramer, *Organizing for Global Competitiveness: The Country Subsidiary Design* (New York: The Conference Board, 1997), 12.
26. Laura B. Pincus and James A. Belohlav, 'Legal Issues in Multinational Business: To Play the Game, You Have to Know the Rules', *Academy of Management Executive* 10, no. 3 (1996), 52–61.
27. John D. Daniels, Robert A. Pitts and Marietta J. Tretter, 'Strategy and Structure of US Multinationals: An Exploratory Study', *Academy of Management Journal* 27 (1984), 292–307.
28. Robert J. Kramer, *Organizing for Global Competitiveness: The Product Design* (New York: The Conference Board, 1994).
29. Robert J. Kramer, *Organizing for Global Competitiveness: The Business Unit Design* (New York: The Conference Board, 1995), 18–19.
30. Based on Robert J. Kramer, *Organizing for Global Competitiveness: The Geographic Design* (New York: The Conference Board, 1993).
31. Sources: Fieldhouse, D. (1978) 'Unilever Overseas: The Anatomy of a Multinational', 1895–1965, Stanford, Hoover Press; Jones, G. (2005), 'Renewing Unilever: Tranformation and Tradition', Oxford, OUP; Jones, G. (2002) 'Unilever – A Case Study' HBS Case Study; Jones, G. and Miskell, P. (2005) 'European integration and corporate restructuring: the strategy of Unilever', c.1957–c.1990, *Economic History Review,* LVIII, 1, 113–139; Zurndorfer, H. (2006), 'Imperialism, Globalization, and the Soap/Suds Industry in Republican China (1912–37): The Case of Unilever and the Chinese Consumer' Global Economic History Working paper 19/06.
32. William Taylor, 'The Logic of Global Business: An Interview with ABB's Percy Barnevik', *Harvard Business Review* (March–April 1991), 91–105; Carla Rappaport, 'A Tough Swede Invades the US', *Fortune* (January 29, 1992), 76–79; Raymond E. Miles and Charles C. Snow, 'The New Network Firm: A Spherical Structure Built on a Human Investment Philosophy', *Organizational Dynamics* (Spring 1995), 5–18; Manfred F. R. Kets de Vries, 'Making a Giant Dance', *Across the Board* (October 1994), 27–32.
33. Antonio Ligi, 'ABB profits on emerging market sales', *International Herald Tribune,* July 27, 2007, p.12.
34. Kramer, *Organizing for Global Competitiveness: The Business Unit Design*, 30–32.
35. 'Marks & Spencer offers international franchises' *Franchise International*, 2006, 2, page 31.
36. Gupta and Govindarajan, 'Converting Global Presence into Global Competitive Advantage'.
37. Jonathan Friedland and Louise Lee, 'The Wal-Mart Way Sometimes Gets Lost in Translation Overseas', *The Wall Street Journal* (October 8, 1997), A1, A12.
38. Robert Frank, 'Withdrawal Pains: In Paddies of Vietnam, Americans Once Again Land in a Quagmire', *The Wall Street Journal* (April 21, 2000), A1, A6.
39. Puffer, S., McCarthy, D. and Zhuplev, A. (1998), 'Doing business in Russia: Lessons from early entrants', *Thunderbird International Business Review,* 40, 461–484.
40. The discussion of these challenges is based on Bartlett and Ghoshal, *Transnational Management*.
41. Ian Katz and Elisabeth Malkin, 'Battle for the Latin American Net', *BusinessWeek* (November 1, 1999), 194–200; and Pamela Drukerman and Nick Wingfield, 'Lost in Translation: AOL's Big Assault in Latin America Hits Snags in Brazil', *The Wall Street Journal* (July 11, 2000), A1.
42. Shirley Leung, 'McHaute Cuisine: Armchairs, TVs, and Espresso – Is It McDonald's?' *The Wall Street Journal* (August 30, 2002), A1, A6.
43. P. Ingrassia, 'Industry is Shopping Abroad for Good Ideas to Apply to Products', *The Wall Street Journal* (April 29, 1985), A1.
44. Based on Gupta and Govindarajan, 'Converting Global Presence into Global Competitive Advantage'.
45. Vijay Govindarajan and Anil K. Gupta, 'Building an Effective Global Business Team', *MIT Sloan Management Review* 42, no. 4 (Summer 2001), 63–71.
46. Charlene Marmer Solomon, 'Building Teams Across Borders', *Global Workforce* (November 1998), 12–17.
47. Charles C. Snow, Scott A. Snell, Sue Canney Davison and Donald C. Hambrick, 'Use Transnational Teams to Globalize Your Company', *Organizational Dynamics* 24, no. 4 (Spring 1996), 50–67.
48. Jane Pickard, 'Control Freaks Need Not Apply', *People Management* (February 5, 1998), 49.
49. Snow et al., 'Use Transnational Teams to Globalize Your Company'.
50. Robert J. Kramer, *Organizing for Global Competitiveness: The Corporate Headquarters Design* (New York: The Conference Board, 1999).
51. These roles are based on Christopher A. Bartlett and Sumantra Ghoshal, *Managing Across Borders: The Transnational Solution*, 2nd ed. (Boston: Harvard Business School Press, 1998), Chapter 11, 231–249.
52. See Jay Galbraith, 'Building Organizations Around the Global Customer', *Ivey Business Journal* (September–October 2001), 17–24, for a discussion of both formal and informal lateral networks used in multinational companies.
53. Geert Hofstede, 'The Interaction Between National and Organizational Value Systems', *Journal of Management Studies* 22 (1985), 347–357; Geert Hofstede, *Cultures and Organizations: Software of the Mind* (London: McGraw-Hill, 1991).

54. Other major studies on national culture differences include Fons Trompenaars and Charles Hampden-Turner (1998), *Riding the waves of culture: understanding cultural diversity in global business*, New York, McGraw-Hill, and 'Culture, leadership, and organizations: the GLOBE study of 62 societies', by Robert J. House, Paul J. Hanges, Mansour Javidan, Peter W. Dorfman and Vipin Gupta, *Culture, Leadership, and Organizations*, London, Sage, 2004.
55. This discussion is based on 'Culture and Organization', Reading 2-2 in Christopher A. Bartlett and Sumantra Ghoshal, *Transnational Management*, 3rd ed. (Boston: Irwin McGraw-Hill, 2000), 191–216, excerpted from Susan Schneider and Jean-Louis Barsoux, *Managing Across Cultures* (London: Prentice-Hall, 1997).
56. Miller, G. (1987), 'Meta-Analysis and the Culture-Free Hypothesis', *Organization Studies*, 8, 309–326.
57. Based on Bartlett and Ghoshal, *Managing Across Borders*, 181–201.
58. Womack, J., Jones, D. and Roos, D. (1990) *The Machine that Changed the World*, New York, Macmillan.
59. Pardi, T. (2005), 'Crise, effets de trajectoire et dynamiques sociales dans l'évolution de Toyota Motor Manufacturing UK', *Sociologie du travail*, 40, 188–204.
60. Schneider S.C. and Barsoux J-L. (2003), *Managing Across Cultures*, Harlow, FT Prentice Hall.
61. Alan M. Rugman (2009), *The Oxford Handbook of International Business*, Oxford, OUP: 773; Brendan McSweeney (2002), 'Hofstede's Model of National Cultural Differences and their Consequences: A Triumph of Faith – a Failure of Analysis', *Human Relations*, 55, 89–118; Ailon, Galit (2008), 'Mirror, Mirror On The Wall: Culture's Consequences In a Value Test of its Own Design', *Academy of Management Review*, 33, 885–904.
62. Huntington, Samuel P. (1996), *The Clash of Civilizations and the Remaking of World Order*, New York, Simon & Schuster.
63. Mahmood Mamdani (2004), *Good Muslim, Bad Muslim: America, the Cold War, and the Roots of Terror*, New York, Pantheon.
64. Sumantra Ghoshal and Christopher Bartlett, 'The Multinational Corporation as an Inter-organizational Network', *Academy of Management Review* 15 (1990), 603–625.
65. The description of the transnational organization is based on Bartlett and Ghoshal, *Transnational Management and Managing Across Borders.*
66. Mathews, J. (2002), *Dragon Multinational. A New Model for Global Growth*, Oxford, OUP.
67. Andrew Davidson, 'Billionaire's boy with ambition', *Sunday Times (London)*, April 20, 2008, p. 8.

PART IV

INTERNAL DESIGN ELEMENTS

CHAPTER 7

MANUFACTURING AND SERVICE TECHNOLOGIES

A LOOK INSIDE

Continental AG

Continental is one of Europe's best known automotive brands. Founded in 1871 in Hanover, the company made its name through processing rubber into various manufactured goods. 'Conti' was the first German company to produce the pneumatic tyre for bicycles, and in 1900 it provided the rubberized material from which the world's first airship was manufactured.[1] The company's association with transportation continues to the present day, and Continental remains the world's fourth-largest tyre manufacturer.

Like many European companies, Continental was deeply affected by the wars and political instability that scarred Europe in the mid twentieth century. The Nazi war effort led to intensified research, particularly into synthetic rubber, but Germany's eventual defeat in the war and subsequent economic dislocation hampered the company in comparison with both France's Michelin and the big American tyre manufacturers.[2] Nevertheless as the economy recovered, the company shared in Germany's rising reputation for high-quality engineered goods; its rubber was fitted on iconic marques such as BMW and Mercedes. From the 1970s the pace of industrial innovation and the heat of competition sharpened. Michelin invented the radial tyre which quickly became the industry standard, and American tyre companies like Goodyear and Uniroyal pushed hard into the European market. Japanese firms like Bridgestone were not far behind, and Conti soon fell into red ink.

After some missteps, the company reorganized along divisional lines, and embarked on a growth and internationalization strategy. Continental neutralized some of its European competition through acquiring Uniroyal's European operations, and entering into a long-term tie-up with Japan's Toyo.[3] By 1992 the company made a major shift into the North American market through acquisition of General Tire. Conti also started moving beyond its traditional reliance on tyres, and into the wider vehicle parts market. As car manufacturers began demanding more modular parts, such as entire braking systems, Conti expanded its manufacture of brakes, both through acquisition and development of its existing operations.[4]

As vehicles became more complex, incorporating sophisticated electronics, Continental moved to capture a share of this market. Its most significant acquisition was of Siemens' automotive electronics business, which Continental bought in 2007 for €11.4 billion.[5] While vehicle electronics might seem a far cry from tyres and brakes, Continental emphasized safety as the common thread. Braking systems are increasingly based on electronics, in which Siemens was a leader, and more broadly, electronic features such as airbag controllers and radar systems also add to safety. Nevertheless, the company acknowledged that a key motivation was to diversify its product lines – into new areas such as in-car entertainment – so that it would be less dependent on a handful of car manufacturers for the bulk of its revenues.

With its many moves to adapt to the twin challenges of globalization and technological change, Continental has managed to keep growing and to remain consistently profitable. By 2008 the company's sales were expected to reach €26 billion, with profits (EBITDA) of about €2.5 billion.[6] Nevertheless, the company itself was a target for acquisition. In August 2008 in a hostile takeover-bid, the privately-held German bearing-manufacturing firm Schaeffler acquired 49.9 per cent of the company, effectively a controlling stake, valuing Continental at just over €12 billion,[7] widely considered a bargain given the combined value of Conti and its recent Siemens electronics acquisition.[8] The combined company looked set to become the world's largest automotive component manufacturer, outflanking fellow German-based Bosch GmbH. The deal was strongly opposed by longtime Continental CEO Manfred Wennemar, who stepped down after failing to convince fellow Conti board members to continue resisting Schaeffler. Wennemar has a reputation as a tough, effective manager who had maintained profitability by cutting costs and moving production to cheaper Eastern European factories, and was selected by *BusinessWeek* magazine as one of its 2005 'Star European Managers'.[9] Still, in the fast-changing world of European industry, last year's accolades provide no protection against this year's reorganization.

Globalization and technological advances have radically altered the manufacturing sector in both developed and developing countries. Where once American and European companies mainly built products for Western consumers in Western countries, now manufacturing is often carried out offshore, with the Western firm mainly concerned with assuring product quality and price competitiveness, and above all building and protecting brand value. Services have become an increasingly greater part of the economy in every developed country. Yet even services are being outsourced to locations where skilled workers can be hired for a fraction of their cost in Western Europe and North America. The restructuring of economic activity on an international and even global basis presents opportunities and challenges for companies in both developed and emerging economies. Even companies that trade on their national identities, like Britain's Reebok and Burberry, or Japan's Toyota have been pushed by the cost factor to move to low-cost manufacturing centres outside Europe and Japan.[10,11]

The transfer of product assembly and simple services offshore is only the first step in a complex and comprehensive restructuring of the global economy. Offshoring of both manufacturing and services also causes major changes and opportunities in emerging economies. Some Western corporations such as American Express, which owns and operates a large customer call centre facility near Delhi, India, choose to establish wholly-owned facilities in emerging economies.[12] Many others choose instead either to enter into joint ventures, or to subcontract part or all of a business process to local companies. This has the effect of transferring technologies and managerial competencies, as well as desperately needed funds that can be used for capital investment, into the emerging economy.

Research shows that the impact of offshoring on emerging economies varies between countries and between industries. In some countries an 'enclave' phenomenon occurs in which the most productive workers are drawn to relatively well-paying offshore jobs while the domestic-market economy remains underdeveloped. Gary Gereffi, whose value-chain theory is discussed in Chapter 6, finds that there will be winners and losers among developing countries from offshoring – with a few larger and stronger emerging economies tending to land most of the benefits.[13]

Whereas a main objective of Western companies' offshoring is to save money, ambitious emerging economy companies are always aiming to move 'up the value chain': to carry out more and more complex and sophisticated processes – whether in manufacturing or services – and eventually to develop and profit from their own process innovations. This sets the stage for a battle between established Western firms and local challengers. The very rapid emergence of Japanese and Korean strength in the automobile industry – one of the more complex and technologically-intensive manufacturing challenges – shows how quickly dominance can be lost when established companies fail to adapt their technologies to meet market challenges.

This chapter explores both service and manufacturing technologies and how technology is related to organizational structure. **Technology** here refers to the work processes, techniques, machines and actions used to transform organizational inputs (materials, information, ideas) into outputs (products and services).[14] Technology is an organization's production process and includes work procedures as well as machinery.

An organization's **core technology** is the work process that is directly related to the organization's mission, such as teaching in a high school, medical services in a health clinic or manufacturing at Continental. For example, at Continental's tyre production facilities, the core technology begins with raw materials (e.g. rubber, steel, etc.). Employees take action on the raw material to make a change in it (they process and mould the natural and synthetic rubbers), thus transforming the raw material into the output of the organization (tyres, etc.). For a service organization like DHL, the core technology includes the production equipment (e.g. sorting machines, package handling equipment, trucks, aeroplanes) and procedures for delivering packages and overnight mail. In addition, as at companies like DHL and Continental, computers and new information technology have revolutionized work processes in both manufacturing and service organizations. The specific impact of new information technology on organizations will be described in Chapter 8.

See online
COUNTERPOINT 7.7

Exhibit 7.1 features an example of core technology for a manufacturing plant. Note how the core technology consists of raw material inputs, a transformation work process (milling, inspection, assembly) that changes and adds value to the raw material and produces the ultimate product or service output that is sold to consumers. In today's large, complex organizations, core work processes vary widely and sometimes can be hard to pinpoint. A core technology can be partly understood by examining the raw materials flowing into the organization,[15] the variability of work activities,[16] the degree to which the production process is mechanized,[17] the extent to which one task depends on another in the workflow[18] or the number of new product or service outputs.[19]

An important theme in this chapter is how core technology influences organizational structure. understanding core technology provides insight into how an organization can be structured for efficient performance.[20]

See online
COUNTERPOINT 7.8

Organizations are made up of many departments, each of which may use a different work process (technology) to provide a good or service within an organization. A **non-core technology** is a work process that is important to the organization but is not directly related to its primary mission. In Exhibit 7.1, non-core work processes are illustrated by the departments of human resources (HR), accounting, research and development (R&C) and marketing. Thus, R&D transforms ideas into new products, and marketing transforms inventory into sales, each using a somewhat different work process. The output of the HR department is people to work in the organization, and accounting produces accurate statements about the organization's financial condition.

See online
COUNTERPOINT 7.9

EXHIBIT 7.1 Core Transformation Process for a Manufacturing Company

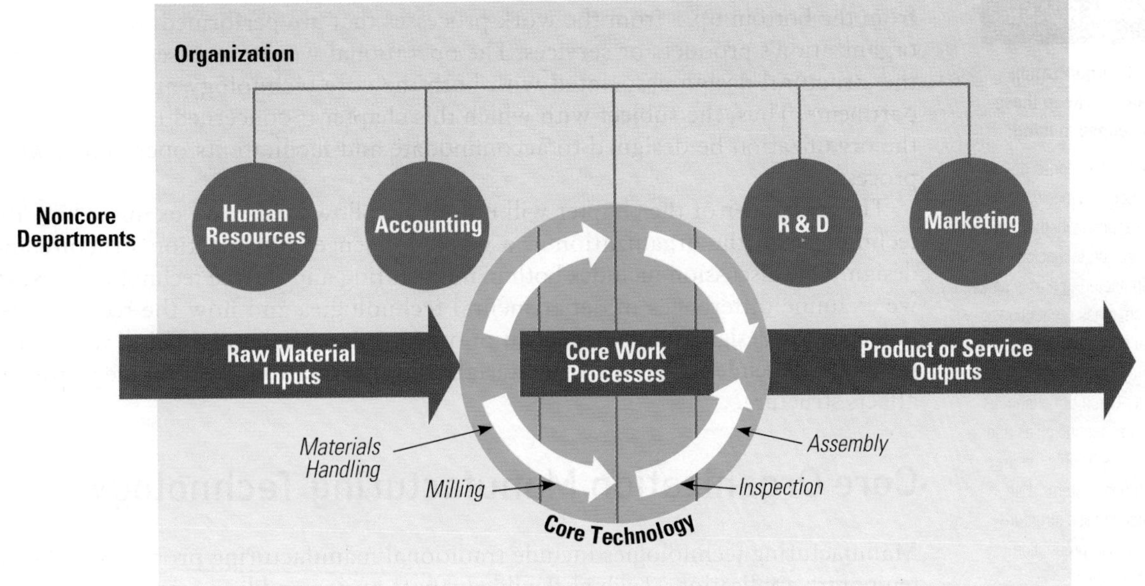

EXHIBIT 7.2 Pressures Affecting Organization Design

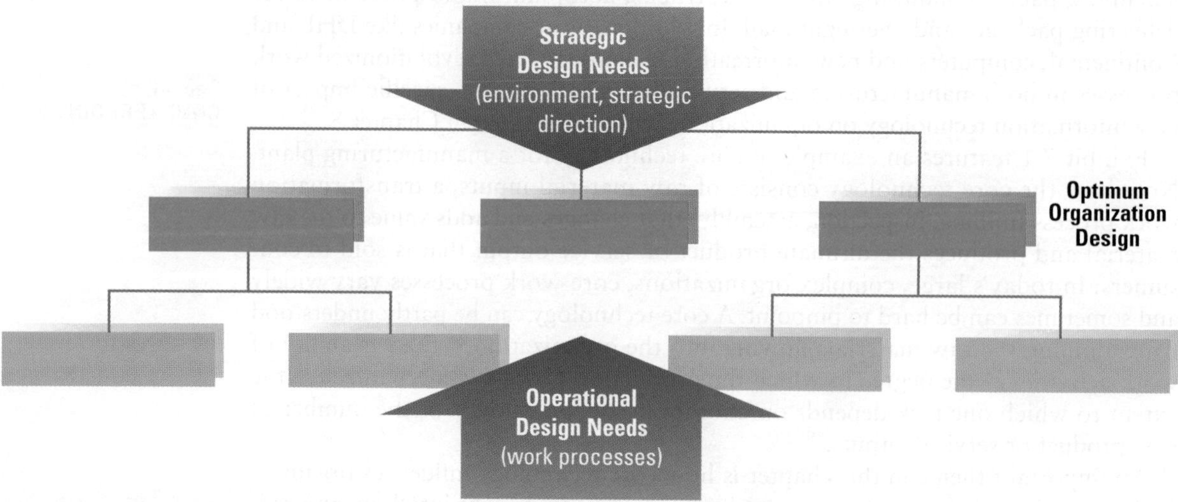

Source: Based on David A. Nadler and Michael L. Tushman, with Mark B. Nadler, *Competing by Design: The Power of Organizational Architecture* (New York: Oxford University Press, 1997), 54.

Purpose of This Chapter

In this chapter, we will discuss both core and non-core work processes and their relationship to designing organization structure. The nature of the organization's work processes must be considered in designing the organization for maximum efficiency and effectiveness. The optimum organization design is based on a variety of elements. Exhibit 7.2 illustrates that forces affecting organization design come from both outside and inside the organization. External strategic demands, such as environmental conditions, strategic direction and organizational goals, create top-down pressure for designing the organization in such a way as to fit the environment and accomplish goals. These pressures on design have been discussed in previous chapters. However, decisions about design should also take into consideration pressures from the bottom up – from the work processes that are performed to produce the organization's products or services. The operational work processes will influence the structural design associated with both the core technology and noncore departments. Thus, the subject with which this chapter is concerned is, 'How should the organization be designed to accommodate and facilitate its operational work processes?'

As an organization manager, keep these guidelines in mind:

Use the categories developed by Woodward to diagnose whether the production technology in a manufacturing firm is small batch, mass production or continuous process. Use a more organic structure with small-batch or continuous-process technologies and with new flexible manufacturing systems. Use a mechanistic structure with mass-production technologies.

The remainder of the chapter will unfold as follows. First, we examine how the technology for the organization as a whole influences organization structure and design. This discussion includes both manufacturing and service technologies. Next, we examine differences in departmental technologies and how the technologies influence the design and management of organizational subunits. Third, we explore how interdependence – flow of materials and information – among departments affects structure.

Core Organization Manufacturing Technology

Manufacturing technologies include traditional manufacturing processes and contemporary applications, such as flexible manufacturing and lean manufacturing.

Manufacturing Firms

The first and most influential study of manufacturing technology was conducted by Joan Woodward, a British industrial sociologist. Her research began as a field study of management principles in south Essex, UK. The prevailing management wisdom at the time (1950s) was contained in what were known as universal principles of management. These principles were 'one best way' prescriptions that effective organizations were expected to adopt. Woodward surveyed 100 manufacturing firms firsthand to learn how they were organized.[21] She and her research team visited each firm, interviewed managers, examined company records and observed the manufacturing operations. Her data included a wide range of structural characteristics (span of control, levels of management) and dimensions of management style (written versus verbal communications, use of rewards) and the type of manufacturing process. Data was also obtained that reflected commercial success of the firms.

Woodward developed a scale and organized the firms according to technical complexity of the manufacturing process. **Technical complexity** represents the extent of mechanization of the manufacturing process. High technical complexity means most of the work is performed by machines. Low technical complexity means workers play a larger role in the production process. Woodward's scale of technical complexity originally had ten categories, as summarized in Exhibit 7.3. These categories were further consolidated into three basic technology groups:

See online COUNTERPOINT 7.10

- *Group I: Small-batch and unit production.* These firms tend to be job shop operations that manufacture and assemble small orders to meet specific needs

EXHIBIT 7.3 Woodward's Classification of 100 British Firms According to Their Systems of Production

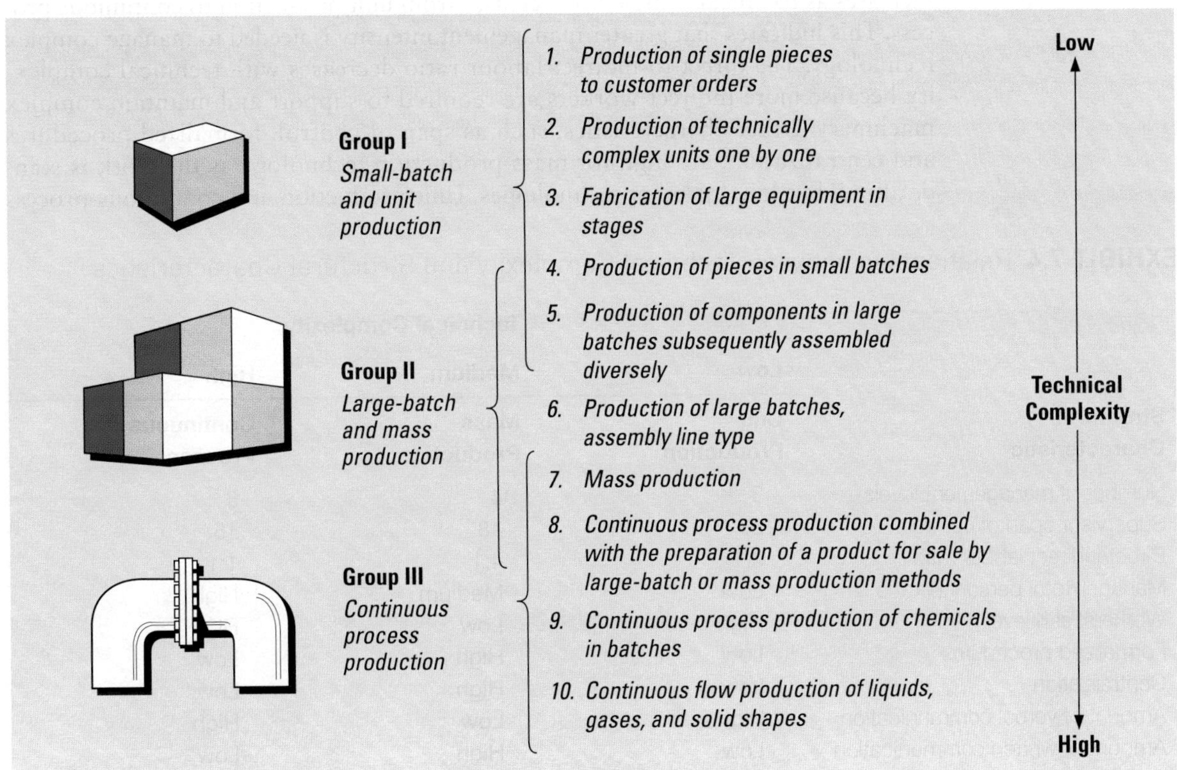

Source: Adapted from Joan Woodward, *Management and Technology* (London: Her Majesty's Stationery Office, 1958). Used with permission of Her Britannic Majesty's Stationery Office.

of customers. Custom work is the norm. **Small-batch production** relies heavily on the human operator; it is thus not highly mechanized. The American firm Rockwell Collins,[22] which makes electronic equipment for aeroplanes and other products, provides an example of small-batch manufacturing. Although sophisticated computerized machinery is used for part of the production process, final assembly requires highly skilled human operators to ensure absolute reliability of products used by aerospace companies, defence contractors and various countries' armed forces. The company's workforce is divided into manufacturing cells, some of which produce only ten units a day. In one plant, 140 workers build Joint Tactical Information Distribution Systems, developed by Rockwell Collins and Britain's BAE Systems, for managing battlefield communications from a circling plane, at a rate of ten a month.[23]

- *Group II: Large-batch and mass production.* **Large-batch production** is a manufacturing process characterized by long production runs of standardized parts. Output often goes into inventory from which orders are filled, because customers do not have special needs. Examples include most assembly lines, such as for automobiles or LCD television monitors.
- *Group III: Continuous-process production.* In **continuous-process production,** the entire process is mechanized. There is no starting and stopping. This represents mechanization and standardization one step beyond those in an assembly line. Automated machines control the continuous process, and outcomes are highly predictable. Examples would include chemical plants, oil refineries, brewing plants, pharmaceuticals and nuclear power plants.

A few of Woodward's key findings are given in Exhibit 7.4. The number of management levels and the manager-to-total personnel ratio, for example, show definite increases as technical complexity increases from unit production to continuous process. This indicates that greater management intensity is needed to manage complex technology. The direct-to-indirect labour ratio decreases with technical complexity because more indirect workers are required to support and maintain complex machinery. Other characteristics, such as span of control, formalized procedures and centralization, are high for mass-production technology as the work is standardized, but low for other technologies. Unit-production and continuous-process

EXHIBIT 7.4 Relationship between Technical Complexity and Structural Characteristics

	Technical Complexity		
	Low	Medium	High
Structural Characteristic	Unit Production	Mass Production	Continuous Process
Number of management levels	3	4	6
Supervisor span of control	23	48	15
Direct/indirect labour ratio	9:1	4:1	1:1
Manager/total personnel ratio	Low	Medium	High
Workers' skill level	High	Low	High
Formalized procedures	Low	High	Low
Centralization	Low	High	Low
Amount of verbal communication	High	Low	High
Amount of written communication	Low	High	Low
Overall structure	Organic	Mechanistic	Organic

Source: Joan Woodward, *Industrial Organization: Theory and Practice* (London: Oxford University Press, 1965). Used with permission.

technologies require highly skilled workers to oversee and maintain the machines, and verbal communication to adapt to changing conditions. Mass production is standardized and routinized, so few exceptions occur, little verbal communication is needed and employees are less skilled.

Overall, the management systems in both unit-production and continuous-process technology are characterized as organic, as defined in Chapter 4. They are more free-flowing and adaptive, with fewer procedures and less standardization. Mass production, however, is mechanistic, with standardized jobs and formalized procedures. Woodward's discovery about technology thus provided substantial new insight into the causes of organization structure. In Joan Woodward's own words, 'Different technologies impose different kinds of demands on individuals and organizations, and those demands had to be met through an appropriate structure'.[24] In short, structure is understood to follow, or adapt to, technology.

Strategy, Technology and Performance

Another portion of Woodward's study examined the success of the firms along dimensions such as profitability, market share, stock price and reputation. As indicated in Chapter 2, the measurement of effectiveness is not simple or precise, but Woodward was able to rank firms on a scale of commercial success according to whether they displayed above-average, average or below-average performance on strategic objectives.

As an organization manager, keep this guideline in mind:

When adopting a new technology, realign strategy, structure and management processes to achieve top performance.

Woodward compared the structure-technology relationship against commercial success and discovered that successful firms tended to be those that had typical configurations of structure and technology – which could be interpreted as being complementary. At any rate, many of the organizational characteristics of the successful firms were near the average of their technology category, as shown in Exhibit 7.4. Below-average firms tended to depart from the more typical structural characteristics for their technology type. Another conclusion was that structural characteristics could be interpreted as clustering into organic and mechanistic management systems. Successful small-batch and continuous process organizations tended to have more organic structures, and successful mass-production organizations had comparatively mechanistic structures. Subsequent research has broadly replicated her findings.[25]

COUNTERPOINT 7.1

One shortcoming of this logic is that it makes no allowance for innovators who depart from standard formulae. At one moment, they may seem to be comparatively unsuccessful and this may be attributed to their deviation from 'the average of their technology' but later they may be regarded as visionary in their unusual deployment of technologies that subsequently transform the industry as they become the new 'norm'. Consider for example the introduction of mass or process production which initially demands a high level of investment without necessarily delivering immediate performance improvements. **Discuss**

What these findings suggest is that effectiveness is contingent upon an alignment of strategy, structure and technology, especially when competitive conditions change.[26] For example, in the computer industry in the 1990s, computer makers had to realign strategy, structure and technology to compete with Dell's technology innovation of direct sales, mass customization and outsourced production in the personal computer market. Manufacturers such as IBM that once tried to differentiate their products and charge a premium price, switched to a low-cost strategy, adopted new technology to enable them to customize PCs, revamped supply chains and began outsourcing manufacturing to other companies that could do the job more efficiently. Eventually, IBM decided that it no longer had a competitive advantage in personal computer manufacture, and sold this part of its business to China's Lenovo.[27]

In recent years it has become almost a rule of thumb that companies should farm out production to other companies. Retailers such as H&M, profiled in Chapter 6, do not produce any of their own merchandise. However, there are examples of corporations, including H&M's largest competitor, Zara, that have chosen to go in the opposite direction by tightly integrating and controlling manufacturing and sales (see Chapter 4).

Failing to adopt appropriate new technologies to support strategy, or adopting a new technology and failing to realign strategy to match it, can lead to below par performance. Today's increased global competition results in more volatile markets, shorter product life cycles and more sophisticated and knowledgeable consumers. Greater structural flexibility and agility to meet these new demands has become a strategic imperative for many companies.[28] Manufacturing companies can adopt new technologies to increase their flexibility. Conversely, highly mechanistic structure tend to hamper flexibility, so preventing the company from reaping the benefits of new technologies.[29] The technological and human systems of an organization are inextricably intertwined. This chapter's Bookmark provides a different perspective on technology by looking at the dangers of failing to understand the human role in managing technological advances.

Contemporary Applications

In the years since Woodward's research, new developments have occurred in manufacturing technology. Manufacturing has dropped steadily as proportion of the gross domestic product (GDP) in Europe and North America for a number of years, although in 2004 it still represented 23 per cent of GDP in Germany, 19 per cent

Bedlam Puzzles

Danny Bamping is managing director of Bedlam Puzzles, a British games company best known for the 'Bedlam Cube', a variation on the famous Rubik's cube puzzle. Until 2007, Bamping outsourced production to China, but started producing them in Britain as a result of rapidly rising costs and long lag time in bringing the goods to market. Just as he was starting production in the UK, a scandal broke about safety issues affecting Chinese-made toys, such as lead found in the paint used for Mattel's Barbie dolls. He acknowledges that this was good timing for his small company, and Bedlam's website now highlights British manufacture and attention to product safety and environmental standards such as a smaller carbon footprint.[30] Bamping has teamed up with another British toy manufacturer to establish UK Manufacture Ltd, offering to produce toys in Britain for other toy companies.[31] Although this is small beginnings, there are increasing signs within both Europe and North America that the outsourcing urge, whether to domestic or emerging market suppliers, might be reaching its peak. In 2008, Mervyn King, governor of the Bank of England, emphasized the need for a 'rebalancing' of the economy in which manufacturing would again play an important role.[32] The same phenomenon is occurring across Europe and North America, where the automobile industry in particular is bringing more production in-house both to contain costs and to ensure quality.[33]

Have you read this book?

Inviting Disaster: Lessons from the Edge of Technology

BY JAMES R. CHILES

Dateline: Paris, France, July 25, 2000. Less than 2 minutes after Air France Concorde Flight 4590 departs Charles DeGaulle Airport, something goes horribly wrong. Trailing fire and billowing black smoke, the huge plane rolls left and crashes into a hotel, killing all 109 people aboard and four more on the ground. It's just one of the technological disasters James R. Chiles describes in his book, *Inviting Disaster: Lessons from the Edge of Technology*. One of Chiles's main points is that advancing technology makes possible the creation of machines that strain the human ability to understand and safely operate them. Moreover, he asserts, the margins of safety are drawing thinner as the energies we harness become more powerful and the time between invention and use grows shorter. Chiles believes that today, 'for every twenty books on the pursuit of success, we need a book on how things fly into tiny pieces despite enormous effort and the very highest ideals'. All complex systems, he reminds us, are destined to fail at some point.

How Things Fly Into Pieces: Examples of System Fractures

Chiles uses historical calamities such as the sinking of the *Titanic* and modern disasters such as the explosion of the space shuttle *Challenger* (the book was published before the 2003 crash of the *Columbia* shuttle) to illustrate the dangers of *system fracture*, a chain of events that involves human error in response to malfunctions in complex machinery. Disaster begins when one weak point links up with others.

- *Sultana* (American steamboat on the Mississippi River near Memphis, Tennessee), April 25, 1865. The boat, designed to carry a maximum of 460 people, was carrying more than 2,000 Union ex-prisoners north – as well as 200 additional crew and passengers – when three of the four boilers exploded, killing 1,800 people. One of the boilers had been temporarily patched to cover a crack, but the patch was too thin. Operators failed to compensate by resetting the safety valve.
- *Piper Alpha* (offshore drilling rig in the North Sea), July 6, 1988. The offshore platform processed large volumes of natural gas from other rigs via pipe. A daytime work crew, which didn't complete repair of a gas-condensate pump, relayed a verbal message to the next shift, but workers turned the pump on anyway. When the temporary seal on the pump failed, a fire trapped crewmen with no escape route, killing 167 crew and rescue workers.
- *Union Carbide (India) Ltd*. (release of highly toxic chemicals into a community), Bhopal, Mahdya Pradesh, India, December 3, 1984. There are three competing theories for how water got into a storage tank, creating a violent reaction that sent highly toxic methyl isocyanate for herbicides into the environment, causing an estimated 7,000 deaths: (1) poor safety maintenance, (2) sabotage, or (3) worker error.

What Causes System Fractures?

There is a veritable catalogue of causes that lead to such disasters, from design errors, insufficient operator training and poor planning to greed and mismanagement. Chiles wrote this book as a reminder that technology takes us into risky locales, whether it be outer space, up a 2,000-foot tower or into a chemical processing plant. Chiles also cites examples of potential disasters that were averted by quick thinking and appropriate response. To help prevent system fractures, managers can create organizations in which people throughout the company are expert at picking out the subtle signals of real problems – and where they are empowered to report them and take prompt action.

Inviting Disaster: Lessons from the Edge of Technology, by James R. Chiles, is published by HarperBusiness.

in Italy, 15 per cent in the UK, and 14 per cent of the GDP and 11 per cent of all employment in the United States.[34,35] Not surprisingly, the factory of today is quite different from the industrial firms Woodward studied in the 1950s. The computer industry – both for corporate and personal use – typically responds to individual customer requirements in a way that would be unthinkable for consumer electronics like television sets, for example. Often, a barebones computer system is produced in a central facility, then shipped out to a local facility for customization.[36] Sometimes this build-to-order (BTO) process involves an international partnership between two manufacturers, as in the collaboration between Hewlett Packard and Sun Moon Star to provide computers to the Taiwanese market.[37]

Computerization has had a massive impact upon continuous production processes, where processes that once required intensive (and error-prone) human supervision and intervention can now be remotely and efficiently monitored. However, it is relevant to note how continuous production requires attention not only to the core process but also to the back-up systems that are needed to support that process, such as instant availability of spare parts, inventory management, etc. Syktyvkarskii LPK, a Russian paper production plant belonging to the Anglo-South African corporation Mondi Business Paper, found that despite holding large and costly inventories of spare parts, maintenance engineers frequently found themselves missing critical components, resulting in production losses. They engaged the Russian IT consultants IBS to design an integrated preventative maintenance (PM) system based on the system integration platform designed by the Swiss software giant SAP. The new system ensures that maintenance planning, process monitoring and parts inventory are better coordinated. Over 200 staff from shop floor workers to top technical experts are involved in entering data into the PM system. The company estimates that computerized integration saves at least €1 million per year.[38]

Mass production manufacturing has seen similar transformations. Two significant contemporary applications of manufacturing technology are flexible manufacturing systems and lean manufacturing.

Flexible Manufacturing Systems

Most of today's factories use a variety of new manufacturing technologies, including robots, numerically controlled machine tools, radio-frequency identification (RFID), wireless technology and computerized software for product design, engineering analysis and remote control of machinery. The ultimate automated factories are referred to as **flexible manufacturing systems** (FMS).[39] Also called *computer-integrated manufacturing, smart factories, advanced manufacturing technology, agile manufacturing* or *the factory of the future*, FMS links together manufacturing components that previously stood alone. Thus, robots, machines, product design and engineering analysis are coordinated by a single computer.

The result has already revolutionized the shop floor, enabling large factories to deliver a wide range of custom-made products at low mass-production costs.[40] Mass customization is one effective response to the dilemma of globalization – how to benefit from the efficiencies of internationalization, while continuing to offer the customer a product that is tailored to her. One example where technology has enabled unique products to be offered to consumers is in ceramic coffee mug imaging. The advent of digital cameras has meant families the world over have many pictures they would like to keep and share with relatives. Through the Internet and advances in photocopy technology, a photograph of the grandchildren can be sent across the world, printed permanently on a coffee mug, and delivered as a present to grandparents, all within a day or two.[41] Flexible manufacturing also enables small enterprises to go toe-to-toe with larger companies and low-cost offshore competitors. Flexible manufacturing is typically the result of three subcomponents:

- *Computer-aided design (CAD)*. Computers are used to assist in the drafting, design and engineering of new parts. Designers guide their computers to draw specified configurations on the screen, including dimensions and component details. Hundreds of design alternatives can be explored, as can scaled-up or scaled-down versions of the original.[42]
- *Computer-aided manufacturing (CAM)*. Computer-controlled machines in materials handling, fabrication, production and assembly greatly increase the speed at which items can be manufactured. CAM also permits a production line to shift rapidly from producing one product to any variety of other products by changing the instruction tapes or software codes in the computer. CAM enables the production line to quickly honour customer requests for changes in product design and product mix.[43]
- *Integrated information network*. A computerized system links all aspects of the firm – including accounting, purchasing, marketing, inventory control, design, production and so forth. This system, based on a common data and information base, enables managers to make decisions and direct the manufacturing process in a truly integrated fashion.

The combination of CAD, CAM and integrated information systems means that a new product can be designed on the computer and a prototype can be produced untouched by human hands. It becomes possible to switch quickly from one product to another, working fast and with precision, without paperwork or record keeping to bog down the system.[44]

One field that has benefited enormously from CAD and CAM is that of dentistry. In the pre-computer era, the discipline of prosthodontics – manufacture of 'false' teeth, bridges, etc., was a matter of artistic design and trial and error. Now, data from dental imaging scans can be automatically inputted into computers and used as a base for accurate design of needed prosthetics. This data can then be directly transferred to the manufacturing process, with an accurate finished product available much sooner, and much more likely to fit well. The success of the Swedish company, Nobel Biocare, which controls many of the best-known brands and processes in dental prosthetics, is based on effective implementation of CAD/CAM in its field.[45,46]

Some advanced factories have moved to a system called *product life-cycle management* (PLM). PLM software can manage a product from idea through development, manufacturing, testing and even maintenance in the field. The PLM software provides three primary advantages for product innovation. PLM (1) stores data on ideas and products from all parts of the company; (2) links product design to all departments (and even outside suppliers) involved in new product development; and (3) provides three-dimensional images of new products for testing and maintenance. PLM has been used to coordinate people, tools, and facilities around the world for the design, development and manufacture of products as diverse as cars produced by Rolls Royce, product packaging for Procter & Gamble consumer products, and Boeing's 787 Dreamliner passenger jet.[47]

Lean Manufacturing

Flexible manufacturing is most productive in its aim to improve quality, customer service and cost cutting when all parts are used interdependently and combined with a system referred to as lean manufacturing. **Lean manufacturing** uses highly trained employees at every stage of the production process, who take a painstaking approach to details and problem solving to cut waste and improve quality. It incorporates technological elements, such as CAD/CAM and PLM, but the heart of lean manufacturing is not machines or software, but people. Lean manufacturing requires changes in organizational systems, such as decision-making processes and management processes, as well as an organizational culture that supports active employee participation. Employees are trained to 'think lean', which means attacking waste and striving for continuous improvement in all areas.[48]

COUNTERPOINT 7.2

'Lean' manufacturing has also been described as 'mean' because in its attempts to remove all slack and waste, it intensifies work. The outcome is that workers suffer from a lack of breaks or respite from the relentless demands of the system. This shortcoming may be adequately compensated by much higher wages that serve to attract and retain personnel. But it may also take its toll on morale and goodwill, producing a workforce that lacks the energy or motivation to participate in the schemes that are a key feature of flexible and lean manufacture. **Discuss**

Japan's Toyota Motor Corporation, which pioneered lean manufacturing, is often considered the premier manufacturing organization in the world. The famous Toyota Production System combines techniques such as just-in-time inventory, product life-cycle management, continuous-flow production, quick changeover of assembly lines, continuous improvement and preventive maintenance with a management system that encourages employee involvement and problem solving. Any employee can stop the production line at any time to solve a problem. In addition, designing equipment to stop automatically so that a defect can be fixed is a key element of the system.[49]

Many organizations worldwide that have studied and introduced the Toyota Production System have seen dramatic improvements in productivity, inventory reduction and quality. MAN Nutzfahrzeuge, the truck and bus manufacturing division of the German industrial giant MAN, has adopted MAN Nutzfahrzeuge Produktionssystem (MNPS), emphasizing lean thinking. Head of production systems Marcus Schnell says that in the cogwheel production area, alone, work-in-progress fell by three-quarters, lead time by 70 per cent, and job set-up times by almost one-third. On the cylinder head assembly line, work-in-progress fell by over one-half, and productivity increased by 20 per cent.[50] Another example was at the Utah, USA plant of Sweden's Autoliv, a major global producer of vehicle safety airbags.

See online COUNTERPOINT 7.11

Despite the success Autoliv has achieved, managers are continuing to make changes under APS. The mantra of lean manufacturing is that there is always room for improvement.

Lean manufacturing and flexible manufacturing systems have paved the way for **mass customization**, which refers to using mass-production technology to quickly and cost-effectively assemble goods that are uniquely designed to fit the demands of individual customers.[51] The idea of mass customization originated in the 1990s[52,53] and was a product of a change in societal thinking towards individualism and differentiation, at the same time as this became possible through the exponential increase in the power of information technologies.[54] Various companies pioneered mass customization in their fields. Nissan Corporation of Japan coined the credo of mass customization, 'Any volume, Anytime, Anybody, Anywhere and Anything'.[55] The idea of mass customization has since expanded to products as diverse as computers, clothing, farm machinery and industrial detergents. Today, you can buy jeans customized for your body, eyeglasses moulded to precisely fit and flatter your face, uPVC windows moulded in the exact shape and size you need for your home, and

Autoliv

Production supervisor Bill Webb thought he was being humble when he suggested to Toyota Motor Corp.'s Takashi Harada that Autoliv ranked around three on a scale of one to ten. He was stunned when Harada replied, 'Maybe a minus-three'. It was the opening lecture for Autoliv's education in the Toyota Production System.

Autoliv has a commanding share of the US market. Toyota was a major customer, though, and, with manufacturing defects rising, Autoliv was more than willing to accept Toyota's offer of help.

One of the first changes Harada made was to set up a system for soliciting and implementing employee suggestions, so that improvements in efficiency and safety began at the bottom. The company also made massive changes in inventory management and production processes.

At the time of Harada's comment, Autoliv was assembling airbag modules on a traditional linear, automated assembly line. The plant held about $23 million in parts – 7 to 10 days worth of inventory – in a giant warehouse. Each day, Webb pushed mountains of inventory onto the assembly floor, but since he was never sure of what was needed, he often pushed a lot of it back at the end of the day. After the introduction of lean manufacturing, software was created to track parts automatically as they were being used. The data were communicated to the warehouse and parts were replenished just as they were needed. At the same time, the information was automatically conveyed to Autoliv's suppliers, so they could ship new stock. Inventory was cut by around 50 per cent. The assembly process was redesigned into eighty-eight U-shaped production cells, each staffed by a handful of employees. Every 24 minutes, loud rock music signals the arrival of more parts and the rotation of each person to a different task. In addition to being trained to perform different tasks, employees were trained to continuously look for improvements in every area.

Autoliv introduced this system, which it coined the Autoliv Production System (APS), in its plants throughout the world. According to Autoliv, APS is built on a foundation of five stones: Team Work, five S[56], Standards, Waste Elimination, TPM[57] and has three 'pillars', Just in Time, Employee Involvement and Quality First.[58]

The shift to APS lean manufacturing has paid off. Defects per million in module parts were cut dramatically, from more than 1,100 in 1998 to just 16 in 2003. In that same year, Autoliv reported profits of $1 billion on revenues of $5.3 billion. 'Their plants are as good as any in the world', said Ross Robson, administrator of the Shingo Prize for Excellence in Manufacturing.[59]

pills with the specific combination of vitamins and minerals you need.[60] In the field of computers, the American-headquartered company used mass customization to successfully break the power of traditional PC makers like IBM and Compaq and become, for a period, the world's largest computer maker.[61] In turn Acer, featured in the Leading by Design box below, broke Dell's dominance by creating a new computing category of the netbook, meeting the IT needs of a growing and highly mobile middle class around the world.

Mass customization has taken hold across the global economy. Sixty per cent of the cars BMW sells in Europe are built to order.[62] Countless new products have been designed, based on the idea of customization. Yogurts that children take to school in their packed lunches have two pouches; one with the basic yogurt, the other containing a topping of chocolate or fudge bits that can be sprinkled on top to taste. The Sharpie pen company allows online customers to choose exactly what colour of ink they would like their pens to contain, and what message will be printed on its side. The French company Ariane Deco offers customers the chance to completely personalize their house linen, from handkerchiefs to pillowcases, to curtains.[63] Numerous national postal services now offer customers the possibility of designing their own postage stamps.[64] These latter examples suggest the direction of mass customization towards what the management futures guru C. K. Prahalad

Acer Computers

It's not so long since the phrase 'no-one ever got fired for choosing IBM' was the watchword of the computer business around the world. Now, IBM is out of the personal computer business altogether, and the major US manufacturers such as HP and Dell are facing serious competition from Asian brands including Lenovo (the purchasers of IBM's PC business) and Acer.

Acer is truly a rags to riches story. Founder Stan Shih started the company in 1976 in Taiwan with 11 employees and a capital investment of $25,000. By 2008, Acer had become the world's largest vendor of notebook computers. The company is in the process of buying Gateway, the world's fifth biggest PC manufacturer, and is already the world's third largest PC manufacturer, with clear designs on number one spot.

Acer is one of a new type of emerging country multinationals discussed in the previous chapter, coined 'dragons' by Australian academic John Mathews. Dragon MNCs differ from traditional MNCs in several ways, including being 'born global'; they are designed from the beginning as global corporations, rather than starting with a focus on the domestic market and then gradually building overseas business.

Acer has been particularly innovative in its business structure, as noted in Chapter Six. While many MNC's have relatively decentralized organizational structures, Acer went further and spun off components of the business into separate businesses, allowing the company to leverage both outside capital and knowledge, but retain the synergies of interconnectedness. Stan Shih's second big innovation was in identifying that value is added in a creative industry such as the IT sector at both ends of what he calls the 'smiling curve' concentrated in research and design on one end, and branding on the other. Manufacturing, on the other hand, tended to generate poor returns.

As a result of Shih's insight, in 2000, Acer spun-off its manufacturing facilities into a separate company, Wistron, which focuses on competitive outsourcing, while Acer concentrated on research and development and branded marketing. It was a bold move, because previously the OEM manufacturing had been seen as a cash cow which funded Acer's efforts to

EXHIBIT 7.5 Stan Shih's 'smiling curve' (graph by Rico Shen, 2007)

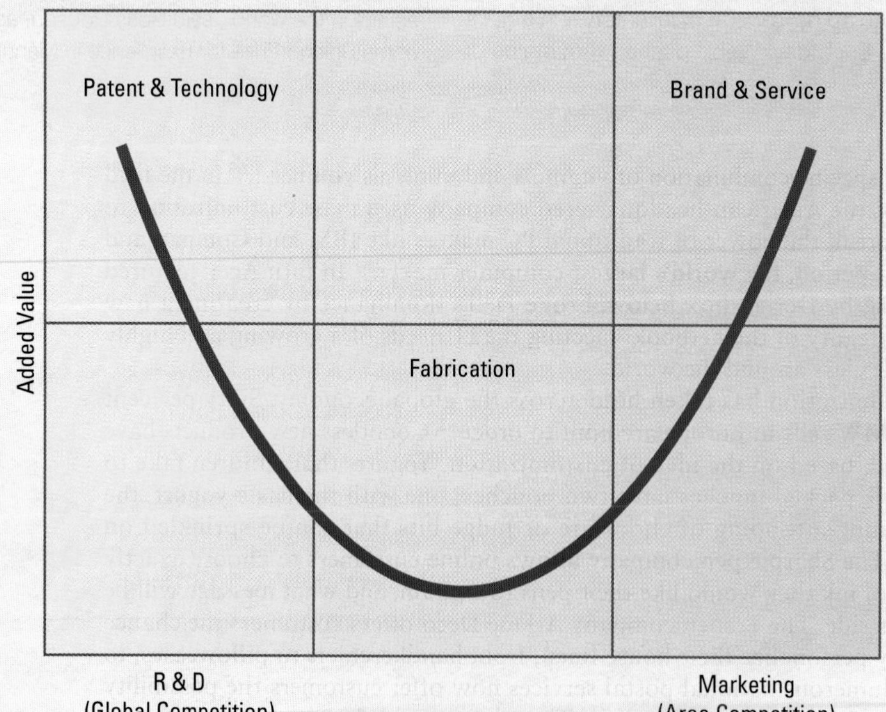

build its brand. Although Shih retired in 2004 the 'smiling curve' vision has been successfully continued under the company's new CEO JT Wang. The breakthrough for Acer's R&D and branding focus came in 2008 as the company established a dominant position in the rapidly emerging 'netbook' market; small, inexpensive, and highly portable machines that bridge the gap between PDAs like the Blackberry, and full-sized laptops. The timing for netbooks' entry was perfect, at the onset of a recession when consumers were looking for less expensive but still-attractive technology. Despite rival Taiwanese firm Asus having been first to mass-market a netbook, Acer's greater branding and marketing capacity allowed it to quickly catch up. By the final quarter of 2008 the company led the global market for netbooks with a 36 per cent share, and solid plans to hit 50 per cent in 2009. The company's long-term goal of overtaking HP as the biggest computer manufacturer in the world is on track, driven by organizational innovation.[65]

calls co-creation.[66] In co-creation, customers are integrated organically in the design process, rather than merely being 'consulted' through focus groups or similar one-off information gathering. Lego of Denmark created a web community of 1,000 to design its new Mindstorms robot. The success of the Mindstorms project led Lego to institutionalize this process with what it calls the Lego Factory, where Lego users can design products and sell them through the Lego website.[67] When Fiat decided to develop a new version of its classic Fiat 500 car, it invited potential customers to participate in designing accessories for the car – it was overwhelmed by the response, in which over 8,000 did so online, many of which, like the idea of a clear glass roof, were put into production.[68,69]

Performance and Structural Implications

One key advantage of flexible manufacturing is that products of different sizes, types and customer requirements freely intermingle on the assembly line. Bar codes imprinted on a part enable machines to make instantaneous changes – such as putting a larger screw in a different location – without slowing the production line. A manufacturer can turn out an infinite variety of products in unlimited batch sizes, as illustrated in Exhibit 7.6. In traditional manufacturing systems studied by Woodward, choices were limited to the diagonal. Small batches allowed for high product flexibility and custom orders, but because of the 'craftsmanship' involved in custom-making products, batch size was necessarily small. Mass production could have large batch size, but offered limited product flexibility. Continuous process could produce a single standard product in unlimited quantities. Flexible manufacturing systems allows plants to break free of this diagonal and to increase both batch size and product flexibility at the same time. When taken to its ultimate level, FMS allows for mass customization, with each specific product tailored to customer specification. This high-level use of FMS has been referred to as *computer-aided craftsmanship*.[70]

Studies suggest that with FMS, machine utilization is more efficient, labour productivity increases, scrap rates decrease and product variety and customer satisfaction increase.[71] Many manufacturing companies around the world are reinventing the factory using FMS and lean manufacturing systems to increase productivity.

Research into the relationship between FMS and organizational characteristics is beginning to emerge, and the patterns are summarized in Exhibit 7.7. Compared with traditional mass-production technologies, FMS has a narrow span of control, few hierarchical levels, adaptive tasks, low specialization and decentralization, and the overall environment is characterized as organic and self-regulative. Employees require the skills to participate in teams; training is broad (so workers are not overly specialized) and frequent (so workers are up-to-date). Expertise tends

EXHIBIT 7.6 Relationship of Flexible Manufacturing Technology to Traditional Technologies

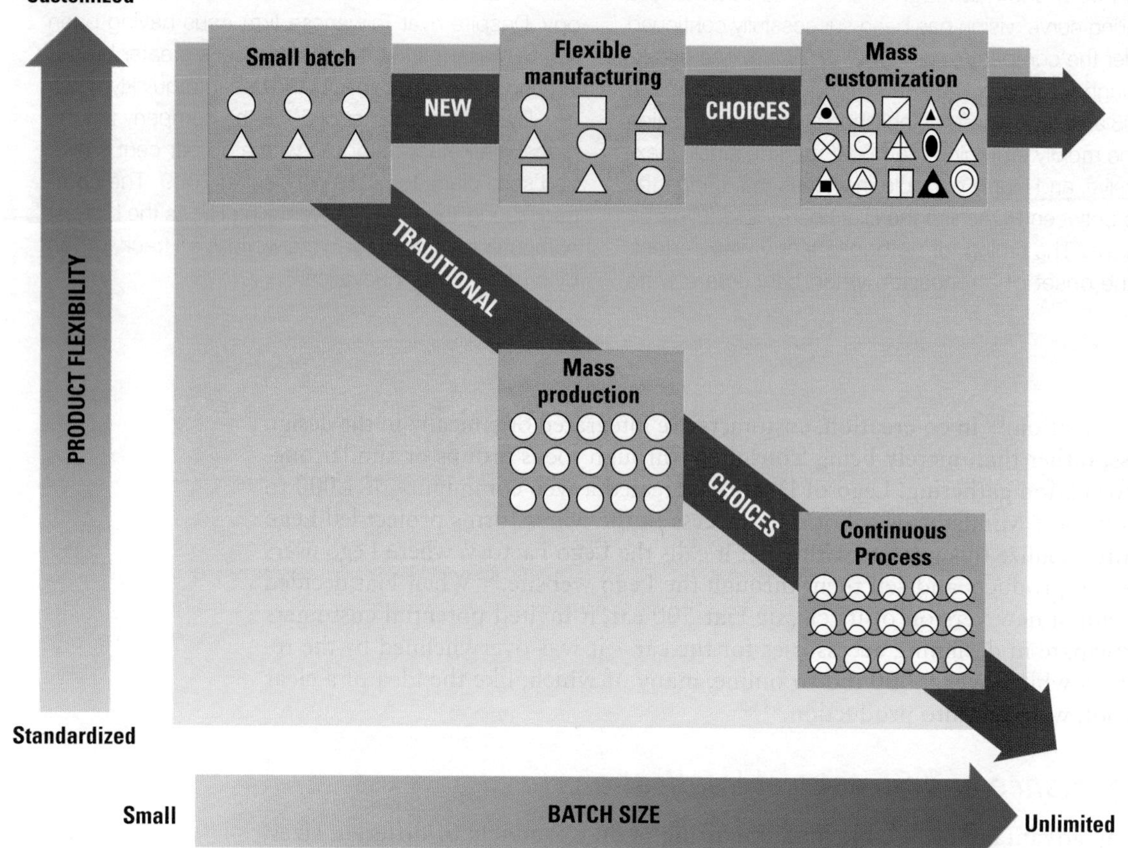

Source: Based on Jack Meredith, 'The Strategic Advantages of New Manufacturing Technologies for Small Firms,' *Strategic Management Journal* 8 (1987), 249–258; Paul Adler, 'Managing Flexible Automation,' *California Management Review* (Spring 1988), 34–56; and Otis Port, 'Custom-made Direct from the Plant,' *BusinessWeek*/21st Century Capitalism (November 18, 1994), 158–159.

to be cognitive so workers can process abstract ideas and solve problems. Interorganizational relationships in FMS firms are characterized by changing demand from customers – which is easily handled with the new technology – and close relationships with a few suppliers that provide top-quality raw materials.[72]

COUNTERPOINT 7.3

Aspects of FMS may be beneficial to employees anxious to update their skills. But lack of specialization renders them more vulnerable to replacement by other, cheaper or more pliable employees. Where there is an element of collective reward associated with teamwork, this can prove demanding and divisive. Demanding because the pressure is on to work 'for the team' rather than exercise some discretion about the level of effort contributed. And divisive because it can set some team members against others who are assessed not to be participating sufficiently fully or not pulling their weight. **Discuss**

Technology alone cannot give organizations the benefits of flexibility, quality, increased production and greater customer satisfaction. Research suggests that FMS can become a competitive burden rather than a competitive advantage unless

EXHIBIT 7.7 Comparison of Organizational Characteristics Associated with Mass Production and Flexible Manufacturing Systems

Characteristic	Mass Production	FMS
Structure		
Span of control	Wide	Narrow
Hierarchical levels	Many	Few
Tasks	Routine, repetitive	Adaptive, craftlike
Specialization	High	Low
Decision making	Centralized	Decentralized
Overall	Bureaucratic, mechanistic	Self-regulating, organic
Human Resources		
Interactions	Standalone	Teamwork
Training	Narrow, one time	Broad, frequent
Expertise	Manual, technical	Cognitive, social Solve problems
Interorganizational		
Customer demand	Stable	Changing
Suppliers	Many, arm's length	Few, close relationships

Source: Based on Patricia L. Nemetz and Louis W. Fry, 'Flexible Manufacturing Organizations: Implications for Strategy Formulation and Organization Design,' *Academy of Management Review* 13 (1988), 627–638; Paul S. Adler, 'Managing Flexible Automation,' *California Management Review* (Spring 1988), 34–56; and Jeremy Main, 'Manufacturing the Right Way,' *Fortune* (May 21, 1990), 54–64.

organizational structures and management processes are redesigned to take advantage of the new technology.[73] However, when top managers make a commitment to implement new structures and processes that empower workers and support a learning and knowledge-creating environment, FMS can help companies be more competitive.[74]

As an organization manager, keep these guidelines in mind:

Use the concept of service technology to evaluate the production process in nonmanufacturing firms. Service technologies are intangible and must be located close to the customer. Hence, service organizations may have an organization structure with fewer boundary roles, greater geographical dispersion, decentralization, highly skilled employees in the technical core and generally less control than in manufacturing organizations.

Core Organization Service Technology

Another big change occurring in the technology of organizations is the growing service sector. As discussed earlier, the percentage of the workforce employed in manufacturing continues to decline throughout the developed countries, while it has increased in emerging economies, particularly China. Some analysts estimate that at 109 million, there are more than twice as many manufacturing workers in China as in all the G7 industrialized countries put together.[75,76] As manufacturing has declined in developed countries, the service sector has rapidly increased in size. More than two-thirds of the European Union workforce, and almost four-fifths of the North American workforce, is employed in services, such as hospitals, hotels, parcel delivery, online services or telecommunications.[77] Service technologies are different from manufacturing technologies and, in turn, require a specific organization structure.

Service Firms

Definition Whereas manufacturing organizations pursue their primary purpose through the production of products, service organizations pursue their primary purpose through the production and provision of services, such as education, health care, transportation, banking and hospitality. Studies of service organizations

EXHIBIT 7.8 Differences between Manufacturing and Service Technologies

Service Technology
1. *Intangible output*
2. *Production and consumption take place simultaneously*
3. *Labour- and knowledge-intensive*
4. *Customer interaction generally high*
5. *Human element very important*
6. *Quality is perceived and difficult to measure*
7. *Rapid response time is usually necessary*
8. *Site of facility is extremely important*

Manufacturing Technology
1. *Tangible product*
2. *Products can be inventoried for later consumption*
3. *Capital asset-intensive*
4. *Little direct customer interaction*
5. *Human element may be less important*
6. *Quality is directly measured*
7. *Longer response time is acceptable*
8. *Site of facility is moderately important*

Service	Product and Service	Product
Airlines	*Fast-food outlets*	*Soft drink companies*
Hotels	*Cosmetics*	*Steel companies*
Consultants	*Real estate*	*Automobile manufacturers*
Health care	*Stockbrokers*	*Mining corporations*
Law firms	*Retail stores*	*Food processing plants*

Source: Based on F. F. Reichheld and W. E. Sasser, Jr., 'Zero Defections: Quality Comes to Services,' *Harvard Business Review* 68 (September–October 1990), 105–111; and David E. Bowen, Caren Siehl, and Benjamin Schneider, 'A Framework for Analyzing Customer Service Orientations in Manufacturing,' *Academy of Management Review* 14 (1989), 75–95.

have focused on the unique dimensions of service technologies. The characteristics of **service technology** are compared to those of manufacturing technology in Exhibit 7.8.

The most obvious difference is that service technology produces an *intangible output*, rather than a tangible product, such as a refrigerator. A service is abstract and often consists of knowledge and ideas rather than a physical product. Thus, whereas manufacturers' products can be inventoried for later sale, services are characterized by *simultaneous production and consumption*. A client meets with a doctor or attorney, for example or students and teachers come together in the classroom or over the Internet. A service cannot be stored, inventoried or viewed as a finished good. If a service is not consumed immediately upon production, it disappears.[78] This typically means that service firms are *labour- and knowledge-intensive*, with many employees needed to meet the needs of customers, in contrast to manufacturing firms that tend to be *capital-intensive*, relying on mass production, continuous process and flexible manufacturing technologies.[79]

Direct interaction between customer and employee is generally very high with services, while there is little direct interaction between customers and employees in the technical core of a manufacturing firm. This direct interaction means that the *human element* (employees) becomes even more important in service firms. Whereas most people never meet the workers who manufactured their cars, they interact directly with the salesperson who sold them their Honda Civic or Renault Clio. The treatment received from the salesperson – or from a doctor, lawyer or hairstylist – affects the perception of the service received and the customer's level of satisfaction. The *quality* of a service is more difficult to measure and compare than the quality of a tangible product. Another characteristic affecting customer satisfaction and perception of quality service is *rapidity of response*. When you take a friend to dinner, you want to be seated and served in a timely manner; you would not be very satisfied if the host or manager keeps you waiting before taking your order or if you are told to come back tomorrow when there would be more tables or servers available to accommodate you.

The final defining characteristic of service technology is that *site selection* is often much more important than with manufacturing. Services are dispersed and located geographically close to customers. For example, fast-food franchises usually disperse their facilities. Most American towns of even moderate size today have two or more McDonald's restaurants rather than one large one in order to provide service where customers want it, (although penetration of fast-food chains is substantially lower in most European countries, where there are cultural and sometimes legal barriers against their expansion[80]).

In reality, it is difficult to find organizations that reflect 100 per cent service or 100 per cent manufacturing characteristics. Some service firms take on characteristics of manufacturers, and vice versa. Many manufacturing firms are placing a greater emphasis on customer service to differentiate themselves and be more competitive. At ASSEAL, a Bradford, UK, based manufacturer of mechanical seals for industries ranging from chemical manufacture to waste water handling, and pulp and paper production, founder Chris Rea realized that in a business where competitors all offer similar quality products, the key to success would be strong customer service. ASSEAL achieved better customer service – and financial success – through setting an industry standard in ready availability of parts. In comparison with competitors who are able to fulfil only 95 per cent of orders immediately, ASSEAL aims for 98 per cent. Production director Richard Cook says: 'It is part of our strategy to be able to supply standard parts the next day, which is why we don't have any big hang-up about carrying stock; if the customer is in trouble that is our chance to say "we can help you" and we don't charge them a premium for quick turn times'. ASSEAL's commitment to customer service helped it to win Britain's Institute of Mechanical Engineers award for Manufacturing Excellence.[81]

In addition to the customer service component that is increasingly integrated in design of the manufacturing operations, manufacturing organizations have departments such as purchasing, HR and marketing that are based on service technology. Organizations such as gas stations, stockbrokers, retail stores and restaurants belong to the service sector, but the provision of a product is a significant part of the transaction. The vast majority of organizations involve some combination of products and services. Organizations can be classified along a continuum that includes both manufacturing and service characteristics, as illustrated in Exhibit 7.7.

New Directions in Services Service firms have always tended to provide some form of *customized output* – that is, providing a service that is responsive to different customer demands. When you visit a hairstylist, you don't automatically get the same cut the stylist gave the three previous clients. The stylist cuts your hair the way you request it. However, the trend toward mass customization that is revolutionizing manufacturing has had a significant impact on the service sector as well. Customer expectations of what constitutes good service are rising.[82] Service companies such as high-end hotels combine traditional hospitality with the use of new technology to build customer loyalty. Britain's Shire group of hotels, which recently won a national award as the country's best hotel chain, has invested in its customer database to ensure that duplicates are removed, that data from all the chain's properties are consistently entered, and that customer preferences are

See online
COUNTERPOINT 7.12

properly recorded.[83] But successful large hotel chains don't rely on technology alone. The Hong Kong-based Shangri-La chain, one of Asia's leading luxury hotel brands, realized when it decided to expand to North America, opening its first hotel in Vancouver, Canada, that 'traditional Asian hospitality' was the chain's USP. Talented, young hospitality professionals from North America were recruited as 'Tigers' – brand hospitality champions – and placed for training in various of the company's Asian properties, where they learned the core Shangri-La values of respect, courtesy, sincerity, helpfulness and humility.[84]

The expectation for better service is also pushing service firms in industries ranging from package delivery to banking to learn from the manufacturing sector. Japan Post, under pressure to cut a $191 million loss on operations, hired Toyota's Toshihiro Takahashi to assist in applying the Toyota Production System to the collection, sorting and delivery of mail. In all, Takahashi's team came up with 370 improvements and reduced the post office's person-hours by 20 per cent. The waste reduction is expected to cut costs by around $350 million a year.[85]

Designing the Service Organization

A feature of service technologies with a distinct influence on organizational structure and control systems is the closeness of technical core employees to the customer.[86] The differences between service and product organizations necessitated by customer contact are summarized in Exhibit 7.9.

The impact of customer contact on the design of organization structure is reflected in the use of boundary roles and structural disaggregation.[87] Boundary roles – that is roles that straddle two or more kinds of activity such as manufacturing and HRM – are used extensively to reduce disruptions for the technical core. Service technology also influences internal organization characteristics used to direct and control the organization. For one thing, the skills of technical core employees typically need to be higher. In service firms, front-line employees require sufficient knowledge and awareness to handle a variety of customer problems directly and effectively, rather than being limited to what knowledge is necessary to perform, standardized mechanical tasks. Much service work requires developed social and interpersonal skills as well as technical skills.[88]

We now turn to another perspective on technology, that of production activities within specific organizational departments. Departments often have characteristics similar to those of service technology, providing services to other departments within the organization.

EXHIBIT 7.9 Configuration and Structural Characteristics of Service Organizations versus Product Organizations

Structural Characteristic	Service	Product
1. Separate boundary roles	Few	Many
2. Geographical dispersion	Much	Little
3. Decision making	Decentralized	Centralized
4. Formalization	Lower	Higher
Human Resources		
1. Employee skill level	Higher	Lower
2. Skill emphasis	Interpersonal	Technical

Pret A Manger

'Would you like fries with that?' The standard line is rattled off by fast-food workers who have been taught to follow a script in serving customers. But at Pret A Manger, a fast-growing chain headquartered in London, England, in which McDonald's has a 33 per cent stake, you won't hear any standard lines. Employees aren't given scripts for serving customers or pigeonholed into performing the same repetitious tasks all day long. Managers want people to let their own personalities come through in offering each customer the best service possible. 'Our customers say, "I like to be served by human beings,"' explains Ewan Stickley, head of employee training. Britain's *Sunday Times* recently ranked Pret A Manger as one of the top fifty companies to work for in the country – the only restaurant to make the cut.

Pret A Manger (faux French for 'ready to eat') operates 118 outlets in the United Kingdom and is expanding into Hong Kong and the United States. 'Nobody has ever gone to America, the home of fast food, with a concept that turned out to be a successful national chain. We think we can do that', says chairman and CEO Andrew Rolfe. Pret's concept is based on organizing a mass-market service business around innovation rather than standardization. The menu is based on salads, fresh-made sandwiches, hot soups, sushi and a variety of yogurt parfaits and blended juices. Menu items are constantly changing, based on what sells and what customers want. Pret A Manger has built in a number of mechanisms for getting fast feedback. The CEO reviews customer and employee comments every Friday. Employees who send in the best ideas for changes to products or procedures can win up to $1,500. Managers spend one day each quarter working in a store to keep in touch with customers and see how their policies affect employees.

In its native UK, Pret A Manger has been a huge hit. Translating that success to the United States is an even bigger challenge. Rather than take on the huge and diverse American market in one bite, Pret settled on the New York market, where lunch habits are fairly close to those in London, with plans to open forty outlets in the next couple of years. Even with McDonald's stake in the company, Pret found itself short of capital for its plans, and in 2008 founders Julian Metcalfe and Sinclair Beecham sold a majority stake to private equity firm Bridgepoint, valuing the firm at £350 million. This was not an insignificant return on a venture started twenty years ago as a student enterprise.[89,90]

Non-Core Departmental Technology

This section considers departments that are not necessarily within the technical core. From a technology perspective, every department has a production process consisting of a distinct technology. A large company such as Toyota Corporation has departments responsible for engineering, R&D, HR, advertising, quality control, finance and dozens of other functions. This section analyzes the nature of departmental technology and its relationship with departmental structure.

A framework that has been particularly influential in understanding departmental technologies was developed by Charles Perrow.[91] It has proved useful for examining a broad range of technologies which makes it directly relevant for examining their role in departmental activities.

Variety

Perrow specified two dimensions of departmental activities that are relevant to organization structure and process. The first is the number of exceptions in the work. This refers to task **variety**, which is the frequency of unexpected and novel events.[92] When employees encounter a large number of unexpected situations, with frequent problems, variety is considered high. When there are few problems, and when day-to-day job requirements are repetitious, technology contains little variety. Variety in departments can range from repeating a single act, such as on a traditional assembly line, to working on a series of unrelated problems or projects.

Analyzability

The second dimension of technology concerns the **analyzability** of work activities. When the process of transforming inputs to the department into outputs for other departments is analyzable, the work can be reduced to mechanical steps and participants can follow an objective, computational procedure to solve problems. Problem solving may involve the use of standard procedures, such as instructions and manuals, or technical knowledge, such as that in a textbook or handbook. On the other hand, some work is not less readily analyzable in this sense. When problems arise, it is difficult to identify the correct solution. There is no store of techniques or procedures to tell a person exactly what to do. The cause of or solution to a problem is not clear, so employees rely on accumulated experience, intuition, and judgement. The effective solution to a problem is often the result of wisdom and experience and not the result of standard procedures. For example, Philippos Poulos, a tone regulator at piano maker Steinway & Sons, has an unanalyzable technology. Tone regulators carefully check each piano's hammers to ensure they produce the proper Steinway sound.[93] These quality-control tasks require years of experience and practice. Standard procedures will not tell a person how to do such tasks.

Framework

The two dimensions of technology and examples of departmental activities on Perrow's framework are shown in Exhibit 7.10. The dimensions of variety and

EXHIBIT 7.10 Framework for Department Technologies

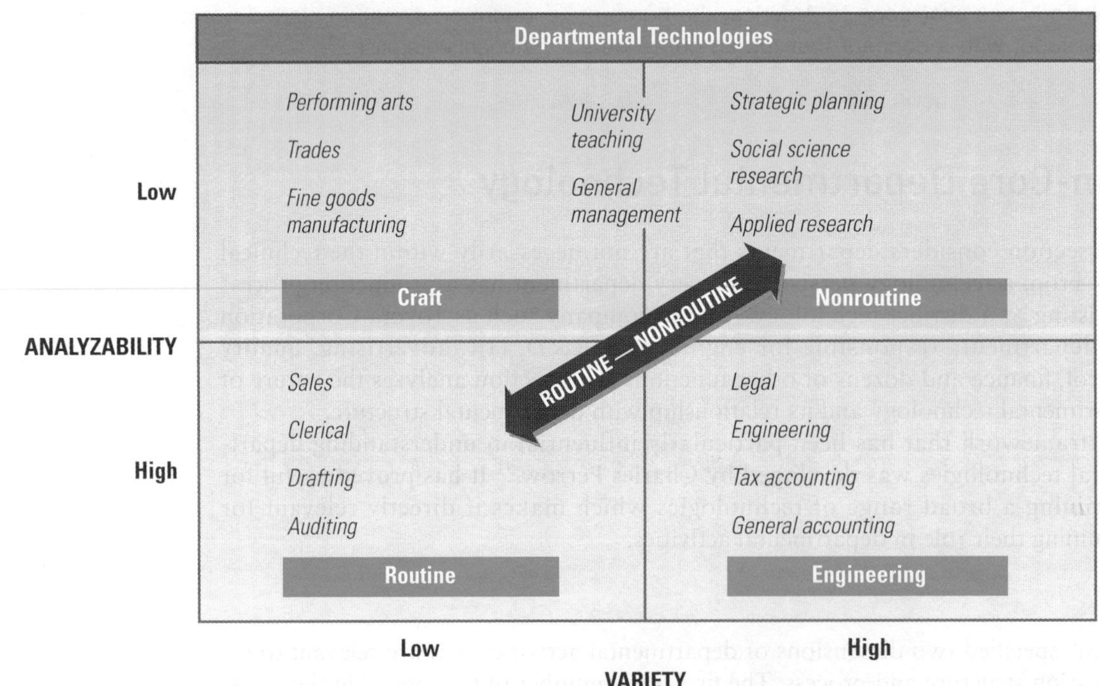

Source: Adapted with permission from Richard Daft and Norman Macintosh, 'A New Approach to Design and Use of Management Information,' *California Management Review* 21 (1978), 82–92. Copyright © 1978 by the Regents of the University of California. Reprinted by permission of the Regents.

analyzability form the basis for four major categories of technology: routine, craft, engineering and nonroutine.

Routine technologies are characterized by little task variety and the use of objective, computational procedures. The tasks are formalized and standardized. Examples include the tasks that comprise an automobile assembly line or a department in which data entry is performed.

Craft technologies are characterized by a fairly stable stream of activities, but the conversion process is not analyzable or well understood. Tasks require extensive training and experience because employees respond to intangible factors on the basis of wisdom, intuition and experience. Although advances in machine technologies seem to have reduced the number of craft technologies in organizations, craft technologies are still important. For example, steel furnace engineers continue to mix steel based on intuition and experience, pattern makers at apparel firms convert rough designers' sketches into salable garments and teams of writers for television series such as Britain's *Eastenders* or Latin America's internationally popular telenovelas (soaps) convert ideas into story lines.

Engineering technologies tend to be complex because there is substantial variety in the tasks performed. Nonetheless, the many of the activities are handled on the basis of established formulas, procedures and techniques. Employees normally refer to a well-developed body of knowledge to handle problems. Many tasks within an HRM department fall into this category.

Nonroutine technologies have high task variety, and the conversion process is not analyzable or well understood. In nonroutine technology, a great deal of effort is devoted to analyzing problems and activities. Several equally acceptable options typically can be found. Experience and technical knowledge are used to solve problems and perform the work. Basic research, strategic planning and other work that involves new projects and unexpected problems are nonroutine. The blossoming biotechnology industry also represents a nonroutine technology. Breakthroughs in understanding metabolism and physiology at a cellular level depend on highly trained employees who use their experience and intuition as well as scientific knowledge. A scientist manipulating the chemical rungs on a DNA molecule has been compared to a musician playing variations on a theme.[94]

Routine versus Nonroutine Exhibit 7.10 also illustrates that variety and analyzability can be combined into a single dimension of technology. This dimension is called *routine versus nonroutine technology*, and it is the diagonal line in Exhibit 7.10. The analyzability and variety dimensions are often correlated in departments, meaning that technologies high in variety tend to be low in analyzability, and technologies low in variety tend to be analyzable. Departments can be positioned along a single dimension of routine versus nonroutine that combines both analyzability and variety, which is a useful shorthand measure for analyzing departmental technology.

The following questions show how departmental technology can be analyzed for determining its placement on Perrow's technology framework in Exhibit 7.10.[95] Employees normally circle a number from one to seven in response to each question.

Variety:

1 To what extent would you say your work is routine?

2 Does almost everyone in this unit do about the same job in the same way most of the time?

3 Are unit members performing repetitive activities in doing their jobs?

Analyzability:

1 To what extent is there a clearly known way to do the major types of work you normally encounter?

2 To what extent is there an understandable sequence of steps that can be followed in doing your work?

3 To do your work, to what extent can you actually rely on established procedures and practices?

If answers to the above questions indicate high scores for analyzability and low scores for variety, the department would have a routine technology. If the opposite occurs, the technology would be nonroutine. Low variety and low analyzability indicate a craft technology, and high variety and high analyzability indicate an engineering technology. As a practical matter, most departments fit somewhere along the diagonal and can be most easily characterized as routine or nonroutine.

Department Design

Once the nature of a department's technology has been identified, a structure appropriate to its technology can be designed. Department technology tends to be associated with a cluster of departmental characteristics, such as the skill level of employees, formalization and pattern of communication. Definite patterns exist in the relationship between work unit technology and structural characteristics which, as we noted earlier when considering Woodward's research, tend to be associated with departmental performance.[96] Key relationships between technology and other dimensions of departments are described in this section and are summarized in Exhibit 7.11.

As an organization manager, keep these guidelines in mind:

Use the two dimensions of variety and analyzability to discover whether the work in a department is routine or nonroutine. If the work in a department is routine, use a mechanistic structure and process. If the work in a department is nonroutine, use an organic management process.

Routine technologies tend to be most strongly associated with a mechanistic structure and processes, with formal rules and rigid management processes. Nonroutine technologies are associated with a more organic structure where department management is more flexible and free-flowing. The differences can be set out in relation to the following dimensions:

1 *Formalization.* Routine technology is characterized by standardization and division of labour into small tasks that are governed by formal rules and procedures. For nonroutine tasks, the structure is less formal and less standardized. When variety is high, as in a research department, fewer activities are covered by formal procedures.[97]

2 *Decentralization.* In routine technologies, most decision making about task activities is centralized to management.[98] In engineering technologies, employees with technical training tend to acquire moderate decision authority because technical knowledge is important to task accomplishment. Production employees who have long experience obtain decision authority in craft technologies as they know how to respond to problems. Decentralization to employees is greatest in nonroutine settings, where many decisions are made by employees.

3 *Worker skill level.* Work staff in routine technologies typically require little education or experience, which is congruent with repetitious work activities. In work units with greater variety, staff are more skilled and often have formal training in technical schools or universities. Training for craft activities, which are less analyzable, is more likely to be through job experience. Nonroutine activities require both formal education and job experience.[99]

4 *Span of control.* Span of control is the number of employees who report to a single manager or supervisor. This characteristic is normally influenced by departmental technology. The more complex and nonroutine the task, the more problems arise in which the supervisor becomes involved. Although the span

EXHIBIT 7.11 Relationship of Department Technology to Structural and Management Characteristics

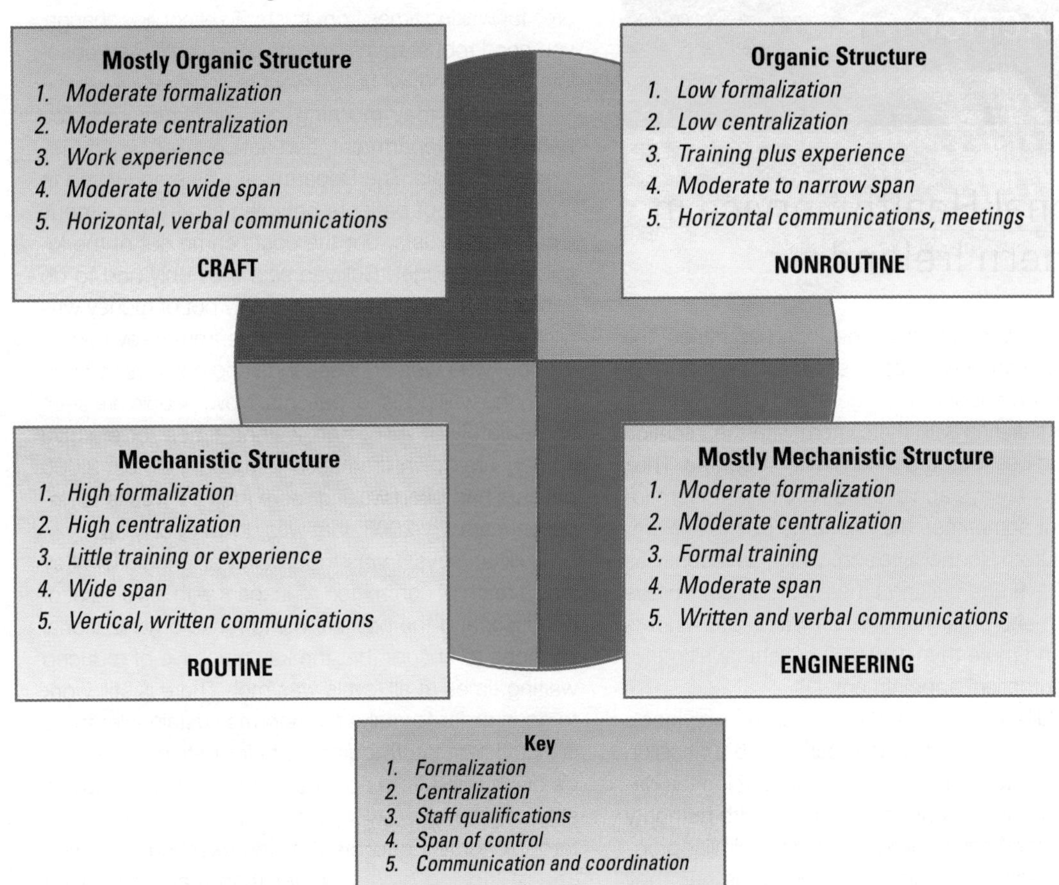

of control may be influenced by other factors, such as skill level of employees, it is typically smaller for complex tasks where the supervisor and subordinate interact frequently.[100]

5 *Communication and coordination*. Communication activity and frequency increase as task variety increases.[101] Frequent problems require more information sharing to solve problems and ensure proper completion of activities. The direction of communication is typically horizontal in nonroutine work units and vertical in routine work units.[102] The form of communication varies by task analyzability.[103] When tasks are highly analyzable, statistical and written forms of communication (memos, reports, rules and procedures) are frequent. When tasks are less analyzable, information typically is conveyed face-to-face, over the telephone, or in group meetings.

Two important points are reflected in Exhibit 7.11. First, differences between departments can be clarified by reference to their workflow technology.[104] Second, structural and management processes differ based on departmental technology. Studies have found that when structure and communication characteristics did not reflect technology, departments tend to be less effective[105] as employees could not communicate with the frequency required to address problems. Consider now how the design characteristics of health services provision in Northern Ireland where the reorganization of core technology brought a transformation in the delivery of key services.

National Health Service in Northern Ireland

In Britain, as in most other developed countries, the state of the country's health services is a matter of intense public debate. Managers and politicians are constantly tinkering with the system with the intention of achieving best outputs within limited budgets. Their efforts don't always achieve the results that were intended, but sometimes they do. One positive example comes from Northern Ireland, which as recently as 2004 had average waiting times on hospital trolleys in Accident and Emergency (A&E) wards of 24 hours or more, and more than 100,000 patients waiting for their first outpatient appointment.

Dean Sullivan, head of planning at the province's health department, says that in early 2005 a decision was made to crack the problem. The first thing the department did was to partner with the health authority in Manchester, England which had faced similar problems and dealt with them effectively. Together, they designed a three-year plan that contained four key elements: performance management, clear targets and goals, robust monitoring and sanctions in case of poor performance. He says that quality data was the foundation of the plan's success: 'When I was director of hospital services, it would take six months to get figures for waiting times from trusts. To effect any change, you need robust monitoring arrangements, and absolute clarity about what you want to achieve.'

Every Monday morning, waiting times were fed back to the Department, and action taken when they exceeded goals. The Department was empowered to move blocks of patients between semi-autonomous local health trusts, but the costs came out of the local trust's budget. Sullivan said they only had to do this once. A separate one-time only pot of money was allocated to pay for hiring doctors from elsewhere in Europe, who worked weekends and holidays to bring down the waiting list of patients. Now, people are seen immediately at A&E, and waiting times for elective surgery are down dramatically. In 2007, almost 2,000 patients had been waiting more than 21 weeks for in-patient care. By 2008, that was down to only 56.

Sullivan says it was 'not rocket science'. The key was a team of committed managers with a clear set of priorities, and the political will to make organizational changes to ensure that the key objective of reduced waiting times at all levels was met. There is still work to do in order to make the reforms sustainable; there is insufficient intermediary care for patients who can be discharged from hospital but are still not ready to stay on their own. Also, there is always the risk with target-oriented reforms that the exercise becomes one of 'ticking boxes' rather than really improving services. But things are going sufficiently well for now that Northern Ireland's richer neighbour to the south, the Republic of Ireland, is studying the example of Parkland Memorial Hospital as a way of ironing out wrinkles in the Republic's health care system.[106]

Workflow Interdependence among Departments

Another characteristic of technology that influences structure is called interdependence. **Interdependence** means the extent to which departments depend on each other for resources or materials to accomplish their tasks. Low interdependence means that departments can do their work with minimal interaction, consultation or exchange of materials with other departments. High interdependence requires the continuous exchange of resources between departments.

Types

James Thompson defined three types of interdependence that influence organization structure.[107] These interdependencies are illustrated in Exhibit 7.12 and are discussed below.

EXHIBIT 7.12 Thompson's Classification of Interdependence and Management Implications

Form of Interdependence	Demands on Horizontal Communication, Decision Making	Type of Coordination Required	Priority for Locating Units Close Together
Pooled (bank) Clients	Low communication	Standardization, rules, procedures Divisional structure	Low
Sequential (assembly line) Client	Medium communication	Plans, schedules, feedback Task forces	Medium
Reciprocal (hospital) Client	High communication	Mutual adjustment, cross-departmental meetings, teamwork Horizontal structure	High

Pooled **Pooled interdependence** is the most basic form of interdependence among departments. In this form, work does not flow between units. Each department is part of the organization and contributes to the common good of the organization, but works independently. Chain restaurants or banks branches are typically examples of pooled interdependence. An outlet in Frankfurt need not interact with an outlet in Munich. Pooled interdependence may be associated with relationships within a *divisional structure*, defined in Chapter 3. Divisions or branches share financial resources from a common pool, and the performance of each division contributes to the fate of the overall organization.

Thompson proposed that pooled interdependence would exist in firms with what he called a mediating technology. A **mediating technology** provides products or services that mediate or link clients and, in so doing, allows each department to work independently. Banks, brokerage firms and real estate offices all mediate between buyers and sellers, but the offices work independently within the organization.

The management implications associated with pooled interdependence are quite simple. Thompson argued that managers should use rules and procedures to standardize activities across departments. If each department is required to use the same procedures and financial statements, the outcomes of all departments can be measured and pooled. Very little day-to-day coordination is required among units.

Sequential When interdependence is of serial form, with parts produced in one department becoming inputs to another department, it is called **sequential interdependence**. The effectiveness of the next department in the chain depends upon the effective performance of the preceding department. This is a higher level

As an organization manager, keep these guidelines in mind:

Evaluate the interdependencies among organizational departments. Use the general rule that, as interdependencies increase, mechanisms for coordination must also increase. Consider a divisional structure for pooled interdependence. For sequential interdependence, use task forces and integrators for greater horizontal coordination. At the highest level of interdependence (reciprocal interdependence), a horizontal structure may be appropriate.

of interdependence than pooled interdependence, because departments exchange resources and depend on others to undertake their tasks. Sequential interdependence creates a greater need for horizontal mechanisms such as integrators or task forces.

Sequential interdependence occurs in what Thompson called **long-linked technology**, which 'refers to the combination in one organization of successive stages of production; each stage of production uses as its inputs the production of the preceding stage and produces inputs for the following stage'.[108] An example of sequential interdependence comes from the shipbuilding industry. Until recently, ship designers made patterns and moulds out of paper and plywood, which were passed on to assembly. Mistakes in measurements or pattern mix-ups, though, often caused errors in the cutting and assembly process, leading to delays and increased costs. Italian-American ship architect Filippo Cali addressed this shortcoming by creating a complex software program that serves as a bridge between design and assembly. The software eliminates the need for paper and plywood moulds by putting that crucial part of the design process inside a computer program.[109] Another example of sequential interdependence would be an automobile assembly line, which must have all the parts it needs, such as engines, steering mechanisms and tyres, to keep production rolling.

The management requirements for sequential interdependence are more demanding than those for pooled interdependence. Coordination among the linked plants or departments is required. This interdependence implies a flow of materials, so extensive planning and scheduling to ensure this flow are generally necessary. Some day-to-day communication is also needed to handle unexpected problems and exceptions as they arise.

Reciprocal The highest level of interdependence is **reciprocal interdependence**. This exists when the output of operation A is the input to operation B, and the output of operation B is the input back again to operation A. The outputs of departments influence those departments in reciprocal fashion. Here there is a two-way flow of materials.

Reciprocal interdependence tends to occur in organizations with what Thompson called **intensive technologies**, which provide a variety of products or services in combination to a client. Hospitals are an example as they provide coordinated services to patients. A patient may move back and forth between X-ray, surgery and physical therapy. A firm developing new products is another example. Intense coordination occurs between design, engineering, manufacturing and marketing in order to combine all their resources in a manner aimed to suit the requirement of the customer.

Because reciprocal interdependence requires that departments work together intimately and be closely coordinated, a horizontal structure may be appropriate. This structure allows frequent horizontal communication and mutual adjustment. Managers from several departments are likely to be jointly involved in face-to-face coordination, teamwork and decision making. Reciprocal interdependence is the most complex form of interdependence and the most demanding to organize effectively.

Structural Priority

As indicated in Exhibit 7.12, because decision making, communication and coordination problems are greatest for reciprocal interdependence, there is a case for its receiving first priority in organization structure. New product development is one area of reciprocal interdependence that is of growing concern to managers as companies face increasing pressure to get new products to market fast. Many firms are revamping the design-manufacturing relationship by closely integrating technologies discussed earlier in this chapter.[110] A horizontal structure, with linked sets of teams working on core processes, can provide the close coordination needed to support reciprocal interdependence. If reciprocally interdependent units are not located close together, coordinating mechanisms can be introduced, such as daily meetings between departments or the use of an intranet to facilitate communication.

Wherever possible and conditional upon their cost, communication tends to improve where its channels are short and simple. For example, the European Airbus company is a joint project of four countries: France, Germany, United Kingdom and Spain. Production of a new plan requires a complex series of negotiations between these countries about who is going to get what piece of the project, followed by the manufacture of the plane as a 'jigsaw' between the four manufacturing bases. Inevitably, the whole process leads to delays and inefficiencies, as the airline industry has found out in the production of the A380, the world's largest superjumbo, with delivery dates repeatedly postponed, and the company facing huge losses because of cost overruns. As a result, Airbus has faced numerous customer cancellations,[111,112] as timeliness of delivery can be more important than the promise of superior product specifications.

Structural Implications

Most organizations experience various levels of interdependence, and structures emerge or are purposefully designed in response to these demands and other contingencies, as illustrated in Exhibit 7.13.[113] In a manufacturing firm, new product development entails reciprocal interdependence among the design, engineering, purchasing,

EXHIBIT 7.13 Primary Means to Achieve Coordination for Different Levels of Task Interdependence in a Manufacturing Firm

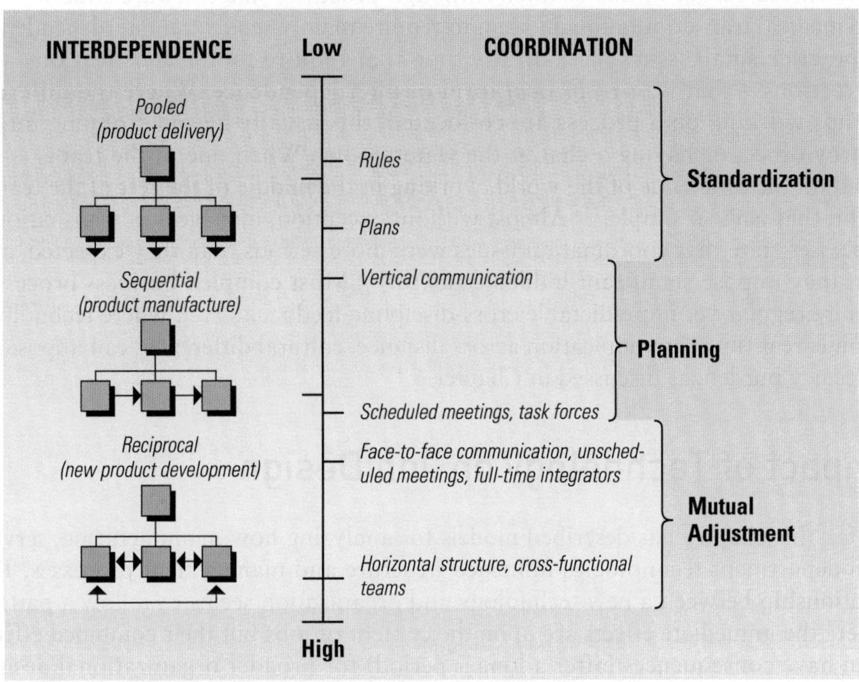

Source: Adapted from Andrew H. Van de Ven, Andre Delbecq, and Richard Koenig, 'Determinants of Communication Modes within Organizations,' *American Sociological Review* 41 (1976), 330.

manufacturing and sales departments. In response to this pattern of interdependence, a horizontal structure or cross-functional teams could be used to handle the back-and-forth flow of information and resources. Once a product is designed, its actual manufacture might then involve sequential interdependence, with a flow of goods from one department to another, such as among purchasing, inventory, production control, manufacturing and assembly. The actual ordering and delivery of products approximates more closely to pooled interdependence, with warehouses working independently. Customers could place an order with the nearest facility, which would not require coordination among warehouses, except in unusual cases such as a stock outage.

COUNTERPOINT 7.4

While this design might be most consistent with the theory propounded earlier in this chapter, many other 'practical' considerations may militate against, or compromise, its application. For example, an established top-down culture of the organization may impede the development of horizontal functional teams. Even where such teams are introduced, decisions may be referred up the hierarchy. **Discuss**

Various new technologies can help permit departmental interdependence even where business processes are outsourced, even offshored across the world. Some aspects of international business processes can speed up interdepartmental communication. For example, due to time differences, software companies can send a task to programmers in Bangalore, India, to be worked on overnight, so that it can be plugged into the bigger project in Europe the next morning.[114] Medical notes and test data can be sent across the world electronically and analyzed in time to be read by a medical consultant before the next patient examination the following day.[115] In practice, however, the number of activities that can be geographically and culturally disconnected is limited by the demands of organizational interdependence, as discussed earlier in this chapter. Although processes like software code writing and medical transcription might seem to require mainly *sequential* interdependence, in practice small issues arise all the time that require minor clarifications and corrections – that is, a *reciprocal* form of interdependence. Where the different groups working on a process are co-located, this usually means dropping into a nearby office, or having a chat at the water cooler. When one of the teams is located on the other side of the world, working in the middle of the rest of the team's night, that isn't so simple.[116] Almost without exception, managers of transnational processes state that coordination issues were more serious than they expected, and that they impose significant hidden costs.[117,118] Most complex business processes require regular yet unpredictable cross-discipline feedback. Even where technology permits real-time communication across distance, cultural differences can impose an efficiency burden, as discussed in Chapter 6.[119]

Impact of Technology on Job Design

So far, this chapter has described models for analyzing how manufacturing, service and department technologies influence structure and management processes. The relationship between a new technology and organization seems to follow a pattern where the immediate effects are upon the content of jobs but their combined effects then have consequences (after a longer period) for broader organizational design. The concepts of job design and sociotechnical systems most directly illuminate the impact of technology on employees.

Job Design

Job design includes the assignment of goals and tasks to be accomplished by employees. Managers may consciously change job design to improve productivity, product or service quality or worker motivation. For example, when workers are involved in performing tasks assessed to be boringly repetitive, managers may introduce **job rotation**, which means moving employees from job to job to give them a greater variety of tasks. However, managers may also unintentionally influence job design through the introduction of new technologies, which can change how jobs are done and the very nature of jobs.[120]

A common theme of new technologies in the workplace is that they in some way substitute machinery for human labour. Automated teller machines (ATMs) have replaced thousands of human bank tellers, for example. In addition to replacing human workers, technology may have several different effects on the jobs that remain. Research has indicated that mass-production technologies tend to result in **job simplification**, which means that the variety and difficulty of tasks performed by a single person are reduced, with a consequent increase in boredom and potential demotivation. More advanced technology, on the other hand, may increase levels of responsibility, recognition and opportunities for growth and development. These technologies create a greater need for employee training and education because higher-level skills and greater competence are required to master the new tasks. For example, ATMs took most of the routine tasks (deposits and withdrawals) away from bank tellers, freeing them up to take on less routine tasks that require higher-level skills and greater customer interaction. However, the overall number of jobs in the banking industry declined as a result of automation.[121,122]

As an organization manager, keep these guidelines in mind:

Be aware that the introduction of a new technology has significant impact on job design. Consider using the sociotechnical systems approach to balance the needs of workers with the requirements of the new technological system.

See online COUNTERPOINT 7.13

See online COUNTERPOINT 7.14

Studies of flexible manufacturing found that it is accompanied by: more opportunities for intellectual mastery and enhanced cognitive skills for workers; more worker responsibility for results; and greater interdependence among workers, enabling more social interaction and the development of teamwork and coordination skills.[123] Such developments are characterized as forms of **job enrichment**. Flexible manufacturing technology may also contribute to **job enlargement**, which is an expansion of the number of different tasks performed by an employee which include those that require additional skill sets.

See online COUNTERPOINT 7.15

With advanced technology, workers have to keep learning new skills where technology is changing so rapidly. Advances in *information technology*, to be discussed in detail in the next chapter, are having a significant effect on jobs in the service industry, including workplaces such as medical clinics, law firms, financial planners and accountants and libraries. Workers may find that their jobs changing repeatedly with the introduction of new software programs, increased use of the Internet, and other advances in information technology.

Sociotechnical Systems

The **sociotechnical systems approach** recognizes the interaction of technical and human elements in effective job design. The *socio* element of the approach refers to the people and groups that work in organizations and how work is organized and coordinated. The *technical* element refers to the materials, tools, machines and processes used to transform organizational inputs into outputs.

Exhibit 7.14 illustrates the three primary components of the sociotechnical systems model.[124] The *social system* includes all human elements – such as individual and team behaviour, organizational culture, management practices and degree of communication openness – that can influence the performance of work. The *technical system* refers to the type of production technology, the level of interdependence,

EXHIBIT 7.14 Sociotechnical Systems Model

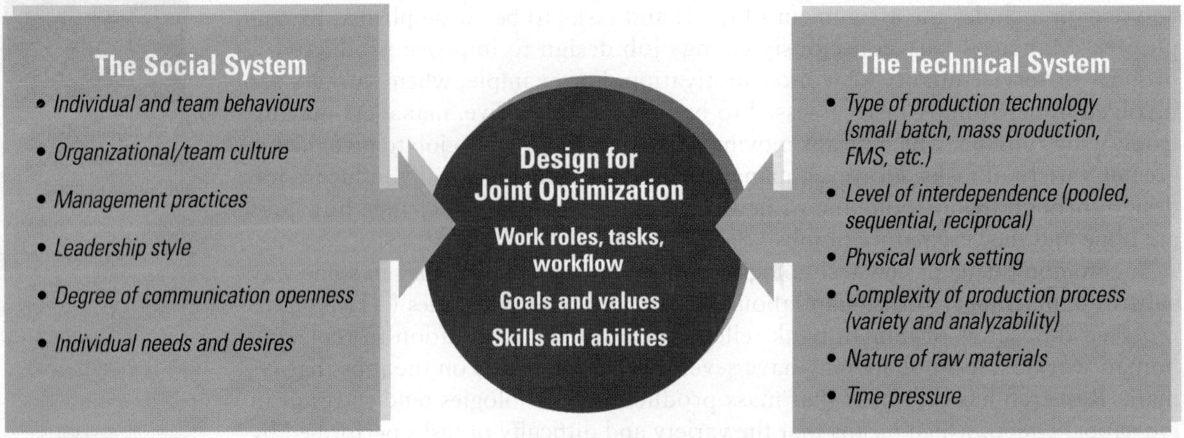

Source: Sources: Based on T. Cummings, 'Self-Regulating Work Groups: A Socio-Technical Synthesis,' *Academy of Management Review* 3 (1978), 625–634; Don Hellriegel, John W. Slocum, and Richard W. Woodman, *Organizational Behavior*, 8th ed. (Cincinnati, Ohio: South-Western, 1998), 492; and Gregory B. Northcraft and Margaret A. Neale, *Organizational Behavior: A Management Challenge*, 2nd ed. (Fort Worth, Tex.: The Dryden Press, 1994), 551.

the complexity of tasks and so forth. The goal of the sociotechnical systems approach is to design the organization for **joint optimization** where the best fit between the social and technical elements of systems is achieved. Conversely, there is a concern to avoid designs that are responsive to the human element but neglect the technical systems, or which concentrate on optimizing the technical element without regard for how human beings will use it. The sociotechnical systems approach attempts to find a sustainable balance between the capacities of employees and the technical requirements of the organization's production system.[125]

COUNTERPOINT 7.5

When expressed in this way, it is evident that 'the technical requirements of the production system' are often given priority. For example, it is decided that competitive survival depends upon changing those requirement by introducing new technical elements. Having made this decision, it is then decided how best to train and organize employees to operate the new technology. An alternative approach would be to start with the capabilities of the employees and assess which technical elements would be provide the best fit so as to maximize productive capability. **Discuss**

One example comes from a museum that installed a closed-circuit TV system. Rather than having several guards patrolling the museum and grounds, the television could easily be monitored by a single guard. Although the technology saved money because only one guard was needed per shift, it led to unexpected performance problems. Guards had previously enjoyed the social interaction provided by patrolling; monitoring a closed-circuit television led to alienation and boredom. When a government agency did an 18-month test of the system, only 5 per cent of several thousand experimental covert intrusions were detected by the guard.[126] The system was ineffective because inadequate account was taken of how human beings would experience and use the new technology. Another study of paper manufacturers found that organizations that put too much faith in machines and technology and pay little attention to the appropriate management of people do not achieve advances in productivity and flexibility.[127]

Sociotechnical principles evolved from the work of the Tavistock Institute, a research organization in Britain, during the 1950s and 1960s.[128] Examples of organizational change using sociotechnical systems principles have occurred in numerous organizations, including Volvo, Procter & Gamble and Switzerland's ABB (Asea Brown Boveri.[129,130] Although there have been failures in some of these innovations, the joint optimization of changes in technology and structure to meet the needs of people as well as efficiency has often improved performance, safety, quality, absenteeism and turnover. As would be expected, in many cases work design did not comply with the optimal application of technical and scientific principles, but worker involvement and commitment more than made up for technical imperfection. Such research illustrates that new technologies do not necessarily have a negative impact on the quality of working life It is sometimes possible to (re)design the sociotechnical system in a way that makes work more satisfying even when it is more demanding in terms of the use of higher-level mental and social skills. Where this possibility is realized, the involvement and commitment of employees may be increased in ways that are valued by both the employee and the organization.

COUNTERPOINT 7.6

Advocates of sociotechnical systems would doubtless claim that the failures are attributable to poor application of the theory. This of course is a standard defence for people whose theories fail to take account of the complex and dynamic field of their application. **Discuss**

Summary and Interpretation

This chapter reviewed several frameworks and key research findings on the topic of technology. The potential importance of technology as a factor in organizational structure was researched during the 1960s. Since then, a flurry of scholarly activity has been undertaken to understand more precisely the relationship of technology to other characteristics of organizations.

Five ideas in the technology literature stand out. The first is Woodward's research into manufacturing technology. Woodward went into organizations and collected practical data on technology characteristics, organization structure and management systems. She found clear relationships between technology and structure in the highest performing organizations that suggest how competitive advantage may be achieved by co-aligning strategy with an appropriate fit between structure and technology.

The second important idea is that there are some key differences between service and manufacturing technologies. Service technologies are characterized by intangible outcomes and direct client involvement in the production process. Service firms tend to have the fixed, machine-based technologies that appear in manufacturing organizations although some do approximate closely to their levels of standardization; hence, organization design often differs as well.

The third significant idea is Perrow's framework applied to department technologies. Understanding the variety and analyzability of a technology gives pointers to how the elements of management style, structure and process might be developed and combined to attain the most effective outcome. Routine technologies are characterized by mechanistic structure and nonroutine technologies by organic structure. Applying the wrong management system to a department increases the risk of dissatisfaction and reduced efficiency.

The fourth important idea is interdependence among departments. The extent to which departments depend on each other for materials, information or other resources affects the amount of coordination required between them. Greater interdependence tends to increase the demands on the organization for coordination. To address these demands, design must accommodate appropriate forms of communication and coordination across departments. The trend towards business process outsourcing, including offshoring, presents challenges in maintaining interdependence across distance, that can be partially, but not fully, handled through new information and communication technologies.

The fifth important idea is that new flexible manufacturing systems are having a significant impact upon organization design. Where technologies replace routine jobs without job losses, give employees more autonomy who want more challenges and/or responsibility, and encourage teamwork when this is not experienced as oppressive, it is probable that the new systems will be highly effective in increasing flexibility and improved response to customer demands. At the same time, there can be significant job losses, particularly at the lower end of the labour market in the developed countries. Where the social conditions for introducing new technologies are less than positive with regard to job losses, etc., interest in greater responsibility, etc., then their impact on productivity will be disappointing In this respect, sociotechnical systems theory, which attempts to design the technical and human aspects of an organization to fit one another, is highly relevant as advances in technology alter the nature of jobs and social interaction in today's companies.

KEY CONCEPTS

analyzability
continuous process production
core technology
craft technologies
engineering technologies
flexible manufacturing systems
intensive technologies
interdependence
job design
job enlargement
job enrichment
job rotation
job simplification
joint optimization
large-batch production
lean manufacturing
long-linked technology
mass customization
mediating technology
non-core technology
nonroutine technologies
pooled interdependence
reciprocal interdependence
routine technologies
sequential interdependence
service technology
small-batch production
sociotechnical systems approach
technical complexity
technology
variety

Discussion Questions

1 Where would your university or college department be located on Perrow's technology framework? Look for the underlying variety and analyzability characteristics when making your assessment. Would a department devoted exclusively to teaching be put in a different quadrant from a department devoted exclusively to research?

2 Explain Thompson's levels of interdependence. Identify an example of each level of interdependence in the university or college setting. What kinds of coordination mechanisms should an administration develop to handle each level of interdependence?

3 Describe Woodward's classification of organizational technologies. Explain why each of the three technology groups is related differently to organization structure and management processes.

4 What relationships did Woodward discover between supervisor span of control and technological complexity?

5 How do flexible manufacturing and lean manufacturing differ from other manufacturing technologies? Why are these new approaches needed in today's environment?

6 What is a service technology? Are different types of service technologies likely to be associated with different structures? Explain.

7 Mass customization of products has become a common approach in manufacturing organizations. Discuss ways in which mass customization can be applied to service firms as well.

8 In what primary ways does the design of service firms typically differ from that of product firms? Why?

9 A top executive claimed that top-level management is a craft technology because the work contains intangibles, such as handling personnel, interpreting the environment and coping with unusual situations that have to be learned through experience. If this is true, is it appropriate to teach management in a business school? Does teaching management from a textbook assume that the manager's job is analyzable, and hence that formal training rather than experience is most important?

10 In which quadrant of Perrow's framework would a mass-production technology be placed? Where would small-batch and continuous process technologies be placed? Why? Would Perrow's framework lead to the same recommendation about organic versus mechanistic structures that Woodward made?

11 To what extent does the development of new technologies simplify and routinize the jobs of employees? How can new technology lead to job enlargement? Discuss.

12 Describe the sociotechnical systems model. Why might some managers oppose a sociotechnical systems approach?

Chapter 7 Workbook Bistro Technology

You will be analyzing the technology used in three different restaurants – McDonald's, a popular national chain of your choice, and a typical local non-chain restaurant. Your instructor will tell you whether to do this assignment as individuals or in a group.

You must visit all three restaurants and infer how the work is done, according to the following criteria. You are not allowed to interview any employees, but instead you will be an observer. Take lots of notes when you are there.

Questions

1 Is the technology used the best one for each restaurant, considering its goals and environment?

2 From the preceding data, determine if the structure and other characteristics fit the technology.

3 If you were part of a consulting team assigned to improve the operations of each organization, what recommendations would you make?

Adapted loosely by Dorothy Marcic from 'Hamburger Technology', in Douglas T. Hall et al., *Experiences in Management and Organizational Behavior*, 2nd ed. (New York: Wiley, 1982), 244–247, as well as 'Behavior, Technology and Work Design' in A. B. Shani and James B. Lau, *Behavior in Organizations* (Chicago: Irwin, 1996), M16–23 to M16–26.

CASE FOR ANALYSIS

Acetate Department

By David L. Hampton, Charles E. Summer & Ross A. Webster

The acetate department's product consisted of about twenty different kinds of viscous liquid acetate used by another department to manufacture transparent film to be left clear or coated with photographic emulsion or iron oxide.

Before the change: The department was located in an old four-story building as in Exhibit 7.15. The workflow was as follows:

1 Twenty kinds of powder arrived daily in 50-pound paper bags. In addition, storage tanks of liquid would be filled weekly from tank trucks.
2 Two or three acetate helpers would jointly unload pallets of bags into the storage area using a lift truck.
3 Several times during a shift, the helpers would bring the bagged material up in the elevator to the third floor, where it would be temporarily stored along the walls.
4 Mixing batches was under the direction of the group leader and was rather like baking a cake. Following a prescribed formula, the group leader, mixers and helpers operated valves to feed in the proper solvent and manually dump in the proper weight and mixture of solid material. The glob would be mixed by giant eggbeaters and heated according to the recipe.
5 When the batch was completed, it was pumped to a finished-product storage tank.
6 After completing each batch, the crew would thoroughly clean the work area of dust and empty bags, because cleanliness was extremely important to the finished product.

To accomplish this work, the department was structured as in Exhibit 7.16.

The helpers were usually young men 18 to 25 years of age; the mixers, 25 to 40; and the group leaders and foremen, 40 to 60. Foremen were on salary; group leaders, mixers and helpers were on hourly pay.

To produce 20 million pounds of product per year, the department operated 24 hours a day, 7 days a week. Four crews rotated shifts: for example, shift foreman A and his two group leaders and crews would work two weeks on the day shift (8:00 A.M. to 4:00 P.M.), then 2 weeks on the evening shift (4:00 P.M. to midnight), then two weeks on the night shift (midnight to 8:00 A.M.). There were 2 days off between shift changes.

EXHIBIT 7.15 Elevation View of Acetate Department before Change

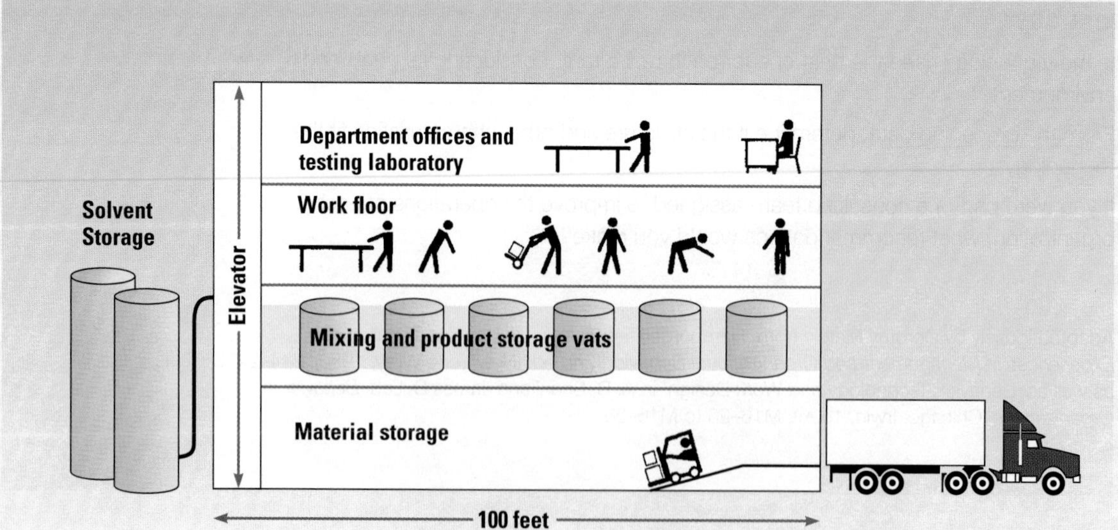

From 'Redesigning the Acetate Department', by David L. Hampton, Charles E. Summer, and Ross A. Webber, *Organizational Behavior and the Practice of Management* (Glenview, Ill.: Scott Foresman and Co., 1982), 751–755. Used with permission.

During a typical shift, a group leader and his crew would complete two or three batches. A batch would frequently be started on one shift and completed by the next shift crew. There was slightly less work on the evening and night shifts because no deliveries were made, but these crews engaged in a little more cleaning. The shift foreman would give instructions to the two group leaders at the beginning of each shift as to the status of batches in process, batches to be mixed, what deliveries were expected, and what cleaning was to be done. Periodically throughout the shift, the foreman would collect samples in small bottles, which he would leave at the laboratory technicians' desk for testing.

The management and office staff (department head, staff engineer, lab technician and department clerk) only worked on the day shift, although if an emergency arose on the other shifts, the foreman might call.

All in all, the department was a pleasant place in which to work. The work floor was a little warm, but well lit, quiet and clean. Substantial banter and horseplay occurred when the crew wasn't actually loading batches, particularly on the evening and night shifts. The men had a dartboard in the work area and competition was fierce and loud. Frequently a crew would go bowling right after work, even at 1:00 A.M., because the community's alleys were open 24 hours a day. Department turnover and absenteeism were low. Most employees spent their entire career with the company, many in one department. The corporation was large, paternalistic and well paying and offered attractive fringe benefits including large, virtually automatic bonuses for all. Then came the change.

The new system: To improve productivity, the acetate department was completely redesigned; the technology changed from batches to continuous processing. The basic building was retained but substantially modified as in Exhibit 7.17. The modified workflow is as follows:

1. Most solid raw materials are delivered via trucks in large aluminum bins holding 500 pounds.
2. One handler (formerly helper) is on duty at all times on the first floor to receive raw materials and to dump the bins into the semiautomatic screw feeder.
3. The head operator (former group leader) directs the mixing operations from his control panel on the fourth floor located along one wall across from the department offices. The mixing is virtually an automatic operation once the solid material has been sent up the screw feed; a tape program opens and closes the necessary valves to add solvent, heat, mix and so on. Sitting at a table before his panel, the head operator monitors the process to see that everything is operating within specified temperatures and pressures.

This technical change allowed the department to greatly reduce its workforce. The new structure is illustrated in Exhibit 7.18. One new position was

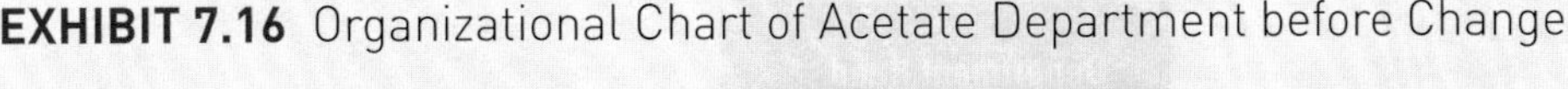

EXHIBIT 7.16 Organizational Chart of Acetate Department before Change

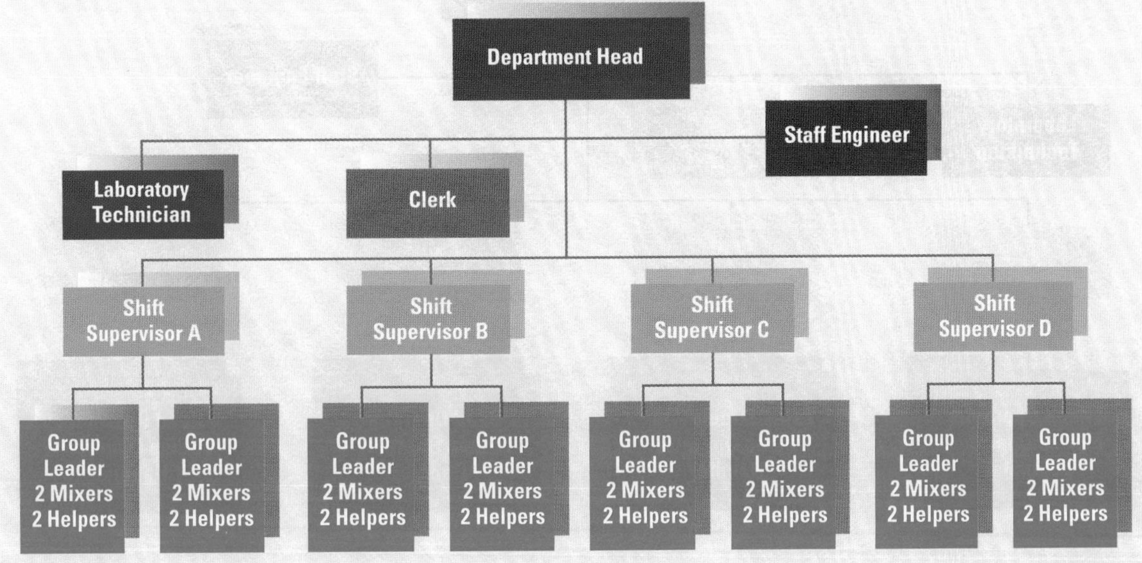

created, that of a pump operator who is located in a small, separate shack about 300 feet from the main building. He operates the pumps and valves that move the finished product among various storage tanks.

Under the new system, production capacity was increased to 25 million pounds per year. All remaining employees received a 15 per cent increase in pay. Former personnel not retained in the acetate department were transferred to other departments in the company. No one was dismissed.

Unfortunately, actual output has lagged well below capacity in the several months since the construction work and technical training were completed. Actual production is virtually identical with that under the old technology. Absenteeism has increased markedly, and several judgemental errors by operators have resulted in substantial losses.

EXHIBIT 7.17 Elevation View of Acetate Department after Change

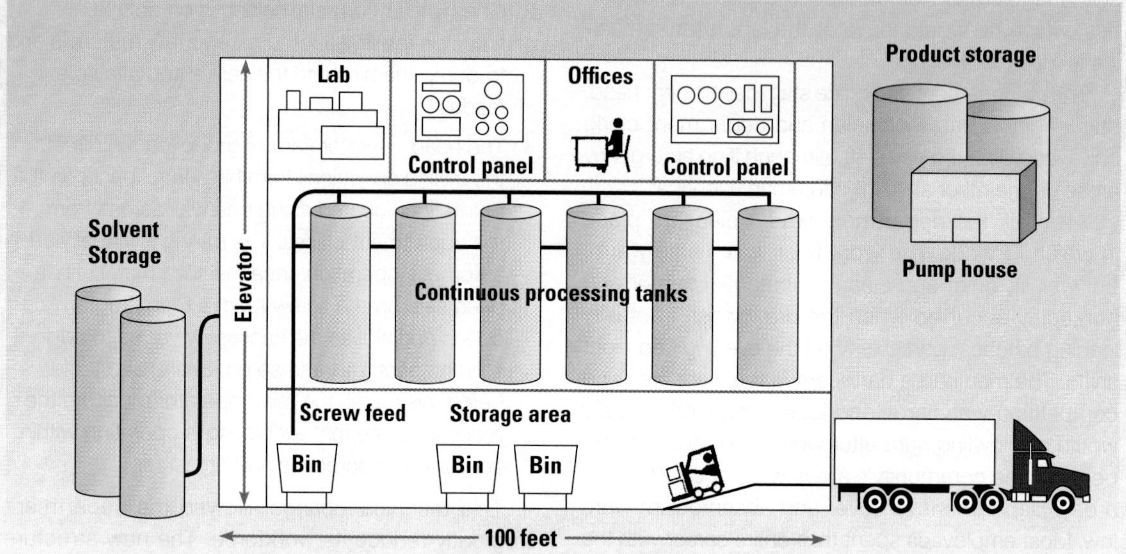

EXHIBIT 7.18 Organizational Chart of Acetate Department after Change

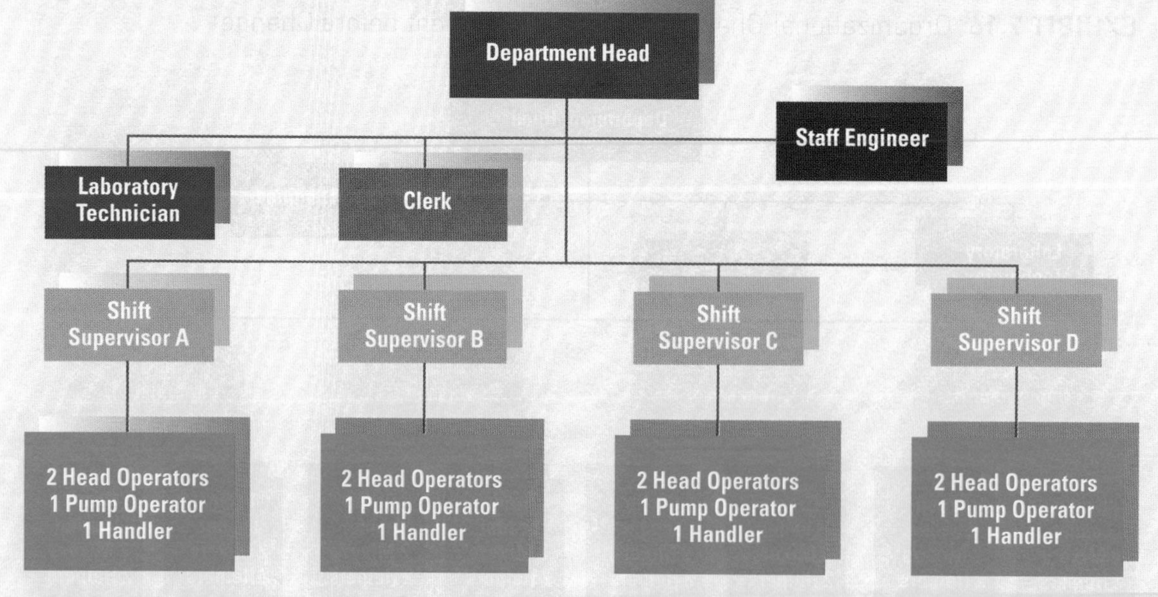

Case Questions:

1 What were the objectives of the production reorganization at Acetate?

2 Why do you think the objectives of the reorganization were not realized, even though no employees lost their jobs, and salaries were increased?

3 Would the company have been better served leaving the production system as it was?

4 Imagine you were hired as an external management consultant to come up with a plan to address the problems at Acetate. How would you go about developing a strategy, and what would that strategy involve?

Notes

1. http://www.conti-online.com/generator/www/us/en/continental/transport/themes/about_continental/conti_ag_history/ag_history_7_en.html accessed on August 25, 2008.
2. Paul Erker (1996) *Competition and Growth: A Contemporary History of the Continental AG*, Dusseldorf, ECON.
3. 'Toyo Ends Deal With Conti', *European Rubber Journal*, June 10, 2002.
4. *New York Times*, 'Continental A.G. in $1.93 Billion Deal', July 28, 1998.
5. *FD (Fair Disclosure) Wire*, 'Continental AG to Acquire Siemens VDO Automotive AG', July 25, 2007.
6. *FD (Fair Disclosure) Wire*, 'Q2 2008 Continental AG Earnings Conference Call', July 31, 2008.
7. *Western Europe Automotive Insights*, 'Continental And Schaeffler Reach A Deal', September 1, 2008.
8. Christiaan Hetzner, 'Continental bidder unlikely to play nice', *International Herald Tribune*, July 28, 2008.
9. *BusinessWeek*, '2005 Stars of Europe – Managers: Manfred Wennemer' May 30, 2005.
10. 'Shoe giants have one foot in India', *Hindustan Times*, February 25, 2007.
11. David Williamson, 'The winners and losers of outsourcing and offshoring', *Western Mail*, September 8, 2006.
12. 'Amex jobs move to other side of world', *Star Tribune* (Minneapolis, MN), May 20, 2002
13. Blonigen, Bruce A. and Wang, Miao (2004), Inappropriate Pooling of Wealthy and Poor Countries in Empirical FDI Studies, NBER Working Paper W10378; Kobrin, S., (1999) 'Development after Industrialisation', in Hood, N., and Young, S., (eds) *The Globalization of Multinational Enterprise Activity and Economic Development,* Basingstoke, Macmillan, 133–154; Gary Gereffi and Olga Memedovic (2003), *The Global Apparel Value Chain: What Prospects for Upgrading by Developing Countries,* Vienna, UNIDO.
14. Charles Perrow, 'A Framework for the Comparative Analysis of Organizations', *American Sociological Review* 32 (1967), 194–208; and R. J. Schonberger, *World Class Manufacturing: The Next Decade* (New York: The Free Press, 1996).
15. Linda Argote, 'Input Uncertainty and Organizational Coordination in Hospital Emergency Units', *Administrative Science Quarterly* 27 (1982), 420–434; Charles Perrow, *Organizational Analysis: A Sociological Approach* (Belmont, Calif.: Wadsworth, 1970); and William Rushing, 'Hardness of Material as Related to the Division of Labour in Manufacturing Industries', *Administrative Science Quarterly* 13 (1968), 229–245.
16. Lawrence B. Mohr, 'Organizational Technology and Organization Structure', *Administrative Science Quarterly* 16 (1971), 444–459; and David Hickson, Derek Pugh, and Diana Pheysey, 'Operations Technology and Organization Structure: An Empirical Reappraisal', *Administrative Science Quarterly* 14 (1969), 378–397.
17. Joan Woodward, *Industrial Organization: Theory and Practice* (London: Oxford University Press, 1965); and Joan Woodward, *Management and Technology* (London: Her Majesty's Stationery Office, 1958).
18. Hickson, Pugh and Pheysey, 'Operations Technology and Organization Structure'; and James D. Thompson, *Organizations in Action* (New York: McGraw-Hill, 1967).
19. Edward Harvey, 'Technology and the Structure of Organizations', *American Sociological Review* 33 (1968), 241–259.
20. Wanda J. Orlikowski, 'The Duality of Technology: Rethinking the Concept of Technology in Organizations', *Organization Science* 3 (1992), 398–427.
21. Based on Woodward, *Industrial Organization and Management and Technology.*
22. FD (Fair Disclosure) Wire, 'Q3 2008 Rockwell Collins, Inc. Earnings Conference Call – Final', July 11, 2008
23. Philip Siekman, 'A Big Maker of Tiny Batches', *Fortune* (May 27, 2002), 152[A]–152[H].
24. Woodward, *Industrial Organization,* vi.
25. William L. Zwerman, *New Perspectives on Organizational Theory* (Westport, Conn.: Greenwood, 1970); and Harvey, 'Technology and the Structure of Organizations'.

26. Dean M. Schroeder, Steven W. Congden and C. Gopinath, 'Linking Competitive Strategy and Manufacturing Process Technology', *Journal of Management Studies* 32, no. 2 (March 1995), 163–189.
27. Steve Lohr, 'U.S. clears IBM sale to Lenovo', *The International Herald Tribune*, March 11, 2005.
28. Fernando F. Suarez, Michael A. Cusumano, and Charles H. Fine, "An Empirical Study of Flexibility in Manufacturing," *Sloan Management Review* (Fall 1995), 25–32.
29. Raymond F. Zammuto and Edward J. O'Connor, 'Gaining Advanced Manufacturing Technologies' Benefits: The Roles of Organization Design and Culture', *Academy of Management Review* 17, no. 4 (1992), 701–728; and Schroeder, Congden, and Gopinath, 'Linking Competitive Strategy and Manufacturing Process Technology.'
30. http://www.bedlampuzzles.com/default.asp accessed on August 26, 2008.
31. 'Toymaker hopes to boost 'UK' tag appeal', *Western Morning News*, 6 December 2007.
32. Tim Webb and Heather Stewart, 'Crunch Times: Why The Future Is Made In Britain: The Factory Floor', *The Observer*, 27 April 2008.
33. Rebecca Wright, France's Bollore Could Invest 30 mil. Euro in Pininfarina, *Global Insight Daily Analysis*, 6 June 2008; 'Italy Antitrust OKs Fiat Group Automobiles Buy of Itca', *ANSA – English Corporate News Service*, 9 May 2007; Tom Murphy, 'Insourcing', *Ward's Auto World*, 1 May 2003.
34. Reported in Grainger David, 'One Truck a Minute,' *Fortune* (April 5, 2004), 252–258.
35. Data calculated dynamically through http://earthtrends.wri.org/ on August 26, 2008.
36. '3 Taiwan Computer Makers in BTO Operations', *Taiwan Business News*, 2 December 1997.
37. John S. McClenahen, 'Bearing Necessitites', *Industry Week* (October 2004), 63ff.
38. 'IBS implements Plant Maintenance Management System at Mondi Business Paper - Syktyvkarskii LPK' *SKRIN Market & Corporate News*, September 14 2006; http://www.ibs-company.com/content/eng/267/2678-article.asp?archive=1, accessed on August 27, 2008.
39. Jack R. Meredith, 'The Strategic Advantages of the Factory of the Future', *California Management Review* 29 (Spring 1987), 27–41; Jack Meredith, 'The Strategic Advantages of the New Manufacturing Technologies for Small Firms', *Strategic Management Journal* 8 (1987), 249–258; and Althea Jones and Terry Webb, 'Introducing Computer Integrated Manufacturing,' *Journal of General Management* 12 (Summer 1987), 60–74.
40. Raymond F. Zammuto and Edward J. O'Connor, 'Gaining Advanced Manufacturing Technologies' Benefits: The Roles of Organization Design and Culture', *Academy of Management Review* 17 (1992), 701–728.
41. Manwiller, Ron, 'Ceramic imaging's digital revolution: digital ceramic printing provides mass customization and has opened a host of new market opportunities', *Ceramic Industry*,1 April 2008.
42. Paul S. Adler, 'Managing Flexible Automation', *California Management Review* (Spring 1988), 34–56.
43. Bela Gold, 'Computerization in Domestic and International Manufacturing'. *California Management Review* (Winter 1989), 129–143.
44. Graham Dudley and John Hassard, 'Design Issues in the Development of Computer Integrated Manufacturing (CIM)', *Journal of General Management* 16 (1990), 43–53.
45. Jeff Wise, 'Plane Dealer,' *FSB* (July–August 2004), 83–84.
46. 'Nobel Biocare Holding AG - SWOT Analysis', *Global Markets Direct Company Profiles*, 4 July 2008.
47. Ibid; and Tom Massung, 'Manufacturing Efficiency', *Microsoft Executive Circle* (Winter 2004), 28–29.
48. Brian Heymans, 'Leading the Lean Enterprise', *Industrial Management* (September–October 2002), 28–33; and Fara Warner, 'Think Lean,' *Fast Company* (February 2002), 40, 42.
49. Peter Strozniak, 'Toyota Alters Face of Production', *IndustryWeek* (August 13, 2001), 46–48.
50. Malcolm Wheatley, 'Lean beacon: German industrial giant pioneers Toyota-style initiative; SAP integration to follow', *Manufacturing Business Technology*, 1 February 2008.
51. B. Joseph Pine II, *Mass Customization: The New Frontier in Business Competition* (Boston: Harvard Business School Press, 1999).
52. Rebecca Duray (2002), 'Mass customization origins: mass or custom manufacturing?', *International Journal of Operations & Production Management*, 22, 314–328.
53. Laetitia Radder and Lynette Louw (1999), 'Mass customization and mass production', *The TQM Magazine*, 11, 35–40.
54. Hart, C. W. L. (1995), 'Mass customization: Conceptual underpinnings, opportunities and limits', *International Journal of Service Industry Management*, 6, 36–45.
55. Joseph B. Pine II (1999), *Mass Customization: The New Frontier in Business Competition*, Cambridge, Harvard Business Press. Cited on page 207.
56. 5 S refers to five Japanese words beginning with 's' that encapsulate the philosophy underpinning lean manufacturing: *seiri, seiton, seiso, seiketsu* and *shitsuke*, signifying order, cleanliness, purity and commitment.
57. TPM – Total Productive Maintenance.
58. 'Autoliv Manufacturing', powerpoint presentation accessed at http://www.besbai.com/OEMWordUpload/2005918162758574.pdf on August 27, 2008.
59. Abrahm Lustgarten, 'Elite Factories', *Fortune,* special section, 'Industrial Management and Technology' (September 6, 2004), 240[B]–240[L].
60. Barry Berman, 'Should Your Firm Adopt a Mass Customization Strategy?' *Business Horizons* (July–August 2002), 51–60.
61. Antone Gonsalves, 'Acer Beats Lenovo For The World's No. 3 Computer Maker Spot: Second-place Dell was the only company in the top five to suffer a decline', *InformationWeek*, June 5, 2007.
62. Erick Schonfeld, 'The Customized, Digitized, Have-It-Your-Way Economy', *Fortune* (September 28, 1998), 115–124.
63. http://www.arianedeco.fr/, accessed on August 27, 2008.
64. These and many other examples posted by Thomas Dusart on 'La Blog de la Mass Customization',

accessed at http://masscustomization.blogspot.com/ on August 27, 2008.

65. Yeh Fang-hsun, 'Building brands key to survival for creative industry', *Central News Agency – Taiwan*, June 20, 2008; 'Acer aims to overtake HP ahead of 2011 goal', The Toronto Star, April 15, 2009; 'Acer expects to grab 50% share of 2009 netbook market', *Digitimes*, November 3, 2008; Stan Shih, J.T. Wang and Arthur Yeung (2006), 'Building Global Competitiveness in a Turbulent Environment: Acer's Journey of Transformation' in William H. Mobley and Elizabeth Weldon, Advances in Global Leadership, Bradford, Emerald Group Publishing, 201–217.
66. Geoffrey Colvin, 'Co-Creation' Is Your Latest Invention', *The Washington Post*, 6 May 2008, D03.
67. Kevin O'Donnell, 'Where Do The Best Ideas Come From? The Unlikeliest Sources; Peers, Suppliers Can Spark Some Great Innovations For Marketers', *Advertising Age*, 14 July 2008.
68. Sven A. Carlsson, 'Enhancing Knowledge Acquisition through the use of ICT', *DSS2004 Conference Proceedings* (2004).
69. Marc Nohr, 'Who says that consumers know best?', *Marketing Direct*, 5 February 2008.
70. Joel D. Goldhar and David Lei, 'Variety Is Free: Manufacturing in the Twenty-First Century', *Academy of Management Executive* no. 4 (1995), 73–86.
71. Meredith, 'The Strategic Advantages of the Factory of the Future'.
72. Patricia L. Nemetz and Louis W. Fry, 'Flexible Manufacturing Organizations: Implementations for Strategy Formulation and Organization Design', *Academy of Management Review* 13 (1988), 627–638; Paul S. Adler, 'Managing Flexible Automation', *California Management Review* (Spring 1988), 34–56; Jeremy Main, 'Manufacturing the Right Way', *Fortune* (May 21, 1990), 54–64; and Frank M. Hull and Paul D. Collins, 'High-Technology Batch Production Systems: Woodward's Missing Type', *Academy of Management Journal* 30 (1987), 786–797.
73. Goldhar and Lei, 'Variety Is Free: Manufacturing in the Twenty-First Century'; P. Robert Duimering, Frank Safayeni and Lyn Purdy, 'Integrated Manufacturing: Redesign the Organization before Implementing Flexible Technology,' *Sloan Management Review* (Summer 1993), 47–56; Zammuto and O'Connor, 'Gaining Advanced Manufacturing Technologies' Benefits'.
74. Goldhar and Lei, 'Variety Is Free: Manufacturing in the Twenty-First Century'.
75. 'Manufacturing's Decline', *Johnson City Press* (July 17, 1999), 9; Ronald Henkoff, 'Service Is Everybody's Business', *Fortune* (June 27, 1994), 48–60; Ronald Henkoff, 'Finding, Training and Keeping the Best Service Workers', *Fortune* (October 3, 1994), 110–122.
76. Judith Banister (2005), 'Manufacturing employment in China', *Monthly Labor Review*, July, 11–29.
77. Antonello D'Agostino, Roberta Serafini and Melanie Ward-Warmedinger, 'Sectoral Explanations of Employment in Europe: The Role Of Services', *European Central Bank Working Paper Series* No. 625, May 2006.
78. Byron J. Finch and Richard L. Luebbe, *Operations Management: Competing in a Changing Environment* (Fort Worth, Tex.: The Dryden Press, 1995), 51.
79. David E. Bowen, Caren Siehl and Benjamin Schneider, 'A Framework for Analyzing Customer Service Orientations in Manufacturing', *Academy of Management Review* 14 (1989), 79–95; Peter K. Mills and Newton Margulies, 'Toward a Core Typology of Service Organizations', *Academy of Management Review* 5 (1980), 255–265; Peter K. Mills and Dennis J. Moberg, 'Perspectives on the Technology of Service Operations', *Academy of Management Review* 7 (1982), 467–478; and G. Lynn Shostack, 'Breaking Free from Product Marketing', *Journal of Marketing* (April 1977), 73–80.
80. Rick Fantasia (1995), 'Fast Food in France', *Theory and Society*, 24, 201–243.
81. 'First Tier Focus: Service seals the deal', *Metalworking Production*, 26 September 2006.
82. Ron Zemke, 'The Service Revolution: Who Won?' *Management Review* (March 1997), 10–15; and Wayne Wilhelm and Bill Rossello, 'The Care and Feeding of Customers', *Management Review* (March 1997), 19–23.
83. Ross Bentley, 'Data with destiny', *Caterer & Hotelkeeper*, 25 August 2005.
84. Schonfeld, 'The Customized, Digitized, Have-It-Your-Way Economy'.
85. Paul Migliorato, 'Toyota Retools Japan', *Business 2.0* (August 2004), 39–41.
86. Richard B. Chase and David A. Tansik, 'The Customer Contact Model for Organization Design', *Management Science* 29 (1983), 1037–1050.
87. Ibid.
88. David E. Bowen and Edward E. Lawler III, 'The Empowerment of Service Workers: What, Why, How and When', *Sloan Management Review* (Spring 1992), 31–39: Gregory B. Northcraft and Richard B. Chase, 'Managing Service Demand at the Point of Delivery', *Academy of Management Review* 10 (1985), 66–75; and Roger W. Schmenner, 'How Can Service Businesses Survive and Prosper?' *Sloan Management Review* 27 (Spring 1986), 21–32.
89. Scott Kirsner, 'Recipe for Reinvention', *Fast Company* (April 2002), 38–42.
90. 'Pret Deal Looks to be on the Table', *Daily Mail*, 21 February 2008.
91. Perrow, 'A Framework for Comparative Analysis' and *Organizational Analysis*.
92. Brian T. Pentland, 'Sequential Variety in Work Processes,' *Organization Science* 14, no. 5 (September–October 2003), 528–540.
93. Jim Morrison, 'Grand Tour. Making Music: The Craft of the Steinway Piano', *Spirit* (February 1997), 42–49, 100.
94. Stuart F. Brown, 'Biotech Gets Productive', *Fortune*, special section, 'Industrial Management and Technology' (January 20, 2003), 170[A]–170[H].

95. Michael Withey, Richard L. Daft and William C. Cooper, 'Measures of Perrow's Work Unit Technology: An Empirical Assessment and a New Scale', *Academy of Management Journal* 25 (1983), 45–63.
96. Christopher Gresov, 'Exploring Fit and Misfit with Multiple Contingencies', *Administrative Science Quarterly* 34 (1989), 431–453; and Dale L. Goodhue and Ronald L. Thompson, 'Task-Technology Fit and Individual Performance', *MIS Quarterly* (June 1995), 213–236.
97. Gresov, 'Exploring Fit and Misfit with Multiple Contingencies'; Charles A. Glisson, 'Dependence of Technological Routinization on Structural Variables in Human Service Organizations', *Administrative Science Quarterly* 23 (1978), 383–395; and Jerald Hage and Michael Aiken, 'Routine Technology, Social Structure and Organizational Goals,' *Administrative Science Quarterly* 14 (1969), 368–379.
98. Gresov, 'Exploring Fit and Misfit with Multiple Contingencies'; A. J. Grimes and S. M. Kline, 'The Technological Imperative: The Relative Impact of Task Unit, Modal Technology and Hierarchy on Structure', *Academy of Management Journal* 16 (1973), 583–597; Lawrence G. Hrebiniak, 'Job Technologies, Supervision and Work Group Structure', *Administrative Science Quarterly* 19 (1974), 395–410; and Jeffrey Pfeffer, *Organizational Design* (Arlington Heights, Ill.: AHM, 1978), Chapter 1.
99. Patrick E. Connor, *Organizations: Theory and Design* (Chicago: Science Research Associates, 1980); Richard L. Daft and Norman B. Macintosh, 'A Tentative Exploration into Amount and Equivocality of Information Processing in Organizational Work Units', *Administrative Science Quarterly* 26 (1981), 207–224.
100. Paul D. Collins and Frank Hull, 'Technology and Span of Control: Woodward Revisited', *Journal of Management Studies* 23 (1986), 143–164; Gerald D. Bell, 'The Influence of Technological Components of Work upon Management Control', *Academy of Management Journal* 8 (1965), 127–132; and Peter M. Blau and Richard A. Schoenherr, *The Structure of Organizations* (New York: Basic Books, 1971).
101. W. Alan Randolph, 'Matching Technology and the Design of Organization Units', *California Management Review* 22–23 (1980–81), 39–48; Daft and Macintosh, 'Tentative Exploration into Amount and Equivocality of Information Processing'; and Michael L. Tushman, 'Work Characteristics and Subunit Communication Structure: A Contingency Analysis', *Administrative Science Quarterly* 24 (1979), 82–98.
102. Andrew H. Van de Ven and Diane L. Ferry, *Measuring and Assessing Organizations* (New York: Wiley, 1980); and Randolph, 'Matching Technology and the Design of Organization Units'.
103. Richard L. Daft and Robert H. Lengel, 'Information Richness: A New Approach to Managerial Behavior and Organization Design', in Barry Staw and Larry L. Cummings, eds., *Research in Organizational Behaviour*, vol. 6 (Greenwich, Conn.: JAI Press, 1984), 191–233; Richard L. Daft and Norman B. Macintosh, 'A New Approach into Design and Use of Management Information', *California Management Review* 21 (1978), 82–92; Daft and Macintosh, 'A Tentative Exploration into Amount and Equivocality of Information Processing'; W. Alan Randolph, 'Organizational Technology and the Media and Purpose Dimensions of Organizational Communication', *Journal of Business Research* 6 (1978), 237–259; Linda Argote, 'Input Uncertainty and Organizational Coordination in Hospital Emergency Units', *Administrative Science Quarterly* 27 (1982), 420–434; and Andrew H. Van de Ven and Andre Delbecq, 'A Task Contingent Model of Work Unit Structure', *Administrative Science Quarterly* 19 (1974), 183–197.
104. Peggy Leatt and Rodney Schneck, 'Criteria for Grouping Nursing Subunits in Hospitals', *Academy of Management Journal* 27 (1984), 150–165; and Robert T. Keller, 'Technology-Information Processing', *Academy of Management Journal* 37, no. 1 (1994), 167–179.
105. Gresov, 'Exploring Fit and Misfit with Multiple Contingencies'; Michael L. Tushman, 'Technological Communication in R&D Laboratories: The Impact of Project Work Characteristics,' *Academy of Management Journal* 21 (1978), 624–645; and Robert T. Keller, 'Technology-Information Processing Fit and the Performance of R&D Project Groups: A Test of Contingency Theory', *Academy of Management Journal* 37, no. 1 (1994), 167–179.
106. 'Healthy advice from the North', *Sunday Business Post*, 27 April 2008.
107. James Thompson, *Organizations in Action* (New York: McGraw-Hill, 1967).
108. Ibid., 40.
109. Gene Bylinsky, 'Shipmaking Gets Modern', *Fortune*, special section, 'Industrial Management and Technology' (January 20, 2003), 170[K]–170[L].
110. Paul S. Adler, 'Interdepartmental Interdependence and Coordination: The Case of the Design/Manufacturing Interface', *Organization Science* 6, no. 2 (March–April 1995), 147–167.
111. Angela Jameson, 'Airbus A380 delay wipes €5bn off the value of EADS', *The Times,* June 15, 2006.
112. Mel Duvall, PLM: Boeing's Dream, Airbus' Nightmare; Product life-cycle management is helping to get Boeing's 787 off the ground, but is a key factor in Airbus' A380 delays, *CIO Insight*, 5 February 2007.
113. Christopher Gresov, 'Effects of Dependence and Tasks on Unit Design and Efficiency', *Organization Studies* 11 (1990), 503–529; Andrew H. Van de Ven, Andre Delbecq and Richard Koenig, 'Determinants of Coordination Modes within Organizations', *American Sociological Review* 41 (1976), 322–338; Linda Argote, 'Input Uncertainty and Organizational Coordination in Hospital Emergency Units'; Jack K. Ito and Richard B. Peterson, 'Effects of Task Difficulty and Interdependence on Information Processing Systems', *Academy of Management Journal* 29 (1986), 139–149; and Joseph L. C. Cheng, 'Interdependence and Coordination in

Organizations: A Role-System Analysis', *Academy of Management Journal* 26 (1983), 156–162.

114. Herbsleb, J.D. and Grinter, R.E. (1999), 'Splitting the Organization and Integrating the Code: Conway's Law Revisited', *In Proceedings of the 21st International Conference on Software Engineering (ICSE'99)*, New York ACM Press, , 85-95; Carmel, E. (1999), *Global Software Teams: Collaborating Across Borders and Time Zones*, New York, Prentice Hall.
115. Ceferino S. Rodolfo (2005), *Sustaining Philippine Advantage in Business Process Outsourcing*, Manila, Philippine Institute for Development Studies, Discussion Paper Series No. 2005-28.
116. Ó Conchúir E, Holmström H, Ågerfalk P J and Fitzgerald B., (2006) *Global Software Development: Never Mind the Problems - Are There Really any Benefits?*, In Proceedings of the 29th Information Systems Research Seminar in Scandinavia, Helsingør, Denmark, 12–15 Aug 2006.
117. Rich Metters (2008), 'A typology of offshoring and outsourcing in electronically transmitted services', *Journal of Operations Management*, 26, 198–211.
118. Jason Cole, The Big Picture, *CIO*, 5 September 2006.
119. Anne Stringfellow, Mary B. Teagarden, Winter Nie (2008), 'Invisible costs in offshoring services work', *Journal of Operations Management*, 26, 164–179.
120. Michele Liu, Héléné Denis, Harvey Kolodny and Benjt Stymne, 'Organization Design for Technological Change', *Human Relations* 43 (January 1990), 7–22.
121. Philip Pangalos, 'One in Five Bank Jobs Will be Lost, Says Lloyds Boss – Sir Brian Pitman', *The Times*, 3 April 1995; 'Skills Review: UK Wholesale Financial Services Summary', Financial Services Skills Council, May 2007, accessed at http://www.fssc.org.uk/cgi-bin/docs.pl/1045/Skills_Review_UK_financial_services_full_report.pdf on August 28, 2008.
122. Antonia Sinden, 'The decline, flexibility and geographical restructuring of employment in British retail banks', *The Geographical Journal*, 1 March 1996, p25.
123. Gerald I. Susman and Richard B. Chase, 'A Sociotechnical Analysis of the Integrated Factory', *Journal of Applied Behavioral Science* 22 (1986), 257–270; and Paul Adler, 'New Technologies, New Skills', *California Management Review* 29 (Fall 1986), 9–28.
124. Based on Don Hellriegel, John W. Slocum, Jr. and Richard W. Woodman, *Organizational Behavior*, 8th ed. (Cincinnati, Ohio: South-Western, 1998), 491–495; and Gregory B. Northcraft and Margaret A. Neale, *Organizational Behavior: A Management Challenge*, 2nd ed. (Fort Worth, Tex.: The Dryden Press, 1994), 550–553.
125. F. Emery, 'Characteristics of Sociotechnical Systems', Tavistock Institute of Human Relations, document 527, 1959; William Pasmore, Carol Francis, and Jeffrey Haldeman, 'Sociotechnical Systems: A North American Reflection on Empirical Studies of the 70s', *Human Relations* 35 (1982), 1179–1204; and William M. Fox, 'Sociotechnical System Principles and Guidelines: Past and Present', *Journal of Applied Behavioral Science* 31, no. 1 (March 1995), 91–105.
126. W. S. Cascio, *Managing Human Resources* (New York: McGraw-Hill, 1986), 19.
127. David M. Upton, 'What Really Makes Factories Flexible?' *Harvard Business Review* (July–August 1995), 74–84.
128. Eric Trist and Hugh Murray, eds., *The Social Engagement of Social Science: A Tavistock Anthology*, vol. II (Philadelphia: University of Pennsylvania Press, 1993); and William A. Pasmore, 'Social Science Transformed: The Socio-Technical Perspective', *Human Relations* 48, no. 1 (1995), 1–21.
129. Ghoshal, Sumantra, Bartlett, Christopher A.1996). 'Rebuilding Behavioral Context: A Blueprint for Corporate Renewal', *Sloan Management Review*, 37(2), 23–36.
130. R. E. Walton, 'From Control to Commitment in the Workplace', *Harvard Business Review* 63, no. 2 (1985), 76–84; E. W. Lawler, III, *High Involvement Management* (London: Jossey-Bass, 1986), 84; and Hellriegel, Slocum, and Woodman, *Organizational Behavior*, 491.

CHAPTER 8

INFORMATION TECHNOLOGY AND CONTROL

The Progressive Group of Insurance Companies

The Progressive Group is the third largest automobile insurance group in the United States, and it just keeps growing. Not bad for a group of companies that got its start as a niche insurer for high-risk drivers and that, as recently as 1990, was only the 15th largest in the United States. How did a relatively small, specialized firm compete with giant insurance companies such as State Farm and Allstate in the larger market for standard and preferred auto insurance? In part, by using information technology to gain a strategic advantage.

Progressive was founded in 1937 and proved itself an innovator from the beginning, when it established the industry's first drive-in claims service. It has been innovating ever since, using technology to provide a more accurate premium rate, a better customer experience and vehicle insurance shopping information not available anywhere else.

Car insurance rates are set, in part, using information about past claims history. An insurance company's ability to understand its claims experience and to use that information to ever more finely segment its customers and its pricing can help to determine its level of success. Progressive has been using technology to better understand its customers at the most granular level for a very long time, and they continue to do so – they won a prestigious award for IT innovation in 2007.[1] From the early 1990s, they began to use that understanding to more accurately price the so-called 'standard and preferred' markets segment. If Progressive was successful in accurately pricing the high-risk, or 'non-standard' segment of the market, they reasoned, why couldn't they apply that talent to the rest of the market?

Progressive introduced other technologies during the 1990s that helped the company grow from $1.2 billion in net premiums in 1990 to nearly $14 billion in 2007. First was the introduction of Immediate Response claims service, which provided the industry's first 24 hours a day, 7 days a week, in-person response to an auto crash. Using mobile technology, claims representatives would arrive wherever customers wished, write an estimate and be able to write them a cheque on the spot. Progressive has since further refined its approach. In a growing number of cities, it offers a 'concierge level' of claims service, which means that the customer need only drop off the car at a specially designated facility and pick up a rental car. The claims representative handles all aspects of the estimate, oversees the repair and inspects the repair before the customer picks up the car. The customer drives away knowing that the work is guaranteed by the shop that repaired the vehicle and by Progressive.

In the early 1990s, Progressive introduced another first – auto insurance comparison rates. Using publicly filed rates and technology, Progressive became the first, and remains the only American auto insurance company providing consumers with comparison rates. Comparison rates were first offered by phone, but, when Progressive launched the world's first auto insurance Web site in 1995, the rates were available using that technology. Today, visitors to the Web site can buy a policy in as little as seven minutes. Customers can also use the Web site to manage their policies, make payments, make changes and print out additional insurance documentation.

Progressive continues to use technology to innovate, for example by making 'e-signatures' available to some of its customers. Electronic signatures eliminate most of the follow-up paperwork, allowing customers to sign applications online, authorize electronic funds transfer for payment or sign forms to decline unwanted coverages.

Insurance isn't the only industry that has been transformed by information technology (IT) and the Internet. Companies such as global consulting firm KPMG, TD Waterhouse, a Canadian-headquartered brokerage firm and Factiva, which provides news, business and corporate information, have long needed to use IT effectively in as a fundamental component of their businesses. But today, IT has become a crucial factor for companies in all industries, to survive and flourish in a global competitive market. Companies, both small and large, are increasingly relying on sophisticated Internet-based systems to manage every link of their supply chains, from suppliers all the way through to their customers' customers.

Part of Britain's Halma group that specializes in industrial safety components, Elfab manufactures bursting discs – devices that provide a fail-safe pressure release – for applications such as oil and gas pipelines. It's a highly specialized business and it's crucial customers can deal directly with knowledgeable sales staff. The problem: Elfab's customers are located all over the world. Many companies would appoint distributors in key regions, but Elfab chose to go in the other direction – setting up a worldwide freephone system so that potential customers can talk directly with someone at Elfab's offices in northern England. Sales staff speak ten different languages, so the vast majority of calls can be handled, and if there are any complex questions, the whole Elfab team is right there. It was a costly and technologically intensive solution, but ultimately it was the best answer for a specialized manufacturer like Elfab. Britain's professional association of mechanical engineers obviously agreed; they awarded Elfab their 2007 award for best customer service in a manufacturing firm.[2,3]

Quanjude, China's most famous roast duck restaurant, has been making the famous dish since 1864, during the Qing dynasty. Traditionally, the duck is cooked in a traditional wood-fired oven. But with nine company restaurants and 61 franchised outlets across the country, Quanjude faced problems of quality control. So it decided to make a giant leap forward into the computer era. In conjunction with a German company, Quanjude designed and installed computer-controlled electric ovens for many of its outlets: 'Computerised ovens, while guaranteeing quality, simplify, standardise and automate the roasting process', said the chain's general manager Xing Ying.[4] While this solved the potential problem of uneven cooking, it disturbed some Chinese traditionalists. Seventy-seven per cent of Beijing residents surveyed by a local newspaper opposed the move, with one saying, 'We commoners not only eat Quanjude duck for its flavour, but also for the hundreds of years of tradition and culture that our ancestors left to us.[5]

See online
COUNTERPOINT 8.7

The rapidly growing use of IT and the Internet presents not only new opportunities, but also new challenges for managers. For one thing, the balance of power has shifted to the customer. With unlimited access to information on the Internet, customers are much better informed and much more demanding, making customer loyalty harder to build.[6] In addition, the concept of electronically linking suppliers, partners and customers is forcing companies to rethink their strategies, organization design and business processes. The pace of business is moving at 'warp speed'.[7] Planning horizons have become shorter, expectations of customers change rapidly and new competitors spring up almost overnight. All this means managers, as well as employees throughout the organization, need quality information at their fingertips.

Highly successful organizations today are typically those that most effectively collect, store, distribute and use information. More than facilities, equipment or even products, it is the information a company has and how it uses it that decides if an organization is successful – some would say even determines organizational survival.[8] Top managers look for ways to manage, leverage and protect what is rapidly becoming the most valuable asset of any organization: information and knowledge.

Purpose of This Chapter

IT is an essential component of successful organizations. Managers spend at least 80 per cent of their time actively exchanging information. They use this information to hold the organization together. For example, the vertical and horizontal information linkages described in Chapter 3 are designed to provide managers with relevant information for decision making, evaluation and control. This chapter examines the evolution of IT. The chapter begins by looking at IT systems applied to organizational operations and then examines how IT is used for decision making and control of the organization. The next sections consider how IT can add strategic value through the use of internal coordination applications such as intranets, enterprise resource planning and knowledge management systems, as well as applications for external collaboration, such as extranets, customer-relationship management systems, e-business and the integrated enterprise. The final sections of the chapter look at possible future trends in IT innovation, and present an overview of how IT affects organization design and interorganizational relationships.

See online COUNTERPOINT 8.8

Information Technology Evolution

The evolution of IT is illustrated in Exhibit 8.1. First-line management is typically mainly concerned with well-defined problems about operational issues and past events. Top management, by contrast, deals mostly with uncertain, ambiguous issues, such as strategy and planning. As the complexity of computer-based IT systems has increased, applications have grown to support effective top management control and decision making about complex and uncertain problems.

COUNTERPOINT 8.1

Many first line managers would not necessarily recognise this description – 'well-defined problems' – in much of what they face. **Discuss**

Initially, IT systems in organizations were applied to operations. These early applications were based on the notion of machine-room efficiency – that is, current operations could be performed more efficiently with the use of computer technology. The goal was to reduce labour costs by having computers take over some tasks. These systems became known as **transaction processing systems** (TPS), which

EXHIBIT 8.1 Evolution of Organizational Applications of IT

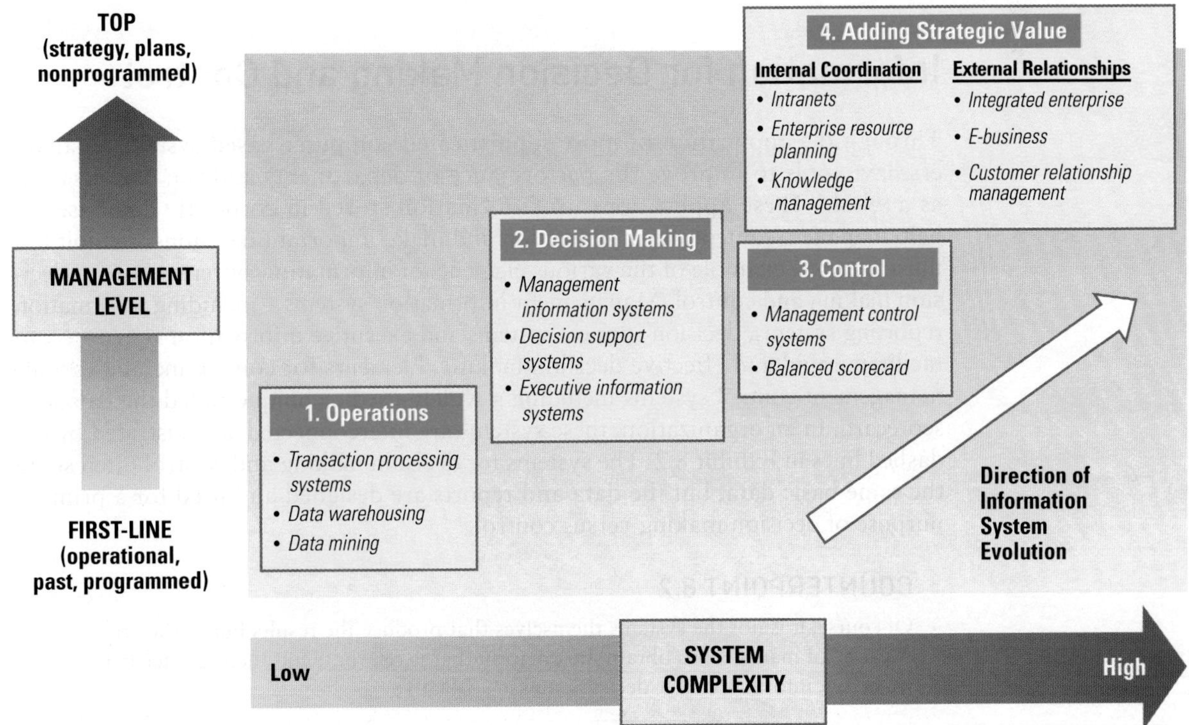

automate the organization's routine, day-to-day business transactions. A TPS collects data from transactions such as sales, purchases from suppliers and inventory changes and stores them in a database. For example, the Greek firm Intralot specializes in setting up computerized gambling and lottery systems around the world, from Australia to Vietnam. Its system not only keeps track of the gambling on countless different events across the world, it is also sophisticated enough to pick up betting patterns which could suggest illegal manipulation of sporting events.[9,10]

In recent years, the use of data warehousing and business intelligence software has expanded the usefulness of this accumulated data. **Data warehousing** is the use of huge databases that combine all of a company's data and allow users to access the data directly, create reports and obtain responses to what-if questions. Building a database at a large corporation is a huge undertaking that includes defining hundreds of gigabytes of data from many existing systems, providing a means of continually updating the data, making it all compatible and linking it to other software that makes it possible for users to search and analyze the data and produce helpful reports. Software for business intelligence helps users make sense of all these data. **Business intelligence** refers to the high-tech analysis of a company's data in order to make better strategic decisions.[11] Sometimes referred to as *data mining*, business intelligence means searching out and analyzing data from multiple sources across the enterprise, and sometimes from outside sources as well, to identify patterns and relationships that might be significant.

Organizations spent over $5 billion on business intelligence software globally in 2007.[12,13] Consider how one Canadian pharmaceutical manufacturer makes profitable use of data warehousing and business intelligence discussed in the *In Practice* box on the next page.

By collecting the right data and using business intelligence to analyze it and spot trends and patterns, managers such as those at Apotex are able to make better informed decisions and increase market share compared to competitors. IT has evolved to more complex systems for managerial decision making and control of the organization, the second stage illustrated in Exhibit 8.1. Further advancements have led to the use of IT to add strategic value, the highest level of application. The remainder of this chapter will focus on these two stages in the evolution of IT.

Information for Decision Making and Control

Through the application of more sophisticated computer-based systems, managers have tools to improve the performance of departments and the organization as a whole. These applications use information stored in corporate databases to help managers control the organization and make important decisions. Exhibit 8.2 illustrates one example of the various elements of information systems used for decision making and control. Management information systems – including information reporting systems, decision support systems and executive information systems – can facilitate rapid and effective decision making. Elements for control include various management control systems including a widely-used technique called the balanced scorecard. In an organization, these systems are interconnected, as illustrated by the dashed lines in Exhibit 8.2. The systems for decision making and control often share the same basic data, but the data and reports are designed and used for a primary purpose of decision making versus control.

COUNTERPOINT 8.2

Of course, it is not the systems themselves that produce the results but, rather, the capacity of managers to obtain information that is relevant, and then to interpret it in ways that inform effective decision making. **Discuss**

Apotex, Inc.

Apotex is Canada's largest pharmaceutical company, and one of the largest generic pharmaceutical manufacturers in the world – generics are pharmaceutical products that are no longer under patent protection. Apotex exports to at least 115 countries. It is a complex and fast-changing business, with numerous twists. There are differences – sometimes subtle, and sometimes large – between each country's drug patent protections, and the constant jockeying between brand-name producers (who seek to extend patent protections as long as possible) and generics (who want to be able to produce popular drugs as quickly as possible) results in frequent changes in the law and legal challenges. Keeping track of all this information, as well as overall market conditions in 115 countries, is a data management challenge. Being on top of the challenge is essential, because being first to the market with a generic product is the key to market share and financial success.

Like many companies, Apotex had various data collection systems operating in different departments. In addition, the company accesses various third-party data sources that provide additional information about market conditions and prescribing patterns in different countries. Because all this information was not integrated, it couldn't easily be used for business decisions, such as deciding to produce a generic for a particular market where a brand-name drug was about to go off-patent.

To address this problem, Apotex decided to integrate its data warehousing and business intelligence using an SAP product, BusinessObjects XI. In addition, the company signed up for SAP's customer relationship management (CRM) package, which integrates information from pharmacists into usable information about market performance that is available to decision-makers company-wide. Michael Davidson, chief information officer of Apotex, says 'we were able to consolidate five separate databases and manual processes onto one common platform. This enables us to effectively track marketing programs and customer activity. The effort reduced our administrative costs and improved our visibility into customer profitability'.[14]

Organizational Decision-Making Systems

A **management information system** (MIS) is a computer-based system that provides information and support for managerial decision making. The MIS is supported by the organization's transaction processing systems and by organizational and external databases. The **information reporting system**, the most common form of MIS, provides managers with reports that summarize data and support day-to-day decision making. For example, when managers make decisions about production scheduling, they can review data on the anticipated number of orders within the next month, inventory levels and availability of human resources. In the service industry, the data can be used to match pricing with demand. For example, the UK-based discount car rental agency Holiday Autos relies on an MIS system to balance rental prices against car availability.[15]

An **executive information system** (EIS) is a higher-level application that facilitates decision making at the more senior levels of management. These systems are typically based on software that can convert large amounts of complex data into pertinent information and provide that information in a timely fashion. Often, MIS and EIS systems are combined through use of the same dataset to provide different reporting levels. SNCF, the French national railway, uses a custom-built system to provide human resource information on the company's 160,000 employees to line managers for day-to-day management and reporting purposes, as well as aggregate data on staff profiles to senior managers who can use the information to assess overall recruitment and training needs.[16]

As an organization manager, keep these guidelines in mind:

Improve the performance of the organization by using IT for better decision making. Implement management information systems, decision support systems and information reporting systems to provide lower- and middle-level managers with reports and information that support day-to-day decision making. Use executive information systems to facilitate better decision making at the highest levels of the organization.

EXHIBIT 8.2 Information Systems for Managerial Control and Decision Making

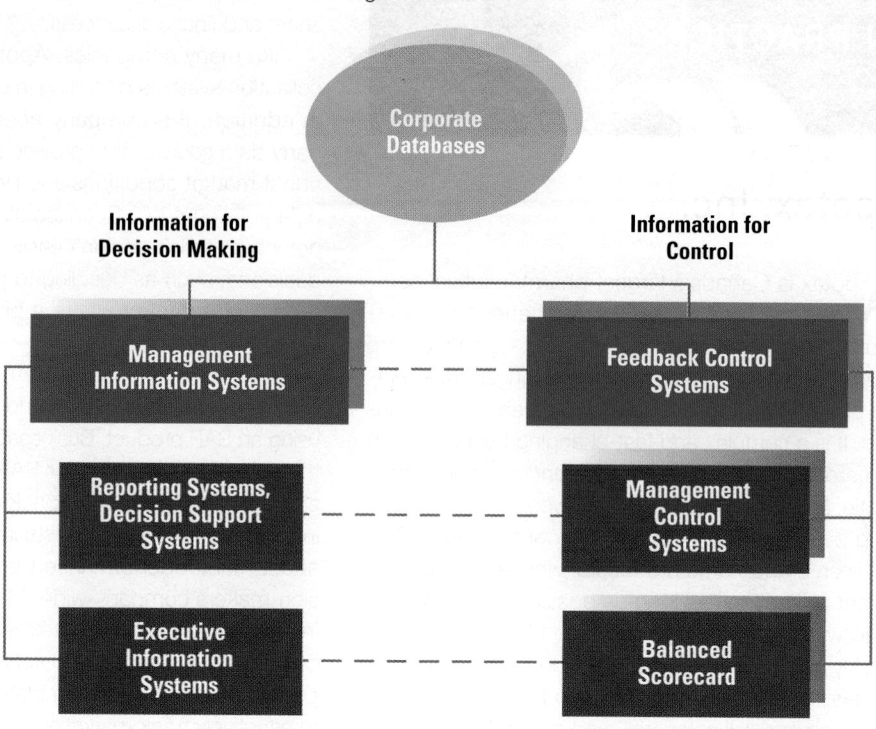

A **decision support system** (DSS) provides specific benefits to managers at all levels of the organization. These interactive, computer-based systems rely on decision models and integrated databases. Using decision support software, users can pose a series of what-if questions to test possible alternatives. Based on assumptions used in the software or specified by the user, managers can explore alternatives and receive information to help them choose the option that promises to deliver the best outcome.

At Tesco, Britain's largest supermarket chain, understanding the purchasing habits of customers is key to success. One of the main tools used by Tesco to understand its customers and to retain their business is the Clubcard, a computerized card that enables customers accumulated points that can be redeemed against future Tesco purchases or for other goods (e.g. discounted hotel deals). The value of the Clubcard to Tesco is that it provides the company with a comprehensive profile of the customer and their shopping patterns. As Giles Pavey, an executive of the marketing firm that runs the Clubcard scheme puts it, 'It's just like standing behind someone in a checkout queue and making assumptions about their lifestyle based on what's in the trolley'.[17]

See online COUNTERPOINT 8.9

Clubcard information is subjected to sophisticated 'segmentation analysis' which identifies types of shoppers and their likely motivations when shopping. This information can be used for many purposes, including targeting advertising, setting product prices and changing the range of goods stocked by specific stores. One example of an application might be to respond to in roads being made by discount retailers like Lidl and Aldi to the 'price-sensitive' segment of Tesco shoppers. Of course, Tesco could simply reduce its prices across the board in order to retain these customers, but this would be very costly, and the price cuts would be wasted on many customers who have no intention of switching to a discount retailer. However, by carefully examining the shopping patterns of the 'price sensitive' group, and applying DSS modelling on likely impact of different customer retention strategies, targeted price cuts could be introduced on lines that are particularly favoured by this group. Alternatively, discount coupons could be delivered on these products, just to the 'price conscious' consumer segment.

Feedback Control Model

Another primary use of information in organizations is for control. Effective control systems involve the use of feedback to determine whether organizational performance meets established standards to help the organization attain its goals. Managers set up systems for organizational control that consist of the four key steps in the **feedback control model** illustrated in Exhibit 8.3.

The cycle of control includes setting strategic goals for departments or the organization as a whole, establishing metrics and standards of performance, comparing metrics of actual performance to standards and correcting or changing activities as needed. Feedback control helps managers make needed adjustments in work activities, standards of performance or goals to help the organization be successful. For example, the South-African based company DigiCore provides client companies with various IT tools enabling them to effectively manage their vehicle fleets – a high-cost operation area where lax control and poor planning can cause substantial losses. DigiCore pioneered the integration of GSM (mobile phone technology) with GPS positioning, enabling companies to keep track minute-by-minute of the progress of their fleets. As one of the first companies in the field, DigiCore was at the forefront when fleet tracking systems became the norm. After surviving the rocky period between product development and mass

As an organization manager, keep this guideline in mind:

Devise control systems that consist of the four essential steps of the feedback control model: set goals, establish standards of performance, measure actual performance and compare to standards and correct or change activities as needed.

EXHIBIT 8.3 A Simplified Feedback Control Model

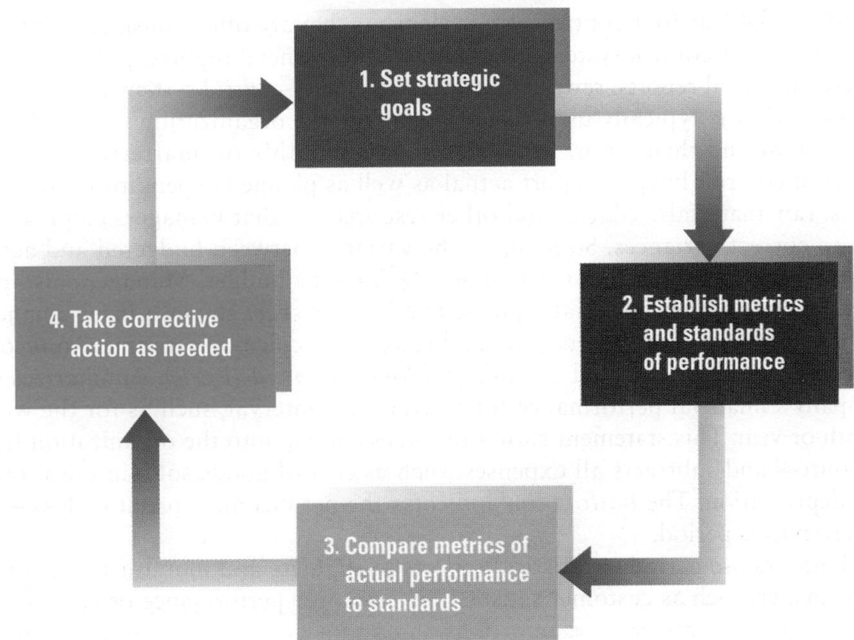

sales, DigiCore has gone from strength to strength, especially in Europe where it has signed fleet management deals with large companies such as Britain's Thames Water.[18]

See online COUNTERPOINT 8.10

Management Control Systems

Management control systems are broadly defined as the formal routines, reports and procedures that use information to maintain or alter patterns in organization activities.[19] These control systems include the formalized information-based activities for planning, budgeting, performance evaluation, resource allocation and employee rewards. Targets are set in advance, outcomes compared to targets and variance reported to managers for corrective action. Advances in IT have dramatically improved the efficiency and effectiveness of these systems. For example, many organizations use *executive dashboards*, which enable managers to see at a glance key control indicators such as sales in relation to targets, number of products on back-order or percentage of customer service calls resolved within a specified time period.[20] Dashboard systems coordinate, organize and display the metrics that managers consider most important to monitor on a regular basis, with software automatically updating the figures. Kuwait's Vodaphone-MTC mobile phone network uses a tailor-made Harris Corporation system monitoring software to deliver an 'executive dashboard' that provides the company's managers with graphical display of network status, usage and Key Performance Indicators (KPIs), all accessible through the Web, and enabling immediate response to problems.[21,22]

COUNTERPOINT 8.3

Of course, the usefulness of these systems depends upon the reliability of the data that is inputed to them. Employees may have their reasons for delaying inputs or in other ways inputing data that is unreliable or even erroneous. Even when the data is complete and uncorrupted, its usefulness always depends upon its ease of accessibility, how it is interpreted and how it is then acted upon. **Discuss**

Exhibit 8.4 lists four control system elements that are often considered the core of management control systems: the budget and financial reports; periodic nonfinancial statistical reports; reward systems; and quality-control systems.[23]

The *budget* is typically used to set targets for the organization's expenditures for the year and then report actual costs on a monthly or quarterly basis. As a means of control, budgets report actual as well as planned expenditures for cash, assets, raw materials, salaries and other resources so that managers can take action to correct variances. Sometimes, the variance between budgeted and actual amounts for each line item is listed as a part of the budget. Managers also rely on a variety of other financial reports. The *balance sheet* shows a firm's financial position with respect to assets and liabilities at a specific point in time. An *income statement*, sometimes called a *profit and loss statement (P&L)*, summarizes the company's financial performance for a given time interval, such as for the week, month or year. This statement shows revenues coming into the organization from all sources and subtracts all expenses, such as cost of goods sold, interest, taxes and depreciation. The *bottom line* indicates the net income – profit or loss – for the given time period.

Managers use periodic statistical reports to evaluate and monitor nonfinancial performance, such as customer satisfaction, employee performance or rate of staff turnover. For e-commerce organizations, important measurements of nonfinancial

EXHIBIT 8.4 Management Control Systems

Subsystem	Content and Frequency
Budget, financial reports	Financial, resource expenditures, profit and loss; monthly
Statistical reports	Nonfinancial outputs; weekly or monthly, often computer-based
Reward systems	Evaluation of managers based on department goals and performance, set rewards; yearly
Quality control systems	Participation, benchmarking guidelines, Six Sigma goals; continuous

Source: Based on Richard L. Daft and Norman B. Macintosh, 'The Nature and Use of Formal Control Systems for Management Control and Strategy Implementation,' *Journal of Management* 10 (1984), 43–66.

performance include metrics such as *stickiness* (how much attention a site gets over time), the *conversion rate*, the ratio of buyers to site visitors, and *site performance data*, such as how long it takes to load a page or how long it takes to place an order.[24] E-commerce managers regularly review reports on conversion rates, customer dropoff and other metrics to identify problems and improve their business. For all organizations, nonfinancial reports typically are computer based and may be available daily, weekly or monthly. The international online auction company eBay provides a good illustration of using both financial and nonfinancial statistical reports for feedback control (see *In Practice* box below).

In addition to performance measurement, eBay also effectively uses the other control system elements listed in Exhibit 8.4 – reward systems and quality control systems. Reward systems offer incentives for managers and employees to improve performance and meet departmental goals. Managers and employees evaluate how well previous goals were met, set new goals and establish rewards for meeting the new targets.

eBay

Meg Whitman, CEO of eBay from 1998 until she stepped down to pursue political ambitions in 2008, has a guiding mantra: 'If you can't measure it, you can't control it'. Whitman built a company that is obsessed with performance measurement from shaky start-up to multi-billion dollar internet giant. She personally monitored performance metrics such as number of site visitors, percentage of new users and time spent on the site, as well as profit and loss statements and the ratio of eBay's revenues to the value of goods traded. Managers throughout the company also monitor performance regularly. Category managers, for example, have clear standards of performance for their auction categories (such as sports memorabilia, jewelry and watches, health and beauty, etc.). They continuously measure, tweak and promote their categories to meet or outperform their targets.

Whitman believes getting a firm grip on performance measurement is essential for a company to know where to spend money, where to assign more personnel and which projects to promote or abandon. The more statistics that are available, the more early warnings managers have about problems and opportunities. But performance isn't just about numbers at eBay. Measuring customer (user) satisfaction requires a mix of methods, such as surveys, monitoring eBay discussion boards and personal contact with customers at regular live conferences.

By defining standards and effectively using financial and statistical reports, eBay managers can identify trouble spots and move quickly to take corrective action when and where it is needed.[25]

Rewards are often tied to the annual performance appraisal process, during which managers assess employee performance and provide feedback to help the employee improve performance and obtain rewards.

COUNTERPOINT 8.4

Reward systems can also incentivize people in ways that can be unintentionally counterproductive and detrimental. One need only think of the incentivized traders in asset-backed securities whose 'exuberance' contributed directly to the financial crisis of 2008. **Discuss**

The final control element listed in Exhibit 8.4 is quality-control systems, which managers use to train employees in quality-control methods, set targets for employee participation, establish benchmarking guidelines and assign and measure *Six Sigma* goals. For example, at eBay, Whitman used benchmarking to measure how the company's Web site performs compared to its peers. She found eBay's site weak in the area of adding new features, so managers have taken action to improve the site's performance in that area. **Benchmarking** means the process of continually measuring products, services and practices against tough competitors or other organizations recognized as industry leaders.[26] **Six Sigma**, originally conceived by Motorola Corporation, is a highly ambitious quality standard that specifies a goal of no more than 3.4 defects per million parts.[27] From this precise definition, Six Sigma has become a generic term for a whole set of control procedures that emphasize a relentless pursuit of higher quality and lower costs. The discipline is based on a methodology referred to as DMAIC (Define, Measure, Analyze, Improve and Control, pronounced de-MAY-ick, for short), which provides a structured way for organizations to approach and solve problems.[28]

As an organization manager, keep these guidelines in mind:

Establish management control systems that use budgets and financial reports, statistical nonfinancial reports, reward systems and quality control systems. Use a balanced scorecard to integrate various control dimensions and get a more complete picture of organizational performance. Select indicators in the areas of financial performance, customer service, internal processes and learning and growth.

Each of the four control systems focuses on a different aspect of the production process. The budget is used primarily to allocate resource inputs. Managers use the budget for planning the future and reducing uncertainty about the availability of human and material resources needed to perform department tasks. Computer-based statistical reports are used to control outputs. These reports contain data about output volume and quality and other indicators that provide feedback to middle management about departmental results. The reward system and quality control systems are directed at the production process. Quality control systems specify standards for employee participation, teamwork and problem solving. Reward systems provide incentives to meet goals and can help guide and correct employee behaviour. Managers also use direct supervision to keep departmental work activities within desired limits.

The Balanced Scorecard

In the past, most organizations tended to rely heavily upon financial accounting measures as the primary basis for measuring organizational performance and control whereas increasingly a more balanced view, incorporating operational as well as financial measures is favoured.

The four control elements listed in Exhibit 8.4 help provide managers with a balanced view. A recent innovation additionally integrates internal financial measurements and statistical reports with a concern for markets and customers as well as employees. The **balanced scorecard** has been developed as a comprehensive management control system that balances traditional financial measures with operational measures relating to what are identified as critical success factors.[29] A balanced scorecard contains four major focal areas, as illustrated in Exhibit 8.5: financial performance, customer service, internal business processes and the organization's

EXHIBIT 8.5 Major Perspectives of the Balanced Scorecard

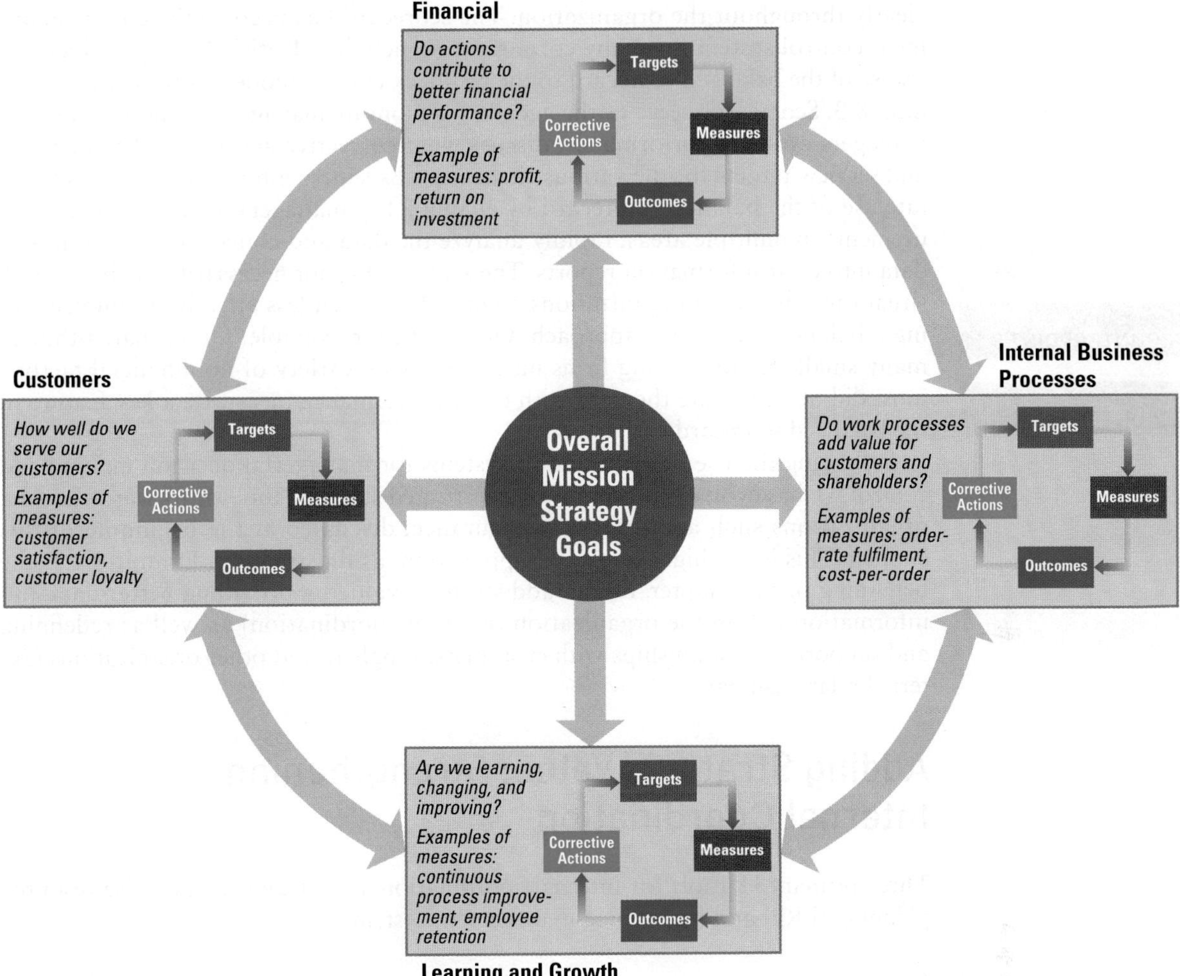

Source: Based on Robert S. Kaplan and David P. Norton, 'Using the Balanced Scorecard as a Strategic Management System,' *Harvard Business Review* (January–February 1996), 75–85; Chee W. Chow, Kamal M. Haddad, and James E. Williamson, 'Applying the Balanced Scorecard to Small Companies,' *Management Accounting* 79, no. 2 (August 1997), 21–27; and Cathy Lazere, 'All Together Now,' *CFO* (February 1998), 28–36.

capacity for learning and growth.[30] Within these four areas, managers identify key performance indicators to be tracked. The *financial perspective* reflects a concern that the organization's activities contribute to improving short- and long-term financial performance. It includes traditional measures such as net income and return on investment. *Customer service indicators* measure such things as how customers view the organization, as well as customer retention and satisfaction. *Business process indicators* focus on production and operating statistics, such as order fulfilment or cost per order. The final component considers the organization's *potential for learning and growth*, focusing on how well resources and human capital are being managed for the company's future. Measurements include such things as employee retention, business process improvements and the introduction of new products. The components of the scorecard are designed in an integrative manner so that they complement and reinforce one another as short-term actions are linked with long-term strategic goals, as illustrated in Exhibit 8.5. Managers can use the scorecard to set goals, allocate resources, plan budgets and determine rewards.[31]

The balanced scorecard helps managers focus on the key strategic measures that define the success of a particular organization over time and communicate them clearly throughout the organization. The scorecard has become the core management control system for many corporations, including British Airways, which ties its use of the balanced scorecard to the feedback control model shown earlier in Exhibit 8.3. Scorecards serve as the agenda for monthly management meetings, where managers evaluate performance, discuss what corrective actions need to be taken and set new targets for the various elements.[32] Executive information systems facilitate use of the balanced scorecard by enabling top managers to easily track measurements in multiple areas, rapidly analyze the data and convert huge amounts of data into clear information reports. The scorecard is not necessarily the best for all situations, and small organizations seem to have been less effective in implementing a balanced-scorecard approach. One study, for example, found that, although many small manufacturing firms measure a wide variety of nonfinancial factors, most did not integrate the data with other performance measures, a key feature of the balanced scorecard.[33]

See online COUNTERPOINT 8.11

See online COUNTERPOINT 8.12

Following the use of information systems for managerial decision making and control, IT has evolved further as a sophisticated strategic tool for forward-thinking organizations such as Progressive Insurance, discussed at the beginning of this chapter. This is the highest level of application, as illustrated in Exhibit 8.1 at the beginning of the chapter. IT can add strategic value by providing better data and information within the organization (internal coordination) as well as redefining and supporting relationships with customers, suppliers and other organizations (external relationships).

Adding Strategic Value: Strengthening Internal Coordination

Three primary IT tools for internal coordination are intranets, enterprise resource planning (ERP) and knowledge-management systems.

Intranets

As an organization manager, keep these guidelines in mind:

Improve internal coordination, integration, and information sharing with intranets, enterprise resource planning (ERP) systems and knowledge management systems. Use ERP to integrate and optimize business processes across the entire firm.

Networking, which links people and departments within a particular building or across corporate offices, enabling them to share information and cooperate on projects, has become an important strategic tool for many companies. For example, in 2008, the Irish Republic's Health Service Executive (HSE), responsible for coordinating the country's universal health care system, consolidated its internal networks into a single **intranet** – Ireland's largest – that provides access to staff news, policy briefings and reports, email and contact directories for all staff and medical libraries. Existing electronic tools, such as the country's Health Atlas, which provides graphical illustrations of health challenges in different parts of Ireland, were also moved onto the intranet.[34,35]

Networks may take many forms, but as in the case of the HSE the most common form of corporate networking is the intranet, a private, company-wide information system that uses the communications protocols and standards of the Internet and the World Wide Web but is accessible only to people within the company. To view files and information, users simply navigate the site with a standard Web browser, clicking on links.[36] Because intranets are Web based, they can be accessed from any type of computer or workstation.

Today, most companies with intranets have moved their management information systems, executive information systems and so forth over to the intranet so they are accessible to anyone in the firm who needs them. In addition, having these systems as part of the intranet means new features and applications can easily be added and accessed through a standard browser.

Intranets can improve internal communications and unlock hidden information. They enable employees to keep in touch with what's going on around the organization, quickly and easily find information they need, share ideas and work on projects collaboratively. The most advanced intranets are linked into the proprietary systems that govern a company's business functions. Portable devices like the BlackBerry and netbooks (see Chapter 7) allow on-the-move employees to stay in touch anywhere in the world, downloading information and filing reports from hotel rooms and airport departure lounges, with data instantly available across the company.[37,38]

COUNTERPOINT 8.5

The usefulness of intranets depends upon the preparedness of employees to share and regularly update (rather than hoard) information, and also their willingness to use an impersonal channel rather than informal networks and word of mouth which are often richer and more nuanced in what they can provide. If information requires little interpretation or finesse, then an intranet can be useful so long as information is easy to find. Otherwise, intranets may be used infrequently and fall into disuse. **Discuss**

See online
COUNTERPOINT 8.13

Enterprise Resource Planning

Another recent approach to information management helps pull together various types of information to see how decisions and actions in one part of the organization affect other parts of the firm. A growing number of companies are setting up broad-scale information systems that take a comprehensive view of the organization's activities. These **enterprise resource planning** (ERP) systems collect, process and provide information about a company's entire enterprise, including order processing, product design, purchasing, inventory, manufacturing, distribution, human resources (HR), receipt of payments and forecasting of future demand.[39] An ERP system can serve as the backbone for an entire organization by integrating and optimizing all the various business processes across the entire firm.[40]

Such a system links all of these areas of activity into a network, as illustrated in Exhibit 8.6. When a salesperson takes an order, the ERP system checks to see how the order affects inventory levels, scheduling, HR, purchasing and distribution. The system replicates organizational processes in software, guides employees through the processes step-by-step and automates as many of them as possible. For example, ERP software can automatically produce an accounts payable cheque as soon as a clerk confirms that goods have been received in inventory, send an online purchase order immediately after a manager has authorized a purchase or schedule production at the most appropriate plant after an order is received.[41]

The world's biggest and best-known travel guidebook company, Australia-based Lonely Planet, has grown from producing a stapled guide to budget travel across Asia in 1973, to selling 6 million guidebooks with 500 different titles a year, publishing in 14 different languages. For a long time the company just grew organically, adding new titles and publishing profits as it went along. But the sheer size of the business and its varied activities meant that important information inevitably fell off the table, and that led to costly errors. By 2003, in the wake of declining sales, Lonely Planet had to lay off staff for the first time. David Sadler, finance and operations director for Lonely Planet's Europe, Middle East and Africa (EMEA) region, was put in charge of developing an ERP system that could improve efficiency by

EXHIBIT 8.6 Example of an ERP Network

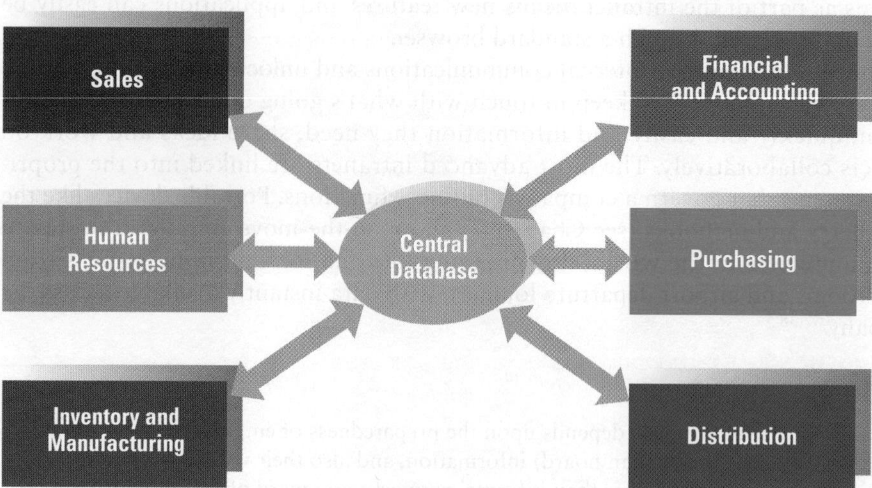

integrating information about all the company's different activities: 'Whether it's sourcing a book, developing content, managing stock, distribution or finances – trying to merge all of that into one is no easy task', says Sadler. However, Lonely Planet moved cautiously. It took more than a year identifying needs and choosing an ERP supplier – in the end choosing Swiss-based SAP. Lonely Planet (LP) decided they needed a full integration of company functions ranging from HR to print contracts, and implemented the project in stages both geographically and by enterprise functions between 2005 and 2007. The new system needed lots of ironing out, and led to further hardware investment, but it helped the company strengthen its financial controls and future planning, particularly in expanding traffic and business through the company's web portal. In October 2007, BBC Worldwide, the business arm of the British Broadcasting Corporation, bought a 75 per cent stake in Lonely Planet for around £75 million, reflecting LP's strong sales, better cost controls and improved profit margins.[42] Not bad for a company started at a kitchen table.[43]

Because ERP systems integrate data about all aspects of operations, managers and employees at all levels can see how decisions and actions in one part of the organization affect other parts, using this information to make better decisions. ERP can provide the kind of information furnished by transaction processing systems, as well as that provided by information reporting systems, decision support systems or executive information systems. The key is that ERP weaves all of these systems together so people can see the big picture and act quickly, helping the organization be smarter and more effective. ERP is not just applicable in the for-profit sector Medecins du Monde, an international aid organization, uses an ERP system to keep precise track of expenses, supplies and needs and enable doctors and volunteers in the field to see what resources are available and where they're most urgently needed.[44]

Knowledge Management

A primary goal for IT systems today is to support efforts to manage and leverage organizational knowledge. Increasingly, intellectual capital is the primary way in which businesses measure their value.[45] Therefore, managers see knowledge as an important resource to manage, just as they manage cash flow, raw materials or other resources. A survey of CEOs attending the World Economic Forum's annual meeting found that 97 per cent of senior executives see knowledge management as a critical issue for their organizations.[46] To learn and change, organizations must effectively acquire, create and transfer knowledge across the company and modify their activities to reflect new knowledge and insight.[47]

Knowledge management is a new way to think about organizing and sharing an organization's intellectual and creative resources. It refers to the efforts to systematically find, organize and make available a company's intellectual capital and to foster a culture of continuous learning and knowledge sharing so that organizational activities build on what is already known.[48] The company's **intellectual capital** is the sum of its knowledge, experience, understanding, relationships, processes, innovations and discoveries. Although most of a company's knowledge is within the formal boundaries of the organization, tapping into the knowledge of outside experts is also important because it brings new knowledge into the organization that can be combined with existing knowledge to highlight problems or opportunities.[49] A variety of new software tools support collaboration and knowledge sharing through services such as Web conferencing, knowledge portals, content management and the use of *wikis*, an emerging collaboration tool. Wikis are an extension of the concept of blogs (Web logs); rather than simply allowing an individual to broadcast his or her views to an online audience, as blogs do, wikis let people edit and add content to the running log.[50]

COUNTERPOINT 8.6

'Knowledge Management' can also be interpreted as the application of Taylorism to employees who work primarily with their heads rather than their hands. From this perspective, its purpose is to rationalize and systematize what had previously been the equivalent of the 'custom and practice' of the 'shopfloor'. Its consequence can be deskilling of work and degradation of work experience, with predictable consequences for morale, goodwill and turnover. **Discuss**

What Is Knowledge? Knowledge is not the same thing as data or information, although it uses both. **Data** are simple, absolute facts and figures that, in and of themselves, may be of little use. A company might have data that show 30 per cent of a particular product is sold to customers in France. To be useful to the organization, the data are processed into finished *information* by connecting them with other data – for example, six out of ten of the products sold in France are bought by people over the age of sixty. **Information** is data that have been linked with other data and converted into a useful context for specific use. **Knowledge** goes a step further; it is a conclusion drawn from the information after it is linked to other information and compared to what is already known. Knowledge, as opposed to information and data, always has a human factor that provides interpretations of the data. Books can contain information, but the information becomes knowledge only when a person absorbs it and puts it to use.[51]

See online COUNTERPOINT 8.14

Organizations deal with both explicit knowledge and implicit, or tacit, knowledge.[52] **Explicit knowledge** is formal, systematic knowledge that can be codified, written down and passed on to others in documents or general instructions. Tacit knowledge, on the other hand, is often difficult to put into words. **Tacit knowledge** is based on personal experience, rules of thumb, intuition and judgement. It includes professional know-how and expertise, individual insight and experience and creative solutions that are difficult to communicate and pass on to others. Explicit knowledge may be equated with *knowing about*; tacit knowledge is equated with *knowing how*.[53]

Finding ways to transfer both explicit and tacit knowledge – the knowing about and the knowing how – across the organization is critical.[54] Although explicit knowledge can easily be captured and shared in documents and through IT systems,

EXHIBIT 8.7 Two Approaches to Knowledge Management

Explicit Provide high-quality, reliable, and fast information systems for access of codified, reusable knowledge		Tacit Channel individual expertise to provide creative advice on strategic problems
People-to-documents approach *Develop an electronic document system that codifies, stores, disseminates, and allows reuse of knowledge*	**Knowledge Management Strategy**	**Person-to-person approach** *Develop networks for linking people so that tacit knowledge can be shared*
Invest heavily in information technology, with a goal of connecting people with reusable, codified knowledge	**Information Technology Approach**	*Invest moderately in information technology, with a goal of facilitating conversations and the personal exchange of tacit knowledge*

Source: Based on Morten T. Hansen, Nitin Nohria, and Thomas Tierney, 'What's Your Strategy for Managing Knowledge?' *Harvard Business Review* (March–April 1999), 106–116.

BRIEFCASE

As an organization manager, keep this guideline in mind:

Establish systems to facilitate both explicit and tacit knowledge sharing to help the organization learn and improve.

as much as 80 per cent of an organization's valuable knowledge may be tacit knowledge that is not easily captured and transferred.[55]

Approaches to Knowledge Management Two distinct approaches to knowledge management are outlined in Exhibit 8.7. The first approach outlined in Exhibit 8.7 deals primarily with the collection and sharing of explicit knowledge, largely through the use of sophisticated IT systems.[56] Explicit knowledge may include intellectual properties such as patents and licences; work processes such as policies and procedures; specific information on customers, markets, suppliers or competitors; competitive intelligence reports; benchmark data; and so forth. When an organization uses this approach, the focus is on collecting and codifying knowledge and storing it in databases where it can easily be accessed and reused by anyone in the organization. With this 'people-to-documents' approach, knowledge is gathered from the individuals who possess it and is organized into documents that others can access and reuse. When money management firm Barclays Global Investors deals with requests for proposals, for example, employees have to answer hundreds of complex questions for clients. A knowledge management system enables them to access and reuse answers to similar questions from previous proposals.[57]

Although IT plays an important role in knowledge management by enabling the storage and dissemination of data and information across the organization, IT is only one piece of a larger puzzle.[58] A complete knowledge management system includes not only processes for capturing and storing knowledge and organizing it for easy access, but also ways to generate new knowledge through learning and to share knowledge throughout the organization. As discussed in this chapter's Bookmark, old-fashioned paper can sometimes play just as important a role in knowledge work as computer technology.

The second approach focuses on leveraging individual expertise and know-how – tacit knowledge – by connecting people face-to-face or through interactive media. Tacit knowledge includes professional know-how, individual insights and creativity and personal experience and intuition. With this approach, managers concentrate on developing personal networks that link people together for the sharing of tacit knowledge. The organization uses IT systems primarily for facilitating conversation and person-to-person sharing of experience, insight and ideas. For

Have you read this book?

The Myth of the Paperless Office

BY ABIGAIL J. SELLEN AND RICHARD H. R. HARPER

At first glance, it seems like a great idea. Get rid of all the paper that clutters desktops and put everything on computers. Especially with the proliferation of handheld gadgets, paper seems redundant. Yet paper sales increase every year because paper is woven into the fabric of our lives and organizations – and for very good reasons, argue Abigail Sellen and Richard Harper, authors of *The Myth of the Paperless Office*. Paper actually enables a certain kind of information processing, as well as supporting collaborative knowledge work. People simply can't *think* the same way when looking at a document on a computer screen.

Why Paper Persists

Sellen and Harper offer a number of reasons why paper persists. Paper has many advantages, they say, for performing certain kinds of cognitive tasks and supporting certain kinds of collaboration.

- *Paper is flexible and easily manipulated for reading.* Most people still prefer to read newspapers or documents on paper rather than on a computer screen. The authors cite four primary reasons for this: paper allows people to flexibly navigate through documents, it facilitates the cross-referencing of more than one document at a time, it allows for easy annotation and it enables the interweaving of reading and writing. Paper allows one to pick up a document or newspaper, flip through it, read bits here and there and quickly get a sense of the overall piece.
- *Paper is a tool for managing and coordinating action among co-workers*. The authors cite a fascinating example of air traffic controllers who, despite the availability and use of highly sophisticated technology, continue to use paper flight strips to support a seamless teamwork, enable easy manipulation to indicate flight variations, give everyone on the team information at a glance and facilitate the rapid pace of work required in this high-pressure environment.
- *Paper supports collaboration and sharing of knowledge*. Paper has interactional properties that are not easy to duplicate with digital media and collaborative tools. People working on collaborative documents that require the professional judgement and contributions of many people typically print drafts to read, mark up and discuss with others while flipping though the pages. Sellen and Harper argue that, without paper drafts, collaborative, iterative knowledge work is much more difficult and time consuming. Paper, they say, 'is a versatile medium that can be co-opted, shaped and adapted to meet the needs of the work'.

The Best of Both Worlds

The authors emphasize that digital technologies have their own advantages. Their point in *The Myth of the Paperless Office* is that managers should understand what paper can do and what computers can do and should know how to get the most out of each medium. 'The real issue for organizations . . . is not to get rid of paper for its own sake, but to have sufficient motivation to understand their own work process and the ways paper plays a role.'

The Myth of the Paperless Office, by Abigail Sellen and Richard Harper, is published by MIT Press.

example, intranets are important for helping employees, especially those who are geographically dispersed, share ideas and tap into expert knowledge throughout the organization.

Organizations typically combine several methods and technologies to facilitate the sharing and transfer of both explicit and tacit knowledge. Consider the example of Toyota, the world's largest and most successful automobile manufacturer.

See online COUNTERPOINT 8.15

Toyota Motor Corporation – developing the Prius

Toyota's success has been an inspiration to numerous other companies, as we saw in the previous chapter's discussion of the Swedish firm Autoliv. One key element that marks Toyota apart from many other companies is its ability to make effective use of tacit knowledge. Rather than send workers on classroom courses, Toyota tends to use hands-on training, whereby employees in new plants will spend several weeks paired with workers in a longer-established facility, often followed by the experienced workers returning to the new facility to model effective work practices. The same emphasis on harvesting tacit knowledge also underpins Toyota's success in product innovation. When Toyota decided to develop a new energy-efficient car in the 1990s – which eventually became the hybrid Prius – it abandoned the traditional incremental and hierarchical approach to product development, and instead established a small team consisting of one or two experts from each area of automobile engineering expertise including body, chassis, engine, drive system and production technology. This team worked intensively together for several years, creating a sense of mutual commitment and frank dialogue. Faced with ambitious targets for fuel economy, traditional ideas that governed individual specialists' thinking about what was possible had to be abandoned. However, individual and team learning still had to be harvested and channelled. One way was achieved through emphasizing 'equal access to information'. New ideas were posted immediately on an email list open to everyone involved in the project, thus creating a dialogue around product developed that spanned across different expertise, and allowed tacit expertise to intermingle and produce advances in explicit knowledge. Engineers were also encouraged to think outside the box; trying out design hunches even if they were unlikely to work properly the first time. And, as Toyota product development had always emphasized, designers were enouraged to put their ideas on a single piece of paper – forcing them to making their thinking approachable to others. Finally, Toyota invested in the most advanced computer aided drafting (CAD) and computer aided engineering (CAE) systems, again encouraging team members to work together on design ideas. These various method of knowledge harvesting enabled Toyota to produce the Prius, a revolutionary design, in only 15 months, compared with the average four years the company takes to design and produce a conventional vehicle, itself an industry-leading standard. A decade later, as high oil prices placed energy conservation and alternative fuels at the top of the political and business agenda, Toyota's foresight in developing the Prius seems almost clairvoyant. The Prius example showed that use of leading edge technology is crucial for successful businesses, but as a support for, not in place of, human ingenuity and determination.[59]

See online COUNTERPOINT 8.16

Adding Strategic Value: Strengthening External Relationships

External applications of IT for strengthening relationships with customers, suppliers and partners include systems for supply chain management and the integrated enterprise, customer relationship management systems and e-business organization design. The extension of corporate intranets to include customers and partners has expanded the potential for external collaboration. An **extranet** is an external communications system that uses the Internet and is shared by two or more organizations. Each organization moves certain data outside of its private intranet, but makes the data available only to the other companies sharing the extranet. For example, the British brewer Greene King has set up an extranet, Pubpartners.net, available to all of the company's 1,600-plus tenanted and leased pubs. Pubpartners is used not only to order products from Greene King, but also as an online information resource. The company posts useful information online, such as the rules for pubs to comply with a recent smoking ban in the British Isles, as well as menu and wine list guidance, marketing updates and personalized weekly sales reports.[60]

The Integrated Enterprise

Extranets play a critical role in today's integrated enterprise. The **integrated enterprise** is an organization that uses advanced IT to enable close coordination within the company as well as with suppliers, customers and partners. One good example of the integrated enterprise is Corrugated Supplies of Chicago, USA, which has linked its entire factory to the Internet, as described in the Leading by Design box. An important aspect of the integrated enterprise is *supply chain management*, which means managing the sequence of suppliers and purchasers covering all stages of processing from obtaining raw materials to distributing finished goods to consumers.[61] For organizations to operate efficiently and provide high-quality items that meet customer needs, the company must have reliable deliveries of high-quality, reasonably priced supplies and materials. It also requires an efficient and reliable system for distributing finished products, making them readily accessible to customers.

As an organization manager, keep this guideline in mind:

Use IT applications such as extranets, systems for supply chain management and enterprise integration and e-business systems to strengthen relationships with customers, suppliers, and business partners.

Information Linkages

The most recent advances involve the use of computer networks or extranets to achieve the right balance of low inventory levels and customer responsiveness. Exhibit 8.8 illustrates horizontal information linkages in the integrated enterprise. By establishing electronic linkages between the organization and key partners for the sharing and exchange of data, the integrated enterprise aspires to create a seamless, integrated line stretching from end consumers to raw materials suppliers.[62] For example, in the exhibit, as consumers purchase products in retail stores, the data are automatically fed into the retail chain's information system. In turn, the chain gives access to this constantly updated data to the manufacturing company through a secure extranet. With knowledge of this demand data, the manufacturer can produce and ship products when needed. As products are made by the manufacturer, data about raw materials used in the production process, updated inventory information and updated forecasted demand are electronically provided to the manufacturer's suppliers, and the suppliers automatically replenish the manufacturer's raw materials inventory as needed.

As an organization manager, keep these guidelines in mind:

Transform your organization into an integrated enterprise by establishing horizontal information linkages between the organization and key outsiders. Create a seamless, integrated line stretching from end consumers to raw materials suppliers that will meet customers' product and time demands.

Horizontal Relationships

The purpose of integrating the supply chain is for everyone to work closely together, moving in lockstep to meet customers' product

EXHIBIT 8.8 The Integrated Enterprise

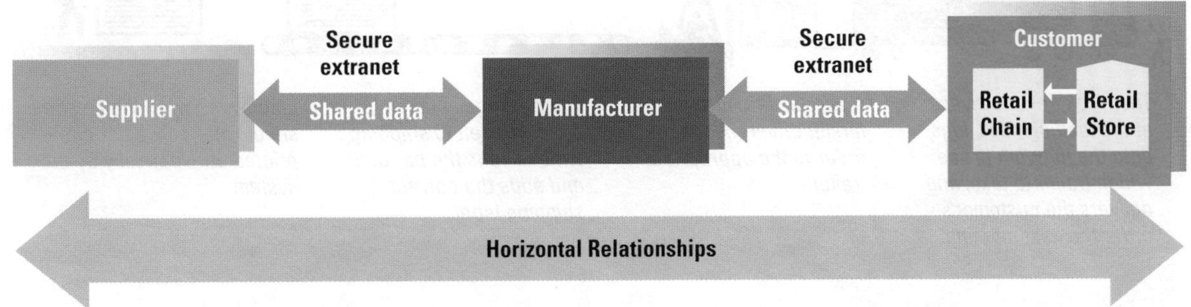

Source: Based on Jim Turcotte, Bob Silveri, and Tom Jobson, 'Are You Ready for the E-Supply Chain?' *APICS – The Performance Advantage* (August 1998), 56–59.

Corrugated Supplies

Rick Van Horne had a vision. What would happen if all his plant's equipment continually fed data to the Internet, where the rest of the company, as well as suppliers and customers, could keep track of what was happening on the factory floor in real time? By using a password, customers could peek into the company's internal workings at any time, calling up Corrugated's production schedules to see exactly where their orders were in the process and when they would arrive. Suppliers could tap into the system to manage their own inventory – inventory they were selling to Corrugated as well as materials stored at Corrugated's plant to sell to someone else.

It cost him millions of dollars, but Van Horne's vision became a reality, making Corrugated one of the world's first completely Web-based production plants. The idea behind the system was to connect all the plant's manufacturing equipment and then link it to the Web; the integrated system is available to everyone, from machinists on the plant floor to customers and suppliers off-site. The diagram shown here illustrates how the system works for a customer placing an order: the customer logs onto the Web site and types in an order for corrugated paper precisely cut and folded for 20,000 boxes. Computers at Corrugated's factory go to work immediately to determine the best way to blend that order with numerous other orders ranging from a few dozen boxes to 50,000. The computer comes up with the optimum schedule – that is, the one that gets the most orders out of a single roll with little leftover paper. A human operator checks the schedule on one of the numerous linked computer screens scattered around the plant and hits the Send button. Computer software directs the massive corrugators, trimmers, slitters and other equipment, which

EXHIBIT 8.9 Corrugated System in Action

A customer order comes in via the Web and the system suggests the optimum schedule. An employee reviews the schedule and downloads it into the database.

At the scheduled time, software downloads the order to production machinery.

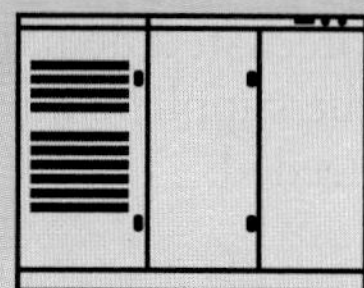

Employees load rolls of paper into the machines, which transform the rolls into corrugated sheets to meet the customer's exact specifications.

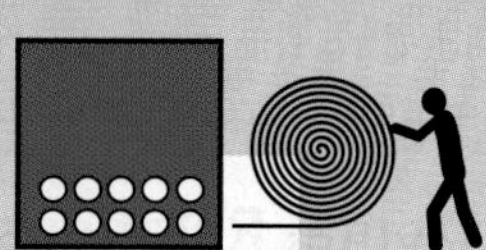

The truck driver arrives at the loading dock, logs onto the network to see which trailer to take, and delivers the customer's order the next morning.

A wireless PC directs the forklift driver to take the order to the appropriate trailer.

The package is taken by conveyor belt to shipping, which scans the bar code and adds the correct shipping label.

Employees wrap the finished sheets and affix a bar code printed automatically by the system.

Source: Adapted from Bill Richards, 'Superplant', *eCompany* (November 2000), 182–196.

begin spewing out paper orders at 250 metres per minute. Computer-controlled conveyor belts carry the order to the loading dock, where forklifts equipped with wireless PCs take the load to the designated trailer. Lorry drivers log onto the Web site and are told which trailer to haul to maximize their trip's efficiency. The order is usually delivered to the customer the very next day.

Today, over 80 per cent of Corrugated's orders are submitted via the Internet and routed electronically to the plant floor. The system saves time and money for Corrugated by automatically scheduling special-order details and cutting out paper waste. For customers, it means faster service and fewer mix-ups. One customer, Gene Mazurek, co-owner of Suburban Corrugated Box Co., says the first thing he does each morning is log onto Corrugated's Web site to see what's running, what's broken, where his order is and when it should arrive. The new system has cut Mazurek's delivery time to his own customers from a week down to 2 days, something larger competitors can't match. It's 'the best thing that's ever happened so far', says Mazurek. 'It's like Rick put his corrugating machine right inside my plant.'

In a second phase of technological upgrading, Corrugated Supplies integrated its proprietary order management system with Sage software's MAS, a standard ERP and management accounting system. This improved the Corrugated Supplies' financial controls and provided further order and financial information to customers. Corrugated has also integrated voice-over-internet-protocol (VOIP) telephone service into its data network. Not only did this result in substantial cost savings over traditional telephone service, it allowed the company's staff to answer calls outside normal office hours.

Corrugated Supplies' integrated web-based approach was so successful that the company decided to create a specialized subsidiary to commercialize the product for use in other paper manufacturing facilities. The spin-off, Blueque Systems, LLC, sells custom-designed systems that, like CSC's own, manage paper companies' order entry, scheduling, manufacturing, production, inventory, warehousing and shipping.[63]

and time demands. Albert Heijn supermarkets, a subsidiary of the Dutch Ahold corporation, uses extranet technologies extensively to do business both with its suppliers and its customers. The extranets are tied into a comprehensive overall business intelligence strategy. The company's suppliers can use the extranet to keep track of the company's orders, while retail customers can shop online and review purchase history. Technology also helps Albert Heijn maintain accurate distribution to its stores; it was one of the first supermarkets in the world to fully automate order picking from its distribution warehouses. The company was chosen as 'Smartest Organization in the Netherlands' by the 2008 Dutch Business Intelligence conference.[64,65]

As with the newer organization designs described in Chapter 3, horizontal relationships get more emphasis than vertical relationships for the integrated enterprise to work. Enterprise integration can create a level of cooperation not previously imaginable if managers approach the practice with an attitude of trust and partnership, as in the interorganizational relationships described in Chapter 5. For example, America's Wal-Mart and Procter & Gamble (P&G) started simply by sharing sales data so P&G goods could be automatically replaced as they were sold off Wal-Mart's shelves. However, this computer-to-computer exchange evolved into a horizontal relationship that had the two firms sharing customer information, shopper loyalty information and other data that provides strategic advantages for both sides of the trading partnership.[66]

See online
COUNTERPOINT 8.17

Customer Relationship Management

Another approach to strengthening external relationships is through the use of **customer relationship** (CRM) management systems. These systems help companies track customers' interactions with the firm and allow employees to call up a

As an organization manager, keep these guidelines in mind:

- Use an in-house e-business division to provide tight integration between the Internet operation and the traditional operation and leverage the brand name, customer information, suppliers and marketing muscle of the parent company.
- Create a spin-off company if the e-business unit needs greater autonomy and flexibility to adapt to rapidly changing market conditions.
- Consider a strategic partnership as a middle ground, but remember that partnerships involve dependency on other firms and require greater time spent managing relationships and resolving potential conflicts.

customer's past sales and service records, outstanding orders or unresolved problems.[67] CRM collects in a database all the customer information that a small-town store owner would keep in his or her head – the names of customers, what they bought, what problems they've had with purchases and so forth. The system helps coordinate sales, marketing and customer service departments so that all are smoothly working together.

E-Business Organization Design

CRM and the integrated enterprise are both components of e-business, a new approach to how organizations conduct their business activities. **E-business** can be defined as any business that takes place by digital processes over a computer network rather than in physical space. Most commonly, it refers to electronic linkages over the Internet with customers, partners, suppliers, employees or other key constituents. The early 2000s, the Internet continues to transform traditional ways of doing business, helping companies in industries from banking to manufacturing to music retailing cut costs, speed innovation and enhance relationships with customers.[68] Many traditional organizations have set up Internet operations to strengthen and improve these external relationships, but managers have to make a decision about how best to integrate *bricks and clicks* – that is, how to blend their traditional operations with an Internet initiative. In the early days of e-business, many organizations set up dot-com initiatives with little understanding of how those activities could and should be integrated with their overall business. As the reality of e-business has evolved, companies have gained valuable lessons in how to merge online and offline activities.[69]

The range of basic strategies for setting up an Internet operation is illustrated in Exhibit 8.10. In principle, there is nothing special about such operations as the same issue is confronted with the strategic options associated with engagement in any novel or non-core area of activity and expertise. At one end of the spectrum, companies can set up an in-house division that is closely integrated with the traditional business. The opposite approach is to create a spin-off company that is totally separate from the traditional organization. Many companies take a third

EXHIBIT 8.10 The Range of Strategies for Integrating Bricks and Clicks

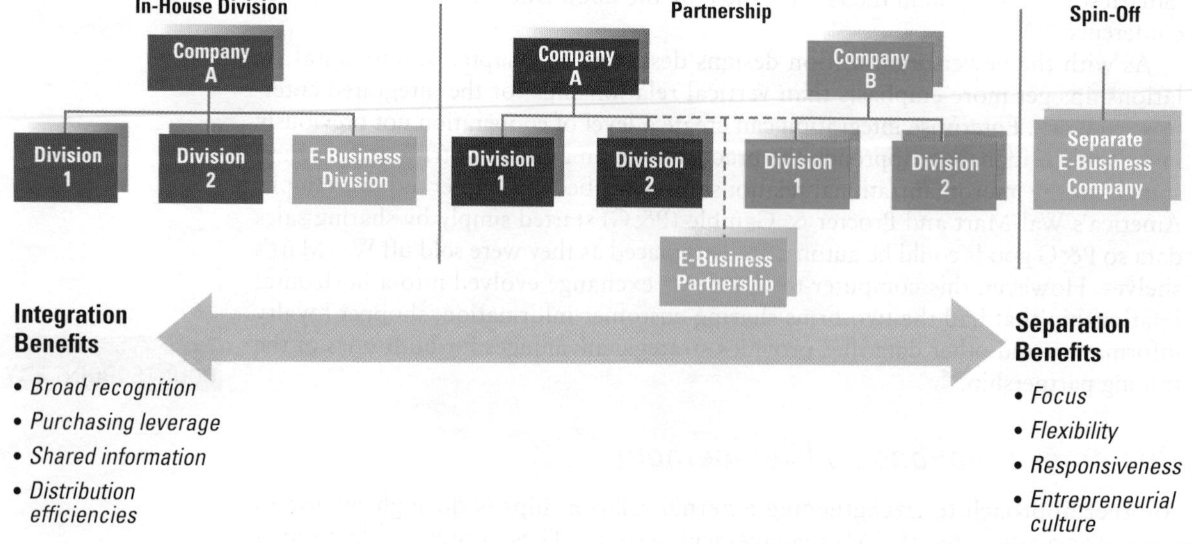

Source: Based on Ranjay Gulati and Jason Garino, 'Get the Right Mix of Bricks and Clicks,' *Harvard Business Review* (May–June 2000), 107–114.

Tesco.com

When Britain's number one supermarket chain, Tesco, decided to launch a dot-com operation, offering a grocery home delivery service, managers evaluated options and decided to set up an in-house division to avoid the huge start-up costs that would be required for a spin-off company. The idea was to start slowly and keep close control over the new operation to maintain profitability. Tesco managers saw their online service as just another way to attract and retain customers.

By being part of the greater Tesco enterprise, Tesco.com was able to ride on the back of the parent company, leveraging its brand, suppliers, advertising and customer database. Tesco started by offering delivery from just one store, gradually rolling out service to other areas. By integrating the new operation with the traditional stores, Tesco didn't have to build new warehouses; the Internet division simply used the established warehouses and distribution systems of the chain and picked goods off supermarket shelves to fill customer orders. Using the store-based picking approach kept start-up costs low. Tesco spent only $58 million on its Internet operation during the first four years, and the operation was profitable from the beginning. Consumer data is collected automatically, and integrated into the Clubcard scheme discussed earlier in this chapter. By the end of 2007, Tesco.com had grown to cover 95 per cent of the United Kingdom and was receiving 250,000 orders per week, although competition was also heating up from rival supermarkets like Sainsbury's and Asda/Wal-Mart.[70,71]

approach that involves forging strategic partnerships with other organizations for their Internet initiative. Each of these options presents distinct advantages and disadvantages.[72]

In-House Division An in-house division offers tight integration between the Internet operation and the organization's traditional operation. The organization creates a separate unit within the company that functions within the structure and guidance of the traditional organization. This approach gives the new division several advantages which include brand recognition, purchasing leverage with suppliers, shared customer information and marketing opportunities and distribution efficiencies. For example, Tesco developed its online grocery delivery by keeping Tesco.com closely integrated with the existing grocery chain.

Tesco's success illustrates many of the advantages of the in-house approach. A potential problem with an in-house division, however, is that the new operation might not have the flexibility and autonomy needed to move quickly in the Internet world.

Spin-Off To give their Internet operations greater organizational autonomy, flexibility and focus, and to cash in on sometimes high valuations of internet stocks, many organizations have chosen to create a separate spin-off company. For example, Sony Japan spun off its ISP and internet portal So-Net into a separately listed company in 2006, with the new company enjoying increased revenues through development of niche content pulling strong advertising interest.[73] Many telephone companies have spun-off part or all of their internet operations, including British Telecom,[74] Portugal Telecom[75] and Hungary's Magyar Telekom.[76] Other companies have gone in the opposite direction; former Canadian publishing giant Thomson sold off most of its print publication properties to focus on electronic information delivery.[77] Advantages of a spin-off can include faster decision making, increased flexibility and responsiveness to changing market conditions, an entrepreneurial culture and management that is totally focused on the success of the online operation. Potential disadvantages include the loss of brand recognition and marketing opportunities, higher start-up costs and loss of leverage with suppliers. The fate of internet spin-offs is also closely linked to volatile investor sentiment about high-tech stocks; for example, US appliance manufacturer Whirlpool's Brandwise.com spinoff, a site designed to help consumers find the best products and value, went under during a dotcom sell-off in 2000.[78]

Strategic Partnership Partnerships, whether through joint ventures or alliances, offer a middle ground, enabling organizations to attain some of the advantages and overcome some of the disadvantages of the purely in-house or spin-off options. For example, Canadian used book distributor Abebooks acts as a portal for independent booksellers to sell their books through the internet. Although consumers can buy their books directly from Abebook's Web site, its books are also listed on Amazon Web sites across the world, as well as other major internet booksellers such as WH Smith in the UK and Buch.de in Germany, thus providing a much larger audience.[79] Another ecommerce partnership option for small and medium sized enterprises is of course eBay, the giant auction site discussed earlier in the chapter. More than 70,000 people in the UK alone earn a full-time living from selling on eBay.[80] It is difficult to argue with the advice of Drew Sharma, managing director of Internet marketing agency Mindfire Interactive, for smaller companies going online: 'If you can stand on the shoulders of giants, then why not?'[81] Disadvantages of partnerships include time spent managing relationships, potential conflicts between partners and a possibility that one company will fail to deliver as promised or go out of business.

IT Impact on Organization Design

As an organization manager, keep this guideline in mind:

With greater use of IT, consider smaller organizational units, decentralized structures, improved internal coordination and greater interorganizational collaboration, including the possibility of outsourcing or a network structure.

Not every organization will become involved in e-business like Tesco, Corrugated Supplies or Abebooks. However, advances in IT are having a tremendous impact on all organizations in every industry. Some specific implications of these advances for organization design are smaller organizations, decentralized structures, improved internal and external coordination and new network organization structures.

1 *Smaller organizations*. Some Internet-based businesses exist almost entirely in cyberspace; there is no formal organization in terms of a building with offices, desks and so forth. One or a few people may maintain the site from their homes or a rented work space. Even for traditional businesses, new IT enables the organization to do more work with fewer people. Nowadays most customers can buy car insurance without ever speaking to an agent or sales rep. In addition, ERP and other IT systems automatically handle many administrative duties, reducing the need for clerical staff. British cattle breeder Alan Swale, who owns a renowned herd, uses the internet to sell top quality semen directly to commercial dairy herds at a reasonable cost – typically around £10 per dose – far less than if a middleman was involved.[82,83] Companies can also make use of internet and other telecommunications technologies to outsource many functions and thus use fewer in-house resources. There is an increasing trend to 'shared services' where functional departments are consolidated internationally and either

outsourced or operated at a lower cost offshore location. For example, many of the back office operations of Standard Chartered, the London-headquartered international bank, are carried out in India by Scope, a subsidiary of Standard Chartered India.[84]

2 *Decentralized organizational structures.* IT enables organizations to reduce layers of management and decentralize decision making. Information that may have previously been available only to top managers at headquarters can be quickly and easily shared throughout the organization, even across great geographical distances. Managers in varied business divisions or offices have the information to make decisions quickly rather than waiting for decisions from headquarters. Technologies that enable people to meet and coordinate online can facilitate communication and decision making among distributed, autonomous groups of workers. In addition, technology allows for telecommuting, whereby individual workers can perform work that was once done in the office from their computers at home or other remote locations. People and groups no longer have to be located under one roof to collaborate and share information. An organization might be made up of numerous small teams or even individuals who work autonomously but coordinate electronically. Although management philosophy informs whether IT is used to decentralize information and authority or to reinforce a centralized authority structure,[85] technology tends to be used to further decentralization within centrally defined parameters.

3 *Improved horizontal coordination.* IT has the potential to improve coordination and communication within the firm. Intranets and other networks can connect people even when their offices, factories or stores are scattered around the world. The British Council, a charity established to build relationships between the UK and other countries, has invested in a comprehensive internal communications system including not just a corporate intranet, but also special software to permit 'virtual meetings', a necessity for an organization with 7,900 staff in 110 countries and territories. Andrew Walker, collaboration consultant at the Council, says that, 'users are very happy as time and effort in completing projects has been reduced and travel cut through digital meetings'.[86]

4 *Improved interorganizational relationships.* IT can also improve horizontal coordination and collaboration with external parties such as suppliers, customers and partners. Extranets are increasingly important for linking companies with contract manufacturers and outsourcers, as well as for supporting the integrated enterprise, as described earlier. Exhibit 8.11 shows differences between traditional interorganizational relationship characteristics and emerging relationship characteristics. Traditionally, organizations had an arms-length relationship with suppliers. However, as we discussed in Chapter 5, suppliers are becoming closer partners, tied electronically to the organization for orders, invoices and payments. In addition, new IT has increased the power of consumers by giving them electronic access to a wealth of information from thousands of companies just by clicking a mouse. Consumers also have direct access to manufacturers, altering their perceptions and expectations regarding convenience, speed and service.

Studies have shown that interorganizational information networks tend to heighten integration and redefine organizational boundaries.[87] One good example of interorganizational collaboration is the Canada Health Infoway. The Infoway, funded by the Canadian federal government, helps ensure best

EXHIBIT 8.11 Key Characteristics of Traditional versus Emerging Interorganizational Relationships

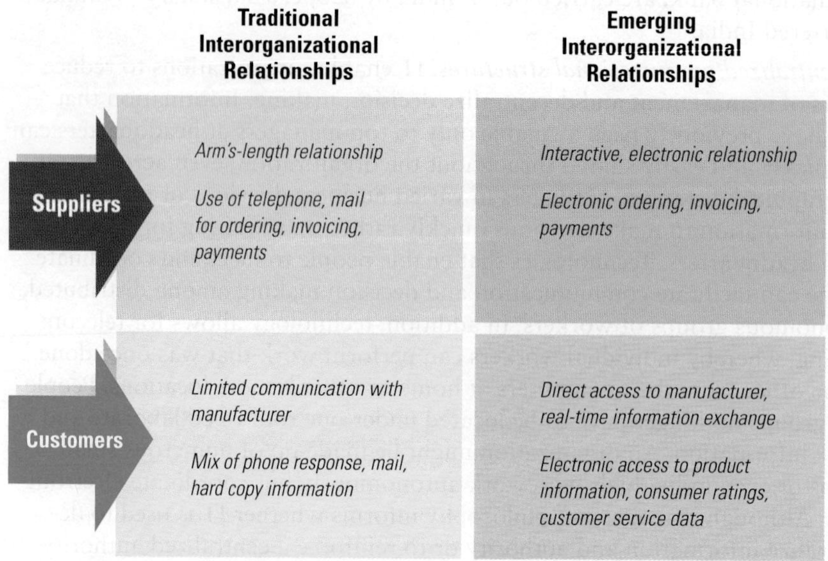

Source: Based on Charles V. Callahan and Bruce A. Pasternack, 'Corporate Strategy in the Digital Age,' *Strategy & Business*, Issue 15 (Second Quarter 1999), 10–14.

practices in health care are shared across the 13 provincial and territorial health care systems that are responsible for operating Canada's national medicare system. In addition, the Infoway will provide early warning in case of infectious disease outbreaks. Infoway is also pioneering the use of electronic health records (EHRs) that, when fully implemented, will give doctors instant access to Canadians' medical records when they seek treatment anywhere in the country, thus ensuring appropriate treatment.[88,89]

5 *Enhanced network structures.* The high level of interorganizational collaboration demanded by a network organization structure, described in Chapter 3, would not be possible without the use of advanced IT. In the business world, these are also sometimes called *modular structures* or *virtual organizations*. Outsourcing has become a major trend, thanks to computer technology that, in principle, can tie companies together into a seamless information flow. For example, Hong Kong's Li & Fung is one of the biggest providers of clothing for retailers such as Abercrombie & Fitch, Guess, Ann Taylor, the Limited and Disney, but the company doesn't own any factories, machines or fabrics. Li & Fung specializes in managing information, relying on an electronically connected web of 7,500 partners in thirty-seven countries to provide raw materials and assemble the clothes. Using an extranet allows Li & Fung to stay in touch with worldwide partners and move items quickly from factories to retailers. It also enables retailers to track orders as they move through production and make last-minute changes and additions.[90] With a network structure, most activities are outsourced, so that different companies perform the various functions needed by the organization. The speed and ease of electronic communication makes the network structure a viable option for companies that want to keep costs low but expand activities or market presence.

Future Trends

The rapid development of internet technologies means that it is very difficult to predict their future business impact. Just as Amazon has revolutionized bookselling, and eBay has created a whole new breed of small-time entrepreneurs, it can be expected that new technologies will emerge in the coming years that will have comparable impacts on both business life and organizational structure.[91]

One major development area in the first decade of the twenty-first century has been the emergence of what is known as Web 2.0.[92] Although Web 2.0 has been defined in different ways, basically it involves different tools for on-line communication, information sharing and collaboration, ranging from the virtual worlds of applications like Second Life, through YouTube with its user-generated video content, to Facebook, MySpace and their myriad rivals. These new internet vehicles differ from previous internet approaches because – to a greater or lesser extent depending on the specific application – users themselves create the environments in which they interact. Some of the applications have become enormously popular, and have attracted very high stock valuations. Facebook, for example, which claims 100 million users, has been variously estimated to be worth up to $15 billion, though its annual revenue is only $300 million.[93] Internet stocks often have very high price/revenue ratios because of the anticipation of rapid and sustained growth.

Web 2.0 technologies are ingenious because much of the work is done by the users themselves; on Facebook for example people take the time to invite friends to join their networks, post pictures and write accounts of their current activities, and it is this user-generated content that attracts traffic to the site. Such Web 2.0 applications are distinctive form of organization in respect of the extent of user involvement in their content.

The problem Web 2.0 initiatives tend to face is how to earn revenue.[94] Some Web 2.0 networking concepts have already faced this crunch; Iyomu, an adult social networking site set up by New Zealand entrepreneurs, folded in 2008 after less than a year in operation, despite attracting 100,000 users.[95] The simplest revenue generating idea is to copy Google's approach through delivering advertising at the side or bottom of the page that is derived from characteristics of the content and conversations in which the users are involved. Like Google, however, Web 2.0 companies must address accusations that the monitoring required to identify suitable advertising is an invasion of privacy. Other Web 2.0 initiatives have found niche approaches to making money. Virtual worlds can be used as a vehicle to promote specific products, such as Barbie.com, which also offers a paid 'VIP' membership to its users.[96] Apart from selling advertising in its virtual world, Second Life has explored marketing the virtual space for corporations to run simulations as part of staff training. Indie musicians have often used MySpace which, in 2008, was still the biggest of the Web 2.0 domains (but rapidly being overtaken by Facebook). Musicians use MySpace to promote their material which in turn provides MySpace with a ready-made audience for ads for music downloads and related paid services.[97]

In theory, however, the greatest value that remains to be unlocked is in the networks themselves. Long before the internet, personal social networks have been used as a business foundation – for example by cosmetics companies Avon and Mary Kay that sell through distributors' own connections. Web 2.0 communities are much larger and potentially more lucrative. Whoever discovers the key to unlock this potential, while avoiding privacy pitfalls, will have a significant impact. Wishful thinking? Possibly, but lots of people said that Google had little business potential.[98] That internet startup recorded a forty-fold increase in revenues between 2002 and 2007, from $400 million to $16 billion, and is still growing, fast.[99]

Summary and Interpretation

The information revolution has had a tremendous impact on organizations in all sectors. Operations applications are applied to well-defined tasks at lower organization levels and help to improve efficiency. These include transaction processing systems, data warehousing and data mining. Advanced computer-based systems are also used for better decision making and control of the organization. Decision-making systems include management information systems, reporting systems, decision support systems and executive information systems, which are typically used at middle and upper levels of the organization. Management control systems include budgets and financial reports, periodic nonfinancial statistical reports, reward systems and quality control systems. The *balanced scorecard* technique provides managers with a more holistic view of the organization by integrating traditional financial measurements and statistical reports with a concern for markets, customers and employees.

Intranets, ERP and knowledge management systems are used primarily to support greater internal coordination, and can aid flexibility. Systems that support and strengthen external relationships include extranets and the integrated enterprise, customer relationship management and e-business. Advanced uses of IT enables close coordination among a company and its suppliers, partners and customers. Customer relationship management systems help companies keep track of their customers' interactions with the organization and provide better service. To establish an e-business, companies have created an in-house division, developed a spin-off or entered a strategic partnership.

Advanced IT is having a significant impact on the design of organizations. Technology enables companies to implement a wider range of organizational design options. It has supported the growth of network organization structures in which a company subcontracts most of its major functions to separate companies that are connected electronically, but it can also enable greater co-ordination and centralization of decision making. Other specific implications of advances in technology for organization design include a tendency toward smaller organizations that concentrate on their core competencies, decentralized organization structures and improved internal and external coordination.

Internet technologies are moving so fast that it is difficult to identify what will be the 'next big thing' five years, two years, or even one year down the road. One rapidly developing area is social networking, where users create their own social spaces in hosted environments. If the revenue potential of these sites can be unlocked in ethically-sound ways, they may form the basis of important new business and organizational models.

KEY CONCEPTS

balanced scorecard
benchmarking
business intelligence
customer relationship management
data
data mining
data warehousing
decision support system
e-business
enterprise resource planning
executive information system
explicit knowledge
extranet
feedback control model
information
information reporting system
integrated enterprise
intellectual capital
intranet
knowledge
knowledge management
management control systems
management information system
networking
Six Sigma
tacit knowledge
Web 2.0
transaction processing systems

Discussion Questions

1 Do you think technology will eventually enable top managers to do their jobs with little face-to-face communication? Discuss.

2 Why might a company consider using an intranet rather than traditional management and executive information systems?

3 How might an enterprise resource planning system be used to improve strategic management of a manufacturing organization?

4 Discuss some ways a large insurance company such as Progressive, described in the chapter opening, might use MIS to improve decision making.

5 Describe how the four management control system elements discussed in the chapter might be used for feedback control within organizations. Compare and contrast this four-part system with use of the balanced scorecard.

6 Describe your use of explicit knowledge when you research and write a term paper. Do you also use tacit knowledge regarding this activity? Discuss.

7 Why is knowledge management particularly important to a company that wants to become a learning organization?

8 What is meant by the integrated enterprise? Describe how organizations can use extranets to extend and enhance horizontal relationships required for enterprise integration.

9 What are some competitive issues that might lead a company to take a partnership approach to e-business rather than setting up an in-house Internet division? What are the advantages and disadvantages of each approach?

10 How might the adoption of IT affect how an organization is designed?

11 What business potential does Web 2.0 have?

Workbook Are You Fast Enough to Succeed in Internet Time?

Does your business have what it takes to move at Internet speed?

What is an Internet year? It's the time in which an e-company needs to accomplish the kind of business goals that once took a year. Conventional wisdom puts an Internet year at anywhere from 60 to 90 days. Regardless, few will argue that companies need to move faster now than ever imagined.

Can you afford the luxury of in-depth analysis, full due diligence, building consensus, test marketing – all the cornerstones of responsible corporate management? Does their value change when you weigh it against the cost to your company's scarcest commodity – time? Kelsey Biggers, executive vice president of Micro Modeling Associates (MMA), offers the following scenarios to help determine whether you are capable of operating at Internet speed. Choose the best course of action from the choices given (answers below):

Question

1 You have met a company that can be a potential strategic partner for marketing your service to a new industry online. The vibes are good, and you want to map out the potential relationship, but to do so you need to share client and billing information. A nondisclosure agreement is necessary, and the company hands you its standard agreement. What do you do?

   a Get a copy of your company's standard nondisclosure agreement and submit it to your potential partner as an alternative to its NDA.

   b Fax or email the agreement to your lawyer and ask him or her to get back to you ASAP with any amendments so you can continue the conversation.

   c Look over the agreement and sign it right away.

2 You're looking for a creative director for your Web site, and you know the position will be critical to your whole look and feel online. You hope to have three or four excellent

candidates to choose from and have considered doing a retained search for the position. Out of nowhere your old university roommate, whom you respect enormously, refers you to an associate for the position. You meet the candidate for breakfast and you are bowled over by the person's credentials and personality. You have three choices:

a Offer the candidate the job before the bill arrives.

b Give the candidate strong positive feedback about the job while you initiate a quick search for a couple of alternative candidates.

c Schedule a round of interviews with your senior colleagues back in the office to confirm your positive instincts, while also identifying one or two alternative candidates for comparison.

3 Your online strategy calls for targeting two vertical markets for your service in the next nine months. Your service can be tailored to meet the buying needs of companies in several industries, so it's a matter of picking the right industries to target. High-growth, dynamic industries are obviously preferred. Which approach would you select?

a Hire an MBA with expertise in finance and marketing to create high-level screening criteria for target industries and identify the five best fits for your services.

b Hire your neighbour, who happens to be a doctor, knows the health care industry and can make several introductions to hospital administrations and pharmaceutical companies.

c Ask an intern to research publicly available information from Forrester Research, Ipsos and other market research organizations for online spending habits in different industries and make recommendations.

4 Your company has been looking to merge with a strategic partner for some time. You have identified three companies that would be good fits, but each has its advantages and disadvantages. Which would you choose?

a Company A offers a service that is perfectly complementary to your own, and the price is right. However, the company has indicated that it doesn't think it has enough scale to do a merger now and would rather wait nine months until after the holiday selling season to complete the transaction.

b Company B is smaller and dynamic, but has grown too fast and has a bad balance sheet. It could be picked up immediately, but your company would have to assume some unwanted debt along with the merger.

c Company C has a great offline presence in its space, but has not yet executed its e-commerce plan. The two companies might be a great fit once Company C has established its online presence by midsummer.

5 Your e-commerce strategy requires a real-time fulfilment system that can process orders straight through and provide data on client buying patterns. You have looked outside your firm for technology support to help bring this capability online and have been presented with three alternatives:

a A senior programmer from your prior firm is now a freelance consultant. He can get started immediately and hire a dozen coders who promise to get a capability up and running in 60 days and grow out the functionality.

b Your internal technology group can staff a team of a dozen people to build out the system in a year and will then have the ability to support and grow the service when it goes live.

c An e-solutions consultancy can project manage and build the entire system, but would want to take 60 days to design the technical architecture before starting development. The consultancy insists this time is necessary to ensure a scalable service.

Answers (Each correct answer is worth one point.)

Question 1

c The objective is to make a decision quickly and to move the process forward without a great deal of red tape and delay. The legal process can oftentimes slow decision making – whether by three weeks or three months – and time is of the essence in the online world. Moreover, when was the last time an NDA about client information materially affected your business? Better to spend your time building trust than protecting against an unlikely downside.

Question 2

a Offer the candidate the job while waiting for the bill. If this person has been vouched for by someone you trust and you love the person's work, grab the candidate while he or she is available and put that person to work. If you think the candidate is a great hire, chances are, so will your competitors.

Question 3

b Hire your neighbour. Any list of dynamic industries you put together is bound to include health care, and your biggest challenge is to find a credible person with industry know-how and contacts who can take you into the industry. Your neighbour can do that. Now start looking for the other industries you want to focus on.

Question 4

b Buy Company B. Company B has proven itself fast-moving and dynamic, and its balance sheet issues makes it open to a favourable price. Companies A and C are both tying their success to future events – a strong holiday selling season or a successful online launch – either of which might not happen and both of which are in the distant Internet future.

Question 5

c The one area a company cannot afford to get wrong is its technical architecture. It must scale and be reliable, or your whole business will be at risk. Programmers without a blueprint cannot ensure a successful online environment, and staffing internally is time-consuming and uncertain. Better to outsource the project immediately while building an internal team to take it over after its launch.

CASE FOR ANALYSIS

Project Tyne: Using an Extranet in Construction

By Kate Kenny, *University of Cambridge*

Introduction

Noel Allen was the design manager in charge of Project Tyne. This was an office facility construction project, based in Hartfield, an hour north of London. The project was £60 million in value and was to house one of the UK's leading mobile phone companies. Noel worked for the main contracting firm on the job, Kent Construction. His job was to oversee and manage both the design of the building and its construction. Unusually, the project was to be 'fast-tracked' for completion in a mere ten months, to meet the requirements of the client company.

Noel knew that it would be difficult to meet this fast-track deadline, given the size and scope of the project. Construction projects, in his experience, were noted for their inefficiencies (see Features of Construction Projects).

Features of Construction Projects

Construction projects involve a number of separate firms coming together to collaborate: the architect, the structural engineer, the building contractor and the services engineer to name but a few.

Communication practices and patterns in the construction sector are quite deeply embedded: there are traditional ways of doing things that are difficult to dislodge. For example, when it comes to document sharing, communication is based on a 'point-to-point' system between firms; typically, when one party completes a document, copies are circulated to the rest of the project team, via post, fax or, sometimes, email. The receiving parties then make corrections and comments on the documents, which are returned to their author for incorporation into the next version.

Each firm typically has its own way of sharing information and documents, along with its own, in-house IT systems. For example, it is common for an architect's office to use Macs, while engineers often use PCs. Similarly, there are a number of computer aided drawing packages (CAD) available, and it is not unusual for collaborating offices to be using different ones: resulting in compatibility issues.

Another source of inefficiency in construction involves the fact that, while other industries have worked hard to develop IT standards (such as what format to use, for saving files), construction has not.

In addition, collaborating firms often have different levels of IT sophistication, with respect both to their systems, and training in the firms.

People working together on a construction project tend not to meet, face-to-face, very often. Given the level of complexity involved in this collaboration work, engagement between firms tends to be surprisingly low; team meetings typically often occur only once per fortnight. This feature of the industry is useful in that it enables firms to become productive quite quickly, once a new project begins: all firms know what is required of them and do not rely too heavily on a period of negotiation around the manner in which work will be carried out (a feature also found in the film production industry).

A short-term outlook on inter-firm collaborations persists. For example, construction industry projects involve short-term alliances, with a new team assembled for each new project. A given contracting firm may never work with the same architect twice. People tend not to concern themselves with developing ongoing inter-firm relationships, and this feature tends to mean relationships are hands-off, with a reluctance to invest time and energy.

In addition, a culture of mistrust can persist between collaborating firms: architects traditionally do not trust contractors, and engineers typically view architects as impractical. These cultural divisions between professions are attributed to clear distinctions introduced early on, at university. The different professions tend to learn very little about other parts of the construction process, and these distinctions are continually reinforced through the ways projects are carried out.

Knowing all of this, Noel's concerns were understandable: coordinating documents and communication between the parties on his team was going to take a lot of effort.

At this point, Noel Allen wondered whether an extranet system would help manage the significant challenges that lay ahead, as the inter-organizational team struggled to build the £60m facility in a mere ten months. He investigated the potential of one software in particular, BuildNet. This software enables the sharing of project information between collaborating firms, via a centrally hosted Internet repository. On such systems, shared information is hosted electronically on a central server, with access being given to relevant members of the project team via username and password (see Extranet Features).

Extranet Features

A customizable 'Project Homepage' with images of the project, latest updates and relevant web links (for example, to media articles on the project, or to material suppliers' websites).

A central document manager where files can be organised and managed by project members.

Built-in viewing software where users can view and add comments to documents, drawings and Computer Aided Design (CAD) files regardless of the software package used to create the file.

An automatic messaging facility that notifies team members when new files have been added to the project site. Members can choose to receive these updates by text message, email or fax.

Online forms that resemble the paper forms normally used in construction. Examples include 'Requests for Information', typically issued by the contractor to the architect if there is a query about an aspect of a design, and 'Submittals' which are issued when a document must be checked by another party on the project.

A facility to maintain a complete audit trail of all activity on the Project Website; e.g. who has opened, saved, edited or added a given document and the date and time that the action in question was carried out.

Server space is typically rented for an annual fee from the software provider, who develops and maintains the web-based interface technology.

By using a centralized collaboration system like BuildNet, with its reporting, 'request for information' and messaging facilities, Noel Allen hoped that Kent's role in coordinating the project would be made easier. He also expressed the hope that the significant administration costs that are associated with a project of this scale might be reduced. In construction, traditional methods of sending around paper versions of drawings, sketches, instructions and meeting minutes are estimated to form 1 per cent of the total project cost (£600,000 st.).

Based on this rationale, Noel Allen approached his bosses, and the client, and asked that the project make use of the BuildNet system. He was supported by Paul Martin, the architect, who agreed that it was worth trying. Paul said that his firm would commit to working with Noel to ensure that the implementation and use of the system was a success. Senior management informed Noel that they were unwilling to make an official decision to approve the use of new and untested software, on a project that was so strategically important. He could 'unofficially' purchase the software, but they would not openly sanction the decision. It was left up to Noel Allen and his team to justify its cost at the end of the project.

Having obtained this indication of support, Noel brought the idea to the wider project team; that a collaboration system would be used going forward. Some agreed that this seemed like a sensible progression. Others expressed reservations. The project team encountered significant hurdles before this software could be implemented successfully. First, there was no culture of co-ordination or trust within the group. While the architect's firm noted that they would like to work with Kent Construction on future projects, this was not certain. In general, there was little emphasis on the formation and development of long-term relationships between the design team firms and the contractor. In addition to these 'cultural issues', working practices around existing technologies proved difficult to leave behind.

The Services Engineer's Perspective

Peter Burton, the project services engineer from Antec, a well-known firm, described how, in his firm, the use of existing technologies had been disrupted by BuildNet. In the short time in which he was working on the project, prior to using the new software, email had developed as the main way in which Antec staff communicated with other design team firms. Even this, according to Peter, had represented a significant progression from previous projects, on which fax or post had chiefly been used. Antec were still struggling to get used to email.

In addition to this *technological* change, the use of BuildNet implied a significant upset to *working practices* for Peter and his organization. As in many engineering firms, workflows in Antec involved incoming project emails and documents being printed off by junior staff and delivered to the engineering manager's desk in paper format for checking and revising. In contrast, BuildNet would require Peter himself to go online, input a username and password, and take the responsibility for downloading and checking the drawings on the system. For Peter, in a busy construction environment, time spent doing what a junior staff member could be doing, such as operating the BuildNet system, was seen as time wasted. In addition, not all PCs at Antec had Internet connections, a common arrangement within engineering firms in Ireland and the UK.

> 'The onus is on *you* to go in and get it (the information) out of the system. Previously, if someone sends you drawings they land on your desk. Now I have to download them and I don't have the resources in-house to do that.' (Peter Burton, Services Engineer)

When it was introduced into this context, the BuildNet system presented an unwelcome source of delay on a job that was already operating under significant time pressure:

> 'It was proposed as a system that would make things quicker but I could see it was the opposite; because of the time taken to get things out of the system. It meant more time in front of the computer rather than doing what you should be doing; designing.' (Peter Burton, Services Engineer)

Furthermore, while many architects, including Paul Martin, are typically responsible for *one* job at a time; within engineering firms like Antec, designers are often working on many projects at once. Standardized processes are difficult to change for just one project while the old way of working remains in place for all others. Peter Burton made the rest of the project team aware of his views on BuildNet, but construction manager Noel Allen chose to push ahead with the system.

The Contractor's Perspective

Noel arranged for full training on the system to be carried out in the offices of all involved. Once training had been completed, both the architect and contracting firms began to promote BuildNet as the only means by which construction drawings and documents would be issued to site. Even with resistance from, for example, the services engineer, Noel Allen actively promoted the system, and insisted that it be used.

Even though Noel was now pushing ahead, the continuing use of the system was not without its problems. Given that much of printing activity had to take place on site, in a prefabricated hut, it was difficult to obtain good data speeds to this makeshiftoffice. This resulted in complaints about the speed of the system:

> 'It is really time wasting to be honest. . . . We just don't have the speed here. If we did then that would be fantastic.' (Lara Wilkes, Design Co-ordinator, Kent Construction)

Nonetheless, Kent's site-based staff used the BuildNet system for all project communication from start to finish. In doing so, they found that they had to innovate and experiment with the way work was carried out in order to keep up with the speed of document exchange on this fast-track project, while still maintaining the integrity of the painfully slow BuildNet system. For example, where a piece of information was needed urgently, it often made more sense to email or fax it. However, the relevant document or message would always be recorded on BuildNet after this was done, in order to maintain the completeness of the electronic project record. Despite labouring under these slow connections, Kent staff spoke about the reduction in administrative work that the BuildNet system provided to them:

> 'You *are* cutting out the distribution time to the contractors and the clients. For someone in my position, I am not copying drawings to everyone; I will just copy one for our engineers, not eight.' (Lara Wilkes, Design Co-ordinator, Kent Construction)

While co-ordination of the design team was Noel Allen's original motive for implementing the BuildNet system, the potential for broader applications of the technology soon became apparent. For example, the opportunity of gaining cost savings in distribution of documents to subcontractors via the software had not been foreseen in advance, but only occurred to him once use of the system was underway. By making all documentation available to subcontractors in electronic format, it was hoped that administration costs, and time involved in printing and distributing documents around the site, would be greatly reduced. This move met with significant resistance from subcontractors. Again, however, Noel actively promoted the system:

> 'Kent spent time and effort and repeatedly stressed to the subcontractors that this is how you are going to get information out of us. If you are not on the system, you are not going to get any information. So if you are expecting these drawings on Tuesday, don't bother ringing us on Wednesday to say you don't have them. The people in Kent were very hard-nosed initially. The response from some subcontractors was; we don't know how to get on the system,

and Kent staff would say, get BuildNet in and get some training.' (Nigel Franklin, Account Manager)

Whenever a subcontractor came to the site office claiming that their Internet connection was 'down for the day', Kent staff would relent and provide a paper version of whatever drawing was required to progress with the work.

'There was a little bit of under the table dealing with little bits of information but it was relatively modest.' (Paul Martin, Architect)

As the project progressed, the amount of leniency shown was reduced.

The Architect's Perspective

Architect Paul Martin made changes to his working practices in order to use the BuildNet system. Specifically, he changed the file formats he was using. His firm was using a different computer aided design (CAD) graphics package to the rest of the design team and so it was problematic to transmit electronic drawings. Having experimented with different possible solutions, Paul decided to convert his files to the common PDF format, which had the advantage of reducing the file size of his drawings. This resulted in quicker upload times to the BuildNet system. PDF format also enabled Paul to determine in advance how the eventual printed document would appear, regardless of the printer or software used to print it. In the rare instance where individuals required the actual files, these would be converted and sent.

For Paul, BuildNet represented a series of unforeseen advantages, including helping him to keep tabs on his own work on the project:

'So what it *does* mean, although it sounds silly, is that every single drawing going onto BuildNet, I've seen, and I've checked and I have uploaded it. Now you could say that an administration assistant or someone else should be doing all of that, but as Project Architect, if I were doing prints, I would be supposed to check all the prints and sign every single drawing that goes out. But the fact that I have uploaded it; BuildNet has a record of every single drawing that it was *me* that uploaded it and exactly when I did it. If I were to get our technicians to upload drawings, how would I know what had gone up; did he put it up? Did he do what I wanted him to do? And I think that that is where companies have to modify their management strategies; of how they do a job.' (Paul Martin, Architect)

Reflecting on the advantages and disadvantages that he and his team had experienced,Paul commented that:

'...So from my point of view, it has made my life possible. I would not want to do another serious job without a system like this.' (Paul Martin, Architect)

The Software Provider's Perspective

Requests were made regularly to the software provider for various enhancements to the functionality. These changes were generally implemented by the software provider a month or two after the initial request came in from Noel Allen.

'We have made some changes; to start with we didn't have the option to look at all the actions linked to a particular piece of information, so we requested this and now you can do this. So that was a good change. We needed that because the previous system we had for managing documents had a checking procedure like this.' (Lara Wilkes, Design Co-ordinator, Kent Construction)

Due to the scale of Kent Construction, and its influence in the UK construction sector, software provider BuildNet reported that they were keen to impress Kent, so that the firm might use BuildNet on other projects in their substantial portfolio.

Summary

It would be simplistic to say that the implementation of BuildNet was a resounding 'success'. Different meanings were clearly attributed to the system by different parties. While some members of the project team, including the architect firm and Kent's own staff, embraced the system and used it actively from the outset, other parties, such as the services engineer and some subcontractors, were more reluctant. Despite the reluctance shown by Peter Burton and others on the project, and despite the slow Internet connection experienced by Kent on the site, by the time design co-ordinator Lara Wilkes joined the project, the system had become almost totally embedded.

'I had just come from another job, and the other job I have been on, everything was paper distributed. Then I came to Hartfield and it just was the norm, it was what they were using. If you didn't use it, you just wouldn't have access to everything you need!' (Lara Wilkes, Design Co-ordinator, Kent Construction)

It is clear that Noel Allen's efforts were successful. He overcame significant challenges to ensure that the technology was implemented, albeit in unforeseen ways, and justified his initial 'leap of faith'. Noel had negotiated and encouraged its use across the project team, and he ensured that adjustments to working practices and the technology itself were carried out when needed. Finally, he had spotted the unexpected opportunity of bringing the subcontractors onto the system. At Project Tyne, this move changed BuildNet from a system facilitating design team work, to a cross-project information repository and communication tool.

Case Questions

1 What were the underlying issues in the construction industry that led to the introduction of BuildNet?

2 What were the key elements of BuildNet?

3 What were the main challenges faced by the different people implementing BuildNet (service engineer, contractor, architect, software engineer)

4 To what extent was BuildNet a success? Could BuildNet have been implemented more efficiently or effectively?

CASE FOR ANALYSIS

Product X

Several years ago the top management of a multi-billion-dollar corporation decided that Product X was a failure and should be disbanded. The losses involved exceeded $100 million. At least five people knew that Product X was a failure six years before the decision was made to stop producing it. Three of those people were plant managers who lived daily with the production problems. The other two were marketing officials who realized that the manufacturing problems were not solvable without expenditures that would raise the price of the product to the point where it would no longer be competitive in the market.

There are several reasons why this information did not get to the top sooner. At first, the subordinates believed that with exceptionally hard work they might turn the errors into successes. But the more they struggled, the more they realized the massiveness of the original error. The next task was to communicate the bad news upward so that it would be heard. They knew that in their company bad news would not be well received at the upper levels if it was not accompanied with suggestions for positive action. They also knew that the top management was enthusiastically describing Product X as a new leader in its field. Therefore, they spent much time composing memos that would communicate the realities without shocking top management.

Middle management read the memos and found them too open and forthright. Since they had done the production and marketing studies that resulted in the decision to produce X, the memos from lower-level management questioned the validity of their analysis. They wanted time to really check these gloomy predictions and, if they were accurate, to design alternative corrective strategies. If the pessimistic information was to be sent upward, middle management wanted it accompanied with optimistic action alternatives. Hence further delay.

Once middle management was convinced that the gloomy predictions were valid, they began to release some of the bad news to the top – but in carefully measured doses. They managed the releases carefully to make certain they were covered if top management became upset. The tactic they used was to cut the memos drastically and summarize the findings. They argued that the cuts were necessary because top management was always complaining about receiving long memos; indeed, some top executives had let it be known that good memos were memos of one page or less. The result was that top management received fragmented information underplaying the intensity of the problem (not the problem itself) and overplaying the degree to which middle management and the technicians were in control of the problem.

Top management therefore continued to speak glowingly about the product, partially to ensure that it would get the financial backing it needed from within the company. Lower-level management became confused and eventually depressed because they could not understand this continued top management support, nor why studies were ordered to evaluate the production and marketing difficulties that they had already identified. Their reaction was to reduce the frequency of their memos and the intensity of their alarm, while simultaneously turning over the responsibility for dealing with the problem to middle-management people. When local plant managers, in turn, were asked by their foremen and employees what was happening, the only response they gave was that the company was studying the situation and continuing its support. This information bewildered the foremen and led them to reduce their own concern.

Case Questions

1 Why did production of Product X continue long after many of the key personnel involved with it had realized it was a failure?

2 Do you think this is a unique example or can you think of other bad decisions which were only reversed years after key actors realized it was a mistake?

3 Can you think of ways in which decision-making in an organization could be better designed so as to ensure that unsuccessful product lines are halted much sooner than in the Product X case?

Excerpted from C. Argyris and D. Schon, *Organizational Learning: A Theory of Action Perspective*. Argyris/Schon, *Organizational Learning*, © 1978, Addison–Wesley Publishing Co., Inc., Reading, Massachusetts. Pages 1–2. Reprinted with permission. Case appeared in Gareth Morgan, *Creative Organization Theory* (1989), Sage Publications.

Notes

1. 'Progressive Group of Insurance Cos. Recognized as IT Innovator' *Colorado Springs Business Journal,* June 15, 2007
2. 'Bursting through to take the award', *MX Magazine*, 2007, 16–17.
3. 'Award for pressure relief', *Food Trade Review*, 1 August 2007.
4. 'How can Peking duck go electric, fume Chinese', *Indo-Asian News Service*, 7 February 2008.
5. 'Purists squawk after Chinese restaurant chain switches from wood ovens to electric', *National Post*, 15 January 2008, A11.
6. Charles V. Callahan and Bruce A. Pasternack, 'Corporate Strategy in the Digital Age', *Strategy & Business*, Issue 15 (Second Quarter 1999), 10–14.
7. Ibid.
8. Bill Richards, 'A Total Overhaul', *The Wall Street Journal* (December 7, 1998), R30.
9. 'Intralot Signs Cooperation Agreement With Fifa's Early Warning System', *Greek Company News Bites – Stock Report*, 26 August 2008.
10. Erik Berkman, 'How to Stay Ahead of the Curve', *CIO* (February 1, 2002), 72–80; and Heather Harreld, 'Pick-Up Artists', *CIO* (November 1, 2000), 148–154.
11. 'Business Intelligence', special advertising section, *Business 2.0* (February 2003), S1–S4; and Alice Dragoon, 'Business Intelligence Gets Smart', *CIO* (September 15, 2003), 84–91.

12 'Gartner Says Worldwide Business Intelligence Platform Market Grew 13 Percent in 2007; Industry Experienced Heavy Consolidation and Slowing Revenue Growth in North America', June 19, 2008, accessed at http://www.gartner.com/it/page.jsp?id=700410&format=print on August 29, 2008.

13. Julie Schlosser, 'Looking for Intelligence in Ice Cream', *Fortune* (March 17, 2003), 114–120.
14. 'SAP Customers Worldwide Tout Early Success With Latest CRM Offering' *PR Newswire (U.S.)*, 30 July 2008; 'SAP case study – Apotex', accessed at http://www.cio.com/solution-centers/sap?item=13&from=cio&src=ciowpl on September 1, 2008.
15. Stephen Hoare, 'The man who went into overdrive – Positive thinking', *The Times*, 19 February 2002.
16. 'French National Railways Improves Efficiency for Tracking 160,000 Employees Using WebFOCUS Business Intelligence', 19 Aug 08. Accessed at http://www.businessintelligence.com/binewsdetail.asp?id=3542 on September 1, 2008.
17. Richard Fletcher, 'Tesco's success puts Clubcard firm on the map', *The Sunday Times*, 19 December 2004; Koschat, M., Ryans, A and Sequeira, S. 'Tesco: Keeping The Hard Discounters At Bay?', *IMD Case Study* 5-0737, 28 March 2008.
18. Ciaran Ryan, 'DigiCore: Tight Focus And Genuine Synergies', *Financial Mail*, 11 November 2005.
19. Robert Simons, 'Strategic Organizations and Top Management Attention to Control Systems', *Strategic Management Journal* 12 (1991), 49–62.
20. Kevin Ferguson, 'Mission Control', *Inc. Magazine* (November 2003), 27–28; and Russ Banham, 'Seeing the Big Picture: New Data Tools Are Enabling CEOs to Get a Better Handle on Peformance Across Their Organizations', *Chief Executive* (November 2003), 46ff.
21. 'MTC-Vodafone Launches Harris Executive Dashboard for Service and Business Monitoring of Entire GSM/3G Network in Kuwait', *PR Newswire Europe*, 14 August 2006.
22. Christopher Koch, 'How Verizon Flies by Wire', *CIO* (November 1, 2004), 94–96.
23. Richard L. Daft and Norman B. Macintosh, 'The Nature and Use of Formal Control Systems for Management Control and Strategy Implementation', *Journal of Management* 10 (1984), 43–66.
24. Susannah Patton, 'Web Metrics That Matter', *CIO* (November 14, 2002), 84–88; and Ramin Jaleshgari, 'The End of the Hit Parade', *CIO* (May 14, 2000), 183–190.
25. Adam Lashinsky, 'Meg and the Machine', *Fortune* (September 1, 2003), 68–78.
26. Howard Rothman, 'You Need Not Be Big to Benchmark', *Nation's Business* (December 1992), 64–65.
27. Tom Rancour and Mike McCracken, 'Applying 6 Sigma Methods for Breakthrough Safety Performance', *Professional Safety* 45, no. 10 (October 2000), 29–32; Lee Clifford, 'Why You Can Safely Ignore Six Sigma', *Fortune* (January 22, 2001), 140.
28. Michael Hammer and Jeff Goding, 'Putting Six Sigma in Perspective', *Quality* (October 2001), 58–62; Michael Hammer, 'Process Management and the Future of Six Sigma', *Sloan Management Review* (Winter 2002), 26–32.
29. 'On Balance', a CFO Interview with Robert Kaplan and David Norton, *CFO* (February 2001), 73–78; Chee W. Chow, Kamal M. Haddad and James E. Williamson, 'Applying the Balanced Scorecard to Small Companies', *Management Accounting* 79, No. 2 (August 1997), 21–27; and Robert Kaplan and David Norton, 'The Balanced Scorecard: Measures That Drive Performance', *Harvard Business Review* (January–February 1992), 71–79.
30. Based on Kaplan and Norton, 'The Balanced Scorecard'; Chow, Haddad and Williamson, 'Applying the Balanced Scorecard'; Cathy Lazere, 'All Together Now', *CFO* (February 1998), 28–36.
31. Debby Young, 'Score It a Hit', *CIO Enterprise*, Section 2 (November 15, 1998), 27ff.
32. Nils-Göran Olve, Carl-Johan Petri, Jan Roy and Sofie Roy, 'Twelve Years Later: Understanding and Realizing the Value of Balanced Scorecards', *Ivey Business Journal* (May–June 2004), 1–7.
33. William Davig, Norb Elbert and Steve Brown, 'Implementing a Strategic Planning Model for Small Manufacturing Firms: An Adaptation of the Balanced Scorecard', *SAM Advanced Management Journal* (Winter 2004), 18–24.

34. John Collins, 'pTools creates Ireland's largest intranet for HSE', *Irish Times*, 2 May 2008.
35. Melanie Warner, 'Under the Knife', *Business 2.0* (January–February 2004), 84–89.
36. Wayne Kawamoto, 'Click Here for Efficiency', *BusinessWeek Enterprise* (December 7, 1998), Ent. 12–Ent. 14.
37. 'Bat keeps data on the move', *Computer Weekly*, 9 October 2007.
38. Esther Shein, 'The Knowledge Crunch', *CIO* (May 1, 2001), 128–132.
39. Derek Slater, 'What is ERP?' *CIO Enterprise*, Section 2 (May 15, 1999), 86; and Jeffrey Zygmont, 'The Ties That Bind', *Inc. Tech* no. 3 (1998), 70–84.
40. Vincent A. Mabert, Ashok Soni and M. A. Venkataramanan, 'Enterprise Resource Planning: Common Myths versus Evolving Reality', *Business Horizons* (May–June 2001), 69–76.
41. Slater, 'What Is ERP?'
42. 'David Sadler, Lonely Planet's globetrotting finance chief – Off the beaten track', *Accountancy Age*, 6 January 2005; Sue Sutton, 'The Lonely Planet Guide to SAP', August 2006, accessed at http://www.saug.com.au/Files/Library/sutton_Lonely%20Planet.pdf on September 2, 2008; Mahesh Sharma, 'Lonely Planet strengthens its web', *The Australian*, 24 July 2007; 'BBC Spends £75m on Lonely Planet', *Daily Mail*, 2 October 2007; Victoria Arnstein, 'Falling prices hit Lonely Planet', *The Bookseller*, 14 May 2008, accessed at http://www.thebookseller.com/news/58579-falling-prices-hit-lonely-planet.html on September 2, 2008.
43. Owen Thomas, 'E-Business Software: Bollinger Shipyards', *eCompany* (May 2001), 119–120.
44. Susannah Patton, 'Doctors' Group Profits from ERP,' *CIO* (September 1, 2003), 32.
45. Research reported in Eric Seubert, Y. Balaji and Mahesh Makhija, 'The Knowledge Imperative', *CIO Advertising Supplement* (March 15, 2000), S1–S4.
46. Andrew Mayo, 'Memory Bankers', *People Management* (January 22, 1998), 34–38; Gary Abramson, 'On the KM Midway', *CIO Enterprise*, Section 2 (May 15, 1999), 63–70.
47. David A. Garvin, 'Building a Learning Organization', in *Harvard Business Review on Knowledge Management* (Boston, Mass.: President and Fellows of Harvard College, 1998), 47–80.
48. Based on Mayo, 'Memory Bankers'; William Miller, 'Building the Ultimate Resource', *Management Review* (January 1999), 42–45; and Todd Datz, 'How to Speak Geek', *CIO Enterprise*, Section 2 (April 15, 1999), 46–52.
49. Vikas Anand, William H. Glick and Charles C. Manz, 'Thriving on the Knowledge of Outsiders: Tapping Organizational Social Capital', *Academy of Management Executive* 16, no. 1 (2002), 87–101.
50. Tony Kontzer, 'Kitchen Sink: Many Collaborative Options', *Information Week* (May 5, 2003), 35; sidebar in Tony Kontzer, 'Learning to Share', *Information Week* (May 5, 2003), 29–37.
51. Richard McDermott, 'Why Information Technology Inspired but Cannot Deliver Knowledge Management', *California Management Review* 41, no. 4 (Summer 1999), 103–117.
52. Based on Ikujiro Nonaka and Hirotaka Takeuchi, *The Knowledge-Creating Company: How Japanese Companies Create the Dynamics of Innovation* (New York: Oxford University Press, 1995), 8–9; and Robert M. Grant, 'Toward a Knowledge-Based Theory of the Firm', *Strategic Management Journal* 17 (Winter 1996), 109–122.
53. Grant, 'Toward a Knowledge-Based Theory of the Firm'.
54. Martin Schulz, 'The Uncertain Relevance of Newness: Organizational Learning and Knowledge Flows', *Academy of Management Journal* 44, no. 4 (2001), 661–681.
55. C. Jackson Grayson, Jr. and Carla S. O'Dell, 'Mining Your Hidden Resources', *Across the Board* (April 1998), 23–28.
56. Based on Morten T. Hansen, Nitin Nohria and Thomas Tierney, 'What's Your Strategy for Managing Knowledge?' *Harvard Business Review* (March–April 1999), 106–116.
57. Kontzer, 'Learning to Share'.
58. Michael A. Fontaine, Salvatore Parise and David Miller, 'Collaborative Environments: An Effective Tool for Transforming Business Processes', *Ivey Business Journal* (May–June 2004); Mary Flood, 'Hawk Vote for California Firm Unanimous', *Houston Chronicle* (May 15, 2001), 15; and 'Firm Finalist for Innovation,' *The Nelson Mail* (May 23, 2003), 4.
59. Hirotaka Takeuchi, Emi Osono and Norihiko Shimizu, 'Contradictions are the drivers of Toyota's success', Business Day (South Africa), 23 June 2008; Japanese scholar explains use of explicit and tacit knowledge in business, Thai News Service, 22 February 2008; Nonaka, I. and Konno, N.. (1998), 'The Concept of 'Ba': Building a Foundation for Knowledge Creation', *California Management Review*, 3, 40–54; Ron Sanchez, 'Tacit Knowledge' versus 'Explicit Knowledge' 'Approaches to Knowledge Management Practice', Copenhagen Business School, IVS/CBS Working Paper 2004-01; Stefan Thomke and Takahiro Fujimoto (2000), 'The effect of 'front-loading' problem-solving on product development performance, *Journal of Product Innovation Management,* 17, 128–142.
60. 'All wired up', *Caterer & Hotelkeeper*, 2 August 2007.
61. Steven A. Melnyk and David R. Denzler, *Operations Management: A Value-Driven Approach* (Burr Ridge, Ill.: Richard D. Irwin, 1996), 613.
62. Jim Turcotte, Bob Silveri and Tom Jobson, 'Are You Ready for the E-Supply Chain?' *APICS – The Performance Advantage* (August 1998), 56–59.
63. "BlueQue Provides Real-Time Visibility", *Official Board Markets*, Nov 27, 2004; CSCLive E-Commerce, *Computerworld Honors 2005*, accessed at http://www.cwhonors.org/search/his_4a_detail.asp?id=5056 on September 2, 2008; Paper supplier calls on Cisco to bridge gap between production machines, facilities, *Manufacturing Business Technology*, 1 February 2005.
64. Katherine Doherty, 'Light Speed; Distributors in Europe are achieving 99.99 percent accuracy in deliveries and reducing headcount with automated material handling systems', *Food Logistics*, 1 December 2005. 'Long-time MicroStrategy Customer Recognized as 'Smartest Organization in the Netherlands', *PR Newswire (U.S.)*, 28 May 2008.

65. Sandra Swanson, 'Get Together', *Information Week* (July 1, 2002), 47–48.
66. Christopher Koch, 'It All Began with Drayer', *CIO* (August 1, 2002), 56–60.
67. Brian Caulfield, 'Facing Up to CRM', *Business 2.0* (August–September 2001), 149–150; and 'Customer Relationship Management: The Good, The Bad, The Future', special advertising section, *BusinessWeek* (April 28, 2003), 53–64.
68. Timothy J. Mullaney, 'E-Biz Strikes Again', *BusinessWeek* (May 10, 2004), 80–90.
69. Christopher Barnatt, 'Embracing E-Business', *Journal of General Management* 30, no. 1 (Autumn 2004), 79–96.
70. 'Tesco.com Under Fire from Rivals Over Home Deliveries' *The Evening Standard,* October 5, 2007.
71. Andy Reinhardt, 'Tesco Bets Small – and Wins Big', *BusinessWeek E.Biz* (October 1, 2001), EB26–EB32; and Patrick Barwise and Sean Meehan, 'The Benefits of Getting the Basics Right', *Financial Times* (October 8, 2004), 4.
72. This discussion is based on Ranjay Gulati and Jason Garino, 'Get the Right Mix of Bricks and Clicks', *Harvard Business Review* (May–June 2000), 107–114.
73. Simon Burns, 'Sony So-net spin-off hits record revenues' *VNUNet United Kingdom*, 30 March 2007.
74. David L. Margulius, 'How to know when to keep great ideas in-house or launch a startup', *InfoWorld*, 4 December 2006.
75. Emeka Obiodu, 'Portugal Telecom Spins Off PT Multimedia', *Global Insight Daily Analysis*, 12 November 2007.
76. Magyar Telekom restructures business divisions along retail, corporate lines, *MTI - EcoNews*, 26 September 2007.
77. Rob Ferguson, 'Thomson moves to sell all its papers except Globe – Former publishing giant concentrates on e-commerce', *The Toronto Star*, 16 February 2000; 'Thomson hunting for new acquisitions', *The Globe and Mail*, 6 December 2006, B12.
78. 'Investors Pull the Rug Out of Brandwise.com', *The Globe and Mail (Canada)*, June 1, 2000.
79. 'In praise of . . . Abebooks', *The Guardian*, 5 October 2006; Michael Gove, 'The net: not guilty of grievous harm to bookshops', *The Times*, April 24, 2007; Abebooks and Amazon pair up, *The Bookseller*, 11 October 2002. On August 1, 2008 Amazon provisionally agreed to buy Abebooks (Amazon Acquires AbeBooks, *FinancialWire*, 3 August 2008).
80. Richard Tyler, 'Home-based work a growing lifestyle', *Daily Telegraph*, 30 October 2007.
81. Andrew Blackman, 'A Strong Net Game', *The Wall Street Journal* (October 25, 2004), R1, R11.
82. 'Alan Swale turns to internet to improve marketing', *Dairy Farmer*, 16 October 2006.
83. Stephanie Overby, 'Paving over Paperwork', *CIO* (February 1, 2002), 82–86.
84. 'India finance: Back office to the world', *Economist Intelligence Unit – Executive Briefing* 310, 20 February 2003.
85. Siobhan O'Mahony and Stephen R. Barley, 'Do Digital Telecommunications Affect Work and Organization? The State of Our Knowledge', *Research in Organizational Behavior* 21 (1999), 125–161.
86. Lisa Kelly, 'Case study: The British Council', *Computing*, 7 August 2008; *Annual Report 2007 / 2008*, British Council.
87. O'Mahony and Barley, 'Do Digital Telecommunications Affect Work and Organization?'
88. Brian Robinson, Canada to build nationwide health surveillance system, *Federal Computer Week*, 14 September 2006; http://www.infoway-inforoute.ca/en/WhatWeDo/Overview.aspx accessed on September 3, 2008; Terrence Belford, 'Physician, upgrade thyself', *The Globe and Mail*, 15 September 2006.
89. Michael A. Fontaine, Salvatore Parise and David Miller, 'Collaborative Environments: An Effective Tool for Transforming Business Processes', *Ivey Business Journal* (May–June 2004).
90. Joanne Lee-Young and Megan Barnett, 'Furiously Fast Fashions', *The Industry Standard* (June 11, 2001), 72–79.
91. Efthymios Constantinides and Stefan J Fountain (2008), 'Web 2.0: Conceptual foundations and marketing issues', *Journal of Direct, Data and Digital Marketing Practice*, 9, 231–244; Roman Högg, Miriam Meckel, Katarina Stanoevska-Slabeva and Robert Martignoni (2006) 'Overview of business models for Web 2.0 communities', Proceedings of GeNeMe 2006, Dresden, 28–29 September, 23–37.
92. Miltiadis D Lytras, Ernesto Damiani and Patricia Ordonez de Pablos (eds.) (2008), *Web 2.0: The Business Model*, Heidelberg, Springer Verlag.
93. Spencer E. Ante, Has Facebook's Value Taken a Hit?, *BusinessWeek*, August 5, 2008; Facebook's 100 million members shows it's out of control, U-Wire, 28 August 2008; Dave Morin, 'We just hit 100,000,000 Facebook users!!!' accessed at http://twitter.com/davemorin/statuses/898779449 on September 4, 2008.
94. Can social networks make money?, *Financial Express*, 22 May 2008; McKinsey Consulting, (2007) 'How business are using Web 2.0: A McKinsey global survey', *The McKinsey Quarterly*, accessed at http://www.mckinseyquarterly.com/Marketing/Digital_Marketing/How_businesses_are_using_Web_20_A_McKinsey_Global_Survey_1913 on April 16, 2009.
95. Claire McEntee, 'Iyomu Founder Prepares To Close Site', *Dominion Post*, 19 May 2008.
96. 'Kid-targeted virtual worlds seek impact, Revenue' *Youth Markets Alert*, 1 May 2008.
97. Aidin Vaziri, 'There's room for everyone on MySpace, from indie rockers to Rupert Murdoch', *The San Francisco Chronicle*, 18 August 2005; 'Virtual Worlds Getting Friendlier For Businesses', *CMP TechWeb*, 3 April 2008.
98. Saul Hansell, 'Google's Toughest Search Is for a Business Model', *The New York Times*, 8 April 2002; Steven Syre, 'Aggressive or Overvalued?', *The Boston Globe*, 27 July 2004.
99. Google Financial Tables accessed at http://investor.google.com/fin_data.html on September 4, 2008.

CHAPTER 9

ORGANIZATION SIZE, LIFE CYCLE AND DECLINE

Interpol

Ron Noble, secretary general of Interpol, manages one of the most complex organizations in the world. Interpol has to work with countries from every corner of the globe, fostering cooperation among people with different cultural values, languages and legal and political systems. Moreover, it must do it all with a budget of about $65 million, about what London's Metropolitan Police spends every four days.[1]

When Interpol works, it works very well, often leading to the quick capture of international terrorists, murderers and other fugitives. But when Noble took over the international police organization, it wasn't working very well. Rather than a fast-moving, crime-fighting organization, Noble found Interpol to be a clumsy, slow-moving, bureaucratic agency that was ill-equipped to respond to the massive challenges of a world increasingly reliant on worldwide coordinated law enforcement to prevent tragedies such as the terrorist attacks on the US of September 2001, the Madrid train bombings of March 11, 2004 or the London bombings of July 7, 2005. If a request for assistance and information on Mohammed Atta, one of the 2001 terrorist leaders, for example, came into Interpol on a weekend, too bad – the agency was closed until Monday morning. Interpol 'Red Notices' (urgent, global wanted-persons alerts) took up to 6 months to process and were sent out by economy post to save postage costs.

Noble knew that kind of slow response had to change. Since taking over as head of Interpol, he has moved the organization forward by leaps and bounds, reducing bureaucracy and transforming Interpol into a modern, fast-moving organization. Keeping Interpol open 24 hours a day, 7 days a week, was one of his first changes. A policy of issuing red alerts for terrorists within 24 hours and notices for less threatening criminals within 72 hours went into effect immediately after September 11, 2001. Noble has reorganized Interpol to increase speed and flexibility and to focus on the 'customer' (law enforcement groups in 179 member countries). Today, the most critical notices are translated immediately, posted online and sent via express delivery service.

The reorganization also includes mechanisms for better coordination and information gathering. Noble's goal is for Interpol to become the number one global police agency, one that coordinates and leads a multidimensional crime-fighting approach. Combatting terrorism and organized crime, Noble knows, requires that everyone have the information they need when they need it and that local police, judicial, intelligence, diplomatic and military services all work together. Another step toward a more coordinated worldwide effort came when Interpol recently appointed its first-ever representative to the United Nations.[2]

As organizations grow large and complex, they need more complex systems and procedures for guiding and controlling the organization. Unfortunately, these characteristics can also cause problems of inefficiency, rigidity and slow response time. Every organization – from international agencies like Interpol to locally owned restaurants and hairdressing salons – wrestles with questions about organizational size, bureaucracy and control. Most entrepreneurs who start a business want their company to grow. Yet, as organizations become larger, they often find it difficult to respond quickly to changes in the environment. Today's organizations, just like Interpol, are looking for ways to be more flexible and responsive to a rapidly changing marketplace.

During the twentieth century, large organizations became widespread and bureaucracy has become a major topic of study in organization theory.[3] Most large organizations have bureaucratic characteristics, which can be very effective. These organizations provide us with abundant goods and services and accomplish astonishing feats – explorations of Mars, overnight delivery of packages to any location in the world, the scheduling and coordination of 85,000 airline flights a day worldwide[4] – that are testimony to their effectiveness. On the other hand, bureaucracy is also accused of many sins, including inefficiency, rigidity and demeaning routinized work that alienates both employees and the customers.

Purpose of This Chapter

In this chapter, we explore the question of large versus small organizations and how size relates to structure and control. Organization size is a contextual variable that influences organizational design and functioning just as do the contextual variables – technology, environment, goals – discussed in previous chapters. In the first section, we look at the advantages of large versus small size. Then, we explore what is called an organization's life cycle and the structural characteristics at each stage. Next, we examine the historical use of bureaucracy as a means to control large organizations and compare bureaucratic control to various other control strategies. Finally, the chapter looks at the causes of organizational decline and discusses some methods for dealing with downsizing. By the end of this chapter, you should be able to recognize when bureaucratic control can make an organization effective and when other types of control are likely to prove more appropriate.

Organization Size: Is Bigger Better?

The question of big versus small begins with the notion of growth and the reasons so many organizations grow in size.

Pressures for Growth

A dream of many businesspeople is to have their company become a member of the FT Global 500 or the *Fortune* 500 lists – to grow fast and to grow big.[5] Sometimes this goal is more urgent than to make the best products or show the greatest profits. A decade ago, analysts and management scholars were heralding a shift away from 'bigness' toward small, nimble companies that could quickly respond in a fast-changing environment. Yet, despite the proliferation of new, small organizations, the giants such as Toyota, Procter & Gamble, Tesco and Wal-Mart have continued to grow.[6] Tesco, for example, accounts for about one-third of all grocery sales in the UK, nearly double its nearest competitor, with 250,000 employees and nearly 2000 stores.[7] The company also holds about $25 billion worth of land for development in the UK, operates stores in 13 countries outside the UK and is the world's fourth largest retailer.[8]

Today, the business world has entered an era of the mega-corporation. Mergers have given rise to industry giants such as Nestle, Citigroup and Vodaphone.[9] The global advertising industry is controlled by four huge agencies – London's WPP Group, Paris-based Publicis Groupe and the Omnicom Group and the Interpublic Group of Companies, both headquartered in New York.[10] These huge conglomerates own scores of companies that soak up more than half the ad industry's revenues and reach into the advertising, direct-mail marketing and public relations of every region on the planet. The growth of these agencies matches that of their clients, who are themselves growing larger and more global. Companies in all industries, from aerospace to consumer products to media, strive for growth to acquire the size and resources needed to compete profitably on a global scale, to invest in new technology and to control distribution channels and secure access to markets.[11]

There are other pressures for organizations to grow. Many executives have found that firms must grow to stay economically healthy. Often, to stop growing is to stagnate. To be stable means that customers may not have their demands fully met or that competitors will increase market share at the expense of your company Lakshmi Mittal, the driving force behind the creation of ArcelorMittal, the world's biggest steel producer, continues to press for further consolidation of the global steel

See online
COUNTERPOINT 9.6

industry.[12] Corporate leaders like Mittal are ingrained with the idea that to stop growing is to stagnate and die.[13] Sabanci Group, the Turkish owners of Teknosa, the country's leading chain of retail electronics shops, is facing increasing competition from European retail giants, as the country's economy integrates with Europe. Sabanci is responding on two levels. They entered into a partnership with French hypermarket giant Carrefour and at the same time invested heavily in bringing Teknosa up to international standards. They also launched the Teknosa Planet concept, featuring large, spacious stores that offer Turkish consumers the possibility of shopping at a familiar, trusted local retailer while enjoying the comfort and service standards that would be expected in Western Europe.[14,15]

Scale is crucial to economic health in marketing-intensive companies such as Orange, Unilever, Nestle and Procter & Gamble.[16] Greater size gives these companies power in the marketplace and thus increases revenues.[17] To the extent that growing organizations are vibrant, exciting places to work, which enables these companies to attract and keep quality employees. When the number of employees is expanding, the company can offer many challenges and opportunities for advancement.

Dilemmas of Large Size

What size organization is better poised to compete in a global environment? The arguments are summarized in Exhibit 9.1.

Large Huge resources and economies of scale are often needed for organizations to compete globally. Only large organizations can build a massive oil and gas pipeline

EXHIBIT 9.1 Differences between Large and Small Organizations

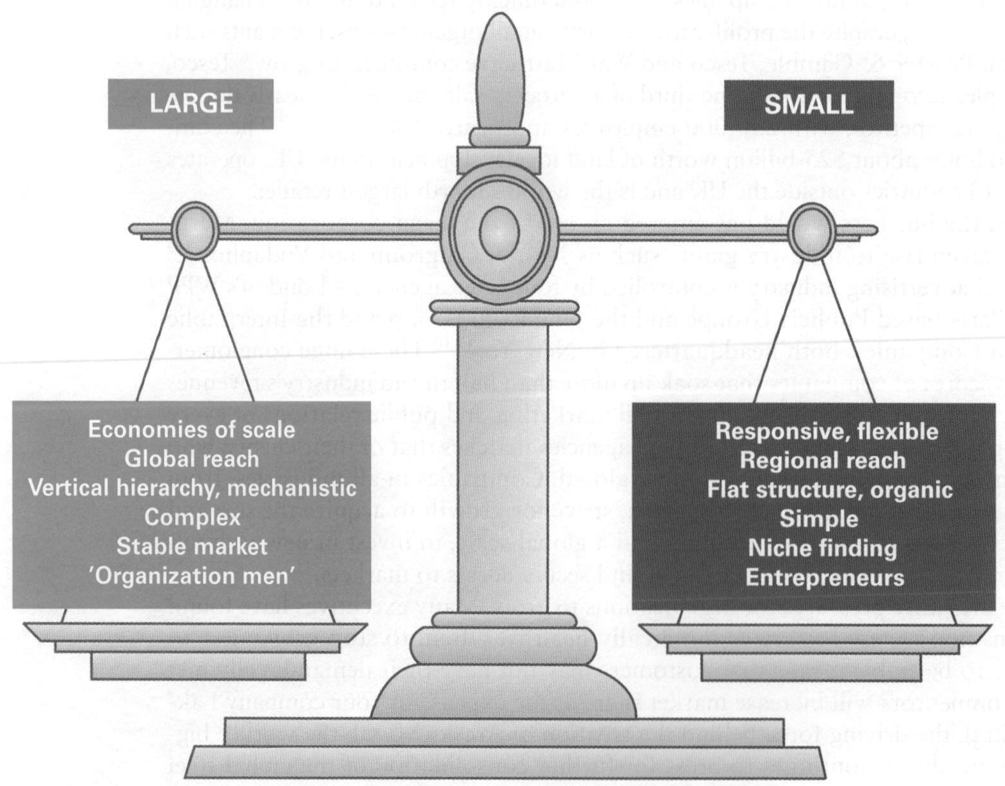

Source: Based on John A. Byrne, 'Is Your Company Too Big?' *BusinessWeek* (March 27, 1989), 84–94.

from Kazakhstan to Europe through the Caucasus. Only a large corporation like Airbus Industrie can build the world's first double-deck passenger aeroplane and only a large airline, such as Singapore Airlines, can afford to buy and operate it. Only a large pharmaceutical company like Germany's Bayer can invest hundreds of millions of euros developing new treatments ranging from Adalat for hypertension to new cancer treatments.[18] In addition, large organizations have the resources to be a supportive economic and social force in difficult times. In 2008, after floods in India's Bihar state killed over 1,000 people and left at least 1.3 million stranded and homeless, the country's largest business conglomerate, Tata Group, sent 100 staff to work full-time on flood relief and in one week built 50 large temporary shelters.[19,20] Similarly, following the collapse of the Canadian airline Zoom in 2008, airline majors Virgin Atlantic and British Airways flew stranded holidaymakers back to the UK at greatly discounted fares.[21,22] Large organizations also are able to get back to business more quickly following a disaster, giving employees a sense of security and belonging during an uncertain time.

Large companies are often standardized, mechanistically run and complex. The complexity offers hundreds of functional specialities within the organization to perform multifaceted tasks and to produce varied and complicated products. Moreover, large organizations, once established, can be a presence that stabilizes a market for years. Managers can join the company and still have reasonable prospects of a career reminiscent of the 'organization men' of the 1950s and 1960s. The organization can provide longevity, raises and promotions.

BRIEFCASE

As an organization manager, keep these guidelines in mind:

Decide whether your organization should act like a large or small company. To the extent that economies of scale, global reach and complexity are important, introduce greater bureaucratization as the organization increases in size. As it becomes necessary, add rules and regulations, written documentation, job specialization, technical competence in hiring and promotion and decentralization.

Small The competing argument says small is beautiful because the crucial requirements for success in a global economy are responsiveness and flexibility in fast-changing markets. Small scale can provide significant advantages in terms of quick reaction to changing customer needs or shifting environmental and market conditions.[23] The largest transnational corporations declined in relation to the overall size of the world economy during the 1990s, though since 2000 their share of global wealth has risen again, driven to a large extent by mergers and acquisition.[24] However, research indicates that few of these mergers live up to their expected performance levels.[25] A study of ten of the largest mergers from 1998 to 2002, including Glaxo/SmithKline, AOL/Time Warner and Daimler/Chrysler, showed a significant decline in shareholder value for eight of the ten combined companies, as illustrated in Exhibit 9.2.[26] There are numerous factors involved in declines in

See online
COUNTERPOINT 9.7

EXHIBIT 9.2 Effect of Ten Mega-Mergers on Shareholder Wealth

Merger	Year of Deal	Value Created or Destroyed As of July 1, 2002
AOL/Time Warner	2001	−$148 billion
Vodafone/Mannesmann	2000	−$299 billion
Pfizer/Warner-Lambert	2000	−$78 billion
Glaxo/SmithKline	2000	−$40 billion
Chase/J.P. Morgan	2000	−$26 billion
Exxon/Mobil	1999	+$8 billion
SBC/Ameritech	1999	−$68 billion
WorldCom/MCI	1998	−$94 billion
Travelers/Citicorp	1998	+$109 billion
Daimler/Chrysler	1998	−$36 billion

Source: Reported in Keith Hammonds, 'Size Is Not a Strategy,' *Fast Company* (September 2002), 78–86.

Have you read this book?

In Search of Management

BY TONY WATSON

In this book Tony Watson, a UK professor of management, explores the working lives of contemporary managers. Through a case study of Ryland, a British engineering firm undergoing rapid changes in response to corporate reorganization and technological innovations, Watson explains how managers are both shaped by their environment – which they find increasingly impossible to control – and also are expected to direct their employees to meet the needs of that ever-changing environment. Watson's key concept is *strategic exchange*; the way in which humans seek both to exercise control over their own working lives while also searching for meaning and security in the external environment.

Watson's research approach is organizational ethnography. While traditionally ethnography has conjured up images of anthropologists living with exotic tribes, it is an approach increasingly used in management research and is particularly useful in understanding the dynamics and complexities of organizational culture. Woodley spent a full year working as a manager inside Ryland, while also observing interactions, participating in daily routines and conducting in-depth interviews with about 60 Ryland managers.

Through the study, Watson explores the meaning of the term management, which he argues covers three different meanings; a function (the overall steering of an organization), activities (the specific actions involved in steering an organization) and the group of people responsible for steering an organization. He argues that weaknesses in the conceptualization and operationalization of the first two meanings of management are often mistakenly diagnosed as failings of the management team. As a result, managers are fired or reassigned, but the structural issues that hamper organizational effectiveness and productivity often go unaddressed.

The study shows how managers hold different and apparently conflicting attitudes to work and the company. When they look at the 'big picture' – continual workplace restructuring, job insecurity and apparent strategic incoherence – they tend to be critical or even negative about the organization. At the same time, however, they tended to be devoted to their own work and to express pride about doing a good job. Watson puts this down primarily to a basic human need for self-esteem. It is simply not sustainable for people to feel they are doing something that is not worthwhile, even if, speaking objectively, they often don't seem to be recognized for their hard work, whether this is with job security, enhanced salaries or even the sense that their ideas are valued and made use of.

Watson describes an organization that is far harder to manage than most textbooks would suggest and indeed an organization where the distinctions between 'good' and 'bad' management are far from clear. While there may be an official organizational culture, this tends to reflect a politically correct designation such as 'the learning organization', while in practice Ryland's managers acknowledged that there was also a culture of cost-cutting and layoffs that, while 'unofficial', in many ways more accurately reflected the dominant concerns of top managers in the company and its corporate parents. Beyond these overarching cultures, the organization was also segmented into various subcultures based on the divisions with which managers worked, their professional designations, their age group, etc. Therefore, organizational cohesiveness is not something that can be planned for through careful design of an organization chart of development of a strategic plan: 'productive cooperation is something that has to be striven for, in a context where conflicts and rivalries are inevitable' (p. 178). Overall, Watson found managers far more pressured and conflicted than the mythology of cool and collected Olympian leaders that is conveyed by popular media and advertising: 'The more I saw of the managers at Ryland, the more I became aware of the extent of human angst, insecurity, doubt and frailty among them'.

Watson's book seems to paint a much darker picture of organizational life than many business texts. But, really, his ethnography demonstrates that organizations cannot be abstracted from ordinary human life, which is full of contradictions, setbacks and conflict, as well as cooperation, harmony and periods of smooth sailing. Above all, organizations, made up of numerous individuals and countless different influences, are complex and ever-changing beasts. The manager will never be able to exercise absolute control, but must rather find the moments and the mechanisms whereby people can be motivated to work together to further both their own agendas and those of the organization for which they work.

In Search of Management, by Tony Watson, is published by Cengage Learning.

value, but clearly, bigness alone doesn't necessarily add up to better performance.[27] This chapter's Bookmark argues that one reason large companies sometimes fail is that top leaders become distant from the nuts and bolts of running the business. Any major strategic initiative, such as a merger, falters without careful planning as well as diligent execution.

Despite the increasing size of many companies, small and mid-sized businesses are crucial to the economic vitality of both the developed and developing world. In the UK, for example, small businesses account for about 60 per cent of GDP.[28] Exporting is becoming a key business strategy for many small businesses around the world, such as in Sweden where the growth rate in exports for small businesses was three times as fast between 2002 and 2006 as for medium and large companies.[29] The growth of the Internet and other information technologies is making it easier for small companies to act big, as described in Chapter 8. The growing service sector also contributes to a decrease in average organization size, as many service companies remain small to better serve customers.

Small organizations typically have a comparatively flat structure and a more organic, free-flowing management style that enables entrepreneurship and innovation. Many of today's innovative drug treatments, for example, were discovered by small firms, such as Holland's PanGenetics, which focuses on developing treatments for immune diseases from the advanced research stage through to 'clinical proof of concept' – when the treatment's viability has been shown and larger companies are willing to invest in the bringing the product to market.[30] To the extent that employees experience a personal involvement in small firms, this can encourage greater motivation and commitment.

As an organization manager, keep this guideline in mind:

If responsiveness, flexibility, simplicity and niche finding are important, subdivide the organization into simple, autonomous divisions that have freedom and a small-company approach.

Big-Company/Small-Company Hybrid The paradox is that the advantages of small companies sometimes enable them to succeed and, hence, grow large. Most of the firms on the *Europe's 500* list of the fastest-growing companies in Europe are small and characterized by an emphasis on being fast and flexible in responding to the environment.[31,32] Small companies, however, can become victims of their own success as they grow large, shifting to a mechanistic structure emphasizing vertical hierarchies and spawning 'organization men' rather than entrepreneurs. Giant companies are 'built for optimization, not innovation'.[33] Big companies tend to become committed to their existing products and technologies and have a hard time supporting innovation for the future.

COUNTERPOINT 9.1

The complexities associated with size, together with increased emphasis upon expanding the sale of existing services or goods, rather than engaging in further innovation, makes a move in the direction of bureaucracy attractive. The challenge is to consolidate to secure reliability without losing dynamism and innovation. Larger companies often rely upon acquisition to provide innovation as this allows the risks of innovation to be externalized. As we note later in this chapter, four-fifths of businesses that make it past the first year still fail within five years because they can't make the transition from the entrepreneurial stage. **Discuss**

One solution is what Jack Welch, the celebrated former chairman of General Electric (GE), called the 'big-company/small-company hybrid' that combines a large corporation's resources and reach with a small company's simplicity and flexibility. Stan Shih's web model of independent but interlinked businesses at Acer, discussed in Chapter 6, also combines the advantages of both small and large firms. Full-service global firms need a strong resource base and sufficient complexity and hierarchy to serve clients around the world. Size is not necessarily at odds with speed and flexibility, as evidenced by large companies such as Toyota, Google, Canada's RIM (manufacturer of the BlackBerry) and Britain's Virgin Group, which all continue to try new things and move quickly to change the rules of business.[34] The divisional structure, described in Chapter 3, is one way some large organizations strive to attain a big-company/small-company hybrid. By reorganizing into smaller autonomous divisions, huge corporations such as Japan's Sony have attempted to capture the mindset and advantages of smallness. In 1994, Sony set up eight divisional companies, each of which would be responsible for all operations, from production to sales. Each divisional president was responsible for most of the functions of a CEO in a fully independent company, reporting to Sony's corporate CEO in the same way as a CEO would report to shareholders at an annual meeting. Sony's then CEO Norio Ohga called it the 'The Company Within a Company System'. These changes were closely associated with Sony's turnaround in the 1990's.[35,36]

See online
COUNTERPOINT 9.8

The development of new organizational forms, with an emphasis on decentralizing authority and cutting out layers of the hierarchy, combined with the increasing use of information technology described in Chapter 8, is making it easier for companies to be simultaneously large and small, thus capturing the advantages of each. The shift can even be seen in how international conflict is organized, in what the social anthropologist Arjun Appadurai calls the transformation from vertebrate to cellular organization.[37,38] Appadurai notes that in contrast to the clear hierarchical structure of the nation state and its military forces, international terrorist organizations operate on a 'cellular' principle, where small groups of militants plan actions based not on the command decision-making structure of a traditional army, but through interpretation of a common set of principles that might be communicated through the internet, in religious sermons and tracts and satellite TV. In response, nation states carry out their 'war on terrorism' based on smaller forces of highly skilled soldiers with access to up-to-the minute information and decentralized decision making, unlike Second World War, for example, which was fought with large masses of soldiers guided by decisions made at top levels.

Big companies also find a variety of ways to act both large and small. Australian cooperative conglomerate Wesfarmers, for example, purchased struggling Australian retailer Coles with the intention of using the advantage of size in areas such as raising capital, while turning around the chain by giving each individual store manager the autonomy to serve customers differently according to their local needs and tastes. Initial results from the 2007 takeover were positive.[39,40] To encourage innovation, the giant corporation Royal Dutch/Shell created a strategy in its exploration-and-production division to set aside ten per cent of the division's research budget for 'crazy' ideas. Anyone can apply for the funds and decisions are made not by managers but by a small group of nonconformist employees.[41] Small companies that are growing can also use these ideas to help their organizations retain the flexibility and customer focus that fuelled their growth.

As an organization manager, keep these guidelines in mind:

Grow when possible. With growth, you can provide opportunities for employee advancement and greater profitability and effectiveness. Apply new management systems and structural configurations at each stage of an organization's development. Interpret the needs of the growing organization and respond with the management and internal systems that will carry the organization through to the next stage of development.

Organizational Life Cycle

A useful way to think about organizational growth and change is the concept of an organizational **life cycle**,[42] which suggests that organizations are born, grow older and eventually die. Organization structure, leadership style and administrative systems follow a fairly predictable pattern through stages in the life cycle. Stages are sequential and follow a natural progression.

Stages of Life Cycle Development

Research on organizational life cycle suggests that organizational development is characterized by several major stages.[43] A four stage model is illustrated in

Exhibit 9.3, along with the problems associated with transition to each stage. Growth is not easy. Each time an organization enters a new stage in the life cycle, it enters a new game with regard to both internal organization and the external environment.[44] For technology companies today, life cycles are getting shorter; to stay competitive, companies ranging from giants like Google to high growth companies like Holland's satnav manufacturer TomTom have to progress effectively through the early stages of the cycle.

1 *Entrepreneurial stage.* When an organization is born, the emphasis is on creating a product or service and surviving in the marketplace. The founders are entrepreneurs and they tend to devote their full energies to the technical activities of production and marketing. The organization is often informal and non-bureaucratic. The hours of work are frequently long. Control is generally based on the owners' personal supervision. Growth is from a creative new product or service. For example, TomTom was founded in the early 1990s by two University of Amsterdam graduates, Peter-Frans Pauwels and Pieter Geelen. Pauwels and Geelen cut their teeth writing aplications for the then popular Psion personal digital assistant (PDA). As improving technologies for handheld devices created new opportunities, they started building navigation software for PDAs, before finally realizing there was a huge market for standalone satnav devices in cars. In 2004 they launched their first TomTom device. By 2007 they were

EXHIBIT 9.3 Organizational Life Cycle

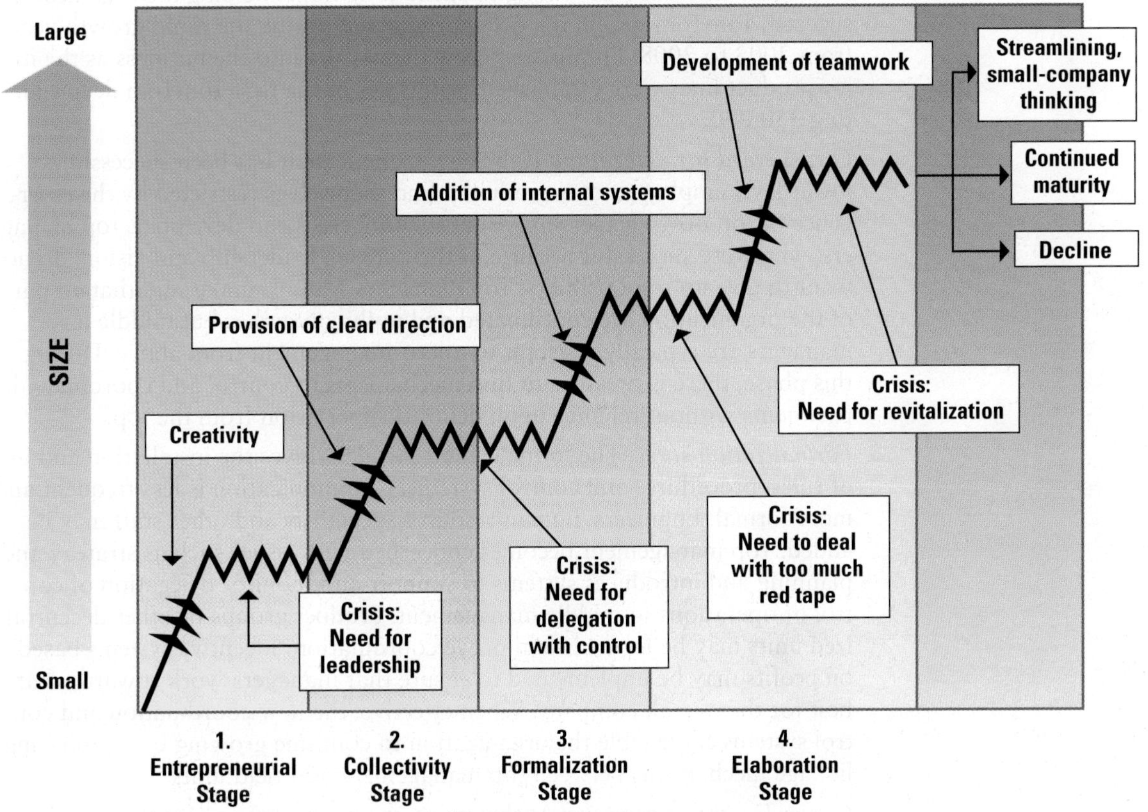

Source: Adapted from Robert E. Quinn and Kim Cameron, 'Organizational Life Cycles and Shifting Criteria of Effectiveness: Some Preliminary Evidence,' *Management Science* 29 (1983), 33–51; and Larry E. Greiner, 'Evolution and Revolution as Organizations Grow,' *Harvard Business Review* 50 (July–August 1972), 37–46.

one of the fastest growing companies in Europe, built from the entrepreneurial and innovative vision of their founders.[45,46] Similarly, Apple Computer, makers of the iconic iPod, was in the **entrepreneurial stage** when it was created by Steve Jobs and Stephen Wozniak in Wozniak's parents' garage.

Crisis: Need for leadership. As the organization starts to grow, the larger number of employees can cause problems. The creative and technically oriented owners are confronted with management issues, but they may prefer to continue to focus their energies on making and selling the product or inventing new products and services. At this time of crisis, entrepreneurs must either adjust the design of the organization to accommodate continued growth or else bring in managers who can do so. When TomTom started to grow, they brought in Harold Goddijn, the former CEO of the early handheld computer manufacturer Psion, someone with solid experience in building a successful technology company.[47]

2 *Collectivity stage*. If the leadership crisis is resolved, the organization begins to develop clear goals and direction. Departments are established along with a hierarchy of authority, job assignments and a division of labour. At Google, founders Larry Page and Sergey Brin devoted their full energy to making sure Google provides the most powerful, fastest and simplest search engine available, then brought in a skilled manager, former Novell CEO Eric Schmidt, to run the company. Google then hired other experienced executives to manage various functional areas and business units as the organization grew.[48] During this collectivity stage, employees may identify strongly with the mission of the organization and be willing to spend long hours helping the organization succeed. TomTom was in the **collectivity stage** during the rapid growth years from 2003 to 2008. Employees threw themselves into the business as the major product lines were established, with sales of the first TomTom device hitting 350,000.

Crisis: Need for delegation. If the new management has been successful, lower-level employees may gradually find themselves restricted by the emergence of top-down leadership. An autonomy crisis can develop as top managers, who were successful because of their strong leadership and vision, do not want to give up responsibility. Top managers want to make sure that all parts of the organization are coordinated and pulling together but middle-level managers are typically resistant to micro-management from above. During this phase, there is pressure to find mechanisms to control and coordinate departments without reliance upon detailed supervision from the top.

3 *Formalization stage*. The **formalization stage** involves the installation and use of rules, procedures and control systems. Communication is less frequent and more formal. Engineers, human resource specialists and other staff may be added. Top management becomes concerned with issues such as strategy and planning and introduces systems to support and monitor delegation of control of operations to middle management. Product groups or other decentralized units may be formed to improve coordination. Incentive systems based on profits may be implemented to ensure that managers work toward what is best for the overall company. When effective, the new coordination and control systems can enable the organization to continue growing by establishing linkage mechanisms between top management and field units.

Crisis: Too much red tape. At this point, the proliferation of systems and programs may begin to stifle initiatives from middle-level executives. Middle management may resent the intrusion of staff. Innovation may be restricted. It was at this stage of Apple's growth that Jobs resigned from the company and a new CEO took control to face the management challenges.

4 *Elaboration stage*. One solution to the red tape crisis is to engender a new sense of collaboration and teamwork. Throughout the organization, managers develop skills for diagnosing problems and working together. Social control and self-discipline can reduce exclusive reliance upon formal controls. Managers learn to work within the bureaucracy without becoming excessively dependent upon it, or adding to it. Formal systems may be simplified and partially replaced by teams and task forces that may operate across functions or divisions of the company. Alternatively, the organization may be split into multiple divisions to maintain a small-company philosophy. Sony, discussed earlier in this chapter, went through this **elaboration stage** of the life cycle in the 1990s.

   Crisis: Need for revitalization. After the organization reaches maturity, it may enter periods of temporary decline.[49] The organization shifts out of alignment with the environment or perhaps becomes slow moving and overbureaucratized. To counter decline, efforts to streamline and innovate may be made. Under pressure from shareholders to revive company fortunes, top managers are often replaced during this period. At Apple, the top spot changed hands a number of times as the company struggled to revitalize. CEOs John Sculley, Michael Spindler and Gilbert Amelio were each ousted by the board as Apple's problems deepened. Steve Jobs returned in mid-1997 to run the company he had founded nearly 25 years earlier. During those 25 years, Jobs had gained management skills and experience he needed to help Apple through its problems. An older and smarter Jobs quickly reorganized the company, weeded out inefficiencies and refocused Apple on innovative products for the consumer market, introducing sleek new iMacs. Even more important, Jobs brought the entrepreneurial spirit back to Apple by moving the company into a whole new direction with the iPod music system. The iPod jump-started growth at Apple as the personal computer market continued to decline. The iPod was then supplemented by the iPhone, which aimed to capture the same customer loyalty as the iPod in the fast-growing mobile phone/PDA market. Sales and profits jumped at Apple thanks to the iPod and iPhone.[50] Nevertheless, the company will have to keep on its toes as it faces a fightback from Nokia on the one hand and the entry of Google into the handset market on the other. All mature organizations have to go through periods of revitalization or they face decline, as shown in the last stage of Exhibit 9.3.

Summary In most countries, four-fifths of businesses that make it past the first year still fail within five years because they can't make the transition from the entrepreneurial stage.[51] The transitions become even more difficult as organizations progress through future stages of the life cycle. Organizations that do not successfully resolve the problems associated with these transitions are restricted in their growth and may even fail. From within an organization, the life cycle crises are very real. For example, Benpres, one of the Philippines' best known conglomerates, nearly went out of business in the late 1990s after playing a leading business role in the country for one hundred years Benpress is featured in the *In Practice* text box on the next page.

Organizational Characteristics during the Life Cycle

As organizations evolve through different stages of the life cycle, changes take place in structure, control systems, innovation and goals. The organizational characteristics associated with different stages are summarized in Exhibit 9.4.

Entrepreneurial Initially, the organization is small, nonbureaucratic and a one-person show. The top manager provides the structure and control system. Organizational

Benpres

Benpres[52] might not be a household name in Western Europe, but it's one of the largest and most successful business groups in the Philippines. Benpres holdings range from television networks to water utilities, toll roads, land development and a major telephone company. In the past, the company operated the country's first passenger airline, a steamship line and even imported double-decker buses from London, plying the streets of a provincial capital, Iloilo, in the 1930s.

The natural life cycle of corporations can be made much more complex in a developing country where business and politics are both intertwined and in conflict. Indeed, the company was built from the assets built up in a sugar hacienda that Eugenio, father of current chairman Oscar Lopez, inherited when his father, a provincial governor, was shot in a political assassination. During this *entrepreneurial* stage, the company began to transform itself from a largely agricultural undertaking into a major business player, although as expected in the classic entrepreneurial phase, there were both successes and failures. The brothers' airline was closed after it suffered too many crashes, but the company's sortie into the power business was a big success. Gradually the company moved into the *collectivity* phase. In 1961, Benpres bought out the American owners of the country's biggest electricity generator, Meralco. Under Benpres, Meralco was both profitable and produced cheap electricity that helped fuel the Philippines' economic development. Emboldened with the success, Benpres soon diversified into manufacturing electrical distribution transformers, again running an internationally-competitive enterprise.

Once again, crisis came in the form of political problems. Eugenio had ambitions to create a media empire and purchased the country's biggest newspaper. Unfortunately this coincided with the rise to power of the dictator Ferdinand Marcos. Marcos took over most of the company's holdings and Eugenio fled to the US, where he died in 1975.

After Marcos himself was forced out of the Phillippines, Oscar Lopez and his brothers came back to try to salvage the various arms of the company that had been seized and run into the ground. This called for a different type of leadership, capable of managing through a rebuilding of the *collectivity stage* but moving towards *formalization*. The Lopez brothers divided up responsibilities for the holdings and brought in a number of professional managers with the expertise needed to turn them around. By and large they were successful: the generating plants in particular were restored to full efficiency and investments made in clean technology.

But once again, Benpres fell into difficulty, this time economic rather than political. The Asian economic crisis of the late 1990s hit the Philippines particularly hard, with economic recession, declining currency and high inflation. Suddenly Benpres's debt burden became unsustainable and Benpres even had to suspend interest repayments for a while. Perhaps the company had become too secure, as can happen with the formalization stage; insufficiently attuned to the danger of sudden downturn. The crisis coincided with the death of Oscar's brother Geny and Oscar's assumption of overall control of Benpres. Oscar's role has been mainly one of *elaboration* – emphasizing the strengthening of managerial skills and controls, rationalizing operation to ensure the business models in place were sustainable, selling off parts of the company that no longer fit a more focused business strategy. In his late 70s in 2008, Oscar was threatening to retire.[53] Would the new generation of managers launch a new phase of *revitalization*, or will the next phase in the life cycle be an end-stage, as Lawrence Miller warns in his seven-stage version of the life-cycle approach?[54]

energy is devoted to survival and the production of a single product or service. The UK-based organization, Shazam, which allows mobile phone users to access a database to identify songs by title and artist, is in the entrepreneurial stage, although it is starting to develop tailored products for specific mobile phone providers and has just made a big breakthrough with Apple agreeing to load the Shazam application on its iPhone.[55] Shazam was described in detail in Chapter 5's Leading by Design box.

EXHIBIT 9.4 Common Organization Characteristics during Four Stages of Life Cycle

Characteristic	1. Entrepreneurial Nonbureaucratic	2. Collectivity Prebureaucratic	3. Formalization Bureaucratic	4. Elaboration Very Bureaucratic
Structure	Informal, one-person show	Mostly informal, some procedures	Formal procedures, division of labour, new specialties added	Teamwork within bureaucracy, small-company thinking
Products or services	Single product or service	Major product or service, with variations	Line of products or services	Multiple product or service lines
Reward and control systems	Personal, paternalistic	Personal, contribution to success	Impersonal, formalized systems	Extensive, tailored to product and department
Innovation	By owner-manager	By employees and managers	By separate innovation group	By institutionalized R&D department
Goal	Survival	Growth	Internal stability, market expansion	Reputation, complete organization
Top management style	Individualistic, entrepreneurial	Charismatic, direction-giving	Delegation with control	Team approach, attack bureaucracy

Source: Adapted from Larry E. Greiner, 'Evolution and Revolution as Organizations Grow,' *Harvard Business Review* 50 (July–August 1972), 37–46; G. L.Lippitt and W. H. Schmidt, 'Crises in a Developing Organization,' *Harvard Business Review* 45 (November–December 1967), 102–112; B. R. Scott, 'The Industrial State: Old Myths and New Realities,' *Harvard Business Review* 51 (March–April 1973), 133–148; Robert E. Quinn and Kim Cameron,'Organizational Life Cycles and Shifting Criteria of Effectiveness,' *Management Science* 29 (1983), 33–51.

Collectivity This is the organization's youth. Growth is rapid and employees are excited and committed to the organization's mission. The structure is still mostly informal, although some procedures are emerging. Strong charismatic leaders like Andrew Fisher at Shazam or Steve Jobs at Apple provide direction and goals for the organization. Continued growth is a major goal.

Formalization At this point, the organization is entering midlife. Bureaucratic characteristics emerge. The organization adds staff support groups, formalizes procedures and establishes a clear hierarchy and division of labour. At the formalization stage, organizations may also develop complementary products to offer a complete product line. Innovation may be achieved by establishing a separate research and development (R&D) department. Major goals are internal stability and market expansion. Top management too delegates, but it also implements formal control systems.

At this stage, for example, Soichiro Honda and Takeo Fujisawa, the entrepreneurial leaders who had built Honda Motor Company into a worldwide force in the quarter-century between 1948 and 1973, handed over the company reins to a collective leadership of younger, professional managers.[56,57]

Elaboration The mature organization is large and bureaucratic, with extensive control systems, rules and procedures. Organization managers attempt to develop a team orientation within the bureaucracy to prevent further bureaucratization. Top managers are concerned with establishing a complete organization. Organizational stature and reputation are important. Innovation is institutionalized through an R&D department. Management may attack the bureaucracy and streamline it.

Summary Growing organizations tend to move through stages of a life cycle and each stage is associated with specific characteristics of structure, control systems, goals and innovation. The life cycle phenomenon is a powerful concept used for understanding problems facing organizations and how managers can respond in a positive way to move an organization to the next stage, although like the human life cycle, many variations and different interpretations are possible.

See online
COUNTERPOINT 9.9

Organizational Bureaucracy and Control

As organizations progress through the life cycle, they usually take on bureaucratic characteristics as they grow larger and more complex. The systematic study of bureaucracy was launched by Max Weber, a sociologist who studied government organizations in Europe and developed a framework of administrative characteristics that would make large organizations rational and efficient.[58] Weber wanted to understand how organizations could be designed to play a positive role in the larger society.

COUNTERPOINT 9.2

Weber was no enthusiast for bureaucracy except for its capacity to deliver 'due process' and thereby eliminate favouritism and nepotism. He was, however, interested in its signifiance for modern societies and therefore attempted to distil its distinctive features (see Exhibit 9.5). In principle, each client of a bureaucracy receives the same treatment – good or bad. Weber's larger concern was the progressive rationalization of modern societies. His interest in bureaucracy arose from this concern. Specifically, Weber identified bureaucracy as simultaneously more efficient and more dehumanizing. The dehumanizing aspects were viewed by him as detrimental to efficient organization as well as damaging to the human spirit. He was not directly interested in how modern organizations could be designed to be more rational. Instead, he was interested in the appeal (e.g. systematic administration) and effects (e.g. depersonalizaiton) that accompanied the growth of this mode of organization. An important virtue of bureaucracy, Weber believed, was its removal of personal patronage and discrimination (see also below). Formalized recuitment and selection procedures increase the likelihood that employees are hired on the basis of their competence, not their skin colour, gender or personal connections. Likewise, customers can expect equal treatment, with no queue jumping or other favours. Critics of bureaucracy tend to emphasise the 'red tape', overlook the positive benefits of its 'impersonality' and conveniently disregard the limitations of alternatives to bureaucracy for dealing effectively and fairly with large, complex adminstrative tasks.
Discuss

What Is Bureaucracy?

Although Weber perceived **bureaucracy** as a potential threat to basic personal liberties, he also recognized it as the most efficient possible system of organizing. He predicted the triumph of bureaucracy because of its ability to ensure more efficient functioning of organizations in both business and government settings. Weber identified a set of organizational characteristics, listed in Exhibit 9.5, that could be found in successful bureaucratic organizations.

EXHIBIT 9.5 Weber's Dimensions of Bureaucracy

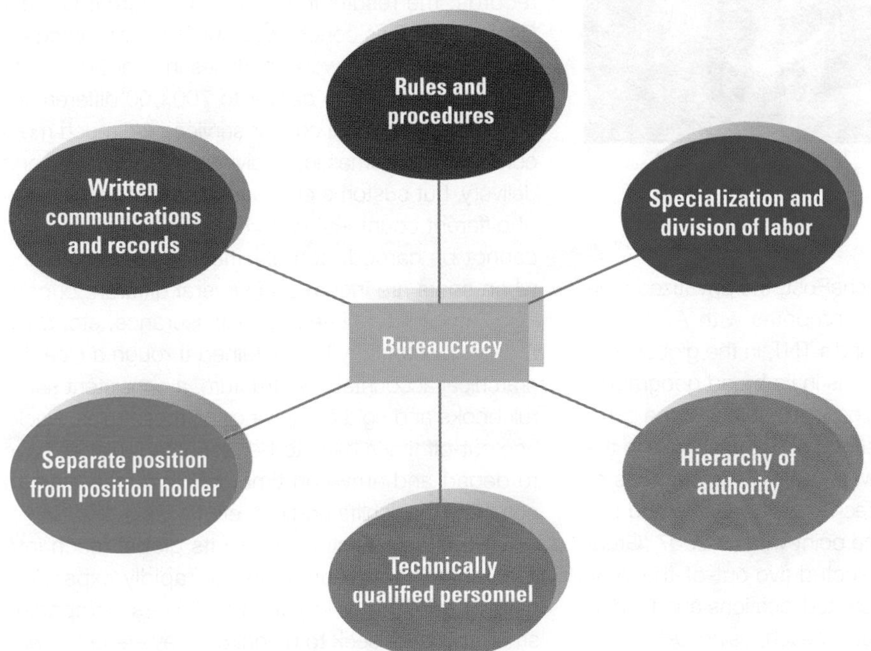

Rules and standard procedures enabled organizational activities to be performed in a predictable, routine manner. Specialized duties meant that each employee had a clear task to perform. Hierarchy of authority provided a sensible mechanism for supervision and control. Technical competence was the basis by which people were hired rather than friendship, family ties and favouritism, which dramatically reduced work performance. The separation of the position from the position holder meant that individuals did not own or have an inherent right to the job, which promoted efficiency. Written records provided an organizational memory and continuity over time.

Although bureaucratic characteristics carried to an extreme are widely criticized today, rational control was a significant idea. Bureaucracy provided many advantages over organization forms based on favouritism, social status, family connections and so on. For example, when he was appointed as commissioner of internal revenue in the Philippines some 30 years ago, Efren Plana found massive corruption, including officials hiring their relatives for high-ranking jobs and tax assessors winning promotions by bribing their superiors.[59] Likewise, Bill Browder, who made a fortune in Russia after the collapse of the Soviet Union, was eventually refused a visa to Russia because he declined to give a bribe to an Interior Ministry official.[60] The tradition of giving government posts to relatives is widespread in many countries, particularly in the developing world. As China's economy develops rapidly and integrates with the world economy, its government is cracking down on such nepotism.[61,62] By comparison, the logical and rational form of organization analyzed by Weber enables pre-bureaucratic inefficiencies to be reduced if not entirely eliminated.

See online
COUNTERPOINT 9.10

The bureaucratic characteristics listed in Exhibit 9.5 can have a positive impact on many large firms. In the *In Practice* feature on the next page, we look at DHL, one of the largest courier companies in the world, now aiming to entrench itself as a big player in the rapidly developing third party logistics (3PL) market.

Bureaucratic characteristics tend to increase with large size. As DHL transitions into a global, knowledge-based logistics business, its managers are obliged to find effective ways to ensure that its bureaucracy serves the company's business goals

DHL

DHL, owned by DeutschePost, the privatized German postal service, competes with America's UPS and Fedex and Holland's TNT, in the global courier market. DHL's strength is in its broad geographic coverage; customers can be pretty sure that the company will be able to deliver a package anywhere in the world, notwithstanding wars, political embargoes or mere isolation. Georgia Tech's Supply Chain and Logistics Institute proved the point with its 2007 'Great Package Race'. They selected five out-of-the-way, dangerous, or politically isolated locations and tried to send packages to contacts in each, using DHL, UPS and Fedex. Only DHL was able to deliver to all five and at a lower overall cost than its competitors. Neither UPS or Fedex accepted packages for Myanmar, probably due to a US government political boycott of that country. UPS lost a package to Samoa somewhere in New Zealand, perhaps because its agents told Georgia Tech that no such country as Samoa exists. Fedex failed to deliver a package to Harare, Zimbabwe, apparently because of an unpaid $1.00 customs fee – the recipient had to go and sort out the problem himself. UPS managed to get a package destined for Tikrit, the Iraq hometown of Saddam Hussein, only as far as Dubai, after which it spent a week in a warehouse in Louisville, Kentucky, before being returned to Georgia Tech. UPS even charged Georgia Tech for the package's long but fruitless journey.

In response to criticism that these delivery locations were very unusual and not a fair test of normal business flows, the Institute also sent a package from Atlanta to Singapore, a major courier destination. Again, DHL delivered before its competitors.[63]

In truth, all four of the major courier companies have remarkable capacities and excellent overall records; the results in other years' 'Great Courier Races' were less conclusive. But DHL's advantage is undoubtedly its network of offices in over 200 countries and its ability to deliver to 700,000 different locations. International courier services are much more complex than domestic, involving not just pick-up and delivery, but customs clearance services, knowledge of different countries' rules regarding what can and cannot be carried, complexities of payment/billing when costs are incurred in several different currencies, intricacies of international insurance, etc. Such a capacity can only be sustained through a clear hierarchical accountability structure, a consistent set of rulebooks and rigid compliance to these rules. Package cut-off times have to be respected, planes have to depart and arrive on time, delivery staff have to complete their shifts on-time, etc.

DHL is now aiming to turn its global reach into a competitive advantage in the rapidly expanding field of third party logistics (3PL). As companies small and large seek to globalize, they are faced with enormous logistical issues. Emerging markets typically lack the kinds of facilities taken for granted in developed countries, like good roads, secure storage facilities, consistent power supplies, transparent customs procedures, etc. The company that tries to set up a supply chain without intimate local knowledge is asking for trouble and will probably find it. Corporations with a global reach and local knowledge like DHL already have a rooted infrastructure, built on a bureaucratic structure of clear rules and operating procedures and can offer that ready-made organizational capacity for sale. DHL's Exel Supply Chain division offers services such as integrated IT solutions, warehouse operations and industry specific product distribution systems.[64]

Increasingly, the bureaucratic structure needed to manage a global logistical operation like that of DHL is intertwined with advanced informational technology systems. DHL has pioneered, for example, the use of RFID (discussed in Chapter 8) to enhance the tracking of packages,[65] and its 3PL arm has helped customers set up their own computer-based supply management systems.

and does not detract from employee initiative. The new technology and emphasis on tailor-made logistics services place more demands on workers, who need flexibility and autonomy to perform well. In particular, the logistics business is moving from 3PL towards what is known as fourth-party logistics (4PL), where the logistics company carries out supply chain analysis, designs and even runs a tailor-made logistics system for the client company. These types of services require flexibility, as the client and service-provider companies essentially integrate their activities in areas such as warehousing and distribution. The key to success becomes the ability to deliver the reliability of a bureaucratically structured service with the flexibility to work with the different requirements of client companies working with diverse product lines, as well as the innovative perspective needed to take advantage of quickly developing technologies.

Now, let's look at some specific ways size affects organizational structure and control.

BRIEFCASE

As an organization manager, keep these guidelines in mind:

As the organization grows, provide greater formalization to achieve standardization and control. Guard against excessive overhead by keeping administrative, clerical and support staff costs low.

Size and Structural Control

In the field of organization theory, organization size has been described as an important variable that influences structural design and methods of control. Should an organization become more bureaucratic as it grows larger? In what size organizations are bureaucratic characteristics most appropriate? More than 100 studies have attempted to answer these questions.[66] Most of these studies indicate that large organizations tend to be different from small organizations along several dimensions of bureaucratic structure, including formalization, centralization and personnel ratios.

Formalization and Centralization **Formalization**, as described in Chapter 1, refers to rules, procedures and written documentation, such as policy manuals and job descriptions, that prescribe the rights and duties of employees.[67] The evidence supports the conclusion that large organizations are usually more formalized, as at DHL. A key reason for this is that large organizations tend to rely on rules, procedures and paperwork to achieve standardization and control across their large numbers of employees and departments, whereas top managers can use personal observation and informal contacts to control a small organization.[68]

Centralization refers to the level of hierarchy with authority to make decisions. In centralized organizations, decisions tend to be made at the top. In decentralized organizations, similar decisions are made at a lower level.

Decentralization represents a paradox. It might seem that, in the perfect bureaucracy, all decisions would be made by the top administrator, who would have perfect control. However, as an organization grows larger and has more people and departments, decisions cannot be passed to the top because senior managers would be overloaded. Thus, the research on organization size indicates that larger organizations permit greater decentralization.[69]

See online
COUNTERPOINT 9.11

In small start-up organizations, on the other hand, the founder or top executive can effectively be involved in every decision, large and small. Consider Honda, where in the early days Soichiro Honda and Takeo Fujisawa used to make every important decision. It was their daring insistence that the company's products could break into international markets that allowed the company to grow from tiny beginnings to become one of the world's great manufacturing enterprises. But, as Honda grew into a global auto maker, the traditional, personal structure started to stand in the way of corporate development. For example, Soichiro Honda was a great believer in air-cooled rather than water-cooled engines. Even when the engineering and business debates had been settled in favour of water-cooled motors, Mr. Honda continued to promote development of the company's commercially unsuccessful air-cooled engines.

When Honda and Fujisawa retired, the new CEO Kiyoshi Kawashima introduced what was called the New Honda Plan (NHP), in which leadership responsibilities would be greatly decentralized, permitting flexibility and early response to shifting circumstances in different parts of the now international firm. Under NHP, the company set up manufacturing plants around the world, a necessity both in terms of efficiency and in order to respond to criticism that the Japanese auto industry was taking jobs away from car workers in Europe and North America. As the company continued to grow, its automobile, motorcycle and power product businesses were carved into separate autonomous divisions. In 1992, the company was further decentralized through establishment of four regional chief operating officers, for Japan, North America, Europe and the rest of the world, who would each have responsibility for production, research, sales and marketing.[70,71]

Personnel Ratios Another characteristic of bureaucracy relates to **personnel ratios** for administrative and professional support staff. The most frequently studied ratio is the administrative ratio.[72] Two patterns have emerged. The first is that the ratio of top administration to total employees is usually smaller in large organizations,[73] indicating that organizations experience administrative economies as they grow larger. The second pattern concerns professional support staff ratios.[74] These tend to *increase* in proportion to organization size, because of the greater need for specialized skills in larger, complex organizations. The transformation of organizational structure as a result of new technology and outsourcing and the consequent dramatic reduction in the proportion of traditional clerical staff, has significantly altered personnel structure and ratios in both the private and public sectors, although research suggests the impact varies according to the societal culture in which organizations operate, with Japanese businesses generally less affected than those in the UK and USA, for example.[75]

Exhibit 9.6 illustrates administrative and support ratios for small and large organizations. As organizations increase in size, the administrative ratio declines and the ratios

EXHIBIT 9.6 Percentage of Personnel Allocated to Administrative and Support Activities

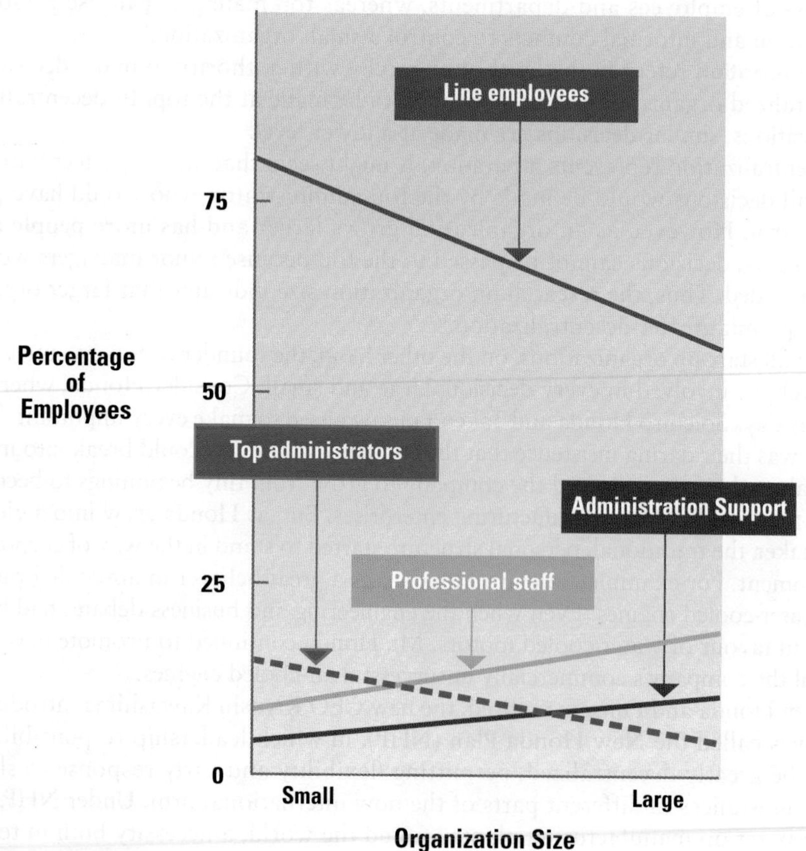

for other support groups increase.[76] The net effect for direct workers is that they decline as a percentage of total employees. In summary, whereas top administrators do not make up a disproportionate number of employees in large organizations, the idea that proportionately greater overhead is required in large organizations is supported. Although large organizations reduced overhead during the difficult economic years of the 1980s, there is anecdotal evidence that overhead costs for corporations began creeping back up again as revenues soared during the late 1990s.[77] Keeping costs for administrative and professional support staff low represents a continuing challenge for large organizations.[78]

See online
COUNTERPOINT 9.12

Bureaucracy in a Changing World

Weber's prediction of the triumph of bureaucracy has proven accurate in some respects.[79] Bureaucratic characteristics have many advantages and have generally worked well in advancing the industrial age.[80] By establishing a hierarchy of authority and specific rules and procedures, bureaucracy provides an effective way to bring order to large groups of people and prevent abuses of power. Impersonal relationships are based on rules rather than the favouritism and nepotism characteristic of many preindustrial organizations. Bureaucracy provides systematic and rational ways to organize and manage tasks too complex to be understood and handled by a few individuals, thus greatly aiding the efficiency and effectiveness of large organizations.

The world is rapidly changing, however and the machinelike bureaucratic system of the industrial age does not necessarily work well as organizations face new challenges including the rise of competitors using different, more flexible business models. Consider the difference between established airlines and their low-cost competitors and the difficulties the former have encountered either in reducing their overheads or establishing low-cost subsidiaries. At the same time, the low-cost competitors must rely upon reliable, bureaucratic procedures for their pared down operations. It is not that they operate without bureaucracy but, rather, that the bureaucracy is minimized by offering 'no-frills'. With global competition and uncertain environments, an alternative for many organizations is to minimize unproductive formalization and staff costs through outsourcing.

There are also significant differences between societies in attitudes towards bureaucracy that influence business and organizational life.[81] In some societies, such as the United States, there is a tradition of individualism and suspicion of large government. The very word bureaucracy is often seen as negative. Some American critics have blamed government bureaucracy for intelligence, communication and accountability failures that helped lead to US disasters as diverse as the 2001 terrorist attacks, the *Columbia* space shuttle explosion, the abuses at Abu Ghraib prison and a slow response to the 2005 Hurricane Katrina devastation. 'Every time you add a layer of bureaucracy, you delay the movement of information up the chain of command ... And you dilute the information because at each step some details are taken out', said Richard A. Posner, a federal appeals court judge who has written a book on intelligence reform.[82] Many Europeans, on the other hand, tend to be more supportive of bureaucratically structured systems, believing that they are more stable and predictable and provide better protection for the less powerful.[83] Nevertheless, at least until the onset of the 2007–2009 recession that cast doubt on the neoliberal model, overall global isomorphic trends still appear to favour market-driven organizations rather than rule-driven bureaucracies.[84]

Organizing Temporary Systems for Flexibility and Innovation

How can organizations overcome the problems of bureaucracy in rapidly changing environments? Some are implementing innovative structural solutions.

One structural concept, called the *incident command system* (ICS), is used by organizations that have to respond rapidly to emergency or crisis situations, such as police and fire services or other emergency management agencies. The **incident command system** was developed to maintain the efficiency and control benefits of bureaucracy yet prevent the problem of slow response to crises.[85] The approach is being adapted by other types of organizations to help them respond quickly to new opportunities, unforeseen competitive threats or organizational crises.

See online COUNTERPOINT 9.13

The basic idea behind the ICS is that the organization can glide smoothly between a highly formalized, hierarchical structure that is effective during times of stability and a more flexible, loosely structured one needed to respond well to unexpected and demanding environmental conditions. The hierarchical side with its rules, procedures and chain of command helps maintain control and ensure adherence to rules that have been developed and tested over many years to cope with well-understood problems and situations. However, during times of high uncertainty, the most effective structure is one that loosens the lines of command and enables people to work across departmental and hierarchical lines to anticipate, avoid and solve unanticipated problems within the context of a clearly understood mission and guidelines.

BRIEFCASE

As an organization manager, keep these guidelines in mind:

Consider using the incident command system to maintain the efficiency and control benefits of bureaucracy but prevent the problem of slow response to rapid environmental change. Enable the organization to glide smoothly from a formalized system during times of stability to a more flexible, loosely structured one when facing threats, crises or unexpected environmental changes.

Much greater attention has been given to effective management in crisis situations since the generalization of large scale terrorist attacks in the US, Spain, India, UK and other countries in the first years of the twenty-first century. The ICS approach has been applied to planning to deal with large scale natural disasters. Weaknesses in the early warning and disaster response systems dealing with the south Asian tsunami of 26 December 2004, which caused over 350,000 deaths, led to development of an Asian ICS involving international collaboration of emergency authorities.[86]

Another type of potential natural disaster is a disease pandemic in which a substantial proportion of the population would become very sick in a short period of time, overstretching the capacities of the healthcare system. Health authorities are particularly concerned about the potential for an influenza pandemic, possibly spread through infected poultry. British health authorities have developed a Pandemic Influenza Plan, which outlines the command system for such a crisis, as well as identifying the health care responses to different levels of pandemic. While the overall care framework is established through the ICS command structure, the Plan emphasizes the need for individual clinicians making the necessary difficult local decisions about what kinds of treatment and to whom, will be offered in a situation where the numbers of sick far exceeds the availability of beds in hospitals.[87]

The international religious charity *The Salvation Army* has long and successful experience dealing with emergencies, from which many private and public organizations could learn. The Salvation Army's approach is discussed in the *Leading by Design* box below.

The Salvation Army

The Salvation Army has been called 'the most effective organization in the world' by a leading management scholar. One reason the organization is so effective and powerful is its approach to organizing, which makes use of the incident command system to provide the right amount of structure, control and flexibility to meet the requirements of each situation. The Salvation Army refers to its approach as 'organizing to improvise'.

The Salvation Army provides day-to-day assistance to the homeless and economically disadvantaged. In addition, the organization rushes in whenever there is a major disaster – whether it be a tornado, flood, hurricane, airplane crash or terrorist attack – to network with other agencies to provide disaster relief. Long after the most desperate moments of the initial crisis have passed, the Salvation Army continues helping people rebuild their lives and communities – offering financial assistance; meeting physical needs for food, clothing and housing; and providing emotional and spiritual support to inspire hope and help people build a foundation for the future. The Army's management realizes that emergencies demand high flexibility. At the same time, the organization must have a high level of control and accountability to ensure its continued existence and meet its day-to-day responsibilities. As a former national commander puts it, 'We have to have it both ways. We can't choose to be flexible and reckless or to be accountable and responsive … We have to be several different kinds of organizations at the same time.'

In the early emergency moments of a crisis, the Salvation Army deploys a temporary organization that has its own command structure. People need to have a clear sense of who's in charge to prevent the rapid response demands from degenerating into chaos. For example, if the Army responds to a flood in Indonesia or a tornado in Oklahoma, manuals clearly specify in advance who is responsible for talking to the media, who is in charge of supply inventories, who liaises duties with other agencies and so forth. This model for the temporary organization keeps the Salvation Army responsive and consistent. In the later recovery and rebuilding phases of a crisis, supervisors frequently give people general guidelines and allow them to improvise the best solutions. There isn't time for supervisors to review and sign off on every decision that needs to be made to get families and communities reestablished.

Thus, the Salvation Army actually has people simultaneously working in all different types of organization structures, from traditional vertical command structures, to horizontal teams, to a sort of network form that relies on collaboration with other agencies. Operating in such a fluid way enables the organization to accomplish amazing results. In the first four months of 2009 alone, the Salvation Army responded to an earthquake in Italy, deadly bushfires in Australia and floods in Papua New Guinea, in addition to many more served by regular day-to-day programmes. It has been recognized as a leader in putting money to maximal use, meaning donors are willing to give because they trust the organization to be responsible and accountable at the same time it is flexible and innovative in meeting human needs.

Sources: www.salvationarmy.org; Peter Walker and Daniel G. Maxwell (2008), *Shaping the Humanitarian World*, London, Taylor & Francis; Robert A. Watson and Ben Brown, *The Most Effective Organization in the U.S.: Leadership Secrets of the Salvation Army* (New York: Crown Business, 2001), 159–181.

Other Approaches to Reducing Bureaucracy

Many organizations are cutting layers of the hierarchy, keeping headquarters staff small and giving lower-level workers greater freedom to make decisions rather than burdening them with excessive rules and regulations. In 2002 Lakshmi Mittal's LNM Corporation, which later went on to form the core of Arcelor Mittal, the world's largest steel manufacturer, had 75,000 employees worldwide but only 25 in its London headquarters.[88,89] The point is not to overload headquarters with lawyers, accountants and financial analysts who inhibit the flexibility and autonomy of divisions.

See online
COUNTERPOINT 9.14

Of course, many companies must be large to have sufficient resources and complexity to produce products for a global environment but most large companies worldwide are striving toward greater decentralization and leanness. They are giving frontline workers more authority and responsibility to define and direct their own jobs, often by creating self-directed teams that find ways to coordinate work, improve productivity and better serve customers.

Another impact on bureaucracy is the increasing *professionalism* of employees. Professionalism is defined as the length of formal training and experience of employees. More employees need college degrees, MBAs and other professional degrees to work as attorneys, researchers or doctors at large firms like Toyota, Tesco and GlaxoSmithKline. In addition, Internet-based companies may be staffed entirely by well-educated knowledge workers. Studies of professionals show that formalization is often not needed because professional training regularizes a high standard of behaviour for employees that acts as a substitute for bureaucracy.[90] Companies also enhance this trend when they provide ongoing training for *all* employees, from the front office to the shop floor, in a push for continuous individual and organizational learning. Increased training substitutes for bureaucratic rules and procedures that can constrain the creativity of employees in solving problems and increases organizational capability.

See online
COUNTERPOINT 9.15

A form of organization called *professional partnership* has emerged that is made up completely of professionals.[91] These organizations include consulting and auditing firms, such as PricewaterhouseCoopers, KPMG and Ernst and Young, management consultants such as Boston Consulting and McKinsey & Company,[92] as well as law firms, engineering partnerships, architectural partnerships, etc. The general finding concerning professional partnerships is that branches have substantial autonomy and decentralized authority to make necessary decisions. They work with a consensus orientation rather than the top-down direction typical of traditional business and government organizations. Thus, the trend of increasing professionalism combined with rapidly changing environments is another factor that appears to be leading to less bureaucracy.

COUNTERPOINT 9.3

The 'autonomy and decentralized' authority of professional partnership tends to be framed within a highly bureaucratic structure. Consider, for example, the processes of recruitment, selection and appraisal which are subject to standardized forms of assessment supplemented by more culturally specific evaluations of applicants' 'suitability'. **Discuss**

Organizational Control Strategies

Even though many organizations are trying to decrease bureaucracy and reduce rules and procedures that constrain employees, every organization needs systems for guiding and controlling the organization. Employees may have more freedom in today's companies, but control is still a major responsibility of management.

Managers at the top and middle levels of an organization can choose among three overall control strategies. These strategies come from a framework for organizational control proposed by William Ouchi of the University of California at Los Angeles. Ouchi suggested three control strategies that organizations could adopt – bureaucratic, market and clan.[93] Each form of control uses different types of information. However, all three types may appear simultaneously in an organization. The requirements for each control strategy are given in Exhibit 9.7.

Bureaucratic Control

Bureaucratic control is the use of rules, policies, hierarchy of authority, written documentation, standardization and other bureaucratic mechanisms to standardize behaviour and assess performance. Bureaucratic control uses the bureaucratic

EXHIBIT 9.7 Three Organizational Control Strategies

Type	Requirements
Bureaucracy	Rules, standards, hierarchy, legitimate authority
Market	Prices, competition, exchange relationship
Clan	Tradition, shared values and beliefs, trust

Source: Based on William G. Ouchi, 'A Conceptual Framework for the Design of Organizational Control Mechanisms,' *Management Science* 25 (1979), 833–848.

characteristics identified by Weber and illustrated in the DHL case. A primary purpose of bureaucratic rules and procedures is to standardize and control employee behaviour.

Recall that as organizations progress through the life cycle and grow larger, they tend to become more formalized and standardized. Within a large organization, thousands of work behaviour and information exchanges take place both vertically and horizontally. Rules and policies evolve through a process of trial and error to regulate these behaviours. Some degree of bureaucratic control is used in virtually every organization. Rules, regulations and directives contain information about a range of behaviour.

To make bureaucratic control work, managers must have the authority to maintain control over the organization. Weber argued that legitimate, rational authority granted to managers was preferred over other types of control (e.g. favouritism or payoffs) as the basis for organizational decisions and activities. Within the larger society, however, Weber identified three types of authority that could explain the creation and control of a large organization.[94]

Rational-legal authority is based on employees' belief in the legality of rules and the right of those elevated to positions of authority to issue commands. Rational-legal authority is the basis for both creation and control of most government organizations and is the most common base of control in organizations worldwide. **Traditional authority** is the belief in traditions and in the legitimacy of the status of people exercising authority through those traditions. Traditional authority is the basis for control for monarchies, churches and some organizations in regions such as Latin America and the Middle East. **Charismatic authority** is based on devotion to the exemplary character or to the heroism of an individual person and the order defined by him or her. Revolutionary military organizations are often based on the leader's charisma, as are some corporations led by charismatic individuals such as the Italian media tycoon and politician Silvio Berlusconi, or the Virgin Group's Richard Branson, who will be discussed later in the chapter. The organization reflects the personality and values of the leader.

More than one type of authority – such as long tradition and the leader's special charisma – may exist in organizations, but rational-legal authority is the most widely used form to govern internal work activities and decision making, particularly in large organizations.

As an organization manager, keep these guidelines in mind:

Implement one of the three basic choices – bureaucratic, clan, market – as the primary means of organizational control. Use bureaucratic control when organizations are large, have a stable environment and use routine technology. Use clan control in small, uncertain departments. Use market control when outputs can be priced and when competitive bidding is available.

Market Control

Market control occurs when price competition is used to evaluate the output and productivity of an organization. The idea of market control originated in economics.[95] A cash price is an efficient form of control, because managers can compare prices and profits to evaluate the efficiency of their corporation. Top managers nearly always use the price mechanism to evaluate performance in corporations. Corporate sales and costs are summarized in a profit-and-loss statement that can be compared against performance in previous years or with that of other corporations.

The use of market control requires that outputs be sufficiently explicit for a price to be assigned and that competition exist. Without competition, the price does not accurately reflect internal efficiency. Governments and even non-profit organizations are increasingly using market control, an approach inspired variously by the American authors Osborne and Gaebler's *Reinventing Government*[96] and New Zealand public sector reform efforts led by Roger Douglas, the country's Finance Minister during much of the 1990s.[97] Market control is central to the concept of New Public Management (NPM) that has been a major influence on public administration in both developed and developing countries.[98] The European Union has placed considerable pressure on its member governments to introduce market mechanisms to many services that were previously run as state monopolies, ranging from postal services to water supply.[99,100]

Market control was once used primarily at the level of the entire organization, but it is increasingly used even in product divisions. Profit centres are self-contained product divisions, such as those described in Chapter 3. Each division contains resource inputs needed to produce a product. Each division can be evaluated on the basis of profit or loss compared with other divisions. Asea Brown Boveri (ABB), a multinational electrical contractor and manufacturer of electrical equipment, includes three different types of profit centres, all operating according to their own bottom line and all interacting through buying and selling with one another and with outside customers.[101] The network organization, also described in Chapter 3, illustrates market control as well. Different companies compete on price to provide the functions and services required by the hub organization. The organization typically contracts with the company that offers the best price and value.

Some firms require that individual departments interact with one another at market prices – buying and selling products or services among themselves at prices equivalent to those quoted outside the firm. To make the market control system work, internal units also have the option to buy and sell with outside companies. Imperial Oil Limited of Canada (formerly Esso) transformed its R&D department into a semiautonomous profit centre several years ago.

Market control can only be used when the output of a company, division or department can be assigned a dollar price and when there is competition. Companies are finding that they can apply the market control concept to internal departments such as accounting, data processing, legal and information services.

Clan Control

Clan control is the use of social characteristics, such as corporate culture, shared values, commitment, traditions and beliefs, to control behaviour. Organizations

Imperial Oil Limited

In the early 1990s, the Canadian oil company Imperial Oil's R&D was a monopoly service provider allocated an annual budget of about $45 million. Imperial Oil felt that this method of operating gave the 200 scientists and staff little incentive to control costs or advance quality.

Today, R&D receives a much smaller budget and essentially supports itself through applied research and lab-services contracts negotiated with internal and external customers. Contracts spell out the costs of each program, analysis, or other service and cost-conscious Imperial-Oil managers can shop for lower prices among external labs.

R&D has even introduced competition within its own small unit. For example, research teams are free to buy some lab services outside the company if they feel their own laboratories are overpriced or inefficient. However, quality and efficiency have dramatically improved at Imperial Oil's R&D and the unit's high-quality, low-cost services are attracting a great deal of business from outside the company. Canadian companies routinely send samples of used motor oil to the R&D labs for analysis. Manufacturers use R&D to autopsy equipment failures. Vehicle makers like General Motors and Ford test new engines at Imperial Oil's R&D's chassis dynamometer lab. According to John Charlton, Imperial Oil's corporate strategic planning manager, applying market control to R&D has led to an increase in the amount of work the unit does, as well as a 12 per cent reduction in internal costs.[102]

that use clan control require shared values and trust among employees.[103] Clan control is important when ambiguity and uncertainty are high. High uncertainty means the organization cannot put a price on its services and things change so fast that rules and regulations are not able to specify every correct behaviour. Under clan control, people may be hired because they are committed to the organization's purpose, such as in a religious organization. New employees may be subjected to a long period of socialization to gain acceptance by colleagues. Clan control is most often used in small, informal organizations or in organizations with a strong culture, because of personal involvement in and commitment to the organization's purpose. For example, St. Luke's Communications Ltd., a London advertising firm committed to equal employee ownership, is especially careful to bring in only new employees who believe in the agency's philosophy and mission. The company even turned down a $90 million contract because it meant rapidly recruiting new employees who might not fit with St. Luke's distinctive culture. Clan control works for St. Luke's; the agency is highly respected and its revenues continue to grow.[104]

Traditional control mechanisms based on strict rules and close supervision are ineffective for controlling behaviour in conditions of high uncertainty and rapid change.[105] In addition, the growing use of computer networks and the Internet, which often leads to a democratic spread of information throughout the organization, may force many companies to depend less on bureaucratic control and more on shared values that guide individual actions for the corporate good.[106]

Virgin Group

When people think of the Virgin Group, two images come to mind. One is the ubiquitous, bright red Virgin logo that dominates the visual imaging of each one of the group's many businesses and the other is Sir Richard Branson, the forever-youthful driving force behind Virgin's success. Branson's image and Virgin's logo are sufficiently appealing in the UK that when he folded his telecommunications interests into the broadband/cable/phone company NTL, the company agreed to pay him £8.5 million a year just to be able to call itself Virgin Media.

Each of Virgin's many enterprises, ranging from the Virgin record label which hit the headlines through signing Mick Jagger, to the Virgin Atlantic airline, are launched with Branson's trademark enthusiasm and commitment, often with a stunt thrown in for good measure. When Virgin Atlantic arrived in India, Branson rode through Delhi on a 'jumbo' elephant and when he launched his Virgin Mobile service in Mumbai seven years later, he first staged his own mock assassination in Bollywood style and then had himself lowered on wires from a 35-storey skyscraper.[107] It is for just these kinds of extrovert qualities that the group's staff are carefully selected. Brett Godfrey, CEO of Virgin Blue, the group's Australian airline, says, 'Culture is about how you go about doing business with your staff, as opposed to how you do business with your customers, so you've just got to get the recruitment right. We probably spend more money on recruitment than any other company I've been associated with.' Highfield, Blue's HR director, adds. 'The culture of the Virgin group is a worldwide phenomenon.' When Virgin Blue was being launched, several managers who had been with the group for a number of years came to Australia and, during the start-up phase, slept on rubber mattresses in shared accommodation with the rest of the dozen-or-so top managers. Highfield describes it as being, 'like family'.

What's remarkable is that Virgin retains an overall positive image despite the fact that many of Branson's enterprises have folded or been involved in various controversies. The company owns one of Britain's regional rail franchises and Virgin Trains has been no more immune than any of the other franchises to the delays and high fares that bedevil the British train network. The list of Virgin businesses that have failed is long indeed, ranging from Virgin vodka to Virgin underwear. The company recently narrowly failed in a bid to take over Britain's ailing Northern Rock bank. But still, Branson and his Virgin group can count on clan loyalty, not only from the group's staff, but also from a healthy chunk of the British population.[108]

COUNTERPOINT 9.4

How narrow this failure was is subject to some contrtoversy. It is not certain whether Virgin Money had the resources or credibility to make a successful bid. But the free publicity involved in demonstrating Virgin's willingness to come to the aid of the government and Northern Rock investors was invaluable. Making the bid was a win-win situation involving minimal investment for maximum return in free publicity as Virgin was spread over the news media during the weeks of the negotiations. **Discuss**

Virgin has successfully used clan control throughout its history, but this story illustrates that large size increases the demands on managers to maintain strong cultural values that support this type of control. Today's companies that are trying to become learning organizations often use clan control or *self-control* rather than relying on rules and regulations. Self-control is similar to clan control, but whereas clan control is a function of being socialized into a group, self-control stems from individual values, goals and standards. The organization attempts to induce a change such that individual employees' own internal values and work preferences are brought in line with the organization's values and goals.[109] With self-control, employees generally set their own goals and monitor their own performance, yet companies relying on self-control need strong leaders who can clarify boundaries within which employees exercise their own knowledge and discretion.

Clan control or self-control may also be used in some departments, such as strategic planning, where uncertainty is high and performance is difficult to measure. Managers of departments that rely on these informal control mechanisms must not assume that the absence of written, bureaucratic control means no control is present. Clan control is invisible yet very powerful. One study found that the actions of employees were controlled even more powerfully and completely with clan control than with a bureaucratic hierarchy.[110] When clan control works, bureaucratic control is not needed.

COUNTERPOINT 9.5

Perhaps the most effective yet insidious form of control involves the self-policing of a group in which no less that total identification with its goals and values is demanded. It is effective because most of its members do not recognize it as control, believing instead that it is a completely voluntary commitment unrelated to anxieties about identity or the desire for absorption into a collective order in the form of a clan. **Discuss**

Organizational Decline and Downsizing

Earlier in the chapter, we discussed the organizational life cycle, which suggests that organizations are born, grow older and eventually die. Every organization goes through periods of temporary decline. In addition, a reality in today's environment is that for some companies, continual growth and expansion may not be possible.

Particularly during economic downturns, we see evidence that some organizations have stopped growing and many are declining. Large organizations such as Britain's Northern Rock, Enron and Bear Stearns[111] in the US and Italy's Parmalat[112] have collapsed partly as a result of rapid growth and ineffective control and governance. The Catholic Church continues to lose membership in many countries following reports of child molestation by priests and the failure in higher levels of the organization to remove molesters and prevent further abuse. Many big companies, including Canada's Nortel Networks and Corel Corporation, Germany's e.on and all the big US car manufacturers have had significant job cuts in recent years. The economic downturn in 2008 led to organizational downsizing and large scale layoffs in major financial centres like London and New York.[113]

In this section, we examine the causes and stages of organizational decline and then discuss how leaders can effectively manage the downsizing that is a reality in today's companies.

Definition and Causes

The term **organizational decline** is used to define a condition in which a substantial, absolute decrease in an organization's resource base occurs over a period.[114] Organizational decline is often associated with environmental decline in the sense that an organizational domain experiences either a reduction in size (such as shrinkage in customer demand or erosion of a city's tax base) or a reduction in shape (such as a shift in customer demand). In general, three factors are considered to cause organizational decline.

1. *Organizational atrophy.* Atrophy occurs when organizations grow older and become inefficient and overly bureaucratized. The organization's ability to adapt to its environment deteriorates. Often, atrophy follows a long period of success, because an organization takes success for granted, becomes attached to practices and structures that worked in the past and fails to adapt to changes in the environment.[115] For example, Blockbuster Inc., which was king of the video-store industry in the 1980s and 1990s, has had trouble adapting to the new world of online film rentals and digital downloading. Blockbuster is way behind upstarts like Britain's Lovefilm and the US-based Netflix because managers had trouble giving up the traditional successful approach of renting out videos in stores and online. Experts warn that companies risk becoming obsolete by sticking to patterns that were successful in the past but might no longer be effective.[116] Some warning signals for organizational atrophy include excess administrative and support staff, cumbersome administrative procedures, lack of effective communication and coordination and outdated organizational structure.[117]
2. *Vulnerability*. Vulnerability reflects an organization's strategic inability to prosper in its environment. This often happens to small organizations that are not yet fully established. They are vulnerable to shifts in consumer tastes or in the economic health of the larger community. Small e-commerce companies that have not yet become established are the first to go out of business when the technology sector goes into a downturn. Some organizations are vulnerable because they are unable to define the correct strategy to fit the environment. Vulnerable organizations typically need to redefine their environmental domain to enter new industries or markets.
3. *Environmental decline or competition*. Environmental decline refers to reduced energy and resources available to support an organization. When the environment has less capacity to support organizations, the organization has

As an organization manager, keep these guidelines in mind:

Understand the causes and stages of decline. Be vigilant to detect signs of decline in the organization and take action as quickly as possible to reverse course. Quick action in the early stages prevents the organization from deteriorating to a stage-4 crisis, when a turnaround becomes much more difficult.

to either scale down operations or shift to another domain.[118] New competition increases the problem, especially for small organizations. The emergence of first Japan and the 'Asian tigers' and now China as major low cost manufacturers has sounded the death knell for huge swathes of Western industry, ranging from home appliances to vehicle parts.[119] Of course, during generalized economic crisis, such as afflicted the global economy starting with the 2007 sub-prime crisis, environmental decline is also generalized and only a few 'counter-cyclical' industries are likely to prosper.[120]

A Model of Decline Stages

Based on an extensive review of organizational decline research, a model of decline stages has been proposed and is summarized in Exhibit 9.8. This model suggests that decline, if not managed properly, can move through five stages resulting in organizational dissolution.[121]

1 *Blinded stage*. The first stage of decline is the internal and external change that threatens long-term survival and may require the organization to tighten up. The organization may have excess personnel, cumbersome procedures or lack of harmony with customers. Leaders often miss the signals of decline at this point and the solution is to develop effective scanning and control systems that indicate when something is wrong. With timely information, alert executives can bring the organization back to top performance.

EXHIBIT 9.8 Stages of Decline and the Widening Performance Gap

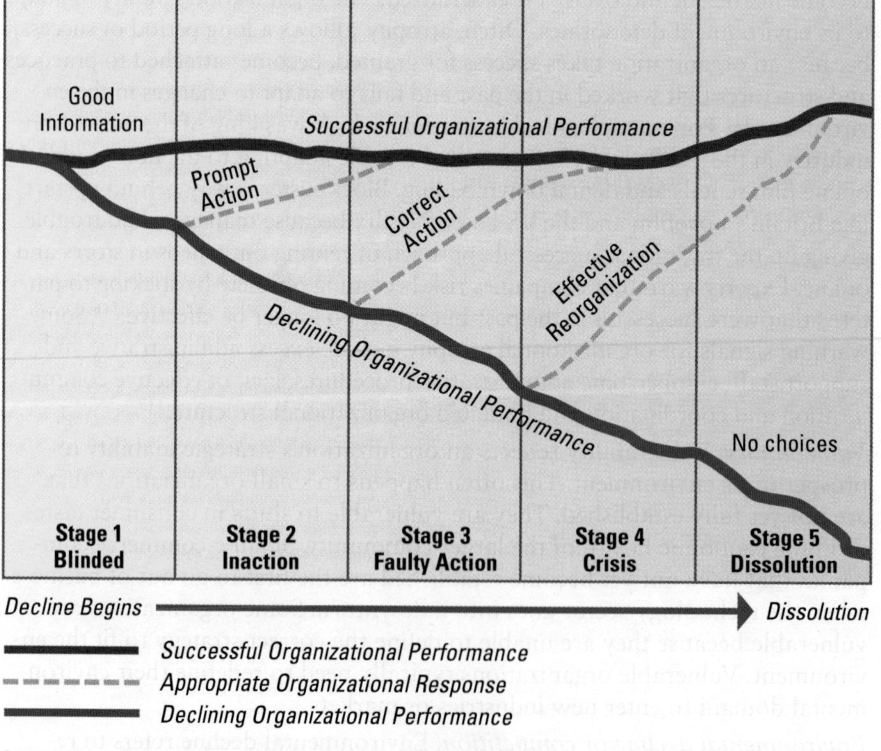

Source: Reprinted from 'Decline in Organizations: A Literature Integration and Extension,' by William Weitzel and Ellen Jonsson, published in *Administrative Science Quarterly*, 34, no. 1 (March 1989), by permission of *Administrative Science Quarterly*. © Johnson Graduate School of Management, Cornell University.

2 *Inaction stage*. The second stage of decline is called inaction in which denial occurs despite signs of deteriorating performance. Leaders may try to persuade employees that all is well. 'Creative accounting' may make things look fine during this period. The solution is for leaders to acknowledge decline and take prompt action to realign the organization with the environment. Leadership actions may include new problem-solving approaches, increasing decision-making participation and encouraging expression of dissatisfaction to learn what is wrong.

3 *Faulty action stage*. In the third stage, the organization is facing serious problems and indicators of poor performance cannot be ignored. Failure to adjust to the declining spiral at this point can lead to organizational failure. Leaders are forced by severe circumstances to consider major changes. Actions may involve retrenchment, including downsizing personnel. Leaders should reduce employee uncertainty by clarifying values and providing information. A major mistake at this stage decreases the organization's chance for a turnaround.

See online
COUNTERPOINT 9.16

4 *Crisis stage*. In the fourth stage, the organization still has not been able to deal with decline effectively and is facing a panic. The organization may experience chaos, efforts to go back to basics, sharp changes and anger. It is best for managers to prevent a stage-4 crisis and the only solution is major reorganization. The social fabric of the organization is eroding and dramatic actions, such as replacing top administrators and revolutionary changes in structure, strategy and culture, are necessary. Workforce downsizing may be severe.

5 *Dissolution stage*. This stage of decline is irreversible. The organization is suffering loss of markets and reputation, the loss of its best personnel and capital depletion. The only available strategy is to close down the organization in an orderly fashion and reduce the separation trauma of employees.

The following example of Alitalia shows how failure to respond to changing circumstances in the airline industry set the company on a downwards spiral to bankruptcy.

As this example shows, properly managing organizational decline is necessary if an organization is to avoid dissolution. Leaders have a responsibility to detect the signs of decline, acknowledge them, implement necessary action and reverse course. As in Alitalia's case, some of the most difficult decisions pertain to downsizing, which refers to intentionally reducing the size of a company's workforce.

As an organization manager, keep these guidelines in mind:

When layoffs are necessary, handle them with care. Treat departing employees humanely, communicate with employees and provide as much information as possible, provide assistance to displaced workers and remember the emotional needs of survivors.

Downsizing Implementation

Downsizing has become a common practice in corporations, particularly in the Anglo-Saxon business world, both in response to business downturns and as part of many change initiatives in today's organizations.[122] Reengineering projects, mergers and acquisitions, global competition and the trend toward outsourcing have all led to job reductions.[123]

Massive downsizing has often not achieved the intended benefits and in some cases has significantly harmed the organization.[124] Large-scale studies have shown that the two major objectives of downsizing – reducing costs and increasing productivity – are achieved in only a minority of cases. Impacts on remaining employees' attitudes towards their jobs are unsurprisingly negative. The rationale for downsizing is often poorly thought out and is associated with excessive reliance on consultants, who have a vested interest in promoting continual organizational

Alitalia

Italy's economy has many post-war success stories, from the emergence of Milan as the style centre of the world, to the country's innovative car industry, to the Agip and Eni oil companies and several successful internet business including the international broadband operator Tiscali.

Alitalia, the country's flagship airline, is not one of those success stories. Like other European flag carriers, Alitalia was founded shortly after the end of the Second World War. In these early days of passenger aviation, the industry was dominated by state-owned carriers of which Alitalia was one. Governments negotiated together to carve up routes between the different airlines, while fares remained high as most companies were in a near monopoly situation. It was an ideal environment and Alitalia flourished after a fashion, growing its network to encompass domestic, European and intercontinental flights. Trade unions, which had long been strong in Italian industry, were able to negotiate generous salaries and conditions. But the situation was not going to last. From the 1980s, pressure for liberalization swept across Europe and in 1992 the European Union liberalized the continent's skies, meaning any country's carrier could fly into any other country. By the end of the decade, Ryanair was spreading its low-cost wings across Europe. It was sink or swim for the national carriers. Some carriers didn't make it: Belgium's Sabena went bankrupt, followed by Swissair. Others, like British Airways, had been privatized as early as 1987 and embarked on an ambitious and generally successful restructuring, reducing workforce to competitive levels and raising capital for new aircraft and new routes. Air France eventually joined in a successful merger with KLM, allowing the combined company to compete globally with the world's biggest airlines.

At Alitalia, the onset of competition had an enervating rather than liberating effect. The company was caught in a seemingly endless vicious cycle of squabbles about needed restructuring, union dissent and industrial action, lost revenues and worsened financial situation. The Italian government bailed out the company several times, but losses just kept mounting and the European Commission frowned upon and eventually forbade further handouts. By the new millennium, Alitalia was losing €2 million a day. The company was restructured in 2004, but the basic problems of overstaffing, poor service and endless strike disruption remained. Efforts were made to sell the company to different consortia, but these came to nothing due to union opposition and political interference.

By late 2008, the company seemed in a hopeless position. Added to Alitalia's own internal problems, the price of jet fuel had risen to hitherto unknown heights and even other, prudently-managed European carriers were in deep trouble. Plans were drawn up for a radical restructuiring involving substantial job loss. Still, Alitalia's unions and management squabbled, even as Italy's bankruptcy commissioner threatened to step in and the company's planes started to run out of fuel.[125]

change. Downsizing is also associated with what van Witteloostuijn describes as 'macho management'; the idea that 'real managers make tough decisions', whether these decisions make sense or not.[126]

Nevertheless, there are times when managers have no choice but to implement downsizing strategies, whether because this is demanded by shareholders who believe this will result in increased profits, or in response to a negative market environment. A number of techniques can help smooth the downsizing process and ease tensions for employees who leave and for those who remain.[127]

1 *Communicate more, not less.* Some organizations seem to think the less that's said about a pending layoff, the better. Not so. Organizational managers should provide advance notice with as much information as possible; in many jurisdictions the law reqires a lengthy notice period for

impending layoffs. At US-headquartered computer networking firm 3Com Corporation, managers drew up a three-stage plan as they prepared for layoffs. First, they warned employees several months ahead that layoffs were inevitable. Soon thereafter, they held on-site presentations at all locations to explain to employees why the layoffs were needed and to provide as much information as they could about what employees should expect. Employees being cut were given their legal entitlement of notice.[128] Managers should remember that it is impossible to 'overcommunicate' during turbulent times. Remaining employees need to know what is expected of them, whether future layoffs are a possibility and what the organization is doing to help coworkers who have lost their jobs.

2 *Provide assistance to displaced workers.* The organization has a responsibility to help displaced workers cope with the loss of their jobs and get reestablished in the job market. The organization can provide training, innovative severance packages, extended benefits and assistance getting started in a new business or line of work. The Luxemburg-headquartered bank Dexia introduced an employee-reduction programme in 2002/2003 to address overstaffing that had built up over a number of years. Rather than simply select the eight per cent of the workforce who were to be let go, Dexia HR staff brainstormed a wide variety of options that could be offered to employees in return for agreeing to depart, ranging from support to carry out charitable projects, seed capital to start up a small business, continuation of the company's generous mortgage subsidy scheme and improved benefits for early retirement. Many employees were content to leave in return for a benefit that suited their needs and interests and the remaining staff's morale was maintained, because they could see that the company had made a real effort to minimize the downsizing programme's human impact.[129]

3 *Help the survivors thrive.* Leaders should remember the emotional needs of survivors as well. Many people experience guilt, anger, confusion and sadness after the loss of colleagues and these feelings should be acknowledged. They might also be concerned about their own jobs and have difficulty adapting to the changes in job duties, responsibilities and so forth. Korea's Samsung responded creatively after having to downsize during the country's deep economic recession in the late 1990's. The company began by reducing the size and power of Samsung Restructuring Headquarters, the company's division that had been responsible for organizing the downsizing, and the company also greatly expanded the value and scope of its charitable donations, providing enhanced opportunities for executives to make a tangible social contribution through volunteer activities.[130,131]

Even the best-managed organizations may sometimes need to lay off employees in a turbulent environment, to revitalize the organization or in response to organizational restructuring due to a merger. Leaders can attain positive results if they handle downsizing in a way that lets departing employees leave with dignity and enables remaining organization members to be motivated, productive and committed to a better future. Seagram, the Canadian spirits and wine group, was acquired by new owners who planned to merge the business into their existing structures, resulting in the closure of the division. Despite the devastating prognosis, Seagram's management was able to effectively use various techniques to help make the process less painful, as we see in the *In Practice* feature on the next page.

Seagram

At the end of the twentieth century, Seagram's was perhaps the best known name in the Canadian liquor trade and a highly profitable part of Montreal businessman Edgar Bronfman's business empire. However, in 2000, Bronfman decided to sell out to the French conglomerate Vivendi. Unfortunately, Vivendi, then building a global media empire, was only interested in Bronfman's pay TV holdings. As soon as it got hold of Seagram's, Vivendi cast around for a buyer. Eventually, it sold out to the British firm Diageo and the French company Pernod Ricard. This was very bad news for Seagram's staff because both companies planned to integrate Seagram's brands into their existing wine and spirits businesses, in the process laying off all but a handful of the existing staff. Ronnie Vansteenkiste, who was a senior HR staff at Seagram's, wrote about what happened next. Surprisingly, it was not as negative a story as it might have seemed at first glance.

The first positive was that Seagram's was a well run and successful operation before its sale. This made a big difference, because the existing management had the confidence of the employees. Management's first action when they found out about the likely developments was to plan various scenarios. They soon realized that winding up the Seagram division was a possibility if not a probability and they were upfront about this with the workers. Managers organized regular communications sessions where they shared their understanding of developments with their staff and they also organized sessions on 'managing change'.

Seagrams managers also knew that, while the new owners were likely to want to close down Seagram's as a separate entity, they wanted the brands they had bought to retain their positive image through the handover. This would require strong manufacturing, distribution and marketing to continue up to the moment of handover/closure. In order to reduce attrition, particularly among key staff, Seagram managers negotiated generous incentive schemes to encourage their key staff to stay on until brand handover. Managers identified staff with key skills or outstanding capacities and recommended them to the new owners. A generous layoff package was developed as soon as possible for the bulk of staff who would be leaving and a great deal of energy was put into helping to manage the emotions of the many Seagrams staff who had years of experience with the firm. The situation was not one that the Seagram's managers would have chosen, but they showed leadership and professionalism in handing it.[132]

Summary and Interpretation

The material covered in this chapter contains several important ideas about organizations. Organizations can be seen to evolve through distinct life cycle stages as they grow and mature. Organization structure, internal systems and management issues are different for each stage of development. Growth creates crises and revolutions along the way. A major task of managers is to guide the organization through the entrepreneurial, collectivity, formalization and elaboration stages of development. As organizations progress through the life cycle and grow larger and more complex, they generally take on bureaucratic characteristics, such as rules, division of labour, written records, hierarchy of authority and impersonal procedures. Bureaucracy is a logical form of organizing that enables firms to deploy resources in a more rational manner. However, in many large corporate and government organizations, bureaucracy has come under attack with attempts to decentralize authority, flatten organization structure, reduce rules and written records and create a small-company mindset. These companies are willing to trade economies of scale for responsive, adaptive organizations. Many companies are subdividing to gain small-company advantages. Another approach to overcoming the problems of bureaucracy is to use a structural concept called the *incident command system*, which promises to enable the organization to glide smoothly between a highly formalized, hierarchical style that is effective during times of stability and a more flexible, loosely structured one needed to respond to unexpected or volatile environmental conditions.

In large organizations, greater support is required from administrative and professional staff specialists. This is a logical outcome of employee specialization and the division of labour. By dividing an organization's tasks and having specialists perform each part, the organization can become more efficient.

All organizations, large and small, rely upon systems of control. Bureaucratic control relies on standard rules and the rational-legal authority of managers. Market control is used where product or service outputs can be priced and competition exists. Clan control and more recently self-control, are associated with uncertain and rapidly changing organization processes. They rely on commitment, tradition and shared values for control. In practice, these control approaches are combined in more or less coherent ways.

Many organizations have stopped growing and some are declining. One of the most difficult decisions pertains to downsizing the workforce. Not only does it threaten the livelihood of those who are cast aside and unsettles those who remain, downsizing has been shown not to result in improved performance in many cases. To smooth the downsizing process, managers can communicate with employees and provide as much reliable information as possible, offer assistance to displaced workers and address the emotional concerns of those who remain with the organization.

KEY CONCEPTS

bureaucracy
bureaucratic control
centralization
charismatic authority
clan control
collectivity stage
downsizing
elaboration stage
entrepreneurial stage
formalization
formalization stage
incident command system
life cycle
market control
organizational decline
personnel ratios
rational-legal authority
traditional authority

Discussion Questions

1 Discuss the key differences between large and small organizations. Which kinds of organizations would be better off acting as large organizations and which are best trying to act as big-company/small-company hybrids?

2 Why do large organizations tend to be more formalized?

3 If you were managing a department of college professors, how might you structure the department differently than if you were managing a department of bookkeepers? Why?

4 Apply the concept of life cycle to an organization with which you are familiar, such as a university or a local business. What stage is the organization in now? How did the organization handle or pass through its life cycle crises?

5 Describe the three bases of authority identified by Weber. Is it possible for each of these types of authority co-exist within an organization?

6 In writing about types of control, William Ouchi said, 'The Market is like the trout and the Clan like the salmon, each a beautiful highly specialized species which requires uncommon conditions for its survival. In comparison, the bureaucratic method of control is the catfish – clumsy, ugly, but able to live in the widest range of environments and ultimately, the dominant species.' Discuss what Ouchi meant with that analogy.

7 Government organizations often seem more bureaucratic than for-profit organizations. Could this partly be the result of the type of control used in government organizations? Explain.

8 The incident command system has been used primarily by organizations that regularly deal with crisis situations. Discuss whether this approach seems workable for a large media company that wants to reduce bureaucracy. How about for a manufacturer of cell phones?

9 Refer to the Xerox case at the beginning of Chapter 1 and discuss how Xerox illustrates the major causes of organizational decline. In what stage of decline does Xerox seem to be?

10 Do you think a 'no growth' philosophy of management should be taught in business schools? Discuss.

Workbook Control Mechanisms

Think of two situations in your life: your work and your school experiences. How is control exerted? Fill out the tables.

Questions

1 What are the advantages and disadvantages of the various controls?
2 What happens when there is too much control? Too little?
3 Does the type of control depend on the situation and the number of people involved?
4 *Optional*: How do the control mechanisms in your tables compare to those of other students?

Workshop Windsock, Inc.

1 *Introduction*. Class is divided into four groups: Central Office, Product Design, Marketing/Sales and Production. Central Office is a slightly smaller group. If groups are large enough, assign observers to each one. Central Office is given 500 straws and 750 pins. Each person reads *only* the role description relevant to that group. *Materials needed*: plastic milk straws (500) and a box of straight pins (750).
2 *Perform task*. Depending on length of class, step 2 may take 30 to 60 minutes. Groups perform functions and prepare for a 2-minute report for stockholders.
3 *Group reports*. Each group gives a 2-minute presentation to stockholders.
4 *Observers' reports (optional)*. Observers share insights with subgroups.
5 Class discussion.
   a What helped or blocked intergroup cooperation and coordination?
   b To what extent was there open versus closed communication? What impact did that have?
   c What styles of leadership were exhibited?
   d What types of team interdependencies emerged?

Roles

Central Office

Your team is the central management and administration of Windsock, Inc. You are the heart and pulse of the organization, because without your coordination and resource allocation, the organization would go under. Your task is to manage the operations of the organization, which is not an easy responsibility because you have to coordinate the activities of three distinct groups of personnel: the Marketing/Sales group, the Production group and the Product Design group. In addition, you have to manage resources including materials (pins and straws), time deadlines, communications and product requirements.

In this exercise, you are to do whatever is necessary to accomplish the mission and to keep the organization operating harmoniously and efficiently.

Windsock, Inc., has a total of 30 minutes (more if instructor assigns) to design an advertising campaign and ad copy, to design the windmill and to produce the first windmill prototypes for delivery. Good luck to you all.

Product Design

Your team is the research and product design group of Windsock, Inc. You are the brain and creative aspect of the operation, because without an innovative and successfully designed product, the organization would go under. Your duties are to design products that compete favorably in the marketplace, keeping in mind function, aesthetics, cost, ease of production and available materials.

In this exercise, you are to come up with a workable plan for a product that will be built by your production team. Your windmill must be light, portable, easy to assemble and aesthetically pleasing. Central Office controls the budget and allocates material for your division.

Windsock, Inc., as an organization has a total of 30 minutes (more if instructor assigns) to design an advertising campaign, to design the windmill (your group's task) and to produce the first windmill prototypes for delivery. Good luck to you all.

Marketing/Sales

Your team is the marketing/sales group of Windsock, Inc. You are the backbone of the operation, because without customers and sales the organization would go under. Your task is to determine the market, develop an advertising campaign to promote your company's unique product, produce ad copy and develop a sales force and sales procedures for both potential customers and the public at large.

For the purpose of this exercise, you may assume that a market analysis has been completed. Your team is now in a position to produce an advertising campaign and ad copy for the product. To be effective, you have to become very familiar with the characteristics of the product and how it is different from those products already on the market. The Central Office controls your budget and allocates materials for use by your division.

Windsock, Inc. has a total of 30 minutes (more if instructor assigns) to design an advertising campaign and ad (your group's task), to design the windmill and to produce the first windmill prototypes for delivery. Good luck to you all.

Production

Your team is the production group of Windsock, Inc. You are the heart of the operation, because without a group to produce the product, the organization would go under. You have the responsibility to coordinate and produce the product for delivery. The product involves an innovative design for a windmill that is cheaper, lighter, more portable, more flexible and more aesthetically pleasing than other designs currently available in the marketplace. Your task is to build windmills within cost guidelines, according to specifications and within a prescribed period, using predetermined materials.

For the purpose of this exercise, you are to organize your team, set production schedules and build the windmills. Central Office controls your budget, materials and specifications.

Windsock, Inc., has a total of 30 minutes (more if instructor assigns) to design an advertising campaign, to design the windmill and to produce the first windmill prototypes (your group's task) for delivery. Good luck to you all.

Adapted by Dorothy Marcic from Christopher Taylor and Saundra Taylor in 'Teaching Organizational Team-Building through Simulations', *Organizational Behaviour Teaching Review* XI(3), 86–87.

CASE FOR ANALYSIS

HOSPI*

***By Henrik Sørensen,** Aarhus University*

HOSPI, a company owned by Italian entrepreneur Fabio Mussaccio, proved a success right from the start although, in retrospect, critics in the industry claimed that it was surprising Mussaccio had not wrecked the company given his unusual approach to management.

HOSPI produces hospital equipment and the company operates in a very turbulent market. Mussaccio has understood from the start, however, that the structure of the company needed to be different from that of traditional companies. The structure had to be far more organic, with many decisions delegated to the employees of the company, because they often repay your trust by permitting the company to be far quicker on the 'trigger' than its competitors. However, many employees were not afraid to make their own decisions and sometimes were willing to 'grease the palms' of a few hospital doctors a bit too liberally in order to have their products prioritized over those of their competitors. On some occasions, Mussaccio has been accused in the media of what could be described as bribery, but each time he had weathered the storm. For example, he fired a particularly eager HOSPI sales rep, who might have gone a little too far. However, in Mussaccio's opinion you do not have to tell the media about everything you do, and he adds 'there is no need to quarrel with your employees'. So the employee who was fired was rehired shortly after in another of Mussaccio's companies. The fired employee received severance pay in HOSPI as well as a better salary in the other Mussaccio company.

In HOSPI, a strong sense of competition reigns among the employees and every employee is, so to speak, fighting with each other as well as against each other. In the course of time, this has created a highly decentralized organization that very often leads to conflicts between the individual employees; gradually an atmosphere has developed where no one is willing to take on responsibility and leadership. At the same time, many believe that as an employee they can do whatever they want because in the end Mussaccio will cover for them. This was particularly evident after the episode of the re-hired employee.

In HOSPI, there is a long series of incidents that clearly demonstrate that the organization is very much left to its own devices. Accordingly, there is limited coordination of the sales effort between the different areas, and the reports prepared by the sales manager Marta Chiabotto are rarely used for anything at all. In reality, the individual employees often define the actions that need to be taken in relation to the customers. For example, a sales rep in one district may find out from her customers that one of her colleagues is making special offers in another district.

And the annual sales meeting often ends in total disaster. The original intention of the meeting was to allow the sales reps to exchange experiences, but instead it seems that each sales rep always tries to single him or herself out as the company's key salesperson, claiming that the problems in the sales division are caused by the other sales reps. If the reps eventually acknowledge that problems of some sort really exist, they inevitably think that these are to be solved by the management.

Another characteristic feature of HOSPI is that all sales reps are dissatisfied with something; and it is a standing joke in the production department that is impossible to meet a sales rep who is not complaining about one issue or another. In other words, there are numerous problems but few solutions – compounded by the fact that Mussaccio seldom interferes.

To be fair, it should however be added that the sales team does in fact function quite well and if you ask Mussaccio it is precisely this dissatisfaction that leads employees to solve problems that emerge. But employees do not always agree with his convenient explanation. Not only do the problems faced by the sales team differ, but the team members' assessments of what is and is not a problem diverge significantly. Giuseppe Carcano – one of the most capable and proactive of the sales reps – said jokingly that the problems of the sales team depend on which of the reps feel inclined to attend the meetings. As the following example may show, there might be some truth in Carcano's statement: for some years there were five sales reps who got along well together and also became personal friends. Of course outside work, they also discussed HOSPI, generally agreeing that since HOSPI functioned in the way it did, they might as well try to take advantage. They decided to raise at every meeting that they considered it a huge problem for HOSPI that there was no direct relation between how well the sales reps supported each other and worked together on one hand, and the remuneration system on the other. They also complained that the division into sales districts often resulted in conflicts between the sales reps.

However, others in the sales division claimed that the districts were in fact the true strength of the company, as they were an excellent way for the individual sales rep to target her efforts toward the customers. They also argued that the issue of customers being aware of offers made by sales reps in other districts was hugely exaggerated.

Nevertheless the group of friends bent Mussaccio's ears as well as the sales manager Marta Chiabotto for several years with their concerns about coordination, eventually causing the other sales reps gave up proving that it was not a problem. There were even sales reps who claimed that as long as the 'Gang of Five', as they were popularly called, concentrated on the coordination issue, which Mussaccio did not want to address, then at least they did not focus on other far more unpleasant issues. The funny thing was that when the 'Gang of Five' gradually left the company, the coordination issue sort of died out, but then there were other sales reps who drew attention to other issues instead.

As the success of HOSPI increased, Mussaccio was gradually forced to acknowledge that he had to pay more attention to the way the sales team operated. Even though he had previously always rejected the existence of problems all together, he now admitted that things needed to change. Nevertheless he found himself in a dilemma which he was unable to solve straight away:

1 Firstly, he felt it was an important strength that the sales reps were able to negotiate directly with the customers. This meant that when the reps found themselves in a specific sales situation and had difficulties selling the products because competing companies were better or cheaper, they were able to negotiate immediately with the customers and make them an offer in order to win the order.

2 Secondly, Mussaccio felt strongly that individual employees should be able to make independent decisions in specific situations. Accordingly, he also felt that by delegating decision-making authority, management had an obligation to back up employees in case anything went wrong. Therefore, for example, he stood by his employees who had gone too far in 'greasing the palms' of the doctors. Only on very rare occasions were the sales reps given a dressing-down. Mussaccio felt it was justifiable if a sales rep took a hasty decision to secure an order even if it turned out later to be a bad decision. 'You rarely learn anything from your successes but you always learn something by your mistakes', was his comment.

3 Thirdly, Mussaccio believed that the fact that the sales reps were making their own decision was to a wide extent contributing to increased sales. If HOSPI didn't give the individual sales reps a wide degree of freedom to conclude the orders themselves, then many of the orders would not be obtained. However, several employees expressed their concern that the huge individual freedom hampered sharing of best practices and learning from mistakes, 'We need to have a sense of community which will allow us to learn from and discuss each other's experiences. Far too often, the individual sales rep misunderstands a customer or misinterprets what the customer wants. Furthermore, great benefits could be gained by helping each other interpret which direction the market is taking. Only if we challenge each other's views on the development will we be able to decipher the impacts of the changes and nuances of the market well enough to make us better than the rest. Great benefits can be gained by helping each other.'

New decision processes

After careful deliberation, Mussaccio decided that HOSPI's decision-making processes should be changed. In future the approach would be far more analytical. He still strongly stressed that the sales reps constituted the fulcrum of the company and that they were the ones creating the company. But the job of the sales reps changed significantly. One major change was the introduction of a number of reporting forms to be completed by the sales reps each week.

One of the new forms concerned new marketing opportunities or changed customer preferences. On this form, the sales reps were to indicate any new marketing opportunities or threats that their customer visits had given rise to during the week. The form was designed so that the sales reps would evaluate all opportunities on a scale starting from 'very easy to implement' through 'relatively easy to implement' to 'very difficult to implement'. Any threats against the company should also be categorized starting from 'significant threats with adverse impact on HOSPI' to 'to threats of marginal importance to HOSPI's sales'.

These forms were then submitted to the sales manager Marta Chiabotto who examined all the forms handed in by the sales reps. Chiabotto's task then was to gather all the information obtained in a special reporting form, which was shown to Mussaccio, the production manager Edmundo Ferrari and other department managers. The management team would then consider whether the information reported by the sales reps was of such magnitude and importance that actions had to be taken.

It soon turned out the individual sales rep did not find it difficult to submit the reports and a few months after the implementation of the system, the sales manager Marta Chiabotto gained significant insight into the challenges faced by HOSPI in the market of hospital equipment.

Only a few months passed before the reporting systems proved of great value to HOSPI. One of the HOSPI sales reps reported that several of the competing companies were making a strategic alliance. He explained that the main motivation for this alliance was to increase the market share in the long run, which would be achieved through cooperation in terms of production, rationalisation and reorganization of the product range, as well as through trimming the sales force. The same sales rep had also been informed by a customer that the new strategic alliance was starting to arrange large professional medical conferences and that the customer had participated in the first one himself. The theoretical topics were top class and furthermore there was an abundance of entertainment during the conference. The alliance partners competing against HOSPI had also managed to sell a fair amount of their products.

Naturally, Marta Chiabotto, the sales manager, immediately reported this information to the management team, but they disagreed among themselves about how to handle the situation. In Mussaccio's opinion, they should let the sales reps be even more aggressive than before and make sure to match or better the offers made by the competing strategic alliance at all times. Chiabotto expressed very strong reservations about this response as she pointed out that due to their cooperation and production coordination, the companies of the strategic alliance would be far more cost-effective than HOSPI, and if they set prices close to their production costs, HOSPI would incur significant losses. Instead Edmundo Ferrari, the production manager, recommended that they copy the idea about medical conferences; but Mussaccio was very sceptical about this: 'We will not be able to compete with the strategic alliance in that context. They have more companies to share the costs of a conference whereas we would be completely on our own in bearing the costs. Furthermore, the sales reps would have to reserve part of their time for participation in the conference and they would have less time for the direct sales effort geared towards customers. As we have customers all over the country, all sales reps would have to participate, as they all want to improve their personal relations with their customers.'

The sales manager Marta Chiabotto felt that it was important not to overreact: 'We will never be able to match the companies of the strategic alliance and if I were you, Mr. Mussaccio, I would take it easy. Let's just wait a few months and allow the strategic alliance time to settle and establish itself in the market. When they have done so, we will purchase one or more of the companies participating in the alliance and gain influence in this way. Later on we might merge HOSPI into the alliance and thereby maintain our market shares. It may also prove an advantage for us to let HOSPI remain independent, while at the same time we participate in the strategic alliance and gain inside information about the initiatives it is planning.'

The management group went completely silent. CEO Fabio Mussaccio, production manager Edmundo Ferrari and the sales manager Marta Chiabotto knew that HOSPI was standing at a crossroads. Not only did they face big threats in the market, the sales rep's report about the alliance had also divided the management team for the first time. And that might prove to be the biggest threat. The management team never succeeded in agreeing on a joint countermove to the competitors' strategic alliance; and when the reps were informed about the outcome of the meeting later that week, Mussaccio had to explain the situation: 'We do not agree about the measures required, but for now it will have no impact on HOSPI. I am still the one in charge and in the end I will be the one making the decision. I own HOSPI, and the only reason why no solution has been found yet is because I am considering the different views.'

However, the sales reps were not satisfied with that answer. They pointed out that a solution was urgently needed and if the management team was not able to produce something sensible, usable and durable, the sales reps would have to take matters into their own hands – just like before the reporting system was introduced.

Without saying it out loud, it actually pleased Mussaccio immensely that the sales reps wanted to take the initiative. If the sales reps took over, he could easily allow them the latitude to be much more aggressive. In this way, he would avoid the difficult discussion with his managers Edmundo Ferrari and Marta Chiabotto. The sales reps immediately started to discuss among themselves and they turned out to be divided into three groups: those who supported Mussaccio's solution, those who supported the production manager Edmundo Ferrari and those who thought that the sales manager Marta Chiabotto had suggested the best solution. So the end result was that both management and the sales reps disagreed about the actions needed.

Mussaccio was not one to give up. But at the same time he was highly affected by the fact that, for the first time in the existence of HOSPI, management and the employees were divided, and his great concern was that this division would prove the downfall of HOSPI. In the short term he particularly feared that the internal division of HOSPI would hamper the operation of the information and monitoring systems required to measure the efficiency of the company.

With management and employees divided into three roughly equal sized groups, would they be able to establish optimal decision processes and foresee conflicts? Mussaccio also feared that HOSPI was on its way into a vicious circle where the company would be unable to react efficiently to opportunities and threats posed by the market. In addition, it was obvious that both management and employees held different views on how to tackle the threats from the their competitors' strategic alliance. Now when unity was most needed, they found themselves more divided than ever before.

Mussaccio feared that HOSPI was heading towards a situation where the range of the problems would increase even if they succeeded in solving some of them. Maybe management would start making the wrong decisions because it did not want to start a conflict, with the result that HOSPI would shrink away from establishing the best structure to meet the current challenges. Last but not least, he worried that his best sales reps would find jobs in the strategic alliance because they saw more opportunities there than in HOSPI.

Therefore, Mussaccio called a meeting for all employees in HOSPI – the remaining part of management and all employees in production, sales, etc. He began the meeting by saying that 'HOSPI is facing serious problems both internally within the company and externally in different markets. It is no secret that all this fuss is created by the strategic alliance. But you know that I am a man of action and that you can trust me.

'Therefore I ask you all within the next month to write down your suggested solutions on a piece of paper and send them to me. It is completely up to you whether you want to send me your personal suggestions or whether you want to work in groups to prepare a joint proposal. When I have received all the suggestions, I will pass them on to an external consultant who is independent of everybody in HOSPI, including myself. The consultant will examine all the suggestions and recommend the most appropriate solution to HOSPI's problems. Therefore I reckon that everybody in HOSPI will join forces to implement the solution suggested.'

The reaction from the employees was unmistakable. Mussaccio received a huge applause and the employees left the meeting in high spirits, well aware however that the outcome could be a solution that they had not suggested themselves. The fighting spirit and the willingness to accept the final decision were, however, obvious. Everybody wanted a stronger HOSPI, and during the month that followed suggestions poured in from the employees. Several employees submitted their own personal suggestions while being contributors to other suggestions at same time. At the same time, HOSPI experienced its best production and sales month ever and it was easy to imagine that HOSPI could best the strategic alliance.

Then Mussaccio hired the consultant. It came as a great surprise when the consultant completely rejected all suggestions made by the employees and chose instead to employ an analytical approach to the future decision model of HOSPI. In his analysis, the consultant chose to focus on the following issues:

1 Market conditions
2 Structure
3 Technology
4 Strategy
5 Culture

Market conditions

The best way to describe the situation in HOSPI was a market with very aggressive competitors. Further, because products are sold mainly to hospitals, the number of potential sales outlets is quite small, and a single doctor may often have crucial influence on the products and suppliers chosen by a hospital. Companies producing and selling hospital equipment are often faced with numerous specific customer requirements. Often a doctor who has chosen a product from one producer meets a colleague from another hospital and they exchange experiences with respect to both products and companies. Often the outcome of this exchange is that one of the doctors changes his product and business preferences; therefore it is always uncertain whether the company will be able to keep a customer. In other words, the industry is characterized by major changes frequent swapping of customers between the companies.

So far, the few companies within this line of business have found it hard to influence or control what happened in the market. The establishment of the strategic alliance should be seen as an initiative by which the competing companies are attempting to achieve a higher degree of control over the surroundings, which is not possible for HOSPI as a single company.

Structure

It very difficult to present a precise outline of the structure in HOSPI and this lack of organizational clarity means that none of the decision-making processes are working efficiently. If the company is to function properly, it needs much greater organizational coherence and consistency between the way the company is organised and how it makes decisions.

The major challenge of the company consists, however, in determining which structure the company should aim for. It has been well known for a long time that Edmundo Ferrari, the production manager, has been opposed to all kinds of initiatives aimed at a more organic structure. Firstly, he saw from a very early stage the dilemmas outlined by Mussaccio above; and secondly, he did not regard an organic structure to be a real structure at all. It is just a place 'where everyone does what they feel like without coordinating anything at all' he once added, 'and consequently HOSPI is completely inefficient'.

The sales manager Marta Chiabotto, and Mussaccio himself, are however of a completely different opinion. Fundamentally, they support a very organic structure where the individual employees to a great extent are responsible for their own actions. They believe that the sales reps should develop teams and these teams need to be able to make rapid and quite far-reaching decisions. In other words, they should not ask before they act; and should they turn out to be wrong, a solution could be found afterwards.

So it will be difficult for the top management team to agree on a basic structure, as well as to implement a clear decision-making process.

Technology

Mussaccio has invested heavily in state-of-art production equipment, and HOSPI has both CAD and CAM facilities. The production facilities of HOSPI are very flexible, with production manager Edmundo Ferrari able to switch production lines without any significant costs. HOSPI does not have separated production lines. Although the employees are divided into production teams, the different teams do not function as independent units, with products often passing through the same team several times. The teams are capable – with some quick adjustments – to change production lines. At the same time the teams do not make many independent decisions; the employees are always told what to do by the production manager Edmundo Ferrari and the individual teams do not make decisions before clearing them with the production manager Edmundo Ferrari.

Ferrari schedules production so that he always has two weeks' rolling production planned in advance. This means that the individual teams always know what to do for the next two weeks. However, sometimes they might be asked by Ferrari to produce for an urgent order.

Strategy

The strategic alliance formed by HOSPI's competitors seems likely to completely change the strategies used so far by the companies across the industry, drawing a completely new picture of how the competition will look in the future. Previously, the industry was characterized by many similar-sized competitors, and everybody was competing against everybody else. Now things would be different.

In the consultant's opinion, the new strategic alliance would quite likely be offering all customers all types of products. He was also convinced that the strategic alliance would generally adopt a low-cost strategy where they would encourage the companies of the alliance that were most efficient at producing a specific product to be in charge of the production of that specific product. This would lead to low-cost advantages. Later on you would probably see a tendency to centralize the production.

The consultant believed HOSPI should abandon the strategy of producing many different products for many different segments and instead try to gain an advantage through differentiation. But the management team, especially the sales manager Marta Chiabotto was not too keen on that idea.

Chiabotto argued:

> 'In future, the dividing line between specialized products and cheap products will be eliminated. In the future, all companies in the industry will be able to produce everything and no one will be able to achieve the same advantages as before. All this will happen because everybody in the industry will introduce flexible production systems as we have always done.
>
> However, I believe we need to think in completely different terms when we plan our corporate strategy. Instead of saying that some companies will win through differentiation and others through low-cost advantages, competition in the future will involve a more progressive market approach.
>
> Some companies will always win by being the first on the market with new products. They win because they are able to charge an extremely high price, which will cover their R&D costs; but they run the risk that other companies in the industry will be quick to copy them. It is essential to have some concealed skills or knowledge that the other companies cannot copy easily. The companies copying them will not have nearly the same amount of R&D costs, but on the other hand they will not be able to price their products so high. I think that the big difference between the two types of companies will depend on how many of the products developed by the first type of company will later prove successful on the market.'

Then Mussaccio proposed an earlier idea of the sales manager, according to which HOSPI should not change that much but just wait for the opportunity to carry out a hostile take-over of one of the companies participating in the alliance. The consultant had been impressed by the sales manager's presentation, and also thought there was merit in the hostile take-over idea. He was starting to doubt whether his own analysis was thorough enough and his conclusions accurate.

Culture

HOSPI's culture might be the area where the consultant would be able to make the most reliable analysis. However, it was not exactly helpful that the consultant was convinced that several more or less incompatible subcultures existed in HOSPI. The most obvious contrasts existed between the production and the sales departments. In the sales department they were used to a culture with huge focus on external circumstances (the customers) and through rapid change and adaptation they had tried to meet the customers' need and requirements. Accordingly, the individual sales rep needed to understand changes in customer requirements and wishes. The consultant also noted that there had been a certain amount of turbulence in the sales team due to the new reporting systems although they had loyally followed the commands of the management. This view was immediately confirmed by the sales manager Marta Chiabotto.

The culture of the production department was in sharp contrast. The production manager Edmundo Ferrari, and for that matter the production staff as a whole, had all come from other companies with highly traditional assembly line methods. When HOSPI introduced the flexible production system, the employees were therefore not used to planning and being in charge of the production themselves. Nor were the employees aware that efficient production at HOSPI was highly dependent on employees' initiative, commitment and active participation in day-to-day production decision-making. Therefore it had been easier for everybody that the production manager Edmundo Ferrari just took over the total responsibility. This method had suited Ferrari and the employees well. The production staff and the production manager Edmundo Ferrari agreed that the production department functions at its best when they were able to pre-program and set up rules for the production processes.

Surprisingly enough, however, the consultant characterized HOSPI's culture as weak overall, to which Mussaccio in particular reacted strongly: 'So far HOSPI has been a well-functioning company and I would like to emphasise that our current problems are not caused by internal inefficiency but rather by external circumstances, because everybody else in the industry has conspired against us. But we will be fighting back.'

The consultant's and management's conclusion

Marta Chiabotto, however, responded calmly to the consultant's statement. 'I am quite convinced that we do have a strong culture, but it is not always supporting the activities that we need to perform and thus we do have problems that need to be solved. I would also like to add that I do not doubt the knowledge and experience of the consultant, but I am aware of how difficult it is to provide a clear picture of HOSPI's market conditions, structure, technology, strategy and culture. By means of the consultant's analysis, we have obtained an explanation as to why we find it so hard to introduce the right decision-making process.

I therefore suggest that we ask the consultant to analyze our market conditions and to make some suggestions based on this analysis as to how we can organize our structure, technology, strategy and culture, which in the end will allow us to implement a decision-making process. Everybody agreed and the consultant began his work backed by the entire management team and the employees.'

Case Questions

1 HOSPI's sales and production departments seem to have different organizational cultures. Can you describe the different characteristics? Are there reasons beyond the personalities of the sales and production manager that these different cultures should have developed?

2 How does the creation of the strategic alliance change competitive conditions for HOSPI?

3 What are the advantages and disadvantages of the organic decision-making approach that has traditionally been practised in the sales department?

4 The consultant does not seem to have a clear idea what to do. Why do you think the company hired him?

5 Mussaccio describes himself as a man of action. Do you think that is accurate? If not, why do you think HOSPI has been a success up until now?

Notes

1. Walt, Vivienne, Global Alert, *Time*, 3 March 2008; MPA Welcomes police budget that pays for even more officers on the streets of London, M2 Presswire, 14 February 2008.
2. Chuck Salter, 'Terrorists Strike Fast…Interpol Has to Move Faster…Ron Noble Is on the Case,' *Fast Company* (October 2002), 96–104; and 'Interpol Pushing to Be UN Globocop,' *The New American* (November 1, 2004), 8.
3. James Q. Wilson, *Bureaucracy* (New York: Basic Books, 1989); and Charles Perrow, *Complex Organizations: A Critical Essay* (Glenview, Ill.: Scott, Foresman, 1979), 4.
4. 'Slowdown in growth rate of flights worldwide', *Daily Travel & Tourism Newsletter* accessed at http://www.traveldailynews.com/pages/show_page/25808 on September 5, 2008.
5. Tom Peters, 'Rethinking Scale,' *California Management Review* (Fall 1992), 7–29.
6. Jerry Useem, 'One Nation Under Wal-Mart,' *Fortune* (March 3, 2003), 65–78.
7. 'Tesco Becomes 4th Largest Global Retailer, Overtakes Metro', accessed at http://www.deloitte.com/dtt/press_release/0,1014,cid%253D196099,00.html on September 5, 2008.
8. 'Tesco, Sainsbury's lose ground – TNS', *just-food.com*, 24 June 2008.
9. Matt Murray, 'Critical Mass: As Huge Companies Keep Growing, CEOs Struggle to Keep Pace,' *The Wall Street Journal* (February 8, 2001), A1, A6.
10. Stuart Elliott, 'Advertising's Big Four: It's Their World Now', *The New York Times* (March 31, 2002), Section 3, 1, 10.
11. Donald V. Potter, 'Scale Matters', *Across the Board* (July–August 2000), 36–39.
12. Martin Flanagan, 'Steel yourself for more consolidation', The Scotsman, 28 November 2006.
13. Jim Collins, 'Bigger, Better, Faster', *Fast Company* (June 2003), 74–78.
14. 'Teknosa Drives Corporate Expansion Strategy', *PR Newswire*, 25 February 2008; John Ryan, Value Zeitgeist, Retail Week, June 13, 2008; Sabanci Holdings, *2007 Annual Report*, accessed at http://www.sabanci.com/pdf/2007en/retail.pdf on September 10, 2008.
15. Adrian Slywotzky and Richard Wise, 'Double-Digit Growth in No-Growth Times', *Fast Company* (April 2003), 66.
16. Sylvester O. Monye (ed) (1999) *The Handbook of International Marketing Communications,* London, Blackwell, 56.
17. James B. Treece, 'Sometimes, You've Still Gotta Have Size', *BusinessWeek/Enterprise* (1993), 200–201 (April, 2003), 66ff.
18. Bayer AG, *Annual Report – 2006*, accessed at http://www.annualreport2006.bayer.com/en/research-and-development.aspx on September 10, 2008.
19. 'Tata offers help to flood-hit Bihar', *Economic Times*, 9 September 2008; Farzand Ahmed and Amitabh Srivastava, 'Bihar's tragedy', *India Today*, September 15, 2008.

20. Alan Murray, 'The Profit Motive Has a Limit: Tragedy', *The Wall Street Journal* (September 7, 2005), A2.
21. Rod Mills, 'Long battle to get home for Zoom's weary passengers', *The Express*, August 30, 2008.
22. John A. Byrne and Heather Timmons, 'Tough Times for a New CEO', *BusinessWeek* (October 29, 2001), 64–70; and Patrick McGeehan, 'Sailing Into a Sea of Trouble', *The New York Times* (October 5, 2001), C1, C4.
23. Frits K. Pil and Matthias Holweg, 'Exploring Scale: The Advantages of Thinking Small', *MIT Sloan Management Review* (Winter 2003), 33–39.
24. David Friedman, 'Is Big Back? Or Is Small Still Beautiful?' *Inc.* (April 1998), 23–28.
25. David Henry, 'Mergers: Why Most Big Deals Don't Pay Off', *BusinessWeek* (October 14, 2002), 60–70.
26. Keith H. Hammonds, 'Size Is Not a Strategy', *Fast Company* (September 2002), 78–86.
27. See Hammonds, 'Size Is Not a Strategy', Henry, 'Mergers: Why Most Big Deals Don't Pay Off', and Tom Brown, 'How Big Is Too Big?' *Across the Board* (July–August 1999), 15–20, for a discussion.
28. Andy Hutson , 'It's No Time To Cry 'Timber!', *Coventry Evening Telegraph*, August 11, 2008.
29. 'Sweden: Greater growth in exports for small businesses', *Dagens Industri*, April 23, 2008.
30. 'BioInnovate 2008: licensing is key to move drugs from bench to clinic in tough climate', *Pharma Marketletter*, June 10, 2008.
31. Entrepreneurs for Growth, *Europe's 500 – 2007*, accessed at http://www.europes500.com/results.html on September 10, 2008.
32. 'The Hot 100', *Fortune* (September 5, 2005), 75–80.
33. Gary Hamel, quoted in Hammonds, 'Size Is Not a Strategy'.
34. 'The World's Most Innovative Companies', *BusinessWeek*, April 24, 2006.
35. Sony Corp., *Sony Since 1946: Company History*, accessed at http://www.sony.net/SonyInfo/CorporateInfo/History/index.html on September 10, 2008.
36. Richard A. Melcher, 'How Goliaths Can Act Like Davids', *BusinessWeek/Enterprise* (1993), 192–201.
37. Arjun Appadurai (2006), *Fear of Small Numbers*, Kolkata, Seagull Press, 87–114.
38. Michael Barone, 'Not a Victory for Big Government', *The Wall Street Journal* (January 15, 2002), A16.
39. Ibid.
40. 'Coles ripe for revival', The Courier Mail (Australia), July 7, 2007; 'Coles posts revenue rise', *Retail Week*, August 29, 2008; Simon Evans, 'How the wolf from the west plans to revive Coles', *The Australian Financial Review,* November 7, 2007.
41. Hammonds, 'Size Is Not a Strategy'.
42. John R. Kimberly, Robert H. Miles and associates, *The Organizational Life Cycle* (San Francisco: Jossey-Bass, 1980); Ichak Adices, 'Organizational Passages – Diagnosing and Treating Lifecycle Problems of Organizations', *Organizational Dynamics* (Summer 1979), 3–25; Danny Miller and Peter H. Friesen, 'A Longitudinal Study of the Corporate Life Cycle', *Management Science* 30 (October 1984), 1161–1183; and Neil C. Churchill and Virginia L. Lewis, 'The Five Stages of Small Business Growth', *Harvard Business Review* 61 (May–June 1983), 30–50.
43. Larry E. Greiner, 'Evolution and Revolution as Organizations Grow', *Harvard Business Review* 50 (July–August 1972), 37–46; and Robert E. Quinn and Kim Cameron, 'Organizational Life Cycles and Shifting Criteria of Effectiveness: Some Preliminary Evidence', *Management Science* 29 (1983), 33–51.
44. George Land and Beth Jarman, 'Moving beyond Breakpoint', in Michael Ray and Alan Rinzler, eds., *The New Paradigm* (New York: Jeremy P. Tarcher/Perigee Books, 1993), 250–266; and Michael L. Tushman, William H. Newman and Elaine Romanelli, 'Convergence and Upheaval: Managing the Unsteady Pace of Organizational Evolution', *California Management Review* 29 (1987), 1–16.
45. 'TomTom history: A history of innovation and category-defining products', accessed at http://investors.tomtom.com/tomtom/overview/history/ on September 11, 2008; Amy Gilroy, Stellar Results For TomTom, Garmin In Q4, *Twice*, February 25, 2008; Deloitte, *Stellar Performers: Technology Fast 500 EMEA Ranking and CEO Survey 2007*, accessed at http://www.deloitte.com/dtt/cda/doc/content/dtt_tmt_EMEAFast500_2007%282%29.pdf on September 11, 2008.
46. David A. Mack and James Campbell Quick, 'EDS: An Inside View of a Corporate Life Cycle Transition', *Organizational Dynamics* 30, no. 3 (2002), 282–293.
47. Rhymer Rigby, 'TomTom maps the future', *World Business*, 1 June 2006.
48. Adam Lashinsky, 'Google Hires a Grown-up', *Business 2.0* (February 2002), 22.
49. David A. Whetten, 'Sources, Responses and Effects of Organizational Decline', in John R. Kimberly, Robert H. Miles and associates, *The Organizational Life Cycle*, 342–374.
50. Brent Schlender, 'How Big Can Apple Get?' *Fortune* (February 21, 2005), 67–76; and Josh Quittner with Rebecca Winters, 'Apple's New Core – Exclusive: How Steve Jobs Made a Sleek Machine That Could Be the Home-Digital Hub of the Future', *Time* (January 14, 2002), 46.
51. Land and Jarman, 'Moving beyond Breakpoint'.
52. Benpres Holdings is part of a complex network of interconnected business holdings, known collectively as the Lopez Group of companies. We refer to Benpres for the sake of simplicity. The current corporate structure of the Lopez Group is documented at http://www.benpres-holdings.com/corpinfo.structure.asp.
53. Elfren Sicangco Cruz. 'The rise and fall of corporations', *BusinessWorld*, August 14, 2007; Oscar M. Lopez, 'Managing Crisis The Lopez Group Way', Leadership in Crisis Forum, Manila, July 29, 2008; '20 Business Revolutionaries', *BusinessWorld*, 28 May 2007; 'Benpres

extends gains on anticipated debt restructuring', *AFX – Asia*, March 11, 2003.

54. Lawrence Miller (1990), *Barbarians to Bureaucrats: Corporate Life Cycle Strategies*, New York, CN Potter.
55. 'Shazam Intros Application For iPhone', *Wireless News*, July 15, 2008.
56. Miho Nagano, 'Soichiro Honda Rode In Front; Step On It', *Investor's Business Daily*, 24 January 2007; Setsuo Mito (1990), *The Honda Book of Management*, London, Athlone.
57. Jay Greene, 'Microsoft's Midlife Crisis', *BusinessWeek* (April 19, 2004), 88–98.
58. Max Weber, *The Theory of Social and Economic Organizations*, translated by A. M. Henderson and T. Parsons (New York: Free Press, 1947).
59. Tina Rosenberg, 'The Taint of the Greased Palm', *The New York Times Magazine* (August 10, 2003), 28.
60. Bill Powell, 'The New Russia Threat: How The Kgb (And Friends) Took Over Russia's Economy', *Fortune*, 15 September 2008.
61. 'China to crack down on nepotism, official abuses', *Reuters News*, 22 January 2007.
62. John Crewdson, 'Corruption Viewed as a Way of Life', *Bryan-College Station Eagle* (November 28, 1982), 13A; Barry Kramer, 'Chinese Officials Still Give Preference to Kin, Despite Peking Policies', *The Wall Street Journal* (October 29, 1985), 1, 21.
63. 'The Great Package Race, 2007', Georgia Tech Supply Chain & Logistics Institute, accessed at http://www2.isye.gatech.edu/%7Ejjb/wh/package-race/2007/2007.html on September 14, 2008; Meghan Reinke, 'The Great Package race: Around the World in ... How Many Days?', *Ground Support Worldwide,* 1 September 2007; 'DHL wins "great package race" contest' *Business Recorder,* 3 May 2007.
64. 'DHL – SWOT Analysis', *Datamonitor Company Profiles*, 18 August 2008; Susanne Hertz and Monica Alfredsson (2003), 'Strategic development of third party logistics providers', *Industrial Marketing Management* 32, 139–149; Sean Murphy, 'The State of the 3PL', *Supply Chain Management Review*, 1 October 2007.
65. Zaheeruddin Asif and Munir Mandviwalla (2005), 'Integrating The Supply Chain With RFID: A Technical And Business Analysis', Working Paper, Temple University School of Business and Management, accessed at http://ibit.temple.edu/programs/RFID/RFIDSupplyChain.pdf on September 13, 2008.
66. Allen C. Bluedorn, 'Pilgrim's Progress: Trends and Convergence in Research on Organizational Size and Environment', *Journal of Management Studies* 19 (Summer 1993), 163–191; John R. Kimberly, 'Organizational Size and the Structuralist Perspective: A Review, Critique and Proposal', *Administrative Science Quarterly* (1976), 571–597; Richard L. Daft and Selwyn W. Becker, 'Managerial, Institutional and Technical Influences on Administration: A Longitudinal Analysis', *Social Forces* 59 (1980), 392–413.
67. James P. Walsh and Robert D. Dewar, 'Formalization and the Organizational Life Cycle', *Journal of Management Studies* 24 (May 1987), 215–231.
68. Nancy M. Carter and Thomas L. Keon, 'Specialization as a Multidimensional Construct', *Journal of Management Studies* 26 (1989), 11–28; Cheng-Kuang Hsu, Robert M. March and Hiroshi Mannari, 'An Examination of the Determinants of Organizational Structure', *American Journal of Sociology* 88 (1983), 975–996; Guy Geeraerts, 'The Effect of Ownership on the Organization Structure in Small Firms', *Administrative Science Quarterly* 29 (1984), 232–237; Bernard Reimann, 'On the Dimensions of Bureaucratic Structure: An Empirical Reappraisal', *Administrative Science Quarterly* 18 (1973), 462–476; Richard H. Hall, 'The Concept of Bureaucracy: An Empirical Assessment', *American Journal of Sociology* 69 (1963), 32–40; and William A. Rushing, 'Organizational Rules and Surveillance: A Proposition in Comparative Organizational Analysis', *Administrative Science Quarterly* 10 (1966), 423–443.
69. Jerald Hage and Michael Aiken, 'Relationship of Centralization to Other Structural Properties', *Administrative Science Quarterly* 12 (1967), 72–91.
70. Doron P. Levin, 'Honda Decentralizes Management', *The New York Times*, 21 May 1992.
71. Steve Lohr and John Markoff, 'You Call This a Midlife Crisis?' *The New York Times* (August 31, 2003), Section 3, 1.
72. Peter Brimelow, 'How Do You Cure Injelitance?' *Forbes* (August 7, 1989), 42–44; Jeffrey D. Ford and John W. Slocum, Jr., 'Size, Technology, Environment and the Structure of Organizations', *Academy of Management Review* 2 (1977), 561–575; and John D. Kasarda, 'The Structural Implications of Social System Size: A Three-Level Analysis', *American Sociological Review* 39 (1974), 19–28.
73. Graham Astley, 'Organizational Size and Bureaucratic Structure', *Organization Studies* 6 (1985), 201–228; Spyros K. Lioukas and Demitris A. Xerokostas, 'Size and Administrative Intensity in Organizational Divisions', *Management Science* 28 (1982), 854–868; Peter M. Blau, 'Interdependence and Hierarchy in Organizations', *Social Science Research* 1 (1972), 1–24; Peter M. Blau and R. A. Schoenherr, *The Structure of Organizations* (New York: Basic Books, 1971); A. Hawley, W. Boland and M. Boland, 'Population Size and Administration in Institutions of Higher Education', *American Sociological Review* 30 (1965), 252–255; Richard L. Daft, 'System Influence on Organization Decision-Making: The Case of Resource Allocation', *Academy of Management Journal* 21 (1978), 6–22; and B. P. Indik, 'The Relationship between Organization Size and the Supervisory Ratio', *Administrative Science Quarterly* 9 (1964), 301–312.
74. T. F. James, 'The Administrative Component in Complex Organizations', *Sociological Quarterly* 13 (1972), 533–539; Daft, 'System Influence on Organization Decision-Making'; E. A. Holdaway and E. A. Blowers, 'Administrative Ratios and Organization Size: A Longitudinal Examination', *American Sociological Review* 36 (1971), 278–286; and John Child, 'Parkinson's Progress: Accounting for the Number of Specialists in Organizations', *Administrative Science Quarterly* 18 (1973), 328–348.
75. Morris, Jonathan, Hassard, John and McCann, Leo (2008), 'The resilience of "institutionalized capitalism": Managing

managers under "shareholder capitalism" and "managerial capitalism"', *Human Relations*, 61, 687–710; Åse Gornitzka and Ingvild Marheim Larsen (2004), 'Towards professionalisation? Restructuring of administrative work force in universities', *Higher Education* 47: 455–471.

76. Richard L. Daft and Selwyn Becker, 'School District Size and the Development of Personnel Resources', *Alberta Journal of Educational Research* 24 (1978), 173–187.
77. Thomas A. Stewart, 'Yikes! Deadwood is Creeping Back', *Fortune* (August 18, 1997), 221–222.
78. Cathy Lazere, 'Resisting Temptation: The Fourth Annual SG&A Survey', *CFO* (December 1997), 64–70.
79. Paul Du Gay (2000), *In praise of bureaucracy: Weber, organization, ethics*, London, Sage.
80. Based on Gifford and Elizabeth Pinchot, *The End of Bureaucracy and the Rise of the Intelligent Organization* (San Francisco: Berrett-Koehler Publishers, 1993), 21–29.
81. B. Guy Peters, *The Politics of Bureaucracy*, London, Routledge, 2001.
82. Scott Shane, 'The Beast That Feeds on Boxes: Bureaucracy', *The New York Times* (April 10, 2005), http://www.nytimes.com.
83. John L. Campbell, John A. Hall, Ove Kaj Pedersen (2006), *National identity and the varieties of capitalism: the Danish experience*. Montreal, McGill-Queen's Press; Peter A. Hall and Kathleen Thelen (2009), 'Institutional change in varieties of capitalism', *Socio-Economic Review*, 7, 7–34.
84. Gili S. Drori, Yong Suk Jang and John W. Meyer (2006), Sources of Rationalized Governance: Cross-National Longitudinal Analyses, 1985–2002, *Administrative Science Quarterly*, 51, 205–229
85. Gregory A. Bigley and Karlene H. Roberts, 'The Incident Command System: High-Reliability Organizing for Complex and Volatile Task Environments', *Academy of Management Journal* 44, no. 6 (2001), 1281–1299.
86. US Indian Ocean Tsunami Warning System (IOTWS), *Program Proceedings: Workshop On The Transition Of The US IOTWS Program To Indian Ocean Partners, December 6-7, 2007*, Bangkok, Thailand, accessed at http://apps.develebridge.net/usiotws/b/US%20IOTWS%20Transition%20Workshop%20Proceedings_Jan08.pdf on September 13, 2008.
87. Kirsty Challen, Andrew Bentley, John Bright and Darren Walter (2007), 'Mass casualty triage – pandemic influenza and critical care', *Critical Care*, 11, 212–218.
88. Philip Johnston, 'Just what is in it for Britain, Mr Blair? Cash for access row', *The Daily Telegraph*, 12 February 2002.
89. Lazere, 'Resisting Temptation'.
90. Philip M. Padsakoff, Larry J. Williams and William D. Todor, 'Effects of Organizational Formalization on Alienation among Professionals and Nonprofessionals', *Academy of Management Journal* 29 (1986), 820–831.
91. Royston Greenwood, C. R. Hinings and John Brown, '"P2-Form" Strategic Management: Corporate Practices in Professional Partnerships', *Academy of Management Journal* 33 (1990), 725–755; Royston Greenwood and C. R. Hinings, 'Understanding Strategic Change: The Contribution of Archetypes', *Academy of Management Journal* 36 (1993), 1052–1081.
92. Most consulting firms are not formally speaking partnerships but rather private corporations, although they operate in a similar manner. Christopher D. McKenna (1995), 'The Origins of Modern Management Consulting', *Business and Economic History,* 24, 51–58; Royston Greenwood and Laura Empson (2003), 'The Professional Partnership: Relic or Exemplary Form of Governance?', *Organization Studies,* 24, 909–933.
93. William G. Ouchi, 'Markets, Bureaucracies and Clans', *Administrative Science Quarterly* 25 (1980), 129–141; idem, 'A Conceptual Framework for the Design of Organizational Control Mechanisms', *Management Science* 25 (1979), 833–848.
94. Weber, *The Theory of Social and Economic Organizations,* 328–340.
95. Oliver A. Williamson, *Markets and Hierarchies: Analyses and Antitrust Implications* (New York: Free Press, 1975).
96. David Osborne and Ted Gaebler (1992), *Reinventing Government,* New York, Addison-Wesley; Philip Collins and Liam Byrne (eds), *Reinventing Government Again,* London, Social Market Foundation.
97. Kelsey, Jane (1996), *The New Zealand Experiment; A World Model for Structural Adjustment?* Wellington, GP Print.
98. Pollitt, C., S. van Thiel & V. Homburg. (eds.), (2007), *New Public Management in Europe: adaptationsand alternatives, Basingstoke,* Palgrave MacMillan.
99. David Cronin, 'Lisbon Treaty May Lead to Privatization of Water', *Inter Press Service,* 8 January 2008.
100. Anita Micossi, 'Creating Internal Markets', *Enterprise* (April 1994), 43–44.
101. Raymond E. Miles, Henry J. Coleman, Jr., and W. E. Douglas Creed, "Keys to Success in Corporate Redesign," *California Management Review* 37, no. 3 (Spring 1995), 128–145.
102. Micossi, 'Creating Internal Markets'.
103. Ouchi, 'Markets, Bureaucracies and Clans'.
104. Anna Muoio, ed., 'Growing Smart', *Fast Company* (August 1998), 73–83.
105. Richard Leifer and Peter K. Mills, 'An Information Processing Approach for Deciding upon Control Strategies and Reducing Control Loss in Emerging Organizations', *Journal of Management* 22, no. 1 (1996), 113–137.
106. Stratford Sherman, 'The New Computer Revolution', *Fortune* (June 14, 1993), 56–80.
107. 'Colourful British tycoon Branson on jumbo stops traffic in New Delhi', *Agence France-Presse,* 10 December 1999; John Arlidge, 'Virgin desire to be taken global', *The Sunday Times,* 25 May 2008.
108. 'Branson Rocks on', *Sunday Business Post,* 2 December 2007; Michael Specter, 'A Modern Knight', *The Australian Women's Weekly*, 31 August 2007; Craig Donaldson (2003), 'Breaking in a new culture: the Virgin Blue story', *Human Resources* (Australia), accessed at http://www.humanresourcesmagazine.com.au/articles/0B/0C01A00B.asp?Type=60&Category=875 on September 14, 2008.
109. Leifer and Mills, 'An Information Processing Approach for Deciding upon Control Strategies'; and Laurie J. Kirsch, 'The Management of Complex Tasks in Organizations: Controlling

the Systems Development Process', *Organization Science* 7, no. 1 (January–February 1996), 1–21.

110. James R. Barker, 'Tightening the Iron Cage: Concertive Control in Self-Managing Teams', *Administrative Science Quarterly* 38 (1993), 408–437.
111. 'Markets fear worst is yet to come as shares plunge after bank's collapse', *Belfast Telegraph,* 18 March 2008.
112. Hugh Dent, 'Parmalat odyssey shakes regulators' world", *Agence France Presse,* 18 January 2004.
113. Patrick McGeehan, 'Layoffs Begin to Show on the Region's Unemployment Rolls', *The New York Times,* 20 June 2008; 'U.K. finance sector weakens', *International Herald Tribune,* 3 September 2008.
114. Kim S. Cameron, Myung Kim and David A. Whetten, 'Organizational Effects of Decline and Turbulence', *Administrative Science Quarterly* 32 (1987), 222–240.
115. Danny Miller, 'What Happens after Success: The Perils of Excellence', *Journal of Management Studies* 31, no. 3 (May 1994), 325–358.
116. Kris Frieswick, 'The Turning Point: What Options Do Companies Have When Their Industries Are Dying?' *CFO Magazine* (April 1, 2005), http://www/cfo.com.
117. Leonard Greenhalgh, 'Organizational Decline', in Samuel B. Bacharach, ed., *Research in the Sociology of Organizations* 2 (Greenwich, Conn.: JAI Press, 1983), 231–276; and Peter Lorange and Robert T. Nelson, 'How to Recognize–and Avoid–Organizational Decline', *Sloan Management Review* (Spring 1987), 41–48.
118. Kim S. Cameron and Raymond Zammuto, 'Matching Managerial Strategies to Conditions of Decline', *Human Resources Management* 22 (1983), 359–375; and Leonard Greenhalgh, Anne T. Lawrence and Robert I. Sutton, 'Determinants of Workforce Reduction Strategies in Organizations', *Academy of Management Review* 13 (1988), 241–254.
119. Timothy Aeppel, 'Die Is Cast; Toolmakers Know Precisely What's the Problem: Price', *The Wall Street Journal* (November 21, 2003), A1, A6.
120. John A. Pearce II and Steven C. Michael (2006), 'Strategies to prevent economic recessions from causing business failure'.
121. William Weitzel and Ellen Jonsson, 'Reversing the Downward Spiral: Lessons from W. T. Grant and Sears Roebuck', *Academy of Management Executive* 5 (1991), 7–21; William Weitzel and Ellen Jonsson, 'Decline in Organizations: A Literature Integration and Extension', *Administrative Science Quarterly* 34 (1989), 91–109.
122. William McKinley, Carol M. Sanchez and Allen G. Schick, 'Organizational Downsizing: Constraining, Cloning, Learning', *Academy of Management Executive* 9, no. 3 (1995), 32–42.
123. Gregory B. Northcraft and Margaret A. Neale, *Organizational Behaviour: A Management Challenge,* 2nd ed. (Fort Worth, Tex: The Dryden Press, 1994), 626; and A. Catherine Higgs, 'Executive Commentary' on McKinley, Sanchez and Schick, 'Organizational Downsizing: Constraining, Cloning, Learning', 43–44.
124. Wayne Cascio, 'Strategies for Responsible Restructuring', *Academy of Management Executive* 16, no. 3 (2002), 80–91; James R. Morris, Wayne F. Cascio and Clifford E. Young, 'Downsizing after All These Years: Questions and Answers about Who Did It, How Many Did It and Who Benefited from It', *Organizational Dynamics* (Winter 1999), 78–86; Stephen Doerflein and James Atsaides, 'Corporate Psychology: Making Downsizing Work', *Electrical World* (September–October 1999), 41–43; and Brett C. Luthans and Steven M. Sommer, 'The Impact of Downsizing on Workplace Attitudes', *Group and Organization Management* 2, no. 1 (1999), 46–70.
125. 'Fuel supply problems could ground Alitalia flights', *Guardian Unlimited,* 13 September 2008; 'Alitalia-Linee Aeree Italiane S.p.A. – SWOT Analysis', *Datamonitor Company Profiles,* 20 July 2004; 'Alitalia-Linee Aeree Italiane S.p.A. – SWOT Analysis', *Datamonitor Company Profiles,* 14 January 2008; Deepa Babington, 'Wanted: Buyer willing to gamble on Alitalia1, *Reuters News,* 6 December 2006; '"Out of control" Alitalia heading to bankruptcy: Italian PM', *Agence France Presse,* 10 October 2006.
126. Guthrie, James P., Datta, Deepak K. (2008), 'Dumb and Dumber: The Impact of Downsizing on Firm Performance as Moderated by Industry Conditions', *Organization Science* 19, 108–123; Sorge, Arndt and van Witteloostuijn, Arjen (2004), 'The (Non)Sense of Organizational Change: An Essai about Universal Management Hypes, Sick Consultancy Metaphors, and Healthy Organization Theories', *Organization Studies,* 25, 1205–1231.
127. These techniques are based on Bob Nelson, 'The Care of the Un-Downsized', *Training and Development* (April 1997), 40–43; Shari Caudron, 'Teach Downsizing Survivors How to Thrive', *Personnel Journal* (January 1996), 38; Joel Brockner, 'Managing the Effects of Layoffs on Survivors', *California Management Review* (Winter 1992), 9–28; Ronald Henkoff, 'Getting beyond Downsizing', *Fortune* (January 10, 1994), 58–64; Kim S. Cameron, 'Strategies for Successful Organizational Downsizing', *Human Resource Management* 33, no. 2 (Summer 1994), 189–211; and Doerflein and Atsaides, 'Corporate Psychology: Making Downsizing Work'.
128. Matt Murray, "Stress Mounts as More Firms Announce Large Layoffs, But Don't Say Who or When" (Your Career Matters column), *The Wall Street Journal* (March 13, 2001), B1, B12.
129. Anna Lindblom, "Dexia BIL: Working Differently", *IMD Case study* 3-1589-90.
130. Kim Ji-hyun, 'Samsung is vanguard of corporate philanthropy: Each group affiliate undertakes unique volunteer work based on customized programs', *The Korea Herald,* 21 March 2006.
131. Caudron, 'Teach Downsizing Survivors How to Thrive'.
132. Ronny Vansteenkiste (2003), 'Who Moved My Drink?: the preparation for the closure of Seagram's spirits and wine business: a personal experience' in Kenneth Paul De Meuse and Mitchell Lee Marks (eds), *Resizing the Organization,* San Francisco, John Wiley.

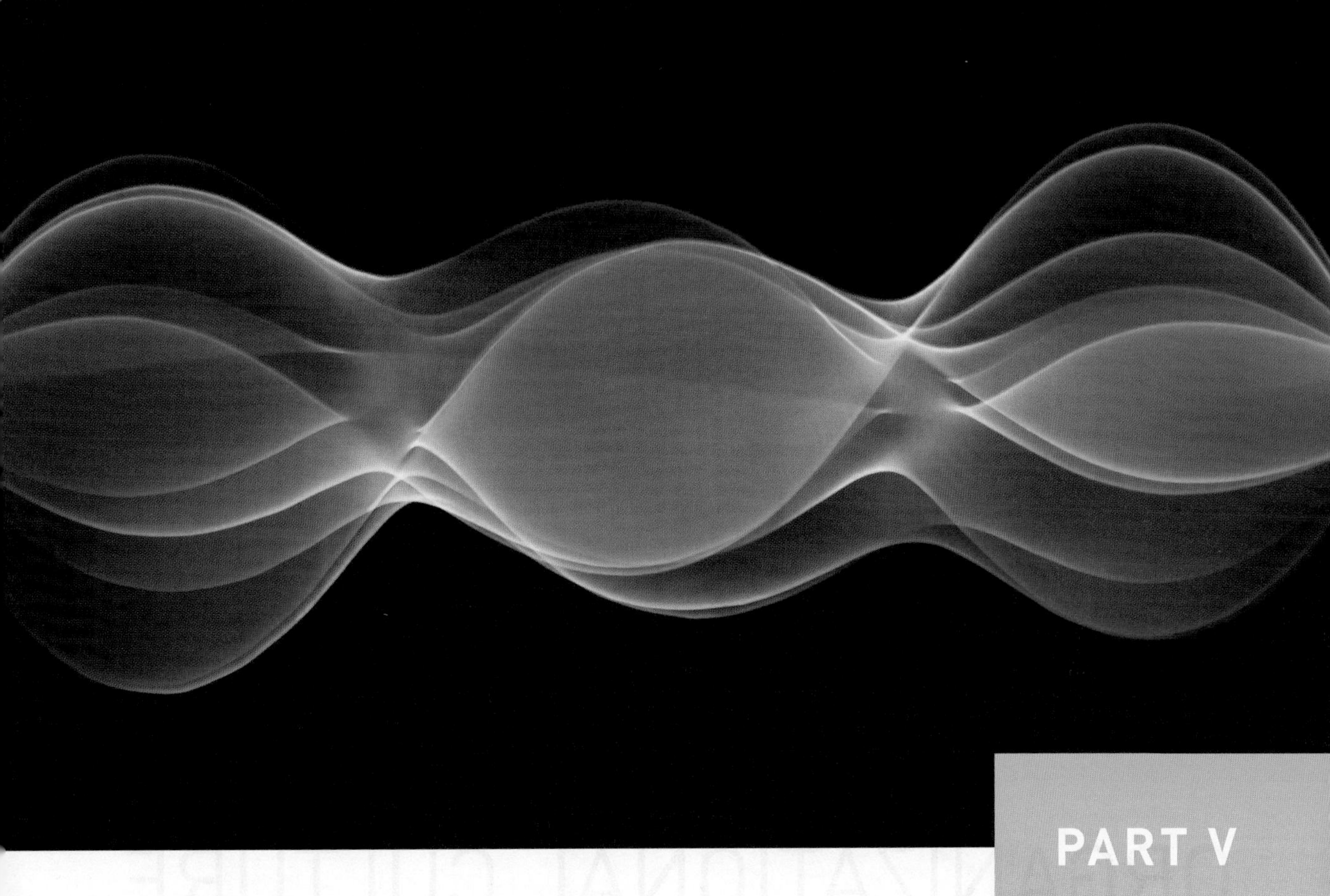

PART V

MANAGING DYNAMIC PROCESSES

CHAPTER 10

ORGANIZATIONAL CULTURE AND ETHICAL VALUES

Organizational Culture
- What Is Organizational Culture?
- Emergence and Purpose of Culture
- Interpreting Culture

Organization Design and Culture
- The Adaptability Culture
- The Mission Culture
- The Clan Culture
- The Bureaucratic Culture
- Culture Strength and Organizational Subcultures

Organizational Culture, Learning and Performance

Ethical Values and Social Responsibility
- Sources of Individual Ethical Principles
- Managerial Ethics and Social Responsibility
- Does It Pay to Be Good?

Sources of Ethical Values in Organizations
- Personal Ethics
- Organizational Culture
- Organizational Systems
- External Stakeholders

How Leaders Shape Culture and Ethics
- Values-based Leadership
- Formal Structure and Systems

Corporate Culture and Ethics in a Global Environment

Summary and Interpretation

Boots Company PLC

Boots. When people in the United Kingdom think of 'Boots', they are usually not thinking of sturdy footwear but rather of the local chemists and tempting shelves stocked with all kinds of health items, cosmetics and toiletries. Boots is a much-loved and trusted retail brand in the United Kingdom, but when Richard Baker took over as chief executive in 2003, the company was looking – well, a bit down at heel. Baker found himself facing one of the most difficult jobs in retailing, helping the troubled company find a way to compete with the growing power of large supermarket chains like Tesco and Asda (Baker's former employer).

Baker immediately recognized many of the problems, such as antiquated distribution and information technology (IT) systems, high costs and inefficient processes, cluttered stores and excessive headquarters personnel. But he soon realized there would be no quick fixes, because the roots of Boots's troubles went very deep, right to the heart of the organization. Indeed, the cultural values at Boots Co. Plc, he found, were woefully out of sync with today's fast-moving, competitive environment.

Baker came to Boots from Asda, which is owned by the US-based discount giant Wal-Mart. At Asda, he had been used to a culture of openness and innovation. Ideas that could promote useful change were encouraged and acted on quickly. At Boots, though, change was almost viewed as the enemy. Boots had its greatest years of success in an era when the world moved more slowly and gently. A 'civil service' culture developed at the firm, with people signing on for lifetime careers and expecting to have a comfortable ride straight to the top. The highly insular culture meant that outsiders and outside ideas often seemed unwelcome. With home-grown managers and a long tradition of doing things a certain way, Boots had grown culturally resistant to change. For example, one previous chairman says his efforts to encourage Boots to concentrate on aspects of the business with the most potential for long-term growth were ignored by a team of long-serving executives who tended to focus on current profits at the expense of the future.

Over the next few years, top management at Boots was changed, and Baker took a number of steps to improve efficiency, spruce up the stores and be more price-competitive. However, the 1,400-store chain continued to struggle. After a promising Christmas 2004 season, sales and profits went flat. Undeterred, Baker continued to restructure the company, culminating in an ambitious merger with the wholesale and retail druggist Alliance Unichem in 2006. The new merged company performed well into 2008, with increased sales and profits.

Despite these successes, managers at Alliance Boots will need to continue to work to change cultural values in the company, and also address resistance to change from both within and outside the company. For example, the company has changed its invoice payment procedures, requiring suppliers to wait up to 75 days for payment, resulting in criticism from the British Federation of Small Businesses, which accused the company of using small businesses as an 'unofficial source of credit'.

The major changes Richard Baker brought to Boots resulted in change for him too. Alliance Boots attracted acquisition interest from various private equity operations, and in 2007 the company was bought out by a consortium including the famous 'corporate raiders' Kohlberg Kravis Roberts & Co (KKR). As a result of the buyout Baker left Alliance Boots, though not empty-handed; he exercised stock options worth about $13 million.[1]

Every organization, like Alliance Boots or Asda, has a set of values that characterize how people behave and how the organization carries out everyday business. Sometimes, these values shift out of alignment with the environment and cause problems for the organization. One of the most important challenges for organizational leaders is to instill and support the kind of values needed for the company to thrive.

Strong cultures can have a profound impact on a company, which can be either positive or negative for the organization. For example, 3M Germany, subsidiary of the US-headquartered 3M Corporation, has been chosen by *Capital* magazine as the 'best employer in Germany' three years in a row, and in 2007 its employees voted it the fourth best large company in Europe to work for. Capital magazine said 3M had, 'credible, competent management, which treated its employees fairly and with respect, and maintained a healthy team-spirit'.[2,3] Negative cultural norms, however, can damage a company just as powerfully as positive ones can strengthen it. Consider the case of America's Enron Corp., where the corporate culture supported pushing everything to the limits: business practices, rules, personal behaviour and laws. Executives drove expensive cars, challenged employees to participate in risky competitive behaviour, and often celebrated big deals by heading off to a bar or dance club. Corporate culture at Enron ultimately led to bankruptcy and criminal convictions for top executives.[4] An internationally-widespread corporate culture in which short-term personal financial gain for executives was valued above all other values including long-term company health is widely thought to have played a key role in the global financial crisis of 2008.[5,6]

See online
COUNTERPOINT 10.8

A related concept concerning the influence of norms and values on how people work together and how they treat one another and customers is called *social capital*. In organizations with a high degree of *social capital*, for example, relationships are based on trust, mutual understandings and shared norms and values that enable people to cooperate and coordinate their activities to achieve organizational goals.[7] Organizations can accumulate varying levels of social capital. *Goodwill* could be viewed as form of social capital. When relationships both within the organization and with customers, suppliers and partners are based on honesty, trust and respect, a spirit of goodwill exists and people willingly cooperate to achieve mutual benefits. A high level of social capital enables smooth social interactions and exchanges that help to facilitate smooth organizational functioning.

Think of eBay, which makes use of social capital in bringing together millions of buyers and sellers on its Web site, leading to forecast annual profits of $2 billion in 2008.[8] The company builds goodwill and trust through mechanisms that include a feedback system enabling buyers and sellers to rate one another, discussion boards that build a sense of community among site users and regular all-day focus groups with representative buyers and sellers. Inevitably, a service such as eBay attracts some people who abuse the system, and the company has to carefully balance the

Different forms of capital?

Until recent years the term 'capital' described economic capital; financial resources resources that are needed in order to establish and develop a business. However, scholars have realized that economic capital alone is insufficient to succeed. Other inputs are needed, including human capital (the education and skills managers and employees bring with them) and social capital (the networking capacities of the people in an organization). Without human capital, economic capital will be under-utilized; machinery will not be properly maintained or deployed, high-tech companies will not develop new applications for sale, etc. But even with ample economic capital and human capital, companies will not succeed unless they can make the necessary connections. Things like building supplier networks depend on staff with contacts and good interpersonal skills. Winning contracts depends on credibility. Dealing with government regulators effectively and efficiently means being able to get along and resolve different interpretations smoothly and in the interests of your organization. These factors are examples of social capital; hard to measure, but essential to success.[9]

advantages of a free-wheeling, low-bureaucracy market with adequate buyer and seller protections. The company has been accused by some European authorities of turning a blind eye towards unscrupulous vendors such as those who sell fake branded goods,[10] accusations that are potentially corrosive of trust and damaging for business.

Another example of a company with high social capital is Microsoft UK. Of employees surveyed by the *Sunday Times*, 89 per cent reported that they 'love working there' and 93 per cent feel that the company 'makes a positive difference to the world we live in'. Although employees work long, hard hours, Microsoft UK has a *Department of People and Culture* to focus on the characteristics that create and strengthen social capital. For example, in 1998, Microsoft UK developed a long-term vision for a culture that fostered 'honesty, openness an entrepreneurial spirit and respect for the customer'.[11] Other organizations also build social capital by being open and honest and cultivating positive social relationships among employees and with outsiders. Relationships based on self-interest, and subterfuge, such as those at Enron, can be devastating to a company and these traits even destabilize an entire economy, as was seen in the global financial crisis that began in 2007, when a culture of self-interested risk taking became the norm in countless financial institutions across North America and Europe, plunging the world into its worst economic crisis since the Great Depression. Social capital is a relevant concept for both corporate culture and ethics, which is the subject matter of this chapter.

See online
COUNTERPOINT 10.9

Purpose of This Chapter

This chapter explores ideas about corporate culture and associated ethical values and how these are influenced by organizations. The first section describes the nature of corporate culture, its origins and purpose and how to identify and interpret culture through ceremonies, stories and symbols. We then examine how culture reinforces the strategy and structural design the organization needs to be effective in its environment and discuss the important role of culture in organizational learning and high performance. Next, the chapter turns to ethical values and social responsibility. We consider how managers implement the structures and systems that influence ethical and socially responsible behaviour. The chapter also discusses how leaders shape culture and ethical values in a direction suitable for strategy and performance outcomes. The chapter closes with a brief overview of the complex cultural and ethical issues that managers face in an international environment.

Organizational Culture

The popularity of the organizational culture topic raises a number of questions. Can we identify cultures? Can culture be aligned with strategy? How can cultures be managed or changed? The best place to start is by defining culture and explaining how it can be identified in organizations.

What Is Organizational Culture?

In the last chapter, we discussed culture as a broader social phenomenon that includes national culture, professional culture and organizational culture. In this chapter we will explore organizational culture in more depth. **Organizational culture** is the set of values, norms, guiding beliefs and understandings that is shared by members of an organization and is taught to new members.[12] It represents the largely unwritten, feeling part of the organization. Everyone participates in culture, but culture generally goes unnoticed. It is often only when organizations try to implement new strategies or programmes that go against basic cultural norms and values that they come face to face with the power of culture.

COUNTERPOINT 10.1

The idea that everyone in an organization subscribes to a shared set of values, norms, etc. is contentious. Within most organizations there is diversity, so the claim of commonality could instead be seen as a form of prescriptive control: it says: 'these are the values that you should have or at least display if you are an employee of this company'. What is interesting is where the idea of a shared set of values comes from – who is it who decides what these are? The probable answer is senior managers (or perhaps consultants hired to identify the values) who select and distil from their experience what they believe or would like the values to be. **Discuss**

Organizational culture exists at two levels, as illustrated in Exhibit 10.1. On the surface are visible artifacts and observable behaviour – the ways people dress and act and the symbols, stories and ceremonies organization members share. The visible elements of culture, however, reflect deeper values in the minds of organization members. These underlying values, assumptions, beliefs and thought processes are

EXHIBIT 10.1 Levels of Corporate Culture

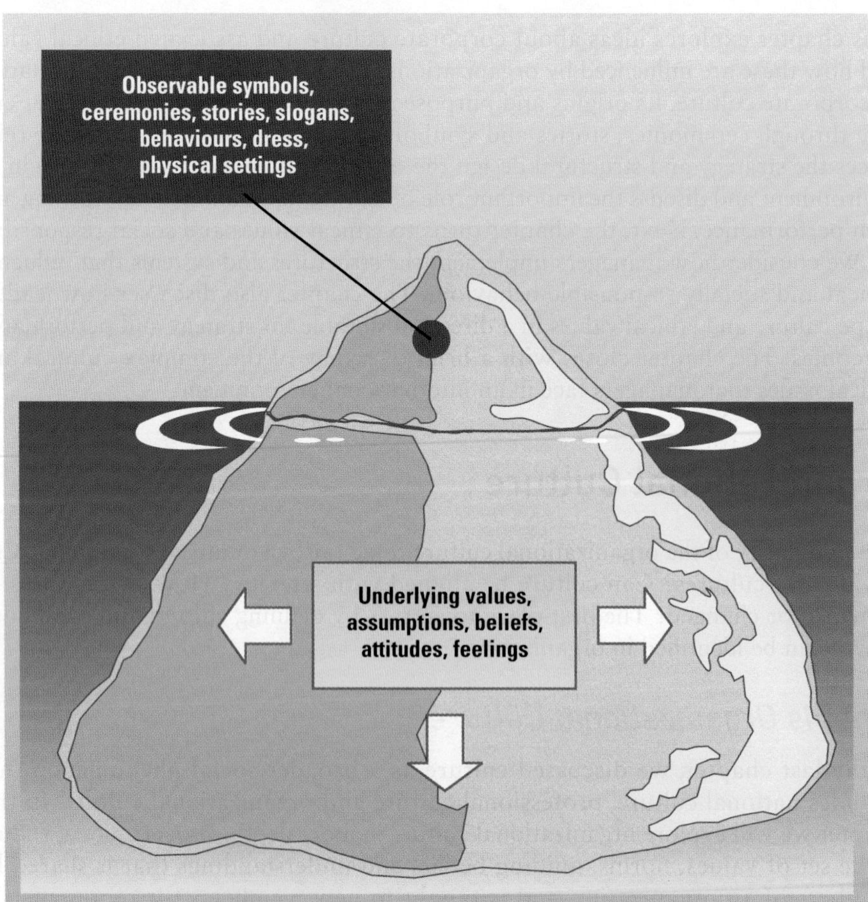

the true culture.[13] For many years, for example, Central and Eastern Europe was dominated by the Soviet Union which imposed a domineering, neo-classical architecture on new buildings, that reflected the omnipotence of the state. When capitalism re-emerged in these countries in the 1990s, early corporate architecture tended to reflect an unimaginative copy of Western-style chrome and glass structures. As a native corporate culture has emerged, local companies are beginning to demand buildings that reflect their own identities. In Hungary, for example, HungaroControl, the country's national air traffic control company, engaged a Hungarian architect to build a new headquarters which has been described as, 'a blocky, bricky slice of earthiness that departs entirely from the international model of dumb glazing and pointless form'.[14] Architecture is just one way that the attributes of culture display themselves as a patterned set of activities carried out through social interaction.[15] Those patterns can be used to interpret organizational culture.

See online
COUNTERPOINT 10.10

Emergence and Purpose of Culture

Culture provides members with a sense of organizational identity and generates in them a commitment to beliefs and values that are larger than themselves. Though ideas that become part of culture can come from anywhere within the organization, an organization's culture generally begins with a founder or early leader who articulates and implements particular ideas and values as a vision, philosophy or business strategy.

See online
COUNTERPOINT 10.11

When these ideas and values lead to success, they become institutionalized, and an organizational culture emerges that reflects the vision and strategy of the founder or leader.[16] For example, Jack Ma, the founder of Alibaba, the successful Chinese B2B auction firm, sweated night and day during the company's early phase to build a corporate culture different from the hierarchical tradition typical in Chinese firms. 'Alibaba's culture is no matter what you do you have pleased the customer', says Ma. At the beginning, he says he slept only two or three hours a day, but now that the company's culture is well embedded in his team, he can play a more strategic role, 'In the past I carried an axe on the battlefield, but now I command my forces on the battlefield'.[17,18]

Cultures serve two critical functions in organizations: (1) to integrate members so that they know how to relate to one another, and (2) to help the organization adapt to the external environment. **Internal integration** means that members develop a collective identity and know-how to work together effectively. It is culture that guides day-to-day working relationships and determines how people communicate within the organization, what behaviour is acceptable or not acceptable, and how power and status are allocated. **External adaptation** refers to how the organization meets goals and deals with outsiders. Culture helps guide the daily activities of workers to meet certain goals. It can help the organization respond rapidly to customer needs or the moves of a competitor. As discussed in this chapter's Bookmark, culture plays a key role in transforming an organization's performance from average to truly great.

COUNTERPOINT 10.2

This idea of culture as 'internal integration' can also be seen as indoctrination – as, for example, at Toyota or IBM. The idea of 'corporate culture' is charged with setting out how people should work together, communicate with each other, adjudicate what is acceptable and determine how allocations of status and power are made. If successful, the outcome is a group of identikit employees – like those at Enron, for example –

who 'work together effectively' but become sect-like in their activities. In the absence of diversity, it is difficult to think critically or to innovate except in ways that comply with 'the culture', whatever this is dictated or designed to be. There is little possibility for gaining any distance from values that are ostensibly all-embracing and sacrosanct.

External adaptation may also result in striving to respond to others' demands – ultimately shareholders if it is a publicly listed company – without regard to the ethics of what is done. Almost any dubious practice can be justified in the name of compliance with 'the culture' – either because it is deemed to be key to 'internal integration' or essential for 'external adaptation'. **Discuss**

The organization's culture also guides employee decision making in the absence of written rules or policies.[19] Thus, both functions of culture are related to building the organization's social capital, by forging either positive or negative relationships both within the organization and with outsiders.

As an organization manager, keep these guidelines in mind:

Pay attention to corporate culture. Understand the underlying values, assumptions and beliefs on which culture is based as well as its observable manifestations. Evaluate corporate culture based on rites and ceremonies, stories and heroes, symbols and language.

Interpreting Culture

To identify and interpret culture requires that people make inferences based on observable artifacts. Artifacts can be studied but are hard to decipher accurately. An award ceremony in one company may have a different meaning than in another company. To decipher what is really going on in an organization requires detective work and probably some experience as an insider. Some of the typical and important observable aspects of culture are rites and ceremonies, stories symbols and language.[20]

Rites and Ceremonies Important artifacts for culture are **rites and ceremonies**, the elaborate, planned activities that make up a special event and are often conducted for the benefit of an audience. Managers can hold rites and ceremonies to provide dramatic examples of what a company values. These are special occasions that reinforce specific values, create a bond among people for sharing an important understanding and anoint and celebrate heroes and heroines who symbolize important beliefs and activities.[21]

Four types of rites that appear in organizations are summarized in Exhibit 10.3. *Rites of passage* facilitate the transition of employees into new social roles. *Rites of enhancement* create stronger social identities and increase the status of employees. *Rites of renewal* reflect training and development activities that improve organization functioning. *Rites of integration* create common bonds and good feelings among employees and increase commitment to the organization. The following examples illustrate how these rites and ceremonies are used by top managers to reinforce important cultural values.

See online COUNTERPOINT 10.12

- In a major bank, election as an officer was seen as the key event in a successful career. A series of activities accompanied every promotion to bank officer, including a special method of notification, taking the new officer to the officers' dining room for the first time and the new officer buying drinks on the Friday after his or her notification.[22] This is a rite of passage.
- Avon, the giant direct sales marketing firm that has made the 'Avon Lady' famous in 140 countries, uses awards ceremonies as a motivating tool for its army of sales consultants. For many, Avon work is a first step back into the world of business after taking time out to raise families. The company's recognition of the achievements of its sales workforce builds loyalty and

Have you read this book?

Gurus, Hired Guns and Warm Bodies

SIMON BARLEY AND GIDEON KUNDA

As we shall see in Chapters 11 and 12, traditional organizational structures, with their stable hierarchies reflected in pyramid-shaped organization charts, are being challenged by various business process innovations. Technological innovations and relaxed regulation of labour markets and of trade permit businesses to extend production process in numerous ways. The traditional workplace, such as the giant automobile plants pioneered by American manufacturers in the 1930s, is being broken up and dispersed into numerous locales, from homes – with teleworking is an increasingly common phenomenon – to across oceans, with service jobs shifted to lower cost labour areas.

Changes in the organization of production – whether of goods or services – do not merely shift the physical location of business activities, but also transform the character of organizations and the relations between people involved in production. Organizations' core activities, previously carried out by regular staff, are to an increasing extent being carried out by contractual workers.

In their book *Gurus, Hired Guns and Warm Bodies,* Barley and Kunda explore the phenomenon of contractualization of key tasks in IT firms in Silicon Valley, California, the centre of the US software industry. Their study, carried out through in-depth dialogue with 71 highly-skilled IT professionals working as contractors, reveals how the transformation in the way production is organized has led to fundamental changes in relationships between organizations and people who work for them.

Unlike many workers, Barley and Kunda's IT contractors are not obvious victims of production re-engineering. They are in high demand, enjoy high earnings and can usually work when and how they choose. Nevertheless their work lives are radically different from counterparts who have continued to work as regular staffers. To begin with, the contractors' success depends on different capacities. While technical skills are a prerequisite for both groups of workers, the contractors need different types of social capital in order to succeed (see above in this chapter for a discussion of social capital). Whereas an effective employee or manager in the firm will tend to be successful when she has strong social capital ties within the organization, the contractor will be more likely to be successful when she has looser but far more dispersed networks; what Barley and Kunda call networks with structural holes.

Similarly, contractors must guess trends for themselves and invest in learning the skills required for new IT skills so that they will profit from such trends. In short, they must *self-manage* in the absence of a traditional management structure that would in earlier times have ensured that a company's workers had up-to-date skills.

EXHIBIT 10.2 Personal Networks with and without Structural Holes

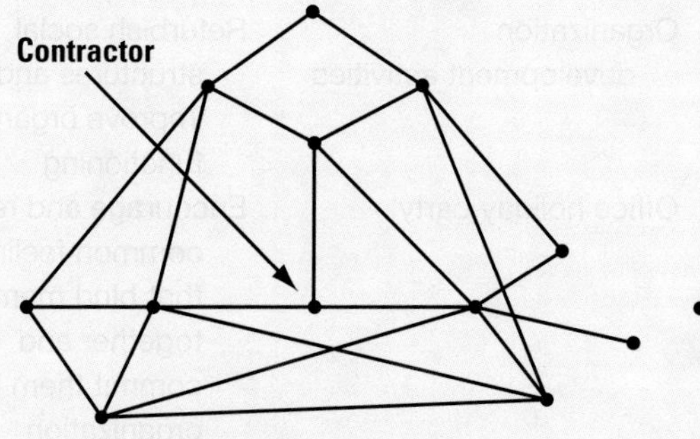

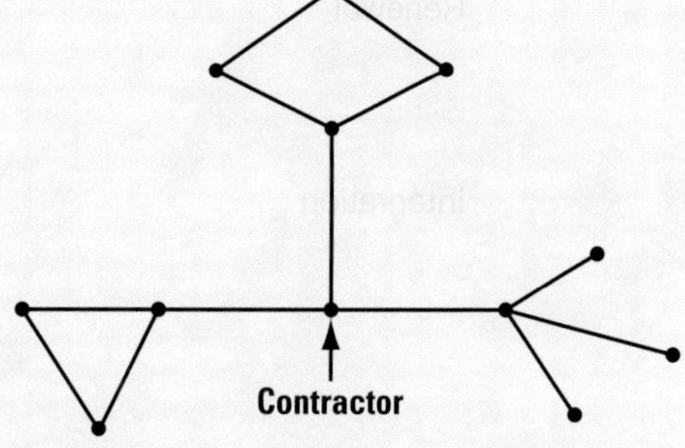

The trend to outsourcing IT professional work also creates new or expanded employment agencies that specialize in matching contractors with companies needing IT expertise for specific projects. The traditional human resource management function, previously carried out by an in-house department, thus also moves outside the organization.

Despite the advantages of greater freedom over when and where they carry out their work, the contractors had to assume responsibility for various costs that are covered the employer in the case of the regular workforce. They are no longer covered by employee-paid benefits such as health care and sick leave, and it is up to them to keep abreast of new technical developments. But the differences don't stop at the financial level. Contractors told Barley and Kunda that their whole lives tended to become monetized. Because they chose when to work or not, they could put an exact price on the times they weren't working; spending time with their children, watching a sports game, etc. As a result, 'many contractors exercised their flexibility by working long hours and forgoing vacations for years at a time' (p. 290). In addition, contractors tended to invest heavily in building social capital through intensive networking, another time-consuming activity on which regular employees focused much less attention.

Barley and Kunda's study suggests that the nature of work and organizations has changed drastically over the past generation, with the flattening of hierarchies, and complex organizations being dismantled in favour of leaner structures relying on short-term networks and alliances with 'free agent' consultants. This new approach does release skilled consultants from a strict nine to five regimen, but ironically the self-employed consultants tended to impose far more onerous working conditions on themselves than their previous employers had done. This phenomenon of self-management appears to be a common feature in contemporary organizations; Willmott amongst others has noted the tendency for organizational discipline to be manifested through the construction of a self-motivating corporate culture rather than through the exercise of hierarchical discipline as was the case in the industrial era.

Willmott, H. (1993), 'Strength is Ignorance; Slavery is Freedom: Managing Culture in Modern Organizations', *Journal of Management Studies,* 30, 515–552.

Gurus, Hired Guns and Warm Bodies, by Simon Barley and Gideon Kunda is published by Princeton University Press.

EXHIBIT 10.3 A Typology of Organization Rites and Their Social Consequences

Type of Rite	Example	Social Consequences
Passage	Induction and basic training, national armed forces	Facilitate transition of persons into social roles and statuses that are new for them
Enhancement	Annual awards night	Enhance social identities and increase status of employees
Renewal	Organization development activities	Refurbish social structures and improve organization functioning
Integration	Office holiday party	Encourage and revive common feelings that bind members together and commit them to the organization

Source: Adapted from Harrison M. Trice and Janice M. Beyer, 'Studying Organizational Cultures through Rites and Ceremonials,' *Academy of Management Review* 9 (1984), 653–659. Used with permission.

commitment. At a recognition ceremony in Birmingham, UK, one award-winner, Natalie Ellis, said that, 'Avon has been a turning point in my life. I've never seen myself as an entrepreneur before, but that's exactly what this job has enabled me to become. I've really surprised myself at how much I've achieved'.[23]

- When Nigeria's Wema Bank emerged from a period of financial difficulties and necessary restructuring, the Bank's leaders organized a colourful relaunching ceremony, including a traditional royal chief, Awujale of Ijebuland, and invited key business and community leaders from the Lagos region. After the chief's speech calling for everyone to work together to support the relaunched bank, he led the invitees in impromptu dancing.[24] This is a rite of renewal.
- When new staff join the Japanese automaker Toyota, they are quickly inculcated in the Toyota Way. Everyone in every Toyota enterprise worldwide, from the humblest cleaner to the top executives, can articulate the company's commitment to respect for people and continuous improvement. Toyota consciously builds a team spirit in which each individual feels they are respected as part of a family. From the company song to the plethora of internal clubs based on sports, hometowns, hobbies, etc.,[25] Toyota supports numerous rites of integration.[26]

Stories **Stories** are narratives based on true events that are frequently shared among organizational employees and told to new employees to inform them about an organization. Many stories are about company **heroes** who serve as models or ideals for serving cultural norms and values. Some stories are considered **legends** because the events are historic and may have been embellished with fictional details. Other stories are **myths**, which are consistent with the values and beliefs of the organization but are not supported by facts.[27] Stories keep alive the primary values of the organization and provide a shared understanding among all employees. Examples of how stories shape culture are as follows:

See online
COUNTERPOINT 10.13

- Stephen Denning was a manager in the African division of the World Bank, a global institution that finances development in poorer countries. He became frustrated that, while Bank staff had lots of knowledge about development issues, it rarely made it down to the grassroots where development workers faced challenges like the explosion of HIV/AIDS cases. After banging his head against the wall trying to make himself heard, he attended a storytelling workshop where he learned how important it is to paint pictures that people can visualize. He started telling the (true) story of how a health worker in Zambia needed some information about AIDS, but unaware of the World Bank, which had lots of expertise located both in-country and globally, she connected to the internet and eventually downloaded information from the Centers for Disease Control in the United States. Most grassroots workers wouldn't have the initiative or technology to go that far in search of information. The story struck a chord with Bank senior staff, and within a couple of years the World Bank had set up a global Knowledge Management division, headed by Denning, that made it its business to ensure that Bank knowledge is effectively disseminated.[28]
- At 3M Corp., the story is told of a vice president who was fired early in his career for persisting with a new product even after his boss had told him to stop because the boss thought it was a stupid idea. After the worker was fired, he stayed in an unused office, working without a salary on the new product idea. Eventually he was rehired, the product was a success, and he was promoted to vice president. The story symbolizes the 3M value of persisting in what you believe in.[29]

COUNTERPOINT 10.3

One problem with corporate storytelling is that the while myths can be powerful and motivate commitment and change, they can also (sometimes at the same time) be misleading and obscure alternative explanations as well as deeper underlying issues. In the case of the World Bank cited above, for example, Stephen Denning's storytelling undoubtedly played a key role in the Bank's decision to invest heavily in 'knowledge management'. The Bank even started to coin itself 'the Knowledge Bank'. But many observers have argued that the information disseminated by the Bank was often little more than self-serving propaganda designed to make the organization seem interested in eradicating global poverty, while the Bank's fiscal programmes that make up the great bulk of its development activity actually lead to deskilling and disinvestment in developing countries, thus actually increasing poverty.[30]

It can also be risky to follow the prescriptions of corporate mythmakers. The Harley-Davison motorbike is famous for having turned around its image from being a heavy, unreliable monster ridden by thugs and leaking oil all over America's highways, to one of the few truly global icons of cool. Harley-Davidson executives naturally like to take credit for the turnaround, telling a story of how they had focused on quality, befriended Harley owners' groups and listened to customers' concerns and even taken to riding the bikes themselves to understand where they could be improved. Douglas Holt convincingly argues that – whether the myth had any basis in truth or not – the actions of executives had nothing to do with Harley's sudden success. Rather, by chance, Harley became a cultural icon through popular culture's mythologization of outlaw culture in movies like *Easy Rider*. Professionals with greying temples and plenty of disposal income saw an opportunity to recapture some of their fading glamour by riding these outlaw machines, and, by fluke, Harley-Davidson Company benefited from a windfall of sales and profits, even though neutral observers say the company was still being badly mismanaged. The company's claim to have masterminded its success might seem harmless enough, except that when executives in other companies try to copy Harley executives' story, they typically end up failing, because that story did not account for the company's success and offers no useful lessons for other companies.[31] **Discuss**

Symbols Another tool for interpreting culture is the **symbol**. A symbol is something that represents another thing. In one sense, ceremonies, stories, slogans and rites are all symbols. They symbolize deeper values of an organization. Another symbol is a physical artifact of the organization. Physical symbols are powerful because they focus attention on a specific item.

In recent years many Korean companies have shifted from bold, aggressive symbols, often based on the company's Roman alphabet initials, towards softer and gentler images designed to communicate a caring company. For example, the Hanwha conglomerate (formerly Hankoook) started in the chemicals industry and developed product lines including military equipment and weapons. It has recently expanded into consumer service industries such as holiday resorts and investment advice, and has adopted a new 'friendly' logo with three hand-drawn circles over the company name printed in gentle, rounded letters (see Exhibit 10.4).[32,33]

See online COUNTERPOINT 10.14

Symbols can also represent negative elements of corporate culture. At Enron, premium parking spots were symbols of power, wealth and winning at any cost. At the company's London office, executives submitted blind e-mail bids for the limited spaces. One top manager paid £4,000 to use a well-placed company spot for a year.[34]

EXHIBIT 10.4 Logo of the Hanwha conglomerate

Language The final technique for influencing culture is **language**. Many companies use a specific saying, slogan, metaphor, motto or other form of language to convey special meaning to employees. Slogans can be readily picked up and repeated by employees as well as customers of the company. The Canadian company Rocky Mountain Soap's slogan, 'Be Kind, Be Real, Be Natural' is not so much a marketing tool as it is a reflection of the company founders' philosophy. Unlike other firms that often misuse words and images of the great outdoors in selling standard industrial products, Rocky Mountain Soap goes to tremendous lengths to remain true to the slogan. Products are developed in the company's small Rocky Mountain headquarters rather than in a laboratory. Only genuine natural ingredients including mountain glacier water are used, and advertising is low key and personal, such as sending customers a free bar of soap on their birthday.[35] Their environmental policy is particularly impressive, and in keeping with products that are 100 per cent natural. The products are biodegradable, do not harm watersheds or eco-systems, there is minimal use of packaging which is selected with sustainability as a priority, they return to the electricity grid an equivalent among of wind power for whatever is used in their workshop and stores, and staff are incentivized to use car-pools or bicycles. Finally, it is acknowledged that the company is not perfect but does try to make its environmental footprint as small as possible. How many other companies, or indeed people, could come anywhere close to making that claim?

Other significant uses of language to shape culture are as follows:

- Before it was acquired by Oracle in a hostile takeover, which had initially been blocked by the US Department of Justice on the grounds that it would break anti-trust laws PeopleSoft Inc. prided itself on a close-knit, family-like culture. Employees called themselves PeoplePeople, shopped at the company PeopleStore, and munched on company-funded PeopleSnacks. The use of this special lingo reinforced the distinctive cultural values. The loss of the culture has been painful for employees, many of whom were laid off after the takeover.[36]

See online COUNTERPOINT 10.15

- Metaphors are often used in order to 'domesticate' corporate activities. For example, when Daimler and Chrysler merged at the end of the twentieth century, phrases such as 'a marriage of equals' and 'a match dictated by chemistry' were used to describe the arrangement, encouraging staff to think positively about the merger as one built on attraction, compatibility and mutual respect. Such use of language can undoubtedly help smooth corporate restructuring, although it always runs the risk of being subverted by disaffected staff; in fact the merger was effectively a Daimler takeover, and some disgruntled Chrysler employees were heard commenting that it was 'more like a shotgun marriage'.[37,38]

See online COUNTERPOINT 10.16

Recall that culture exists at two levels – the underlying values and assumptions and the visible artifacts and observable behaviour. The slogans, symbols and ceremonies just described are artifacts that reflect underlying company values. These visible artifacts and behaviour can be used by managers to shape company values and to strengthen organizational culture.

Organization Design and Culture

Corporate culture should reinforce the strategy and structural design that the organization needs to be effective within its environment. For example, if the external environment requires flexibility and responsiveness, such as the environment for Internet-based companies like Alibaba, the culture should encourage adaptability. The correct relationship among cultural values, organizational strategy and structure and the environment can enhance organizational performance.[39]

See online COUNTERPOINT 10.17

Culture can be assessed along many dimensions, such as the extent of collaboration versus isolation among people and departments, the importance of control and where control is concentrated or whether the organization's time orientation is short range or long range.[40] Here, we will focus on two specific dimensions: (1) the extent to which the competitive environment requires flexibility or stability; and (2) the extent to which the organization's strategic focus and strength are internal or external. Four categories of culture associated with these differences, as illustrated in Exhibit 10.5, are adaptability, mission, clan and bureaucratic.[41] These four categories relate to the fit among cultural values, strategy, structure and the environment. Each can be successful, depending on the needs of the external environment and the organization's strategic focus.

The Adaptability Culture

The **adaptability culture** is characterized by strategic focus on the external environment through flexibility and change to meet customer needs. The culture encourages

EXHIBIT 10.5 Relationship of Environment and Strategy to Corporate Culture

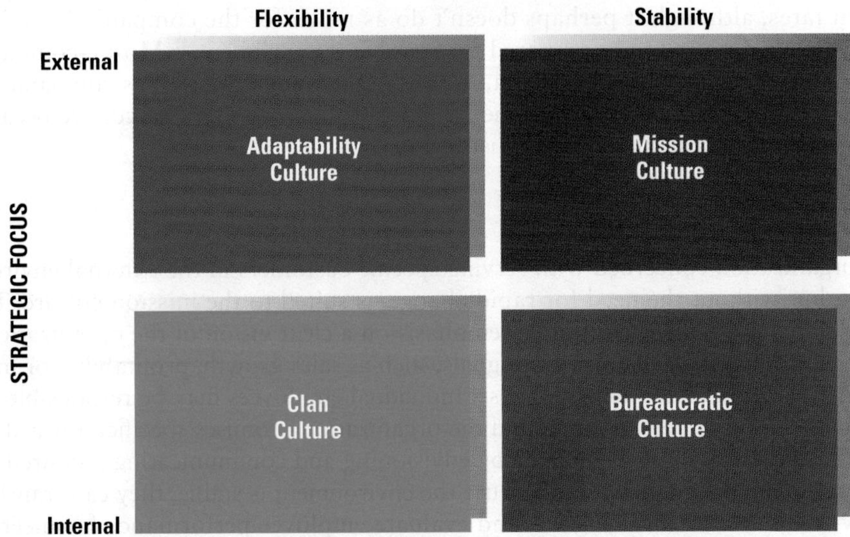

Source: Based on Daniel R. Denison and Aneil K. Mishra, 'Toward a Theory of Organizational Culture and Effectiveness,' *Organization Science* 6, no. 2 (March–April 1995), 204–223; R. Hooijberg and F. Petrock, 'On Cultural Change: Using the Competing Values Framework to Help Leaders Execute a Transformational Strategy,' *Human Resource Management* 32 (1993), 29–50; and R. E. Quinn, *Beyond Rational Management: Mastering the Paradoxes and Competing Demands of High Performance* (San Francisco: Jossey-Bass, 1988).

entrepreneurial values, norms and beliefs that support the capacity of the organization to detect, interpret and translate signals from the environment into new behaviour responses. This type of company, however, doesn't just react quickly to environmental changes – it actively creates change. Innovation, creativity and risk taking are valued and rewarded.

Technology companies need to have an adaptability culture. The pace of change is so fast that any company failing to adapt quickly to competitive innovations will soon be a casualty left behind on information superhighway. The concept of the 'real time enterprise' emerged from the high-tech sector, and reflects the goal of responding instantly to emerging issues. Partly this is possible through technology; BTexact started off as British Telecom's internal business support division but has quickly become a major money-earner helping companies reorganize their back-office functions to save money. That involves smart use of new technology to monitor blockages in processes, such as delays in transferring patient data between doctors' surgeries and hospitals. But success also requires adaptability culture; there is no point spending money on high-tech fixes if staff are unwilling to change. Much of BTexact's work involves working with staff in institutions such as the National Health Service, training them both to use new technology and work more flexibly and efficiently.

Business models are increasing built upon flexibility. The low-cost carrier (LCC) in the airline industry is a good example, so successful indeed that traditional full-service airlines are being priced out of short-haul air travel, particularly in Europe. At companies like Ireland's Ryanair, Hungary's WizzAir and Britain's EasyJet, routes are started up as soon as a business opportunity is sensed, and shut down again

As an organization manager, keep these guidelines in mind:

Make sure corporate culture is consistent with strategy and the environment. Culture can be shaped to fit the needs of both. Four types of culture are adaptability culture, mission culture, clan culture and bureaucratic culture.

See online
COUNTERPOINT 10.18

just as quickly if revenues don't meet expectations. Every possible service except the bare seat on the plane is 'unbundled' and charged separately, from baggage to pillows to refreshments. A small staff team is responsible for multiple functions, with as many ancillary services outsourced as possible. The model works well in keeping down fares, although it perhaps doesn't do as much for the companies' employees, who always need to be prepared for possible retrenchment.[42] Most e-commerce companies, such as China's Alibaba, Amazon and Google, as well as companies in the marketing, electronics and cosmetics industries, use this type of culture because they must move quickly to satisfy customers.

The Mission Culture

An organization concerned with serving specific customers in the external environment, but without the need for rapid change, is suited to the mission culture. The **mission culture** is characterized by emphasis on a clear vision of the organization's purpose and on the achievement of goals, such as sales growth, profitability or market share, to help achieve the purpose. Individual employees may be responsible for a specified level of performance, and the organization promises specified rewards in return. Managers shape behaviour by envisioning and communicating a desired future state for the organization. Because the environment is stable, they can translate the vision into measurable goals and evaluate employee performance for meeting them. In some cases, mission cultures reflect a high level of competitiveness and a profit-making orientation.

Sports teams aim to build a mission culture; for their fans success is easily measured in terms of trophies won, which in turn builds the value of the franchise. Teams that have languished in relative obscurity will make special efforts to create enthusiasm and determination throughout the organization. In Birmingham, England Aston Villa FC is a good example. The team has a storied past but in recent years it has tended to finish in mid-table in England's Premier League. In 2007 the team 'relaunched' itself with an updated crest, a corporate slogan 'Proud History – Bright Future', and a manual outlining consistent messaging that everyone from players to executives to office staff were expected to follow. As the slogan suggests, the mission is built around the idea that the team remains proud of its moment of greatest glory – winning the 1982 European Cup – and determined to recapture that glory. In 2007 – 2008, the season after Villa established this new mission, the team finished in sixth place, its best in the past five years, and good enough to enter the UEFA Cup, Europe's secondary club championship. Whether that relative success owed most to the vision or the club's canny manager Martin O'Neill, is a debate that could enliven many an evening at pubs in Britain's Midlands.[43]

COUNTERPOINT 10.4

The other, 'overlooked' key ingredient for success in the English premier league is the financing of the club. Although teams such as Hull (promoted in successive seasons from lower divisions) have demonstrated that the money of Manchester United and Chelsea is not the sole key to success, the capacity to buy in the best players in the world certainly helps. That said, the capacity to win or draw a football match is not dependent upon individual players but the ability of a team, including the coach, to identify and exploit the weaknesses of its opponents in addition to the balance of good fortune in benefiting from deflections and so on. **Discuss**

Marks and Spencer

Marks and Spencer is a venerable British brand, but for the past few decades it had an image not dissimilar from that of its home country; a formerly great power whose best days seemed to be behind it. While upstart high street chains captured the imagination of Britain's youth, Marks seemed to cater to an ever greyer and staider clientele, an image perhaps encapsulated when the country's redoubtable 1980s Prime Minister Margaret Thatcher declared that M&S was where she liked to shop for her underwear. The company remained well enough loved in the UK, but when executives attempted to replicate the model overseas, the result was a resounding thud. Just because foreigners liked to watch reruns of *Fawlty Towers* and *Yes Minister* did not mean they wanted to dress in the same clothes as the shows' lead characters. When CEO Stuart Rose took over in 2004, the company was bleeding red ink and had retreated wounded from its forays overseas. Rose soon revamped the company's image, sharpening the pencil on prices and targeted a younger clientele to compete with chains like H&M. Exclusive designers were hired, such as Patricia Field, who had styled the clothes for the successful *Sex and the City* TV series. The 1960s model Twiggy came back to model a range of hip clothes for mature women. By 2008, profits were once again above £1 billion, and Rose started to carefully plan another overseas venture, with the company opening its first store in mainland China in October of that year. Unfortunately that coincided with that autumn's financial and stock market meltdown. Even the clearest mission can be brought down by extraneous events.[44]

The Clan Culture

The **clan culture** has a primary focus on the involvement and participation of the organization's members and on rapidly changing expectations from the external environment. This culture is similar to the clan form of control described in Chapter 9. More than any other, this culture focuses on the needs of employees as the route to high performance. Involvement and participation create a sense of responsibility and ownership and, hence, greater commitment to the organization.

In a clan culture, an important value is taking care of employees and making sure they have whatever they need to help them be satisfied as well as productive. Companies in the fashion and retail industries often adopt this culture because it releases the creativity of employees to respond to rapidly changing tastes. Wegmans, a New York, USA-based chain of supermarkets, has succeeded with a clan culture. Employee commitment and satisfaction is considered key to success. Wegmans pays good wages, sends employees on learning trips and offers university scholarships for both full- and part-time employees. Employees are empowered to use their own initiative and creativity in serving customers.[45] Wegmans consistently comes near the top in polls of the best companies to work for in America, and manages at the same time to consistently make good profits.[46]

See online
COUNTERPOINT 10.19

The Bureaucratic Culture

The **bureaucratic culture** has an internal focus and a consistency orientation for a stable environment. This organization has a culture that supports a methodical approach to doing business. Symbols, heroes and ceremonies support cooperation, tradition and following established policies and practices as ways to achieve goals. Personal involvement is somewhat lower here, but that is outweighed by a high level of consistency, conformity and collaboration among members. This organization succeeds by being highly integrated and efficient.

For many years, bureaucratic cultures have suffered a bad press as the corporate environment has favoured flexibility and continuous reinvention. With the global economic troubles that began in 2008, however, some people began to reevaluate this perspective. For example, in Britain, the cautious and conservative building societies – mutual associations that take in deposits from mainly small investors and lend out to home buyers – have mainly been in the decline since the 1980s, when financial services were liberalized. Many building societies converted themselves to banks. The old-time building societies operated according to strict – and 'bureaucratic' – income criteria to decide whether a person would be issued a mortgage to buy a house. In contrast, the new banks lent at ever-higher income ratios, sometimes even handing out mortgage loans of over 100 per cent of the value of the houses on which they were secured, and then went out onto the global money markets in search of cheap, but 'hot', short-term funding for those mortgages. All seemed to work well as house prices continued to rise, but when problems developed in the American financial markets and credit dried up in 2008, several of the new banks quickly went to the wall, and disaster was only averted by enormous and costly government bail-outs.[47]

Culture Strength and Organizational Subcultures

A strong organizational culture can have a powerful impact on company performance. **Culture strength** refers to the degree of agreement among members of an organization about the importance of specific values. If widespread consensus exists about the importance of those values, the culture is cohesive and strong; if little agreement exists, the culture is weak.[48]

A strong culture is typically associated with the frequent use of ceremonies, symbols, stories, heroes and slogans. These elements increase employee commitment to the values and strategy of a company. In addition, managers who want to create and maintain strong corporate cultures often give emphasis to the selection and socialization of employees.[49] Tech Target, a Massachusetts, USA interactive media company, uses a painstaking hiring process to find the kind of employees who will mesh with the company's unique values. Tech Target has an 'open-leave' policy, meaning that employees are free to come and go as they please. The culture emphasizes individual autonomy and personal responsibility; founder and CEO Greg Strakosch tries to hire people who are independent, achievement oriented, conscientious and capable of managing their own time.[50]

However, culture is not always uniform throughout the organization, particularly in large companies. Even in organizations that have strong cultures, there may be several sets of subcultures. **Subcultures** develop to reflect the common problems, goals and experiences that members of a team, department or other unit share. An office, branch or unit of a company that is physically separated from the company's main operations may also take on a distinctive subculture.

For example, although the dominant culture of an organization may be a mission culture, various departments may also reflect characteristics of adaptability, clan or bureaucratic cultures. The manufacturing department of a large organization may thrive in an environment that emphasizes order, efficiency and obedience to rules, whereas the research and development (R&D) department may be characterized by employee empowerment, flexibility and customer focus. This is similar to the concept of differentiation described in Chapter 4, where employees in manufacturing, sales and research departments studied by Paul Lawrence and Jay Lorsch[51] developed different values with respect to time horizon, interpersonal relationships and formality in order to perform the job of each particular department most effectively. Differentiation is particularly common – and necessary – in multinational corporations, where companies need to respond to differing market conditions, cultural differences, regulatory environments and business climates in their operations around the world. When differentiation succeeds, whether in a national or multinational company, it can leverage maximum productivity and revenues from the different capacities within the company. Poorly managed, however, it can result in culture clash or in the loss of proper systems of internal control. Some organization theorists argue that, where the required culture within a particular corporate subdivision varies too greatly from the corporate norm, it can be preferable to spin off that subsidiary into a separate company. The Anglo-Dutch company Unilever, featured in the *In Practice* text box below, is famous for diversity in its products, corporate culture and geographic reach, which at different times has proven both a help and a hindrance to the company's success.

COUNTERPOINT 10.5

This assumes that management is, or should be, in a position to control culture as if it were something that exists independently of their own activities. It may be that 'poor management' is itself a facet of the culture of the company, and one that cannot necessarily be corrected by changing the management. Ultimately, the effectiveness of 'systems of internal control', for example, will depend upon the perceived legitimacy – something that is culturally dependent. **Discuss**

Unilever Plc

Unilever products are available in every country of the world, and one household in every two across the globe has at least one Unilever product in the home. This global reach is in itself an indication of the company's success, which has been built on a far more decentralized corporate strategy than most other large multinationals. Back in 1963 then Chairman George Cole put it succinctly, 'Unilever is not a ship, it is a fleet – several fleets, several hundred subsidiary companies – and the ships are of many different sizes, doing all kinds of different things, all over the place'.

Whereas other companies have focused on the biggest markets in the wealthiest countries, Unilever, with its origins in the colonial era, has been selling in developing countries since the beginning. Given wildly different consumer tastes and different-sized wallets, the only way to succeed was to give the company's national subsidiaries considerable autonomy, allowing them to develop internal cultures and business strategies suitable to the environments in which they were operating. Now that many developing countries are becoming more affluent 'emerging markets', the company's attention to these formerly small markets is paying off in spades; 38 per cent of the company's revenues came from emerging markets in 2005, more than all of Europe. India's Hindustan Unilever, for example, is that emerging giant's largest consumer products company, with an enormous reservoir of goodwill built up over three-quarters of a century of operations. Many of India's top executives cut their teeth at Hindustan Unilever, and the company was chosen fourth-best company in the world for leadership development in 2007 in a Fortune/Hewitt Associates survey.

Nevertheless, Unilever's overall financial performance has been relatively sluggish compared with more centralized competitors like Procter & Gamble, due in part, claim critics, to an inability to draw the line between creative differentiation and local inefficiencies. Patrick Cescau, who took over as CEO in 2005, saw greater corporate coherence as one of his top priorities, 'We have to be culturally relevant, but delivering to a global strategy'. When Cescau retired in 2008, Unilever's board chose for the first time to hire its leader from outside the company, selecting a top executive from Procter & Gamble, further sign that the balance between differentiation and global coordination would continue to be tilted in the latter direction.[52]

Subcultures typically include the basic values of the dominant organizational culture plus additional values unique to members of the subculture. However, subcultural differences can sometimes lead to conflicts between departments, especially in organizations that do not have strong overall corporate cultures. When subcultural values become too strong and outweigh the corporate cultural values, conflicts may emerge and hurt organizational performance. Conflict will be discussed in detail in Chapter 13.

See online
COUNTERPOINT 10.20

Organizational Culture, Learning and Performance

As an organization manager, keep this guideline in mind:

Consciously manage culture to shift values toward high performance and goal accomplishment.

Culture can play an important role in creating an organizational climate that enables learning and innovative response to challenges, competitive threats or new opportunities. A strong culture that encourages adaptation and change enhances organizational performance by energizing and motivating employees, unifying people around shared goals and a higher mission and shaping and guiding employee behaviour so that everyone's actions are aligned with strategic priorities. Thus, creating and influencing an adaptive culture is one of the most important jobs for organizational leaders. The right culture can drive high performance.[53] Singapore Airlines, described the Leading by Design box on the next page, has achieved phenomenal success partly because of its strong adaptive culture.[54] A number of studies have found a positive relationship between culture and performance.[55] *In Corporate Culture and Performance,* Kotter and Heskett provided evidence that companies that intentionally managed cultural values outperformed similar companies that did not. Until recently, the culture within South Korean companies were typically hierarchical and male-dominated, reflecting norms running through a society that for many years had been dominated by the country's military and paternalistic business leaders. But as the country has democratized and opened to the world, values are changing along with corporate needs. With Korean companies' success in global markets, they need to embrace talent and youth and new ideas. Workforces are becoming more diverse with many more women and young people in management positions. Large companies such as Samsung and Hyundai have consciously changed their corporate cultures. Excessive formality in addressing managers has been eliminated, salary and promotion are based on performance rather than longevity and workers are being encouraged to put in quality work time rather than just making sure they stay at the office as long as their bosses. Effective campaigns have been implemented against sexual harassment, with even senior officials disciplined. 'If men insist on the old way, they'll be in trouble', said Cho Yoon Hee, 28, who works at Hyundai Capital, 'we women won't take it any more'.[56,57]

See online
COUNTERPOINT 10.21

A danger for many successful organizations is that the culture becomes set and the company fails to adapt as the environment changes, as we saw in the chapter-opening example of Alliance Boots PLC. When organizations are successful, the values, ideas and practices that helped attain success become institutionalized. As the environment changes, these values may become detrimental to future performance. Many organizations become victims of their own success, clinging to outmoded and even destructive values and behaviour. Thus, the impact of a strong culture is not always positive. Typically, healthy cultures not only provide for smooth internal integration but also encourage adaptation to the external environment. Nonadaptive cultures encourage rigidity and stability. Strong adaptive cultures often incorporate the following values:

1 *The whole is more important than the parts and boundaries between parts are minimized.* People are aware of the whole system, how everything fits together and the relationships among various organizational parts. All members consider how their actions affect other parts and the total organization. This emphasis on the whole reduces boundaries both within the organization and with other companies. Although subcultures may form, everyone's primary attitudes and behaviour reflect the organization's dominant culture. The free flow of people, ideas and information allows coordinated action and continuous learning.

2 *Equality and trust are primary values.* The culture creates a sense of community and caring for one another. The organization is a place for creating a web

Singapore Airlines

Singapore is one of Asia's great success stories, and Singapore Airlines (SIA) is a jewel in the crown of the successful city-state located at the southern tip of the Malay Peninsula. Visitors to Singapore today almost invariably comment on its affluence, sparkling cleanliness and sense of order, but Singapore's success, like that of its flagship airline, is built on careful planning and rigorous discipline. Singapore Airlines was created in 1972, a few years after the country achieved independence from Malaysia. From its earliest days, SIA managers focused on building the ariline's competitive edge as offering uniquely high levels of customer service, building on south-east Asia's reputation for hospitality with the carefully imaged 'Singapore girl' cabin crew. At the same time, the company has always operated at a profit, unlike most other airlines in a highly volatile and competitive industry, demonstrating what one research report describes as the ability to be 'hard' while also being 'soft'. SIA aims to be at the forefront of technological change and innovation in the industry, and has been first to introduce many services that later became industry norms, such as internet booking, web and SMS check-in and a whole range of high-end services to attract and keep the lucrative business executive traveller. At the same time, the company has responded to changing social mores. As women have assumed a larger and more equal role in society, SIA faced increasing criticism from women's groups that SIA's Singapore girl was a sexist and even insulting stereotype of women. Despite denying that it was bowing to pressure, in 2007 the company put out a tender for an image revamp that most expected would result in a more formally professional image for its cabin crew.[58] SIA is in many ways, therefore, an excellent example of the adaptive organization discussed earlier in this chapter. This adaptive approach also extends to the company's activities in corporate social and environmental responsibility. In the post September 11, 2001 world, Singapore Airlines is aiming to be the first to effectively use biometrics to speed a passenger through check-in, baggage drop, and security and on to their flight within a few minutes.

As one of a handful of world-class Singaporean enterprises, SIA makes it its business not merely to practise CSR, but to be at its forefront. The airline operates a number of charitable projects in the Asia – Pacific Region, such as supporting schooling for children from low-income families in the Philippines, as well as various projects such as visiting for the elderly within Singapore. On a more strategic level, the company is invariably represented on committees for national activities such as the Singapore Compact for CSR, which ties in with the United Nations' Global Compact, and offers comprehensive CSR training for smaller and midsize Singaporean companies.[59] Like many projects in the country, the Singapore Compact is a tripartite (government, company, union) initiative. SIA itself is majority-owned by Temasek Holdings, the Singapore government's investment holding vehicle. The biggest corporate image challenge being faced by SIA, along with other world airlines, is climate change and the argument that air travel is a significant contributor to the problem. Once again, Singapore Airlines was out in front of the issue, producing an annual environmental responsibility report for the past seven years, and rejuvenating its fleet.[60] The company was the first in the world to acquire the huge A380 Airbus, which uses less fuel per passenger than smaller planes, but which is viewed with mixed feeling by environmental campaigners because of the additional runway infrastrusture needed to support its enormous weight.

Singapore Airlines' combination of adaptive culture and attention to social and environmental values consistently push the company to the top of global rankings. In 2007 SIA ranked 17th in Fortune's list of the top companies globally, and second in the world in the airline subcategory.[61] In 2008 the company was ranked best airline by the World Airline Awards, the third time in the last ten years that it had bagged that honour.[62]

Singapore Airlines operates in a different social environment than Western companies, Singaporean society is directed by government to a much greater extent than in most western countries, and this gives the company some advantages. For example, in the mid-1990s, when pilots were threatening industrial action, they were warned by Lee Kuan Yew, the 'retired' founder of Singapore, not to step too far out of line. One of the union leaders, who is not a Singaporean citizen, even had his residency permit revoked.[63] Nevertheless, overall Singapore Airlines' high rankings for both customer service and social and environmental responsibility are easily justified.

As an organization manager, keep these guidelines in mind:

To support a learning orientation, emphasize cultural values of openness and collaboration, equality and trust, continuous improvement and risk taking. Build a strong internal culture that encourages adaptation to changing environmental conditions.

of relationships that allows people to take risks and develop to their full potential. The emphasis on treating everyone with care and respect creates a climate of safety and trust that allows experimentation, frequent mistakes and learning. Managers emphasize honest and open communications as a way to build trust.

3 *The culture encourages risk taking, change and improvement.* A basic value is to question the status quo. Constant questioning of assumptions opens the gates to creativity and improvement. The culture rewards and celebrates the creators of new ideas, products, and work processes. To symbolize the importance of taking risks, an adaptive culture may also reward those who fail in order to learn and grow.

As illustrated in Exhibit 10.6, adaptive corporate cultures have different values and behaviour patterns than nonadaptive cultures.[64] In adaptive cultures, managers are concerned with customers and employees as well as with the internal processes and procedures that bring about useful change. Behaviour is flexible and managers initiate change when needed, even if it involves risk. In unadaptive cultures, managers are more concerned about themselves or their own special projects, and their values discourage risk taking and change. Thus, strong, healthy cultures, such as those in learning companies, help organizations adapt to the external environment, whereas strong, unhealthy cultures can encourage an organization to march resolutely in the wrong direction.

EXHIBIT 10.6 Adaptive versus Nonadaptive Corporate Cultures

	Adaptive Corporate Cultures	Nonadaptive Corporate Cultures
Core Values	Managers care deeply about customers, stockholders, and employees. They also strongly value people and processes that can create useful change (for example, leadership initiatives up and down the management hierarchy).	Managers care mainly about themselves, their immediate work group, or some product (or technology) associated with that work group. They value the orderly and risk-reducing management process much more highly than leadership initiatives.
Common Behaviour	Managers pay close attention to all their constituencies, especially customers, and initiate change when needed to serve their legitimate interests, even if it entails taking some risks.	Managers tend to be somewhat isolated, political, and bureaucratic. As a result, they do not change their strategies quickly to adjust to or take advantage of changes in their business environments.

Source: Adapted and reprinted with the permission of The Free Press, a division of Simon & Schuster Adult Publishing Group, from *Corporate Culture and Performance* by John P. Kotter and James L. Heskett. Copyright © 1992 by Kotter Associates, Inc. and James L. Heskett.

Ethical Values and Social Responsibility

Of the values that make up an organization's culture, ethical values are now considered among the most important. Corporate accounting scandals, allegations that top managers of some organizations made personal use of company funds, and charges of insider trading have blanketed the media in recent years. Top corporate managers are under scrutiny from the public as never before, and even small companies are finding a need to put more emphasis on ethics to restore trust among their customers and the community.

Sources of Individual Ethical Principles

Ethics is the code of moral principles and values that governs the behaviour of a person or group with respect to what is right or wrong. Ethical values set standards as to what is good or bad in conduct and decision making.[65] Ethics are personal and unique to each individual, although in any given group, organization or society there are many areas of concensus about what constitutes ethical behaviour.[66] Exhibit 10.7 illustrates the varied sources of individual ethical principles. Each person is a creation of his or her time and place in history. National culture, religious heritage, historical background and so forth lead to the development of societal morality, or society's view of what is right and wrong. Societal morality is often reflected in norms of behaviour and values about what makes sense for an orderly society. Some principles are codified into laws and regulations, such as laws against drunk driving, robbery or murder.

EXHIBIT 10.7 Sources of Individual Ethical Principles and Actions

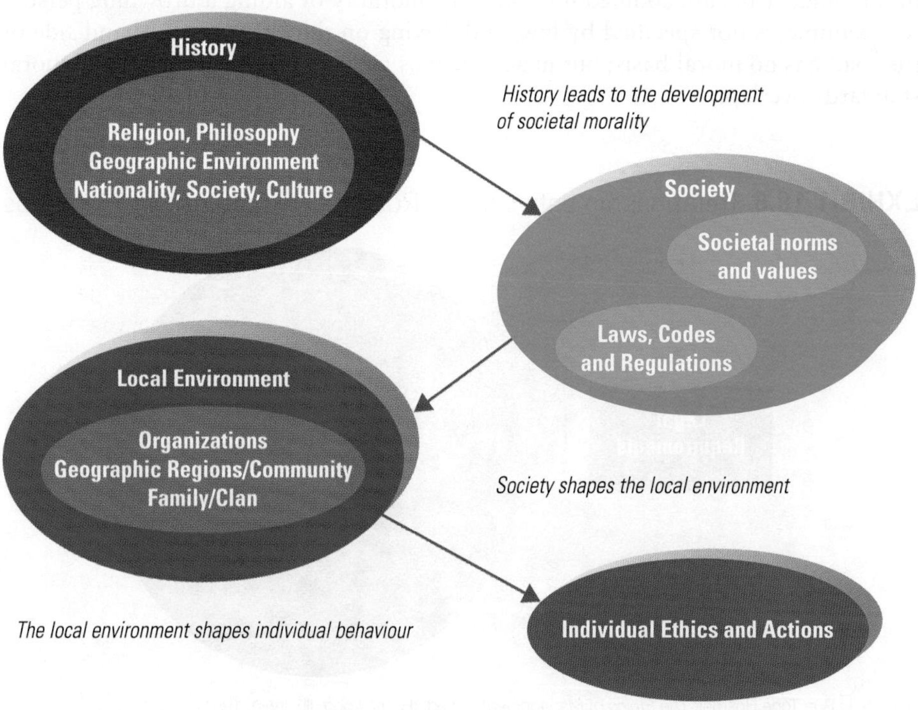

Thanks to Susan H. Taft and Judith White for providing this exhibit.

These laws, as well as unwritten societal norms and values, shape the local environment within which each individual acts, such as a person's community, family and place of work. Individuals absorb the beliefs and values of their family, community, culture, society, religious community and geographic environment, typically discarding some and incorporating others into their own personal ethical standards. Each person's ethical stance is thus a blending of his or her historical, cultural, societal and family backgrounds and influences.

It is important to look at individual ethics because ethics always involve an individual action, whether it be a decision to act or the failure to take action against wrongdoing by others. In organizations, an individual's ethical stance may be affected by peers, subordinates and supervisors, as well as by the organizational culture and broader social norms. Organizational culture often has a profound influence on individual choices and can support and encourage ethical actions or promote unethical and socially irresponsible behaviour.

See online COUNTERPOINT 10.22

As an organization manager, keep these guidelines in mind:

Take control of ethical values in the organization. Ethics is not the same as following the law. Ethical decisions are influenced by management's personal background, by organizational culture and by organizational systems.

Managerial Ethics and Social Responsibility

Recent events have demonstrated the powerful influence of organizational standards on ethical behaviour. Strict ethical standards are becoming part of the formal policies and informal cultures of many organizations, and courses in ethics are taught in many business schools. Many of the recent scandals in the news have dealt with people and corporations that broke the law. But it is important to remember that ethics goes far beyond behaviour governed by law.[67] The **rule of law** arises from a set of codified principles and regulations that describe how people are required to act, that are generally accepted in society and that are enforceable in the courts.[68]

The relationship between ethical standards and legal requirements is illustrated in Exhibit 10.8. Ethical standards for the most part apply to behaviour not covered by the law, and the rule of law applies to behaviour not necessarily covered by ethical standards. Current laws often reflect combined moral judgements, but not all moral judgements are codified into law. The morality of aiding a drowning person, for example, is not specified by law, and driving on the left- or right-hand side of the road has no moral basis; but in acts such as robbery or murder, rules and moral standards overlap.

EXHIBIT 10.8 Relationship between the Rule of Law and Ethical Standards

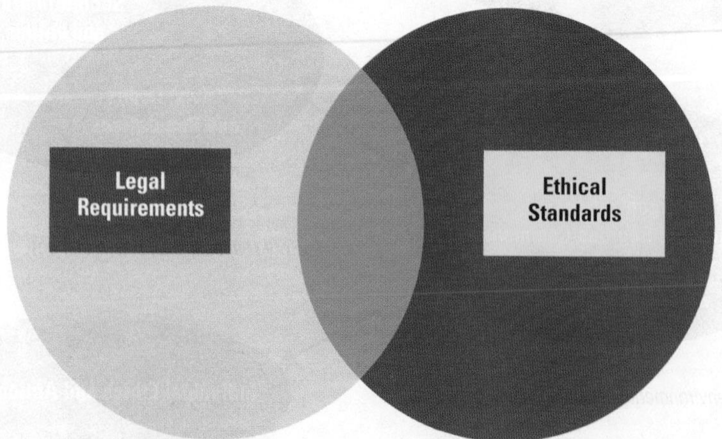

Source: LaRue Tone Hosmer, *The Ethics of Management*, 2d ed. (Homewood, Ill.: Irwin, 1991).

Unethical conduct in organizations is surprisingly widespread. More than 54 per cent of human resource (HR) professionals polled by the US-headquartered Society for Human Resource Management and the Ethics Resource Center reported observing employees lying to supervisors or coworkers, falsifying reports or records or abusing drugs or alcohol while on the job.[69] Many people believe that if you are not breaking the law, then you are behaving in an ethical manner, but this is incorrect. Many deviant behaviours have not been legally codified, and managers must be sensitive to emerging norms and values about those issues. It can even be the case that complying with a law (particularly in an undemocratic regime) may breach a manager's ethical standards. For example, the former apartheid government in South Africa mandated discrimination against the majority black population in various ways including through banning black people from holding certain skilled positions.[70] A manager who blindly administered such an offensive and discriminatory policy would share ethical responsibility for its impact on the black majority population. **Managerial ethics** are principles that guide the decisions and behaviour of managers with regard to whether they are right or wrong. The notion of **social responsibility** is an extension of this idea and refers to management's obligation to make choices and take action so that the organization contributes to the welfare and interest of all organizational stakeholders, such as employees, customers, shareholders, the community and the broader society.[71]

Examples of ethical issues are as follows:[72]

- Top executives are considering promoting a rising sales manager who consistently brings in $70 million a year and has cracked open new markets in places like Brazil and Turkey that are important to the organization's international growth. However, female employees have been complaining for years that the manager is verbally abusive to them, tells offensive jokes and throws temper tantrums if female employees don't do exactly as he says.
- The manager of a beauty supply store is told that she and her salespeople can receive large bonuses for selling a specified number of boxes of a new product, a permanent-wave solution that costs nearly twice as much as what most of her salon customers typically use. She orders the salespeople to store the old product in the back and tell customers there's been a delay in delivery.
- The project manager for a construction planning project wondered whether some facts should be left out of a report because the community where the facility would be built might object if they discovered certain environmental aspects of the project.
- An American manufacturer operating abroad was asked to make cash payments (a bribe) to government officials and was told it was consistent with local customs and the practices of firms from some European countries, despite being illegal in the United States.

See online COUNTERPOINT 10.23

As these examples illustrate, ethics and social responsibility is about making decisions. Managers make choices every day about whether to be honest or deceitful with suppliers, treat employees with respect or disdain and be a good or a harmful corporate citizen. Some issues are exceedingly difficult to resolve and often represent ethical dilemmas. An **ethical dilemma** arises in a situation concerning right and wrong in which values are in conflict.[73] Right or wrong cannot be clearly identified in such situations. For example, for a salesperson at the beauty supply store, the value conflict is between being honest with customers and adhering to the boss's expectations. The manufacturing manager may feel torn between following local customs and being competitive with practices of a European firm, or adhering to US laws concerning bribes. Sometimes, each alternative choice or behaviour seems undesirable.

See online COUNTERPOINT 10.24

Ethical dilemmas are not easy to resolve, but top executives can aid the process by establishing organizational values that provide people with guidelines for making the best decision from a moral standpoint.

Does It Pay to Be Good?

The relationship of an organization's ethics and social responsibility to its performance concerns both organizational managers and organization scholars. Studies have provided varying results but most have found that there is a small positive relationship between ethical and socially responsible behaviour and financial results.[74] It may be, however, that well-managed and successful companies tend to pay attention to corporate ethics, rather than corporate ethics having a direct impact on profitability.[75,76]

As discussed earlier in the chapter, companies with high levels of social capital are more likely to enjoy long-term organizational success. One way that companies can accumulate social capital is through building a reputation for honesty, fairness and doing the right thing. Researchers have found that people prefer to work for companies that demonstrate a high level of ethics and social responsibility, so these companies can attract and retain high-quality employees.[77] Many companies now evaluate their top executives not only on the financial bottom line but also on their effectiveness in demonstrating the corporation's social responsibility.[78] Particularly in fast-growing economies, such as China, retaining capable, committed employees can be a challenge, and large firms such as Standard Chartered and Manulife Financial stress corporate integrity and social responsibility in recruitment campaigns.[79,80]

Many customers pay attention, too, and gear their purchases to companies they view as ethical. However, research shows that while most consumers will state that they have a preference for doing business with ethical companies, not all will translate that preference into actual purchasing habits, and companies designing social responsibility initiatives with a view to attracting and retaining customers would need to identify those segments of the purchasing public likely to be motivated by specific strategies.[81] At the same time, there is some research evidence that many consumers are relatively sceptical about corporations' motives for engaging in ethical activities; overall, consumers are more likely to support companies they believe have an authentic commitment to social responsibility rather than those that simply view it as a marketing ploy.[82,83]

See online COUNTERPOINT 10.25

Companies that put ethics on the back burner in favour of short-term profits ultimately suffer, while those that stick to high ethical standards tend to win out in the longer term. During the Asian economic crisis of the late 1990s, PT Denpoo Mandiri Indonesia (DMI), an Indonesian appliance manufacturer, had a tough decision to make. The crisis led to a dramatic drop in the value of the Indonesian currency, the rupiah, and made appliances much more expensive to manufacture. As a result, contracts it had signed with retailers suddenly became money-losing. Many Indonesian firms reneged on their contracts, which saved money in the short term. DMI, however, decided to bite the bullet. 'As a brand name, we must be trustworthy', says Yeane Keet, DMI's marketing director, 'Even though we had to sell our products at a loss, we continued to honor orders already placed'. As a result, she said, retailers' trust in the company grew and their loyalty repaid the short term losses many times. In 2004, DMI was able to expand its production and sales overseas and is now a big player in several countries in southeast Asia.[84,85]

See online COUNTERPOINT 10.26

Sources of Ethical Values in Organizations

Ethics in organizations is both an individual and an organizational matter. The standards for ethical or socially responsible conduct are embodied within each employee as well as within the organization itself. In addition, external stakeholders can

EXHIBIT 10.9 Forces That Shape Managerial Ethics

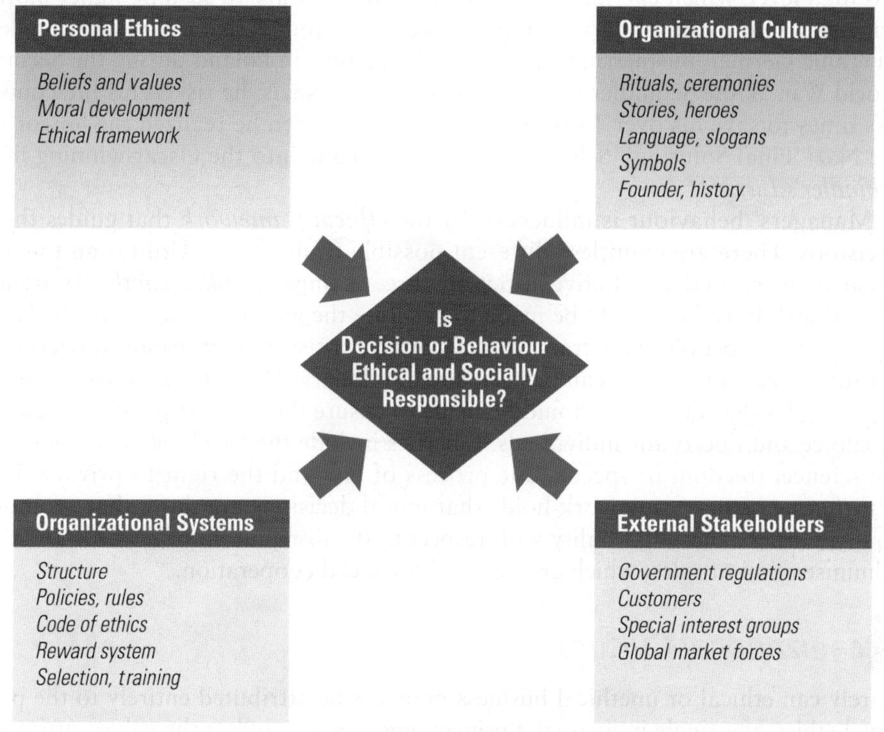

influence standards of what is ethical and socially responsible. The immediate forces that impinge on ethical decisions in organizations are summarized in Exhibit 10.9. Individual beliefs and values, a person's ethical decision framework and moral development influence personal ethics. Organizational culture, as we have already discussed, shapes the overall framework of values within the organization. Moreover, formal organization systems influence values and behaviour according to the organization's policy framework and reward systems. Companies also respond to numerous stakeholders in determining what is right. They consider how their actions may be viewed by customers, government agencies, shareholders and the general community, as well as the impact each alternative course of action may have on various stakeholders. All of these factors can be explored to understand ethical and socially responsible decisions in organizations.[86]

Personal Ethics

Every individual brings a set of personal beliefs and values into the workplace. Personal values and the moral reasoning that translates these values into behaviour are an important aspect of ethical decision making in organizations.[87]

As we discussed earlier, the historical, cultural, family, religious and community backgrounds of managers shape their personal values and provide principles by which they carry out business. In addition, people go through stages of moral development that affect their ability to translate values into behaviour. For example, children have a low level of moral development, making decisions and behaving to obtain rewards and avoid punishment. At an intermediate level of development, people learn to conform to expectations of good behaviour as defined by colleagues and society. Most managers are at this level, willingly upholding the law and responding to societal expectations. At the highest level of moral development are people who develop an internal set of standards. These are self-chosen ethical principles that are more important to decisions than external expectations. Only a few people reach this high level, which can mean breaking laws if necessary to sustain higher moral principles. One extraordinary example of such behaviour is that of Oskar Schindler, an ethnic German businessman who owned a factory in Poland during the Second World War. While Schindler initially supported the Nazis, he risked his life countless times to save his over 1,000 Jewish employees when he realized the horror of the Nazi 'Final Solution'. Schindler's story was made into the Oscar-winning film *Schindler's List*.[88,89]

See online COUNTERPOINT 10.27

Managers' behaviour is influenced by the *ethical framework* that guides their decisions. There are countless different possible frameworks. Utilitarian theory, personal liberty and distributive justice are three examples. *Utilitarian theory* argues that ethical decisions should be made to generate the greatest benefits for the largest number of people. This framework is often consistent with business decisions because costs and benefits can be calculated in dollars. The *personal liberty* framework argues that decisions should be made to ensure the greatest possible freedom of choice and liberty for individuals. Liberties include the freedom to act on one's conscience, freedom of speech, due process of law and the right to privacy. The *distributive justice* framework holds that moral decisions are those that promote equity, fairness and impartiality with respect to the distribution of rewards and the administration of rules, which are essential for social cooperation.[90]

Organizational Culture

Rarely can ethical or unethical business practices be attributed entirely to the personal ethics of a single individual. Business practices also reflect the values, attitudes and behaviour patterns of an organization's culture and in turn of the broader society in which it operates. To promote ethical behaviour in the workplace, companies should make ethics an integral part of the organization's culture. The British surfwear company Finisterre makes ethics and environmental friendliness central to its business model. Founder Tom Kay sells only renewable or recyclable fabrics, and has pulled production out of China because of that country's human rights issues, preferring to source his products from sources such as nuns in Columbia and a women's self-help project.[91]

Organizational culture has a powerful impact on individual ethics because it helps to guide employees in making daily decisions. When the culture supports wrongdoing, it is easier for individual employees to go along. One young Enron employee explained how he slid into unethical decisions and practices in his job: 'It was easy to get into, Well, everybody else is doing it, so maybe it isn't so bad'.[92]

Organizational Systems

The third category of influences that shape managerial ethics is formal organizational systems. This includes the basic architecture of the organization, such as whether ethical values are incorporated in policies and rules; whether an explicit code of ethics is available and issued to members; whether organizational rewards, including praise, attention and promotions, are linked to ethical behaviour; and whether ethics is a consideration in the selection and training of employees. These formal efforts can reinforce ethical values that exist in the informal culture.

Many companies have established formal ethics programmes, sometimes after facing bad publicity. For example, the British defence firm BAE Systems has been widely criticized for unethical conduct in various arms deals, including accusations that it paid bribes to foreign government officials to secure business. While BAE has denied acting unlawfully, it attempted to address the criticism by appointing a former Chief Justice to conduct an ethical review of the company's activities. Lord Woolf made 23 recommendations for a comprehensive ethics programme, including a comprehensive register of all the hospitality provided by the company to its clients and third parties, as well as a regular external audit of the ethics of its business activities. BAE's new CEO promised to implement all 23 recommendations within three years. The company continued to receive criticism for failing to address past conduct, demonstrating how hard it is to rebuild reputations that have already been damaged.[93,94]

External Stakeholders

Managerial ethics and social responsibility are also influenced by a variety of external stakeholders, groups outside the organization that have a stake in the organization's performance. Ethical and socially responsible decision making recognizes that the organization is part of a larger community and considers the impact of a decision or action on all stakeholders.[95] Important external stakeholders are government agencies, customers and special-interest groups such as those concerned with the natural environment.

Companies must operate within the limits of government regulations, including environmental protection requirements, workers' health and safety rules and many other laws and regulations. Numerous companies have come under investigation by financial regulatory bodies such as the Securities and Exchange Commission (SEC) in the United States and the various similar financial oversight authorities around the world for violating laws related to financial controls and accounting practices. In the wake of the global financial meltdown of 2008, the SEC launched more than 50 investigations into the subprime mortgage industry in the US, whose collapse sparked worldwide financial panic. Nevertheless, there was widespread criticism that the SEC, and even more so the European regulatory authorities, acted only after the full-blown crisis had emerged.[96]

Customers are another important stakeholder group. Customers are primarily concerned about the quality, safety and availability of goods and services. For example, fast-food restaurants such as McDonald's, Burger King and Kentucky Fried Chicken have been pressured to reduce or eliminate the presence of trans-fatty acids in in their products in response to growing customer concerns about health risks. Some jurisdictions such as New York in the US and Calgary in Canada have entirely banned trans fats in response to pressure from consumers and the medical profession.[97,98]

Special-interest groups continue to be one of the largest stakeholder concerns that companies face. Today, those concerned with corporate responsibility to the natural environment are particularly vocal. Thus, environmentalism is becoming an integral part of organizational planning and decision making for leading companies. The concept of *sustainable development*, a dual concern for economic growth and environmental sustainability, has been gaining ground among many business leaders. The public is no longer comfortable with organizations focusing solely on profit at the expense of the natural environment. Environmental sustainability – meaning that what is taken out of the environmental system for food, shelter, clothing, energy and other human uses is restored to the system in waste that can be reused – is a part of strategy for companies like Canon, Unilever, Toyota, Nike and IKEA. In 2006 Toyota announced that it was committed to becoming a carbon-neutral company and producing zero emissions, and other carmakers such as BMW quickly followed suit (though none has yet to come close to that goal).[99]

How Leaders Shape Culture and Ethics

Top management have a key role in providing commitment, leadership and examples for ethical behaviour.[100] The CEO and other top managers must be committed to specific values and provide constant leadership in tending and renewing the values. Values can be communicated in a number of ways – speeches, company publications, policy statements and, especially, personal actions. Top leaders are responsible for creating and sustaining a culture that emphasizes the importance of ethical behaviour for all employees every day. When the CEO engages in unethical practices or fails to take firm and decisive action in response to the unethical practices of others, this attitude filters down through the organization. Formal ethics codes and training programmes are worthless if leaders do not set and live up to high standards of ethical conduct.[101]

The following sections examine how managers signal and implement values through leadership as well as through the formal systems of the organization.

Values-based Leadership

As an organization manager, keep these guidelines in mind:

Act as a leader for the internal culture and ethical values that are important to the organization. Influence the value system through values-based leadership, including the use of ceremonies, slogans, symbols and stories. Communicate important values to employees to enhance organizational effectiveness, and remember that actions speak louder than words.

The underlying value system of an organization cannot be managed in the traditional way. Issuing an authoritative directive, for example, has little or no impact on an organization's value system. Organizational values are developed and strengthened primarily through **values-based leadership**, a relationship between a leader and followers that is based on shared, strongly internalized values that are advocated and acted upon by the leader.[102]

Leaders influence cultural and ethical values by clearly articulating a vision for organizational values that employees can believe in, communicating the vision throughout the organization and institutionalizing the vision through everyday behaviour, rituals, ceremonies and symbols, as well as through organizational systems and policies. Anita Roddick, the founder of the Body Shop beauty product chain who died suddenly in 2007, was the pioneer of corporate social activism. Her business was phenomenally successful, with over 2,000 stores in 55 countries. However, she never deviated from her commitment to sell only natural products that had not been tested on animals and her belief in a fairer world. She sought to operationalize her values through the company; the Body Shop was one of the first companies in the world to report regularly and comprehensively on its performance meeting its ethical and social responsibility goals. Roddick also espoused radical politics – she had no hesitation in joining protestors who shut down World Trade Organization meetings in Seattle in 1999, and was active in several campaigning NGOs including Greenpeace. Roddick's success and popularity made corporate social responsibility fashionable in the UK and internationally.[103]

COUNTERPOINT 10.6

This presumes that employees are seeking values or a vision they can believe in. Might they not already have their own values and visions? If they are 'ethically developed' then it is probable that they will be sceptical about leaders' efforts to 'institutionalize' values which they may feel are being imposed upon them. The outcome is as likely to ferment resentment or compliance as it is to increase commitment. **Discuss**

Managers need to lead by example. Typically, companies that fall victim to large scale employee wrongdoing are found to have weak ethical leadership. At Société Générale, the major French bank, a junior 'rogue trader' lost nearly €5 billion in 2008 through unauthorized trades, While Société Générale CEO Daniel Bouton initially called the errant trader a 'terrorist', Bouton was eventually forced to step down when government and independent investigators found that internal controls were lax. The accused trader claimed that he was under pressure to deliver large trading profits, that company officials knew what he was doing, and that other traders routinely made similar financial bets. At the same time, Société Générale executives were embroiled in a court case involving alleged money laundering between Israel and France. The story was familiar to Nick Leeson, the trader whose failed financial market gambles caused the collapse of Baring's Bank 13 years earlier. Leeson claims that because of the huge profits he seemed to be making, he became a celebrity at Baring's: 'The management of the bank holds you up as an example of how they want things to be done'. British financial journalist Jules Stewart summarizes the problem: 'Due to corporate greed...the people who should have known better turned a blind eye to what were obvious danger signals'.[104]

Employees learn about values, beliefs and goals from watching managers, just as students learn which topics are important for an exam and how to get a good grade from their teachers. To be effective values-based leaders, executives often use symbols, ceremonies, speeches and slogans that match the values. Siemens, the giant German technology group, was shaken by a bribery scandal uncovered in 2006. Apparently, for many years and in many different countries, the company had been providing illegal bribes and kick-backs to win contracts; it was a way of doing business that had become ingrained. It was crucial that Siemens act decisively to restore faith in the company. Although the previous CEO and other top managers denied wrongdoing, they stepped down. The board hired a top New York law firm as outside investigators of the scandal; their independence made it possible to dig into what had happened over a period of many years, thus ensuring transparency.

The new Siemens CEO Peter Loescher is Austrian, the first time the company has chosen a non-German leader, another sign that the board was determined to mark a break with an inward-looking and self-justifying corporate culture that had hitherto marked Siemens and German industry as a whole. Loescher, former head of pharmaceutical giant Merck, quickly took several decisive steps to draw a line under the scandal. To begin with, he made clear the new rule by which Siemens was going to play: 'From Day One, what I have clearly communicated to everyone is that we have a Zero Tolerance policy; that there is absolutely no grey zone and that Siemens stands for clean business everywhere, and at all times. So you establish this principle, and you clearly lead it from the top. And this is what both my colleagues and myself are doing every day, reinforcing this leadership principle in the organisation.' Loescher also appointed a general counsel at management board level, who is responsible for compliance. All control functions were centralized (many of the bribery accusations came from different national subsidiaries), and the company's global operations in general were placed under strong central leadership, rather than the previous decentralized model that may have encouraged a 'hear no evil, see no evil' attitude towards national subsidiaries at corporate headquarters.[105]

See online
COUNTERPOINT 10.28

Values-based leaders engender a high level of trust and respect from employees, based not only on their stated values but also on the courage, determination and self-sacrifice they demonstrate in upholding them. Leaders can use this respect and trust to motivate employees toward high-level performance and a sense of purpose in achieving the organizational vision. When leaders are willing to make personal sacrifices for the sake of values, employees also become more willing to do so. This element of self-sacrifice puts a somewhat spiritual connotation on the process of leadership. Indeed, one writer in organization theory, Karl Weick, has said that 'managerial work can be viewed as managing myth, symbols and labels; because managers traffic so often in images, the appropriate role for the manager may be evangelist rather than accountant'.[106]

John Tu and David Sun, cofounders of Kingston Technology Co., are first generation immigrants to the US from Taiwan, who provide an example of values-based leadership.

Kingston Technology Co.

'Business is not about money', says David Sun, vice president and chief operating officer of Kingston Technology Co., a US-headquartered company with production facilities on three continents. Kingston manufactures memory products for personal computers, laser printers, digital cameras and other products. 'It's about relationships.' Sun and his cofounder, president John Tu, strive to develop deep, caring, trusting relationships with employees. 'They are part of the team', says one employee of the partnership that workers feel with leaders at Kingston. 'They are not owners; they are employees. And that value system is passed on'.

Sun and Tu believe everyone in the company is a leader, so they share the wealth with employees. When the two sold 80 per cent of Kingston to Softbank Corp. of Japan for $1.5 billion in 1996, they set aside $100 million of the proceeds for employee bonuses. The initial distribution of $38 million went to about 550 employees who were with the company at the time of its sale. Another $40 million has since been divvied up among the company's current 4,000 workers. Sun and Tu seem genuinely puzzled by people's astonishment that they would give $100 million to employees. It seems only right to them. In 1999, John Tu and David Sun bought back the 80 per cent of Kingston owned by Softbank for $450 million.

Despite this generosity, when people talk about why they like working for Kingston, they rarely mention money and benefits. Instead, they talk about personal acts of gentleness or kindness performed by the two top leaders. There are many stories of these leaders quietly offering money, time, other resources – or just genuine concern – to employees who were dealing with family or personal troubles. This approach to leadership creates an emotional bond with employees that builds mutual trust and respect. Employees feel that they are part of a caring family. And because employees are treated with kindness, care and respect, they pass that attitude on in their relationships with each other and with customers, suppliers and other outsiders. Employees are highly motivated to meet organizational goals and keep the company's reputation for doing the right thing. Says one, 'We try to keep the family name a good name'.[107]

Kingston Values

The Kingston spirit reflects an individual commitment, based on teamwork and loyalty, to reach a standard of exceptional quality, reliability and service in providing system enhancements to our customers worldwide.

Respect... for one another in our culturally diverse environment.

Loyalty... for our long-term partnerships.

Integrity & Fairness... in all aspects of business.

Flexibility & Adaptability... in responding to our customers' needs.

Investing in Our Employees... to continuously improve our most valuable resource.

Having fun... working in the company of friends.

http://www.kingston.com/company/values.asp

Formal Structure and Systems

Another set of tools leaders can use to shape cultural and ethical values is the formal structure and systems of the organization. These systems have been especially effective in recent years for influencing managerial ethics.

Structure Managers can assign responsibility for ethical values to a specific position, as was the case with Siemens, noted above. This not only allocates organization time and energy to the problem but symbolizes to everyone the importance of ethics. One example is an **ethics committee**, which is a cross-functional group of executives who oversee company ethics. The committee provides rulings on questionable ethical issues and assumes responsibility for disciplining wrongdoers. By appointing top-level executives to serve on the committee, the organization signals the importance of ethics.

COUNTERPOINT 10.7

Recognizing the significance of ethics within the structure of a company can signal their importance. But it can also be a substitute, rather than an impetus, for reflection upon the institutionalized ethics of a company. To what extent do ethics codes, committees and hotlines actively encourage scrutiny of the ethics of the company's treatment of its employees or its impact upon the environment? Or could it be that these elements are introduced mainly to ensure that the company minimizes its exposure to exceptional recklessness or bad publicity? **Discuss**

Today, many large organizations have ethics departments that manage and coordinate all corporate ethics activities. These departments are headed by a **chief ethics or chief compliance officer**, a high-level company executive who oversees all aspects of ethics, including establishing and broadly communicating ethical standards, setting up ethics training programmes, supervising the investigation of ethical problems and advising managers on the ethical aspects of corporate decisions.[108] This position was almost unheard of twenty years ago, but recent ethical and legal problems have created a growing demand for these specialists. Between 1992 and 2008, membership in the Ethics and Compliance Officer Association, a US-based trade group with membership on six continets, soared from only twelve companies to over 1,300. There are similar business ethics associations based in Europe and Asia, as well as a global network of organizations promoting business ethics.[109,110]

Ethics offices sometimes also work as counselling centres to help employees resolve difficult ethical dilemmas. The focus is as much on helping employees make the right decisions as on disciplining wrongdoers. Many ethics offices have confidential **ethics hotlines** that employees can use to seek guidance as well as report questionable behaviour. One organization calls its hotline a 'Guide Line' to emphasize its use as a tool for making ethical decisions as well as reporting lapses.[111] Some organizations such as Singapore International Airlines (SIA) operate their ethics hotline in-house. SIA's ethics hotline can be reached by telephone or email 24 hours a day, and is for staff, vendors, suppliers and anyone else who deals with the airline. Other organizations such as Japan's Pioneer Corporation electronics group contract with outside organizations to run their hotline; Pioneer's is an email service run by Integrex, a Japanese firm that specializes in running ethics hotlines and similar services. The hotline at Pioneer feeds into a high-level Business Ethics Committee chaired by the company President and CEO and including among its members company officers, division managers, board members including outside directors and corporate auditors.[112]

As an organization manager, keep these guidelines in mind:

Use the formal systems of the organization to implement desired cultural and ethical values. These systems include an ethics committee, a chief ethics officer, disclosure mechanisms, a code of ethics, a mission statement and training in ethical decision-making frameworks.

Disclosure Mechanisms A confidential hotline is also an important mechanism for employees to voice concerns about ethical practices. Holding organizations accountable depends to some degree on individuals who are willing to speak up if they suspect illegal, dangerous or unethical activities. Organizations can establish policies and procedures to support and protect *whistle-blowers*. **Whistle-blowing** is employee disclosure of illegal, immoral or illegitimate practices on the part of the organization.[113] One value of corporate policy is to protect whistle-blowers so they will not be transferred to lower-level positions or fired because of their ethical concerns. A policy can also encourage whistle-blowers to stay within the organization – for instance, to quietly blow the whistle to responsible managers.[114] Whistle-blowers have the option to stop organizational activities by going to newspaper or television reporters, but as a last resort. As ethical problems in the corporate world increase, many companies are looking for ways to protect whistle-blowers. In addition, calls are increasing for stronger legal protection for those who report illegal or unethical business activities.[115] When there are no protective measures, whistle-blowers suffer and the company may continue its unethical or illegal practices.

See online COUNTERPOINT 10.29

Many whistle-blowers suffer financial and personal loss to maintain their personal ethical standards. Katherine Gun, a translator at Britain's secretive General Communications Headquarters (GCHQ) was fired when she leaked an email said to come from US authorities that discussed a plan to arrange illegal wiretapping of United Nations delegates in order to support the US plan to invade Iraq. Gun was initially charged with breaching Britain's Official Secrets Act. The British government eventually dropped the charges. Gun went on to form the Truth-Telling Coalition, an international association devoted to protecting whistle-blower s in similar situations.[116]

See online COUNTERPOINT 10.30

Corporate whistle-blowers are often in an even weaker situation than those in the public sector. Corporations can often claim that whistle-blowers have damaged their commercial interests and/or failed to pursue all avenues within the company, even where the whistle-blower legitimately fears that complaining internally about some unethical practice will merely result in the company covering up the misdeed and getting rid of the whistle-blower. Sherron Watkins, a former executive with Enron, complained to CEO Kenneth Lay about the huge holes in company finances that were being covered up.[117] An internal enquiry was held that largely dismissed her claims, which were of course justified when the company collapsed a few months later.

Whistle-blowers are better protected in the US than in most other countries; the Sarbanes-Oxley Act of 2002, which was enacted in the wake of Enron and other corporate scandals, provides for severe criminal penalties against anyone victimizing a whistle-blower. Increasingly, companies will blow the whistle on each other when they realize that they have engaged in illegal activity such as price-fixing, that is likely to come to light. This is because the corporate whistle-blower is often granted immunity in return for testifying against their competitors and erstwhile price-fixers. In 2007, Virgin Atlantic, Britain's second largest long-haul airline, approached the Office of Fair Trading with details of a scheme it had been running with British Airways, the country's biggest airline, to set the fuel surcharge charged by the two airlines, which operate a near duopoly on many routes. In return for blowing the whistle on its competitor, Virgin avoided a fine and criminal prosecution of participating executives. British Airways, on the other hand, was fined £271.5 million and four executives were charged with criminal price-fixing.[118]

Despite the obvious temptation to cover up scandal, enlightened companies will strive to create a climate and a culture in which employees feel free to point out problems and managers take swift action to address concerns about unethical or illegal activities. Organizations should view whistle-blowing as a benefit to the company, helping to prevent the kind of disasters that have hit companies such as Enron, Parmalat and Arthur Andersen, and make dedicated efforts to encourage and protect whistle-blowers.

Code of Ethics In the 1980s about three-quarters of large American companies had separate codes of ethics, and by the end of the 1990s that had risen to over 90 per cent. Codes of ethics were less widespread although still very common in European-based firms, with more than half of British and German firms having codes, although French firms lagged behind at less than one-third.[119] A **code of ethics** is a formal statement of the company's values concerning ethics and social responsibility; it clarifies to employees what the company stands for and its expectations for employee conduct. At Toyota, for example, the code of ethics is contained in two interlinked documents, the Guiding Principles of Toyota, which sets out the company's broad long-term goals, and the Toyota Code of Conduct, which outlines what is expected of employees on a daily basis; the first clause of the latter document requires employees to, 'honor the language and spirit of the law of every nation and undertake open and fair corporate activities to be a good corporate citizen of the world'.[120] The code specifies the types of behaviour expected to honour the Guiding Principles of Toyota, and encourages employees to use available company resources to help make ethical choices and decisions.[121] Codes of ethics may cover a broad range of issues, including statements of the company's guiding values; guidelines related to issues such as workplace safety, the security of proprietary information or employee privacy; and commitments to environmental responsibility, product safety and other matters of concern to stakeholders. Research comparing companies' ethics codes has found that European companies are more likely than North American to have ethics codes that go beyond strict legal compliance and mandate compliance with broader norms of ethical responsibility.[122]

See online
COUNTERPOINT 10.31

Written codes of ethics are important because they clarify and formally state the company's values and expected ethical behaviour. However, it is essential that top managers support and reinforce the codes through their actions, including rewards for compliance and discipline for violations. Otherwise, a code of ethics is nothing more than a piece of paper. Indeed, one study found that companies with a written code of ethics are just as likely as those without a code to be found guilty of illegal activities which suggests that, on their own, codes, committees and hotlines are not particularly effective in engendering ethical conduct.[123] Many companies that run into trouble with regulatory authorities and the formal legal system had well-developed codes of ethics, but managers failed to support and enforce ethical values. For example the US firm Halliburton, which is accused of having bribed officials to win contracts in Nigeria, and having overcharged the US government for goods and services in Iraq, has a comprehensive code of business conduct, as does British Airways, despite its involvement in the price fixing scandal mentioned above.[124]

Training Programmes To ensure that ethical issues are considered in daily decision making, companies can supplement a written code of ethics with employee training programmes.[125] At GlaxoSmithKline new employees receive ethics information and training as part of their induction.[126,127] BP has established a comprehensive ethical business programme with key elements including a layered roll-out to ensure buy-in from key communicators within the organization, an annual compliance and ethics certification process, ethical code integration into all employees' performance evaluation processes and a number of other programme elements.[128,129]

In an important step, ethics programmes also include frameworks for ethical decision making, such as the utilitarian approach described earlier in this chapter. Learning these frameworks helps managers act autonomously and still think their way through a difficult decision. In a few companies, managers are also taught about the stages of moral development, which helps to bring them to a high level of ethical decision making. This training has been an important catalyst for establishing ethical behaviour and integrity as critical components of strategic competitiveness.[130]

These formal systems and structures can be highly effective. However, they alone are not sufficient to build and sustain an ethical company. Ethics should be integrated into the organizational culture, and leaders need to support and renew ethical values through their words and actions.

See online
COUNTERPOINT 10.32

Corporate Culture and Ethics in a Global Environment

Singapore Airlines – discussed in detail in the Learning by Design box – is proof that the global environment is a place of both cultural convergence and continuing divergence. Managers find this to be true not only in terms of economics or HR issues, but also in terms of cultural and ethical values. Organizations operating in many different areas of the world have to be extremely flexible to successfully deal with diverse cultural and market factors. The greater complexity of the environment and organizational domain create a greater potential for ethical problems or misunderstandings.[131] In Europe, for example, there is strong public and regulatory resistance to companies sharing data about their customers, whereas such sensibilities are less prevalent in North America.[132] Strong and effective organizational cultures are key to success, but they may be less effective in a widely divergent global environment. How can companies develop ethics codes or other ethical structures and systems that address the complex issues associated with doing business on a global scale?

Corporate culture and national culture are intertwined, as discussed in Chapter 9, and the global diversity of many of today's companies presents a challenge to managers trying to build a strong organizational culture. Employees who come from different countries often have varied attitudes and beliefs that can make it difficult to establish a sense of community and cohesiveness based on the corporate culture. In fact, some research has indicated that national culture has a greater impact on employees than does corporate culture.[133] For example, a study of effectiveness and cultural values in Russia found that flexibility and collectivism (working together in groups), which are key values in the national culture, are considerably more important to organizational effectiveness than they are for most US-based companies.[134] When these values are not incorporated into the organizational culture, employees tend not to perform as well. Another recent study found that differences in national cultural values and preferences also create significant variance in ethical attitudes among people from different countries.[135]

Some companies have been successful in developing a broad global perspective that permeates the entire organizational culture. For example, Omron, a global company with headquarters in Kyoto, Japan, has offices on six continents. However, until a few years ago, Omron had always assigned Japanese managers to head them. Today, it relies on local expertise in each geographical area and blends the insights and perspectives of local managers into a global whole. Global planning meetings are held in offices around the world. In addition, Omron established a global database and standardized its software to ensure a smooth exchange of information among its offices worldwide. It takes time to develop a broad cultural mind-set and spread it throughout the company, but firms such as Omron try to bring a multicultural approach to every business issue.[136]

Professor Vijay Govindarajan, who teaches at Dartmouth College, USA, offers some guidance for managers trying to build a global culture. His research indicates that, even though organizational cultures may vary widely, there are specific components that characterize a global culture. These include an emphasis on multicultural rather than national values, basing status on merit rather than nationality, being open to new ideas from other cultures, showing excitement rather than trepidation when entering new cultural environments and being sensitive to cultural differences without being limited by them.[137]

Global ethics is also challenging today's organizations to think more broadly. Many are using a wide variety of mechanisms to support and reinforce their ethics initiatives on a global scale. One of the most useful mechanisms for building global ethics is the **social audit**, which measures and reports the ethical, social and environmental impact of a company's operations.[138] While many companies carry out one or other type of social audit, Social Accountability International, an NGO, has established a standardized measure, the Social Accountability 8000, or SA8000,[139] which provides some consistency in measuring corporate social impact throughout. The system is designed to work like the ISO 9000 quality-auditing system of the International Standards Organization.

Many companies are taking steps to ensure that their factories and suppliers meet SA8000 standards, especially where they operate in developing countries where formal corporate regulation may be weak or non-existent. While most companies seeking SA8000 audits are multinationals, domestic firms in emerging markets are starting to make use of the audits. China First Division Construction and Development Company, a State-owned enterprise in China, recently became the first construction company in the country to achieve the standard.[140,141] Companies can also ask an outside company to perform an independent social audit to measure how well the company is living up to its ethical and social values and how it is perceived by different stakeholder groups.

In the coming years, organizations will continue to evolve in their ability to work with varied cultures, to combine them into a cohesive whole, to live up to high social and ethical standards worldwide and to cope with the conflicts that may arise when working in a multicultural environment.

Summary and Interpretation

This chapter covered a range of material on corporate culture, the importance of cultural and ethical values and techniques managers can use to influence these values. Cultural and ethical values can help determine the organization's social capital, and the right values can contribute to organizational success.

Organizational cultures can serve to integrate members so that they know how to relate to one another and adapt their productive capabilities to the external environment. Culture is enacted through rites and ceremonies, stories and heroes, symbols and language.

Organizational culture may reflect and reinforce or be in tension with the strategy and structure of the organization and its members efforts to adapt to, or control, its environment. Four types of culture that may exist in organizations are adaptability culture, mission culture, clan culture and bureaucratic culture. When widespread consensus exists about the importance of specific values, the organizational culture is characterized as strong and may have a cult-like cohesiveness. However, even in organizations with strong cultures, several sets of subcultures may emerge.

Ethical decision making in organizations is shaped by many factors: personal characteristics, which include personal beliefs, moral development and the adoption of ethical frameworks for decision making; organizational culture, which is the extent to which values, heroes, traditions and symbols reinforce ethical decision making; organizational systems, which pertain to the formal structure, policies, codes of ethics and reward systems that reinforce ethical or unethical choices; and the interests and concerns of external stakeholders, which include government agencies, customers and special interest groups.

Values-based leadership embraces the idea that leaders define a vision of proper values, communicate it throughout the organization and institutionalize it through everyday behaviour, rituals, ceremonies and symbols. We also noted how formal systems are important for shaping ethical values. Formal systems include the existence of an ethics committee, disclosure mechanisms for whistle-blowing, ethics training programmes and a code of ethics. Social audits can also provide a useful tools for companies trying to maintain ethical standards on a global basis.

As business increasingly crosses geographical and cultural boundaries, leaders face difficult challenges in establishing ethical values with which employees can readily accept. Companies that develop global cultures emphasize multicultural values, emphasize merit rather than nationality, rise to the challenge of new cultural environments, remain open to ideas from other cultures and are sensitive to different cultural values without being limited by them.

KEY CONCEPTS

adaptability culture
bureaucratic culture
chief ethics officer
clan culture
code of ethics
culture
culture strength
ethical dilemma
ethics
ethics committee
ethics hotlines
external adaptation
heroes
internal integration
language
legends
managerial ethics
mission culture
myths
rites and ceremonies
rule of law
social audit
social capital
social responsibility
stories
subcultures
symbol
values-based leadership
whistle-blowing

Discussion Questions

1 Describe observable symbols, ceremonies, dress or other aspects of culture and the underlying values they represent for an organization where you have worked.

2 What might be some of the advantages of having several subcultures within an organization? The disadvantages?

3 Explain the concept of social capital. Name an organization currently in the business news that seems to have a high degree of social capital and one that seems to have a low degree.

4 Do you think a bureaucratic culture would be less employee oriented than a clan culture? Discuss.

5 Why is values-based leadership so important to the influence of culture? Does a symbolic act communicate more about company values than an explicit statement? Discuss.

6 Are you aware of a situation in which either you or someone you know was confronted by an ethical dilemma, such as being encouraged to inflate an expense account? Do you think the person's decision was affected by individual moral development or by the accepted values within the company? Explain.

7 Why is equality an important value to support learning and innovation? Discuss.

8 What importance would you attribute to leadership statements and actions for influencing ethical values and decision making in an organization?

9 How do external stakeholders influence ethical decision making in an organization? Discuss why globalization has contributed to more complex ethical issues related to external stakeholders.

10 Codes of ethics have been criticized for transferring responsibility for ethical behaviour from the organization to the individual employee. Do you agree? Do you think a code of ethics is valuable for an organization?

11 Top executives at numerous technology companies, including Nortel Networks, Sun Microsystems and Cisco, made millions of dollars from the sale of stock during the 'bubble years' of 1999–2001. When the bubble burst, ordinary investors lost 70 to 90 per cent of their holdings. Do you see anything wrong with this from an ethical standpoint? How do you think this affects the social capital of these organizations?

Workbook Shop 'til You Drop: Corporate Culture in the Retail World

To understand more about corporate culture, visit two retail stores and compare them according to various factors. Go to one discount or low-end store, such as Lidl or Primark, and to one high-end store, such as Harrod's or Waitrose, or their equivalents in your country. Do not interview any employees, but instead be an observer or a shopper. After your visits, fill out the following table for each store. Spend at least 2 hours in each store on a busy day and be very observant.

Questions

1. How does the culture seem to influence employee behaviour in each store?
2. What effect does employees' behaviour have on customers?
3. Which store was more pleasant to be in? How does that relate to the mission of the store?

Workshop The Power of Ethics

This exercise will help you to better understand the concept of ethics and what it means to you.

1. Spend about 5 minutes individually answering the questions below.
2. Divide into groups of four to six members.
3. Have each group try to achieve consensus with answers to each of the four questions. For question 3, choose one scenario to highlight. You will have 20 to 40 minutes for this exercise, depending on the instructor.
4. Have groups share their answers with the whole class, after which the instructor will lead a discussion on ethics and its power in business.

Questions

1. In your own words, define the concept of ethics in one or two sentences.
2. If you were a manager, how would you motivate your employees to follow ethical behaviour? Use no more than two sentences.
3. Describe a situation in which you were faced with an ethical dilemma. What was your decision and behaviour? How did you decide to do that? Can you relate your decision to any concept in the chapter?
4. What do you think is a powerful ethical message for others? Where did you get it from? How will it influence your behaviour in the future?

Adapted by Dorothy Marcic from Allayne Barrilleaux Pizzolatto's 'Ethical Management: An Exercise in Understanding Its Power', *Journal of Management Education* 17, no. 1 (February 1993), 107–109.

CASE FOR ANALYSIS

TARCO GmbH*

By Henrik Sørensen, *Aarhus University*

TARCO GmbH is a medium-sized Germany-based manufacturer of domestic appliances. TARCO has quite a comprehensive product range, but the emphasis is on washing machines, refrigerators and deep freezers. The company has experienced solid growth in recent years and now has an annual turnover of approximately €100 million.

Up until a few years ago, TARCO bought most of its components from small component suppliers and accordingly the company's factory functioned primarily as an assembly plant. The relationship between the two main suppliers and TARCO had initially been fine, but gradually TARCO had become more and more dependent on them. About two years ago, TARCO took an opportunity to acquire two of these component suppliers. The initiative came from the two founding directors of TARCO, Mr Metzelder and Mr Adler, who believed that by buying the suppliers they could ensure more stable deliveries of components as well as capture the profit margin of the component suppliers.

Soon after, Metzelder and Adler decided that they would step down from day to day management and only participate in the company's supervisory board. A new managing director, Mr. Kahn, was employed who would be responsible for the three factories (TARCO and the two component suppliers) as well as administration and management. Each of the three factories had a production manager and Mr Wiese was appointed manager of the 'old' TARCO factory, whereas Mr Schmidt and Mr Möller, the former directors of the component supplier factories, were appointed factory managers at the newly acquired companies.

In addition, new managers were appointed for the sales and finance and accounting departments. Ranking directly under Mr. Kahn are Ms Brunner the sales manager, a finance and accounting manager, an IT manager and a human resource manager, the intention being that each of them should be in charge of their respective units in all three companies. The managing director is supported by a central administrative unit.

Response was positive when the new organisational changes were presented to the employees. The employees at the former component suppliers were all pleased, since job security had improved, and Schmidt and Möller were also happy because they had received a good price for their companies. Some even claimed that the price paid to the two component suppliers was so good that neither Schmidt nor Möller needed to worry about the future. The employees of TARCO were thrilled that Wiese had become factory manager. He was admired by everyone for his personal charisma and his excellent ability to foresee difficult situations.

One of the first saving measures carried out, when the three factories were combined, was a reduction in the stock of the component factories. The new administrative director managed to reduce the stocks by a total of €3 million, representing a saving in interest costs alone of nearly €275,000 per year.

However, TARCO GmbH soon encountered problems. Although the sale of the company's products had always been characterized by seasonal fluctuations, this had not caused any problems previously, as the component suppliers had always been able to deliver the required components at a day's notice. After the amalgamation with TARCO GmbH, the two component factories often had difficulties in keeping up despite frequent overtime work. Furthermore, the production conversion costs had increased significantly due to the production of small series. Finally, production generally generated too much waste.

TARCO GmbH had never carried out any actual production planning – neither before nor immediately after the amalgamation with the two component factories. Any problems occurring were resolved through informal conversations. However, Mr. Wiese, TARCO's factory manager decided that a more systematic production planning process should be introduced and the following procedures were implemented:

Once a week, an inventory count of finished goods is made at the assembly plant. Based on the stocks available, a plan is made for the coming week. This plan is broken down up into plans for the component production which are distributed to the two component factories. The factory managers, Schmidt and Möller, are then responsible for ensuring that the production is carried out according to the weekly plans. Furthermore, they are responsible for purchasing raw materials for their productions.

In order to rationalize production, the maximum time needed to produce each component was determined based on 'time and motion' studies. Standards specify how efficient the use of raw materials ought to be under normal circumstances. The production of cabinets can be used as a typical example of the importance of the utilization of raw materials: The cabinets are punched out of large rectangular metal plates. It is impossible to utilize 100% of these plates, but through skilful production planning, 90% utilization of raw material is possible. Standards for time to be spent and standards for the utilization of raw materials are prepared by the accounting department.

To be able to check that production has progressed according to plan, TARCO's factory manager developed a reporting system:

As mentioned already, the planning process began by preparing weekly plans at the assembly plant for the production of finished goods required for the coming week. Based on these weekly plans, the production manager of the assembly factory prepares plans specifying the type and number of components to be delivered by the two component factories. The plans for a given week's production of components are sent from the production manager on Thursday of the preceding week. A copy of the weekly plans is sent to the IT department.

At the end of the week, all three factories prepare a list of actual production performed during the week; plus a list of the inputs including labour time spent and raw materials used. These lists, which are prepared manually, are usually finished on Monday or Tuesday of the following week, and then sent to the IT department. Based on these lists and copies of the weekly plans received earlier, the IT department prepares two production statistics.

A statistical analysis is prepared showing planned and realized production of components as well as finished goods at the assembly plant. The statistics include information for the different item numbers about planned or realized production, deviations from planned and realized production as well as deviation from planned estimates.

Another analysis is prepared showing labour used for each item number as well as the utilization of raw materials. This information is compared to the planned figures.

The production statistics are sent to the three factory managers Mr. Wiese, Mr. Schmidt and Mr Möller, as well as to Mr. Kahn, the managing director, who is formally to coordinate the production of the three factories.

The Situation Today

The planning and information system described has now been in operation for almost a year since the takeover. However, discontent has begun to spread through the various departments. To illustrate the points of view of the individual managers, an extract of a discussion that took place at the last management meeting is quoted below:

Ms. Brunner, the Sales Manager:

'One of our biggest problems is that we are often unable to deliver. Delivery time is longer than it used to be. Furthermore the number of complaints from our customers has increased. What actions does the production department actually take to ensure a uniform quality of finished goods?'

TARCO Factory Manager, Mr Wiese:

'To ensure quality, we have prepared careful specifications of how each component should be produced and assembled. But actual compliance with the specifications is not checked. The biggest problem however, is that the deliveries from the two component factories are inconsistent. Often components are delivered late causing unnecessary interruptions of the assembly lines. This has, among other things, led to some employee dissatisfaction because it reduces their earnings under the piecework system.'

Component Supply Factory Manager Mr Schmidt:

'Our working conditions are inadequate. First of all, we have far too little influence on the production plans. Moreover, the weekly plans are sent at short notice and the range of items requested by plans varies too much to allow smooth production.

We also have problems purchasing raw materials. The production manager demands that the stock of raw materials is as low as possible and therefore we have to make frequent purchases. The raw materials needed to fulfil the weekly plans are purchased based on the norms prepared by the accounting department. However, this has often led to shortages. The adopted standards are almost ideal standards that are impossible to comply with in practice.'

The Accounting Department Manager:

'Our standards are planned very carefully based on time and motion studies, etc. If these standards cannot be fulfilled, it must be because the factories are not careful enough in maintaining production standards.'

TARCO Factory Manager, Mr Möller:
'We do not have particularly favourable conditions for incorporating feedback from the monitoring statistics, as the report from the IT department arrives at least one week too late and then it is too late to correct the errors. Finally, all too frequently corrections for the weekly plan are delivered by phone in the middle of the week. This makes it difficult to plan the production and at the same it reduces the possibility of follow-up as the IT department's follow-up statistics are based on the original production plans. I believe we are producing a lot of unnecessary paper through the follow-up monitoring system.'

Mr. Kahn, the Managing Director:
'The question is whether the entire takeover is already doomed to fail with all this bickering. I would prefer that we either prepare a carefully planned strategy together or consider whether it is possible to divest the two component factories and make cooperation agreements with them instead.'

The Discussion Continues
But Mr. Wiese, TARCO manager, does not entirely agree. 'No one should imagine that you can just buy two component suppliers and everything will succeed from day one.' There might already be heated discussion at the management meeting, but it was nothing compared to the uproar set off by the factory manager's comment. Directly addressed to Wiese, the component supplier factory manager Mr. Schmidt said, 'I find it absolutely unbelievable that you can get away with making one crazy plan after another without a board member or the managing director Mr. Kahn saying anything. You have implemented a planning process that only considers the interests of the old TARCO factory, whereas you let the two former component factories solve all the problems, with the result that all the problems fall back on us. You simply have to learn that one company needs to be treated as a single entity and it is unfortunate that neither the managing director nor the board makes you toe the line. You need to start thinking about your place in the organization.'

Wiese was not a man to surrender just because he encountered a little resistance. He immediately replied: 'Dear Schmidt, I thought that you had been here long enough to understand that the old TARCO is the fulcrum of the company and the part of the company with direct contact to the customers, whereas the two old component suppliers just need to adapt to what happens in TARCO'.

Now Möller, manager of the other component factory, plunged into the debate: 'I find it very discouraging to hear that you only focus on one part of the company and that you do not realize how dependent you are on other parts of the company. You cannot get the old TARCO to function if we do not make the components, if the human resource department does not employ the right people, if the sales department does not sell the products produced by TARCO and so on.'

Now Kahn, the managing director, also joined the debate: 'Please be calm! I regard it as my job to coordinate the procedures between the different departments, and I must admit that I have previously done this based primarily on the needs of TARCO. But this will change in the future. We need to see the company as a whole, and if someone feels that he has been treated unfairly, we need to talk about it and correct the situation.

TARCO founders Metzelder and Adler also participated in the meeting. They backed up their managing director and the effect soon made itself felt. This reassured Mr Kahn, allowing him to speak with much more authority and weight. At the same time, Wiese knew that he did not have full support for his crusade against the two component factories. The immediate effect was that Wiese calmed down and showed much more willingness to make concessions.'

Then Mr. Kahn, the managing director, told them all how important it is to show respect for each other in the management team and at the same time be able to freely express one's opinion. Kahn also declared that he had taken note of the discussion and he would soon present a draft for a new planning system. Then the management meeting ended and everybody left feeling positive. Not Wiese, however, who was furious about the outcome.

The Staff Meeting and the Lie
The employees in TARCO were very anxious to know what had happened at the management meeting. They knew very well that their boss Mr. Wiese might have been exposed to too much pressure from the remaining management team, and several employees were conscious of the fact that the current situation could not go on forever. At a staff meeting held shortly after the management meeting, Wiese announced

that everyone in the management team appreciated the old factory as setting the trend in TARCO and that he had managed to convince the managing director that nothing could happen without his support.

The employees applauded spontaneously, and Wiese immediately felt more confident than he had right after the management meeting. This new confidence was, however, short-lived as a new and relatively young employee asked Wiese: 'I am very impressed by what you have done for the company, but I think it is a huge problem that we have this negative approach to the other departments.

If we want the company to function as optimally as possible and in this way create secure jobs, then we all have to contribute to our common good, and it does not seem right that our prime objective is to outcompete the other departments?'

There was silence in the room because no one had ever asked Wiese a question like that. Wiese agreed with his opinion, but said that the other departments agreed that TARCO should take the lead, and therefore the competition implied did not really exist. Then Wiese ended the meeting, but many of the TARCO employees left the meeting feeling sceptical, and they realized that their young colleague had a good point. Actually, many of the old employees in TARCO also did not really understand why they fought against the component suppliers in the way they did.

Wiese was well aware that he had a problem. The scepticism of the management team and the employees was growing and he knew that personally he had to do something. The big question was how Wiese should tackle the situation.

Wiese's Salvation: the Weekend Seminar

But when the situation seemed most critical, Wiese's luck changed. Ms. Brunner, the sales manager, had run into serious problems dealing with BigBox, one of Europe's major retail chains, as competitors had become more aggressive. Accordingly, Brunner decided that TARCO should increase its engagement with the customer. The sales department therefore invited BigBox's management team to a weekend technical workshop. Business was mixed with pleasure, and TARCO used the opportunity to inform the chain's representatives about its product range, while two external consultants spoke on topics relevant for the industry. From TARCO, Metzelder and Adler participated together with the managing director, the three factory managers and, of course, some sales reps as well as the sales manager, Ms. Brunner.

The presentation of the product range was a particularly critical issue for the sales department. Purchasers for leading retail chains had strongly criticized TARCO for its lack of innovation in its products and Ms. Brunner, TARCO's sales manager, exhibited a rather nervous body language when Wiese began to speak and delivered a long sales speech lasting at least 45 minutes. During his speech, he explained very specifically the great advantages of TARCO's product range compared to their competitors. Not least, he mentioned, was the new digital warning system that flagged for the consumer and repair engineers different functional errors and the need to clean various filters on products such as washing machines, refrigerators and deep freezers. Wiese also revealed that his department was working on a completely new generation of washing machines, refrigerators and deep freezers with advanced self-cleaning and self-defrosting properties. All of this was based on a technology to be patented during the next six months, after which production would start immediately.

At the end of his speech, Wiese also promised BigBox's representatives that if they continued to deal with TARCO during the year up until the new product range was ready, he would deliver the new products to them one month before all other retail chains; and as an extra twist to his speech he invited BigBox to nominate one of its people to join TARCO's product development team to provide input into the new product range.

The retailer's representatives were impressed. Their managing director praised Wiese for his innovative and collaborative approach, and he was eager to start the cooperation. Metzelder, Adler, managing director Kahn, the two component factory managers and the sales manager Ms. Brunner were speechless. All they could do was to participate in the enthusiasm and hope that everything that Wiese had said was true.

Half an hour later, Metzelder and Adler had the opportunity to be alone with Wiese, and they immediately asked him whether it was all pure gimmick or whether his promises had a basis in fact. Wiese replied, 'We are less than three months away from completing the development of the new products, but only a small handful of people know about this. You can ask yourself why the R&D costs of TARCO have exploded and where Berthold, Matthäus, Hottiger and Brunner have been hiding for the past year. They have been working on this top-secret project. TARCO's staff weekend in two months will not start with the usual excursion, but with a presentation delivered by me. I could not just stand idly by and watch us lose customers, so I hope I have your understanding for forging ahead without consulting widely.

Wiese was proud of his achievement in turning around the relationship with TARCO's key customer. He suggested that everyone should enjoy the entertainment for the rest of the weekend. The managing director of BigBox quickly replied that that was the best thing he had heard – other than the proposed cooperation regarding the new product line – and he raised his glass and congratulated Wiese.

Next Management Meeting

The effect was unmistakable. When the entire TARCO management arrived at work the following Monday, Metzelder and Adler had called the management team to an urgent meeting. Metzelder began by complimenting Wiese for his speech at the weekend arrangement, but at the same time he scolded Wiese for not having informed the remaining management team about the project. Wiese would not tolerate this, however.

He told Metzelder that he had previously been harshly accused of saying that the two component factories should just conform to the old TARCO factory. Had he (Wiese) revealed the project earlier, they would just have started to discuss who should contribute what and when. Instead he had chosen a model where he just ordered the components needed and pretended as if the components were used for the current production.

Möller, manager of one of the component the factories, gave his almost unqualified support to Wiese. I must confess, he said, that the entire management of this company, except for Wiese, seems to have been sleeping on their watch. It is remarkable that none of us discovered that such a significant development had reached such an advanced stage. Ms. Brunner, who had been unaware of the extent of customer dissatisfaction, sat at the meeting feeling embarrassed. She admitted, 'I find it highly commendable that a production manager, who does normally not have anything to do with the customers, is able to spot such a need'.

However Mr. Schmidt, the manager of the other component factory, sat in silence listening to the discussion, and when the managing director asked about his opinion, he answered that he did not understand Möller: 'I don't think anyone should initiate a development project of this magnitude without informing at least the management team. The entire chain of events proves that Wiese is someone who has not understood that teamwork is essential in order for the company to work, and if you ask me I think that he ought to be fired. He might have put himself in the lead of the development and he might have saved TARCO during the weekend meetings. But that does not justify such solitary approach. I can't just sit idly by and watch the impact of his individualistic approach to planning. It has to end.'

Kahn, the managing director, fully supported Möller: 'I am the managing director and I seem to remember that we agreed at the last management meeting that I should launch an entirely new planning system that would take all factories, departments and employees into consideration.'

Now Adler, who together with Metzelder constituted the supervisory board, spoke, 'Don't do that. I think that, through the failure of the planning system for which you are responsible, your lack of in-depth knowledge about the real circumstances of the company, you have demonstrated that you are not capable of handling the job as managing director. You are simply too weak and I think that we should appoint Wiese as managing director.'

Now Ms. Brunner interjected:

> 'Let's all calm down. I don't think that we should worsen the conflict; and the rule about respecting each other still applies, doesn't it? Let's admit that Mr. Wiese has been very, very far-sighted, and that he can be given full credit for the fact that we are not in a completely hopeless situation after the weekend meeting with our retail customer. On the other hand, he should also acknowledge that great results are only achievable if we all work together in the same direction towards a common goal.
>
> We should all understand that this conflict has existed in TARCO for some time, and it is not just my problem, Mr. Metzelder and Mr. Adler's problem, the employees' or for that matter Wiese's problem. The problem concerns us all, and we all have a common interest in dealing with the problem.
>
> I have spent some time thinking about the situation, and about why we have these conflicts with each other in management. I think we should try to understand that Wiese needs to have one set of production principles, whereas Schmidt and Möller quite naturally should have a completely different set of production principles. Perhaps Schmidt and Möller should take the time to learn more about how

Wiese runs the old TARCO factory, whereas Wiese for his part should acquaint himself with the way in which Schmidt and Möller run their component factories. This might lead to a common understanding of the areas in which the three factory managers can help each other determine different, but complementary goals for each of the three factories, and in this way create a better mutual understanding.'

Metzelder spoke, 'Hear, hear!', he said. 'I agree with Ms. Brunner', and the other management team members nodded their heads in support. Meanwhile Kahn, the managing director, had to go along with the consensus.

Wiese is challenged

Wiese returned to his factory knowing that he had saved TARCO. In his opinion the management meeting had clearly reinforced his formal as well as informal power in the company. Although several people in the management group has expressed their hesitation as to Wiese's management methods, no one doubted that he was the one running TARCO.

But a big surprise awaited Wiese when he entered the factory. All the employees were very agitated and the production stood still. When he asked the first one he met, what was wrong, the employee answered, 'At the last staff meeting you were asked whether you considered it a huge problem that we have a negative approach to the other departments. You replied that the other departments agreed that the old factory should take the lead and the contradiction implied by the new employee did not exist.'

'We have found out that in reality there is major disagreement within the management team. Furthermore, there is a rumour that both Schmidt and Möller are angry with you – to say the least – because you have imposed a planning system on them which makes them totally dependent on us. And that is not exactly "in agreement with", is it?'

Wiese did remember the young staff member's question and his more or less untruthful reply. He felt the earth starting to burn beneath his feet. Several of the employees who had backed him loyally since the takeover of the two component factories were quite furious that he had lied. One of them, Studer, who had been working for TARCO more than 36 years, was so angry that he approached Wiese directly and said, 'I have known you for 36 years. I have always backed you up and looked up to you. But you ruined that. I have no wish to fight the other departments. To me Schmidt and Möller are highly respectable people.'

Wiese was under so much pressure that he did not stand up on the old beer crate, like he usually did, when he had something to say to the production workers. To everybody's surprise the managing director Mr. Kahn, who had followed Wiese into the production hall unnoticed, pulled out the beer crate. He climbed onto the crate and said, 'My dear employees! You are right that we have had many tough discussions in the management team about how to run the business. It is also a fact that we sometimes strongly disagree and that we are in a deep managerial crisis at the moment. I therefore ask you not to let us down. When management is not functioning properly, it is important the employees support the company because in the end you constitute the company and are its greatest asset.'

The managing director continued: 'I understand that you are not completely satisfied with the answers that Wiese has given you. I am not the one to judge that. But I know that Wiese has been under severe pressure for the past half year and I beg you to support him. TARCO needs him. This weekend, we held a seminar for our biggest customer. It did not start out very well, but then Wiese took over and splendidly managed to put us on the right track again. Instead of being close to losing the customer, we have now extended our cooperation; so you can thank him for assuring your jobs. Promise me that you will give him your full support. I can also inform you that within a few months, we will be presenting to you something completely new and groundbreaking; this will require a new strategy, a new structure and, hopefully, a much stronger market position. But please support Wiese and the management from now on. I would like to repeat that your jobs are not in danger – thanks to Wiese.'

The employees responded to the managing director's speech with a huge applause. It seemed as if the applause would never end, and when it finally did, the employees kept shouting 'Wiese, Wiese, Wiese'; which was their way of declaring their renewed faith in their manager. At the same time, Wiese realized he was indebted to Mr. Kahn. A certain equilibrium had been attained.

Case Questions

1 Please identify in list form the challenges that TARCO is facing. Which are the most important? Are they interlinked?

2 Mr. Wiese chose to develop the new product line without consulting his management colleagues. What was his rationale for this? Do you think he was justified?

3 Was Wiese right to lie to his employees about the attitude of the component factories to the TARCO factory's leadership within the overall company? In general, what would you described as Mr Wiese's strengths and weaknesses as a manager.

4 There are continuing differences of opinion between the managers of TARCO's main factory and its component supply factories. Are these inevitable? Was it a mistake to have purchased the supply factories?

5 What are the advantages and disadvantages of involving BigBox in the new product development process?

6 Whose intervention was the most important in resolving the conflict within the management team? Why?

7 At the end of the case study, Mr. Kahn stepped in and supported Mr. Wiese. Given that Wiese was clearly a threat to him, why do you think Kahn did this? Can Wiese now assume that Mr. Kahn will be a strong ally of his in the future?

Notes

1. 'Alliance Boots' Baker tabbed best global retailer', *Chain Drug Review*, 1 January 2007; 'Small Businesses Take Boots to Task over Stalled Payment', *Chemist and Druggist*, 26 July 2008; 'In wake of buyout, Boots CEO Baker exits', *Chain Drug Review*, 23 July 2007; Murrah Ahmud, 'Alliance Boots to Move Head Office Out of UK', *The Times*, June 9, 2008; 'Small businesses take Boots to task over stalled payments', *Chemist & Druggist*, 26 July 2008.
2. Julia Boorstin, 'Secret Recipe: J. M. Smucker', *Fortune* (January 12, 2004), 58–59.
3. Stefan Stern, 'Old Europe fighting back', *Financial Times*, 28 May 2008.
4. Anita Raghavan, Kathryn Kranhold and Alexei Barrionuevo, 'Full Speed Ahead: How Enron Bosses Created a Culture of Pushing Limits', *The Wall Street Journal* (August 26, 2002), A1, A7.
5. Mark C. Bolino, William H. Turnley and James M. Bloodgood, 'Citizenship Behaviour and the Creation of Social Capital in Organizations', *Academy of Management Review* 27, no. 4 (2002), 505–522; and Don Cohen and Laurence Prusak, *In Good Company: How Social Capital Makes Organizations Work* (Boston, Mass.: Harvard Business School Press, 2001), 3–4.
6. David Nicklaus, 'Convictions in Enron case mark end to shameful era', *St. Louis Post-Dispatch*, 28 May 2006.
7. Eric Lichtblau, David Johnston and Ron Nixon, 'F.B.I. Struggling To Handle Wave Of Finance Cases', *The New York Times*, 19 October 2008; Jim Mateja, 'Former Chrysler boss attacks corporate greed; World is out of whack, Lee Iacocca says in his book', *Chicago Tribune*, 27 April 2007; Anatole Kaletsky and Robin Blackburn, 'Should capitalism be transformed?' *Prospect Magazine*, 23 October 2008.
8. '*Fortune* 1,000 Ranked within Industries', *Fortune* (April 18, 2005), F-46–F-69; Erick Shonfeld, 'eBay's Secret Ingredient', *Business 2.0* (March 2002), 52–58.
9. Bourdieu, P. (1994), *Raisons Pratiques: Sur la théorie de l'action*, Paril, Seuil; Putnam, Robert D. (2007) 'E Pluribus Unum: Diversity and Community in the Twenty-first Century', *Scandinavian Political Studies* 30, 137–174. For critiques of human capital and social capital see, Samuel Bowles & Herbert Gintis (1975), 'The Problem with Human Capital Theory – A Marxian Critique', *American Economic Review*, 65(2), pp. 74–82, and Ben Fine (2001), 'Social capital versus social theory: political economy and social science at the turn of the millennium', London, Routledge.
10. James Quinn, 'IBM and eBay shrug off gloom'. '*The Daily Telegraph'* April 17 2008; Pierre-Antoine Souchard, 'France Faults eBay Over Fake Goods; Web Site to Appeal $61 Million Court Decision Favoring Luxury Brands', The *Washington Post*, 1 July 2008.
11. Joy Persaud, 'Keep the Faithful', *People Management* (June 2003), 37–38.
12. W. Jack Duncan, 'Organizational Culture: "Getting a Fix" on an Elusive Concept', *Academy of Management Executive* 3 (1989), 229–236; Linda Smircich, 'Concepts of Culture and Organizational Analysis', *Administrative Science Quarterly* 28 (1983), 339–358; and Andrew D. Brown and Ken Starkey, 'The Effect of Organizational Culture on Communication and Information', *Journal of Management Studies* 31, no. 6 (November 1994), 807–828.
13. Edgar H. Schein, 'Organizational Culture', *American Psychologist* 45 (February 1990), 109–119.
14 Edwin Heathcote, 'Architecture: E Europe redefines its identity', *Financial Times*,10 March 2008
15. Harrison M. Trice and Janice M. Beyer, 'Studying Organizational Cultures through Rites and Ceremonials', *Academy of Management Review* 9 (1984), 653–669; Janice M. Beyer and Harrison M. Trice, 'How an Organization's Rites Reveal Its Culture', *Organizational Dynamics* 15 (Spring 1987), 5–24; Steven P. Feldman, 'Management in Context: An Essay on the Relevance of

Culture to the Understanding of Organizational Change', *Journal of Management Studies* 23 (1986), 589–607; and Mary Jo Hatch, 'The Dynamics of Organizational Culture', *Academy of Management Review* 18 (1993), 657–693.

16. This discussion is based on Edgar H. Schein, *Organizational Culture and Leadership*, 2d ed. (Homewood, Ill.: Richard D. Irwin, 1992); and John P. Kotter and James L. Heskett, *Corporate Culture and Performance* (New York: Free Press, 1992).
17. He Huafeng, 'Alibaba founder keeps focus on customers corporate culture', *The Wall Street Journal Asia*, 18 October 2007.
18. Cheryl Dahle, 'Four Tires, Free Beef', *Fast Company* (September 2003), 36.
19. Larry Mallak, 'Understanding and Changing Your Organization's Culture', *Industrial Management* (March–April 2001), 18–24.
20. For a list of various elements that can be used to assess or interpret corporate culture, see '10 Key Cultural Elements', sidebar in Micah R. Kee, 'Corporate Culture Makes a Fiscal Difference', *Industrial Management* (November–December 2003), 16–20.
21. Charlotte B. Sutton, 'Richness Hierarchy of the Cultural Network: The Communication of Corporate Values' (unpublished manuscript, Texas A&M University, 1985); and Terrence E. Deal and Allan A. Kennedy, 'Culture: A New Look through Old Lenses', *Journal of Applied Behavioural Science* 19 (1983), 498–505.
22. Thomas C. Dandridge, 'Symbols at Work' (working paper, School of Business, State University of New York at Albany, 1978), 1.
23. 'Avon lady is sitting pretty after awards', *Derby Evening Telegraph*, 2 September 2008.
24. Tunde Olofintila, 'Wema Bank – Better Days Are Here', *Daily Independent*, 23 October 2008.
25. Don Hellriegel and John W. Slocum, Jr., *Management*, 7th ed. (Cincinnati, Ohio: South-Western, 1996), 537.
26. Jack Smith, 'Driving continuous improvement', *Plant Engineering*, 1 December 2006; Hirotaka Takeuchi, Emi Osono and Norihiko Shimizu, 'Contradictions are the drivers of Toyota's success', *Business Day* (South Africa), 23 June 2008.
27. Trice and Beyer, 'Studying Organizational Cultures through Rites and Ceremonials'.
28. Stephen Denning, 'Telling Tales', *Harvard Business Review*,
29. Sutton, 'Richness Hierarchy of the Cultural Network'; and Terrence E. Deal and Allan A. Kennedy, *Corporate Cultures: The Rites and Rituals of Corporate Life* (Reading, Mass.: Addison-Wesley, 1982).
30. Jonathan Murphy (2008), *The World Bank and Global Managerialism*, London, Routledge.
31. Douglas B. Holt (2004), *How Brands Become Icons*, Cambridge, Mass., Harvard Business Press, pp. 155–189.
32. 'Caring Corporations and Their Sensitive New Logos', *Chosun Ilbo*, 30 November 2006.
33. 'FYI', *Inc.* (April 1991), 14.
34. Raghavan, Kranhold, and Barrionuevo, 'Full Speed Ahead'.
35. 'Climbing the Ladder: There's more than one way to turn a regional hit into a national retail brand. How do you know which is right for you?' *National Post*, 1 February 2007.
36. David Bank, 'Fund Helps PeopleSoft Ex-Workers', *The Wall Street Journal* (April 4, 2005), B4.
37. Fitzgibbon, J. E. , Seeger, M. (2002) 'Audiences and Metaphors of Globalization in the Daimler Chrysler Merger', *Communication Studies*, 53, 40–55.
38. Higgins and McAllaster, 'Want Innovation?'
39. Jennifer A. Chatman and Sandra Eunyoung Cha, 'Leading by Leveraging Culture', *California Management Review* 45, no. 4 (Summer 2003), 20–34; and Abby Ghobadian and Nicholas O'Regan, 'The Link between Culture, Strategy, and Performance in Manufacturing SMEs', *Journal of General Management* 28, no. 1 (Autumn 2002), 16–34.
40. James R. Detert, Roger G. Schroeder and John J. Mauriel, 'A Framework for Linking Culture and Improvement Initiatives in Organizations', *Academy of Management Review* 25, no. 4 (2000), 850–863.
41. Based on Daniel R. Denison, *Corporate Culture and Organizational Effectiveness* (New York: Wiley, 1990), 11–15; Daniel R. Denison and Aneil K. Mishra, 'Toward a Theory of Organizational Culture and Effectiveness', *Organization Science* 6, no. 2 (March–April 1995), 204–223; R. Hooijberg and F. Petrock, 'On Cultural Change: Using the Competing Values Framework to Help Leaders Execute a Transformational Strategy', *Human Resource Management* 32 (1993), 29–50; and R. E. Quinn, *Beyond Rational Management: Mastering the Paradoxes and Competing Demands of High Performance* (San Francisco: Jossey-Bass, 1988).
42. Helen Kelly, 'How BT Exact retrained an in-house support division with flexible skills', *Personnel Today*, 27 February 2007; Management – The real story behind a real-time enterprise, *Computing*, 31 July 2003; Robert Wall and Jens Flottau, 'Turbulent Skies; Europe's low-fare sector faces uncertainty, but remains set on expansion', *Aviation Week & Space Technology*, 19 November 2007; 'Teaching Airlines To Think More Like Marketers, Teaching Travelers To Expect Less But Pay More; Lessons to Be Had in Ancillary Revenue Creation', *M2 Presswire*, 5 December 2007; Valencia Loses 750,000 Passengers And 750 Jobs As Ryanair Closes Base, *M2 Presswire*, 24 October 2008.
43. Emma Pinch, 'New logo and vision to achieve Villa's goals', *Birmingham Post*, 3 May 2007.
44. 'Marks & Spencer's Rose faces tougher challenge', *Reuters News*, 12 May 2008; 'Marks and sparks: Shopping in the 21st century', *The Independent*, May 27, 2007.
45. Matthew Boyle, 'The Wegmans Way', *Fortune* (January 24, 2005), 62–68.
46. Tom Dochat, 'Wegmans grocery chain keeps it all in the family', *The Patriot-News*, 9 September 2007.
47. BBC News, 'Northern Rock to be nationalized', 17 February 2008, accessed at http://news.bbc.co.uk/1/hi/business/7249575.stm on October 24, 2008; David Prosser 'The Return of the Building Society: Credit Crisis, What Credit Crisis?', *The Independent,* November 23, 2007.

48. Bernard Arogyaswamy and Charles M. Byles, 'Organizational Culture: Internal and External Fits', *Journal of Management* 13 (1987), 647–659.
49. Chatman and Cha, 'Leading by Leveraging Culture'.
50. Patrick J. Sauer, 'Open-Door Management', *Inc.* (June 2003), 44.
51. Paul R. Lawrence and Jay W. Lorsch, *Organization and Environment* (Homewood, Ill.: Irwin, 1969).
53. 'Five Asian firms among global elite in leadership', *Bangkok Post*, 1 October 2007; Simon Caulkin, 'The colossal cares of Unilever revisited' *Management Today*, September 2006; Haig Simonian and Tom Braithwaite, 'Unilever goes outside for chief', *Financial Times*, September 4, 2008;
53. Chatman and Cha, 'Leading by Leveraging Culture'; Jeff Rosenthal and Mary Ann Masarech, 'High-Performance Cultures: How Values Can Drive Business Results', *Journal of Organizational Excellence* (Spring 2003), 3–18.
54. Loizos Heracleous, Jochen Wirtz Robert Johnston, (2005) 'Kung-fu service development at Singapore Airlines', *Business Strategy Review*, Volume 16, Issue 4 , 26–31
55. Ghobadian and O'Regan, 'The Link between Culture, Strategy and Performance'; G. G. Gordon and N. DiTomaso, 'Predicting Corporate Performance from Organisational Culture', *Journal of Management Studies* 29, no. 6 (1992), 783–798; and G. A. Marcoulides and R. H. Heck, 'Organizational Culture and Performance: Proposing and Testing a Model', *Organization Science* 4 (1993), 209–225.
56. Choe Sang-Hun, 'In South Korea, 'the old way' is crumbling. Major companies lead push to abandon male-oriented, top-down business culture', *International Herald Tribune*, 25 October 2008.
57. Tressie Wright Muldrow, Timothy Buckley, and Brigitte W. Schay, 'Creating High-Performance Organizations in the Public Sector', *Human Resource Management* 41, no. 3 (Fall 2002), 341–354.
58. Loizos Heracleous, Jochen Wirtz and Robert Johnston (2005), 'Kung-fu service development at Singapore Airlines', *Business Strategy Review*, Winter 2005; 'Singapore Compact', website accessed at http://www.csrsingapore.org/index.html on October 28, 2008; David Fullbrook, 'Have We Seen the Back of the Singapore Girl' *Asia Sentinel*, Friday, 9 March 2007.
59. Penelope Phoon, 'Gaining momentum in Singapore', *The Edge Malaysia*, 7 May 2007.
60. Singapore Airlines, Environmental Report 2007–08, accessed at http://www.singaporeair.com/saa/en_UK/docs/company_info/environment/SIA_EnvReport2007-08.pdf on October 28, 2008.
61. Fortune, 'World's Most Admired Companies 2007', accessed at http://money.cnn.com/magazines/fortune/globalmostadmired/2007/snapshots/8155.html on October 28, 2008.
62. World's Best Airline Awards, accessed at www.worldairlineawards.com/Awards_2008/AirlineYear-2008.htm on October 28, 2008.
63. Garry Rodan, 'Singapore in 2004: Long-Awaited Leadership Transition', *Asian Survey*, January/February 2005, 45, 140–145.
64. John P. Kotter and James L. Heskett, *Corporate Culture and Performance* (New York: The Free Press, 1992).
65. Gordon F. Shea, *Practical Ethics* (New York: American Management Association, 1988); Linda K. Treviño, 'Ethical Decision Making in Organizations: A Person–Situation Interactionist Model', *Academy of Management Review* 11 (1986), 601–617; and Linda Klebe Treviño and Katherine A. Nelson, *Managing Business Ethics: Straight Talk about How to Do It Right*, 2nd ed. (New York: John Wiley & Sons, Inc., 1999).
66. Thanks to Susan H. Taft, Kent State University, and Judith White, University of Redlands, for this overview of the sources of individual ethics.
67. Dawn-Marie Driscoll, 'Don't Confuse Legal and Ethical Standards', *Business Ethics* (July–August 1996), 44.
68. LaRue Tone Hosmer, *The Ethics of Management*, 2d ed. (Homewood, Ill.: Irwin, 1991).
69. Geanne Rosenberg, 'Truth and Consequences', *Working Woman* (July–August 1998), 79–80.
70. Horwitz, Frank M., Browning, Victoria, Jain, Harish and Steenkamp, Anton J. (2002), 'Human resource practices and discrimination in South Africa: overcoming the apartheid legacy', *The International Journal of Human Resource Management*, 13, 1105–1118.
71. N. Craig Smith, 'Corporate Social Responsibility: Whether or How?' *California Management Review* 45, no. 4 (Summer 2003), 52–76; and Eugene W. Szwajkowski, 'The Myths and Realities of Research on Organizational Misconduct', in James E. Post, ed., *Research in Corporate Social Performance and Policy*, vol. 9 (Greenwich, Conn.: JAI Press, 1986), 103–122.
72. Some of these incidents are from Hosmer, *The Ethics of Management*.
73. Linda K. Treviño and Katherine A. Nelson, *Managing Business Ethics: Straight Talk about How to Do It Right* (New York: John Wiley & Sons, Inc., 1995), 4.
74. Curtis C. Verschoor and Elizabeth A. Murphy, 'The Financial Performance of Large U.S. Firms and Those with Global Prominence: How Do the Best Corporate Citizens Rate?' *Business and Society Review* 107, no. 2 (Fall 2002), 371–381; Homer H. Johnson, 'Does It Pay to Be Good? Social Responsibility and Financial Performance', *Business Horizons* (November–December 2003), 34–40; Quentin R. Skrabec, 'Playing By the Rules: Why Ethics Are Profitable', *Business Horizons* (September–October 2003), 15–18; Marc Gunther, 'Tree Huggers, Soy Lovers and Profits', *Fortune* (June 23, 2003), 98–104; Dale Kurschner, '5 Ways Ethical Business Creates Fatter Profits', *Business Ethics* (March–April 1996), 20–23. Also see various studies reported in Lori Ioannou, 'Corporate America's Social Conscience', *Fortune,* special advertising section (May 26, 2003), S1–S10.
75. McWilliams A., and Siegel D. (2000), 'Corporate social responsibility and financial performance: Correlation or misspecification?' *Strategic Management Journal*, 21, 603–609; Marc Orlitzky, Frank L. Schmidt and Sara L. Rynes (2003) 'Corporate Social and Financial Performance: A Meta-Analysis', *Organization Studies*, 24, 403–441.
76. Gretchen Morgenson, 'Shares of Corporate Nice Guys Can Finish First', *The New York Times* (April 27, 2003), Section 3, 1.

77. Daniel W. Greening and Daniel B. Turban, 'Corporate Social Performance as a Competitive Advantage in Attracting a Quality Workforce', *Business and Society* 39, no. 3 (September 2000), 254.
78. Alison Maitland, 'Tools to build a reputation', *Financial Times*, 20 January 2003.
79. Andrea Li 'Keeping staff happy key to success', *South China Morning Post*, 21 February 2008.
80. Christopher Marquis, 'Doing Well and Doing Good', *The New York Times* (July 13, 2003), Section 3, 2; and Joseph Pereira, 'Career Journal: Doing Good and Doing Well at Timberland', *The Wall Street Journal* (September 9, 2003), B1.
81. Lois A. Mohr, Deborah J. Webb, Katherine E. Harris, 'Do Consumers Expect Companies to be Socially Responsible? The Impact of Corporate Social Responsibility on Buying Behaviour', *Journal of Consumer Affairs*, 35, 45–72.
82. Julie Pirsch, Shruti Gupta, Stacy Landreth Grau (2007) 'A Framework for Understanding Corporate Social Responsibility Programs as a Continuum: An Exploratory Study', *Journal of Business Ethics*, 70, 125–140.
83. 'The Socially Correct Corporate Business', segment in Leslie Holstrom and Simon Brady, 'The Changing Face of Global Business', *Fortune*, special advertising section (July 24, 2000), S1–S38.
84. T. Hidayat, 'Yeane Keet: If employees are happy, customers will be happy', *The Jakarta Post*, 28 May 2008.
85. Carol Hymowitz, 'CEOs Must Work Hard to Maintain Faith in the Corner Office' (In the Lead column), *The Wall Street Journal* (July 9, 2002), B1.
86. Linda Klebe Treviño, 'A Cultural Perspective on Changing and Developing Organizational Ethics', in Richard Woodman and William Pasmore, eds., *Research and Organizational Change and Development*, vol. 4 (Greenwich, Conn.: JAI Press, 1990); and Lynn Sharp Paine, 'Managing for Organizational Integrity', *Harvard Business Review* (March/April 1994), 106–117.
87. James Weber, 'Exploring the Relationship between Personal Values and Moral Reasoning', *Human Relations* 46 (1993), 435–463.
88. Herbert Steinhouse, 'The Real Oskar Schindler', *Saturday Night*, April 1994.
89. L. Kohlberg, 'Moral Stages and Moralization: The Cognitive-Developmental Approach', in T. Likona, ed., *Moral Development and Behaviour: Theory, Research, and Social Issues* (New York: Holt, Rinehart & Winston, 1976).
90. Hosmer, *The Ethics of Management*.
91. Lucy Siegle, 'The Ethical Issue: Green at heart', *Observer Magazine*, 8 June 2008.
92. John A. Byrne with Mike France and Wendy Zellner, 'The Environment Was Ripe for Abuse', *BusinessWeek* (February 25, 2002), 118–120.
93. Matt Dickinson, Recommendations Made To BAE, *Press Association National Newswire*, 6 May 2008; David Leigh, 'BAE Systems admits to ethical failings as investigations into corruption continue', *The Guardian*, 7 May 2008.
94. Jennifer Bresnahan, 'For Goodness Sake', *CIO Enterprise*, Section 2 (June 15, 1999), 54–62.
95. David M. Messick and Max H. Bazerman, 'Ethical Leadership and the Psychology of Decision Making', *Sloan Management Review* (Winter 1996), 9–22; Dawn-Marie Driscoll, 'Don't Confuse Legal and Ethical Standards', *Business Ethics* (July–August 1996), 44; and Max B. E. Clarkson, 'A Stakeholder Framework for Analyzing and Evaluating Corporate Social Performance', *Academy of Management Review* 20, no. 1 (1995), 92–117.
96. 'SEC's Cox Defends Agency, Seeks More Authority', *Dow Jones News Service*, 23 October 2008; EU Calls for Tougher Rules to Fix Crippled Financial System, *Deutsche Welle*, 1 October 2008; EU business: Deregulation hits the buffers, *Economist Intelligence Unit*, 24 October 2008.
97. 'New York City restaurants go trans-fat-free', *Reuters News*, 1 July 2008.
98. Roger Parloff, 'Is Fat the Next Tobacco?' *Fortune* (February 3, 2003), 51–54.
99. Toyota Motor Corporation, 'aim: zero emissions', Toyota Environmental Brochure 2006, accessed at http://www.toyota.eu/Images/Brochure_tcm416-493730.pdf on October 27 2008; 'BMW unveils plans for a zero-emissions future', *Guardian Unlimited*, 27 September 2007.
100. *Corporate Ethics: A Prime Business Asset* (New York: The Business Round Table, February 1988).
101. Andrew W. Singer, 'The Ultimate Ethics Test', *Across the Board* (March 1992), 19–22; Ronald B. Morgan, 'Self and Co-Worker Perceptions of Ethics and Their Relationships to Leadership and Salary', *Academy of Management Journal* 36, no. 1 (February 1993), 200–214; and Joseph L. Badaracco, Jr., and Allen P. Webb, 'Business Ethics: A View from the Trenches', *California Management Review* 37, no. 2 (Winter 1995), 8–28.
102. This discussion is based on Robert J. House, Andre Delbecq and Toon W. Taris, 'Value Based Leadership: An Integrated Theory and an Empirical Test' (working paper).
103. Frank Vogl, 'The proud legacy of a corporate ethics pioneer', *Financial Times*, 13 September 2007; 'Dame Anita Roddick', *Guardian Unlimited*, 11 September 2007.
104. Jules Stewart, 'Break the bank', *Financial Director*, 1 April 2005; Cristina McEachern, Confessions of a Rogue Trader, *Advanced Trading*, 1 April 2008; Societe Generale boss admits faults in control systems, *Agence France Presse*, 10 June 2008; Minister faults bank controls in Societe Generale scandal, *Agence France Presse*, 4 February 2008; 'Societe Generale scandal: Unanswered questions Who knew what?', *The Guardian*, 26 January 2008; 'Societe Generale Scandal Presents Lessons in Operational Risk Management', *PR Newswire*, 22 February 2008; Doreen Carvajal and James Kanter, 'Société Générale: A Quest for Glory and a Bonus Ends in Disgrace', *New York Times*, January 29, 2008.
105. 'Siemens battles bribery probes on many fronts', *Reuters News*, 8 November 2007; Mike Esterl and David Crawford, 'Why Siemens Bribery Probe Slogs On – Decentralization, Stonewalling Make Quick Resolution Unlikely', *The Wall Street Journal*, 16 August 2007; Michael D. Goldhaber, 'How the massive Siemens bribery scandal made U.S.–style internal investigations the new model for Europe',

American Lawyer, 1 May 2008; Carter Dougherty, 'The Sheriff at Siemens, at Work Under the Justice Dept.'s Watchful Eye', *The New York Times*, 8 October 2008.
106. Karl E. Weick, 'Cognitive Processes in Organizations', in B. M. Staw, ed., *Research in Organizations*, vol. 1 (Greenwich, Conn.: JAI Press, 1979), 42.
107. Richard Osborne, 'Kingston's Family Values', *IndustryWeek* (August 13, 2001), 51–54.
108. Alan Yuspeh, 'Do the Right Thing', *CIO* (August 1, 2000), 56–58.
109. 'Ethics & Compliance Officer Association (ECOA) Elects New Board Officers', *Business Wire*, 29 May 2008; http://www.theecoa.org/AM/Template.cfm?Section=Global_Ethics_and_Compliance, accessed on 28 October 2008.
110. Information in Amy Zipkin, 'Getting Religion on Corporate Ethics', *The New York Times* (October 18, 2000), C1, C10; and *http://www.eoa.org,* accessed April 20, 2005.
111. Treviño and Nelson, *Managing Business Ethics*, 212.
112. Karamjit Kaur, 'Ethics hotline' for SIA', *Straits Times*, 28 October 2005; Dale Hug, 'Pioneer Opens E-Mail Based 'Business Ethics Hotline', *Japan Corporate News Network*, 13 June 2003.
113. Janet P. Near and Marcia P. Miceli, 'Effective Whistle-Blowing', *Academy of Management Review* 20, no. 3 (1995), 679–708.
114. Richard P. Nielsen, 'Changing Unethical Organizational Behaviour', *Academy of Management Executive* 3 (1989), 123–130.
115. Jene G. James, 'Whistle-Blowing: Its Moral Justification', in Peter Madsen and Jay M. Shafritz, eds., *Essentials of Business Ethics* (New York: Meridian Books, 1990), 160–190; and Janet P. Near, Terry Morehead Dworkin and Marcia P. Miceli, 'Explaining the Whistle-Blowing Process: Suggestions from Power Theory and Justice Theory', *Organization Science* 4 (1993), 393–411.
116. Martin Bright 'Follow my lead, says whistleblower', *The Observer*, 12 September 2004; Katharine Gun, 'The truth must out', *The Observer*; 19 September 2004; Martin Bright, 'The woman who nearly stopped the war', *The New Statesman*, March 19, 2008.
117. Lesley Curwen, 'The corporate conscience', *The Guardian*, 21 June 2003.
118. 'British Airways executives charged over price-fixing scandal', *Guardian Unlimited*, 7 August 2008
119. Linda Klebe Treviño, Gary R. Weaver, David G. Gibson and Barbara Ley Toffler, 'Managing Ethics and Legal Compliance: What Works and What Hurts?' *California Management Review* 41, no. 2 (Winter 1999), 131–151.
120. 'Toyota Code of Conduct 2006', Toyota Motor Company, accessed at http://www.toyota.co.jp/en/vision/code_of_conduct/code_of_conduct.pdf on October 28, 2008.
121. 'Setting the Standard', Lockheed Martin's Web site, *http://www.lockheedmartin.com/exeth/html/code/code.html*, accessed August 7, 2001.
122. Stohl, Cynthia, Stohl, Michael and Popova, Lucy. 'A New Generation of Global Corporate Codes of Ethics?', paper presented at the annual meeting of the International Communication Association, San Francisco, CA, May 23, 2007.
123. Ronald E. Berenbeim, *Corporate Ethics Practices* (New York: The Conference Board, 1992).
124. For British Airways code of conduct, see http://www.britishairways.com/cms/masterEN/content/company_information/community_and_environmental/code_of_conduct.pdf accessed on October 28 2008, and for Halliburton see http://www.halliburton.com/Default.aspx?navid=344&pageid=731, accessed on October 28, 2008. Some of Halliburton's ethical challenges are detailed in Russell Gold, 'Halliburton Ex-Official Pleads Guilty In Bribe Case', *The Wall Street Journal*, 4 September 2008.
125. James Weber, 'Institutionalizing Ethics into Business Organizations: A Model and Research Agenda', *Business Ethics Quarterly* 3 (1993), 419–436.
126. 'Code of conduct', GlaxoSmithKline, accessed at http://www.gsk.com/responsibility/cr_issues/be_code_conduct.htm on October 28, 2008.
127. Landon Thomas Jr. 'On Wall Street, a Rise in Dismissals over Ethics', *The New York Times* (March 25, 2005), http://www.nytimes.com.
128. Crystal E. Ashby, Paul Basson, Donna C. Boehme and Jean-Claude Najar, 'Global Harmonization of Codes of Conduct', accessed at http://www.acc.com/vl/public/ProgramMaterial/loader.cfm?csModule=security/getfile&pageid=20242 on October 28, 2008.
129. Mark Henricks, 'Ethics in Action', *Management Review* (January 1995), 53–55; Dorothy Marcic, *Management and the Wisdom of Love* (San Francisco: Jossey-Bass, 1997); and Beverly Geber, 'The Right and Wrong of Ethics Offices', *Training* (October 1995), 102–118.
130. Susan J. Harrington, 'What Corporate America Is Teaching about Ethics', *Academy of Management Executive* 5 (1991), 21–30.
131. Jerry G. Kreuze, Zahida Luqmani and Mushtaq Luqmani, 'Shades of Gray', *Internal Auditor* (April 2001), 48.
132. David Scheer, 'For Your Eyes Only; Europe's New High-Tech Role: Playing Privacy Cop to the World', *The Wall Street Journal* (October 10, 2003), A1, A16.
133. S. C. Schneider, 'National vs. Corporate Culture: Implications for Human Resource Management', *Human Resource Management* (Summer 1988), 239.
134. Carl F. Fey and Daniel R. Denison, 'Organizational Culture and Effectiveness: Can American Theory Be Applied in Russia?' *Organization Science* 14, no. 6 (November–December 2003), 686–706.
135. Terence Jackson, 'Cultural Values and Management Ethics: A 10-Nation Study', *Human Relations* 54, no. 10 (2001), 1267–1302.
136. Gail Dutton, 'Building a Global Brain', *Management Review* (May 1999), 34–38.
137. Ibid.
138. Homer H. Johnson, 'Corporate Social Audits–This Time Around', *Business Horizons* (May–June 2001), 29–36.
139. http://www.sa-intl.org, accessed on October 28, 2008.
140. Guan Xiaofeng, 'Building Worker Rights', *China Business Weekly*, 2 April 2007.
141. Cassandra Kegler, 'Holding Herself Accountable', *Working Woman* (May 2001), 13; Louisa Wah, 'Treading the Sacred Ground', *Management Review* (July–August 1998), 18–22.

CHAPTER 11

INNOVATION AND CHANGE

Toyota Motor Corporation

In auto manufacturing, Japanese companies rule, and one manufacturer outshines them all. Toyota increasingly dominates the global auto market, while the former giants of the global vehicle market like America's General Motors and Ford teeter at the edge of bankruptcy. The basis of Toyota's supremacy lies primarily in its steady stream of technological and product innovation. Toyota executives created the doctrine of *kaizen*, or continuous improvement, and the company applies it relentlessly. Toyota hands the responsibility for continuous improvement to every employee. People on the shop floor can get cash rewards for searching out production glitches and finding ways to solve them.

Although thinking big can be important, Toyota knows that sweating the details is just as critical for driving innovation. Consider this: several years ago, Toyota made a small change to its production lines by using a single master brace to hold automobile frames in place as they were welded, instead of the dozens of braces used in a standard auto factory. It seemed almost insignificant in the context of the company's complex manufacturing system, yet it was a radical manufacturing innovation. That one change, referred to now as the Global Body Line system, slashed 75 per cent off the cost of retrofitting a production line and made it possible for Toyota to produce different car and truck models on a single line. The result has been billions of dollars in annual cost savings.

For developing new models, Toyota applies the concept of *obeya*, which literally means 'big room'. To make sure all the critical factors are considered from the beginning, product development teams made up of manufacturing and product engineers, designers, marketers and suppliers hold regular face-to-face brainstorming sessions. New software programs, including the product life cycle management software discussed in Chapter 8, also make it possible for these cross-functional teams to collaborate digitally, viewing product design changes and associated costs. That way, if a designer makes a change that conflicts with manufacturing's needs or a supplier's capability, it can be noted and adjusted immediately. This collaborative process created Toyota's sturdy small truck, the Hilux, which is extremely popular in developing countries (it was the favoured vehicle of the Taliban and their opponents alike in Afghanistan[1] and is also favoured by oil companies and other organizations working in areas where a breakdown can mean life or death). A new version of the Hilux is one of the keys to Toyota's strategy of maintaining its dominance in the world auto market.[2]

Today, every company must change and innovate to survive. New discoveries and inventions quickly replace standard ways of doing things. Organizations like Toyota, Microsoft, Nokia and Procter & Gamble are searching for any innovation edge they can find. Some companies, like 3M, the maker of Post-it Notes, Thinsulate insulation, Scotch-Brite scouring pads and thousands of other products, are known for innovation. 3M's culture supports a risk-taking and entrepreneurial spirit that keeps it bubbling over with new ideas and new products. However, many large, established companies have a hard time being entrepreneurial and continually look for ways to encourage change and innovation to keep pace with changes in the external environment.

See online **COUNTERPOINT 11.7**

The pace of change is revealed in the fact that the parents of today's college-age students grew up without debit cards, video on demand, iPods, self-service supermarket checkout systems, mobile phones, instant messaging and the Internet. The idea of communicating instantly with people around the world was unimaginable to most people as recently as a couple of decades ago.

Purpose of This Chapter

This chapter will explore how organizations change and how managers direct the innovation and change process. The next section describes the difference between incremental and radical change, the four types of change – technology, product, structure, people – occurring in organizations, and how to manage change successfully. The organization structure and management approach for facilitating each type of change is then discussed. Management techniques for influencing both the creation and implementation of change are also covered.

Innovate or Perish: The Strategic Role of Change

If there is one theme or lesson that emerges from previous chapters, it is that organizations run fast to keep up with changes taking place all around them. Large organizations find ways to act like small, flexible organizations. Manufacturing firms reach out for new, flexible manufacturing technology and service firms for new information technology (IT). Today's organizations position themselves to innovate and change, not only to prosper but merely to survive in a world of increased competition.[3] As illustrated in Exhibit 11.1, a number of environmental forces drive major organizational change. Powerful forces associated with advancing technology, international economic integration, the maturing of domestic markets and the shift to capitalism in formerly communist regions have brought about a globalized economy that affects every business, from the largest to the smallest, creating more

EXHIBIT 11.1 Forces Driving the Need for Major Organizational Change

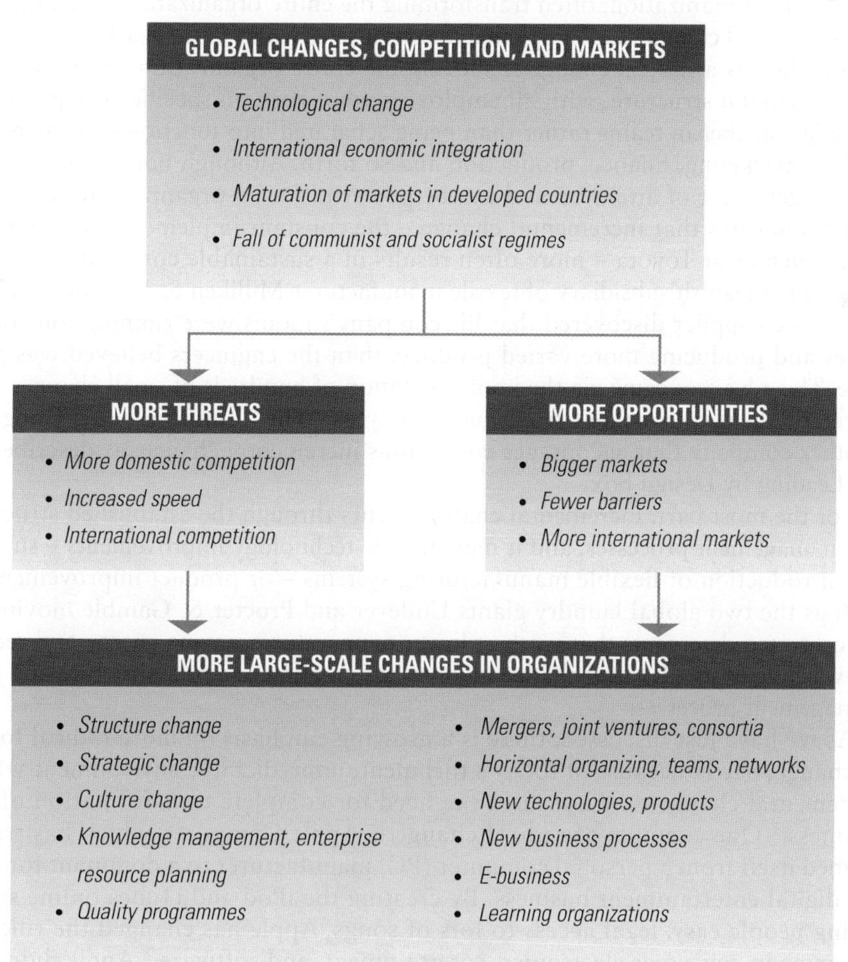

Source: Based on John P. Kotter, *The New Rules: How to Succeed in Today's Post-Corporate World* (New York: The Free Press, 1995).

threats as well as more opportunities. To recognize and manage the threats and take advantage of the opportunities, today's companies are undergoing dramatic changes in all areas of their operations.

As we have seen in previous chapters, many organizations are responding to global forces by adopting self-directed teams and horizontal structures that enhance communication and collaboration, streamlining supply and distribution channels and overcoming barriers of time and place through IT and e-business. Others become involved in joint ventures or consortia to exploit opportunities and extend operations or markets internationally. Some adopt structural innovations such as the virtual network approach to focus on their core competencies while outside specialists handle other activities. In addition, today's organizations face a need for dramatic strategic and cultural change and for rapid and continuous innovations in technology, services, products, and processes.

Incremental versus Radical Change

The changes used to adapt to the environment can be evaluated according to scope – that is, the extent to which changes are incremental or radical for the organization.[4] As summarized in Exhibit 11.2, **incremental change** represents a series of continual progressions that maintain the organization's general equilibrium and often affect only one organizational part. **Radical change**, by contrast, breaks the frame of reference for the organization, often transforming the entire organization. For example, an incremental change is the implementation of sales teams in the marketing department, whereas a radical change is shifting the entire organization from a vertical to a horizontal structure, with all employees who work on specific core processes brought together in teams rather than being separated into functional departments such as marketing, finance, production and so forth. Although bold, transforming change gets a lot of attention and can be powerful for an organization, recent research indicates that incremental change – the constant implementation of small ideas, such as at Toyota – more often results in a sustainable competitive advantage. At the Danish subsidiary of textile manufacturer Milliken & Co., for example, a machine supplier discovered that his company's looms were running four times faster and producing more varied products than the engineers believed was possible. The advances came via the implementation of hundreds of small changes suggested by the textile maker's front-line employees.[5] The California-based Google is another company that encourages continuous incremental change, as described in the Leading by Design box.

For the most part, incremental change occurs through the established structure and management processes, and it may include technology improvements – such as the introduction of flexible manufacturing systems – or product improvements – such as the two global laundry giants Unilever and Procter & Gamble moving to concentrated detergents that wash at lower temperatures, saving energy and reducing washing costs.[6] Radical change involves the creation of a new structure and new management processes.

As we have just discussed, there is a growing emphasis on more radical forms of change, partly because of today's turbulent, unpredictable environment where incremental change may not meet the need for complete transformation of the business.[7] One example of radical change is Apple Computer, which has transformed itself from a personal computer (PC) manufacturer to a dominant force in the digital entertainment business. By creating the iPod and iTunes online store, giving people easy, legal access to lots of songs, Apple has changed the rules of the game in consumer electronics, entertainment, and software.[8] Apple didn't sit back on its laurels, next introducing the iPhone. Corporate transformations and

EXHIBIT 11.2 Incremental versus Radical Change

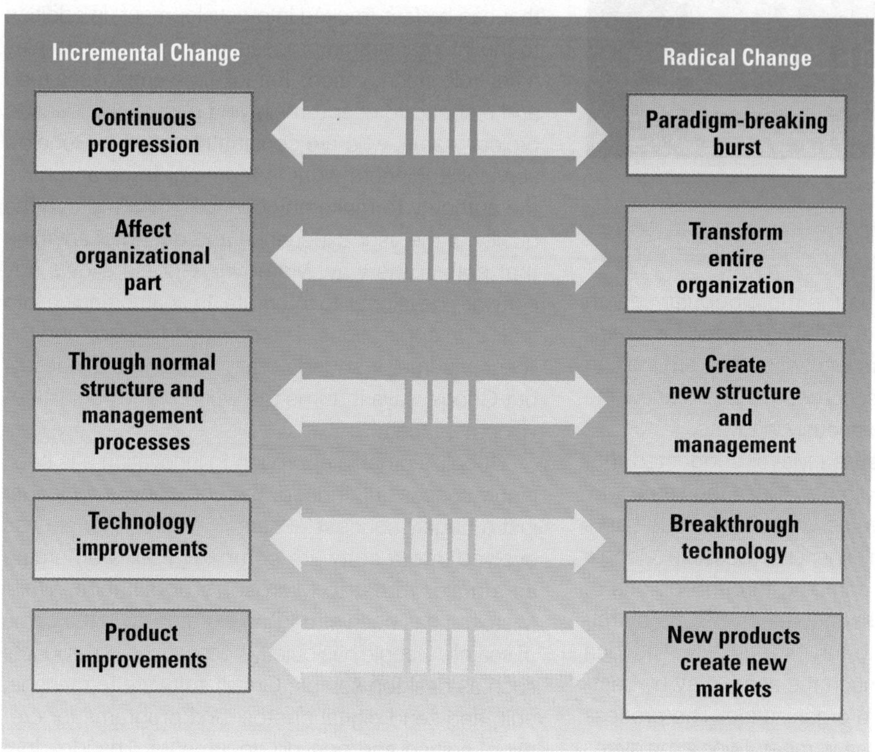

Source: Based on Alan D. Meyer, James B. Goes, and Geoffrey R. Brooks, 'Organizations in Disequilibrium: Environmental Jolts and Industry Revolutions,' in George Huber and William H. Glick, eds., *Organizational Change and Redesign* (New York: Oxford University Press, 1992), 66–111; and Harry S. Dent, Jr., 'Growth through New Product Development,' *Small Business Reports* (November 1990), 30–40.

turnarounds, such as Sergio Marchionne's turnaround of Fiat[9] or Jorma Ollila's transformation of Nokia from a manufacturer of rubber boots and toilet paper to the world's biggest mobile manufacturer,[10] are also considered radical change. Major turnarounds involve changes in all areas of the organization, including structure, management systems, culture, technology and products or services.

It's important not to confuse radical and rapid forms of change, although they are sometimes needed at the same time. Nokia's transformation from a sprawling multidivisional company to a cutting edge mobile telephony business took over 30 years, but it was definitely a radical transformation.[11]

Strategic Types of Change

Managers can focus on four types of change within organizations to achieve strategic advantage. These four types of change are summarized in Exhibit 11.3 as products and services, strategy and structure, culture and technology. We touched on overall leadership and organizational strategy in Chapter 2 and in the previous chapter on corporate culture. Each company has a unique configuration of products and services, strategy and structure, culture and technologies that can be focused for maximum impact upon the company's chosen markets.[12]

As an organization manager, keep this guideline in mind:

Recognize that the four types of change are interdependent and that changes in one area often require changes in others.

Technology changes are those in an organization's production process, including its knowledge and skill base, that enable distinctive competence. These changes are typically designed to make production more efficient or to produce greater volume.

LEADING BY DESIGN

Google

Google quickly became the most popular search engine on the Internet with its smarter, faster approach to providing users with what they are looking for. But to maintain that success, managers knew the company needed to continuously innovate.

Product manager Marissa Mayer suggested that the company come up with new ideas the same way its search engine scours the Web. To provide users with the best Web search experience possible, Google searches far and wide, combing through billions of documents. Then it ranks the search results by relevance and zaps them to the user quickly. The idea search process works much the same way by casting a wide net across the organization. The process begins with an easy-to-use intranet. Even employees with limited technology expertise can quickly set up a page of ideas. 'We never say, "This group should innovate and the rest should just do their jobs,"' says Jonathan Rosenberg, vice president of product management. 'Everyone spends a fraction of [the] day on R&D'. The intranet has also tapped into more ideas from technologically savvy Google employees who may not be very vocal or assertive in meetings. Mayer says some engineers had lots of good ideas but were shy about putting them forth in open meetings. Now, employees can post their ideas on the intranet and see what kind of response they get.

Mayer searches the site each day to see which ideas are generating the most excitement and comments. Once a week, she sits down with a team to hash over the ideas and flesh out at least six or seven that can be fast-tracked into development. In addition to the internal search process, users continue to play a key role in innovation. Ten full-time employees read and respond to user e-mails and pass along ideas to project teams, who are constantly tweaking Google's service. Engineers work in teams of three and have the authority to make any changes that improve the quality of the user experience and get rid of anything that gets in the way. Moreover, Google allows any software developer to integrate its search engine into their own applications. The download is easy and the licence is free. It sounds crazy to some businesses, but Google says it 'turns the world into Google's development team'.

Google's organic approach to innovation has been highly successful. Indeed, the company is no longer just a hugely successful search engine. Google has evolved into a software company that is emerging as a major threat to Microsoft's dominance. While Microsoft has been struggling to catch up in the game of search, Google has quietly been launching products such as desktop search; Gmail; software to manage, edit, and send digital photos; and programs for creating, editing and posting documents. The idea that Google could one day marginalize Microsoft's operating system and bypass Windows applications is being taken seriously by Microsoft managers. Microsoft is still much larger than Google and has plenty of cash with which to compete. But Microsoft leaders know that, for now, Google's innovation process gives it an edge. 'Here Microsoft was spending $600 million a year in R&D for MSN, $1 billion a year for Office, and $1 billion a year for Windows, and Google [got] desktop search out before us', said a Microsoft executive. 'It was a real wake-up call'.

Source: Fara Warner, 'How Google Searches Itself', *Fast Company* (July 2002), 50–52; Fred Vogelstein, 'Search and Destroy', *Fortune* (May 2, 2005), 72–82; and Keith H. Hammonds, 'How Google Grows . . . and Grows . . . and Grows', *Fast Company* (April 2003), 74.

Changes in technology involve the techniques for making products or services such as work methods, equipment and workflow. For example, a technology change at the global courier firm DHL automatically returns details of a package's progress from handheld scanners to the company database, via Wi-fi and GPRS technology, so that vendors can instantly tell a package has been delivered.[13,14]

Product and service changes involve the product or service outputs of an organization. New products include small adaptations of existing products or entirely new product lines. New products and services are normally designed to increase the

EXHIBIT 11.3 The Four Types of Change Provide a Strategic Competitive Wedge

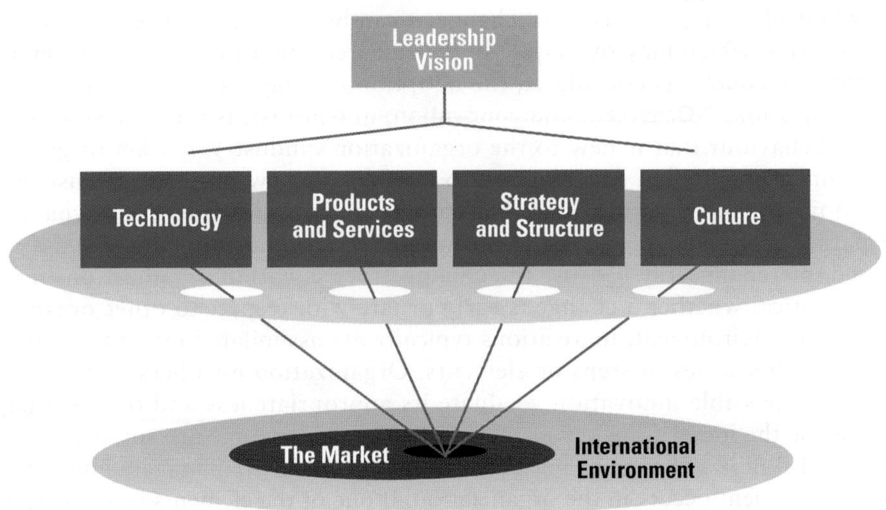

Source: Joseph E. McCann, 'Design Principles for an Innovating Company,' *Academy of Management Executive* 5 (May 1991), 76–93. Used by permission.

market share or to develop new markets, customers, or clients. Toyota's Hilux truck was a new product introduced to increase market share, whereas Asus's Eee mini netbook computer is a new product that created a new market for the company. An example of a new service designed to reach new markets and customers is Korean mobile phone operator SK Telecom's introduction of technology permitting customers to view and record television programmes on their telephones.[15,16]

Strategy and structure changes pertain to the administrative domain in an organization. The administrative domain involves the supervision and management of the organization. These changes include changes in organization structure, strategic management, policies, reward systems, labour relations, coordination devices, management information and control systems and accounting and budgeting systems. Structure and system changes are usually top-down, that is, mandated by top management, whereas product and technology changes may often come from the bottom up. A system change instituted by management in a university might be a new merit pay plan. Corporate downsizing and the shift to horizontal teams are other examples of top-down structure change.

Culture changes refer to changes in the values, attitudes, expectations, beliefs, abilities and behaviour of employees. Culture changes pertain to changes in how employees think; these are changes in mind-set rather than technology, structure or products.

The four types of change in Exhibit 11.3 are interdependent – a change in one often means a change in another. New products may require changes in the production technology, or a change in structure may require new employee skills. For example, when Jong-Yung Yun took over as President and CEO of Samsung Electronics in 1996, he found the company's product division structure stood in the way of taking advantage of technological convergence. A typical case was the company's refrigerators, which had been simple machines but now included specialized semiconductors, made by another division that was not in tune with the white goods department. Over the next years Yun restructured the company to bring core divisions together.[17] The structural change was an outgrowth of the technology change.

Elements for Successful Change

As an organization manager, keep these guidelines in mind:

Make sure every change undertaken has a definite need, idea, adoption decision, implementation strategy and resources. Avoid failure by not proceeding until each element is accounted for.

Regardless of the type or scope of change, it can be analysed as a series of stages of innovation which may overlap.[18] In the research literature on innovation, **organizational change** is considered the adoption of a new idea or behaviour by an organization.[19] **Organizational innovation**, in contrast, is the adoption of an idea or behaviour that is new to the organization's industry, market or general environment.[20] The first organization to introduce a new product is considered the innovator, and organizations that copy it are considered to adopt changes. For purposes of managing change, however, the terms *innovation* and *change* will be used interchangeably because the **change process** within organizations tends to be identical whether a change is early or late with respect to other organizations in the environment. Innovations typically are assimilated into an organization through a series of steps or elements. Organization members first become aware of a possible innovation, evaluate its appropriateness and then evaluate and choose the idea.[21] The key elements of successful change are summarized in Exhibit 11.4. For a change to be successfully implemented, managers must make sure each element occurs in the organization. If one of the elements is missing, the change process will be likely to fail.

COUNTERPOINT 11.1

Sequential models can be helpful in simplifying what is often a complex and even chaotic process. Innovation and change are frequently contested and resisted as they may be promoted and welcomed by some groups but viewed as a threat by others. Processes of change and innovation are often lumpy and recursive. Developments occur in fits and starts; and stages of 'awareness' and 'evaluation' are revisited as new understandings emerge and re-assessments are made. **Discuss**

EXHIBIT 11.4 Sequence of Elements for Successful Change

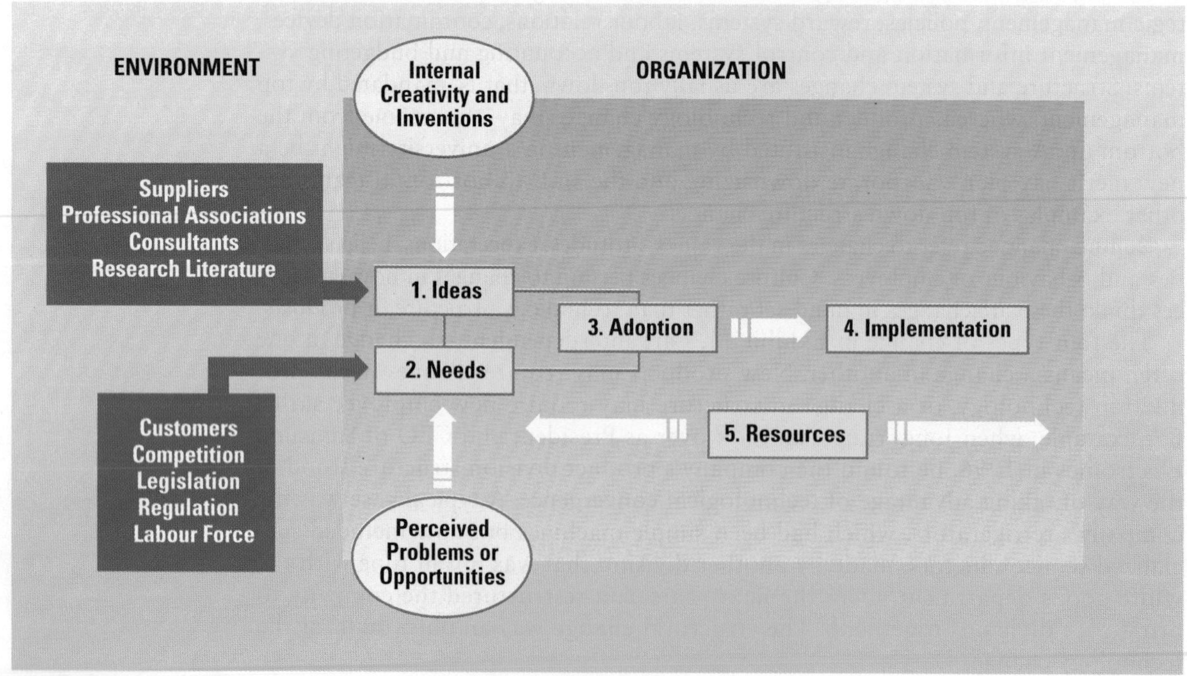

1 *Ideas.* No company can remain competitive without new ideas; change is the outward expression of those ideas.[22] An idea is a new way of doing things. It may be a new product or service, a new management concept or a new procedure for working together in the organization. Ideas can come from within or from outside the organization. Internal creativity is a dramatic element of organizational change. **Creativity** is the generation of novel ideas that may meet perceived needs or respond to opportunities. Yahoo! Corporation organizes regular programming competitions for its staff, where they are encouraged to think 'outside the box' about new applications. Several of the ideas have made it onto Yahoo's portal, including MapMixer, which lets users take maps on the Web and overlay them onto the same locations on Yahoo Maps – creating hybrid maps working independently of the underlying structure of the different maps. MapMixer allows non-technical users to merge a map – for example a historical map of a town – with a Yahoo road or satellite map.[23,24] At Samsung's India subsidiary, employees receive rewards for interesting innovative ideas, with extra bonuses if the innovation is implemented. The concept has been so popular that the company's 300 employees generate 1,800 ideas a month.[25,26]

2 *Need.* Ideas are generally not seriously considered unless there is a perceived need for change. A perceived need for change occurs when managers see a gap between actual performance and desired performance in the organization. Managers try to establish a sense of urgency so that others will understand the need for change. Sometimes a crisis provides an undoubted sense of urgency. In many cases, however, there is no crisis, so managers have to recognize a need and communicate it to others.[27] A study of innovativeness in industrial firms, for example, suggests that organizations that encourage close attention to customers and market conditions and support for entrepreneurial activity produce more ideas and are more innovative.[28] Jeffrey Immelt, since 2000 the CEO of American-headquartered General Electric (GE), has focused on creating just those conditions at the sprawling industrial giant, which had grown in recent years largely through acquisition. By combining an emphasis on marketing, a renewed basic research effort and a company-wide focus on learning and sharing ideas, Immelt is recharging GE into a house of technological innovation, calling for constant reinvention to generate more growth from internal operations. The company has regularly been named one of the world's most innovative by business executives, and is currently investing heavily in green tecnologies.[29,30]

COUNTERPOINT 11.2

The 'need for change' is something that may not be perceived by all managers or employees. Some may well prefer the status quo, not just because it is familiar but because it is tried and tested. Change in itself is not necessarily a 'good thing'. It may be ill-thought through and it may have unanticipated and deleterious consequences. All too often, changes are introduced to 'make an impact', often led by a CEO who may have moved on before the full effects have been felt.

Change may be supported by 'key managers' without them agreeing that it is desirable if they anticipate that their jobs or credibility is put at risk by challenging the proposals. If this occurs, then adoption may be conditional or half-hearted. The outcome may be that the proposed change is incompletely or inadequately implemented. This may not necessarily be a 'bad thing' if the proposed idea is itself poorly thought through or if it has the effect of undermining established strengths. **Discuss**

3 *Adoption*. Adoption occurs when decision makers choose to go ahead with a proposed idea. Key managers and employees need to be in agreement to support the change. For a major organizational change, the decision might require the signing of a legal document by the board of directors. For a small change, adoption might occur with informal approval by a middle manager.

See online COUNTERPOINT 11.8

4 *Implementation*. Implementation occurs when organization members actually use a new idea, technique or behaviour. Materials and equipment may have to be acquired, and workers may have to be trained to use the new idea. Implementation is of course the most important step because without it, previous steps are to no avail. Implementation of change is often the most difficult part of the change process. Until people use the new idea, no change has actually taken place.

5 *Resources*. Human energy and activity are required to bring about change. Change does not happen on its own; it requires time, resources and energy, for both creating and implementing a new idea. Someone must develop a proposal and provide the time and effort to implement it. India's software and business process outsourcing (BPO) giant Wipro has a central innovation council that funds innovative ideas. The company has a special unit, the 'quantum innovation centre' where outside consultants help to bring new ideas to market. Each year five or six ideas are operationalized to build the range of process re-engineering services Wipro offers its clients. Wipro's CEO Azim Premji says, 'Analysts are saying we will do around $4 billion in revenues this year: nine to ten per cent of those revenues will come from innovation, and that's a substantial amount. We are not talking small investments; some of these projects will pay back this year, while some others the year after.[31]

One point about Exhibit 11.4 is especially important. Needs and ideas are listed simultaneously at the beginning of the change sequence. Either may occur first. Many organizations adopted the computer, for example, because it seemed a promising way to improve efficiency. The search for a vaccine against the AIDS virus, on the other hand, was stimulated by a severe need.

Technology Change

As an organization manager, keep these guidelines in mind:

Facilitate frequent changes in internal technology by adopting an organic organizational structure. Give technical personnel freedom to analyze problems and develop solutions or create a separate, organically structured department or venture group to conceive and propose new ideas.

In today's business world, any company that isn't continually developing, acquiring, or adapting new technology will likely be out of business in a few years. However, organizations face a contradiction when it comes to technology change, because the conditions that promote new ideas are not generally the best for implementing those ideas for routine production. An innovative organization is often characterized by flexibility and empowered employees and the absence of rigid work rules.[32] As discussed earlier in this book, an organic, free-flowing organization is typically associated with change and is considered the best organization form for adapting to a chaotic environment.

The flexibility of an organic organization is attributed to opportunities to be creative and introduce new ideas. Organic organizations encourage a bottom-up innovation process. Ideas bubble up from middle- and lower-level employees when they have the freedom to propose ideas and to experiment. A mechanistic structure, in contrast, tends to stifle innovation with its emphasis on rules and regulations, even though it may be the best structure for efficiently producing routine products. The challenge for managers is to create both organic and mechanistic conditions within the organization to achieve both innovation and efficiency. To attain both aspects of technological change, many organizations use the ambidextrous approach.

The Ambidextrous Approach

Recent thinking has refined the idea of organic versus mechanistic structures with respect to innovation creation versus innovation utilization. An organic structure may generate innovative ideas but is not necessarily the best structure for using those ideas.[33] In other words, the initiation and the utilization of change are different kinds of processes. Organic characteristics such as decentralization and employee freedom are conducive for initiating ideas; but these same conditions often make it hard to implement a change because employees are less likely to comply. Decentralization and a generally loose structure may mean that employees can ignore the innovation.

How does an organization solve this dilemma? One remedy is for the organization to use an **ambidextrous approach** – to incorporate structures and management processes that are appropriate to both the creation and the implementation of innovation.[34] Another way to think of the ambidextrous approach is to look at the organization design elements that are important for *exploring* new ideas versus the design elements that are most suitable for *exploiting* current capabilities. Exploration means encouraging creativity and developing new ideas, whereas exploitation means implementing those ideas to produce routine products. The organization can be designed to behave in an organic way for exploring new ideas and in a mechanistic way to exploit and use the ideas. Exhibit 11.5 illustrates how one department is structured organically to explore and develop new ideas and another department is structured mechanistically for routine implementation of innovations. Research has shown that organizations that use an ambidextrous approach by designing for both exploration and exploitation are significantly more successful in launching innovative new products or services.[35]

For example, a study of long-established Japanese companies such as Honda and Canon that have succeeded in breakthrough innovations found that these companies use an ambidextrous approach.[36] To develop ideas related to a new technology, the companies assign teams of young staff members who are not entrenched in the 'old way of doing things' to work on the project. The teams are headed by an esteemed elder and are charged with doing whatever is needed to develop new ideas and products, even if it means breaking rules that are important in the larger organization for the process of implementing the new ideas.

Techniques for Encouraging Technology Change

Some of the techniques used by companies to maintain an ambidextrous approach are switching structures, separate creative departments, venture teams and corporate entrepreneurship.

EXHIBIT 11.5 Division of Labour in the Ambidextrous Organization

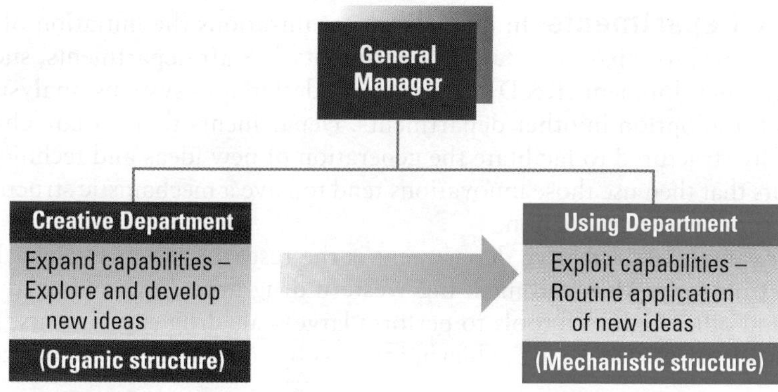

Switching Structures Switching structures occurs when, for example, a mechanistic organization creates an organic structure for the initiation of new ideas.[37] Some of the ways organizations have switched structures to achieve the ambidextrous approach are as follows:

- Electrolux, the Swedish home appliance maker, was facing declining sales. Its products, typically designed by the engineering department, were taking too long to get to market and were failing to capture consumers' attention. CEO Hans Straberg knew the problem needed a radical solution, and called in the chief of the Consumer Innovation division, Johan Hjertonsson. Hjertonsson had developed a reputation for radical solutions when facing up to the challenge of cheaper Chinese goods in the late 1990s. His approach was to abandon engineer-driven product development and instead set up cross-functional innovation teams made up of designers, engineers, marketers and salespeople working together to come up with products that excite consumers even if they are more expensive than the bog-standard imported competition. The entire company's strategy has now been revamped in order to focus on higher end, higher profit margin products, de-emphasizing lower priced, 'commoditized' products. The product development system keeps employees engaged and helps them to avoid 'silo' thinking where they become focused only on the culture and dynamics of their own divisions.[38]
- The Japanese car maker Nissan recently opened a new innovation facility, the Nissan Advanced Technology Centre (NATC), designed to bring together R&D teams from around the company to work together more closely and more collaboratively in product development. The centre, which is focused primarily on developing green technologies and bringing them to market, was physically designed to encourage not only cross-functional collaboration but also to involve external engineers and visiting academics and researchers. Engineers from production factories from around the world are seconded to the centre, providing them a different perspective on the company's business, and ensuring that nuts and bolts production issues are addressed early in the development process The whole centre is physically designed with an 'open' concept, for example including 'collaboration rooms' that can accommodate up to 200 people, fitted with vehicle lifts. The facility interior is designed to permit an unobstructed view from much of the building of the testing going on in the vehicle pit-lane on the first floor, again contributing to the collaborative process.[39]

Both of these organizations found creative ways to be ambidextrous, establishing organic conditions for developing new ideas in the midst of more mechanistic conditions for implementing and using those ideas.

Creative Departments In many large organizations the initiation of innovation is assigned to separate **creative departments**.[40] Staff departments, such as research and development (R&D), engineering, design and systems analysis, create changes for adoption in other departments. Departments that initiate change are organically structured to facilitate the generation of new ideas and techniques. Departments that then use those innovations tend to have a mechanistic structure more suitable for efficient production.

One example of a creative department is the research lab at Oksuka Pharmaceutical Company. Although most big Western drug firms have switched to using robots and other high-tech tools to perform large-scale drug experiments, Japanese companies such as Oksuka are achieving success by continuing to emphasize human creativity. To get the kind of creative spirit that is willing to try new things and look for the unexpected, Oksuka's president Tatsuo Higuchi says its research labs 'put a high value on weird people'.[41] However, in the department that manufactures drugs, where routine and precision is important, a pharmaceutical company probably favours the employment of less unusual people who are comfortable following rules and standard procedures.

Another type of creative department is the **idea incubator**, an increasingly popular way to facilitate the development of new ideas within the organization. An idea incubator provides a safe harbour where ideas from employees throughout the organization can be developed without interference from company bureaucracy or politics.[42] The incubator gives people throughout the organization a place to go rather than having to shop a new idea all over the company and hope someone will pay attention. Companies as diverse as Intel India, Microsoft, and Netherlands-based Philips NV use incubators to support the development of creative ideas.[43]

Venture Teams **Venture teams** are a technique used to give free rein to creativity within organizations. Venture teams are often given a separate location and facilities so they are not constrained by organizational procedures. A venture team is like a small company within a large company. Numerous organizations have used the venture team concept to free creative people from the bureaucracy of a large corporation. Shell Oil established its GameChanger unit to increase innovation within the company's exploration business, providing a vehicle that channels promising employee ideas into projects funded with the parent company's capital. One of the earliest and most successful venture units is Innovacom, set up by France Telecom in 1988. Innovacom operates as its parent's in-house venture capital-plus outfit. It provides capital to early-stage inventors and entrepreneurs in the fields of telecom hardware, telecom software, enterprise software and internet content and services. Crucially, it links start-ups with experts within France Telecom's numerous telecommunication companies, allowing new companies to learn from the operations of a mature company, while providing an injection of entrepreneurial enthusiasm to the collaborating division. Successful ventures may be sold-off or brought under the France Telecom umbrella.[44,45]

COUNTERPOINT 11.3

A cautionary tale about the importance of setting up venture teams early, and the need to think 'outside-the-box' of the parent business comes from the newspaper business. Newspapers around the world have been rocked by the challenge of the internet, where information is often available free – and instantaneously. Developing an internet strategy is a matter of survival for the industry, and in most cases companies have set up internet-based operations as venture teams to explore and develop the new technology. One major challenge has been to find ways for internet operations to replace revenues from declining paper sales as readers shifted to online access. Many papers like Canada's *Globe and Mail*, the *New York Times*, and the *Irish Times* tried to charge for internet content by forcing readers to buy a subscription in the same way that they had for their paper copies. However they quickly found out that the internet is a different kind of business. Readers simply went elsewhere for their news, with the result that online newspapers were in a vicious cycle of declining subscription revenues and falling readership, leading to lower advertising revenues. One-by-one they have almost all abandoned this approach, accepting that the internet requires an entirely different revenue strategy even though the content may be identical to what consumers are prepared to purchase for cash from a newsagent. Internet newspaper ventures now depend almost exclusively on advertising, but the rates are much lower than for hard-copy advertising. It's a dilemma internet newspaper venture groups will have to resolve soon, as the printed versions of newspapers sell fewer and fewer copies. Britain's *Telegraph* group manages to get 20 per cent of its advertising revenues from the internet, but it was one of the first major papers to go online in 1994. Other papers that started online later are struggling.[46] **Discuss**

One type of venture team is called a *skunkworks*.[47] A **skunkworks** is a separate, small, informal, highly autonomous and often secretive group that focuses on breakthrough ideas for the business. The original skunkworks was created by America's Lockheed Martin aerospace manufacturer more than 50 years ago and is still in operation. The essence of a skunkworks is that highly talented people are given the time and freedom to let creativity reign. Michelin has set up a skunkworks in Switzerland to go one step further than the Toyota Prius and develop a zero-pollution car. Team leader Pierre Varenne says that the apparently counter-intuitive decision to set up in a small town in a country with no automobile industry is not an accident; it allows the team to work away from the pressure of car companies and oil conglomerates that might negatively influence the project back home in France.[48]

A variation of the venture team concept is the **new-venture fund**, which provides financial resources for employees to develop new ideas, products or businesses. In order to tap into its employees' entrepreneurial urges, Lockheed Martin allows workers to take up to two years' unpaid leave to explore a new idea, using company labs and equipment and paying company rates for health insurance. If the idea is successful, the corporation's venture fund invests about $250,000 in the start-up company. One successful start-up has been Genase, which created an enzyme that 'stone-washes' denim.[49]

Corporate Entrepreneurship Corporate entrepreneurship attempts to develop an internal entrepreneurial spirit, philosophy and structure that will produce a higher-than-average number of innovations. Corporate entrepreneurship may involve the use of creative departments and new venture teams, but it also attempts to release the creative energy of all employees in the organization. Managers can create systems and structures that encourage entrepreneurship. For example, at the giant oil company BP, top executives establish contracts with the heads of all BP's business units. The unit managers are given free rein to deliver on the contract in whatever way they see fit, within clearly identified constraints.[50]

An important outcome of corporate entrepreneurship is to facilitate **idea champions**. These go by a variety of names, including *advocate, intrapreneur*, or *change agent*. Idea champions provide the time and energy to make things happen. They fight to overcome natural resistance to change and to convince others of the merit of a new idea.[51] Idea champions need not be within the organization. Some companies have found that fostering idea champions among regular customers can be a highly successful approach.[52] An example is Britain's Anglian Water, where every innovation project has a sponsor or champion who is a customer seeking a solution to a specific problem.[53] The business strategy of Johor Corporation (JCorp), a Malaysian state-owned regional economic development company, is built around 'intrapraneurship' with a social goal of increasing entrepreneurship among the ethnic Malay population. JCorp executives are encouraged to develop and implement business ideas in partnership with outside entrepreneurs, and can access venture funds from JCorp, which usually takes a majority ownership stake in the venture. The ventures have turned a profit overall for both JCorp and its intrapreneurs.[54,55]

Idea champions usually come in two types. The **technical champion**, or *product champion*, is the person who generates or adopts and develops an idea for a technological innovation and is devoted to it, even to the extent of risking position or prestige. The **management champion** acts as a supporter and sponsor to shield and promote an idea, such as a new project or a change of structure, within the organization.[56] The management champion sees the potential application and has the prestige and authority to get the idea a fair hearing and to allocate resources to it. Numerous studies have identified the importance of idea champions as a factor in the success of new products. US fabric and clothing manufacturer W.L. Gore, featured in the *In Practice* box below, is a leading example of a company that fosters and benefits from idea champions.[57]

New Products and Services

Although the ideas just discussed are important to product and service as well as technology changes, other factors are also important. In many ways, new products and services are a special case of innovation because they are used by customers outside the organization. Since new products are designed for sale in an uncertain environment, doubts about the suitability and success of an innovation are high.

New Product Success Rate

Research has explored the enormous uncertainty associated with the development and sale of new products.[58] To understand what this uncertainty can mean to organizations, just consider such flops as Sony's Betamax video recording format, which lost out to VHS after an epic 25 year battle,[59] or IPC publishing company's *Nova*

W.L. Gore

W. L. Gore, a privately held American company best known as the maker of Gore-Tex fabric, is so good at innovating that it has become a major player in areas as diverse as guitar strings, dental floss, fuel cells and medical devices. Everyone at Gore is expected to become an idea champion at some time in their career with the company. Gore provides the environment for that to happen by letting employees figure out what they want to do.

Gore's employees, known as associates, don't have job titles or bosses. Rather than being assigned to tasks, people make commitments to work on projects where they think they can make the biggest contribution. That means employees tend to be 'very passionate about what they're doing', says company researcher Jeff Kolde. Kolde himself is an excellent example of an idea champion. Gore researchers had developed an improved kind of ionic membrane that separates positive and negative ions, but the company wasn't sure what to do with it. Kolde got excited about the potential use in the fuel cell industry and began sending out prototypes. The fuel cell industry got really excited too. W. L. Gore became the first commercial supplier of membrane-electron assemblies (MEAs), a critical technology for fuel cells. But Kolde first had to convince others that the project was worth their time and effort, no easy task in a new area like fuel cells. His passion for the project enabled him to recruit people from around the company, including two Ph.Ds.

Gore research associates get to spend 10 per cent of their time as 'dabble time', developing their own ideas. A senior colleague serves as a mentor and guide; if the idea is promising and the associate is passionate about it, the mentor becomes a management champion to make sure the project gets the attention and resources needed to pursue it. Gore has found that having associates recruit volunteers to work on projects turns out to be a pretty good indication of whether an innovation is likely to succeed.[60]

women's magazine which actually failed twice. It had been an iconic UK fashion title in the 1960s that lost readership and stopped publication in 1975, only to be revived in 2000 before failing again less than 12 months later.[61] Swiss drug manufacturer Novartis dropped $235 in development costs for the Aurograb antibiotic before it failed its second round of clinical tests.[62] Developing and producing products that fail is a part of business in all industries. Companies spend billions on R&D for new products such as Canada's Dr. Care aerosol toothpaste (that parents feared would be too popular with their children), Blue Circle Cement's abortive entry into the lawnmower market, and IBM's doomed attempt to take on Microsoft Windows with its OS/2 operating system.[63] Thousands of new products and service concepts fail each year.

Experts estimate that about 80 per cent of new products fail upon introduction and another ten per cent disappear within five years. Considering that, depending on the product and the market, it can be hugely costly to successfully launch a new product, new product development is a risky, high-stakes game for organizations. Nevertheless, without new product development, companies will inevitably wither and die, and so most large corporations devote energy and resources to developing new products.[64]

COUNTERPOINT 11.4

Similar figures are regularly cited for failures of organizational innovation where change programmes fail to deliver their promises. Change may be regarded as a necessity but it is also very frequently ineffective or abandoned.

- Two-thirds of Total Quality Management (TQM) programmes fail, and reengineering initiatives fail 70 per cent of the time (Senge, 1999, pp. 5-6).[65]
- A seminal study found a 64 per cent failure rate among new technological innovations introduced into municipal public service programmes (Yin, 1978, p. vi).[66]
- Change initiatives crucial to organizational success fail 70 per cent of the time (Miller, 2002, p. 360).
- Major corporate investments in technology are not used as intended or abandoned within six months 80 per cent of the time (Gartner Group in Miller, 2002, p. 360).[67]
- Leaders of the corporate reengineering movement report that the success rate for Fortune 1000 companies is below 50 per cent, possibly only 20 per cent (Strebel, 1996, p. 86).[68] **Discuss**

A survey some years ago examined 200 projects in nineteen chemical, drug, electronics and petroleum laboratories to learn about success rates.[69] To be successful, the new product had to pass three stages of development: technical completion, commercialization and market success. The findings about success rates are given in Exhibit 11.6. On the average, only 57 per cent of all projects undertaken in the R&D laboratories achieved technical objectives, which means all technical problems were solved and the projects moved on to production. Of all projects that were started, less than one third (31 per cent) were fully marketed and commercialized. Several projects failed at this stage because production estimates or test market results were unfavourable.

Finally, only 12 per cent of all projects originally undertaken achieved economic success. Most of the commercialized products did not earn sufficient returns to cover the cost of development and production. This means that only about one project in eight returned a profit to the company.

EXHIBIT 11.6 Probability of New Product Success

	Probability
Technical completion (technical objectives achieved)	.57
Commercialization (full-scale marketing)	.31
Market success (earns economic return)	.12

Source: Based on Edwin Mansfield, J. Rapaport, J. Schnee, S. Wagner, and M. Hamburger, *Research and Innovation in Modern Corporations* (New York: Norton, 1971), 57.

Reasons for New Product Success

The next question to be answered by research was, 'Why are some products – both physical products and service – more successful than others? Why has the United Arab Emirates-headquartered Thuraya satellite phone service remained profitable while US-based Iridium and Globalstar have both had to declare Chapter 11 bankruptcy protection? Why did Sony's Blu-Ray format for high density data disks succeed while rival Toshiba's HD-DVD standard fall by the wayside?'[70] Further studies indicated that innovation success is often related to collaboration between technical and marketing departments. Successful new products and services seem to be technologically sound and also carefully tailored to customer needs.[71] A study called Project SAPPHO examined seventeen pairs of new product innovations, with one success and one failure in each pair, and concluded the following:

1. Successful innovating companies had a much better understanding of customer needs and paid much more attention to marketing.
2. Successful innovating companies made more effective use of outside technology and outside advice, even though they did more work in-house.
3. Top management support in the successful innovating companies was from people who were more senior and had greater authority.

Thus there is a distinct pattern of tailoring innovations to customer needs, making effective use of technology, and having influential top managers support the project. These ideas taken together indicate that the effective design for new product innovation is associated with horizontal coordination across departments.

Horizontal Coordination Model

The organization design for achieving new product innovation involves three components – departmental specialization, boundary spanning and horizontal coordination. These components are similar to the horizontal coordination mechanisms discussed in Chapter 3, such as teams, task forces and project managers, and the differentiation and integration ideas discussed in Chapter 4. Exhibit 11.7 illustrates these components in the **horizontal coordination model**.

As an organization manager, keep this guideline in mind:

Encourage marketing, research and production departments to develop linkages to each other and to their environments when new products or services are needed.

Specialization The key departments in new product development are R&D, marketing and production. The specialization component means that the personnel in all three of these departments are highly competent at their own tasks. The three departments are differentiated from each other and have skills, goals and attitudes appropriate for their specialized functions.

EXHIBIT 11.7 Horizontal Coordination Model for New Product Innovations

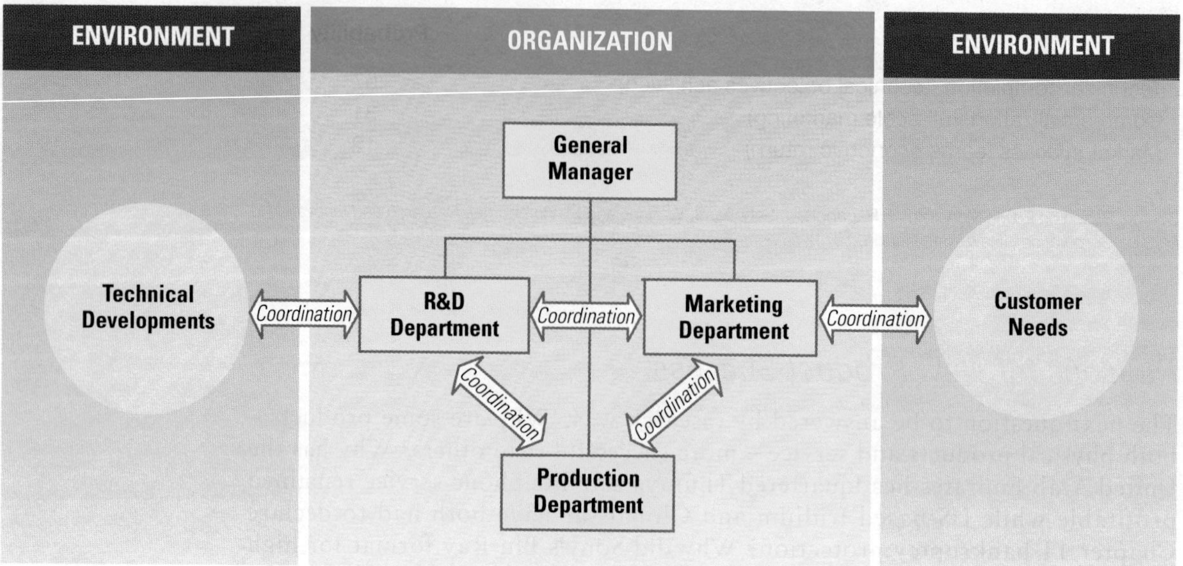

Boundary Spanning This component means each department involved with new products has excellent linkage with relevant sectors in the external environment. R&D personnel are linked to professional associations and to colleagues in other R&D departments. They are aware of recent scientific developments. Marketing personnel are closely linked to customer needs. They listen to what customers have to say, and they analyze competitor products and suggestions by distributors. For example, Charles Rolls and Tim Warrilow launched UK-based Fever-Tree in 2001 when they observed that the big drinks mixer manufacturers like Schweppes were focusing on high volume mixes based on cheap, artificial ingredients: the victory of company laboratories and accountants over consumer focus. Fever-Tree developed six premium drinks mixes based on natural ingredients, and distributed through high-end bars, and premium supermarkets such as the UK's Waitrose.[72]

Horizontal Coordination This component means that technical, marketing and production people share ideas and information. Research people inform marketing of new technical developments to learn whether the developments are applicable to customers. Marketing people provide customer complaints and information to R&D to use in the design of new products. People from both R&D and marketing coordinate with production because new products have to fit within production capabilities so costs are not exorbitant. The decision to launch a new product is ultimately a joint decision among all three departments. Horizontal coordination, using mechanisms such as cross-functional teams, increases both the amount and the variety of information for new product development, enabling the design of products that meet customer needs and circumventing manufacturing and marketing problems.[73]

Recall the chapter-opening example of Toyota, which uses a product development technique called *obeya*. The idea behind *obeya* is to change the way people think about product innovation and development by changing how they share information. 'There are no taboos in *obeya*', explains Takeshi Yoshida, chief engineer for the 2003 Corolla. 'Everyone in that room is an expert. They all have a part to play in building the car'.[74] Consumer products firm Unilever is also taking a bold new approach to innovation.

See online COUNTERPOINT 11.9

Companies such as Unilever and, W. L. Gore routinely turn to customers and other organizations for advice. Gore worked with physicians to develop its thoracic graft.[75] During development of new planes such as the Airbus A380, engineers from Airbus

Unilever

Anglo-Dutch firm Unilever is one of the two giants of the global consumer products industry, along with America's Procter & Gamble. However, like many long-established and successful firms, by the beginning of the twenty-first century Unilever was in a downward cycle of tired brands and declining profits. In 2005 new CEO Patrick Cescau launched a turnaround strategy that focused on eliminating declining brands, reducing layers of bureaucracy, investing in the more profitable emerging markets and making the company far more nimble in developing product innovations and bringing them to market.[76] Unilever sold off its North American laundry products, which had consistently lost market share to Procter & Gamble's products, on the latter's home turf.

The key to Unilever's recent successes in product innovation has been to emphasize consumer-driven product development. As noted earlier in this chapter, consumers are becoming increasingly sensitive to environmental issues. For example, breakthroughs have been achieved in concentrating liquid detergent such as *Persil Small and Mighty*, which saves energy that would have been wasted transporting the excess water in traditional more diluted detergents, as well as making it easier for the consumer to haul the product home from the supermarket.[77] Unilever is working to achieve recognition of many of its products as environmentally sound. The company is a major tea producer, and is working with the Rainforest Alliance, an environmental NGO, to have all its tea plantations in East Africa certified as environmentally and socially sustainable.[78]

The company has also successfully leveraged its decentralized structure; its products are present in about 150 countries, and product development occurs all over the globe. Whereas previously national units of Unilever worked almost independently, Cescau has worked to encourage local innovation but take greater advantage of locally-developed innovations.[79] One of a number of recent successes in this area has been high-calcium ice cream, which was first developed in Asian markets and then successfully introduced in Europe.[80]

Unilever has also worked closely with its advertising agencies to ensure they are producing their cutting edge campaigns for Unilever, whose products had tended to be supported by cautious, conservative advertising. Unilever Chief Marketing Officer Simon Clift says the company and its advertising agencies were once 'a bit like a married couple who had great sex . . . just not with each other'. In other words, Unilever had great products that were not always backed up by great advertising campaigns, while its advertising agencies ran great campaigns, just not necessarily for Unilever. By shifting some of its accounts and restructuring its relationships with other advertising agencies, the company has produced an edgier advertising image that not only has brought several Cannes Grand Prix awards but also delivered higher sales for several products. The approach also involves careful analysis of markets. Whereas European consumers tend to appreciate racy advertisement, the same may not be true in the US, for example. A campaign for its Axe male grooming line implies that young women will lose sexual inhibition when they smell Axe products being worn by their male friends; Clift says Unilever have delayed introducing its Axe line in the States at the cost of several hundred million dollars in potential revenues, partly because 'we find this overt sexual reference in advertising might not go down too well in the Bible Belt'.[81]

and the purchasing airlines work closely with flight attendants, pilots and frequent flyers, to make sure the plane is designed for maximum functionality and customer satisfaction.[82,83]

Successful companies typically use this concept of horizontal coordination to achieve competitive advantage. Innovation failures – such as Kellogg's initial efforts to introduce cornflakes to India or Chrysler Corporation's early (and in retrospect, patronizing) effort to market to women with the 'LaFemme' model car[84] – usually violate the horizontal linkage model. Employees fail to connect with customer needs and market forces or internal departments fail to adequately share needs and coordinate with one another. Recent research has confirmed a connection between effective boundary spanning that keeps the organization in touch with market forces, smooth coordination among departments and successful product development.[85]

Achieving Competitive Advantage: The Need for Speed

The rapid development of new products is becoming a major strategic weapon in the shifting international marketplace.[86] To remain competitive, companies are learning to develop ideas into new products and services incredibly fast. Whether the approach is called the *horizontal linkage model, concurrent engineering, companies without walls, the parallel approach or simultaneous coupling of departments*, the point is the same – get people working together simultaneously on a project rather than in sequence. Many companies are learning to sprint to market with new products.

Time-based competition means delivering products and services faster than competitors, giving companies a competitive edge. Tekes, the Finnish government technology agency, has set up RAPID, a special programme to help the country's major corporations develop products and put them on the market more quickly, essential in quickly changing global markets. Most of the country's major corporations have benefited from the programme. Finland has been a leader in the high-tech sector, with companies like Nokia regularly outstripping competitors in speed to market and thus capturing and protecting market share in highly competitive markets.[87]

Some companies use what are called *fast cycle teams* as a way to support highly important projects and deliver products and services faster than competitors. A fast cycle team is a multifunctional, and sometimes multinational, team that works under stringent timelines and is provided with high levels of company resources and empowerment to accomplish an accelerated product development project.[88,89] By using the Internet to collaborate on new designs among various functional departments and with suppliers, teams at the US-headquartered plumbing accessory manufacturer Moen take a new kitchen or bath faucet from drawing board to store shelf in only 16 months. The time savings means Moen's teams can work on three times as many projects as previously and introduce up to fifteen new designs a year for today's fashion-conscious consumers.[90] Similarly, as we noted in Chapter 8, Toyota used a variety of innovative team approaches to develop the innovative Prius in only 15 months, in comparison with an industry standard of four years for the development of a new car model.[91]

Another critical issue is designing products that can compete on a global scale and successfully marketing those products internationally. Companies such as the ice cream maker Häagen Dazs are trying to improve horizontal communication and collaboration across geographical regions, recognizing that they can pick up winning product ideas from customers in other countries. A new Häagen Dazs flavour, *dulce de leche*, developed primarily for sale in Argentina, quickly became a favourite in the rest of the world.[92,93]

Many new product development teams today are global teams because organizations have to develop products that will meet diverse needs of consumers all over the world.[94] Unilever, profiled earlier in this chapter, established the Centre of Excellence Assembled Foods, a global product development centre, located on campuses in Italy and the UK, where multinational expert teams will be responsible for scouting innovations worldwide and developing new 'composite food products' for the company, such as meals, salads, snacks and bakery goods.[95]

Strategy and Structure Change

The preceding discussion focused on new production processes and products, which are based in the technology of an organization. The expertise for such innovation lies within the technical core and professional staff groups, such as research and engineering. This section turns to an examination of strategy and structure changes.

All organizations need to make changes in their strategies, structures and administrative procedures from time to time. In the past, when the environment was relatively stable, most organizations focused on small, incremental changes to solve immediate problems or take advantage of new opportunities. However, over the past couple of decades, with globalization and technological innovations upending traditional organizational models, companies throughout the world have faced the need to make radical changes in strategy, structure and management processes to adapt to new competitive demands.[96] Many organizations are cutting out layers of management and decentralizing decision making. There is a shift toward more horizontal structures, with teams of front-line workers empowered to make decisions and solve problems on their own. Some companies are breaking totally away from traditional organization forms and shifting toward virtual network strategies and structures. Numerous companies are reorganizing and shifting their strategies as the expansion of e-business changes the rules. Global competition and rapid technological change will likely lead to even greater strategy-structure realignments over the next decade.

These types of changes are the responsibility of the organization's top managers, and the overall process of change is typically different from the process for innovation in technology or new products.

The Dual-Core Approach

The **dual-core approach** to organizational change compares administrative and technical changes. Administrative changes affect the design and structure of the organization itself, including restructuring, downsizing, teams, control systems, information systems and departmental grouping. Research into administrative change suggests two things. First, administrative changes occur less frequently than do technical changes. Second, administrative changes occur in response to different environmental sectors and follow a different internal process than do technology-based changes.[97] The dual-core approach to organizational change identifies the unique processes associated with administrative change.[98]

Organizations – schools, hospitals, city governments, welfare agencies, government bureaucracies and many business firms – can be conceptualized as having two cores: a *technical core* and an *administrative core*. Each core has its own employees, tasks and environmental domain. Innovation can originate in either core.

The responsibility of the administrative core includes the structure, control and coordination of the organization itself and concerns the environmental sectors of government, financial resources, economic conditions, human resources and

As an organization manager, keep this guideline in mind:

Facilitate changes in strategy and structure by adopting a top-down approach. Use a mechanistic structure when the organization needs to adopt frequent administrative changes in a top-down fashion.

competitors. The technical core is concerned with the transformation of raw materials into organizational products and services and involves the environmental sectors of customers and technology.[99]

The point of the dual-core approach is that many organizations – especially not-for-profit and government organizations – must adopt frequent administrative changes and need to be structured differently from organizations that rely on frequent technical and product changes for competitive advantage.

Organization Design for Implementing Administrative Change

The findings from research comparing administrative and technical change suggest that a mechanistic organization structure is appropriate for frequent administrative changes, including changes in goals, strategy, structure, control systems and personnel.[100] In many government organizations that are bureaucratically structured, administrative changes in policy, regulations or control systems are more critical than technical changes. Organizations that successfully adopt many administrative changes often have a larger administrative ratio, are larger in size, and are centralized and formalized compared with organizations that adopt many technical changes.[101] The reason is the top-down implementation of changes in response to changes in the government, financial or legal sectors of the environment. Research into civil service reform found that the implementation of administrative innovation was extremely difficult in organizations that had an organic technical core. The professional employees in a decentralized agency could resist civil service changes. By contrast, organizations that were considered more bureaucratic in the sense of high formalization and centralization adopted administrative changes more readily.[102]

The innovation approaches associated with administrative versus technical change are summarized in Exhibit 11.8. Technical change, such as changes in production techniques and innovation technology for new products, is facilitated by an organic structure, which allows ideas to bubble upward from lower- and middle-level employees. Organizations that must adopt frequent administrative changes, in contrast, tend to use a top-down process and a mechanistic structure. For example, policy changes, such as the adoption of no-smoking policies, sexual harassment policies or new safety procedures, are usually implemented through a top-down approach. Downsizing and restructuring are nearly always managed top down, for example when New Zealand's privatized telecommunications operator, Telecom, laid off 230 staff in 2006–2007 under the leadership of chief executive Theresa Gattung.[103,104]

What about business organizations that are normally technologically innovative in bottom-up fashion but suddenly face a crisis and need to reorganize? Or a technically innovative, high-tech firm that must reorganize frequently to accommodate changes in production technology or the environment? Technically innovative firms may suddenly have to restructure, reduce the number of employees, alter pay systems, disband teams or form a new division.[105] One answer is to use a top-down change process. In a top-down process, the authority for strategy and structure change lies with top management, who initiate and implement the new strategy and structure to meet environmental circumstances. Employee input may be sought, but top managers have the responsibility to direct the change. Top down decision-making is often necessary to put an organization back on its feet when dealing with unexpected economic shocks. This was the situation facing the Anglo-Australian mining giant Rio Tinto Group when world commodity prices fell sharply in the 2008 slump.

See online COUNTERPOINT 11.10

EXHIBIT 11.8 Dual-Core Approach to Organization Change

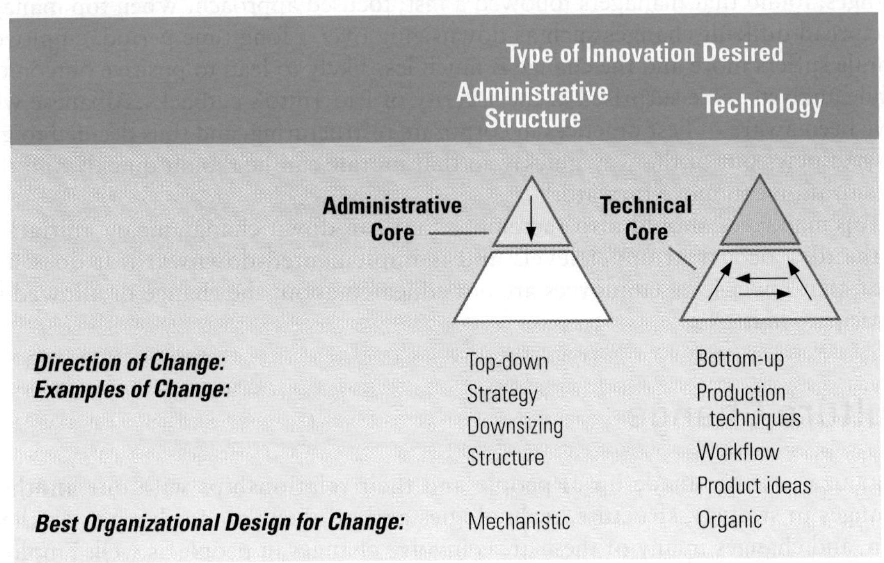

Rio Tinto Group

Rio Tinto is one of the storied names in world mining. The company dates back to 1873 when Rothschild family companies in London and Paris came together to buy the Spanish government's Rio Tinto copper mines in southern Spain (hence the company's name). By 2008 the company was a major miner of various minerals, including bauxite, iron ore, copper and diamonds. Rio Tinto is also the world's third-largest coal producer.

As the long global boom that began in the 1990s reached a crescendo in the first years of the twenty-first century, the commodities produced by Rio Tinto ballooned in value. Rapidly expanding economies like China and India were consuming ever-increasing quantities of metals and other minerals, and increased demand fed into higher prices. Rio Tinto expanded aggressively, including purchase of the major Canadian aluminium producer Alcan in 2007. Rio Tinto shares seemed on a one-way upwards escalator, fuelled both by the commodity prices and a hostile takeover bid from rival BHP Billiton.

Suddenly, however, the bottom fell out of the market for Rio Tinto's main products. Between January and December 2008, the price of both copper and aluminium dropped by two-thirds, and iron ore by one-third. Rio Tinto's own stock price also plunged; between May and December 2008 the company's shares declined by almost 90 per cent. BHP withdrew its bid for Rio Tinto. The company's near $40 billion in debt, mainly accumulated from the Alcan purchase, worried investors. Rio CEO Tom Albanese needed to do something quickly to reduce overcapacity, rein in costs, reduce debt, restage capital investments to the longer term and thus improve investor confidence. In December 2008 he announced a wide-ranging package including 14,000 redundancies worldwide, a cut of more than 50 per cent in planned spending during 2009 including putting several mine projects on hold, a freeze on dividends and an asset sale to raise cash. Albanese commented, 'By taking these tough decisions now we will be well positioned when the recovery comes'. The immediate reaction of stock markets was positive, but employees and communities around the world were worried. Albanese's next task will be to maintain morale as the cuts bite.[106]

A study of successful corporate transformations, which frequently involve painful changes, found that managers followed a fast, focused approach. When top managers spread difficult changes such as downsizing over a long time period, employee morale suffers more and the change is much less likely to lead to positive outcomes. While analysts were surprised at the severity of Rio Tinto's cutbacks, Albanese will have been aware of best practices in corporate restructuring, and thus decided to get the bad news out of the way quickly so that morale can be rebuilt quickly and the organization can move forward.[107]

Top managers should also remember that top-down change means initiation of the idea occurs at upper levels and is implemented downward. It does not mean that lower-level employees are not educated about the change or allowed to participate in it.

Culture Change

Organizations are made up of people and their relationships with one another. Changes in strategy, structure, technologies and products do not happen on their own, and changes in any of these areas involve changes in people as well. Employees must learn how to use new technologies, or market new products, or work effectively in a team-based structure. Sometimes achieving a new way of thinking requires a focused change in the underlying corporate cultural values and norms. Changing corporate culture fundamentally shifts how work is done in an organization and generally leads to renewed commitment and empowerment of employees and a stronger bond between the company and its customers.[108]

Forces for Culture Change

A number of recent trends have contributed to a need for cultural makeovers at companies such as Marks and Spencer, IBM and DHL. Some of the primary changes requiring a shift in culture and employee mind-set are reengineering and the move toward horizontal forms of organizing, greater employee and customer diversity and the shift to the learning organization.

Reengineering and Horizontal Organizing As described in Chapter 3, reengineering involves redesigning a vertical organization along its horizontal workflows. This changes the way managers and employees need to think about how work is done and requires greater focus on employee empowerment, collaboration, information sharing and meeting customer needs. In his book *The Reengineering Revolution*, Michael Hammer refers to people change as 'the most perplexing, annoying, distressing and confusing part' of reengineering.[109] Managers may confront powerful emotions as employees react to rapid, massive change with fear or anger.

In the horizontal organization, managers and front-line workers need to understand and embrace the concepts of teamwork, empowerment and cooperation. Managers shift their thinking to view workers as colleagues rather than cogs in a wheel; and workers learn to accept not only greater freedom and power, but also the higher level of responsibility that comes with them. Mutual trust, risk taking and tolerance for mistakes become key cultural values in the horizontal organization.

One of the biggest challenges in reengineering is the shift underway in China and several other formerly communist countries in Asia, which have now adopted capitalist models. Traditionally, organizations were very hierarchical, and staff had limited opportunities to provide their input to decisions. Ironically the first generation of capitalist business leaders may even have exacerbated this attitude, as they built companies based on their own charisma and capacity to act decisively. However, as organizations mature and become more complex, effective information sharing and making best use of all the talents in the company becomes crucial. Louis Liu, a Hong Kong-based human resource management consultant, says, 'There are a lot of brilliant businessmen in the mainland. They are brilliant at doing business, but they don't even know how to hold a meeting properly. They ask their colleagues to give their report, then give each of them some verbal instructions and call that a meeting'. Gradually, though, a new generation of human resource managers is helping to foster contemporary management skills, drawing attention to the subtleties of organizational culture and not only the short term bottom line.[110]

Diversity Diversity is a fact of life for today's organizations, and many are implementing new recruiting, mentoring and promotion methods, diversity training programmes, tough policies regarding sexual harassment and racial discrimination and new benefits programmes that respond to a more diverse workforce. Organizations are moving beyond the concept of 'managing diversity', which emphasizes the difficulties associated with a diverse workforce, towards 'diversity leadership', where companies take a lead in fostering and supporting diversity both within and outside the organization. The Toronto, Canada office of accounting major Ernst and Young is actively involved in community programmes to support minority and immigrant youth succeed in employment. Jeanine Pereira, the firm's inclusiveness leader, says this pays off for Ernst and Young, 'We recruit worldwide, and if you can show that you help immigrants integrate into Canadian society, it is a lot easier for you to attract and retain skilled accountants from around the world'.[111]

The Learning Organization The learning organization involves breaking down boundaries both within and between organizations to create companies that are focused on knowledge sharing and continuous learning. Recall from Chapter 1 that shifting to a learning organization involves changes in a number of areas. For example, structures become horizontal and involve empowered teams working directly with customers. There are few rules and procedures for performing tasks, and knowledge and control of tasks are located with employees rather than supervisors. Information is broadly shared rather than being concentrated with top managers. In addition, employees, customers, suppliers and partners all play a role in determining the organization's strategic direction. Clearly, all of these changes require new values, new attitudes and new ways of thinking and working together. A learning organization cannot exist without a culture that supports openness, equality, adaptability and employee participation.

As noted above, many Chinese organizations are in the process of cultural change, instituting internal reforms aimed at creating a learning organization. Zhujiang Iron and Steel Company, featured in the *In Practice* box on the next page, is a case in point.[112]

As an organization manager, keep this guideline in mind:

Work with organization development consultants for large-scale changes in the attitudes, values or skills of employees, and when shifting to a learning organization culture.

Organization Development Culture Change Interventions

Managers use a variety of approaches and techniques for changing corporate culture, some of which we discussed in Chapter 10. One method of quickly bringing about culture change is known as **organization development** (OD), which focuses on the human and social aspects of the organization as a way to improve the organization's ability to adapt and solve problems. OD emphasizes the values of human development, fairness, openness, freedom from coercion and individual autonomy that allows workers to perform the job as they see fit, within reasonable organizational constraints.[113] In the 1970s, OD evolved as a separate field that applied the behavioural sciences in a process of planned organization-wide change, with the goal of increasing

IN PRACTICE

Zhujiang Iron and Steel Company (ZISCo) is a specialist steel producer, set up by the Chinese state in 1997 as part of its industrial upgrading programme in the country's ninth Five Year Plan. Although the company was established long after the Communist era and was organized on business rather than political lines, its operations still reflected a productivist orientation. In other words, there was an emphasis on production quantity rather than price and profit margins, and efforts to improve the bottom line were usually made through cost reduction rather than improvements to quality leading to increased revenues. The company tended to be driven by its engineers rather than professional managers. Typically as in other Chinese firms, human resources was an underdeveloped area.

Ruoshen Zhang, president of ZISCo between 2003 and 2006, is an MBA-educated professional manager. He was well aware of modern management techniques and quickly built a reform strategy around the concept of value creation, with three elements; creating value to customers through higher quality and better marketing, to the company through more efficient production and to employees through remuneration and advancement opportunities tied to performance. The company introduced longer-term agreements with suppliers, a professionalised HR team, a more engaged middle management and a better system for cross-functional coordination. One of the most important innovations was investing time and resources in better understanding the customer. This paid off handsomely, as ZISCo found it could substantially reduce production waste by planning for steel offcuts to be used to make smaller parts its customers needed, rather than just being thrown in the scrap bin.

In 2006, Zhang was promoted to president of Guangzhou Iron and Steel Enterprises (GISE), ZISCo's parent company. One of his senior managers took his place. The prospects for ZISCo looked good, but Zhang was aware that he had personally driven many of the management innovations. It would be crucial in the next phase of corporate development for the whole management team to adopt a strategic orientation. The value creation approach was one step towards systematizing strategic thinking, but Zhang and his senior colleagues at GISE would need to ensure that this became a principle underlying continuous learning, rather than just a mantra repeated to satisfy senior management.

organizational effectiveness. Today, the concept has been enlarged to examine how people and groups can change to a learning organization culture in a complex and turbulent environment. Organization development is not a step-by-step procedure to solve a specific problem but a process of fundamental change in the human and social systems of the organization, including organizational culture.[114]

OD uses knowledge and techniques from the behavioural sciences to create a learning environment through increased trust, open confrontation of problems, employee empowerment and participation, knowledge and information sharing, the design of meaningful work, cooperation and collaboration between groups and the full use of human potential.

OD interventions involve training of specific groups or of everyone in the organization. For OD interventions to be successful, senior management in the organization must see the need for OD and provide enthusiastic support for the change. Techniques used by many organizations for improving people skills through OD include the following.

Large Group Intervention Most early OD activities involved small groups and focused on incremental change. However, in recent years, there has been growing interest in the application of OD techniques to large group settings, which are more attuned to bringing about radical or transformational change in organizations operating in complex environments.[115] The **large group intervention** approach[116] brings together participants from all parts of the organization – often including key stakeholders from outside the organization as well – in an off-site setting to discuss problems or opportunities and plan for change. A large group intervention might involve 50 to 500 people and last for several days. The off-site setting limits interference and distractions, enabling participants to focus on new ways of doing things. General Electric's 'Work Out' programme, an ongoing process of solving problems, learning and improving, begins with large-scale off-site meetings that get people talking across functional, hierarchical and organizational boundaries. Hourly and salaried workers come together from many different parts of the organization and join with customers and suppliers to discuss and solve specific problems.[117] The process forces a rapid analysis of ideas, the creation of solutions and the development of a plan for implementation. Over time, Work Out creates a culture where ideas are rapidly translated into action and positive business results.[118]

Team Building **Team building** promotes the idea that people who work together can work as a team. A work team can be brought together to discuss conflicts, goals, the decision-making process, communication, creativity and leadership. The team can then plan to overcome problems and improve results. Team-building activities are also used in many companies to train task forces, committees and new product development groups. These activities enhance communication and collaboration and strengthen the cohesiveness of organizational groups and teams.

Interdepartmental Activities Representatives from different departments are brought together in a mutual location to expose problems or conflicts, diagnose the causes and plan improvements in communication and coordination. This type of intervention has been applied to union – management conflict, headquarters – field office conflict, interdepartmental conflict and mergers.[119] A box-storage business, which stores archived records for other companies, found interdepartmental meetings to be a key means of building a culture based on team spirit and customer focus. People from different departments met for hour-long sessions every two weeks and shared their problems, told stories about their successes, and talked about things they'd observed in the company. The meetings helped people understand the problems faced in other departments and see how everyone depended on each other to do their jobs successfully.[120]

One current area in which OD can provide significant value is in spurring culture change toward valuing diversity.[121] In addition, today's organizations are continuously adapting to environmental uncertainty and increasing global competition, and OD interventions can respond to these new realities as companies strive to create greater capability for learning and growth.[122]

Strategies for Implementing Change

Managers and employees can think of inventive ways to improve the organization's technology, creative ideas for new products and services, fresh approaches to strategies and structures or ideas for fostering adaptive cultural values, but until the ideas are put into action, they are worthless to the organization. Implementation is the most crucial part of the change process, but it is also the most difficult. Change is frequently disruptive and uncomfortable for managers as well as employees. The Bookmark explores how managers can improve change implementation by understanding the emotional aspects of the change process. Change is complex, dynamic and messy, and implementation requires strong and persistent leadership. In this final section, we briefly discuss the role of leadership for change, some reasons for resistance to change, and techniques that managers can use to overcome resistance and successfully implement change.

Have you read this book?

The Change Monster: The Human Forces That Fuel or Foil Corporate Transformation and Change

BY JEANIE DANIEL DUCK

The change monster is lurking in every organization, just waiting to gobble up unsuspecting managers who are striving to implement new strategies, accomplish reorganizations, or complete mergers. Jeanie Daniel Duck uses the term *change monster* in her book by the same name to refer to all the complex human emotions and social dynamics that emerge during major change efforts. Many managers, she says, simplify or ignore the people issues of change, a sure prescription for failure.

Mastering the Change Curve

Duck says that major organizational change typically follows a change curve – a roller-coaster ride that brings out myriad unexpected and conflicting emotions.

- *Stagnation*. This is the period during which the organization has lost direction or is moving in the wrong direction. The change monster is generally quiet – people feel comfortable and safe. However, it is the job of managers to recognize stagnation and create a sense of urgency for change.
- *Preparation*. In this stage, Duck says, 'the change monster is rudely awakened from its hibernating slumber and stretches itself, causing all kinds of emotional tremors'. This is the period during which change leaders define and refine their vision for change and begin to involve others in the change process. Emotions range from excitement and hopefulness to anxiety and betrayal. Everyone is jittery and distracted.
- *Implementation*. This phase is the actual tactical start of the change journey, and as such is the longest and typically the most painful. There is an explosion of emotions, both positive and negative, in the organization. During this phase, employees often feel in limbo. Everything has changed, and yet the changes haven't been solidified. Many people feel uncertain about their ability to function in the new environment.
- *Determination*. During this period, Duck says, the change monster is roaming the hallways, ready to do its worst damage. Many managers think the change has been accomplished and turn their attention elsewhere right at the time when reinforcement is most needed. People often exhibit *retroactive resistance*, a sort of change fatigue and a desire to revert to the old familiar patterns.
- *Fruition*. Ahhhh…the time when all the hard work pays off at last. In this phase, the changes have become a part of the accepted way of doing things. The whole organization may feel new and different. Employees have gained confidence and are optimistic and energized. The change monster has been corralled.

Coming Full Circle

It is the goal of every change initiative to reach fruition. But Duck cautions that a new period of stagnation is just around the corner. When an organization accomplishes a major change, people need to take time to bask in the success. But managers must be on guard that basking doesn't turn to napping. Managers can teach their organizations how to perpetually adapt and help them muster the will to do so. 'When an organization sees itself as a hearty band of monster slayers, change becomes a challenge they're ready to meet rather than a threat that signals retreat.'

The Change Monster: The Human Forces That Fuel or Foil Corporate Transformation and Change, by Jeanie Daniel Duck, is published by Crown Business.

Leadership for Change

The need for change within organizations and the need for leaders who can successfully manage change continues to grow. The leadership style of the top executive sets the tone for how effective the organization is at continuous adaptation and innovation. One style of leadership, referred to as *transformational leadership*, is particularly suited for bringing about change. Top leaders who use a transformational leadership style enhance organizational innovation both directly, by creating a compelling vision, and indirectly, by creating an environment that supports exploration, experimentation, risk taking and sharing of ideas.[123]

Successful change can happen only when employees are willing to devote the time and energy needed to reach new goals, as well as endure possible stress and hardship. Having a clearly communicated vision that embodies flexibility and openness to new ideas, methods and styles sets the stage for a change-oriented organization and helps employees cope with the chaos and tension associated with change.[124] Leaders also build organization-wide commitment by taking employees through three stages of the change commitment process, illustrated in Exhibit 11.9.[125] In the first stage, *preparation*, employees hear about the change through memos, meetings, speeches or personal contact and become aware that the change will directly affect their work. In the second stage, *acceptance*, leaders should help employees develop an understanding of the full impact of the change and the positive outcomes of making the change. When employees perceive the change as positive, the decision to implement is made. In the third stage, the true *commitment* process begins. The commitment stage involves the steps of installation and institutionalization. Installation is a trial process for the change, which gives leaders an opportunity to discuss problems and employee concerns and build commitment to action. In the final step, *institutionalization*, employees view the change not as something new but as a normal and integral part of organizational operations.

COUNTERPOINT 11.5

Sadly, the way companies handled large-scale layoffs in the severe global economic recession that began in 2007 revealed that many have failed to learn the lessons outlined in this chapter about how to deal with difficult restructuring decisions. In 2008, Ford emailed about 500 Canadian staff who had recently been hired, telling them that their new jobs no longer existed.[126] In the US, RadioShack laid off 400 workers in 2007, also notifying them by email.[127] In 2008, Citigroup in the UK fired

EXHIBIT 11.9 Stages of Commitment to Change

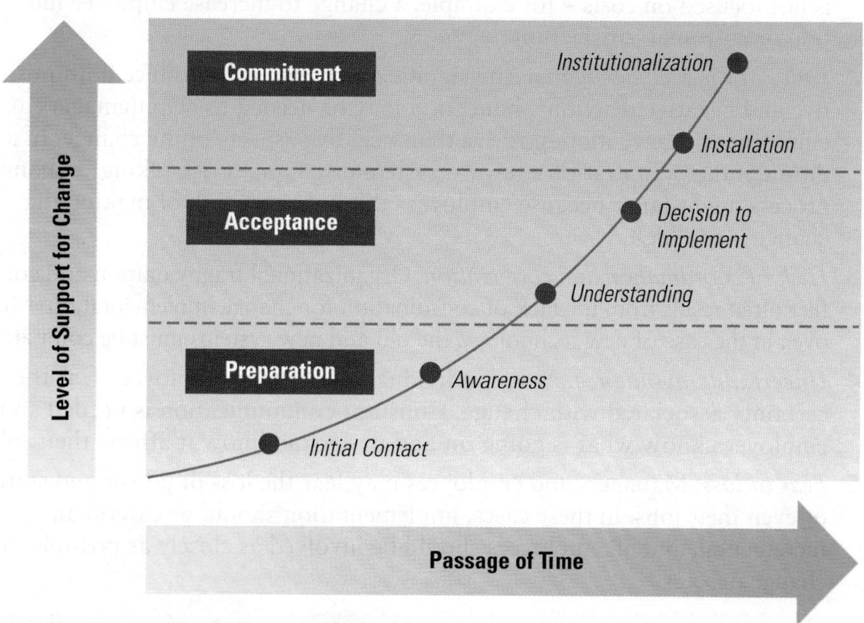

Source: Adapted from Daryl R. Conner, *Managing at the Speed of Change* (New York: Villard Books, 1992), 148. Used with permission.

all its personal loans staff during a conference call.[128] Robbs, a shop in the British market town of Hexham, set off a fire alarm and once the workforce had assembled in the car park, informed them they no longer had jobs.[129] Few, however, could top the management consultancy Pricewaterhouse Coopers, however, which in 2003 sent a text message to 2,400 employees of failed UK insurance company The Accident Group, telling them they would not be paid and that they had lost their jobs.[130] Are such examples indicative of incompetence or simply a failure to be professional by adopting 'best practice'? An alternative interpretation is that they are symptomatic of managerial distance from, and perhaps indifference to, employees. Or it may be interpreted as managers' unwillingness to deal with the face-to-face responses of employees to such news. Emailing spares executives the pain of facing the personal consequences of such decisions. **Discuss**

The pressures on organizations to change will probably increase over the next few decades. Leaders must develop the personal qualities, skills and methods needed to help their companies remain competitive. Indeed, some management experts argue that to survive the upheaval of the early twenty-first century, managers must turn their organizations into *change leaders* by using the present to actually create the future – breaking industry rules, creating new market space and routinely abandoning outmoded products, services and processes to free up resources to build the future.[131]

Barriers to Change

Visionary leadership is crucial for change; however, leaders should expect to encounter resistance as they attempt to take the organization through the three stages of the change commitment process. It is normal for people to resist change in situations where they feel vulnerable, and many barriers to change exist at the individual and organizational levels.[132]

1. *Excessive focus on costs*. Management may possess the mind-set that costs are all-important and may fail to appreciate the importance of a change that is not focused on costs – for example, a change to increase employee motivation or customer satisfaction.
2. *Failure to perceive benefits*. Any significant change will produce both positive and negative reactions. Education may be needed to help managers and employees perceive more positive than negative aspects of the change. In addition, if the organization's reward system discourages risk taking, a change process might falter because employees think that the risk of making the change is too high.
3. *Lack of coordination and cooperation*. Organizational fragmentation and conflict often result from the lack of coordination for change implementation. Moreover, in the case of new technology, the old and new systems must be compatible.
4. *Uncertainty avoidance*. At the individual level, many employees fear the uncertainty associated with change. Constant communication is needed so that employees know what is going on and understand how it affects their jobs.
5. *Fear of loss*. Managers and employees may fear the loss of power and status – or even their jobs. In these cases, implementation should be careful and incremental, and all employees should be involved as closely as possible in the change process.

Implementation can typically be designed to overcome many of the organizational and individual barriers to change.

COUNTERPOINT 11.6

Careful attention to implementation can reduce avoidable resistance but it is unlikey to 'overcome' it. A more realistic approach is to anticipate that change programmes will be partial in their effeciveness and will result in unintended consequences – negative as well as positive. In many situations it will simply not be possible – because of lack of resources, skills and climate – to introduce the measures suggested below under technique 5. **Discuss**

Techniques for Implementation

Top leaders articulate the vision and set the tone, but managers and employees throughout the organization are involved in the process of change. A number of techniques can be used to successfully implement change.[133]

As an organization manager, keep these guidelines in mind:

Lead employees through the three stages of commitment to change – preparation, acceptance and commitment – and use techniques to achieve successful implementation. These include obtaining top management support, implementing the change in a series of steps, assigning change teams or idea champions and overcoming resistance by actively communicating with workers and encouraging their participation in the change process.

1 *Establish a sense of urgency for change.* Once managers identify a true need for change, they need to thaw resistance by creating a sense of urgency that change is really needed. Organizational crises can help unfreeze employees and make them willing to invest the time and energy needed to adopt new techniques or procedures. For example, British Airways, like all other airlines, was badly affected by the decline in air travel and oppressive security measures put in place after the September 11, 2001 terrorist attacks. Managers worked with the whole staff in order to implement necessary downsizing, and BA emerged from the crisis relatively stronger than many of its competitors.[134] However, in many cases there is no public crisis and managers have to make others aware of the need for change.

2 *Establish a coalition to guide the change.* Change managers have to build a coalition of people throughout the organization who have enough power and influence to steer the change process. For implementation to be successful, there must be a shared commitment to the need and possibilities for change. Top management support is crucial for any major change project, and lack of top management support is one of the most frequent causes of implementation failure.[135] In addition, the coalition should involve lower-level supervisors and middle managers from across the organization. For smaller changes, the support of influential managers in the affected departments is important.

3 *Create a vision and strategy for change.* Leaders who have taken their companies through major successful transformations often have one thing in common: They focus on formulating and articulating a compelling vision and strategy that will guide the change process. Even for a small change, a vision of how the future can be better and strategies to get there are important motivations for change.

4 *Find an idea that fits the need.* Finding the right idea often involves search procedures – talking with other managers, assigning a task force to investigate the problem, sending out a request to suppliers or asking creative people within the organization to develop a solution. The creation of a new idea requires organic conditions. This is a good opportunity to encourage employee participation, because employees need the freedom to think about and explore new options.[136] Belgacom, Belgium's largest telecom company, has introduced special idea management software encouraging employees to come up with ideas for new products and services, as well as more efficient practices. Wim De Meyer, Strategy & Business Development Director at Belgacom's landline department says 'Belgacom wanted to develop a corporate culture of innovation where anyone in any job function – sales, support, field

service, administration – can share their ideas and help shape the future of the company. An intelligent and creative workforce is one of Belgacom's most valued assets'.[137]

5 *Develop plans to overcome resistance to change*. Many good ideas are never used because managers failed to anticipate or prepare for resistance to change by consumers, employees or other managers. No matter how impressive the performance characteristics of an innovation, its implementation will conflict with some interests and jeopardize some alliances in the organization. To increase the chance of successful implementation, management must acknowledge the conflict, threats and potential losses perceived by employees. Several strategies can be used by managers to overcome the resistance problem:

- *Alignment with needs and goals of users*. The best strategy for overcoming resistance is to make sure change meets a real need. Employees in R&D often come up with great ideas that solve nonexistent problems. This happens because initiators fail to consult with the intended users. Resistance can be frustrating for managers, but moderate resistance to change is good for an organization. Resistance provides a barrier to frivolous changes and to change for the sake of change. The process of overcoming resistance to change normally requires that the change be good for its users.
- *Communication and training*. Communication means informing users about the need for change and the consequences of a proposed change, preventing rumours, misunderstanding and resentment. In one study of change efforts, the most commonly cited reason for failure was that employees learned of the change from outsiders. Top managers concentrated on communicating with the public and shareholders but failed to communicate with the people who would be most intimately involved with and most affected by the change – their own employees.[138] Open communication often gives management an opportunity to explain what steps will be taken to ensure that the change will have no adverse consequences for employees. Training is also needed to help employees understand and cope with their role in the change process.
- *An environment that affords psychological safety*. Psychological safety means that people feel a sense of confidence that they will not be embarrassed or rejected by others in the organization. People need to feel secure and capable of making the changes that are asked of them.[139] Change requires that people be willing to take risks and do things differently, but many people are fearful of trying something new if they think they might be embarrassed by mistakes or failure. Managers support psychological safety by creating a climate of trust and mutual respect in the organization. 'Not being afraid someone is laughing at you helps you take genuine risks', says Andy Law, one of the founders of St. Luke's, an advertising agency based in London.[140]
- *Participation and involvement*. Early and extensive participation in a change should be part of implementation. Participation gives those involved a sense of control over the change activity. They understand it better, and they become committed to successful implementation. One study of the implementation and adoption of technology systems at two companies showed a much smoother implementation process at the company that introduced the new technology using a participatory approach.[141] The team-building and large group intervention activities described earlier can be effective ways to involve employees in a change process.

- *Forcing and coercion.* As a last resort, managers may overcome resistance by threatening employees with the loss of jobs or promotions or by firing or transferring them. In other words, management power is used to overwhelm resistance. In most cases, this approach is not advisable because it leaves people angry at change managers, and the change may be sabotaged. However, this technique may be needed when speed is essential, such as when the organization faces a crisis. It may also be required for needed administrative changes that flow from the top down, such as downsizing the workforce.[142]

6 *Create change teams.* Throughout this chapter the need for resources and energy to make change happen has been discussed. Separate creative departments, new-venture groups and ad hoc teams or task forces are ways to focus energy on both creation and implementation. A separate department has the freedom to create a new technology that fits a genuine need. A task force can be created to see that implementation is completed. The task force can be responsible for communication, involvement of users, training and other activities needed for change.

7 *Foster idea champions.* One of the most effective weapons in the battle for change is the idea champion. The most effective champion is a volunteer champion who is deeply committed to a new idea. The idea champion sees that all technical activities are correct and complete. An additional champion, such as a manager sponsor, may also be needed to persuade people about implementation, even using coercion if necessary.

Summary and Interpretation

Organizations face a dilemma. Managers prefer to organize day-to-day activities in a predictable, routine manner. However, change – not stability – is the natural order of things in today's global environment. Thus, organizations need to build in change as well as stability, to facilitate innovation as well as efficiency.

Most change in organizations is incremental, but there is a growing emphasis on the need for radical change. Four types of change – technology, products and services, strategy and structure, and culture – may give an organization a competitive edge, and managers can make certain each of the necessary ingredients for change is present.

For technical innovation, which is of concern to most organizations, an organic structure that encourages employee autonomy works best because it encourages a bottom-up flow of ideas. Other approaches are to establish a separate department charged with creating new technical ideas, establish venture teams or idea incubators and encourage idea champions. New products and services generally require cooperation among several departments, so horizontal linkage is an essential part of the innovation process.

For changes in strategy and structure, a top-down approach is typically best. These innovations are in the domain of top administrators who take responsibility for restructuring, for downsizing and for changes in policies, goals, and control systems.

Culture changes are also generally the responsibility of top management. Some recent trends that may create a need for broad-scale culture change in the organization are reengineering, the shift to horizontal forms of organizing, greater organizational diversity and the learning organization. All of these changes require significant shifts in employee and manager attitudes and ways of working together. One method for bringing about this level of culture change is organization development (OD). OD focuses on the human and social aspects of the organization and uses behavioural science knowledge to bring about changes in attitudes and relationships.

Finally, the implementation of change can be difficult. Strong leadership is needed to guide employees through the turbulence and uncertainty and build organization-wide commitment to change. A number of barriers to change exist, including excessive focus on cost, failure to perceive benefits, lack of organizational coordination and individual uncertainty avoidance and fear of loss. Managers can thoughtfully plan how to deal with resistance to increase the likelihood of success. Techniques that will facilitate implementation are to establish a sense or urgency that change is needed; create a powerful coalition to guide the change; formulate a vision and strategy to achieve the change; and overcome resistance by aligning with the needs and goals of users, including users in the change process, providing psychological safety and, in rare cases, forcing the innovation if necessary. Change teams and idea champions are also effective.

KEY CONCEPTS

ambidextrous approach
change process
creative departments
creativity
culture changes
dual-core approach
horizontal coordination model
idea champion
idea incubator
incremental change
large group intervention
management champion
new-venture fund
organization development
organizational change
organizational innovation
product and service changes
radical change
skunkworks
strategy and structure changes
switching structures
team building
technical champion
technology changes
time-based competition
venture teams

Discussion Questions

1 How is the management of radical change likely to differ from the management of incremental change?

2 How are organic characteristics related to changes in technology? To administrative changes?

3 Describe the dual-core approach. How does administrative change normally differ from technology change? Discuss.

4 How might organizations manage the dilemma of needing both stability and change? Discuss.

5 Why do organizations experience resistance to change? What steps can managers take to overcome this resistance?

6 'Bureaucracies are not innovative.' Discuss.

7 A noted organization theorist said, 'Pressure for change originates in the environment; pressure for stability originates within the organization'. Do you agree? Discuss.

8 Of the five elements required for successful change, which element do you think managers are most likely to overlook? Discuss.

9 How do the underlying values of organization development compare to the values underlying other types of change? Why do the values underlying OD make it particularly useful in shifting to a learning organization?

10 The manager of R&D for a drug company said that only five per cent of the company's new products ever achieve market success. He also said the industry average is ten per cent and wondered how his organization might increase its success rate. If you were acting as a consultant, what advice would you give him concerning organization structure?

11 Review the stages of commitment to change illustrated in Exhibit 11.9 and the seven techniques for implementing change discussed at the end of the chapter. At which stage of change commitment would each of the seven techniques most likely be used?

Workbook Innovation Climate

In order to examine differences in the level of innovation encouragement in organizations, you will be asked to rate two organizations. The first should be an organization in which you have worked, or the university. The second should be someone else's workplace, that of a family member, a friend or an acquaintance. You will have to interview that person to answer the questions below. You should put your own answers in column A, your interviewee's answers in column B and what you think would be the ideal in column C.

Innovation Measures

Questions

1 What comparisons in terms of innovation climates can you make between these two organizations?
2 How might productivity differ between a climate that supports innovation and a climate that does not?
3 Where would you rather work? Why?

Adapted by Dorothy Marcic from Susanne G. Scott and Reginald A. Bruce, 'Determinants of Innovative Behaviour: A Path Model of Individual Innovation in the Workplace', *Academy of Management Journal* 37, no. 3 (1994), 580–607.

CASE FOR ANALYSIS

Technology and change at Universal Training

Case by Craig Prichard, *Department of Management, Massey University, Palmerston North New Zealand.*

Universal Training is a local authority-owned training and development services company that provides mostly public sector organizations (e.g. health, education and local authority) with training and organizational development services. Universal was 'spun off' as part of public sector changes in the early 1990s and is owned by a consortium of local authorities who remain its major clients. Universal employs about 30 staff including trainers, developers and support staff. Some work part-time or on short contracts. It has a senior management team of four. This includes Brenda, John and Carl, who manage training and development teams, and Steve, who manages a support team of eight providing IT, HR, accounts and communication support for the staff. Universal's chief executive, Harold, was the previous head of training with one of the owning local authorities and has been in the post since Universal went independent.

Typically, Universal signs long term contracts to provide its client organizations with a range of off-the-shelf and tailored programmes. The off-the-shelf programmes typically deal with skill development areas (supervisory management, employment relations, project management and managing contracts) and statutory compliance processes such as health and safety. Tailored work includes organization development work.

Andrew is a new business studies graduate. He recently joined Universal as a junior consultant. He is the newest member of Universal's Training team, most of whom, including Sandy, have more than ten years' experience with the firm. Andrew worked in the main office for about six months before going on his first 'live' job, which included a health and safety audit and training with a local authority. Since completing this assignment he was asked to update the delivery of Universal's Health and Safety courses and to investigate the use of new web-based technologies.

Sandy is a 30-something trainer and organization development specialist. Sally now shares an office with Andrew. Here's Sally account of how the change project developed.

Sally: *Before Andrew got moving he would get really frustrated and regularly tell me he was leaving. He would describe Universal as a machine designed to grinding new ideas into little pieces so they can be blown away by the wind. Initially it was quite entertaining but gradually he became a really pain. I'd tell him he was taking things too personally and he should think how to work the system more effectively. I guess I was playing a kind of older sister role with him. He was particularly frustrated with his relationship with Brenda – our joint boss. Actually it was a combination of his naivety and her well honed political skills. She played him like a fish – beautifully. He'd go to see her about something and she'd say something like 'aarrh Andrew just the person I want to see', which was pretty close to a bare faced lie. Then she'd say something really cuttingly sarcastic like 'what brilliant idea do you have for me today' all with a big smile on her face – what a crocodile aye! He just didn't 'get it'. So I'd say to him 'Look', you've got two options. You can resign and go up the road to the other company that's really into these new technologies. They had some whiz bang application for running web meetings and presentations and online quizzes, that kind of thing, and Andrew thought all this was pretty cool. Or, and this was the other option, he could get into the politics of place and try and get the change effort moving. You'd think with his business qualification and all that he'd have a pretty good idea what I was talking about. Well eventually the penny seemed to drop and away he went. It was a big relief for me actually. He use to sit around complaining about what others weren't doing but now he's getting there.'*

Case Questions

1 *Planning for change*. Andrew decides to take Sandy's advice. Using the seven step approach identified in the 'Techniques for Implementation' in the chapter above prepare the change plan

that you think Andrew would have developed for the introduction of new web-based learning technologies at Universal Training. In particular, prepare a resistance management plan that includes appropriate mix of tactics and responses to the features identified in the chapter above: *'Alignment with needs and goals of users', 'Communication and training', 'An environment that affords psychological safety', 'Participation and involvement' and 'Forcing and coercion'.*

2 *What happened next?* In the months following the above discussion Andrew makes progress on the change plan he devised. Imagine that Andrew has a conversation with Sandy some months later in which he outlines how he worked with Brenda as part of the change process. Write that conversation.

Notes

1. John F. Burns, 'Trucks of the Taliban: Durable, Not Discreet', *The New York Times*, 23 November 2001.
2. Robert D. Hof, 'Building an Idea Factory', *BusinessWeek* (October 11, 2004), 194–200; Brian Bremner and Chester Dawson, 'Can Anything Stop Toyota?' *BusinessWeek* (November 17, 2003), 114–122; and Norihiko Shirouzu and Jathon Sapsford, 'Heavy Load; For Toyota, a New Small Truck Carries Hopes for Topping GM', *The Wall Street Journal* (May 12, 2005), A1, A6.
3. Based on John P. Kotter, *Leading Change* (Boston, Mass.: Harvard Business School Press, 1996), 18–20.
4. David A. Nadler and Michael L. Tushman, 'Organizational Frame Bending: Principles for Managing Reorientation', *Academy of Management Executive* 3 (1989), 194–204; and Michael L. Tushman and Charles A. O'Reilly III, 'Ambidextrous Organizations: Managing Evolutionary and Revolutionary Change', *California Management Review* 38, no. 4 (Summer 1996), 8–30.
5. Alan G. Robinson and Dean M. Schroeder, *Ideas Are Free: How the Idea Revolution Is Liberating People and Transforming Organizations* (San Francisco: Berrett-Koehler, 2004), as reported in John Grossman, 'Strategies: Thinking Small', *Inc. Magazine* (August 2004), 34–35.
6. 'War of the whites', *Marketing Week*, 5 June 2008; http://www.unilever.co.uk/ourcompany/newsandmedia/pressreleases/2007/small_pack_mighty_profits.asp accessed on November 24, 2008.
7. William A. Davidow and Michael S. Malone, *The Virtual Corporation* (New York: HarperBusiness, 1992); and Gregory G. Dess, Abdul M. A. Rasheed, Kevin J. McLaughlin and Richard L. Priem, 'The New Corporate Architecture', *Academy of Management Executive* 9, no. 3 (1995), 7–20.
8. Brent Schlender, 'How Big Can Apple Get?' *Fortune* (February 21, 2005), 66–76.
9. 'The miracle of Turin – Recovery at Fiat', *The Economist*, 26 April 2008.
10. Dan Steinbock, 'The rise and rise of Nokia', *The Economist*, 2 June 2001.
11. Nokia Corporation (2008), "Nokia Firsts in Telecommunications", accessed at http://www.nokia.com/NOKIA_COM_1/About_Nokia/Sidebars_new_concept/Nokia_firsts/Firsts.pdf on April 20 2009.
12. Joseph E. McCann, 'Design Principles for an Innovating Company', *Academy of Management Executive* 5 (May 1991), 76–93.
13. 'DHL adopts new-gen Wi-Fi scanning systems', *New Zealand Transport & Logistics Business Week*, 25 January 2007.
14. Kelly Barron, 'Logistics in Brown', *Forbes* (January 10, 2000), 78–83; and Scott Kirsner, 'Venture Vérité: United Parcel Service', *Wired* (September 1999), 83–96.
15. SanDisk, SK Telecom launch new platform for mobile TV, *Middle East North Africa Financial Network*, 13 February 2008.
16. Robert D. Hof, 'Building an Idea Factory'.
17. 'The Strategist', *Latin Trade*, 1 March 2008.
18. Richard A. Wolfe, 'Organizational Innovation: Review, Critique and Suggested Research Directions', *Journal of Management Studies* 31, no. 3 (May 1994), 405–431.
19. John L. Pierce and Andre L. Delbecq, 'Organization Structure, Individual Attitudes and Innovation', *Academy of Management Review* 2 (1977), 27–37; and Michael Aiken and Jerald Hage, 'The Organic Organization and Innovation', *Sociology* 5 (1971), 63–82.
20. Richard L. Daft, 'Bureaucratic versus Non-bureaucratic Structure in the Process of Innovation and Change', in Samuel B. Bacharach, ed., *Perspectives in Organizational Sociology: Theory and Research* (Greenwich, Conn.: JAI Press, 1982), 129–166.
21. Alan D. Meyer and James B. Goes, 'Organizational Assimilation of Innovations: A Multilevel Contextual Analysis', *Academy of Management Journal* 31 (1988), 897–923.
22. Richard W. Woodman, John E. Sawyer and Ricky W. Griffin, 'Toward a Theory of Organizational Creativity', *Academy of Management Review* 18 (1993), 293–321; and Alan Farnham, 'How to Nurture Creative Sparks', *Fortune* (January 10, 1994), 94–100.
23. 'Yahoo Programmers Mix It Up', *PC Magazine*, 13 September 2007; Julia L Todd, 'GIS and libraries: a cross-disciplinary approach', *Online*, 1 September 2008.

24. Robert I. Sutton, 'Weird Ideas That Spark Innovation', *MIT Sloan Management Review* (Winter 2002), 83–87; Robert Barker, 'The Art of Brainstorming', *BusinessWeek* (August 26, 2002), 168–169; Gary A. Steiner, ed., *The Creative Organization* (Chicago, Ill.: University of Chicago Press, 1965), 16–18; and James Brian Quinn, 'Managing Innovation: Controlled Chaos', *Harvard Business Review* (May–June 1985), 73–84.
25. Rajeshwari Sharma, 'Banking on ideas to grow', *Mint*, 11 June 2007.
26. Thomas M. Burton, 'Flop Factor: By Learning from Failures, Lilly Keeps Drug Pipeline Full', *The Wall Street Journal* (April 21, 2004), A1, A12.
27. Kotter, *Leading Change*, 20–25; and John P. Kotter, 'Leading Change', *Harvard Business Review* (March–April 1995), 59–67.
28. G. Tomas M. Hult, Robert F. Hurley and Gary A. Knight, 'Innovativeness: Its Antecedents and Impact on Business Performance', *Industrial Marketing Management* 33 (2004), 429–438.
29. Jena McGregor, '25 Most Innovative Companies: Smart Ideas for Tough Times', *BusinessWeek*, 28 April 2008.
30. Erick Schonfeld, 'GE Sees the Light', *Business 2.0* (July 2004), 80–86.
31. Pankaj Mishra, 'Enlightened owners don't shoot themselves in the foot', *Mint*, 29 May 2007.
32. D. Bruce Merrifield, 'Intrapreneurial Corporate Renewal', *Journal of Business Venturing* 8 (September 1993), 383–389; Linsu Kim, 'Organizational Innovation and Structure', *Journal of Business Research* 8 (1980), 225–245; and Tom Burns and G. M. Stalker, *The Management of Innovation* (London: Tavistock Publications, 1961).
33. James Q. Wilson, 'Innovation in Organization: Notes toward a Theory', in James D. Thompson, ed., *Approaches to Organizational Design* (Pittsburgh, Penn.: University of Pittsburgh Press, 1966), 193–218.
34. Charles A. O'Reilly III and Michael L. Tushman, 'The Ambidextrous Organization', *Harvard Business Review* (April 2004), 74–81; M. L. Tushman and C. A. O'Reilly III, 'Building an Ambidextrous Organization: Forming Your Own "Skunk Works"', *Health Forum Journal* 42, no. 2 (March–April 1999), 20–23; J. C. Spender and Eric H. Kessler, 'Managing the Uncertainties of Innovation: Extending Thompson (1967)', *Human Relations* 48, no. 1 (1995), 35–56; and Robert B. Duncan, 'The Ambidextrous Organization: Designing Dual Structures for Innovation', in Ralph H. Killman, Louis R. Pondy, and Dennis Slevin, eds., *The Management of Organization*, vol. 1 (New York: North-Holland, 1976), 167–188.
35. C. A. O'Reilly III and M. L. Tushman, 'The Ambidextrous Organization'.
36. Tushman and O'Reilly, 'Building an Ambidextrous Organization'.
37. Edward F. McDonough III and Richard Leifer, 'Using Simultaneous Structures to Cope with Uncertainty', *Academy of Management Journal* 26 (1983), 727–735.
38. Ariane Sains and Stanley Reed , 'Electrolux Redesigns Itself; Johan Hjestonsson's drive for change', *BusinessWeek*, 27 November 2006.
39. 'Nissan opens technology centre', *Just-Auto*, 15 May 2007.
40. Judith R. Blau and William McKinley, 'Ideas, Complexity, and Innovation', *Administrative Science Quarterly* 24 (1979), 200–219.
41. Peter Landers, 'Back to Basics; With Dry Pipelines, Big Drug Makers Stock Up in Japan', *The Wall Street Journal* (November 24, 2003), A1, A7.
42. Sherri Eng, 'Hatching Schemes', *The Industry Standard* (November 27–December 4, 2000), 174–175.
43. Carl Mortished, 'Philips changes the mood with bold move into the bedroom', *The Times*, 6 September 2008; 'Nurture your inner entrepreneurs', *Computer Weekly*, 11 December 2007; PP Thimmayya and J Padmapriya, 'Intel India logs in inhouse entrepreneurial ventures', *The Economic Times*, 29 November 2007.
44. Julian Birkinshaw and Susan A. Hill (2005), 'Corporate Venturing Units: Vehicles for Strategic Success in the New Europe', *Organizational Dynamics*, 34, 247–257; Michel Ferrari (2008), 'Strategic spin-off: a new incentive contract for managing R&D researchers, *The Journal of Technology Transfer*, Volume 33, Number 6 (in press).
45. Christine Canabou, 'Fast Ideas for Slow Times', *Fast Company* (May 2003), 52.
46. Manfreda Cavazza, 'Can online save newspapers?', *Media Week*, 2 September 2008; Peter John Meiklem, 'Good Times for one Irish editor . . . but are the storm clouds gathering?', *Sunday Herald*, 8 June 2008.
47. Christopher Hoenig, 'Skunk Works Secrets,' *CIO* (July 1, 2000), 74–76.
48. Bruno Giussani, 'Driving Michelin's Zero-Pollution Car', *BusinessWeek*, 9 May 2007.
49. Phaedra Hise, 'New Recruitment Strategy: Ask Your Best Employees to Leave', *Inc.* (July 1997), 2.
50. Daniel F. Jennings and James R. Lumpkin, 'Functioning Modeling Corporate Entrepreneurship: An Empirical Integrative Analysis', *Journal of Management* 15 (1989), 485–502; and Julian Birkinshaw, 'The Paradox of Corporate Entrepreneurship', *Strategy & Business,* issue 30 (Spring 2003), 46–57.
51. Jane M. Howell and Christopher A. Higgins, 'Champions of Technology Innovation', *Administrative Science Quarterly* 35 (1990), 317–341; and Jane M. Howell and Christopher A. Higgins, 'Champions of Change: Identifying, Understanding, and Supporting Champions of Technology Innovations', *Organizational Dynamics* (Summer 1990), 40–55.
52. Peter F. Drucker, 'Change Leaders', *Inc.* (June 1999), 65–72; and Peter F. Drucker, *Management Challenges for the 21st Century* (New York: HarperBusiness, 1999).
53. Stuart Crainer and Des Dearlove, 'Water Works', *Management Review* (May 1999), 39–43.
54. Dalila Abu Bakar, 'The intrapreneur way', *Malaysian Business*, 1 February 2007.
55. Thomas J. Peters and Robert H. Waterman, Jr., *In Search of Excellence* (New York: Harper & Row, 1982).
56. Peter J. Frost and Carolyn P. Egri, 'The Political Process of Innovation', in L. L. Cummings and Barry M. Staw, eds.,

Research in Organizational Behavior, vol. 13 (New York: JAI Press, 1991), 229–295; Jay R. Galbraith, 'Designing the Innovating Organization', *Organizational Dynamics* (Winter 1982), 5–25; and Marsha Sinatar, 'Entrepreneurs, Chaos and Creativity – Can Creative People Really Survive Large Company Structure?' *Sloan Management Review* (Winter 1985), 57–62.

57. See Lionel Roure, 'Product Champion Characteristics in France and Germany', *Human Relations* 54, no. 5 (2001), 663–682 for a recent review of the literature related to product champions.
58. Ann Harrington, 'Who's Afraid of a New Product?' *Fortune* (November 10, 2003), 189–192.
59. Christopher Power with Kathleen Kerwin, Ronald Grover, Keith Alexander and Robert D. Hof, 'Flops', *BusinessWeek* (August 16, 1993), 76–82; Modesto A. Maidique and Billie Jo Zirger, 'A Study of Success and Failure in Product Innovation: The Case of the U.S. Electronics Industry', *IEEE Transactions in Engineering Management* 31 (November 1984), 192–203.
60. 'Bye-bye, Betamax', *The Japan Times*, 8 September 2002.
61. Claire Billings, 'IPC closes Nova magazine after 12 months', *Brand Republic*, 3 May 2001.
62. 'Novartis plans $235M charge after dropping drug', *Associated Press*, August 29, 2008.
63. Paul B. Carroll and Chunka Mui, '7 Ways to Fail Big', *Harvard Business Review*, Vol. 86 Issue 9, pp. 82-9; Paul B. Carroll and Chunka Mui (2008), *Billion-Dollar Lessons: What You Can Learn from the Most Inexcusable Business Failures of the Last 25 Years*, Knoxville TN, Portfolio; Sangita Joshi. 'Getting the recipe right', *Business Line*, 13 November 2003; Robert McMath and Thomas Forbes (2000), *What Were They Thinking?: Marketing Lessons I've Learned from Over 80,000 New Products*, New York, Times Books.
64. Cliff Edwards, 'Many Products Have Gone Way of the Edsel', *Johnson City Press* (May 23, 1999), 28, 30; Paul Lukas, 'The Ghastliest Product Launches', *Fortune* (March 16, 1998), 44; Robert McMath, *What Were They Thinking? Marketing Lessons I've Learned from Over 80,000 New-Product Innovations and Idiocies* (New York: Times Business, 1998).
65. Senge, P. (1999). *The dance of change.* New York: Currency Doubleday.
66. Yin, R. K. (1978). *Changing urban bureaucracies: how new practices become routinized.* Santa Monica: Rand Corporation.
67. Miller, D. (2002). Successful change leaders: what makes them? what do they do that is different?, *Journal of Change Management,* 2(4), 359–368.
68. Strebel, P. (1996). Why Do Employees Resist Change? *Harvard Business Review*, 74(3), 86–92.
69. Edwin Mansfield, J. Rapaport, J. Schnee, S. Wagner and M. Hamburger, *Research and Innovation in Modern Corporations* (New York: Norton, 1971); and Antonio J. Bailetti and Paul F. Litva, 'Integrating Customer Requirements into Product Designs', *Journal of Product Innovation Management* 12 (1995), 3–15.
70. 'Blu-ray aplasta a HD- DVD en el mercado japonés de grabadoras', *Gaceta de los Negocios*, 19 January 2008.
71. Shona L. Brown and Kathleen M. Eisenhardt, 'Product Development: Past Research, Present Findings, and Future Directions', *Academy of Management Review* 20, no. 2 (1995), 343–378; F. Axel Johne and Patricia A. Snelson, 'Success Factors in Product Innovation: A Selective Review of the Literature', *Journal of Product Innovation Management* 5 (1988), 114–128; and Science Policy Research Unit, University of Sussex, *Success and Failure in Industrial Innovation* (London: Centre for the Study of Industrial Innovation, 1972).
72. 'Brand innovators', *Marketing Week*, 24 April 2008.
73. Brown and Eisenhardt, 'Product Development'; Dan Dimancescu and Kemp Dwenger, 'Smoothing the Product Development Path', *Management Review* (January 1996), 36–41.
74. Fara Warner, 'In a Word, Toyota Drives for Innovation', *Fast Company* (August 2002), 36–38.
75. Ann Harrington, 'Who's Afraid of a New Product?' *Fortune* (November 10, 2003), 189–192.
76. Deborah Ball, 'Unilever's sales, margins increase', *The Wall Street Journal*, 2 August 2007.
77. 'War of the whites', *Marketing Week*, 5 June 2008
78. Toby Webb, 'Unilever's CEO: Social innovation and sustainability the only game in town', *Ethical Corporation*, 30 May 2007.
79. Andrew Saunders, 'Britain's Most Admired Companies: Tough Times turn Tables', *Management Today*, 1 December 2008.
80. 'Innovation helps Unilever take the cream', *Citywire*, 3 May 2007.
81. 'CCFC to Unilever: Ax the Axe Campaign if You Care about "Real Beauty"', accessed at http://commercialfreechildhood.org/pressreleases/axtheaxe.htm on December 15, 2008.
82. 'Riding on the A380', *Channel NewsAsia*, 16 October 2007.
83. Melissa A. Schilling and Charles W. L. Hill, 'Managing the New Product Development Process', *Academy of Management Executive* 12, no. 3 (1998), 67–81; and J. Lynn Lunsford and Daniel Michaels, 'New Orders; After Four Years in the Rear, Boeing Is Set to Jet Past Airbus', *The Wall Street Journal* (June 10, 2005), A1, A5.
84. Matt Haig (2003), *Brand failures*, London, Kogan Page.
85. Kenneth B. Kahn, 'Market Orientation, Interdepartmental Integration, and Product Development Performance', *The Journal of Product Innovation Management* 18 (2001), 314–323; and Ali E. Akgün, Gary S. Lynn and John C. Byrne, 'Taking the Guesswork Out of New Product Development: How Succcessful High-Tech Companies Get That Way', *Journal of Business Strategy* 25, no. 4 (2004), 41–46.
86. John A. Pearce II, 'Speed Merchants', *Organizational Dynamics* 30, no. 3 (2002), 191–205; Kathleen M. Eisenhardt and Behnam N. Tabrizi, 'Accelerating Adaptive Processes: Product Innovation in the Global Computer Industry', *Administrative Science Quarterly* 40 (1995),

84–110; Dougherty and Hardy, 'Sustained Product Innovation in Large, Mature Organizations'; and Karne Bronikowski, 'Speeding New Products to Market', *Journal of Business Strategy* (September–October 1990), 34–37.

87. 'Rapid Product Development - RAPID 1996–1999', Government of Finland, Tekes, accessed at http://www.tekes.fi/english/programmes/rapid/rapid.html on December 15, 2008.
88. VK Narayanan, B Kemmerer, FL Douglas, B Guernsey (2003), 'The Social Construction of Organizational Capabilities: A Multilevel Analysis' in Bala Chakravarthy, Strategic Management Society, Guenter Mueller-Stewens, and Peter Lorange *Strategy Process: Shaping the Contours of the Field*, Oxford, Blackwell, 137–163.
89. V. K. Narayanan, Frank L. Douglas, Brock Guernsey and John Charnes, 'How Top Management Steers Fast Cycle Teams to Success', *Strategy & Leadership* 30, no. 3 (2002), 19–27.
90. Faith Keenan, 'Opening the Spigot', *Business-Week e.biz* (June 4, 2001), EB17–EB20.
91. Steve Konicki, 'Time Trials', *Information Week* (June 3, 2002), 36–44.
92. http://www.haagen-dazs.co.uk/collection/pints/index.htm accessed on December 15, 2008.
93. David Leonhardt, 'It Was a Hit in Buenos Aires – So Why Not Boise?' *BusinessWeek* (September 7, 1998), 56, 58.
94. Edward F. McDonough III, Kenneth B. Kahn and Gloria Barczak, 'An Investigation of the Use of Global, Virtual, and Colocated New Product Development Teams', *The Journal of Product Innovation Management* 18 (2001), 110–120.
95. 'Unilever opens global centres', *Food Trade Review*, 1 October 2008.
96. Raymond E. Miles, Henry J. Coleman, Jr. and W. E. Douglas Creed, 'Keys to Success in Corporate Redesign', *California Management Review* 37, no. 3 (Spring 1995), 128–145.
97. Fariborz Damanpour and William M. Evan, 'Organizational Innovation and Performance: The Problem of "Organizational Lag"', *Administrative Science Quarterly* 29 (1984), 392–409; David J. Teece, 'The Diffusion of an Administrative Innovation', *Management Science* 26 (1980), 464–470; John R. Kimberly and Michael J. Evaniski, 'Organizational Innovation: The Influence of Individual, Organizational and Contextual Factors on Hospital Adoption of Technological and Administrative Innovation', *Academy of Management Journal* 24 (1981), 689–713; Michael K. Moch and Edward V. Morse, 'Size, Centralization and Organizational Adoption of Innovations', *American Sociological Review* 42 (1977), 716–725; and Mary L. Fennell, 'Synergy, Influence, and Information in the Adoption of Administrative Innovation', *Academy of Management Journal* 27 (1984), 113–129.
98. Richard L. Daft, 'A Dual-Core Model of Organizational Innovation', *Academy of Management Journal* 21 (1978), 193–210.
99. Daft, 'Bureaucratic versus Nonbureaucratic Structure'; Robert W. Zmud, 'Diffusion of Modern Software Practices: Influence of Centralization and Formalization', *Management Science* 28 (1982), 1421–1431.
100. Daft, 'A Dual-Core Model of Organizational Innovation'; Zmud, 'Diffusion of Modern Software Practices'.
101. Fariborz Damanpour, 'The Adoption of Technological, Administrative, and Ancillary Innovations: Impact of Organizational Factors', *Journal of Management* 13 (1987), 675–688.
102. Gregory H. Gaertner, Karen N. Gaertner and David M. Akinnusi, 'Environment, Strategy and the Implementation of Administrative Change: The Case of Civil Service Reform', *Academy of Management Journal* 27 (1984), 525–543.
103. Sue Allen, 'Telecom axes 230 in restructure', *The Press* (Christchurch), 16 January 2007.
104. Steve Hamm, 'Is Oracle Finally Seeing Clearly?' *BusinessWeek* (August 3, 1998), 86–88.
105. Claudia Bird Schoonhoven and Mariann Jelinek, 'Dynamic Tension in Innovative, High Technology Firms: Managing Rapid Technology Change through Organization Structure', in Mary Ann Von Glinow and Susan Albers Mohrman, eds., *Managing Complexity in High Technology Organizations* (New York: Oxford University Press, 1990), 90–118.
106. Tanalee Smith, 'Rio Tinto to cut 14,000 jobs to cope with slump', *Associated Press*, 10 December 2008; 'Rio to axe 14,000 and cut spending', *The Gold Coast Bulletin*, 11 December 2008; Tom Jennemann, 'Alcan in focus as Rio slashes debt, cuts jobs', *Metal Bulletin News Alert Service*, 10 December 2008; Vivek Tulpule, *Commodity markets report*, London, Rio Tinto, December 2008.
107. Stan Pace, 'Rip the Band-Aid Off Quickly', *Strategy & Leadership* 30, no. 1 (2002), 4–9.
108. Benson L. Porter and Warrington S. Parker, Jr., 'Culture Change', *Human Resource Management* 31 (Spring–Summer 1992), 45–67.
109. Quoted in Anne B. Fisher, 'Making Change Stick', *Fortune* (April 17, 1995), 122.
110. May Chan, 'Put staff through paces: Companies in the mainland need to train their next generation of leaders to compete', *South China Morning Post*, 27 September 2008.
111. Trevor Phillips, 'A diverse workforce makes business sense', *Financial Times*, 21 July 2008; 'Diversity Management is out: Diversity Leadership is in', *Canada NewsWire*, 29 April 2008.
112. 'Brief introduction of Zhujiang Steel', accessed at http://www.gise-zis.com/english/english.htm on December 17, 2008; Huang, X., 'Strategic Management at Zhujiang Iron And Steel Company', Case 307-392-1, Asia Case Research Centre, The University of Hong Kong.
113. W. Warner Burke, 'The New Agenda for Organization Development', in Wendell L. French, Cecil H. Bell, Jr. and Robert A. Zawacki, *Organization Development and Transformation: Managing Effective Change* (Burr Ridge, Ill.: Irwin McGraw-Hill, 2000), 523–535.
114. W. Warner Burke, *Organization Development: A Process of Learning and Changing*, 2nd ed. (Reading, Mass.: Addison-Wesley, 1994); and Wendell L. French and Cecil H. Bell, Jr., 'A History of Organization Development', in

French, Bell and Zawacki, *Organization Development and Transformation*, 20–42.

115. French and Bell, 'A History of Organization Development'.
116. The information on large group intervention is based on Kathleen D. Dannemiller and Robert W. Jacobs, 'Changing the Way Organizations Change: A Revolution of Common Sense', *The Journal of Applied Behavioral Science* 28, no. 4 (December 1992), 480–498; Barbara B. Bunker and Billie T. Alban, 'Conclusion: What Makes Large Group Interventions Effective?' *The Journal of Applied Behavioral Science* 28, no. 4 (December 1992), 570–591; and Marvin R. Weisbord, 'Inventing the Future: Search Strategies for Whole System Improvements', in French, Bell and Zawacki, *Organization Development and Transformation*, 242–250.
117. J. Quinn, 'What a Workout!' *Performance* (November 1994), 58–63; and Bunker and Alban, 'Conclusion: What Makes Large Group Interventions Effective?'
118. Dave Ulrich, Steve Kerr and Ron Ashkenas, with Debbie Burke and Patrice Murphy, The GE Work Out: How to Implement GE's Revolutionary Method for Busting Bureaucracy and Attacking Organizational Problems – Fast! (New York: McGraw-Hill, 2002).
119. Paul F. Buller, 'For Successful Strategic Change: Blend OD Practices with Strategic Management', *Organizational Dynamics* (Winter 1988), 42–55.
120. Norm Brodsky, 'Everybody Sells', (Street Smarts column), *Inc. Magazine* (June 2004), 53–54.
121. Richard S. Allen and Kendyl A. Montgomery, 'Applying an Organizational Development Approach to Creating Diversity', *Organizational Dynamics* 30, no. 2 (2001), 149–161.
122. Jyotsna Sanzgiri and Jonathan Z. Gottlieb, 'Philosophic and Pragmatic Influences on the Practice of Organization Development, 1950–2000', *Organizational Dynamics* (Autumn 1992), 57–69.
123. Bernard M. Bass, 'Theory of Transformational Leadership Redux', *Leadership Quarterly* 6, no. 4 (1995), 463–478; and Dong I. Jung, Chee Chow and Anne Wu, 'The Role of Transformational Leadership in Enhancing Organizational Innovation: Hypotheses and Some Preliminary Findings', *The Leadership Quarterly* 14 (2003), 525–544.
124. Ronald Recardo, Kathleen Molloy and James Pellegrino, 'How the Learning Organization Manages Change', *National Productivity Review* (Winter 1995/96), 7–13.
125. Based on Daryl R. Conner, *Managing at the Speed of Change* (New York: Villard Books, 1992), 146–160.
126. Linda Diebel, 'Layoff by email: Ford's latest innovation', *Toronto Star*, July 28, 2008.
127. 'RadioShack lays off employees via e-mail', *USA Today*, March 2, 2007.
128. 'You're fired – by conference call', *The Evening Standard (London)*, May 21, 2008.
129. Sathnam Sanghera, 'There really is no easy way to say this', *The Times*, May 3, 2008.
130. 'Dealing with mass redundancies', *Contract Journal*, June 13, 2007; 'Bust company sacks workers by text', *BBC News*, 30 May 2003, accessed at http://news.bbc.co.uk/1/hi/business/2949578.stm on April 20, 2009.
131. Drucker, *Management Challenges for the 21st Century*; Tushman and O'Reilly, 'Ambidextrous Organizations'; Gary Hamel and C. K. Prahalad, 'Seeing the Future First', *Fortune* (September 4, 1994), 64–70; and Linda Yates and Peter Skarzynski, 'How Do Companies Get to the Future First?' *Management Review* (January 1999), 16–22.
132. Based on Carol A. Beatty and John R. M. Gordon, 'Barriers to the Implementation of CAD/CAM Systems', *Sloan Management Review* (Summer 1988), 25–33.
133. These techniques are based partly on John P. Kotter's eight-stage model of planned organizational change, Kotter, *Leading Change*, 20–25.
134. Burke Warner (2008), *Organization Change: Theory and Practice*, London, Sage Publications; 'Change: well begun is half done', *Financial Express*, 13 January 2006.
135. Everett M. Rogers and Floyd Shoemaker, *Communication of Innovations: A Cross Cultural Approach*, 2d ed. (New York: Free Press, 1971); Stratford P. Sherman, 'Eight Big Masters of Innovation', *Fortune* (October 15, 1984), 66–84.
136. Richard L. Daft and Selwyn W. Becker, *Innovation in Organizations* (New York: Elsevier, 1978); and John P. Kotter and Leonard A. Schlesinger, 'Choosing Strategies for Change', *Harvard Business Review* 57 (1979), 106–114.
137. 'Belgacom Standardizes on Imaginatik's Idea Central Global to Foster Culture of Innovation', *Business Wire*, 19 October 2004.
138. Peter Richardson and D. Keith Denton, 'Communicating Change', *Human Resource Management* 35, no. 2 (Summer 1996), 203–216.
139. Edgar H. Schein and Warren Bennis, *Personal and Organizational Change via Group Methods* (New York: Wiley, 1965); and Amy Edmondson, 'Psychological Safety and Learning Behavior in Work Teams', *Administrative Science Quarterly* 44 (1999), 350–383.
140. Diane L. Coutu, 'Creating the Most Frightening Company on Earth; An Interview with Andy Law of St. Luke's', *Harvard Business Review* (September–October 2000), 143–150.
141. Philip H. Mirvis, Amy L. Sales and Edward J. Hackett, 'The Implementation and Adoption of New Technology in Organizations: The Impact on Work, People, and Culture', *Human Resource Management* 30 (Spring 1991), 113–139; Arthur E. Wallach, 'System Changes Begin in the Training Department', *Personnel Journal* 58 (1979), 846–848, 872; and Paul R. Lawrence, 'How to Deal with Resistance to Change', *Harvard Business Review* 47 (January–February 1969), 4–12, 166–176.
142. Dexter C. Dunphy and Doug A. Stace, 'Transformational and Coercive Strategies for Planned Organizational Change: Beyond the O.D. Model', *Organizational Studies* 9 (1988), 317–334; and Kotter and Schlesinger, 'Choosing Strategies for Change'.

CHAPTER 12

DECISION-MAKING PROCESSES

A LOOK INSIDE

Oroton Group

Every Australian woman, and most of their partners, knows about Oroton handbags. Founded in Sydney 70 years ago by Boyd Lane, Oroton became a household fashion name in the early 1950s with the introduction of its iconic mesh handbags. The company continued to expand in the intervening years, selling through the major Australian department store David Jones, opening a chain of more than 30 company stores in Australia and New Zealand and even briefly venturing into the US market. Oroton gradually expanded its range of fashion accessories, selling jewelery, watches, purses and wallets and make-up accoutrements. Oroton also began accumulating Australian franchises of global retail brands, including the Canadian shoe outlet Aldo, and the American preppie clothiers Polo Ralph Lauren. In addition, Oroton picked up several well-respected Australian brand outlets such as Morrissey, named after Peter Morrissey, the country's best known fashion designer, and designer of uniforms to Australia's flagship airline Qantas. Although Oroton group went public in 1987, the Lane family continued to play a key management role, with the founder's grandson Ross Lane holding managing director and CEO positions until 2006.

Despite the value of the Oroton brand in Australasia, the company's efforts at expansion enjoyed mixed success. Oroton pulled out of the US market back in 1997 after poor trading results. From the early 2000s, Aldo shoe stores performed poorly, and results were disappointing at Morrissey. In 2006, as the Australian retail market tightened, the company dipped into the red, and the board realized something needed to be done. A strategic review was ordered, which concluded that the company's different brands lacked synergy, and management focus was dissipated between too many different endeavours. The company underwent a significant restructuring and downsizing. Sally Macdonald, a Harvard MBA, former executive with US retailer Banana Republic, came on board, first as a management consultant with Boston Consulting Group working on the restructuring, then directly as group CEO. The company would focus on the strong Oroton and Polo/Ralph Lauren brands, while Macdonald says a tough decision was made 'to put the other kids in a foster home'. In other words Aldo and Morrissey were sold off.

Internally, several Lane family members stepped off the board, and Ross Lane moved up to Chairman, leaving day-to-day decisions in Macdonald's hands. Headquarters staff were cut significantly in line with the focused, slimmed-down company. As Macdonald puts it: 'Too much time was spent in lower profitability aspects of the business; corporate overheads were blooming, there were too many layers of management and a splintered focus – it was too siloed and too functional'. A performance-based pay structure was introduced, and several lower performing stores closed, but a new flagship shop in Sydney was opened, along with an on-line sales portal. Despite the tough decisions, efforts have been made to encourage innovative thinking in the company, with improved communication and a less hierarchical structure. Headquarters was redesigned on an open plan concept, and a 360-degree staff feedback system introduced: 'It gives workers a sense of power and was important to culture change. It's not for everyone but it's more honest, more direct', says Macdonald.

The early results have been very promising. The company was back in the black in 2007 despite the upheaval. In FY 2007–2008 profits doubled to A$16 million. Like-for-like sales were up 20 per cent in the Oroton stores and 17 per cent at Polo/Ralph Lauren. In the last quarter of 2008, sales jumped another 10 per cent compared with the previous year. The company is cautiously planning expansion despite the global economic downturn, with eight new Oroton and three new Polo stores planned. New international licensing agreements have been signed for the Oroton bags, including in the lucrative Japanese market. However, restructuring is no cure for a bleak overall business environment. Despite the strong sales figures, and a high annualized dividend rate of 7.1 per cent, Oroton shares hit 52 week lows on nine different occasions in the the last quarter of 2008, reflecting investor sentiment that no matter how effective Oroton's turnaround strategy has been, luxury goods will inevitably be hit in the global recession. Sally Macdonald and her colleagues still have lots of choppy water ahead of them.[1]

Every organization grows, prospers or fails at least in part as a result of decisions by its managers, and decisions can be risky and uncertain, without any guarantee of success. Sometimes, decision making is a trial-and-error process, in which top managers continue to search for appropriate ways to solve complex problems. At Oroton, Sally Macdonald and her management team continue to evaluate the market environment and adjust the company's strategies to deal with the environment. Decision making is carried out amid constantly changing factors, unclear information and conflicting points of view. The 2002 decision to merge two American IT giants Hewlett-Packard (HP) and Compaq, for example, was highly controversial. Former HP CEO Carly Fiorina and her supporters believed it was essential for HP's future success, but other managers and board members argued that it was insane to risk HP's printer business and move the company more deeply into the highly competitive computer world. Fiorina's side ultimately won out, but results of the merger were disappointing. Hewlett-Packard's board ousted Fiorina in early 2005, partly due to issues related to the Compaq merger. Now, CEO Mark Hurd faces his own challenges, with managers, consultants and observers offering different, often conflicting, views of what is needed to get HP back on track. He has had to take tough decisions, initially cutting the company's workforce by 10 per cent and in late 2008 announcing a further 24,600 redundancies worldwide over the next three years in a bid to improve the company's focus and bottom line.[2,3] Nevertheless, in mid-2009, HP was still selling more personal computers than any other company worldwide.[4]

Many organizational decisions turn out to be serious mistakes. Britain's RBS banking group, for example, embarked on a highly ambitious expansion strategy under CEO Fred Goodwin. Under Goodwin's leadership what had been a small Scottish bank briefly made it into the ranks of the world's ten largest banks. Through a combination of acquisitions, including the much larger NatWest Bank, and ruthless cost-cutting (for which he earned the title Fred the Shred), RBS became fast-growing, highly profitable but also highly-leveraged. The final chapter in the expansion was the £46 billion buyout in 2007 of Dutch banking major ABN-Amro, in alliance with Belgium's Fortis and Spain's Santander banks. Goodwin announced that the deal had catapulted his bank, 'to the top of the premier league', but the US subprime mortgage crisis was already beginning to shake credit markets, and it was not long before he was being openly criticized. RBS shares slumped from over £7 in early 2007 to less than 50 pence by the time the company was forced to accept partial nationalization by the UK government in late 2008 in order to avoid total collapse. Goodwin was forced to resign, telling shareholders he was 'extremely sorry' for the errors he and fellow managers had made.[5,6]

The problems at RBS and much of the rest of the British banking sector pale in comparison with problems in the Icelandic business sector that emerged in 2008. All major Icelandic banks collapsed as a result of being heavily over-leveraged when the credit crunch hit in 2008. In 2007 alone they had made loans equivalent to nine times the size of the entire Icelandic economy, and the failure of the banks is expected to cost the Icelandic state more than 80 per cent of the country's annual GDP. Furthermore, the crisis badly hit several business empires that had grown enormously in an era of easy credit and infectious ambition among Iceland's business leaders. Largest amongst these groups is Baugur, a retail empire with worldwide holdings, but concentrated in the UK, where it owns all or part of many household names including House of Fraser, Iceland supermarkets, Hamley's and Moss Bros. Britain's *Financial Times* describes Baugur's plight, 'The Icelandic banks highly leveraged their borrowings to holding companies [such as Baugur] to make leveraged acquisitions of companies that were dependent on leveraged consumers and that's why it unravelled so quickly'. By the end of 2008, much of Baugur's once mighty retail empire was on the selling block, a victim of overambition, and in early 2009 Baugur had to seek bankruptcy protection.

See online
COUNTERPOINT 12.7

Yet managers also make many successful decisions every day. NXP Electronics, a chip manufacturer spin-off from Philips, built its business during 2008 despite the global slowdown, through a series of astute partnerships and product development strategies, particularly expanding into the fast-growing wireless technology sector.[7] Meg Whitman made eBay a model of what an Internet company should be by keeping the company focused on nurturing its community of buyers and sellers. In October 2008 it announced the lay-off of 10 per cent of its workforce while at the same time expanding through the acquisition of Bill Me Later and the Danish classified advertising companies Den Bla Avis and BilBasen. At Japan's Nissan, Carlos Ghosn implemented structural, management and product changes that transformed the company from being directionless and debt-ridden into one of the most dynamic and profitable automakers in the world.[8] And Ed Robinson and Matt Smith of Britain's Viral Factory pioneered the viral advertising concept, successfully skating the boundaries of the permissible in edgy ads for companies such as Diesel jeans and Trojan condoms.[9]

Purpose of This Chapter

At any time, an organization may be identifying problems and implementing alternatives for hundreds of decisions. Managers and organizations somehow muddle through these processes.[10] The purpose here is to analyze these processes to learn what decision making is actually like in organizational settings. Decision-making processes can be thought of as the brain and nervous system of an organization. Decision making is the end use of the information and control systems described in Chapter 8. Major decisions are made about organization strategy, structure, innovation and acquisitions. This chapter explores how organizations can and should make decisions about these issues.

The first section defines decision making. The next section examines how individual managers make decisions. Then several models of organizational decision making are explored. Each model is used in a different organizational situation. The final section in this chapter combines the models into a single framework that describes when and how they should be used and discusses special issues, such as decision mistakes.

Definitions

Organizational decision making is formally defined as the process of identifying and solving problems. The process has two major stages. In the **problem identification** stage, information about environmental and organizational conditions is monitored to determine if performance is satisfactory and to diagnose the cause of shortcomings. The **problem solution** stage is when alternative courses of action are considered and one alternative is selected and implemented.

As an organization manager, keep these guidelines in mind:

Adapt decision processes to fit the organizational situation. Understand how processes differ for programmed and nonprogrammed decisions.

Organizational decisions vary in complexity and can be categorized as programmed or nonprogrammed.[11] **Programmed decisions** are repetitive and well defined, and procedures exist for resolving the problem. They are well structured because criteria of performance are normally clear, good information is available about current performance, alternatives are easily specified and there is relative certainty that the chosen alternative will be successful. Examples of programmed decisions include decision rules, such as when to replace an office photocopier, when to reimburse managers for travel expenses or whether an applicant has sufficient qualifications for an assembly-line job. Many companies adopt rules based on experience with programmed decisions. For example, a rule for large hotels staffing banquets is

See online COUNTERPOINT 12.8

to allow one server per thirty guests for a sit-down function and one server per forty guests for a buffet.[12]

Nonprogrammed decisions are novel and poorly defined, and no procedure exists for solving the problem. They are used when an organization has not seen a problem before and may not know how to respond. Clear-cut decision criteria do not exist. Alternatives are fuzzy. There is uncertainty about whether a proposed solution will solve the problem. Typically, few alternatives can be developed for a nonprogrammed decision, so a single solution is custom-tailored to the problem.

COUNTERPOINT 12.1

It may be potentially misleading to say that nonprogrammed decisions are always novel or poorly defined: they may have been seen before; they may be amenable to definition. What makes them 'nonprogrammed' is the absence of any predetermined, systematic way of proceeding. That may be because there is no strong inclination to develop a procedure or because there is a conflict, manifest or latent, over how to proceed. **Discuss**

Many nonprogrammed decisions involve strategic planning, because uncertainty is great and decisions are complex. One example is the situation faced by water utility organizations both in the private and public sectors. The pipes and other infrastructure have to be replaced on a regular basis, and every utility has an upgrading schedule. However unexpected problems such as pipe breaks can occur at any time, even where company projections suggest the infrastructure is not due for repair or renewal. The problem may be a single fault due for example to poor installation, which can simply be repaired with focus then restored to planned upgrading elsewhere in the system. Alternatively it could however reflect a bigger problem that will require diversion of resources from previously-planned upgrading. Utility and other companies responsible for complex infrastructure need to have strategies for dealing with unexpected difficulties which are inevitable in complex systems.[13] The Metronet consortium that was contracted by London Underground to rehabilitate and maintain part of London's aging Underground system was hit by a flood of nonprogrammed issues ranging from ballooning staffing costs to unexpectedly difficult engineering challenges. The company had inadequately planned for such unforeseen challenges and folded, resulting in losses both for its investors and the state-owned Transport for London organization that had contracted the private-public partnership (PPP) project.[14,15]

Particularly complex nonprogrammed decisions have been referred to as 'wicked' decisions, because simply defining the problem can turn into a major task. Wicked problems are often associated with manager conflicts over objectives and alternatives, rapidly changing circumstances and unclear linkages among decision elements. Managers dealing with a wicked decision may hit on a solution that merely proves they failed to correctly define the problem to begin with.[16]

Today's managers and organizations are dealing with a higher percentage of nonprogrammed decisions because of the rapidly changing business environment. As outlined in Exhibit 12.1, today's environment has increased both the number and complexity of decisions that have to be made and has created a need for new decision-making processes. Managers in rapidly changing e-business departments, for example, often have to make quick decisions based on very limited information. Another example is the impact of globalization. The trend toward business process outsourcing to low-wage countries has managers in most Western countries struggling with complex decisions concerning the advantages and disadvantages of moving part or all of their operations offshore. These decisions include not only strict cost-benefit analysis but also ethical considerations about working conditions in developing countries and the impacts of job losses in the company's home environment. These issues can reflect

EXHIBIT 12.1 Decision Making in Today's Environment

Today's Business Environment

- *Demands more large-scale change via new strategies, reengineering, restructuring, mergers, acquisitions, downsizing, new product or market development and so on*

Decisions Made Inside the Organization

- *Are based on bigger, more complex, more emotionally charged issues*
- *Are made more quickly*
- *Are made in a less certain environment, with less clarity about means and outcomes*
- *Require more cooperation from more people involved in making and implementing decisions*

A New Decision-Making Process

- *Is required because no one individual has the information needed to make all major decisions*
- *Is required because no one individual has the time and credibility needed to convince lots of people to implement the decision*
- *Relies less on hard data as a basis for good decisions*
- *Is guided by a powerful coalition that can act as a team*
- *Permits decisions to evolve through trial and error and incremental steps as needed*

Source: Reprinted by permission of Harvard Business School Press. From *Leading Change* by John P. Kotter. Boston, MA, 1996, p. 56.

poorly on the company's image. For example, the sports apparel company Reebok has been sharply criticized in Canada – where ice hockey has the same exalted status as football in much of the rest of the world – for moving production of hockey jerseys to China and other low-cost Asian countries. In fact, almost all of the athletic footwear for which Reebok (now owned by German sportswear giant Adidas) is most famous is manufactured in low cost Asian countries – China (51 per cent of total footwear production), Indonesia (21 per cent), Vietnam (17 per cent) and Thailand (7 per cent).[17]

See online COUNTERPOINT 12.9

Individual Decision Making

Individual decision making by managers can be described in two ways. First is the **rational approach**, which suggests how managers should try to make decisions. Second is the **bounded rationality perspective**, which describes how decisions actually have to be made under severe time and resource constraints. The rational approach is an ideal managers may work towards but never reach.

See online COUNTERPOINT 12.10

Rational Approach

The rational approach to individual decision making stresses the need for systematic analysis of a problem followed by choice and implementation in a logical, step-by-step sequence. The rational approach was developed to guide individual decision making because many managers were observed to be unsystematic and arbitrary in their approach to organizational decisions.

Although the rational model is an ideal not fully achievable in the real world of uncertainty, complexity and rapid change highlighted in Exhibit 12.1, the model does help managers think about decisions more clearly and rationally. Managers should use systematic procedures to make decisions whenever possible. When managers have a deep understanding of the rational decision-making process, it can help them make better decisions even when there is a lack of clear information. Military organizations typically aim to use rational decision-making in order to handle complex problems quickly and decisively.

COUNTERPOINT 12.2

What the rational approach struggles to model is the complex interdependency and interaction of different factors. It also tends to assume a non-dynamic context so that seemingly 'ideal' solutions are calculated for circumstances that, as a consequence of change, no longer exist. Often so-called tacit knowledge based upon experience can be more instructive than additional amounts of information that can simply flood the process. A sub-optimal quick decision is often more effective than a delayed decision that is accompanied by increased uncertainty and lack of direction. **Discuss**

According to the rational approach, decision making can be broken down into eight steps, as illustrated in Exhibit 12.2.[18]

EXHIBIT 12.2 Steps in the Rational Approach to Decision Making

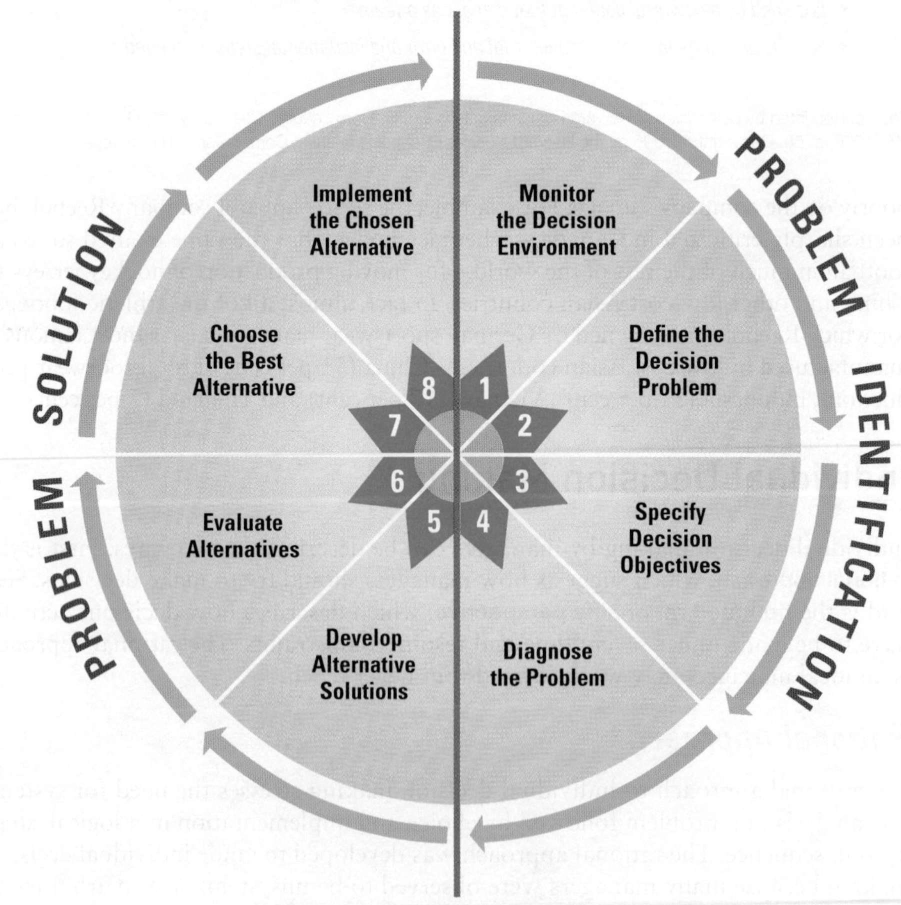

1 *Monitor the decision environment.* In the first step, a manager monitors internal and external information that will indicate deviations from planned or acceptable behaviour. He or she talks to colleagues and reviews financial statements, performance evaluations, industry indices, competitors' activities and so forth. Increasingly, environmental monitoring is supported by specialist software. For example, Switzerland's Cablecom was becoming increasingly concerned by the proportion of customers it was losing. As Federico Cesconi, Cablecom's director of business intelligence noted: 'It's very difficult to win back customers after they've left you. And in Europe, the win-back rate is only about 10 per cent to 15 per cent. So, our intent was to assess the satisfaction of every single customer.'

2 *Define the decision problem.* The manager responds to deviations by identifying essential details of the problem: where, when, who was involved, who was affected and how current activities are influenced. For Cablecom, this might mean defining whether customers are lost early in their relationship with the company, what groups have customers have the highest and lowest levels of 'churn', etc. Cablecom's data analysis found that complaints started rolling in about nine months in to customer contracts on average, and customers were mostly lost in the 12 to 14 month period.

3 *Specify decision objectives.* The manager determines what performance outcomes should be achieved by a decision.

4 *Diagnose the problem.* In this step, the manager digs below the surface to analyze the cause of the problem. Additional data might be gathered to facilitate this diagnosis. Understanding the cause enables appropriate treatment. For Cablecom, the problem seemed to be a combination of excessively pressuring sales pitches, and a lack of follow-up response to complaints.

5 *Develop alternative solutions.* Before a manager can move ahead with a decisive action plan, he or she must have a clear understanding of the various options available to achieve desired objectives. The manager may seek ideas and suggestions from other people. Cablecom's options included ensuring sales pitches also included attractive new product offers, and following up customer complaint calls to see if the customer was now satisfied.

6 *Evaluate alternatives.* This step may involve the use of statistical techniques or personal experience to gauge the probability of success. The merits of each alternative are assessed, as well as the probability that it will reach the desired objectives.

7 *Choose the best alternative.* This step is the core of the decision process. The manager uses his or her analysis of the problem, objectives and alternatives to select a single alternative that has the best chance for success. At Cablecom, decisions were made both to roll out new product offerings such as personal video recorders (PVR) and an online video library that can be delivered through cable's superfast broadband connection.

8 *Implement the chosen alternative.* Finally, the manager uses managerial, administrative and persuasive abilities and gives directions to ensure that the decision is carried out. The monitoring activity (step 1) begins again as soon as the solution is implemented. For Cablecom's Federico Cesconi, the decision cycle is a continuous process, with new decisions made daily based on monitoring the environment for problems and opportunities.[19]

The first four steps in this sequence are the problem identification stage, and the next four steps are the problem solution stage of decision making, as indicated in

Alberta Consulting

1 *Monitor the decision environment*. It is Monday morning, and Joe DeFoe, Alberta's accounts receivable supervisor, is absent again.

2 *Define the decision problem*. This is the fourth consecutive Monday DeFoe has been absent. Company policy forbids unexcused absenteeism, and DeFoe has been warned about his excessive absenteeism on the last two occasions. A final warning is in order but can be delayed, if warranted.

3 *Specify decision objectives*. DeFoe should attend work regularly and establish the invoice collection levels of which he is capable. The time period for solving the problem is two weeks.

4 *Diagnose the problem*. Discreet discussions with DeFoe's co-workers and information gleaned from DeFoe indicate that DeFoe has a drinking problem. He apparently uses Mondays to dry out from weekend benders. Discussion with other company sources confirms that DeFoe is a problem drinker.

5 *Develop alternative solutions*. (1) Fire DeFoe. (2) Issue a final warning without comment. (3) Issue a warning and accuse DeFoe of being an alcoholic to let him know you are aware of his problem. (4) Talk with DeFoe to see if he will discuss his drinking. If he admits he has a drinking problem, delay the final warning and suggest that he enrol in Alberta's new employee assistance programme for help with personal problems, including alcoholism. (5) Talk with DeFoe to see if he will discuss his drinking. If he does not admit he has a drinking problem, let him know that the next absence will cost him his job.

6 *Evaluate alternatives*. The cost of training a replacement is the same for each alternative. Alternative 1 ignores cost and other criteria. Alternatives 2 and 3 do not adhere to company policy, which advocates counselling where appropriate. Alternative 4 is designed for the benefit of both DeFoe and the company. It might save a good employee if DeFoe is willing to seek assistance. Alternative 5 is primarily for the benefit of the company. A final warning might provide some incentive for DeFoe to admit he has a drinking problem. If so, dismissal might be avoided, but further absences will no longer be tolerated.

7 *Choose the best alternative*. DeFoe does not admit that he has a drinking problem. Choose alternative 5.

8 *Implement the chosen alternative*. Write up the case and issue the final warning.[20]

Exhibit 12.2. A manager normally goes through all eight steps in making a decision, although each step may not be a distinct element. Managers may know from experience exactly what to do in a situation, so one or more steps will be minimized. The *In Practice* illustrates how the rational approach is used to make a decision about a personnel problem.

In the Alberta Consulting *In Practice* example above, issuing the final warning to Joe DeFoe was a programmed decision. The standard of expected behaviour was clearly defined, information on the frequency and cause of DeFoe's absence was readily available and acceptable alternatives and procedures were described. The rational procedure works best in such cases, when the decision maker has sufficient time for an orderly, thoughtful process. Moreover, Alberta Consulting had mechanisms in place to implement the decision, once made.

See online **COUNTERPOINT 12.11**

When decisions are nonprogrammed, ill-defined and piling on top of one another, the individual manager should still try to use the steps in the rational approach, but he or she often will have to take shortcuts by relying on intuition and experience. Deviations from the rational approach are explained by the bounded rationality perspective.

COUNTERPOINT 12.3

'Intuition' and 'experience' are not helpfully characterized as 'short cuts'. It might be more relevant to call rational decision-making 'long-winded' and 'clunky'. **Discuss**

Bounded Rationality Perspective

The point of the rational approach is that managers should try to use systematic procedures to arrive at good decisions. When organizations are facing little competition and are dealing with well-understood issues, managers generally use rational procedures to make decisions.[21] Yet research into managerial decision making shows that managers often are unable to follow an ideal procedure. Many decisions must be made very quickly. Time pressure, a large number of internal and external factors affecting a decision, and the ill-defined nature of many problems make systematic analysis virtually impossible. Managers have only so much time and mental capacity and, hence, cannot evaluate every goal, problem and alternative. The attempt to be rational is bounded (limited) by the enormous complexity of many problems. There is a limit to how rational managers can be. For example, an executive in a hurry may have a choice of fifty ties on a rack but will take the first or second one that matches his suit. The executive doesn't carefully weigh all fifty alternatives because the short amount of time and the large number of plausible alternatives would be overwhelming. The manager simply selects the first tie that solves the problem and moves on to the next task.

See online
COUNTERPOINT 12.12

As an organization manager, keep these guidelines in mind:

Use rational decision processes when possible, but recognize that many constraints may impinge on decision makers and prevent a perfectly rational decision. Apply the bounded rationality perspective and use intuition when confronting ill-defined, nonprogrammed decisions.

Constraints and Tradeoffs Not only are large organizational decisions too complex to fully comprehend, but several other constraints impinge on the decision maker, as illustrated in Exhibit 12.3. For many decisions, the circumstances are ambiguous, requiring social support, a shared perspective on what happens and acceptance and agreement. For example, the decision to outsource production to low labour cost countries is typically based on a limited cost benefit analysis of savings that can be realized by replacing high cost in-house staffing with lower cost contracted labour overseas. However, moving parts of the business process not only outside the company, but also outside the home country business environment greatly increases the unknowns.[22] Trust between the contracting parties is typically limited, especially in the critical early stages of outsourcing, and can rarely be fully replaced by comprehensive contract terms and conditions. Trust is built up over time through close working interaction which is difficult to replicate in distant outsourced units.

Numerous other unknowns can impinge on the outcomes of an outsourcing strategy, ranging from currency exchange risk for example (the Indian rupee increased in value by 20 per cent against the British pound between 2007 and 2008, while it lost 20 per cent against the US dollar) to end-user resistance (particularly in the case of outsourced call centres). Finally, some analysts argue that outsourcing leads inherently to *asymmetric power relationships*, with the supplier often in the ascendancy over the outsourcing organization. UK academic Chris Lonsdale believes that it is 'risible' to think that British National Health Service (NHS) commercial managers, for example, each responsible for managing hundreds of service contracts, could effectively foresee issues likely to arise in each of the contracts. In contrast the supplier companies to the NHS are often multinationals with highly professional sales and marketing teams able to structure advantageous contracts and skate over potential pitfalls.[23]

EXHIBIT 12.3 Constraints and Trade-offs during Nonprogrammed Decision Making

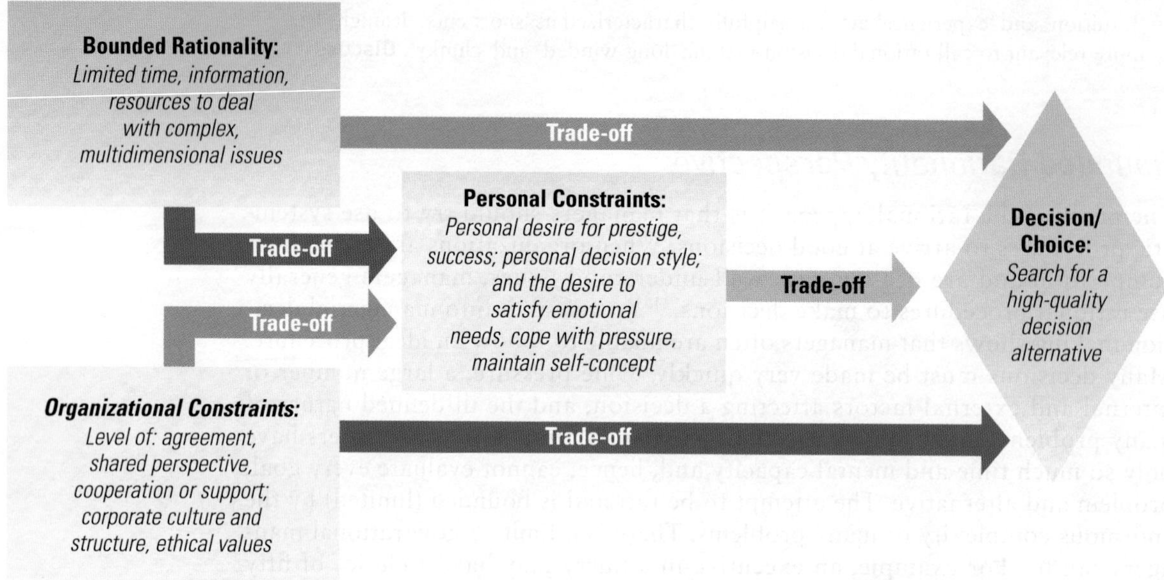

Source: Adapted from Irving L. Janis, *Crucial Decisions* (New York: Free Press, 1989); and A. L. George, *Presidential Decision Making in Foreign Policy: The Effective Use of Information and Advice* (Boulder, Colo.: Westview Press, 1980).

Even in cases where the outsourcing strategy is well-planned and generally successful, such as Danish medical supplies company Coloplast, which decided to outsource volume production to Hungary between 2005 and 2008, managers can be surprised by the number of unexpected challenges that arose. These ranged from inefficiencies caused by the location of the distribution warehouse close to the Danish headquarters, meaning goods produced in Hungary had to be transported all the way to northern Europe for centralized distribution, to the complexity of transferring tacit knowledge underpinning the production process.[24] Managerial decisions, small and large, are made in the context of imperfect knowledge, and of bounded rationality.[25]

See online COUNTERPOINT 12.13

Corporate culture and ethical values also influence decision making, as discussed in Chapter 10. In the best cases, such as at the late Anita Roddick's Body Shop, companies have primary goals of improving the world while enhancing the lives of employees and customers. Managers also often make decisions within a context of trying to please upper managers, people who are perceived to have power within the organization, or others they respect and want to emulate.[26] Personal constraints – such as decision style, work pressure, desire for prestige, or simple feelings of insecurity – may constrain either the search for alternatives or the acceptability of an alternative. All of these factors constrain a perfectly rational approach that should lead to an obviously ideal choice.[27] Even seemingly simple decisions, such as selecting a job on graduation from college, can quickly become so complex that a bounded rationality approach is used. Graduating students have been known to search for a job until they have two or three acceptable job offers, at which point their search activity rapidly diminishes. Hundreds of firms may be available for interviews, and two or three job offers are far short of the maximum number that would be possible if students made the decision based on perfect rationality.

The Role of Intuition The bounded rationality perspective is often associated with intuitive decision processes. In **intuitive decision making**, experience and judgment rather than sequential logic or explicit reasoning are used to make decisions.[28] Intuition is not arbitrary or irrational because it is based on years of practice and hands-on experience, often stored in the subconscious. 'When managers use their intuition based on long experience with organizational issues, they more rapidly perceive and understand problems, and they develop a gut feeling or hunch about which alternative will solve a problem, speeding the decision-making process.[29] The value of intuition for effective decision making is supported by a growing body of research from psychology, organizational science, and other disciplines.[30] Indeed, many universities are offering courses in creativity and intuition so business students can learn to understand and use these processes.

See online
COUNTERPOINT 12.14

In a situation of great complexity or ambiguity, previous experience and judgement are needed to incorporate intangible elements at both the problem identification and problem solution stages.[31] A study of manager problem finding showed that thirty of thirty-three problems were ambiguous and ill-defined.[32] Bits and scraps of unrelated information from informal sources resulted in a pattern in the manager's mind. The manager could not prove a problem existed but knew intuitively that a certain area needed attention. A too-simple view of a complex problem is often associated with decision failure.[33] Intuition plays an increasingly important role in problem identification in today's fast-paced and uncertain business environment.

Intuitive processes are also used in the problem solution stage. Executives frequently make decisions without explicit reference to the impact on profits or to other measurable outcomes.[34] As we saw in Exhibit 12.3, many intangible factors – such as a person's concern about the support of other executives, fear of failure and social attitudes – influence selection of the best alternative. These factors cannot be quantified in a systematic way, so intuition guides the choice of a solution. Managers may make a decision based on what they sense to be right rather than on what they can document with hard data. A 2006 survey of American CEO's found that six in ten acknowledge that 'gut feeling' is highly influential in their decision-making. Similar results have been found in New Zealand and elsewhere.[35,36]

COUNTERPOINT 12.4

It may be a mistake to conflate a sense of 'what is right' with 'gut feeling'. 'Gut feeling' is as likely to be accommodating of self-interest or with staying in the comfort zone as it is with taking decisions that turn out to be 'right'. **Discuss**

Take the case of Austrian motorbike manufacturer KTM Fahrrad GmbH. Stefan Pierer took over in 2002 as CEO of the company after it emerged from bankruptcy. Once he had put the company back on its feet he took a leap into the unknown, steering KTM, long-famous for its off-road models, into the competitive world of street bikes. The gut decision has been a huge success, by 2006 KTM had become Europe's second biggest motorbike manufacturer on the back of 15 years during which the company averaged 25 per cent annual revenue growth. Street bikes now make up almost one-third of KTM's revenues, Pierer says, 'When it comes to really serious business decisions I ultimately rely on my intuition. It's sometimes the case that rational arguments speak for or against something, but then somehow the decision still won't leave me in peace. I wake up in the night and have the feeling that I should do it differently after all'.[37] However, there are also many examples of intuitive decisions that turned out to be complete failures.[38] This chapter's Bookmark discusses how managers can give their intuition a better chance of leading to successful decisions.

Have you read this book?

Blink: The Power of Thinking without Thinking

BY MALCOLM GLADWELL

Snap decisions can be just as good as – and sometimes better than – decisions that are made cautiously and deliberately. Yet they can also be seriously flawed or even dangerously wrong. That's the premise of Malcolm Gladwell's *Blink: The Power of Thinking without Thinking*. Gladwell explores how our 'adaptive unconscious' arrives at complex, important decisions in an instant – and how we can train it to make those decisions good ones.

Sharpening Your Intuition

Even when we think our decision making is the result of careful analysis and rational consideration, Gladwell says, most of it actually happens subconsciously in a split second. This process, which he refers to as 'rapid cognition', provides room for both amazing insight and grave error. Here are some tips for improving rapid cognition:

- *Remember that more is not better*. Gladwell argues that giving people too much data and information hampers their ability to make good decisions. He cites a study showing that emergency room doctors who are best at diagnosing heart attacks gather less information from their patients than other doctors do. Rather than overloading on information, search out the most meaningful parts.
- *Practice thin-slicing*. The process Gladwell refers to as *thin-slicing* is what harnesses the power of the adaptive unconscious and enables us to make smart decisions with minimal time and information. Thin-slicing means focusing on a thin slice of pertinent data or information and allowing your intuition to do the work for you. Gladwell cites the example of a Pentagon war game, in which an enemy team of commodities traders defeated a US Army that had 'an unpredented amount of information and intelligence' and 'did a thoroughly rational and rigorous analysis that covered every conceivable contingency'. The commodities traders were used to making thousands of instant decisions an hour based on limited information. Managers can practise spontaneous decision making until it becomes second nature.
- *Know your limits*. Not every decision should be based on intuition. When you have a depth of knowledge and experience in an area, you can put more trust in your gut feelings. Gladwell also cautions to beware of biases that interfere with good decision making. *Blink* suggests that we can teach ourselves to sort through first impressions and figure out which are important and which are based on subconscious biases such as stereotypes or emotional baggage.

Conclusion

Blink is filled with lively and interesting anecdotes, such as how firefighters can 'slow down a moment' and create an environment where spontaneous decision making can take place. Gladwell asserts that a better understanding of the process of split-second decision making can help people make better decisions in all areas of their lives, as well as help them anticipate and avoid miscalculations.

Blink: The Power of Thinking without Thinking, by Malcolm Gladwell, is published by Little, Brown.

Managers may walk a fine line between two extremes: on the one hand, making arbitrary decisions without careful study, and on the other, relying obsessively on numbers and rational analysis.[39] Remember that the bounded rationality perspective and the use of intuition apply mostly to nonprogrammed decisions. The novel, unclear, complex aspects of nonprogrammed decisions mean hard data and logical procedures are not available. One study of executive decision making found that managers simply could not use the rational approach for nonprogrammed decisions, such as when to buy a computed tomography (CT) scanner for an osteopathic

Rough Trade

It all started because Geoff Travis couldn't find the records that he liked, back in 1976 when big labels were king and if you didn't fit their formula you didn't have a chance. Travis set up a small record store and stocked it with his kind of music, alternative, edgy material. He freely admits he was lucky, because musical taste was on the cusp of a revolution. The musical lull of the early 1970s was about to be shaken up by the advent of punk. Travis started by selling his huge collection of alternative music records he had bought while hitchhiking across America the previous year, where bands like the Ramones had already started to shake things up. His West London location turned out to be at the epicentre of the European scene, 'The Clash lived up the road, and The Sex Pistols would come in trying to sell us all the records they'd nicked from somewhere else', Travis recalls.

It wasn't long before Travis's friends who owned similar stores across London started to source hard-to-find music through him, and soon he formed the core of a national network of independent record stores and the myriad fledgling labels that were producing singles by new artists. Rough Trade records was born two years later in 1978, with early successes like The Fall and Stiff Little Fingers. The first band Rough Trade chaperoned to the big time was The Smiths, and by 2008 some of the names featuring on the label's 30 year anniversary tour were The Strokes, Belle & Sebastian, Arcade Fire and Jarvis Cocker.

Rough Trade has seen its ups and downs. In the early 1990s the distribution arm of the business folded, and Travis sold off the record label in order to ensure artists, who risked losing desperately-needed record sales revenues in the bankruptcy, would be paid. But after working for another label for a while, Travis bought Rough Trade back and relaunched it in 2000. Since then things have gone well, underpinned by Travis's firm commitment to choose bands according to his intuition, rather than a prepackaged marketing formula.

hospital or whether a city had a need for and could reasonably adopt an enterprise resource planning system.[40] In those cases, managers had limited time and resources, and some factors simply couldn't be measured and analyzed. Trying to quantify such information could cause mistakes because it may oversimplify decision criteria. Intuition can also balance and supplement rational analysis to help organization leaders make better decisions. Geoff Travis, founder of Rough Trade, the British indie record label, relied on his intuition, his innate feel for 'the next thing' in music, to build a successful label that also freed young musicians from the suffocating control of the big record companies.[41]

Organizational Decision Making

Organizations are composed of managers who make decisions using both rational and intuitive processes; but organization-level decisions are not usually made by a single manager. Many organizational decisions involve several managers. Problem identification and problem solution involve many departments, multiple viewpoints and even other organizations, which are beyond the scope of an individual manager.

The processes by which decisions are made in organizations are influenced by a number of factors, particularly the organization's own internal structures and the degree of stability or instability of the external environment.[42] Research into organization-level decision making has identified four primary types of organizational decision-making processes: the management science approach, the Carnegie model, the incremental decision process model and the garbage can model.

As an organization manager, keep this guideline in mind:

Use a rational decision approach – computation, management science – when a problem situation is well understood.

Management Science Approach

The **management science approach** to organizational decision making is the analogue to the rational approach by individual managers. Management science came into being during the Second World War.[43] At that time, mathematical and statistical techniques were applied to urgent, large-scale military problems that were beyond the ability of individual decision makers.

Mathematicians, physicists and operations researchers used systems analysis to develop artillery trajectories, antisubmarine strategies and bombing strategies such as salvoing (discharging multiple shells simultaneously). Consider the problem of a battleship trying to sink an enemy ship several miles away. The calculation for aiming the battleship's guns should consider distance, wind speed, shell size, speed and direction of both ships, pitch and roll of the firing ship and curvature of the earth. Methods for performing such calculations using trial and error and intuition are not accurate, take far too long and may never achieve success.

This is where management science came in. Analysts were able to identify the relevant variables involved in aiming a ship's guns and could model them with the use of mathematical equations. Distance, speed, pitch, roll, shell size and so on could be calculated and entered into the equations. The answer was immediate, and the guns could begin firing. Factors such as pitch and roll were soon measured mechanically and fed directly into the targeting mechanism. Today, the human element is completely removed from the targeting process. Radar picks up the target, and the entire sequence is computed automatically.

Management science yielded success for many military problems. This approach to decision making diffused into corporations and business schools, where techniques were studied and elaborated. Today, many corporations have assigned departments to use these techniques. The computer department develops quantitative data for analysis. Operations research departments use mathematical models to quantify relevant variables and develop a quantitative representation of alternative solutions and the probability of each one solving the problem. These departments also use such devices as linear programming, Bayesian statistics, PERT charts and computer simulations.

Management science is an excellent device for organizational decision making when problems are analyzable and when the variables can be identified and measured. Mathematical models can contain a thousand or more variables, each one relevant in some way to the ultimate outcome. Management science techniques have been used to correctly solve problems as diverse as finding the right spot for a church camp, test-marketing the first of a new family of products, drilling for oil and radically altering the distribution of telecommunications services.[44] The *In Practice* example on the next page describes how Germany's Labour Agency, the Bundesagentur für Arbeit used management science techniques to set up its Virtual Labour Market (VAM).

Despite the positive outcomes, VAM's development had its share of controversy, which is very common in a complex system. Cost overruns in the final development phase led to allegations of corruption in awarding contracts. An enquiry showed this was not the case but that more could have been done to keep costs closer to original estimates.[45]

Management science can accurately and quickly solve problems that have too many explicit variables for human processing. This system is at its best when applied to problems that are analyzable, are measurable and can be structured in a logical way. Increasingly sophisticated computer technology and software programs are allowing the expansion of management science to cover a broader range of problems than ever before. For example, most large retailers, including Zara, Marks and Spencer and Gap, use software to analyze current and historical sales data and

Germany's Virtual Labour Market[46]

Despite the successes of the German economy in the post-war period, the country still faces stubbornly high unemployment, particularly among youth. At the same time, as in most countries, employers continue to say that they cannot find the right people to fill certain positions. The German government labour agency responsible for helping unemployed people get matched with work opportunities, the Bundesagentur für Arbeit (BfA), set about developing an IT-based system that would match workers with available opportunities. The new system consists of internal and external online portals, with links to private firms' HR departments, as well as commercial and government employment services. VerBIS, the intranet (internal) portal, supports the 100,000 counsellors and placement workers located in BfA's employment offices throughout Germany. These internal users make about 40 million hits on the portal every day.

VAM has helped BfA to improve the quality and efficiency of its work. Its centralized database of all job opportunities in Germany makes it a useful resource not only for the unemployed but for employed workers seeking better jobs. The system has substantially reduced the time taken to match qualified candidates against available employment opportunities, with about 800,000 jobs posted and 5.5 million job seekers registered at any one time. Over two million job matches are identified every week. In addition, the system maintains updated records of all workers seeking employment, which can be accessed by any BfA counsellor across the country. This contrasts positively with the previous system where personnel files were held by individual counsellors, with information frequently being lost when counsellors changed or the jobseeker moved.

The internet side of the VAM provides new services both to employers and jobseekers. Employers can directly enter information about positions available, and for the first time job seekers can access a nationwide database of positions available, either from home through an internet connection, or at one of the terminals located in all BfA offices. The system helps job seekers take greater control over their job search, and reduces the time BfA workers have to devote to each case.

The new system is part of labour market reforms that the German government has put in place in an effort to reduce long-term unemployment. It is linked to training and social benefits databases and thus helps ensure people receive the benefit to which they are entitled. The more efficient matching service gets people back into the workforce more quickly, thus improving government finances. But the most important aspect of the system is the help it provides for people seeking rewarding work. Markus Michel, formerly unemployed, worked with his BfA placement agent to find his current job using the system's enhanced matching technology – it is a position requiring skills which he had acquired by self-study but for which he had no formal qualification: 'I would have fallen through the cracks [before] because the only possible job search would have been the search for a job title'. The virtual labour market concept has been adopted in other countries, including the UK.[47]

determine when, where and how much to mark down prices. Airlines and hotel chains now use yield management software to set prices according to factors such as passenger load and occupancy rates, respectively. The success of European low-cost carrier Ryanair is largely based on sophisticated use of yield management systems. Passengers booking well in advance for unseasonal destinations, such as seaside resorts in midwinter, can snag fares as low as one euro, but those wishing to travel at short notice on well-subscribed flights can expect to pay top prices.[48] Former Ryanair executives Jim McMahon and Seamus Moriarty set up an aviation consultancy that specializes in helping other airlines to take best advantage of yield management systems to maximize their seat revenues.[49,50] Yield management pricing is now being used in many different sectors from car rentals to do-it-yourself equipment rental. Railway companies across Europe now use yield management with positive results; France's state-owned SNCF railway company first introduced the system for its high-speed TGV trains but is now planning to extend the approach to the regional TER services.[51]

Companies need to address potential negative customer sentiment when considering using yield management.[52] This can take various forms. Customers who have paid top prices for a holiday package may well feel ripped-off if they find that fellow travellers who booked at the last minute paid far less than they did. Further, customers are aware that costs to provide a service such as a hotel room tend to be similar despite tariffs varying widely according to load factors. Loyal customers who always use a particular company may object if they suddenly find they have to pay an exorbitant rate for a service because they are using it at a popular time, and will be more likely to 'counter-attack' by searching for a cheaper alternative with another company. Yield management can thus damage customer loyalty, another important weapon in a company's competitive arsenal.[53]

Management science has, to go along with its successes, produced many failures.[54] In recent years, many banks have begun using computerized scoring systems to rate those applying for credit, but some argue that human judgement is needed to assess an individual's real creditworthiness. Many analysts place part of the responsibility for the global credit system meltdown of 2007–2008 on banks' withdrawal from personal relationships with their clients in favour of outsourced models where companies – frequently based in India and other offshore locations – were paid to identify potential borrowers through telephone canvassing. Although a rudimentary financial qualification assessment was conducted, usually on the telephone, obviously the loan-originating companies were most interested in getting their fee for finding a customer. Banks and other financial institutions then 'securitized' these loans by packaging them up in bundles which were then assigned a market value based on the supposed solidity of the underlying security – such as customers' houses. These financial instruments were then swapped amongst the banks and sold off to various investors in an increasingly complex series of arrangements. The complexity of the system was such that banks and other investors lost track of the underlying value of the securities. Investors and banks panicked when it became clear that the house price boom in countries like the US and UK was coming to an end and that significant numbers of customers could not afford to repay their loans and mortgages. Banks knew that many of the bundled loans and mortgages they held were worthless but did not know which ones. The credit explosion turned overnight into a credit freeze and numerous financial institutions in Europe, the USA and the rest of the world, either went bankrupt or had to be bailed out at enormous cost to taxpayers.[55] The computerized infrastructure that managed the credit system, from customer credit assessment through to loan bundling and securitization, appeared sophisticated but obscured the absence of both internal and external oversight.

The dangers of complex, poorly understood, poorly regulated, computerized financial markets are also demonstrated by the collapse of Bernard L. Madoff Investment Securities in late 2008.[56] Madoff, a former chairman of the NASDAQ stock exchange and highly regarded figure in US financial circles, apparently concocted a scheme in which he purported to manage investors' funds using a complex and secretive computerized investment model. In fact it appears he paid existing investors their dividends using new investors' resources, as well as leaching off substantial amounts of money to support his extravagant lifestyle. The US Securities and Exchange Commission, which should have overseen his activities, failed to detect the fraud despite numerous tip-offs. Once the final tallies were made, losses were expected to exceed $25 billion, and the incident sent shockwaves through stock markets already depressed by the impacts of the credit meltdown described above.[57,58]

Apart from complexity and the consequent tendency for lack of transparency, another problem with the management science approach is that quantitative data are not rich and do not convey tacit knowledge, as described in Chapter 8. Informal cues that indicate the existence of problems have to be sensed on a more personal basis by managers.[59] The most sophisticated mathematical analyses are of no value if the important factors cannot be quantified and included in the model. Such things as competitor reactions, consumer tastes and product warmth are qualitative dimensions. In these situations, the role of management science is to supplement manager decision making. Quantitative results can be given to managers for discussion and interpretation along with their informal opinions, judgement and intuition. The final decision can include both qualitative factors and quantitative calculations.

Carnegie Model

The **Carnegie model** of organizational decision making is based on the work of Richard Cyert, James March and Herbert Simon, who were all associated with Carnegie-Mellon University in Pittsburgh, USA.[60] Their research helped formulate the bounded rationality approach to individual decision making, as well as provide new insights about organizational decisions.

As an organization manager, keep these guidelines in mind:

Use a coalition-building approach when organizational goals and problem priorities are in conflict. When managers disagree about priorities or the true nature of the problem, they should discuss and seek agreement about priorities.

Until their work, research in economics assumed that business firms made decisions as a single entity, as if all relevant information were funnelled to the top decision maker for a choice. Research by the Carnegie group indicated that organization-level decisions involved many managers and that a final choice was based on a coalition among those managers. A **coalition** is an alliance among several managers who agree about organizational goals and problem priorities.[61] It could include managers from line departments, staff specialists and even external groups, such as powerful customers, bankers or union representatives.

Management coalitions are needed during decision making for two reasons. First, organizational goals are often ambiguous, and operative goals of departments are often inconsistent. When goals are ambiguous and inconsistent, managers disagree about problem priorities. They must bargain about problems and build a coalition around the question of which problems to solve.

COUNTERPOINT 12.5

While attention to coalition building is undoubtedly important, it requires a close appreciation of what enables coalitions to be built. How, for example, is credibility and legitimacy established? To what extent do coalitions represent the outcome of established power relations? What kinds of 'solutions' are simply never contemplated because those occupying privileged positions have effectively closed them off? Coalition building does not mean that the resulting decisions are better ones, only that they have been agreed by a dominant coalition. What is probable is that the decision broadly reflects the preconceptions, fears, hopes and values of the coalition members. **Discuss**

The second reason for coalitions is that individual managers intend to be rational but function with human cognitive limitations and other constraints, as described earlier. Managers do not have the time, resources or mental capacity to identify all dimensions and to process all information relevant to a decision. These limitations lead to coalition-building behaviour. Managers talk to each other and exchange points of view to gather information and reduce ambiguity. People who have relevant information or a stake in a decision outcome are consulted. Building a coalition will lead to a decision that is supported by interested parties.

The process of coalition formation has several implications for organizational decision behaviour. First, decisions are made to *satisfice* rather than to optimize problem solutions. **Satisficing** means organizations accept a satisfactory rather than a maximum level of performance, enabling them to achieve several goals simultaneously. In decision making, the coalition will accept a solution that is perceived as satisfactory to all coalition members. Second, managers are concerned with immediate problems and short-run solutions. They engage in what Cyert and March called *problemistic search*.[62]

Problemistic search means managers look around in the immediate environment for a solution to quickly resolve a problem. Managers don't expect a perfect solution when the situation is ill-defined and conflict-laden. This contrasts with the management science approach, which assumes that analysis can uncover every reasonable alternative. The Carnegie model says that search behaviour is just sufficient to produce a satisfactory solution and that managers typically adopt the first satisfactory solution that emerges. Third, discussion and bargaining are especially important in the problem identification stage of decision making. Unless coalition members perceive a problem, action will not be taken.

The decision process described in the Carnegie model is summarized in Exhibit 12.4. The Carnegie model points out that building agreement through a managerial coalition is a major part of organizational decision making. This is especially true at upper management levels. Discussion and bargaining are time consuming, so search procedures are usually simple and the selected alternative satisfices rather than optimizes problem solution. When problems are programmed – are clear and have been seen before – the organization will rely on previous procedures and routines. Rules and procedures prevent the need for renewed coalition formation and political bargaining. Nonprogrammed decisions, however, require bargaining and conflict resolution.

Organizations suffer when managers are unable to build a coalition around goals and problem priorities, as illustrated by the *In Practice* case of Encyclopaedia Britannica.

The Carnegie model is particularly useful at the problem identification stage. However, a coalition of key department managers is also important for smooth implementation of a decision, particularly a major reorganization. Top executives at Britannica realized the importance of building coalitions for decision making

EXHIBIT 12.4 Choice Processes in the Carnegie Model

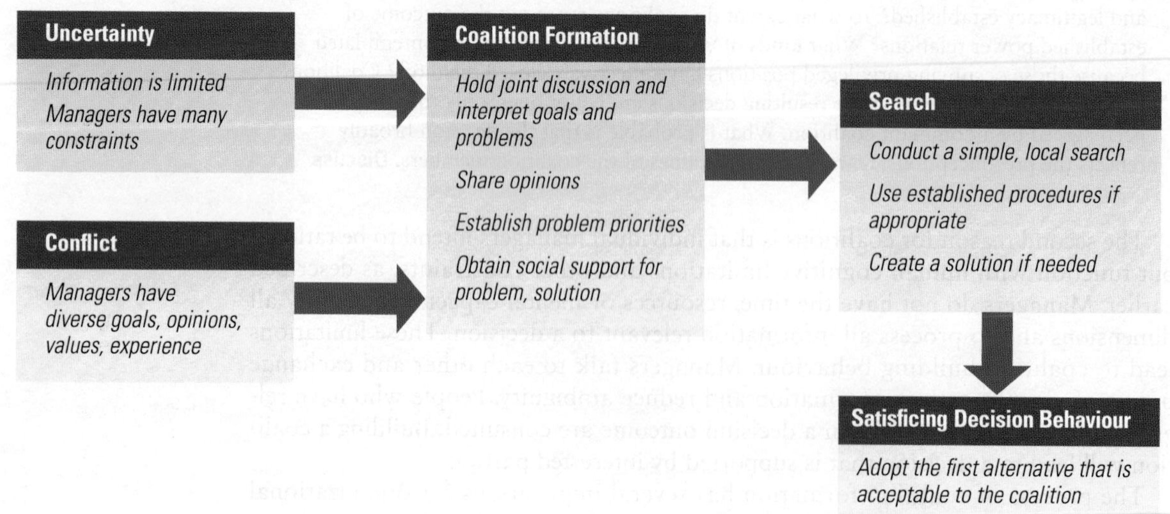

Encyclopaedia Britannica

For most of its 231-year history, the *Encyclopaedia Britannica* had been viewed as an illustrious repository of cultural and historical knowledge. Generations of students and librarians relied on the *Britannica* – but that was before CD-ROMs and the Internet became the study tools of choice. Suddenly, the thirty-two-volume collection of encyclopedias, stretching four feet on a bookshelf and costing as much as a personal computer (PC), seemed destined to fade into history.

When Swiss-based financier Joseph Safra bought Britannica, he discovered one of the reasons. For nearly a decade, managers had bickered over goals and priorities. Some top executives believed the company needed to invest more in electronic media, but others supported Britannica's traditional direct-to-home sales force. Eventually, the company's Compton unit, a CD-ROM pioneer now being used by millions of consumers, was sold, leaving Britannica without any presence in the new market. In the 1980s, Microsoft had approached Britannica to develop a CD-ROM encyclopedia; when it didn't work out, Microsoft went with Funk & Wagnalls and developed Encarta. Microsoft arranged to have Encarta preinstalled on PCs, so the CD-ROM was essentially free to new PC buyers. When Britannica finally came out with its CD-ROM version, however, it was priced at a staggering $1,200. The squabbling among managers, owners and editors about product development, pricing, distribution and other important decisions contributed to the company's decline.

The first step in Safra's turnaround strategy was to install a new top management team, led by one of his longtime advisors. The team immediately coalesced around the important problem of establishing a presence in the world of electronic media. With this goal, the company rushed out a revamped, lower-cost CD-ROM package and launched the Britannica.com Web site, which allows users to call up encyclopedia entries online as well as get a list of links to related Web sites. The team also created a separate digital media division to focus on new product development, such as for wireless Web technology. Managers are looking toward the wireless Web as the best route to a successful future and have teamed up with numerous wireless carriers and licensed Britannica's content to other Web sites.

Building a coalition focused on common goals rather than having managers pushing and pulling in different directions got Britannica off the critical list by helping it cross the bridge to the digital era. Now, managers are in the process of evaluation to see what new decisions need to be made to help the company thrive in the digital world.[63]

to keep the company moving forward. When top managers perceive a problem or want to make a major decision, they need to reach agreement with other managers to support the decision.[64]

As an organization manager, keep these guidelines in mind:

Take risks and move the company ahead by increments when a problem is defined but solutions are uncertain. Try solutions step by step to learn whether they work.

Incremental Decision Process Model

Henry Mintzberg and his associates at McGill University in Montreal, Canada approached organizational decision making from a different perspective. They identified twenty-five decisions made in organizations and traced the events associated with these decisions from beginning to end.[65] Their research identified each step in the decision sequence. This approach to decision making, called the **incremental decision process model**, places less emphasis on the political and social factors described in the Carnegie model, but tells more about the structured sequence of activities undertaken from the discovery of a problem to its solution.[66]

Sample decisions in Mintzberg's research included choosing which jet aircraft to acquire for a regional airline, developing a new supper club, developing a new container terminal in a harbour, identifying a new market for a deodorant, installing a controversial new medical treatment in a hospital and firing a star radio announcer.[67] The scope and importance of these decisions are revealed in the length of time taken to complete them. Most of these decisions took more than a year, and one third of them took more than two years. Most of these decisions were nonprogrammed and required custom-designed solutions.

One discovery from this research is that major organization choices are usually a series of small choices that combine to produce the major decision. Thus, many organizational decisions are a series of nibbles rather than a big bite. Organizations move through several decision points and may hit barriers along the way. Mintzberg called these barriers *decision interrupts*. An interrupt may mean an organization has to cycle back through a previous decision and try something new. Decision loops or cycles are one way the organization learns which alternatives will work. The ultimate solution may be very different from what was initially anticipated.

The pattern of decision stages discovered by Mintzberg and his associates is shown in Exhibit 12.5. Each box indicates a possible step in the decision sequence. The steps take place in three major decision phases: identification, development and selection.

Identification Phase The identification phase begins with *recognition*. Recognition means one or more managers become aware of a problem and the need to make a decision. Recognition is usually stimulated by a problem or an opportunity. A problem exists when elements in the external environment change or when internal performance is perceived to be below standard. In the case of firing a radio announcer, comments about the announcer came from listeners, other announcers and advertisers. Managers interpreted these cues until a pattern emerged that indicated a problem had to be dealt with.

See online
COUNTERPOINT 12.15

The second step is *diagnosis*, in which more information is gathered if needed to define the problem situation. Diagnosis may be systematic or informal, depending upon the severity of the problem. Severe problems do not allow time for extensive diagnosis; the response must be immediate. Mild problems are usually diagnosed in a more systematic manner.

Development Phase In the development phase, a solution is shaped to solve the problem defined in the identification phase. The development of a solution takes one of two directions. First, *search* procedures may be used to seek out alternatives within the organization's repertoire of solutions. For example, in the case of firing a star announcer, managers asked what the radio station had done the last time an announcer had to be let go. To conduct the search, organization participants may look into their own memories, talk to other managers or examine the formal procedures of the organization.

The second direction of development is to *design* a custom solution. This happens when the problem is novel so that previous experience has no value. Mintzberg found that in these cases, key decision makers have only a vague idea of the ideal solution. Gradually, through a trial-and-error process, a custom-designed alternative will emerge. Development of the solution is a groping, incremental procedure, building a solution brick by brick.

Selection Phase The selection phase is when the solution is chosen. This phase is not always a matter of making a clear choice among alternatives. In the case of custom-made solutions, selection is more an evaluation of the single alternative that seems feasible.

Evaluation and choice may be accomplished in three ways. The *judgement* form of selection is used when a final choice falls upon a single decision maker, and the

EXHIBIT 12.5 The Incremental Decision Process Model

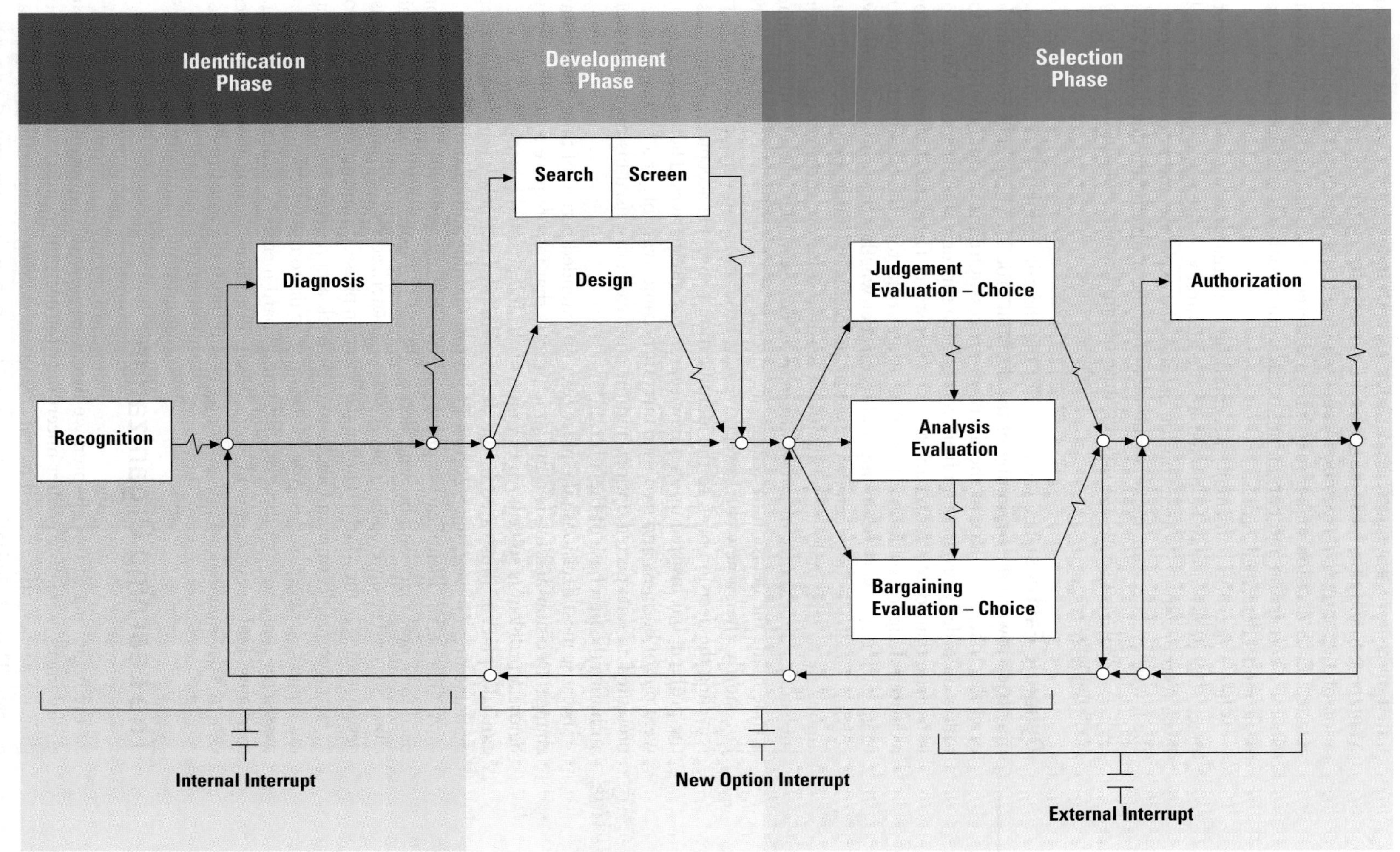

Source: Adapted and reprinted from 'The Structure of Unstructured Decision Processes' by Henry Mintzberg, Duru Raisinghani, and André Théorêt, published in *Administrative Science Quarterly* 21, no. 2 (1976), 266, by permission of The *Administrative Science Quarterly*. Copyright © 1976 Cornell University.

choice involves judgement based upon experience. In analysis, alternatives are evaluated on a more systematic basis, such as with management science techniques. Mintzberg found that most decisions did not involve systematic analysis and evaluation of alternatives. *Bargaining* occurs when selection involves a group of decision makers. Each decision maker may have a different stake in the outcome, so conflict emerges. Discussion and bargaining occur until a coalition is formed, as in the Carnegie model described earlier.

When a decision is formally accepted by the organization, *authorization* takes place. The decision may be passed up the hierarchy to the responsible hierarchical level. Authorization is often routine because the expertise and knowledge rest with the lower-level decision makers who identified the problem and developed the solution. A few decisions are rejected because of implications not anticipated by lower-level managers.

Dynamic Factors The lower part of the chart in Exhibit 12.5 shows lines running back toward the beginning of the decision process. These lines represent loops or cycles that take place in the decision process. Organizational decisions do not follow an orderly progression from recognition through authorization. Minor problems arise that force a loop back to an earlier stage. These are decision interrupts. If a custom-designed solution is perceived as unsatisfactory, the organization may have to go back to the very beginning and reconsider whether the problem is truly worth solving. Feedback loops can be caused by problems of timing, politics, disagreement among managers, inability to identify a feasible solution, turnover of managers or the sudden appearance of a new alternative. For example, when a small Canadian airline made the decision to acquire jet aircraft, the board authorized the decision, but shortly after, a new chief executive was brought in who cancelled the contract, recycling the decision back to the identification phase. He accepted the diagnosis of the problem but insisted upon a new search for alternatives. Then a foreign airline went out of business and two used aircraft became available at a bargain price. This presented an unexpected option, and the chief executive used his own judgement to authorize the purchase of the aircraft.[68]

See online
COUNTERPOINT 12.16

Because most decisions take place over an extended period of time, circumstances change. Decision making is a dynamic process that may require a number of cycles before a problem is solved. An example of the incremental process and cycling that can take place is illustrated in the decision to create a new razor of global razor manufacturer Gillette, since 2005 a Procter & Gamble subsidiary.

At Gillette, the identification phase occurred because executives were aware of the need for a new razor and became alert to the idea of using three blades to produce a closer shave. The development phase was characterized by the trial-and-error custom design leading to the Mach3. During the selection phase, certain approaches were found to be unacceptable, causing Gillette to cycle back and redesign the razor, including using thinner, stronger blades. Advancing once again to the selection phase, the Mach3 passed the judgement of top executives and board members, and manufacturing and marketing budgets were quickly authorized. This decision took more than a decade. Gillette's decision-making process for its new rasors is discussed *In Practice* below.

The Learning Organization

At the beginning of this chapter, we discussed how the rapidly changing business environment is creating greater uncertainty for decision makers. Some organizations that are particularly affected by this trend are shifting to the learning organization concept. These organizations are marked by a tremendous amount of uncertainty at

Gillette Company

The Gillette Company uses incremental decision making to perfect the design of razors such as the Mach3 high-tech family of razors. While searching for a new idea to increase sales in Gillette's mature shaving market, researchers at the company's British research lab came up with a bright idea to create a razor with three blades to produce a closer, smoother, more comfortable shave (recognition and diagnosis). Ten years later, the Mach3 reached the market, after thousands of shaving tests, numerous design modifications and a development and tooling cost of $750 million, roughly the amount a pharmaceutical firm invests in developing a blockbuster drug.

The technical demands of building a razor with three blades that would follow a man's face and also be easy to clean had several blind alleys. Engineers first tried to find established techniques (search, screen), but none fit the bill. Eventually a prototype called Manx was built (design), and in shaving tests it greatly outperformed Gillette's Sensor Excel, the company's best-selling razor at the time. However, Gillette's CEO insisted that the razor had to have a radically new blade edge so the razor could use thinner blades (internal interrupt), so engineers began looking for new technology that could produce a stronger blade (search, screen). Eventually, the new edge, known as DLC for diamond-like carbon coating, would be applied atom by atom with chip-making technology (design).

The next problem was manufacturing (diagnosis), which required an entirely new process to handle the complexity of the triple-bladed razor (design). Although the board gave the go-ahead to develop manufacturing equipment (judgement, authorization), some members became concerned because the new blades, which are three times stronger than stainless steel, would last longer and cause Gillette to sell fewer cartridges (internal interrupt). The board eventually made the decision to continue with the new blades, which have a blue indicator strip that fades to white and signals when it's time for a new cartridge.

The board gave final approval for production of the Mach3 to begin in the fourth quarter of 1997. The new razor was introduced in the summer of 1998 and began smoothly sliding off shelves. Gillette recovered its huge investment in record time. Gillette then started the process of searching for the next shaving breakthrough all over again, using new technology that can examine a razor blade at the atomic level and high-speed video that can capture the act of cutting a single whisker. The company has again moved ahead in increments and rolled out its five-bladed Fusion in 2006. Fusion became Procter & Gamble's fastest growing brand ever, while Mach3 in its various permutations, as well as the earlier Sensor, continue to sell well to loyal consumers.[69,70]

both the problem identification and problem solution stages. Two approaches to decision making have evolved to help managers cope with this uncertainty and complexity. One approach is to combine the Carnegie and incremental process models just described. The second is a unique approach called the garbage can model.

Combining the Incremental Process and Carnegie Models

The Carnegie description of coalition building is especially relevant for the problem identification stage. When issues are ambiguous, or if managers disagree about problem severity, discussion, negotiation and coalition building are needed. Once agreement is reached about the problem to be tackled, the organization can move toward a solution.

The incremental process model tends to emphasize the steps used to reach a solution. After managers agree on a problem, the step-by-step process is a way of trying various solutions to see what will work. When problem solution is unclear, a trial-and-error solution may be designed. For example, in 1999, executives from three of the world's largest music companies formed a coalition to provide online

As an organization manager, keep these guidelines in mind:

Apply both the Carnegie model and the incremental process model in a situation with high uncertainty about both problems and solutions. Decision making may also employ garbage can procedures. Move the organization toward better performance by proposing new ideas, spending time working in important areas and persisting with potential solutions.

consumers with a legal alternative to the digital piracy of internet song-swapping services. However, making the joint venture MusicNet an appealing choice was a challenge. As originally conceived, the service didn't provide music lovers with the features they wanted, so managers took an incremental approach to try to make MusicNet more user-friendly. After a brief period of success, MusicNet, now part of MediaNet Digital, fell back in the face of increased competition. The music industry is still casting about for effective responses to illegal file-sharing. For several years music companies tried a combination of negotiating legal file-sharing contracts with various providers including Apple's iTunes, and legal action against people illegally sharing their files through 'torrent' software. In late 2008 the biggest industry association, the Recording Industry Association of America, decided to discontinue the lawsuit strategy, which had created some bad publicity for the industry without significantly affecting the illegal file-sharing problem. Instead, the US and European music industry has focused on internet service providers (ISPs). ISPs also don't like illegal file-sharing as it uses up a huge amount of internet bandwidth. Instead of launching lawsuits, the music industry will identify abusers and contact their ISP, who can issue warnings and even cut abusers' internet service altogether.[71] As one executive put it, 'This is a business of trial and error'.[72]

The two models do not disagree with one another. They describe how organizations make decisions when either problem identification or solution is uncertain. The application of these two models to the stages in the decision process is illustrated in Exhibit 12.6. When both parts of the decision process are simultaneously highly uncertain, which is often the case in learning organizations, the organization is in an extremely difficult position. Decision processes in that situation may be a combination of Carnegie and incremental process models, and this combination may evolve into a situation described in the garbage can model.

Garbage Can Model

The **garbage can model** is not directly comparable to the earlier models because the garbage can model deals with the pattern or flow of multiple decisions within organizations, whereas the incremental and Carnegie models focus on how a single decision is made. The garbage can model helps you think of the whole organization and the frequent decisions being made by managers throughout.

Organized Anarchy The garbage can model was developed to explain the pattern of decision making in organizations that experience extremely high uncertainty, such as the growth and change required in a learning organization. Michael Cohen, James March and Johan Olsen, the originators of the model, called the highly uncertain

EXHIBIT 12.6 Decision Process When Problem Identification and Problem Solution Are Uncertain

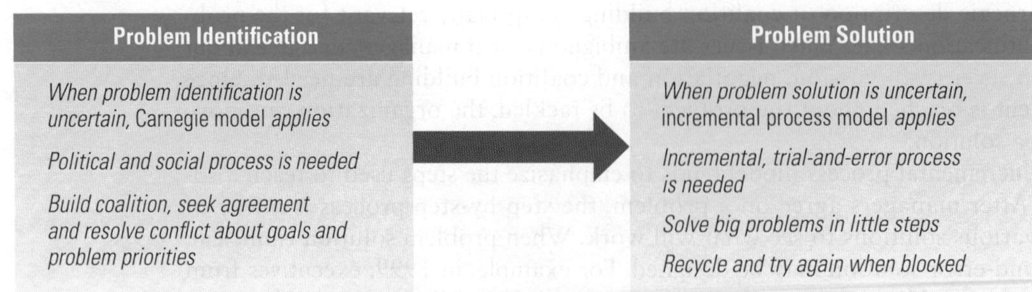

conditions an **organized anarchy**, which is an extremely organic organization.[73] Organized anarchies do not rely on the normal vertical hierarchy of authority and bureaucratic decision rules. They result from three characteristics:

1 *Problematic preferences*. Goals, problems, alternatives and solutions are ill-defined. Ambiguity characterizes each step of a decision process.
2 *Unclear, poorly understood technology.* Cause-and-effect relationships within the organization are difficult to identify. An explicit database that applies to decisions is not available.
3 *Turnover*. Organizational positions experience turnover of participants. In addition, employees are busy and have only limited time to allocate to any one problem or decision. Participation in any given decision will be fluid and limited.

An organized anarchy is characterized by rapid change and a collegial, nonbureaucratic environment. No organization fits this extremely organic circumstance all the time, although learning organizations and today's internet-based companies may experience it much of the time. Many organizations will occasionally find themselves in positions of making decisions under unclear, problematic circumstances. The garbage can model is useful for understanding the pattern of these decisions.

Streams of Events The unique characteristic of the garbage can model is that the decision process is not seen as a sequence of steps that begins with a problem and ends with a solution. Indeed, problem identification and problem solution may not be connected to each other. An idea may be proposed as a solution when no problem is specified. A problem may exist and never generate a solution. Decisions are the outcome of independent streams of events within the organization. The four streams relevant to organizational decision making are as follows:

1 *Problems*. Problems are points of dissatisfaction with current activities and performance. They represent a gap between desired performance and current activities. Problems are perceived to require attention. However, they are distinct from solutions and choices. A problem may lead to a proposed solution or it may not. Problems may not be solved when solutions are adopted.
2 *Potential solutions*. A solution is an idea somebody proposes for adoption. Such ideas form a flow of alternative solutions through the organization. Ideas may be brought into the organization by new personnel or may be invented by existing personnel. Participants may simply be attracted to certain ideas and push them as logical choices regardless of problems. Attraction to an idea may cause an employee to look for a problem to which the idea can be attached and, hence, justified. The point is that solutions exist independent of problems.
3 *Participants*. Organization participants are employees who come and go throughout the organization. People are hired, reassigned and fired. Participants vary widely in their ideas, perception of problems, experience, values and training. The problems and solutions recognized by one manager will differ from those recognized by another manager.
4 *Choice opportunities*. Choice opportunities are occasions when an organization usually makes a decision. They occur when contracts are signed, people are hired or a new product is authorized. They also occur when the right mix of participants, solutions and problems exists. Thus, a manager who happened to learn of a good idea may suddenly become aware of a problem to which it applies and, hence, can provide the organization with a choice opportunity. Match-ups of problems and solutions often result in decisions.

With the concept of four streams, the overall pattern of organizational decision making takes on a random quality. Problems, solutions, participants and choices all flow through the organization. In one sense, the organization is a large garbage can in which these streams are being stirred, as illustrated in Exhibit 12.7. When a problem, solution and participant happen to connect at one point, a decision may be made and the problem may be solved; but if the solution does not fit the problem, the problem may not be solved.

Thus, when viewing the organization as a whole and considering its high level of uncertainty, one sees problems arise that are not solved and solutions tried that do not work. Organization decisions are disorderly and not the result of a logical, step-by-step sequence. Events may be so ill-defined and complex that decisions, problems and solutions act as independent events. When they connect, some problems are solved, but many are not.[74]

COUNTERPOINT 12.6

The garbage can model illuminates the messy, disorderly quality of much complex decision-making. What it does not do is account for the role of power broking in the process of proposing solutions, making choices and even ensuring that decisions are not made or indefinitely deferred. In other words, in common with other decision-making approaches discussed in this chapter, including the Carnegie school, it does not shed much light on how power operates to define what and how problems are identified or ignored, and what possible solutions are considered or excluded. **Discuss**

EXHIBIT 12.7 Illustration of Independent Streams of Events in the Garbage Can Model of Decision Making

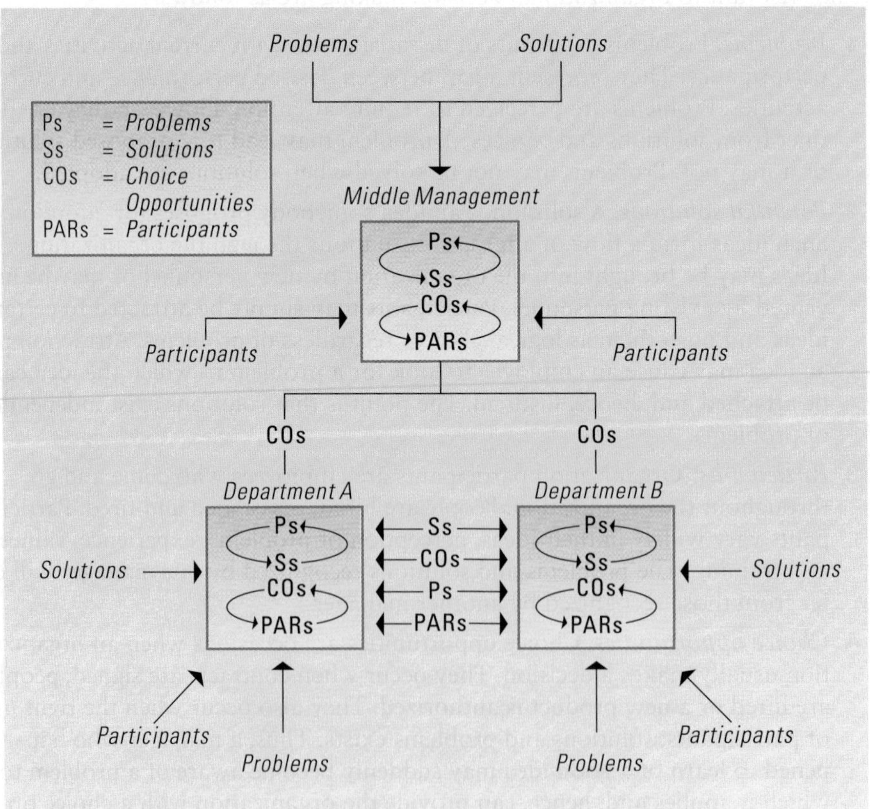

Consequences There are four specific consequences of the garbage can decision process for organizational decision making:

1 *Solutions may be proposed even when problems do not exist.* An employee might be sold on an idea and might try to sell it to the rest of the organization. An example was the adoption of computers by many organizations during the 1970s. The computer was an exciting solution and was pushed by both computer manufacturers and systems analysts within organizations. The computer did not solve any problems in those initial applications. Indeed, some computers caused more problems than they solved.

2 *Choices are made without solving problems.* A choice such as creating a new department may be made with the intention of solving a problem; but, under conditions of high uncertainty, the choice may be incorrect. Moreover, many choices just seem to happen. People decide to quit, the organization's budget is cut, or a new policy bulletin is issued. These choices may be oriented toward problems but do not necessarily solve them.

3 *Problems may persist without being solved.* Organization participants get used to certain problems and give up trying to solve them; or participants may not know how to solve certain problems because the technology is unclear. A university in Canada was placed on probation by the American Association of University Professors because a professor had been denied tenure without due process. The probation was a nagging annoyance that the administrators wanted to remove. Fifteen years later, the nontenured professor died. The probation continues because the university did not acquiesce to the demands of the heirs of the association to reevaluate the case. The university would like to solve the problem, but administrators are not sure how, and they do not have the resources to allocate to it. The probation problem persists without a solution.

4. *A few problems are solved.* The decision process does work in the aggregate. In computer simulation models of the garbage can model, important problems were often resolved. Solutions do connect with appropriate problems and participants so that a good choice is made. Of course, not all problems are resolved when choices are made, but the organization does move in the direction of problem reduction.

The effects of independent streams and the rather chaotic decision processes of the garbage can model can be seen in many organizational processes, including the ways United Nations peacekeeping missions are agreed upon and organized, discussed in the *In Practice* box.

In the exceptionally complex environment of global governance, a garbage-can decision making model is probably inevitable. However the fact that it has worked passably well for international peacekeeping in recent years is no guarantee it will succeed in the future. Success is dependent on a combination of a fluid decision-making environment, openness to policy alternatives, and effective policy 'champions' or entrepreneurs. As the international environment shifts and the United Nations changes over time, the decision-making arena may be less open to experimentation, or worse, policy entrepreneurs may pull less positive options out of the 'primeval policy soup', as was the case with American neoconservatives' attempts to enforce democratic transitions in the Middle East through US military power.[75]

United Nations Peacekeeping

The United Nations organization was created in the aftermath of the Second World War as a means to ensure international cooperation, thus avoiding the bloody military disasters of the two great wars of the twentieth century. The UN has many different functions and agencies, dealing with issues as diverse as child poverty, economic development, democratic governance and the environment. However the UN is perhaps most famous for its 'blue helmet' peacekeeping operations in various troubled parts of the world. During the Cold War, peacekeeping missions were relatively infrequent, small scale, emphasized neutrality between the conflicting parties, and primarily involved monitoring of the situation. Between 1947 and 1988 only 13 missions were undertaken.

As the Cold War ended, the UN became much more active, and much more proactive, stretching traditional peacekeeping principles of consent, neutrality and limited use of force. In only seven years after 1988, 27 missions were organized, more than double the total in the previous thirty years. Furthermore, the new, 'second generation' missions tended to get directly involved in the *enforcement* of peace agreements. The UN started to take an active role in building state institutions after conflict.

Although the change in the UN's role has been generally welcomed as preferable to the Cold War era when human suffering through conflict often went unaddressed because of the stand-off between the US and USSR, until recently there has been little analysis of how this change actually came about. Michael Lipson, a Montreal academic, analyzed the processes underlying the shift to second generation peacekeeping and found that the 'garbage can model' provided a good explanation.

As discussed above, the garbage can model applies in situations of 'organized anarchy'. The UN, with its 190-plus members states and complex decision-making processes, is a classic organized anarchy. During the Cold War this anarchy was tempered, because many states owed allegiance to one or other of the superpowers, meaning that the balance of forces in decision-making was fairly consistent.[76] As the Soviet bloc disintegrated, this certainty of voting patterns disappeared. Although the Americans expected to assume a dominant role, this didn't happen, as states realized they no longer needed the protective umbrella of a superpower, and made their choices more independently. The UN organization itself is not a unitary actor, with its various commissions, agencies and authorities each having their own missions, mandates and particular interests. The UN as a whole, therefore, encounters *problematic preferences*.

The UN also has to deal with *unclear technology* (remember that technology in organization science refers to the way decisions are made). Although in theory an organizational chart could be drawn, in practice decisions are made through ever-changing processes and alliances. Even Boutros Boutros-Ghali, former head of the UN, admitted that he did not really understand the intricate workings of the organization. Finally, the UN in recent years has had very *fluid participation*. The number of state-members of the UN increased significantly as countries like the former USSR, Yugoslavia and others broke up into smaller units, each with a UN seat. Within the UN administration, waves of internal restructuring have continually changed the bureaucratic dynamics, so that a clear hierarchical decision-making process is absent.

When deciding what to do about conflicts in various parts of the world, the 'organized anarchy' of the UN has been faced with *ambiguity* on several levels, in which 'alternative interpretations or perspectives on the situation are available, and the basis for choosing among them is unclear'. UN decision-makers were unsure about, 'the nature and causes of interstate, ethnic and civil conflicts, the nature of post – Cold War order, the role of the United Nations, and the implications for peacekeeping'.[77] Although the number of conflicts globally has not increased since the end of the Cold War, the expectation that the UN will deal effectively with them has increased greatly.

In the absence of a rational method for deciding *how* to act effectively, UN policy makers dipped into what one analyst calls the 'policy primeval soup'.[78] This soup is made up of all the different peacekeeping options that have been tried, or even proposed and discarded, in the past of international organizations. For example, in planning for the first 'second generation' peacekeeping effort in post-apartheid Namibia at the end of the 1980s, officials looked back as far as the United Nations' predecessor, the League of Nations, which had been given a mandate to govern the disputed Saar region between France and Germany after the First World War. They also explored ambitious earlier UN peacekeeping missions such as in Congo in the 1960s.

Whereas most of these efforts had been classified as failures, post-Cold War optimism about the possibilities for peace and democratic transformation meant that a mutation and recombination of ideas from the 'policy soup' could be tried by the UN's Transition Assistance Group (UNTAG) for Namibia. The successful outcome of the Namibia transition was an impetus for further peacekeeping interventions that included activities like overseeing disarmament, demobilization, and reintegration (DD&R), humanitarian relief and working to develop the political foundations for new state institutions like governments and parliaments. In the late 1980s and early 1990s, these new peacekeeping approaches were tried in various countries including Cambodia, Nicaragua, Haiti, El Salvador and Angola.

Not all the 'second-generation' peacekeeping initiatives tried by the UN have been successful; the continuing failure to establish a stable government in Somalia is a case in point. However, on the whole, a more active and intense involvement of the UN in not only monitoring peace agreements but also through helping in rehabilitation and building stable post-conflict institutions, has reduce the dangers of violence reigniting, and has improved the lives of people affected by conflict.

Contingency Decision-Making Framework

This chapter has covered several approaches to organizational decision making, including management science, the Carnegie model, the incremental decision process model and the garbage can model. It has also discussed rational and intuitive decision processes used by individual managers. Each decision approach is a relatively accurate description of the actual decision process, yet all differ from each other. Management science, for example, reflects a different set of decision assumptions and procedures than does the garbage can model.

One reason for having different approaches is that they appear in different organizational situations. The use of an approach is contingent on the organization setting. Two characteristics of organizations that determine the use of decision approaches are (1) problem consensus and (2) technical knowledge about the means to solve those problems.[79] Analyzing organizations along these two dimensions suggests which approach will be used to make decisions.

See online
COUNTERPOINT 12.17

Problem Consensus

Problem consensus refers to the agreement among managers about the nature of a problem or opportunity and about which goals and outcomes to pursue. This variable ranges from complete agreement to complete disagreement. When managers agree, there is little uncertainty – the problems and goals of the organization are clear, and so are standards of performance. When managers disagree, organization direction and performance expectations are in dispute, creating a situation of high uncertainty. Problem uncertainty frequently occurs over competing visions for the use of scarce natural resources. For example, several different interests conflicted over use of a mountainous area in Switzerland. Recreational users wanted access to skiing and hiking opportunities, which would generate tourism revenues. The area was also the site of an important international highway, and there was pressure from road planners and users to expand the road. Finally, environmentalists felt that this fragile area with unique biodiversity needed to be left alone to protect its habitat. Advocates for all three positions could be found within the local government.[80]

Problem consensus tends to be low when organizations are differentiated, as described in Chapter 4. This would apply where different departments within the same government have different missions, as in the Swiss case above. Recall that uncertain environments cause organizational departments to differentiate from one another in goals and attitudes to specialize in specific sectors. This differentiation leads to disagreement and conflict, so managers must make a special effort to build coalitions during decision making. For example, the American space agency NASA has been criticized for failing to identify problems with the *Columbia* space shuttle that might have prevented the February 2003 disaster. Part of the reason was high differentiation and conflicting opinions between safety managers and scheduling managers, in which pressure to launch on time overrode safety concerns. In addition, after the launch, engineers three times requested – and were denied – better photos to assess the damage from a piece of foam debris that struck the shuttle's left wing just seconds after launch. Investigations now indicate that the damage caused by the debris may have been the primary physical cause of the explosion. Mechanisms for hearing dissenting opinions and building coalitions can improve decision making at NASA and other organizations dealing with complex problems.[81]

Problem consensus is especially important for the problem identification stage of decision making. When problems are clear and agreed on, they provide clear standards and expectations for performance. When problems are not agreed on, problem identification is uncertain and management attention must be focused on gaining agreement about goals and priorities.

Technical Knowledge about Solutions

Technical knowledge refers to understanding and agreement about how to solve problems and reach organizational goals. This variable can range from complete agreement and certainty to complete disagreement and uncertainty about cause–effect relationships leading to problem solution. For example, international organization managers disagree with each other about how to achieve some of the Millennium Development Goals, as discussed in Chapter 2. On the universal education goals, World Bank and International Monetary Fund managers argue that the problem is that teachers are too costly, and they have put pressure on developing country governments to introduce low-priced contract teachers. Experts at UN gencies like the United Nations Childrens Fund (UNICEF) and UNESCO believe that this will be counterproductive in producing more education but of a lower standard, and that holistic approaches employing community empowerment and lifelong learning strategies will have a better long-term result.[82] The disagreement about causes and solutions has led to conflicting policy implementation in developing countries.

When means are well understood, the appropriate alternatives can be identified and calculated with some degree of certainty. When means are poorly understood, potential solutions are ill-defined and uncertain. Intuition, judgement and trial and error become the basis for decisions.

Contingency Framework

Exhibit 12.8 describes the **contingency decision-making framework**, which brings together the two dimensions of problem consensus and technical knowledge about solutions. Each cell represents an organizational situation that is appropriate for the decision-making approaches described in this chapter.

Cell 1 In cell 1 of Exhibit 12.8, rational decision procedures are used because problems are agreed on and cause–effect relationships are well understood, so there is little uncertainty. Decisions can be made in a computational manner. Alternatives

EXHIBIT 12.8 Contingency Framework for Using Decision Models

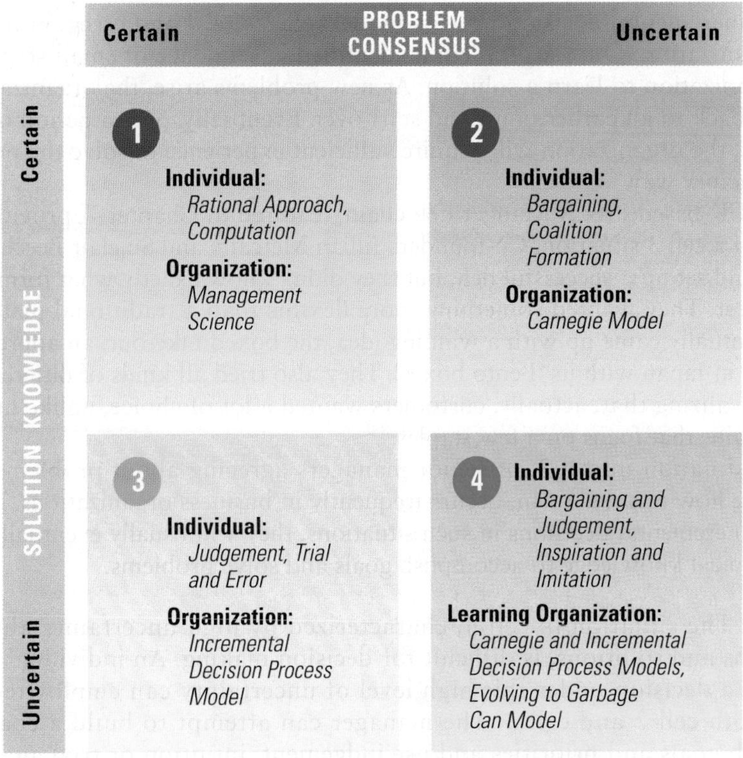

can be identified and the best solution adopted through analysis and calculations. The rational models described earlier in this chapter, both for individuals and for the organization, are appropriate when problems and the means for solving them are well defined.

Cell 2 In cell 2, there is high uncertainty about problems and priorities, so bargaining and compromise are used to reach consensus. Tackling one problem might mean the organization must postpone action on other issues. The priorities given to respective problems are decided through discussion, debate and coalition building.

Managers in this situation should use broad participation to achieve consensus in the decision process. Opinions should be surfaced and discussed until compromise is reached. The organization will not otherwise move forward as an integrated unit. In the Swiss mountain region case, a strategy was developed so that the interests of the different users of the area could be reconciled.

The Carnegie model applies when there is dissension about organizational problems. When groups within the organization disagree, or when the organization is in conflict with constituencies (government regulators, suppliers, unions), bargaining and negotiation are required. The bargaining strategy is especially relevant to the problem identification stage of the decision process. Once bargaining and negotiation are completed, the organization will have support for one direction.

Cell 3 In a cell 3 situation, problems and standards of performance are certain, but alternative technical solutions are vague and uncertain. Techniques to solve a problem are ill defined and poorly understood. When an individual manager faces this situation, intuition will be the decision guideline. The manager will rely on past experience and judgement to make a decision. Rational, analytical approaches are not effective because the alternatives cannot be identified and calculated. Hard facts and accurate information are not available.

The incremental decision process model reflects trial and error on the part of the organization. Once a problem is identified, a sequence of small steps enables the organization to learn a solution. As new problems arise, the organization may recycle back to an earlier point and start over. Eventually, over a period of months or years, the organization will acquire sufficient experience to solve the problem in a satisfactory way.

The UK-based Pret A Manger deli chain, featured in Chapter 7, provides an example of a cell 3 situation, Co-founders Julian Metcalfe and Sinclair Beecham knew they could set up a successful deli, but they didn't know exactly what format would work best. They wanted something more flexible than a traditional plate service, and eventually came up with a winning idea, the boxed take-out; an approach long popular in Japan with its 'Bento boxes'. They also tried all kinds of different fillings before realizing that, actually, customers wanted a lot of choice, unlike many fast-food chains that focus on a few staples.[83]

The situation in cell 3, of senior managers agreeing about problems but not knowing how to solve them, occurs frequently in business organizations. If managers use incremental decisions in such situations, they will usually eventually acquire the technical knowledge to accomplish goals and solve problems.

Cell 4 The situation in cell 4, characterized by high uncertainty about both problems and solutions, is difficult for decision making. An individual manager making a decision under this high level of uncertainty can employ techniques from both cell 2 and cell 3. The manager can attempt to build a coalition to establish goals and priorities and use judgement, intuition or trial and error to solve problems. Additional techniques, such as inspiration and imitation, also may be required. **Inspiration** refers to an innovative, creative solution that is not reached by logical means. Inspiration sometimes comes like a flash of insight, but – similar to intuition – it is often based on deep knowledge and understanding of a problem that the unconscious mind has had time to mull over.[84] **Imitation** means adopting a decision tried elsewhere in the hope that it will work in this situation.

For example, in one university, accounting department faculty members were unhappy with their current circumstances but could not decide on the direction the department should take. Some faculty members wanted a greater research orientation, whereas others wanted greater orientation toward business firms and accounting applications. The disagreement about goals was compounded because neither group was sure about the best technique for achieving its goals. The ultimate solution was inspirational on the part of the dean. An accounting research centre was established with funding from major accounting firms. The funding was used to finance research activities for faculty interested in basic research and to provide contact with business firms for other faculty. The solution provided a common goal and unified people within the department to work toward that goal.

When an entire organization is characterized by high uncertainty regarding both problems and solutions, as in learning organizations, elements of the garbage can model will appear. Managers may first try techniques from both cells 2 and 3, but logical decision sequences starting with problem identification and ending with problem solution will not occur. Potential solutions will precede problems as often as problems precede solutions. In this situation, managers should encourage widespread discussion of problems and idea proposals to facilitate the opportunity to make choices. Eventually, through trial and error, the organization will solve some problems.

Research has found that decisions made following the prescriptions of the contingency decision-making framework tend to be more successful. However, the study noted that nearly six of ten strategic management decisions failed to follow the framework, leading to a situation in which misleading or missing information decreased the chance of an effective decision choice.[85] Managers can use the contingency framework in Exhibit 12.8 to improve the likelihood of successful organizational decisions.

See online
COUNTERPOINT 12.18

Different Types of Decision-Making Approaches

The approaches discussed in this chapter relate to different types and levels of decision-making. Some approaches are geared to the *individual* manager and others apply to an *organization* as a whole. Some approaches are *prescriptive*; in other words an approach is described that a manager could learn – or an organization could adopt – and apply in suitable circumstances. Other decision-making models that have been discussed are *descriptive*: they are not models that a company could adopt, but simply describe how decisions are made in certain circumstances. To give a couple of examples, a rational decision-making model applies to an *individual* and is *prescriptive*; it is a model a manager can choose to follow. On the other hand, the garbage can model applies to an *organization*, and is *descriptive*; organizations do not choose to apply a garbage can model, it just happens, as discussed in the example of United Nations peacemaking operations. Exhibit 12.9 categorizes the different models we have discussed in this chapter according to the individual/organization and prescriptive/descriptive criteria.

Special Decision Circumstances

In a highly competitive world beset by global competition and rapid change, decision making seldom fits the traditional rational, analytical model. Today's managers have to make high-stakes decisions more often and more quickly than ever before

EXHIBIT 12.9 Summary of decision-making models

Approach	Individual or Organizational	Prescriptive or descriptive
Rational	Individual	Prescriptive
Bounded rationality	Individual	Descriptive
Management Science	Organizational	Prescriptive
Carnegie	Mainly organizational	Descriptive
Incremental	Organizational	Descriptive
Combining Carnegie and incremental	Organizational	Descriptive
Garbage can	Organizational	Descriptive
Contingency	Individual	Prescriptive

Figure courtesy of Dirk Akkermans, Assistant Professor, Department of International Economics and Business, Faculty of Economics and Business, University of Groningen, the Netherlands.

in an environment that is increasingly less predictable. For example, interviews with CEOs in high-tech industries found that they strive to use some type of rational process, but the uncertainty and change in the industry often make that approach unsuccessful. The way these managers actually reach decisions is through a complex interaction with other managers, subordinates, environmental factors, and organizational events.[86]

Three issues of particular concern for today's decision makers are coping with high-velocity environments, learning from decision mistakes and avoiding escalating commitment.

High-Velocity Environments

As an organization manager, keep this guideline in mind:

Track real-time information, build multiple alternatives simultaneously, and try to involve everyone – but move ahead anyway when making decisions in a high-velocity environment.

In some industries today, the rate of competitive and technological change is so extreme that market data are either unavailable or obsolete, strategic windows open and shut quickly, perhaps within a few months and the cost of poor decisions is company failure. Research has examined how successful companies make decisions in these **high-velocity environments**, especially to understand whether organizations abandon rational approaches or have time for incremental implementation.[87]

A comparison of successful with unsuccessful decisions in high-velocity environments found the following patterns:

- Successful decision makers tracked information in real time to develop a deep and intuitive grasp of the business. Two to three intense meetings per week with all key players were usual. Decision makers tracked operating statistics about cash, scrap, backlog, work in process and shipments to constantly feel the pulse of what was happening. Unsuccessful firms were more concerned with future planning and forward-looking information, with only a loose grip on immediate happenings.
- During a major decision, successful companies began immediately to build multiple alternatives. Implementation of alternatives sometimes ran in parallel before they finally settled on a final choice. Companies that made decisions slowly developed just one alternative, moving to another only after the first one failed.
- Fast, successful decision makers sought advice from everyone and depended heavily on one or two savvy, trusted colleagues as counsellors. Slow companies were unable to build trust and agreement among the best people.
- Fast companies involved everyone in the decision and tried for consensus; but if consensus did not emerge, the top manager made the choice and moved ahead. Waiting for everyone to be on board created more delays than was warranted. Slow companies delayed decisions to achieve a uniform consensus.
- Fast, successful choices were well integrated with other decisions and the overall strategic direction of the company. Less successful choices considered the decision in isolation from other decisions; the decision was made in the abstract.[88]

See online COUNTERPOINT 12.19

When speed matters, a slow decision is as ineffective as the wrong decision. As we discussed in Chapter 11, speed is a crucial competitive weapon in a growing number of industries, and companies can learn to make decisions quickly. To improve the chances of a good decision under high-velocity conditions, some organizations stimulate constructive conflict through a technique called **point–counterpoint**, which divides decision makers into two groups and assigns them different, often competing responsibilities.[89] The groups develop and exchange proposals and debate options until they arrive at a common set of understandings and recommendations.

Groups can often make better decisions because multiple and diverse opinions are considered. In the face of complexity and uncertainty, the more people who have a say in the decision making, the better. At the leading computer chip maker Intel Corp., the decision-making process typically involves people from several different areas and levels of hierarchy, 'jousting with one another about the pros and cons of this or that', says board chairman Craig Barrett.[90]

In group decision making, a consensus may not always be reached, but the exercise gives everyone a chance to consider options and state their opinions, and it gives top managers a broader understanding. Typically, those involved support the final choice. However, if a very speedy decision is required, top managers are willing to make the decision and move forward. Once a decision has been made at Intel, for example, it is everyone's responsibility to be involved and commit, even if they disagree. As Barrett says, 'No backbiting, no second-guessing. We make a decision, we charge ahead.'[91]

Decision Mistakes and Learning

Organizational decisions result in many errors, especially when made in conditions of great uncertainty. Managers simply cannot accurately determine or predict which alternative will solve a problem. In these cases, the organization must make the decision – and take the risk – often in the spirit of trial and error. If an alternative fails, the organization can learn from it and try another alternative that better fits the situation. Each failure provides new information and insight. The point for managers is to move ahead with the decision process despite the potential for mistakes. 'Chaotic action is preferable to orderly inaction'.[92]

In some organizations, managers are encouraged to instil a climate of experimentation to facilitate creative decision making. If one idea fails, another idea should be tried. Failure often lays the groundwork for success, such as when technicians at 3M developed Post-it Notes based on a failed product – a not-very-sticky glue.

Stanley Kalms (properly speaking, Lord Kalms of Edgware), whose DSGi group is the largest electronics retailer in Europe, freely acknowledges that many of his efforts have fallen flat. Since his dad started out with a single small photography shop in Southend, UK, the evolving family-led company has constantly tried new business angles. Many of his initiatives worked, but others haven't. Kalms was the first retailer to focus heavily on marketing products from the burgeoning Asian electronics industry back in the 1970s, when sturdy but costly German brands like Leica and Grundig still ruled European markets. Freeserve, his early entry in the internet service provider (ISP), also paid off handsomely when he sold out to French giant Wanadoo in 2000 for £1.65 billion. But the 1987 purchase of Silo, one of the early US 'big box' retailers was a failure, and he bailed out in 1993 shortly before the US chain went under.[93] The acquisition of the UK's biggest electronics chain, Curry's, in 1984, has been a success, but the shift to online purchasing in the early 2000s forced DSGi to cut back on its retail presence and try to quickly build online success against internet specialists like Amazon. The Europe-wide recession that began in 2008 is sure to hit DSGi hard, but Kalms, even at 76 years of age, is ready to work with DSGi managers to come up with innovative ways to stay out of trouble, and if possible, find ways to benefit from the downturn, all the while staying true to his motto: 'Bend the rules, gentlemen; rules are for bending. There are only two rules that should never be bent: say what you mean, mean what you say; and don't steal'.[94]

Only by making mistakes can managers and organizations go through the process of decision learning and acquire sufficient experience and knowledge to perform more effectively in the future. Sinclair Beecham of Pret a Manger says, 'It's

BRIEFCASE

As an organization manager, keep these guidelines in mind:

Do not persist in a course of action that is failing. Some actions will not work if uncertainty is high, so encourage organizational learning by readily trying new alternatives. Seek information and evidence that indicates when a course of action is failing, and allocate resources to new choices rather than to unsuccessful ventures.

important not to kill ideas in the making. We've made zillions of mistakes, yet making and recognizing mistakes is the way we've gone forward.'

Escalating Commitment

A much more dangerous mistake is to persist in a course of action when it is failing, a tendency referred to as **escalating commitment**. Research suggests that organizations often continue to invest time and money in a solution despite strong evidence that it is not working. Two explanations are given for why managers escalate commitment to a failing decision. The first is that managers block or distort negative information when they are personally responsible for a negative decision. They simply don't know when to pull the plug. In some cases, they continue to throw good money after bad even when a strategy seems incorrect and goals are not being met.[95]

A second explanation for escalating commitment to a failing decision is that consistency and persistence are valued in contemporary society. Consistent managers are considered better leaders than those who switch around from one course of action to another. Even though organizations learn through trial and error, organizational norms value consistency. These norms may result in a course of action being maintained, resources being squandered and learning being inhibited. Escalating commitment is a common issue where a company has already sunk a lot of money, and particularly managers' passion, into a business idea. Guy Laliberté, founder of Québec, Canada's world famous Cirque du Soleil circus, had longed dreamed of having an iconic headquarters building in the circus's home town of Montreal.[96] In conjunction with the provincial lottery agency, Loto Quebec, Laliberté drew up plans for a huge Cirque-themed casino and hotel, which would be the centrepiece of a redevelopment of the city's rundown waterfront area. However, the proposal drew strong criticism from anti-poverty groups, whose objections included fears the casino would worsen gambling problems among the poor. Cirque du Soleil had no financial downside on the project, but the bad publicity was one of the first big threats to the company's positive reputation. Despite strong backing from Montreal's business community, after a couple of years of wrangling, Laliberté decided to pull out. It was a big blow to the company's development strategy and to Laliberté's ego; he had even restructured Cirque and hired a top private sector manager to execute the company's shift beyond a circus into operator of entertainment complexes. But ultimately, Laliberté had identified a dangerous escalating commitment to a losing project, and pulled the plug in time.

Failure to admit a mistake and adopt a new course of action is far worse than an attitude that tolerates mistakes to encourage learning. The next time Cirque du Soleil had a chance to develop an entertainment complex, this time in Miami, they quickly identified the same type of barriers that they had seen in Montreal, and decided to end their involvement much earlier in the process.

Based on what has been said about decision making in this chapter, one can expect companies to be ultimately successful in their decision making by adopting a learning approach toward solutions. They will make mistakes along the way, but they will resolve uncertainty through the trial-and-error process.

Summary and Interpretation

The most important idea in this chapter is that most organizational decisions are not made in a logical, rational manner. Most decisions do not begin with the careful analysis of a problem, followed by systematic analysis of alternatives, and finally implementation of a solution. On the contrary, decision processes are characterized by conflict, coalition building, trial and error, speed and mistakes. Managers operate under many constraints that limit rationality; hence, intuition and hunch often are the criteria for choice.

Another important idea is that individuals make decisions, but organizational decisions are not made by a single individual. Organizational decision making is a social process. Only in rare circumstances do managers analyze problems and find solutions by themselves. Many problems are not clear, so widespread discussion and coalition building take place. Once goals and priorities are set, alternatives to achieve those goals can be tried. When a manager does make an individual decision, it is often a small part of a larger decision process. Organizations solve big problems through a series of small steps. A single manager may initiate one step but should be aware of the larger decision process to which it belongs.

The greatest amount of conflict and coalition building occurs when problems are not agreed on. Priorities must be established to indicate which goals are important and what problems should be solved first. If a manager attacks a problem other people do not agree with, the manager will lose support for the solution to be implemented. Thus, time and activity should be spent building a coalition in the problem identification stage of decision making. Then the organization can move toward solutions. Under conditions of low technical knowledge, the solution unfolds as a series of incremental trials that will gradually lead to an overall solution.

The most novel description of decision making is the garbage can model. This model describes how decision processes can seem almost random in highly organic organizations such as learning organizations. Decisions, problems, ideas and people flow through organizations and mix together in various combinations. Through this process, the organization gradually learns. Some problems may never be solved, but many are, and the organization will move toward maintaining and improving its level of performance.

Finally, many organizations must make decisions with speed, which means staying in immediate touch with operations and the environment. Moreover, in an uncertain world, organizations will make mistakes, and mistakes made through trial and error should be encouraged. Encouraging trial-and-error increments facilitates organizational learning. On the other hand, an unwillingness to change from a failing course of action can have serious negative consequences for an organization. Norms for consistency and the desire to prove one's decision correct can lead to continued investment in a useless course of action.

KEY CONCEPTS

bounded rationality perspective
Carnegie model
coalition
contingency decision-making framework
decision learning
escalating commitment
garbage can model
high-velocity environments
imitation
incremental decision process model
inspiration
intuitive decision making
management science approach
nonprogrammed decisions
organizational decision making
organized anarchy
point–counterpoint
problem consensus
problem identification
problem solution
problemistic search
programmed decisions
rational approach
satisficing
technical knowledge

Discussion Questions

1 When you are faced with choosing between several valid options, how do you typically make your decision? How do you think managers typically choose between several options? What are the similarities between your decision process and what you think managers do?

2 A professional economist once told his class, 'An individual decision maker should process all relevant information and select the economically rational alternative'. Do you agree? Why or why not?

3 Do you think intuition is a valid way to make important business decisions? Why or why not? Can you think of a time when you used intuition to make a decision?

4 The Carnegie model emphasizes the need for a political coalition in the decision-making process. When and why are coalitions necessary?

5 What are the three major phases in Mintzberg's incremental decision process model? Why might an organization recycle through one or more phases of the model?

6 An organization theorist once told her class, 'Organizations never make big decisions. They make small decisions that eventually add up to a big decision.' Explain the logic behind this statement.

7 How would you make a decision to select a building site for a new waste-treatment plant in the Philippines? Where would you start with this complex decision, and what steps would you take? Explain which decision model in the chapter best describes your approach.

8 Why would managers in high-velocity environments worry more about the present than the future? Discuss.

9 Describe the four streams of events in the garbage can model of decision making. Do you think those streams are independent of each other? Why?

10 Why are decision mistakes usually accepted in organizations but penalized in college courses and exams that are designed to train managers?

Workbook Decision Styles

Think of some recent decisions that have influenced your life. Choose two significant decisions that you made and two decisions that other people made. Fill out the following table, using Exhibit 12.8 to determine decision styles.

Questions

1 How can a decision approach influence the outcome of the decision? What happens when the approach fits the decision? When it doesn't fit?

2 How can you know which approach is best?

Adapted by Dorothy Marcic from 'Action Assignment' in Jennifer M. Howard and Lawrence M. Miller, *Team Management* (Miller Consulting Group, 1994), 205.

CASE FOR ANALYSIS

The Collapse of Barings' Bank

By Helga Drummond, *University of Liverpool*

'It was the last thing I expected'
(Peter Baring giving evidence to Treasury Committee 15 May 1996: 29)

On Thursday 23 February 1995 the directors of Barings' bank hosted a lunch for City magnates. The conversation was animated, much of it focused on Barings new venture in Mexico. 'They had no idea', said a guest afterwards.

The directors had 'no idea' that Barings, one of the oldest and most respectable houses in the City of London, was about to collapse thanks to the unauthorized trading of a relatively junior employee named Nick Leeson based in Singapore. Yet there were warning signs of malfeasance including:

- An apparent long standing reconciliation problem of £100 million.
- The discovery of an illicit £50 million transaction about six weeks before the bank collapsed.
- Trading rising when it should have been falling.
- The knowledge that Leeson was largely unsupervised and that he was both trading contracts and processing paperwork – roles that are normally segregated as a basic precaution against malfeasance.
- Leeson failing to account properly for millions of pounds remitted from London as collateral (margin) to support his trading.
- Markets in the Far East ablaze with rumours of impending catastrophe.

Why did it happen and how can we learn to make better decisions?

'A Structure That Will Prove Disastrous . . .'

Nick Leeson was seconded to Singapore in March 1992 to 'Head up our Simex [Singapore Stock Exchange] operation and also act as floor manager . . . he will report to Simon Jones and Gordon Bowser' (Board of Banking Supervision 1995: 31).

James Bax Area Manager for Singapore was not pleased as Bowser was based in London. He wanted Leeson to be solely responsible to Jones the local manger. Bax wrote to his hierarchical superiors in London 'Once again we are in danger of setting up a structure which will subsequently prove disastrous. . . . In my view it is critical that we should keep clear reporting lines' (Board of Banking Supervision 1995: 31).

The letter was ignored.

Leeson's duties were to manage the back office where the paperwork for trades is processed and payments (known as settlements) issued and to execute financial contracts for colleagues based in Japan by stepping into the trading pit. From the start, Leeson seemed to have a magical ability to beat market rates. In fact, he was deliberately underpricing business in order to impress his colleagues. Leeson's colleagues were indeed impressed. Eventually they trusted him so much that they stopped specifying contract prices enabling Leeson to quietly become a de facto trader.

The resultant losses were hidden in a secret account. By September 1992 the amount had become too big to hide indefinitely so Leeson tried to try and trade his way back into profit. Since Leeson had no authority to risk Barings' capital, he told Barings he was conducting arbitrage. For example, if oranges cost 10p in London and 11p in Amsterdam, the arbitrageur buys a quantity in London and sells them on in Amsterdam. As Barings understood that Leeson's positions were matched (contract to buy matched with an equal and opposite contract to sell) Barings deemed arbitrage to be 'essentially without risk' (Secretary of State versus Tuckey) or to paraphrase Gapper and Denton (1996: 10) like 'shooting fish in a barrel'.

The author gratefully acknowledges financial support from the University of Liverpool and the Economic and Social Research Council. Helga Drummond is Professor of Decision Sciences at the University of Liverpool Management School. She is a Lay Member of the General Optical Council Fitness to Practice Committee and of the Bar Standards Board. Professor Drummond is a former Non-Executive Director of the Veteran's Agency, the Armed Forces Personnel Administration Agency and latterly the Service Personnel and Veteran's Agency. Professor Drummond serves the Royal Institution of Chartered Surveyors in a non-executive capacity. She is also a member of the Defence Scientific Advisory Council.

In practice, arbitrage in financial markets is difficult because price differentials are both wafer thin and fleeting – as Leeson's colleagues in Japan had discovered having lost money on it. Leeson's situation was apparently different, however. As Barings understood it, Leeson's knowledge of customers' orders enabled him to anticipate the emergence of price differentials and arbitrage profitably – a practice known as 'front running' a customer – insider trading in other words.

In fact, Leeson was secretly selling options. An option gives another party the right, but not the obligation, to buy or sell a given quantity at some date in the future in return for payment of a premium, for example, to buy 1000 oranges at 10p each in nine months' time. If at the end of nine months the price of oranges has fallen to 9p, the option expires worthless. However, if the price of oranges has risen to 11p, the option is exercised. Options' trading is extremely risky because the party granting the option is obliged to supply the oranges at the contracted price regardless of how far the market may have moved in the meantime (Gapper and Denton 1996: 24).

Options are mainly bought as insurance against currency fluctuations. Leeson was forbidden to expose Barings to such risk but he could buy and sell for Barings' customers. That was precisely what Leeson was doing – only the customer was Barings. Leeson eluded detection because he controlled both trading and settlement and because there was no one close enough to notice as neither Jones nor Bowser took much interest in him.

'He is a star!'

Since the premium obtained from those illicit options sales was booked as pure profit, Leeson's alleged arbitrage business seemed highly profitable. In 1993 Leeson contributed £10 million of the £35 million that Barings' earned in Asia – making him an important contributor to the bonus pool. That 'fact' would become increasingly apparent in London during the first half of 1994 to both Ron Baker Head of Financial Products Group and Mary Waltz Global Head of Equity Financial Products. Excited by the possibilities Baker quietly resolved to become Leeson's line manager so that Leeson's profits would become part of his group's accounts (Ministry for Finance, Singapore 1995: 36). Baker told Barings' Chief Executive Peter Norris that Leeson was someone Norris should 'care about . . . . He is a star!' (Secretary of State versus Baker np) and recommended Leeson for a bonus of £320 000.

'A Significant General Risk . . .'

In July 1992 Barings noticed that they seemed to have paid out about £10 million more in collateral (margin) to Singapore than they had collected from customers. Since clients are required to repay margin advanced on their behalf promptly, the problem should not exist. A subsequent investigation proved inconclusive and the discrepancy was attributed to time lags between London and Singapore. By early 1994, however, the unreconciled amount was nearing £100 million so Barings ordered an internal audit.

It was a nerve wracking experience for Leeson but he need not have worried. No detailed testing of records was undertaken and consequently the auditors discovered nothing amiss, 'They completely missed what was staring me in the face every time I went back to my desk', said Leeson (1996: 121).

The auditors' report was published in October 1994. It was largely reassuring as Leeson's arbitrage business was pronounced generally sound. Yet the auditors relied on information supplied by Leeson:

> Leeson spoke rapidly about crossing a leg here and giving a tick here. Baker (the auditor) would ask him to go over it again, struggling to grasp enough to write an explanation in plain English. He unwittingly became Leeson's ghost-writer in a work of fiction (Gapper and Denton 1996: 255).

Not all of the audit report was fiction. The auditors noted that it was possible for non-existent trades to be booked and extra margin called as there was no check to ensure that amounts requested by Leeson actually matched trades. Leeson argued that frequent reconciliation was impossible because of the timing differences. After some internal squabbling the recommendation was dropped. The audit concluded:

> While the individual controls over BFS's system and operations are satisfactory, there is a significant general risk that controls could be overridden by the general manager (Board of Banking Supervision 1995: 146).

No one was alarmed by this weakness in internal controls. The report recommended that trading and settlement be segregated but nothing was done. Indeed, hardly anyone in Barings read the report.

'The wrong thing to do to this guy . . .'
In early January 1995 the external auditors Coopers and Lybrand (Singapore) discovered a £50 million 'hole' in Leeson's accounts and reported it to London. 'This was the call that would kill me', said Leeson (1996: 224).

Indeed the news caused uproar in London. Leeson claimed that he had sold a financial contract 'over the counter' (OTC) to a firm of Brokers named Spear Leeds and Kellogg (SLK). That was bad enough as Leeson had no authority to conduct such a trade. Even worse, Leeson said that he had forgotten to collect the money. He should have been sacked and if he had been the bank would have been saved – albeit badly damaged as Leeson's losses were now over £200 million and the bank's capital was only about £450 million. Yet when Tony Hawes, Barings Head of Treasury tried to investigate this alleged 'booking error' Waltz and Baker responded aggressively. For example, Waltz warned Hawes against asking, 'Time consuming or difficult questions' adding she did not want, 'every morning to be a giant investigation into Nick's life', because it was: 'The wrong thing to do to this guy . . . when he is making a million bucks a day. . . .' (Board of Banking Supervision 1995: 130).

'That premise was never doubted. . . .'
On 17 January 1995 an earthquake struck Japan. The resultant wave of selling on the stock market forced Leeson to buy massive quantities in a desperate effort to force the index to rise and stop his losses from spiralling out of control. On Monday, 23 January 1995 Leeson's reported profits were a stunning £3.3 million. The reality was a £100 million loss in a single day.

By now Barings had paid out over £221 million in margin calls, of which less than £30 million matched known customer positions. The explanations provided by Leeson for his margin requests were strikingly brief. Everyone in the settlements knew that Leeson's accounts of how the money was being used were fiction but they assumed that Leeson was so busy trading that he was neglecting settlements. Staff talked about awaiting the breakdown from 'buddy Nick . . . once they creatively allocate the numbers' (Secretary of State versus Gamby).

On 25 January Hawes reported to ALCO (Asset and Liability Committee) that Barings had almost broken their overdraft limit with Citibank. This was a serious issue of credibility and ALCO immediately instructed Leeson not to increase his positions. Leeson's trading promptly doubled.

ALCO then discussed how they would ensure sufficient funds would be available to meet sudden margin calls at any time of day and arranging extra overdraft facilities. No one asked why Leeson's positions had suddenly doubled. Norris who chaired ALCO said, 'Discussion . . . started with a reconfirmation that all our positions were fully matched. That premise was never doubted. . . .' (Board of Banking Supervision 1996: 137).

'They wanted to believe it was all true . . .'
On Monday 6 February 1995 Peter Norris made a special verbal report to MANCO highlighting Leeson's £3.2 million ($9 million) profit for the previous week. One of the directors, Diarmid Kelly was sceptical, 'You do not make $9 million in a week with no risk', he said (Gapper and Denton 1996: 291). Kelly's comment was politely ignored. Deputy Chairman Andrew Tuckey said:

> It was not our practice with senior colleagues to interrogate them as to what steps they had actually taken to bring themselves into a state of confidence and satisfaction.... Our culture was particularly inconsistent with that. (Secretary of State versus Tuckey).

Around 15 February Kelly learned that Morgan Stanley and Goldman Sachs were warning their customers to be careful about dealing with Barings as they were incurring massive exposure to a mystery customer. Kelly telephoned Baker to ask who Leeson's mystery customer was. Baker stalled though in fact he did not know either. Again, starting from the premise that Leeson's positions were matched, the two men decided that since one stock exchange published trades and the other did not, financial markets in the Far East were seeing only half of the equation.

Meanwhile Hawes and a junior from the settlements office named Tony Railton had travelled to Singapore to investigate the reconciliation problem. Railton wrestled with Leeson's accounts for a fortnight. No matter how he added the figures, there was a £95 million shortfall. 'If you close out [sell up] all these positions there is absolutely no way on God's earth that you could return all the yen', said Railton (Fay 1996: 188).

Railton persisted for another week. Meanwhile a further US$169 million was remitted by the London settlements office to Singapore. Of that sum, $110 million was posted in the last two days of Barings' existence. Leeson said, 'As each day went on, and my requests continued to be met, the explanation dawned on me: they wanted to believe it was all true' (Leeson 1996: 217).

All of the margin funding was lost.

'None of us believed was that this business would last . . .'

Barings' last hope lay with the Management Committee (MANCO) chaired by Peter Baring. Peter Baring was not surprised by Leeson's unusual profits. He had seen it all before:

> We had a number of businesses that were low risk and relatively high profitability; the most pronounced example of this was the Japanese warrant trading business. . . . What none of us believed was that this business would last. The basic instinct . . . that there is something about this business that defied gravity is something which we shared; but it was in terms of its durability. . . . In our experience, these businesses could last for a period but then they would go. That would happen to us again and again (Treasury Committee 1996, 15 May: 22).

There was alarm of sorts. Peter Baring said, 'When I finally saw the January 1995 figures, which I saw a number of days before the crisis broke, those figures seemed to me alarming in . . . that I believed this could not last' (Treasury Committee 1996, 15 May: 21).

Yet without Leeson's alleged profits Barings were making a loss. Latterly the management committee discussed was whether, '. . . other opportunities could be developed using similar concepts elsewhere' (Secretary of State versus Tuckey). In other words, could Barings continue to outwit competitors by practising Leeson's style of arbitrage in other markets? It must have seemed a tantalizing possibility.

Meanwhile, Railton was growing more alarmed daily by his continuing failure to solve the reconciliation problem. He needed Leeson to explain things but Leeson was proving elusive. Eventually Railton enlisted help from Jones and they insisted upon Leeson meeting with them. It was Thursday 23 February. The Nikkei index had fallen resulting in a £143 million loss in one day alone. After a few minutes, Leeson mumbled an excuse and left the meeting.

Discussion Points

1 **Problem definition**
Assuming Leeson's positions were matched, Barings saw their problem as ensuring sufficient funding was available to support Leeson's trading. It was the **rational approach** to decision-making yet wrong. What can we learn from this mistake?

2 **Programmed decisions**
Barings were destroyed by the automatic payment of margin calls. Programmed decisions attract comparatively little attention precisely because they are routine. Yet they can have serious unintended and unwanted consequences. What occurs in Barings' case is a form of passive escalation. Can you think of other ways in which programmed decisions could precipitate disaster?

3 **Intuition**
Recall some managers prefer to rely on intuition when making important decisions. Intuition can be uncannily accurate. Yet no one in Barings (even Kelly) sensed impending catastrophe. On the contrary managers were discussing expansion hours before the bank collapsed. Why might their intuition have failed?

4 **Structure and formalization**
No one explicitly authorized Leeson to trade. No one decided that he should control trading and settlement. How far is the **garbage can** metaphor helpful in explaining those developments?

5 **Decision-making and politics**
How far do political perspectives on decision-making explain why Leeson became untouchable?

References

Board of Banking Supervision, (1995) *Report of the Inquiry into the Circumstances of the Collapse of Barings,* London, HMSO.

Fay, S. (1996) *The Collapse of Barings,* London, Arrow.

Gapper, J. and Denton, N. (1996) *All That Glitters: The Fall of Barings,* Penguin, Harmondsworth.

Leeson, N. (1996) *Rogue Trader,* London, Warner.

'Secretary of State's case against Mr Baker', *In the High Court of Justice Chancery Division*, 3 March 1998.

'Secretary of State's case against Mr Gamby,' *In the High Court of Justice Chancery Division*, 3 March 1998.

'Secretary of State's case against Mr Tuckey,' *In the High Court of Justice Chancery Division*, 3 March 1998.

Treasury Committee (1996) *Barings Bank and International Regulation: Minutes of Evidence,* 15 May, London, HMSO.

Further Reading

Brown, A. D. (2005) 'Making sense of the collapse of Barings' bank,' *Human Relations,* 58, 1579–1604.

Drummond, H. (2008) *The Dynamics of Organizational Collapse: The Case of Barings,* Routledge, Abingdon.

Stein, M. (2000) 'The risk-taker as shadow: a psychoanalytic view of the collapse of Barings' *Journal of Management Studies,* 37, 1215–1259.

Notes

1. 'Polo and Oroton sales up 10%', *Inside Retailing*, 15 December 2008; OrotonGroup, *2006 Annual Report*; OrotonGroup, *2007 Annual Report*; OrotonGroup, *2008 Annual Report*; Lyn White, 'OrotonGroup results signal turnaround success', *Inside Retailing*, 29 September 2008; OrotonGroup, 'Major restructuring and focus on core Oroton and Polo business – New CEO appointed', company announcement, September 25, 2006; 'OrotonGroup announces sale of Aldo in Australia and New Zealand', company announcement, 20 September 2006; 'OrotonGroup adds 2.8% on high volume', *Australian Company News Bites – Trading Floor*, 15 December 2008. Jenny Napier, Oroton Int'l Posts Lower Interim Net Profit, Asia Pulse, 11 March 1997.
2. Carol J. Loomis, 'Why Carly's Big Bet Is Failing', *Fortune* (February 7, 2005), 50–64; David Bank and Joann S. Lublin, 'For HP, No Shortage of Ideas; Turnaround Experts Offer Wide Range of Conflicting Strategies', *Asian Wall Street Journal* (February 14, 2005), M5; and James B. Stewart, 'Common Sense: Finding a New CEO Won't Help Unless HP Finds New Products', *The Wall Street Journal* (February 23, 2005), D3.
3. 'Hewlett Packard Company', *Hoover's Company Reports – In-Depth Report*, November 10, 2008, HP anuncia mais 9000 despedimentos na Europa, *EuroNews*, 25 September 2008
4. 'PC sales down 7%, Dell toppled in the US', *Guardian Unlimited*, April 16, 2009.
5. 'A year on from ABN Amro Goodwin is facing flak', *Birmingham Post*, 24 April 2008; Moody's downgrades ratings of Royal Bank of Scotland to Aa1/B', *Moody's Investors Service Press Release*, 27 June 2008; Erikka Askeland 'RBS admits 'deal too far' as shareholders vote for bail-out', *The Scotsman*, 21 November 2008; 'fred is shredded', *Irish Independent*, 18 October 2008; Victor Mallet, 'Still standing', *Financial Times*, 16 December 2008.
6. Adam Horowitz, Mark Athitakis Mark Lasswell and Owen Thomas, '101 Dumbest Moments in Business', *Business 2.0* (January–February 2005), 103–112.
7. 'NXP Named by Business Watch as One of the Top Ten Fast Reaction Companies of 2008', *ENP Newswire*, 12 December 2008.
8. Saul Hansell, 'Meg Whitman and eBay, Net Survivors', *The New York Times* (May 5, 2002), 17; Michael V. Copeland and Owen Thomas, 'Hits (& Misses)', *Business 2.0* (January–February 2004), 126; Carlos Ghosn, 'Saving the Business without Losing the Company', *Harvard Business Review* (January 2002), 37–45.
9. 'The top ten viral ad campaigns: Adverts so good people choose to watch them? Send them to their friends, even?', *Times Online*, July 25, 2007; Claire Beale, 'Can you create a buzz around a sex toy without saying what it is?', *The Independent*, 29 September 2008.
10. Charles Lindblom, 'The Science of "Muddling Through,"' *Public Administration Review* 29 (1954), 79–88.
11. Herbert A. Simon, *The New Science of Management Decision* (Englewood Cliffs, N.J.: Prentice-Hall, 1960), 1–8.
12. Paul J. H. Schoemaker and J. Edward Russo, 'A Pyramid of Decision Approaches', *California Management Review* (Fall 1993), 9–31.
13. P. Torterotot, M. Rebelo, C. Werey and J. Craveiro (2004), 'Rehabilitation of water networks : analysis of the decision making processes', paper presented at 4th IWA World Water Congress – Marrakech, 19–24 September.
14. Dan Milmo, 'Tube repairs at risk as cost overrun hits £750m', *Guardian*, 19 April 2007; Pippa Crerar, 'Tube Partnership Investigated Over Metronet Collapse', *The Evening Standard*, 29 August 2007.
15. Rick Brooks, 'Sealing Their Fate; A Deal with Target Put Lid on Revival at Tupperware', *The Wall Street Journal* (February 18, 2004), A1, A9.
16. Michael Pacanowsky, 'Team Tools for Wicked Problems', *Organizational Dynamics* 23, no. 3 (Winter 1995), 36–51.
17. 'Canada's National Sport not so Canadian', *Canada NewsWire*, 27 November 2008; 'New goal for NHL jerseys', *The Hamilton Spectator*, 29 November 2008.
18. Earnest R. Archer, 'How to Make a Business Decision: An Analysis of Theory and Practice', *Management Review* 69 (February 1980), 54–61; and Boris Blai, 'Eight Steps to Successful Problem Solving', *Supervisory Management* (January 1986), 7–9.
19. Christopher Hosford, 'Cablecom mines text to satisfy clients', *B to B*, 14 July 2008; Cablecom offers new services, *Inside Satellite TV*, 27 August 2008; 'Cablecom brings out HD PVR', *Broadband TV News,* 5 November 2008.
20. Adapted from Archer, 'How to Make a Business Decision', 59–61.
21. James W. Dean, Jr. and Mark P. Sharfman, 'Procedural Rationality in the Strategic Decision-Making Process', *Journal of Management Studies* 30 (1993), 587–610.
22. Michelle Perry, 'Outsourcing – Scrutinised, demonized', *Accountancy,* 22 January 2007; Nancy Feig, 'Transformational Outsourcing: Strategies for the 21st Century', *Bank Systems + Technology*, 1 August 2007; 'the recipe for success', *Computer Weekly*, 10 July

2007; 'Outsourcing is making its mark', *Computing*, 7 November 2007; Ephraim Schwartz, 'Painful lessons from IT outsourcing gone bad', *InfoWorld Daily News*, 25 August 2008.

23. Chris Lonsdale (2006), 'Risk Mitigation and Outsourcing: Alternative Models for Managing Supply Risk', in Peter Barrar and Roxane Gervais (eds.), *Global Outsourcing Strategies: An International Reference on Effective Outsourcing Relationships,* London, Gower.
24. Bo Nielsen, Torben Pedersen and Jacob Pyndt (2008), 'Coloplast A/S: Organizational Challenges in Offshoring', Case 9B08M031, London ON, Richard Ivey School of Business.
25. Farnaz Fassihi, Greg Jaffe, Yaroslav Trofimov, Carla Anne Robbins and Yochi J. Dreazen, 'Winning the Peace; Early US Decisions on Iraq Now Haunt American Efforts', *The Wall Street Journal* (April 19, 2004), A1, A14.
26. Art Kleiner, 'Core Group Therapy', *Strategy & Business*, issue 27 (Second Quarter, 2002), 26–31.
27. Irving L. Janis, *Crucial Decisions: Leadership in Policymaking and Crisis Management* and (New York: The Free Press, 1989); and Paul C. Nutt, 'Flexible Decision Styles and the Choices of Top Executives', *Journal of Management Studies* 30 (1993), 695–721.
28. Herbert A. Simon, 'Making Management Decisions: The Role of Intuition and Emotion', *Academy of Management Executive* 1 (February 1987), 57–64; and Daniel J. Eisenberg, 'How Senior Managers Think', *Harvard Business Review* 62 (November–December 1984), 80–90.
29. Sefan Wally and J. Robert Baum, 'Personal and Structural Determinants of the Pace of Strategic Decision Making', *Academy of Management Journal* 37, no. 4 (1994), 932–956; and Orlando Behling and Norman L. Eckel, 'Making Sense Out of Intuition', *Academy of Management Executive* 5, no. 1 (1991), 46–54.
30. Gary Klein, *Intuition at Work: Why Developing Your Gut Instincts Will Make You Better at What You Do* (New York: Doubleday, 2002); Milorad M. Novicevic, Thomas J. Hench and Daniel A. Wren, '"Playing By Ear . . . In an Incessant Din of Reasons": Chester Barnard and the History of Intuition in Management Thought', *Management Decision* 40, no. 10 (2002), 992–1002; Alden M. Hayashi, 'When to Trust Your Gut', *Harvard Business Review* (February 2001), 59–65; Brian R. Reinwald, 'Tactical Intuition', *Military Review* 80, no. 5 (September–October 2000), 78–88; Thomas A. Stewart, 'How to Think with Your Gut', *Business 2.0* (November 2002), accessed at *http://www.business2.com/articles* on November 7, 2002; Bill Breen, 'What's Your Intuition?' *Fast Company* (September 2000), 290–300; and Henry Mintzberg and Frances Westley, 'Decision Making: It's Not What You Think', *MIT Sloan Management Review* (Spring 2001), 89–93.
31. Thomas F. Issack, 'Intuition: An Ignored Dimension of Management', *Academy of Management Review* 3 (1978), 917–922.
32. Marjorie A. Lyles, 'Defining Strategic Problems: Subjective Criteria of Executives', *Organizational Studies* 8 (1987), 263–280; and Marjorie A. Lyles and Ian I. Mitroff, 'Organizational Problem Formulation: An Empirical Study', *Administrative Science Quarterly* 25 (1980), 102–119.
33. Marjorie A. Lyles and Howard Thomas, 'Strategic Problem Formulation: Biases and Assumptions Embedded in Alternative Decision-Making Models', *Journal of Management Studies* 25 (1988), 131–145.
34. Ross Stagner, 'Corporate Decision-Making: An Empirical Study', *Journal of Applied Psychology* 53 (1969), 1–13.
35. 'CEOs More Likely to Rely on Intuition than Metrics When Making Business Decisions', *Business Wire*, November 6, 2006; Jabulani Sikhakhane, 'Managers can benefit from an overlooked resource: the gut', *The Star*, 6 September 2007; 'SME Survey: Gut feeling rules in small businesses', *The Independent Financial Review*, 21 February 2007.
36. Reported in Eric Bonabeau, 'Don't Trust Your Gut', *Harvard Business Review* (May 2003), 116ff.
37. Hamish Cooper, 'KTM's rocket for the road', *The Courier-Mail* (Australia), 19 April 2008; Kurt Matzler, Franz Bailom and Todd A. Mooradian (2007), 'Intuitive Decision Making', *MIT Sloan Management Review*, October 1,
38. Bonabeau, 'Don't Trust Your Gut'.
39. Ann Langley, "Between 'Paralysis by Analysis' and 'Extinction by Instinct,'" *Sloan Management Review* (Spring 1995), 63–76.
40. Paul C. Nutt, 'Types of Organizational Decision Processes', *Administrative Science Quarterly* 29 (1984), 414–450.
41. Brian Boyd, 'Magic maker', *Irish Times*, 8 October 2007; David Sinclair, 'Rough Trade: The label that changed music history', *The Independent*, 8 September 2006; Fiona Shepherd, 'Rough diamonds', *The Scotsman*, 25 November 2008; Nadine Mcbay. 'Roughing it around Britain', *Metro*, 25 November 2008.
42. Nandini Rajagopalan, Abdul M. A. Rasheed and Deepak K. Datta, 'Strategic Decision Processes: Critical Review and Future Decisions', *Journal of Management* 19 (1993), 349–384; Paul J. H. Schoemaker, 'Strategic Decisions in Organizations: Rational and Behavioural Views', *Journal of Management Studies* 30 (1993), 107–129; Charles J. McMillan, 'Qualitative Models of Organizational Decision Making', *Journal of Management Studies* 5 (1980), 22–39; and Paul C. Nutt, 'Models for Decision Making in Organizations and Some Contextual Variables Which Stimulate Optimal Use', *Academy of Management Review* 1 (1976), 84–98.
43. Hugh J. Miser, 'Operations Analysis in the Army Air Forces in World War II: Some Reminiscences', *Interfaces* 23 (September–October 1993), 47–49; Harold J. Leavitt, William R. Dill and Henry B. Eyring, *The Organizational World* (New York: Harcourt Brace Jovanovich, 1973), chap. 6.
44. Stephen J. Huxley, 'Finding the Right Spot for a Church Camp in Spain', *Interfaces* 12 (October 1982), 108–114; James E. Hodder and Henry E. Riggs, 'Pitfalls in Evaluating Risky Projects', *Harvard Business Review* (January–February 1985), 128–135.
45. 'Labour Agency report on creating 'virtual labour market', *German News*, 3 November 2004, accessed at, http://www.germnews.de/archive/dn/2004/11/03.html on December 23, 2008.
46. The Computerworld Honors Program, 'Germany's Labour Agency (Bundesagentur für Arbeit): Virtual Labour

Market (VAM)', accessed at http://www.cwhonors.org/viewCaseStudy.asp?NominationID=204 on December 23, 2008.

47. Rajeshree Sisodia, 'Jobless welcome hi-tech option', *The Journal* (Newcastle, UK), 21 February 2003.
48. Alistair Osborne, 'Ryanair protests too much', *Daily Telegraph*, 7 June 2007.
49. 'Ex-Ryanair duo set up aviation consultancy', *Irish Independent*, 18 January 2008.
50. Julie Schlosser, Markdown Lowdown, '*Fortune* (January 12, 2004), 40; Christina Binkley, 'Numbers Game; Taking Retailers' Cues, Harrah's Taps Into Science of Gambling', *The Wall Street Journal* (November 22, 2004), A1, A8.
51. 'Les TER, prochain chantier de la politique tarifaire de la compagnie ferroviaire', *Les Echos*, 29 October 2008.
52. Barry Berman (2005), 'Applying yield management pricing to your service business', *Business Horizons*, 48, 169–179.
53. Peter Jarvis (2002), 'Introducing yield management into a new industry' *Journal of Revenue and Pricing Management*, Vol. 1, 67–75; Jochen Wirtz, Jeannette Ho, Pheng Theng and Paul Patterson, 'Yield Management: Resolving Potential Customer and Employee Conflicts' (2001), Working Paper 0126, National University of Singapore Business School.
54. Harold J. Leavitt, 'Beyond the Analytic Manager', *California Management Review* 17 (1975), 5–12; and C. Jackson Grayson, Jr., 'Management Science and Business Practice', *Harvard Business Review* 51 (July–August 1973), 41–48.
55. Larry Elliott and Dan Atkinson (2008), *The Gods That Failed: How Blind Faith in Markets Has Cost Us Our Future*, London, Bodley Head; 'The foreclosure epidemic: the costs to families and communities of the predictable mortgage meltdown: an interview with Allen Fishbein', *Multinational Monitor,* 1 May 2007.
56. Amir Efrati, 'The Madoff Fraud Case: Scope of Alleged Fraud Is Still Being Assessed', *The Wall Street Journal*, 18 December 2008; Marcy Gordon, 'Madoff fraud case raises questions about SEC's scrutiny of operations, response to alarms', *Associated Press Newswires*, 13 December 2008; 'The Madoff Fraud Case: Victims of Scandal Reflect on Shocking Turnabout', *The Wall Street Journal*, 20 December 2008.
57. James Auger, 'Madoff Fraud Scandal Further Undermines Confidence in US. Financial System, Regulation', *Global Insight Daily Analysis*, 15 December 2008.
58. David Wessel, 'A Man Who Governs Credit Is Denied a Toys 'R' Us Card', *The Wall Street Journal* (December 14, 1995), B1.
59. Richard L. Daft and John C. Wiginton, 'Language and Organization', *Academy of Management Review* (1979), 179–191.
60. Based on Richard M. Cyert and James G. March, *A Behavioural Theory of the Firm* (Englewood Cliffs, N.J.: Prentice-Hall, 1963); and James G. March and Herbert A. Simon, *Organizations* (New York: Wiley, 1958).
61. William B. Stevenson, Joan L. Pearce and Lyman W. Porter, 'The Concept of 'Coalition' in Organization Theory and Research', *Academy of Management Review* 10 (1985), 256–268.
62. Cyert and March, *A Behavioural Theory of the Firm*, 120–222.
63. Pui-Wing Tam, 'One for the History Books: The Tale of How Britannica Is Trying to Leap from the Old Economy Into the New One', *The Wall Street Journal* (December 11, 2000), R32; and Richard A. Melcher, 'Dusting Off the *Britannica*', *BusinessWeek* (October 20, 1997), 143–146.
64. Lawrence G. Hrebiniak, 'Top-Management Agreement and Organizational Performance', *Human Relations* 35 (1982), 1139–1158; and Richard P. Nielsen, 'Toward a Method for Building Consensus during Strategic Planning', *Sloan Management Review* (Summer 1981), 29–40.
65. Based on Henry Mintzberg, Duru Raisinghani and André Théorêt, 'The Structure of 'Unstructured' Decision Processes', *Administrative Science Quarterly* 21 (1976), 246–275.
66. Lawrence T. Pinfield, 'A Field Evaluation of Perspectives on Organizational Decision Making', *Administrative Science Quarterly* 31 (1986), 365–388.
67. Mintzberg et al., 'The Structure of 'Unstructured' Decision Processes'.
68. Ibid., 270.
69. 'Gillette Fusion Case Study Demonstrates Developing a $1US Billion Brand', *Business Wire*, August 1, 2008; William C. Symonds, 'Gillette's 5 Blade Wonder', *Business Week*, September 15, 2005.
70. William C. Symonds with Carol Matlack, 'Gillette's Edge', *BusinessWeek* (January 19, 1998), 70–77; William C. Symonds, 'Would You Spend $1.50 for a Razor Blade?' *BusinessWeek* (April 27, 1998), 46; and Peter J. Howe, 'Innovative; For the Past Half Century, "Cutting Edge" Has Meant More at Gillette Co. Than a Sharp Blade,' *Boston Globe* (January 30, 2005), D1.
71. Garrett Downing, 'Music-sharing lawsuits ending; Illegal downloading still will draw warning', *The Columbus Dispatch*, 23 December 2008; 'Will warning file-sharers curb their behaviour?', *New Media Age*, 31 July 2008; Sean Crotty, 'Why file sharers should beware', *Daily Post (Liverpool)*, 23 September 2008; John McKinlay, 'File-sharers under fire', *Silicon.com*, 3 September 2008.
72. Anna Wilde Mathews, Martin Peers and Nick Wingfield, 'Off-Key: The Music Industry Is Finally Online, but Few Listen', *The Wall Street Journal* (May 7, 2002), A1, A20; and *http://www.musicnet.com.*
73. Michael D. Cohen, James G. March and Johan P. Olsen, 'A Garbage Can Model of Organizational Choice', *Administrative Science Quarterly* 17 (March 1972), 1–25; and Michael D. Cohen and James G. March, *Leadership and Ambiguity: The American College President* (New York: McGraw-Hill, 1974).
74. Michael Masuch and Perry LaPotin, 'Beyond Garbage Cans: An AI Model of Organizational Choice', *Administrative Science Quarterly* 34 (1989), 38–67.
75. Francis Fukuyama (2007), *America at the Crossroads: Democracy, Power, and the Neoconservative Legacy*, New Haven CT, Yale University Press; Arthur A. Goldsmith (2008), 'Making the World Safe for Partial Democracy? Questioning the Premises of Democracy Promotion', *International Security*, 33, 120–147.

76. William M. Newmann (1998), 'Foreign policy decision making, garbage cans and policy shifts: the Eisenhower administration and the "Chances for Peace" speech' *American Review of Public Administration*, 28, 187–212.
77. Michael Lipson (2007), 'A 'Garbage Can Model' of UN Peacekeeping', *Global Governance* 13, 79–97, p. 96.
78. John Kingdon (1993), 'How do issues get on public policy agendas?', in John Kingdon (ed.) *Sociology and the Public Agenda*, London, Sage, 40–50.
79. Adapted from James D. Thompson, *Organizations in Action* (New York: McGraw-Hill, 1967), chap. 10; and McMillan, 'Qualitative Models of Organizational Decision Making', 25.
80. Johannes Heeb and Karin Hindenlang (2008), 'Negotiating Landscape in the Swiss Alps: Experience with Implementation of a Systemic Landscape Development Approach', *Mountain Research and Development*, 28, 105–109.
81. Beth Dickey, 'NASA's Next Step', *Government Executive* (April 15, 2004), 34ff; and Jena McGregor, 'Gospels of Failure', *Fast Company* (February 2005), 61–67.
82. Jonathan Murphy (2008), *The World Bank and Global Managerialism*, London, Routledge, 108–117,
83. Dave Waller, 'From little acorns', *Management Today*, July 1, 2007, p.42.
84. Mintzberg and Wheatley, 'Decision Making: It's Not What You Think'.
85. Paul C. Nutt, 'Selecting Decision Rules for Crucial Choices: An Investigation of the Thompson Framework', *The Journal of Applied Behavioural Science* 38, no. 1 (March 2002), 99–131; and Paul C. Nutt, 'Making Strategic Choices', *Journal of Management Studies* 39, no. 1 (January 2002), 67–95.
86. George T. Doran and Jack Gunn, 'Decision Making in High-Tech Firms: Perspectives of Three Executives', *Business Horizons* (November–December 2002), 7–16.
87. L. J. Bourgeois III and Kathleen M. Eisenhardt, 'Strategic Decision Processes in High Velocity Environments: Four Cases in the Microcomputer Industry', *Management Science* 34 (1988), 816–835.
88. Kathleen M. Eisenhardt, 'Speed and Strategic Course: How Managers Accelerate Decision Making', *California Management Review* (Spring 1990), 39–54.
89. David A. Garvin and Michael A. Roberto, 'What You Don't Know about Making Decisions', *Harvard Business Review* (September 2001), 108–116.
90. Janes Surowiecki, The Wisdom of Crowds: Why the Many Are Smarter Than the Few and How Collective Wisdom Shapes Business, Economies, Societies and Nations (New York: Doubleday, 2004); Doran and Gunn, 'Decision Making in High-Tech Firms'.
91. Doran and Gunn, 'Decision Making in High-Tech Firms'.
92. Karl Weick, *The Social Psychology of Organizing*, 2d ed. (Reading, Mass.: Addison-Wesley, 1979), 243.
93. Matt Roush, 'How Fretter fell: 'Whole bunch of things' led to demise of appliance icon,' *Crain's Detroit Business*, December 2, 1996.
94. Dave Waller, 'Stanley Kalms turned an ailing photographic studio into Dixons, the mighty consumer electronics chain', *Management Today*, 1 November 2007; Charlotte Hardie, 'Voices of experience', *Retail Week*, 5 September 2008; 'Dixons through the ages', *Daily Telegraph*, 6 April 2006; James Hall 'Whatever happened to dear old Dixons?' *The Sunday Telegraph*, 8 April 2007; James Hall, 'It's time to recharge the batteries', *The Sunday Telegraph*, 3 June 2007.
95. Helga Drummond, 'Too Little Too Late: A Case Study of Escalation in Decision Making', *Organization Studies* 15, no. 4 (1994), 591–607; Joel Brockner, 'The Escalation of Commitment to a Failing Course of Action: Toward Theoretical Progress', *Academy of Management Review* 17 (1992), 39–61; Barry M. Staw and Jerry Ross, 'Knowing When to Pull the Plug', *Harvard Business Review* 65 (March–April 1987), 68–74; and Barry M. Staw, 'The Escalation of Commitment to a Course of Action', *Academy of Management Review* 6 (1981), 577–587.
96. Konrad Yakabuski, The Greatest Canadian Company on Earth; From hippies on stilts to global champion, *Globe and Mail*, 31 August 2007; James Mennie, 'Tourism, business boards ready to roll dice on new casino locale', *The Montreal Gazette*, 13 October 2005.

CHAPTER 13

CONFLICT, POWER AND POLITICS

Intergroup Conflict in Organizations
- Sources of Conflict
- Rational versus Political Model

Power and Organizations
- Individual versus Organizational Power
- Power versus Authority
- Vertical Sources of Power
- Horizontal Sources of Power

Political Processes in Organizations
- Definition
- When Is Political Activity Used?

Using Power, Politics and Collaboration
- Tactics for Increasing Power
- Political Tactics for Using Power
- Tactics for Enhancing Collaboration

Summary and Interpretation

Lenovo

In 2005, the Chinese computer manufacturer Lenovo shocked the IT world when it purchased IBM's personal computer business for about $1.3 billion. IBM, which was focused increasingly on IT consulting services, had been losing market share to personal computer (PC) manufacturing specialists like Dell. Lenovo, which is part-owned by the Chinese state, had been growing rapidly since being set up by the Chinese Academy of Sciences in 1984 and by the time of the IBM takeover was the ninth-biggest PC manufacturer in the world, while IBM was third. Nevertheless, many industry-watchers were sceptical. Lenovo's strength was in the Chinese market where it sold low-end machines, whereas IBM was best known for its high-end machines, particularly the ThinkPad range which was popular with high-flying global executives. Furthermore, would Lenovo, until the IBM purchase almost unknown in the West, be able to hold on to IBM's best employees, who were used to the prestige and privileges associated with working for one of the top global corporations? Many of the big computer firm mergers have faced big problems, as we saw in the previous chapter with HP and Compaq, where the two firms cannabilized each other's sales and morale and profits plummeted. HP CEO Carly Fiorino, the mastermind of that merger, paid for those problems with her job. Indeed, at the beginning, things were shaky at Lenovo. Online computer user forums were full of stories (probably mainly mythological) about how the quality of the ThinkPad machines had gone down as soon as Lenovo (or, 'the Chinese') took over. A major sale of computers to the US defence department was scrapped by the US government, supposedly due to security concerns. Former IBM staffers were nervous, wondering what corporate culture their new bosses would bring along with them.

Indeed, there were huge differences in the ways the two firms were managed. The Chinese firm had been used to operating with militaristic discipline. Twice a day calisthenic exercises were broadcast over the loadspeaker system at Lenovo with staff expected to stop work and do their stretches. Managers arriving late to meetings had to stand at the front of the meeting room with their head bowed for a full minute while their colleagues watched in silence. On the other hand, Chinese executives felt their American colleagues tended to wastefully hog meeting time: 'The Americans would just talk and talk', says Qiao Jian, a vice president of human resources, 'Then they'd say "How come you don't want to add value to this meeting?"'.

Lenovo brought in William Amelio, a top American computer executive as CEO in an effort to convince American corporate purchasers that nothing had changed from the old days when it was famously said that 'Nobody ever got fired for buying IBM'. Amelio, himself a former 18-year IBM veteran, had previously been Dell VP for the Asia region. Along with company president Yang Yanqing, he decided to tackle the cultural issues head-on organizing a cultural audit of employees. As they suspected, they found that former IBM employees often didn't really trust their new Lenovo colleagues, while the Lenovo managers found the new American staff undisciplined, used to being let off the hook too easily for missing targets or blowing deadlines.

Lenovo HR chief Ken DiPietro agrees that problems often originated in communication. 'Westerners tend to speak first, then listen and easterners tend to listen, then speak', he explains. But while the former IBM executives said they valued straight talk and communicating openly, the Chinese staff didn't see things that way. A Chinese colleague told Mr Amelio: 'You know what straight talk really means in China? It means an excuse for Westerners to be rude'. The incident helped bring home to Amelio that trust is required for effective communication. A workshop dubbed 'East Meets West', was organized which addressed topics including Western and Eastern history and religion. It was a great success and has been expanded into a four-day programme for all Lenovo managers.

Amelio built on this groundwork to foster genuine openness within the company, 'by having an open and straight talk about what straight talk is all about, everybody, including the Chinese side, came to realise, "Wow, that's a good way to solve problems". Internal meetings are more efficient now because people put their concerns on the table and get to the point', he says. 'It has become a value everybody aspires to. Throughout the company you now find lots of straight talkers – from both cultures.' Still, the Westerns tended to talk more, so in 2007 a rule was instituted that during conference calls, the American managers can talk for a maximum of five minutes at a time and the Chinese for ten.

The problem of differing attitudes to targets and deadlines was addressed by delving into different management practices in the two firms. Amelio says, 'The China side was a rigorous, metrics-driven, fact-based organisation – very edgy. They would put goals in place and do whatever it took to achieve them. They would argue hard at the start as to where the goal post should be. But once the goal post was set, they would make sure commitments were kept.' On the other hand, in the old IBM business, 'typically, the finance department would hand targets to the team that would usually be 120 per cent of what was actually do-able. So a culture started to build up where if you could explain why you couldn't do 120 per cent and 90 per cent was good enough, you were OK. But that's insidious. You don't keep a performance-based culture when that kind of mentality starts to seep through an organisation.' So the whole firm, including the former IBM team, moved to a performance-based culture that sets realistic targets but also ensures people are accountable for what they say they are going to do.

The salary structure in the merged business was also carefully examined. At IBM, sales staff had been paid about 80 per cent in base salary, with around 20 per cent for performance, whereas at Lenovo most salary was performance-related. When the companies were integrated, the Chinese Lenovo managers often found they were making far less than staff they supervised who had come over from IBM. The salary structure was brought into alignment, although this has to be balanced against the much lower cost of living in China compared with the US.

Overall, the massive effort put into ironing out conflicts and misunderstandings has helped to build a successful orgaization. Lenovo has continued to grow its business and avoided the disastrous mistakes of the HP-Compaq merger. However, problems still exist. The company still has a double personality; as a mass market, consumer brand in China, and an up-market, enterprise-oriented brand in the West. Amelio is aiming to recapture the consumer segment in the West, which IBM had deserted in the late 1990s. In the context of a global recession, it won't be easy, but at least the firm has built a culture of dialogue and common understanding with which to tackle the challenges ahead.[1]

All organizations are a complex mix of individuals and groups with different backgrounds and perspectives and pursuing various goals and interests. Conflict is a natural and inevitable outcome of the close interaction of people who may have diverse opinions and values, pursue different objectives and have differential access to information and resources within the organization. Individuals and groups will use power and political activity to handle their differences and manage conflict.[2]

COUNTERPOINT 13.1

This conception of conflict could also be seen, however, as reducing it to the opinions and values of individuals instead of appreciating how such differences arise – for example, as a consequence of occupying different positions in the hierarchy or because they come for different social or cultural backgrounds. In other words, individual differences in *organizations* are often understandable by paying attention to differences within and between *societies*. **Discuss**

Too much conflict can be harmful to an organization. However, conflict can also be a positive force because it challenges the status quo, encourages new ideas and approaches, and leads to change.[3] Some degree of conflict occurs in all human relationships – between friends, romantic partners, and teammates, as well as between parents and children, teachers and students and bosses and employees. Conflict is not necessarily a negative force; it results from the normal interaction of varying human interests. Within organizations, individuals and groups frequently have different interests and goals they wish to achieve through the organization. In learning organizations, which encourage a democratic push and pull of ideas, the forces of conflict, power and politics may be particularly evident. Managers in all organizations regularly deal with conflict and struggle with decisions about how to get the most out of employees, enhance job satisfaction and team identification and realize high organizational performance.

See online
COUNTERPOINT 13.9

Purpose of This Chapter

In this chapter we discuss the nature of conflict and the use of power and political tactics to manage and reduce conflict among individuals and groups. The notion of conflict has appeared in previous chapters. In Chapter 3, we talked about horizontal linkages such as task forces and teams that encourage collaboration among functional departments. Chapter 4 introduced the concept of differentiation, which means that different departments pursue different goals and may have different attitudes and values. Chapter 10 discussed the emergence of subcultures and in Chapter 12, coalition building was proposed as one way to resolve disagreements among departments.

The first sections of this chapter explore the nature of intergroup conflict, characteristics of organizations that contribute to conflict and the use of a political versus a rational model of organization to manage conflicting interests. Subsequent sections examine individual and organizational power, the vertical and horizontal sources of power for managers and other employees and how power is used to attain organizational goals. The latter part of the chapter looks at politics, which is the application of power and authority to achieve desired outcomes. We also discuss some tactics managers can use to enhance collaboration among people and departments.

Intergroup Conflict in Organizations

Intergroup conflict requires three ingredients: group identification, observable group differences and frustration. First, employees have to perceive themselves as part of an identifiable group, such as a department.[4] Second, there has to be an observable group difference of some form. Groups may be located on different floors of the building, members may have different social or educational backgrounds or members may work in different department with different responsibilities within the organization. The ability to identify oneself as a part of one group and to observe differences in comparison with other groups is necessary for conflict.[5]

The third ingredient is frustration. Frustration means that if one group achieves its goal, the other will not; it will be blocked. Frustration need not be severe and only needs to be anticipated to set off intergroup conflict. Intergroup conflict will appear when one group tries to advance its position in relation to other groups. **Intergroup conflict** can be defined as the behaviour that occurs among organizational groups when participants identify with one group and perceive that other groups may block their group's goal achievement or expectations.[6] In the chapter-opening example, managers from the two halves of the new Lenovo company found communication frustrating. This was not merely because of different styles of dialogue, but also because the two companies had pursued different business strategies and because the former Lenovo executives had inferior compensation packages compared with former IBM staff, even though the pre-merger Lenovo business had been more profitable than the IBM PC operation. Conflict means that groups clash directly, that they are in fundamental opposition. Conflict is similar to competition but more severe. **Competition** is rivalry among groups in the pursuit of a common prize, whereas conflict presumes direct interference with goal achievement. In general, conflict hampers the organization's achievement of its goals or mission, whereas in some circumstances competition may be harnessed to increase an organization's overall productivity. When groups within an organization clash, the result is often a 'zero-sum game', where neither side in the conflict wins, but the organization as a whole is weakened.

See online
COUNTERPOINT 13.10

Intergroup conflict within organizations can occur horizontally across departments or vertically between different levels of the organization.[7] The production department of a manufacturing company may have a dispute with quality control because new quality procedures reduce production efficiency. Teammates may argue about the best way to accomplish tasks and achieve goals. Workers may clash with bosses about new work methods, reward systems or job assignments. Another typical area of conflict is between groups such as unions and management, franchise owners and headquarters and managers and investors. For example, Germany's Deutsche Telekom has been involved in conflicts for several years with staff over job cuts and restructuring aimed at making the privatized company more competitive.[8] Australia's Bank of Queensland, which sold off branches to owner-managers as franchises, ended up in court as many of the franchisees lost money even as the Bank itself was turning record profits. Also in Australia, the investor Souls Private Equity wrote off the entire value of its A$18.8 million investment in 24 per cent of the country's Krispy Kreme doughnut chain because it felt the company's aggressive store-opening policy was unwise given the global recession, even as CEO John McGuigan insisted that 'We are just getting on with the game and running the business. We have a different degree of confidence in current performance'.[9]

Conflict can also occur between different divisions or business units within an organization, such as between the auditing and consulting units of big firms such as PricewaterhouseCoopers and Deloitte.[10] In global organizations, conflicts between regional managers and business division managers, among different divisions or between divisions and headquarters are common because of the complexities of international business, as described in Chapter 6.

As an organization manager, keep these guidelines in mind:

Recognize that some interdepartmental conflict is natural and can benefit the organization. Associate the organizational design characteristics of goal incompatibility, differentiation, task interdependence and resource scarcity with greater conflict among groups. Expect to devote more time and energy to resolving conflict in these situations.

Sources of Conflict

Some specific organizational characteristics can generate conflict. These **sources of intergroup conflict** include goal incompatibility, differentiation, task interdependence and limited resources. These characteristics of organizational relationships are determined by the contextual factors of environment, size, technology, strategy and goals and organizational structure, which have been discussed in previous chapters. These characteristics, in turn, help shape the extent to which a rational model of behaviour versus a political model of behaviour is used to accomplish objectives.

Goal Incompatibility Goal incompatibility is probably the greatest cause of intergroup conflict in organizations.[11] The goals of each department reflect the specific objectives members are trying to achieve. The achievement of one department's goals often interferes with another department's goals. University security staff, for example, have a goal of providing a safe and secure campus. They can achieve their goal by locking all buildings on evenings and weekends and not distributing keys. Without easy access to buildings, however, progress toward the science department's research goals will proceed slowly. On the other hand, if scientists come and go at all hours and security is ignored, the security team's goals for security will not be met (and valuable property of the university might be stolen). Goal incompatibility throws the departments into conflict with each other.

EXHIBIT 13.1 Marketing-Manufacturing Areas of Potential Goal Conflict

	MARKETING versus	MANUFACTURING
Goal Conflict	**Operative Goal is Customer Satisfaction**	**Operative Goal is Production Efficiency**
Conflict Area	**Typical Comment**	**Typical Comment**
1. Breadth of product line	'Our customers demand variety.'	'The product line is too broad – all we get are short, uneconomical runs.'
2. New product introduction	'New products are our lifeblood.'	'Unnecessary design changes are prohibitively expensive.'
3. Product scheduling	'We need faster response. Our customer lead times are too long.'	'We need realistic commitments that don't change like wind direction.'
4. Physical distribution	'Why don't we ever have the right merchandise in inventory?'	'We can't afford to keep huge inventories.'
5. Quality	'Why can't we have reasonable quality at lower cost?'	'Why must we always offer options that are too expensive and offer little customer utility?'

Source: Based on Benson S. Shapiro, 'Can Marketing and Manufacturing Coexist?' *Harvard Business Review* 55 (September–October 1977), 104–114; and Victoria L. Crittenden, Lorraine R. Gardiner, and Antonie Stam, 'Reducing Conflict between Marketing and Manufacturing,' *Industrial Marketing Management* 22 (1993), 299–309.

The potential for conflict is often greater between marketing and manufacturing than between other departments because the goals of these two departments are frequently at odds. Exhibit 13.1 shows examples of goal conflict between typical marketing and manufacturing departments. Marketing strives to increase the breadth of the product line to meet customer tastes for variety. A broad product line means short production runs, so manufacturing has to bear higher costs.[12] Other areas of goal conflict are quality, cost control and new products or services. Designers of Indian car manufacturer Tata's new Nano car, aimed at making car ownership affordable for the burgeoning middle classes in developing countries, had to cut corners in order to break the $2,500 (100,000 rupee) barrier. For example, the car lacks some basic features which are considered standard and even legally required in developed countries, such as air bags, side impact beams and anti-lock brakes.[13] These savings may well make it impossible to sell the car in countries with higher safety standards than India.

Differentiation *Differentiation* was defined in Chapter 4 as 'the differences in cognitive and emotional orientations among managers in different functional departments'. Functional specialization requires people with specific education, skills, attitudes and time horizons. For example, people may join a sales department because they have ability and aptitude consistent with sales work. After becoming members of the sales department, they are influenced by departmental norms and values.

Departments or divisions within an organization often differ in values, attitudes and standards of behaviour and these subcultural differences lead to conflicts.[14] Consider an encounter between a sales manager and a research and development (R&D) scientist about a new product:

The sales manager may be outgoing and concerned with maintaining a warm, friendly relationship with the scientist. He may be put off because the scientist seems withdrawn and disinclined to talk about anything other than the problems in which he is interested. He may also be annoyed that the scientist seems to have such freedom in choosing what he will work on. Furthermore, the scientist is probably often late for appointments, which, from the salesman's point of view, is no way to run a business. Our scientist, for his part, may feel uncomfortable because the salesman seems to be pressing for immediate answers to technical questions that will take a long time to investigate. All the discomforts are concrete manifestations of the relatively wide differences between these two men in respect to their working and thinking styles.[15]

A lack of trust within the organization can magnify these natural differences and increase the potential for conflict among departments and with top managers, as a new CEO discovered at Guidant (now part of Boston Scientific). Her solution was to build a new culture of honesty, as discussed in this chapter's Leading by Design, although as Counterpoint shows 13.3, the new culture did not necessarily extend to the company's disclosures to doctors and patient users of the company's devices.

COUNTERPOINT 13.2

Lack of trust is often associated with conflict. Lack of trust indicates a lack of respect for the other person or group which, in turn, indicates doubts about the legitimacy of their claims or even their existence. If executives are not willing openly to share all information with employees, what does this say about trust? What does it say about divergent or convergent interests? **Discuss**

Managing Dynamic Processes

Guidant[16] (now part of Boston Scientific) was the darling of the medical devices industry. The company, established by US pharmaceutical giant Eli Lilly, reached $100 million in sales within five years of launching its first product and revolutionized the field of angioplasty by producing one innovation after another. But when Ginger Graham took over as president and CEO of the medical device manufacturer, she realized that something was terribly wrong. Even though top managers were still touting Guidant's strong internal and external relationships as key to the company's success, the reality was that these relationships were increasingly marked by conflict and discord rather than harmony and cooperation.

When Graham gave her first address to the company, she decided to tell the truth: 'I've always heard about what a wonderful company Guidant is', she began, 'but frankly, that's not what I see. What I see is deteriorating morale, disillusioned customers and finger-pointing. I see a place where R&D and manufacturing are practically at war. You folks in sales blame manufacturing. R&D blames marketing. We're all so busy blaming each other that nothing gets done.' The response of employees – standing and cheering their approval – confirmed Graham's suspicions. People just wanted to hear that someone at the top knew the truth and was willing to admit it. From that moment, Graham began building a culture at Guidant in which everyone feels free to tell the truth without fear of negative consequences.

Guidant established a number of practices fostering open and honest communications. To start, Graham reversed the top-down communication structure in an immediately visible way. Each top manager was assigned a coach from lower ranks of the organization. The coaches were trained to ask questions and gather specific information from everyone throughout the organization about the manager's openness and honest communication skills. Managers met with their coaches once a quarter. Because it had support from the top, the coaching programme worked to close the communication gap between managers and employees. Managers also began sharing all information with employees – good and bad – and asking for their help in solving company problems. Employees who went above and beyond the call of duty to meet organizational goals were recognized and rewarded.

Rallying everyone around company goals rather than departmental goals helped alleviate much of the tension and conflict between departments. The war between R&D and manufacturing, however, had become so entrenched that stronger methods were needed.

Even though it cost the company dearly, Graham shut down product development altogether while representatives from R&D, manufacturing, clinical and marketing worked with a professional facilitator to confront the issues head-on and come up with a new approach to product development. The process meant that no new products went out the door for 18 months, but the results were worth it. The company repeatedly launched innovative new products every year, produced enough to supply the entire market in a matter of weeks, completed clinical studies in record-setting time and improved quality while cutting costs.

Source: Ginger L. Graham, 'If You Want Honesty, Break Some Rules', *Harvard Business Review* (April 2002), 42–47.

As an organization manager, keep these guidelines in mind:

Use the rational model of organization when alternatives are clear, when goals are defined and when managers can estimate the outcomes accurately. In these circumstances, coalition building, cooptation or other political tactics are not needed and will not lead to effective decisions.

Task interdependence Task interdependence refers to the dependence of one unit on another for materials, resources or information. As described in Chapter 7, *pooled interdependence* means there is little interaction; *sequential interdependence* means the output of one department goes to the next department; and *reciprocal interdependence* means that departments mutually exchange materials and information.[18]

Generally, as interdependence increases, the potential for conflict increases.[19] In the case of pooled interdependence, units have little need to interact. Conflict is at a minimum. Sequential and reciprocal interdependence require employees to spend time coordinating and sharing information. Employees must communicate frequently and differences in goals or attitudes will surface. Conflict is especially likely to occur when agreement is not reached about the coordination of services to each other. Greater interdependence means departments often exert pressure for a fast response because departmental work has to wait on other departments.[20]

Limited Resources Another major source of conflict involves competition between groups for what members perceive as limited resources.[21] Organizations have limited money, physical facilities, staff resources and human resources to share among departments. In their desire to achieve goals, groups want to increase their resources. This throws them into conflict. Managers may develop strategies, such as inflating budget requirements or working behind the scenes, to obtain a desired level of resources.

Resources also symbolize power and influence within an organization. The ability to obtain resources enhances prestige. Departments typically believe they have a legitimate claim on additional resources. However, exercising that claim results in conflict. For example, in almost every organization, conflict occurs during the annual budget exercise, often creating political activity.

Rational versus Political Model

The sources of intergroup conflict are listed in Exhibit 13.2. The degree of goal incompatibility, differentiation, interdependence and conflict over limited resources determines whether a rational or political model of behaviour is used within the organization to accomplish goals.

When goals are in alignment, there is little differentiation, departments are characterized by pooled interdependence and resources seem abundant, managers can use a **rational model** of organization, as outlined in Exhibit 13.2. As with the rational approach to decision making described in Chapter 12, the rational model of organization is not fully achievable in the real world and indeed assumes common agreement on an organization's objectives that is highly unlikely in all but the smallest organization.

EXHIBIT 13.2 Sources of Conflict and Use of Rational versus Political Model

Sources of Potential Intergroup Conflict
• *Goal incompatibility*
• *Differentiation*
• *Task interdependence*
• *Limited resources*

When Conflict is Low, Rational Model Describes Organization		When Conflict is High, Political Model Describes Organization
Consistent across participants	*Goals*	*Inconsistent, pluralistic within the organization*
Centralized	*Power and control*	*Decentralized, shifting coalitions and interest groups*
Orderly, logical, rational	*Decision process*	*Disorderly, result of bargaining and interplay among interests*
Norm of efficiency	*Rules and norms*	*Free play of market forces; conflict is legitimate and expected*
Extensive, systematic, accurate	*Information*	*Ambiguous; information used and withheld strategically*

In the rational organization, behaviour is not random or accidental. Goals are clear and choices are made in a logical way. When a decision is needed, the goal is defined, alternatives are identified and the choice with the highest probability of success is selected. The rational model is also characterized by centralized power and control, extensive information systems and an efficiency orientation.[22] The opposite view of organizational processes is the **political model**, also described in Exhibit 13.2. When differences are great organization groups have separate interests, goals and values. Disagreement and conflict are normal, so power and influence are needed to reach decisions. Groups will engage in the push and pull of debate to decide goals and reach decisions. Information is ambiguous and incomplete. Typically, rational and political processes co-exist in organizations. In most organizations, neither the rational model nor the political model characterizes things fully, but each will be used some of the time. Jeff Bezos, the founder and CEO of global online bookseller Amazon.com, emphasizes a rational approach to planning and decision making whenever possible. 'The great thing about fact-based decisions', he says, 'is that they overrule the hierarchy. The most junior person in the company can win an argument with the most senior person with a fact-based decision.' For decisions and situations that are complex, ill-defined and controversial, however, Bezos uses a political model, discussing the issues with people, building agreement among senior executives and relying on his own judgement.[23]

COUNTERPOINT 13.3

For some observers, there is a tendency to regard the rational model as non-political. But if 'rational' decisions are always guided by assumptions and values that fill in for missing information, don't they shade into political decisions? Also, how often is a rational decision made *post hoc*? That is to say, rationality is invoked to justify the decision rather than to make it. When Bezos says that there are 'fact-based decisions', he is arguably referring to the kinds of facts that he is prepared to recognise and endorse – that is, facts that are usable in a way that he judges to be good (e.g. for securing his postion of for the profitable growth of the company). Politics is indeed 'needed to accomplish objectives' and the most potent form of politics is that which appears to be non-political or 'rational'. **Discuss**

Managers may strive to adopt rational procedures but will find that politics is needed to accomplish objectives. The political model means managers learn to acquire, develop and use power to accomplish objectives.

Power and Organizations

Power is an intangible force in organizations. It cannot be seen, but its effect can be felt. *Power* is often defined as the potential ability of one person (or department) to influence other people (or departments) to carry out orders[24] or to do something they would not otherwise have done.[25] Other definitions stress that power is the ability to achieve goals or outcomes that power holders desire.[26] The achievement of desired outcomes is the basis of the definition used here: **Power** is the ability of one person or department in an organization to influence other people to bring about desired outcomes. It is the potential to influence others within the organization with the goal of attaining desired outcomes for power holders.

See online COUNTERPOINT 13.11

Power exists only in a relationship between two or more people and it can be exercised in either vertical or horizontal directions. The source of power often derives from an exchange relationship in which one position or department provides scarce or valued resources to other departments. When one person is dependent on another person, a power relationship emerges in which the person with the resources has greater power.[27]

COUNTERPOINT 13.4

It could also be argued that the person or group with the greatest power is the person who is least vulnerable to the dependency of others. The person or group who is commonsensically seen to have the most power is not ultimately powerful if s/he depends upon others to sustain that power or is obliged to ensure others' subjugation in order to maintain that power. Consider the example of the football owners and managers in the following paragraph. The owners are desperate for results and silverware. They have the resources. But they are dependent upon managers and ultimately the players to realize their dreams. **Discuss**

When power exists in a relationship, the power holders can achieve compliance with their requests. Powerful individuals are often able to get bigger budgets for their departments, more favourable production schedules and more control over the organization's agenda.[28]

As an illustration, consider how power has shifted in the game of football. Seasoned team managers, who typically base their decisions on instinct and experience, are losing power to wealthy owners who purchase teams and tend both to estimate their own capacities very highly and to expect very rapid results (and returns on their investments). For example, Manchester City's Manager Sven-Goren Eriksson was fired by new owner Thaksin Shinawatra in 2008 after only one season, even though the club's results under Eriksson were the best in fifteen years. Subsequently, the team was resold to an Abu Dhabi-based company linked with the local royal family. Despite a new manager, further injections of cash, and high-profile purchases the team's performance worsened the next year. Within months, rumours had started that the new owners were about to change managers yet again. Manchester City managers have fared better than those of the Scottish team Heart of Midlothian, purchased in 2005 by Lithuanian multi-millionaire Vladimir Romanov. After three years at the helm, Romanov was already on his eighth manager.[29,30]

Individual versus Organizational Power

In popular literature, power is often described as a personal characteristic, and a frequent topic is how one person can influence or dominate another person.[31] You probably recall from an earlier management or organizational behaviour course that managers have five sources of personal power.[32] *Legitimate power* is the authority granted by the organization to the formal management position a manager holds. *Reward power* stems from the ability to bestow rewards – a promotion, raise or pat on the back – to other people. The authority to punish or recommend punishment is called *coercive power. Expert power* derives from a person's greater skill or knowledge about the tasks being performed. The last, *referent power*, is derived from personal characteristics: people admire the manager and want to be like or identify with the manager out of respect and admiration. Each of these sources may be used by individuals within organizations.

Power in organizations, however, is often the result of structural characteristics.[33] Organizations are large, complex systems that contain hundreds, even thousands, of people. These systems have a formal hierarchy in which some tasks are more important regardless of who performs them. In addition, some positions have access to greater resources or their contribution to the organization is more critical. Thus, the important power processes in organizations reflect larger organizational relationships, both horizontal and vertical.

Power versus Authority

Anyone in an organization can exercise power to achieve desired outcomes, though of course the amount of power that individuals hold in an organization varies substantially. Toyota executive Takeshi Uchiyamada grasped his opportunity to drive change when he was put in charge of organizing the company's various research centres. He got interested in the possibilities for developing a fuel-efficient car and in 1996 was appointed chief engineer of the team developing the new Prius, which was released in December 1997. The car has shifted the paradigm of automobile development away from bigger and faster to cleaner and greener.[34] As a result, Uchiyamada is viewed within Toyota and throughout the global automobile industry as the leader of a transport revolution.[35]

The concept of formal authority is related to power but is narrower in scope. **Authority** is also a force for achieving desired outcomes, but only as prescribed by the formal hierarchy and reporting relationships. Three properties identify authority:

1. *Authority is vested in organizational positions.* People have authority because of the positions they hold, not because of personal characteristics or resources.
2. *Authority is accepted by subordinates.* Subordinates comply because they believe position holders have a legitimate right to exercise authority.[36] In most organizations around the world, employees accept that supervisors can legitimately tell them what time to arrive at work, the tasks to perform while they're there and what time they can go home.

3 *Authority flows down the vertical hierarchy.*[37] Authority exists along the formal chain of command and positions at the top of the hierarchy are vested with more formal authority than are positions at the bottom.

Organizational power can be exercised upward, downward and horizontally in organizations. Formal authority is exercised downward along the hierarchy and is the same as legitimate power. In the following sections, we will examine vertical and horizontal sources of power for employees throughout the organization.

See online COUNTERPOINT 13.12

As an organization manager, keep this guideline in mind:

Understand and use the vertical sources of power in organizations, including formal position, resources, control of decision premises and information and network centrality.

Vertical Sources of Power

All employees along the vertical hierarchy have access to some sources of power. Although a large amount of power is typically allocated to top managers by the organization structure, employees throughout the organization often obtain power disproportionate to their formal positions and can exert influence in an upward direction, as Takeshi Uchiyamada did at Toyota. There are four major sources of vertical power: formal position, resources, control of decision premises and information and network centrality.[38]

Formal Position Certain rights, responsibilities and prerogatives accrue to top positions. People throughout the organization accept the legitimate right of top managers to set goals, make decisions and direct activities. Thus, the power from formal position is sometimes called *legitimate power*.[39] Senior managers often use symbols and language to perpetuate their legitimate power. For example, many large corporations have private jet aircraft for the use of their top executives. Canada's Bombardier, the market leader in corporate and private jets, predicts that the global market for corporate jets will almost double from 12,800 to 24,800 jets between 2007 and 2017. The jets not only allow executives to get around their empires more quickly than by commercial carrier, but also demonstrate the corporate power and wealth in their control.[40]

COUNTERPOINT 13.5

Sometimes the line between legitimate displays of authority and unreasonable excess can be hard to define. For example, money managers for the super-rich are expected to show their own style and class in order to attract clients and make them feel at ease. Russ Prince, who runs a consultancy that studies the habits of the super rich, says, 'If you want to deal with the super-rich, it is important to have some measure of success of your own. A man in a mansion is not going to take advice from a man who lives in a hovel.' Global banking giant Citigroup's Todd Thomson, who headed the company's wealth management division, took this advice at face value. He had the division's boardroom decked out in marble flooring and polished wood cabinets, and installed a tropical fish tank, Persian rugs, and a wood-burning fireplace in his 50th floor office overlooking New York's Central Park. Unfortunately for Thomson, by 2007 Citigroup's finances were already starting to tighten in advance of the global credit crunch, and the company's top managers decided he had gone too far, firing him for lack of judgement.[41] Thomson's case was not unique. Merrill Lynch's CEO, John Thain, spent $1.2m of company funds to refurbish his office, including a waste paper basket costing over $1000. **Discuss**

The amount of power provided to middle managers and lower-level participants can be built into the organization's structural design. The allocation of power to middle managers and staff is important because power enables employees to be productive. When job tasks are nonroutine and when employees participate in self-directed teams and problem-solving task forces, this encourages employees to be flexible and creative and to use their own discretion. Allowing people to make their own decisions increases their power.

Power is also increased when a position encourages contact with high-level people. Access to powerful people and the development of a relationship with them provide a strong base of influence.[42] For example, in some organizations an administrative assistant to the president might have more power than a department head because the assistant has access to the senior executive on a daily basis and can act as a gate-keeper.

The logic of designing positions for more power assumes that an organization does not have a limited amount of power to be allocated among high-level and low-level employees. Based on this assumption, the total amount of power in an organization can be increased by designing tasks and interactions along the hierarchy so everyone can exert more influence. Winnipeg, Canada-based haulage company Bison Transport has grown over the past twenty years from just 18 trucks to over 1,000, based on employee empowerment at all levels of the organization. Empowerment is built on effective, two-way communication, with a heavy emphasis on using new technologies allowing drivers to pass information back and forth with their colleagues and supervisors wherever they might be in North America. 'Throughout our business we endeavour to train people to make good decisions and we then allow and encourage them to make good decisions, so there's an empowerment for the driver to decide when the truck moves', says Don Streuber, the company's president and CEO. The company management is committed to genuinely listen to its employees and use their input to improve the organization. 'Our employees have expressed concerns about our commitment to the environment', says Mr. Streuber. Management took note – and worked with staff to take action through modifications to vehicles and driving practices. Bison has been recognized with a special award from the US Environmental Protection Agency for its commitment to sustainability and environmental responsibility, in addition to being named one of Canada's 50 best managed companies for the past fifteen years consecutively.[43]

Resources Organizations allocate huge amounts of resources. Buildings are constructed, salaries are paid and equipment and supplies are purchased. Each year, new resources are allocated in the form of budgets. These resources are allocated downward from top managers. Top managers often own stock, which gives them property rights over resource allocation. However, in many of today's organizations, employees throughout the organization also share in ownership, which increases their power.

In most cases, top managers control the resources and, hence, can determine their distribution. Resources can be used as rewards and punishments, which are additional sources of power. Resource allocation also creates a dependency relationship. Lower-level participants depend on top managers for the financial and physical resources needed to perform their tasks. Top management can exchange resources in the form of salaries and bonuses, personnel, promotions and physical facilities for compliance with the outcomes they desire. The board of PCCW, Hong Kong's largest telecommunications form, was concerned that the company's shares lagged well behind the local Hang Seng stock market index, limiting shareholder value. Therefore, a new bonus scheme was drawn up in 2007 that tied executive directors' and senior managers' bonuses to the company's share value as well as to internal goals such as numbers of subscribers and revenue per customer. Initial results were positive, with the company outperforming the Hang Seng during the first half of

2007. However the shares slumped again during 2008, suggesting the stock price-linked bonus scheme had not worked.[44]

During the global economic downturn beginning in 2007–2008, considerable negative attention was focused on the impact of bonus schemes, particularly in the financial sector, which reward short term performance over long-term viability. In the UK, bankers received £13.2 billion in bonuses in the first five months of 2008, when only a few months later the British government was forced to implement a huge bailout package including partial privatization of several banks in order to avoid the total collapse of the country's banking system. Richard Lambert, head of Britain's employer association the CBI, singled out the bonus culture as a main cause of the global financial crisis, saying that it 'has encouraged some employees to take spectacular short-term risks, confident that if things work out well they will reap huge rewards and that if they don't they won't be around to pay the price'.[45]

Control of Decision Premises and Information Control of **decision premises** means that top managers place constraints on decisions made at lower levels by specifying a decision frame of reference and guidelines. In one sense, top managers make big decisions, whereas lower-level participants make small decisions. Top management decides which goal an organization will try to achieve, such as increased market share. Lower-level participants then decide how the goal is to be reached. In one company, top management appointed a committee to select a new marketing vice president. The CEO provided the committee with detailed qualifications that the new vice president should have. He also selected people to serve on the committee. In this way, the CEO shaped the decision premises within which the marketing vice president would be chosen. Top manager actions and decisions such as these place limits on the decisions of lower-level managers and thereby influence the outcome of their decisions.[46]

See online
COUNTERPOINT 13.13

The control of information can also be a source of power. Managers in today's organizations recognize that information is a primary business resource and that by controlling what information is collected, how it is interpreted and how it is shared, they can influence how decisions are made.[47] In many of today's companies, especially in learning organizations, information is openly and broadly shared, which increases the power of people throughout the organization.

COUNTERPOINT 13.6

Even in the most 'enlightened' and 'progressive' of 'learning organizations', it is doubtful that all information is openly shared or even available to consult. The limited availability of this information, despite the existence of intranets and so on, is perhaps indicative of the limited trust and significant social distance that exists between different groups of employees. It is this distance that recurrently impedes and undermines cooperation. **Discuss**

However, top managers generally have access to more information than do other employees. This information can be released as needed to shape the decision outcomes of other people. In one organization, Clark, Ltd., the senior information technology (IT) manager controlled information given to the board of directors and thereby influenced the board's decision to purchase a sophisticated computer system.[48] The board of directors had formal authority to decide from which company the system would be purchased. The management services group was asked to recommend which of six computer manufacturers should receive the order. Jim Kenny was in charge of the management services group and Kenny disagreed

EXHIBIT 13.3 Information Flow for Computer Decision at Clark, Ltd.

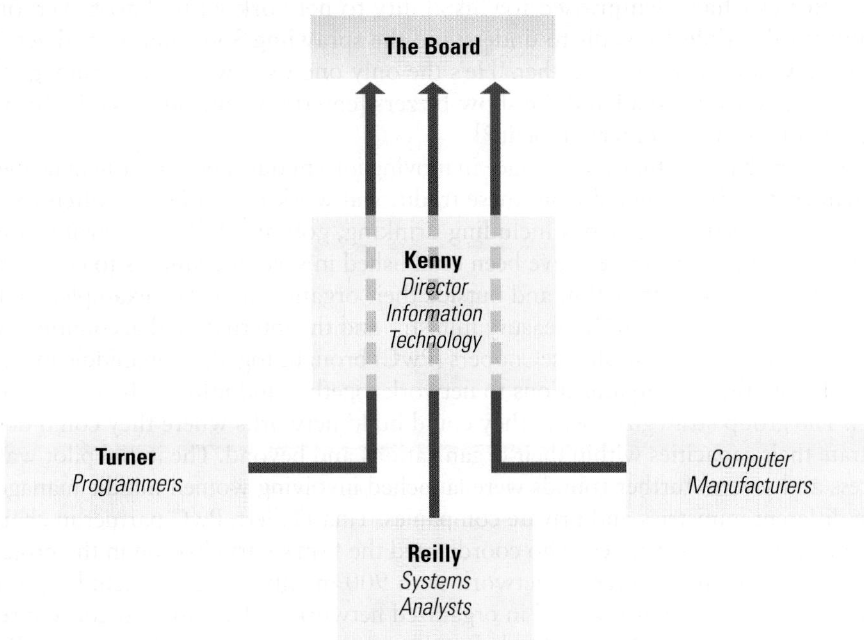

Source: Andrew M. Pettigrew, *The Politics of Organizational Decision-Making* (London: Tavistock, 1973), 235, with permission.

with other managers about which system to purchase. As shown in Exhibit 13.3, other managers had to go through Kenny to have their viewpoints heard by the board. Kenny shaped the board's thinking toward selecting the system he preferred by controlling information given to them.

Control of information can also be used to shape decisions for self-serving, unethical and even illegal purposes. For example, at Hollinger International, Inc., which owned major newspapers around the world including the UK *Daily Telegraph*, Canada's *National Post*, the *Chicago Sun-Times* and Israel's *Jerusalem Post*, the board approved a series of transactions that allowed Canadian-born CEO Conrad Black and his colleagues to improperly draw off millions of dollars from the company for personal gain. Although the board has been criticized for its lax governance, directors insisted that their decisions were based on false, skewed or misleading information provided by Black. Black was eventually convicted of fraud and obstruction of justice by a US court and sentenced to six and a half years in prison, fined US$125,000 and ordered to pay $6.1 million in restitution.[49,50]

Middle managers and lower-level employees may also have access to information that can increase their power. A secretary to a senior executive can often control information that other people want and will thus be able to influence those people. Top executives depend on people throughout the organization for information about problems or opportunities. Middle managers or lower-level employees may manipulate the information they provide to top managers in order to influence decision outcomes.

Network Centrality **Network centrality** means being centrally located in the organization and having access to information and people that are critical to the company's success. Top executives are more successful when they put themselves at the centre of a communication network, building connections with people throughout the company. Sir Howard Stringer, the CEO of Sony, is known as a skilled corporate politician who builds trust and alliances across different divisions and hierarchical levels. Stringer has been praised for his ability to network with almost everyone. He needs these political skills to understand the sprawling Sony empire and get the various divisions working together. 'He's the only one I know who can manage the Japanese [electronics side] and the show-bizzers [entertainment side]', said a former head of Sony Pictures Entertainment.[51]

One of the barriers that women face in moving into middle and senior management is a tendency to be excluded from these traditional work networks that often rotate around male-focused activities including drinking, golf and following professional sports. Effective programmes have been established in several countries to encourage women to network both within and outside their organizations. For example, a pilot partnership between Britain's Treasury ministry and the international accounting and consultancy firm PricewaterhouseCoopers (PwC) brought together ten middle managers each from the two organizations to network together and informally mentor each other. The group strategized ways they could build networks where they could demonstrate their capacities within their organizations and beyond. The initial pilot was a success and several further rounds were launched involving women middle managers from different ministries and private companies. Tina Hallett, PwC partner in charge of women-in-work initiatives, who coordinated the firm's participation in the project, chairs PwCwomen, an internal network with 900 members – even including some men. Hallett says she got involved in organized networking because: 'I'd got to a reasonably senior level and I wanted to help other people to maximise their potential'.[52]

Employees also have more power when their jobs are related to current areas of concern or opportunity. When a job pertains to pressing organizational problems,

Arla Foods

Arla Foods, a major Danish-Swedish cooperative dairy company, was unexpectedly caught up in the controversy over publication in a Danish newspaper in 2005 of cartoons of the Prophet Mohammed that some Moslems found offensive. Although Arla had absolutely nothing to do with the cartoons, it was immediately caught up in the dispute because of its high profile brand identities in the Middle East, for example selling Lurpak, the region's most popular brand of butter. In addition, the company is closely identified with Denmark, normally not the most controversial of countries, for example through sponsoring the country's football team. Arla was subjected to a boycott in which 50,000 stores in 20 Moslem countries pulled its products, action that was soon costing the company $1.8 million a day in lost sales. Opinion was divided within Arla about what to do. Finn Hansen, responsible for international sales, insisted that the company needed to respond to the boycott, despite other executives at Arla and other Danish firms preferring a lower profile. The company printed two large advertisements in Saudi newspapers distancing itself from the cartoon publication. Although there was little immediate improvement in the situation, a few weeks later the International Committee for the Support of the Prophet recommended the boycott be lifted, praising the measures Arla had taken to distance itself from the Prophet Mohammad caricatures. By 2008, Hansen was pleased to note that 'our position is just as good as it was before the Mohammad crisis'. There are still occasional flare-ups and temporary sales slumps in the Middle East whenever the cartoons are reprinted by Danish newspapers keen to emphasize the importance of free speech, but company officials are happy to leave the response to Hansen's steady hands, He says that the company now makes a consistent effort to communicate with its retailers, consumers and employees in the Middle East, so that 'Everyone knows that Arla has nothing to do with these drawings' and boycott talk quickly fades away.[53]

power is more easily accumulated. For example, managers at all levels who possess crisis leadership skills have gained power in today's world of international tensions and misunderstandings, major natural disasters and economic uncertainty.

Employees like Arla's Finn Hansen increase their network centrality by becoming knowledgeable and expert about certain activities or by taking on difficult tasks and acquiring specialized knowledge that makes them indispensable to managers above them. People who show initiative, work beyond what is expected, take on undesirable but important projects and show interest in learning about the company and industry often find themselves with influence. Physical location also helps because some locations are in the centre of things. Central location lets a person be visible to key people and become part of important interaction networks.

People Top leaders often increase their power by surrounding themselves with a group of loyal executives.[54] Loyal managers keep the top leader informed and in touch with events and report possible disobedience or troublemaking in the organization. Top executives can use their central positions to build alliances and exercise substantial power when they have a management team that is fully in support of their decisions and actions.

This works in the opposite direction too. Lower-level people have greater power when they have positive relationships and connections with higher-ups. By being loyal and supportive of their bosses, employees sometimes gain favourable status and exert greater influence.

Although it is natural for senior executives to surround themselves with loyal employees, and for staff to cultivate positive relationships with their superiors, this all too often degenerates into sycophancy, where subordinates publicly agree with their superiors even when they privately know that errors are being made. Many recent corporate collapses and scandals have their origins in a culture of top management inability to encourage and accept constructive criticism from subordinates.[55]

At Lenovo, the chapter-opening example, a healthier approach was adopted. As we saw, senior company officials emphasized building open lines of communication as a means to break down barriers between the mainly Chinese continuing Lenovo employees and the former IBM staff who joined them after the takeover. An additional positive effect of this approach is that staff are encouraged to make constructive criticism of company directions, even when this implies criticism of other managers. CEO William Amelio tells his managers, 'You have to make sure you tell me what's not working well ... if I find out later on that something was busted and you didn't include it . . . we have a problem'. As an example, during one senior management meeting in 2008, several participants were shocked that consumer sales boss consumer chief Liu Jun sharply questioned Gerry P. Smith, Lenovo's head of supply chain, about shortages of the popular new netbook PCs. Although the tone was a little inappropriate and Jun later apologized, putting it down to poor English, Smith says 'I sat there and smiled and took it', and the incident left no hard feelings.[56]

Horizontal Sources of Power

Horizontal power pertains to relationships across departments or divisions. All vice presidents are usually at the same level on the organization chart. Does this mean each department has the same amount of power? No. Horizontal power is not defined by the formal hierarchy or the organization chart. Each department makes a unique contribution to organizational success. Some departments will have greater say and will achieve their desired outcomes, whereas others will not. For example, Charles Perrow surveyed managers in several industrial firms.[57] He bluntly asked, 'Which department has the most power?' among four major departments: production, sales and marketing, R&D and finance and accounting. Partial survey results are given in Exhibit 13.4.

EXHIBIT 13.4 Ratings of Power among Departments in Industrial Firms

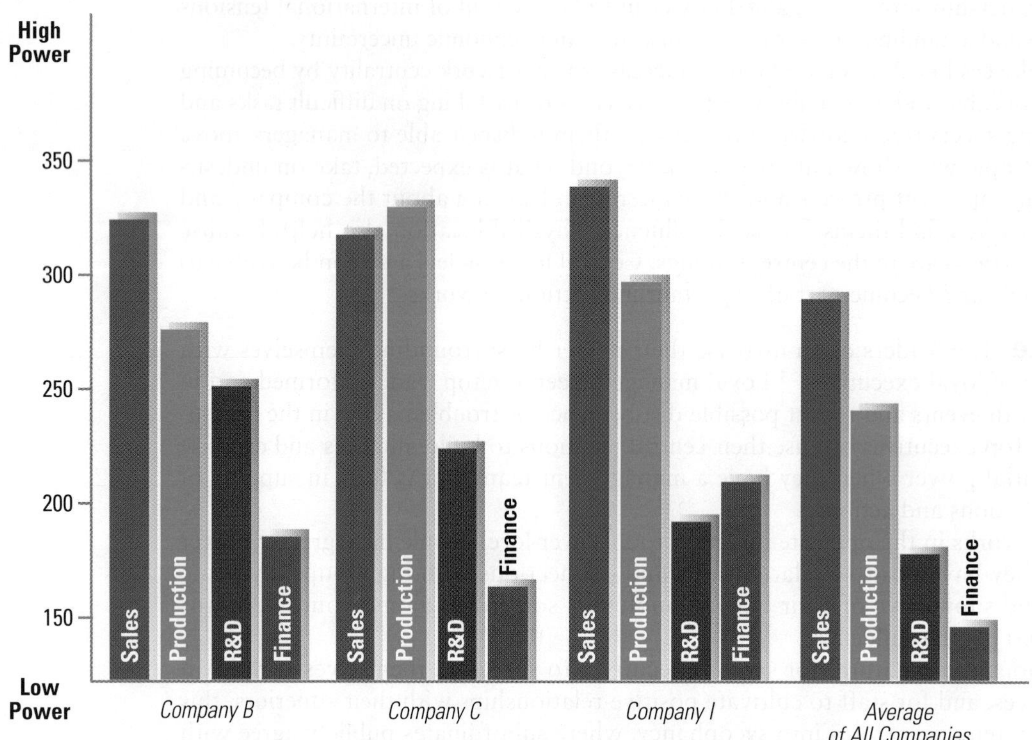

Source: Charles Perrow, 'Departmental Power and Perspective in Industrial Firms,' in Mayer N. Zald, ed., *Power in Organizations* (Nashville, Tenn.: Vanderbilt University Press, 1970), 64.

In most firms, sales had the greatest power. In a few firms, production was also quite powerful. On average, the sales and production departments were more powerful than R&D and finance, although substantial variation existed. Differences in the amount of horizontal power clearly occurred in those firms. Today, IT departments have growing power in many organizations.

See online COUNTERPOINT 13.14

Horizontal power is difficult to measure because power differences are not defined on the organization chart. However, some initial explanations for departmental power differences, such as those shown in Exhibit 13.4, have been found. The theoretical concept that explains relative power is called strategic contingencies.[58]

Strategic Contingencies **Strategic contingencies** are events and activities both inside and outside an organization that are essential for attaining organizational goals. Departments involved with strategic contingencies for the organization tend to have greater power. Departmental activities are important when they provide strategic value by solving problems or crises for the organization. For example, if an organization faces an intense threat from lawsuits and regulations, the legal department will gain power and influence over organizational decisions because it copes with such a threat. If product innovation is the key strategic issue, the power of R&D can be expected to be high.

See online COUNTERPOINT 13.15

The strategic contingency approach to power is similar to the resource dependence model described in Chapters 4 and 5. Recall that organizations try to reduce dependency on the external environment. The strategic contingency approach to power suggests that the departments most responsible for dealing with key resource issues and dependencies in the environment will become most powerful.

EXHIBIT 13.5 Strategic Contingencies that Influence Horizontal Power among Departments

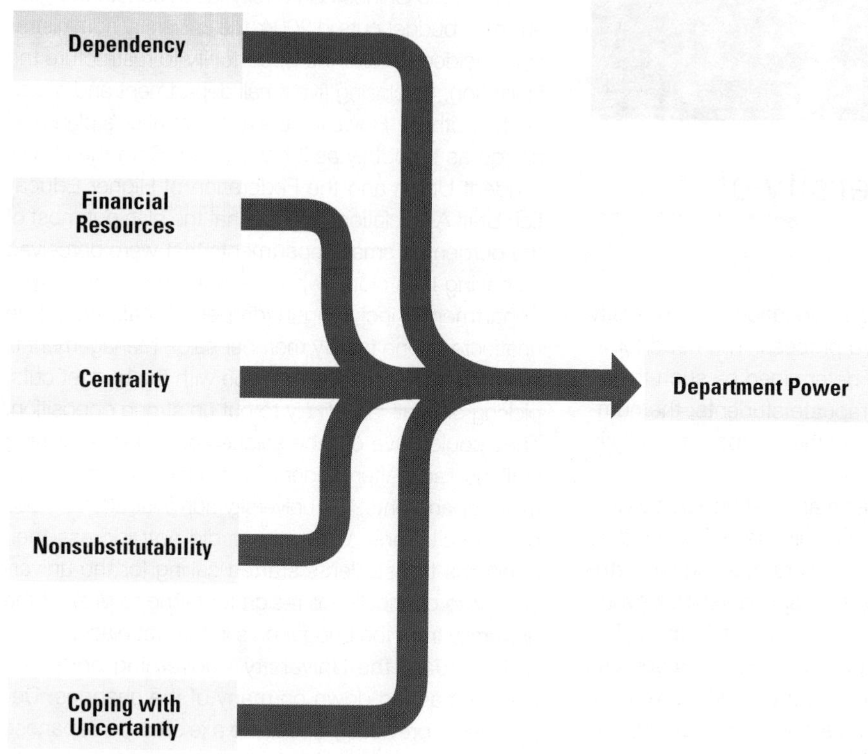

Power Sources Jeffrey Pfeffer and Gerald Salancik, among others, have been instrumental in conducting research on the strategic contingency theory.[59] Their findings indicate that a department rated as powerful may possess one or more of the characteristics illustrated in Exhibit 13.5.[60] In some organizations these five **power sources** overlap, but each provides a useful way to evaluate sources of horizontal power.

1 **Dependency.** Interdepartmental dependency is a key element underlying relative power. Power is derived from having something someone else wants. The power of department A over department B is greater when department B depends on department A.[61] Materials, information and resources may flow between departments in one direction, such as in the case of sequential task interdependence (see Chapter 7). In such cases, the department receiving resources is in a lower power position than the department providing them. The number and strength of dependencies are also important. When seven or eight departments must come for help to the engineering department, for example, engineering is in a strong power position. In contrast, a department that depends on many other departments is in a low power position. Likewise, a department in an otherwise low power position might gain power through dependencies. If a factory cannot produce without the expertise of maintenance workers to keep the machines working, the maintenance department is in a strong power position because it has control over a strategic contingency.

2 **Financial resources.** There's a new golden rule in the business world: 'The person with the gold makes the rules'.[62] Control over resources is an

Chinese University of Hong Kong

You might expect budget allocation in a university to be a straightforward process. The need for financial resources can be determined by such things as the number of undergraduate students, the number of graduate students and the number of faculty in each department.

In fact, resource allocation at most universities is a highly political process. The Chinese University gets most of its resources from the state, along with students' fees and some business sponsorship. Beyond that, some funds come from research grants. The larger departments, that provide the most resources to the university, tend to have the most power, but this is complicated because some smaller departments, like Religion, provide a lot of 'service' courses to students from other departments. In addition, departments with high quality students bring prestige to the institution which is helpful in funding negotiations.

When the Chinese University faced substantial government budget cuts in 2004, the university administration decided to take the opportunity to restructure the institution, by closing five small department and merging four others. However, the administration's plans did not go as smoothly as it had hoped. Both the CUHK Student Union and the Federation of Higher Education Staff Associations argued that the plan put most of the burden on small departments that were perceived as having little clout, while inefficiencies within larger departments, including incompetent staff, would be unaffected. One faculty member said, 'Management is just finding an easy way to cope with the budget cuts, picking on staff least likely to put up strong opposition. They could have cut the salaries of underperforming staff instead'. After students threatened sit-ins to save their departments, the university administration agreed on consultations. When these did not address their concerns the students started calling for the university's vice chancellor to resign for failing to protect the university from the budget cuts in the first place.

Eventually the University's governing body, the senate, backed down on many of the changes. Departments previously under the axe such as Japanese Studies were allowed to access external support to continue operations, while others slated for merger, such as Religion, were allowed to continue offering specialized degrees.[63]

important source of power in organizations. Money can be converted into other kinds of resources that are needed by other departments. Money generates dependency; departments that provide financial resources have something other departments want. Departments that generate income for an organization have greater power. Exhibit 13.4 showed sales as the most powerful unit in most industrial firms. This is because salespeople find customers and bring in money, thereby removing an important problem for the organization. An ability to provide financial resources also explains why certain departments are powerful in other organizations, such as universities.

See online COUNTERPOINT 13.16

In their study of the budgeting process at the University of Illinois in the USA, Pfeffer and Salancik concluded that 'Power derived from acquiring resources is used to obtain more resources, which in turn can be employed to produce more power – the rich get richer'.[64] The case of the Chinese University, discussed in the *In Practice* box above, confirms their conclusion, but only up to a point. While larger departments were initially in a stronger position to demand resources than smaller ones, a determined fightback by the smaller departments, supported by students' and faculty organizations, was able to ensure the pain of budget cuts was spread more evenly across the institution than the university administration initially intended.

3 **Centrality.** Centrality reflects a department's role in the primary activity of an organization.[65] One measure of centrality is the extent to which the work of the department affects the final output of the organization. For example, the production department is more central and usually has more power than staff groups (assuming no other critical contingencies). Centrality is associated with power because it reflects the contribution made to the organization. The corporate finance department of an investment bank generally has more power than the stock research department. By contrast, in the manufacturing firms described in Exhibit 13.4, finance tends to be low in power. When the finance department has the limited task of recording money and expenditures, it is not responsible for obtaining critical resources or for producing the products of the organization. Today, however, finance departments have greater power in many organizations because of the greater need for controlling costs.

4 **Nonsubstitutability.** Power is also determined by *nonsubstitutability,* which means that a department's function cannot be performed by other readily available resources. Similiarly, if an employee cannot be easily replaced, his or her power is greater. If an organization has no alternative sources of skill and information, a department's power will be greater. This can be the case when management uses outside consultants. Consultants might be used as substitutes for staff people to reduce the power of staff groups.

The impact of substitutability on power was studied for programmers in computer departments.[66] When computers were first introduced, programming was a rare and specialized occupation. Programmers controlled the use of organizational computers because they alone possessed the knowledge to program them. Over a period of about ten years, computer programming became a more common activity. People could be substituted easily, and the power of programming departments dropped, although the power of computer network planners grew as companies began depending on more and more complex IT systems.

5 **Coping with Uncertainty.** Elements in the environment can change swiftly and can be unpredictable and complex. In the face of uncertainty, little information is available to managers on appropriate courses of action. Departments that reduce this uncertainty for the organization will increase their power.[67] When market research personnel accurately predict changes in demand for new products, they gain power and prestige because they have reduced a critical uncertainty. But forecasting is only one technique. Sometimes uncertainty can be reduced by taking quick and appropriate action after an unpredictable event occurs.

As an organization manager, keep these guidelines in mind:

Be aware of the important horizontal power relationships that come from the ability of a department to deal with strategic contingencies that confront the organization. Increase the horizontal power of a department by increasing involvement in strategic contingencies.

Departments can cope with critical uncertainties by (1) obtaining prior information, (2) prevention, and (3) absorption.[68] *Obtaining prior information* means a department can reduce an organization's uncertainty by forecasting an event. Departments increase their power through *prevention* by predicting and forestalling negative events. *Absorption* occurs when a department takes action after an event to reduce its negative consequences. Consider the following case from the British health care industry.

Because of the risks of cost overrun, the contract negotiating and legal teams at the NHS were in a high power position. They coped with a critical uncertainty by obtaining prior information and through prevention. However, room for absorption after problems appeared – including cost delays and the pullout of key contracts – was limited, as the NHS was caught between ballooning costs and delays on the one hand, and the refusal by contractors to continue working unless their additional costs were covered on the other hand. The situation is discussed in the *In Practice* box on the next page.

NHS and the National Programme for IT[69]

The British National Health Service (NHS) is one of the longest-operating universal health service systems in the world. Every British citizen is entitled to comprehensive health care coverage, in most cases without any charge. Although the NHS is operated as a public service, many services have always been provided by private contractors, including for example groups of doctors operating family practice clinics. In recent years the process of outsourcing has expanding with many ancillary services such as IT support being tendered to outside companies. So, when the NHS decided it needed to establish a new computer network for the whole service, including a comprehensive patient database that would allow service providers anywhere in England to access a patient's full medical records, it decided to outsource the project to a number of private service suppliers. The project, begun in 2004, is called the National Programme for Information Technology (NPfIT). It quickly became the world's largest non-military IT project, with a total cost possibly exceeding £20 billion.[70]

There are a number of different departments and interests involved in decision-making for such a project. Politicians from outside the NHS had ultimate authority over the institution and were clearly enthusiastic about the concept of 'joined-up services'. However they were perhaps naïve about the challenges involved in making a coordinated IT system work in such a large institution with numerous legacy systems being used, and the potential for substantial resistance from GPs and other staff more concerned with day-to-day patient care than the long-term potential of IT. The NHS established a special unit, Connecting for Health (CfH), which would be responsible for implementing NPfIT. This unit included NHS internal IT experts who were very supportive of the project and would be responsible for designing the overall system architecture. However CfH also contains a Central Commercial Team (the 'beancounters') responsible for drawing up the contracts with outside contractors and monitoring their performance.

The relationship between government services and outside contractors is often fraught with difficulties, especially when, as in the case of the NHS, the systems being outsourced are extremely complex and difficult to specify. Cost overruns are common, and critics frequently accuse outside contractors of fleecing the public purse with unnecessary expenditures and frequent demands for contract amendments and increased payments.[71] These criticisms greatly strengthened the power of the beancounters. They ensured that the NPfIT contracts were tightly worded, with tough penalties for failure to deliver, and payments made only once the patient records and other data systems were operational. As the head of NPfIT, Richard Granger, put it, the system, 'shifted a vast amount of the risk associated with the project to service providers, which have to demonstrate that their systems work before being paid'. Four main contracts were signed with outsourcing consultants, including one with Accenture valued at about £2 billion and another with Fujitsu worth about £1 billion.

Perhaps predictably, the project ran into difficulties from an early stage. The complexity of the system led to difficulty meeting the needs of all stakeholders. There were more legacy computer systems in place than the contractors expected, and folding them into the new NPfIT proved very time consuming. Integration of the various elements of the new IT system was much more complex than had been anticipated. Some of the expert IT subcontractors that the contractor companies like Accenture and Fujitsu had hired were unable to produce operational software.

Because of the tight contracts that had been signed, the cost of the implementation delays fell on the contractors and subcontractors. By 2006, Accenture had already lost £400 million, even though it was by far the most successful of the contractors in putting its parts of the IT systems into place. Accenture's bosses decided to cut their losses and negotiated a pull-out from the contract, avoiding most of the very heavy penalties they could have been assessed. By 2007, Fujitsu also found itself in difficulties. Its project chief was suspended for telling an industry conference of his concerns: 'It isn't working, and it isn't going to work', said Andrew Rollerson. 'There is a belief that the national programme is somehow going to propel transformation in the NHS simply by delivering an IT system. Nothing could be further from the truth. A vacuum, a chasm, is opening up.' In 2008 Fujitsu tried to renegotiate its contract with the NHS, but without success. It, too, pulled out, saying, 'In the end the terms the NHS were willing to agree to we could not have afforded.... There was a limit beyond which we could not go.' The result was that only two main contractors remained. This seriously weakens the bargaining position of the NHS, because the remaining contractors know that the NHS's options are limited, and that the government cannot afford the embarrassment of allowing the project to fail. Richard Granger left NPfIT in 2008 amid rumours he was exhausted by the enormity of the project and the delays and cost overruns. The project continues, but there are mixed views about whether it will ever be fully realized.

The strength of the NHS beancounters in the NPfIT process derived from the NHS's legitimate need to control costs on an extremely complex project. But did the rigid focus on payment-for-results mean that the real stakeholders – patients and health care providers – didn't get their concerns heard, and thus resisted participating in it? Or was the project simply too ambitious to ever succeed?[72,73]

It is less obvious what was happening internally at Accenture and Fujitsu, as private corporations' business matters are closed to public scrutiny. But in all likelihood the political attractiveness of gaining these huge and prestigious contracts drove corporate leaders to agree to contracts without adequate prior information and prevention. Health care IT experts within the firms, like Fujitsu's Andrew Rollerson, probably realized early on that the project would be problematic and a potential big money loser. The fact Rollerson spoke out publicly about the problems and was disciplined suggests his views were not heard early enough within the company. Eventually, however, Fujitsu's beancounters must have put down their feet and insisted on a contract renegotiation. When that didn't happen, Fujitsu reluctantly pulled out.

Horizontal power relationships in organizations change as strategic contingencies change, as for example Fujitsu came to confront the financial black hole the NPfIT project had become.

In a health care system dealing with a major health crisis, the communications department might gain power, for example, by soothing public fears and keeping people informed about the health department's efforts to control the spread of disease. As another example, in the late 1990s the World Bank, which provides developing countries with development financing, faced major criticism from civil society activists who said that many of the projects it supported made things worse for poor people in developing countries, even though the World Bank's overall mandate is to reduce global poverty. The Bank was put into crisis mode, until its external relations (communications) department embarked on an extensive, costly and substantially effective campaign to build links with civil society and to improve the image of the organization.[74] As in the World Bank example, the communications department can gain power by helping the organization present a positive side to the story and counteract the arguments of protestors. Departments that help organizations cope with new strategic issues will have greater power.

Political Processes in Organizations

Politics, like power, is intangible and difficult to measure. It is hidden from view and is hard to observe in a systematic way. Two surveys uncovered the following reactions of managers toward political behaviour.[75]

1 Most managers have a negative view toward politics and believe that politics will more often hurt than help an organization in achieving its goals.
2 Managers believe that political behaviour is common in practically all organizations.
3 Most managers think that political behaviour occurs more often at upper rather than lower levels in organizations.
4 Political behaviour arises in certain decision domains, such as structural change, but is absent from other decisions, such as handling employee grievances.

Based on these surveys, politics seems more likely to occur at the top levels of an organization and around certain issues and decisions. Moreover, managers do not approve of political behaviour. The remainder of this chapter explores more fully what political behaviour is, when it should be used, the type of issues and decisions most likely to be associated with politics, and some political tactics that may be effective.

COUNTERPOINT 13.7

An alternative possible explanation of managers' aversion to references to 'politics' is that it undermines their sense of professionalism and authority. Instead of the image of impartial, rational professionalism which they like to project, managers are portrayed as 'political fixers'. Yet, the rough and tumble of management is all about coping with uncertainty and endeavouring to 'fix' problems on the basis of limited information, often with an eye to how it will play with the boss, and ultimately with regard to how it will be received by shareholders. **Discuss**

Definition

Power has been described as the available force or potential for achieving desired outcomes. *Politics* is the use of power to influence decisions in order to achieve those outcomes. The exercise of power and influence has led to two ways to define politics – as self-serving behaviour or as a natural organizational decision process. The first definition emphasizes that politics is self-serving and involves activities that are not sanctioned by the organization.[76]

COUNTERPOINT 13.8

What these definitions tend to overlook is how power becomes institutionalized – notably in social and organizational hierarchies. Simply occupying an elevated position in a hierarchy provides access to resources and a degree of legitimacy. Much is done routinely that serves to reproduce this position. At the same time, there is always the possibility that the institution will be challenged – by competitors or from within by resistance or incompetence. So whatever power is vested in institutions and hierarchical position, it is dependent upon subordinates' ability and willingness to reproduce their dependence. Paradoxically, it is the person or group that is least dependent upon others has the greatest (personal or collective) power. **Discuss**

In this view, politics involves deception and dishonesty for purposes of individual self-interest and leads to conflict and disharmony within the work environment. This dark view of politics is widely held by laypeople, and political activity certainly can be used in this way. Recent studies have shown that workers who perceive this kind of political activity within their companies often have related feelings of anxiety and job dissatisfaction. Studies also support the belief that inappropriate use of politics is related to low employee morale, inferior organizational performance and poor decision making.[77] This view of politics explains why managers in the aforementioned surveys did not approve of political behaviour.

See online COUNTERPOINT 13.17

Although politics can be used in a negative, self-serving way, the appropriate use of political behaviour can serve organizational goals.[78] The second view sees politics as a natural organizational process for resolving differences among organizational interest groups.[79] Politics is the process of bargaining and negotiation that is used to overcome conflicts and differences of opinion. In this view, politics is similar to the coalition-building decision processes defined in Chapter 12.

See online COUNTERPOINT 13.18

The organization theory perspective views politics as described in the second definition – as a normal decision-making process. Politics is simply the activity through which power is exercised in the resolution of conflicts and uncertainty. Politics is neutral and is not necessarily harmful to the organization. The formal definition of organizational politics is as follows: **Organizational politics** involves activities to acquire, develop and use power and other resources to obtain the preferred outcome when there is uncertainty or disagreement about choices.[80]

See online COUNTERPOINT 13.19

Political behaviour can be either a positive or a negative force. Politics is the use of power to get things accomplished – good things as well as bad. Uncertainty and conflict are natural and inevitable, and politics is the mechanism for reaching agreement. Politics includes informal discussions that enable participants to arrive at consensus and make decisions that otherwise might be stalemated or unsolvable.

When Is Political Activity Used?

Politics is a mechanism for arriving at consensus when uncertainty is high and there is disagreement over goals or problem priorities. Recall the rational versus political models described in Exhibit 13.2. The political model is associated with conflict over goals, shifting coalitions and interest groups, ambiguous information and uncertainty. Thus, political activity tends to be most visible when managers confront nonprogrammed decisions, as discussed in Chapter 12, and is related to the Carnegie model of decision making. Because managers at the top of an organization generally deal with more nonprogrammed decisions than do managers at lower levels, more political activity will appear at higher levels. Moreover, some issues are associated with inherent disagreement. Resources, for example, are critical for the survival and effectiveness of departments, so resource allocation often becomes a political issue. Rational methods of allocation do not satisfy participants. Three **domains of political activity** (areas in which politics plays a role) in most organizations are structural change, management succession and resource allocation.

As an organization manager, keep these guidelines in mind:

Expect and allow for political behaviour in organizations. Politics provides the discussion and clash of interests needed to crystallize points of view and to reach a decision. Build coalitions, expand networks, control decision premises, enhance legitimacy and make a direct appeal to attain desired outcomes.

Structural reorganizations strike at the heart of power and authority relationships. Reorganizations such as those discussed in Chapter 3 change responsibilities and tasks, which also affects the underlying power base from strategic contingencies. For these reasons, a major reorganization can lead to an explosion of political activity (although of course reorganizations are themselves often the outcome of political activity!).[81] Managers may actively bargain and negotiate to maintain the responsibilities and power bases they have. Mergers and acquisitions also frequently create tremendous political activity. Organizational changes such as hiring new executives, promotions and transfers have great political significance, particularly at top organizational levels where uncertainty is high and networks of trust, cooperation and communication among executives are important.[82] Hiring decisions can generate uncertainty, discussion and disagreement. Managers can use hiring and promotion to strengthen network alliances and coalitions by putting their own people in prominent positions.

The third area of political activity is resource allocation. Resource allocation decisions encompass all resources required for organizational performance, including salaries, operating budgets, employees, office facilities, equipment, use of the company aeroplane and so forth. Resources are so vital that disagreement about priorities exists, and political processes help resolve the dilemmas.

Using Power, Politics and Collaboration

One theme in this chapter has been that power in organizations is not primarily a phenomenon of the individual. It is related to the resources that departments command, the role departments play in an organization and the environmental contingencies with which departments cope. Position and responsibility, more than personality and style, determine a manager's influence on outcomes in the organization.

Power is used through individual political behaviour, however. Individual managers seek agreement about a strategy to achieve their departments' desired outcomes. Individual managers negotiate decisions and adopt tactics that enable them to acquire and use power. In addition, managers develop ways to increase cooperation and collaboration within the organization to reduce damaging conflicts.

To fully understand the use of power within organizations, it is important to look at both structural components and individual behaviour.[83] Although the power comes from larger organizational forms and processes, the political use of power involves individual-level activities. For instance, all managers use tactics to exert influence, but research indicates that managers in HR departments may use softer, more subtle approaches than do managers in more powerful finance departments. In one study, HR executives, who were not seen as having centrality to the firm's mission, took a low-key approach to try to influence others, whereas finance executives, who had a more central and powerful position, used harder, more direct influence tactics.[84] The following sections briefly summarize various tactics that managers can use to increase the power base of their departments, political tactics they can use to achieve desired outcomes, and tactics for increasing collaboration. These tactics are summarized in Exhibit 13.6.

EXHIBIT 13.6 Power and Political Tactics in Organizations

Tactics for Increasing the Power Base	Political Tactics for Using Power	Tactics for Enhancing Collaboration
1. Enter areas of high uncertainty. 2. Create dependencies. 3. Provide scarce resources. 4. Satisfy strategic contingencies. 5. Make a direct appeal.	1. Build coalitions and expand networks. 2. Assign loyal people to key positions. 3. Control decision premises. 4. Enhance legitimacy and expertise. 5. Create superordinate goals.	1. Create integration devices. 2. Use confrontation and negotiation. 3. Schedule intergroup consultation. 4. Practise member rotation.

Tactics for Increasing Power

Four **tactics for increasing power** for the organization are as follows:

1. *Enter areas of high uncertainty.* One source of departmental power is to cope with critical uncertainties.[85] If department managers can identify key uncertainties and take steps to remove those uncertainties, the department's power base will be enhanced. The contracting and legal teams in the NHS example above initially enhanced their power through promising to remove uncertainties with a tough negotiating strategy. In a manufacturing plant, uncertainties could arise from stoppages on an assembly line, from the quality demanded of a new product, or from the inability to predict a demand for new services. Once an uncertainty is identified, the department can take action to cope with it. By their very nature, uncertain tasks will not be solved immediately. Trial and error will be needed, which is to the advantage of the department. The trial-and-error process provides experience and expertise that cannot easily be duplicated by other departments.
2. *Create dependencies.* Dependencies are another source of power.[86] When the organization depends on a department for information, materials, knowledge or skills, that department will hold power over others. This power can be increased by incurring obligations. Doing additional work that helps out other departments will obligate the other departments to respond at a future date. The power accumulated by creating a dependency can be used to resolve future disagreements in the department's favour. An equally effective and related strategy is to reduce dependency on other departments by acquiring necessary information or skills. IT departments have created dependencies in many organizations because of the rapid changes in this area. Employees in other departments depend on the IT unit to master complex software programs, changing use of the Internet and other advances so that they will have the information they need to perform effectively.
3. *Provide scarce resources.* Resources are always important to organizational survival. Departments that accumulate resources and provide them to an organization in the form of money, information or facilities will be powerful. University departments with the greatest power tend to be those that obtain external research funds for contributions to university overhead. Likewise, sales departments are powerful in industrial firms because they bring in financial resources.
4. *Satisfy strategic contingencies.* The theory of strategic contingencies says that some elements in the external environment and within the organization are especially important for organizational success. A contingency could be a critical event, a task for which there are no substitutes, or a central task that is interdependent with many others in the organization. An analysis of the organization and its changing environment will reveal strategic contingencies. To the extent that contingencies are new or are not being satisfied, there is room for a department to move into those critical areas and increase its importance and power.

In summary, the allocation of power in an organization is not random. Power is the result of organizational processes that can be understood and to a degree predicted. The abilities to reduce uncertainty, increase dependency on one's own department, obtain resources and cope with strategic contingencies all enhance a department's power. Once power is available, the next challenge is to use it to attain helpful outcomes.

Political Tactics for Using Power

The use of power in organizations requires both skill and willingness. Many decisions are made through political processes because rational decision processes do not fit. Uncertainty or disagreement is too high. **Political tactics for using power** to influence decision outcomes include the following:

1. *Build coalitions and expand networks.* Coalition building means taking the time to talk with other managers to persuade them to your point of view.[87] Most important decisions are made outside of formal meetings. Managers discuss issues with each other and reach agreement. Effective managers are those who huddle, meeting in groups of twos and threes to resolve key issues.[88] Effective managers also build networks of relationships across hierarchical and functional boundaries. Networks can be expanded by (1) reaching out to establish contact with additional managers and (2) coopting dissenters. A research project found that the ability to build networks has a positive impact on both employees' perception of a manager's effectiveness and the ability of the manager to influence performance.[89] Establishing contact with additional managers means building good interpersonal relationships based on liking, trust and respect. Reliability and the motivation to work with rather than exploit others are part of both networking and coalition building.[90] The second approach to expanding networks, cooptation, is the act of bringing a dissenter into one's network. One example of cooptation involved a university committee whose membership was based on promotion and tenure. Several professors who were critical of the tenure and promotion process were appointed to the committee. Once a part of the administrative process, they could see the administrative point of view. Cooptation effectively brought them into the administrative network.[91]
2. *Assign loyal people to key positions.* Another political tactic is to assign trusted and loyal people to key positions in the organization or department. Top managers as well as department heads often use the hiring, transfer and promotion processes to place in key positions people who are sympathetic to the outcomes of the department, thus helping to achieve departmental goals.[92] Top leaders frequently use this tactic, as we discussed earlier. For example, the Australian-born media baron Rupert Murdoch has had his son James appointed to senior positions within the News Corp. empire.[93] James Murdoch has gained a reputation as a savvy businessman with a mind of his own, but the same was not the case with late British media mogul Robert Maxwell, whose sons Kevin and Ian were in senior company positions when their father died mysteriously leaving behind a collapsing business empire. An inquiry found Kevin 'bears a heavy responsibility in respect of many of the events' leading to the business collapse which left hundreds of workers without company pensions.[94] When he became CEO at US investment bank Merrill Lynch & Co., Stan O'Neal removed a whole generation of top talent and moved in other managers who supported his vision and goals for the organization. O'Neal was eventually forced to leave Merrill Lynch after the bank lost at least $3.7 billion in bad investments on sub-prime mortgages. The bank came close to failing and had to be taken over by the Bank of America to avoid bankruptcy.[95,96]
3. *Control decision premises.* To control decision premises means to constrain the boundaries of a decision. One technique is to choose or limit information provided to other managers. A common method is simply to put your department's best foot forward, such as selectively presenting favourable criteria.

A variety of statistics can be assembled to support the departmental point of view. A university department that is growing rapidly and has a large number of students can make claims for additional resources by emphasizing its growth and large size. Such objective criteria do not always work, but they are a valuable step.

Decision premises can be further influenced by limiting the decision process. Decisions can be influenced by the items put on an agenda for an important meeting or even by the sequence in which items are discussed.[97] Items discussed last, when time is short and people want to leave, will receive less attention than those discussed earlier. Calling attention to specific problems and suggesting alternatives also will affect outcomes. Stressing a specific problem to get it – rather than problems not relevant to your department – on the agenda is an example of agenda setting.

4 *Enhance legitimacy and expertise.* Managers can exert the greatest influence in areas in which they have recognized legitimacy and expertise. If a request is within the task domain of a department and is consistent with the department's vested interest, other departments will tend to comply. Members can also identify external consultants or other experts within the organization to support their cause.[98] For example, a financial vice president in a large retail firm wanted to fire the director of HR management. She hired a consultant to evaluate the HR projects undertaken to date. A negative report from the consultant provided sufficient legitimacy to fire the director, who was replaced with a director loyal to the financial vice president.

5 *Make a direct appeal.* If managers do not ask, they seldom receive. Political activity is effective only when goals and needs are made explicit so the organization can respond. Managers should bargain aggressively and be persuasive. An assertive proposal may be accepted because other managers have no better alternatives. Moreover, an explicit proposal will often receive favourable treatment because other alternatives are ambiguous and less well defined. Effective political behaviour requires sufficient forcefulness and risk taking to at least ask for what you need to achieve desired outcomes.

The use of power, however, should not be obvious.[99] If you formally draw on your power base in a meeting by saying, 'My department has more power, so the rest of you have to do it my way', your power will be diminished. Power works best when it is used quietly. To call attention to power is to lose it. People know who has power. Explicit claims to power are not necessary and can even harm the department's cause.

If managers are perceived to be throwing their weight around or pursuing goals that are self-serving rather than beneficial to the organization, they will lose respect. On the other hand, managers must recognize the relational and political aspect of their work. It is not sufficient to be rational and technically competent. Politics is a way to reach agreement. This chapter's Bookmark describes some basic psychological principles that underlie successful political influence tactics. Managers can use this understanding to assert influence and get things done within the organization. When managers ignore political tactics, they may find themselves failing without understanding why. This is partly the reason Tim Koogle failed to accomplish a key acquisition at Yahoo!.

BRIEFCASE

As an organization manager, keep these guidelines in mind:

If conflict becomes too strong, use tactics for enhancing collaboration, including integration devices, confrontation, intergroup consultation, member rotation and superordinate goals. Select the technique that fits the organization and the conflict.

Tactics for Enhancing Collaboration

Power and political tactics are important means for getting things done within organizations. Most organizations today have at least moderate inter-unit conflict.

Have you read this book?

Against Management

BY MARTIN PARKER

Throughout this book we have talked about management as something that is inevitable and important, indeed pivotal in the life of organizations. Managers are presented as able to build a great organization, or lead an organization to ruin, depending on their capacities and their ability to select the right organization theory and design strategies. But actually, do managers really have as much power as we often imagine, and even if they do, is it desirable for the world to be 'managed'?

In this provocative and influential book, Martin Parker takes aim at the idea that perfecting management is a desirable goal. He argues that managerialism is a dogmatic ideology insisting that only markets run by professional managers can efficiently organize human interaction. In fact, the actual results of this system are often dehumanizing. He says 'organizations are getting too big to be human', they are offering an 'increasingly homogenized set of choices for consumers,' and they have constructed a world in which the artifice of brands has become more important and more valuable than the products upon which the brand logo is applied.

Parker is critical of efforts to humanize managerial capitalism, originating from within business schools. For example, he argues that the field of 'business ethics' when taught in business schools is a figleaf that covers up the need for a deeper political debate about what kind of a society we want to construct, and what types of organizations are needed in order to facilitate a more human-oriented society. In general, he believes that academia, which emphasizes the importance of a mythological 'neutrality', is less effective than civil society campaigners in identifying and rooting out the negative features of business activity.

Given the importance of organizations in many people's lives, Parker explores whether they could play a more positive, holistic role if they were stripped of their managerialist focus on market efficiency. He speculates about the possibility of 'orgunities'; organizations that would act as places of spiritual belonging and of productive enterprise. Of course, organizations are exclusive institutions with entry criteria and the ever-present possibility of enforced exit. Thus, transferring citizenship to them from the universal level of the state could restrict rather than enhance freedoms, an issue Parker somewhat skates over.

Ultimately, Parker argues for 'demanagerialization' of society, so that the normative goals of organizations would be as important as their 'efficiency', which is currently measured solely from the point of view of their success in generating profits. He calls for an expansion of grassroots, community level organizations that would meet local needs, such as for quality child care and environmentally sustainable transportation. Rather than devoting themselves to a single corporate identity, people should be encouraged to nurture our multifaceted identities, through multiple and decentred community memberships.

Parker's critique may seem radical and his solutions Utopian. It is important, however, that we keep open the possibility for alternative ways of thinking about organizations and also that we are open to criticism when organizations, stray far from their ultimate purpose, which is to serve the needs of people.

Klein, N. (2000), *No Logo: No Space, No Choice, No Jobs: Taking Aim at the Brand Bullies*, London, Flamingo.

Murphy, J. (2004), 'Managerialism Meets its Nemesis' *Organization*, 11, 315–319.

Against Management by Martin Parker, is published by Polity.

An additional approach in many organizations is to overcome conflict by stimulating cooperation and collaboration among departments to support the attainment of organizational goals. **Tactics for enhancing collaboration** include the following:

1 *Create integration devices.* As described in Chapter 3, teams, task forces and project managers who span the boundaries between departments can be used

Yahoo!

In late March of 2000, Yahoo! began negotiating to buy online auction leader eBay Inc. Tim Koogle, Yahoo!'s CEO at the time, was fully in support of the deal, believing it would enable the company to beef up its e-commerce revenues and bring needed new blood to the increasingly insular Yahoo! culture. But the deal never happened, and while Yahoo!'s fortunes flagged, eBay's revenues and net income continued to climb.

What happened? Jeffrey Mallett, Yahoo!'s president, opposed the acquisition of eBay, and he used political tactics to quash it. Koogle had always been a consensus-style manager. He believed the top leaders would debate the pros and cons of the acquisition and arrive at the best decision. In addition, he felt sure the merits of the eBay deal would ultimately win the day. But Mallett, who insiders say was already angling to take over the CEO job, began courting co-founders Jerry Yang and David Filo. Eventually, he convinced them that the eBay culture was a poor fit with Yahoo!. With Koogle outnumbered, the deal fell apart. A former Yahoo! manager called it management by persuasion.

By failing to build a coalition, Koogle allowed Mallett to control this important decision. It's only one example of several that ultimately led to Koogle being pushed out as CEO. Despite Mallett's political moves, he was passed over for the top job in favour of an outsider who board members felt could turn the struggling company around. Koogle took the decision to seek a new CEO calmly and blamed himself for not keeping a closer eye on Mallett.[100]

as integration devices. Bringing together representatives from conflicting departments in joint problem-solving teams is an effective way to enhance collaboration because representatives learn to understand each other's point of view.[101] Sometimes a full-time integrator is assigned to achieve cooperation and collaboration by meeting with members of the respective departments and exchanging information. The integrator has to understand each group's problems and must be able to move both groups toward a solution that is mutually acceptable.[102]

Teams and task forces reduce conflict and enhance cooperation because they integrate people from different departments. Integration devices can also be used to enhance cooperation between labour and management, as the example of German-based car manufacturer Volkswagen and union IG Metall demonstrates (In the *In Practice* box on the next page).

Labour–management teams, which are designed to increase worker participation and provide a cooperative model for solving union–management problems, are used at many companies throughout the world. For example in 2006 Transnet, the South African state company responsible for the country's national airline, railways and ports, set up teams with the industries' main trade unions in order to work out a restructuring plan that would meet the needs of the country, company, workers and transport users.[103]

2 *Use confrontation and negotiation.* **Confrontation** occurs when parties in conflict directly engage one another and try to work out their differences. **Negotiation** is the bargaining process that often occurs during confrontation and that enables the parties to systematically reach a solution. These techniques bring appointed representatives from the departments together to work out a serious dispute. For example, in 2006 and 2007, Chilean copper miners were engaged in disputes with their employer, Codelco, over

Volkswagen and IG Metall

Germany has risen from catastrophic defeat in the Second World War to become Europe's pre-eminent manufacturing centre. This success is built on a unique system of labour–management cooperation called codetermination in which workers are entitled to significant representation in company decision-making processes. One of the strongest partnerships has been at the automaker Volkswagen, the world's third largest automobile maker.

Like other major automakers, Volkswagen has gone through a series of highs and lows, depending on the strength of the company's product offer, as well as competitors' strategies. In contrast with other European car companies which have tended to engage in mass layoffs, VW has usually been able to agree on less radical measures with IG Metall, the major union representing most German VW workers. For example, when the company came close to bankruptcy in 1993 and 1994, workers agreed on a package of reduced salaries and short-hours working in order to save costs. Again, in 2004, as VW attempted to restructure in order to respond to heightened competition from Asian carmakers, the union was able to agree on a pay freeze in return for seven years job security.

Beginning in the 1980s, Volkswagen has acquired a number of foreign automakers, including Spain's SEAT, and Skoda from the Czech Republic. VW workers worried that their jobs would be at risk given these countries' lower labour costs. However the company and union agreed on setting up first a European Works Council including representation from workers and management across the company's European plants, and then a World Works Council including representation from the company's plants overseas, including in Latin America where VW is a major player. The international works councils have not removed all frictions between management and workers over attempts to reduce costs by moving production to lower wage countries, but Volkswagen has maintained a much higher proportion of its manufacturing capacity within Germany and other high wage European countries than is the case for many other companies.

The co-operative approach is constantly under threat, however, given globalization and pressures to lower costs. In 2009, Porsche, traditionally much less sympathetic to unions, took effective control of Volkswagen. In addition, some of the good relationships between management and union representatives were not built on an entirely honourable foundation; evidence emerged that the company had paid for prostitutes for works council members on a junket to Brazil.[104]

wages and labour conditions, which they eventually resolved after tough negotiations.[105,106]

Confrontation and negotiation involve some risk. There is no guarantee that discussions will focus on a conflict or that emotions will not get out of hand. However, if members are able to resolve the conflict on the basis of face-to-face discussions, they will find new respect for each other, and future collaboration becomes easier. The beginnings of relatively permanent attitude change are possible through direct negotiation.

Confrontation and negotiation are more likely to be successful when managers engage in a *win–win strategy.* Win–win means both sides adopt a positive attitude and strive to resolve the conflict in a way that will benefit each other.[107] If the negotiations deteriorate into a strictly win–lose strategy (each group wants to defeat the other), the confrontation will usually be ineffective. The differences between win–win and win–lose strategies of negotiation are shown in Exhibit 13.7. With a win–win strategy – which includes defining the problem as mutual, communicating openly and avoiding threats – understanding can be changed while the dispute is resolved.

EXHIBIT 13.7 Negotiating Strategies

Win–Win Strategy	Win–Lose Strategy
1. Define the conflict as a mutual problem.	1. Define the problem as a win–lose situation.
2. Pursue joint outcomes.	2. Pursue own group's outcomes.
3. Find creative agreements that satisfy both groups.	3. Force the other group into submission.
4. Be open, honest, and accurate in communicating the group's needs, goals, and proposals.	4. Be deceitful, inaccurate, and misleading in communicating the group's needs, goals, and proposals.
5. Avoid threats (to reduce the other's defensiveness).	5. Use threats (to force submission).
6. Communicate flexibility of position.	6. Communicate strong commitment (rigidity) regarding one's position.

Source: Adapted from David W. Johnson and Frank P. Johnson, *Joining Together: Group Theory and Group Skills* (Englewood Cliffs, N.J.: Prentice-Hall, 1975), 182–183.

One type of negotiation, used to resolve a disagreement between workers and management, is referred to as **collective bargaining.** The bargaining process is usually accomplished through a union and results in an agreement that specifies each party's responsibilities for the next several years, as with the contract between VW and IG Metall.

3 *Schedule intergroup consultation.* When conflict is intense and enduring, and department members are suspicious and uncooperative, top managers may intervene as third parties to help resolve the conflict or bring in third-party consultants from outside the organization.[108] This process, sometimes called *workplace mediation,* is a strong intervention to reduce conflict because it involves bringing the disputing parties together and allowing each side to present its version of the situation. The technique has been developed by such psychologists as Robert Blake, Jane Mouton and Richard Walton.[109]

Department members attend a workshop, which may last for several days, away from day-to-day work problems. This approach is similar to the organization development (OD) approach described in Chapter 11. The conflicting groups are separated, and each group is invited to discuss and make a list of its perceptions of itself and the other group. Group representatives publicly share these perceptions, and together the groups discuss the results.

Intergroup consultation can be quite demanding for everyone involved. Although it is fairly easy to have conflicting groups list perceptions and identify discrepancies, exploring their differences face-to-face and agreeing to change is more difficult. If handled correctly, these sessions can help department employees understand each other much better and lead to improved attitudes and better working relationships for years to come.

4 *Practice member rotation.* Rotation means that individuals from one department can be asked to work in another department on a temporary or permanent basis. The advantage is that individuals become submerged in the values, attitudes, problems and goals of the other department. In addition, individuals can explain the problems and goals of their original departments to their new colleagues. This enables a frank, accurate exchange of views and information. Rotation works slowly to reduce conflict but is very effective for changing the underlying attitudes and perceptions that promote conflict.[110]

5 *Create shared mission and superordinate goals.* Another strategy is for top management to create a shared mission and establish superordinate goals that require cooperation among departments.[111] As discussed in Chapter 10, organizations with strong, adaptive cultures, where employees share a larger vision for their company, are more likely to have a united, cooperative workforce. Studies have shown that when employees from different departments see that their goals are linked together, they will openly share resources and information.[112] To be effective, superordinate goals must be substantial, and employees must be granted the time and incentives to work cooperatively in pursuit of the superordinate goals rather than departmental subgoals.

Summary and Interpretation

The central message of this chapter is that conflict, power and politics are natural outcomes of organizing. Differences in goals, backgrounds and tasks are necessary for organizational excellence, but these differences can throw groups into conflict. Managers use power and politics to manage and resolve conflict. Two views of organization were presented. The rational model of organization assumes that organizations have specific goals and that problems can be logically solved. The other view, the political model of organization, is the basis for much of the chapter. This view assumes that the goals of an organization are not specific or agreed upon. Departments have different values and interests, so managers come into conflict. Decisions are made on the basis of power and political influence. Bargaining, negotiation, persuasion and coalition building decide outcomes.

The chapter also discussed the vertical and horizontal sources of power. Vertical sources of power include formal position, resources, control of decision premises and network centrality. In general, managers at the top of the organizational hierarchy have more power than people at lower levels. However, positions all along the hierarchy can be designed to increase the power of employees. As organizations face increased competition and environmental uncertainty, top executives are finding that increasing the power of middle managers and lower-level employees can help the organization be more competitive. Research into horizontal power processes has revealed that certain characteristics make some departments more powerful than others. Such factors as dependency, resources and nonsubstitutability determine the influence of departments.

Managers can use political tactics such as coalition building, expanded networks and control of decision premises. Tactics for enhancing collaboration include integration devices, confrontation and negotiation, intergroup consultation, member rotation and shared mission and superordinate goals.

KEY CONCEPTS

authority
centrality
collective bargaining
competition
confrontation
coping with uncertainty
decision premises
dependency
domains of political activity
financial resources
intergroup conflict
labour–management teams
negotiation
network centrality
nonsubstitutability
organizational politics
political model
political tactics for using power
power
power sources
rational model
sources of intergroup conflict
strategic contingencies
tactics for enhancing collaboration
tactics for increasing power

Discussion Questions

1 Give an example from your personal experience of how differences in tasks, personal background and training lead to conflict among groups. How might task interdependence have influenced that conflict?

2 A noted expert on organizations said that some conflict is beneficial to organizations. Discuss.

3 In a rapidly changing organization, are decisions more likely to be made using the rational or political model of organization? Discuss.

4 What is the difference between power and authority? Is it possible for a person to have formal authority but no real power? Discuss.

5 Discuss ways in which a department at an insurance company might help the organization cope with the increased power of large hospital systems by obtaining prior information, prevention or absorption.

6 In Exhibit 13.4, R&D has greater power in company B than in the other firms. Discuss possible strategic contingencies that give R&D greater power in this firm.

7 State University X receives 90 per cent of its financial resources from the state and is overcrowded with students. It is trying to pass regulations to limit student enrollment. Private University Y receives 90 per cent of its income from student tuition and has barely enough students to make ends meet. It is actively recruiting students for next year. In which university will students have greater power? What implications will this have for professors and administrators? Discuss.

8 A bookkeeper at HealthSouth Corp., which is currently embroiled in a financial scandal, tried for several years to expose fraud in the organization's accounting department, but he couldn't get anyone to pay attention to his claims. How would you evaluate this employee's power? What might he have done to increase his power and call notice to the ethical and legal problems at the firm?

9 The engineering college at a major university brings in three times as many government research dollars as does the rest of the university combined. Engineering appears wealthy and has many professors on full-time research status. Yet, when internal research funds are allocated, engineering gets a larger share of the money, even though it already has substantial external research funds. Why would this happen?

10 Which do you believe would have a greater long-term impact on changing employee attitudes toward increased collaboration – intergroup consultation or confrontation and negotiation? Discuss.

Chapter 13 Workbook How Do You Handle Conflict?

Think of some disagreements you have had with a friend, relative, manager or co-worker. Then indicate how frequently you engage in each of the following behaviours. There are no right or wrong answers. Respond to all items using the following scale from 1 to 7:

Scale

Always	Very often	Often	Sometimes	Seldom	Very seldom	Never
1	2	3	4	5	6	7

_____ 1 I blend my ideas to create new alternatives for resolving a disagreement.
_____ 2 I shy away from topics that are sources of disputes.
_____ 3 I make my opinion known in a disagreement.
_____ 4 I suggest solutions that combine a variety of viewpoints.
_____ 5 I steer clear of disagreeable situations.
_____ 6 I give in a little on my ideas when the other person also gives in.
_____ 7 I avoid the other person when I suspect that he or she wants to discuss a disagreement.
_____ 8 I integrate arguments into a new solution from the issues raised in a dispute.
_____ 9 I will go 50–50 to reach a settlement.
_____ 10 I raise my voice when I'm trying to get the other person to accept my position.

_____ 11 I offer creative solutions in discussions of disagreements.
_____ 12 I keep quiet about my views in order to avoid disagreements.
_____ 13 I give in if the other person will meet me halfway.
_____ 14 I downplay the importance of a disagreement.
_____ 15 I reduce disagreements by making them seem insignificant.
_____ 16 I meet the other person at a midpoint in our differences.
_____ 17 I assert my opinion forcefully.
_____ 18 I dominate arguments until the other person understands my position.
_____ 19 I suggest we work together to create solutions to disagreements.
_____ 20 I try to use the other person's ideas to generate solutions to problems.
_____ 21 I offer tradeoffs to reach solutions in disagreements.
_____ 22 I argue insistently for my stance.
_____ 23 I withdraw when the other person confronts me about a controversial issue.
_____ 24 I sidestep disagreements when they arise.
_____ 25 I try to smooth over disagreements by making them appear unimportant.
_____ 26 I insist my position be accepted during a disagreement with the other person.
_____ 27 I make our differences seem less serious.
_____ 28 I hold my tongue rather than argue with the other person.
_____ 29 I ease conflict by claiming our differences are trivial.
_____ 30 I stand firm in expressing my viewpoints during a disagreement.

Scoring and Interpretation: Three categories of conflict-handling strategies are measured in this instrument: solution oriented, nonconfrontational and control. By comparing your scores on the following three scales, you can see which of the three is your preferred conflict-handling strategy.

To calculate your three scores, add the individual scores for the items and divide by the number of items measuring the strategy. Then subtract each of the three mean scores from seven.

Solution oriented: Items 1, 4, 6, 8, 9, 11, 13, 16, 19, 20, 21 (total = 11)

Nonconfrontational: Items 2, 5, 7, 12, 14, 15, 23, 24, 25, 27, 28, 29 (total = 12)

Control: Items 3, 10, 17, 18, 22, 26, 30 (total = 7)

Solution-oriented strategies tend to focus on the problem rather than on the individuals involved. Solutions reached are often mutually beneficial, with neither party defining himself or herself as the winner and the other party as the loser.

Nonconfrontational strategies tend to focus on avoiding the conflict by either avoiding the other party or by simply allowing the other party to have his or her way. These strategies are used when there is more concern with avoiding a confrontation than with the actual outcome of the problem situation.

Control strategies tend to focus on winning or achieving one's goals without regard for the other party's needs or desires. Individuals using these strategies often rely on rules and regulations in order to win the battle.

Questions

1 Which strategy do you find easiest to use? Most difficult? Which do you use more often?
2 How would your answers have differed if the other person was a friend, family member or co-worker?
3 What is it about the conflict situation or strategy that tells you which strategy to use in dealing with a conflict situation?

From 'How Do You Handle Conflict?' in Robert E. Quinn et al., *Becoming a Master Manager* (New York: Wiley, 1990), 221–223.

CASE FOR ANALYSIS

Closing Tuatech Web Design

By Craig Prichard, *Department of Management, Massey University, Palmerston North, Aotearoa/New Zealand*

Tuatech is a software company based in Auckland, New Zealand, with a global reputation in computer graphics. The firm was founded in the mid-1990s by two software engineers and a technology manager. The technology manager brought with him to the new firm a successful website design and development practice. In Tuatech's early years the web design business was highly profitable and provided much of the early capital for software development. Since then the website design and hosting business has lost ground to larger and more specialized web agencies. The company's software products have, meanwhile, received international acclaim and significant licensing contracts have been signed with global software houses. In mid-2006 the former technology manager, who had overseen the company's operations, including its web design office, sold his share of the business to the two other directors and retired. In response the directors promoted the company's web sales person to the post of web design unit manager. This new manager struggled to adjust to his new role. He continued to book work for the design team but conflicts erupted between himself and some members of the unit's six staff (four developers, a graphic designer and a part-time trainer). The performance of the web design group plummeted. The manager resigned abruptly in the midst of these difficulties. Realizing that they were out of their depth, the company's two directors successfully advertised and appointed both a new manager for the web design business, Radha Singh, and a new general manager for the firm, Sam Little. Both new managers started work on the same day.

Sam worked previously as a technology services manager for a large public sector organization. He was determined to make a success of his work with the much smaller but highly regarded Tuatech. Before he started work he developed, for his own use, an analysis and plans for the firm that included notes on how he might deal with the web design unit. Sam identified significant weaknesses in the performance of the design group – for which Radha was to become responsible. In the first two weeks on the job he put a lot of time into getting to know and supporting Radha. He then introduced Radha to the owners of another web design company in the local area, Mana Web Design, whom he knew was looking for new staff. Sam also discussed whether Mana Web Design would be able to take on any new work that Tuatech's web design office received – the firm was enthusiastic. Two weeks later Sam met with Tuatech's two directors for their regular monthly meeting. At that meeting Sam announced that Radha had resigned her position as manager of the firm's web design studio and taken a position with Mana Web Design. The directors were surprised.

'Really, she's gone?' said Brendon.

'Yes, unfortunately. She left yesterday', replied Sam.

'Oh dear! Just a month in the job', said Peter, Tuatech's other director. 'Those guys can be trouble. Is Haiden's up to his old tricks then?'

'It's complicated', said Sam. 'Gender differences, cultural background. As you know Radha's a recent migrant. She struggled with some of our less endearing local customs. She tried to get on with the staff, they might have overwhelmed her a bit; I offered some ideas but didn't want to meddle too much.'

Brendon interrupted: 'What concerns me right now are all these complaints from customers the web group has accumulating. Everything is running late, they have promised a heap and delivered next to nothing, and do we also have some cash flow problems as well?'

'Yes', said Sam. 'There's some urgency there.' Sam followed up: 'I've done some analysis using a systems approach I picked up a little while back. We seem to have three options: battle through, appoint another manager or shut the unit down. I'd like to run over the analysis and then perhaps we could agree a final decision late next week. In the meantime I need to meet the design group, let them know we are considering options, and get their input – they might have some good ideas! Also I'm going to get some advice

A number of details of the case have been changed to protect both the identity of the firm and those involved.

from a local HR consultant about restructuring and redundancy – just so that we don't get into hot water.'

Under New Zealand employment law any efforts by managers or owners to make changes to employees' jobs and work arrangements must be discussed with those potentially affected by these changes BEFORE formal decisions are made. Sam's move to discuss the options, but not the final decision, with the directors, and then to hold formal meetings with employees over the issue is in line with these provisions. After his meeting with the directors Sam sent individual letters about the first meeting to all the members of the web design team. Present at the Monday meeting were the developers (Haiden, Chandra, Jin and Reese), the graphic artist (Jen) and the trainer (Georgia). Sam took along Janine, the directors' secretary, to take notes. When he and Janine entered the room the design staff were sitting in silence.

Haiden suddenly stood up smiling. 'And here comes our new boss', he said. 'Can we have a big round of applause for Sam, the savoir of Tuatech web design and development, hip hip hooray!' The design team turned and watched Sam and Janine walk toward them and sit at the large table around which they had gathered.

'Thanks Haiden', said Sam, unfazed at the sarcasm. 'I'll get straight to it.'

Sam told the group that there had been a significant decline in the number of new web design and support customers and a reduction in the number of new initiatives from existing customers. In response the directors were reluctant to continue financing the deficit in this operation and were considering making positions in the web services group redundant. However the directors were very keen to hear any options and suggestions the web group could table.

Each of the meetings with the web group was difficult and heated at times as tempers flared. The closure process took 18 months to run its course and concluded in mid-2008 with two redundancies. During that period three of the web design team moved to Mana Web Design where they work with Radha as their manager.

Case Questions

1. What were the reasons that Tuatech's top management decided to shut down its Web design unit?
2. Do you think the decision to shut down the unit was handled well?
3. Radha's departure from Tuatech seems to have been a pivotal moment. Why did Tuatech's Web design unit perform poorly while Radha managed it, while she seemed to be successful in the same position at Manha Web Design?
4. Are there lessons for Tuatech in this case study that it should apply to other departments within the company?

CASE FOR ANALYSIS

Selecting a New Dean for a University Faculty

By Tuomo Peltonen, *University of Oulu*

Veijo Karhila is sitting in his professorial office. He has to make a difficult decision whether to run for the dean of the faculty of economics at the Lakeside University. Things have escalated quickly since his colleague Kari Miettinen was chosen as the new vice-rector for the whole university. Miettinen had acted as the dean of the faculty for many years and now has to step down because it is not acceptable to hold a double position in the university hierarchy. In fact, Miettinen has been the only dean the faculty has had since its inauguration about ten years ago. He was recently elected for another three-year post as the other professors were reluctant to take the task, fearing the responsibilities it carries with it. But now the situation has changed. Veijo Karhila knows that he and the rest of the marketing department will not accept Matti Virtanen, a colleague from economics, to be selected as the new dean. Yet, running for the post means that he has to engage with the other groups of the faculty to secure the required support. Becoming a dean would mean a farewell to the life of a regular department professor and a new challenge in an administrative task. At the same time he knows that, in reality, as the head of the largest department he has no other option but to run for the leadership of the faculty.

Lakeside is a relatively large university in the middle of Finland. It is governed in the similar way as all the other Finnish universities, namely by a combination of bureaucracy and representative democracy. The university is composed of faculties, which all have a faculty council that is formally charged with making most of the administrative decisions. Some operative issues such as the grading of dissertations are handled at the departmental level. In addition, there is a university board that decides on the overall strategy of the organization. The university board is chaired by the rector of the university, who is normally a tenured professor. Typical for the Finnish system is the absence of professional managers in the governing bodies. The faculty council consists of representatives of different employee groups, who participate as elected officials in the decision-making. Thus, for example the dean of the faculty, one of the tenured professors, works in a position of trust rather than in a dedicated managerial position. Faculty council consists of three segments representing three different personnel groups: professors, other faculty staff and students. Members are elected democratically among each group represented in the council. Professors have the biggest single number of seats in each council but they do not have the majority, meaning that for controversial issues there is a need to build coalitions across three representative groups.

The faculty of economics is the smallest of the five faculties within the Lakeside University. It is organized into four departments: economics, accounting, management and marketing. Professor of economics Kari Miettinen has been the head of the faculty for some ten years. He is also the oldest of the tenured professors. In the recent years, the economics department has been suffering from a loss of students at the same time as accounting and marketing have grown in size. Marketing makes up almost the half of the faculty in terms of number of staff. The management department is a more fragmented unit, where several miniature disciplines are organized into an administrative whole. There is an informal division between different disciplines that reflects their methodological and scientific preferences: economics, accounting and finance, all based on quantitative research approaches, reside in the second floor whereas more qualitatively oriented marketing and management occupy the third floor. Yet at the same time there are differences between individual subject areas within each floor that in turn illustrate substantial divergences in orientations towards research and teaching. Marketing and accounting are for example more practice-oriented than economics, which tends to focus on broader macroeconomic issues and methodology. However, despite these divides the faculty was enjoying a relatively stable working climate. Difficult issues were normally negotiated before they were allowed to escalate into visible conflicts. The dean exerted his leadership in questions that required conciliation between diverging interests.

Things started to roll when Dean Kari Miettinen was chosen as the vice-rector of university. He had to step down from the office of the faculty dean, leaving the rest of the staff a couple of weeks to fill the position. Quite soon, Matti Virtanen, another professor from economics, announced his willingness to run for deanship. Virtanen was known to be close to Dean Miettinen, both professionally and socially. This announcement was met with a response from the marketing department that they would not accept a situation where both vice-rector, still influential in his new role, and the new dean, would represent economics and the quantitative disciplines. Professors from the management department were also reluctant to accept Virtanen as the new dean, fearing that a bias in decision-making would result.

However, despite the opposition from the marketing discipline, Veijo Karhila, the head of the marketing department, was not keen to run for deanship because of his other ongoing projects and commitments. At the same time it was he who would be the obvious counter-candidate for Virtanen. It took some time for Karhila to make up his mind about the candidacy. As he hesitated, his colleagues at the management department made an effort to try and convince him that his candidacy was needed. Only after one of the professors indicated that unless Karhila stands for office, he will be running instead, Karhila made up his mind and announced that he will be running for deanship.

Important decisions were normally primed before the faculty council sessions in an informal meeting of professors. The routine was to form a consensus around an issue that was then pursued in the formal council sessions so as to avoid unnecessary conflict. This time there was no consensus in the meeting. Both Matti Virtanen and Veijo Karhila insisted on staying as candidates for the post. They both assured everyone that they had the needed support from the faculty council members. The meeting ended without any solution to the competition between the rival candidates and their support groups. The atmosphere was becoming increasingly tense as the faculty began dividing into two opposing camps each supporting the different agenda of each of the candidates.

At this point, the coalition behind Veijo Karhila activated. Virtanen had a group of supporters in the faculty council. They would probably vote for him. However, there were a number of uncertain members, including professors and students who had not decided on whom to vote. Management department professors, keen to support the runner from the marketing department, started lobbying individual council members. Head of management department, who had been relatively neutral in many other issues, propagated openly for Karhila. Some hesitating professors were persuaded to support Karhila. The main argument was that selecting Virtanen would lead to a power imbalance in favour of a small clique that does not represent the collective will of the faculty.

It soon became evident that the students would hold the balance of power in the selection. Student members come from different disciplines but they also represent the more general student voice in matters related to teaching and the treatment of students by the staff. Some of the students were hesitant about who to promote. They have been satisfied with the current dean who was seen to be easy to access. Students would have liked to see the same trend to continue also during the following dean. In this sense, Virtanen would be an attractive candidate. Karhila, instead, was viewed as somewhat less student-friendly although his accomplishments in the development of the faculty were widely appreciated.

With Karhila being limited in his negotiating power with the students, a management department professor turned directly to one of the student members of the council he knew. The student was in a key position as an active member of the student union. The management department professor expressed the fears among the faculty that the selection of Virtanen would mean a fracture in the harmonious relations between the different departments within the faculty. Karhila would bring stability. In addition to talking directly to a student, supporters of Karhila asked a former colleague of theirs to make an additional plead to the student. The former colleague and the key student were kinsfolk.

There was also a series of manoeuvres on the other side. Virtanen had contacted several council members to talk about his potential support in case of a ballot. He was especially active among some of the members representing the non-professorial staff in the second group. The group consisted of lecturers and administrative faculty members. Many of these were in support of Virtanen who they viewed as more impartial than Karhila who was in the eyes of many a slightly authoritarian leader. Non-professorial staff work under the supervision of professors, and it is the nature of this hierarchical relationship that affects the way in which professors are evaluated as foremen. Virtanen and his supporters wanted to see faculty being run on the basis of jointly agreed rules and regulations rather than on the grounds of the whims of the few professors each pursuing their own narrow academic and disciplinary agenda. There were also concerns about the marketing department taking over other departments on the issues related to the contents of research and teaching as well as in how academic work was to be organized in the faculty. Especially some older lecturers were afraid of the possible restructurings that would make them obsolete as new degree programmes would be introduced to replace the traditional curricula.

Karhila and his coalition, instead, perceived Virtanen and his supporters as defenders of their own vulnerable position. They thought that the opposing group was on the losing side as the faculty was evolving from an economics department into a modern business school. In their eyes, the rival group just wanted to use bureaucratic rules and regulations to delay the reforms that were in any way necessary in the near future. There was for example a widespread belief that Virtanen was running for deanship to be able to retreat from the departmental or operative problems looming ahead. The group itself wanted to emphasize the freedom of academic research in the face of what was seen as an intensifying bureaucratisation of university life. Some also perceived the tendency to lean on the formal administrative principles as an attempt to control those academics that are active in consulting, management education and other extra-departmental tasks.

Then the council meeting day came. There was a lot of tension in the air as the two candidates presented themselves. Both had prepared a short formal programme speech outlining how they would develop faculty. Brief discussion was followed by a ballot. The votes were counted and with a slight surprise in his face, the administrative clerk announced the result. Karhila had received eight votes and Virtanen five, meaning that Karhila was elected as the new dean of the faculty. As the meeting dissembled, many open questions were left in the air. The supporters of Virtanen were baffled with the result. They noticed that some of the regular student members were missing and deputy members had been called to participate in the meeting. Perhaps there was a secret conspiracy between the students and the coalition that had turned the result in the favour of Karhila. Suspicions of foul play abound. Similarly, the supporters of the new dean reflected later on the events of the day, sharing their feelings about the ideas of the opposing camp. The coalition was particularly disoriented about the way in which Virtanen displayed his eagerness to move from a faculty job to a full-time administrative position. This confirmed to them the belief that Virtanen was not defending the interests of the faculty as a whole. They were convinced that the right candidate had won.

As the Election Day came to a close, many were wondering about what exactly had happened during the preceding weeks. How was it possible that a smallish university unit was suddenly transformed into a battleground between opposing viewpoints and groups? And how were the participants of this political drama were to go on in their daily work now as the illusion of unity was so severely broken? Nobody knew just how the workplace would function after the dust settled and the life at the faculty would return to business as usual. One thing was though sure: these divides would affect the relations between individual members of the faculty community for years to come.

Case Questions

1. How would you explain the emergence of divides in the case organization? What were the background social and cultural structures accounting for the surfacing of different interest groups within the faculty?
2. What kinds of political tactics did the different interest groups pursue in order to influence faculty council decision-making? How would you describe the effectiveness of various tactics used?

Notes

1. Amit Roy Choudhury, ' Lessons from the cultural divide', *Business Times Singapore*, 11 October 2008; Karlin Lillington 'Learning about Lenovo', *Irish Times*, 25 July 2008; Rick Newman Lenovo's Great Leap, *U.S. News & World Report* October 15, 2007; Jane Spencer and Loretta Chao, 'Lenovo goes global, with bumps', *The Wall Street Journal Asia*, 5 November 2008; 'The IBM/ Lenovo Deal: Victory For China?', *Knowledge@Wharton*, accessed at http://knowledge.wharton.upenn.edu/ article.cfm?articleid=1106 on January 5, 2009; Rebecca Buckman, 'Lenovo Gets Its Yin-Yang On; The new face of globalism means having an office everywhere and nowhere', *Forbes*, 22 December 2008; Venkatesha Babu, 'Lenovo is at a Tipping Point', Business Today, 22 April 2007; Elaine Chan, 'Chen crosses cultures to make Lenovo global', *South China Morning Post*, 21 April 2008.

2. Lee G. Bolman and Terrence E. Deal, *Reframing Organizations: Artistry, Choice and Leadership* (San Francisco: Jossey-Bass, 1991).
3. Paul M. Terry, 'Conflict Management', *The Journal of Leadership Studies* 3, no. 2 (1996), 3–21; and Kathleen M. Eisenhardt, Jean L. Kahwajy and L. J. Bourgeois III, 'How Management Teams Can Have a Good Fight', *Harvard Business Review* (July–August 1997), 77–85.
4. Clayton T. Alderfer and Ken K. Smith, 'Studying Intergroup Relations Imbedded in Organizations', *Administrative Science Quarterly* 27 (1982), 35–65.
5. Muzafer Sherif, 'Experiments in Group Conflict', *Scientific American* 195 (1956), 54–58; and Edgar H. Schein *organizational Psychology*, 3d ed. (Englewood Cliffs, N.J.: Prentice-Hall, 1980).
6. M. Afzalur Rahim, 'A Strategy for Managing Conflict in Complex Organizations', *Human Relations* 38 (1985), 81–89; Kenneth Thomas, 'Conflict and Conflict Management', in M.D. Dunnette, ed., *Handbook of Industrial and Organizational Psychology* (Chicago, Ill.: Rand McNally, 1976); and Stuart M. Schmidt and Thomas A. Kochan, 'Conflict: Toward Conceptual Clarity', *Administrative Science Quarterly* 13 (1972), 359–370.
7. L. David Brown, 'Managing Conflict among Groups', in David A. Kolb, Irwin M. Rubin and James M. McIntyre, eds. *Organizational Psychology: A Book of Readings* (Englewood Cliffs, N.J.: Prentice-Hall, 1979), 377–389; and Robert W. Ruekert and Orville C. Walker, Jr., 'Interactions between Marketing and R&D Departments in Implementing Different Business Strategies', *Strategic Management Journal* 8 (1987), 233–248.
8. Mike Esterl, 'Deutsche Telekom, Union Clash', *Wall Street Journal*, September 12, 2008.
9. Giles Parkinson, 'Is Krispy getting Kremed?', *Business Spectator*, 23 September 2008.
10. Nanette Byrnes, with Mike McNamee, Ronald Grover, Joann Muller and Andrew Park, 'Auditing Here, Consulting Over There', *BusinessWeek* (April 8, 2002), 34–36.
11. Thomas A. Kochan, George P. Huber and L. L. Cummings, 'Determinants of Intraorganizational Conflict in Collective Bargaining in the Public Sector', *Administrative Science Quarterly* 20 (1975), 10–23.
12. Victoria L. Crittenden, Lorraine R. Gardiner and Antonie Stam, 'Reducing Conflict between Marketing and Manufacturing', *Industrial Marketing Management* 22 (1993), 299–309; and Benson S. Shapiro, 'Can Marketing and Manufacturing Coexist?' *Harvard Business Review* 55 (September–October 1977), 104–114.
13. Peter Wells, 'Finding Nano: the significance of Tata's long-awaited one lakh car', *Automotive World*, 15 January 2008; Hiroshi Kotani, 'Tata's Nano raises hopes, eyebrows', *Nikkei Weekly*, 21 January 2008.
14. Eric H. Neilsen, 'Understanding and Managing Intergroup Conflict', in Jay W. Lorsch and Paul R. Lawrence, eds., *Managing Group and Intergroup Relations* (Homewood, Ill.: Irwin and Dorsey, 1972), 329–343; and Richard E. Walton and John M. Dutton, 'The Management of Interdepartmental Conflict: A Model and Review', *Administrative Science Quarterly* 14 (1969), 73–84.
15. Jay W. Lorsch, 'Introduction to the Structural Design of Organizations', in Gene W. Dalton, Paul R. Lawrence and Jay W. Lorsch, eds. *organization Structure and Design* (Homewood, Ill.: Irwin and Dorsey, 1970), 5.
16. Guidant went through several name changes since being formed, originally Cardiac Pacemakers Inc., then Advanced Cardiovascular Systems, and finally Guidant, now part of Boston Scientific. We have used Guidant throughout for the sake of simplicity.
17. 'FDA Says Guidant Defi brillator Failure Rate Higher Than Reported', *American Health Line*, 23 June 2006; Barry Meier, Maker of Heart Device Kept Flaw From Doctors, *The New York Times*, 24 May 2005; 'Boston Scientific Posts $4.26 Billion Loss', *The New York Times*, July 28, 2006; Barry Meier, 'Inquiry Arranged by Guidant May Aid Lawsuits and Critics', *The New York Times*, 22 March 2006.
18. James D. Thompson, *organizations in Action* (New York: McGraw-Hill, 1967), 54–56.
19. Walton and Dutton, 'The Management of Interdepartmental Conflict'.
20. Joseph McCann and Jay R. Galbraith, 'Interdepartmental Relations', in Paul C. Nystrom and William H. Starbuck, eds., *Handbook of Organizational Design*, vol. 2 (New York: Oxford University Press, 1981), 60–84.
21. Roderick M. Cramer, 'Intergroup Relations and Organizational Dilemmas: The Role of Categorization Processes', in L. L. Cummings and Barry M. Staw, eds., *Research in Organizational Behavior*, vol. 13 (New York: JAI Press, 1991), 191–228; Neilsen, 'Understanding and Managing Intergroup Conflict', and Louis R. Pondy, 'Organizational Conflict: Concepts and Models', *Administrative Science Quarterly* 12 (1968), 296–320.
22. Jeffrey Pfeffer, *Power in Organizations* (Marshfield, Mass.: Pitman, 1981).
23. Alan Deutschman, 'The Mind of Jeff Bezos', *Fast Company* (August 2004), 53–58.
24. Robert A. Dahl, 'The Concept of Power', *Behavioral Science* 2 (1957), 201–215.
25. W. Graham Astley and Paramijit S. Sachdeva, 'Structural Sources of Intraorganizational Power: A Theoretical Synthesis', *Academy of Management Review* 9 (1984), 104–113; Abraham Kaplan, 'Power in Perspective', in Robert L. Kahn and Elise Boulding, eds., *Power and Conflict in Organizations* (London: Tavistock, 1964), 11–32.
26. Gerald R. Salancik and Jeffrey Pfeffer, 'The Bases and Use of Power in Organizational Decision-Making: The Case of the University', *Administrative Science Quarterly* 19 (1974), 453–473.
27. Richard M. Emerson, 'Power-Dependence Relations', *American Sociological Review* 27 (1962), 31–41.
28. Rosabeth Moss Kanter, 'Power Failure in Management Circuits', *Harvard Business Review* (July–August 1979), 65–75.
29. Hughes under Sven's shadow as he tries to overcome Manchester City 'hysteria', 'Guardian Unlimited', 26

December 2008; Robert Millward, 'Reversal of fortunes; Manchester City is sliding toward relegation as Villa rebounds', *The Hamilton Spectator*, 26 December 2008; Angus Wright, 'Romanov 'reaping what he has sown' as Rober turns down post', *The Scotsman*, 29 June 2008.

30. Sam Walker, 'On Sports: Meet the Micro Manager', *The Wall Street Journal* (July 11, 2003), W12.
31. Examples are Robert Greene and Joost Elffers, *The 48 Laws of Power* (New York: Viking, 1999); Jeffrey J. Fox, *How to Become CEO* (New York: Hyperion, 1999).
32. John R. P. French, Jr. and Bertram Raven, 'The Bases of Social Power', in *Group Dynamics*, D. Cartwright and A. F. Zander, eds. (Evanston, Ill.: Row Peterson, 1960), 607–623.
33. Ran Lachman, 'Power from What? A Reexamination of Its Relationships with Structural Conditions', *Administrative Science Quarterly* 34 (1989), 231–251; and Daniel J. Brass, 'Being in the Right Place: A Structural Analysis of Individual Influence in an Organization', *Administrative Science Quarterly* 29 (1984), 518–539.
34. Innovator Profiles – Takeshi Uchiyamada', *EE Times*, 28 October 2005, accessed at http://www.eetimes.com/disruption/profiles/uchiyamada.jhtml on January 5, 2009.
35. 'Leading a global revolution', *New Zealand Herald*, 3 November 2007; 'Toyota engineers reflect as Prius approaches 10th birthday', *The Japan Times*, 22 May 2007.
36. A. J. Grimes, 'Authority, Power, Influence and Social Control: A Theoretical Synthesis', *Academy of Management Review* 3 (1978), 724–735.
37. Astley and Sachdeva, 'Structural Sources of Intraorganizational Power'.
38. Jeffrey Pfeffer, *Managing with Power: Politics and Influence in Organizations* (Boston, Mass.: Harvard Business School Press, 1992).
39. Robert L. Peabody, 'Perceptions of Organizational Authority', *Administrative Science Quarterly* 6 (1962), 479.
40. Corporate Jet Market Forecasted to Double in 10 Years, *Maeil Business Newspaper*, 22 July 2008.
41. Stephen Foley, 'The new masters of the universe', *The Independent*, 26 February 2007; Siobhan Kennedy, 'Ex-Citigroup boss tells of "smear campaign"', *The Times*, 8 November 2007; Dominic Rushe, 'Money honey brings down bank high-flyer', *The Sunday Times*, 28 January 2007; 'Citigroup Announces Departure of Head of Global Wealth Management Division', *M2 Presswire,* 23 January 2007.
42. Richard S. Blackburn, 'Lower Participant Power: Toward a Conceptual Integration', *Academy of Management Review* 6 (1981), 127–131.
43. 'On the right road with safety focus', *National Post*, 21 July 2008; the safe choice; 'Bison Transport is not only one of Canada's Best Managed Companies, but also the nation's safest fleet', *Canadian Transportation and Logistics*, 1 April 2008.
44. Frederick Yeung, 'PCCW links executive bonuses to share price Incentive seeks to end years of underperformance', *South China Morning Post*, 1 June 2007; '$1.9bn plan to take PCCW private', *Financial Times,* 4 November 2008.
45. David Teather, 'What credit crunch? City bankers receive pounds 13bn bonuses this year', *The Guardian*, 26 May 2008; Mark Milner, 'Brown and City regulator clamp down on bonuses', *The Guardian*, 14 October 2008.
46. Pfeffer, *Power in Organizations.*
47. Erik W. Larson and Jonathan B. King, 'The Systemic Distortion of Information: An Ongoing Challenge to Management', *Organizational Dynamics* 24, no. 3 (Winter 1996), 49–61; and Thomas H. Davenport, Robert G. Eccles and Laurence Prusak, 'Information Politics', *Sloan Management Review* (Fall 1992), 53–65.
48. Andrew M. Pettigrew, *The Politics of Organizational Decision-Making* (London: Tavistock, 1973).
49. 'A chronology of events in the Conrad Black fraud case', *The Canadian Press*, 3 March 2008; Stephen Foley, 'Lord Fraud: Conrad Black faces jail after being convicted on four counts of fraud and obstruction', *Belfast Telegraph*, 14 July 2007.
50. Robert Frank and Elena Cherney, 'Paper Tigers; Lord Black's Board: A-List Cast Played Acquiescent Role', *The Wall Street Journal* (September 27, 2004), A1.
51. Lorne Manly and Andrew Ross Sorkin, 'At Sony, Diplomacy Trumps Technology', *The New York Times* (March 8, 2005), http://www.nytimes.com.
52. Mark Hunter, 'Where women want to work', *The Times*, 8 October 2008; Carol Lewis, 'Life's all about making connections', *The Times,* 4 October 2006; Roland Gribben, 'Sisters are doing it for themselves, *The Daily Telegraph,* 6 September 2007.
53. Andrew Higgins, 'Cartoon puts Danish firms on the spot – Hit by Muslim fury, businesses weigh sales against values', *The Wall Street Journal Europe*, 14 February 2006; 'Arla Products Back In Saudi Stores After Boycott Lifted', *Dow Jones International News*, 6 April 2006; 'Arla Foods and the Cartoon Crisis', Richard Ivey Business School Case Study 9B08M005, 13 February 2008; 'When markets melt away – Consumer boycotts', *The Economist,*11 February 2006; Martin Burlund, 'Denmark's Arla yet to see Prophet cartoon boycott', *Reuters News*, 4 March 2008.
54. Astley and Sachdeva, 'Structural Sources of Intraorganizational Power'; and Noel M. Tichy and Charles Fombrun, 'Network Analysis in Organizational Settings', *Human Relations* 32 (1979), 923–965.
55. Aoife White, 'Fortis falls hard after trying to fly too high', *Associated Press Newswires*, 29 September 2008; Clive Horwood, 'Board stupid', *Euromoney*, 1 February 2008; Ruth Sunderland, 'Inside the minds of men who want to get rich quick', *The Observer*, 21 December 2008.
56. Rebecca Buckman, 'Lenovo Gets Its Yin-Yang On; The new face of globalism means having an office everywhere and Nowhere', *Forbes*, 22 December 2008.
57. Charles Perrow, 'Departmental Power and Perspective in Industrial Firms,' in Mayer N. Zald, ed., *Power in Organizations* (Nashville, Tenn.: Vanderbilt University Press, 1970), 59–89.

58. D. J. Hickson, C. R. Hinings, C. A. Lee, R. E. Schneck and J. M. Pennings, 'A Strategic Contingencies Theory of Intraorganizational Power', *Administrative Science Quarterly* 16 (1971), 216–229; and Gerald R. Salancik and Jeffrey Pfeffer, 'Who Gets Power – and How They Hold onto It: A Strategic-Contingency Model of Power', *Organizational Dynamics* (Winter 1977), 3–21.
59. Pfeffer, *Managing with Power*; Salancik and Pfeffer, 'Who Gets Power'; C. R. Hinings, D. J. Hickson, J. M. Pennings and R. E. Schneck, 'Structural Conditions of Intraorganizational Power', *Administrative Science Quarterly* 19 (1974), 22–44.
60. Carol Stoak Saunders, 'The Strategic Contingencies Theory of Power: Multiple Perspectives', *Journal of Management Studies* 27 (1990), 1–18; Warren Boeker, 'The Development and Institutionalization of Sub-Unit Power in Organizations', *Administrative Science Quarterly* 34 (1989), 388–510; and Irit Cohen and Ran Lachman, 'The Generality of the Strategic Contingencies Approach to Sub-Unit Power', *Organizational Studies* 9 (1988), 371–391.
61. Emerson, 'Power-Dependence Relations'.
62. Pfeffer, *Managing with Power*.
63. Teddy Ng, 'University denies giving in to students', *The Standard*, 25 February 2004; Linda Yeung, 'Students consulted in Chinese U rejig', *South China Morning Post*, 7 February 2004; Linda Yeung, 'Chinese U minnows face mauling under strict budget constraints', *South China Morning Post*, 17 January 2004; May Chan, 'CUHK students want head to stand down', *South China Morning Post*, 21 February 2004; Marek Kwiek (2006) 'Academic Entrepreneurship vs. Changing Governance and Institutional Management Structures at European Universities' (a theme paper for the European Commission EUEREK project).
64. Salancik and Pfeffer, 'Bases and Use of Power in Organizational Decision-Making', 470.
65. Hickson et al., 'A Strategic Contingencies Theory'.
66. Pettigrew, *The Politics of Organizational Decision-Making*.
67. Hickson et al., 'A Strategic Contingencies Theory'.
68. Ibid.
69. Laton McCartney, 'Prescription for Disaster', *CIO Insight*,13 November 2006.
70. Nic Fleming, 'Bill for hi-tech NHS soars to £20 billion', *Daily Telegraph*, 12 October 2004.
71. Allyson M Pollock (2005), *NHS Plc: The Privatisation of Our Health Care*, London, Verso; David Craig and Richard Brooks, *Plundering the Public Sector*, London, Constable.
72. Mark Ballard, 'NPfIT champion suspended after speaking out', *The Register*, 8 March 2007; Lucy Sherriff, 'Fujitsu man condemns NPfIT as failure', *The Register*, 13 February 2007; Simon Bowers, 'Accenture to quit NHS technology overhaul', *The Guardian*, 28 September 2006; 'Accenture feels the squeeze on NHS contracts', *E-Health Insider*, 8 April 2005; Chip Means, 'Fujitsu ends contract with NHS IT project', *Healthcare I.T. News EU*, 30 May 2008; Paul Crompton (2007), 'The National Programme for Information Technology – An Overview', *Journal of Visual Communication in Medicine*, 30, 72–77; Nick Heath, 'The 10 projects at the heart of NHS IT', *Silicon.com*, 10 November 2008; John Oates, 'NHS IT: what went wrong, what will go wrong', *The Register*, 30 May 2008; Laton McCartney, 'Prescription for Disaster', *CIO Insight*, 13 November 2006; Jane Hendy et al. (2005), 'Challenges to implementing the national programme for information technology (NPfIT)', *British Medical Journal*, 331, 331–336; The National Programme for IT in the NHS, 'Procurement approach document', NHS, 2003; 'Accenture's NHS losses grow as NPfIT delays mount', *E-Health Insider*, 29 March 2006; Nicholas Timmins 'NHS narrows down field for £2.3bn IT contracts', *Financial Times*, 6 August 2003; Rosalie Marshall, Outlook for NHS IT is far from healthy, *Computing*, 13 November 2008; UK National Audit Office, 'NHS Connecting for Health Process Capability Appraisal', report CR050700, 28 April 2005; Second full NAO review of NPfIT to be carried out, E-Health Insider, 26 April 2007.
73. Barbara Martinez, 'Strong Medicine; With New Muscle, Hospitals Squeeze Insurers on Rates', *The Wall Street Journal* (April 12, 2002), A1; James V. DeLong, 'Rule of Law: Just What Crime Did Columbia/HCA Commit?' *The Wall Street Journal* (August 20, 1997), A15; and Lucette Lagnado, 'House Panel Begins Inquiry into Hospital Billing Practices', *The Wall Street Journal* (July 17, 2003), B1.
74. Jonathan Murphy (2008), *The World Bank and Global Managerialism*, London, Routledge, pp. 76–98.
75. Jeffrey Gantz and Victor V. Murray, 'Experience of Workplace Politics', *Academy of Management Journal* 23 (1980), 237–251; and Dan L. Madison, Robert W. Allen, Lyman W. Porter, Patricia A. Renwick and Bronston T. Mayes, 'Organizational Politics: An Exploration of Managers' Perception', *Human Relations* 33 (1980), 79–100.
76. Gerald R. Ferris and K. Michele Kacmar, 'Perceptions of Organizational Politics', *Journal of Management* 18 (1992), 93–116; Parmod Kumar and Rehana Ghadially, 'Organizational Politics and Its Effects on Members of Organizations', *Human Relations* 42 (1989), 305–314; Donald J. Vredenburgh and John G. Maurer, 'A Process Framework of Organizational Politics', *Human Relations* 37 (1984), 47–66; and Gerald R. Ferris, Dwight D. Frink, Maria Carmen Galang, Jing Zhou, Michele Kacmar and Jack L. Howard, 'Perceptions of Organizational Politics: Prediction, Stress-Related Implications and Outcomes', *Human Relations* 49, no. 2 (1996), 233–266.
77. Ferris et al., 'Perceptions of Organizational Politics: Prediction, Stress-Related Implications and Outcomes'; John J. Voyer, 'Coercive Organizational Politics and Organizational Outcomes: An Interpretive Study', *Organization Science* 5, no. 1 (February 1994), 72–85; and James W. Dean, Jr. and Mark P. Sharfman, 'Does Decision Process Matter? A Study of Strategic Decision-Making Effectiveness', *Academy of Management Journal* 39, no. 2 (1996), 368–396.

78. Jeffrey Pfeffer, *Managing with Power: Politics and Influence in Organizations* (Boston, Mass.: Harvard Business School Press, 1992).
79. Amos Drory and Tsilia Romm, 'The Definition of Organizational Politics: A Review', *Human Relations* 43 (1990), 1133–1154; and Vredenburgh and Maurer, 'A Process Framework of Organizational Politics'; and Lafe Low, 'It's Politics, As Usual', *CIO* (April 1, 2004), 87–90.
80. Pfeffer, *Power in Organizations*, 70.
81. Madison et al., 'Organizational Politics'; Jay R. Galbraith *Organizational Design* (Reading, Mass.: Addison-Wesley, 1977).
82. Gantz and Murray, 'Experience of Workplace Politics'; Pfeffer, *Power in Organizations*.
83. Daniel J. Brass and Marlene E. Burkhardt, 'Potential Power and Power Use: An Investigation of Structure and Behaviour', *Academy of Management Journal* 38 (1993), 441–470.
84. Harvey G. Enns and Dean B. McFarlin, 'When Executives Influence Peers, Does Function Matter?' *Human Resource Management* 4, no. 2 (Summer 2003), 125–142.
85. Hickson et al., 'A Strategic Contingencies Theory'.
86. Pfeffer, *Power in Organizations*.
87. Ibid.
88. V. Dallas Merrell, *Huddling: The Informal Way to Management Success* (New York: AMACON, 1979).
89. Ceasar Douglas and Anthony P. Ammeter, 'An Examination of Leader Political Skill and Its Effect on Ratings of Leader Effectiveness', *The Leadership Quarterly* 15 (2004), 537–550.
90. Vredenburgh and Maurer, 'A Process Framework of Organizational Politics'.
91. Pfeffer, *Power in Organizations*.
92. Ibid.
93. Stephen Brook, 'Murdochs make the headlines', *Guardian Unlimited*, 14 July 2008.
94. 'Maxwell inquiry indicts son and bank', *Irish Times*, 31 March 2001.
95. Bank of America to buy Merrill Lynch for 50 billion, *Agence France Presse*, 15 September 2008; Dominic Walsh and Suzy Jagger, 'Morgan Stanley takes Dollar 3.7bn sub-prime hit', *The Times*, 8 November 2007.
96. Ann Davis and Randall Smith, 'Merrill Switch: Popular Veteran Is In, Not Out', *The Wall Street Journal* (August 13, 2003), C1.
97. Pfeffer, *Power in Organizations*.
98. Ibid.
99. Kanter, 'Power Failure in Management Circuits'; Pfeffer, *Power in Organizations*.
100. Ben Elgin, 'Inside Yahoo!' *BusinessWeek* (May 21, 2001), 114–122.
101. Robert R. Blake and Jane S. Mouton, 'Overcoming Group Warfare', *Harvard Business Review* (November–December 1984), 98–108.
102. Blake and Mouton, 'Overcoming Group Warfare'; Paul R. Lawrence and Jay W. Lorsch, 'New Management Job: The Integrator', *Harvard Business Review* 45 (November– December 1967), 142–151.
103. 'Transnet strike off as unions agree to talk', *FT Now*, 25 March 2006; Transnet, Unions Sign Restructuring Accord, South African Press Association, 16 May 2006.
104. Stephen Power and Matthew Karnitschnig, 'Risky Business: VW's Woes Mount Amid Claims Of Sex Junkets for Union Chiefs – Scandal Rocks Auto Giant As Its Luxury Push Fades; New Blow to Germany Inc.,' *The Wall Street Journal*, 17 November 2005; BBC News, 'IG Metall deal averts VW strike', accessed at http://news.bbc.co.uk/1/hi/business/3978405.stm on January 7, 2009; Ian Greer and Marco Hauptmeier (2008), 'Political Entrepreneurs and Co-Managers: Labour Transnationalism at Four Multinational Auto Companies', *British Journal of Industrial Relations*, 46, pp. 76–97; Paul Newton, 'VW and IG Metall Agree to Continue Restructuring Talks', *Global Insight Daily Analysis,* 14 July 2006; Jack Ewing, 'Volkswagen Rolls the Dice on Tennessee', Der Spiegel Online, 11 December 2008; 'Declaration on Social Rights and Industrial Relationships at Volkswagen', accessed at http://www.fes.or.kr/Industrial_Relations/Vw-de.htm on January 7, 2009; 'VW taken over by Porsche; Luxury car maker's move sends stocks soaring', *Vancouver Province*, 7 January 2009.
105. 'Chile Codelco reaches wage agreement with workers', *Reuters News*, 21 February 2007; Paul Harris, 'Codelco Norte union threatens strike', *Metal Bulletin News Alert Service*, 21 February 2007; 'Codelco Norte Closes Negotiations With Unions', *Corporate Chile*, December 21, 2006.
106. White, et al., 'UAW Is Facing Biggest Battles in Two Decades'.
107. Robert R. Blake, Herbert A. Shepard and Jane S. Mouton, *Managing Intergroup Conflict in Industry* (Houston: Gulf Publishing, 1964); Doug Stewart, 'Expand the Pie before You Divvy It Up', *Smithsonian* (November 1997), 78–90.
108. Patrick S. Nugent, 'Managing Conflict: Third-Party Interventions for Managers', *Academy of Management Executive* 16, no. 1 (2002), 139–155.
109. Blake and Mouton, 'Overcoming Group Warfare'; Schein, *Organizational Psychology*; Blake, Shepard and Mouton, *Managing Intergroup Conflict in Industry;* and Richard E. Walton, *Interpersonal Peacemaking: Confrontation and Third-Party Consultations* (Reading, Mass.: Addison-Wesley, 1969).
110. Neilsen, 'Understanding and Managing Intergroup Conflict'; McCann and Galbraith, 'Interdepartmental Relations'.
111. Neilsen, 'Understanding and Managing Intergroup Conflict'; McCann and Galbraith, 'Interdepartmental Relations'; Sherif et al., *Intergroup Conflict and Cooperation*.
112. Dean Tjosvold, Valerie Dann and Choy Wong, 'Managing Conflict between Departments to Serve Customers', *Human Relations* 45 (1992), 1035–1054.

INTEGRATIVE CASES

1.0

INTEGRATIVE CASE 1.0

CIRCUS OZ (A)

We have to think very carefully about...whether the values and the culture of our organization can engage with the corporate sector in a way that furthers the aims of our company without diluting them.
—Linda Mickleborough, General Manager, Circus Oz

In early 2002, Linda Mickleborough, general manager of Australia's Circus Oz, had to decide how to respond to an offer by its major government sponsor (the Australia Council) to fund the creation of a new position of director of development. The decision should have been an easy one for a number of reasons. First, the Australia Council had strongly encouraged the country's major performing arts organizations to hire development professionals to expand their funding from corporate donors – at least partly as a way to reduce these organizations' reliance on government support. Second, the council was offering to underwrite the cost of the position for a period of two years. Third, Mickleborough had found the ideal candidate for the position in Paul McGill, a senior management consultant at Deloitte & Touche who had done *pro bono* consulting for Circus Oz in the past. During her interview with McGill, his passion for Circus Oz and his excitement about the prospect of developing the company's strategic alliances and partnerships with corporate sponsors was transparent.

The problem for Circus Oz, however, was that a competitive salary for a talented development professional like McGill could easily be close to twice what the highest paid performers or managers at Circus Oz currently received – a fact confirmed by the suggestions offered by the Australia Council about the level of compensation necessary to attract the calibre of person it envisioned in such a position. In its early years, all employees of Circus Oz were paid the same salary. Though this changed over time, even in 2002 the highest paid person earned about 50 per cent more than the lowest paid. Mickleborough was acutely aware of the potential damage a larger disparity might wreak on the company's morale and culture. While Circus Oz had grown professionally, artistically, and financially over the years, this success had been based on deeply held egalitarian and democratic values that had shaped both the artistic and operational practices of the company.

Despite the fact that Paul McGill might easily bring in contributions many times his salary, hiring him at anything close to the going rate seemed to fly in the face of everything Circus Oz stood for. Aside from the concerns about salary, Mickleborough also faced nagging questions about whether McGill's corporate background would fit with, and be accepted by, the rest of the staff at Circus Oz. Anticipating the havoc that such a departure from Circus Oz's bohemian culture and egalitarian wage structure might wreak on the company, Mickleborough recounted the image that her colleague, Artistic Director Mike Finch, had conjured up as they contemplated the type of person who might be hired as a director of development: 'They'll be driving up in a new BMW and dropping in for a couple of hours to hand over the corporate cheque that they'd gathered that week and then cruising off again to the beach house . . . while all the artists and performers are still struggling along on basic equity wages'.

A final complication surrounding the position was the actual decision-making process. As general manager of Circus Oz, Mickleborough was the primary person responsible for dealing with the administrative and financial issues facing the organization. However, consistent with the company's strong egalitarian ethos, its governance was based on norms of broad participation and a tradition of consensus building. Hence, any decision about the development position and/or Paul McGill would have to be approved by the member-dominated board of directors.

Hilary Stockton prepared this case under the supervision of Professor James Phills as the basis for class discussion rather than to illustrate either effective or ineffective handling of an administrative situation. It is intended to be used in conjunction with the videocase *Circus Oz*: *The Development* Director SI-69V.

Overview of Circus Oz

After more than 23 years of existence, Circus Oz was Australia's premier international circus, having performed in 26 countries on five continents, ranging from New York's Kennedy Center to Denmark's Tivoli Gardens to a glass opera house in the middle of a Brazilian rain forest. Circus Oz had broken box office records at the Edinburgh Fringe Festival, represented Australia at scores of international festivals, and was the first circus in history to perform on three continents in one year. Circus Oz's international success flowed from several factors: its cutting-edge acts, with their natural drama and inherent risk; the wide range of tradition and performance forms Circus Oz encompassed and borrowed from, such as cabaret, popular music, knockabout comedy, music theatre and traditional circus; and not least, the quintessentially Australian combination of social satire, inclusiveness, strident egalitarianism and self-deprecating humour that imbued Circus Oz performances.

Coupled with its international and artistic success, Circus Oz in early 2002 was in its strongest financial position since the company's inception. Unlike several of Australia's other premier performing arts companies, Circus Oz was making a profit, and had an accumulated surplus of AUD$1,169,313. In recent years, the company had also increased the percentage of its revenue generated from the box office, relative to the portions coming from performance fees, grants and sponsorships.

Founding and Early History

Circus Oz, founded in 1977, was the product of two established and well-known circuses, Soapbox Circus, a road show set up by the Melbourne-based Australian Performing Group (APG), and the New Ensemble Circus, based in Adelaide. Both groups embodied the ideals of the new Australian theatre of the late sixties and early seventies – ensemble playing and group creativity; exuberant physicality; breaking down the barriers between spectator and performer; an exploration of comedy, populism and political commentary; egalitarianism; and the development of a unique Australian voice – and these ideas also became integral to the Circus Oz philosophy.

None of the original 25 members of Circus Oz had a traditional circus background; however, some had worked in circuses to learn particular skills first-hand. As Finch explained:

> *It was a group of left-wing theatre people, most of them university educated, living in Melbourne, which is probably the most cultural city in Australia. Luckily they had some circus skills…a few of them could walk tight wire and do trapeze, so it did have the credibility that allowed it to become a circus, but the driving force behind it was the late seventies' radical politics…the strong feminist movement, anti-nuclear movement, indigenous rights.*[1]

The original members' goal in forming Circus Oz was as much to create the kind of communal, egalitarian life they wanted, as to perform a thrilling and uniquely Australian show, utilizing their individual and collective talents. One of the first things they did as a company was to work together to sew a tent with whatever pieces of canvas they could get their hands on. The performances themselves were remarkable in part due to the multiple skills of the performers – the acrobats played music in the band in addition to their performances, while the musicians helped with the production and rigging of the show. Another feature of Circus Oz was the de-emphasis of traditional gender roles. Many of the costumes were unisex, and female performers were trained to perform acts requiring considerable strength, just as male performers were encouraged to be graceful and beautiful in performance. Within the first year of its existence, Circus Oz was invited to perform in Europe, and after a successful tour, they returned to Australia to play a 32-week season at Melbourne's Last Laugh Theatre Restaurant. Other key developments in Circus Oz's early history were the master classes the company took with Chinese acrobats in 1983–1984 and again in 1985, which built such core skills as hoop diving, pole climbing and group bicycle; and the strengthening of the group's relationship with the Flying Fruit Fly Circus. In the early 1980s, Circus Oz's relationship with the 'Fruities', a regionally based children's circus, proved beneficially symbiotic: not only did the two circus groups share a big top, but many Circus Oz members coached Flying Fruit Fly Circus members, while many of the second generation Circus Oz performers were former Fruit Fly performers.

Although only three of the original members were still with Circus Oz in 2002, and over 700 individuals had worked with the company over the years, the overall tenor of the performances had changed little over time. As one brochure described the style:

> *The show is a non-stop mix of new ridiculousness and finely tuned absurdity. There's someone trapped in a giant hamster wheel, a brand new skill from Scandinavia via Germany and Russia; a classical musician called Paul in search of an orchestra; a sense of national identity in a clash of the classical and the eclectic, and the fearless precision skydivers*

[1] All quotations in this case, unless otherwise noted, are from the authors' interviews.

1.0

now open the show in a blizzard of laundry and a tangle of limbs...

In a review of Circus Oz's London tour in early 2000, the *Guardian* raved:

> *Circus Oz are a spectacular international success story, breathing creative life into the tired world of the big top. Over the last 20 years the company has been one of contemporary circus's leading trailblazers. Fusing traditions such as altitude acrobatics, tightrope-walking, strong women, freaks with satire, modern-day pyrotechnics, innovation and tremendous live musical scores, Australia's Circus Oz is credited as the first contemporary circus. The company's breathtaking shows are not only 'sexy and sophisticated', like Cirque du Soleil's, but also contain a wonderfully seditious edge.*[2]

There were usually 11 to 14 performers (generally including at least two specialist musicians) who performed an energetic mélange of graceful, brash, satirical eclectic and daring spectacle, accompanied by live music and even involving the musicians. The multiple skills employed by each performer, which resulted in the appearance of everyone doing everything, continued as a performance hallmark.

Culture and Mission

Circus Oz's unique start, from a group of idealistic and politically left-wing university theatre students, was reflected not only in its eclectic performance but in its mission, which was to create a post-modern, breathtaking performance with a uniquely Australian wackiness and sense of humour that would entertain, inspire and challenge a diverse audience. This overarching mission was fleshed out in some of the specific goals for the show:

Circus Oz aims to create a show:

- In which performers engage with the audience in equally shared and interacting experiences and in which members of the audience delight in taking an active role in the relationship with the performers and with other members of the audience
- Which expresses an analytical and critical view of society
- Which expresses a positive and optimistic position derived from faith in and belief in humanity[3]

For a complete list of Circus Oz Aims, see **Exhibit 2**.

Circus Oz's mission, with its emphasis on inspiring and challenging a diverse audience, also reflected the company's core values of encouraging performers' creative expression and contribution to decisions affecting their work; conducting the company as a joint enterprise, under a shared vision; conducting training and workshops to develop members' skills; and paying core employees as much as the company could afford.[4]

The culture of Circus Oz was consistently inclusive, embracing, curious, eclectic and democratic.[5] Finch expressed the Circus Oz core values this way:

> *Democracy's probably the first thing on the list, innovation in terms of coming up with new things that are highly regarded amongst other circus performers. Another key value is that we're distinctly Australian and being funny and irreverent is a core value too.*

(For more on Circus Oz culture, see excerpts of reviews of Circus Oz's 2000 tour in **Exhibit 1**.)

Mickleborough emphasized the importance of each individual in the Circus Oz organization, and the multiple skills each member needed to stage a performance:

> *Circus Oz is an organization that has been built on its people...and it's special because of every single individual within the organization, both the people that you see on stage, and the people that you see behind the scenes, and the sort of incredible range of areas that everyone covers through a sort of multi-skilling system. We feel that that culture enables us to create the sorts of performances that we do and...to function as we do very successfully.*

One incident that exemplified Circus Oz's tradition of independence and critical social commentary occurred early in 1990. Due to a very unsuccessful season, Circus Oz found itself without the cash or the reserves to fund the upcoming season. A major chemical company offered to underwrite the season as a corporate sponsor. Without the proffered funds, Circus Oz would have had to cancel the season, throwing the performers and technicians out of work. Nevertheless, Mickleborough recounted how the performers elected not to accept the sponsorship, because many were offended by the company's poor environmental record:

> *Without that money we couldn't do the season, and it meant that people would lose their jobs. But [these same people] elected not to take that money. And – instead, we cancelled the season.*

---

[2] M. Keating, 'Circus Oz', The Guide Friday: The Rest, *The Guardian*, 2000, August 11, p. 15.

[3] Circus Oz Business Plan for 2002–2004, p. 6.

[4] Core employees were defined as financial company members of Circus Oz, who became eligible after having worked continuously at Circus Oz for three years (Circus Oz Business Plan for 2004–2006, p. 39).

[5] Circus Oz Business Plan, October 2001, p. 9.

Despite being out of work, the company members eventually regrouped and committed themselves to developing financial reserves to insure that something like this would never happen again.

Circus Oz members' decision to turn down the chemical company sponsorship reflected an underlying aversion to engaging in any kind of partnership with organizations whose products or policies the Circus Oz members believed were damaging in some way. This might be because the products themselves were unhealthy, or because the means used to produce them resulted in environmental degradation, or in exploitation of the workers. In addition, the company had a longstanding policy against touring to countries characterized by politically repressive regimes, with a poor human rights record. The company even avoided regions where there was political turmoil, unless Circus Oz felt it could effect positive change in those countries. As a result, although Circus Oz was pursued for several years by the Jerusalem Festival, the company declined to participate until Itzhak Rabin became prime minister of Israel and the Israeli-Palestinian peace process appeared to be moving forward. Moreover, Circus Oz insisted on performing at a Palestinian refugee camp, in addition to its appearance at the Jerusalem Festival.

Decisions about whether or not to partner with a particular company or perform in a given country were rarely clear-cut. Mickleborough described the process engendered by the company's democratic style of decision making:

> *Get us in a room together and there will be 30 opinions and we will thrash things out, and we will argue and we'll try to convince people to come over to our side. And at times that's sort of difficult and frustrating and drives you completely insane. But I think that that means there is an ongoing creativity and renewal and that when you do make a decision, you know that you've looked at all your options.*

Finch agreed that this aspect of the collective ideal was still alive and well in 2002:

> *[The collective has] slowly evolved into a more corporate hierarchy that's still very flat. The expectations of the group [are] that information will be shared, that decisions will be made for the good of the group, rather than the good of the organization, that no one will be paid drastically more than anyone else unless they've done drastically more time at the company....*

Financials

In 2000, Circus Oz achieved its strongest financial performance in company history, increasing the company's profit to AUD$573,743, up more than 18-fold from AUD $30,587 in 1999 and resulting in an accumulated surplus of AUD$1,104,066. The strong financial position resulted from extensive international touring (the company performed more than double the number of shows given in 1999), increased box office sales for Circus Oz's self-produced seasons[6] and a tight rein on expenses, although this last tactic meant that additional investment would be needed in future years. From 1998 to 2000, Circus Oz met and exceeded its goal of maintaining working capital reserves of 20 per cent of average annual turnover. This success followed a period from 1992 to1998 when Circus Oz's earned income increased significantly relative to government funding. Over the same period, the annual growth of government funding for Circus Oz had increased 6.4 per cent, the second highest of all Sydney and Melbourne based companies profiled in the 1999 Australia Council report, 'Securing the Future'.

Circus Oz's income in 2001 declined, due to a combination of factors including fewer shows, a decline in ticket sales and reduction in sponsorship revenue. In particular, Circus Oz's European tour produced lower revenue due to market contraction post-September 11th, and a number of sponsors cut back. Network 7 reduced its contribution to the Melbourne season from AUD$87,620 in 2000 to $31,753 in 2001, and eliminated its sponsorship of the Sydney season. MIX FM and *Sun Herald* eliminated their sponsorships entirely in 2001. (See **Exhibit 4** for excerpts from the 1998–2000 financial statements and targets for 2001–2004 and **Exhibit 5** for actual and target performance and audience figures.)

Circus Oz Organizational Structure and Leadership

Governance

Circus Oz was organized as a nonprofit Limited Liability Corporation (LLC), comprised of members who paid nominal annual dues (AUD$2) and were eligible to attend the annual meeting, participate in policy discussions and elect the company's board of directors. Only members were qualified to serve as directors. Company membership was open to those who had worked for Circus Oz continuously over a three-year period, or to selected outsiders who were asked to join the board and, concurrently, invited to become members. These individuals

[6] Circus Oz defined self-produced, or self-entrepreneured seasons as those seasons produced and marketed by Circus Oz itself in Australia, typically Sydney and Melbourne. Locally promoted seasons were those purchased and marketed by Australian or international presenters or agents.

1.0

retained their membership even after ceasing to be active performers or staff with Circus Oz. As a result, the membership included a larger group of former performers than current performers. In 2003, approximately half the creative team had become company members of Circus Oz.[7]

In 2001, the Circus Oz board of directors consisted of nine members, the maximum number allowed by the Circus Oz Articles of Association[8]: five outside directors with specific skills or expertise; two directors who had been financial members of the company for five years or more; and two directors elected as representatives of the current working group. The standing committees of the Circus Oz board consisted of the executive committee, the board membership committee, the finance committee, the wages committee and the sponsorship committee.

In a 2001 meeting with Circus Oz, representatives of the Major Performing Arts Board and Arts Victoria commented that Circus Oz appeared to contradict the general rule that entrenched boards tend to perform poorly at increasing a company's profitability and dynamism. Although Circus Oz had a long-lived board with little turnover of directors, the company was acknowledged to be financially stable and creatively vibrant. The Circus Oz board noted differences between its role and that of a corporate board, where the focus was on profitability and might call for a change in the entrenched culture in order to steer in a more profitable direction. Indeed, the Circus Oz Business Plan for 2002–2004 stressed:

> *In Circus Oz, there is little difference between the 'culture' of the organization and its 'product'. Circus Oz is selling its culture as its product, and recognizes the board's important role in maintaining that culture.*[9]

Despite its apparently successful record of effective governance, the Circus Oz board had begun to examine the question of whether its strong history and insider composition might constrain its future development. In particular, board members pondered how they could balance their role as caretakers of the company's culture and values against the need to ensure continued, even expanded access to the resources for its continued growth and development.

Company Management

The organization was managed by an executive team that included the artistic director (Mike Finch), general manager (Linda Mickleborough), and senior circus artist (Tim Coldwell). Additional staff included performers, workshop teachers, technicians and administrative professionals, and was considered the working group. Technicians worked under a production manager, while a workshop coordinator managed workshop teachers. On the business side, Mickleborough supervised administration. (See **Exhibit 3** for the organization's structure.)

The 11 to 14 performers worked with Finch and an associate artistic director. However, the collaborative and creative process of putting together a show meant that responsibility for the artistic direction of the company was not vested solely in the artistic director, but rather shaped by the contributions of the performers and technicians. Circus Oz believed this approach to building the show was necessary, due to the limited number of circus directors in Australia who had experience with a company and show on the scale of Circus Oz. The model depended on maintaining both significant senior level experience and a balance and stability within the performance and technician ensemble. As a result, the organization tried to limit turnover among the performers to no more than two each year – though in some recent years turnover had exceeded this goal.

Background on the Australia Performing Arts Industry

Australia's performing arts industry included about 30 major dance, music, opera and theatre companies with at least AUD$1 million per year of revenue from grants or ticket sales. The artistic and economic contribution and funding of these leading companies was disproportionate to their actual number. Although in 1997 these major performing arts companies were only 17 per cent of the total number of subsidized performing arts organizations, they received 49 per cent of government funding to the sector, reached 71 per cent of the paying audience, provided 86 per cent of the employment opportunities and earned 79 per cent of the sector's income. In 1997, this 79 per cent of the performing arts sector income amounted to $124 million: $96 million from box office and performing arts fees, $17 million from sponsorship

[7] Circus Oz Business Plan 2004–2006, p. 43.

[8] Articles 34 in the Circus Oz Memorandum and Articles of Association provided for the following structure of the board: The number of directors shall be not less than four (4) and not more than nine (9) and each director shall hold office until he or she resigns or is removed or vacates office as provided in these Articles. Only members of the company are qualified to be directors.

[9] Circus Oz Business Plan for 2002–2004, p. 28.

and fundraising and $11 million from miscellaneous activities.[10] Geographically, most of these top companies were based in Australia's capital cities, particularly Sydney (9), Melbourne (5), Brisbane (4) and Perth (4). Nevertheless, many also toured in the other capital cities of Adelaide, Hobart, Canberra and Darwin. In addition to touring within Australia, eight of the companies toured internationally during 1998 on 16 tours, of which 10 were in the Asia Pacific region.

Government Funding

Federal and state governments provided critical direct and indirect support for the performing arts in Australia. Direct government support through grants amounted to AUD$86.6 million in 1997. Additionally, some companies received support in the form of goods and services, such as venue rental and/or maintenance at less than market rates, or legal, building, human resource and financial services at discounted rates. Payroll and/or sales tax exemptions were a further source of direct implicit government support. Indirect government support was provided through government arts and management practice training programmes, and via the Australia Foundation for Culture and the Humanities, whose mission was to work with the private sector to encourage its understanding and philanthropic support of the arts. In 1997, earned income exceeded government funding for fewer than half of the top 27 arts companies, with companies based outside Sydney and Melbourne showing greater reliance on government funding than Sydney and Melbourne based companies.

The Major Performing Arts Inquiry

Context of the Inquiry

In December 1996 at a meeting of the Cultural Ministers' Council (CMC) of the Australia Federal and State Government, concerns over the financial pressures faced by major performing arts companies and the associated challenges to these companies' artistic vitality were raised. In September 1997, the 17 performing arts companies funded by the Australia Council Major Organisations Fund (MOF) asked the MOF to analyze the financial pressures and challenges the companies were facing. The MOF responded by obtaining assistance from McKinsey and Company, whose work formed the basis for the MOF 'Managing for the Future' report. This was presented to a meeting of the state and federal government funding agencies and major performing arts companies on June 5, 1998. The participants endorsed the report and asked MOF to examine potential solutions to the challenges faced by the companies discussed in the report. Senator Richard Alston, the Minister for Communications, Information Technology and the Arts, formally announced the MOF's study on December 15, 1998. The Inquiry, know formally as the Australian Major Performing Arts Inquiry, was charged with reporting on:

- The current financial position of Australia's major government subsidized performing arts companies, including the managerial and governance capabilities of the companies; their cost and revenue dynamics; the extent to which the financial health of the companies enhanced or impeded their ability to achieve artistic outcomes; and the extent of their accessibility across Australia;
- The forces driving further change in the sector, including the impact of global and local competition, new technologies, and governments' funding policies on the sector;
- Structural, financial, managerial and governance barriers that might impede the sector's sustainability and development; and
- Measures for action by the companies, Commonwealth and State/Territory Governments to ensure an artistically vibrant and financially stable sector, including structural, financial, managerial and organizational initiatives.

Inquiry Findings

The AMPA Inquiry findings were released in two documents, the Discussion Paper released in August 1999 and a Final Report, released in December 1999. The Discussion Paper outlined the financial position of the performing arts companies studied, the driving forces in the sector, the factors impeding the industry's development, and over 90 options for grappling with the challenges faced by the companies. The Final Report recommended actions to be taken by the companies and by the Commonwealth and State Governments over an implementation time frame of three years. The following three challenges faced by Australian performing arts companies were emphasized in the Discussion Paper: artistic innovation, access and financial viability.

[10] 'Securing the Future,' Australia Council Final Report, p. 122.

1.0

Artistic Innovation

The Inquiry found that innovation in most companies was undermined by financial weakness, resulting in a decline in new works from 50 to 32 between 1997 and 1998; fewer productions of existing works; less artistic risk-taking, as measured by a decline in production of works by new playwrights or choreographers; reduced ensemble sizes; use of less experienced artists; and, for all the companies in the Inquiry, cutbacks or elimination of their development programs for young artists.

Access

Several factors indicated reduced geographic and demographic access by audiences to the performances of the Australian performing arts companies profiled in the report. The number of regional seasons declined 10 per cent between 1997 and 1998, and the number of companies touring to regional areas decreased 7 per cent over the same period. Touring to smaller capital cities also declined. Especially striking were the low audience participation rates in some cities: 34 per cent in Sydney, 26 per cent in Melbourne, 16 per cent in Canberra, 15 per cent in Adelaide, 14 per cent in Brisbane, 13 per cent in Darwin, and 11 per cent in Hobart and Perth. The Inquiry also found low youth participation; less than 20 per cent of the companies' audiences were under the age of 25, although 38 per cent of the actual population was under this age. Similarly, ethnic minorities were underrepresented in performing arts audiences.

Financial Viability

The Inquiry found that the financial dynamics of the Australian performing arts sector were unsustainable, with costs outpacing the growth in earned income, private sector and government funding. While expenses increased at 4.1 per cent per year between 1992 and 1998, box office revenue increased only 3.4 per cent per year, and government funding rose 3.7 per cent. Private sector funding grew 8.9 per cent, but constituted on average only 13 per cent of a performance company's budget. Further findings were revealing if contradictory. Many companies lacked the critical mass to employ an adequate number of staff with the skills to increase the company's earned income. Cost reduction opportunities existed for companies to cooperate with each other and thereby lower salary and production costs, as well as to increase buying power in advertising rates. Inappropriate incentives existed in the then-current government funding scheme, which failed to provide incentives for companies to build reserves, while providing incentives to stretch already limited company resources on additional, usually not fully funded, activities.

Inquiry Recommendations

The findings of the Inquiry resulted in 94 recommendations for the Commonwealth and State Governments and the companies. The recommendations for the federal and state governments were grouped in the following main categories:

- Agree on the strategy for the sector;
- Clearly define funding and managerial responsibilities between the Commonwealth and State Governments and within the Commonwealth (Australia Council and DOCITA[11]);
- Assist with the stabilization and repositioning of the sector, as well as with initiatives to increase artistic vibrancy and improve box office and private sector support;
- Agree on clear and appropriate performance objectives with each company; and
- Ensure cost-effective access for all Australians.

The recommendations for the companies fell under the following broad mandates:

- Ensure artistic vibrancy;
- Provide access; and
- Change existing financial dynamics by:
  - Enhancing art form cooperation
  - Enhancing geographic cooperation
  - Improving box office and fee income
  - Strengthening private sector support
  - Reducing costs
  - Strengthening the balance sheet
  - Implementing best practice management and governance.

Among these recommendations, those pertaining to strengthening private sector support proposed a shift towards increased private sector philanthropy and corporate sponsorship that was quite new for most of the Australian companies. In the U.S., 30 to 50 per cent of a music or theatre company's revenues might come from private or corporate sponsors, with much of the balance coming from mostly from box office sales. Typically less than six per cent came from government sources. In Australia, by contrast, the largest Australian performing arts organizations drew only 6–15 per cent of their revenues from private sources, and 13–53 per cent of their revenues from government funding, with the remainder coming from ticket sales (see **Exhibit 6**).

[11] DOCITA is the acronym for Australia's Department of Communications, Information Technology and the Arts.

One specific private sector support recommendation advised smaller companies to take advantage of an offer by the Commonwealth Government to fund development staff for up to two years to increase the companies' private sector sponsorship income.[12] In addition, the report suggested that companies planning to hire development staff should commit to sending them to a high quality training program, with the assistance of the Major Performing Arts Board, as a prerequisite for receiving commonwealth funding for this position. Beyond adding dedicated development staff, the report laid out guidelines for the organization's boards of directors, advocating the inclusion of a number of board members with high level corporate connections, and at least one board member with marketing and/or development experience. The report also stipulated that boards should support the development of relationships with sponsors that were sensitive to the company's art form (see **Exhibit 7**).

Impact of The Recommendations on Circus Oz

The most relevant AMPA Inquiry recommendations for Circus Oz were the ones dealing with board composition, increasing earned income and garnering greater private sector support. However, the issues of greater corporate representation on the Circus Oz board and the hiring of a dedicated development officer were the areas of greatest potential concern for Mickleborough, Finch and Colwell. Mickleborough described the ongoing question of whether to add more corporate representation to the board:

> *Circus Oz has a very non-corporate board in comparison to any of the other organizations . . . even amongst our external people we have people who've been associated with Circus Oz for a very long time . . . we will look at whether there is any value that we think can be had in appointing . . . corporate people to the board . . . we'll be looking at whether we can find people who share our value system and who may be able to build networks and make contacts for us.*

A related concern for Mickleborough was the directive to increase corporate sponsorships and funding for Circus Oz. Her initial conversations with the Australia Council indicated that the going salary for dedicated development officers was quite high, and that many arts organizations were finding that they needed to pay their development officers more than anyone else in the organization. This would be a significant challenge to Circus Oz's flat wage structure. Mickleborough explained:

> *The very flat wage structure enables us to pay as much as we can possibly afford, but also enables us to control wage growth, [which] is not an individual negotiation situation because everyone knows everyone else is in the same position, pretty much. And so we were very worried that if we had someone come into the organization from outside who was paid an enormous amount more than the people within the organization, it would do two things: it would send a message to the people already in the organization that they weren't worth as much. And it would completely destroy the egalitarian wage structure that we had, and therefore affect the company culture.*

The Development Director Decision

Mickleborough focused again on the decision about whether to accept the Australia Council's offer of funding for a new director of development, and if so, whether to offer the position to Paul McGill, and how much to pay him.

In many ways, if Circus Oz were to accept the offer and create the position, McGill, with his extensive experience and wealth of corporate connections, was the ideal candidate. He was certainly far more qualified than anyone Circus Oz had expected to find. But given the uncertainty about the premise of an expanded development role, Mickleborough had not even broached the compensation issue with McGill. Although she had heard that some organizations paid their development officers more than the CEO, Circus Oz had a seniority-based compensation scheme where, in addition to skills and experience, length of service to the company was rewarded.

On the one hand, Mickleborough recognized that making an exception to this structure for one person could easily lead to an open rebellion within the company. Moreover, she knew that the board was likely to be strongly opposed to violating the traditional wage structure. On the other hand, Mickleborough imagined how McGill's desire to transition from the corporate world to a nonprofit circus might wither if he

[12] 'Securing the Future', Major Performing Arts Sector Final Report, December 1999, p. 71.

were offered a salary within the existing wage structure. She was also worried about how the Australia Council might react to a half-hearted effort to hire McGill, a clear decision not to hire him or even a choice not to create a development position at all. At a time when the Council provided 60 per cent of Circus Oz grant funding, it was clear that much more was at stake than the AUD$109,000 the government entity had offered to fund the development position.

EXHIBIT 1 Circus Oz 2000 Tour Press Excerpts

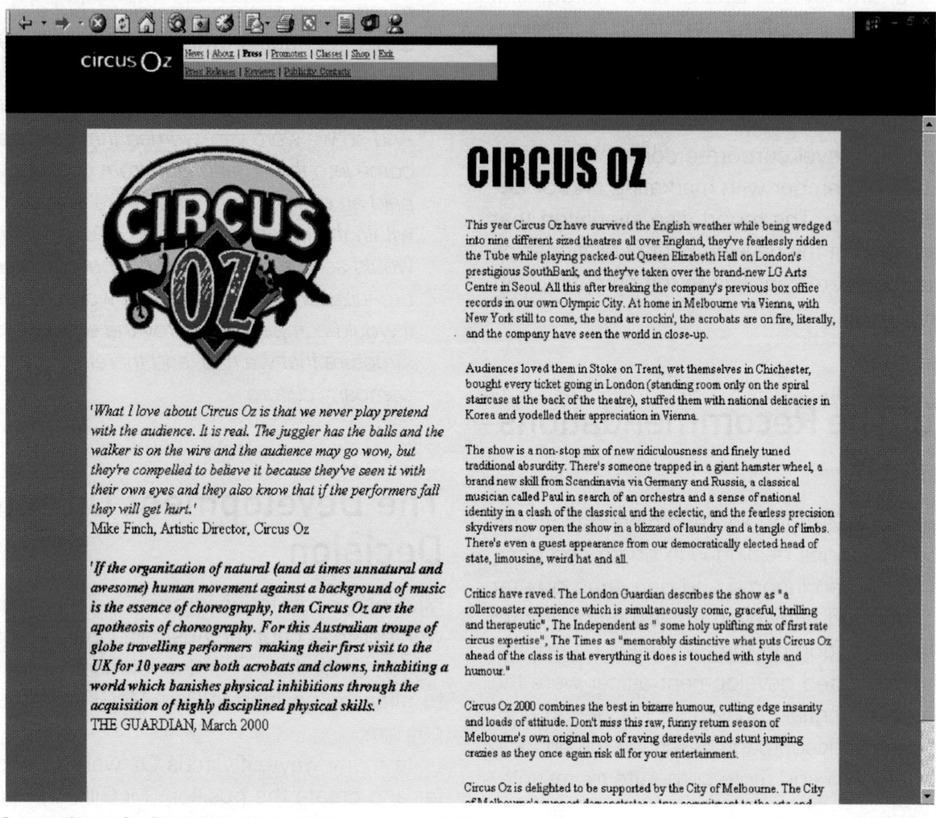

circus Oz

News | About | **Press** | Promoters | Classes | Shop | Exit

Press Releases | Reviews | Publicity Contacts

'What I love about Circus Oz is that we never play pretend with the audience. It is real. The juggler has the balls and the walker is on the wire and the audience may go wow, but they're compelled to believe it because they've seen it with their own eyes and they also know that if the performers fall they will get hurt.'

Mike Finch, Artistic Director, Circus Oz

'If the organization of natural (and at times unnatural and awesome) human movement against a background of music is the essence of choreography, then Circus Oz are the apotheosis of choreography. For this Australian troupe of globe travelling performers making their first visit to the UK for 10 years are both acrobats and clowns, inhabiting a world which banishes physical inhibitions through the acquisition of highly disciplined physical skills.'

THE GUARDIAN, March 2000

CIRCUS OZ

This year Circus Oz have survived the English weather while being wedged into nine different sized theatres all over England, they've fearlessly ridden the Tube while playing packed-out Queen Elizabeth Hall on London's prestigious SouthBank, and they've taken over the brand-new LG Arts Centre in Seoul. All this after breaking the company's previous box office records in our own Olympic City. At home in Melbourne via Vienna, with New York still to come, the band are rockin', the acrobats are on fire, literally, and the company have seen the world in close-up.

Audiences loved them in Stoke on Trent, wet themselves in Chichester, bought every ticket going in London (standing room only on the spiral staircase at the back of the theatre), stuffed them with national delicacies in Korea and yodelled their appreciation in Vienna.

The show is a non-stop mix of new ridiculousness and finely tuned traditional absurdity. There's someone trapped in a giant hamster wheel, a brand new skill from Scandinavia via Germany and Russia, a classical musician called Paul in search of an orchestra and a sense of national identity in a clash of the classical and the eclectic, and the fearless precision skydivers now open the show in a blizzard of laundry and a tangle of limbs. There's even a guest appearance from our democratically elected head of state, limousine, weird hat and all.

Critics have raved. The London Guardian describes the show as "a rollercoaster experience which is simultaneously comic, graceful, thrilling and therapeutic", The Independent as " some holy uplifting mix of first rate circus expertise", The Times as "memorably distinctive what puts Circus Oz ahead of the class is that everything it does is touched with style and humour."

Circus Oz 2000 combines the best in bizarre humour, cutting edge insanity and loads of attitude. Don't miss this raw, funny return season of Melbourne's own original mob of raving daredevils and stunt jumping crazies as they once again risk all for your entertainment.

Circus Oz is delighted to be supported by the City of Melbourne. The City

Source: Circus Oz. Reprinted with permission.

EXHIBIT 2 Circus Oz Aims

Circus Oz aims to create a show:

- In which performers engage with the audience in equally shared and interacting experiences and in which members of the audience delight in taking an active role in the relationship with the performers and with other members of the audience
- Which expresses an analytical and critical view of society
- Which expresses a positive and optimistic position derived from faith in and belief in humanity
- Which is devised for presentation in a tent and can also be adapted for presentation in theatres and non theatrical spaces
- Which presents a multi-skilled ensemble involved in all aspects of the show
- Which presents an ensemble with equal numbers of women and men, where all performers can engage in acts of strength and grace
- Which has a lively comic element and quirky bent edge
- Which acknowledges the importance of music as being integral to the performance
- Which has a recognizable stance on social issues expressed through irreverent wit and humour
- Which has an intrinsic Australian quality, reflecting the cultural diversity of Australian society
- Which will appeal to audiences both in Australia and overseas.

Further, Circus Oz aims to:

- Encourage individual creative expression and establish an environment in which the company will be open to new ideas and change through analysis of past and present performance
- Provide a working environment that enables each of the group's members to contribute to decisions affecting their work and encourages everyone to develop a range of skills to the highest possible standard
- Conduct the company as a joint enterprise, with all members sharing a vision, acknowledging, with trust and respect, each person's role in setting out to achieving our goals and objectives
- Conduct training and workshop programmes in the skills required to excel in circus craft, acrobatics, music, comedy, theatrical arts, design, technical aspects of theatre, management and administration
- Pay award, or better, wages to all employees, and pay core employees as much as Circus Oz can afford.

Source: Circus Oz

1.0

EXHIBIT 3 Circus Oz Organizational Structure

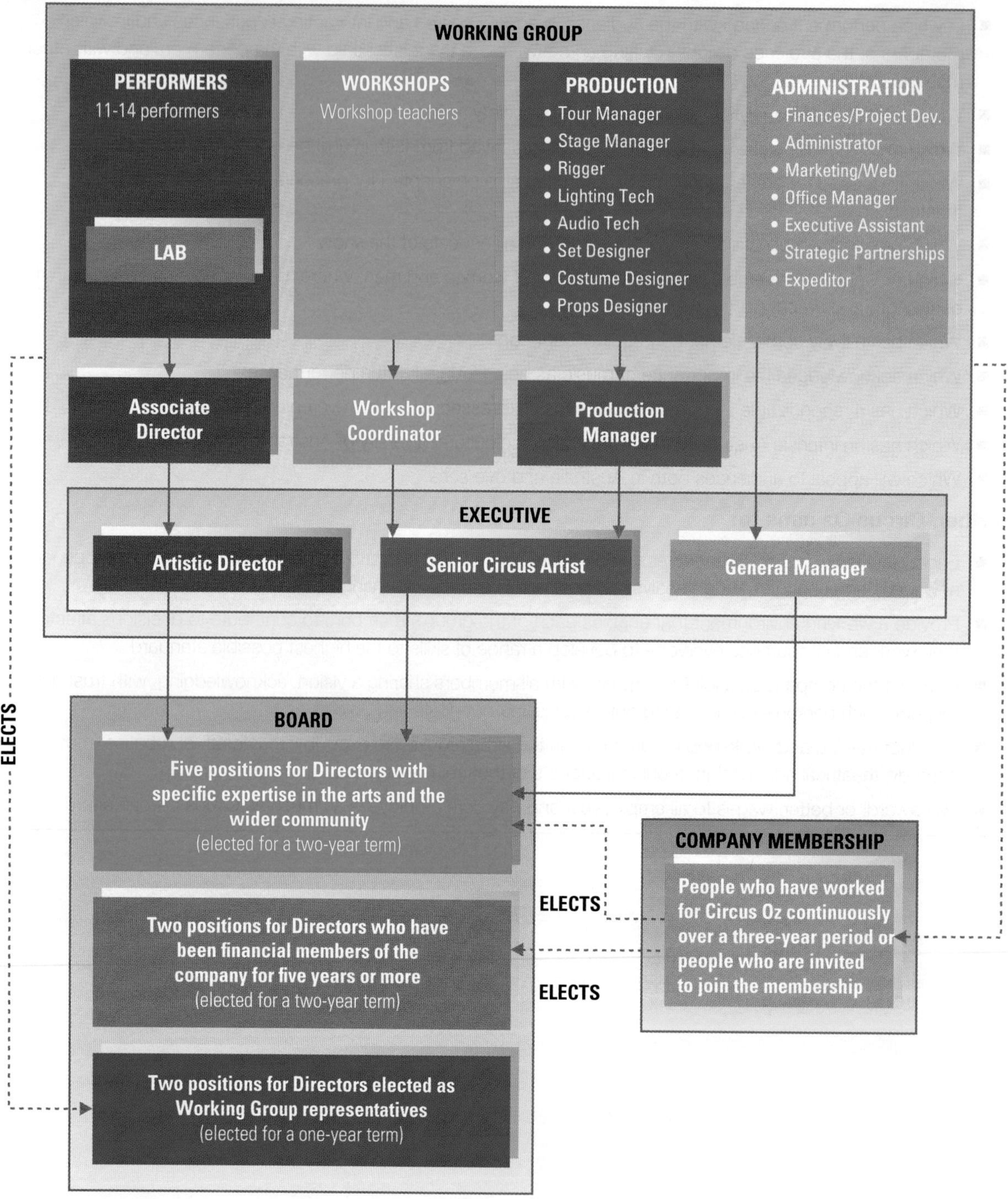

Source: Circus Oz

EXHIBIT 4 Circus Oz Statements of Financial Performance 1995–2001

	2001	2000	1999	1998	1997	1996	1995
INCOME	AUD $	AUD $	AUD $	AUD	AUD $	AUD $	AUD $
Grants	$ 1,092,222	$ 1,083,519	$ 851,831	$ 731,539	$ 824,713	$ 880,999	$ 493,813
Sponsorships	$ 51,298	$ 406,880	$ 194,115	$ 336,527	$ 347,055	$ 263,217	$ 165,000
Production Income	$ 2,072,319	$ 3,454,692	$ 1,186,067	$ 808,983	$ 1,248,145	$ 714,713	$ 1,158,913
Trading Income	$ 78,754						
Net Trading Income		$ 58,638	$ 17,509	$ 12,013	$ 42,551	$ 17,319	$ 72,709
Donations	-	$ 17,133					
Interest	$ 64,719	$ 48,336	$ 33,746				
Other Income	$ 56,281	$ 58,185	$ 64,452	$ 71,540	$ 141,287	$ 85,636	$ 55,085
Capital Grant	-	$ 28,710					
	3,415,593	5,156,093	2,347,720	1,960,602	2,603,751	1,961,884	1,945,520
EXPENDITURE							
Wages and Salaries	$ 1,864,912	$ 2,180,329	$ 1,263,972	$ 1,097,817	$ 1,291,399	$ 1,062,745	$ 1,052,622
Administration Overheads	$ 451,946	$ 220,542	$ 197,966	$ 193,595	$ 219,171	$ 177,560	$ 162,893
Production Costs	$ 803,478	$ 1,462,761	$ 481,212	$ 375,087	$ 575,102	$ 422,781	$ 225,394
Publicity Costs	$ 166,730	$ 718,718	$ 373,983	$ 258,500	$ 402,359	$ 290,651	$ 227,481
Trading Cost of Sales	$ 63,880						
	$ 3,350,946	$ 4,582,350	$ 2,317,133	$ 1,924,999	$ 2,488,031	$ 1,953,737	$ 1,668,390
OPERATING SURPLUS FOR THE YEAR	$ 64,647	$ 573,743	$ 30,587	$ 35,603	$ 115,720	$ 8,147	$ 277,130
Accumulated Surplus (Beginning of year)	$ 1,104,666	$ 530,923	$ 500,336	$ 459,733	$ 344,013	$ 335,866	$ 58,736
Adjustments (Asset revaluation reserve)				$ 5,000			

Source: Circus Oz

1.0

EXHIBIT 5 Actual and Target Audience Development

	ACTUALS			TARGETS			
	1998	1999	2000	2001	2002	2003	2004
AUDIENCE DEVELOPMENT							
Number of Venues	22	11	17	28	13	12	17
Number of Shows	91	88	198	153	149	156	183
Audience Numbers	56,473	58,836	167,564	81,347	95,038	104,076	117,780
SELF ENTREPRENEURED SEASONS							
Number of Venues	2	2	2	1	3	3	3
Number of Shows	26	43	58	26	56	56	84
Audience Numbers	25,505	35,493	44,930	17,160	38,760	40,460	54,600
LOCALLY PROMOTED SEASONS (Australian Regional and Met. Centres)							
Number of Venues	14	8	0	22	7	6	10
Number of Shows	54	18	N/A	55	21	28	27
Audience Numbers	24,286	10,177	N/A	20,987	8,758	11,676	11,340
LOCALLY PROMOTED SEASONS OUTSIDE AUSTRALIA							
Number of Venues	2	1	15	4	4	4	4
Number of Shows	11	27	140	72	68	72	72
Audience Numbers	6,682	13,166	122,634	43,200	47,520	51,840	51,840
PUBLIC CLASSES PROGRAMME							
Number of Classes	194	321	294	250	250	250	250

Source: Circus Oz

EXHIBIT 6 Interenational Benchmarks: 1997 Composition of Revenue (% of Total Revenue)

Artform	Company	Box	Private	Government	Other
Ballet	**The Australian Ballet**	**55**	**15**	**17**	**13**
	American Ballet Theatre	48	46	2	4
	Houston Ballet	46	30	3	21
	English National Ballet	38	2	56	4
	Royal Ballet	38	6	44	12
Opera	**Opera Australia**	**57**	**10**	**27**	**7**
	The Metropolitan	51	49	0	N/A
	Canadian Opera Company	25	50	25	N/A
	English National Opera	38	5	57	N/A
	Royal Opera House	55	12	33	N/A
Music	**Sydney Symphony Orchestra**	**39**	**7**	**53**	**1**
	Minnesota	29	35	3	33
	San Francisco	35	37	4	24
	City of Birmingham	57	6	3	34
Theatre	**Sydney Theatre Company**	**76**	**6**	**13**	**5**
	Melbourne Theatre Company	**75**	**7**	**14**	**4**
	Goodman Theatre	62	32	2	4
	Seattle Repertory Theatre	56	30	6	8
	Stratford Festival	73	15	5	7
	Canadian Stage Company	40	24	32	4
	Shaw Festival	74	19	7	N/A
	Royal National Theatre	30	8	43	19

Notes: Minnesota, City of Birmingham and San Francisco Orchestras' other revenue includes endowment income. Other revenue for overseas opera companies is absorbed into Box Office, Private and Government income.

Source: Compiled by Author from 1997 Circus Oz audited financial statements.

1.0

EXHIBIT 7 Inquiry Recommendations to Grow Private Sector Support for Australian Arts Companies

15.1 Create a Receptive Environment

Recommendation 15.1.1 The companies should work with the Australia Foundation for Culture and the Humanities, the Major Performing Arts Board and the Commonwealth and State Governments to support initiatives to build a better understanding among corporate Australia of the value of arts sponsorship.

The Inquiry supports this recommendation because more work is needed to demonstrate to corporate Australia how arts sponsorship can be leveraged as a marketing tool. The companies have an important role to play in helping create a receptive environment, as do other key players.

15.2 Build the Required Skills

Recommendation 15.2.1 Selected smaller companies should take advantage of the Inquiry's initiative for the Commonwealth Government to fund development staff for up to two years to encourage the growth of private sector income. After two years, the income generated should cover the cost of the companies maintaining the positions.

The Inquiry supports this recommendation because it enables smaller companies, particularly those based in the less populous states, to pursue private sector income opportunities more effectively. A company's ability to raise private sector revenue is strongly related to its having dedicated development staff.

Recommendation 15.2.2 The companies collectively (assisted by the Major Performing Arts Board) should send their development staff to a high quality training programme developed with a major tertiary institution aimed at improving the approach to generating greater corporate sector and private philanthropic support. Attendance at such a programme should be a prerequisite for any company in receipt of seed funding for development staff.

The Inquiry supports this recommendation because there simply is no alternative for companies wanting to secure private sector support than to be highly sophisticated in their approach – particularly in understanding the marketing needs of the corporate sector. Education programmes from a high quality education institution can help achieve that understanding.

Recommendation 15.2.3 The board of each company should help with the growth of private sector income by ensuring:

15.2.3.1 it has a number of board members with high level corporate connections;
15.2.3.2 it has at least one board member with marketing and/or development expertise; and
15.2.3.3 it supports the development of a culture in the company of working with sponsors in a way that is sensitive to the art form.

The Inquiry supports this recommendation because the board must show leadership in initiatives to raise significant private sector income. While full-time professional development staff are essential, the board has an important role to play in creating a culture that supports private sector income generation.

Source: Department of Communications, Information Technology and the Arts, Australian Government, 'Securing the Future – Inquiry into the Major Performing Arts,' 1999, http://www.dcita.gov.au/__data/assets/pdf_file/10700/Securing_the_Future_-_Inquiry_into_the_Major_Performing_Arts.pdf (September 19, 2006).

INTEGRATIVE CASE 2.0

HOSPITAL SOFTWARE SOLUTIONS (A)

2.0

'Sometimes we just have to do things we don't want to do. Now come on, Natalie, stop complaining. I'm busy and you should be too! Get back to work!'

With her manager's words still ringing in her ears after a disastrous meeting, Natalie MacLachlan fell into her chair with a sigh. It was August 2005, and MacLachlan was three months into her tenure at Hospital Software Solutions. Things were not going well – how could MacLachlan's superiors seemingly perceive her as the office 'slacker'? This was certainly not what she had planned for her first job after graduation, and MacLachlan knew she had to fix the situation fast ... before she was fired.

Natalie MacLachlan

Being labelled as a poor performer was something new for MacLachlan. Before accepting her position at Hospital Software Solutions, she had always been a conscientious student and a high achiever. Originally from Ottawa, Ontario, MacLachlan was attracted to The University of Western Ontario (Western) by the honours business administration (HBA) programme at the Richard Ivey School of Business (Ivey), one of Canada's most respected business schools. Because of her strong academic performance and extensive community involvement throughout high school, MacLachlan was pre-accepted into the HBA programme before arriving at Western.[1]

[1] The HBA program was a '2+2' curriculum wherein students undertook two years of university in a field other than business and then entered the HBA programme for their third and fourth years of university. Students with exemplary academic and extra-curricular performance could apply at the end of secondary school to have a spot initially reserved for them in the HBA programme. Final acceptance into the HBA programme was dependent on the maintenance of a high standard of academic and extra-curricular performance in the first two years of university.

During her four years at Western, MacLachlan excelled. She was the recipient of numerous scholarships and awards, including a victory in the Business 020 case competition in her first year. MacLachlan's colleagues at Ivey described her as a good teammate, which was very important in the HBA programme, since group work was an important component of the curriculum. Peers considered MacLachlan down-to-earth, articulate, dependable and even-tempered. It was rare to find someone with whom she did not get along. She was ambitious and wanted to do well, but she was not someone who played games to succeed at the expense of others.

MacLachlan extended this sense of thoughtfulness to her activities outside of school. She was active in many charitable, cultural and community organizations in the London area, and she continued to work on behalf of the community when she moved back to Ottawa to begin working for Hospital Software Solutions.

Hospital Software Solutions

History

Hospital Software Solutions (HSS) was founded in 1999 by ten University of Ottawa software engineering classmates in response to the challenges Ontario hospitals were experiencing when integrating technology into their operations. Deep provincial government budget cuts were forcing hospitals to develop innovative solutions to provide effective and efficient patient care, while keeping costs as low as possible. Many hospitals in Ontario were still using paper systems for tasks such as nursing histories, patient records and medical literature databases.[2] Technology could help streamline these

[2] Canadian Institute for Health Information. *Hospital Report 2002: Acute Care*, pp. 17–18.

Jason Stornelli wrote this case under the supervision of Elizabeth M. A. Grasby solely to provide material for class discussion. The authors do not intend to illustrate either effective or ineffective handling of a managerial situation. The authors may have disguised certain names and other identifying information to protect confidentiality.

2.0

processes and greatly improve service delivery. HSS's customized software solutions promised hospitals an end to the days of lost charts, illegible handwriting and unused capacity with hospital equipment.

Once hospital administrators and physicians were convinced that the computer systems would be as reliable and as easy to use as paper-based methods, HSS's business started to boom. Indeed, the company had uncovered an excellent business opportunity that was easily scalable beyond Ontario. Hospitals around the world were facing similar challenges, and HSS grew very quickly as it expanded into markets in the United States, the United Kingdom and Europe. Much of the company's growth was accomplished through acquisition as the company bought competitors and integrated their operations into the HSS family. By 2005, HSS's financial results were very strong, and the prospects looked good for its future success.

Office Culture

Although HSS had grown significantly, the culture at its Ottawa headquarters had not changed significantly. HSS was still run very much as it had been when the company started – like a small business. Because the original 10 partners knew the business best, all strategic decisions had to be cleared through their offices. They worked very hard, putting in long hours and sacrificing their personal lives to put HSS first. It was not unusual to hear the partners talking about missing an anniversary or a child's birthday, and a few had even come to work on the morning of their wedding day. This devotion to the company was what helped to make HSS a success, and the partners expected everyone on staff to work equally hard to move the company forward. Given the business's success to date, the partners believed they had a winning formula, so they had a strong desire to run the company 'as it always had been'.

Outside of the partners' offices, the culture at HSS was rather individualistic. Everyone concentrated on their own work, and interaction between employees was infrequent. Most staff communicated through instant messaging programs over the computer, and there were few team meetings. Employees received information on the company's strategic direction through a monthly newsletter, which served as the primary link between the company's partners and its employees.

Unexpected Beginnings

Recruiting season during her final year in the HBA programme had been a challenge for MacLachlan. She wanted to work for a company that would give her a position with a significant amount of responsibility and would provide opportunity for advancement within the organization. A few friends of MacLachlan had accepted monotonous jobs, such as data entry, and she knew that she would not be happy unless she was being challenged. MacLachlan had also just married, and a position in Ottawa would allow her and her spouse to be close to both sides of their family.

When MacLachlan saw HSS's posting for a project manager position, she was elated:

> *The project manager position had exactly what I wanted. The responsibilities were fantastic, and I could really see myself getting into my work on a daily basis. I've always been interested in computers and technology, and I worked on a large project during HBA that uncovered problems with the installation of a new computer system in a hospital in London, so I was already familiar with the industry. Compensation was more than what I was seeking, which I thought would certainly help with paying back my student loans, and the job was in Ottawa. Not only were our families there, but also, the Ottawa technology community was both tight-knit and growing. I thought the position at HSS would be a great opportunity to make contacts in the industry that would really help me in the future. At the time, I couldn't have asked for anything more.*

MacLachlan's interviews with Derek Chow (vice-president, customer care), Marcus Nardi (manager, customer care) and Allan Densmore (vice-president, human resources) went well. All three men expressed numerous times during the interview process how perfect MacLachlan would be for the position. For the most part, the company appeared very laid-back and relaxed, although Chow and Densmore each had to step out of the room a few times to answer phone calls during the interview. MacLachlan left the interview convinced that HSS would be a good fit for her personality.

At the beginning of February 2005, MacLachlan received an offer over the telephone for the project manager position, effective July 1, 2005. Even though the company advised her to take a few weeks to consider, MacLachlan believed the job would be perfect for her, and she insisted on accepting over the telephone. She cancelled her upcoming interviews with other firms the next day.

A few weeks later, Densmore called MacLachlan to tell her that the company was changing its offer: they were now planning to hire her as a Customer Care Team Lead, which was a newly created role. Densmore assured MacLachlan that the team lead position was more prestigious than a project manager job, but he could not to provide her with many details on her expected responsibilities because the job was so new. MacLachlan was reluctant to accept the team lead position:

> *It was unclear what I would be doing as a team lead, and I really liked the project manager role. I think Densmore could tell I was upset – he kept saying on the phone how the team lead job was much better, but he could not give me a firm reason why. I reluctantly accepted, on the condition that they would provide me with a full written job description within two weeks. I don't like to start things when I don't know what I'm getting into.*

When MacLachlan received the customer care team lead job description (see Exhibit 1), she had a few concerns, chiefly that she did not have the required three years of support experience with customer service applications; however, she decided not to say anything, fearing Densmore would realize his mistake and rescind the offer.

In early May, MacLachlan and one of her classmates, who had also been hired at HSS, received e-mails from Chow requesting that they start immediately – the office was short-staffed and a client was requesting a complicated software installation. MacLachlan had purposefully booked travel plans before the starting date in her offer, and she really did not want to cancel them. She also wanted to attend her HBA convocation, which was taking place in mid-June. When MacLachlan explained why she would be unable to start work right away, Chow became rather upset. MacLachlan apologized but, at the same time, reminded him that her contract did not begin until July 1. Thankfully, MacLachlan's classmate responded that he was at the end of his vacation and he had a flexible airline ticket, so he could start early. MacLachlan's classmate later told her that Chow had made a point of thanking him for his devotion to the company.

The First Month

No Supervisor

On July 1, MacLachlan arrived at HSS headquarters. Despite the initial issues, MacLachlan was excited to begin the first day of her career; however, her enthusiasm soon waned when she arrived at the reception desk to ask for her manager, Marcus Nardi. She was told he had been fired three weeks earlier. Given her difficulties with Densmore and Chow, Nardi was the only member of the interview team she had not yet disappointed. MacLachlan was told that Chow would be supervising her for the next month until Nardi's replacement, April Worthington, returned from her maternity leave (see Exhibit 2).

MacLachlan proceeded to her desk. Due to a shortage of space, her work area was next to the programming staff area, on the other side of the building from the rest of the customer care team (see Exhibit 3). Chow stopped by soon thereafter; he appeared very rushed and flustered, but he did not mention or appear upset about her refusal to start the job early. Chow told MacLachlan that, unfortunately, he did not have time to train her, since there were too many outstanding projects awaiting completion. In the interim, he was not quite sure what to do with her, so she would have to work on data entry and database cleanup tasks for a few weeks. MacLachlan was disappointed. She believed these menial tasks did not fit with the customer care team lead job description Densmore had given her, and she had been looking forward to developing those required skills right away. Nevertheless, Chow seemed like a reasonable person, and MacLachlan did not want to risk further hindering her relationship with him.

Data Entry

Like most people beginning a new position, MacLachlan frequently had questions about her tasks, especially surrounding the HSS computer systems, and she often stopped by Chow's office to ask for clarification. He would usually interrupt his typing or phone call to give her a one-word answer and then go right back to work. MacLachlan thought this was odd, but she deduced that Chow was just busy.

After approximately three weeks, MacLachlan was much more comfortable with her tasks. She devised some time-saving measures to make the data entry more efficient, and she was particularly proud of herself when she was able to clean a significant amount of redundant data off the system. Excited about her progress, MacLachlan sent Chow an e-mail highlighting her efforts to date and asking for his feedback on her performance, but Chow replied with a short response reminding her of the importance of following established procedures (see Exhibit 4).

Shortly thereafter, serious problems began to develop with the systems on which MacLachlan was working. She was certain the issues did not relate to her work; nevertheless, she heard from others in the office that Chow was unhappy with her performance. Since she had already asked for feedback in an e-mail and felt that she was bothering Chow, MacLachlan chose not to say anything further.

MacLachlan looked at the pile of data entry sheets sitting on her desk. She believed the established processes Chow had reminded her to follow were redundant, and they were

2.0

clearly a waste of time. For example, they required a lot of manual checking of figures, when the program had the capability to do that automatically. Chow had asked her to go back and check all her numbers again, which basically meant doing the past three weeks' work over again, even though she knew the numbers were right. 'What a waste of my time ... I don't think I'll bother,' she whispered under her breath. This wasn't even what she had signed on for – the customer care team lead position was supposed to help her build skills and give her a significant degree of responsibility, not force her to sit in front of a computer and type in numbers all day.

MacLachlan was very frustrated and, since her work did not require collaboration with others, she decided to start working from home. She assumed this was not a problem, since Chow seemed too busy to spend any time with her and the programming staff (who sat around her) had flexible schedules, often arriving and leaving at odd hours.

The Second Month

April Worthington

A few days into MacLachlan's second month at HSS, she met her supervisor, April Worthington, who had returned from her maternity leave.

Worthington had worked at HSS for her entire career (about ten years), joining the company directly from high school. She held a correspondence diploma in management from a local community college. She had held a number of different positions at the same level within the company over the past three years. As one of the managers of customer care, Worthington was responsible for overseeing many different functions, including sales, technical support and complaint resolution. This responsibility required her to develop skills in a number of different areas and, as a result, she often felt overloaded.

Worthington was a very hard worker, and she appeared very dedicated to the company and its processes. It was not unusual to find her at the office late at night after a 12-hour day. Although she had children and a family, she always put her career first. Every task was urgent in Worthington's mind, and she expected the same urgency from her subordinates. She was very ambitious and had mentioned her keen interest in moving up through the organization.

In their first few weeks of working together, the relationship between MacLachlan and Worthington was cordial. Upon Worthington's return to work, MacLachlan was not clear about who she was now working for – Worthington was supposed to be her immediate supervisor, but she still had outstanding projects from Chow. Because she knew both managers were quite busy, MacLachlan decided not to say anything to either Worthington or Chow, and instead decided to complete all her delegated tasks from home, where there were fewer distractions.

The Phone Call

A few days before the end of her second month at HSS, MacLachlan was working through data entry on her home computer when she received a phone call from Worthington. She seemed particularly agitated that MacLachlan was not in the office, and told her that it would be in her best interest to be at her desk immediately. MacLachlan rushed to the office, only to find Worthington standing at her cubicle, waiting for her:

MacLachlan:

'Hi April. Was there something you needed to talk to me about? The weather wasn't too great this morning, so I felt like working from home today. I have so much on my plate right now.'

Worthington:

'Why don't you know you're not supposed to be working from home? I expect you to be here when I'm here. I really needed your help yesterday and today on the presentation to the executive board, and I haven't been able to find you. You knew this seminar was very important.'

MacLachlan:

'Well, nobody told me I couldn't log in from home. After all, the programmers do it all the time. I think this is going a bit far. I'm kind of wasting my time at the office doing this data entry stuff anyhow. Do you really want a time sheet from me?'

Worthington:

'No, I don't think I'm that controlling. However, to be honest with you, maybe I should be. I hear your work on the Ontario hospitals database was very disappointing. I've heard you're not following any of the proper procedures.'

MacLachlan:

'Well, I wasn't trained. Besides, I was just trying to make things more efficient. I came into this job expecting to take a leadership role, and I was trying to do that by improving the processes. Data entry isn't really what I was expecting, given my job description.'

Worthington:

'Your job description is two sentences long. Sometimes we just have to do things we don't want to do. Now come on, Natalie, stop complaining. I'm busy and you should be too. Get back to work!'

As MacLachlan was about to show Worthington the two-page job description from Densmore, Worthington snarled, 'If you really want to do something different, do a system format! Have it done by this afternoon.' She then stormed off.

Dejected, MacLachlan sat down at her desk. As she turned on her computer, an e-mail from Chow arrived saying that the system problems were getting worse. There appeared to be serious problems with the integrity of the data that needed her immediate attention. In addition to the fact her superiors thought she was a slacker, MacLachlan was now faced with conflicting instructions from two bosses. There was no way she could complete the work for both managers on time.

To add to her troubles, in the course of her data entry, MacLachlan had found problems with the way some of the system processes had been created by the programmers. These processes were unrelated to the data she was entering, but they still affected the computer system as a whole. MacLachlan thought this might be the cause of the problems that had been occurring lately, so she documented her findings. Chow and Worthington probably had no idea there was any problem with the processes, since they had so many other tasks to focus on. Regardless, she was not particularly motivated to share her concerns with either of the two managers, given their recent behaviour toward her.

What Next?

'Now what?' MacLachlan thought to herself. She knew a town-hall meeting[3] with HSS's president was coming up in a week and that the executive team had specifically asked for feedback on management styles and work processes. This was a meeting for non-management staff only, so Worthington and Chow would not be attending. MacLachlan had met the president a few times in passing, and he seemed like a nice man. She had heard from her colleagues that he was easy to talk to, and he genuinely wanted to do anything that would improve the company. MacLachlan had many ideas about how to improve the workflow at HSS, and she was eager to share them with someone who would listen. She wondered whether she should approach the president at the town hall meeting and raise her concerns. Could this be her chance to make a difference?

'Or maybe I should just talk to Worthington and Chow', thought MacLachlan. After all, a lot of the problems seemed to stem from misunderstandings. After all, Worthington had specifically mentioned that MacLachlan's job description was two sentences long, which was not the case. Had Chow and Worthington thought she was recruited to be doing something different? Maybe a good chat would clear things up. But, what would MacLachlan say? What would be the best way to approach the situation? Should she be threatening? Conciliatory?

MacLachlan knew she could quit, but that would leave her without a job, and she was still paying bills from her wedding and her school debt. It would be very difficult to make ends meet financially. The information technology community in Ottawa was also small, and news of her poor performance and early departure from HSS would surely spread quickly.

MacLachlan knew she had to act quickly. Whatever she decided, she wanted to have a detailed plan of action, with no more mistakes. How could she get herself out of this mess?

---

[3] 'Town-hall' meetings are designed to provide a public link between upper management and front-line personnel. They are usually open to all employees and are often used by management to share corporate strategy or receive feedback from employees in a public forum.

2.0

EXHIBIT 1 Team Lead Job Description

Customer Care – Team Lead

Basic Purpose

This position requires a self-motivated, highly organized and independent individual, responsible for working with Sales and Operations team members to deliver outstanding Customer Service to our Top 150 Public Health Care Accounts. The incumbent will demonstrate productivity, profitability and quality, ensuring excellent customer service is provided to clients at all levels. The incumbent will develop strategies to improve overall Customer Satisfaction Scores. As the 'voice of the Customer', the successful person will develop processes to improve internal communication and optimize Help Desk policies and procedures. Key initiatives that derive high value-creating benefit for our customers need to be defined, implemented and measured for their effectiveness. Develop streamlined reporting statistics for Account Management, and work with the Sales Team to articulate the value proposition of maintenance revenues. The successful candidate will have excellent customer service skills and communication skills, coupled with strong technical skills and a positive team player attitude.

Essential Duties and Responsibilities

1. Leadership / Management

- Streamline processes, increase productivity, gain efficiencies and enhance value.
- Develop and communicate a clear vision of goals and objectives, philosophies about growth, revenue generation and profitability, in particular the corporate customer care agenda relating to the 'Customer is No. 1'.
- Generate, maintain and review with management, annual, quarterly and monthly revenue statistics (leading and lagging indicators) that represent customer satisfaction trends, financial statistics, productivity rates and overall improvement trends.
- Maintain communications on daily activities, issues and potential challenges.

2. Customer Support / Sales

- Deliver an effective long-term customer care programme for top 150 clients, and implement and maintain client support initiatives.
- Facilitate in-house training sessions, client training sessions and regional conferences for clients and potential clients.
- Assist company personnel in the collection and assessment of Customer Care generated client information, and produce documentation relating to program usage, special function, instruction and promotions.
- Assist in the development and maintenance of competitive intelligence programs and generate industry direction reports to support the development of new features and products.
- Approve and co-ordinate the administration of customer satisfaction and information gathering surveys and other communication tools.

3. Controlling / Internal

Review with Management:

- Annual, quarterly and monthly revenue results/forecasts and costs.
- Participate in the development of special projects, as well as relationships with various levels of government organizations, other private/public sect or organizations (e.g. FTA, State, local government).
- Participate in the development of internal department policies and programs to support quality and growth.

(Continued)

EXHIBIT 1 *(Continued)*

Education and Work Experience

Bachelor's degree in business or technical field (engineering or IT).
Typically requires minimum three years of customer applications support experience.

Technical and Functional Skills

Excellent customer service skills, including a patient courteous manner and a clear voice.
Excellent oral and written communication skills.
Managing project-related activities.
Defining and improving processes.
Demonstrated team leadership.
Ownership of issues through to resolution.
Ownership of customer satisfaction and improving scores.
Excellent knowledge of all HSS products, documentation, add-ons and reports.

Equipment and Applications

Knowledge of Hyperion, MS Office, MS Project, Lotus Notes and Maximizer.
Previous experience with incident reporting/bug reporting/call tracking systems an asset.

Work Environment and Physical Demands

General office environment.
Moderate levels of stress may occur at times.
Irregular hours at times.
No special physical demands required.
Travel may be required.

Source: Company files.

2.0

EXHIBIT 2 Partial Hospital Software Solutions Organizational Chart

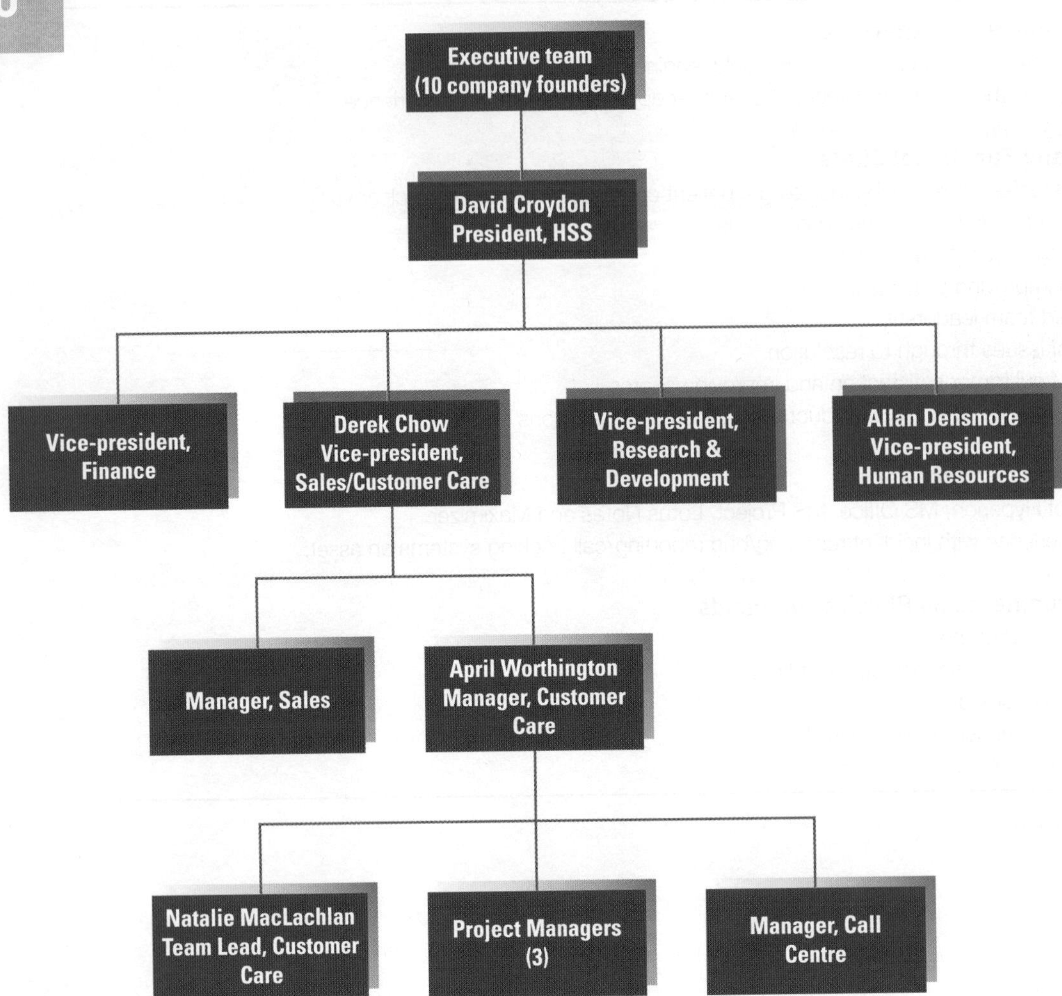

Source: Field

EXHIBIT 3 Floor Plan of Hospital Software Solution's Ottawa Headquarters

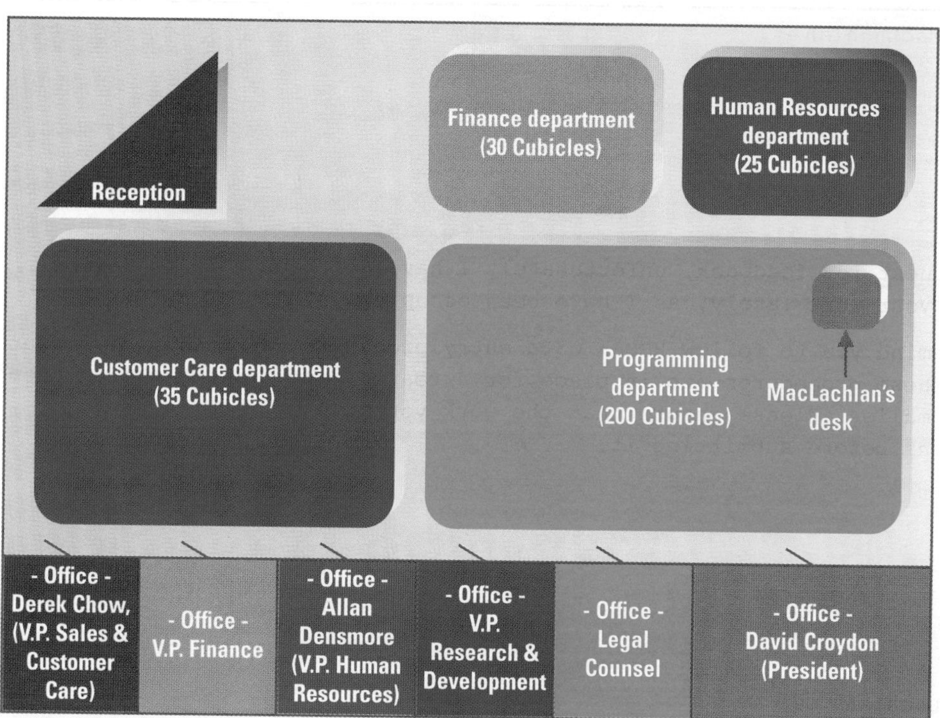

2.0

EXHIBIT 4 E-Mail Correspondence Between Derek Chow and Natalie Maclachlan

TO: Natalie MacLachlan

FROM: Derek Chow

SUBJECT: Re: My performance?

Natalie,

Regarding your request for feedback, unfortunately I have not been able to devote much attention to your work lately, as I have been occupied with other matters.

However, I will remind you to follow HSS's data entry procedures as outlined in your employee manual. These procedures are in place for a reason, and deviating from them may cause data anomalies. Please ensure that the work you have done conforms to these specifications before submitting it.

Regards,

Derek Chow

TO: Derek Chow

FROM: Natalie MacLachlan

SUBJECT: My performance?

Hi Derek,

Just wondering if you could give me some feedback on my performance as of late. I have been working hard on the data entry tasks you gave me, and I think I have come up with a way to tabulate the information without requiring a manual check. This makes the process significantly faster. I have attached the files for your review.

Thanks,
Natalie

Natalie MacLachlan, HBA
Team Lead, Customer Care Hospital
Software Solutions

Source: Field

HOSPITAL SOFTWARE SOLUTIONS (B)

2.0

Three months into her tenure at Hospital Software Solutions (HSS), Natalie MacLachlan had had just about all she could take. Her tasks had been limited to data entry and database cleanup, which was certainly not the experience she had envisioned when she signed on to be a customer care team lead. Furthermore, MacLachlan had developed a reputation among her supervisors as the team slacker, even though she was doing work outside of her job description and trying to improve the way HSS handled data. Yet, nobody seemed to want to listen to her. To add to her frustrations, the computer systems MacLachlan was working on were starting to display more problems, and she was receiving conflicting instructions from two managers in the office. She knew she needed a plan of action to get herself out of this mess – fast.

The Town Hall Meeting

MacLachlan believed the best way to solve her concerns quickly was to attend the town hall meeting[1] and speak to the company president. She did not want to be blamed for the system problems that were occurring, and she was worried that if she voiced her concerns to the two managers, Derek Chow and April Worthington, they would simply dismiss her concerns as more complaining. As well, the programming team would be attending the meeting so it would be a good opportunity for collaboration to solve the problems quickly. MacLachlan considered telling the president about her frustrations with the misalignment between her job description and actual tasks, but she decided against it, believing it was a matter that should stay between her and her direct supervisors.

At the town hall meeting, MacLachlan voiced her concerns about the system processes, making sure not to blame anyone. The programmers were very pleased that their error had been uncovered, and thanked MacLachlan for her work on the project. They specifically commented that they would not have had the opportunity to hear from her if she had not spoken up at the town hall meeting, since the programming and customer care teams rarely shared information. The president also seemed impressed. He made a point of approaching MacLachlan after the meeting to commend her on a job well done. MacLachlan thought this would be an excellent opportunity to start building a relationship with someone influential at HSS, so she decided to send the president an e-mail shortly after the meeting, thanking him for the opportunity to be heard (see Exhibit 1).

April Worthington

MacLachlan continued to try to work with Worthington in an attempt to resolve the issues between them, chiefly the disconnect between MacLachlan's job description and her day-to-day tasks. MacLachlan scheduled a meeting with Worthington to go over the job description she had originally received. She also tried to involve Densmore, the vice-president of human resources, who had developed the position, but she found out that he had left the company. Following a review of the job description, Worthington assured MacLachlan that she would try to find her some more varied tasks; however, she cautioned that doing so would be difficult, given that Densmore had hired MacLachlan while Worthington was on maternity leave and she was not aware of the

[1] 'Town hall' meetings are designed to provide a public link between upper management and front-line personnel. They are usually open to all employees and are often used by management to share corporate strategy or receive feedback from employees in a public forum.

Jason Stornelli wrote this case under the supervision of Elizabeth M. A. Grasby solely to provide material for class discussion. The authors do not intend to illustrate either effective or ineffective handling of a managerial situation. The authors may have disguised certain names and other identifying information to protect confidentiality.

team lead position until her return. Over the next few months, Worthington continued to promise MacLachlan training opportunities and different tasks, but nothing materialized. MacLachlan wondered whether Worthington believed Densmore had made a poor hiring choice.

MacLachlan had observed that Worthington would appear very friendly and willing to help her staff progress within the company, but she was not very supportive of them if they ran into difficulty. She would often say that the job of her subordinates was 'to make me look good'. She also did not take criticism well. MacLachlan and her colleagues wondered whether the nice behaviour was an act, especially when they were on the receiving end of one of Worthington's tirades if a task was not completed correctly.

Because she found it difficult to work with Worthington, MacLachlan would avoid her whenever possible. She preferred to work with Chow – although he was busy, he at least made an effort to be civil. Often, MacLachlan still received conflicting requests to perform work from both managers, and she would usually choose to complete Chow's work first, even though Worthington was her direct supervisor. In fact, MacLachlan frequently deferred Worthington's tasks until Worthington asked for them, at which time MacLachlan would rush to finish them. At the same time, MacLachlan was making some great progress with her assigned work from Chow. She was also working closely with the programmers to ensure things were running smoothly, and she was finally gaining some leadership experience.

The Performance Review

Regular performance reviews were conducted every six months for all employees at HSS. These evaluations affected pay and were often a major factor in determining whether an employee would stay with the company past their first year of employment. There were three parts to a typical performance review. First, the manager noted the employee's performance in a written report that would be placed in the employee's file. Managers were asked to examine a number of dimensions, including an employee's fit with the HSS culture, performance of job tasks, potential for future development, etc. After the written report was completed, the manager discussed his or her findings with the employee in a formal meeting. Finally, the employee completed a '360-degree review', which was an opportunity for the employee to provide feedback to his or her manager.

In December 2005, Worthington met with MacLachlan in the HSS conference room to discuss her performance over the past six months:

Worthington:

'Natalie, I'm rather concerned about your performance. Over the past six months, you have done little to improve.'

MacLachlan:

'Well, April, I haven't really had the opportunity ... I'm still doing data entry. You promised I could go on the Leading Change training course three months ago, and I still have not been able to.'

Worthington:

'You haven't had the opportunity because every time I ask you to do something, it isn't done.'

MacLachlan:

'Well, I've been working on stuff for Derek Chow.'

Worthington:

'Natalie, I'm your boss. Not Chow. I expect you to do what I ask you to do, and for you to stay as long as I need you to stay. As a result, I'm going to be rating you as a 'Needs Improvement' on your completion of job tasks. Since I rarely see you, you will also be receiving a 'Needs Improvement' on your interaction with me and the rest of the team.'

MacLachlan:

(Sputtering) 'But ... April! That's not fair! Chow knows I have been working ...'

Worthington:

(Cuts off MacLachlan) 'And another thing: don't ever go over my head again. I've seen your e-mail to the executive team, and I know you're complaining about how I manage this department. Let me remind you I've been with this company for nearly 11 years and you've been here less than one. Your lack of enthusiasm and insubordination are definitely being noted in your personnel file.'

To end the meeting, Worthington threw down a copy of MacLachlan's e-mail that she had sent to the president after the town hall meeting and left the room.

MacLachlan was shocked. She was certainly not complaining about Worthington to her superiors – in fact, she had made a point of not doing so. The town hall meeting had led to positive changes in the customer care department, so why was Worthington making such an issue? MacLachlan knew she could not stand to have statements like these in her personnel file, statements that she felt were blatant lies about her performance.

As she stood up to leave the conference room, MacLachlan wondered what to do next.

EXHIBIT 1 Email from MacLachlan to Hospital Software Solutions' President

FROM: NATALIE MACLACHLAN (TEAM LEAD - CUSTOMER CARE)
DATE: AUGUST 5, 2005
TO: DAVID CROYDON (PRESIDENT, HOSPITAL SOFTWARE SOLUTIONS)

SUBJECT: THANKS FOR LISTENING!
MESSAGE:
Hi David,

I just wanted to thank you for the opportunity to air my concerns that we've been facing lately in the Customer Care unit. It's great to have a leader who is willing to address staff concerns and work with us to reach constructive solutions!

Thanks again,
Natalie MacLachlan

Natalie MacLachlan, HBA
Team Lead, Customer Care Hospital
Software Solutions

Source: Field

3.0

INTEGRATIVE CASE 3.0 AIRASIA: THE SKY'S THE LIMIT

'Now everyone can fly' – AirAsia had been drumming South-east Asians to take to the skies by making air travel affordable to the masses. In October 2004, AirAsia successfully attracted over USD 200 million in fresh capital through an Initial Public Offer (IPO) of its shares.[1] In December 2004, it announced its decision to purchase up to eighty Airbus A320s (Defence-aerospace 2005). Arguably, AirAsia not only enabled many ordinary people to travel by air, but also stirred up competition and encouraged the formation of several low-cost airlines in South-east Asia (SEA). The financial market recognized its impressive financial performance, and Morgan Stanley Capital International Inc. (MSCI) included AirAsia Bhd's[2] shares, which were listed on the Kuala Lumpur Exchange, in its global index, the MSCI Standard Index Series (The Star Online 2005). By February 2005, its shares were traded at a 50 per cent premium (RM 1.78) to its offer price (The Star Online 2005). How did AirAsia achieve such spectacular success?

Company Background

AirAsia was incorporated in 1993, with Hicom Berhad and Mofaz Air as shareholders. In 1996, it became Malaysia's second national carrier and commenced full-service domestic operations with two Boeing 737–300s. It initially flew from Kuala Lumpur (the capital of Malaysia) to four destinations – three in East Malaysia (Kota Kinabalu, the capital of Sabah; Labuan, the Federal Territory and an offshore financial centre; and Kuching, the capital of Sarawak) and one in West Malaysia (Langkawi, a duty-free island and holiday destination). In December 2001, Tune Air acquired AirAsia from DRB-HICOM Bhd.[3] for RM1 (USD 0.26) and assumed its debt of RM 40 million (USD 10.5 million). The management team, headed by its CEO, Tony Fernandes, transformed AirAsia into a successful low-cost carrier and within two years expanded its fleet nearly eightfold to fifteen aircraft. Exhibit 1 shows the milestones of AirAsia's progress. By 30 June 2003, despite its limited operational and financial resources, AirAsia achieved a net profit of RM35 million (USD 9.2 million) on the back of RM 400 million in revenues – a major turnaround from a profit of RM 232,000 (USD 61,000) in 2002 and a loss of RM 19.1 million (USD 5.0 million) a year earlier. Within three years, AirAsia had built a brand and become a household name, not only in Malaysia, but also in Thailand, and increasingly in Singapore and Indonesia.

AirAsia's main operations remained in Malaysia, but it had shareholding interests in Thailand through Thai AirAsia (a low-cost carrier based in Bangkok, Thailand) and in PT AWAir (a low-cost carrier based in Jakarta, Indonesia). AirAsia operated from four hubs: Kuala Lumpur International Airport (KLIA) in Sepang near Kuala Lumpur; Senai, near Johor Bahru in the southern part of West Malaysia, close to Singapore; Don Muang Airport (DMA), near Bangkok, Thailand; and Soekarno–Hatta International Airport, near Jakarta, Indonesia. Exhibit 2 shows the air routes of the AirAsia group. Exhibit 3 provides a

[1] Based on the price of RM 1.25 per share for institutional investors (560,407,500 shares) and RM 1.16 per share for retail investors (140,101,900 shares) – as reported in Airline Industry Information Online (M2 Communications Ltd). 1USD at RM 3.8.

[2] Bhd is an abbreviation of the Malay word 'Berhad', which means 'limited'. Bhd is thus used to indicate limited companies.

[3] DRB-HICOM was the result of a merger between two companies, DRB and HICOM.

profile of the AirAsia group; and Exhibit 4 details income, cost of sales and expenses.

Low-Cost Carriers Industry Background

Low-cost air travel was not a new phenomenon. Approximately 25 per cent of the domestic departing passengers in the United States of America (USA) and Australia travelled by low-cost carriers. In South-east Asia, there was thus room for low-cost carriers to increase their market share. A low-cost carrier, as the name suggests, was run on the principle of minimizing the costs of operations and maximizing sales revenues. Cost minimization was the core business principle that drove the business. This business principle did not imply that the products of a low-cost airline were always the cheapest in the market or that its products were of low quality. 'Low-cost' as a business principle simply emphasized the need to keep operating costs low. A low-cost business may have used high technology and costly equipment. The product proposition that low-cost carriers offered to customers was 'value', by delivering basic product functionality, that is, a cost effective means of transport. Carriers or airlines that adopted this principle included the 'original' low-cost carrier, Southwest Airlines (USA), as well as Ryanair (based in Ireland) and EasyJet (based in the United Kingdom).

Low-Cost Air Travel Markets in South-East Asia

AirAsia was the first low-cost carrier in South-east Asia. In Malaysia, MAS (Malaysian Airline System, the national airline of Malaysia) was AirAsia's main competitor. MAS was a full-service carrier that provided multi-class scheduled services to a network of more than 100 domestic and international destinations. It provided complimentary in-flight meals, a frequent-flyer programme and airport lounges for business and first class customers. In the past, MAS had offered 'Supersaver Fares' on almost all its routes within Malaysia. Supersavers enabled passengers to save up to 50 per cent of the usual economy class fares. On shorter routes, namely Kuala Lumpur to Senai and from Kuala Lumpur to Penang or Alor Star (two cities in the north of West Malaysia), AirAsia was in competition with ground transportation such as trains, express buses and self-driven cars. Driving time from Kuala Lumpur to these cities took less than five hours.

In addition to MAS, the AirAsia group also faced competition from carriers based in neighbouring countries. Thai AirAsia faced competition from Thai Airways International (THAI), Nok Air (a budget airline associated with THAI) and One-Two-Go (a budget airline associated with Orient Thai). On certain routes like, for example, Bangkok to Singapore, AirAsia faced fierce competition from scheduled airlines that chose to exercise their 'Fifth Freedom Right'[4] to fly and pick up passengers. Along this route, AirAsia was in direct competition against two budget and twelve full-service airlines. Exhibit 5 shows the major players in the aviation market, including low-cost carriers in South-east Asia. Exhibit 6 compares AirAsia's operational data with two of its main competitors, the scheduled airlines; Thai Air and MAS. Although the cost and revenue per ASK[5] for both of these scheduled airlines was relatively higher than that of AirAsia, the net revenue per ASK of AirAsia was almost the same as that achieved by Thai Air. Arguably, this shows that a low-cost model can produce a reasonable, if not better, net revenue than the traditional full service model.

According to the S–A–P Group LLC (an independent aviation consulting company engaged by the AirAsia Group), intra-regional passenger volumes in South-east Asia were expected to grow at an annual rate of 8.6 per cent per year between 2003 and 2008.[6] Five factors that were expected to drive the aviation activities in South-east Asia were cited:

i *A large demographic area*: South-east Asia was a large demographic area with a relatively 'good' per capita income growth. S-A-P, in its study, found that the number of air travels (passenger round trips) was positively related to per capita GDP (Gross Domestic Product). Exhibit 7 shows the relationship between per capita GDP and air travel in selected countries of Asia-Pacific. In South-east Asia, more than half of the population lived within a five and six hours flying radius from Bangkok and Kuala Lumpur respectively.

ii *Liberalized aviation industry*: Countries in South-east Asia had liberalized their aviation markets.

4 '*Fifth Freedom of The Air* – the right or privilege, in respect of scheduled international air services, granted by one State to another State to put down and to take on, in the territory of the first State, traffic coming from or destined to a third State (also known as the *Fifth Freedom Right*)' – International Civil Aviation Organizations (ICAO).

5 Available Seat Kilometers (ASK) is the total number of seats available on scheduled flights multiplied by the number of kilometers those seats are flown.

6 This was reported in AirAsia's IPO prospectus.

Thailand and China, for example, agreed to open their skies to each other's airlines. Nearly unrestricted airline operations were allowed between the two countries through the 'open skies agreement'. Additionally, China relaxed its travel restrictions and became more willing to issue exit visas for independent and group travel. Thailand also entered into an 'open-skies' agreement with India.

iii *The geography of South-east Asia*: Many parts of South-east Asia were separated by water and Indonesia had many islands. Surface (land and sea) transportation was not extensively developed and low-cost air transport services were an attractive substitute for land surface transport services.

iv *Growing numbers of business travellers*: Further expansion in the economies of South-east Asian countries and China increased the business activities within the region. On certain air routes, such as between capital and commercial cities – most notably along the Bangkok–Kuala Lumpur/Bangkok–Singapore corridor – low-cost air travel, when combined with increased frequency and reliable air schedules, was an attractive proposition to business travellers.

v *Increase in urbanization*: There was a strong trend towards urbanization in Southeast Asia. Growth in cities and the general population generated higher demand.

What was the potential market size and growth rate for air travel in South-east Asia? This could be anyone's guess, but the statistics seemed to point towards growth. The markets of AirAsia could be seen from many different angles: nationality of travellers, purposes of travel, types of needs (which required different products, for example, excess baggage and air freight facilities) and destinations that involved intra and inter-country travel by people from within the country and abroad. In this case, we highlight AirAsia's markets in terms of the countries where potential air travellers are based.

Market 1 – Malaysia

Malaysia comprised West and East Malaysia, which were separated by the South China Sea. By 12 October 2004, AirAsia operated 322 flights from Kuala Lumpur International Airport (KLIA) to fourteen domestic and eight international destinations (three in Thailand and five in Indonesia) and another sixty-three flights from Senai to four domestic and two international destinations. Malaysia had a total population of approximately 24.3 million with a per capita Gross Domestic Product (GDP) of USD 3,905.[7] Malaysia's per capita GDP in 2005, in terms of PPP (Purchase Power Parity) was equivalent to USD 10,449 (International Monetary Fund 2005). With a relatively high per capita GDP, Malaysians could afford to travel more frequently. AirAsia had so far managed to get a fair share of domestic passenger movement within Malaysia. From January 2002 to June 2004, AirAsia's share on all routes was 23.1 per cent (1.35 million persons) but this translated into a higher share of 24.1 per cent on the routes that AirAsia flew. By 2015, the proportion of urban population in Malaysia was expected to increase to 66 per cent, from a current share of 59 per cent of the whole population. Knowing that AirAsia was based in Malaysia, foreign tourists might consider using Malaysia as their base to travel within South-east Asia. Malaysia was among the world's top fifteen tourist destinations, which in 2002 attracted 13.3 million visitors (World Tourism Organization 2005).

Market 2 – Thailand

Thailand had a population of 61.6 million and a per capita GDP of USD 2,060. Thailand's per capita GDP in 2005, in terms of PPP, was equivalent to USD 7,851 (International Monetary Fund 2005). It covered a land area of 513,115 sq km and it offered many tourist attractions (Tourism Thailand 2005). From its hub in Don Muang Airport (DMA), Bangkok, Thai AirAsia commenced operations in February 2004. In the first five months of operations, Thai AirAsia carried 380,400 passengers to or from DMA, the majority of which (86.7 per cent) were travelling on Thailand's domestic routes. Within five months of operations, Thai AirAsia managed to build a market share of 11.9 per cent of domestic passenger movement. Domestic passenger movements at Thailand's major airports (Bangkok, Phuket, Chiang Mai, Chiang Rai, and Hat Yai) grew at a compounded average annual growth rate of 10.6 per cent between 1985 and 2003. This growth rate gave Thai AirAsia a tremendous opportunity to carry more passengers. In the international market, Thai AirAsia was in a competitive position to serve destinations in India, Burma, Bangladesh, Cambodia, Vietnam and Southern China. In 2002, 10.9 million foreign tourists entered Thailand (World Tourism Organization 2005). Moreover, Thailand's open

---

7 In 2002, based on S-A-P's report and quoted in the AirAsia IPO prospectus.

sky policy was likely to facilitate airlines in bringing in more foreign tourists.

Market 3 – Indonesia

Indonesia was a populous country. It had a population of 211.7 million (three and a half times that of Thailand) and per capita GDP of USD 817. Indonesia's per capita GDP in 2005, in terms of PPP, was equivalent to USD 3,661 (International Monetary Fund 2005). It had a land area of over 1 million sq km (twice that of Thailand) and was the largest archipelago in the world, with over 17,500 islands spread in an area between the Asian continent and Australia, and between the Pacific and the Indian oceans (Tourism Indonesia 2005). Indonesia's urban population, which was AirAsia's potential market, accounted for 43 per cent of its total population (World Bank 2005).

Market 4 – Singapore

Even though Singapore had a comparatively small population of 4.16 million, it was among those countries with the world's highest per capita GDP. Singapore's per capita GDP in 2005, in terms of PPP, was equivalent to USD 25,385 (International Monetary Fund 2005). It was a city-state and a well known international destination. More than forty airlines flew in and out of Singapore (World Airport Guide 2005).

Although AirAsia did not fly into Singapore, travellers could, for about USD 1 (RM 4), take a shuttle bus from Senai Airport to City Lounge in Johor Bahru and then change to another bus that would take them to Kranji (mass rapid transit (MRT)—a rail service) station in Singapore (Senai Airport 2005).

Market 5 – Other Countries

Several other untapped markets could also be served by AirAsia. These included Cambodia, Vietnam, Laos, Southern China, Burma, Sri Lanka, Bangladesh, Southern India, the Philippines and even Western Australia. Hubs in East Malaysia, Thailand and Indonesia could serve destinations in these countries. News clips in Exhibit 8 show that AirAsia arranged to fly to China and the Philippines in April 2005. Thai AirAsia was also planning to fly to seven other southern China destinations, that is, Guangzhou, Naning, Kun-ming, Wuhan, Chengdu, Chongqing and Hankou by the end of 2005 (The Star Online 2005). In 2003, China was among the world's top air passenger markets, registering 21.9 million passengers, and that was expected to grow at an annual rate of 12.5 per cent until 2008, according to the International Air Transport Association's (IATA) forecast (IATA 2005).

AirAsia Business Strategies

3.0

AirAsia targeted markets (destinations) within a three-and-a-half hour flight-time from its hubs. These destinations covered virtually the whole of South-east Asia. It was estimated that approximately 500 million people would be able to travel through these destinations. Short flight-time air routes would enable AirAsia to optimize the utilization of its aircrafts and other ground support assets. AirAsia optimized both the frequency and turnaround time (time between arrival and departure). It was one of the airlines that had the world's lowest cost per ASK (Available Seat Kilometers, which is the total number of seats available on scheduled flights multiplied by the number of kilometers those seats are flown) at US 2.5 cents.

AirAsia believed that it had six business strengths:

Single-class, No Frills Service

There was only one class in all AirAsia flights, and the service did not provide free in-flight meals, in-flight entertainment, airport lounges or other amenities. Neither did it have a loyalty programme for its customers. However, customers could purchase a wide range of items aboard AirAsia flights, such as snacks and merchandise. AirAsia priced its one-way travel seats based on expected demand and time of booking. On every route, its fare structure comprised twelve tiers of fares, and offered customers savings depending on how far in advance a particular booking was made and the level of demand for the seats. Purchased seats were non-refundable and changes, when allowed, involved an administration fee.

High Aircraft Utilization and Efficient Operations

AirAsia maximized the utilization of the Boeing 737–300, which it operated in a number of ways. It fitted an additional sixteen seats to the typical 132 seats on a two-class configuration. It operated on a longer working day, which commenced at 0700 hrs, and it maintained a low turnaround time of approximately 25 minutes compared to the 45–120 minutes that was typical of full-service airlines. AirAsia planned its routes and operations so that on average its aircrafts were used for a 12–13 hour block, compared to the 8 hour block typical of full-service airlines. This higher aircraft utilization rate enabled AirAsia to mount five additional round trips per aircraft per week or more than 200 per aircraft per year. AirAsia also multi-tasked by hiring employees who were capable of carrying out varied jobs.

3.0

Low Fixed Costs

AirAsia negotiated and obtained lower lease charges for its aircrafts, lower rates for long-term maintenance contracts, lower airport fees and lower rates on its insurance fees, because of its high safety and maintenance standards. Employees were not unionized and a large portion of their remuneration was tied to their productivity. Pilots were provided with incentives to keep flight and operation times to a minimum and to cover as many flight sectors as possible on a given day. Cabin crews were rewarded for punctuality, availability for duty and standby, and fewer leaves. Ground crew remuneration was based on both basic salary and productivity-related compensation, which was measured by performance and commission from the sale of seats, as well as linked to factors such as service skills, product knowledge, attendance, punctuality and the ability to perform multiple tasks. In addition to basic salary, type-rating allowances were awarded to the engineers in recognition of the individual's technical qualifications. In the area of information technology, AirAsia invested in the necessary technology that would not only improve efficiency but also cost less to use. Instead of purchasing software, AirAsia subscribed for it on an annual basis, using OpenSkies for inventory and sales management, Microsoft's Axapta for financial management, the Geneva Optimum Airline Performance for flight scheduling and crew rostering, and ASPrecise's Engineering Software Solution for managing aircraft maintenance engineering and logistics.

Low Product Distribution Costs

AirAsia did not issue tickets, and that helped save administrative costs and related expenses. It sold its seats through the Internet, its agents, sales offices, mobile phone SMS and a Nationwide Call Centre (NCC). Customers, however, had to pay a nominal surcharge on bookings made through the mobile phone SMS and call centre. Seats sold through the Internet were priced at a discount to seats sold through other channels. By August 2004, the Internet channel accounted for 50 per cent of all bookings/sales. Customers could also pay for their seats through credit cards, or through cash at banks, post offices and other third party outlets in various countries, such as mobile telecommunication operators. In addition to this, AirAsia also maintained a network of 'preferred' travel agents, 'sky agents', sales stations and sales offices located at airports and throughout Malaysia, as well as in the countries it operated in. 'Preferred' travel agents were those that had registered with AirAsia. They maintained a pre-paid account with AirAsia, from which purchases were made while customer payments were secured. 'Sky agents' did not have accounts with AirAsia but they could book and pay for purchased seats with their own credit cards or the credit cards of their customers. 'Preferred' and 'sky' agents did not earn any commission from AirAsia, but they were allowed to charge customers for their services.

Using a Single Aircraft Type

AirAsia operated a fleet of similar aircrafts, that is, Boeing 737–300s. Simplified maintenance (that resulted from using one type of aircraft and engine) and reduced spare parts inventory requirements helped AirAsia to increase cost savings.

Maximizing the Benefits of Regional Media Coverage

AirAsia's success in South-east Asia attracted publicity and the group used these opportunities to promote and increase its brand awareness without additional promotional costs. It was awarded 'Superbrand' status in Malaysia by Superbrands International.

AirAsia continued to find ways to reduce its cost of operations without compromising safety and customer service. Like other airlines, fuel was a major component of its cost of operations, and AirAsia implemented a number of strategies to keep its fuel costs to a minimum. For example, it hedged its fuel purchases (approximately 83 per cent of its purchases in the year 2003–04). Whenever permissible, its aircraft carried minimum fuel, and purchased fuel from suppliers at destinations where it was less expensive. AirAsia paid for its fuel upfront, which gave it bargaining power to obtain better prices. It also had clear policies and guidelines covering all areas of flight operations that, among others, aimed at minimizing fuel consumption. For instance, its pilots took their aircrafts to their optimum height within the shortest period of time and they took straight-line paths. AirAsia also decreased the overall weight of its aircrafts by eliminating unnecessary load, such as ovens in aircraft galleys and built-in steps. Its efforts in reducing costs resulted in a 50 per cent overall reduction in cost per ASK (from USD 0.050 or ½ cent, to USD 0.025 or ¼ cent within the four years and three months from March 2000 to June 2004). However, during the same period, lower average fares resulted in a 30.7 per cent reduction in revenue per RPK, from RM 0.205 (USD 0.0539) to RM 0.142 (USD 0.0374).

In addition to the above, AirAsia prided itself on building a strong, team-focused corporate culture. AirAsia's core strategy involved maintaining low costs while achieving high productivity. It also had a proven management team that had been together since the company commenced operations in 2002. The Centre of Asia Pacific Aviation awarded AirAsia the title of 'Asia Pacific Airline of the Year' in 2003. Since June 2002, AirAsia employed over 1,800 people in Malaysia and 322 in Thailand.

What was Next?

AirAsia's goal was to establish itself as a leading low-cost carrier in Asia. It had seven strategies:

Stimulating Demand by Offering Low Fares

It believed that its success in attracting air travellers and building customer loyalty depended on the ability to continue to offer low fares – fares that were, on average, substantially lower than the published fares of full-service competitor airlines in the countries in which it operated.

Expand within Asia

AirAsia planned to do this by focusing on routes that were under-served by other airlines within Malaysia, Thailand, Indonesia and other countries in South-east Asia and China.

Increase Flight Frequencies

AirAsia considered this as a key strategy because it expected that air travellers would not only want low fares, but would wish to benefit from convenience in terms of the availability of flights. It planned to increase the frequency of flights in its established markets, and those with high growth potential.

Continue to Minimize Operating Costs

Cost minimization could be achieved by several measures. The first was to encourage air travellers to book their flights online. Second, it would continue to contract out aircraft maintenance services, ground handling and ground support services at airports in Indonesia, Macau and Singapore. Contracts would be awarded through a competitive bidding process or negotiation. Third, it would continue to adhere strictly to its 'low-cost carrier model' and leverage its economies of scale to further reduce the per unit cost of input by negotiating better terms with suppliers and airports.

Invest and Enhance AirAsia's Brand

AirAsia regarded its brand as an important asset. It planned to refine its branding strategy and increase brand awareness, particularly in Malaysia, Thailand, Indonesia and Singapore. AirAsia wanted to be 'the people's airline' and its tag line 'Now everyone can fly' underscored that objective. It was very selective in choosing its media of communication – it normally used print, supported by radio and outdoor advertising. It also participated in community and charity projects, and helped to promote local and international artists. AirAsia allocated up to 3 per cent of its revenue for marketing campaigns and activities.

Continued Focus on Customer Service

Despite its low fares, AirAsia emphasized high-quality service that was friendly and personal. This was achieved through effective recruitment and staff training. AirAsia embarked on initiatives that sped-up bookings and check-ins, improved handling services, and provided rapid and effective responses to customer feedback. It monitored its punctuality performance and published it on its website.

Optimization of Revenue and Development of New Revenue Streams

AirAsia used a revenue management system that was geared to optimize revenue from passenger seat sales. It also worked towards increasing revenues from other sources, such as freight and charter services, holiday packages and hotel rooms. It sold food and beverages under its own brand, 'SnackAttack', and worked towards acquiring exclusive or more advantageous concessions at airports, particularly those airports where AirAsia contributed more than 50 per cent of the total traffic. In addition, AirAsia also worked in alliance with other organizations. It teamed up with RHB Bank in Malaysia to launch AirAsia Credit Cards; and with Singapore's DBS to issue debit cards, credit cards and charge cards bearing the AirAsia logo. In its efforts to attract corporate customers, AirAsia launched 'GoCorporate' – a product, which offered services to companies that purchased more than 500 point-to-point sectors a year. Corporate customers not only enjoyed cost savings on fares, but also flexibility and convenience when they chose to purchase AirAsia's fully flexible fares. In addition, AirAsia's system allowed companies to track and manage their employees' travel details. Advertising was another source of income. 'TIME dotcom Berhad', for instance, paid RM 800,000 (USD 210,000) to use AirAsia aircrafts as its 'flying billboard' for three years. Other revenues came from excess baggage fees, administration fees, and cancellation charges.

There were a number of risks faced by AirAsia, particularly increased competition. Aircraft maintenance costs could also increase and there was a risk that its ground support service contractors might not be able to deliver services that were integral to its international business operations. For the year ending June 2004, fuel costs accounted for approximately 31 per cent of AirAsia's cost of sales. Its ability to contain this cost was crucial to its future success. AirAsia relied on the Internet to minimize its distribution

3.0

costs, but the group's primary markets, particularly new markets in Thailand and Indonesia, had low Internet penetration and credit card usage. Historically, South-east Asia's economy had experienced economic upturns and downturns, as well as currency depreciations and appreciations. A recurrence of economic upheavals in the South-east Asia regions was potentially devastating. Finally, yet importantly, demand for air travel was sensitive to adverse news such as terrorism, or the recurrence of illnesses like SARS (Severe Acute Respiratory Syndrome) and the bird flu.

The Future

AirAsia had decided to acquire eighty Airbus 320s through forty purchase obligations and forty purchase options (Defence-aerospace 2005). Delivery of the new aircraft was to commence in 2006. In the light of growing competition from other low-cost carriers, semi-low-cost carriers and full-service airlines (see Exhibit 5), the air travel market had, in general, become more competitive. There were mixed comments from travellers who had used AirAsia (see Exhibit 8). The airline now faced a number of issues that could enhance or inhibit future growth. First, it had to identify further opportunities to reduce costs, so that it could continue to offer lower prices. Second, it had to identify new markets, so that it could increase the number of customers and revenues. Third, it had to find new sources of revenue other than from fares.

The Sky's the Limit! What further specific actions could AirAsia take?

Please address all correspondence to Dr Rizal Ahmad and Dr Mark Neal at Department of Marketing, Sultan Qaboos University, Oman. E-mail address: rizal@squ.edu.om, markneal@squ.edu.om

EXHIBIT 1 The Milestones of AirAsia's Progress

2001

- Lease agreements for two aircrafts are renegotiated resulting in a significant reduction of average monthly aircraft leasing costs.

2002

- AirAsia's Nationwide Call Center (NCC) at Kelana Square commences operations, enabling guests to pay for their reservations by phone.
- Ticketless services are launched.
- Internet booking and on-line payment services commence operations.
- Fleet expands to four Boeing 737–300 aircraft by leasing two additional aircraft.
- Operations at Kuala Lumpur International Airport (KLIA) commence.

2003

- Fleet expands to eleven aircraft, nine of which are leased and two of which are purchased.
- IDBIF Malaysian Investments Ltd, Crescent AirAsia Investments II, Ltd (CAAL) and Deucalion Capital II Ltd (DCL) acquire a 26 per cent shareholding for RM 98.8 million.
- The world's first airline booking by SMS from a guest's mobile phone is introduced.
- AA International Ltd (AAIL) forms a joint venture with Shin Corporation[8] to invest in Thai AirAsia.
- Operations from Senai commence.
- International flights between Kuala Lumpur and Thailand begin.

(Continued)

[8] Shin Corporation: a Public Limited Company based in Thailand.

EXHIBIT 1 *(Continued)*

2004

- Fleet expands to twenty-four aircraft (of which sixteen aircraft are operated by AirAsia, four leased to and operated by Thai AirAsia and four are expected to be in operation, two in Malaysia and two in Thailand, by the beginning of November 2004) of which eighteen are leased and six are purchased.
- Thai AirAsia, managed by AirAsia, commences operations with flights to Chiang Mai, Phuket, Hat Yai, Khon Kaen and Singapore.
- AirAsia commences international flights to Indonesia.
- AirAsia acquires a 99.8 per cent interest in AA International Ltd.

Awards and Accolades

The Group and its CEO, Tony Fernandes, have received the following awards and accolades:

AirAsia

- Asia Pacific Airline of the Year 2003 by the Centre for Asia Pacific Aviation, an independent private aviation consultancy company.
- Air Finance Journal's Development Airline of the Year 2003.
- Top 100 Company, CIO 100 2004, by CIO Asia, a subsidiary of International Data Group.
- www.airasia.com voted as the most popular website for online shopping in the 11th Malaysia Internet User Survey conducted by AC Nielsen Consult.
- Awarded Malaysian SuperBrand status by SuperBrands International based on an evaluation by professionals from the branding and media industry and, more importantly, results from a consumer evaluation from a regional study conducted by SuperBrands International.

Tony Fernandes, CEO of the Group

- Emerging Entrepreneur of the Year 2003, Ernst & Young Entrepreneur of The Year Malaysia 2003.
- CEO of the Year 2003, American Express Corporate Services & Business Times.
- International Herald Tribune award for the Visionaries & Leadership Series in 2003.

Source: AirAsia's IPO prospectus, 2004.

EXHIBIT 2 The Air Routes of AirAsia Group as of 12 June 2004

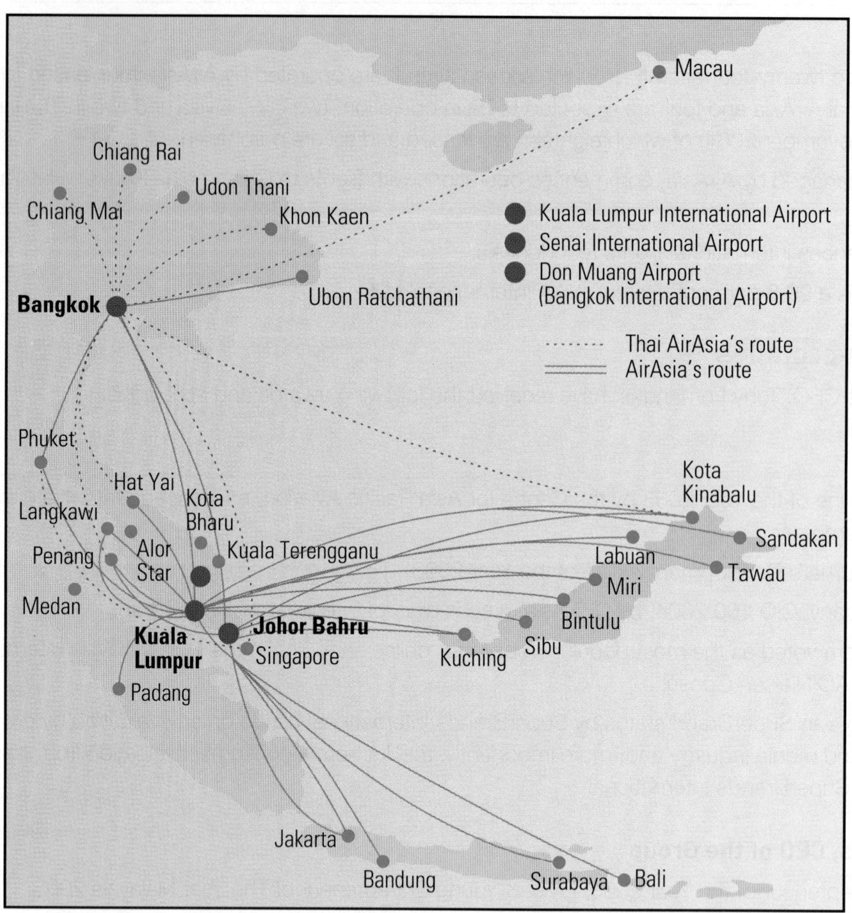

Source: AirAsia's IPO prospectus, 2004.

EXHIBIT 3 Corporate Structure of AirAsia Berhad

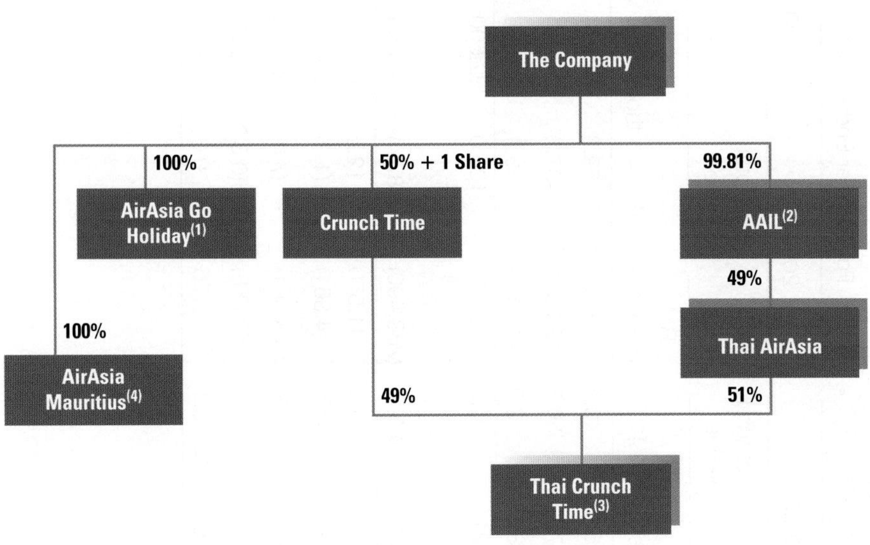

Notes:

(1) Operating company for 'Go Holiday' and 'Get A Room'

(2) Effective July 1 2004, the Company will equity account for Thai AirAsia's results (Please refer to Section 13.2.7 'Management's discussion and analysis of financial condition and results of operations – Results of Significant Associate')

(3) Thai Crunch Time is effectively 49.4% owned by the Company

(4) Leasing entity

No. of aircraft AirAsia operates as of 30 June 2004: 13.

No. of employees as of 30 June 2004: 1,382. This includes AirAsia's cabin crew and pilots seconded (loaned) to Thai AirAsia and Crunch Time employees.

[Thai AirAsia has 436 employees including Thai AirAsia's cabin crew and pilots seconded to AirAsia.
Additionally, AirAsia and Thai AirAsia have arrangements for sharing and/or loaning their pilots and cabin crews to each other, as when that becomes necessary].

No. of destinations: 28 (18 domestic and 10 International). In addition, Thai AirAsia serves 10 destinations (7 domestic and 3 international destinations).
No. of hubs: 2 in Malaysia. (Thai AirAsia has a hub in Bangkok).

Source: AirAsia Berhad IPO prospectus, October 2004, p. 66.

EXHIBIT 4 Details on Income, Costs of Sales and Operating Expenses

13.3 Income Statement

The table below shows AirAsia's, income statement, the components of which are expressed as a percentage of total revenue, for the periods indicated.

	For the Year Ended March 31,				For the 15 Months Ended June 30,		For the Year Ended June 30,			
	2000		2001		2002[1]		2003		2004	
		% of total revenue		% of total revenue		% of total revenue		% of total revenue		% of total revenue
Revenue:	(RM thousands)	(%)	(RM thousands)	(%)	(RM thousands)	(%)	(RM thousands)	(%)	(RM thousands)	(%)
Passenger seat sales................	41,181	27.6	44,041	26.3	87,856	40.4	195,864	59.3	347,971	88.6
Chartered flight revenue............	105,844	70.9	118,409	70.6	123,179	56.7	123,061	37.3	24,514	6.3
Other revenue	2,260	1.5	5,299	3.1	6,386	2.9	11,115	3.4	20,205	5.1
Total	149,285	100.0	167,749	100.0	217,421	100.0	330,040	100.0	392,690	100.0
Cost of sales	(171,994)	(115.2)	(176,463)	(105.2)	(208,147)	(95.7)	(288,490)	(87.4)	(279,119)	(71.1)
Gross (loss)/profit	(22,709)	(15.2)	(8,714)	(5.2)	9,274	4.3	41,550	12.6	113,571	28.9
Sales and marketing expenses	(640)	(0.4)	(409)	(0.2)	(1,499)	(0.7)	(4,361)	(1.3)	(9,411)	(2.4)
Administration expenses	(2,862)	(1.9)	(3,523)	(2.2)	(7,936)	(3.6)	(23,061)	(7.0)	(34,351)	(8.7)
Other operating expenses	(2,573)	(1.8)	(2,048)	(1.2)	(1,445)	(0.7)	(3,758)	(0.3)	(4,563)	(3.3)
Other operating income	566	0.4	136	0.1	307	0.1	1,175	0.3	4,563	1.1

EXHIBIT 4 *(Continued)*

	For the Year Ended March 31,				For the 15 Months Ended June 30,		For the Year Ended June 30,			
	2000		2001		2002[1]		2003		2004	
		% of total revenue		% of total revenue		% of total revenue		% of total revenue		% of total revenue
Revenue:	(RM thousands)	(%)	(RM thousands)	(%)	(RM thousands)	(%)	(RM thousands)	(%)	(RM thousands)	(%)
(Loss)/profit from operations..........................	(28,218)	(18.9)	(14,558)	(8.7)	(1,299)	(0.6)	11,545	3.5	61,318	15.6
Finance costs........................	(3,075)	(2.1)	(4,559)	(2.7)	(308)	(0.1)	(84)	-	(3,131)	(0.8)
Share of losses of an associated company............	-	-	-	-	-	-	-	-	(116)	-
(Loss)/profit before taxation	(31,293)	(21.0)	(19,117)	(11.4)	(1,607)	(0.7)	11,461	3.5	58,071	14.8
Taxation	(35)	-	(21)	-	(56)	-	7,375	2.2	(9,052)	(2.3)
(Loss)/profit after taxation	(31,328)	(21.0)	(19,138)	(11.4)	(1,663)	(0.7)	18,836	5.7	49,019	12.5
Minority interests....................	-	-	-	-	-	-	2	-	48	-
(Loss)/profit attributable to shareholders	(31,628)	(21.0)	(19,138)	(11.4)	(1,663)	(0.7)	(18,838)	5.7	49,067	12.5

EXHIBIT 4 *(Continued)*

13.3.2 Cost of Sales and Operating Expenses

The following table presents AirAsia's cost of sales and operating expenses, which are also expressed as a percentage of total cost of sales and operating expenses, for the periods indicated.

	For the Year Ended March 31,				For the 15 Months Ended June 30,		For the Year Ended June 30,			
	2000		2001		2002[1]		2003		2004	
		% of toal cost of sales and operating expenses		% of toal cost of sales and operating expenses		% of toal cost of sales and operating expenses		% of toal cost of sales and operating expenses		% of toal cost of sales and operating expenses
Cost of Sales and Operating expenses	RM Thousands	%	RM Thousands	%	RM Thousands	%	RM Thousands	%	RM Thousands	%
Cost of sales										
Aircraft fuel expenses	34,477	19.4	41,417	22.7	63,980	29.2	93,581	29.3	102,707	30.6
Aircraft operating lease expenses	68,898	38.7	72,858	39.9	74,492	34.0	78,989	24.7	42,790	12.7
Maintenance and overhaul expenses	19,598	11.0	17,828	9.8	13,804	6.3	55,876	17.5	73,778	22.0
Staff costs	8,248	4.6	8,340	4.6	10,626	4.9	25,496	8.0	48,403	14.4
User charges and station expenses	23,287	13.1	18,669	10.2	24,071	11.0	21,837	6.7	9,579	2.9
Others	17,486	9.8	17,351	9.5	21,174	9.6	12,714	4.0	1,862	0.5
Total cost of sales	171,994	96.6	176,463	96.7	208,147	95.0	288,490	90.2	279,119	83.1
Operating expenses										
Sales and marketing expenses	640	0.4	409	0.2	1,499	0.7	4,361	1.4	9,411	2.8
Administration expenses	2,862	1.6	3,523	1.9	7,936	3.6	23,061	7.2	34,351	10.2
Other operating expenses	2,573	1.4	2,048	1.2	1,445	0.7	3,758	1.2	13,054	3.9
Total operating expenses	6,075	3.4	5,980	3.3	10,880	5.0	31,180	9.8	56,816	16.9
Total cost of sales and operating expenses	178,069	100.0	182,443	100.0	219,027	100.0	319,670	100.0	335,935	100.0

Note: (1) In 2002, the company changed its financial year-end from March 31 to June 30 to coincide with the financial year end of Tune Air.
Source: Airasia's IPO prospectus, 2004

EXHIBIT 5 Major Players in the South-east Asia Aviation Market Including Low-cost Carriers

Current Low-Cost Carriers and Low-fare Carrier Market Shares (Estimated)
Departing Seats
As at June 1, 2004

	Domestic Activity		International Activity (a)	
Country	Share	Carriers Included	Share	Carriers Included
India	1%	Air Deccan	-	-
Indonesia	21%	Lion Air	8%	AirAsia, Lion Air, Valuar
Malaysia	25%	Air Aisa	5%	AirAsia, Lion Air
Philippines	33%	Cebu Pacific Air	-	-
Singapore	n.a	-	2%	Thai Air Asia, Lion Air, Valuair
Thailand	20%	Orient Thai (b), Thai Air Asia	2%	Air Asia, Thai Lion Air, Valuair

Notes: (a) within Southeast Asia region, (b) operating as One-Two-Go. n.a. = not applicable
Source: AirAsia's IPO prospectus, 2004.

Low-cost airlines in Asia

Thailand: Bangkok Airways, NOK Air, and One-Two-Go.

Singapore: JetStar Asia, Value Air, and Tiger Airways.

Indonesia: Adam Air, Lion Air, and Citi Link.

Philippines: Air Philippines and Cebu Pacific Air.

Pakistan: Aero Asia and Air Blue.

India: Air Deccan, Air India Express, Kingfisher, and Spicejet.

Japan: Air Do, Air Next, Ibex Airlines, JAL Express, Skymark Airlines, and Skynet Asia Airways.

Source: http://www.attitudetravel.com/lowcostairlines/asia/

3.0

EXHIBIT 6 Comparative Operational Data on AirAsia, MAS and THAI*

	AirAsia [1]		Malaysia Airline Syatem (MAS)[2]		Thai Airways International (THAI)[3]	
	2004 (as of June 30)	2003 (as of June 30)	2004 (as of 31 March)	2003 (as of 31 March)	2004 (as of Sept 30)	2003 (as of Sept 30)
No. of aircraft	13	7	109	99	83	8
No. of types of aircraft	1	1	8	9	9	9
No. of passengers carried (*000)	2,839	1,481	15,375	16,325	19,540	17,048
ASK (mil)	3,592	2,086	55,692	54,266	69,830	63,826
RPK (mil)	2,771	1,539	37,659	37,653	50,633	44,396
Cost per	RM 0.094	RM 0.109	RM 0.154	RM 0.163	THB 1.837	THB 1.893
ASK	USD 0.025	USD 0.029	USD0.041	USD 0.041	USD 0.037	USD 0.038
Revenue	RM 0.142	RM 0.151	RM 0.233	RM 0.235	THB 3.014	THB 3.030
per RPK	USD 0.037	USD 0.040	USD 0.061	USD 0.062	USD 0.061	USD 0.061
Revenue	RM 0.029	RM 0.029	RM 0.042	RM 0.043	THM 0.042	THB 0.044
per Ask	USD 0.029	USD 0.029	USD 0.042	USD 0.043	USD 0.042	USD 0.044
Difference between Revenue and Cost per ASK	USD 0.004	USD 0.000	USD 0.001	USD 0.002	USD 0.005	USD 0.006

Notes: *Exchange rate used = 1 USD = RM 3.8 = THB 49.594.

1. Figures were obtained and, when relevant, calculations were based on data published in AirAsia IPO prospectus, 2004, p. 73. The stated figures were based on AirAsia's operating information for its scheduled flights to and from KLIA and Senai – its hubs in Malaysia.
2. Figures were obtained and, when relevant, calculations were based on data obtained from Malaysia Airline Annual Report 2004. (Also available on http://hq.malaysiaairlines.com/mys/eng/about_ us/investor_relations/annual_reports/annual_reports.asp, accessed 2 July 2005.) In calculating Cost and Revenue per ASK and per RPK, revenues refers to total revenue; and operating expenses refers to total expenditure stated under the performance highlights.
3. Figures were obtained and, when relevant, calculations were based on data obtained from Thai Airways International Annual Report 2004. (Also available on http://www.thaiair.com/About_ Thai/Investor_Relations/annual_reports.htm, accessed 2 July 2005.) In calculating Cost and Revenue per ASK and per RPK, revenues refers to total operating revenue; and operating expenses refers to operating costs stated in the account.

3.0

EXHIBIT 7 The Relationship between Per Capita GDP and Air Travel in Selected Countries of the Asia-Pacific

The figure below highlights this relationship for 13 countries in the Asia-Pacific region.

RELATIONSHIP BETWEEN PER CAPITA GROSS DOMESTIC PRODUCT (GDP) AND AIR TRAVEL

Select Countries in Asia-Pacific Per Capita 2002

Country	Per Capita GDP (in Current US$)	Total passenger roundtrips
Australia	$ 20,822	1.11
Brunei	$ 18,151	1.29
China	$ 989	0.04
India	$ 487	0.01
Indonesia	$ 817	0.05
Japan	$ 31,407	0.55
Malaysia	$ 3,905	0.42
New Zealand	$ 14,872	1.53
Pakistan	$ 408	0.02
Philippines	$ 975	0.08
Singapore	$ 20,886	3.30
South Korea	$ 10,006	0.42
Thailand	$ 2,060	0.26

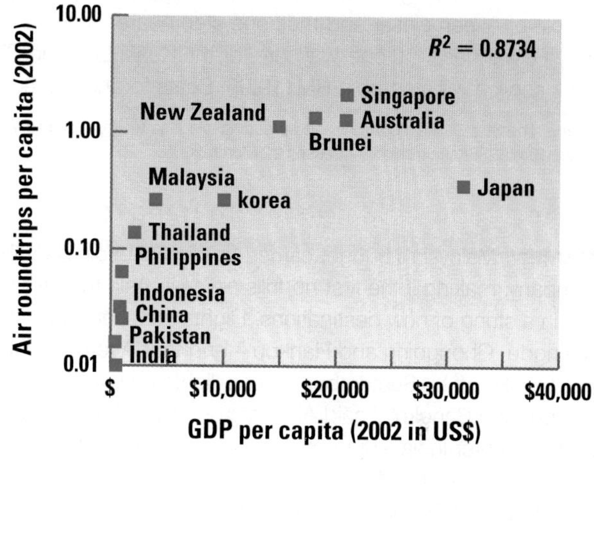

Notes: Amounts include domestic and international air travel to/from reporting airports in the countries shown and may include some transfer passengers. Roundtrips represent double one-way passenger movements.

Source: S-A-P Group LLC, reported in AirAsia's IPO prospectus, 2004.

3.0

EXHIBIT 8 Selected News Clips on AirAsia

AirAsia spreading wings to Philippines

PETALING JAYA: AirAsia will commence flights to Diosdado Macapagal International Airport (formerly the Clark Angeles Airport) in Manila beginning April 5. According to a statement, daily flights for this new service would begin simultaneously out of KL International Airport and Kota Kinabalu International Airport. 'By connecting Clark to Malaysia, and linking it to our network of flights serving Thailand, Indonesia, and Macau, AirAsia is indirectly bringing the people of Asean closer and thus one step nearer to achieving a borderless Asean policy,' said the airline group CEO Tony Fernandes. The one-way fare for the Kuala Lumpur–Clark route starts from RM129.99 while the Kota Kinabalu–Clark service will start from RM119.99. Seats for the respective flights would be available for sale from March 19.

Source: The Star Online (2005), AirAsia spreading wings to Philippines, http://www.thestar.com.my/news/story.asp?file=/2005/3/22/nation/10479833&sec=nation. Accessed 22 March 2005.

AirAsia to fly to Xiamen from Bangkok

XIAMEN: Malaysia's budget carrier AirAsia will begin daily flights to this Chinese city next month through its Thai sister company, making it the first no-frills airline in Asia to enter China. The Bangkok–Xiamen route, starting April 25, is the first in a string of new destinations. Flights to seven cities in southern China— Guangzhou, Naning, Kunming, Wuhan, Chengdu, Chongqing and Hankou – and four Asean countries – the Philippines, Laos, Cambodia and Vietnam – are due to take off by September. 'These flights may take off from Kota Kinabalu and Penang as well, not just from Kuala Lumpur and Bangkok,' said AirAsia group CEO Tony Fernandes. 'Coming to China is a huge step. Another major step will be to enter India – but not right now,' he said, adding that Thai AirAsia was offering 8,888 seats at a special launch fare of 388 yuan (RM178) or 1,899 baht for one way. These fares, which exclude airport tax and fees, are valid from April 25 to Oct 29, he told a press conference, after a ceremony to announce the airline's entry into China, here yesterday. Fernandes said the company had secured most of the aircrafts required for its new routes. On the company's inroads into China, he said: 'The market is right, the airport (Xiamen) is right, Thai AirAsia is strong.'

Source: The Star Online (2005), AirAsia to fly to Xiamen from Bangkok, http://archives.thestar.com.my/ last30days/default.asp?Query=airasia&NewSearch=True. Accessed 21 March 2005.

AirAsia considers flying to Darwin from Kota Kinabalu

AirAsia and Australia's Northern Territory officials are willing to hold talks on flights between Sabah and Darwin. 'We never turn down any offer. We are keeping an open mind,' AirAsia executive director Kamarudin Meranun told *Agence France-Presse*. Kamarudin said the route between Sabah capital Kota Kinabalu and Darwin in the Northern Territory is within the three-hour time horizon of the carrier. Meanwhile, Northern Territory International Trade Director Quentin Kilian told *AFP* such a link would promote tourism and trade and help make state capital Darwin a departure point for Australian tourists. 'We're certainly interested in discussing it ... everything hinges on it being a commercial reality,' Kilian said. 'The opportunity is very much there,' he added. Northern Territory officials were in talks with a number of airlines about expanding Darwin's currently limited international reach of direct flights to Singapore, Denpasar in Bali and Brunei only, he added. 'What we want to do is open up both trade and tourism links within the near region,' he said, adding that this could include Malaysia and Brunei. Kamarudin said AirAsia's Indonesian unit, PTAWAIR International (AWAIR), was also keen to launch flights from Bali to Darwin. 'We can also do the Bali–Darwin route,' he said, adding that AirAsia would have to conduct a feasibility study before making a decision. AirAsia operates in Malaysia, Thailand, Indonesia, the Philippines and Macau and will become the first no-frills foreign airline to fly to China next month with daily services between Bangkok and Xiamen in Southeastern China. – AFX-Asia

Source: The Star Online (2005), AirAsia and Australia ready to discuss Kota Kinabalu–Darwin flights, Wednesday 30 March 2005. http://biz.thestar.com.my/news/story.asp?file=/2005/3/30/business/ 10543154&sec=business. Accessed 30 March 2005.

(*Continued*)

EXHIBIT 8 *(Continued)*

Passenger opinions

AirAsia – by Wouter Gijs

5 August 2004

We used AirAsia on 3 internal flights. Booking was done through the internet which was swift and correct. At the airport, you just show the booking printout and the passports. You get a flimsy boarding pass looking like a supermarket bill. They are serious about overweight luggage because you are allowed just 15 kg – but the extra charge is just 50 baht/kg. Airplanes are modern Boeing 737s. One class configuration, all leather seats. Seat pitch is narrow. Families with children board first. The seats are not allocated. Drinks and snacks (and even AirAsia souvenirs) are sold at economical rates. Toilets are clean, the airplane is clean enough. Staff is friendly and correct. Prices were 300 baht to Udorn and 500 baht on the Phuket stretch. These prices seem to have increased a bit recently. Be aware about the fact that AirAsia doesn't guarantee connections on their own flights. You have to get out of the airplane and check-in again for the next flight. This forced us to take a Nokair ticket on the Phuket–Bangkok–Udorn Thani stretch – otherwise we would have had to wait 5 hours! AirAsia advertises itself as 'now everyone can fly'. It is very economical and the quality is there. Good alternative from Nokair and Orient Thai (and Valuair on the Singapore stretch for visa runs). Each flight the plane was full. Each flight had a small departure delay of about 10–20 minutes. But arrival times were almost correct. You can book by phone, internet and also at regional small offices. Domestic terminals of Bangkok, Phuket and Udorn Thani are small and convenient.

AirAsia – by K. Kwan

18 September 2004

I've flown with AirAsia a few times. Their airfares are the talk of the town and I must agree these are rock bottom prices; hence, this is the main reason I chose to fly with them. Services rendered, on board and ground, are comparable to more established airlines. Their call centres for ticket bookings are efficient and helpful. However, I've noticed that AirAsia has one blatant flaw that's given the airline immensely bad publicity. This airline will simply postpone or cancel a scheduled flight at the very 11th hour. Most of this occurs either during when its patrons are on their way to the airport or during check-in. I've experienced this 'stunt' twice myself and it messed up one of my family vacations. No apology was given, they will simply put you in the next flight out. And when I questioned them about the incident, the check-in staff simply replied that they've sent a text message to my mobile to inform me about the delay. I was given no option but to accept this unacceptable explanation and then tortured myself by waiting for a few more hours for the next flight. I really hope that AirAsia can seriously look into this matter, as people hate it when their trip itinerary is ruined, be it a vacationer or a business traveller.

AirAsia – by Stephen Blakey

5 January 2005

Despite sending frequent emails to AirAsia since December 1st, requesting information on a specific scheduled routing for April 2005, I have still not received the courtesy of a reply or an acknowledgement from them. This draws into question how customer focused they may be in other areas as well and I would therefore be very wary of booking with them.

AirAsia – by Al Patok

28 January 2005

I've flown AirAsia around 10 times, international, domestic Malaysian, and domestic Thai, including just last weekend (BKK–UTH–BKK for less than US$30 return). I have usually been quite happy: the value for money is amazing by any standard. Usually flights depart on time and everything goes like clockwork, but like all low-cost carriers, the tight scheduling can cause problems: a single mechanical problem (even on a different plane) can cause multi-hour delays to cascade through the schedule for the rest of the day. Don't take AK/FD if you have a tight connection to catch, but for leisure travel it's more than OK in my book.

(Continued)

3.0

EXHIBIT 8 *(Continued)*

AirAsia – by Paul Hotchan

2 February 2005

I flew AirAsia from MFM (Macau)–KLIA–MFM on the 27th of Jan. The reason why I chose this flight is because its timings allowed me to have two full days in KL for meetings whilst only staying one night. Make sure you get an early check-in from your hotel! Outbound from Macau, the flight left bang on time. Very competent and personable cabin and flight crew. Full of smiles and laughs which was surprising as they were turning around after a 4 hour flight from KUL. Hot meals (Nasi Lemak) were available for purchase, in addition to the usual drinks & snacks. Noticed that the majority of passengers were mainland Chinese who probably expected a full service airline – many of them asked for blankets, and were surprised to see a menu with prices. Return flight was a different story however. Flight delayed over 45 minutes due to technical problems. Boarding was very confused and chaotic as there was a flight to Kuching departing after us from the same gate. However, the Kuching passengers were in the boarding area together with us. The boarding screens showed that the Macau flight was on final call whilst the Kuching flight was not yet boarding according to the monitors – but in fact it was the other way round. Many of the Macau passengers boarded the Kuching flight. Once the ground crew realized what was happening, they had to check everyone on the Kuching flight and this led to a further delay. The crew onboard this flight wasn't as professional as the previous flight.

AirAsia – by Karin Ho

23 February 2005

I have flown with AirAsia 6 times and suffered no delays yet. Booking through their online website was convenient and time saving. I would like to add that since this IS a BUDGET Airline, do NOT expect first class bells and whistles service. Paying peanuts and expecting a SIA/MAS full service is not fair to AirAsia. I like the crew's crisp red uniforms and the Thai AirAsia's leather seats. Just wish we could meet the pilots. I just returned from Bangkok on Feb 18, 2005 and will be flying to Trengganu on Feb 28. April 25, 2005 will be my maiden flight to Macao. Thank you AirAsia for providing us with an affordable way to fly.

AirAsia – by Roger Mathastein

7 March 2005

Would like to agree wholeheartedly with Karin Ho. Recently flew with my wife from Bangkok to Chiang Mai and return. On time both journeys. No faults at all as far as I am concerned. It is a budget airline. Some of the budget airlines closer to home could learn a lot from AirAsia. Very pleasant experience. Would book again with absolutely no hesitation.

AirAsia – by Dominik Choy

15 March 2005

HKT-KUL and KUL-BKK.[9] Both flights departed and arrived on time. Check-in staff was efficient, friendly and helpful, for a moment you thought it was a non-budget airline. The staff was very efficient in turning the aircraft around – 20 mins back to back. The seats were comfortable enough, no complaint because we paid only £5 to KUL and £60 to BKK – my fault booked it last minute.

Source: Airlinequality.com (2005), Airline forum on AirAsia, http://www.airlinequality.com/Forum/ air_asia.htm. Accessed 24 March 2005.

[9] HKT = Hong Kong. KUL = Kuala Lumpur. BKK = Bangkok.

References

Defence-aerospace. 2005. 'Air Asia Seals 80 Aircraft, Deal—Airbus A320 Picked for New Fleet', http://www.defence+aerospace.com/cgi+bin/client/modele.pl? prod=50651 & session + dae.9820346. 1109677751. QIRWE 80a9d UAACMV SoE & Modele = jdc_1, accessed 1 March 2005.

IATA. 2005. 'Internation Cargo and Passenger Forecasts 2004 to 2008, 15 December 2004' http:// www.iata.org/pressroom/industry - stats/2004-12-03.htm, accessed 25 March 2005.

International Monetary Fund. 2005. http://www.imf.org on wikipediahttp://en.wikipedia.org/wiki/ list-of-countries by GDP-% 28PPP% 29-per-capita, accessed 22 March 2005.

Senai Airport. 2005. http://www.senaiairport.com/city-lounge.html, accessed 22 March 2005.

The Star Online. 2005, 'Air Asia Added to the MSCI Standard Index Series' http://biz.thestar.com.my/ news/story.asp? File1/2005/2/16/ business/10174525 & sec=business, accessed 18 February 2005.

——. 2005. 'CEO:AirAsia up to the Challenge, 25 March', http://biz.thestar.com.my/news/ story.asp? File=/2005/3/25/ business/10488065&sei=business, accessed 25 March 2005.

——. 2005. 'RM 4 Billion Value for Successful AirAsia Business Model', The Star, 19 February 2005, http://biz.the star.com.my/ news/story.asp? file=/2005/2/19/business/10208988 7 sec=business, accessed 1 March 2005.

Tourism Thailand. 2005. 'Facts at a Glance' http://www.tourismthailand.org/about_thailand.php? Module=plan& file = plan 01

Tourism Indonesia. 2005. 'General Information', http://www.tourismindonesia.com/index.php? Option = com.content & task = view & Iternid = 41, accessed 25 March 2005.

World Airport Guide. 2005. http://www.singapore—sin.com/airlines.html, accessed 22 March 2005.

World Tourism Organization. 2005. 'Inbound Tourism – World's Top Tourist Destinations, http://www.world-tourism.org/facts/tmt.html, accessed 24 March 2005.

World Bank. 2005. 'Indonesia Social Indicators', http://sitesources.worldbank.org/INTINDONESIA/Resources/Country=Data/ SocialIndicators.pdf, accessed 25 March 2005.

http://www.findarticles.com/p/articles/mi-mocwu/is.2004-Oct-29/ ai_N 6274688, accessed 21 March 2005.

http://www.icao.int/cgi/goto.pl? icao/en/trivia/freedoms-air.htm

4.0

INTEGRATIVE CASE 4.0
MATT COFFIN

Lunchtime: Los Angeles, January 11, 2005. Following the early morning birth of his daughter Orchid, Matt Coffin was back on his BlackBerry keeping close tabs on his other baby; LowerMyBills.com. His company was poised to post its first million-dollar revenue day, and the talented motivator was doing what he did best: charging around among his 250 'best of the best' employees to inspire passion and extreme wins.

What better day to be selling his business? That night, at a favoured Hollywood diner, he'd be meeting with one of his key people to detail the sale to a corporate buyer that was prepared to pay a sizable fortune for the closely held venture.

So why was Matt filled with such trepidation about the harvest? Was this really the time to sell, or were there better options?

Down East Roots

Matt Coffin, the oldest of three enterprising children, grew up on the coast of Northern Maine, not far from the Canadian border. His parents, Greg and Marcia, were hardware store proprietors, and Matt witnessed early on the challenges and benefits of business ownership. By his teens he'd become fascinated by the creative process of building a profitable enterprise from nothing more than an innovative idea.

Drawn to the small-school environment and its focus on entrepreneurship, Matt attended Babson College in Wellesley, Massachusetts. Not one to wait for anything like graduation to get down to business, he developed a dorm room venture called Boston's Best Storage – a summertime operation that served to defray many of his college expenses.

In a new venture creation module at Babson, Matt developed a business plan for a jobs newsletter listing summer employment in places that were the place to be: Nantucket, Cape Cod, Martha's Vineyard and the like. Although he never launched the business, those investigations served to spark an interest in publishing and creative advertising vehicles.

From Boston Bars to New York Fashion

Matt graduated from Babson in 1990 with a steady mate (Natasha Esch, a fellow Babson student with a similar interest in enterprise), and a unique idea:

> *Right after I graduated, I started a business placing display ads and billboards in local bars – inside the bathrooms where I figured I'd have a captive audience. I signed up around 15 bars and nightclubs in Boston, and then went out and found advertisers. The biggest challenge, of course, was that on Friday and Saturday nights college kids being crazy would deface and even tear down my boards, so every week I had to run around replacing them. We got sales and it got off the ground, but it wasn't a success.*
>
> *It was a great example of 'not a big idea'. An interesting one, but not big. And it really showed me; wow, I didn't know the first thing about building a real business.*

Intent on enhancing his advertising and sales skills, Matt accepted a job from Natasha's father at a small marketing firm in New York City. After she graduated, Natasha joined him in NYC to run Wilhelmina Models, an agency her father had purchased. While Matt enjoyed his work, it wasn't long before he was off on a new challenge:

> *The bar thing was an early instigator around advertising and media, and that experience led me to start a magazine in New York called* Fashion Reporter. *The idea was* Entertainment Weekly *meets* Women's Wear Daily. *Glossy paper, lots of brief articles geared for short attention spans and a trade focus in the fashion business.*

This case was prepared by Carl Hedberg under the direction of Professor William Bygrave. Funding provided by Babson College.

The modest publishing venture was a partnership with Brett Markinson, a friend from Babson who had graduated a year earlier than Matt. Brett, who was doing well building his own business interests out in Los Angeles, was able to serve as Matt's primary financial supporter. Matt raised a total of $200,000, hired a competent team, and after a few very challenging months, was able to break even. By that time, however, Matt felt that he'd gained a clearer understanding of what constitutes an attractive opportunity:

> *Fashion Reporter was a great and amazing experience, but I didn't know anything about fashion and I didn't care. I was really just chasing the money and trying to grow it so I could sell it off. We had raised about a tenth of what we should have, we had a limited upside-potential, and we were in an industry that was massively consolidating in response to the emerging Internet.*

After a series of accolades in the press, *Fashion Reporter stabilized*. Ad revenue climbed, and to his delight, Matt began to receive general interest from a few potential buyers – including a consolidating publisher who would come to play a dramatic role in Matt's career trajectory.

Natasha was feeling burnt out as well:

> *I had been running Wilhelmina for five years. The company was doing well, but I wasn't having much fun at it. Any business that is talent-oriented is going to be a really tough place to manage – primarily because the expectations and demands of the talent are often completely unreasonable.*
>
> *Matt was saying that if I was up for quitting my job, we could move to LA and he could run* Fashion Reporter *from there until he was able to find a buyer. We returned home to a garbage strike in New York City. The street to our apartment was lined with trash. We looked at each other and knew we were out of there.*

When Matt informed Bob Miller of the decision to move west, the publisher offered him a job as director of development at MPG. Bob added that although he was not interested in acquiring *Fashion Reporter*, he did like the idea of adding a hard-core startup entrepreneur to his corporate group of former Time Inc veterans. Matt easily decided to close down his small venture so that he could give full attention to his work at MPG.

New Horizons

Based in Los Angeles, Bob Miller had been a highly regarded publishing executive at Time Inc when he began his own company, Miller Publishing Group (MPG), by purchasing *Vibe*, Spin, Where, and four other special-interest magazines from The New York Times Company. Matt set up an appointment to pitch *Fashion Reporter* to MPG, and in the fall of 1997, he and Natasha flew out to Southern California. While Matt was unable to close the deal, the visit marked a sea change in his thinking:

> *After seeing Bob's operation, I came to the conclusion that I wasn't getting any pleasure out of bootstrapping. Being the owner of an underfinanced, marginally profitable magazine in a non-high-growth category just wasn't a lot of fun. I wanted a situation like MPG where I could attract the greatest people – real killers.*
>
> *Often times in a bootstrap situation it is really tough to find excellent people because killers tend to be doing big things, they have family obligations, and they have a base of experience they expect to get paid for. At that time, only the dot-coms were able to attract superior talent for short money and promises.*

Pain-Point and Opportunity

Working at MPG proved very enlightening. Internet companies were all the rage, and e-versions of established magazines were fetching as much as twice the price of the printed parents that had spawned them. During this time, Matt was getting calls from recruiters with 'big' opportunities in a variety of dot-coms; he always turned them down and got back to work.

Matt and Natasha were married in May of 1999. Life in LA was far from cheap, and substantial bills began to roll in – including their hefty new mortgage and a cell phone charge fattened to $1,300 by roaming fees. Matt recalled the situation:

> *I was looking at our bills relative to how much I was making, and said 'Whoa, this is not good!' So I started calling a bunch of cell phone providers and mortgage companies to find out their rates. I have always been good with numbers, so I figured it wouldn't be hard to create a spreadsheet that would help me determine the best deals.*
>
> *After calling lots of companies, hanging on hold for hours, and tracking all of the figures I had gathered, I still didn't seem any closer to a solution.*

4.0

I screamed, 'This is so painful! I have to do something about these bills; I have to lower my bills...'

I decided to search for a one-stop service where I could comparison shop to get a better deal and lower my bills. What would such a business be called? Lower My Bills. I typed that into my browsers and got nothing.

Remember; this is 1999, at the peak of the Internet boom. So I bought LowerMyBills.com, LowerYourBills.com, as well as a few misspellings. My initial investment was about $70.

Matt added that his fevered Internet opportunity investigation resulted in a pair of pivotal calls:

I thought maybe there is a storefront business called Lower My Bills. I dialled 411 for LA and for NY, figuring that if something like that existed it would be there.

Both operators said the exact same thing. They started laughing and said, 'No we don't have it, but I need that, so when you find it you call me back'. It was uncanny. Almost immediately, I decided to quit my job.

But before he gave up his steady income at a job he enjoyed, Matt decided to investigate a bit further. What he discovered was all good:

I flew to New York for my MPG work, and in my off-time I took a meeting with a venture capitalist that a friend had introduced me to. There were a few young Ivy League MBAs there, and before I had gotten back to LA, one of them had called a friend of his who worked for the largest investor in Miller Publishing. That guy called Bob Miller to let him know that I was thinking about starting a business.

Matt got a heads up on what his boss knew, and immediately set up a time to talk:

Bob was so gracious. He said, 'I hired you to come here and think about new ideas, and the risk of doing that was that you'd come up with one that didn't fit with what we're doing.' Then about my idea, he said, 'I get it; good luck'.

Rising with the Tide

Matt charged ahead on Internet time. Within a couple of days he had parlayed lunch with a friend who founded e-hobbies into a meeting with Sky Dayton; the founder of Earthlink and e-companies, a high-profile incubator. Using 10 basic PowerPoint slides, Matt presented his idea to the investor arm at e-companies. Less than two weeks later, he received a $4 million term sheet[1] – but not before he'd had an odd encounter on the way to the money:

As an entrepreneur there are funny things you have to fight through. We were talking about saving people money on a wide range of different categories of bills, and one of their analysts wanted to know why we're not also in drinking water. He harps on that one thing; poking at it, poking at it. I started to argue with him – but only for about a minute before I realized that you don't need to convince everyone in the world that you're right. One of their team members however, Len Vickers, a long time ad industry expert, said 'I get it. I don't get many of these dot-coms, but Lower My Bills could be on a billboard and consumers will get it instantly.'

Matt accepted the investment but declined their offer to start up as a tenant within the incubator:

The incubator terms were not something that I was interested in. They were asking for a much larger equity stake than I wanted to give up. The space and technical expertise they were offering might have been very helpful, but really expensive if your company takes off. Plus, I am a squeaky wheel, so I would just prod them for free help whenever I needed it.

Instead, I found some really cheap office space in North Hollywood. It was so run down that on one side the heat worked, and on the other side the air conditioning worked. It was one or the other. That space built into the culture of LowerMyBills; we were going to focus on the stuff that was really important– and everyone could see that I was ridiculously on top of the numbers.

Matt had grown to dislike two aspects of new venturing; negative cash flows, and trading equity for investment capital. Even so, he was not interested in high-concept solutions:

Everybody was encouraging us to go and sign a multi-million dollar deal with someone like America Online, or to concentrate mainly on building revenue. We didn't do any of that. Instead, I hired the best

[1] Earlier, Matt had received a $250,000 commitment from an investor group that included fellow Babson graduates Brett Markinson and Konstantin Glasmacher. He had not called the money until the deal with e-companies was finalized. Although the $4 million deal with Dayton's group significantly increased the pre-money valuation of the company, Matt rolled the $250,000 investment into the deal at the original valuation of $2.5 million.

people I could find who were connected with our mission of becoming profitable as soon as possible.

Matt described an aggressive hiring technique that had proved highly effective:

I was hiring teams rather than individuals. Our initial tech team, for example, was seven guys from US Web who were interested in a more entrepreneurial challenge. That was a big win for us because they walked in and were able to help us make a lot of fast headway.

Some owners see a talented team of four and feel they can only afford to hire two of them. But if you hire all four, you'll get the power of six. It's a smart investment.

Matt pointed out that his role as the lead entrepreneur reflected the fact that his hires were passionate individuals who understood their areas of expertise a lot better than he did:

What I can do that no one else can do at the company is to run around and pump people up. I am passionate, and from the beginning I have been rallying employees to get wins every day. That evolved to the idea of 'krushing'; we know we are getting wins, but are we getting extreme wins? Now every employee goes through an orientation programme called Krushing 101.

LowerMyBills was a free online service that worked by enabling consumers to enter their pertinent information, which was then used to match them with participating companies across 18 categories, including home mortgage, home equity loans, purchase loans, debt consolidation loans, credit cards, auto loans, insurance and cell phones (see Web site: www.lowermybills.com). Revenues were derived by charging those service companies on a pay for performance basis, either for a new customer, or a lead. LowerMyBills.com utilized aggressive direct business-to-business selling tactics to build a base of local and national players in each category. To attract consumers to the site, LowerMyBills developed a wide range of colourful and creative pop-ups and banner ads.

Before long, others began to spot the opportunity. A Massachusetts company, *Essential.com* had raised nearly $75 million, and a Harvard Business School group was providing a similar bill-reduction service with their venture *Get-connected*. Matt recalled that for a long while he was too busy to think about what his challengers were up to:

Early on it's not as much about the competitors as it is about you. You have to stay focused. Running a high-growth start-up is like being a driver in a NASCAR race. During the race those cars get really beat up, and everyone out there is leaking oil. So what the race comes down to is being able to pull into the pit stops to quickly fix fix fix and get back out there. Winning the race is not about having the most expensive or the prettiest car, it's about having a great team that knows how to execute under pressure – and win.

Matt explained that he developed a culture of peak performance by setting the bar high:

When I talk to my teams or to individuals, I am always asking how we can double that aspect of the business. In Vegas it's called doubling down. If you double down on the things that are working, and keep doubling down, you can grow a lot faster.

For instance, a momentum strategy that works for me is: We have two sales people, let's go to four. Four? Let's go to eight. Eight? Take it to sixteen... The idea is to double-down until you hit a wall. The key to doubling down is to make sure you have great metrics to measure so that you know what to focus your efforts on.

In 2000, LowerMyBills lost $8 million on revenues of $600,000. By the third quarter of 2001, the company had cut its loss-rate in half while generating revenues in excess of $5 million. Seed investor Brett Markinson noted that these significant improvements were related to an opportunity focus:

Interest rates were coming come down, the real estate market was cooking, and people were flocking to refinance their homes. All the stars were aligned.

LowerMyBills was providing a service for people to lower their bills across a broad series of categories, but they had not been getting much traction. After looking at the relationship between their revenue lines and the growth lines relative to all of the other components of the business, Matt singularly focused on the mortgage niche. As soon as he began pouring a lot of focus into that domain, his business started to take off.

LowerMyBills had become an Internet star with over 50 employees and a need for additional capital. That's when things got a bit ugly.

Adverse Change

When the capital markets softened in 2001, the irrational exuberance for Internet-related concepts evaporated almost overnight. No matter that Matt had never

4.0

subscribed to the 'revenues now, profits whenever' culture that had contributed to the market downturn; with its dot-com affiliation, LowerMyBills was entirely out of favour. Although he had come a long way towards building a solid, profitable operation, suddenly he found himself in survival mode:

> *This was the toughest situation I had ever dealt with. Investors didn't care that we were doing well; Internet companies were the devil. They wouldn't even return my phone calls. I was driving to work with a stomach ache every day for about nine months.*
>
> *It was so awful! I was going into the office and pumping people up, 'Are we getting wins?' Then I'd go back to the room with my finance guy and see that in very little time we weren't going to be able to make payroll. Early-stage venture money was being diverted to prop up existing portfolio investments, even my current investors were shying away.*

In the late summer of 2001, Matt attracted the interest of Jim Simons at St. Paul Ventures. Just after they had presented a term sheet, Matt received a most unwelcome call from his bank:

> *In the late 90s we had established a million-dollar line through Silicon Valley Bank – which at the time was giving out credit lines like candy. We had drawn down that line and now our cash balance was $750,000 – less than what we owed them.*
>
> *So they sent over what they call an* adverse change notice. *At the time I had signed the documents I didn't even know what that meant; yeah sure, just give me the million dollars.*
>
> *Now I realized that an adverse change notice is a small print clause that allows the bank to demand immediate repayment of the outstanding balance – pretty much at any time they felt like it. If you can't do that, they can take all the cash on hand and begin calling in assets. So now, instead of running my business and raising money, I was meeting with lawyers and fighting with my bank just to stay alive. Over time, it became clear that they were basically trying to squeeze me for more – that is, warrant coverage as a per cent of the loan.*

Seeing how dire the situation was becoming at LowerMyBills – and how close the venture had been to turning the corner – original investors came forward to help out. Investor Brett Markinson said that they all understood that Matt was the type of individual to support in a down market:

> *Everyone, including myself, had gotten sucked into the idea of raising as much money as you could and spending it on making noise. Matt had focused on raising as little as possible; he just kept his head down and concerned himself with driving value.*
>
> *Since Matt hadn't raised too much money, and had maintained a lean infrastructure, he was in a good position to really take advantage of the circumstances. While everyone else was cutting back or going out of business, Matt was able to rent space at a great price, and hire excellent talent at a great price.*

With a couple of investors putting in their own money, LowerMyBills was able to pay off the bank and secure the round. In the last quarter of 2001, LowerMyBills posted its first profit. Investor financing totalled $13 million, and Matt still owned nearly 33 per cent of the company. While he and his team saw profitability as a significant milestone for the business, they also understood that their big win was still a long way off.

High Speed Turns

The early 2000s at LowerMyBills became a long series of cliffhangers – each a test of the company's ability to remain flexible and execute on the fly. Rob Gabel, one of Matt's first hires,[2] recalled one such critical turning point:

> *By 2002, eighty per cent of our business was coming from pop-under ad units on the Internet. All of a sudden, Microsoft announces that the next version of Internet Explorer will have a pop-up blocker. Oh my gosh; losing eighty per cent of new customer inflow while you're trying to double the business each year isn't going to work...*

[2] Rob, an MBA from Stanford, who served as VP of Product & Consumer Experience, explained how he chose LowerMyBills from a number of other promising opportunities: 'I was interested in the model where you didn't need to ship a box or have any physical goods. I had met with GoTo which later became Overture, and a couple of other companies. One of the people at GoTo referred me to Matt as a generalist who could help him grow the business. Matt and I met on a Saturday at his office and had a free-ranging conversation for a couple of hours. He knew a lot about the Internet; he had some opinions and wanted to know my opinions as well. It was a conversation about searching for a better joint understanding about the market and what models were going to win. Matt is one of the most curious people I've ever met, and one of the fastest learners.'

We quickly got focused on getting active in the search space and in designing other types of banner units – and that reliance we had on pop-ups went away pretty quickly.

We were always coming up against fundamental challenges like that. In fact, if you took any point in the last five years – if we had stayed as the same business and mode then as we were – we would have not made it. You have to grow and change, or die by getting sucked up and supplanted by your competition.

A similar situation arose as the revenue from one customer topped 50 per cent of sales. The company swung into focused action, and within 12 months that customer contribution had been brought down significantly. Once again, Matt attributed the win to the team he had assembled:

Something that Google is really good at is attracting really smart, high brain-horsepower people who can think outside of the box. You need to be able to hire good mental athletes, and we have tons of people like that here.

But those people aren't cheap; you have to pay them and you have to motivate them so they don't get picked off by some other opportunity. I never realized that when you get your company to this level, you become the biggest target for recruiters trying to steal away your best employees.

In 2003, Matt broke from his own doubling tactic and increased the size of the tech department substantially in a short amount of time – from 10 to 50 employees. The problems stemming from that move – including a dip in morale and a severe lessening of effectiveness – nearly brought the company down. On the other side of that growth surge chasm, however, Matt and his team would arrive at the place they'd been pushing so hard to reach.

In the Money

In the last quarter of 2003, LowerMyBills posted a $2.3 million profit on sales of $17 million (see Exhibit 1). While Matt was now certain that he'd built a business of considerable value, at the same time he was concerned about his exposure to risk:

By 2004, I knew personally that I was way in the money, but I also knew that I had 99 per cent of my net worth tied up in the business. Back when the Internet crashed, I had a bunch of friends that had started online companies that had gone up and come down fast. One guy who had turned down an offer for $700 million went bankrupt a year later.

Investment banks were calling me like crazy to say it was time for us to go public. We looked at the possibility of raising additional capital from new investors – recapitalize with new shareholders so that current stakeholders could get some liquidity. There was also the option of selling to a corporate buyer while staying on in some sort of earn-out arrangement.

The team hired an investment bank and considered all of its strategic alternatives. The team began the process with the partial buyout route, gave eight presentations, and within short order had received five offers from private equity funds Private equity firms that were interested in a partial buyout were putting forward valuations that were lower than what the acquirers were offering. Matt added that his decision was about a lot more than financial gain.

Every employee owns stock in this business, and they have worked really hard to get us to this point. We did need some sort of harvest, but I also knew that we still had a lot of growth ahead of us, and every option has its own set of risks and potential ramifications.

From his vantage point, VP Rob Gabel noted that while the corporate buyers were willing to pay more, the risk of losing something special was higher as well:

By selling to a corporation, we all stand to make a significant amount of money. But then what happens to the culture when Matt lies four to five layers deep on an org chart – reporting to a guy who reports to a woman who reports to a guy in London? There are plenty of examples of companies getting acquired and becoming ghost towns as talent leaves in search of the type of culture we have here right now. With competitors like Barry Diller[3] out there, the last thing we need is to lose our edge.

Harvest Time?

The sun was low and bright as Matt hustled across Santa Monica Boulevard. With Natasha and Orchid

[3] Barry Diller was a long-time media magnate and CEO of IAC/InterActiveCorp. One of the many online businesses in his group was LendingTree, a leading financial services marketplace that provided consumers with 'the tools to efficiently manage their finances and access competitive financial products and services through a single online destination'. Consumers could explore a range of products including mortgages, home equity loans, auto loans and credit cards.

resting comfortably at the hospital, he was now on his way to meet with what he had determined was the best fit of eight corporate suitors.

It wasn't that he had any qualms about cashing out for millions, but what then? He was already making an excellent income running exactly the type of business he'd set out to create – and, today would be their first million dollar day. And what if this was all a fluke – more the result of an alignment of market factors rather than his prowess as an entrepreneur? If selling to a multinational doused the flame, could he do it again; build a dynamic company from nothing more than an innovative idea? And if he did leave, what would become of LowerMyBills and the team he'd assembled?

Matt walked into *Jerry's Famous Deli* in West Hollywood, still uncertain as to the outcome of this pivotal scene in his life. He took another deep breath and thought of the feedback Natasha had given him; *just do whatever you feel is best…*

Questions

1. Apply the Timmons entrepreneurship framework (entrepreneur-opportunity-resources) to frame this case. Pay particular attention to the Matt Coffin's traits, experience, mindset, leadership and team building skills and to how he pursued the opportunity and attracted resources.
2. Discuss the issues that Matt is facing with regard to the harvest. Is this the right time to be selling?
3. Discuss their competitive position in this market and strategies for maintaining it.

EXHIBIT 1 Income Statement

	2000	2001	2002	2003	2004
Revenues	$569,812	$7,090,527	$18,440,227	$49,618,508	$93,632,254
Expenses					
Sales and marketing	$3,914,799	$7,053,959	$12,084,566	$28,058,426	$61,156,561
Technology and Website	1,595,917	1,891,605	2,056,469	5,516,200	8,460,278
General and administrative	2,837,239	2,087,691	2,617,218	5,332,908	9,878,977
Total operating expenses	$8,347,955	$11,033,255	$16,758,253	$38,907,534	$79,495,816
Income from operations	($7,778,143)	($3,942,728)	$1,681,974	$10,710,974	$14,136,438
Other income (expense)					
Interest expense	($151,422)	($179,352)	($155,461)	($49,546)	($40,187)
Interest and other income	79,091	167,164	28,656	54,288	129,928
Total other income	($72,331)	($12,188)	($126,805)	$4,742	$89,741
Income before taxes	($7,850,474)	($3,954,916)	$1,555,169	$10,715,716	$14,226,179
Income tax (provision) benefit	$0	$0	($35,206)	$100,230	($5,972,188)
Net income	($7,850,474)	($3,954,916)	$1,519,963	$10,815,946	$8,253,991
Other financial information					
Depreciation and amortization	443,820	114,600	233,370	328,283	1,320,169
EBITDA	(7,334,323)	(3,828,128)	1,915,344	11,039,257	15,456,607
Cash flow from operations	(5,753,646)	(4,208,114)	1,970,923	10,861,857	10,911,811

INTEGRATIVE CASE 5.0
CONSULTING TEAM

5.0

Consulting Team: Chris Cummings

Omni Consulting, a large American IT-services provider, has contracted to perform a systems-implementation project for a large Canadian telecom company. In particular, Omni is responsible for customizing, installing and testing software that supports the client's new Web-enabled supply-chain initiative. Thus, Omni's off-the-shelf client-server software needs to be extensively customized to meet the client's needs.

These systems-implementation projects tend to be massive: many subteams working in different areas of the company. Subteams include professionals with a variety of skills. Consultants (typically, MBAs) work with client staff to ensure that the completed system will meet the company's business requirements. Programmers customize the software accordingly. Projects are large and the work is complex. Coordination between groups is essential.

The Canadian telecom project started four months ago. Subteams have completed their work in several areas of the company, and new teams have been formed to work in new areas. One subteam was formed three weeks ago to serve the client's order-processing department, which handles everything from when an order is placed until the service is provided and the customer pays.

Pat Lettner, a Canadian national, heads the programmers for the order-processing sub-team. Pat has worked at Omni Canada for five years, since graduating from college with a computer-science degree. Pat's group of programmers has worked together at this client for four months on a variety of subteams.

Robin Haskell, an American, just joined Omni after receiving an MBA the previous spring. The order-processing subteam is Robin's first project with Omni. On the subteam, Robin is responsible for working with the client staff to define business requirements.

Paul Bennett is the American partner for the entire project, and is ultimately responsible for Omni's work for the telecom client.

You, Chris Cummings, a Canadian, have been with Omni for several years, ever since receiving an MBA, and have risen from consultant to manager.

Today, you're scheduled to meet with Pat and Robin at Omni's local office. Could be a challenging conversation.

Chris's Perspective

You've been pulled into something a little unusual involving two Omni professionals.

Apparently, some bad blood has developed between Pat Lettner and Robin Haskell, which has come to a head this week. You got a call from Paul Bennett, the partner on their project. Paul said that there was some sort of problem, and that he simply didn't have time to deal with it himself. He asked you to see what you could do.

You've asked both of them to meet with you back at the office to try to resolve this problem. You hope it'll be fairly straightforward. Pat and Robin are both on a subteam working on a big systems-implementation project at a telecom client. In general, the authority on these subteams tends to be a little unclear. Technically, an Omni partner leads a collection of sub-teams. But obviously they're too busy to make every decision. So sometimes there are conflicts between team members over decisions.

You've worked with Pat on a few projects, and you met Robin during a few recruiting events. Robin seems like a typical MBA – a little aggressive, ready to take charge. And it's typical of programmers who've been made manager – like Pat – to feel a little protective of their new authority. So, in the case of Pat and Robin, it appears that their overlapping responsibilities have created some tension, and the tension is interfering with the business decisions they have to make.

You're up for promotion, which just adds to the pressure. Let's face it: this is a good opportunity to show the partner your stuff. Or at least an opportunity *not* to screw up. This really should get resolved today. You certainly don't want Paul to come back on Monday and find out it's still a problem. On the other

This case was prepared by David P. Pinto (MBA/JD '01) under the supervision of Dana R. Clyman. It was written as a basis for class discussion rather than to illustrate effective or ineffective handling of an administrative situation.

5.0

hand, you can't impose a solution by fiat. These two have to work together throughout this project. Any outcome they reach has to address the current concerns of both of them. And it has to be sustainable. Otherwise, things will just blow up again – and that would make you look even worse.

Consulting Team: Pat Lettner

Omni Consulting, a large American IT-services provider, has contracted to perform a systems-implementation project for a large Canadian telecom company. In particular, Omni is responsible for customizing, installing and testing software that supports the client's new Web-enabled supply-chain initiative. Thus, Omni's off-the-shelf client-server software needs to be extensively customized to meet the client's needs.

These systems-implementation projects tend to be massive: many subteams working in different areas of the company. Subteams include professionals with a variety of skills. Consultants (typically, MBAs) work with client staff to ensure that the completed system will meet the company's business requirements. Programmers customize the software accordingly. Projects are large and the work is complex. Coordination between groups is essential.

The Canadian telecom project started four months ago. Subteams have completed their work in several areas of the company, and new teams have been formed to work in new areas. One subteam was formed three weeks ago to serve the client's order-processing department, which handles everything from when an order is placed until the service is provided and the customer pays.

You, Pat Lettner, a Canadian national, head the programmers for the order-processing subteam. You've worked at Omni Canada for five years, since graduating from college with a computer-science degree. Your group of programmers has worked together at this client for four months on a variety of subteams.

Robin Haskell, an American, just joined Omni after receiving an MBA the previous spring. The order-processing subteam is Robin's first project with Omni. On the subteam, Robin is responsible for working with the client staff to define business requirements.

Paul Bennett is the American partner for the entire project, and ultimately responsible for Omni's work for the telecom client.

Chris Cummings, a Canadian, has been with Omni for several years, ever since receiving an MBA, and has risen from consultant to manager.

Today, you're scheduled to meet with Robin and Chris back at Omni's office. You're not looking forward to the meeting.

Pat's Perspective

Robin Haskell is going to run Omni out of business. What a jerk. A typical MBA. But never mind the incompetence and the poor judgment: it's time that Robin treated you with some respect.

Omni treats the MBAs like they're royalty or something. When a new MBA starts on a project, the whole team takes him or her out to a really fancy dinner. Expensive bottles of wine, the whole thing. When a new programmer starts? They might get lunch at a deli. When your team started at order processing three weeks ago, they were veterans of three previous subteams. They knew the routine, and they were ready to get down to work. But because this is Robin's first project, the whole team had to drop everything and troop out for Robin's 'welcome dinner' at the end of the first week.

That's when you discovered that Robin takes 'stuffed-shirt MBA' to a whole new level. Talk about being full of oneself! Robin asked a few questions about you, and then proceeded to lecture you on 'leveraging the synergistic paradigms of the telecom industry' and other MBA garbage. But the scary thing is that Robin is supposed to determine what the system you're installing will need to support the client's business requirements. You could tell that God's gift to American business certainly doesn't know a thing about software design and implementation.

This was even worse than the e-mail Robin had sent, the one offering a 'vision' for the project from a 'strategy perspective': 'I don't actually know anything, but I'm going to pretend that I do . . . and I certainly know more about everything than you do'. The e-mail had plenty of bullet points and 'action items'. But there was not much there that was actually useful to anyone. In your four months with this client, you've made good friends with some of the IT staff. They weren't at the dinner, but you showed them the e-mail. (Robin had recommended that you 'share this vision with client staff,' right?) You all had some laughs. They have to deal with MBAs, too. (You actually feel a little bad about talking about an Omni teammate like that. But what you say to your friends is your business. And if Robin ends up looking like a jackass, it's hardly surprising; it's not as if it's not well deserved.)

But the real headache was yet to come. Robin's job is to analyze the client's 'business requirements' and make sure the new system supports them. You and the IT folks have already talked through most of this. Robin should be focusing on the few details left to be ironed out. Instead, Robin starts over, talks to a couple of client managers, and now wants to make several major changes to the system. For example, adding a new category of orders, called 'upgrades', that would be treated differently within the system; and creating a new report that calculates cycle time for orders, from entry to service provisioning. This is brand new to you, and this type of thing would be considerably more work for your programming group. Sure, it could be done, but it would have to be finished in three weeks in order to keep the project on schedule. That would take a lot of overtime, and even then, there's no guarantee that it would be done on time. It would be much easier – and far less risky – to stick to the timeline that you and the client's IT staff had already agreed upon. And really: why should your team go out on a limb for Robin?

Clearly, pushing to make these changes in the time Robin proposes is a bad idea. But even worse is how you found out about it: through an e-mail Robin sent to your entire team on Monday afternoon – four days ago – simply telling them to make the changes. As if it's a done deal. How incredibly arrogant. Robin has no authority to do this – Robin isn't the boss around here.

And not a word to you beforehand – how insulting. You're a manager now, not just a programmer. Robin should at least have come to talk to you directly, to find out the implications of the proposed change. You know things Robin doesn't, and, at a minimum, you deserve to be consulted and treated like a colleague.

First thing Tuesday morning, you went to set Robin straight. You tried to explain why the changes would be too difficult. Robin had no understanding of the situation. It was like talking to a brick wall. Finally, Robin said, 'Look, I'm the one in charge of the client's business needs', as if that somehow gives final authority. You pointed out that client needs are important to you, too. And that was that. Clearly, this wouldn't be resolved anytime soon.

Or so you thought. On Wednesday, there was a client meeting with Michelle Foster, the head of order management. You and Robin were there, plus Michelle's staff and some of the client IT staff. Michelle asked about how things were going with customizing the system. Before you could respond, Robin said, 'Michelle, those changes we discussed will be made – no problem'. What a power-hungry jerk! That decision hadn't been made – still hasn't. Where did Robin get off saying it had? And what a way to put you on the spot! Everybody in the room could tell that Robin was just trying to stick it to you.

You couldn't speak up and directly contradict Robin, of course. Not in front of Michelle. But fortunately, one of your IT friends from the client side, with whom you'd commiserated over a beer, was there to bring Robin back to reality. He told Robin that he didn't think the team would be able to make the changes in the time promised. You appreciated the support. But Robin had still put you in an incredibly awkward position and made you look bad, especially when Michelle turned to you and asked you whether the changes could be made. What an opportunity to slam Robin. But you didn't. Instead, you gave the most professional response you could: the changes would be difficult under the current schedule, so the team would have to study them further. And that was that.

Did Robin thank you afterwards for covering up the faux pas? No way. Instead, you heard a string of invective, screaming, and shouting that you couldn't believe. There's no way you can work with this wet-behind-the-ears jerk.

You finally went to Paul Bennett (the partner) and told him the situation was entirely intolerable, that someone needed to teach this new MBA how to work on a team. He asked you and Robin to speak with a senior manager, Chris Cummings, back at the office today, Friday. You've worked with Chris on a few projects. No complaints. But let's face it: Chris will probably support Robin, as they're both MBAs and part of the consulting staff. You'll watch Chris carefully for any signs of favouritism, and go right back to Paul if you see any.

MBAs can be a pain, but Robin takes the cake. Someone really made a mistake when they hired this one. Pushing through those changes to the system just shows how little practical sense Robin has. Apparently, it's just a power grab, an attempt to take over the project to make a big impression. Well, that's too much. Robin's got to go. At the very least, you need an acknowledgment that Robin must treat you and the other members of the team with respect, and consult with you and not make unilateral decisions. And Robin needs to apologize for putting you on the spot like that with the client, and treating you as nothing more than a programmer rather than a manager. And finally, you want some kind of promise that this behaviour will stop. If you get that apology and promise – and it's credible – then you'll know that Robin can be trained, can become someone you can work with. If not, you won't even consider whether it's feasible to make the changes Robin is proposing, much less discuss it.

Consulting Team: Robin Haskell

Omni Consulting, a large American IT-services provider, has contracted to perform a systems-implementation project for a large Canadian telecom company. In particular, Omni is responsible for customizing, installing and testing software that supports the client's new Web-enabled supply-chain initiative. Thus, Omni's off-the-shelf client-server software needs to be extensively customized to meet the client's needs.

These systems-implementation projects tend to be massive: many subteams working in different areas of the company. Subteams include professionals with a variety of skills. Consultants (typically, MBAs) work with client staff to ensure that the completed system will meet the company's business requirements. Programmers customize the software accordingly. Projects are large and the work is complex. Coordination between groups is essential.

The Canadian telecom project started four months ago. Subteams have completed their work in several areas of the company, and new teams have been formed to work in new areas. One subteam was formed three weeks ago to serve the client's order-processing department, which handles everything from when an order is placed until the service is provided and the customer pays.

Pat Lettner, a Canadian national, heads the programmers for the order-processing sub-team. Pat has worked at Omni Canada for five years, since graduating from college with a computer-science degree. Pat's group of programmers has worked together at this client for four months on a variety of subteams.

You, Robin Haskell, are an American who just joined Omni after receiving an MBA the previous spring. The order-processing subteam is your first project with Omni. On the sub-team, you're responsible for working with the client staff to define business requirements.

Paul Bennett is the American partner for the entire project, and is ultimately responsible for Omni's work for the telecom client.

Chris Cummings, a Canadian, has been with Omni for several years, ever since receiving an MBA, and has risen from consultant to manager.

Today, you're scheduled to meet with Pat and Chris back at Omni's office. You're not looking forward to the meeting.

Robin's Perspective

When Omni came to campus last year, they said their number-one priority was client service. So what is Pat Lettner doing here?

Pat is obstructionist and unprofessional. And, on a personal level, Pat has undermined your authority and made you look like a fool, with both the client and Omni staff. No, *not* a great way to start your first project at Omni.

It had all seemed so promising a few weeks ago. OK, so order processing is a little dull. But it's a big project at a hot client. And you established yourself early as the strategy expert, the one who gets things done. During the first week, you sent an e-mail to the entire subteam, laying out a vision for the project, and you received some very positive responses; the partner thought it was dynamite.

Then things started falling apart. Your first real chance to talk to Pat came at the big team dinner at the end of the first week. That's when you realized: this is a programmer, a technician-type – clearly knows computers, but not aggressive enough. And not someone you'd want to put in front of a client. You tried giving Pat some pointers on business at that first dinner, to smooth out the rough spots. Maybe a mistake. Because, since then, it's been one thing after another. First, you got wind that Pat had been making fun of you over drinks with some buddies on the client's IT staff. Totally unprofessional, of course. It looks pretty bad to a client to have one Omni professional disparaging another. And, on a personal level, it certainly couldn't help your reputation on the client side. But what programmers talk about is their business; you're above that sort of thing. So you didn't confront Pat about it.

Instead, you tried to stick to doing your job. Over the last few weeks, you've held meetings with client staff members to determine their business requirements and define necessary modifications to the system. Then, on Monday afternoon – four days ago – you sent an e-mail to the programming team describing the necessary changes. For example, with the client, you identified a need to add a new category of orders, called 'upgrades', that would be treated differently within the system. You also identified a need for the system to include a new report that calculates cycle time for orders, from entry to service provisioning. Necessary stuff. Not that big of a deal.

But guess who went ballistic? Tuesday morning, Pat showed up, all angry, complaining that making the changes would be too much work. Too much work? Of course it'll take effort, and maybe some overtime, but the budget can support it and the schedule has room for it. And these changes are required by the client's business needs, which this system is *supposed* to support. The changes can definitely be done within three weeks – as required – and still have the project stay on schedule. OK, so they'll have to work hard, but come on. They'll be paid overtime, and that's what they're paid for.

You told all of this to Pat, but it did no good. In the end, you had to remind Pat that you're the one in charge of representing the client's business needs, and so you get the final say. Pat didn't like it much, but you figured the message had gotten through. It was your decision, you'd made it, and that was the end of it.

You'd scheduled a client meeting for the next day – Wednesday – with Michelle Foster, the client's head of order management, as well as her staff, some client IT staff, and Pat. During the meeting, Michelle wanted reassurances that the changes to the system would be made. Having made the decision, you told her it wouldn't be a problem. And then suddenly one of Pat's friends on the client IT staff chimes in. He says that he doesn't see how Pat's team can possibly make the changes in the time you've promised. And then he drops the bomb: 'In B-school, it may seem like you can just snap your fingers and make things happen, but it doesn't work that way in the real world'. The real world? The nerve! And then, when Michelle turned to Pat to ask if it could be done, Pat didn't support you. Instead, Pat caught your eye and said that the changes would be difficult to make, and that the subteam would 'have to study it further'.

What a disaster. You would have been open to a professional discussion about the matter. Why couldn't Pat have been direct with you? Using a friend on the client staff to undermine you like that – it's simply not the way things should be done. What kind of credibility do you have with Michelle Foster after this? And with the rest of the staff?

After that, you sat down with Pat and let loose with a piece of your mind – undermining you like that in front of the client! Pat retorted that you were the one doing the undermining, making promises you couldn't deliver. The meeting ended in a shouting match.

So you finally called Paul Bennett (the partner), and left a message asking for an appointment. You didn't explain much, just said that you wanted some advice on a personal and professional conflict you were having with Pat. Paul responded by voice mail that he was too busy to talk to you himself, but that he had asked Chris Cummings, a senior manager not on the project, to give you a call *and* try to help. Then you got a call from Chris asking if you and Pat could meet with Chris back at the office today, Friday. So now there's no chance to get some quiet advice, and yet another person has been brought into this mess. This is looking worse and worse every minute.

Apparently, the goal of the meeting is to 'fix' the situation. But that's absurd. You're in danger of having your consulting career go seriously off-track. And if you back down now, it's over. Pat needs to acknowledge her mistake and apologize for having undermined your authority with the client – embarrassing both you and the firm. And what's more, Pat needs to promise not to do it again. Having Pat apologize will help guarantee that this behaviour won't recur. Once you get this well-deserved apology, you and Omni need some reassurance that Pat will be more focused on client-service concerns. The best way to do that would be for Pat to accept your decision on the changes to the system.

6.0

INTEGRATIVE CASE 6.0 LIVERPOOL CITY COUNCIL (A): THE ICT OUTSOURCING DECISION

It was October 1999, and David Henshaw looked back with satisfaction on the achievements of the last four months. Appointed chief executive of Liverpool City Council in July 1999, he had inherited an organization in collapse, third from the bottom out of 426 local authorities in terms of service quality, and with the highest local tax in the United Kingdom. By implementing radical organizational and cultural changes, he had turned the council around and restored employees' confidence. Nevertheless, there was still a long way to go to achieve the recently elected council's goal of 'making Liverpool a premier European city again'.

Henshaw knew that more improvements were needed. Delivery of social services such as housing, medical care, educational support and financial benefits was slow and inefficient. Each transaction generated streams of paper forms and was error-prone, slow and expensive. Henshaw wanted to re-engineer the council's services around the needs of its customers, stripping out bureaucracy and focusing on front-line service delivery. Information and communication technology (ICT) was integral to this vision of improving service, quality and cost.

Traditionally, local councils had to choose between two ICT procurement options: invest from their own resources or outsource to a private sector company via a contractual arrangement. Each solution had its limitations. In addition, central government was encouraging Henshaw to move away from these traditional models.

Whichever solution he chose, Henshaw knew he was walking a tightrope. The unions were watching, and employees were having difficulty keeping up with the pace of change. Nevertheless, he was determined to continue his improvement efforts. He knew he would have to make a recommendation on whether, and if so how, to outsource ICT at the next ratification committee, scheduled in 48 hours.

The City of Liverpool and Its Council

A Rich Heritage but Socio-Economic Difficulties

Liverpool, situated on the northwest coast of England, is the sixth largest city in the United Kingdom. Famous as the home of the Beatles and Liverpool Football Club, the city, with its revitalized waterfront and rich cultural and architectural heritage, was internationally renowned and attracted millions of visitors each year.

Despite this rich heritage, Liverpool's recent past had been characterized by population loss and economic recession. Once a dominant trading centre in Europe, the city experienced growing levels of unemployment during the second half of the 20th century as the shipping industry in which it had its roots became more automated. The population of 468,000 was decreasing. The outward migration of younger, skilled people had resulted in a higher proportion of dependent people. In 1998, 33 per cent of the population was unemployed, retired or unable to work because of invalidity. Nationally, Liverpool had the highest concentration of deprivation than any other local authority, with 72 per cent of its residents living in areas that were among the 10 per cent most deprived in the country.[1]

[1] Office for Standards in Education (Ofsted). *Inspection of Liverpool Local Authority*. Office of Her Majesty's Chief Inspector of Schools. In conjunction with the Audit Commission, May 1999.

Research Associate Henri Bourgeois prepared this case under the supervision of Professor David Robertson as a basis for class discussion rather than to illustrate either effective or ineffective handling of a business situation.

Yet Liverpool also had many assets. With one of the world's most important ports, an international airport and excellent rail and road links with other UK cities, the city was well connected to the rest of the UK and to Europe. In addition to the port and distribution activities, Liverpool also had strong activity in the life sciences, automotive, food and ICT sectors.

Liverpool City Council (LCC)

LCC's role was to provide public services to the local community. It was a significant local employer, accounting for around 23,500 jobs. It was also a major local investor and purchaser. The council's gross expenditure was £1.2 billion, the net revenue budget over some £600 million and the annual capital programme £142 million.

The Labour Party had controlled LCC for many years. Yet a history of high council taxes and poor performance had caused much of the electorate to lose confidence in LCC's members. In elections in 1998 the Liberal Democrats, led by Mike Storey, won 70 of the 99 council seats on a mandate not to increase council tax. Labour then formed the main opposition. The Liberal Democrats promised to improve LCC's operations and cost effectiveness, but quickly found out that this would not be easy. The council was in very poor shape: it was third from the bottom (out of 426 local authorities) in terms of quality of services, despite charging the highest council tax in the country. LCC's operational performance, financial health and overall image in 1998 were poor.

Inefficient Processes and Surging Costs

In June 1999 LCC showed a record £23 million deficit. Internal systems were cumbersome, expensive and fraught with operational and functional problems.

For example, the Revenues and Benefits Department, which collected taxes and administered housing and other benefits, was in complete disarray. Citizens were being summonsed for non-payment of taxes, while waiting to receive benefit payments. At its worst, there was a backlog of 60,000 queries waiting to be answered. The existing processes had transformed the office into a massive warehouse of more than 600,000 files occupying several floors of office space, all infested with vermin. It was an unpleasant working environment, and finding a file could take more than 30 minutes.

The situation in many other services was little better. The Education Awards Service, whose mission was to inform citizens about educational grants, schools meals and transport costs, could not answer more than 4 per cent of the incoming calls. As for the Payroll Service, its costs were so high and the quality of its services so low that other departments were seriously considering finding outside agencies for payroll administration.

To make matters worse, absenteeism within the council had reached an average of 16 days a year per employee, six days more than the national average. Henshaw described the general climate at the time:

> *When I was hired, I saw all the signs of an organization in collapse. It was significant system breakdown and a general sense of powerlessness of the staff. Nothing could be changed. People's main role was to make sure they would not get blamed.*

A variety of inspections confirmed the poor performance of LCC's operations:

- **The Local Government Improvement and Development Agency** (a peer group) found that LCC, as a whole, was failing its stakeholders and was suffering from chronic departmentalism. They produced a scathing report that criticized LCC's corporate governance, cost effectiveness and service quality.
- **The Ofsted inspection of education services** reported in May 1999 that the Liverpool Local Education Authority's weaknesses outweighed its strengths. Some fundamental services were unsatisfactory and poorly managed. 'Strategic planning was weak and in general schools were not receiving the support they needed.' Consultants employed jointly by the city council and the Department for Education and Employment confirmed these problems and recommended large-scale outsourcing of education services.[2]
- **The pilot Best Value inspection of ICT services**, completed by Deloitte & Touche in June 1999, highlighted a lack of investment in ICT and a fragmented approach to ICT development. This, along with the lack of an organization-wide approach to standards or ICT strategy, led to operational inefficiency and poor service for the council's customers.[3]

The Liberal Democrat controlled council realized that a quantum leap was needed and proclaimed the following mission:

> *To make Liverpool a premier European city by developing a more competitive economy, building*

---

[2] Office for Standards in Education (Ofsted). *Inspection of Liverpool Local Authority*. Ofsted, October 2002.

[3] 4ps (local government project procurement agency). *Liverpool City Council: Embracing the Electronic Age. Co-sourcing ICT, customer contact, revenues and benefits, payroll and human resources*. London, 2001.

healthier, safer and more inclusive communities and enhancing individual life chances.[4]

More precisely, the council identified five major goals:

- Improve services, giving guarantees of service quality, value for money and doing things right first time.
- Ensure that Liverpool citizens are well educated by improving the quality of education for people of all ages and helping schools to raise attainment.
- Make Liverpool a healthier, cleaner, greener, safer place – enhancing residential areas, protecting open spaces, promoting community safety and giving special attention to the city centre.
- Create an enterprise culture, to enable local people to get jobs, and a business-friendly environment so that businesses invest in the city and its people.
- Achieve best value[5] – deliver these aims while keeping council tax as low as possible.

Soon after, the political leadership of LCC decided to bring in a new chief executive to implement this vision. His main mission would be to improve the quality of services dramatically, while reducing costs and lowering council tax charges.

New Organization and Leadership

David Henshaw, born and educated in Liverpool, was appointed council chief executive designate in July 1999 and formally took up office on 4 October 1999. Henshaw and his team knew they were at the bottom end of the spectrum when compared to other councils, and shared the political leaders' view that the changes had to be radical:

There was a long way to go between where we were and where we wanted to go. The question for us was: Do we want to reach for the average, or do we want to make a big leap from our poor platform to be at the leading edge? We chose the latter.

Henshaw believed that a city like Liverpool worked on confidence. If he and his team managed to restore confidence among the staff, the work climate would improve and with it the quality of service. His actions were driven by two priorities:

- First, get the basics right. Go from poor performance to competent performance. Henshaw's goal was to reach the top quartile of local council performance over a period of two years.
- Second, focus the staff on a vision of Liverpool as a premier European city. Henshaw wanted the council staff to stop judging themselves by the past and focus instead on their potential future. As a result of growing confidence, they would start to look at what they could do, not what they had done.

Henshaw focused his efforts on three areas: (1) restructuring the council to improve its ability to make decisions and manage its operations; (2) measuring and reporting results; and (3) improving the council's internal operations.

Restructuring the Council

When the new council took over in 1998, the staff had been organized into nine directorates, all run separately and competing with each other. There were ten HR services: one for each of the nine directorates and another for the central group. This highly autonomous departmental structure looked to Henshaw more like a series of different councils:

It was the nature of an organization in decline, with a series of silos or departments, not very well connected and interacting with one another occasionally. There was a parading management style, where barons were more preoccupied with defending their territories than serving our customers.

In an attempt to modernize and streamline the decision making process, Henshaw decided to adopt a more integrated management structure. The nine directorates were reduced to five portfolios (*refer to* ***Exhibit 1*** *for the new organizational structure*). The entire management team was replaced, except for one original director. Acknowledging that the council was overstaffed, Henshaw offered a voluntary severance package to those who did not share his vision. It resulted in the loss of over 2,000 staff.

An executive board was created, chaired by Henshaw. The board was not legally empowered to make decisions but could make recommendations. Members were

[4] 'Liverpool City Council Markets'. Best Value Inspection, October 2001, p. 5.

[5] The Best Value Program, launched in 2000 by the UK government, required local authorities to deliver services to clear cost and quality standards through the most efficient and effective means possible. It required authorities to publish annual Best Value Performance Plans and their performance according to a variety of Best Value Performance Indicators (BVPIs). For example, BVPI #157 monitored councils' progress towards the target of 100 per cent electronic service delivery by 2005.

'portfolio holders' with strategic service responsibilities. They were accountable to select scrutiny committees, which mirrored their area of responsibility. The key decision making forum was the small, politically balanced ratification committee, which met weekly to consider the executive board's recommendations. The full council took all major budget and policy decisions.[6]

Henshaw also established a **City Council project team** to drive change. The team members came from across the council and were responsible for carrying out improvement projects, reengineering processes and acting as champions for change.

In parallel, Henshaw created an **improvement and best value team** that reported directly to him. It was responsible for performance management overall. The team developed a comprehensive performance management framework, which included monitoring and reporting of performance to the executive management team.

Measuring Performance

In addition to the BVPIs required as part of the national Best Value Program, Henshaw decided that each LCC portfolio would also measure its performance with a more detailed set of Key Performance Indicators (KPIs). KPIs, although optional, had been set by the government to assist local authorities to meet the requirements of the BVPIs. They also facilitated comparisons between organizations and were regarded as indicators of the health and effectiveness of local council services.[7]

Henshaw met with each senior manager monthly to discuss how the organization had performed on each KPI. He held each manager personally accountable for bringing every KPI into the upper quartile of UK council performance within two years. Success was widely broadcast in the council, as was underperformance.[8]

Using ICT as a Change Agent

The third major thrust of Henshaw's improvement effort was a drive to 'embrace the electronic age' and improve LCC's use of ICT. Henshaw wanted to invest in information technology to reduce the flood of paper, save money and improve performance.

Alyson Myles, who was in charge of IT for Social Services, elaborated on how a customer request used to be handled by the department and how it could be improved:

> *Someone would ring Social Services and say: 'I am concerned about the child next door'. We would then go and fill in a paper. The form would be faxed to a social worker who would fill in another form. He would initiate a care plan, and then apply for funding. All the information was written on paper.*

Each service had its own version of a given form. As a result, a single incident would generate multiple forms, capturing largely the same information over and over. Despite all these redundancies, some forms were still incomplete and others ultimately were lost somewhere during the back and forth process between staff and suppliers.

> *With an electronic version of the form, we would have only one document, online, and the information would be captured once and for all. Everybody could access the form, even third parties, and the form could be stored in a database and upgraded later. We could also monitor progress and estimate how much work each person had to do.*

It was estimated that £5 million a year could be saved by eliminating this 'endless paper chase' across the council services, especially for procurement, financial transactions and benefit applications. In addition, scanning thousands of filing cabinet documents and storing them on CDs would free around one million square feet of office space.

An Outdated and Inefficient ICT Platform

Reflecting on the 1999 pilot best value review findings, Peter Cosgrove, head of Revenues and Benefits, admitted:

> *[Before 1998] the investment in technology was virtually non-existent. There was a lack of overall strategy; each directorate had its own IT agenda, with a vast number of systems that did not talk to each other. We even had two different e-mail protocols . . .*

'We had different pockets of IT people all over the place', confirmed Pauline Owens, the ICT strategy director. Of the nine directorates, five of them possessed their own ICT department. There was also a central ICT department. When the central department initiated changes, the local departments would listen but could decide whether to comply or not, arguing that they were closer to the businesses and could better understand

---

[6] 4ps (local government project procurement agency). *Liverpool City Council: Embracing the Electronic Age. Co-sourcing ICT, customer contact, revenues and benefits, payroll and human resources*. London, 2001.

[7] www.socitm.gov.uk

[8] NLGN and I&DeA. *E-government and Organizational Transformation: Lessons from Liverpool and Hertfordshire*. London, 2002.

6.0

local needs. This lack of strategy and decentralized management of IT over the years had resulted in the coexistence of two mainframes, over 170 different servers, over 250 independent applications, 500 major different databases, and five incompatible e-mail protocols.

The view of the customer had, an IT officer argued, 500 blind spots, with all the inherent costs and lost opportunities.

Henshaw, to emphasize the importance of ICT, added a sixth goal to the council's mission: 'To place the city at the forefront of delivering services electronically'. He explained:

We wanted to move towards a model of an intelligence-led organization. The new IT platform should give us the ability to capture the customer profile, information and experience in a 360° sense. By organizing around the customers and their different needs, we would offer them a high quality of service at a cost they could afford.

Henshaw saw ICT not only as a means to improve the efficiency of operations, but also as a 'way to establish closer links between council management and staff, our customers and the business community'. To reach this goal, he envisaged a two-step approach: (1) in the short term, improve the ICT infrastructure and the services that depended on it (*refer to* ***Exhibit 2*** *for a description of IT intensive services*); (2) in the longer term, re-engineer business processes across the council from front to back office.

The Council's E-Vision

LCC considered improving ICT to be a 'technological vision' (*refer to* ***Exhibits 3*** *and* ***4*** *for a detailed description of the council's strategic and technological vision*).

The basic elements of the council's vision included using the Internet and advanced call centre technology to improve communication with customers, and a centralized customer relationship management (CRM) system and data warehouses to track the interactions and ensure good service.

This would require a huge investment – around £50 million, according to Deloitte & Touche estimates. Securing such funding would take a lot of time, so Henshaw and his team identified several 'quick wins' that did not require capital investment and could improve basic processes and morale.

Small Changes that Make a Big Difference

Kevin Murtagh, former head of IT for education services, recalled how he and Owens proceeded:

We first looked at the workflows ICT dealt with and tried to quantify them. We then built a structure based on the services we would have to deliver. Basically, we reorganized in a way that made much more sense to our customers.

All ICT people were brought under the same roof and interviewed. Having identified all the skills at hand, Murtagh tried to match them with the newly created posts, in an effort to keep as many people as possible. Ultimately, some 156 posts were created (as an initial review) out of the existing 200 (100 in the central IT department, around 100 in the directorates).

These structural changes, combined with the introduction of basic performance management, showed immediate results. The ICT backlog of 700 unanswered requests was cleared within two months. The major KPI for ICT – the percentage of calls answered – jumped from 35 per cent to 75 per cent in the same period.

The Outsourcing Decision

In parallel with these short-term improvements, LCC considered a number of procurement options to address the dramatic ICT improvements needed to re-engineer its business processes across front and back office. (***Exhibit 5*** *summarizes ICT's functions in 1999 and some of the envisioned improvements.*)

Generally, public services had two main options when it came to improving an internal service that did not meet expectations:

- Keep the service in-house, get rid of underperforming people, and restructure the service process to improve performance
- Outsource the failing activity via a private sector contractual agreement.

Deloitte & Touche's Best Value review had clearly recommended outsourcing. This solution was backed by those in the council who believed, 'It is so bad here that it cannot be worse in the private sector'. More generally, the Conservative central government had encouraged outsourcing since the early 1980s. Still, Henshaw was not convinced:

The best value review was a flawed process, where you presume an outcome and build the case to achieve it. There are several examples out there where public services outsourced a problem and ended up with an outsourced problem.

Indeed, several local councils, especially in the London boroughs, were in the process of bringing back in-house services for which improvements had failed to materialize. In Liverpool, the outsourcing of refuse collection services in the mid-1980s had left severe scars. Toni Byrnes, former secretary for the Joint Trade Union of Liverpool, recalled:

> *There were picket lines, demonstrations and fights in the streets. The workers and the quality of service suffered, not the private companies. Since then, unions have always had a negative opinion of outsourcing. It usually meant downsizing and a decline in work conditions.*

In addition, there were strict guidelines protecting the benefits of employees when work was outsourced (*refer to* ***Exhibit 6*** *for some of the regulations governing the Transfer of Undertakings (Protection of Employment), or TUPE*).

Keeping the service in-house would reassure the unions and be much cheaper to implement. Of course, the council lacked key skills such as change management and IT solution expertise, but they could be acquired through external recruiting. Phil Halsall, LCC's executive director, was not convinced either:

> *We could not afford the highly skilled IT people we needed. In addition, our investments are controlled by the central government. Money on IT rarely wins over money on education and social services.*

Henshaw considered the pros and cons of the two alternatives:

	In-house	**Traditional outsourcing**
Advantages	■ Builds morale by recognizing existing skills in the council: 'we can do it' ■ Potentially cheaper solution ■ Preserves control of finance and budget ■ Less disruptive solution, employees would have more time to adapt ■ Keeps unions happy	■ Pressure for it after the Best Value review ■ A private company can invest £50 million more easily ■ Would facilitate a rapid change in work culture ■ Would provide access to change management and IT skills
Disadvantages	■ Hard to convince government to invest £50 million in IT ■ Public salaries too low to attract the needed ICT expertise ■ More difficult to implement a radical change	■ Risk of strike or other resistance by unions ■ Council would lose control of outsourced services ■ Significant risk: outsourcing had failed for other councils ■ TUPE regulations put significant constraints on solution

Encouraged by the new Labour central government to come up with innovative ways of dealing with outsourced services, Henshaw was guided by the principle, 'We don't want an outsourced problem, but rather aim to insource a solution'.

If Liverpool did outsource its IT operations, the main challenge would be to build a collaborative partnership with the outsourcing vendor. Council staff had useful skills and knowledge that would be valuable if properly managed. At the same time, a private partner could potentially bring the £50 million capital investment and extensive ICT knowledge.

Time was of the essence. Henshaw needed to maintain the momentum for change that he and his team had been fostering in the last few months. Staff morale was up and relationships with the unions were improving. Those who did not share his vision had left through voluntary severance. The staff who had stayed acknowledged the need for change, but remained concerned that outsourcing might affect their quality of work life, benefits, job security and pension plan.

Henshaw sat in his chair and weighed up his options:

- Keep the ICT services in-house. Centralization had already brought significant improvements, but could the council develop the necessary expertise and resources to make the radical changes that were required?
- Outsource operations. If he chose this option, would he be able to avoid alienating the unions? Could he prevent the costly adversarial behaviour between council and vendor he had seen in other local councils?

- Come up with a new framework of partnership between public and private sector. This partnership should satisfy both the council's vision for service delivery and the legitimate profit orientation of its commercial partner. Were these goals compatible? And if so, how to best satisfy both parties?

If the council did decide to outsource, Henshaw also had to decide at what level. Should it outsource only the operation and management of the shared ICT hardware and software? This would primarily affect the 200 ICT staff. Or should it outsource the processing of transactions and delivery of IT-supported services for the council? If so, the jobs of around 1,100 employees would be outsourced, and the negotiations with the unions would be much more difficult.

EXHIBIT 1 Liverpool City Council Structure in March 2003

Chief Executive
David Henshaw

Housing and Social Services Annie Shepherd	Central Services David McElhinney	Resources Phil Halsall	Education and Lifelong Learning Colin Hilton	Regeneration Charlie Parker
• Housing Management • Neighbourhood Services • Community Safety • Adult's Social Services • Children's Social Services	• Marketing • Human Resources • IT • Revenue and Benefit • Liverpool Direct Call Centre • One Stop Shops • Communication • Payroll • E-government • Business Process Re-engineering	• Financial Control • Procurement • Audit • External Funding	• School Effectiveness • Educational Support Services • Policy and Strategy • Leisure Services	• Development and New Companies • Regeneration and New Initiatives • Policy and Strategy • Procurement • Performance Business • Finance • Environmental Health • Trading Standards

Source: Liverpool City Council

6.0

EXHIBIT 2 IT Intensive Services in 2000

Services	Summary of Services
Revenues and Benefits 400 employees	The key functions of the Revenues and Benefits service were: ■ Benefits: administration and processing of all Housing Benefit and council tax benefit claims ■ Billing and collections: administration and collection of council tax, business rate and overpaid benefits ■ Cashiering: receipt, allocation and reconciliation of customer payments to the council ■ Customer services: providing services to personal callers at the city centre one-stop shop
Liverpool Direct 300 employees	Liverpool Direct was Liverpool's call centre, a front-line service providing information and services to both citizens and staff. As a first contact point for queries from the public, it was increasingly taking responsibility for managing communication from a single point. It was also responsible for: ■ Proactive customer surveying on behalf of other departments ■ A degree of back-end administration to support services performed ■ Direct face-to-face customer contact for some services provided Most of the staff were generalists, aiming to answer queries at the first point of contact whenever possible. The service emphasized human contact with callers.
Payroll and	Payroll was an in-house service running on a council mainframe. The operation was devoted to each directorate, with a central payroll section managing the payroll processing and liaison with external bodies. Each directorate was responsible for collecting and inputting employees' pay-related data. Some integrated these tasks with the local HR administration work.
Human Resources 210 employees combined	HR services dealt with: ■ Personnel information ■ Absence monitoring ■ Training and development ■ Organization capacity planning and risk management ■ Resignations, redundancies and retirements ■ Management information and reporting

Source: 4ps (local government project procurement agency). *Liverpool City Council: Embracing the Electronic Age. Co-sourcing ICT, customer contact, revenues and benefits, payroll and human resources.* London, 2001.

EXHIBIT 3 Liverpool Council Vision: Strategic Vision

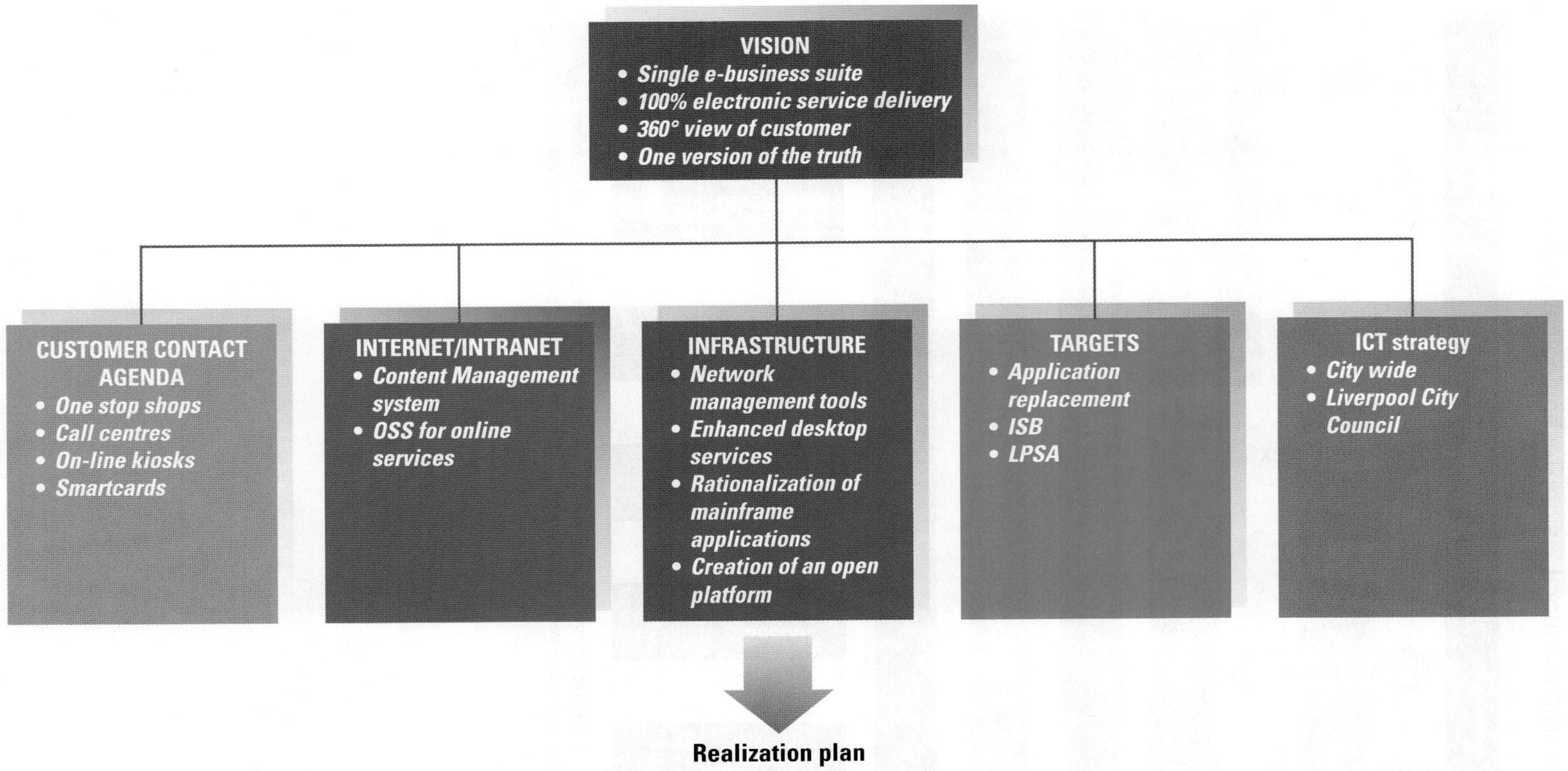

VISION
- *Single e-business suite*
- *100% electronic service delivery*
- *360° view of customer*
- *One version of the truth*

CUSTOMER CONTACT AGENDA
- *One stop shops*
- *Call centres*
- *On-line kiosks*
- *Smartcards*

INTERNET/INTRANET
- *Content Management system*
- *OSS for online services*

INFRASTRUCTURE
- *Network management tools*
- *Enhanced desktop services*
- *Rationalization of mainframe applications*
- *Creation of an open platform*

TARGETS
- *Application replacement*
- *ISB*
- *LPSA*

ICT strategy
- *City wide*
- *Liverpool City Council*

Realization plan

Source: Implementing Electronic Government Return 2003, www.liverpool.gov.uk

EXHIBIT 4 Liverpool Council Vision: Technological Vision

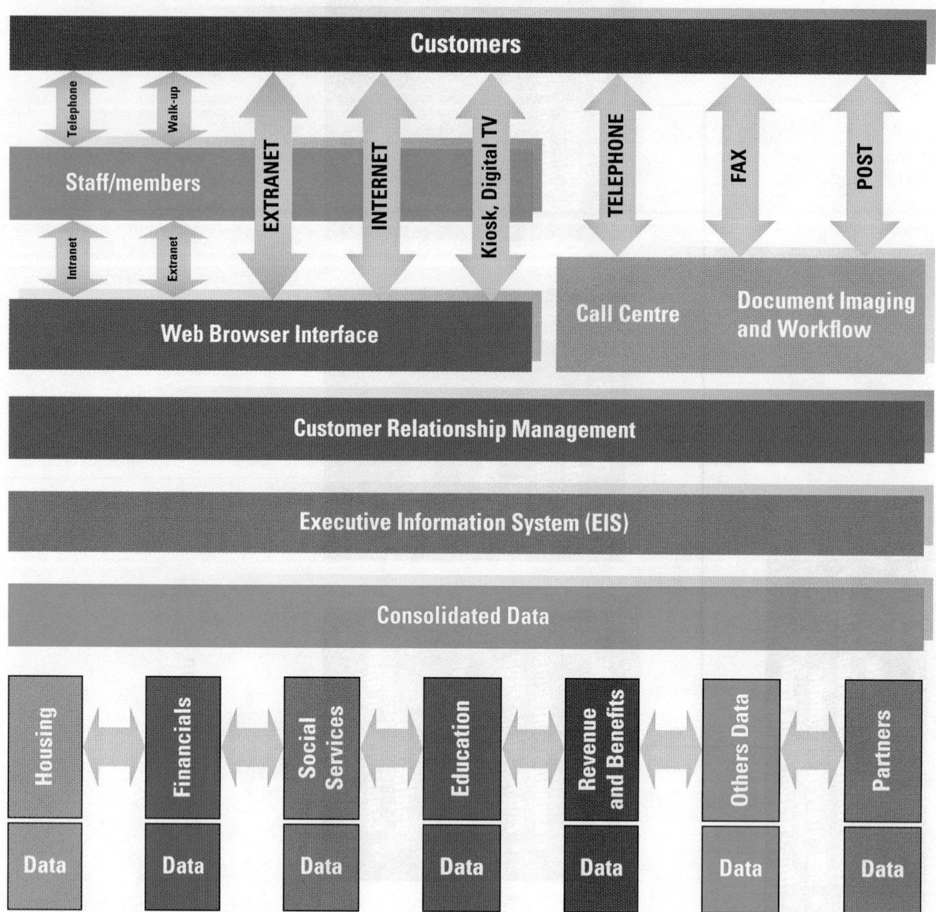

Source: 4ps (local government project procurement agency). *Liverpool City Council: Embracing the Electronic Age. Co-sourcing ICT, customer contact, revenues and benefits, payroll and human resources*. London, 2001.

EXHIBIT 5 ICT: Summary of Services and Envisioned Improvements

Service content	Planned improvements
All staff and services were managed and delivered through a centralized service. There were 199 staff working in ICT, with external service providers used to supplement this capability. Central ICT provided: ■ A service desk as a single point of contact ■ Operational services, including the support of corporate and portfolio applications ■ Technical infrastructure services (WAN, Internet access) ■ Telephone systems ■ Business systems support ■ Project management ■ Business development	■ Server rationalization ■ Planned continual technical updates ■ Mainframe replacement ■ Introduction and continuous support for e-CRM ■ Delivering the ICT required to support the council's developing call centre and one-stop-shop strategy ■ Rolling out document management across the council ■ Supporting the use of laptop computers (at home, on business) ■ Electronic payment/collections ■ Implementing voice mail capability ■ Address-matching across the council ■ Introducing video conferencing facilities

Source: 4ps (local government project procurement agency). *Liverpool City Council: Embracing the Electronic Age. Co-sourcing ICT, customer contact, revenues and benefits, payroll and human resources*. London, 2001.

6.0

EXHIBIT 6 TUPE Regulation (Extracts)

The regulations preserve employees' terms and conditions when a business or undertaking, or part of one, is transferred to a new employer . . .

Employees employed by the previous employer when the undertaking changes hands automatically become employees of the new employer on the same terms and conditions. It is as if their contracts of employment had originally been made with the new employer. Thus employees' continuity of employment is preserved, as are their terms and conditions of employment under their contracts of employment (except for certain occupational pension rights).

Representatives of employees . . . affected have the right to be informed about the transfer. They must also be consulted about any measure which the old or new employer envisages taking concerning affected employees. [. . .]

The new employer takes over the contract of all employees who were employed in the undertaking immediately before the transfer, or who would have been so employed if they had not been unfairly dismissed for a reason connected with the transfer. An employer cannot just pick and choose which employees to take on.

The new employer takes over all rights and obligations arising from those contracts of employment, except criminal liabilities and rights and obligations relating to provisions about benefits for old age, invalidity or survivors in employees' occupational pension schemes.

The new employer takes over any collective agreements made on behalf of the employees and in force immediately before the transfer.

Neither the new employer nor the previous one may fairly dismiss an employee because of the transfer or a reason connected with it, unless the reason for the dismissal is an economic, technical or organisational reason entailing changes in the workforce. If there is no such reason, the dismissal will be unfair. If there is such a reason, the dismissal will be fair provided an employment tribunal decides that the employer acted reasonably in the circumstances in treating that reason as sufficient to justify dismissal. If, in this case, there is a redundancy situation, the usual redundancy procedures will apply.

The new employer may not, unless the contract of employment so provides, unilaterally worsen the terms and conditions of employment of any transferred employee.

'The previous and new employers must consult representatives of the employees.'

Source: 'TUPE, an Introduction Part 1'. TSSA Reps Bulletin, September 2001, www.tssa.org.uk

LIVERPOOL CITY COUNCIL (B): CO-SOURCING PUBLIC SERVICES THROUGH A JOINT VENTURE WITH BT

On July 13, 2002 British Telecom (BT) and Liverpool City Council (LCC) celebrated the first birthday of their £350 million ground-breaking joint venture, Liverpool Direct Limited (LDL).

One year earlier, to mark the birth of LDL, BT had presented 21 newborn babies with a brand new computer and the latest software to help them develop technology skills from day one. Now the 'BT babies' were returning to the Town Hall to celebrate a year of growth and development for them and LDL.

The past year had indeed witnessed significant achievements for LDL. The council's revenues and benefits, HR, payroll, ICT and call centre functions had been brought in to LDL, which had been using the latest technology to revolutionize council services. Early results were promising. The number of council staff had been reduced from 23,500 to 19,800, while the quality of services had sharply improved; 75 per cent of the council's key performance indicators (KPIs) had improved from rock bottom to the upper quartile of local government performance. Moreover, LCC was about to announce a 3 per cent reduction in council tax.

David Henshaw, chief executive of LCC, stated:

> *This is not just about improving our operations. This is about leading a city differently. Our e-government agenda aims to put the customer at the heart of everything we do.*

Rob McVicker, commercial director of LDL and seconded from BT, was also enthusiastic:

> *The success of our partnership with LCC demonstrates that BT understands the needs of local government . . . We look forward to taking this partnership from strength to strength in the future.*

Liverpool Direct Limited

The Joint Venture and Its Governance

The LDL joint venture was launched on July 13, 2001. LDL began services for ICT and the call centre. Revenues and benefits, HR and payroll functions were all transferred by December 2001.

This joint venture company model supported the aspiration of both partners to create and sustain a long-term strategic partnership. It was designed to provide the benefits of realistic risk and reward sharing, with both partners sharing responsibility for the delivery of services[1] *(refer to **Exhibit 1** for a graphic representation of the partnership)*. Elaborating on this model, Henshaw explained:

> *We did not want to bind ourselves through a traditional outsourcing contract in which as soon as something goes wrong, you reach for your lawyer instead of looking for a solution. So I came up with a joint venture model. I call it the drunken man scenario: if one falls down, both fall down.*

A prominent feature of the partnership was a shared approach to the future strategy and growth of the

[1] Liverpool Direct Limited, Office of the Deputy Prime Minister, September 2002.

Research Associate Henri Bourgeois prepared this case under the supervision of Professor David Robertson as a basis for class discussion rather than to illustrate either effective or ineffective handling of a business situation.

6.0

company, ensuring that the new organization could evolve to meet changing needs. In this respect, the council held a minority stake of 19.9 per cent in LDL which granted it veto rights on key decisions such as the scope of future business activities, a change in the name of the company, or its closure. BT owned the remaining 80.1 per cent. The intellectual property and assets rested with the City Council! The capital value of the company was split equally 50/50.

LDL was managed via a joint venture board made up of the CEO, four BT directors, and two Liverpool City Council representatives (*refer to* ***Exhibit 2*** *for a summary of the management arrangements*).[2] Members of this board met quarterly to develop strategy and monitor the performance of LDL. There was also a strategy group comprising senior executives from LCC, BT and LDL.

LDL's operational management team included all service directors. They met fortnightly and reported directly to the LDL board via the CEO. Finally, a number of functional teams met regularly to discuss the daily management of the five services running the transferred services (*refer to* ***Exhibit 3*** *for the organizational structure of LDL*). Because of the size and complexity of the partnership, the council had recognized the importance of putting in place robust management and monitoring arrangements to ensure continued service delivery. Accordingly, LDL as underpinned by a series of contractual agreements that provided a legal framework for the venture.

A Flexible Contract for an Evolving Partnership

David Henshaw commented on the structure of the contract:

> *The flexibility is built into the contract. It is both explicit and implicit. The board of representatives that drives the business includes members of the two organizations, and there is transparent open-book accounting. As long as you have this approach, you naturally go for win-win solutions.*

The main contract was the Joint Venture and Shareholders Agreement between BT and LCC. The 26-clause document covered issues such as funding, board meetings and how company strategy was determined. More importantly, it regulated the way the two parties should behave towards each other in a formal company relationship.

Under this agreement, LCC would pay £30 million a year to the joint venture for the ten years of the contract. This annual payment represented LCC's estimate of how much it would cost the council to run the five services co-sourced with LDL. BT received the annual £30 million payment, less the cost of LCC employees' salaries and the interest on the operating lease. The remaining sum had to cover BT's own costs and generate a profit if BT obtained savings from operational improvements.

Another key document was the Service Provision Agreement signed by LCC and LDL. It defined the price, quality and performance levels for the services LDL would deliver (*refer to* ***Exhibit 4*** *for examples of performance measures*). Should a service fall below the minimum service level, LDL would incur default points reflecting the loss to the council arising out of the poor performance. When the total of default points exceeded a maximum level agreed in the contract, an escalation procedure would begin that could result in partial or full termination of the contract. Both partners expected LDL to expand in the future as it re-engineered both existing service delivery processes and internal support processes to exploit new technology. Other departments in LCC, as well as organizations outside the city, contract with LDL to supply services.

Finally, both parties signed a Secondment Agreement. According to this arrangement, staff (from both BT and LCC) who joined LDL would remain employees of their respective companies, would retain their existing salary and benefits and would have the right to end their secondment after an initial period of six months. Henshaw considered this last issue to be critical – the experience of LCC employees who had been outsourced in the past was poor; this escape clause would create a more positive climate for service provision improvements.

In addition to the secondment arrangement and performance agreement, the contractual agreements governed two other areas of the partnership: IT investment and profit allocation.

IT Investment

As part of the joint venture contract, BT agreed to invest £60 million in new IT equipment and systems, with £30 million available over the first two years of the partnership. LCC would own the equipment at the end of the contract. To accomplish this, BT sold the equipment to a third funding party, which then entered into a lease agreement with LCC (LCC chose an operating lease as it did not want to include the equipment in its asset allocation). This off-balance sheet agreement also prevented a high negative cash flow for LDL in the first two years of the contract. The parties also agreed that LDL would pay the cost of determining the system requirements and replac-

[2] 4ps (local government project procurement agency). *Liverpool City Council: Embracing the Electronic Age. Co-sourcing ICT, customer contact, revenues and benefits, payroll and human resources*. London, 2001.

ing obsolete system components. The third-party funder (BTCR) would pay for the new system development and system re-engineering, in return for an increase in lease payments (*refer to* ***Exhibit 1*** *for the financial flows between LCC, BT, LDL and the funder*).

Risk and Profit Allocation

The two partners developed a shared risk register in order to identify and address key risks, whether they were contractual, financial, HR-related or technical. The identified risks were then allocated after intense negotiations. LCC would not take any financial risk and would not be liable for any losses of LDL. BT took on all financial risk, but was entitled to all financial rewards from efficiency improvements.

The financial rewards for BT would take the form of efficiency savings and headcount reduction. As the productivity of LDL staff rose, LDL would release employees back to LCC and would keep more of the £30 million annual payment. Another way of generating profit was to create new business with third parties. In this case, the profits would be shared between the two partners and would result in a reduction of the contract fee for LCC and a 'return' for BT. McVicker explained:

> *A total of 880 people have been seconded to LDL from the council, 30 from BT. We look at the financial equivalent of taking 350 people out by the end of the contract. In terms of new business, it will be done on a case by case basis. For example on ticket sales, we share the profit 50/50, while the increased business of the call centre will enable LCC to reduce its payments to LDL.*

The secondment of employees created risks for LCC. The council retained its obligations to the employees seconded to LDL, such as ensuring that benefits were delivered and providing an Ombudsman to help resolve problems. Yet seconded council staff were also guaranteed certain rights and privileges under the traditional form of a TUPE[3] agreement, and these rights had to be respected even though the seconded staff were managed by personnel from LDL. Therefore, both partners spent a lot of time defining a contractual arrangement that allowed daily management of seconded staff by LDL managers, while maintaining the contractual relationship between the employees and LCC.

[3] Transfer of Undertakings (Protection of Employment). TUPE applies in the case of traditional outsourcing, a situation the council had promised the unions to avoid at all costs.

More than just Cost Savings

6.0

The IT Infrastructure Transformation

LDL's first move was to rationalize and standardize the IT infrastructure. The council's 500 different databases are being consolidated into a single database. Standards for hardware were defined for all new PCs and peripherals. Software standards ensured compatibility among services and facilitated the transfer of information.

This IT infrastructure transformation had visible impacts on the services LDL delivered. For revenues and benefits, LDL re-engineered the business process and introduced a Document Management System. The result was immediate, with the backlog being reduced from 60,000 queries to 4,000 – a reduction of about a year's worth of work.[4] Revenue collection also improved, resulting in an estimated gain of £1.5 million from high rent debtors who had disputes with the council.

The call centre was seen as a central instrument in turning residents' perceptions of the council around and offering them best service. To achieve this, LDL implemented a new CRM system to redirect most inquiries to the call centre. In June 2002 the call centre handled and resolved 90 per cent of them at the first point of contact. Abandoned calls dropped from 25 per cent to 12 per cent. In parallel, the service grew from 80 seats taking 40,000 calls per month during office hours to a 24/7 operation, with 225 seats handling 160,000 calls. Talks were even underway to build a new 500-seat call centre with a capacity to take eight million calls a year, creating 300 new jobs for the city.

BT also recommended a total re-engineering of the HR and payroll systems to provide an integrated process. This was achieved by implementing an ERP system to replace the old paper-based processes. The new system offered self-administration of transactions via the intranet, and the number of staff was reduced by 50 per cent.

Finally, the reforms were not confined to the inner workings of the council. LCC, with the help of LDL, rolled out self-service kiosks and 'one-stop shops' to facilitate contact between residents and the council. The city was awarded Beacon Status[5] for this initiative and praised by the local government minister:

[4] 'Liverpool City Direct Ltd.' BT Ignite press release, June 2002.

[5] The British government awards Beacon Status for excellence in a particular service or cross-cutting service area. Councils also need to demonstrate good performance overall, and make a commitment to share their best practice during their Beacon year. This dissemination of good practice includes taking part in showcase events, holding open days and running other learning events.

6.0

The city council will now help other authorities learn from its experience so that authorities across the country might provide services that meet the standards of the best.

All this was accomplished by a central IT staff of 120 people. In the past, LCC's less efficient processes had required 186 staff.

Redeployment and Retraining

For Henshaw, the investment in technology had to be accompanied by a cultural change in LCC. The joint venture was an important part of that change. By partnering with BT, the council hoped to learn about change management from the company, which invested considerable resources in retraining employees. For example, the 28 employees chose to work in the first one-stop shop took part in a 13-week multidisciplinary training course. By watching this and other efforts, Henshaw hoped to bring change management expertise into LCC.

Shared Benefits

The benefits of this partnership were obvious for the council. The joint venture brought cost reductions, increased flexibility, and major improvements in service delivery. The council expected these benefits to extend and grow over time.

The secondment arrangement was also important, as it had smoothed the transition of services. Staff continued to enjoy their existing benefits and BT was avoiding the bad publicity that can accompany downsizing. Headcount had been reduced from 23,500 to 19,500. Increased morale had resulted in a six-day cut in annual absenteeism rates, from 16 days to the national average of 10 days per person.

Of course, BT remained a profit-seeking company and planned to achieve a significant return on its investment over the ten-year period of the contract, funded from actual cost reductions and new business sales. And through LDL, BT was gaining experience as a business solution provider for local authorities, paving the way for future business with other local authorities. McVicker summarized the prevailing thoughts at BT:

The success of our ground-breaking partnership with LCC demonstrates that BT understands the needs of local government and knows how to create a solution that will really make a difference in the way that services are delivered to local citizens.[6]

[6] 'Liverpool City Direct.' Ltd www.btglobalservices.com/en/casestudy

EXHIBIT 1 The Joint Venture Partnership Model

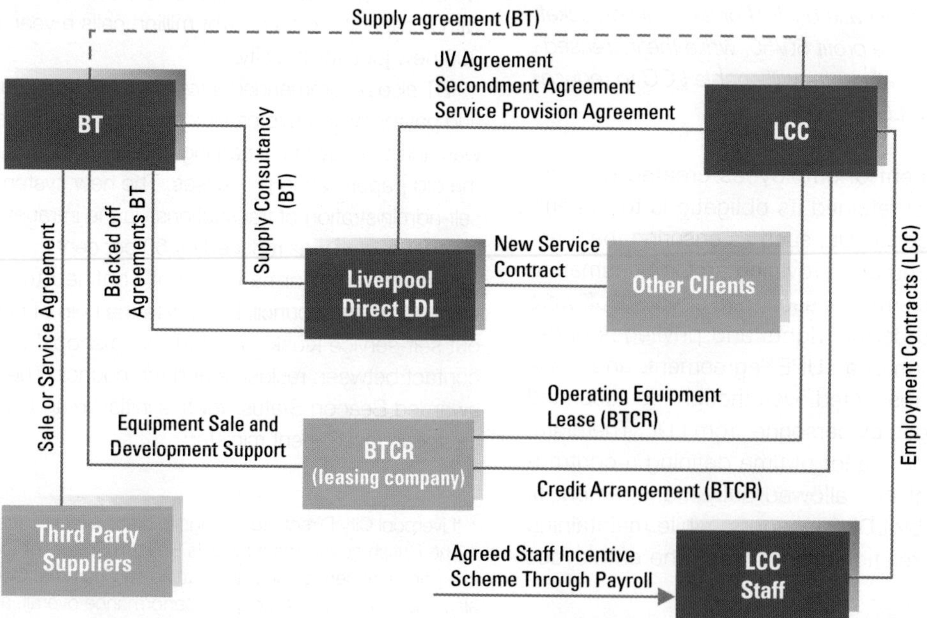

Source: Strategic Partnering Taskforce.

EXHIBIT 2 Management Arrangement of the JV between LCC and BT

Vehicle	Membership	Role	Report to
Board of Directors (meets quarterly)	■ Leader of the council (LCC) ■ Chief Executive (LCC) ■ Chief Executive (LDL) ■ Director Global Solutions (BT) ■ General Manager Local Government (BT) ■ Director of Finance Global Solution (BT) ■ General Manager (Global Solutions)	■ Determine LDL policy and strategy ■ Undertake all legal responsibilities as Directors of a company	■ Liverpool City Council ■ BT Corporate Management
Strategy Group (meets monthly)	■ Executive Director Resources (LCC) ■ Chief Executive (LDL) ■ General Manager (Global Solutions)	■ Make recommendations for overall LDL strategy ■ Define IT strategy for LDL ■ Review and prioritize proposed major initiatives ■ Consider opportunities for economic development ■ Promote LDL ■ Oversee performance of LDL	■ LDL Board of Directors ■ Liverpool City Council ■ BT Corporate Management ■ LDL Management Team

EXHIBIT 3 LDL Organizational Structure

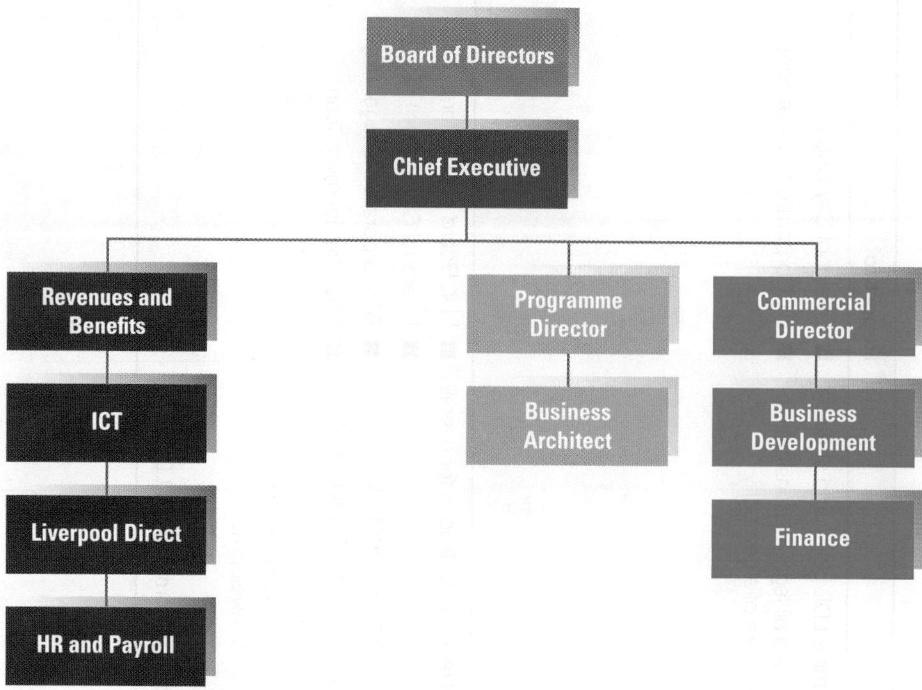

Source: Strategic Partnering Taskforce.

EXHIBIT 4 Examples of Service Level Agreements Used to Monitor LDL Services

ICT	REVENUES and BENEFITS
■ Percentage of working hours that end users have access to technical infrastructure and applications ■ Customer satisfaction with ICT service ■ Percentage of helpdesk calls resolved at first point of contact ■ Availability of online catalogue service procurement	■ Council tax collection rates ■ Business tax collection rates ■ Turnaround times from receipt to payment of new and renewal benefit claims ■ Accuracy of benefit assessment ■ Overpayment recovery ■ Fraud incentive achievement
LIVERPOOL DIRECT – call centre	**PAYROLL and HR**
■ Percentage of calls answered ■ Percentage of calls answered within 20 seconds ■ Customer satisfaction	■ Accuracy of payments ■ Use of ICT ■ Customer satisfaction

Source: 4ps (local government project procurement agency). *Liverpool City Council: Embracing the Electronic Age. Co-sourcing ICT, customer contact, revenues and benefits, payroll and human resources*. London, 2001.

INTEGRATIVE CASE 7.0

LARSON IN NIGERIA

David Larson, vice-president of international operations for Larson Inc., was mulling over the decisions he was required to make regarding the company's Nigerian operation. He was disturbed by the negative tone of the report sent to him on January 4, 2004, by the chief executive officer (CEO) of the Nigerian affiliate, George Ridley (see Exhibit 1). Larson believed the future prospects for Nigeria were excellent and was concerned about what action he should take.

Company Background

Larson Inc. was a New York-based multinational corporation in the wire and cable business. Wholly-owned subsidiaries were located in Canada and the United Kingdom, while Mexico, Venezuela, Australia and Nigeria were the sites of joint ventures. Other countries around the world were serviced through exports from the parent or one of its subsidiaries.

The parent company was established in 1925 by David Larson's grandfather. Ownership and management of the company remained in the hands of the Larson family and was highly centralized. The annual sales volume for the corporation worldwide approximated $936 million in 2003. Revenue was primarily generated from the sale of power, communication, construction and control cables.

Technical service was an important part of Larson Inc.'s product package; therefore, the company maintained a large force of engineers to consult with customers and occasionally supervise installation. As a consequence, licensing was really not a viable method of serving foreign markets.

Background on Nigeria

Nigeria is located in the west-central part of the African continent. With 134 million people in 2003, it was the most populous country in Africa and the ninth most populous nation in the world. Population growth was estimated at 2.5 per cent annually. About 44 per cent of the population was under 15 years of age. A majority of the labour force in Nigeria worked in agriculture but there was a trend of more people moving to urban centres.

The gross domestic product in 2003 was about $55 billion. While per capita GDP was only about $433, on a purchasing power parity basis it was substantially higher at $900. GDP had grown from 1998 to 2003 at about two per cent to three per cent annually. This increase was fuelled in part by growth in agriculture and the export sales of Nigeria's oil reserves.

During the 1998 to 2003 period, Nigeria's annual inflation rate had ranged between 10 and 11.7 per cent. This high level had contributed to the change in the value of the naira from 85.3 to the U.S. dollar in 1998 to 129.8 to the U.S. dollar in 2003.

The Nigerian Operation

Larson Inc. established a joint venture in Nigeria in 1994 with a local partner who held 25 per cent of the joint venture's equity. In 1999, Larson Inc. promised Nigerian authorities that the share of local ownership would be increased to 51 per cent within the next five to seven years. Such indigenization requests from developing country governments were quite common.

Sales revenue for the Nigerian firm totalled $45 million in 2003. Of this revenue, $39.4 million was realized in Nigeria, while $5.6 million was from exports. About 40 per cent of the firm's Nigerian sales ($16 million) were made to various enterprises and departments of the government of Nigeria. The company was making a reasonable profit of 10 per cent of revenue, but with a little bit of luck and increased efficiency, it was believed it could make a profit of 20 per cent.

Professor Paul W. Beamish and Harry Cheung revised this case (originally prepared by Professor I.A. Litvak) solely to provide material for class discussion. The authors do not intend to illustrate either effective or ineffective handling of a managerial situation. The authors may have disguised certain names and other identifying information to protect confidentiality.

7.0

The Nigerian operation had become less attractive for Larson Inc. in recent months. Although it was widely believed that Nigeria would become one of the key economic players in Africa in the 2000s and that the demand for Larson's products would remain very strong there, doing business in Nigeria was becoming more costly. Furthermore, Larson Inc. had become increasingly unhappy with its local partner in Nigeria, a lawyer who was solely concerned with quick 'paybacks' at the expense of reinvestment and long-term growth prospects.

David Larson recognized that having the right partner in a joint venture was of paramount importance. The company expected the partner or partners to be actively engaged in the business, 'not business people interested in investing money alone'. The partner was also expected to hold a substantial equity in the venture. In the early years of the joint venture, additional funding was often required and it was necessary for the foreign partner to be in a strong financial position.

The disillusionment of George Ridley, the Nigerian firm's chief executive officer (CEO), had been increasing since his early days in that position. He was an expatriate from the United Kingdom who, due to his background as a military officer, placed a high value upon order and control. The chaotic situation in Nigeria proved very trying for him. His problems were further complicated by his inability to attract good, local employees in Nigeria, while his best expatriate staff requested transfers to New York or Larson Inc.'s other foreign operations soon after their arrival in Nigeria. On a number of occasions, Ridley was prompted to suggest to head office that it reconsider its Nigerian commitment.

The Decision

David Larson reflected on the situation. He remained convinced that Larson Inc. should maintain its operations in Nigeria; however, he had to design a plan to increase local Nigerian equity in the venture to 51 per cent. Larson also wondered what should be done about Ridley. On the one hand, Ridley had been with the company for many years and knew the business intimately; on the other hand, Larson felt that Ridley's attitude was contributing to the poor morale in the Nigerian firm and wondered if Ridley had lost his sense of adaptability. Larson knew Ridley had to be replaced, but he was unsure about the timing and the method to use, since Ridley was only two years away from retirement.

Larson had to come to some conclusions fairly quickly. He had been requested to prepare an action plan for the Nigerian operation for consideration by the board of directors of Larson Inc. in a month's time. He thought he should start by identifying the key questions, whom he should contact, and how he should handle Ridley in the meantime.

EXHIBIT 1 The Ridley Report

In response to the request from head office for a detailed overview of the Nigerian situation and its implications for Larson Inc., Ridley prepared the following report in December, 2003. It attempts to itemize the factors in the Nigerian environment that have contributed to the problems experienced by Larson's joint venture in Nigeria.

Repatriation of Capital

1 While the Nigerian Investment Promotions Commission (NIPC) has removed time constraints and ceilings on repatriation, the divesting firm still has to submit evidence of valuation. In most cases the valuation is unrealistically low. This has represented substantial real-capital asset losses to the overseas companies concerned.

Remittance

2 A problem regarding remittances has arisen as a result of the Nigerian Insurance Decree No. 59, under which cargoes due for import to Nigeria have to be insured with a Nigerian-registered insurance company. For cargoes imported without confirmed letters of credit, claims related to cargo loss and damage are paid in Nigeria; however, foreign exchange for remittance to pay the overseas suppliers is not being granted on the grounds that the goods have not arrived.

Problems Affecting Liquidity and Cash Flow

3 A number of problems have arisen during the last two years that are having a serious effect upon liquidity and cash flow, with the result that the local expenses can be met only by increasing bank borrowing, which is not only an additional cost but also becoming more difficult to obtain.

(Continued)

EXHIBIT 1 *(Continued)*

a Serious delays exist in obtaining payment from federal and state government departments for supplies and services provided, even in instances where payment terms are clearly written into the contract concerned. This is particularly true for state governments where payment of many accounts is 12 months or more in arrears. Even after payment, further delays and exchange-rate losses are experienced in obtaining foreign currency for the part that is remittable abroad. This deterioration in cash flow from government clients had, in turn, permeated through to the private clients.

b There is a requirement that a 100 per cent deposit be made on application for foreign currency to cover letters of credit.

c In order to clear the cargo as soon as possible and to avoid possible loss at the wharf, importers normally pay their customs duty before a ship arrives.

d Most company profits are taxed at a flat rate of 30 per cent. Firms operating in Nigeria must contend with a number of arbitrary levies and taxes, imposed mainly by state governments eager to augment their extremely thin revenue bases. The federal government attempted to put a halt to such practices by specifying which taxes all three (federal, state and local) tiers of government can collect, but it has not been entirely successful in enforcing compliance. Tax authorities are constantly trying to 'trip up' companies in the course of inspections or audits, through their 'interpretation' of the tax legislation. Consequently, net earnings after tax are insufficient to cover increased working capital requirements.

Incomes and Prices Policy Guidelines

4 Many of the guidelines issued by the Productivity, Prices and Incomes Board are of direct discouragement, as they make operations in Nigeria increasingly less attractive in comparison with other areas in the world. Although these guidelines were removed in 1987, increases for wage, salary, fees for professional services and auditing are still subject to final government approval.

Offshore Technical and Management Services

5 Restrictions on the reimbursement of expenses to the parent company for offshore management and technical services are a cause of great concern, since such services are costly to provide.

Professional Fees

6 The whole position regarding fees for professional services provided from overseas is most unsatisfactory. Not only are the federal government scales substantially lower than those in most other countries, but also the basis of the project cost applied in Nigeria is out of keeping with normally accepted international practice. The arbitrary restriction on the percentage of fees that may be remitted is a further disincentive to attracting professional services. Moreover, payment of professional fees in themselves produces cash flow problems exacerbated by long delays in payments and remittance approvals.

Royalties and Trademarks

7 The National Office of Technology Acquisition and Promotion (NOTAP) restricts the payment of royalties for the use of trademarks for a period of ten years, which is out of keeping with the generally accepted international practice. This can be extended only under special cases. Limits for licensing and technical service fees are between one per cent to five per cent of net sales. Management fees are chargeable at two per cent to five per cent of a company's profit before tax (or one per cent to two per cent of net sales when no profits are anticipated during the early years). The maximum foreign share of consulting fees is five per cent. Such applications, however, are only granted for advanced technology projects for which indigenous technology is not available. Further, service agreements for such projects have to include a schedule of training for Nigerian personnel for eventual takeover and Nigerian professionals are required to be involved in the project from inception.

Quotas, Work Permits, and Entry Visas

8 It must be recognized that expatriate expertise is a very important element for this business, but expatriate staff is very costly. Unfortunately, at the present time there are a number of difficulties and frustrations, such as the

(Continued)

EXHIBIT 1 *(Continued)*

arbitrary cuts in expatriate quotas, the delays in approving quota renewal, and in some cases, the refusal of entry visas and work permits for individuals required for work in Nigeria. Expatriate quotas are usually granted for two to three years subject to renewal.

Expatriate Staff

9 In general, the conditions of employment and life in Nigeria are regarded as unattractive when compared with conditions in many other countries competing for the same expertise. These differences are due to: the general deterioration in law and order; the restrictions on salary increase and home remittance; the difficulties in buying air tickets; the poor standard of health care; the unsatisfactory state of public utilities such as electricity, water and telecommunications; the harassment from the police, airport authorities and other government officials; the general frustrations related to visas and work permits mentioned above. The situation has now reached a stage where not only is recruitment of suitably qualified, skilled experts becoming increasingly difficult, but we are also faced with resignations and refusals to renew contracts even by individuals who have worked and lived here for some years. Furthermore, the uncertainty over the length of time for which employment in Nigeria will be available (due to doubts whether the necessary expatriate quotas will continue to be available to the employer) is most unsettling to existing staff. This and the restriction of contracts to as little as two years are important factors in deterring the more highly qualified applicants from considering posts in Nigeria. These factors are resulting in a decline in the quality of expatriate staff it is possible to recruit.

Local Staff

10 Nigeria has one of the strongest national unions in Africa – the National Labour Congress (NLC). It is almost impossible to discipline a worker without attracting confrontation with the union. On certain occasions, some union members can be very militant. The union is also continuously attacking the employment of expatriates and trying to replace them with Nigerian staff.

11 Inadequate local technical training leads to low quality workers who tend to be lazy and not quality conscious.

12 The desirability of maintaining a tribal balance in the work force limits the options in recruiting the best workers.

13 Nigerian companies suffer heavily from pilferage, which normally accounts for two per cent of sales.

Public Utilities

14 The constant interruption in public utility services not only affects the morale of all employees but also has a very serious impact upon the operation of the business itself. Unless reasonable and continuing supplies of electricity, water, petroleum products and telecommunications can be assured, and the highway adequately maintained, the costs related to setting up and operating escalate.

Continuity of Operating Conditions

15 The general and growing feeling of uncertainty about the continuity of operating conditions is a matter of considerable concern. It would seem that this uncertainty is engendered by a whole range of matters related to: short notice changes (sometimes even retrospective) in legislation and regulations; imprecise definition of legislation and regulations, which leads to long periods of negotiation and uncertainty; delays between public announcement of measures and promulgation of how they are to be implemented; and sometimes inconsistent interpretation of legislation and regulations by Nigerian officials.

Government Officials

16 Foreign partners have to rely on their Nigerian counterpart to handle the government officials. But it is impossible to measure its performance nor to control its expense in these activities. In addition, carefully cultivated relationships with officials could disappear, as they are transferred frequently.

Bribery

17 Surrounding many of the problems previously listed is the pervasive practice of bribery, known locally as the *dash*. Without such a payment it is very difficult to complete business or government transactions with native Nigerians.

INTEGRATIVE CASE 8.0
L'ORÉAL THAILAND (A)

I was officially appointed Managing Director of L'Oréal Thailand in early April 2000. Although I'm originally from the UK, I have worked overseas since my MBA in 1984. I had already lived in Asia for seven years when I joined L'Oréal in 1996. In my previous position as L'Oréal's Deputy Managing Director for Asia, I was already quite familiar with the situation of our Thai business.... Since the Asian Crisis of 1997, market share, sales and profitability had all been under sustained pressure and targets were being missed again and again. My boss asked me to move to Bangkok to further evaluate the situation and fix it. The results for the first quarter of 2000 were already five per cent below budget in units and ten per cent below for value. On April 15, I called a Management Committee meeting to review the situation and discuss the next steps with my team!

Chris Martin

L'Oréal in Thailand

Thailand, with 63 million inhabitants, was the world's seventeenth most populous country and the thirtieth largest economy but ranked only sixtieth in gross domestic product per capita. With an area of 513,000 km^2, the Kingdom of Thailand was as large as France, with almost the same population (refer to Exhibit 4 for a global perspective of Thailand).

L'Oréal products had been distributed in Thailand since the early fifties through local agents. By the early nineties, two different L'Oréal entities existed in Bangkok: Siampar and Thailor. Siampar, the oldest, was a joint venture with a local conglomerate. Due to high import duties on luxury products, Siampar manufactured some Lancôme products locally and imported the rest of the line. It then distributed Lancôme through counters in top department stores, together with several other luxury brands owned by the L'Oréal Group. In 1998 L'Oréal was able to buy out its partner's share of the joint venture. L'Oréal at once decided to discontinue the local production of Lancôme in Thailand.

Thailor, the second company, was created in 1992 to directly manage the importation and distribution of L'Oréal's mass consumer and professional hair salon products. The Thailor product line included hair colour, make-up and skin care products.

Although both were part of the L'Oréal Group, the two companies maintained their offices in different locations, had different internal cultures, different processes and different policies, especially regarding pay and benefits, due to the local partner's desire to minimize expenses.

In 1999, as part of a market-opening package implemented in return for International Monetary Fund (IMF) aid, the Thai government abolished the requirement that foreign-invested companies must have an equity structure with substantial local Thai ownership. Lindsay Owen-Jones, Chairman and CEO of the L'Oréal Group, decided to create a single, wholly owned subsidiary in Thailand. Consequently, Siampar was merged with Thailor to create a single multi-division entity: L'Oréal Thailand Ltd.

Martin recalled:

> *When I arrived in Bangkok, Thailor and Siampar had already moved into the same building. However, the two former companies were located on two different floors and did not really talk to each other! Both were suffering major losses, used a lot of cash resources, were under-capitalized and still managed under the 'Thai exception' since things were supposed to be uniquely different in this country ... Thailand was our seventh largest market in Asia, on a par with Singapore and well behind*

Professor Dominique Turpin prepared this case as a basis for class discussion rather than to illustrate either effective or ineffective handling of a business situation. All names and data have been disguised.

8.0

Japan, China, Korea, Taiwan, Hong Kong and Malaysia. Together with a fresh team of young L'Oréal executives who had recently been sent to Bangkok, my mission was to create a truly 'L'Oréalized' company which espoused the Group's long-term values and would deliver healthy profitable growth.

One of the key challenges for L'Oréal in Thailand had been the effect of the 1997 Asian crisis triggered by excessive fixed asset investment and reckless borrowing by over-ambitious local corporations and undisciplined financial institutions. Since then, L'Oréal's operations in Thailand had been hurt by stagnant markets for mass retail products, and aggressive attempts by local and international competitors to win market share. Key issues for the business included:

- Import duties and taxes were among the highest in the world for beauty products, ranging from 20 per cent to 75 per cent.
- The Food and Drug Administration regulation of cosmetics, which was quite bureaucratic and inflexible (for example, packaging and advertising claims were still highly regulated).
- The government tended to be more protective of local companies and had recently announced a new 'Buy Thai' campaign.

The Thai Beauty Market

At the beginning of 2000 Martin estimated the size of the total Thai beauty market as Bt 26.6 billion[1] at retail prices, of which L'Oréal in Thailand had a seven per cent share (refer to Exhibit 5).

Roberto Shimizu had just been appointed general manager of the Consumer Products Division. Shimizu estimated that the strategic categories of Skin Care, Make-Up and Hair Colouration in Thailand were well developed compared with other Southeast Asian markets. Among other categories, Hair Care was considered to be in line with other countries, while Fragrance was significantly underdeveloped, especially compared with Malaysia.

L'Oréal in Thailand mainly targeted the core group of women between 20 and 44 years of age. Thai consumers who regularly bought L'Oréal products were concentrated in the urban areas of Central Thailand (four million people) and Greater Bangkok (ten million people), where the average monthly wage was estimated at Bt 7,000 and average monthly household expenditure on personal care and health at Bt 650.[2]

Cosmetics Distribution in Thailand

Since the Asian crisis of 1997, total store count had declined due to the closure of marginally viable sites, particularly in the local department store and traditional store/stall sectors. Foreign retailers began to enter the market in a big way after the government lifted protective restrictions under pressure from the IMF. The fastest growing formats were foreign-invested hypermarkets, supermarkets and personal care stores, which were rapidly replacing traditional wet/dry markets and 'mom and pop' operations. Personal care stores (similar to US/UK drug stores), a totally new concept in Thailand, first appeared in 1996.

The L'Oréal sales force in Thailand covered retail formats which accounted for 53 per cent weighted distribution (WD) by value of the total beauty market (refer to Exhibit 6). Direct sales (15 per cent WD) were an important channel for make-up and skin care products, and it was covered by many local beauty companies and by Unilever Thailand. Unlike the latter, L'Oréal did not have deep coverage of the traditional trade formats, as its strategy had historically been to focus on the higher end of the beauty market.

According to Martin and Shimizu, a retail revolution had started in Thailand. Traditionally, the industry had been dominated by large Thai groups, sometimes with minority foreign partners, often lacking modern management techniques and with many marginal sites. Since 1998, international retailers had come to dominate all sectors, usually via a buy-out of their Thai partner. Competition and professionalism had increased dramatically as a result. However, local retailers were lobbying hard for the government to limit the growth of foreign retailers, especially hypermarkets (refer to Exhibit 7 for L'Oréal customer 'hit parade').

Only two Thai companies remained in effective control of their retail operations: Central and The Mall. Consequently, department stores were a local duopoly, but all other formats were wide open, with international retailers (mainly European) making rapid progress. The only top international retailer not present in Thailand was Wal-Mart. However, the property arms of both Central and The Mall owned most of the upscale retail locations across the country.

[1] US$ 1 = Bt 42 = €1.02.

[2] About 13 per cent (8 million) of the Thai population was estimated to live in poverty (less than Bt 890 per month).

The cosmetics sections of department stores were still under-developed due to the popularity of duty-free shops (both at international airports and downtown Bangkok). Cosmetic counters inside department stores still lacked the sophistication found in more developed markets in terms of display, ambiance and merchandising.

Martin had also noticed that there was bitter rivalry between L'Oréal's key accounts in each retail sector: Central vs The Mall, Boots vs Watsons, Tesco vs Carrefour, Tops vs Foodlion, etc.

Competitors in the Thai Beauty Industry

L'Oréal's overall business was estimated to rank No. 4 in terms of turnover in the Thai beauty industry (refer to Exhibit 8 for a ranking of the competitors) and No. 700 in the total Thai corporate ranking. Unilever had been operating in Thailand well before World War II and commanded a 16 per cent market share, well ahead of the No. 2 player, Procter & Gamble (P&G). Local firms such as Better Way, Skyline Unity and others accounted for 28 per cent of the Thai beauty market. Their focus was on make-up and skin care products via direct sales. Japan was their main source of innovation via contract manufacture and/or licensing tie-ups.

The most significant local non-direct sales operation was International Cosmetics Corporation (better known under the acronym of ICC). ICC's top brand was Pias for skin care and make-up products. Its brand name had been licensed from a private Japanese company, but its products were specific to Thailand.

Over recent years, local brands had been almost driven out of the retail hair care and skin care markets by the big international players. A total of fifty-five local brands shared 35 per cent share of the hair colour segment. Only in the make-up segment did local brands really resist, with 285 local brands battling for a 61 per cent share of this business.

Lever and P&G

Unilever (or Lever for short) and P&G were both remodeling their Thai operations. Both companies were major players in beauty and non-beauty sections (such as detergents, personal hygiene and food), whereas L'Oréal had remained focused on the beauty industry. Lever's Thailand factory was being developed into a key export hub (supplying 20 per cent of Unilever's Asian volume) especially for liquid products and ice cream.

In the beauty market, Thailand was a key innovation center for Lever. A Personal Care R&D Centre had recently been relocated from Indonesia to Thailand to join a long-standing Hair Care R&D Centre. Thailand had also been the first Asian Lever operation to enter the hair colour segment (with its Sunsilk Procolour brand) as well as direct sales (with the Aviance make-up and skin care brand).

P&G had relocated its hair care R&D centre from Japan to Thailand and had opened a huge new US$ 150 million factory to make hair care and skin care products for nineteen countries, generating exports of over $100 million per year. However, P&G's marketing development had been centralized in Singapore with only trade marketing remaining in-country.

The L'Oréal Brand Portfolio

Martin strongly believed that L'Oréal's business was very much about brand management. In fact, four brands accounted for 80 per cent of its business in Thailand. These brands were segmented by price and, consequently, by distribution channel (refer to Exhibit 9). Out of the fourteen brands sold in 2000, Biotherm, the six PCI (a French abbreviation standing for Prestige & Collection International) brands, Kerastase, Helena Rubinstein and Lancôme covered the very high end of the market; L'Oréal Paris and L'Oréal Professional, the high end; and Maybelline and Garnier were more mass market. Consequently, distribution of Helena Rubinstein was restricted to six major department stores, Lancôme to thirty-four; L'Oréal Paris was distributed in 1,200 outlets and Maybelline and Garnier in about 5,000 stores. In comparison, P&G and Unilever were present in 5,000 to 30,000 stores depending on the product categories.

- **Biotherm** offered skin care products exclusively, **Kerastase** only hair care, and **PCI** only fragrances and ancillary products. **Helena Rubinstein** and **Lancôme** both offered skin care and make-up products.[3] This last category included foundations, lipsticks, eye and nail colouring.
- **L'Oréal Paris** covered four categories: Hair Colouring with the L'Oréal Excellence and L'Oréal Feria brands; Skin Care with the L'Oréal Plénitude brand; L'Oréal Make-Up; and a crowded category called Hair Care products, which included shampoos and styling aids. However, this last category was becoming increasingly commoditized by the competition

[3] Lancôme also offered fragrances such as Trésor.

with lower prices and slimmer margins. L'Oréal Paris was very much the umbrella brand for the brands in the different categories, aimed at bringing a promise of quality to the Thai customers.

- **L'Oréal Professional** (hair colouring and hair care treatment) was sold exclusively in 2,000 top professional salons to build the image and credibility of the L'Oréal brand and to enhance awareness of L'Oréal quality to assist the mass-market L'Oréal Paris products.
- **Maybelline** was used exclusively for make-up products and did not carry the L'Oréal signature. Maybelline products were on average 20 per cent cheaper than those of L'Oréal Paris and were intended to compete with Pias and other local products in the mass-market segment.
- **Garnier** covered hair colour only and was also targeted at the mass market.

L'Oréal's Three Divisions

In early 2000 L'Oréal in Thailand operated three business divisions: Luxury (the old Siampar company), Consumer and Professional Products (the old Thailor company). (The Active Cosmetics brands – the Group's fourth division – had not yet been introduced in Thailand.)

The Luxury Division

This division accounted for about 20 per cent of L'Oréal's turnover in Thailand and encompassed four major businesses: Lancôme, Biotherm, Helena Rubinstein and a group of smaller prestigious fragrance brands such as Paloma Picasso, Lanvin, Cacharel, Guy Laroche, Giorgio Armani and Ralph Lauren, grouped under the PCI label.

Alessandra Badini had recently been appointed general manager of the Luxury Division. Like Martin and Shimizu, Badini had not been in Bangkok for long, arriving at the end of 1999. The young Italian had quickly found that the local luxury business was characterized by a high retail price structure (+20 per cent premium over Singapore and duty-free shops) due to Thailand's heavy duty rates.[4] Consequently, 50 per cent of selective beauty purchases were made outside the country.[5] Distribution in Thailand was very much restricted to the duopoly of the Central Group (56 per cent of sales) and The Mall (27 per cent), with the top two outlets alone (both belonging to Central) accounting for 30 per cent of the market.

Other key facts gathered by Badini were that the customer base for her business was still relatively small (just 300,000 consumers) and that skin care represented 56 per cent of the market; make-up 36 per cent; and fragrance eight per cent.

In the luxury segment of the beauty industry, four major international competitors accounted for 70 per cent of the Thai market:

The US-based Lauder Group with brands such as Estée Lauder, Clinique, Mac, Bobbi Brown, La Mer, Prescriptives, Origins, DKNY, Stilla and Aveda had conquered 33.5 per cent of the luxury segment.

- Shiseido of Japan, with the brands Shiseido, 5S, Clé de Peau and Ipsa, accounted for 16.5 per cent.
- L'Oréal with five major brands (Lancôme, Biotherm, Helena Rubinstein, Giorgio Armani and Ralph Lauren) maintained a 16 per cent share. However, brands such as Paloma Picasso and Lanvin were in decline.
- Finally, the other French-based Group LVMH (Moët Hennessy-Louis Vuitton) accounted for 5.1 per cent of the market with two key brands: Dior and Guerlain.

The Consumer Division

Shimizu, who had arrived in Bangkok only a few months before Martin, headed the Consumer Division. He found that sales had been flat over the last four years. Several local managers explained to him that this trend reflected the overall evolution of the market, with a steady drop in make-up being offset by a persistent upward trend in skin care. Shimizu remained unconvinced by these arguments. The Consumer Division accounted for about 65 per cent of L'Oréal's total turnover in Thailand.

This division handled three categories of products: skin care, hair colour and make-up.

- Skin Care: In this category, Plénitude was L'Oréal's leading brand. However, it only accounted for 4.1 per cent in value market share vs 28 per cent for Ponds, the category leader. During 1999 other competitors such as Nivea had grown share, Neutrogena had made a little progress, and Ponds and Olay were broadly stable.
- Hair Colour: This product category was the original core business of L'Oréal, with Excellence and Natea its key leading brands in Thailand. Excellence was targeted at women over 35 who

[4] Between 30 per cent and 40 per cent depending on the country of origin.

[5] L'Oréal survey of 1,200 Lancôme customers.

needed to cover grey hairs, while Natea was targeted at the 15 to 35 age group. However, because of a lack of media support, Shimizu was not sure if this positioning was totally clear in the minds of Thai consumers. The brands accounted for 10.3 per cent and 2.9 per cent, respectively, of the market (in value terms). However, Thailand was a test for Lever's Sunsilk Procolour brand (13.3 per cent in market value), while Clairol from Bristol-Myers had a 12.1 per cent value share.

- Make-Up: In this category, Maybelline held a 2.7 per cent value share, and L'Oréal Paris had a very limited impact with a 0.8 per cent share. The L'Oréal franchise was fairly well spread across the categories, but Maybelline was more focused on eye products, such as mascara.

The Professional Products Division

The Professional Products Division, headed by Seng Wee (John) Chua, who had just been promoted to General Manager, represented 15 per cent of L'Oréal Thailand's turnover. The results from the Professional Products Division had been relatively stable and were slowly regaining their pre-1997 crisis levels, except for Perm products, which were declining among older users.

L'Oréal's two major Professional Products brands, L'Oréal Professional and Kerastase, were market leaders thanks to an excellent image among the top professional salon owners. L'Oréal constantly reinforced this reputation through rapid innovation and true technical superiority.

The Challenges

At the end of April 2000 Martin called a new meeting of the Management Committee, which consisted of the head of each division together with Pablo Gomez, Deputy Managing Director in charge of Finance and Operations. The Human Resources Director was also a member of the committee. However, the previous incumbent had resigned in December 1999 and Martin had decided to take on this role directly for the time being, in addition to his responsibilities as Managing Director. Gomez, a Mexican by birth, had arrived in Bangkok in September 1999. Unlike the other members of the Management Committee, Gomez was not a 'typical' L'Oréal man, in the sense that he was a newcomer to the Group. A chartered accountant by training, he had just completed six months of initial familiarization, learning L'Oréal's business and control systems. He had previously worked in a major bank in New York and London, then joined Ciba Geigy to become chief financial officer of their operations in Taiwan before becoming a country manager for a Swiss pharmaceutical company. In his new position in L'Oréal Thailand, Gomez supervised all financial and operations functions (customer service, logistics, warehousing, information technology, registrations with the local authorities).

Gomez started the discussion: With the exception of Kerastase and L'Oréal Professional, none of our brands is making real money. Overall, our sales are flat or declining, margins are down and our cash flow is negative. We have been cutting on marketing expenses to improve the bottom line but I do not think this is healthy for our long-term business.

Badini: For me, another major problem is semi-consignment, whereby we issue invoices to the department stores but receive no payments until well after they have actually sold the stock. Although the sales of my division grew three times from Bt 100 million to Bt 332 million between 1993 and 1998, accounts receivable grew from seventy to 154 days! As a result of the 1997 crisis, the market has suddenly dropped by ten per cent. This has generated an automatic overstock in products at the retail level. Stocks that were at three-and-a-half months with an expected market growth of +20 per cent have turned 'mechanically' to more than six months. Right now my accounts receivable have further increased to 203 days and are getting worse by the minute! Although Lancôme sales reached Bt 241 million in 1998, by the end of the 1999, we were at −11 per cent and all my other brands were flat, at barely 1 per cent growth.

Martin: Things are even worse than the numbers indicate. Because of the stores that expect us to supply them on semi-consignment terms, we have been invoicing customers for sales that have not even materialized at the consumer level.

For Shimizu, results at the end of 1999 reflected the continuing lack of a strong brand/consumer franchise that could consistently generate competitive levels of marketing means.

Shimizu: We are heavily out-spent by our competitors, in an environment where too many brands and too many retailers are fighting for a consumer base of only 4 million women with a disposable income of €2,000. Our brands tend to overlap and don't have a clear positioning in the minds of our customers. For us it may be clear, but with limited media support, I doubt it is the case for our customers. We have too many niche brands and too many new brand launches.

Martin: The year-to-date results for 2000 are disappointing: 11 per cent below budget due to destocking of retailers by both the Consumer and the Luxury divisions. We are now flat versus 1999, with a challenging catch up of 32 per cent if we are to achieve our full year budget – and look at our working capital figures, they are just terrible. Without the bank loans guaranteed by our parent company, we'd be out of business (Refer to Exhibits 10 and 11)

Shimizu: Let me bring you another challenge! We were ranked No. 35 in overall media spending at the end of 1999. Total media spending by all advertisers in Thailand has increased 25 per cent since January 2000, following a decline of nine per cent in 1998 and a growth of 25 per cent in 1999. Within the beauty industry of this country, L'Oréal is ranked No. 4 in media spending by company, with our biggest brand – L'Oréal Paris – coming in at No. 8 in brand ranking. Lever is spending ten times what we are for the same category. Against a share of voice of three per cent for L'Oréal Paris, Lever's Sunsilk brand has a 17 per cent share. All international competitors increased media spending by 50 per cent to 100 per cent in 1999. Pablo, I would need another Bt 50 million to start playing catch-up with Lever and P&G – can I have this money? (Refer to Exhibit 12).

Gomez (*jokingly*): You must be kidding Roberto. As you know, any extra budget will have to come from Paris.

Shimizu: Yes and I know that I'd better have a good plan – because I know the management in Paris is sick and tired of sending us extra money.

Martin: You are very right, Roberto, but tell me one thing, although L'Oréal, Maybelline and Garnier are nowhere near 'top of mind' for our consumers, I am really concerned by how we will maintain, let alone increase, the awareness of these brands (Refer to Exhibit 13).

Shimizu: This will be tough. We don't have the money to go on TV and our visibility in print media is almost zero. All we have been doing recently is running promotions, offering temporary price reductions or giving away free gifts!

Badini: Two magazines, *Dichan and Praew*, can cover 45 per cent of our customer target.

Shimizu: We can take advantage of our great international ambassadors: Claudia Schiffer, Andie McDowell and Milla Jovovich.

Chua: Well, I am not so sure Thai consumers can really identify with these Western stars. I am not even sure we have the right products for them. While some international competitors make special products for Asian women, do we?

Shimizu: Good point! What is our real competitive advantage, by the way? We like to say that we have the best technology, but do our retailers really care about our technology or are they more concerned about either being out of stock or overstocked all the time?! One thing is for sure, we should be faster to meet their needs.... Our organization is much leaner and much less bureaucratic than our major international competitors.

Martin: I have one more major concern and it has to do with the ambiance and morale of this organization. As you all know, the turnover rate remains high as we continue to lose staff. Many are people who cannot adapt to our demands for increased professionalism, but we are also losing good people who wonder if L'Oréal has any future in Thailand (Refer to Exhibit 14). All these resignations are placing stress on the organization, due to gaps that need to be covered until new staff are brought on board, and due to the need for constant training and retraining. I recently received some data from a panel of eleven multinationals that show that we had the second highest turnover rate during 1999, with 23 per cent of staff leaving versus an average of 13 per cent. Turnover is highest in the support functions. As you all know, the search for a HR Director has become totally stale, with no outstanding candidates recently. I will temporarily suspend the search and take personal charge of the HR team. What do you think Pablo?

Gomez (*nodding*): As you said last time, Chris, in the past our hiring criteria have been too focused on a very narrow band of candidates who tend to come from highly privileged backgrounds.

Chua: Right! This leads to a lack of in-depth understanding of real Thai consumers, a constant outflow related to 'stop working' or 'family business' obligations, and an overall lack of maturity, motivation and drive, especially in the marketing teams.

Shimizu: If I may add to this ... I had dinner with a friend last Monday who works for a major international headhunting firm. He does not want to work with us because he thinks our reputation is zero: 'You have no name,' he said to me! Who has heard of Siampar and Thailor? On top of that, he told me that the image of our company here was that we had no vision, no results and no rewards.

Martin: I know, I know. This organization has grown a 'loser mentality'. Only positive results can change that. We also have these huge disparities in salaries between the two former Siampar and Thailor entities.

Shimizu: Yes! And we are totally out of touch with what the market pays. One of my controllers is making one-fourth of what his counterpart is making with Unilever Thailand! We can't attract good talent if we pay peanuts! All my people are young and cheap. As a result, the sales forecasts I am getting from my people are unrealistic or too simplistic – we are always either without stock or with too much inventory.

Badini: Same thing with my team. We need to review the skills and competences of many of our people.

Gomez: And the reward system, and the motivation. The mentality so far has been to cut expenses in order to deliver the bottom line. When I arrived here last September, sales people had to share hotel rooms when they were on the road.... Back in November last year, I was even told to travel economy class from Bangkok to Paris for my first meeting at the headquarters. And look at these offices, they are so cramped, so dark, so uninspiring!

Martin: These issues are real. We need to further professionalize and stimulate our teams. The cultures of the two old companies are at odds with each other. I hate this 'tribal mentality' between the two sides of the organization. This has been going on for too long.

Next Steps

Martin concluded:

> *The difficulty may not be so much in framing a new finance, marketing and HR strategy; we also need to make sure we can execute it correctly. Except for John, all of us here have been in Thailand for six months at the most, and we don't have a single Thai executive with us in this room because all the senior local people from the old companies have left. As foreign expatriates, I hope we don't make any cultural mistakes either in communicating with our local staff or in shaping the future of this company. Several of my colleagues in other parts of the Group have already been asking me why I agreed to become 'Captain of the* Thai-tanic'. *One thing is sure: the five of us will either survive or sink together!*

Please address all correspondence to Dominique Turpin, IMD – International Institute for Management Development, PO Box 915, CH 1001 Lausanne, Switzerland. E-mail address: dominique. turpin@imd.ch

8.0

EXHIBIT 1 Consolidates Group Sales

Published consolidated total

	1996	1997	1998	1998 (pro forma)	1999	2000
€ millon	9,200	10,537	11,498	9,588	10,751	12,671
FFr million	60,347	69,121	75,421	62,892	70,520	83,116

Consolidated sales by sector (€ million)

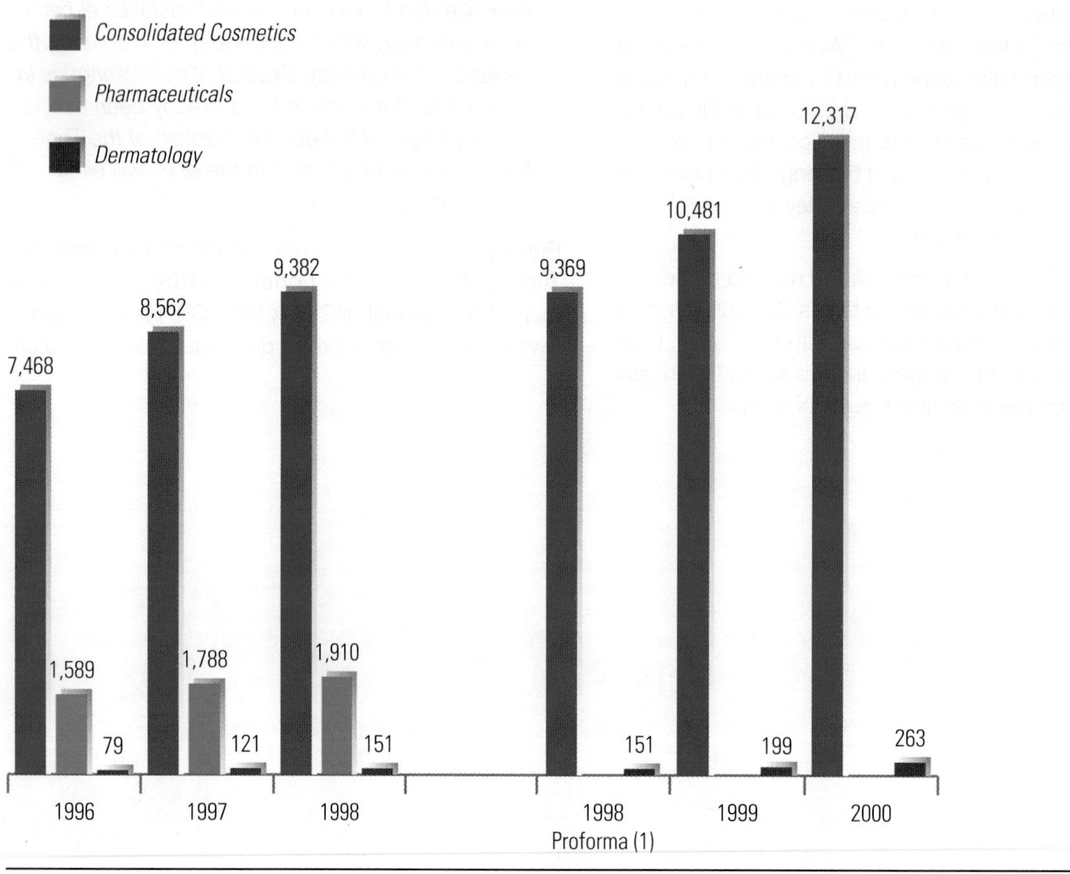

(1) After reclassification of sales according to sector following the spin-off of Synthélabo, a pharmaceuticals company.

Source: Company information.

EXHIBIT 2 Breakdown of Consolidated Cosmetics Sales* by Division for 2000

	€ Million	Growth	
		Published Figures	**Like-for-like Basis**
Consumer products	6,745	+14.8 (%)	+6.5 (%)
Luxury products	3,385	+19.8 (%)	+10.8 (%)
Professional products	1,518	+27.7 (%)	+8.5 (%)
Active cosmetics	574	+15.1 (%)	+12.0 (%)
Other cosmetics	95	+4.0 (%)	+1.8 (%)
Total cosmetics sales	**12,317**	**+17.5** (%)	**+8.1** (%)

*Including sales generated by agents, 2000 group cosmetics sales stood at € 12.5 billion.

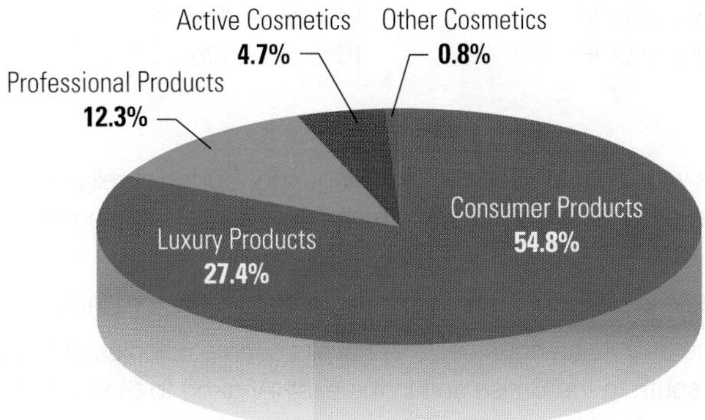

Source: Company information.

EXHIBIT 3 Breakdown of Consolidated Cosmetics Sales by Geographical Zone for 2000

	€ Million	Growth	
		Published Figures	**Like-for-like Basis**
Western Europe	6,234	+6.0 (%)	+5.1 (%)
North America	3,733	+31.4 (%)	+8.0 (%)
Rest of the world	2,350	+33.4 (%)	+17.3 (%)
Total cosmetics sales	**12,317**	**+17.5** (%)	**+8.1** (%)

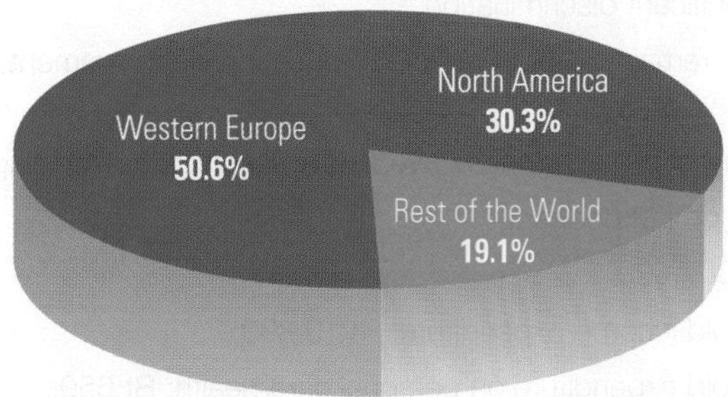

Source: Company information.

EXHIBIT 4 Thailand Global Perspective 2000

World Ranking

- Seventeenth most populous country
- Thirtieth largest economy
- Sixtieth in gross domestic product (GDP) per head

Vital Statistics

Area 513,000 km^2, 63 million inhabitants, +1% annual population growth (similar to France, same population as Turkey).

GDP per head is US$ 1,950 (similar to Turkey and Russia)

Main Industries

Agriculture	11% of GDP	48% of workforce
Manufacturing/assembly	28% of GDP	14% of workforce
Tourism	9% of GDP	10% of workforce

History

- Thailand has close historical links with India (shared Sanskrit language, Buddhist religion), China (migration from Yunnan and, more recently, Fujian and Hainan) and Japan (mercenary soldiers in the fifteenth/sixteenth centuries, World War II alliance).
- Thai people were originally nomadic and are found across Indochina from Eastern India to Vietnam.
- Thailand, Japan and China are the only Asian countries that never became colonies of foreign powers. However, Thailand had to cede land in the south to the British and in the east (Angkor) to the French.
- Since the beginning of the modern era in 1932 (coup d'état and establishment of constitutional monarchy), there has been tension between military (conservative) and civilian (progressive) power bases. Military governments were the norm until 1973. Brief military regimes were established in 1976–80 and 1991–92, but widespread public opposition sent the military back to barracks in 1992.
- Civilian democracy is now quite well established, following the enactment of the People's Constitution in 1997.
- Thailand was a founder member of Association of Southeast Asian Nations (ASEAN) and, since 1998, has quietly replaced Indonesia as the 'large country driving force' behind regional integration.
- Historical tensions with Burma (Thailand's traditional enemy) have worsened recently due to the Burmese government's acquiescence in large-scale narcotics production and smuggling into Thailand.

Society

- Stable, traditional and deferential. No major internal tensions. Ethnic and income inequalities are much better tolerated than in many other Asian countries. Chinese (11 per cent), Lao (11 per cent) and Muslim (4 per cent) minorities do not face significant discrimination.
- Feudalism and corruption remain major influences. Educational achievement, especially post-primary, is low: 53 per cent global enrolment rate.
- Urbanization is recent – most urban families have strong links to a home village or farming district.
- Urban population: 14 million (22 per cent).
- Average monthly wage: Bt 7,000.*
- Average monthly household income/expenditure: Bt 10,800.
- Average monthly household expenditure on personal care/health: Bt 650.

(Continued)

EXHIBIT 4 *(Continued)*

Government

- Constitutional monarchy since 1932.
- Democratically elected government headed by prime minister.
- Free and vibrant public media.
- Coalition politics and multiplicity of government agencies with overlapping responsibilities makes decisive, rapid implementation of change difficult.
- Strong tradition of protection of local business.

*Bt 41 (baht) = € 1

Source: Company information.

EXHIBIT 5 Market Size in 2000

	Volume (million pieces)	Value (Bt billion)	Growth vs 1999
Skin care	72.4	9	+8 (%)
Make-up	43.6	6.2	–7 (%)
Hair colour	18.7	1.7	0
Hair care	340	9.1	–4 (%)
Fragrance	0.3	0.6	–10 (%)
Total beauty	**475**	**26.6**	**–2** (%)

US $1 = Bt 42 = €1.02

Source: Company information.

8.0

EXHIBIT 6 Cosmetics Distribution in Thailand

Retail Format	Store Count	Weighted Distribution
Premium department stores*	**15**	**6 (%)**
Popular department stores*	**65**	**7 (%)**
Personal care stores*	121	5 (%)
Pharmacies**	2,000	7 (%)
Hypermarkets*	77	17 (%)
Supermarkets*	81	16 (%)
Convenience stores	1,800	2 (%)
Traditional stores	20,000	11 (%)
Stalls	150,000	9 (%)
Premium hair salons*	**2,500**	**2 (%)**
Other hair salons	30,000	3 (%)
Direct sales		15 (%)

*Covered by L'Oréal Thailand sales operations.

** Have full time pharmacists. In addition, there are 3,000 stores with a pharmacist present three hours/day and 7,000 registered 'pharmacies' with no pharmacist present at all. These 10,000 outlets are included in the traditional stores type in our classification.

Source: Company information.

EXHIBIT 7 Customer Hit Parade

Retail Format	Store Count	Weighted Distribution
Central department stores*	12	14 (%)
The mall department stores*	7	**9 (%)**
Watsons personal care stores	54	**9 (%)**
Tops supermarkets	41	**6 (%)**
Boots pharmacy/Personal care stores	61	**6 (%)**
Tesco hypermarkets	27	**4 (%)**
Big C (casino) hypermarkets	23	**4 (%)**
Robinson popular department stores*	18	4 (%)
Carrefour hypermarkets	11	**3 (%)**
Makro hypermarkets	20	**2 (%)**

*Thai ownership. Central and Robinson are associated companies.

Source: Company information.

EXHIBIT 8 Breakdown of Market Product Share of Major Competitors by Segment

% Market Share	Skin Care	Make-Up	Colouration	Hair Care	Fragrance
Unilever	46 (%)	0	10 (%)	41 (%)	10 (%)
P&G	29 (%)	0	0	24 (%)	0
Better way	11 (%)	8 (%)	0	0	0
L'Oréal	**7 (%)**	**17 (%)**	**19 (%)**	**0**	15 (%)
ICC (Pias)	3 (%)	8 (%)	0	0	0
All others	4 (%)	67 (%)	71 (%)	35 (%)	75 (%)

Source: Company information.

EXHIBIT 9 L'Oréal Brand Portfolio and Channel Strategy

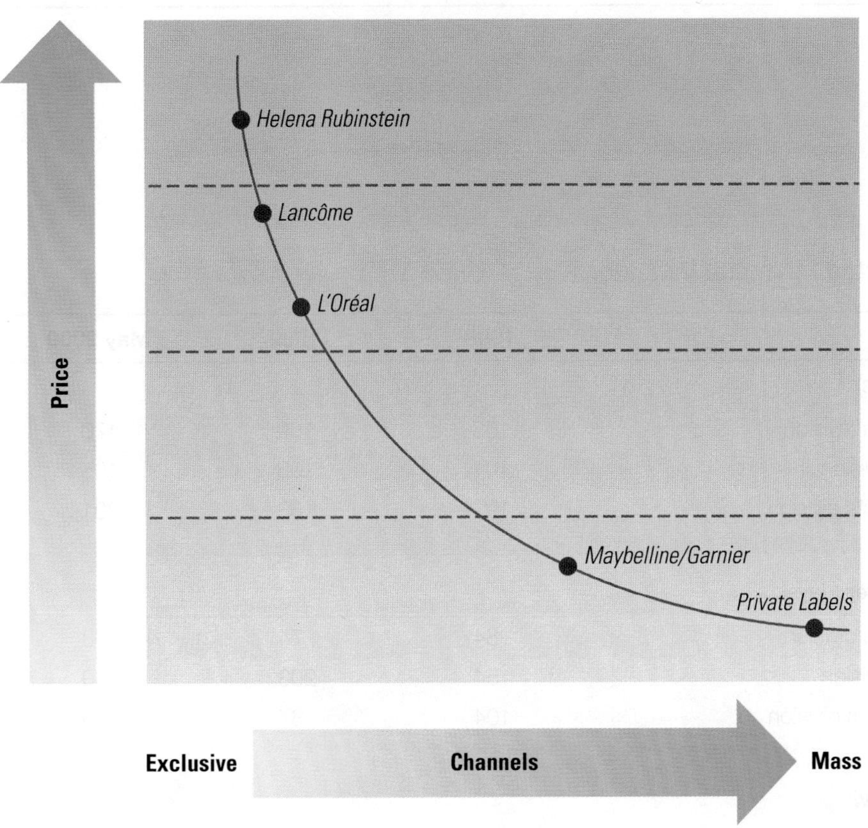

Source: Company information.

8.0

EXHIBIT 10 Working Capital

	Total	Consumer	Luxury	Professional
Stocks				
End March 2000 (in days)	145	165	132	128
End 1999 (in days)	146	160	106	168
Budget end 2000	120	140	90	120
Receivables				
End March 2000 (in days)	104	76	184	69
End 1999 (in days)	113	74	203	87
Budget end 2000	95	72	130	85
Payables				
End March 2000 (in days)	45			
End 1999 (in days)	40			
Budget end 2000	60			

Source: Company information

EXHIBIT 11 Selected Financial Indicators

	1998	1999	May 2000
Inventory cover (days)			
Consumer products division	153	160	170
Luxury products division	101	106	105
Professional products division	197	168	201
Cosmetic active	-	-	-
Customer credit cover (days)			
Consumer products division	84	74	78
Luxury products division	154	203	180
Professional products division	104	87	78
Cosmetic active	-	-	-
Operational cash flow			
(Bt million)	(261)	(103)	(82)
Net equity (Bt million)	(140.6)	(169.5)	(170.2)
Operating profits (Bt million)	(126.5)	(120.9)	(122.1)

Source: Company information.

EXHIBIT 12 Media Investments in 1999

Company	Spending (Bt mn)	Changes vs YAG	Share of Voice, SOV
Lever	2,825	+16 (%)	5 (%)
P&G	935	(–11) (%)	2 (%)
Better way	297	+96 (%)	1 (%)
L'Oréal Thailand	243	+40 (%)	1 (%)

Brand	Spending (Bt mn)	Changes vs YAG	Share of Voice, SOV
Sunsilk	661	+46 (%)	17 (%)
Ponds	347	+13 (%)	9 (%)
Mistine	295	+114 (%)	7 (%)
Clinic	264	+120 (%)	7 (%)
Pantene	202	–38 (%)	5 (%)
L'Oréal Paris	124	+28 (%)	3 (%)

Source: Company information.

EXHIBIT 13 Brand Awareness 2000

	Top of mind	Unaided	Aided
Sunsilk	31	68	100
Ponds	12	30	99
Pantene	7	31	100
Mistine	6	26	100
Avon	5	21	99
L'Oréal	1	6	79
Maybelline		2	63
Lancôme		2	28
Garnier		1	51

Source: Company information.

EXHIBIT 14 Staffing

Permanent Contracts	Total	Consumer	Luxury	Professional	Other
End March 2000	349	63	162	30	94
Resignations Qtr 1	26	5	15	1	5
Recruitment Qtr 1	17	3	10	1	3

Source: Company information.

8.0

INTEGRATIVE CASE 8.0 L'ORÉAL THAILAND (B)

This is the first of a two case series (IMD-5-0612 and IMD-5-0613). Over several years, market share, sales and profitability at L'Oréal Thailand had all been under sustained pressure and targets had been missed again and again. Participants are put in the position of the new managing director and are asked to decide on a whole range of top management issues to restore the company's profitability and its competitive position. A video (IMD-5-0612-V) is available to accompany this case series.

Keywords: Turnaround, marketing, general management, global management, brand management, cross-cultural management, Thailand, Asia

Although we had been appointed to our respective positions only a few months earlier, the key challenges to be solved were very clear to me and the rest of the management team. We had to quickly turn around the business by tackling three issues simultaneously: people, finance and marketing. The first priority was to bring the L'Oréal and Lancôme brands into profitability to restart a virtuous spiral for the Thai organization. Once profitable, these brands, which account for 68 per cent of our turnover, would generate the cash needed for future investment in the business and to recreate a winning team spirit.

Chris Martin, Managing Director
L'Oréal Thailand

The People Issue

In the absence of a human resources manager, Martin decided to act as HR director. He mobilized his entire Management Committee to greatly speed up the assessment of the talent in the organization as well as the recruitment process. Within three months, two work groups had been created in HR—one to specialize in hiring and systems, the other in training and retention. Another step was to begin career development via interdivisional transfers, to widen the opportunities available and break down the 'tribal fiefdoms' that had been a feature of the previous organization. 'As a symbolic measure, we also banned our people from using the names Siampar and Thailor!' Martin added.

By 1 July 2000, a new entity – L'Oréal Thailand Ltd – had been officially inaugurated. At the end of the year, Martin took advantage of the dramatic fall in rent triggered by the Asian crisis to relocate the offices to a brand-new, prestigious (but much cheaper) building.

'We had to decide who was going to make it into the new organization and who would not,' Martin explained.

We quickly identified the key people who were essential to keep the business running, such as the manager in charge of government relations, the head of information technology, the manager of the warehouse, etc. In a single shot and in the nicest possible way, we sought the resignations of all those of whom we had no hope or who did not fit with the L'Oréal culture. We decided to do our utmost to keep all the others, even if we had some doubts about their ability to grow with the business. Then we focused on a group of about six local people who we as a team felt could one day become the leaders of the company. We decided we would not accept the loss of a single one of these high potentials.

This was not an easy task at all, because of the message we had sent internally and externally by asking some people to leave. Thailand is an extremely close-knit society and we already had a poor reputation in the job market. The people we decided

Professor Dominique Turpin prepared this case as a basis for class discussion rather than to illustrate either effective or ineffective handling of a business situation. All names and data have been disguised.

to keep quickly became overburdened as they had to take over the work of the ones who had left. Unfortunately, several people we very much wanted to retain in important jobs (such as the warehouse manager) decided to quit. But we kept every one of the high potentials, despite some very tough moments when we needed all our persuasiveness and creativity to motivate people to reject good offers from outside.

Martin continued:

We also had to revisit the reward system. Pablo and I called it the 'Cultural Revolution', an ironic reference to my experience in China in the early nineties when the country was transitioning from Communism to capitalism and needed to balance two systems. We had – on average – a 30 per cent difference in salaries between the Siampar and Thailor people. All the Thailor top managers had a company car, a standard practice at our international competitors such as Unilever and P&G but a benefit that the former local partner in Siampar had adamantly rejected each time it was proposed by L'Oréal. However, we could not immediately give a company car to every executive, nor could we raise salaries by 30 per cent right away. Firstly, we did not have the money. Secondly, it is a well-known HR management principle that, in this kind of situation, it is better to spread the wage increase over time than to do it overnight in one single shot. We didn't want to give our people the sense that they had been 'exploited' for years. We explained to the people we wanted to retain that they were our best people and that their hard work and dedication would be well rewarded. A bonus system linked to retention was also put in place to motivate the best talents to stay with us.

In the meantime, Pablo Gomez, the Deputy Managing Director in charge of Finance and Operations, worked with Martin, Roberto Shimizu and Alessandra Badini (heads of the Consumer and Professional divisions, respectively) to restore cash flow and profitability. Gomez commented:

It was very soon apparent to me that while our customers paid us only when they felt like it, we were paying our own bills remarkably quickly! Just matching our payments to our suppliers with the length of time it took to get the money from our customers produced a quick and significant improvement in cash flow. That was an easy, quick 'win'. However, the L'Oréal Paris and Lancôme brands together represented the bulk of our business in Thailand and were the clear priorities of the turnaround.

Turning the Consumer Division Around

Shimizu recalled:

The key issue was to deal with the very large quantities of stock dating from 1996 to 1998 that was obsolete or had expired. We needed to fix it in an orderly and cost-effective way by rethinking our logistics, our inventory management, our sales forecasts and working very closely with retailers. Consequently my priorities became: understanding the market, getting the right products, communicating more effectively with consumers and getting the right resources to implement the strategy.

Understanding the Market

Shimizu continued:

Three department stores, two major drug stores and five key food chains were contributing 70 per cent of my turnover. By listening carefully to our retailers, we were able to design tailor-made strategies for each one of them.

For example, drug stores needed to create an environment where consumers would find both very rational and highly emotional benefits from beauty products. These large drug stores are generally located close to the foodstore chains, for which price is key. Therefore, these drug stores had to compete with foodstore chains through unique product or merchandizing innovations. For example, Carrefour's major competitor was clearly Tesco. Consequently, we decided to help Carrefour revamp its beauty space and since Carrefour is a fast implementer, we could help it get an edge over its main competitor. Tesco's main concern was category management. Since L'Oréal is the leader of the skin care and colouring categories, we could help them better understand the emotional value of beauty products. Our competitors – P&G and Unilever – were better at helping them sell commodity products, such as soaps and shampoos.

In every retail segment, the business has become so competitive that each player is forced to get business from its closest competitor. In this market, you have strong winners and strong losers. Since the Thai retailing industry was in total flux, we also had to get our priorities right: more professionalism in dealing with retailers, clearer ideas in terms of product positioning and a better understanding of the market to launch the right products with the support of the right communications strategy.

Getting the Right Products

Consumer research was telling us that we lacked the right products and that our communications were unconvincing. For example, in skin care we did not have good whitening products – they make up 50 per cent of this category. Consumer insights also confirmed that there was too much overlap between the different positioning of our brands. As a result, we immediately clarified the positionings of L'Oréal Paris, Maybelline and Garnier by redefining our pricing strategy.

We also dramatically increased the number of stock keeping units (SKUs) in the hair colour category. While Sunsilk (Unilever), our major competitor in this segment had only seven SKUs, we increased our SKUs from fifteen to twenty within nine months. The results were immediate. Almost overnight, our shelf space at Watsons (one of the major drug store chains in Bangkok) went up from 50 per cent to 90 per cent. The reason for this success was simple. Consumers in this category are looking for the exact match between the colour they have in mind and the offer presented on the shelves. While Sunsilk decided to respond by attacking us on price, we decided to respond by matching their offer but never undercutting them. We also clarified the positioning of our two main brands by targeting Natea at 15 to 35-year-olds and Excellence at consumers over 35.

Communicating More Effectively with Consumers

Shimizu acknowledged:

We also found that we did not have a convincing local ambassador. Our image was inconsistent. The local stars we had been using in our commercials were perceived as boring and lacking in self-confidence in comparison with our international ambassadors, such as Claudia Schiffer, who in turn were seen as glamorous and talented but totally removed from the realities of Thailand. I know from experience that when we are consistent, consumers tend to reward us, but when we are inconsistent, they punish us! Accordingly, we thought of recruiting a well-known local star who enjoyed widespread respect and credibility for achievements on an international level but who could also demonstrate a commitment to Thailand.

Another challenge was our media mix and the financial resources necessary to support our new communications campaign. Back in 1999, our communications budget was spent mainly on promotions (primarily consumer give-aways) and very little on print media. At the beginning of 2000, the competition was still spending almost ten times more than we were. We decided to rethink our media mix and to emphasize print media, invest more in the point-of-sale and reduce consumer promotions. TV was just too costly but we were under-investing in magazines. The print media was very appropriate to explain our technical innovations. We could not get leadership in terms of share of voice on television, but we could get it with print, and we did!

The decision to put more emphasis on point-of-sale meant spending more on shelf space and merchandizing. We knew that many Thai consumers made their final purchasing decision at the point-of-sale, especially when we had great product innovations. With a new media mix privileging print more than TV, we were also achieving a balance in line with the global L'Oréal communications strategy.

Getting the Right Resources

Shimizu continued:

Of course, the key issue was the money! With the support of Chris and Pablo, I decided to present our new marketing strategy to Paris and ask for a final subsidy grant from headquarters. After some tough negotiations with headquarters, the CEO and Chairman, Lindsay Owen-Jones, approved a last and final transfer of BT 50 million.[1] *Owen-Jones also made it very clear to us that this would be the last gift from Paris and that the money would have to be spent exclusively on communications and communications only!*

We were also fortunate in being able to recruit a great local ambassador by the name of Areeya Sirisopa, but known to everyone as 'Pop'. The Thais are very proud people, so using a person from another Asian country would not have been as convincing. Moreover, before 1999 L'Oréal products were perceived as foreign while P&G's and Unilever's were perceived as local. To compensate for this weakness, I rebalanced my communications budget 50:50 using famous international and local beauty ambassadors. In our communications we also used the argument that Thai women are highly sophisticated and do understand beauty. This was of course a very well-received argument!

[1] Bt 25 = US$ 1; Bt 28 = €1.

Implementation

The implementation would not have succeeded without the active involvement of both our people and the retailers. We selected the best elements of our previous sales and marketing teams and recruited additional talents. We went to explain our strategy to every one of our retailers, stressing the extra value that our tailor-made services would bring them. In other words, we tried to make them part of our winning strategy.

One of our key strengths against big competitors has also been the flexibility of our organization. Because we are much smaller and focused exclusively on beauty products, we used speed and our image as specialist as key competitive advantages. We were able to move fast in the market with good innovations, adjust our plans and react quickly if necessary.

In summary, I would say that the turnaround of the Consumer Division was achieved by three simple principles: listening to the market, bringing the right products and communicating effectively with our target consumers.

Turning the Luxury Division Around

Most of the turnaround strategy that had been devised for the Consumer Division also applied to the Luxury Division, headed by Badini. In early 2000 this division represented 20 per cent of turnover.

Badini explained:

My first objective was to get rid of the semi-consignment system. We reduced the stock coverage at the counters from 5.2 months in December 1999 to a more acceptable 2.5 months a year later, and moved our account receivables from 203 to 130 days during the same period of time. As a result, operational cash flow significantly improved.

However, these efforts took their toll on the operating results. Sales dropped 40 per cent during the first quarter of 2000, followed by another 13 per cent during the second quarter, before increasing to +33 per cent and 23 per cent in the last two quarters of the year 2000.

Since sales of the Luxury Division were concentrated on just two major outlets, it made sense to focus our investments on those two locations first. Working closely with both customers, we brought to Bangkok some designers from Paris and London to help develop the best beauty counters in the country. Our merchandizing is now in line with the top department stores of New York, London, Paris and Tokyo, and the results are there too. Six months after renovation, sales were up 55 per cent in the biggest store and 69 per cent in the second. Coupled with the introduction of product innovations, Lancôme reported a growth rate double that of competitors Estée Lauder and Shiseido. Similar results were also achieved with our Biotherm and Helena Rubinstein product lines! We completely restructured our fragrance brands to better align them with the limited market size by withdrawing Paloma Picasso and Lanvin and concentrating resources on Ralph Lauren and Armani. Ralph Lauren grew by eight per cent within a year and remained the most popular fragrance in Thailand.

Professional Products Division

Although the Professional Products Division had not experienced the same disappointing results as the other two divisions in 1999, it nevertheless clearly benefited from the revival of the company. Martin was succeeding in breaking the old 'tribe' mentality between the three divisions. In particular, he had strongly encouraged the sharing of best practices by running regular meetings between the three teams. Exciting, innovative products had helped increase the division results by an additional 17 per cent. However, Martin believed that most of the difference was due to the strong teams that had been put in place.

The Results

Nine months after the start of their 'Cultural Revolution', Martin and his team were proud of the results achieved (refer to Exhibits 1 to 3). At the end of 2000 L'Oréal Thailand had grown by 21 per cent in units and 19 per cent in value. Despite generally flat consumer markets, the new entity had grown shares of all its strategic brands. After ten years of losses Thailand would generate positive cash flows and profits for 2001. The strong results achieved by L'Oréal and Lancôme, the main engines of the company, supplied the cash necessary for all new investments in L'Oréal Thailand, which transformed the negative spiral of the 1990s into a positive spiral for the new millennium. There was also a huge change in organizational capability and morale. By the end of 2000 L'Oréal Thailand had recruited more people than would have been necessary merely to replace those who had resigned, and had rebuilt the teams, greatly reducing

8.0

the stress caused by under-manning due to the previously high staff turnover. The L'Oréal name was becoming an asset in attracting new talents, since the brand was better known than the old Siampar and Thailor names. Since September 2000 resignations had averaged four per cent, even after the period of year-end bonus eligibility had passed. Martin concluded:

> *This was an encouraging sign that the reorganization conducted during the spring and summer of 2000 had been effective and had not undermined the spirit of those who were identified as being strong contributors. Even more encouragingly, the quality of new hires began to improve dramatically. We are starting to have real stars in the company, who are ready to develop their careers via inter-divisional transfers and overseas assignments.*
>
> *We were able to launch the fourth division (Active Cosmetics) by mid-2001, with a 'home-grown' Thai person transferred from the Professional Products Division as its General Manager. The L'Oréal Group has made several international acquisitions in the last few years and we were able to assimilate their local Thai operations smoothly into L'Oréal Thailand and start to grow them quickly and aggressively. The brands can be separated into two groups: the 'small and beautiful' strong niche players with high margins that effectively fund additional investments in 'the big and the bold', such as Garnier, which we are expanding rapidly as main engines of growth by adding new categories such as skin care.*
>
> *Thailand is now clearly established as L'Oréal's most important and strategic market in Southeast Asia. I have moved on to a new assignment now, but I still carefully follow their results. The day when a Thai national is named Managing Director will be a moment of great emotion and pride for all of us who made up the 2000 turnaround team.*

Please address all correspondence to Dominique Turpin, IMD – International Institute for Management Development, PO Box 915, CH 1001 Lausanne, Switzerland. E-mail Address: dominique. turpin@imd.ch

EXHIBIT 1 Indicators

	1998	1999	2000	2001
Inventory cover (days)				
Consumer products division	153	160	173	99
Luxury products division	101	106	108	139
Professional products division	197	168	196	125
Cosmetic active	–	–	–	100
Customer credit cover (days)				
Consumer products division	84	74	77	76
Luxury products division	154	203	134	69
Professional products division	104	87	76	68
Cosmetic active	–	–	–	47
Operational cash flow (Bt million)	(261)	(103)	(62)	32
Net equity (Bt million)	(140.6)	(169.5)	(163.8)	(21.7)
Operating profits (Bt million)	(126.5)	(120.9)	(94.4)	59.9

Source: Company information.

EXHIBIT 2 Financial Results (Bt million)

	1997	1998	1999	2000	2001
Net turnover	900	1,081	1,085	1,283	1,630
Other customer allowances	15	23	35	43	46
Cost of goods/royalties	300	397	385	469	538
Product contribution	585	662	663	772	1,045
Advertising, promotion, production	343	385	391	445	527
General marketing expenses	31	23	43	30	29
Marketing contribution	211	255	229	297	489
Operating expenses	235	281	293	333	387
Variances/OIE*/Financing	(12)	(12)	15	28	53
Reserve	–	–	–	–	31
Operating result	(12)	(14)	(78)	(64)	18
Operational cash flow	(376)	(261)	(103)	(62)	32

	Value End 2001	Change vs 31/12/00	Days End 2001	Change vs 31/12/00
Inventories				
Consumer	122	–23	99	–74
Luxury	38	–1	139	+31
Professional	26	–3	125	–71
Total entity	**186**	**–27**	**118**	**–38**
Receivables				
Consumer	179	–15	76	–1
Luxury	159	–20	69	–65
Professional	46	–2	68	–8
Total entity	**384**	**–37**	**73**	**–16**

*OIE = Other income and expenses

Source: Company information.

EXHIBIT 3 Brand Presence

Brands	%Evolution*	Outlets	Launch	% of Entity
L'Oréal	+30 (%)	1,048	1992	39 (%)
Lancôme	+32 (%)	31	1950s	17 (%)
L'Oréal Professional	+30 (%)	1,750	1992	12 (%)
Maybelline	+12 (%)	741	1995	11 (%)
Garnier	+20 (%)	1,234	1999	8 (%)
Biotherm	+23 (%)	12	1997	3 (%)
Kerastase	+50 (%)	90	1995	3 (%)
PCI	–14 (%)	20	1960s	3 (%)
Helena Rubinstein	+27 (%)	6	1999	2 (%)
Shu Uemera	N.A.	3	2001	1 (%)
La Roche Posay	N.A.	N.A.	2001	1 (%)

*%evolution 2001 vs 2000.

Source: Company information.

COUNTERPOINTS – RECOMMENDED SUPPLEMENTARY READING

The following books are recommended for exploring the alternative perspectives in the Counterpoints that appear in *Organization Theory and Design* and its accompanying web-based materials. Common to these texts is their location within a broad, alternative approach to the study of management and organization known as critical management studies (CMS) which forms one of the divisions within the Academy of Management (see http://www.aomonline.org/aom.asp?id=18).

Textbooks range from introductory (little previous specialist knowledge required) to advanced (substantial specialist knowledge required). Edited collections contain previously published material including journal articles and extracts from books that can be variable in their level of difficulty. Handbooks provide state-of-the art reviews and tend to be comparatively advanced. In addition to these sources, articles published in good (tightly refereed) academic journals are a relevant resource for advanced students. The recommended texts generally have indexes which can be searched for key words. Google Scholar (www.scholar.google.com/) is a useful tool for searching for relevant articles and books; the number of citations received by a book or an article can provide an indication of a text's influence and scholarly standing.

Textbooks

Introductory

Knights, D. and Willmott, H.C. (2006), *Introducing Organizational Behaviour and Management*, London: Cengage Learning
Wilson, F. M. (2003), *Organizational Behaviour and Gender*, Gower: Ashgate

Intermediate

Barry, J. , Chandler, J. and Clark, H. (2009), *Organizational Behaviour: A Critical Text*, London: Cengage Learning
Clegg, S.R, Pitsis, T. and Kornberger, M. (2008), 2nd ed., *Managing and Organizations: An Introduction to Theory and Practice*, London: Sage
Fulop. L., Linstead, S. and Lilley, S. (2004), *Management and Organization: A Critical Text*, London: Macmillan Palgrave
Grey, C. (2008), 2nd ed., *A Very Short Fairly Interesting and Reasonably Cheap Book About Studying Organizations*, London: Sage
Hatch, M-J. with Cunliffe, A. (2006), 3rd ed., *Organization Theory: Modern, Symbolic, and Postmodern Perspectives*, Oxford University Press
Thompson, P. and McHugh, D. (2009), 4th ed., *Work Organizations: A Critical Approach*, London: Palgrave Macmillan

Advanced

Alvesson, M. and Willmott, H.C. (1996), *Making Sense of Management*, London: Sage
Jackson, N. and Carter, P. (2004), 2nd ed., *Rethinking Organizational Behaviour: A Poststructuralist Framework*, London: Prentice-Hall
McAuley, J., Duberley, J. and Johnson, P. (2007), *Organization Theory: Challenges and Perspectives*, London: FT Prentice-Hall

Edited collections

Alvesson, M. and Willmott, H.C. (2003), *Studying Management Critically*, London: Sage
Clark, H., Chandler, J. and Barry, J. (1994), *Organizations and Identities: Text and Readings in Organizational Behaviour*, London: Cengage Learning
Knights, D. and Willmott, H.C. (2010), *Organizational Analysis*, London: Cengage Learning

Handbooks

Barry, D. and Hansen, H. (2008), *The Sage Handbook of New Approaches in Management and Organization*, London: Sage
Clegg, S., Hardy, C., Lawrence, T. and Nord, W.R. (2006), *The Sage Handbook of Organization Studies*, London: Sage

GLOSSARY

A

adaptability culture a culture characterized by strategic focus on the external environment through flexibility and change to meet customer needs.

administrative principles a closed systems management perspective that focuses on the total organization and grows from the insights of practitioners.

ambidextrous approach a characteristic of an organization that can behave in both an organic and a mechanistic way.

analyzability a dimension of technology in which work activities can be reduced to mechanical steps and participants can follow an objective, computational procedure to solve problems.

analyzer a business strategy that seeks to maintain a stable business while innovating on the periphery.

authority a force for achieving desired outcomes that is prescribed by the formal hierarchy and reporting relationships.

B

balanced scorecard a comprehensive management control system that balances traditional financial measures with operational measures relating to an organization's critical success factors.

benchmarking process whereby companies find out how others do something better than they do and then try to imitate or improve on it.

boundary spanning roles activities that link and coordinate an organization with key elements in the external environment.

bounded rationality perspective how decisions are made when time is limited, a large number of internal and external factors affect a decision and the problem is ill-defined.

buffering roles activities that absorb uncertainty from the environment.

bureaucracy an organizational framework marked by rules and procedures, specialization and division of labour, hierarchy of authority, technically qualified personnel, separate position and incumbent and written communications and records.

bureaucratic control the use of rules, policies, hierarchy of authority, written documentation, standardization and other bureaucratic mechanisms to standardize behaviour and assess performance.

bureaucratic culture a culture that has an internal focus and a consistency orientation for a stable environment.

bureaucratic organization a perspective that emphasizes management on an impersonal, rational basis through such elements as clearly defined authority and responsibility, formal recordkeeping and uniform application of standard rules.

business intelligence high-tech analysis of large amounts of internal and external data to identify patterns and relationships.

C

Carnegie model organizational decision making involving many managers and a final choice based on a coalition among those managers.

centrality a trait of a department whose role is in the primary activity of an organization.

centralization refers to the level of hierarchy with authority to make decisions.

centralized decision making is limited to higher authority.

change process the way in which changes occur in an organization.

chaos theory a scientific theory that suggests that relationships in complex, adaptive systems are made up of numerous interconnections that create unintended effects and render the environment unpredictable.

charismatic authority based in devotion to the exemplary character or heroism of an individual and the order defined by him or her.

chief ethics officer high-level company executive who oversees all aspects of ethics, including establishing and broadly communicating ethical standards, setting up ethics training programmes, supervising the investigation of ethical problems and advising managers in the ethical aspects of corporate decisions.

clan control the use of social characteristics, such as corporate culture, shared values, commitments, traditions and beliefs, to control behaviour.

clan culture a culture that focuses primarily on the involvement and participation of the organization's members and on rapidly changing expectations from the external environment.

closed system a system that is autonomous, enclosed and not dependent on its environment.

coalition an alliance among several managers who agree through bargaining about organizational goals and problem priorities.

code of ethics a formal statement of the company's values concerning ethics and social responsibility.

coercive forces external pressures such as legal requirements exerted on an organization to adopt structures, techniques or behaviours similar to other organizations.

collaborative network an emerging perspective whereby organizations allow themselves to become dependent on other organizations to increase value and productivity for all.

collective bargaining the negotiation of an agreement between management and workers.

collectivity stage the life cycle phase in which an organization has strong leadership and begins to develop clear goals and direction.

competing values approach a perspective on organizational effectiveness that combines diverse indicators of performance that represent competing management values.

competition rivalry between groups in the pursuit of a common prize.

confrontation a situation in which parties in conflict directly engage one another and try to work out their differences.

consortia groups of firms that venture into new products and technologies.

contextual dimensions traits that characterize the whole organization, including its size, technology, environment and goals.

contingency a theory meaning one thing depends on other things; the organization's situation dictates the correct management approach.

contingency decision-making framework a perspective that brings together the two organizational dimensions of problem consensus and technical knowledge about solutions.

continuous process production a completely mechanized manufacturing process in which there is no starting or stopping.

cooptation occurs when leaders from important sectors in the environment are made part of an organization.

coping with uncertainty a source of power for a department that reduces uncertainty for other departments by obtaining prior information, prevention and absorption.

core technology the work process that is directly related to the organization's mission.

craft technology technology characterized by a fairly stable stream of activities but in which the conversion process is not analyzable or well understood.

creative departments organizational departments that initiate change, such as research and development, engineering, design and systems analysis.

creativity the generation of novel ideas that may meet perceived needs or respond to opportunities.

culture the set of values, guiding beliefs, understandings and ways of thinking that are shared by members of an organization and are taught to new members as correct.

culture changes changes in the values, attitudes, expectations, beliefs, abilities and behaviour of employees.

culture strength the degree of agreement among members of an organization about the importance of specific values.

customer relationship management systems that help companies track customer interactions with the firm and allow employees to call up a customer's past sales and service records, outstanding orders or unresolved problems.

D

data the input of a communication channel.

data mining software that uses sophisticated decision-making processes to search raw data for patterns and relationships that may be significant.

data warehousing the use of a huge database that combines all of an organization's data and allows users to access the data directly, create reports and obtain answers to 'what-if' questions.

decentralized decision making and communication are spread out across the company.

decision learning a process of recognizing and admitting mistakes that allows managers and organizations to acquire the experience and knowledge to perform more effectively in the future.

decision premises constraining frames of reference and guidelines placed by top managers on decisions made at lower levels.

decision support system a system that enables managers at all levels of the organization to retrieve, manipulate and display information from integrated databases for making specific decisions.

defender a business strategy that seeks stability or even retrenchment rather than innovation or growth.

departmental grouping a structure in which employees share a common supervisor and resources, are jointly responsible for performance and tend to identify and collaborate with each other.

dependency one aspect of horizontal power: when one department is dependent on another, the latter is in a position of greater power.

differentiation the cognitive and emotional differences among managers in various functional departments of an organization and formal structure differences among these departments.

direct interlock a situation that occurs when a member of the board of directors of one company sits on the board of another.

divisional grouping a grouping in which people are organized according to what the organization produces.

divisional structure the structuring of the organization according to individual products, services, product groups, major projects or profit centres; also called *product structure* or *strategic business units.*

domain an organization's chosen environmental field of activity.

domains of political activity areas in which politics plays a role. Three domains in organizations are structural change, management succession and resource allocation.

domestic stage the first stage of international development in which a company is domestically oriented while managers are aware of the global environment.

downsizing intentionally reducing the size of a company's workforce by laying off employees.

dual-core approach an organizational change perspective that identifies the unique processes associated with administrative change compared to those associated with technical change.

E

e-business any business that takes place by digital processes over a computer network rather than in physical space.

economies of scale achieving lower costs through large volume production; often made possible by global expansion.

economies of scope achieving economies by having a presence in many product lines, technologies or geographic areas.

effectiveness the degree to which an organization achieves its goals.

efficiency the amount of resources used to produce a unit of output.

elaboration stage the organizational life cycle phase in which the red tape crisis is resolved through the development of a new sense of teamwork and collaboration.

electronic data interchange (EDI) the linking of organizations through computers for the transmission of data without human interference.

empowerment the delegation of power or authority to subordinates; also called *power sharing*.

engineering technology technology in which there is substantial variety in the tasks performed, but activities are usually handled on the basis of established formulas, procedures and techniques.

enterprise resource planning (ERP) sophisticated computerized systems that collect, process and provide information about a company's entire enterprise, including order processing, product design, purchasing, inventory, manufacturing, distribution, human resources, receipt of payments and forecasting of future demand.

entrepreneurial stage the life cycle phase in which an organization is born and its emphasis is on creating a product and surviving in the marketplace.

escalating commitment persisting in a course of action when it is failing; occurs because managers block or distort negative information and because consistency and persistence are valued in contemporary society.

ethical dilemma when each alternative choice or behaviour seems undesirable because of a potentially negative ethical consequence.

ethics the code of moral principles and values that governs the behaviour of a person or group with respect to what is right or wrong.

ethics committee a group of executives appointed to oversee company ethics.

ethics hotline a telephone number that employees can call to seek guidance and to report questionable behaviour.

executive information system (EIS) interactive systems that help top managers monitor and control organizational operations by processing and presenting data in usable form.

explicit knowledge formal, systematic knowledge that can be codified, written down and passed on to others in documents or general instructions.

external adaptation the manner in which an organization meets goals and deals with outsiders.

extranet private information network.

F

factors of production supplies necessary for production, such as land, raw materials and labour.

feedback control model a control cycle that involves setting goals, establishing standards of performance, measuring actual performance and comparing it to standards and changing activities as needed based on the feedback.

financial resources control over money is an important source of power within an organization.

flexible manufacturing systems (FMS) using computers to link together manufacturing components such as robots, machines, product design and engineering analysis to enable fast switching from one product to another.

focus an organization's dominant perspective value, which may be internal or external.

focus strategy a strategy in which an organization concentrates on a specific regional market or buyer group.

formalization the degree to which an organization has rules, procedures and written documentation.

formalization stage the phase in an organization's life cycle involving the installation and use of rules, procedures and control systems.

functional grouping the placing together of employees who perform similar functions or work processes or who bring similar knowledge and skills to bear.

functional matrix a structure in which functional bosses have primary authority and product or project managers simply coordinate product activities.

functional structure the grouping of activities by common function.

G

garbage can model model that describes the pattern or flow of multiple decisions within an organization.

general environment includes those sectors that may not directly affect the daily operations of a firm but will indirectly influence it.

generalist an organization that offers a broad range of products or services and serves a broad market.

global company a company that no longer thinks of itself as having a home country.

global geographical structure a form in which an organization divides its operations into world regions, each of which reports to the CEO.

global matrix structure a form of horizontal linkage in an international organization in which both product and geographical structures are implemented simultaneously to achieve a balance between standardization and globalization.

global product structure a form in which product divisions take responsibility for global operations in their specific product areas.

global stage the stage of international development in which the company transcends any one country.

global teams work groups made up of multinational members whose activities span multiple countries; also called *transnational teams*.

globalization strategy the standardization of product design and advertising strategy throughout the world.

goal approach an approach to organizational effectiveness that is concerned with output and whether the organization achieves its output goals.

H

Hawthorne Studies a series of experiments on worker productivity begun in 1924 at the Hawthorne plant of Western Electric Company in Illinois; attributed employees' increased output to managers' better treatment of them during the study.

heroes organizational members who serve as models or ideals for serving cultural norms and values.

high-velocity environments industries in which competitive and technological change is so extreme that market data is either unavailable or obsolete, strategic windows open and shut quickly and the cost of a decision error is company failure.

horizontal coordination model a model of the three components of organizational design needed to achieve new product innovation: departmental specialization, boundary spanning and horizontal linkages.

horizontal grouping the organizing of employees around core work processes rather than by function, product or geography.

horizontal linkage the amount of communication and coordination that occurs horizontally across organizational departments.

horizontal structure a structure that virtually eliminates both the vertical hierarchy and departmental boundaries by organizing teams of employees around core work processes; the end-to-end work, information and material flows that provide value directly to customers.

human relations model emphasis on an aspect of the competing values model that incorporates the values of an internal focus and a flexible structure.

hybrid structure a structure that combines characteristics of various structural approaches (functional, divisional, geographical, horizontal) tailored to specific strategic needs.

I

idea champions organizational members who provide the time and energy to make things happen; sometimes called *advocates, intrapreneurs* and *change agents.*

idea incubator safe harbour where ideas from employees throughout the organization can be developed without interference from company bureaucracy or politics.

imitation the adoption of a decision tried elsewhere in the hope that it will work in the present situation.

incident command system developed to maintain the efficiency and control benefits of bureaucracy yet prevent the problems of slow response to crises.

incremental change a series of continual progressions that maintain an organization's general equilibrium and often affect only one organizational part.

incremental decision process model a model that describes the structured sequence of activities undertaken from the discovery of a problem to its solution.

indirect interlock a situation that occurs when a director of one company and a director of another are both directors of a third company.

information that which alters or reinforces understanding.

information reporting systems the most common form of management information system, these computerized systems provide managers with reports that summarize data and support day-to-day decision making.

inspiration an innovative, creative solution that is not reached by logical means.

institutional environment norms and values from stakeholders (customers, investors, boards, government, etc.) that organizations try to follow in order to please stakeholders.

institutional perspective an emerging view that holds that under high uncertainty, organizations imitate others in the same institutional environment.

institutional similarity the emergence of common structures, management approaches and behaviours among organizations in the same field.

integrated enterprise an organization that uses advanced information technology to enable close coordination within the company as well as with suppliers, customers and partners.

integration the quality of collaboration between departments of an organization.

integrator a position or department created solely to coordinate several departments.

intellectual capital the sum of an organization's knowledge, experience, understanding, processes, innovations and discoveries.

intensive technologies a variety of products or services provided in combination to a client.

interdependence the extent to which departments depend on each other for resources or materials to accomplish their tasks.

intergroup conflict behaviour that occurs between organizational groups when participants identify with one group and perceive that other groups may block their group's goal achievements or expectations.

interlocking directorate a formal linkage that occurs when a member of the board of directors of one company sits on the board of another company.

internal integration a state in which organization members develop a collective identity and know how to work together effectively.

internal process approach an approach that looks at internal activities and assesses effectiveness by indicators of internal health and efficiency.

internal process emphasis an aspect of the competing values model that reflects the values of internal focus and structural control.

international division a division that is equal in status to other major departments within a company and has its own hierarchy to handle business in various countries.

international stage the second stage of international development, in which the company takes exports seriously and begins to think multidomestically.

interorganizational relationships the relatively enduring resource transactions, flows and linkages that occur among two or more organizations.

intranet a private, company-wide information network that uses the communications protocols and standards of the

Internet but is accessible only to people within the company.

intuitive decision making the use of experience and judgement rather than sequential logic or explicit reasoning to solve a problem.

J

job design the assignment of goals and tasks to be accomplished by employees.

job enlargement the designing of jobs to expand the number of different tasks performed by an employee.

job enrichment the designing of jobs to increase responsibility, recognition and opportunities for growth and achievement.

job rotation moving employees from job to job to give them a greater variety of tasks and alleviate boredom.

job simplification the reduction of the number and difficulty of tasks performed by a single person.

joint optimization the goal of the sociotechnical systems approach, which states that an organization will function best only if its social and technical systems are designed to fit the needs of one another.

joint venture a separate entity for sharing development and production costs and penetrating new markets that is created with two or more active firms as sponsors.

K

knowledge a conclusion drawn from information that has been linked to other information and compared to what is already known.

knowledge management the efforts to systematically find, organize and make available a company's intellectual capital and to foster a culture of continuous learning and knowledge sharing so that organizational activities build on existing knowledge.

L

labour–management teams a cooperative approach designed to increase worker participation and provide a cooperative model for union-management problems.

language slogans, sayings, metaphors or other expressions that convey a special meaning to employees.

large-batch production a manufacturing process characterized by long production runs of standardized parts.

large group intervention an approach that brings together participants from all parts of the organization (and may include outside stakeholders as well) to discuss problems or opportunities and plan for change.

lean manufacturing uses highly trained employees at every stage of the production process who take a painstaking approach to details and continuous problem solving to cut waste and improve quality.

learning organization an organization in which everyone is engaged in identifying and solving problems, enabling the organization to continuously experiment, improve and increase its capability.

legends stories of events based in history that may have been embellished with fictional details.

legitimacy the general perspective that an organization's actions are desirable, proper and appropriate within the environment's system of norms, values and beliefs.

level of analysis in systems theory, the subsystem on which the primary focus is placed; four levels of analysis normally characterize organizations.

liaison role the function of a person located in one department who is responsible for communicating and achieving coordination with another department.

life cycle a perspective on organizational growth and change that suggests that organizations are born, grow older and eventually die.

long-linked technology the combination within one organization of successive stages of production, with each stage using as its inputs the production of the preceding stage.

low-cost leadership a strategy that tries to increase market share by emphasizing low cost when compared with competitors' products.

M

management champion a manager who acts as a supporter and sponsor of a technical champion to shield and promote an idea within the organization.

management control systems the formalized routines, reports and procedures that use information to maintain or alter patterns in organizational activity.

management information system a comprehensive, computerized system that provides information and supports day-to-day decision making.

management science approach organizational decision making that is the analog to the rational approach by individual managers.

managerial ethics principles that guide the decisions and behaviours of managers with regard to whether they are morally right or wrong.

market control a situation that occurs when price competition is used to evaluate the output and productivity of an organization.

mass customization the use of computer-integrated systems and flexible work processes to enable companies to mass produce a variety of products or services designed to exact customer specification.

matrix structure a strong form of horizontal linkage in which both product and functional structures (horizontal and vertical) are implemented simultaneously.

mechanistic an organization system marked by rules, procedures, a clear hierarchy of authority and centralized decision making.

mediating technology the provision of products or services that mediate or link clients from the external environment and allow each department to work independently.

meso theory a new approach to organization studies that integrates both micro and macro levels of analysis.

mimetic forces under conditions of uncertainty, the pressure to copy or model other organizations that appear to be successful in the environment.

mission the organization's reason for its existence.

mission culture a culture that places emphasis on a clear vision of the organization's purpose and on the achievement of specific goals.

multidomestic company a company that deals with competitive issues in each country independent of other countries.

multidomestic strategy one in which competition in each country is handled independently of competition in other countries.

multifocused grouping a structure in which an organization embraces structural grouping alternatives simultaneously.

multinational stage the stage of international development in which a company has marketing and production facilities in many countries and more than one-third of its sales outside its home country.

myths stories that are consistent with the values and beliefs of the organization but are not supported by facts.

N

negotiation the bargaining process that often occurs during confrontation and enables the parties to systematically reach a solution.

network centrality top managers increase their power by locating themselves centrally in an organization and surrounding themselves with loyal subordinates.

networking linking computers within or between organizations.

new-venture fund a fund that provides financial resources to employees to develop new ideas, products or businesses.

niche a domain of unique environmental resources and needs.

non-core technology a department work process that is important to the organization but is not directly related to its central mission.

nonprogrammed decisions novel and poorly defined, these are used when no procedure exists for solving the problem.

nonroutine technology technology in which there is high task variety and the conversion process is not analyzable or well understood.

nonsubstitutability a trait of a department whose function cannot be performed by other readily available resources.

normative forces pressures to adopt structures, techniques or management processes because they are considered by the community to be up-to-date and effective.

O

official goals the formally stated definition of business scope and outcomes the organization is trying to achieve; another term for *mission*.

open system a system that must interact with the environment to survive.

open systems emphasis an aspect of the competing values model that reflects a combination of external focus and flexible structure.

operative goals descriptions of the ends sought through the actual operating procedures of the organization; these explain what the organization is trying to accomplish.

organic an organization system marked by free-flowing, adaptive processes, an unclear hierarchy of authority and decentralized decision making.

organization development a behavioural science field devoted to improving performance through trust, open confrontation of problems, employee empowerment and participation, the design of meaningful work, cooperation between groups and the full use of human potential.

organization structure designates formal reporting relationships, including the number of levels in the hierarchy and the span of control of managers and supervisors; identifies the grouping together of individuals into departments and of departments into the total organization; and includes the design of systems to ensure effective communication, coordination and integration of efforts across departments.

organization theory a macro approach to organizations that analyzes the whole organization as a unit.

organizational behaviour a micro approach to organizations that focuses on the individuals within organizations as the relevant units for analysis.

organizational change the adoption of a new idea or behavior by an organization.

organizational decision making the organizational process of identifying and solving problems.

organizational decline a condition in which a substantial, absolute decrease in an organization's resource base occurs over a period of time.

organizational ecosystem a system formed by the interaction of a community of organizations and their environment, usually cutting across traditional industry lines.

organizational environment all elements that exist outside the boundary of the organization and have the potential to affect all or part of the organization.

organizational form an organization's specific technology, structure, products, goals and personnel.

organizational goal a desired state of affairs that the organization attempts to reach.

organizational innovation the adoption of an idea or behaviour that is new to an organization's industry, market or general environment.

organizational politics activities to acquire, develop and use power and other resources to obtain one's preferred outcome when there is uncertainty or disagreement about choices.

organizations social entities that are goal-directed, deliberately structured activity systems linked to the external environment.

organized anarchy extremely organic organizations characterized by highly uncertain conditions.

outsourcing to contract out certain corporate functions, such as manufacturing, information technology or credit processing, to other companies.

P

personnel ratios the proportions of administrative, clerical and professional support staff.

point–counterpoint a decision-making technique that divides decision makers into two groups and assigns them different, often competing responsibilities.

political model a definition of an organization as being made up of groups that have separate interests, goals and values in which power and influence are needed to reach decisions.

political tactics for using power these include building coalitions, expanding networks, controlling decision premises, enhancing legitimacy and expertise and making a direct appeal.

pooled interdependence the lowest form of interdependence among departments, in which work does not flow between units.

population a set of organizations engaged in similar activities with similar patterns of resource utilization and outcomes.

population ecology perspective a perspective in which the focus is on organizational diversity and adaptation within a community or population or organizations.

power the ability of one person or department in an organization to influence others to bring about desired outcomes.

power distance the level of inequality people are willing to accept within an organization.

power sources there are five sources of horizontal power in organizations: dependency, financial resources, centrality, nonsubstitutability and the ability to cope with uncertainty.

problem consensus the agreement among managers about the nature of problems or opportunities and about which goals and outcomes to pursue.

problem identification the decision-making stage in which information about environmental and organizational conditions is monitored to determine if performance is satisfactory and to diagnose the cause of shortcomings.

problem solution the decision-making stage in which alternative courses of action are considered and one alternative is selected and implemented.

problemistic search occurs when managers look around in the immediate environment for a solution to resolve a problem quickly.

process organized group of related tasks and activities that work together to transform inputs into outputs that create value for customers.

product and service changes changes in an organization's product or service outputs.

product matrix a variation of the matrix structure in which project or product managers have primary authority and functional managers simply assign technical personnel to projects and provide advisory expertise.

programmed decisions repetitive and well-defined procedures that exist for resolving problems.

prospector a business strategy characterized by innovation, risk-taking, seeking out new opportunities and growth.

R

radical change a breaking of the frame of reference for an organization, often creating a new equilibrium because the entire organization is transformed.

rational approach a process of decision making that stresses the need for systematic analysis of a problem followed by choice and implementation in a logical sequence.

rational goal emphasis an aspect of the competing values model that reflects values of structural control and external focus.

rational-legal authority based on employees' belief in the legality of rules and the right of those in authority to issue commands.

rational model a description of an organization characterized by a rational approach to decision making, extensive and reliable information systems, central power, a norm of optimization, uniform values across groups, little conflict and an efficiency orientation.

reactor a business strategy in which environmental threats and opportunities are responded to in an ad hoc fashion.

reasons organizations grow growth occurs because it is an organizational goal, it is necessary to attract and keep quality managers or it is necessary to maintain economic health.

reciprocal interdependence the highest level of interdependence, in which the output of one operation is the input of a second, and the output of the second operation is the input of the first (for example, a hospital).

reengineering redesigning a vertical organization along its horizontal workflows and processes.

resource dependence a situation in which organizations depend on the environment but strive to acquire control over resources to minimize their dependence.

resource-based approach an organizational perspective that assesses effectiveness by observing how successfully the organization obtains, integrates, and manages valued resources.

retention the preservation and institutionalization of selected organizational forms.

rites and ceremonies the elaborate, planned activities that make up a special event and often are conducted for the benefit of an audience.

role a part in a dynamic social system that allows an employee to use his or her discretion and ability to achieve outcomes and meet goals.

routine technology technology characterized by little task variety and the use of objective, computational procedures.

rule of law that which arises from a set of codified principles and regulations that describe how people are required to act, are generally accepted in society and are enforceable in the courts.

S

satisficing the acceptance by organizations of a satisfactory rather than a maximum level of performance.

scientific management a classical approach that claims decisions about organization and job design should be based on precise, scientific procedures.

sectors subdivisions of the external environment that contain similar elements.

selection the process by which organizational variations are determined to fit the external environment; variations that fail to fit the needs of the environment are 'selected out' and fail.

sequential interdependence a serial form of interdependence in which the output of one operation becomes the input to another operation.

service technology technology characterized by simultaneous production and consumption, customized output, customer participation, intangible output and being labour intensive.

simple-complex dimension the number and dissimilarity of external elements relevant to an organization's operation.

Six Sigma quality standard that specifies a goal of no more than 3.4 defects per million parts; expanded to refer to a set of control procedures that emphasize the relentless pursuit of higher quality and lower costs.

skunkworks separate, small, informal, highly autonomous and often secretive group that focuses on breakthrough ideas for the business.

small-batch production a manufacturing process, often custom work, that is not highly mechanized and relies heavily on the human operator.

social audit measures and reports the ethical, social and environmental impact of a company's operations.

social capital the quality of interactions among people, affected by whether they share a common perspective.

social responsibility management's obligation to make choices and take action so that the organization contributes to the welfare and interest of society as well as itself.

sociotechnical systems approach an approach that combines the needs of people with the needs of technical efficiency.

sources of intergroup conflict factors that generate conflict, including goal incompatibility, differentiation, task interdependence and limited resources.

specialist an organization that has a narrow range of goods or services or serves a narrow market.

stable-unstable dimension the state of an organization's environmental elements.

stakeholder any group within or outside an organization that has a stake in the organization's performance.

stakeholder approach also called the *constituency approach,* this perspective assesses the satisfaction of stakeholders as an indicator of the organization's performance.

standardization a policy that ensures all branches of the company at all locations operate in the same way.

stories narratives based on true events that are frequently shared among organizational employees and told to new employees to inform them about an organization.

strategic contingencies events and activities inside and outside an organization that are essential for attaining organizational goals.

strategy the current set of plans, decisions and objectives that have been adopted to achieve the organization's goals.

strategy and structure changes changes in the administrative domain of an organization, including structure, policies, reward systems, labour relations, coordination devices, management information control systems and accounting and budgeting.

structural dimensions descriptions of the internal characteristics of an organization.

structure the formal reporting relationships, groupings and systems of an organization.

struggle for existence a principle of the population ecology model that holds that organizations are engaged in a competitive struggle for resources and fighting to survive.

subcultures cultures that develop within an organization to reflect the common problems, goals and experiences that members of a team, department or other unit share.

subsystems divisions of an organization that perform specific functions for the organization's survival; organizational subsystems perform the essential functions of boundary spanning, production, maintenance, adaptation and management.

switching structures an organization creates an organic structure when such a structure is needed for the initiation of new ideas.

symbol something that represents another thing.

symptoms of structural deficiency signs of the organization structure being out of alignment, including delayed or poor-quality decision making, failure to respond innovatively to environmental changes and too much conflict.

system a set of interacting elements that acquires inputs from the environment, transforms them, and discharges outputs to the external environment.

T

tacit knowledge knowledge that is based on personal experience, intuition, rules of thumb and judgement, and cannot be easily codified and passed on to others in written form.

tactics for enhancing collaboration techniques such as integration devices, confrontation and negotiation, intergroup consultation, member rotation and shared mission and superordinate goals that enable groups to overcome differences and work together.

tactics for increasing power these include entering areas of high uncertainty, creating dependencies, providing resources and satisfying strategic contingencies.

task a narrowly defined piece of work assigned to a person.

task environment sectors with which the organization interacts directly and that have a direct effect on the organization's ability to achieve its goals.

task force a temporary committee composed of representatives from each department affected by a problem.

team building activities that promote the idea that people who work together can work together as a team.

teams permanent task forces often used in conjunction with a full-time integrator.

technical champion a person who generates or adopts and develops an idea for a technological innovation and is devoted to it, even to the extent of risking position or prestige; also called *product champion.*

technical complexity the extent of mechanization in the manufacturing process.

technical knowledge understanding and agreement about how to solve problems and reach organizational goals.

technology the tools, techniques and actions used to transform organizational inputs into outputs.

technology changes changes in an organization's production process, including its knowledge and skills base, that enable distinctive competence.

time-based competition delivering products and services faster than competitors, giving companies a competitive edge.

traditional authority based in the belief in traditions and the legitimacy of the status of people exercising authority through those traditions.

transaction processing systems (TPS) automation of the organization's routine, day-to-day business transactions.

transnational model a form of horizontal organization that has multiple centres, subsidiary managers who initiate strategy and innovations for the company as a whole and unity and coordination achieved through corporate culture and shared vision and values.

U

uncertainty occurs when decision makers do not have sufficient information about environmental factors and have a difficult time predicting external changes.

uncertainty avoidance the level of tolerance for and comfort with uncertainty and individualism within a culture.

V

values-based leadership a relationship between a leader and followers that is based on strongly shared values that are advocated and acted upon by the leader.

variation appearance of new organizational forms in response to the needs of the external environment; analogous to mutations in biology.

variety in terms of tasks, the frequency of unexpected and novel events that occur in the conversion process.

venture teams a technique to foster creativity within organizations in which a small team is set up as its own company to pursue innovations.

vertical information system the periodic reports, written information and computer-based communications distributed to managers.

vertical linkages communication and coordination activities connecting the top and bottom of an organization.

virtual network grouping organization that is a loosely connected cluster of separate components.

virtual network structure the firm subcontracts many or most of its major processes to separate companies and coordinates their activities from a small headquarters organization.

virtual team made up of organizationally or geographically dispersed members who are linked through advanced information and communications technologies. Members frequently use the Internet and collaborative software to work together, rather than meeting face-to-face.

W

whistle-blowing employee disclosure of illegal, immoral or illegitimate practices on the part of the organization.

SUBJECT INDEX